ACTA CONVENTUS
NEO-LATINI BARIENSIS

MEDIEVAL & RENAISSANCE

TEXTS & STUDIES

VOLUME 184

ACTA CONVENTUS
NEO-LATINI BARIENSIS

*Proceedings of the Ninth International Congress
of Neo-Latin Studies*

Bari 29 August to 3 September 1994

GENERAL EDITOR

Rhoda Schnur

EDITED BY

J. F. Alcina, John Dillon, Walther Ludwig,
Colette Nativel, Mauro de Nichilo,
and Stephen Ryle

Medieval & Renaissance Texts & Studies
Tempe, Arizona
1998

A generous grant from Pegasus Limited for the Promotion
of Neo-Latin Studies has helped meet publication costs of this book.

Library of Congress Cataloging-in-Publication Data

International Congress of Neo-Latin Studies (9th : 1994 : Bari, Italy)
  Acta Conventus Neo-Latini Hafniensis : proceedings of the ninth International
Congress of Neo-Latin Studies, Barie, 29 August to 3 September, 1994 / general
editor, Rhoda Schnur ; edited by J.F. Alcina . . . [et al.].
    p. cm. — (Medieval & Renaissance texts & studies ; v. 184)
  Includes Bibliographical references (p.) and index.
  ISBN 0–86698–226–4 (alk. paper)
    1. Latin literature, Medieval and modern — History and criticism — Congresses.
2. Latin philology, Medieval and modern — Congresses. 3. Learning and scholarship
— History — Congresses. 4. Civilization, Medieval — Congresses. 5. Renaissance —
Congresses. 6. Classicism — Congresses. 7. Humanists — Congresses. I. Schnur,
Rhoda. II. Alcina Rovira, Juan. III. Title. IV. Series.
PA8002.I57 1994
870.9'003—dc21   98–23345
                                                                   CIP

100 29571 61

T

This book is made to last.
It is set in Bembo, smythe-sewn
and printed on acid-free paper
to library specifications.

Printed in the United States of America

International Association for Neo-Latin Studies

Ninth International Congress

Bari, 29 – 3 September 1994

PROGRAMME

The Impact of Italian Humanism:
Continuations and Transformations

Sponsors

Università degli Studi di Bari, Dipartimento di Italianistica
Consiglio Nazionale delle Richerce
Comune di Bari

Instituto Nazionale de Studi sul Rinascimento Meridionale
Università degli Studi di Lecce, Dipartimento di Filologia, Linguistica e
Letteratura, Dipartimento di Beni Culturali
Regione Puglia, Assessorato alla Cultura e al Turismo
Comune di Ruvo di Puglia
Comune di Trani

Advisory Committee
for the Ninth International IANLS Congress

Professor Ch. Béné
Université de Grenoble

Professor J. Chomarat
Université de Paris

Professor J. Ijsewijn
Universiteit Leuven

Professor I. Kajanto
University of Helsinki

Professor J.-C. Margolin
Centre d'études supérieures de la Renaissance

Professor Judith Rice Henderson
University of Saskatchewan

Professor R. Simonds
The American University

Professor J. Starnawski
Uniwersytet Lodz

Professor C. Vasoli
Università di Firenze

Monday, 29 August

15.30 Registration

17.30 Opening Meeting

18.30 Plenary Paper
G. TOURNOY, Neo-Latin Satire in the Low Countries
from an Italian Perspective

19.30 Buffet offered by the Università degli Studi di Bari

Tuesday, 30 August

9.00–11.00 Papers I

Section A, France↔Italy   Chair: C. Nativel
P. FORD, The *Mithologiae* of Natalie Conti and the Pléiade
C. DEMAIZIÈRE, Les Relations entre humanistes lombards et lyonnais au XVIème siècle: le
rôle de Gaudenzio Merula et Sébastien Gryphe
M. GRÜNBERG-DRÖGE, Little Italy on the Rhône: A Look at Lyons from an Emblematic
Point of View
M. DÉRAMAIX, Sannazar entre Marsile Ficin et Guy Lefèvre de la Boderie: la première
traduction française du *De partu Virginis* et le succes du platonisme florentino.

Section B, Ethics and Politics   Chair: L. Valcke
C.M.MURPHY, Humanist Values in Thomas More's Life of Giovanni Pico della Mirandola
J. LINDHARDT, Martin Luther and Laurentius Valla on Free Will
H.-J. VAN DAM, *Summa potestas:* Grotius and the Italians
P. J. OSMOND, Constantius Felicius Durantinus, *De coniuratione Catilinae liber* (1518): Anti-
Sallustian Criticism and Renaissance Ciceroniansim

Section C, Low Countries↔Italy   Chair: G. Tournoy
A. J. E. HARMSEN, Sannazaro nella letteratura olandese
M. SKAFTE JENSEN, Italian Influence on the Latin Poetry of Zacharias Lund (1608–1667)
M. VAN DER POEL, Gerolamo Cardano's *Neronis encomium* (1562) and Its Reception, with
Some Remarks on the Dutch Translation by I. H. Glaremaker (1649)

Section D, Mimesis and Drama   Chair: W. Ludwig
M. LAUSBERG, Neulateinische "mimetische" Gedichte
G. EHRSTINE, *Scaenica Faceta:* The Choral Odes in Johannes Reuchlin's *Scaenica Progym-
nasmata (Henno)*
E. V. GEORGE, Vives and Mimetic Prose: Notes on Two Dialogues
H. B. NORLAND, Gager's *Ulysses Redux:* Tragoedia Nova

Section E, Translations   Chair: R. Green
M. PADE, The Humanist Translations of Plutarch's *Lives* and Their Dissemination in Europe
in the Fifteenth and Sixteenth Centuries

M. DE NICHILO, Teodoro Gaza traduttore dell'*Ars rhetorica* dello pseudo Dionigi d'Alicarnasso

Section F, Epistolography   Chair: J. Rice Henderson

L. QUAQUARELLI, Carteggi umanistici ed epistolografia cancelleresca nella Bologna del Quattro e Cinquecento

J. AXER, La corrispondenza di Johannes Dantiscus (1485–1548): fonti italiane

R. KÖSSLING, Die Korrespondenz der Olympia Morata (1526–1555) als Dokument italodeutscher Begegnung

11.30 Plenary Paper
G. MARC'HADOUR, Jean Pic de la Mirandole et son influence
au nord des Alpes (1498–1560)

16.00–17.30 Papers II

Section A, Historiography   Chair: J. Costas

A. MOSS, Literary History, a Humanist Invention

B. POZUELO CALERO, Le historiografía humanista del Quattrocento y Juan Ginés de Sepúlveda

L. B. MORTENSEN, Andreas Velleius' *De scribenda historia Danica* (1579) and Its European Background

Section B, Patronage and Literature   Chair: R. J. Schoeck

P. ZEEBERG, The Literary Patronage of Heinrich Rantzau (1526–1599)

K. SKOVGAARD-PETERSEN, Two Trends of Historiography at the Court of Christian IV of Denmark (1588–1648): Traditional Humanism and Contemporary Antiquarianism

R. W. CARRUBBA, Pastor H. G. Weland's Latin Compositions on Engelbert Kaempfer

Section C, Italian Humanism and Europe I   Chair: C. Heesakkers

N. VAN YZENDOORN, Petrarch and Boccaccio in 18th-Century Finland

O. MERISALO, La crisi dell'Umanesimo tradizionale nella Finlandia settecentesca

G. M. ANSELMI, Letteratura inglese e tradizione neolatina dell'Umanesimo italiano

Section D, Spain⇔Italy   Chair: L. Gualdo Rosa

J. SOLANA PUJALTE, Quelques notes sur la présence de Maffeo Vegio en Espagne

F. J. MAÑAS VINIEGRA, Angeli Politiani *Silvae*. Cum scholiis Francisci Sancti Brocensis

Section E, Chorography   Chair: K. Enenkel

D. DEFILIPPIS, Descrivere la Terra: le fonti classiche negli scritti geografici di Antonio De Ferrariis Galateo

E. HAYWOOD, Paolo Giovio's *Descriptio Hibernae:* Humanist Chorography or Political Manifesto?

J. CLOSA FARRÉS, Italian Humanistic Tradition in the *Libro de las grandezas y cosas memorables de la metropolitana, insigne y famosa ciudad de Tarragona* by Micer Luys Pons de Ycart (Lérida, 1572)

Section F, Humanism in Germany   Chair: M. Lausberg

C. JEUDY, L'Humaniste allemand Johannes Caesarius (ca. 1460–1550)

J. RAMMINGER, Die Dichterkrönung des Georgius Sibutus

18.00–19.30 Papers III

Section A, Italian Humanism and Europe II   Chair: R. Schnur

A. MAZZOCCO, The Spread of Italian Humanism in Europe: The Case of Biondo Flavio

A. LAIRD, Politian's Influence and the Reception of Homer

F. ROUGET, Le Séjour d'Olivier de Magny à Rome (mars 1555–octobre 1556) et l'influence de l'Humanisme italien sur ses *Odes* de 1559

Section B, Philosophy and Science   Chair: C. M. Murphy
L. VALCKE, De la mathématique à le physique chez Jean Pic de la Mirandole
K. A. NEUHAUSEN, De ineditis operibus iis, quae quidem Latine Dominicus quidam Cyllenius Graecus in Italia decimo sexto conscripserit saeculo
T. VAN HOUDT, On "Medium" and "Message" in Late Scholastic Moral Theology: The Economic and Ethical Writings of Robert Bellarmine and Leonard Lessius

Section C, Reception of the Classics   Chair: A. Wesseling
E. BORZA, Sofocle nell'Umanesimo italiano: una fortuna troppo sconosciuta
R. P. H. GREEN, Prudentius in the Renaissance
A. IURILLI, L'opera di Orazio fra editoria e scuole umanistiche

Section D, Women in Neo-Latin Literature   Chair: B. Hosington
J.LARSENKLEIN, "Ne suffreth nat that men yow doon offence": A Feminist Reading of the Griselda Story in Boccaccio, Petrarca, and Chaucer
A. M. O'DONNELL, Classical Women in the Letters of Erasmus

Section E, Poetry   Chair: P. Ford
S. F. RYLE, The Celebrations for the Marriage of Sigismund I of Poland and Bona Sforza, Duchess of Bari
R. SARASTI-WILENIUS, Latin Wedding Poetry in Finland
J. PASCUAL BAREA, La poesia latina del genovès Franco Leardo en Sevilla

Session F, Humanism in the New World   Chair: E. McCutcheon
G. L. GIGLIOTTI, Towards a New World *Senatus doctorum:* The Liminary Verse of the *Magnalia Christi Americana*
R. HEREDIA CORREA, El neolatín en los orígenes de nuestra identidad nacional

19.30 Visit to Medieval Bari

Wednesday, 31 August

8.30 Departure to Trani
9.30-11.30 Seminars

Seminar A: Humanism in the   F. Akkerman, University of Groningen
Northeastern Parts of the Low Countries before Erasmus
F. AKKERMAN, Rudolph Agricola and Italy: Reality and Fiction in the Sources
P.SCHOONBEEG, *Scribe quod innuptae possint memorare puellae:* A Comparison between Neo-Latin Poetry from Italy and from the Milieu of the "Adwert Academy"
A. H. VAN DER LAAN, The *Familiarium epistolarum compendium* by Antonius Liber

Seminar B: El Humanismo italiano y sus   J. Costas, University of Madrid
relaciones con el humanismo hispano
J. F. ALCINA, La poesía humanística italiana y su difusión en España a través de la imprenta
L. CARRASCO REIJA, Traducciones de auctores clásicos latinos en el humanismo italiano y español
M. CONDE SALAZAR, Las ideas pedagógicas en los tratados de humanistas españoles e italianos
J. COSTAS RODRÍGUEZ, La teoría historiográfica humanista en Italia y España
M. A. DIAZ GITO, Una visión libresca de la isla de Córcega: el poema *Corsica* de J. C. Calvete de Estrella

J. GONZALEZ VAZQUEZ, La influencia del humanismo italiano en la Granada renacentista

D. LÓPEZ-CAÑETE QUILES, El *De Hispania instaurata* de Jaime Falcó y la *Gerusalemme Liberata* de Tasso

M. J. LÓPEZ DE AYALA, Ideas sobre la paz y la guerra entre los humanistas italianos y españoles

J. M. MAESTRE MAESTRE, La influencia de Italia y sus humanistas en la literatura latina del Renacimiento hispano

J. L. NAVARRO LÓPEZ, El *Supplementum ad Aeneidos librum XII* de M. Vegio y la versión castellana de Hernández de Velasco

C. T. PABÓN DE ACUÑA, Las canciones de amor chipriotas de inspiración petrarquiana y obras paralelas castellanas: diferencias y semejanzas

J. PASCUAL BAREA, Poetas latinos de Sevilla y sus relaciones con Italia

E. DEL PINO GONZÁLEZ, Los humanistas italianos en el *Epistolario* de Juan de Verzosa

B. POZUELO CALERO, El petraquismo en Francisco Pacheco

S. RAMOS MALDONADO, Roma y los humanistas italianos en los *Commentariorum de Sale libri quinque* del alcañizano Bernardino Gómez Miedes

C. RAMOS SANTANA, Aspectos de la obra de Lucio Marineo Sículo

E. RODRÍGUEZ PEREGRINA, Primeros historiadores italianos en la corte de los Reyes Católicos

J. SALVADÓ RECASENS, La estancia en Italia de Juan Partenio Tovar

A. SERRANO CUETO, ¿Influencias de la edición aldina de las fábulas de Esopo en Fernando de Arce?

M. TRASCASAS CASARES, Traducciones de autores clásicos griegos en el humanismo italiano y español

Seminar C: Biography and Portrait   K. Enenkel, University of Leiden
in Renaissance Humanism

K. ENENKEL, The Starting Point of Humanistic Biography: Boccaccio's *Vita Petrarce* and Petrarch's *Epistola posteritati*

W. BERSCHIN, Rudolph Agricolas Petrarca-Biographie

J. L. DE JONG, Portraits of Condottieri

A. BODAR, *Amicitiae nostrae monumentum:* Erasmus and Portraiture

12.00 Visit to Cathedral

**13.00 Buffet offered by the
Istituto Nazionale di Studi sul Rinascimento Meridionale**

15.00 Excursion to Castel del Monte

**18.00 Ruvo di Puglia, Cathedral
Plenary Paper**
M. MIGLIO, La teorizzazione dell'*Ars historica* tra tardo Medioevo
ed Età moderna
19.00 visit to Museo Jatta

**21.00 Buffet offered by the
Civica Amministrazione di Ruvo di Puglia**

Thursday, 1 September

9.00 Plenary Paper
F. RÄDLE, Frische Luft in Italien: Deutsche Humanisten Jenseits der Alpen

10.30 Business meeting

16.00–17.30 Papers IV

Section A, Humanism in Rome I   Chair: J. IJsewijn

M.LAUREYS, Andrea Fiocchi's *De Romanorum sacerdotiis et magistratibus:* Roman Antiquarian Studies under Martin V and Eugenius IV

G. SOLARO, Un corso lucreziano di Pomponio Leto

M.G.BLASIO, Gerarchia delle discipline e *studia humanitatis:* l'orazione di Bartolomeo Platina a Pio II *De laudibus bonarum artium*

Section B, Humanism and Education   Chair: J. Starnawski

J. OKOŃ, Umanesimo gesuita nella Polonia del Cinquecento tra Occidente e Oriente

J. GLOMSKI, Italian Influences on Early Humanist Educational Theory at Cracow (1495–1530)

J. K. KROUPA, The Impact of Italian Humanism on the Bohemian Lands

Section C, *Imitatio* and *aemulatio*   Chair: A. Moss

F. J. NICHOLS, Navagero's *Lusus* and the Pastoral Tradition

D. SACRÉ, *Varis* et *Syphilis* sive de Gadsone Coopmans Hieronymi Fracastorii imitatore

P. C. DUST, Petrarchism and George Herbert's *Memoriae Matris Sacrum*

Section D, Commentaries   Chair: R. W. Carrubba

C. KALLENDORF, Ascensius, Landino, and Virgil: Continuity and Transformation in Renaissance Commentary

A. FRITSEN, Renaissance *Fasti* Commentaries and Antiquarianism

M. C. RAMOS SANTANA, El *In Ciceronis librum de fato commentarium* de Giorgio Valla y el *Liber de parcis* de Lucio Marineo Sículo

Section E, Germany⇔Italy   Chair: F. Rädle

C. DRÖGE, The Pope's Favorite Humanist in the Land of Reformation: On the Reception of the Writings of the Florentine Humanist Giannozzo Manetti (1396–1459) in Sixteenth-Century Germany

F.PALLADINI, Gli umanisti italiani in una biblioteca tedesca del '600. Il caso di S. Pufendorf

R. JOHNSON, Paulus Niavis pedagogo sassonico e lo spirito italiano

18.00–19.30 Papers V

Section A, Humanism in Rome II   Chair: M. Miglio

W. O'NEAL, *De gentilium deorum imaginibus* of Lazzarelli: Why Two?

S. REVARD, Lampridio and the Poetic Sodalities in Rome in the Early Sixteenth Century

Section B, Early Humanism   Chair: D. Marsh

P. M. CLOGAN, Italian Humanism at the Court of King Robert of Anjou

D. GILMAN, Petrarch's Sophonisba: Stereotypical Seductress or Tragic Heroine?

L. GUALDO ROSA, Padova 1420: un commento universitario di Gasparino Barzizza ad alcune orazioni ciceroniane scoperte da Poggio

Section C, Humanism in England   Chair: A. Mazzocco

R. J. SCHOECK, The Humanistic Works Given by Bishop Richard Fox to Corpus Christi College, Oxford, in 1528

M. VESSEY, An English Humanist, His College, and His Books: The *Vita et Epicedion Iohannis Claymundi* of John Shepery in Its Institutional Setting

Section D, Editors   Chair: V. Ussani

J.-L. CHARLET, L'Édition du *Cornu Copiae* de N. Perotti

J. STARNAWSKI, L'Édition d'Horace dedié par Bernardino Partenio da Spilim-bergo au roi polanais Étienne Bathory (1584)

M. D. RINCÓN GONZÁLEZ, Presenza dell'elemento italiano nella stampa di libri spagnoli o di tematica spagnola in tipografie tedesche del XV secolo e degli inizi del XVI

Section E, Poetics   Chair: J. Dillon

L. BEK, Alberti's Humanistic Art Theory and the Rules and Precepts of the European Academies of Art

L. CHINES, La fortuna della *Poetica* di Girolamo Vida tra didattica e poesia

R. PITKÄRANTA, Pangrammatischer Manierismus in der akademischen lateinischen Dichtung Finnlands des 17. Jh.s

21.00 Concert

Friday, 2 September

9.00 Plenary Paper
E. McCUTCHEON, The Humanism of Thomas More:
Continuities and Transformations in Latin Letters

10.30 Colloquium on Neo-Latin Lexicography

16.00–17.30 Papers VI

Section A, Rhetoric   Chair: C. Kallendorf

J. RICE HENDERSON, The Impact of Italian Humanism on the *Ars dictaminis:* Manuals of Letter-Writing Printed in Northern Europe

C. NATIVEL, Les Jardins de l'éloquence: la description des jardins de Saint-Germain dans les *Vacationes autumnales* de Louis de Cressoles (1620)

Section B, Erasmus and Italy   Chair: G. Marc'hadour

A. WESSELING, Advertizing the *Adagia:* Erasmus in Venice

T. O. TUNBERG, Observations on the Latinity of Erasmus' Prose and Its Debt to the Italian Humanists

Section C, Humanism in Southern Italy   Chair: E. Haywood

J. DILLON, Pastoral Tradition and Passionate Double-entendre: Generic Modulation in the Polyphemus Poems of Pontano

I. NUOVO, Mito e natura nel *De hortis Hesperidum* di Giovanni Pontano

R. GIRARDI, L'eredità umanistica nella lirica meridionale del secolo XVI. Spunti su L. Paterno

Section D, Satire and Parody   Chair: K. A. Neuhausen

D. MARSH, L'elogio satrico degli umanisti

D. BEECHER, Parody and Schwankzyklus as Structural Principles in the Latin Solomon and Marcolphus

Section E, Italian Humanism and Europe III   Chair: F. Akkerman

R. JURGELĖNAITĖ, The Impact of Italian Poetical Tradition in Lithuania

E. WITKOWSKA-ZAREMBA, Il pensiero italiano e la mediazione tedesca nella musicografia latina del Cinquecento polacco

20.30 Banquet (Barion Club, Bari)

Saturday, 3 September

8.15 Departure to Lecce

10.00 Visit to Town

12.30 Università di Lecce, Dipartimento di Beni Culturali
Monastero degli Olivetani:
Official Greeting of the University Authorities
F. Tateo, Studi neo-latini e Umanesimo nel Salento

13.30 Buffet offered by the Università degli Studi di Lecce

15.30 Departure to Otranto

16.00 Visit to Cathedral

18.30 Departure to Monopoli

20.00 Masseria La Spina—Dinner

§§§

Executive Committee
President: Prof. Francesco Tateo, Università di Bari
Past President: Prof. Walther Ludwig, Universität Hamburg
First Vice President: Prof. Brenda Hosington, Université de Montréal
Second Vice President: Prof. Mauro de Nichilo, Università di Bari
Chair of Publications: Mrs. Rhoda Schnur, St. Gallen
Treasurer: Prof. Chris Heesakkers, University of Amsterdam-Leiden
Secretary: Mr. Roger Green, University of St. Andrews

Organizing Committee
Dipartimento di Italianistica, Università di Bari:
Prof. Francesco Tateo
Prof. Mauro de Nichilo
Dott. Domenico Cofano
Dott. Domenico Defilippis
Prof. Grazia Distaso
Dott. Maria A. Mastronardi
Dott. Isabella Nuovo
Dott. Pietro Sisto

Dipartimento di Linguistica, Letteratura e Filologia Moderna,
Università di Bari:
Dott. Antonio Iurilli

Collaborators
Dipartimento di Italianistica, Università di Bari:
Dott. Daniele Pegorari
Dott. Giovanni Pirrelli
Dott. Paolo Testone

Dott. Sebastiano Valerio
Dott. Giovanna Verna
Sig. Guiseppe Delle Grazie

Agenzia SYMPOSIA
Studio e organizzazione di Congresse
70125 Bari via Fanelli 206/25
Telephone: 080.813757
Fax: 5587155

ACTA CONVENTUS
NEO-LATINI BARIENSIS

S. RAMOS MALDONADO, M. N. RAMOS SANTANA, E. RODRÍGUEZ PEREGRINA,
J. SALVADÓ RECASENS, A. SERRANO CUETO, M. TRASCASAS CASARES
REDACTOR: J. F. ALCINA ROVIRA

COMMUNICATIONS

ACTA CONVENTUS
NEO-LATINI BARIENSIS

Saluto del Presidente
Studi neo-latini e Umanesimo nel Salento

FRANCESCO TATEO

Illustri colleghi della "Societas internationalis neolatinis studiis provehendis," amici e studiosi convenuti al IX Congresso dell'Associazione, l'Università di Bari, in particolare il Dipartimento di Italianistica e la Facoltà di Lettere e Filosofia che hanno organizzato la manifestazione, il Comune e la Provincia di Bari, l'Assessorato alla Cultura e al Turismo della Regione Puglia, che hanno sostenuto l'iniziativa, vi porgono il benvenuto e vi ringraziano per aver voluto onorare questa città e questa regione d'Italia.

Non è un caso che la Puglia abbia ospitato uno dei momenti della riflessione sulla vitalità del risorto latino, tornato ad essere in Europa, nell'età moderna, un forte vincolo di coesione culturale nonostante l'approfondirsi delle differenziazioni nazionali. Questa regione infatti partecipa, sul piano della cultura letteraria, più alla *koiné* latina che eredita e diffonde il rinnovamento umanistico nelle scuole e nelle corti europee, che alla emancipazione del volgare quale distintivo delle diverse nazioni. Se infatti l'Associazione si è proposta il recupero della cultura scritta latina oltre il primo secolo dell'Umanesimo, valorizzando gli elementi di continuità che sussistono in un arco di tempo che va dal XIV al XVII secolo, o le manifestazioni del volgare che rientrino nell'orizzonte della cultura neo-latina, il fenomeno umanistico quale appare nella raccolta di testi uscita in questa occasione, ad opera di studiosi della nostra Università, sotto il titolo di *Puglia neolatina* risulta parallelo rispetto ai numerosi fenomeni europei risvegliati in questi lunghi anni di vita dell'Associazione attraverso gli incontri periodici dei congressi e la continuità di un lavoro di scavo, di ricognizione e di approfondimento quale si rispecchia esemplarmente negli *Humanistica Lovaniensia* di J. IJsewijn.

D'altra parte l'edificio nel quale ci troviamo, questo castello svevo che eredita in parte le linee normanne, e la combinazione cronologica con l'anno federiciano mi inducono a ricordare come in questa regione, all'alba della rinascita neo-latina, la pratica religiosa dell'ordine benedettino da un lato e l'opera politica e legislativa di Federico II dall'altra abbiano segnato alcuni aspetti rilevanti della risorta latinità d'Occidente.

Sarebbe inopportuno affrontare *per incidens* il problema delle origini dell'Umanesimo nel cuore della civiltà mediolatina, e discutere dell'identità culturale e politica di Federico che il Burckhardt, un classico da non dimenticare, colloca nel primo capitolo della sua *Civiltà del Rinascimento in Italia*, ma non possiamo trascurare, in questa circostanza, che questo castello ha visto dal XII al XVI secolo l'avvicendarsi di tre fenomeni legati alla rinascita neo-latina, il regno normanno di Guglielmo di Altavilla, il regno svevo di Federico II e il ducato di Bari di Bona Sforza regina di Polonia.

Nella tradizione dei nostri studi regionali la presenza romana e medievale e quella ecclesiastica dell'età moderna sopravanzano di gran lunga quella dell'Umanesimo, per cui l'occasione di questo Convegno può diventare una data storica, perché sancisce una inversione di tendenza tesa ad integrare la cultura letteraria pugliese dei secoli XV–XVII entro le linee complesse e variegate del Rinascimento nell'Italia meridionale, cui un illustre studioso tedesco degli inizi del secolo, Eric Gothein, prestò tanta attenzione, tanta intelligenza e cura, avviando la ricerca che tuttora è in atto.

Il richiamo alla nostra città e alla nostra regione non intende ridurre l'orizzonte del Congresso, ma solo giustificare la sua presenza in un angolo d'Italia significativo, dove non hanno ragione di essere i primati tradizionali che condizionano l'interpretazione storica del complessivo fenomeno umanistico. Solo il superamento di alcuni pregiudizi potrà adeguare lo studio dell'Umanesimo ad un'esigenza che avvertiamo quanto mai viva proprio in questo periodo di ricostruzione dell'unità europea.

E' per questo che il titolo di questo Congresso, pur conservando l'ampiezza tematica che caratterizza i nostri incontri, è stato particolarmente definito come l'"impatto fra Umanesimo italiano e Umanesimo europeo." Molti interventi riguarderanno specificamente questo problema e sono accorpati nelle sezioni Francia ⇔ Italia, Germania ⇔ Italia, Inghilterra ⇔ Italia, Paesi Bassi ⇔ Italia, Spagna ⇔ Italia; altri si muoveranno su questo sfondo ma affrontando aspetti dell'Umanesimo nelle varie nazioni o in un centro significativo dell'Umanesimo europeo come Roma; altri affronteranno tematiche tipiche della cultura umanistica, perfezionate dalla metodologia attuale, quali la ricezione della letteratura classica, la retorica, la poetica, i generi letterari nuovi e rinnovati; altri interventi si concentreranno su figure emblematiche quali Erasmo o Pontano, per tanti versi distanti, per tanti altri effettivamente vicine e perfino analoghe. Perché proprio la considerazione storica di questo differenziarsi, accanto alla considerazione apparentemente contraddittoria della integrazione e della unitarietà del fenomeno, costituisce—a mio parere—il principio attivo degli studi promossi dalla nostra Associazione e la funzionalità del suo contributo scientifico.

Il *colloquium* sulla lessicografia neolatina rappresenta uno dei maggiori impegni dell'Associazione, la creazione degli strumenti più indispensabili allo studioso della letteratura latina, ma anche un segno dell'identità dei nostri studi. Salutiamo con calore il seminario sui rapporti fra Spagna e Italia, un tema che ha avuto nel passato momenti significativi e che attende un approfondimento filologico proprio nell'area della letteratura umanistica. Il seminario sulla "biografia" s'inserisce in un momento favorevole degli studi sulla storiografia umanistica, cogliendone uno dei lati più complessi e problematici: lo vedremo infatti intrecciarsi con l'arte figurativa del ritratto.

Anche la scelta di questi luoghi ha un senso nel genere di Congresso che celebriamo. Trani ci accoglierà in un'antica abbazia benedettina che dovette mantener viva in età umanistica la sua funzione educativa, se nella città s'insediò più tardi la prima tipografia stabile della provincia; ma la città è famosa per essere stata fra le prime a promulgare uno statuto della navigazione, preludio della rinascita del diritto romano e dell'organizzazione laica dei comuni. Castel del Monte ricorda, alla pari di questo Castello, il regno laico e moderno di Federico II, che diede un altro grande contributo alla rinascita del diritto romano con le Costituzioni promulgate nella non lontana Melfi; ma ricorda, Castel del Monte, anche l'opera dei Templari e gli incunaboli della scienza astronomica che tanta parte ha avuto nella cultura neo-latina. Ruvo di Puglia conserva, accanto ad una delle più belle cattedrali romaniche, una delle più prestigiose raccolte di arte ceramica antica, proveniente da questa regione: e la Magna Grecia—come è ben noto—rappresenta uno dei più importanti punti di riferimento dell'Umanesimo antiquario. La città di Lecce, dove si concluderà il nostro congresso, è al centro di quella regione salentina che ancora nei secoli XV e XVI rivela un cospicuo legame con la tradizione bizantina, ed elabora un Umanesimo particolare, in cui la componente religiosa e quella naturalistica rappresentano l'ambiguo impatto con il mondo orientale, per un verso osteggiato e per l'altro assorbito. Otranto, che ricorda con un tragico evento questo ambiguo impatto, non costituisce soltanto un episodio della difesa dell'Umanesimo occidentale, ossia il rovescio della crociata umanistica sognata da Pio II, ma la continuità fra la conservazione dei classici in ambiente monastico e la rinascita delle lettere latine e greche. Né può trascurarsi la funzione svolta dal monastero di Casole, collocato sulla stessa sponda salentina, quale tramite fra un Medioevo illuminato e la nuova filologia umanistica, se la dispersione del suo tesoro librario non fu soltanto dovuta ad un fenomeno fisiologico di decadenza o alla barbarie, ma al passaggio del cardinale Bessarione e quindi all'incremento di quella che sarà la Biblioteca Marciana. Un fatto apparentemente negativo, che ha un suo risvolto positivo, e comunque un significato storico nell'ambito di un'altra contraddittoria vicenda del Rinascimento sulla sponda adriatica, che registra un notevole rapporto fra Venezia e le cittadine del litorale pugliese.

Nella prospettiva della storia dell'arte italiana Lecce significa il Barocco, e quest'ultimo, sempre in quella prospettiva, rappresenta tradizionalmente in Italia la rottura dell'equilibrio classicistico del Rinascimento e per molti versi il distacco dallo strumento linguistico del latino. In realtà, quali che siano le origini prossime di questo fenomeno artistico e i confronti analogici con i fenomeni contemporanei che lo storico dell'arte può tesservi, l'*ornatus* dei monumenti leccesi è radicato in una cultura e in una abilità artigianale che esalta i *flores* e la preziosità dei particolari senza intaccare la struttura fondamentalmente classica tramandata dall'arte romanica. Il discorso delle continuità e delle trasformazioni si presta sempre ad una *quaestio infinita* ed è quindi da evitare, ma io ho inteso soltanto accennare ad una delle possibili letture di un fenomeno spesso considerato separatamente dalla cultura scritta, e quindi soggetto ad interpretazioni unilaterali.

La scrittura salentina dei secoli XVI e XVII, di cui proprio in questa provincia della Puglia si va recuperando da qualche decennio la produzione più significativa, rivela una propensione all'uso del volgare che sembra allinearsi alla battaglia in favore dei moderni contro gli antichi e perciò contribuire all'abbandono dell'esperienza più tipica dell'Umanesimo. Il problema investe la funzione svolta dagli ordini religiosi in questa regione, dove l'organizzazione culturale è un fenomeno della Riforma cattolica ed è concomitante con gli sviluppi della Riforma protestante negli altri paesi europei. Questa organizzazione o riorganizzazione culturale, che vede in prima linea i Gesuiti con le loro scuole che impostano l'insegnamento su basi ciceroniane, i Francescani che sviluppano la formazione in senso spirituale, gli Olivetani che ereditano la cultura benedettina e che si ispirano ai valori della crociata in quanto recupero spirituale dei luoghi santi, costituisce in effetti un *revival*, come lo era stato l'Umanesimo, anzi il *pendant* religioso, ritardato quanto si vuole, della *renovatio* umanistica, o meglio la interpretazione in termini più schiettamente ecclesiastici, e talora mistici, della svolta in senso cristiano che accusa il Rinascimento nella sua versione "romana" durante il secolo XVI.

Che questo *revival* concorrenziale con il Rinascimento possa apparire sia nel rilancio del volgare, sia nel recupero di forme letterarie quali la predicazione o la cronaca rispetto all'oratoria e alla storiografia, uno spostamento verso l'asse tardomedievale più che verso l'asse classicistico, dipende prevalentemente dalla severa distinzione che la moderna storiografia letteraria ha fatto, forse troppo condizionata dal modello delle arti visive, fra aspetti più decisamente laici e aspetti più decisamente religiosi a cominciare proprio da quei secoli XIII e XIV che costituiscono gli incunaboli dell'Umanesimo.

Solo attraverso un ripensamento che tenga conto di questa complessa serie di problemi, di questa particolare evoluzione, possiamo comprendere una figura di primo piano, né locale né solo nazionale, come Roberto Caracciolo da Lecce, il frate predicatore che ebbe fortuna anche europea. L'interesse recente per la storia della lingua e per il volgare ha fatto giustamente rivolgere una particolare attenzione alle sue prediche volgari, ma in una prospettiva storica più avveduta, quella della rinascita neo-latina insomma, bisogna riconoscere il carattere secondario e divulgativo di quella esperienza volgare, quantunque essa testimoni il rapporto del frate con il centro napoletano allora investito in pieno dal movimento umanistico. La vasta produzione latina del predicatore va considerata con minore impazienza di quanto si sia soliti fare; perché essa è certo quella che più direttamente ha nutrito la formazione degli scrittori sacri fioriti in sintonia con la Riforma degli ordini religiosi.

Contemporaneo degli intellettuali che rappresentano il momento più autenticamente secolare dell'Umanesimo, Roberto Caracciolo è stato sempre annoverato fra le glorie salentine quando prevaleva una semplicistica prospettiva erudita e locale; ma ora che è stato messo in evidenza l'atteggiamento ostile verso di lui, al pari che verso Bernardino da Siena, da parte di certa intellettualità laica, e dopo l'insistenza sull'aspetto secolare del movimento umanistico quattrocentesco, si ha qualche perplessità a collocare il frate conventuale di Lecce accanto ai Pontano e perfino ai Galateo. I tempi non sono ancora maturi per una diversa sistemazione di questi autori, specialmente in territori che hanno lungamente subìto l'emarginazione dalla storia letteraria ufficiale. Una ricostruzione storica che sia meno esclusivamente condizionata dagli elementi ideologici e dalle dichiarazioni programmatiche e si fondi maggiormente sull'analisi effettiva delle istituzioni formative e dello strumento linguistico; che consideri con maggiore attenzione la compresenza di linguaggi e generi diversi, e allo stesso tempo consideri i travasi dall'uno all'altro come importanti fenomeni fisiologici di organismi complessi e contraddittori, gioverà alla ricerca delle aree più oscure, superando l'accumulazione erudita senza cedere ad un metodo pericolosamente selettivo.

Due volumi significativi sotto questo aspetto hanno visto la luce recentemente nella collana di Scrittori salentini, gli *Scrittori di pietà* a cura di Mario Marti e le *Epistole eroiche* di Antonio Bruni a cura di Gino Rizzo. Possiamo assumerli come recuperi esemplari di quella duplice e concomitante tendenza implicita nella *renovatio* umanistica, cui si accennava. La mistica dell'eroismo e lo slancio della pietà hanno certo un esito più evidente nella maniera baroccheggiante degli scrittori secenteschi. Ma fra Quattro e Cinquecento l'Umanesimo salentino aveva elaborato appunto una stretta relazione fra i motivi della rinascita classicistica e le aspirazioni religiose rinfocolate anche dalla questione orientale.

Oggi è difficile, di fronte alle complesse e delicate relazioni col mondo musulmano, alla diversa e cangiante realtà rappresentata dalla Grecia e dalla Turchia attuali, rileggere con distacco storicistico i testi umanistici scritti sotto l'impressione di un pericolo che pareva coinvolgere tutta la latinità. Ma non possiamo non comprendere l'atteggiamento culturale di chi viveva sulle sponde più esposte all'attacco dei nemici della romanità. Altrove la polemica antimusulmana poteva smorzarsi in un confronto scientifico sui metodi di tradurre Aristotele, o dileguarsi in un'ambigua spiegazione del pericolo turco come uno dei flagelli divini, o trovare un correttivo nella necessità di non interrompere i rapporti commerciali e favorire con i pellegrinaggi il flusso mercantile. Nel Salento l'immagine dell'Oriente era quella che ancora nel secolo XVII faceva rappresentare la vittoria cristiana, davanti al portale di Santa Croce, con i Turchi al posto dei mostri delle chiese romaniche.

Come non collegare questa sensibilità nutrita anche da episodi drammatici come quello della caduta di Otranto in mano dei Turchi con la difesa della lingua latina e della sua tradizione più pura, in una linea che va da un medico che assorbe, riempiendola di contenuti ideologici, la lezione di Ermolao Barbaro (mi riferisco ad Antonio Galateo) ad un grammatico che trasforma in metodo scolastico e in funzione ecumenica la lezione dell'Amaseo (mi riferisco a Quinto Mario Corrado)? E come non collegare l'esperienza della sconfitta cristiana sul fronte orientale con il disagio che trapela nelle ambiguità e nelle contraddizioni dei due letterati salentini, ai quali si rifà direttamente un bizzarro personaggio quale Bernardino Bonifacio, che finisce i suoi giorni e il suo patrimonio girando per l'Europa con l'identità duplice di riformatore e di libertino?

Abbiamo così scandito tre generazioni che costituiscono l'asse principale dell'Umanesimo nel Salento. Una successione cronologica e generazionale che assume quasi il significato simbolico di una trasformazione nella continuità (è il tema del nostro Convegno) dell'adesione alla rinascita del latino, sulle linee del fenomeno europeo. Dalla riconquista della lingua latina e dei valori etici dell'antico, alla meditazione sulla funzione moderna dei testi antichi e sulla integrazione fra romanità e cristianesimo; dalla battaglia contro la barbarie alla riflessione sulla residua o riaffiorante barbarie interna alla latinità cristiana, o meglio alla cristianità latina. Infine dal recupero dell'etica e della politica classica all'utopia di una rinnovata società cristiana. Gli studi neo-latini dovrebbero ricostruire attorno a queste ormai note figure eccellenti il contesto culturale in cui si collocano, come verifica dell'ipotesi storiografica che si è andata delineando in questi ultimi decenni.

Questi umanisti autentici si confrontano con i temi più vivi, non importa ora con quale esito, presenti nell'opera di Erasmo, il punto di riferimento più certo dell'Umanesimo dopo la crisi dei centri tradizionali italiani. Si può dire (ed il compito di un approfondimento spetta appunto a questi studi che si auspicano) che in questo itinerario non compare la filologia, che sembra aliena dall'orizzonte culturale pugliese e in genere del Mezzogiorno d'Italia dell'età del Rinascimento, se si escludono quelle particolari versioni della filologia che sono, in campi diversi da quello letterario, l'antiquaria da un lato e la giurisprudenza dall'altro.

Non cercheremo ora le ragioni di questa conformazione particolare, se si vuole mutila, degli *studia humanitatis*; ma val la pena di riflettere, mentre si va rinnovando profondamente, su basi paleografiche, lo studio dell'eredità bizantina nel Salento, val la pena di riflettere alla crisi dei rapporti con l'Oriente bizantino che ha investito questa regione proprio durante l'età umanistica che segna invece in altri centri italiani l'acquisizione della dimensione filologica degli studi letterari attraverso l'apporto dei dotti venuti dall'Oriente.

L'Umanesimo insomma assumeva nel Salento una sua identità, e mediante questa sua identità svolgeva la sua funzione al di là dei limiti della scrittura latina. Anche la fortuna del Tasso passava attraverso quel particolare umanesimo e diventava recupero delle ascendenze normanne e delle glorie autoctone nel poema epico intitolato a *Tancredi* da Ascanio Grandi. Il più illustre poeta del Seicento leccese, sepolto presso il monastero degli Olivetani di Lecce, ci rammenta l'ultima dimora napoletana del Tasso e il culmine del suo poema, il monte Oliveto. E il Tasso rappresenta con la sua epopea della riconquista la trasposizione, in termini epici e religiosi, di un tema centrale della cultura umanistica, quale la *instauratio*.

Università di Bari

Plenary Papers

Jean Pic de la Mirandole
et son influence au nord des Alpes (1498–1560)*

GERMAIN MARC'HADOUR

L'an de grâce 1494 fut pour l'Italie une année de disgrâce, un *annus horribilis*. Selon l'historien Guichardin, l'invasion française déclencha une longue période de calamité en tous domaines, entre autres ce mal hideux autant que nouveau: la syphilis, et en 1527 les brutalités impies du Sac de Rome.[1] A Florence, fleuron de la péninsule, Angelo Poliziano mourut le 24 septembre 1494, trois jours après le sermon de Savonarole prophétisant l'arrivée du nouveau Cyrus, Charles VIII, qui punirait et purgerait la société corrompue. Politien avait 40 ans; c'est à 31 ans que s'éteignit son ami Giovanni Pico,[2] le 17 novembre, jour même où "le Roi Très-Chrétien" faisait son entrée triomphale dans Florence, acclamé par une population que l'usure du pouvoir médicéen avait rendue avide de changement.

Charles VIII devait se tuer bêtement, moins de cinq ans plus tard, plus jeune encore que Pic, et le chagrin de cette mort poussa le vieux Robert Gaguin à se plonger dans les *Opera Ioannis Pici,* ou peut-être dans les *Epistolae Aureae* souvent publiées séparément:[3] une de ces lettres lui parut si belle qu'il en réalisa et publia une traduction française. Ce sera un des morceaux sur lesquels je m'arrêterai au cours d'un survol qui se veut sélectif et plutôt comparatif qu'exhaustif.

Vous l'aurez deviné, ce qui m'attira personnellement vers Pic est le fait que

---

* Parmi les experts que j'ai consultés, je remercie spécialement Paul Oskar Kristeller, Robert Walter, et Louis Valcke, ainsi que Marc Laureys, rencontré au Congrès de Bari alors qu'il s'apprêtait à parler de Pic à la Mirandole.

[1] Francesco Guicciardini dans *Historia d'Italia*. Paradoxalement, le mythe de l'âge d'or faisait florès: on a souvent cité les *Saturnia regna* que Gilles de Viterbe salue dans une lettre à Ficin, et l'*Oraculum de novo saeculo* prononcé à Florence par Giovanni Nesi à la gloire de Savonarole le 1er septembre 1486, et imprimé le 8 mai 1497.

[2] Les noms des deux amis sont fréquemment associés dans la littérature des décennies suivantes, et l'on souligne presque toujours leur jeunesse.

[3] Le titre est d'ordinaire suivi des mots *piae non minus quam elegantes,* les deux critères favoris des pédagogues.

Thomas More inaugura sa carrière d'écrivain anglais par *The Life of John Picus*. Imprimé à une date que les experts ne parviennent pas à fixer, cet opuscule commence par une lettre de More le dédiant à Joyeuse Lee, jeune clarisse dont la famille appartenait à la même paroisse que lui. La "Vie" est une traduction fort libre de la *Vita Ioannis Pici* par laquelle Gianfrancesco Pico avait préfacé les *Oeuvres* de son oncle. More n'en signale pas l'auteur, peut-être en raison des libertés qu'il prend avec le texte.[4]

L'anthologie qui occupe la moitié de l'ouvrage appartient principalement à la littérature édifiante. Elle inclut trois lettres de direction spirituelle; le commentaire du psaume 15: *Conserva me, Domine*; une série de 36 avis groupés en "dodécalogues";[5] enfin une *elegia deprecatoria ad Deum*, souvent publiée avec les épîtres choisies. Mû par un sûr instinct didactique, Pic a condensé son art de vivre chrétiennement en 'capsules' d'ingestion commode: les douze règles du combat spirituel, les douze armes de ce combat, et les douze propriétés de l'amour vrai, autrement dit une stratégie, une panoplie, et une psychologie. More en tire 61 strophes de sept vers, 427 vers en tout. D'une ligne il traduit chaque arme avant de la versifier. Certaines expriment des lieux communs, ce qui ne les discrédite nullement à ses yeux. "*Vita somnus et umbra*: This life a dream and a shadow" (arme 4). "*Mors instans et improvisa*: The death at our hand and unware" (arme 5). La huitième, "The nature and dignity of man," reprend la thèse majeure de l'*Oratio de Homine*. More la développe avec ces apostrophes qu'il affectionne, et dont une au moins semble sortir d'un sermon de Noël de Saint Léon: "Regard, o man, thine excellent nature!" (CW1, 112/3). More traite chaque "condition ou propriété" de l'amant en deux strophes: la première applique à l'amour humain un des douze traits relevés par Pic; la seconde en tire un corollaire pour l'amour entre Dieu et l'homme. L'amoureux est jaloux, Dieu ne l'est pas moins: "Il ne veut pas une part, mais tout ou rien: part will he none, but either all or nought" (CW1, 114/16).

Ecrivant pour un public peu cultivé, More fournit un minimum d'explications. Il préface chacune des trois lettres et présente, non pas Marthe et Marie, symboles familiers à des lecteurs nourris des mystiques anglais et rhénans, mais Circé l'enchanteresse. "La voie molle et spatieuse" est, précise-t-il, celle qui, "selon le Christ dans l'évangile, mène à l'enfer—that leadeth to hell."[6]

---

[4] Les omissions, nombreuses et parfois substantielles, portent notamment sur le "pedigree" du héros, sur les sources ésotériques de son érudition et sur les aspects sociaux de sa carrière. La première addition, *de vera nobilitate*, montre que l'attrait exercé par le jeune Comte est dû à sa vertu, non à ses ancêtres. Le texte entier de *Ioannis Pici Vita* est reproduit en appendice à "The Life of John Picus," ed. Clarence H. Miller, *Complete Works of St. Thomas More*, vol. 1 (New Haven: Yale Univ. Press, 1997). Je renvoie, dans cet article, à cette édition sous le sigle CW1, en indiquant la page et la ligne.

[5] Terme emprunté à J. B. Trapp, qui consacre des pages brillantes à Pic dans *Erasmus, Colet and More* (London: The British Library, 1991), 123–136.

[6] On reconnaît Mat 7.13 et plus encore Luc 13.24. Un peu plus tard, préfaçant sa traduction de Lucien de Samosate, More dira *"arcta illa atque angusta via quae ducit ad vitam"* (CW3, Part I, 4/5): *illa* souligne que ce chemin était proverbial en chrétienté, en opposition à "the voluptuous

Dans les *Opera* de son oncle, Gianfrancesco a inclus une lettre où Ficin résume pour Germain de Ganay les trois projets de Pic: concilier Aristote et Platon, rêve déjà de Boèce et du Cusain; commenter les Saintes Ecritures; réfuter les astrologues. Au second projet on doit le psaume *Conserva me*: More l'a retenu pour son florilège. Il cite en latin tout ce qui provient de la Vulgate: cette source majeure de Pic est familière à toute la chrétienté de l'époque; et il n'est pas besoin d'être clerc pour en comprendre les phrases essentielles, par exemple *Deus meus es tu*, que More, suivant son modèle, rencontre à six reprises, et traduit à chaque fois par "My God art thou."[7] Citant la Bible de mémoire, Pic la modifie parfois inconsciemment: ainsi l'*Oportet oboedire Deo* de S. Pierre devient *Oportet placere Deo*; bien loin de corriger ce libellé, More l'enregistre et le répétera sous sa propre responsabilité.[8]

Dans l'*Apologia*, dédiée à Laurent de Médicis, Pic cite beaucoup les Pères de l'Eglise, mais aussi les scolastiques, et surtout Saint Thomas d'Aquin. Dans le *De ente et uno*, il va plus loin, puisqu'à Politien, le poète et rhéteur, il dit *Thomas tuus*, "ton cher Thomas." More après Fisher, défendant le Docteur Angélique contre le mépris de Luther et de Tyndale, rappellera le consensus des doctes vénérant en lui "le fleuron de la théologie."[9]

Que la pensée de Pic ait coloré l'*Utopie* de More est hors de doute. Le narrateur, Raphaël Hythlodée, a lui aussi donné tout son patrimoine à un sien neveu; pour être libre, il a renoncé au mariage comme au service de la chose publique. Cette option a pu tenter le jeune traducteur de Pic avant qu'il ne choisisse les servitudes et les risques de l'engagement. Le chapitre 8 de l'*Apologia* a pour thèse que "l'acte de croire est un acte libre: *Actus credendi est actus liber*"; le roi Utopus est d'accord, et a décrété que nul ne serait forcé d'épouser la religion dominante.[10]

L'*Adversus astrologos* n'a pu que nourrir la haine de More envers ce pseudo-savoir ou 'art' qui ôte à l'homme le sens de sa responsabilité morale. Lorsqu'en 1503 mourut, âgée de 37 ans, la reine Elizabeth, à qui l'astrologue de Henry VII avait promis qu'elle dépasserait sa 80e année, More composa une *Lamentation* dans laquelle la défunte gémit: "O false astrology and divinatrice!" Ces termes décalquent ceux de Pic, popularisés à partir de 1495 par le court traité où Savonarole condense les douze livres de son jeune dirigé.[11]

---

broad way that leadeth to hell" (CW1, 65/23). Dans une prière autographe de ses dernières années, More demande la grâce "to walk the narrow way that leadeth to life" (CW13 226/28).

[7] CW1, 96/3–24. Nous retrouverons plus loin ce souci morien de conserver l'ordre des mots latins lorsque la structure de l'anglais le permet.

[8] Actes 5.29, "We must rather please God than men" (CW1, 81/16) se retrouve presque inchangé (man au lieu de men) en 1532 dans la Préface à *The Confutation* (CW8, 32/35).

[9] "*Theologiae florem passim appellarunt*," écrit John Fisher dans *Defensio regiae assertionis* (Cologne: Quentell, 1525), f. XVIIIv, parlant de Pic et autres doctes.

[10] L'*Utopie*, édition bilingue d'André Prévost (Paris: Mame, 1978), 595; remarquer l'emploi de l'expression *humanae naturae dignitate* (p. 596). Dominic Baker-Smith consacre deux pages à dresser un bilan de cette influence dans *More's Utopia* (London: HarperCollins, 1991), 219–220. José V. de Pina Martins a souligné plus d'une fois l'air de famille qui fait de Hythlodée un proche cousin de Pic.

[11] L'épouse de Henry VII mourut en couches le 11 février 1503, quelques semaines après la

Succès des œuvres morales et spirituelles

La motivation profonde des premiers diffuseurs est on ne peut plus clairement exprimée par le prêtre alsacien Jacob Wimpfeling dans sa Préface à l'édition strabourgeoise des *Opera Pici* (J. Prüss, mars 1504). Lisons plutôt:

> Gaude, candidissime lector, habere te in manibus opera Pici iucunda lectu et utilia tum tibi ipsi, tum rei publicae christianae, in quibus accendi poteris ad amorem omnis philosophiae et divinarum litterarum lectionem, quandoquidem illustris comitis filius nobilitate insignis, viribus corporis elegans, facie ornamentissimus a teneris annis eis artibus inservivit, quae Dei naturam, animae immortalitatem, futurae vitae certitudinem bonorumque morum affectum docent. Solae Pici epistolae sanctissimis sententiarum floribus respersae aurum aequant et argentum. Adde quod *duodecim in astrologos libri* sacris litteris maximisque theologis innixi magno pretio aestimari digni sunt.[12]

Je paraphrase: ces œuvres sont "agréables à lire et utiles," les deux qualités ensemble font la perfection; elles conduisent à aimer tout savoir, et à lire les "lettres divines," c'est à dire l'Ecriture; noble, beau de corps et surtout de visage, leur auteur "s'est appliqué dès ses tendres années aux lettres qui enseignent la nature de Dieu, l'immortalité de l'âme, la certitude de la vie future et le souci des bonnes mœurs." Les épîtres de Pic ainsi que ses douze livres contre les astrologues constituent un double pactole.

Wimpfeling ne signale pas ici les "Douze armes du combat spirituel": point n'en est besoin, puisqu'il les a déjà reproduites, sans commentaire, dans *Adolescentia* (Strasbourg, 1500), manuel scolaire fréquemment réédité, avec révisions, jusqu'en 1515. Une phrase en exprime l'intention: *cum peccandi libido hominem invasit.* En 1507, Johannes Murmellius les reprend dans ses *Elegiae morales*; le livre 3, intitulé "De duodecim spiritualis pugnae armis," déploie chacune des armes en une élégie, que le poète adresse à ses amis de Münster.[13] Cette amplification poétique est, à très peu près, contemporaine de celle de More.

---

prognostication de Noël 1502, où l'astrologue William Parron, attaché à la cour, lui promettait d'atteindre 80 ans. Dans *A Rueful Lamentation,* la défunte flétrit l'impiété des faux-savants qui prétendent connaître "les secrets de Dieu" (CW1, 10/23–29). Dans les épigrammes latines de More, oeuvre de jeunesse pour la plupart, non moins de onze ont les astrologues pour cible, voir *Latin Poems,* CW3, Part II, épig. n° 60sq. Le commentaire (p. 349) cite un *De astrorum vi fatali* de Parron (1499), attaquant l'*Adversus astrologos.* Une minorité d'experts fit bon accueil à la thèse de Pic, entre autres Simon de Phares, qui dédia à Charles VIII (mort en avril 1498) un *Elucidaire* où il salue "ce noble Comte Picus . . . , qui a esté tenu pour le plus grand clerc de la terre" (Dorez-Thuasne, p. 179). L'opuscule vulgarisateur de Savonarole, publié d'abord en toscan, avait paru dès 1495 en traduction latine.

[12] C'est le n° 156 de la correspondance—*Briefwechsel*—de Wimpfeling, éd. par Otto Herding et Dieter Mertens (Fink, 1990), 455–456. La meilleure biographie de l'éducateur alsacien demeure, je crois, *Jakob Wimpfeling* (1450–1528), de Joseph Knepper (Fribourg-en-Brisgau: Herder, 1902).

[13] Cité par Marc Laureys, dans sa communication d'octobre 1994 au Congrès de La Mirandola, "The Reception of Giovanni Pico in the Low Countries."

Les épîtres au neveu

S'il ne nomme pas Gianfrancesco en tant que biographe, More le présente comme destinataire de deux lettres sur les trois qu'il a sélectionnées. La première, "the first epistle of Picus unto his nephew John Francis," est privilégiée par sa position dans les *Opera*, ce qui contribua sans aucun doute à sa fortune. Avant More, Robert Gaguin la traduisit pour son réconfort personnel et la publia en avril 1498 sous le titre de *Conseil profitable contre les ennuys et tribulations du monde*.[14] Voici en quels termes il la présente:

> S'ensuit une épistole moult pleine de saincte et salutaire doctrine pour bien vivre selon Dieu, envoyée par un moult grand philosophe et bon théologien nommé Picus Mirandula, comte de Concorde, à son neveu François Mirandula, auquel ledit Picus avoit délaissé sa Comté et seigneurie terrienne, et se estoit de tout donné aux lettres et doctrines pour vaquer en icelles sans occupation et empeschement de choses mondaines et corruptibles.

Hommage touchant si l'on songe que Pic n'avait pas trente ans lorsqu'il signa cette épître, et que son traducteur en a 65, qu'il est doyen de la Faculté de Décret à l'Université de Paris et Général de son Ordre, les Trinitaires; qu'il a été en mission diplomatique auprès des grands d'Europe, en Italie, en Angleterre, en Allemagne; qu'il jouit d'un grand prestige comme historien et comme prédicateur. Indépendamment de Gaguin, je suppose, son cadet Wimpfeling, né en 1450 (Gaguin en 1433), réalisa et fit imprimer à Strasbourg, en mai 1509, une traduction allemande de cette épître du 15 mai 1492, sous le titre:

> Ein Sendtbrief des wohlgeborenen Grafen Ioannis Pici von Mirandel zu seinem Vettern, ihn zu ermahnen zu christenlichem Leben und zu Lehre der heiligen Geschrift.

Faut-il traduire? "Lettre du noble comte Jean Pic de la Mirandole à son neveu [comme l'est *cousin* en Tudor English, *nepos* est un terme élastique] pour l'engager à vivre en chrétien et à étudier l'Ecriture Sainte." Le prêtre alsacien insiste sur le fait que Pic est "bien né" (wohlgeboren) car c'est sur la noblesse qu'il compte pour réformer la société en abandonnant la chasse pour l'étude. Le conseil d'étudier la Bible, qu'il monte en épingle, n'occupe dans l'épître que ces quelques lignes:

> Nihil Deo gratius, nihil tibi utilius facere potes, quam si non cessaueris litteras sacras nocturna versare manu, versare diurna. Latet enim in illis caelestis uis quaedam uiua & efficax quae legentis animum, si modo illas pure humiliterque tractauerit, in diuinum amorem mirabili quadam potestate transformat (CW1, 348/4–9).

Ce que Pic prêche ici, il le vit, à en juger par ses innombrables emprunts aux deux testaments. Et puisque More fait preuve d'une non moins étonnante familiarité avec

---

[14] *Roberti Gaguini Epistolae et Orationes*, éd. Louis Thuasne (Paris: Bouillon, 1903), 136–137.

la Bible,[15] on peut imaginer qu'au seuil de sa vie professionnelle, très séculière, il prit à cœur cet appel pressant d'un autre laïc. Voici comment il le traduit:

> Thou mayst do nothing more pleasant to God, nothing more profitable to thyself, than if thine hand cease not day nor night to turn and read the volumes of Holy Scripture. There lieth privily in them a certain heavenly strength, quick and effectual, which with a marvellous power transformeth and changeth the reader's mind into the love of God, if they be clean and lowly entreated (CW1, 84/3–9).

Le jeune traducteur fait à son modèle le compliment d'une fidélité minutieuse: *privily*, "secrètement," explicite la connotation de *latet*; *transformeth, entreated, effectual* décalquent *transformat, tractauerit et efficax*. Quant aux doublets "turn and read," "transformeth and changeth," ils représentent l'abondance orale qui caractérise les traducteurs anglais de l'ère Tudor.

Les règles du combat spirituel

Si chaque arme du combat spirituel, comme chaque propriété de l'amant vrai, tient dans une ligne, il en va autrement des règles, dont l'expression occupe au moins trois lignes, et jusqu'à une page pour la quatrième. Le titre *Duodecim regulae partim excitantes partim dirigentes homines in spirituali pugna* est fidèlement rendu par More: "Twelve rules of John Picus, Earl of Mirandula, partly exciting partly directing a man in spiritual battle." Mais puisqu'il amplifie les règles en strophes, More s'écarte forcément du mot à mot. La dixième règle, par sa longueur comme par son inspiration à la fois biblique et classique, constituera un bon spécimen:

> Decima regula: ut in tentationibus semper in principio occurras & allidas paruulos Babylonis ad petram (*petra autem est Christus*), quia sero medicina paratur (CW1, 374/19–21).

Les contraintes du vers expliquent sans doute que More ait renoncé à l'écho de Saint Paul dans les mots soulignés.[16] "Les petits enfants de Babylone," à la fin du psaume 137 (136 selon la numérotation de la Vulgate), sont par l'exégèse traditionnelle (depuis au moins Origène) interprétés comme les semences d'iniquité au cœur de l'homme, ou les premières suggestions de péché que nous souffle le Tentateur.[17]

---

[15] Voir mon *Thomas More et la Bible* (Paris: Vrin, 1967), et mon répertoire-bilan en 5 tomes intitulé *The Bible in the Works of Thomas More* (Nieuwkoop: B. de Graaf, 1969–1972).

[16] *Petra erat Christus,* selon la Vulgate en 1 Co 10.4, que la tradition exégétique reliera très vite à la *petra* de Ps 136.9. More se souvient peut-être des *regulae* lorsqu'en 1534, dans *History of the Passion*, il exhorte ses lecteurs à fracasser les suggestions du démon contre "the stone, that is our sure strong Savior Christ" (CW13, 10/33).

[17] Erasme, employant cette même interprétation dans le canon 9 de son *Enchiridion* (1503), est très probablement influencé par la règle 10 de Pic, mais tous deux ont pu la trouver dans Origène ou Saint Jérôme, voir la note d'André Godin recensant l'*Enchiridion* (éd. Festugière), dans *Moreana* n° 34 (mai 1972): 89–90, n. 2.

Voici la traduction de More:

> In all temptation withstand the beginning:
> The cursed infants of wretched Babylon,
> To suffer them wax is a jeopardous thing;
> Beat out their braines therefore at the Stone:
> Perilous is the canker that catcheth the bone.
> Too late cometh the medicine if thou let the sore
> By long continuance increase more and more
>
> (CW1, 107/21–28).

La version d'Elyot en facilitera la lecture pour qui n'est pas habitué à la prosodie anglaise:

> In all temptations resist the beginning, and beat the children of Babylon against the Stone, which Stone is Christ, and the children be evil thoughts and imaginations. For in long continuing of sin, seldom worketh medicine or remedy.[18]

On le voit, Elyot conserve les mots importants identifiant la Pierre avec le Christ. Il explicite l'allégorie: "les enfants sont les mauvaises pensées et imaginations." More, en revanche, développe la métaphore médicale qui lui est chère:[19] "Périlleux est le chancre qui atteint l'os, etc." Elyot a connu la traduction de More, dont il était l'ami et le collègue dans le service du roi. Issu, comme More, de la bourgeoisie dévote qui fréquentait les couvents, il dédia le "petit traité" de Pic, en juillet 1534, à une de ses parentes qui, veuve, s'est consacrée à Dieu. Les lignes introductoires méritent d'être citées:

> I have added hereto a little treatise but wonderful fruitful, made by the virtuous and noble prince John Picus, Earl of Mirandula, who in abundance of learning and grace incomparably excelled all other in his time and since, whose picture I would to God were in all noble men's chambers, and his grace and virtues in their souls and manners.

S'agissant de Pic, les mots "virtuous," "noble," et "learning" sont inévitables. Reste la "grâce," qui me paraît se référer non au style, mais à l'âme de Pic: en savoir et en grâce, il n'a pas eu d'égal "en son temps et depuis," un depuis qui inclut Erasme et More. Elyot souhaite voir le portrait de ce héros dans les chambres de tous les nobles, sa grâce et ses vertus dans leur âme et leurs mœurs: c'est pousser l'éloge beaucoup plus loin que ne le fait More.

La prose d'Elyot s'est voulue à la fois fidèle et accessible. La structure prosodique a autorisé More à employer une langue proche encore du 15ᵉ siècle, et non exempte d'archaïsmes: *I wis* (st. 2), *threst* (st. 6), *eke* au sens de "aussi" (st. 13), etc. Les 22

---

[18] J. M. Rigg a reproduit "The Rules of a Christian Life" à la note 40 de son *Thomas More: Giovanni Pico* (London: David Nutt, 1850), 89–93. Notre extrait se trouve à la p. 92.

[19] Voir mon article "Thomas More et la médecine," *Pellis* n° 13 (août 1991): 28–38.

strophes de More eurent en fait moins de succès que les deux ou trois pages d'Elyot, reproduites jusqu'en 1585, y compris dans la ville de Rouen à l'usage des "récusants," ces catholiques anglais réfugiés sur le Continent pour échapper à l'Uniformité anglicane.[20] Elyot, humaniste consommé, s'est également inspiré de Pic dans son *Book of the Governor* (1531), une sorte de vademecum pour les membres du gouvernement.

La France s'intéressa plus tard au *tractatulus* de Pic. En 1570, Fédéric Morel l'Aîné (1523–1583) publia *Les douze reigles de M. Jean Pic de la Mirandole, comprenant en brief les choses plus requises pour vivre chrestiennement* (Rouault, p. 38). Le juriste lyonnais Jean de Coras préfaça en 1559 une traduction de l'entière trilogie pichienne, qu'il dédia à sa fille. Voici comme spécimen la première phrase de la dixième règle: "Il est besoin d'obvier du commencement, et froisser les enfants de Babylone à la pierre. ..."[21]

Elegia deprecatoria ad Deum

Les *Opera Pici* ne contiennent que deux poèmes; l'un, très mythologique, de 27 distiques, où Pic félicite Florence d'avoir un Jérôme Benivieni, est reproduit par Rigg (XXXIV–XXXV). L'autre consiste en 31 distiques adressés au Dieu de majesté, un et trine, qui, par l'incarnation et la passion du Christ, a révélé qu'il est Père encore plus que Seigneur. Cette *deprecatoria* a souvent été incluse dans les morceaux choisis de Pic. Sa qualité, n'en déplaise à Rigg, n'a pas impressionné le seul Thomas More, puisque au moins trois écrivains de la génération suivante l'ont traduite en vers, soit français, soit grecs. Louis des Masures (1510–1580), en latin Ludovicus Masurius, publia à Lyon, en 1557, la "Prière à Dieu, prise du latin de Jean Picus." La version de Joachim du Bellay parut en 1561, l'année d'après sa mort, sous le titre de "Hymne Chrestien," sans indication de source. On l'imagine réalisée durant la période où l'Angevin, malade, sent approcher sa mort prématurée. Avec 62 alexandrins, c'est lui qui serre de plus près le texte latin. Les quatre derniers vers permettront de comparer nos traducteurs:

Picus: Vt cum mortalis perfunctus munere uitae
          Ductus erit Dominum spiritus ante suum,
          Promissi regni felici sorte potitus
          Non Dominum, sed te sentiat esse Patrem.

More: That when the journey of this deadly life
          My sely ghost hath finishèd, and thence

---

[20] L'initiative en revint à Robert Parsons, S.J., cheville ouvrière de mainte édition clandestine. Les "12 rules" y jouxtent l'*Epistola aurea* de Saint Bernard et l'*Imitatio Christi* traduites par Richard Whitford, ce Gallois de Londres qu'Erasme et More connurent comme précepteur du jeune Mountjoy. En 1872, Wilfrid Raynal, O.S.B., a également reproduit *The Rules of a Christian Life* en appendice à l'*Imitation*; il croit citer More, mais il cite Elyot (London: Richardson, 1872), 405–413.

[21] Jean de Coras (1513–1572) ne mentionne que les "douze règles" après le titre d'un ouvrage dont la première partie, la plus copieuse, est *Discours des parties et office d'un bon et entier juge* (Lyon: Vincent, 1565, et autres éditions: j'ai consulté celle de 1605). Il adresse la seconde partie "à Jeanne de Coras ma fille pour engraver soigneusement dans son coeur."

Departen must, without his fleshly wife,
Alone into his Lordès high presènce,
He may thee find, O well of indulgènce,
In thy lordship not as a Lord, but rather
As a very tender loving Father.

Du Bellay: Afin qu'ayant parfait le cours de notre vie,
Lorsque devant son Roy l'âme sera ravie,
De son partage heureux jouissant avec toi,
Tu lui sois comme Père, et non pas comme Roi.

Des Masures: A celle fin qu'estant fini le cours
De cette vie, à l'heure terminée,
Quand au partir l'âme sera menée
Devant son Dieu, son Juge, et son recours,
Là sus, alors, par un sort plus heureux,
Vivante au règne éternel et prospère,
Elle te sente amiable et bon Père,
Non Seigneur rude, ou Juge rigoureux.

Dans les sept vers de More, j'ai marqué d'un accent les voyelles, aujourd'hui muettes, qui sont essentielles au rythme ou à la rime. Noter que l'oxymoron *mortalis uitae* subsiste dans "deadly life." L'épithète *sely* est devenue *silly*, qui en anglais moderne dénote la sottise. Chez More elle reste proche du *selig* initial, qui signifie "béat, bienheureux"—évolution sémantique parallèle à celle de *benêt*, venant de *benedictus*, et désignant d'abord la sottise de l'innocent (qui a la chance de ne pouvoir pécher) et à celle de *crétin*, venant de *chrétien*, et postulant l'indulgence fraternelle pour le handicapé mental qui, de par son baptême, est membre à part entière de la Chrétienté. L'âme du purgatoire est bienheureuse d'être assurée du paradis, mais exposée nue aux regards du Juge, comme l'*animula nudula* de l'empereur romain, sans cette "épouse charnelle: fleshly wife" qu'est le corps dans l'anthropologie platonicienne; *sely* qualifiait habituellement les *silly* souls de "l'Eglise souffrante," sécures mais prisonnières, dont More en 1529 fera entendre la voix dans *La Supplique des Ames.*[22] L'amplification qui, des 31 distiques, a fait 84 pentamètres anglais (douze strophes de sept vers) culmine dans le vers final, correspondant au seul mot de *Patrem*: "very" dans l'anglais de More n'est pas adverbe d'intensité, mais adjectif signifiant "véritable"; "tender loving" peut s'interpréter comme "tendrement aimant." Trente ans plus tard, écrivant à ses enfants depuis la Tour de Londres, More reprend ces mots pour se dire, au moins trois fois, "Your tender loving father."[23]

Chez du Bellay, "Roi" pour *Dominus* reflète bien la réalité de la "seigneurie" dans la France de Henry II, et "âme" pour *spiritus* est le français usuel quand on prie pour

---

[22] L'épithète de nature se présente dès la phrase initiale de *The Supplication of Souls*: "poor prisoners of Good, the sely souls in purgatory" (CW7, 111/6).

[23] *The Correspondence of Sir Thomas More,* ed. Elizabeth F. Rogers (Princeton: Princeton Univ. Press, 1947), lettre 507/8; 509/50; 559/150.

les défunts. Une variante du dernier vers, "Tu lui sois bénin Père, et non sévère Roy," est plus riche, mais s'écarte davantage de l'original.

Louis des Masures, protégé du Cardinal Jean du Bellay, était ami de Joachim. Il devint pasteur calviniste, ce qui pourrait éclairer son double emploi de "Juge" ici. Il demeure présent dans nos lettres françaises par ses *Tragédies saintes,* notamment la trilogie "David Combattant, David Triomphant, David Fugitif," qui a connu plus d'une réédition au 20ᵉ siècle.[24] Notre extrait de huit vers, doublant la longueur de l'original, représente. assez bien l'ensemble de sa traduction, qui frise parfois la paraphrase.

A des Masures, Joachim avait dédié le sonnet 148 des *Regrets*: est-ce pour ne pas sembler donner l'impression de rivaliser avec lui qu'il laissa inédite sa propre version, plus pieusement fidèle à Pic? Il connaissait l'œuvre latine de More, ainsi que les épitaphes pleurant son martyre, celles notamment de Janus Secundus. Mais, bien que le Cardinal du Bellay eût commencé sa carrière diplomatique à Londres du vivant de More (1527–1534), il est peu probable qu'il ait lu quoi que ce soit en anglais. C'est à Pic lui-même que le poète est relié par Sylvie Mirandola, arrière-petite-nièce de Giovanni Pico, devenue Mᵐᵉ de La Rochefoucauld, et dont l'arrière-petit-fils sera l'auteur des *Maximes.* Quand elle meurt, en septembre 1557, du Bellay lui consacre quatre épitaphes, une en français, trois en latin—où l'illustre Comte est évoqué avec ferveur. La défunte est la réplique féminine de Giovanni Pico:

> La vertu, le sçavoir, la jeunesse et la grâce,
> Et la merveille encor' du surnom de ta race.

Plus visiblement que *merveille* ici, un *miratur* du latin joue sur *Mirandola*; l'univers *admire* les *immensa monumenta laboris* de "ce divin Picus,"

> Duquel, comme Italie et tout le monde encore
> Les immortels labeurs lit, apprend et adore.[25]

A la même famille appartient le Cardinal de La Rochefoucauld, ce qui explique la plaquette luxueuse imprimée par Claude Morel en 1620, et contenant, outre des vers de Marc-Antoine Muret, une traduction, en 31 distiques grecs, de l'*Elegia deprecatoria par Fédéric Morel II* (1558–1630), *protodidaskalos* royal, c'est-à-dire au Collège de France. Cette *paraphrasis metrica* fait face au texte latin, et s'intitule *Ioannou Pikou . . . hè pros Theon euchè*: noter l'article *hè,* c'est "la" prière bien connue.[26] Un sizain latin

---

[24] Ces pièces furent éditées à Genève, Anvers et Paris, au moins sept fois en trente ans (1566–1595). David est le héros le plus aimé de toute l'Histoire Sainte, et avec sa fronde il représente le petit troupeau réformé affrontant le Goliath et le Saül que sont le pape et le roi de France.

[25] Joachim du Bellay, *Oeuvres Poétiques,* tome V, éd. Henri Chamard (Paris, 1923), 341, pour le français; tome VII, éd. Geneviève Demerson (Paris, 1984), 173, pour le latin.

[26] Rouault reproduit le texte intégral, p. 47–48. J'ai obtenu, en montrant patte blanche, de consulter un exemplaire de l'original à la Bodleian Library. Un sizain final honore, en même temps que Pic, le Cardinal Franciscus Augustus Rupifucaldius: on reconnaît la famille La Rochefoucauld, dans laquelle sont entrées, par mariage, deux soeurs Mirandola, demoiselles d'honneur de la reine Catherine de Médicis.

ajoute que désormais on entendra le philosophe prier Dieu *utraque lingua*.

Des lecteurs prévenus ont cru déceler dans ce poème des accents de Lucrèce, à qui Pico emprunte des ornements tels que *flammantia moenia mundi*. More a sagement amorti ces échos, et plutôt amplifié l'évocation de Jésus Sauveur, "avec l'eau et le sang qui ruissellent des plaies grand-ouvertes dans ton flanc béni" (st. 9). Vraie prière chrétienne, donc, et qu'on retrouve copiée, avant 1551, par un curé de campagne, au nord de l'Angleterre, qui s'adapte non sans peine à sa nouvelle identité de pasteur anglican.[27]

Sed vide, mi Angele ...

Si More n'a traduit aucune page philosophique de Giovanni Pico, il a rencontré dans sa *Vita* la seule phrase empruntée par le biographe aux *Opera* de son oncle. Cette exclamation lyrique, rompant la trame austère du traité *De ente et uno,* a été mille fois citée,[28] ce qui me paraît une invitation à la reproduire ici; ce sera un hommage aussi à Politien en cette année de son Cincentenaire car c'est vers lui, dédicataire de l'ouvrage, que l'auteur se tourne pour s'écrier:

"Sed vide, mi Angele, quae nos insania teneat! amare Deum dum sumus in corpore plus possumus quam vel eloqui vel cognoscere; amando plus nobis proficimus, minus laboramus, illi magis obsequimur. Malumus tamen semper quaerendo per cognitionem nunquam inuenire quod quaerimus, quam amando possidere id quod non amando frustra etiam inueniretur." Illud quoque divi Francisci, *Tantum scit homo quantum operatur,* illius in ore frequens fuerat (CW1, 326/11–17).

Chose surprenante, More, qui pourtant aimait Saint François et ses Frères Mineurs, omet la maxime que nous mettons en italique. Mais il traduit l'apostrophe pichienne avec une fidélité exemplaire:

But now behold, o my well-beloved Angel, what madness holdeth us! Love God (while we be in this body) we rather may than either know him, or by speech utter him. In loving him also we more profit ourself, we labor less and serve him more. And yet had we lever alway by knowledge never find that thing that we seek than by love to possede that thing which also without love were in vain found (CW1, 67/19–25).

More respecte l'ordre des mots. Il décalque en *possede* ce *possidere* que Pic emploie aussi dans sa fameuse lettre à Alde Manuce: "*Philosophia veritatem quaerit, theologia*

---

[27] Voir A. S. G. Edwards, "Robert Parkyn's Transcript of More's 'Prayer of Picus Mirandula unto God'," *Moreana* 101–102 (mai 1990): 133–138.

[28] Gianfrancesco l'a sertie en 1516 dans un *De amore divino libri quattuor* qu'il dédie à Léon X, et il l'introduit par ces mots: "Scripsit haec verba sapientissime Io. Picus patruus." L'oeuvre de son oncle qu'il cite le plus souvent est la lettre du 15 mai 1492; il reprend notamment l'exhortation à feuilleter la Bible assidûment, de main diurne et nocturne.

inuenit, religio possidet"[29]—les mêmes verbes qu'ici, et que trop peu de traducteurs s'ingénient à conserver.

Si l'expression est vigoureuse et soignée, si le contexte lui donne une allure dramatique, et si Politien (l'interpellé) nous en apparaît moins profane qu'il ne semble quand on l'aborde sous d'autres angles, la thèse elle-même n'est pas nouvelle. Logeant à la chartreuse de Londres, l'étudiant More avait pu la lire dans *Le Nuage de l'Inconnaissance* (ou *La Nuée du non-savoir*), le fameux *Cloud of Unknowing* d'un auteur anonyme: "Love may reach to God in this life, but not knowing."[30] Colet, après une période d'intense cogitation nourrie par le platonisme florentin et les élucubrations ésotériques de Reuchlin, écrit à Erasme que seuls comptent, en définitive, "l'amour fervent et l'imitation du Christ."[31] Et cette capacité d'imiter le Fils de Dieu, en répondant à son plan d'amour, n'aboutissait à rien de moins qu'une divinisation. En résultait la "dignité de l'homme," déjà chantée dans les psaumes, et devenue leitmotiv de la spiritualité chrétienne; Pic se distingua surtout par l'orchestration poétique qu'il fournit au thème, et en exaltant la liberté qu'avait l'homme de descendre ou de monter sur l'échelle de la création.[32]

Theologus summus?

Quand on lut devant l'Université de Paris, le 28 janvier 1488, le bref pontifical condamnant 13 *Conclusions* de Pico, Robert Gaguin ne cacha pas son mécontentement. La proposition déclarant "plus raisonnable de croire Origène sauvé que de le croire damné" paraissait à presque tous les chrétiens une quasi-évidence: le grand Alexandrin demeurait pour toute l'Eglise latine une noble figure de savoir et de piété. Peut-être est-ce pourquoi cette *quaestio 7a de salute Origenis* eut l'honneur d'occuper durant des mois un des théologiens qui jugèrent Pic par commission d'Innocent VIII: Henri Crouzel présente le fruit de ce labeur dans *Une Controverse sur Origène à la Renaissance: Jean Pic de la Mirandole et Pierre Garcia*.[33] Ce Garcia, déjà évêque durant le procès, sera promu en 1490 au siège de Barcelone, où en mourant (1505) il laissera le souvenir d'un pasteur éclairé et dévoué. Ayant reçu à Paris sa maîtrise en théologie (1478), il est un de ces *magistri nostri* si constamment vilipendés par Erasme et ses

---

[29] Dans la même lettre du 11 février 1490, Pic dit aussi à l'humaniste-éditeur vénitien de se souvenir qu'il n'y a pas de philosophie, ou mieux que "nulle est la philosophie qui nous détournerait de la vérité des mystères: nullam esse philosophiam quae a musteriorum veritate nos auocet." Ce précieux billet, mille fois cité, l'est notamment par J. V. de Pina Martins dans l'*Utopie: catalogue de l'Exposition bibliographique* (Paris: Centre Culturel Portugais, 1977).

[30] "L'amour peut atteindre Dieu en cette vie, mais pas le savoir," feuillet XVI d'un exemplaire manuscrit que j'ai consulté à la chartreuse de Parkminster.

[31] *Opus Epistolarum Des. Erasmi,* ed. P. S. Allen (Oxford: Oxford Univ. Press, 1906–1952), vol. 2, lettre 593, 599/15–21.

[32] More, qui n'a pas jugé bon de traduire l'*Oratio de homine,* en a néanmoins développé un thème dans son prologue à la première épître, à propos de Circé, en insistant moins sur l'ange que sur la bête.

[33] Paris: Vrin, 1977. Dans sa préface, le P. Henri de Lubac y voit "un échantillon parfait, et parfaitement expliqué, de la plus mauvaise théologie de l'époque" (p. 5), propre "à montrer ce que pouvait être, en cette fin du XVe siècle, une scolastique dégénérée" (p. 6).

frères d'armes dans le combat pour régénérer les sciences sacrées. Une idée du chemin parcouru en une génération est fournie par la remarque d'Erasme invoquant en 1522 le plébiscite de la chrétienté en faveur du Mirandolien:

> An non turpissimum est, a magnis olim theologis apud Italos damnatas fuisse Pici Mirandulani conclusiones ut impias et haereticas, quae nunc ut christianae piaeque leguntur ab omnibus, non sine applausu theologorum?

> "N'est-ce pas une honte que de grands théologiens en Italie aient condamné comme impies et hérétiques des conclusions de Pic de la Mirandole qui sont maintenant lues comme chrétiennes et pieuses par tout le monde, non sans l'applaudissement des théologiens?"[34]

La dette d'Erasme, docteur en théologie, envers les *duodecim arma* et les *duodecim regulae* a été souvent démontrée: "en les développant avec une émouvante conviction," écrit Raymond Marcel, il a fait du ch. 7 "un véritable traité à l'intérieur de l'*Enchiridion.*"[35] Dès 1500, dans la préface aux *Adagia*, Erasme dotait Pic d'une *diuina quadam ingenii felicitate*. Il reprendra la même épithète 28 ans plus tard, avec *indolem plane diuinam*, dans le *Ciceronianus*, où la théologie est accusée, en même temps que la philosophie et les langues orientales, d'avoir "quelque peu gâté son style: *dictionem nonnihil vitiauit.*"[36]

Erasme vise naturellement ce *modus parisiensis* que Pic a adopté pour ses traités, et qu'il défend vigoureusement dans une lettre-manifeste adressée à Ermolao Barbaro: Louis Valcke y consacre plus de vingt pages dans un article récent.[37] Johannes Major, Ecossais qui arriva à Paris dès 1493, et publia des ouvrages tout en préparant son doctorat en théologie (passé en 1506), était une sommité de la Sorbonne quand parut son *Commentaire sur le Quart Livre des Sentences* (Paris: Pigouchet, 1509). Il dédie cet in-folio au primat d'Ecosse, Alexander Stewart, jeune prélat de sang royal qui avait eu Erasme pour mentor en Italie. "Maison de marbre," écrit Major, la théologie n'a que faire du badigeon des élégances. Comme toute science, elle revendique le

---

[34] *Erasmi Opera,* ed. J. Clericus (Leyde, 1703 s.), tome VI, dans les pages d'introduction ★★★3r.

[35] "*L'Enchiridion militis Christiani,*" *Colloquia Erasmiana Turonensia* (Paris: Vrin, 1972), 630, après avoir énuméré (p. 629) the *duodecim arma* de Pic. Anne O'Donnell, dans l'édition critique de la première version anglaise de l'*Enchiridion* (1523), détaille les correspondances au fil de son Commentaire, citant in extenso les règles 4, 5, 7, 8, 10, 11 et 12: *Enchiridion Militis Christiani: An English Version* (Oxford: Early English Text Society, 1981), 283–288. Dans Erasme et l'Espagne de Marcel Bataillon, nouvelle édition en 3 vol. (Genève: Droz, 1991), Ivan Pusino relève des parallèles frappants entre l'*Enchiridion* et la première lettre à Jean-François et Silvana Seidel-Menchi note que Pic a devancé Erasme dans l'emploi du topos *Sileni Alcibiadis* (p. 79–80).

[36] "*Quid Ioannem Picum Mirandulae?,*" demande Bulephorus. Et Nosoponus répond: "Indolem plane diuinam narras, ingenium ad omnia factum, sed huius quoque dictionem nonnihil vitiauit linguarum ac philosophiae atque etiam theologiae cura" (ASD I–2, p. 663–664). La forme *Mirandulae* surprend, car, dans le *De conscribendis epistolis,* Erasme estime meilleur latin (*latinius*) l'adjectif *Mirandulanus* (ASD I–2, p. 281).

[37] "Jean Pic et le retour au 'style de Paris': portée d'une critique littéraire," *Rinascimento* 32 (1992): 253–273.

droit d'employer une terminologie propre. On a beau jeu d'appeler nos hommes *barbaros* parce qu'ils négligent les grâces du langage: *"Joannes Picus,* qui ne manque pas d'élégance, n'a pas rougi de les lire, et de les relire à fond, et dans une lettre à Ermolao Barbaro il s'applique à les défendre."[38]

Paris, où le jeune Pic a passé une année scolaire—avant d'y revenir comme prisonnier à Vincennes—lui porte l'affection d'une *alma mater,* mais l'Angleterre se mettra davantage à son école. More, on l'a vu, l'a élu comme maître spirituel, sans doute avec les encouragements de son propre directeur, le Doyen de Saint-Paul's Cathedral, John Colet, docteur en théologie. Robert Weiss, en 1963, inclut Colet dans le "premier sondage" qu'il offre sur "Pic et l'Angleterre"; d'autres ont inventorié la dette multiple de Colet envers l'*Heptaplus* et l'*Apologia.*[39] Moins connue est l'admiration de John Fisher, théologien plus professionnel que le Doyen, et plus équilibré. Remerciant, en 1515, Erasme de lui avoir envoyé le *De arte cabbalistica* de Reuchlin, Fisher ajoute: "L'érudition de cet homme me plaît énormément, car aucun autre, je crois, ne s'approche davantage de Jean Pic."[40] Erasme escompte que Reuchlin, qui est maintenant sexagénaire, sera flatté de recevoir, par cet accessit, la seconde place après le *nec plus ultra* qu'est Pic. A la différence de Colet, Fisher n'exprimera pas de désenchantement à l'égard de la Cabbale, qu'il est sans doute le premier Anglais à exploiter, et cela jusque dans un sermon en langue anglaise.[41]

La *Germania* est richement présente par les éditions des *Opera Pici* à Strasbourg et plus encore à Bâle; de ses *Aureae epistolae* dans plusieurs villes des Pays-Bas; de sa *Deprecatoria* à Vienne (1511 et 1516). Beatus Rhenanus (*Briefwechsel,* rpt. Nieuwkoop, 1966) mentionne trois membres de la famille Pico; il félicite Reuchlin d'être cité, à propos du nom JESUS, en même temps que Pic dans le *Psalterium Quincuplex de Lefèvre d'Etaples* (1509) et parle de l'Heptaplus en 1536. Wimpfeling, dans sa *Vita Geileri* (1510), nous apprend que Johann Geiler parlait de Pic dans ses sermons de Strasbourg, affirmant que "si la nature avait doublé le cours de sa vie, il n'eût guère été inférieur (*vix inferiorem*) à Saint Augustin et à Saint Jérôme sur le terrain des Ecritures." Reuchlin connaissait personnellement et Giovanni et Gianfrancesco: celui-ci reçut un accueil chaleureux en Alsace, où certains de ses écrits parurent en *editio princeps.*

---

[38] Malcolm Sinclair m'a copié la page de dédicace de l'*In Quartum Sententiarum,* et l'excellent article de John Durkan présentant Major (Ian Mair) dans *Innes Review* 1, 2 (Dec. 1950): 131–157.

[39] Voir John Gleason, dans *John Colet* (Berkeley: Berkeley Univ. Press, 1989), 71–84. Colet ne semble avoir rencontré ni Pic, ni Ficin (avec qui il correspondit). Trois autres amis de More: Linacre, Grocyn et Latimer, avaient séjourné à Florence.

[40] Voir n. 11 pour *flos theologiae* appliqué à l'Aquinate; Allen, vol. 2, ép. 324 du 1er mars 1515: "qui vicinius ad Ioannem Picum accesserit, alium extare neminem credam" (p. 49). Fisher fait également appel à Gianfrancesco Pico pour excuser Savonarole (*Defensio,* fol. Vv).

[41] Dans son sermon du 12 mai 1531, défendant la tradition orale contre le scriptura sola de Luther, l'évêque dit: "Our fathers the Jews, of whom we spiritually descended, have their Cabala, which is derived from man to man by mouth only and not by writing," *The Works of John Fisher,* ed. John E. B. Mayor (Oxford: Early English Text Society, 1876), 321. Plus loin il dit, parlant des prophètes, "their Cabala, that is to say their secret eruditions not written in the Bible" (p. 336).

La fortune de Pic aux Pays-Bas inclut une pléiade distinguée, avec Mosellanus, Barlandus, de Schepper, Geldenhouwer, etc., et une étoile de première grandeur: Juan Luis Vives. Notre Espagnol découvrit Pico durant ses études à Paris. Parmi les grands de l'humanisme, lui seul fut pleinement à l'unisson du Mirandolien: le laïc mobilisé dans la cause du Christ, le penseur qui sait écrire mais ne sacrifie jamais le fond à la forme, ni ne rejette les auteurs médiévaux pour l'amour de l'antiquité.

Ces grands noms d'avant la Réforme nous préparent de loin à l'abondante moisson de gros ouvrages où nos contemporains analysent la pensée de Pic, toujours hantée par les mystères qui, tout en relevant de la théologie, "passent l'homme" et lui demeurent inaccessibles sans un *afflatus* surnaturel.

Conclusion

Cette exploration jubilaire m'a fait redécouvrir "le Phénix des génies" tel que l'ont fait sortir de son urne, par des emprunts ou par la traduction, des écrivains aussi variés que Lefèvre d'Etaples, Erasme, Reuchlin, Fisher, More, Gaguin, Wimpfeling, Vives, Elyot, du Bellay, des Masures, Morel père et fils.

L'âge avancé auquel Wimpfeling et surtout Gaguin ont traduit Pic m'a frappé par analogie avec celui du P. de Lubac, qui avait 78 ans quand parut son volumineux *Pic de la Mirandole* (Paris: Aubier-Montaigne, 1974), si vibrant d'admiration, si véhément dans la dénonciation des caricatures, si pichien aussi par l'ampleur des comparaisons, avec Pascal notamment. Dès 1730, un Anglais, Mr. Jessup, publia *The Lives of Picus and Pascal: A Parallel between These Two Christian Worthies* (London: Hooke), qui eut plusieurs éditions. Le parallèle est multiple: deux génies très précoces et morts prématurément, restés laïcs mais célibataires, et dont la curiosité universelle, quelque peu agressive au départ, fit place à un zèle ardent au service de leur foi chrétienne. *Worthy* se rendrait bien par preux, et ces deux vies sont riches en prouesses. Jessup cite volontiers The *Life of Picus* de More, qui est devenu un classique, au point d'être pris comme texte de départ pour d'autres traductions, allemande et française.[42] J'ai privilégié More parce que les longues heures qu'il passa avec le "Christian Worthy" florentin suffiraient à démontrer la grandeur exceptionnelle de Pic, et quant à la matière et quant à la manière. Il retient sans l'atténuer le *consummatus* de Gianfrancesco: "Yet a child and beardless he was both reputed and was in deed both a perfect philosopher and a perfect divine" (CW1, 56/18–20)—"encore enfant et imberbe il était considéré—et était en fait—à la fois philosophe accompli et théologien accompli." Sans compter l'accolade d'apôtre (*piscator hominum*) reçue de Ficin, et l'accolade de poète reçue de Politien et de Baptiste Mantouan.

Université Catholique de l'Ouest

---

[42] La française est le mémoire de maîtrise d'Odile Le Ny à l'Université Catholique de l'Ouest (1975). L'allemande occupe 23 pages avant la traduction de l'*Oratio de homine* par H. W. Reisel: *Die Würde des Menschen* (Fribourg en Brisgau: Pantheon, 1940), 19–41.

Études qui intéressent mon essai

Barone, Giuseppe. *Giovanni Pico della Mirandola*. Milano: Gastaldi, 1948.

———. *L'umanesimo filosofico di Giovanni Pico della Mirandola*. Milano: Gastaldi, 1949.

Dorez, Léon, et Louis Thuasne. *Pic de la Mirandole en France 1485–1488*. Paris: Leroux, 1897.

Gabrieli, Vittorio. "Giovanni Pico and Thomas More," *Moreana* nº 15–16 (nov. 1967), 43–57.

Jayne, Sears, editor. Giovanni Pico Pico della Mirandola, *Commentary on a Canzone of Bieniveni*. New York: Lang, 1984.

Roulier, Fernand. *Jean Pic de la Mirandole*. Genève: Slatkine, 1989. Comporte 28 pages de bibliographie.

Thuasne, voir sous Dorez.

Valcke, Louis. "Jean Pic lu par Thomas More." *Moreana* nº 100 (1989), 77–98.

Weiss, Robert. "Pico e l'Inghilterra." *L'opera e il pensiero di Giovanni Pico della Mirandola nella storia dell' umanesimo*. Vol. I, *Relazioni* (Firenze: Istituto Rinascimento, 1965), 143–158 (en comptant les 5 pages de réactions des congressistes).

The Humanism of Thomas More:
Continuities and Transformations in His Latin Letters

ELIZABETH McCUTCHEON

The letter, like the dialogue, was a favorite humanist genre, whether in its open or public form, where it lent itself to discussion and debate on intellectual and polemical issues and constituted something like a letter-essay,[1] or in its more personal form, as the familiar epistle, with which the humanists were particularly engaged.[2] A personal and private (or quasi-private) form, associated with the study, the familiar epistle was thought of, in Demetrius's classic formulation, as a conversation carried on in absence between good friends and as a gift, "designed to be the heart's good wishes in brief."[3] Mindful of pseudo-Libanius, Erasmus offered an even

---

[1] For extended discussions, see Ronald Witt, "Medieval 'Ars Dictaminis' and the Beginnings of Humanism: A New Construction of the Problem," *Renaissance Quarterly* 35 (1982): 1–35; Judith Rice Henderson, "Erasmus on the Art of Letter Writing," in *Renaissance Eloquence: Studies in the Theory and Practice of Renaissance Rhetoric*, ed. James J. Murphy (Berkeley, 1983), 331–355; Daniel Kinney, "Introduction," *In Defense of Humanism*, ed. Daniel Kinney, The Complete Works of St. Thomas More, vol. 15 (New Haven, 1986), xciii–cxviii.

[2] See such studies as Aloïs Gerlo, "The *Opus de conscribendis epistolis* of Erasmus and the Tradition of the *Ars Epistolica*," in *Classical Influences on European Culture A.D. 500–1500*, ed. R. R. Bolgar (Cambridge, 1971), 103–114; Cecil H. Clough, "The Cult of Antiquity: Letters and Letter Collections," in *Cultural Aspects of the Italian Renaissance: Essays in Honour of Paul Oskar Kristeller*, ed. Cecil H. Clough (Manchester and New York, 1976), 33–67; Marc Fumaroli, "Genèse de l'épistolographie classique: Rhétorique humaniste de la lettre, de Pétrarque à Juste Lipse," *Revue d'Histoire Littéraire de France* 78 (1978): 886–905; Gilbert Schrenck, "Profile d'humanistes: Budé, Erasme, More, d'après leur correspondance (1500–1530)," *Travaux de Linguistique et de Littérature* 21 (1983): 105–119; Judith Rice Henderson, "Defining the Genre of the Letter: Juan Luis Vives' *De Conscribendis Epistolis*," *Renaissance and Reformation* n.s. 7 (1983): 89–105; John F. Tinkler, "Renaissance Humanism and the *genera eloquentiae*," *Rhetorica* 5 (1987): 279–309.

[3] Demetrius, *On Style*, trans. W. Rhys Roberts, in *Aristotle, "Longinus," and Demetrius*, Loeb Classical Library (Cambridge and London, 1973), 4: 224, 225, and 231. On the familiar letter in general in the Renaissance, see Wesley Trimpi's magisterial survey, "The Epistolary Tradition," in his *Ben Jonson's Poems: A Study of the Plain Style* (Stanford, 1962), 60–75. For a study stressing the

terser definition, calling the familiar letter "a kind of mutual exchange of speech between absent friends": "epistola absentium amicorum quasi mutuus sermo."[4] When Thomas More wrote William Budé, circa 1520, he played upon a similar definition: "Literas tuas, quibus hanc absentiam tuam faceres mihi minus grauem, nisi vehementer me cupiditas vrgeret, non auderem petere."[5]

Implicit in these definitions by Demetrius and Erasmus and in More's witty transformation is the complex versatility that attracted the humanists and that a recent study of what Janet Altman calls "epistolarity" spells out, albeit in another context. Altman is concerned with the familiar letter in later manifestations, as it turned into the epistolary novel of the eighteenth century. By contrast, the familiar letter of the sixteenth-century humanists is less "personal" and has close affinities with the dialogue and with satire, comedy, and epigram, other classical and Renaissance modes traditionally written, like the familiar letter, in a plain (or at least a "plainer") style.[6] And where the eighteenth-century letter typically privileges erotic themes, the humanists were concerned with friendship, education, and other cultural issues. Yet Altman's points let us sharpen the significance of the familiar letter for humanists like Erasmus and More.[7]

Paradoxical and fictive, the familiar letter tries to close the gulf between presence and absence, candor and dissimulation; it emphasizes speech acts, yet is written out. As a "connector" between two distant points and a bridge between sender and receiver,[8] it raises fundamental questions about the nature of speech (sermo) and communication between two (or more) persons, and it invites reflection upon the relation of language to writer, circumstances, subject matter, and reader—pervasive concerns for the humanists, who rejected scholastic modes of argument and dialectic for something more flexible, oriented towards the needs of human beings and the

---

rhetorical, rather than the stylistic dimension, see Judith Rice Henderson, "On Reading the Rhetoric of the Renaissance Letter," in Renaissance-Rhetorik: Renaissance Rhetoric, ed. Heinrich F. Plett (Berlin, 1993), 143–162.

[4] De Conscribendis Epistolis, ed. Jean-Claude Margolin, Opera Omnia Desiderii Erasmi Roterodami recognita et adnotatione critica instructa notisque illustrata, 1–2: 225; cf. Lisa Jardine, Erasmus, Man of Letters: The Construction of Charisma in Print (Princeton, 1993), 149–153.

[5] The Correspondence of Sir Thomas More, ed. Elizabeth Frances Rogers (Princeton, 1947), 245. Subsequent citations from this edition will be incorporated in the text as "Rogers." Cf. translation in St. Thomas More: Selected Letters, ed. Elizabeth Frances Rogers (New Haven, 1961), 144: "If it were not for the vehemence of my desires, I would not dare to ask you to lessen the pain of your absence by writing to me." Subsequent citations from this collection will be incorporated in the text as "SL."

[6] Cf. Trimpi, 83–85.

[7] Space does not permit a discussion of definitions here; see Craig R. Thompson, "The Humanism of More Reappraised," Thought 52 (1977): 231–248; Paul Oskar Kristeller, "Thomas More as a Renaissance Humanist," Moreana 17 (1980): 5–22; Charles Trinkaus, "Thomas More and the Humanist Tradition: Martyrdom and Ambiguity," in The Scope of Renaissance Humanism (Ann Arbor, 1983), 422–436; and Vito R. Giustiniani, "Homo, Humanus, and the Meanings of 'Humanism'," Journal of the History of Ideas 46 (1985): 167–195.

[8] Janet Gurkin Altman, Epistolarity: Approaches to a Form (Columbus, Ohio, 1982), 13.

social and moral needs of the community.[9] A flexible form, it can accommodate the personal concerns of friendship, real or feigned, the exchange of information and news, the promotion of values, and the exploration of philosophical questions and controversies without freezing discussion or becoming monologic, since the letter, by definition, is part of an ongoing dialogue and a larger exchange.

From one point of view the letter is personal, grounded in the human voice and speech act—hence its presumed value, in the sixteenth century, for its revelation of character and personality. But if the letter is psychological, it is also audience-directed, rhetorical, and performative in this and other ways. It invites a response from its reader (the original addressee) and may well have other readers (or over-readers), persons privileged to see the original communication, and a larger audience still, if the letter circulates in manuscript or is printed, perhaps as originally written or, as often happened, in a revised or edited version. However much it disclaims art and insists on its plainness, its spontaneity, and its improvisatory nature, then, the letter is not unmediated. And it implicitly reveals aesthetic as well as cultural values— indeed, though the letter may not seem "literary," it involves issues at the heart of all writing.[10] Hence its multiple attraction for Erasmus, More, and other Renaissance humanists, who moved between ideas and lived life, past and present, art and life, and manipulated the letter, whether in its open and public or more familiar form, for a variety of purposes, projecting a sense of self, establishing and maintaining a coterie while promoting cultural values and the idea of a larger community, exchanging information, feelings, attitudes, and ideas, and seeking social, moral, and philosophical truths—what Wesley Trimpi more precisely calls "the individual and psychological search for philosophic truth."[11] This deepens the traditional notion of the Renaissance humanist as a "man of letters," for his letters, and the letters of his fellow humanists (More calls them "literas *tuas*" [Rogers 245; emphasis mine], using the personal form of *your*) were an essential part of their discourse and their lives.

Obvious exemplars include Petrarch, Salutati, Pico della Mirandola, and Erasmus, with some sixteen hundred familiar letters and his works on the art of the letter. By contrast, only ninety-three of More's Latin letters (among them four written under pseudonyms) survive,[12] counting the familiar, the public, and everything in between.[13] More also translated three Latin letters by Pico della Mirandola into

---

[9] Here and subsequently I am drawing upon material from Elizabeth McCutcheon, *My Dear Peter: "The Ars Poetica" and Hermeneutices for More's "Utopia"* (Angers, 1983).

[10] Altman, 188, 212.

[11] Trimpi, 91; cf. Fumaroli, 889–901; 904–905.

[12] At the congress in Bari, Abbé Germain Marc'hadour asked whether some of the letters for which we have only a Latin text (namely those in Stapleton's *Vita*) might have been translated from English originals. It is possible; however, the topics, the occasions, and the independent existence of other correspondence with the same persons in Latin suggest that More wrote most (perhaps all) in Latin, which the humanists consciously used as part of the cultural world they were fashioning.

[13] Besides works cited earlier, see the following on aspects of epistolary form: Hubertus Schulte Herbrüggen, "Einführung," in Sir Thomas More, *Neue Briefe,* ed. H. Schulte Herbrüggen

English, important early evidence of his interest in the genre and his debt to the older Italian humanist.[14]

Some of More's letters were suppressed, lost, or destroyed for political reasons, which makes the recent discovery of a manuscript bundle that belonged to Frans van Cranevelt and includes seven hitherto unknown letters by More an extraordinary event.[15] But More himself, in this respect unlike Erasmus, does not seem to have tried to publish his letters (or have them published) as a *collection*, although clearly he kept copies. In fact, on occasion he withheld publication. In 1520, for instance, he wrote William Budé and asked him not to publish his letters to him, at least until he had revised them, explaining that his Latin might well not measure up to Budé's and that he was afraid that he had not written circumspectly enough about peace, war, manners and morality, marriage, the clergy, the people, etc., and would invite censure.[16] More's caution suggests both the power and the danger he attributed to the letter as a form, his sensitivity to his own political situation, and the potential value of his letters (in their original versions, at least) as clues to his attitudes and ideas.

In any case, More's situation differed from someone like Erasmus's, despite his connections with him. More wrote some of his best-known familiar letters (and most of his official letters) in English, not Latin. Additionally, he was a busy lawyer, judge, administrator, and statesman; humanism was never the whole of his life, and his projections of self and life are multiple, even disparate. To put this another way, More depended much less than Erasmus did upon representing himself as a man of letters,[17] although he was attracted to that sort of life. In fact only twenty-four of More's letters were published—that is, printed—during his lifetime, and many of his familiar letters were printed for the first time in 1588 by Thomas Stapleton, who had access to More's manuscript correspondence through connections with the family. But almost all the Latin letters that were printed or otherwise circulated before More was executed are linked with Erasmus and/or Erasmian humanism. Despite the many gaps and their relatively small number, then, More's extant Latin letters are an integral part of his humanism and his humanist self or selves.

(Münster, 1966), xiii–xliv; Richard J. Schoeck, *The Achievement of Thomas More: Aspects of His Life and Works* (Victoria, 1976), 25–38.

[14] James McConica, "The Patrimony of Thomas More," in *History & Imagination: Essays in Honour of H. R. Trevor-Roper*, ed. Hugh Lloyd-Jones, Valerie Pearl, and Blair Worden (London, 1981), 56–71, is perceptive on More's relation to Pico. For a broader study of Pico and England, see Robert Weiss, "Pico e l'Inghilterra," in *L'opera e il pensiero di Giovanni Pico della Mirandola* (Firenze, 1965), 144–158; More is discussed specifically, 146–147.

[15] See Hubertus Schulte Herbrüggen, "A Hundred New Humanists' Letters: More, Erasmus, Vives, Cranevelt, Geldenhouwer and Other Dutch Humanists," *Bibliothèque d'Humanisme et Renaissance* 52 (1990): 65–76. These are calendared in J. and L. IJsewijn, D. Sacré, G. Tournoy, "Literae ad Craneveldium Balduinianae," *Humanistica Lovaniensia* 39 (1990): 369–374. See too H. Schulte Herbrüggen, "Seven New Letters from Thomas More," *Moreana* 27, n. 103 (1990): 49–66.

[16] Cf. Rogers, 246.

[17] Jardine shows just how carefully Erasmus fashioned this representation of himself.

More wrote his first Latin letter we know of in about 1501 and his last one in 1535, while imprisoned in the Tower of London; this means that they span almost his entire adult life. But most are dated between 1515 and 1524, when he was most fully engaged as a humanist and was closely associated with Erasmus. Numerically, too, Erasmus is the most important of some thirty addressees: twenty-four Latin letters are addressed to him.[18] Cranevelt follows, with thirteen, then More's daughter, Margaret Roper, with his other children (in some instances) or his "school," with nine. Then the count drops; there are four to Budé and John Cochlaeus and three to John Fisher, Peter Giles, Edward Lee, and Cuthbert Tunstall. Formally there is a great range: brief notes and compliments; many longer familiar or quasi-familiar letters, among them letters of dedication, prefaces to published works, and partly or wholly fictional letters; a verse epistle; and six extremely long essay-letters—that is, extended open letters on intellectual, literary, and religious issues. Of these, only three, to Lee, an unnamed monk (actually, John Batmanson), and Germanus Brixius, were printed contemporaneously, all in 1520, while a fourth (to Martin Dorp) circulated in manuscript in humanist circles and passages from it appeared in Juan Luis Vives's *In Pseudodialecticos* (also published in 1520).[19] More used a fifth, to the University of Oxford, as a text in his "school"—his daughters translated it[20]—and withheld publication of a sixth, to John Bugenhagen.[21] Probably this is the text More circumspectly mentions in his last surviving letter to Erasmus, when he says that he will follow Erasmus's advice "and make no reply to the person about whom you wrote, although I have held a lengthy letter in readiness for some time now." He goes on to explain that he does not want to have to write replies to "outsiders" (*externis*) when it is more urgent for him to answer those in his own country (*domesticis*).[22]

The young humanist-scholar-wit is easily recognizable in early letters to two mentors, John Holt, a grammarian and teacher, and John Colet, founder of St. Paul's School. Writing around 1501, More, who has sent much of his writing to Holt, claims that he lives as he pleases—"ita viuimus vt volumus" (Rogers 3), adding that

---

[18] For two views of their correspondence, see Margaret Mann-Phillips, "The Correspondence of Erasmus and Thomas More," in *Thomas More 1477–1977*, Aloïs Gerlo, allocution (Brussels, 1980), 27–37; and Thomas I. White, "Legend and Reality: The Friendship between More and Erasmus," in *Supplementum Festivum: Studies in Honor of Paul Oskar Kristeller*, ed. James Hankins, John Monfasani, and Frederick Purnell, Jr. (Binghamton, N.Y., 1987), 489–504.

[19] See *Juan Luis Vives against the Pseudodialecticians: A Humanist Attack on Medieval Logic*, ed. Rita Guerlac (Dordrecht, 1979); Jardine, 14–23; and Daniel Kinney, "More's *Letter to Dorp*: Remapping the Trivium," *Renaissance Quarterly* 34 (1981): 179–210.

[20] Thomas Stapleton, *The Life and Illustrious Martyrdom of Sir Thomas More*, trans. Philip E. Hallett, ed. E. E. Reynolds (New York, 1966), 92.

[21] See discussion in *Letter to Bugenhagen, Supplication of Souls, Letter against Frith*, The Complete Works of St. Thomas More, vol. 7, ed. Frank Manley, Germain Marc'hadour, Richard Marius, and Clarence H. Miller (New Haven, 1990), xxxiii–xxxvi.

[22] *SL* 180–181; *Opus Epistolarum Des. Erasmi Roterodami*, ed. P. S. Allen, H. M. Allen, and H. W. Garrod (Oxford, 1906–1958), 10: 260. Subsequent citations from this edition (which contains the Latin texts of More's letters to Erasmus) will be incorporated in the text.

he is doing very well in his studies, having turned from Latin "to take up the study of Greek" (*SL* 2), although he hasn't quite completed the transition—at which point he tactfully changes the subject. To Colet he writes, some three years later, about the welfare of his soul. Representing himself as someone in exile—a favorite classical motif that here seems to suggest a felt sense of isolation (perhaps political) on More's part—and as a Eurydice bereft of her Orpheus, he begs Colet to return to London, which he portrays as a quasi-hell, where even the roofs block out much of the light (Rogers 7). Like More's other writing, these letters are dramatic, hyperbolic, bursting with details and classical allusions, and self-consciously performative.

The deeper humanist issues they embed—the nature of the good life, the uses of *otium,* and the tension between learning or retirement and an active life—are fundamental for More.[23] And they loom large in the three letters by Pico della Mirandola that More appended to his translation of Gianfrancesco Pico's biography of his uncle, which he sent in 1505 as a New Year's gift to Joyeuce Leigh (Lee), a cloistered nun of the Poor Clares, for "the happy continuance and graciouse encreace of vertue in your soule."[24] Besides translating these letters, More paraphrased and edited them, thereby reshaping them, a sign of how quickly he saw the familiar letter as a way to explore ideas and values. He also rearranged the letters (all dated 1492) to emphasize their narrative and dramatic impulse; he sandwiches the well-known letter to Andrew Corneus (October 15) between two letters to Pico's nephew—one dated May 15, the other July 2. They share a common problem—how to resist temptation—and their present order lets More highlight the question of the nature of human nature, the need for perseverance in one's chosen way of life, and a critical dilemma that he, like so many humanists, faced—the *via activa* vis-à-vis the *via contemplativa.*[25]

All three letters encourage the pursuit of virtue and the life of the mind and spirit, energizing the soul as it "*laborest* to heauenwarde" (Kullnick, 121:340; emphasis mine). And Pico's letter to Corneus explores a related question of particular interest, given More's subsequent life and works. Here Pico adamantly refuses to merchandise philosophy or sell himself for the favor of the court—a position echoed by Raphael Hythlodaeus in Book I of More's *Utopia.* Instead Pico holds forth the hope of "some bokes of myne own to the common profit" (Kullnick, 121:334), trying to find a balance point between action and repose by stressing the labor and travail involved in the pursuit of wisdom.

A year later More publicly assumes a similar role, or more precisely a joco-serious variation of it, with the publication of the *Luciani Opuscula* (1506), a joint work by Erasmus and More. This volume was very popular in sixteenth-century Europe. With

---

[23] And for the humanists in general. Tinkler, "Renaissance Humanism," 286–291, discusses the poles of specialized learning and professional action between which the humanists moved.

[24] "Thomas Morus' 'Picus Erle of Mirandula'," ed. Max Kullnick, *Archiv für das Studium der neueren Sprachen und Literaturen* 121 (1908): 47–75, 316–340, and 122 (1909): 27–50 is my source for this and subsequent citations, which will be included parenthetically in the text as "Kullnick." The present citation is from 121:56.

[25] There is a fine overview of these letters in Dominic Baker-Smith, *More's "Utopia"* (London and New York, 1991).

More's epigrams and the *Utopia*, it accounts for much of his early reputation as a humanist, and the prefatory letter was the first of More's letters to be printed. Dedicating his translations of Lucian from Greek to Latin to Thomas Ruthall, the royal secretary, More defends what he calls the first fruits of his Greek studies. Pico and Lucian can seem a world apart, but More turns first to Horace (and later to St. John Chrysostom), insisting that Lucian "fulfilled the Horatian maxim and combined delight with instruction."[26] Lucian, he continues, eschewed both "the arrogant pronouncements of the philosophers" and the "wanton wiles of the poets," and "everywhere reprimands and censures, with very honest and at the same time very entertaining wit, our human frailties."[27] A Lucianic impulse is an important element in both Erasmus's and More's humanist writing, which values irony, drama, and seriocomic wit, testing and exercising its readers. But the Horatian element is also important; like Horace and later humanists, More is "conversational, epistolary, idiomatic, ironic, satiric" and concerned with the dramatic and performative aspects of all discourse.[28]

A major difference between Pico and More shows up three years later in a second dedicatory letter—this time to Henry VIII. It was first printed in 1518, with More's Latin epigrams, but is part of an illuminated manuscript containing five Latin poems written in honor of the king's coronation on June 24, 1509. The letter is both a gift and an apology. In an epigrammatic vein More claims that the illuminator had an attack of gout, which is why his gift is so late: "Itaque ... haud scio, maioremne gratiam uersiculis nostris pictoris manus adiecerint, an pedes ademerint."[29] But the handsomely illustrated manuscript, complete with the Tudor Rose tellingly surmounted by an *imperial* crown, must be a bid for royal favor—a bid seemingly unanswered until years later.[30]

More's most productive period as a humanist falls roughly between 1515 and the early 1520s, and the majority of his extant Latin letters, including many of his substantively most important ones, were written then as well. In fact, between 1509 and the fall of 1515, the date of More's long manuscript letter to Dorp, we have only a fragment of a letter to Colet. Following the letter to Dorp, the number (insofar as we can document it) increases rapidly. Erasmus is More's most important corres-

---

[26] *Translations of Lucian*, The Complete Works of St. Thomas More, vol. 3, part I, ed. Craig R. Thompson (New Haven, 1974), 3.

[27] *Translations of Lucian*, 3.

[28] For a comprehensive treatment of the Lucianic, see, e.g., Douglas Duncan, *Ben Jonson and the Lucianic Tradition* (Cambridge, 1970), 52–76. I have adapted my description of the Horatian from William K. Wimsatt Jr. and Cleanth Brooks, *Literary Criticism: A Short History* (New York, 1957), 751.

[29] *Latin Poems*, The Complete Works of St. Thomas More, vol. 3, part II, ed. Clarence H. Miller, Leicester Bradner, Charles A. Lynch, and Revilo P. Oliver (New Haven, 1984), 96–97. Subsequent references will be included in my text as "*CW* 3, 2."

[30] Dale Hoak's lecture on Bale's *King John* and the politics of imperial kingship, at the William Tyndale Conference in Washington, D.C., July 16, 1994, called the significance of the *imperial* form of the crown to my attention. For the crown and Tudor rose, see *CW* 3, 2: between 107–108.

pondent, but other humanists, administrators, and churchmen appear—including Tunstall, Giles, Bishop Warham, an anonymous member of the royal court, Antonio Bonvisi, More's daughters, their tutor, William Gonell, Budé, Reginald Pole, and John Clement, together with the addressees of his humanist defenses. *Utopia*, its publication, promotion, and reception by its first readers, is a major topic. The education of his children and wards and their intellectual development is another recurrent concern; Margaret virtually becomes a model for the new learning in women, and More's letter to one of her tutors, Gonell, is an extremely important early text on the new learning. Numerous details project the densely textured life of a humanist and administrator, and friendship and communication (and the dangers of misunderstanding or being misunderstood) are pervasive concerns. The cause of humanism, particularly Erasmian humanism, dominates the open letters, and More's preoccupations—how to balance the public and the private life, the nature of interpretation and reading—appear in both the familiar letters and the letter-essays, connecting them. Additionally, he often relates these problems to an altogether-too-human tendency to privilege one's own ego-centered ideas.

I have space to discuss just three of the familiar—or quasi-familiar—letters from this period. First, a private one (first printed by Stapleton in 1588) to Cuthbert Tunstall, a statesman and ecclesiastic whom More frequently names—he was anxious for his reactions to the *Utopia*. Tunstall licensed him to respond to heretical writings in English, and More singles him out on the inscription for his tomb. Circa 1517 he wrote Tunstall to acknowledge his expression of gratitude for More's services to friends of his and thank him for a piece of amber—"a precious sepulcher for flies" (*SL* 91). More interprets the amber iconographically, making much of its shape, "a heart, a sort of symbol of your love for me" (*SL* 91). He continues: "As the fly, winged like Cupid [literally, the son of Venus] and as fickle, is so shut up and entangled in the substance of the amber that it cannot fly away, so embalmed in the aromatic juice that it cannot perish, so your love will never fly away and always remain unchanged" (*SL* 91). This is More at his most epigrammatic and most eloquent on a favorite humanist theme—friendship (here as so often including patronage), now encapsulated emblematically.[31]

In another letter—to Erasmus in 1520—friendship appears both overtly and obliquely by way of More's promotion of the liberal arts and his attack on scholastic logic; there is also a lavish panegyric of Juan Luis Vives, a young humanist, whom, the letter insinuates, More does not know. But most of this letter is far less candid than it appears to be, for a letter Erasmus wrote to More on March 8, 1517, presupposes that he already knew Vives: "If Vives has been with you often, you will easily guess what I have suffered in Brussells. . . ."[32] And even if they had not met,

---

[31] Friendship as a theme in More's letters to Erasmus is treated by both Mann-Phillips and White.

[32] *The Correspondence of Erasmus*, Collected Works of Erasmus, vol. 4, trans. R. A. B. Mynors and D. F. S. Thomson, annotated James K. McConica (Toronto, 1977), 274–275 and n. 16; Guerlac; Jardine, 18.

the similarities that More claims to find amazing between Vives's *In Pseudodialecticos* and More's earlier analysis, in his letter to Dorp, are readily explained by the younger scholar's knowledge and use of More's work, already circulating in humanist circles. This letter seems to have been written to order, then, to help Vives in his search for a place and thus promote the larger cause of humanism.[33] Not surprisingly, it was published the same year in Barlandus's edition of a selection of Erasmian *Epistolae.*

My third example is the long letter More addressed to Peter Giles, chief secretary of the city of Antwerp, and a humanist, editor, and patron of the arts.[34] More wrote it sometime before September 3, 1516, as a preface for the *Utopia*, and it is a superb example of More's joco-seriousness, paradoxicality, irony, and love of feigning—important aspects of his sort of humanism. He writes what appears to be a letter to a dear friend, creating the putative circumstances of their discussions with the wholly fictive Raphael Hythlodaeus—discussions that have taken More (who claims merely to be the reporter of the text that follows) an unreasonably long time simply to write out. It is not always easy, or possible, to separate fiction from fact here—More is an expert at what the Renaissance would have called *evidentia.* But More met Giles for the first time in 1515, while abroad on his so-called Utopian embassy in Flanders, and Giles, a good friend of Erasmus's, is in some sense a stand-in for him.

More makes much of his reportorial guise while parodying his life as busy lawyer, judge, arbitrator, and family man. As he explains it, indeed, he is so busy that "relinquo mihi, hoc est literis, nihil"—"I leave for myself, that is for literature, nothing."[35] Hyperbolic? Of course. Yet its deeper point resonates throughout More's life: so often an activist, yet hungering for the life of the mind, More comes closest here, perhaps, to identifying himself as a man of letters—an identity that is an essential part of his being and yet he later plays down. Even here, albeit wittily, he denies himself any creative role, representing himself as a candid and conscientious reporter and treating his assertions and fabrications with wide-eyed literalism and seeming gravity and plainness: the consummate tongue-in-cheek speaker, More delights in projecting a sense of self as slow-witted, clumsy, something of a fool, notions that the sophisticated irony, ambiguities, and paradoxes of his text undermine.

As I have argued in *My Dear Peter*, the letter contains a concealed *ars poetica,* and learning how to read it also lets us experience More's hermeneutics for the *Utopia.* For here, as in a second letter to Giles (published at the end of the second edition of *Utopia*, in 1517), More invites reflections on the relationship of the scribe and writer to the work, the formal craft and art of its making (structure, style, etc.), the ontological status of the narrative, differences between a bad reader or critic and a good one, and reader-writer-text relationships that, we discover, are unfolded in this order in the course of the first letter. As in his polemical works, both humanist and religious, More is extremely concerned with the processes of reading and interpre-

---

[33] So Jardine argues, 17–20.

[34] I am condensing material to be found in greater length in McCutcheon, *My Dear Peter.*

[35] Cited from my translation in *My Dear Peter*, 92, 93.

tation, the ways that reading goes awry, and the need for good readers—readers, that is, who are good both ethically and intellectually.

Richard Sylvester, Richard Schoeck, and Daniel Kinney have already made the case for More's open letters to Dorp, Oxford, Lee, and a monk as a "Defense of Humanism" in which, Kinney argues, More works out "a truly progressive prescription for the continual renewal and refinement of the 'living gospel of faith'."[36] To these letters we can add More's to Brixius, which constitutes something like an *ars poetica*.[37] Each letter grew out of a particular occasion or situation. Maartin van Dorp, a theologian and humanist at Louvain, had objected to Erasmus's *Moria* and to his plan to publish a new translation of the New Testament; a preacher at Oxford had attacked the study of Greek there; Edward Lee, a churchman and a friend of More's, was circulating a manuscript volume attacking Erasmus's translation of the New Testament; a London Carthusian had written a general attack on Erasmus; and, in 1520, Brixius published his *Antimorus*, attacking the style and substance of More's epigrams, which included a satiric demolition of some of Brixius's.

Each of the letters has its own style, and More is sometimes dialogic and exploratory, sometimes apologetic, sometimes very formal, and sometimes polemic as he answers the various charges leveled at Erasmus and his works and defends his own epigrams and integrity. But, increasingly, he becomes defensive, even vitriolic. His personal letter to Dorp—whose actual situation vis-à-vis Erasmus and other humanists is open to a variety of interpretations—is flexible, informal, dialogic, and carefully nuanced. Five years later, in 1520, when he attacks the monk and Brixius, More is obviously rhetorical; as Kinney puts this, "In defense of Erasmian dialogue he begins to sound almost as peremptory as those who condemn it: epistolary discussion begins to give way to one-sided polemic."[38] For More, always the lawyer, the best defense was often an offense—obviously a temperamental difference from Erasmus. A similar pattern recurs in More's later English defenses of the traditional Church against the reformers between 1528 and 1533; in both cases More becomes increasingly aggressive, at times violent, as he responds to what must have felt to him like increasingly provocative, dangerous, and unjustified attacks on the persons, institutions, ideas, and values he held dearest. At the same time, there are contradictions in his position: by the late 1520s More is defending ceremonies and practices he had earlier (like Erasmus) treated derisively, and his defense of the Catholic Church becomes global.

This is a perennial problem in More studies—one that remains unsolved. But I do want to point out a critical moment that falls between the first and second versions of More's first Latin work against heresy, his *Responsio ad Lutherum* (1523). This curious combination of joco-serious humanism and Catholic polemics is a turning

---

[36] Richard Sylvester, "Thomas More: Humanist in Action," in *Medieval and Renaissance Studies,* ed. O. B. Hardison, Jr. (Chapel Hill, 1966), 125–137; see also Schoeck, 25–38; Kinney, "Introduction" to *In Defense of Humanism,* xix–cxxxii: specific citation from lxxvii.

[37] For a discussion of More's letter as both an *ars* and a polemic, see Daniel Kinney, "*More's Letter to Brixius,*" Appendix C in *CW* 3, 2: 551–592.

[38] Kinney, "Introduction" to *In Defense of Humanism,* cxvii–cxviii.

point in More's works. More wrote it (at the king's request) to defend Henry VIII's book "asserting" the seven sacraments against Martin Luther's *De Captivitate Baby-lonica Ecclesiae* (1521) and to answer Luther's subsequent counter-blast against the king (in 1522). But only after finishing the first version did More fully realize the centrali-ty of the controversy over the nature of the church, and he added a long chapter on this issue, suppressing the initial version of the *Responsio* shortly after it was published. He likewise wrote new versions of the letters, in each case fictional, that introduce the text—carrying over a strategy from the *Utopia*—and he changed his pseudonym and persona. In the first version the work is attributed to a Spaniard, Ferdinand Bara-vellus, a learned man who is at home at the university; in the later, more biting ver-sion, the writer is an Englishman, William Ross, who has been living in Italy. And this is just the beginning of a complicated preliminary narrative with dialogue that More invents as a cover and "prejudicial introduction"[39] for the defense that fol-lows: by writing these letters More establishes an inner circle of readers who are ex-pected to laugh at that clown Luder, fool and Satanist from Hell, "Dominus doctor Martinus."[40]

Only two other Latin letters that More wrote after 1520 were published during his lifetime. More actually had a number of correspondents, however—both old and new, among the latter Conrad Goclenius, John Cochlaeus, John Sinapius, and (nota-bly) Frans van Cranevelt, a lawyer who held important administrative offices, first in Bruges and later in Mechelen, and was also a translator, editor, and assiduous letter-writer. Thirteen of More's letters to Cranevelt, written between 1520 and 1528, have been edited (seven very recently), and they speak to many of More's humanist in-terests in the 1520s.[41] They are all short—in a few cases very short—but they touch on major matters of the period for the humanists: war and peace, Luther, the marriage of Vives, the question of the real author of a pamphlet written against Erasmus's writings on confession (attributed to "Taxander" but actually written by four Dominicans), the death of Dorp. There are likewise more personal concerns—candlesticks and a portrait of the Virgin Mary that More had ordered, the house and furniture he will need if he is a member of the embassy supposed to be going to Bruges after Easter 1521, and so on.

---

[39] Rainer Pineas, *Thomas More and Tudor Polemics* (Bloomington, 1968), 15.

[40] *Responsio ad Lutherum*, The Complete Works of St. Thomas More, vol. 5, ed. John M. Headley (New Haven, 1969), 584.

[41] Materials supplementing n. 13 include *Literae uirorum eruditorum ad Franciscum Cranveldium: 1522–1528*, ed. Henry de Vocht (Louvain, 1928); *Litterae ad Craneveldium Balduinianae: A Preliminary Edition*, ed. Jozef IJsewijn with G. Tournoy, D. Sacré, Line IJsewijn-Jacobs, and Monique Mund-Dopchie, *Humanistica Lovaniensia* 41 (1992): 1–85; 42 (1993): 1–51; and (with addition of M. Verweij) 43 (1994): 15–68, edition in progress; Clarence H. Miller, "Thomas More's Letters to Frans van Cranevelt: Including Seven Recently Discovered Autographs: Latin Text, English Translation, and Facsimiles of the Originals," *Moreana* 31, n. 117 (1994): 3–66. I am indebted to Professor IJsewijn for sending me the offprints from *Humanistica Lovaniensia*, facilitating a comparison of texts with Miller's in *Moreana*. Both are indispensable, but I cite Miller's because it contains all the letters.

As important as the specific subject, however, which is rarely fully developed, are still broader humanist concerns. By writing these letters, More maintains his connections with Cranevelt and, through him, with the large number of fellow humanists whose letters flowed through Cranevelt's house or were held by him for safekeeping. In 1521, for instance, More writes a quick note on a scrap of paper to say that he is returning Cranevelt's book along with "a bundle of letters which Erasmus sent me to read. He neither wants them published nor is there any need or usefulness in doing so, unless his adversary continues his insane antics in some way or other. For which eventuality I deposit them with you for safekeeping, just as Erasmus himself told me to do."[42]

Similarly, More dramatizes the friendship motif that binds them and characterizes the letters he is writing. Friendship is one of humanism's favorite themes and one More repeatedly employed in his letters and his life. As Erasmus remarked, More "seems born and designed" for friendship.[43] More apologizes for his silence, thanks Cranevelt for books, sends him and his wife several consecrated rings, and (in his letter of August 10, 1524) self-consciously reflects on the process of writing and reading the letters that he has received. What, he says, could be more agreeable than to receive letters from Cranevelt—"*the dearest of all men?*" He continues:

> Unless someone could provide the opportunity to speak with the man himself in person—although whenever I read what you have written, I am so affected by it that while I am reading I seem to be talking with you face to face. Therefore nothing grieves me more distinctly than that your letter is not longer, although for that defect I could also find a sort of remedy: I read the ones I receive over and over, and slowly at that, so that quick reading does not take away the pleasure [*voluptatem*] too quickly. (Miller 35)

More also writes numerous variations upon a conceit, epigrammatic and ultimately formulaic in nature, that plays upon an imagined relationship with Cranevelt and his wife, the mother of at least eleven children. In February 1521 she is simply "dulcissima coniuge matrona omnium prudentissima atque honestissima" (Miller 7). But less than two months later she is "dominam meam uxorem tuam aut potius dominam tuam uxorem meam" (Miller 17), and four years later she is "vxore diurna mea; nocturne tua; domina uero communi" (Miller 43). More continues to ring changes on the formula; in 1527 he sends his greetings to "dominae uxori tue matronae prestantissime" (Miller 51), and (more self-reflexively still), "Dominam meam coniugem tuam (nam ordinem non audeo rursus interuertere)" (Miller 54). It seems that More, like other humanists, is responding to a new and awkward situation, wherein the man of letters is also a married man with a family, their place and role ambiguous.[44] At

---

[42] Miller's translation, *Moreana* 31 (1994): 23. Subsequent citations will be incorporated into my text as "Miller."

[43] From the famous 1519 letter to Ulrich van Hutten; see *The Correspondence of Erasmus*, Collected Works of Erasmus, vol. 7, trans. R. A. B. Mynors, annotated Peter G. Bietenholtz (Toronto, 1987), 18.

[44] See his letter of August 10, 1524, in Miller, 37. Schrenck, "Profile d'humanistes," p. 113,

the same time, these self-conscious variations echo an impulse behind the familiar letter, which often is erotic in other contexts: in these instances, however, it seems intended to link More more fully to the Cranevelts, although the perspective is unfortunately "old boy" or clubby.

But there is still another way to read much of this material—as a cover or filler for what More does *not* write but which is conveyed by the carrier of the letter. More himself suggests as much in his letter of July 14, 1527. Writing from Calais, he speaks of a truly "reliable letter-carrier" and explains that

> this carrier is a servant of Erasmus, now returning directly to him, highly commended by him as very loyal and close-mouthed. If you want to communicate to Erasmus anything that you do not wish to commit to a letter, you can very safely entrust it to this man. If there is anything else I wish you to know, you will learn it from this letter-carrier. (Miller 51)

Cagey as ever, More prefaces his own behavior with a telling "si," a signal of just how coded his letters could become; in some instances, what is not there may be more important than what is.

Only four Latin letters postdate May 16, 1532, when More resigned the Lord Chancellorship and withdrew, at least nominally, from public life: in fact he became even more active in his verbal warfare against heresy and remained a figure of high visibility. On June 14, 1532, he wrote to both John Cochlaeus, More's "client" and one of Luther's most vitriolic opponents, and Erasmus, to tell them about his retirement. He attributes it to ill health and resolves to "devote to intellectual things and to God the leisure graciously granted" him by the king (*SL* 178). While what he says about his health is probably true, it is not the whole truth, but a face-saving strategy that protects both his reputation and the partly feigned relationship with the king that More constructs here and in subsequent letters.

His letter to Erasmus is longer, more playful, and more vitally humanist than is the one to Cochlaeus. More begins by invoking a perennial dream of leisure (that is, withdrawal from public life) that he had first articulated over thirty years earlier, in his letter to Holt, and which, he says, Erasmus has always enjoyed. An extended defense and eulogy of Erasmus and his many publications follows; More imagines him as a heroic figure who has persevered despite his many detractors and encourages him to continue his brave work—echoing Pico's letter to Corneus. Erasmus himself probably did not need to hear all this at such great length, even though his detractors were real enough: More is writing for a larger public. It almost seems that he is constructing a dual biography and public apology, in fact—one for Erasmus and his life work and one for himself and the works he hopes to write—works which will prove to be more vitriolic than Erasmus's.

---

identifies family life as a theme newly found in humanist writing; for the tension traditionally understood between the scholar and the family man, see the treatment of philosophic misogamy in Katharina M. Wilson and Elizabeth M. Makowski, *Wykked Wyves and the Woes of Marriage: Misogamous Literature from Juvenal to Chaucer* (Albany, 1990).

Rogers, following Allen, tentatively dates More's second letter to Erasmus, one that even Margaret Mann-Phillips found "opaque," to June? 1533;[45] I think it is slightly earlier. It includes business (Erasmus's financial problems are never far from More's mind) and news. More passes on information about Melanchthon's visit to Paris as he obtained it from a copy of William Tyndale's January 1533 letter to John Frith, who was then in the Tower of London and subsequently executed for heresy.[46] More adds the epitaph he wrote for his own tomb, now in Chelsea Old Church. He calls it "a public declaration of the actual facts" (SL 179) and certainly it is an "official" or public autobiography—one that he wants to see published, for he assures Erasmus (albeit somewhat disingenuously) of the king's good will and encourages him to print this letter and his earlier one so as to refute rumors that he was dismissed from office.

More downplays his literary endeavors (in litteris vtcunque versatus is his only overt reference) and represents himself as a successful and well-connected public administrator and the obedient servant of the king and his own father: conscientious, loyal, deferential, eager for peace, and "a source of trouble [molestus] to thieves, murderers, and heretics" (SL 181). He would then have been in the midst of writing his harshest polemical works against Tyndale and other heretics, and this statement is both personal and political; he assures Erasmus that the king is "more antagonistic [acrior] toward heretics than even the bishops are" (SL 179). He could hardly write more forthrightly about the heretics than he does to Cochlaeus or here in this letter: "How those people fret over this matter [the eucharist] as if God had commissioned them to give the whole world its fundamental instructions in the faith!" (SL 179). Erasmus published both letters the next year, including them with some of his own at the end of his De Praeparatione ad Mortem and setting off and thus highlighting the inscription.[47]

More ends his inscription on a Picoesque note of resignation and steadfast piety, anxious to contemplate the eternity of life to come. Characteristically, though, he follows this somber and authoritative, if theatrical (and potentially ironic) inscription—given its insistence on the king as the defender of the faith—with his personal and witty epigram about his two wives and their possible relationship as a threesome: "O, how happily we could have lived all three together if fate and morality [relligio, CW 3, 2: 270] had permitted" (SL 183). It seems that More himself could not altogether let go of a younger, freer, humanist self, or renounce his love of literature. He wrote the epigram sometime between 1511 and 1518 (it was the last poem in the first edition of his epigrams in 1518 [CW 3, 2: 411]), and it implicitly projects a multi-

---

[45] Rogers, 464; Mann-Phillips, 36.

[46] More, who obtained a copy of this letter, paraphrased another part of it in his Apology, published a little before Easter, 1533; see The Apology, The Complete Works of St. Thomas More, vol. 9, ed. J. B. Trapp (New Haven, 1979), 91. I assume, then, that More wrote Erasmus while the letter and the news were still fresh. For the text of this letter, see The Acts and Monuments of John Foxe, ed. The Rev. George Townsend (n.d.; rpt. New York, 1965), 5: 133–134.

[47] Des. Erasmi Roterodami Liber cvm Primis pivs, De Praeparatione ad Mortem (Basel, 1534), 109–111.

faceted, more subtle and comic image of More than the inscription itself does.

More's last Latin letter substantiates the continuity and depth of the humanist impulse in his life. In or around June 1535, less than a month before he was put to death, he wrote to an old friend and patron, Antonio Bonvisi.[48] Bonvisi, a merchant banker, humanist, and generous benefactor, had come to London in 1505 to join other family members in the London branch of a great financial empire centered in Lucca. Over the years he was of considerable help to More; he was well connected and a knowledgeable source of information from abroad, he enjoyed the protection of the king and had easy access to those in power, probably he lent money to More's family after he was imprisoned, and he stood by the More circle then and later. Moreover, Bonvisi and More shared intellectual interests and religious attitudes: Bonvisi's name turns up at critical moments in More's life.

Now More writes what is, in some sense, a paean of friendship, thanking Bonvisi for his many kindnesses and saying goodbye. To an unparalleled degree, this letter enacts the younger More's claim that "a loving letter represents the mind (*reddat amans animum littera* [*CW* 3, 2: 298])." Using the language of his international, humanist self, with its urbane conceits and formulas of polite and elegant conversation, More portrays his own personality and consciousness even as he acknowledges their imminent annihilation from the point of view of this world and witnesses, just this side of death, to his identity as he himself defined it. Making friendship both his lens and focal point, he writes, throughout, as one who owes a debt he can never repay. He describes himself as *addictum,* one sentenced to prison for unpaid debts, and he repeatedly plays upon the multiple meanings of *fortuna* and *prosperitas,* counterpoising his fortune, or rather misfortune, with Bonvisi's *fortuna* (including his fortune or wealth), his *improspero naufragio* with the *prosperitas* of Bonvisi's faithful friendship. Even before he was imprisoned, he says, he was only a barren lover (*sterilem amatorem*). But now that his resources are exhausted, he will never be able to discharge his debt. But the letter itself is, in some sense, a gift, as More well knows. As he re-enacts Bonvisi's inexhaustible generosity by hyperbolic expressions of thanks, the letter overflows with words like *iucunditate, delectatus sum, deglutiebam, suauitas.* His language is the language of love, his values at once classical and Christian. More characteristically portrays the joys of heaven in terms of love, communion, and community between and among good friends, who "maie merily meete in heauen" (Rogers 564). Perhaps the most moving and poignant part of this letter is when More negates his present situation to imagine meeting Bonvisi:

> Where there will be no need for letters, where no wall will separate us, where no porter will prevent us from talking together, but with God the Father unbegotten, and his only-begotten Son, our Lord and Redeemer Jesus Christ,

---

[48] Here and hereafter I am drawing on my extended study and new translation of More's letter to Bonvisi: " 'The Apple of My Eye': Thomas More to Antonio Bonvisi: A Reading and a Translation," *Moreana* 18, n. 71–72 (1981): 27–56. Citations from my translation will be included parenthetically in the text as "Bonvisi."

and the Holy Spirit of them both, the Comforter proceeding from them both, we shall fully enjoy eternal joy. (Bonvisi 56)

But I run the risk of overemphasizing the sweetness of this letter, which ends on a very different note, as More signs his name, perhaps for the last time, concluding, "Nor am I now such, that it matters whose I am" (Bonvisi 56)—the anger, frustration, and sense of betrayal reminding us of his polemics.

Unlike Erasmus, More never wrote an art of the letter. But his Latin letters give us the many faces of his humanism as well as many different representations of the self. His defensive postures and his commitment to Erasmian humanism, whose interests he advanced through his powerful humanist defenses, are well represented, and we can see how important the letter was in the development of a coterie and in the promotion of humanist ideas. At the same time, any number of other voices are present—there is the young intellectual, the wit and jokester, the man of letters, the educator, the father and family man, the mature scholar-critic, the patron, the busy administrator, the tenacious opponent of heresy, the man facing his own imminent death. Beyond all else, the Latin letter proved to be, for More, an extraordinarily flexible and creative vehicle for reflection upon friendship, communication, and community, while he represented himself as the good friend. What we have experienced in these letters we can see in Quentin Metsys's famous diptych of Erasmus and Peter Giles, commissioned by them in 1517 as a gift for More.[49] More is an absent presence, adumbrated by the letter that Giles holds in his left hand. In a letter to Giles, More begs for this letter, so he can put it alongside the picture. Otherwise, he says, he will try to "imitate the man who imitates my hand so well."[50] In this brief moment—where the artist, the intellectual, the humanist, and the friend coalesce— we catch a glimpse of the dynamic and open-ended exchange that the letter optimally constituted for More.

University of Hawaii

---

[49] The two pictures are reproduced in *CW* 3, 2: between 299 and 300.

[50] *The Correspondence of Erasmus*, The Complete Works of Erasmus, vol. 5, trans. R. A. B. Mynors and D. F. S. Thomson, annotated Peter G. Bietenholz (Toronto, 1979), 151.

La teorizzazione dell'ars historica
tra tardo Medioevo ed età moderna

MASSIMO MIGLIO

Nel 1971, a Lovanio, al primo Congresso internazionale di studi neolatini, tentavo di cogliere, all'interno della storiografia pontificia, la presenza di una "coscienza critica negli scrittori di storia." L'argomento scelto in questa occasione sembrerebbe indicare una volontà di continuità: se allora l'ambito era rigidamente quello pontificio, a quasi venticinque anni di distanza paiono cadere limitazioni e barriere geografiche nella presunzione di un'analisi globale della teorizzazione dell'*ars historica* tra Medioevo ed età moderna.[1]

In realtà non vi è stata nella scelta alcuna volontà di indicare una continuità di ricerca o ricorrenze di percorsi biografici, quanto piuttosto una forte necessità personale che sicuramente vizierà questa relazione. Quale senso ha, oggi, leggere Bruni, Biondo, Valla o qualsiasi altro storico o cronista? E' possibile recuperare e trasmettere una nostra coscienza critica della storia confrontandola con la loro coscienza storiografica? Venticinque anni di storia contemporanea di un villaggio globale mettono ognuno di noi di fronte a una riflessione che non può essere solo un bilancio personale, che è banale ricondurre a una *laudatio temporis acti*, che soltanto per fede è possibile riferire alla provvidenza. Anche negli scrittori di storia che leggiamo ottimismo e pessimismo finiscono per essere categorie storiografiche a scapito delle teorizzazioni.

Le novità della storiografia italiana tra '400 e '500 sono riconducibili più al contesto ideologico di riferimento che non ai contenuti o alle forme. Gli uni e le altre hanno come presupposto la consapevolezza di aver superato un'età che è sentita di transizione e la cosciente elaborazione del concetto di Medioevo, in un'età segnata

---

[1] Massimo Miglio, "La storiografia pontificia del Quattrocento," in *Acta Conventus Neo-Latini Lovaniensis*. Proceedings of the First International Congress of Neo-Latin Studies, Louvain 23–28 August 1971, ed. J. IJsewijn-F. Kessler (München, 1973), 411–432, repr. in *Storiografia pontificia del Quattrocento* (Bologna, 1975), 1–30.

dalla crisi di impero e di papato, dove le monarchie non sono più tali per diritto divino, dove la storia non è più scandita dalle sei età del mondo. La prospettiva storica è completamente mutata.

E' possibile individuare gli aspetti formali e istituzionali in qualche pagina dedicata all'*ars historica*, e in una in particolare che tento di tradurre abbastanza letteralmente: "La storia è il racconto degli avvenimenti degni di ricordo, sia in pace che in guerra. Tre sono i compiti dello storico: raccontare cose vere, in modo chiaro e con brevità. La verità degli avvenimenti si ha solo quando siano state investigate diligentemente la loro antichità e oscurità, e quando vengano riferiti, dopo l'analisi, in piena libertà, cioè senza paura, compiacenza o invidia. La storia è trasparente se gli avvenimenti vengono spiegati, così come necessita, secondo i tempi, secondo i luoghi, secondo le azioni; deve essere soprattutto breve, senza inserire nulla di inutile o futile, esprimendo i concetti con poche parole, senza inutili giri di frasi. La storia deve essere piacevole e accattivante e questo avviene con la varietà degli argomenti, con metafore (?), con le immagini, con il ricorso a nuove parole, con la scelta attenta dei concetti; è piacevole e accattivante se è addensata in una struttura concisa. Il fine della storia è la conoscenza, per sapere cosa fare o cosa non fare, o per servircene nel discorso."[2]

Possiamo saltare le ultime brevi battute di questa teorizzazione, per svelare subito, leggendo il testo in originale, un piccolo bluff:

> Historia est rerum gestarum et dignarum memoria relatio: ea versatur aut in rebus bellicis aut in negotiis civilibus, id est pacis. Hitorici officii sunt tria: ut veras res, ut dilucide, ut breviter exponat. Verae res sunt, si rerum actarum vetustas et obscuritas diligenter exploretur, si explorata libere, id est sine metu aut gratia aut invidia referatur. Lucida fit historia, si ut oportet res pro temporibus, pro locis, pro actibus structura simplici et perfecta explanetur; brevis autem, si nichil vel supervacaneum, vel leve interponatur, si singulis verbis sententiae exprimantur, si non longo circuitu elocutio terminetur. Est et illa virtus ut grata sit, quod fieri solet, si varietate, si translationibus, si figuris, si novis verbis, si cultu sententiarum, si concinnatiore structura concinnetur. Opus historiae est, ut nos notitia rerum instruat, finis autem, id est τὸ τέλος, ut ex ea sequendas aut fugiendas res cognoscamus aut ad usum eloquentiae adiuvemur. . . .

La sensibilità di chi ascolta avrà colto che il *De historia* che ho letto non è una teorizzazione d'età umanistica. E' un testo, poco noto e poco utilizzato dalla letteratura storiografica, tràdito in un manoscritto in scrittura beneventana della fine del secolo VIII, un codice cassinese miscellaneo, copiato durante il soggiorno di Paolo Diacono, dai forti interessi per le arti del trivio, dipendente da un modello di Fulda, con elementi tipicamente insulari e con un apparato decorativo legato alla cultura tardoantica e paleocristiana. La fortuna di questo manoscritto nei secoli successivi è ancora tutta da studiare, ma è importante ricordare che fu sicuramente visto da Lorenzo Valla.[3]

---

[2] Traduco da Karl Halm, *Rhetores Latini minores* (Lipsiae, 1863), 588–589.

[3] Vedi sopra n. 2, e cf. Santo Mazzarino, *Il pensiero storico classico*, II/2 (Bari, 1966), 3–15. Per

E' proprio in questo anonimo trattatello altomedioevale una se pur parziale conferma che nella trattatistica rinascimentale relativa alla storia le novità non furono molte e non soltanto dal punto di vista formale. Del resto le fonti classiche relative, greche e latine, sono state ripetutamente investigate dalla ormai abbondante, e nota, letteratura storiografica in proposito, e saranno in questa sede sostanzialmente sottintese.[4] Si ha invece, nel Quattrocento, la volontà, ma non sempre la capacità, da parte di un ceto intellettuale, di imporre la storia, e lo scrittore di storia, come il momento più alto delle discipline letterarie e della gerarchia sociale. Sembrava favorire questo tentativo la crisi e il rinnovamento degli organismi istituzionali, oltre che ovviamente la situazione culturale profondamente modificata.

Il primo elemento da indicare come caratterizzante l'*historica* umanistica è l'eterogeneità. La sua trattazione è legata a epistole, introduzioni e corsi universitari, prefazioni, lettere di dedica, orazioni, dialoghi; non ha mai uno sviluppo autonomo. E' vero che la teorizzazione dell'*ars historica* non coincide e non si sovrappone alle diverse forme scritte, e che da queste è possibile ricavare, *a posteriori*, ulteriori *artes historicae*, ha pure ugualmente un senso che fino alla prima metà del Cinquecento i tentativi di teorizzazione della storia non abbiano una loro autonomia, pur senza perdere una propria identità. E' una lettera quella di Coluccio Salutati a Fernández de Herédia, lettera quella di Lapo da Castiglionchio il Giovane a Biondo Flavio e quella di Guarino; prefazione quella del Valla (ma tante altre potrebbero essere citate in tal senso); dialogo quello del Pontano.[5] Forme diverse di scrittura dovute forse al peso vincolante del modello antico, all'assenza di un pubblico che non fosse quello degli specialisti e infine alla mancata autonomia accademica della storia.

Seguiamo velocemente Coluccio Salutati. Ad apertura di pagina troviamo l'indicazione della funzione degli storici: "rerum gestarum memoriam studium fuit posteris tradere, ut regum, nationum, et illustrium virorum exemplis per imitationem possent maiorum virtutes vel excedere vel equare ... quoniam rerum gestarum scientia monet principes, docet populos et instruit singulos quid domi quidque foris, quid secum, quid cum familia, quid cum civibus et amicis, quidque privatim vel publice sit agendum."[6]

La storia fa vivere quanto non si è vissuto (*ante oculos posuit*) e a dimostrazione Coluccio cita una lunga serie di esempi, perché: *historie docent* ed insegnano attraverso gli esempi. Non c'è "aliquis virtutis splendor seu deformitas vitiorum, nulla gerendorum

---

il ms., Par. lat. 7530, cf. E. A. Loew, *The Beneventan Script: A History of the South Italian Minuscule*, ed. W. Brown (Roma, 1980[2]), 114–115.

   [4] Vasta la recente bibliografia sulla storiografia umanistica; potrà bastare il rinvio alle relazioni contenute in *La storiografia umanistica*. Convegno internazionale di studi, Messina 22–25 ottobre 1987, 3 vols. (Messina, 1992 ma 1993), e a Mariangela Regoliosi, "Riflessioni umanistiche sullo scrivere storia," *Rinascimento* 31 (1991): 3–37.

   [5] Regoliosi, "Riflessioni," 8, n. 13, anche se la valutazione complessiva sulla letteratura storiografica è solo parzialmente condivisibile.

   [6] *Epistolario di Coluccio Salutati*, ed. F. Novati, vol. 2 (Roma, 1893), 289–292; cf. A. Luttrell, "Coluccio Salutati's Letter to Juan Fernández de Heredia," *Italia Medioevale e Umanistica* 13 (1970): 235–243.

varietas, nulla cautio nullaque deceptio, nullaque denique consilia que non possint ex historyis elici et exemplis illustribus confirmari."[7]

Sono evidenti in queste parole di Coluccio oltre che le forti reminiscenze classiche, la fortissima memoria di un altra lettera di Francesco Petrarca tutta insistita sul ruolo dell'esemplarità. Esemplarità che è funzionale alle necessità personali e sociali: *ad usum humane vite prudentiorem,* perché non c'è chi non possa capire la storia, chi *talium rerum narratio non delectet, qui non possit ex ipsis elicere documentum fugiendi vitium aut imitande virtutis exemplum.*[8]

La funzione etica e politica della storia, che è l'aspetto che interessa in questa sede, non sembra mutata rispetto all'esile teorizzazione dell'anonimo altomedioevale, così come non cambierà a decenni di distanza, alla fine del primo trentennio del Quattrocento, in Lapo da Castiglionchio.

La fedeltà ai modelli era portata da Coluccio alle estreme conseguenze in una totale laicizzazione della storia. Teorizzare la valenza assoluta dell'esemplarità significava presupporre una storia dell'umanità che si ripete, sul modello biologico, ciclicamente; una storia racchiusa in cicli conclusi in sé stessi, che nei secoli precedenti aveva trovato la sua espressione nell'immagine simbolo della ruota della fortuna. Una ripetitività che era colta anche nell'intervento divino, in quanto tale anch'esso prevedibile: "Ut sine contentione fatendum sit concionatoris illud, non solum in naturalibus aut Dei providentia, sed etiam in rebus gestis: 'nichil sub sole novum, nec valet quisquam dicere: hoc recens est'" (Eccl. 1.9–10).[9]

La storia del passato serviva quindi per dare ordine al presente e congetturare sul futuro (*dare presentibus ordinem et coniecturam sumere de futuris*).[10] La riflessione sul passato serve a mettere ordine nella società presente e a preparare il futuro. In questa formula potremmo racchiudere il senso di un'opera, capolavoro tra i più alti, scritta pochi anni prima della lettera di Coluccio ma dedicata tutta e soltanto alla storia contemporanea, opera che l'Anonimo romano o, come ha proposto recentemente Giuseppe Billanovich, Bartolomeo di Iacovo da Valmontone, dedicava a Roma, a Cola di Rienzo e alla propria biografia.[11] Storia contemporanea, ma storia in volgare. Storia dove gli esempi del passato servono a misurare il presente nella volontà, tesa e amara, di sperare in giorni migliori.

Non interessa in questo contesto leggere nel densissimo proemio dell'Anonimo gli echi degli antichi e la ribadita epidittica della storia: "moito belli e buoni esempî; donne porrao omo alcuna cosa pericolosa schifare, alcuna porrao eleiere e adoperare, sì che lo leiere de questa opera non passarao senza frutto de utilitate,"[12] quanto piuttosto fermarci ancora una volta sulla interpretazione della vita umana che ne è alla base. La prima ragione della scrittura della *Cronica* è che in essa "omo trovarao alcuna

---

[7] *Epistolario di Coluccio Salutati,* 292–294 (294).

[8] *Epistolario di Coluccio Salutati,* 295–296.

[9] *Epistolario di Coluccio Salutati,* 294–295.

[10] *Epistolario di Coluccio Salutati,* 295.

[11] Cf. Miglio, "Convegni," *RR. Roma nel Rinascimento* 1993: 239–242.

[12] Anonimo Romano, *Cronica,* ed. G. Porta (Milano, 1979), 4.

cosa scritta la quale se revederao avenire in simile, donne conoscerao che llo ditto de Salomone ène vero. Dice Salomone: 'Non è cosa nova sotto lo sole, ché cosa che pare nova stata è'."[13] Tutto si ripete, e il racconto degli avvenimenti della storia d'Europa alla metà del Trecento potrà essere utile al lettore futuro. L'Anonimo romano sceglie volutamente come argomento quello che Petrarca aveva rifiutato.

Nei decenni seguenti il volgare fu demonizzato, la *Cronica* non fu letta. Non venne meno però la necessità di confrontarsi con la storia contemporanea. E' questo uno degli elementi distintivi della storiografia umanistica. Ribadire la necessità di scrittura della storia contemporanea, racchiudere la storia dei propri tempi nel dettato delle regole storiografiche antiche. Ma questo sembra rimanere per molti anche un nodo irrisolto, tanto da ricorrere a una distinzione lessicale, *commentari* non *storie*, per risolvere le contraddizioni della società in cui vivevano e le proprie discrasie metodologiche.[14]

Sull'importanza della storia contemporanea insiste molto Lapo da Castiglionchio nella lettera/recensione alle *Decadi* di Biondo Flavio.[15] La funzione della storia era la stessa indicata dal Salutati: "Hinc tamquam ex aliquo fonte uberrimo in omnes vitae partes praecepta elici possunt: quae ratio sit domesticae rei administrandae, quo pacto regenda et gubernanda res publica, quibus causis bella suscipienda ... Hinc illa uberrima dicendi copia suppeditatur nobis cum volumus homines ab aliquo vitio deterrere aut impellere ad virtutem. ..." (e tralascio quanto altro aggiunge in proposito).[16] L'esempio è lo strumento didattico per eccellenza. La storia del Biondo è superiore a quella del Bruni, perché solo fiorentina quest'ultima, mentre l'altra coinvolgeva l'Italia intera, e quindi risultava più funzionale *ad communem utilitatem*. Ma la

---

[13] Anonimo, *Cronica*, 4. Per l'Anonimo Romano cf. Miglio, "Anonimo Romano," in *Il senso della storia nella cultura medievale italiana. 1100–1340.* XIV Convegno internazionale di studi, Pistoia 14–17 maggio 1993 (Pistoia, 1995), 175–187.

[14] Gary Ianziti, "Storiografia e contemporaneità. A proposito del *Rerum suo tempore gestarum commentarius* di Leonardo Bruni," *Rinascimento* 30 (1990): 3–28; idem, "I 'Commentarii': appunti per la storia di un genere storiografico quattrocentesco," *Archivio storico italiano* 150 (1992): 1029–1063; idem, "Storiografia come propaganda: il caso dei 'Commentarii' rinascimentali," *Società e storia* 22 (1983): 909–918; idem, "Humanism's New Science: The History of the Future," *I Tatti Studies* 4 (1991): 59–88.

[15] Miglio, *Storiografia pontificia*, 31–59, 187–201. Per Lapo da Castiglionchio cf., recentemente, Vincenzo De Caprio, "Sulle autoproiezioni dell'Umanesimo curiale. Alcune questioni di metodo," in *Roma capitale (1447–1527)*, ed. S. Genzini. Centro di studi sulla civiltà del Tardo Medioevo. San Miniato, Collana di studi e ricerche, vol. 5 (Pisa, 1994), 505–518; e il contributo riedito in John F. D'Amico, *Roman and German Humanism. 1450–1550,* ed. P. Grendler. Collected Studies Series (Alderschot-Brookfield, 1993), III.

In un recense intervento, che ho visto solo dopo la stesura di questo lavoro, Giuliana Crevatin, "Il protagonismo nella storiografia petrarchesca," in *Preveggenze umanistiche di Petrarca.* Atti delle giornate petrarchesche di Tor Vergata, Roma–Cortona, 1–2 giugno 1992 (Pisa, 1994), 27–56, interpreta la lettera di Lapo come indicativa della rimozione dell'opera petrarchesca: "Nella mente di Lapo dunque la grandezza della storiografia del Biondo sta nell'aver risposto al *De viris* del Petrarca con l'argomento che anche il tempo presente ha i suoi *viri illustres* ..." (p. 55).

[16] Miglio, *Storiografia pontificia*, 193.

superiorità del Biondo non é solo nell'aver abbandonato una storiografia d'ambito municipale, ma anche nell'aver scelto di trattare, "non inertia sed consilio," gli avvenimenti a lui contemporanei abbandonando il passato già tanto trattato. Argomento delle *Decadi* è l'età presente "contempta in obscuritate quadam ac tenebris scriptorum inopia"; la scelta di scrivere storia contemporanea costringerà tutti a riflettere che "si qua strenue recteque aut contra nequiter et perperam facerent, ea non modo vivos latere non posse, sed etiam nota posteritati fore."[17]

Lapo non rinuncia, naturalmente, a indicare quali siano le leggi della storia, ripetute, e questo è l'elemento più sorprendente, tenendo presente l'anonimo trattato altomedievale *De historia*: "Ut ne quid falsum admiscere audeant, ne quid verum pretermittant, ne *invidia, gratia, metu,* spe, odio, cupiditate a vera ac recta sententia deducantur,"[18] dove l'anonimo più concisamente aveva dettato: "explorata libere, id est sine *metu* aut *gratia* aut *invidia* referatur." Merito del Biondo, inoltre, era stato aver raccontato gli avvenimenti secondo: "*ordinem temporum, locorum descriptiones,* tum consilia, *acta,* eventus,"[19] così come l'Anonimo aveva affermato che la chiarezza della storia era data dal racconto degli avvenimenti: "*pro temporibus, pro locis, pro actibus.*"

L'elogio della storia è ormai totale; Lapo può giungere ad affermarne la superiorità su ogni altra disciplina; filosofia, geometria, musica, astrologia sono discipline settoriali e sterili, utili solo a chi si dedichi a studi specifici. La storia è totalizzante, sintesi di ogni sapere sviluppa qualsiasi argomento possibile, è *cognitio*/conoscenza che soddisfa l'innata sete di sapere dell'uomo. E' utile e dilettevole anche per la moltitudine delle persone non erudite. La storia sviluppa tutti gli aspetti degli avvenimenti ricordati, che scorrono davanti ai nostri occhi come se noi fossimo presenti (Coluccio Salutati); da essa possiamo scegliere una fonte inesauribile di *praecepta* (nell'Anonimo *sententiae*), e quanto ha raccontato può essere di insegnamento per ogni fase della vita umana e per tutti i momenti della *res publica*, in guerra e in pace e nella vita privata (nell'anonimo: *aut in rebus bellicis, aut in negotiis civilibus, id est pacis*).

Gli *exempla* della storia sono guida nelle scelte quotidiane; il desiderio di gloria che ha ispirato gli attori della storia diventerà il nostro desiderio. La consapevolezza che verrà scritta la storia di quanto si compie sarà un deterrente dal commettere ingiustizie e terrà lontani dai vizi.

La storia è superiore a qualsiasi altra arte: gli avvenimenti ai quali ci fa partecipare quasi visivamente sono veri, esempi storici veri, non *res fictae*, come per le favole della poesia o per le immagini della pittura.[20]

La presunta superiorità della storia innescava una seconda presunzione, forse meno pericolosa, ma individualmente traumatica, che è possibile cogliere in qualche biografia umanistica. E' in discussione ora lo statuto dello storico all'interno della società

---

[17] Miglio, *Storiografia pontificia,* 198.

[18] Miglio, *Storiografia pontificia,* 54, 199. In Roberto Cardini, *Mosaici. Il "nemico" dell'Alberti* (Roma, 1990), 50, n. 4, é proposta la derivazione da Luciano di alcuni passi della lettera di Lapo.

[19] Miglio, *Storiografia pontificia,* 199.

[20] Miglio, *Storiografia pontificia,* 199–201; Paola Casciano, "Storia di un *topos* della storiografia umanistica: *exempla* e *signa*," in *Storiografia umanistica,* 1: 75–92.

contemporanea, la sua dimensione sociale, la sua compartecipazione alla gestione del potere. La superiorità della storia si trasforma spesso nella superiorità dello storico. Non tanto dell'intellettuale, quanto proprio dello storico.

Dopo Lapo altri ancora scriveranno di *ars historica*, o indicheranno i principi ai quali hanno informato il loro lavoro: Guarino, Valla, Pomponio, Platina, Giorgio da Trebisonda, Bartolomeo Fonzio, Poliziano, per nominarne solo alcuni.[21] Trattazioni che sarebbe errato omologare le une alle altre, diversificate come sono dalle sensibilità personali, dalle culture individuali, dai contesti storici e politici. Ma se è vero che ognuno, nella scelta delle sue fonti, intarsiava pagine che finivano per essere sostanzialmente diverse, è altrettanto reale che nessuno rinunciava a indicare la superiorità della storia. Con un retropensiero, che non è difficile individuare altrettanto presente: la funzione primaria ed essenziale dello storico nella società contemporanea. Una primazia svilita e annullata, più che dalla sordità intellettuale dei signori e delle *élites* dirigenti alle quali quelle opere erano consciamente o inconsciamente dedicate, dalla diversa e oramai articolata gestione del consenso che era patrimonio comune.

Riferita alla situazione politica italiana l'*historica* teorizzata si innesta su una contraddizione di fondo: viene pensata come perfettamente funzionale ai nuovi stati regionali, quali quelli che si affermeranno nella prima metà del Quattrocento, sarà vanificata dalla crisi quasi immediata di questi stessi stati, anche se, come conseguenza di questa stessa crisi, verrà irradiata in Europa.

Ritorno per un attimo alla storiografia pontificia individuando nel papato quattrocentesco il più raffinato utente di modelli di comunicazione ideologica, da tutti imitato.

La polemica di ambienti pieschi contro le scelte a tal proposito di Paolo II era costruita con una dura contestazione dei contenuti di quel desidero di gloria che i teorizzatori dell'*ars historica* avevano indicato come una delle motivazioni forti della storia. L'Ammannati invitava il pontefice a incanalare la sua "magna aeternitatis cupido" in una vita incorrotta; nella riforma degli studi ecclesiastici, della disciplina e della libertà del clero, nella preoccupazione per gli infedeli; nella realizzazione della pace tra i popoli; nella pratica di una serie di qualità morali. Era esplicito e violento, al limite dell'invettiva, il rifiuto di quelle che erano le scelte di immagine del pontefice: il desiderio di eternità non si ottiene con monete commemorative, epigrafi, giostre e banchetti: "Ignosce Paule. Veram laudem ista non habent."[22]

All'Ammannati fa da controcanto Giovan Antonio Campano che esprime al pontefice il suo desiderio di scrivere una storia, mai scritta, del suo pontificato, ed elenca i vantaggi della storia: la sola disciplina che crei consenso, senza inventare nulla, che non dica il falso raccontando ogni cosa in modo chiaro e limpido. La storia è: "Fidelis nuntius, testis verus, benignus interpres, diuturnum monumentum, firma indubitaque memoria ...";[23] quanto scelto da Paolo II dà invece solo una temporanea

---

[21] L'attenzione su Pomponio é stata anche recentemente richiamata in Pomponio Leto, *Lucrezio*, ed. G. Solaro (Palermo, 1995), 25.

[22] Miglio, *Storiografia pontificia*, 151–152.

[23] Miglio, *Storiografia pontificia*, 123–124, 149–150.

popolarità: "aedes et statuae et trophea et triumphales arcus et huiusmodi caetera quamvis itura in longum videantur, uno tamen affixae loco, neque tam vagantur late, neque tam diu durant, neque aliquam praesertim tantam afferunt notitiam neque certa sunt et propria ... Sola est historia cui credatur. ..." La verità della storia viene proposta come elemento primario della fruizione: viene letta perché vera; è una verità che dura in eterno, è ubiqua; se la verità si identifica con la storia, la storia si identifica con il suo protagonista.[24]

Anche in questa circostanza gli argomenti fortemente polemici, utilizzati da Campano, perfettamente identici a quelli dell'Ammannati, non sono una novità. Quello che nella prospettiva di entrambi vuole avere un forte significato di contestazione, e cioè il ricorso del pontefice a veicoli ideologici, come palazzi, raccolte statuarie, scritture d'apparato, scenografie effimere, viene ricondotto a elemento di superiorità della storia, a momento della sua teorizzazione. Ricollegandosi pure in questo a una tradizione non certo recente. La superiorità della storia scritta rispetto a quella narrata per immagini era stata affermata da Cicerone e Sallustio, ribadita da Giovanni di Salisbury e Boncompagno da Signa, confusamente accennata dall'Anonimo romano, accentuata da Francesco Petrarca, ripresa da Coluccio Salutati e Lapo da Castiglionchio, ricordata da Leonardo Bruni, esplicitata da Guarino, ancora una volta collegandola direttamente al desiderio di gloria: "Postremo si gloriae ut sic dicam instrumenta conferre libet, annales quamlibet imaginem statuamque praecellunt; hae siquidem corpora dumtaxat, illi vero animos etiam effingunt; hae mutae, illi voce sua terras implent et maria; hae paucis item in locis figi possunt, illi per universum terrarum orbem facile pervagantur disseminarique valent."[25]

Gli strumenti della gloria, del potere e del consenso, nella raffinata arte del governo nel Quattrocento non potevano più essere delegati alla sola storia scritta. I committenti preferirono diversificare in maniera articolata i loro investimenti; se fosse possibile un'analisi comparata vedremmo forse che nella società rinascimentale la fetta di bilancio destinata agli storici è assolutamente marginale, minima la committenza esplicita, dichiarata, diretta, voluta di annali, cronache e biografie.

L'illusione di Lapo, che sarà anche di tanti altri, che la storia governasse gli uomini e che la storia fosse a fondamento di ogni dottrina, che lo ricollegava inconsapevolmente, forse, a Ugo di San Vittore, si annacquava nella realtà contemporanea; ma l'illusione del privilegio della storia e degli storici diventerà patrimonio comune delle culture successive, tanto da lamentare da parte degli uomini di cultura l'insufficienza delle teorizzazioni dell'*ars historica*.

Una brevissima appendice. Nel volume *Puglia neo-latina* compaiono anche le *Lodi della storia*, già pubblicate a Madrid nel 1649 da Paolo Emilio di Tarsia, in testa ai suoi *Historiarum Cupersanensium libri III*. La guida è Cicerone, i motivi quelli tante volte ricordati della funzione della storia e della sua superiorità: "Precipitano sotto gli occhi le cose caduche, scorrono i giorni e le notti: noi non conosciamo gli avvenimenti futuri, quelli presenti non riusciamo a trattenerli, né quelli passati potrebbero tornare

---

[24] Miglio, *Storiografia pontificia*, 47–50.

[25] Miglio, *Storiografia pontificia*, 150; Casciano, "Storia di un *topos*."

alla memoria, se non cavassimo le immagini dall'immenso serbatoio della storia."[26] Insomma, per utilizzare le parole della puntuale introduzione: "Muovendo dunque dal concetto ciceroniano dell'*historia magistra vitae* e dunque da quella visione esemplare, pedagogica e parenetica della storia, che aveva connotato tanta parte del dibattito umanistico, da Petrarca a Salutati, a Guarino e dalla rivendicazione del ruolo primario che la storia e la storiografia dovrebbero avere presso la corte . . . [il Tarsia] propone un modello di storia locale."[27]

Quanto a me interessa notare è che anche gli storici dell'Umanesimo, di un periodo che è oramai sentito come fosse l'antichità, e le loro biografie, diventano ormai un *exemplum*. Spiega infatti il Tarsia che ". . . non solo la storia ma anche gli storici devono essere amati dai principi e da essi accolti." E l'esempio che viene citato è quello di Biondo Flavio, che Pietro Loredan volle presso di sé "come scrive l'Egnazio 'con grandissimi regali lo trascinò a Brescia e lo volle tra i suoi segretari e insieme ad altri onori gli conferì la cittadinanza veneziana'."[28] *Non meno per l'utile che per l'onore*, scriveva ai Medici uno storico marginale ma non minore del Quattrocento, e utile e onore erano le parole guida della storiografia umanistica, ma anche degli storici.

Università "La Tuscia"

---

[26] Maria Aurelia Mastronardi, "Paolo Antonio Tarsia," in *Puglia Neo-Latina. Un itinerario del Rinascimento fra autori e testi*, eds. F. Tateo, M. de Nichilo, P. Sisto (Bari: Cacucci, 1994), 369–399: 384–385.

[27] Mastronardi, "Paolo Antonio Tarsia," 378.

[28] Mastronardi, "Paolo Antonio Tarsia," 386–387.

Heitere Luft und frischer Geist in Italien: Deutsche Humanisten jenseits der Alpen

FIDEL RÄDLE

"Komm unverzüglich nach Italien![1] Du siehst doch, wie das beschwerliche Alter für dich allmählich näherrückt, und wenn du dann Italien nicht gesehen hast, wirst du deines Lebens nie mehr froh werden."

Italiam e vestigio pete. Videsne ingravescentem tibi etatem irripere, que Italia invisa numquam tibi futura est iocunda.[2]

---

[1] Der ursprüngliche mündliche Charakter dieses Beitrags sollte und konnte auch in seiner hier veröffentlichten Fassung nicht getilgt werden. Die zitierte Sekundärliteratur stellt nur eine (auch durch Platzmangel erzwungene) Auswahl aus einer kaum übersehbaren Masse neuer Forschungsergebnisse dar. Bequemen Zugang zu weiteren Arbeiten findet man jetzt in vielen Fällen über die sehr nützlichen neuen Autorenlexika: *Literaturlexikon. Autoren und Werke deutscher Sprache*, hg. von Walther Killy, Band 1–15 (München, 1988–1992); *Deutsche Dichter der frühen Neuzeit (1450–1600). Ihr Leben und Werk*, hg. von Stephan Füssel (Berlin, 1993). Ausgezeichnete Beiträge über die südwestdeutschen Humanisten enthält: *Humanismus im deutschen Südwesten. Biographische Profile*, hg. von Paul Gerhard Schmidt (Sigmaringen, 1993). Für unser Thema sind weiter einschlägig: Jozef IJsewijn, *Companion to Neo-Latin Studies* (Amsterdam, New York, und Oxford, 1977); ders.: *Companion to Neo-Latin Studies, Part 1, Second Entirely Rewritten Edition* (Leuven, 1990); *L'humanisme allemand (1480–1540). XVIIIᵉ Colloque International de Tours.* Humanistische Bibliothek. Reihe I: Abh. 38. (München, 1979); Erich Meuthen, "Charakter und Tendenzen des deutschen Humanismus," in: *Säkulare Aspekte der Reformationszeit*, hg. von Heinz Angermeier unter Mitarbeit von Reinhard Seyboth. Schriften des Historischen Kollegs, Kolloquien 5 (München und Wien, 1983), 217–276; Lewis W. Spitz, *The Religious Renaissance of the German Humanists* (Cambridge, Mass., 1963); ders., "The Course of German Humanism," in: *Itinerarium Italicum*, edd. by H. A. Oberman / Th. A. Brady, Jr. (Leiden, 1975), 371–436; Eckhard Bernstein, *Die Literatur des deutschen Frühhumanismus.* Sammlung Metzler 168 (Stuttgart, 1978).

[2] Ludwig Bertalot, "Humanistisches Studienheft eines Nürnberger Scholaren aus Pavia (1460)," in: ders., *Studien zum italienischen und deutschen Humanismus 1*, hg. von Paul Oskar Kristeller (Rom, 1975), 137.

Dies schreibt gegen Ende des 15. Jahrhunderts ein unbekannter deutscher Student der
Rechte von Padua aus an den magister artium Johannes Berge in Erfurt. Berge hatte
sich zuvor erkundigt, mit welchen Kosten man pro Jahr zu rechnen habe, wenn man
sich "zum Erwerb humanistischer Bildung" (disciplinarum capiendarum gracia) an
italienischen Universitäten aufhalten wolle. Die Antwort ist präzise: "Wenn du sehr
bescheiden leben willst, genügen 25 Rheinische Gulden, für durchschnittlichen Auf-
wand 32, für einen großzügigen Lebensstil höchstens 40."

> Si frugali vitam agere velis, XXV renani aurei, modico vero homini XXXII,
> liberali autem XL ad summum sufficient.[3]

Und dann zählt er seinem Freund auf, was ihn alles in Italien erwartet: er kann Rom
erleben, er kann feine Manieren lernen, er kann sich alle möglichen Tricks[4] aneig-
nen, er kann besseren und billigeren Wein trinken als den "kranken" Wein von
Erfurt, und er wird wunderbare Paläste und Gärten vorfinden: der Schreiber jedenfalls bewohnt mit zwei weiteren Personen ein schöneres Gebäude als der Adressat in
Erfurt mitsamt der Belegschaft seines Kollegiums, "auch wenn es sich nicht eines so
himmlischen Namens erfreut. . . ."[5]

> Cupis urbis videre limina: hic sunt. Cupis mores perdiscere: Italia te reddit
> moratum. Sin vis diversucias intelligere: hec te docebit. Vino libens uteris, scio:
> hic emuntur minoris quam tuus infirmus (ut dicitis). Petis si domos aut hortos
> amenissimos, scito me cum duobus splendidiores incolere edes (quamquam ce-
> lesti careant nomine) quam tua porta celi tota. . . .[6]

Dieser Brief, der, wie man leicht sieht, ein nicht genau abzuschätzendes Maß an
typisch humanistischen Scherzen und auch an Ironie enthält, ist ein Alltagszeugnis[7]
für ein bedeutsames Phänomen der deutschen Kulturgeschichte: in der zweiten Hälfte
des 15. und Anfang des 16. Jahrhunderts gehen die Deutschen in großer Zahl nach
Italien, um den dort bereits blühenden Renaissancehumanismus kennen zu lernen
und nach Möglichkeit über die Alpen zu exportieren. Auch wenn es schon früher
wichtige Kulturkontakte mit Italien, etwa durch Petrarca und Cola di Rienzo unter

---

[3] Bertalot, "Humanistisches Studienheft eines Nürnberger Scholaren," 137.

[4] "Diversucia," sonst nicht belegt, hängt vermutlich mit "versucia" zusammen.

[5] Berge wohnte im Erfurter Universitätskolleg "Porta coeli."

[6] Bertalot, "Humanistisches Studienheft eines Nürnberger Scholaren," 138.

[7] Sehr ähnlich klingt Rudolph Agricolas einladender Brief (aus Pavia) an Johannes Vredewolt:
nonne tibi pulchrum Italiam ipsam videtur, dominatricem quondam principemque gentium,
intueri? unde virtutis illi viri, unde sanctissima, maxima, severissima ingenia prodiere. Ego quidem
vidisse eam tanti puto, ut etiam tibi censeam vel propter hoc solum videndam, ut videris. Nihil de
moribus hominum, nihil de studiis, nihil de reliquis id genus rebus dico. . . . (ed. Karl Hartfelder,
"Unedierte Briefe von Rudolf Agricola. Ein Beitrag zur Geschichte des Humanismus" [1886]),
jetzt in: ders., *Studien zum Pfälzischen Humanismus,* hg. von Wilhelm Kühlmann und Hermann
Wiegand (Heidelberg, 1993, 356f.). Der letzte Satz des Zitats dürfte eine gewisse Reserve gegen-
über dem zeitgenössischen Italien andeuten.—Auch über die Kosten eines Italienaufenthalts gibt
Agricola (ibidem, 357) Auskunft.

Karl IV. gegeben hat—ohne diese neuen Impulse aus persönlichen Italienaufenthalten ist nach allgemeiner Ansicht[8] der deutsche Humanismus nicht zu erklären. Ludwig Bertalot, der den vorliegenden Brief aus einer Berliner Handschrift ediert hat, nennt die entscheidenden Akteure dieses Vorgangs: es waren vor allem "Studenten, die in ihren italienischen Universitätsjahren an der humanistischen Modeliteratur Gefallen fanden und außer juristischen [hier könnte man ergänzen: und medizinischen] Kenntnissen und akademischen Graden auch literarischen Geschmack in die Heimat zurückbrachten."[9]

Bevor ich das Thema meines Vortrags etwas verdeutliche, möchte ich aus eben dieser Arbeit Bertalots eine weitere, wie ich glaube, illustrative Briefstelle zitieren. Der Münchener Caspar Schmidhauser berichtet im September 1460 aus Ferrara dem Schreiber des Kaiserlichen Landgerichts in Nürnberg, Lorenz Schaller, daß er von verschiedenen Seiten getadelt werde, weil er als Jurist "den humanistischen Disziplinen so beharrliches Interesse" entgegenbringe (quod hisce humanitatibus tam assiduam navo operam); seine Antwort darauf sei: Juristen könne man leicht finden und zwar an jeder Universität höchst qualifizierte, hingegen sei es schwierig und gelinge selten, einen hervorragenden "poeta" und "orator" aufzuspüren. "Doch," so fährt er fort, "sie werden mich mit ihren Verleumdungen nicht von meinem Kurs abbringen, bis ich, soweit es an mir ist, den Hafen erreiche. Ich will nämlich meinen Lehrer Guarino, der eine wahre Quelle jeglicher 'humanitas' und aller humanistischen Disziplinen ist, so lange wie möglich genießen. Doch leider ist er schon sehr alt . . . und wird bald sterben."

... responderem . . . , iure consultos posse inveniri facile et quidem in singulis gymnasiis prestantissimos, difficile vero et raro poetam aut oratorem egregium inveniri. Illi tamen suis maledictis cursum meum non impedient, priusquam, quantum in me est, in portum pervenero. Totius namque humanitatis et omnium bonarum disciplinarum fonte preceptore meo Guarino frui volo, quo usque licebit. Sed heu senectute oppressum . . . mors intempestiva rapiet.[10]

Die Zahl deutscher Studenten von der Art des Caspar Schmidhauser in Italien war beträchtlich, wie uns die italienischen Universitätsarchive lehren können und wie vor allem die unerschöpflichen Arbeiten von Agostino Sottili[11] immer neu belegen.

---

[8] Vgl. Otto Herding, "Über einige Richtungen in der Erforschung des deutschen Humanismus seit etwa 1950," in: *Humanismusforschung seit 1945*, Kommission für Humanismusforschung, Mitteilung II, hg. von der deutschen Forschungsgemeinschaft (Boppard, 1975), 76.

[9] Bertalo, "Humanistisches Studienheft eines Nürnberger Scholaren" (wie Anm. 2), 83.

[10] "Humanistisches Studienheft eines Nürnberger Scholaren," 132. Guarino starb tatsächlich noch im Dezember desselben Jahres 1460.

[11] Jetzt gesammelt in: Agostino Sottili, *Università e cultura. Studi sui rapporti italo-tedeschi nell'età dell'Umanesimo*. Bibliotheca Eruditorum 5 (Goldbach, 1993); wichtig sind für unser Thema vor allem die folgenden Aufsätze: "Tunc floruit Alamannorum natio: Doktorate deutscher Studenten in Pavia in der zweiten Hälfte des 15. Jahrhunderts," ibidem, 61*–80*; "La Natio Germanica dell' Università di Pavia nella storia dell' Umanesimo," ibidem, 201*–218*; "Nürnberger Studenten an italienischen Renaissance-Universitäten mit besonderer Berücksichtigung der Universität Pavia,"

Freilich haben nur die wenigsten dieser Studenten literarische Zeugnisse hinterlassen, und die Zahl derer, die in nennenswerter Weise den deutschen Humanismus mitbestimmt haben, bleibt natürlicherweise begrenzt. Ich möchte heute aus der Gruppe dieser deutschen Humanisten der früheren Zeit einige charakteristische Individuen beobachten, die ihre leibhaftige Italienberührung literarisch und "ideologisch" bekennen oder zumindest nicht verleugnen können. Dabei klammere ich manche Namen, wie Erasmus, wegen ihrer einschüchternden Überlebensgröße bewußt aus. Das gilt auch etwa für Hermann von dem Busche, dessen *Vallum humanitatis* (Köln 1518) ein bedeutendes Zeugnis für italienisch fundierte, aber deutsch verarbeitete Humanismus-Konzeptionen darstellt.[12] Ebenso lasse ich die in das 16. Jahrhundert gehörenden großen poetischen Italienreisen der Georgius Sabinus, Georgius Fabricius und Petrus Lotichius Secundus sowie die italienisch beeinflußte Lyrik eines Paulus Melissus Schedius unerwähnt. Diese Autoren sind, mit Ausnahme von Schedius, bereits bei Ellinger[13] ausführlich zu Wort gekommen und haben neuerdings in Hermann Wiegand,[14] Bernhard Coppel[15] und Eckart Schäfer[16] ihre kompetenten Interpreten gefunden.

Ich möchte meinerseits, wie gesagt, aus der früheren Epoche ein paar durch Italien geprägte Autoren betrachten und damit einige Möglichkeiten vorführen, wie man als Deutscher auf Italien reagieren konnte. Dabei ergibt sich implizit auch ein Blick auf humanistische Bildungsprogramme (z. B. bei Rudolph von Langen[17] oder Celtis[18]), die in Deutschland offenbar stärker als anderswo pädagogisch funktionalisiert worden sind. Ich nenne vorweg in der Reihenfolge ihres Auftretens einige Namen, die nun eine gewisse Rolle spielen sollen: Conrad Celtis, Rudolph Agricola, Joachim Vadianus, Giovanni Antonio Campano, Jacob Locher Philomusus, Rudolph

---

ibidem, 319*–373*. In der *Flora* des Hermann von dem Busche findet sich eine ganze Litanei italienischer Universitäten, wohin der Autor der Kölner Studentenschaft zu gehen rät. (Vgl. *Humanismus und Renaissance in den deutschen Städten und an den Universitäten*, hg. von Hans Rupprich [Leipzig, 1935], 146f., V. 222–263.)

[12] Vgl. James V. Mehl, "Hermann v. dem Busche's Vallum humanitatis (1518): A German Defense of the Renaissance Studia Humanitatis," *Renaissance Quarterly* 42 (1989): 480–506.

[13] Georg Ellinger, *Geschichte der neulateinischen Literatur Deutschlands im sechzehnten Jahrhundert*, Band 2 (Berlin und Leipzig, 1929).

[14] Hermann Wiegand, *Hodoeporica. Studien zur neulateinischen Reisedichtung des deutschen Kulturraums im 16. Jahrhundert*. Saecula Spiritalia 12 (Baden-Baden, 1984). Diese Untersuchung ist für unser Thema grundlegend.

[15] Vgl. zuletzt Bernhard Coppel, "Petrus Lotichius Secundus," in: *Deutsche Dichter der frühen Neuzeit* (wie Anm. 1), 529–544.

[16] Vgl. Eckart Schäfer, "Paulus Melissus (Schede)," ibidem, 545–560; ders., "Paulus Melissus Schedius (1539–1602). Leben in Versen," in: *Humanismus im deutschen Südwesten* (wie Anm. 1), 239–263.

[17] Über den im wesentlichen auf ihn gegründeten westfälischen Humanismus vgl. jetzt Wilhelm Righegge, "Westfälische Humanisten (I. Teil)," *Wolfenbütteler Renaissance Mitteilungen* 17 (1993): 107–116; (II. Teil) ibidem 18 (1994): 1–10.

[18] Vgl. dazu u. a. Kurt Adel, "Rodolphus Agricola und Conrad Celtis," in: *Rodolphus Agricola Phrisius 1444–1485*, ed. by F. Akkerman and A. J. Vanderjagt (Leiden etc., 1988), 149–157.

von Langen, Enea Silvio Piccolomini, schließlich, in einem Ausblick, Nikodemus Frischlin.

Das Überqueren der Alpen mit dem Ziel Italien—oder besser gleich mit dem Ziel Rom—war dem Mittelalter so geläufig, daß es sogar ein eigenes Verb dafür gab: "transalpinari" findet man verzeichnet und erklärt im *Catholicon* des Johannes Balbus von Genua aus dem Ende des 13. Jahrhunderts:

> transalpinor, transalpinaris id est ultra alpes ire. Et producitur pi.[19]

Der Gang über die Alpen zur Kurie als der Entscheidungsinstanz der Katholischen Kirche, bereits im 12. Jahrhundert von den Satirikern nicht minder scharf kommentiert[20] als zur Zeit der Reformation, war über Jahrhunderte eine selbstverständliche Übung, und der Unterschied zwischen deutschen Humanisten auf dem Weg nach Italien, Klerikern, die in kirchlichem Auftrag in Rom zu tun hatten, und einfachen frommen Rompilgern ist vor und um 1500 nach außen kaum erkennbar. Die Intentionen differierten, die äußeren, technischen Bedingungen des Reisens und die Begegnung mit dem physischen Italien, waren durchaus vergleichbar. Ob es Zeugnisse von dieser Begegnung gibt und welcher Art sie sind, hängt natürlich von der jeweiligen Funktion der Reise, vom Naturell des Reisenden und ganz besonders vom Zufall der Überlieferung ab.[21]

Dichter haben sicherlich andere Möglichkeiten und Interessen, ihre Reiseerlebnisse festzuhalten, als kirchliche Funktionäre, und auch diese verhalten sich unterschiedlich. Von dem Lübecker Domherrn Albert Krummediek, der im Jahre 1462 wegen des sogenannten Lüneburger Prälatenkrieges an die Kurie reiste, besitzen wir einen hochinteressanten Bericht,[22] in dem allerdings keine einzige emotionale Reaktion des humanistisch sonst durchaus interessierten Verfassers auf das Bildungserlebnis Italien erkennbar wird, während jede einzelne geschäftliche Aktion dieser Reise peinlich genau registriert ist: welche wichtige Person er wann endlich angetroffen hat, wo ihm ein Pferd auf den vereisten Wegen durch die Berge eingegangen ist, wo er für wieviel Geld seinem Begleiter Stiefel gekauft hat, welchen Botenlohn

---

[19] D. h.: die Silbe *pi* ist lang. Vgl. Joannes Balbus, *Catholicon* (first published in Mainz 1460, republished by Gregg International Publishers, 1971).

[20] Vgl. dazu Helga Schüppert, *Kirchenkritik in der lateinischen Lyrik des 12. und 13. Jahrhunderts*. Medium Aevum 23 (München, 1972).

[21] Besonders beklagenswert ist der Verlust der Dokumente, die Conrad Celtis von seiner Italienreise mitgebracht haben muß und die auf seiner Rückreise von Krakau in Breslau verloren gegangen sein dürften. Vgl. dazu Kurt Leopold Preiß, *Konrad Celtis und der italienische Humanismus* (Wien, 1951, Diss. masch.), 53ff. Auffallend wenig bekannt ist auch über Agricolas 10-jährigen Italienaufenthalt. Vgl. Agostino Sottili, "Notizie per il soggiorno in Italia di Rodolfo Agricola," in: *Rodolphus Agricola* (wie Anm. 18), 79–95.

[22] Ed. Dieter Brosius, "Eine Reise an die Kurie im Jahre 1462. Der Rechenschaftsbericht des Lübecker Domherrn Albert Krummediek," *Quellen und Forschungen aus italienischen Archiven und Bibliotheken* 58 (1978): 411–440.

bzw. welches Schmiergeld er dem oder jenem gezahlt hat ("propinare" ist der Terminus dafür). Man gewinnt hier den wahrscheinlich realistischen Eindruck einer mühsamen, von fast übermenschlichem Streß gekennzeichneten Reise durch ein schlecht organisiertes, ja gefährliches Land, und man liest danach die panegyrischen Italien-Gedichte, die von einem Stadtlob in das andere taumeln, mit einem etwas kritischeren Bewußtsein.

Im Gegensatz zu diesem Lübecker Domherrn liegt die Dienst- und Pilgerreise eines anderen kirchlichen Funktionärs aus Deutschland, des Augustinereremiten Martinus Luther, für uns, was die Realien angeht, völlig im Dunkeln. Luther wurde, vermutlich um die Jahreswende 1510/1511, im sog. Staupitz-Streit nach Rom geschickt, aber er hat diese Reise auf keine Weise dokumentiert (genaue Daten, Stationen und Begleiter sind unbekannt). Er hat sich freilich, wie man weiß, das eine oder andere für später gemerkt. Seine Urteile über Rom und die Erinnerungen an den Eindruck, den das heilige Rom aus der Ferne beim überwältigenden ersten Anblick, und den das verdorbene Rom aus der Nähe auf den damals ahnungslos frommen Mönch gemacht hat, stammen alle aus viel späterer Zeit.[23]

Zurück zu den Humanisten und ihren spontanen Äußerungen über Italien. Der Titel dieses Vortrags nimmt implizit Bezug auf eine berühmt gewordene Metapher, mit der Erasmus die humanistischen Pioniertat des Rudolph Agricola bewertet hat. In seinem Brief an Johannes Botzheim vom 30. Januar 1523 schreibt Erasmus: "Als ich ein Knabe war, hatten in Italien die 'bonae litterae' wieder zu sprießen begonnen, aber weil die Kunst des Buchdrucks noch nicht erfunden bzw. erst ganz wenigen bekannt war, kam nichts an Büchern bis zu uns herauf, und es regierten in aller Ruhe jene weiter, die überall ihre ganz und gar geistlose Literatur lehrten. Als erster von allen hat Rudolph Agricola ein kleines Lüftchen (einen Hauch) von der besseren Literatur aus Italien bis zu uns gebracht."[24]

Nam me puero repullulascere quidem coeperant apud Italos bonae literae, sed ob typographorum artem aut nondum repertam aut paucissimis cognitam nihil ad nos librorum perferebatur, et altissima quiete regnabant ubique qui literas docebant illiteratissimas. Rodolphus Agricola primus omnium aurulam quandam melioris litteraturae nobis invexit ex Italia.[25]

---

[23] Wie man sich dem humanistisch-säkularen Erlebnis "Italien" um seines Seelenheiles willen verschließen kann, zeigt das Beispiel des Ignatius von Loyola und seiner Gefährten, die Rom und Italien nur berührten, um über die Begegnung mit dem Papst rasch weiter nach Jerusalem zu kommen. Die beim Bau seiner römischen Niederlassung gefundenen antiken Baudenkmäler verkaufte Ignatius, "um den Erlös guten Zwecken zuzuführen." Vgl. dazu Miquel Batllori, "Zwischen Mittelalter und Renaissance. Ignatius im Strom seiner Zeit," in: *Ignatius von Loyola und die Gesellschaft Jesu 1491–1556*, hg. von Andreas Falkner und Paul Imhof (Würzburg, 1990), 19–30, hier 22.

[24] Eine ähnliche Erfahrung, aus geographischen Gründen von der aktuellen humanistischen Kultur ausgeschlossen zu sein, beschreibt Agricola selbst in einem Brief vom 1. Oktober 1484 an Adolf Rusch (ed. Hartfelder [wie Anm. 7], 381).

[25] *Opus Epistolarum Des. Erasmi Roterodami*, denuo recognitum et auctum per P. S. Allen (Oxonii, 1906), Nr. I, S. 2. Über das Verhältnis Agricola—Erasmus vgl. R. J. Schoeck, "Agricola

Ganz ähnlich wie Erasmus hat sich Joachim Vadianus in seinem historisch-poetologischen Werk *De poetica et carminis ratione* (gedr. Wien 1518) über Agricolas Verdienste für den Humanismus nördlich der Alpen geäußert und bei dieser Gelegenheit die problematische, nämlich trennende Funktion eben dieser Alpen explizit angesprochen. Ich schiebe diese Überlegung vorgreifend ein, weil sie zu unserem gleich zu behandelnden Problem physisch-kultureller Relationen gut paßt. Vadian schreibt über Agricola: "Er war der erste, der durch die Lauterkeit seines Geistes die wahren Musen veranlaßte, jene Alpen zu überqueren, die Deutschland vorher das Recht verweigert hatten, die 'litterae' zur Kenntnis zu nehmen—teils wegen ihrer Höhe und ihrer Unwegsamkeit, die zwar für das Römische Reich sehr günstig war, wie wir aus dem dritten Buch des Plinius[26] wissen, sich für uns jedoch als schädlich erwies, weil durch sie die Gelegenheit zu raschem kulturellen Zugriff unterbunden wurde, teils auch (um die Wahrheit zu sagen) wegen der siegreichen Waffengewalt der Deutschen."

> Primus enim fuit [scil. Rudolphus Agricola], qui Musas ingenuas animi sui candore ultra Alpes illas, ut irent, provocavit, quae Germaniae antea ius nullum litteras agnoscendi praestiterunt: partim ob altitudinem et locorum difficultatem, quae ut Romano imperio saluberrima fuit autore Plinio lib. 3., ita certe noxia nobis visa, quod per eam doctrinarum festina occasio intercepta est; partim (ut id, quod verum est, dicam) ob armorum apud Germanos victricem potentiam.[27]

Während das "Lüftchen von der besseren Literatur" (aurula melioris litteraturae) aus Italien bei Erasmus eindeutig metaphorisch zu verstehen ist, beschreibt Vadianus dasselbe Problem in einem konkreten, nämlich geographischen Zusammenhang. In dem von der Natur gesegneten Italien wohnen fraglos die "Musae ingenuae," die nördlichen Völker aber sitzen buchstäblich "hinterm Berg," ausgeschlossen und abgesperrt durch die Alpen. Diese müssen von jedem, der wie Agricola den Geist der neuen Zeit erleben will, erst einmal physisch überwunden werden, und so kommt es, daß der "Zugang" zu den Ideen des Humanismus immer zusammenfällt mit dem Kontrast-Erlebnis des paradiesischen, nicht nur von der Kultur, sondern auch von der Natur gesegneten Italien jenseits der Alpen. Dadurch sind die Italienbilder wie die realen Italienerlebnisse der aus dem Norden kommenden Humanisten in einem besonderen und auffallenden Maße immer durch die Ethnogeographie oder auch durch die Meteorologie bestimmt.[28] Und das gilt nicht nur für die Humanisten: ich

---

and Erasmus. Erasmus' Inheritance of Northern Humanism," in: *Rodolphus Agricola* (wie Anm. 18), 181–188.

[26] Plinius, *Naturalis Historia* III, IV, 5: . . . pars Galliarum, . . . amne Varo ab Italia discreta Alpiumque vel saluberrimis Romano imperio iugis. . . .

[27] J. Vadianus, *De poetica et carminis ratione*, in: *Humanismus und Renaissance*, ed. Rupprich (wie Anm. 11), 306.

[28] Vgl. Zahlreiche poetische Zeugnisse für derartige innere Befreiung durch *Natur und Kultur* Italiens in humanistischer Zeit sind gesammelt und interpretiert von Pierre Laurens, "Rome et la Germanie chez les poètes humanistes allemands," in: *L'humanisme allemand* (wie Anm. 1), 339–355.

zitiere hier—auch als Kompliment an unsere Gastgeber—leider nur kurz Goethe. Am Beginn der *Italienischen Reise*, unter dem 11. September 1786 (zwischen Bozen und Trient) notiert Goethe:

> Und nun, wenn es Abend wird, bei der milden Luft wenige Wolken an den Bergen ruhen, am Himmel mehr stehen als ziehen, und gleich nach Sonnen-untergang das Geschrille der Heuschrecken laut zu werden anfängt, da fühlt man sich doch einmal in der Welt zu Hause und nicht wie geborgt oder im Exil. Ich lasse mir's gefallen, als wenn ich hier geboren und erzogen wäre und nun von einer Grönlandsfahrt, von einem Walfischfange zurückkäme. . . . Wenn mein Entzücken hierüber jemand vernähme, der in Süden wohnte, von Süden herkäme, er würde mich für sehr kindisch halten. Ach, was ich hier ausdrücke, habe ich lange gewußt, so lange, als ich unter einem bösen Himmel dulde. . . .[29]

Als Kommentar zu Goethe muß man hier unbedingt ein Epigramm des Giovanni Antonio Campano[30] mit dem Titel *In reditu e Germania* zitieren. Campano hatte in Begleitung des Kardinals Francesco Piccolomini-Todeschini, eines Neffen des Enea Silvio, im Jahre 1471 am Reichstag von Regensburg teilgenommen, auf dem die Türkengefahr erörtert wurde, und das Gedicht schildert, gewissermaßen als ein ein-ziger Schwur "Nie wieder Deutschland!," seine Gefühle, als er, wie Goethe, die Alpen in Richtung Süden überwunden hatte und endlich in der Heimat war. Die ersten Verse lauten:

> Linquo Tridentinas Alpes et Rhaetica saxa
> nunquam oculis posthac aspicienda meis.
> Accipe Campani, sterilis Germania, terga,
> accipe nudatas, barbara terra, nates.[31]

Der hier spricht, ist ironischerweise derselbe, der auf dem erwähnten Reichstag in einer Rede, die freilich nicht gehalten wurde, mit Zitaten aus der *Germania* des Taci-tus an die bewährte Tapferkeit der Deutschen appelliert hatte, um sie zum Kampf gegen die Türken zu bewegen.[32]

Ein relativ spätes Dokument aus den fünfziger Jahren des 16. Jahrhunderts ist Jan Kochanowskis Elegie 3,4 (vgl. *Renaissance Latin Verse. An Anthology*, edd. A. Perosa und J. Sparrow [Duckworth: 1979], 551–553, "The Glories of Italy").

[29] Johann Wolfgang von Goethe, *Italienische Reise*, in *Goethe: Werke*. Hamburger Ausgabe, Band 11, hg. von Erich Trunz (München, 8. Auflage 1974), 26.

[30] Über ihn vgl. F. Di Bernardo, *Un vescovo umanista alla corte pontificia: G. Campano (1429–1477)*. Miscellanea Historiae Pontificiae 39 (Roma, 1975).

[31] Perosa und Sparrow (wie Anm. 28), 66.

[32] Vgl. Ludwig Krapf, *Germanenmythos und Reichsideologie. Frühhumanistische Rezeptionsweisen der taciteischen Germania* (Tübingen, 1979), 45–47 und 53–60, vor allem 54, Anm. 14. Zu Campanos verächtlichen brieflichen Äußerungen über die kulturlosen Deutschen vgl. Preiß (wie oben Anm. 21), 204: Campano schreibt u. a.: "Nihil tam foetidum quam Germania, aspectu sunt omnia iniu-cunda, tactu refuga, olfactu graviora." ". . . Taedia Germanica infinita sunt . . . incredibilis est hic

Goethes "böser Himmel," der von der—nach überstandenem Sommer—"milden Luft" im heiteren und fruchtbaren Italien abgelöst wird, ist hier, wie man sieht, humanistisch variiert: "sterilis Germania," "barbara terra," das sind nicht nur Schimpfworte dieses frustrierten Italieners, es sind die faktisch-physischen Tatsachen, die schon seit der Antike literarisch festgestellt waren, speziell im Vergleich mit dem etwa von Vergil gelobten Land Italien, und sie wurden von allen wie selbstverständlich auch metaphorisch verstanden—nämlich auf die Kulturfähigkeit der Deutschen bezogen—und so zu belastenden Bewußtseinstatsachen. Die Deutschen: ein prädestiniertes Nicht-Kulturvolk! Wir werden sehen, wie gerade Conrad Celtis an diesem "ingenuus morbus" der Deutschen, an dieser "vetus Germanorum infamia,"[33] wie er voller Bitterkeit in seiner Ingolstädter Rede vom Jahre 1492 formulierte, gelitten hat und wie er, durch seinen Italienaufenthalt offensichtlich traumatisiert, für den Rest seines Lebens dagegen ankämpfte.

Ein Schüler des Celtis, Jakob Locher Philomusus,[34] der in Italien eine bewegte Studentenzeit verbracht hatte, schrieb bei seinem Abschied aus Bologna (1495?) ein wehmütiges Gedicht an seinen Freund Schoenleben. Er spürt, daß sein poetisches Feuer mit dem Weggang aus Italien erloschen ist:

> Est exstincta mei penitus scintilla furoris
> quo placui Latiis Felsineisque viris.
> 25   terram mutavi Latiam caelumque disertum,
> eloquii sub quo flumina larga fluunt.
> ah, careo studii sociis invitus amoenis
> et te praecipue, qui mihi carus eras.
> inter Teutonicos cogor versare colonos
> 30   atque deas cantu sollicitare novem.[35]

Ich möchte Sie ausdrücklich aufmerksam machen auf das metonymische "caelum disertum" (V. 25), das mir sehr willkommen ist, weil es die enge Relation zwischen physischem und kulturellem "Klima" unterstreicht, um die es in meinem Vortrag

---

ingeniorum barbaries, rarissimi norunt litteras, nulli elegantiam. Nec putes habitare hic Musarum aliquam."

[33] *Oratio in gymnasio in Ingelstadio publice recitata*, in *Selections from Conrad Celtis 1459–1508*, ed. with translation and commentary by Leonard Forster (Cambridge, 1948), 44 bzw. 42: Tollite veterem illam apud Graecos, Latinos et Hebraeos scriptores Germanorum infamiam, qua illi nobis temulentiam, immanitatem, crudelitatem et si quid aliud, quod bestiae et insaniae proximum est, ascribunt.

[34] Über ihn vgl. Bernhard Coppel, "Jakob Locher Philomusus (1471–1528). Musenliebe als Maxime," in: *Humanismus im deutschen Südwesten* (wie Anm. 1), 151–178, vor allem "Locher und Italien," 168–177.

[35] Aus *Elegidium ad Fredericum Bellavita alias Schoenleben*, V. 23–30 (im Anhang des Drucks *Epitoma rhetorices graphicum*, vgl. Coppel, wie Anm. 34, 178), aus Ellinger übernommen in *Lateinische Gedichte deutscher Humanisten*, ausgewählt, übersetzt und erläutert von Harry C. Schnur (Stuttgart, 1967), 244.

noch eine ganze Weile gehen wird. Locher hat, wie man bei Bernhard Coppel[36] lernen kann, nach der Rückkehr aus Italien sein Versprechen, die Musen in Deutschland zu mobilisieren, wahr gemacht. Er schreibt dazu seinem ehemaligen Lehrer Johannes Vetter in einem 1495 gedruckten Brief folgende Sätze: "Ich habe auf einem weiten Weg quer durch die Schulen Italiens versucht, durch Lesen und Schreiben den nahezu ausgelöschten deutschen Namen wieder zum Leben zu erwecken, und ich freue mich über die Maßen, daß jetzt Männer auftreten, welche die Grobheit und Verwilderung der Sprache weit fort aus unserem Land verjagen."

> Feci periculum longe per Latias palaestras, ut et legendo et scribendo nomen Germanicum paene exstinctum suscitarem. Gaudeo plurimum ac laetor iam ortos esse, qui crassam intractabilemque sermonis barbariem procul a finibus nostris propellerent.[37]

Man erkennt hier den vor allem von Celtis propagierten Impetus einer nationalen Anstrengung der Deutschen, kulturell den Anschluß an das arrivierte Italien zu gewinnen—"kulturell" bedeutet hier: nach den humanistischen Normen, die sich vor allem auf die Pflege der lateinischen Sprache bezogen.

Zunächst hatten die deutschen Humanisten, noch ohne an Konkurrenz zu denken, verehrend und sehnsüchtig die begnadete Superiorität Italiens akzeptiert. "Reinen Lufthauch wird er einatmen, wenn er von den zerklüfteten Alpen aus Italien erblickt," schreibt Rudolph von Langen aus Münster, Kommilitone des Rudolph Agricola, in einem Propempticon für seinen Freund Johannes Listhigus:

> Afflatum capiet naribus integrum
> Cernens italiam faucibus alpium . . .[38]

Der Autor erwartet von diesem Freund, daß er den Beutel, den er ihm zur Abreise schenkt, prall gefüllt mit "Gold aus Italien" zurückbringt:

> Ad peram eidem Jo. listigo dono datam:
> Ausonio redeas distentum follibus auro
> Cum domino, munus nobile, marsupium.[39]

Rudolph von Langen hatte 1466 in Rom selber Kontakte zu italienischen Humanisten geknüpft, seine Bibliothek systematisch durch Bücher aus Italien erweitert und die humanistische Reform der Domschule in Münster begründet.[40] Es ist klar, was für Gold er aus Italien erwartete. Die zitierte Sammlung seiner Ge-

---

[36] Wie Anm. 34, 156f.

[37] Ibidem, 156.

[38] "Ad praeclarissimum Iuuenem Iohannem Listhigum Romam e patria sua repetentem Rhodolphi Longii amici sui pro fausto felicique itinere Comprecatio," in: *Rhodolphi Longii. Ca. Monasteriensis Carmina*, 1486 (in der Druckerei des Johannes Limburg), faksimilierter Neudruck, leider ohne Paginierung (Münster, 1991) mit deutschen Übersetzungen von Herman Hugenroth.

[39] Ibidem.

[40] Vgl. dazu Anm. 17.

dichte aus dem Jahre 1486 war übrigens der erste Druck zeitgenössischer humanistischer Lyrik in Deutschland.

Aus Rom hatte Langen zusammen mit dem Statius-Kommentar des Domitio
Calderino ein junges Lorbeerbäumchen geschenkt bekommen. Es wollte, wie der
Geehrte in der Vorbemerkung zu seinem Gedicht über diesen tief symbolischen
Gegenstand bemerkt, "unter diesem kalten Himmel" (sub hoc frigido . . . caelo) nur
mühsam Wurzel schlagen. Daß es dann doch gelang, deutet Langen als günstiges
Zeichen für die bevorstehenden Siege des durchlauchtigsten Herzogs von Österreich,
des späteren Kaisers Maximilian.[41] Auch diese Verse sind gekennzeichnet durch die
fixe Vorstellung von dem harten, unfruchtbaren Boden und dem finsteren, "bösen"
Himmel, die dem Lorbeer, dem Attribut des Herrschers und des Dichters, von Natur
nicht hold sind:

> Roma potens dederat quamvis plantaria viva
>   Germinet ut dura hac inclyta laurus humo:
> Sub tetrico magni valeat coalescere caelo
>   Laurigerae ducis hoc commeruere comae. . . .

Das—im Blick auf Italien kränkende—Bewußtsein, als Deutscher unter einem in
mehrfacher Hinsicht "bösen Himmel" zu leben,[42] hat niemand deutlicher zum
Ausdruck gebracht und also schmerzlicher verspürt als der schon öfter genannte
Conrad Celtis.[43] Er war der ethno-geographischste unter allen deutschen Humanisten: sein Weltbild wurde von der Geographie und Ethnographie in einem ebenso
universalen Sinn wie von der Astronomie bestimmt.[44] Kulturelle Leistungen waren
für ihn noch weit mehr als für die Antike Leistungen eines Landes, eines Stammes
oder einer Nation, zumindest gehörten sie nicht einer einzelnen Person, auch wenn
persönlicher Ruhm für ihn natürlich immer ein verlockender Gedanke gewesen ist.
Die Entdeckung der Buchdruckerkunst hat er, wie noch zu zeigen sein wird, immer
der deutschen Nation gutgeschrieben, einmal sogar dem Rhein.[45]

---

[41] "In iam dictae lauri arbusculam Roma adductam egre hic coalescentem: quasi tamen in
Illustrissimi ducis Austriae futuras laetasque victorias sub hoc frigido germinat caelo: quam et cir-
cumsatum ocymum basilicae herba exuberantissime pullulans magnam frondosamque fore promisit"
(wie Anm. 38).

[42] Am Beispiel des Gregor Heimburg schildert Arnold Esch, Pius II. referierend, den zur
unbedingten Italienliebe der Deutschen komplementären "Rom-Koller," der im vorliegenden Fall
durch das notorisch problematische Sommerklima in Rom mitbedingt ist: Arnold Esch, "Rom
und Bursfelde: Zentrum und Peripherie," in: *900 Jahre Kloster Bursfelde. Reden und Vorträge zum
Jubiläum 1993*, hg. von Lothar Perlitt (Göttingen, 1994), 56. Über Du Bellay's zuletzt mühsamen
Romaufenthalt vgl. Jozef IJsewijn, "Joachim du Bellay's 'Patriae Desiderium'," *Humanistica Lovaniensia* 40 (1991): 244–261, bes. 245f.

[43] Für seine Beziehung zu Italien durchaus ergiebig: Preiß (wie Anm. 21).

[44] Vgl. dazu besonders Rosmarie Füllner, *Natur und Antike. Untersuchungen zu Dichtung,
Religion und Bildungsprogramm des Conrad Celtis* (Göttingen, 1956, Diss. masch.), 136–144.

[45] Vgl. *Fünf Bücher Epigramme von Konrad Celtis*, hg. von Karl Hartfelder (Berlin, 1881,
Nachdruck Hildesheim, 1963); *Epigr.* 2, 56: "Ad Rhenum, qui artem imprimendi invenerit." (S.
35)

In seinem zuletzt erwähnten Gedicht hatte sich Rudolph von Langen dankbar gezeigt, daß sein Lorbeerbäumchen aus Rom in Westfalen Wurzel geschlagen hat: Celtis dagegen fordert in seiner berühmtesten Ode Apollo, den Gott des Lorbeers, auf, gleich selber nach Deutschland zu kommen. Sie lautet:[46]

Ode ad Apollinem repertorem poetices:
ut ab Italis cum lyra ad Germanos veniat

Phoebe, qui blandae citharae repertor,
Linque delectos Heliconque Pindum
Et veni nostris vocitatus oris
    Carmine grato.

Cernis ut laetae properent Camenae
Et canant dulces gelido sub axe;
Tu veni incultam fidibus canoris
    Visere terram.

Barbarus, quem olim genuit vel acer
Vel parens hirtus, Latii leporis
Nescius, nunc sit duce te docendus
    Pangere carmen.

Quod ferunt dulcem cecinisse Orpheum,
Quem ferrae atroces agilesque cervi
Arboresque altae celeres secutae
    Plectra moventem.

Tu celer vastas aequoris per undas
Laetus a Graecis Latium videre
Invehens Musas voluisti gratas
    Pandere et artes.

Sic velis nostras, rogitamus, oras
Italas ceu quondam aditare terras,
Barbarus sermo fugiatque, ut atrum
    Subruat omne.[47]

---

[46] Es erschien zuerst im Jahre 1486 im Anhang zur *Ars versificandi et carminum*. Vgl. dazu Franz Josef Worstbrock, "Die 'Ars versificandi et carminum' des Konrad Celtis," in: *Studien zum städtischen Bildungswesen des späten Mittelalters und der frühen Neuzeit*, hg. von Bernd Moeller, Hans Patze und Karl Stackmann (Göttingen, 1983), 467; dort (Anm. 23) sind die zahlreichen Interpretationen dieses Gedichts verzeichnet; seither kamen hinzu: Eckart Schäfer, "Conrad Celtis' Ode an Apoll," in: *Gedichte und Interpretationen. Band 1: Renaissance und Barock*, hg. von Volker Meid (Stuttgart 1982), 81–93, und Dieter Wuttke, "Conradus Celtis Protucius," in: *Deutsche Dichter* (wie Anm. 1), 177–179.

[47] Nach dem bei Schäfer und Wuttke (vgl. Anm. 46) abgedruckten Text, dessen vierte Strophe von der in Schnurs Sammlung (vgl. Anm. 35), S. 54f., wiedergegebenen Fassung abweicht.

Schon Peter Luder, der früheste deutsche Wanderhumanist, hatte für sich in Anspruch genommen, als erster die Musen von Italien, ihrem seit langem angestammten Sitz, in sein Vaterland gebracht zu haben:

> Primus ego in patriam deduxi vertice Musas
> Italico mecum, fonte Guarine tuo.[48]

Das Distichon variiert Vergils Verse aus dem dritten Buch der *Georgica* (10f.):

> Primus ego in patriam mecum, modo vita supersit,
> Aonio rediens deducam vertice Musas.[49]

Was Celtis in seiner Ode an Apollo ausspricht, ist allerdings viel kühner—und zudem ein später ernsthaft verfolgtes kulturpolitisches Programm. Er betreibt nichts Geringeres als die Abwerbung Apollos aus Italien nach Deutschland, und dieser postulierte Vorgang der "translatio studii" ist für ihn vergleichbar mit dem epochalen Übergang der griechischen Kulturmacht auf die Römer in der Antike.[50]

---

[48] Frank Baron, *The Beginnings of German Humanism: The Life and Work of the Wandering Humanist Peter Luder* (Berkeley, 1966), 16f. und 208. Vgl. auch ders., "Peter Luder," in: *Deutsche Dichter* (wie Anm. 1), 83–95, hier 84.

[49] Auch Celtis variiert diese Verse, z. B. in *Epode* 12, V.7f. Vgl. Conradus Celtis Protucius, *Liber odarum quattuor. Liber Epodon. Carmen saeculare*, ed. Felicitas Pindter (Leipzig, 1937), 111f.

[50] Panegyrisch relativiert, als Wunsch und feierliche Beschwörung, ist das "Programm" des Celtis auch im ersten Gedicht seiner Odensammlung "Ad Fridericum Caesarem pro laurea proseutice" enthalten. Die wichtigsten Verse, deren Inhalt dem der Einladung an Apollo z. T. sehr nahe kommt, lauten (ed. Pindter [wie Anm. 49], S. 1f.):

	Germanis populis te duce maximus
10	Laudis surgit honos, dum fugit horrida
	Morum barbaries, foedaque saecula
	Commutata nitent per vaga sidera.
	Saltamus, canimus nec male pingimus
	Et chordas resonas pollice tangimus.
15	Nil nobis peregre est difficile aut modo
	Rimantes variis artibus abditam
	Naturae seriem, Dorica et Itala
	Miscentes pariter non sine gloria.
	Te vivo Latiis gloria litteris
20	Antiquumque decus iam redit artibus,
	In lucem veniunt cum modo singula,
	Quae Grai et Latii condiderant viri....
25	Hinc caelum omne patet terraque cognita est
	Et, quid quadrifidis continet angulis,
	In lucem veniunt arte Alemanica,
	Quae pressis docuit scribere litteris.
	Te vivo lyricos iam canimus modos
30	Et laudata viris plectra prioribus
	Concinnis fidibus pollice tangimus.
35	... Hoc Grai studio nomen ad aethera

Auf Apollo wartet in Deutschland eine schwere Aufgabe. Zwar eilen die Musen schon herbei und singen bereits unter dem kalten Himmel, doch das meiste bleibt noch zu tun: die "inculta terra"[51] ist vom Gott der Kultur erst in Besitz zu nehmen. Ihre barbarischen Bewohner wissen nichts von römischer Eleganz und müssen darum im Dichten noch "unterrichtet" werden, damit die unkultivierte Sprache verschwinde und "alles Düstere" entfalle. "atrum omne" ist ein Sammelbegriff für das, was der aus dem Norden kommende Italienreisende bei seiner Begegnung mit dem italienischen Licht schmerzlich als sein Teil empfindet. Er beschreibt im Sinne der antiken Ethnographie zugleich die klimatische wie die psychologisch-kulturelle Bedingung menschlichen Lebens nördlich der Alpen.[52]

Man könnte in den Schriften der deutschen Humanisten weitere Adjektive ähnlicher Bedeutung und Funktion finden.[53] Celtis gebraucht oft "rigidus" ("sub caelo rigido")[54] und bezeichnet sich selber als den dem rauhen Klima entsprechenden "rigidus vates."[55] Ein Schlüssel—und Sehnsuchtswort in der Poesie des Celtis ist auf der anderen Seite "nitidus"—"hell und frisch strahlend."

> Fuderunt Italis inde sequacibus.
> Et nos nunc facili tenuia barbito,
> Illorum celeres dum sequimur pedes,
> Caelo sub rigido carmina spargimus. . . .

[51] Es ist hier zu betonen (und gilt für diesen Beitrag insgesamt), daß es im Bewußtsein der Deutschen—und zumal des Celtis—wie auch der betroffenen Italiener beträchtliche Unterschiede in der Bewertung der einzelnen Landschaften der "Germania" gab. Vgl. dazu Esch [wie Anm. 42], 37f. und 48.

[52] Stellvertretend für viele ein Zeugnis solchen Bewußtseins bei Celtis, *Carm.* 2, 12 (V. 13–20):

> Rara haec sub oris gloria Teutonis
> Prisco creatos sanguine nobiles
>   Musarum et optandae sophiae
>   Ingenuas habuisse curas.

> Effrenis obstat mentibus impetus
> Et blanda Bacchum quae sequitur Venus,
>   Aut barbari mores, gelato
>   Frigida quae dedit Ursa caelo. . . .

(ed. Pindter [wie Anm. 49] S. 44)

[53] Z. B. tetricus, tristis, asper.

[54] Vgl. z. B. *Carm.* 1, 1, 39; 1, 2, 3; 1, 2, 67; 2, 11, 15f.; 2, 12, 17–20 etc.

[55] Vgl. *Carm.* 2, 11, 15f. Eine entsprechende Vorstellung kommt auch in den folgenden an Celtis adressierten Versen des Angelus Rampler zum Ausdruck:

> Tu modo Celtis, Latias Camaenas
> Italas terras, placidasque gentes
> Dereliquisti, rigidas petisti;
>   Plaudite, Musae!

(*Der Briefwechsel des Konrad Celtis*, gesammelt, hg. u. erläutert von Hans Rupprich [München, 1934], S. 337, 91ff.).

Wenn die deutschen Humanisten—im Vergleich mit Italien—das "atrum," das "tetricum" und "rigidum" ihres physischen und kulturellen Milieus konzedieren, so ergeben sie sich damit vor allem auch den herrschenden Bewußtseinstatsachen, die nicht zuletzt deshalb unkorrigierbar erscheinen, weil sie durch die antiken Klassiker bestätigt sind. Vergil hatte im zweiten Buch der *Georgica* sein Lob Italiens gesungen, den ewigen Frühling dieses Landes gepriesen und seine natürliche wie geistige Fruchtbarkeit gerühmt (2,149 und 173f.):

> Hic ver assiduum atque alienis mensibus aestas. . .
> Salve, magna parens frugum, Saturnia tellus
> magna virum.

Dagegen ließ sich nichts sagen und nichts machen.[56] "Germania" kommt bei Vergil nur dreimal vor, zweimal davon im Zusammenhang mit Krieg.

Ein anderer antiker Gewährsmann, an dem man als Deutscher auf dem Weg nach Italien nicht vorbeikam, Tacitus, ist viel expliziter.[57] Der in unserm Zusammenhang fürchterlichste Satz des Tacitus steht im zweiten Kapitel der *Germania* und lautet: "Wer würde, ganz abgesehen von der Gefahr, den das schreckende und unbekannte Meer bietet, Asien, Afrika oder Italien verlassen, um nach Germanien zu ziehen mit seinen häßlichen Landschaften, dem rauhen Klima, dem trostlosen Äußeren—es sei denn, es ist seine Heimat?"

> Quis porro praeter periculum horridi et ignoti maris Asia aut Africa aut Italia
> relicta Germaniam peteret, informem terris, asperam caelo, tristem cultu
> aspectuque, nisi si patria sit?[58]

Conrad Celtis hat sich mit der *Germania* des Tacitus in Vorlesungen befaßt und im Jahre 1500 in Nürnberg eine Edition dieses Werks veranstaltet. Seit 1493, also nach seiner Rückkehr aus Italien, wo er die humanistische Idee einer Beschäftigung mit nationaler Geschichte kennen lernen konnte, trug er sich mit dem Gedanken, eine *Germania illustrata* (nach dem italienischen Modell des Flavio Biondo) zu schaffen. Einzelne Stücke dieses "großen patriotischen Projekts"[59] einer poetischen Beschreibung Deutschlands haben sich erhalten, und ihre innere Verbindung mit Tacitus, der in diesen Gedichten zumindest implizit korrigiert wird, dokumentiert sich allein schon darin, daß Celtis sie seiner Edition der *Germania* des Tacitus bei-

---

[56] Schon für das Mittelalter waren die Superlative maßgebend, mit denen Isidor von Sevilla (*Etym.* 14, 4, 18) Italien bedacht hatte: "(Italia) . . . ab occiduo Alpium iugis finitur, terra omnibus in rebus pulcherrima, soli fertilitate, pabuli ubertate gratissima. . . ."

[57] Vgl. zu diesem Komplex Krapf (wie Anm. 32) und Jacques Ridé, *L'image du Germain dans la pensée et la littérature allemandes de la redécouverte de Tacite à la fin du XVIe siècle. Contribution à l'étude de la génèse d'un mythe*, 3 vols. (Lille, 1977), besonders Kapitel IV: "Les Germains dans l'oeuvre de K. Celtis (Caractéristique et fonction d'une image)," 1: 229–259.

[58] Tacitus, *Germania* 2.

[59] Dazu Jacques Ridé, "Un grand projet patriotique: 'Germania illustrata'," in: *L'humanisme allemand* (wie Anm. 1), 99–111.

gab.[60] Unter den erhaltenen Teilen dieser poetischen Celtis-*Germania* finden sich 18 Verse über die *qualitas telluris per Germaniam*, die fast wie Vergils Lob Italiens beginnen:

> Terra hominum pecudumque ferax quaeque ubere gleba
> Spiciferam Cererem multo cum fenore reddit
> Pascua florigeris extendens pinguia pratis
> Ingentesque lacus. . . .[61]

Das klingt nicht nur nach Vergil, es ist z. T. Vergil: wenigstens der erste Vers variiert Aeneis 1, 531 (terra antiqua, potens armis atque ubere glaeba), und es muß eine Ironie des Zufalls oder des Celtis sein, daß bei Vergil damit Italien beschrieben wird (nunc fama minores / Italiam dixisse ducis de nomine gentem . . . , V. 532f.) Gleichzeitig sind diese Verse erkennbar eine Antwort auf Tacitus, der den Germanen nicht nur die natürlichen Ressourcen, sondern vor allem jede zivilisatorische und kulturelle Begabung abgesprochen hatte. Gerade diese rühmt Celtis nun in den folgenden Versen fast trotzig, und es ist halb Zustandsbeschreibung und halb Appell oder Versprechen[62] wenn er sagt: "So können sich die verschiedenen Arten, das Land zu bebauen, entfalten, die Städte verfügen über den Schutz von ansehnlichen Mauern, und es entsteht ein milderes Volk im Bereich Germaniens, nachdem die wilde Rohheit verbannt ist, die früher der ungebildete Waldbewohner in den sumpfigen Gebirgswäldern noch bewahrt hatte."

> Hinc varii cultus cultisque in moenibus urbes,
> Mitior et populus Germano nascitur orbe
> Explosa ruditate fera, quam barbarus olim
> Silvicola in riguis servabat saltibus ortus.[63]

Ein wenig klingt hier noch die Ode an Apollo nach, aber die Verse sind, wie schon gesagt, eine implizite Richtigstellung des Tacitus. Dabei kann sich Celtis auf einen Italiener, auf Enea Silvio Piccolomini, stützen, der im zweiten Buch seiner *Germania*[64] auf der Folie der frühen Zustandsbeschreibung des Tacitus die unglaubliche zivilisatorische Entwicklung Germaniens dargestellt hatte, die ganz dem segensreichen Wirken ("beneficium") des apostolischen Stuhles zuzuschreiben sei.[65] Celtis

---

[60] Die Stücke sind ediert von Kurt Adel, *Conradi Celtis quae Vindobonae prelo subicienda curavit opuscula* (Leipzig, 1966), 55–72; zu den Überlieferungsverhältnissen vgl. ebenda S. 49–54.

[61] V. 1–4, ed. Adel (wie Anm. 60), 63.

[62] Bei den Humanisten ist, wie Worstbrock (vgl. Anm. 46), 464, formuliert, die "Inkongruenz von Programm und Erfüllung" durchaus "nicht selten."

[63] V. 10–14, ed. Adel (wie Anm. 60), 64. Vgl. dazu auch Hermann Hamelmann, "Oratio de quibusdam Westphaliae viris claris, qui *explosa barbarie* puritatem Romanae Linguae toti Germaniae attulerunt" (Lemgo, 1563).

[64] Adolf Schmidt (Hg.), *Aeneas Silvius: "Germania" und Jakob Wimpfeling: "Responsa et Replicae ad Eneam Silvium"* (Köln / Graz, 1962).

[65] ". . . ostendendum imprimis est, quenam fuerit olim Germania et que sit hodie" (ibidem, 45).

ist da natürlich anderer Ansicht: die machtvolle Entfaltung des Heiligen Römischen Reichs deutscher Nation ist ein Resultat der inneren Kraft der deutschen Stämme.[66] Der mit Stolz geäußerte Anspruch auf diese historische Leistung und die Besinnung auf die vollends, nämlich durch humanistische Kultur, zu mobilisierende geistige Kraft der Deutschen—das ist der Kern des Bildungsprogramms, das Celtis in seiner Ingolstädter Rede vom Jahre 1492 entwarf.

Die "aemulatio" mit dem stolzen Italien, ein allgemeines Signum und Movens des deutschen Humanismus,[67] ist bei Celtis besonders scharf ausgeprägt, und es ließe sich mit vielen seiner Äußerungen—auch aus der Ingolstädter Rede—zeigen, daß diese "aemulatio" durch die persönliche Italien-Erfahrung noch einen Schuß Aggressivität erhalten hat.[68] Celtis sieht einen unausrottbaren Gegensatz zwischen den beiden Völkern und meint, man könne froh sein, daß die Alpen zwischen ihnen

---

[66] Vgl. dazu Krapf (wie Anm. 32), vor allem im Kapitel III ("Die Rezeption der 'Germania' im frühen deutschen Humanismus") die Abschnitte "1 c. Celtis' humanistische Kulturkritik (simplicitas als ästhetisches Problem)," S. 91ff., und "1 d. Die Synthese von Zeitkritik und humanistischer Programmatik (simplicitas = simplicitas morum und simplicitas = barbaries)," S. 93ff. Krapfs entschieden positive Bewertung von "simplicitas" als "Sittlichkeit" (und als einer der beiden "Zielvorstellungen" des Celtis, neben der "humanistischen Bildung") bedürfte einer Korrektur: die von Celtis angestrebte Sittlichkeit ist gewiß liberaler, antik-rhetorischer, sozusagen Ciceronischer gedacht, als es eine lediglich vom Makel der "barbaries" geheilte germanische "simplicitas" werden könnte.

[67] vgl. Celtis, *Epigr.* 4, 60 (ed. Hartfelder [wie Anm. 45], 87):

> Ad imaginem Philosophiae in aula Viennensi
> Philosophia triplex, triplici circumdata lingua
> Hic habito, Italicis aemula facta scholis.

Im Jahre 1520 schrieb Johannes Caesarius in der Widmung seiner *Dialektik* an Hermann von Neuenahr: Vel forte adeo stupida sit nostra praecipue Germania, ut sua non norit bona [vgl. Vergil, *Georgica* 2, 459], praesertim hac tempestate, qua (si verum fateri licebit, citra tamen aliarum nationum iniuriam) una Germania, si Italiam non superat, ei tamen cedere ut non debet ita non vult, non tam imperii (quod sibi ante annos septingentos viribus et virtute sua peperit) ratione, quam doctissimorum virorum foecunditate et incredibili propemodum studiorum foetura. (*Humanismus und Renaissance*, ed. Rupprich [wie Anm. 11], 158f.). Krapf (wie Anm. 32), 93, spricht vom "Wettkampf mit den italienischen Humanisten, der zu einem Trauma der deutschen Frühhumanisten wurde."

[68] Vgl. den 1491 in Ingolstadt an Sixtus Tucher geschriebenen Brief, in dem Celtis seine kulturpolitischen Bestrebungen in einem ausdrücklich unfreundlichen Wetteifer mit Italien formuliert. Er strenge sich an, schreibt er, "ut aliquid excuderem, quod, etsi Italicis ingeniis impar foret, Germanos tamen nostros, qui me doctrina et ingenio et multum haec duo fulcientibus opibus praestarent, impellerem expergefaceremque, quo Itali in suam gloriam effusissimi fateri cogerentur non solum Rhomanum imperium et arma, sed et litterarum splendorem ad Germanos commigrasse." (ed. Rupprich, wie Anm. 55, Nr. 15); einen ähnlichen Tenor hat das am 28. März 1492 an König Maximilian adressierte Widmungsschreiben zur *Epitoma in utramque Ciceronis Rhetoricam* (ed. Rupprich, ibidem, Nr. 25). Das "Aufwecken" der Deutschen wird übrigens später ein (scharf gegen Italien gerichtetes) Hauptanliegen Ulrichs von Hutten sein.

lägen.[69] Auch für Celtis war die Erfindung des Buchdrucks, die er stolz "ars Alemanica" nennt, die triumphalste kulturelle Errungenschaft der Deutschen.[70] Es ist immer wieder überraschend zu sehen, wie beflissen die deutschen Humanisten mit diesem Pfund zu wuchern suchten. Die Richtung des Imponiergehabes war dabei immer Italien: "ne Italo cedere videamur"—"Es soll nicht der Eindruck entstehen, als stünden wir dem Italiener nach," so lautete das Motto des Augsburger Druckers Gunther Zainer.[71]

Ich werfe zum Abschluß einen Blick in das Jahr 1583. Der schwäbische Humanist Nikodemus Frischlin,[72] immer etwas spät dran, brachte in diesem Jahr an der Universität Tübingen ein lateinisches Schauspiel mit dem Titel *Julius Redivivus*[73] auf die Bühne. Gemeint war damit Julius Cäsar.

Das Redivivus-Motiv, literarisch und vor allem didaktisch oft von überraschender, auch komischer Wirkung, konnte Frischlin bei einem uns bereits vertrauten Autor und in einem uns bereits vertrauten Zusammenhang vorfinden: in der *Germania* des Enea Silvio. Dieser rühmte, wie bereits dargestellt, im Vergleich mit der *Germania* des Tacitus die imponierende zivilisatorische Entwicklung des neuen Deutschland, die dem Christentum, also der römischen Kurie, zu verdanken sei, und er stellt sich vor, wie wohl ein alter Germane reagieren würde, wenn er heute in dieses Land käme. Enea Silvio schreibt: "Es wäre zu wünschen, daß einer der alten Germanen von den Toten auferstünde.... Denn wenn man einen von ihnen heute vernehmen könnte,

---

[69] Pudeat, nobiles viri, in sugillationem et amaram cavillationem Germani nominis modernis quorundam historiis, qui se novarum Decadum editione illud priscum Romanum imperium aequasse gloriantur, clarissimos principes nostros natalicio illorum nomine suppresso barbaros tantum vocari: tantum potuit vetus et inexpiabile inter nos odium et antiqua discordia numinum, quam nisi provida natura Alpibus et elatis in sidera scopulis diremisset, a mutuis caedibus pro hostili utrimque spiritu nunquam temperaretur (*Oratio*, ed. Forster [wie Anm. 33], 44). Die Empörung des Celtis, daß italienische Historiker die Deutschen verhöhnten und ihre Fürsten nicht mit dem Geburtsnamen, sondern mit dem Appellativum "Barbaren" bezeichneten, bezieht sich auf die *Historiae rerum Venetarum ab urbe condita libri XXIII* (Venedig, 1487) des Marcus Antonius Coccius Sabellicus, dem Celtis nach Ausweis seiner Vita in Italien persönlich begegnet war.

[70] Vgl. dazu das an Kaiser Friedrich gerichtete erste Gedicht der Odensammlung (V. 25–28), das oben in Anm. 50 zitiert ist, und *Carm.* 3, 9; außerdem *Epigr.* 2, 56, sowie u. a. *Epigr.* 5, 64 (ed. Hartfelder [wie Anm. 45], 115):

In inventorem artis typographicae
Qualem te memorem, talem qui inveneris artem
Italicis, Graiis plus memorande viris?

[71] In der Tendenz vergleichbar: Sebastian Brants *Ad dominum Iohannem Bergmann de Olpe, de praestantia artis impressoriae a Germanis nuper inventae Elogium* (ed. Schnur [wie Anm. 35], 16). Vgl. auch Herding (wie Anm. 8), 90, und den stolzen Satz des Johannes Caesarius: . . . una Germania, si Italiam non superat, ei tamen cedere ut non debet ita non vult . . . (zit. in Anm. 67).

[72] Über ihn zuletzt Wilhelm Kühlmann, "Nicodemus Frischlin (1547–1590)," in: *Humanismus im deutschen Südwesten* (wie Anm. 1), 265–288, und Richard E. Schade, "Philipp Nicodemus Frischlin," in: *Deutsche Dichter* (wie Anm. 1), 613–625.

[73] Nicodemus Frischlinus, *Julius Redivivus*, hg. von Walther Janell. Lateinische Litteraturdenkmäler 19 (Berlin, 1912).

würden wir von ihm die Behauptung hören, dieses Land, das er so zivilisiert sehe, könne unmöglich Germania sein."

Vellemus a mortuis aliquis ex illis veteribus resurgeret.... Nam si quis horum nunc audiri posset, audiremus eum profecto Germaniam non esse asseverantem terram ipsam, quam tam bene cultam videret.[74]

Frischlin stellt sich in seinem Tübinger *Julius Redivivus* umgekehrt die Frage, was wohl die alten *Römer* zum neuen Deutschland sagen würden, und er erfüllt seinen deutschen Landsleuten wenigstens auf der Theaterbühne den alten Wunsch,[75] der in der Wirklichkeit nur selten in Erfüllung gegangen war: daß nämlich Italiener nach Deutschland kamen[76] und sich von der deutschen Kultur beeindruckt zeigten.[77] Die beiden "Italiener" bzw. Römer, die Frischlin auftreten ließ, waren das Beste, was man sich als Humanist ausdenken konnte: Cäsar und Cicero. Diese beiden kommen aus der Unterwelt herauf und müssen sich tief beeindruckt, z. T. ungläubig, ansehen, was Deutschland im 16. Jahrhundert zu bieten hat: die schönen deutschen (süddeutschen) Städte, die mit Schießpulver operierenden Waffen und Kriegsmaschinen und, natürlich, eine Buchdruckerei. Zufällig hören Cäsar und Cicero einen italienischen Gastarbeiter, einen Kaminfeger ("Caminarius," V. 1503ff.), reden und sind entsetzt darüber, was aus der lateinischen Sprache in Italien geworden ist; zur gleichen Zeit hören sie ganz überwältigt den deutschen Humanisten Eobanus Hessus wunderbar, "Romano more" (V. 1423), lateinisch sprechen, und Cicero stellt endlich fest, was alle schon immer hören wollten: "Was bedeutet das alles? Doch nichts anderes, als daß Italien und Griechenland die Alpen überquert haben."

> CAESAR: O dii, quid audio?
> CICERO: Quid enim, nisi quod Alpes hasce Italia / Et
> Graecia transvolarunt.[78]

Universität Göttingen

---

[74] Aeneas Silvius, *Germania* (wie Anm. 64), 65f.

[75] Man vergleiche den poetischen Brief (ed. Rupprich [wie Anm. 55], Nr. 2), den Celtis an Fridianus Pighinutius, den aus Lucca stammenden Erzieher und Orator des Erzbischofs von Magdeburg, Ernst von Sachsen, im Jahre 1486 von Leipzig aus schreibt. Celtis ist geradezu gerührt und dankbar, daß ein Italiener die Mühe und Entbehrung auf sich nimmt, in das unwirtliche Deutschland zu kommen und sich des nur schwer bildbaren Deutschen anzunehmen ("indocilem Almanum et erudiisse velis").

[76] Hermann Wiegand (wie Anm. 14), 27, schreibt zu dem auffallenden Mangel an Hodoeporica italienischer Autoren: "Die Dichter geben selbst ein Erklärung dafür: als Italiener hat man keine Veranlassung, wenigstens größere Reisen in das 'Barbarenland' zu machen. Ja, man sieht sich—wenn man reist—veranlaßt, sich zu rechtfertigen."

[77] Eine der wenigen Ausnahmen ist Filippo Beroaldo's *Endecasyllabon in Germaniam*, in dem nicht nur die Tapferkeit und Gesundheit der Menschen, sondern Fruchtbarkeit und Reichtum des Landes und die geistige Begabung ihrer Bewohner (dokumentiert in der Erfindung des Buchdrucks) und ein gutes Bildungssystem gerühmt werden. (Vgl. Preiß [wie Anm. 21], 206.)

[78] Ed. Janell (wie Anm. 73), V. 1426f.

Neo-Latin Satire in the Low Countries
from an Italian Perspective

GILBERT TOURNOY

When, in autumn 1992, I had the honour of being invited to deliver one of the main lectures at this conference, I had not yet made up my mind properly about attending this event. At that time I was in the midst of preparing a piece of work for the celebration of Juan Luis Vives at Valencia, as well as thinking about a Vives exhibition of our own at Louvain. Furthermore I had promised shortly before to speak about Neo-Latin satire in the Low Countries at the Brussels colloquium on humanistic satire scheduled for spring 1993.

In the previous two decades I had put together a lot of material concerning Neo-Latin writers of satires, and already it was clear to me that my Brussels paper could cover only a small part of the subject matter, even within the limits of the Low Countries. The invitation from Bari was therefore very tempting; it provided me with the opportunity to develop my theme further, and to deal with one of its most promising aspects: the impact of Italian humanism on writers of formal verse satire. I should make it clear from the start, however, that this discussion will bear mainly upon the first century of humanism in the Low Countries, even if I allow myself the occasional excursus into a later period.

Twenty years ago, the present honorary president of this association devoted two fine papers to Neo-Latin satire.[1] In the very first lines of each he stressed that satire was without doubt to be counted among the lesser known genres of Neo-Latin literature. The situation has somewhat improved, especially in the field of Menippean satire, it seems. In general, however, interest in satire is still rather limited. A quick glance at the published proceedings of previous Neo-Latin conferences confirms this tendency: whilst a few papers have dealt with Neo-Latin Menippean satires, only one

---

[1] Jozef IJsewijn, "Neo-Latin Satire in Eastern Europe," *Ziva Antika* 25 (1975): 190–196; and "Neo-Latin Satire: *Sermo* and *Satyra Menippea*," in *Classical Influences on European Culture, AD 1500–1700*, ed. R. R. Bolgar (Cambridge, 1976), 41–55.

has focused upon a formal verse satire, viz. Buchanan's satirical poem against the Cardinal of Lorraine (1572).[2]

Several reasons may be adduced for this rather limited attention to satire—reasons which hold true for Neo-Latin as well as for classical Roman satire. To begin with, in the formal classification of Latin literature by genres, Roman satire was of very low value in the hierarchy of genres, even if it was entirely Roman, as Quintilian proudly boasted in his *Institutio oratoria*: "satura quidem tota nostra est" (10, 1, 93).

In many cases a satire, like an epigram, was aimed at specific persons in precise situations, so that for almost anyone not living at the same time and not moving in the same circles, it is impossible to grasp the author's exact meaning. Take for instance the six satires of Persius, which altogether amount to no more than six hundred and fifty hexameters. The recent very extensive commentary by Walter Kissel covers almost eight hundred pages but still leaves many questions unanswered. The same is true for Juvenal, and to a lesser extent for Horace, who moves on a more general level, and whose satires, therefore, are less time-specific and easier to understand.

The same arguments apply also to Neo-Latin satires, the difficulties of which are not to be underestimated. Their authors often seem to consider complexity, highly allusive imagery, and obscurity of style to be specific qualities of the genre. Modern scholars may consider themselves fortunate if they come across Neo-Latin satires published with an adequate commentary. The case of John Barclay's *Euphormionis Lusinini Satyricon* (Paris, 1605–1607), which was readily circulated with a handwritten key, is well known. For the Low Countries the most elaborate commentary I know of is the one on the satires of the Antwerp patrician Petrus Scholirius (1583–1635), published by Albert Le Roy along with a new edition of Scholirius's *Sermones* some sixty years (1683) after their first publication (1623–1627).

Let me now summarize the contents of my Brussels paper, before going a step further. In it, I limited myself to the very beginnings of Neo-Latin satire in the Low Countries and mainly to its external history. The first thing I had to do was to rule out Erasmus. As a youth Erasmus had written a few elegiac poems, calling them "satires." He himself corrected his error in the authorized edition of his *Progymnasmata* (printed by Martens at Louvain in January or in the very first days of February 1521), by changing the title of every poem from "satyra" to "elegia." Apart from one isolated satire by Kempo Thessaliensis (or Kempo from Texel), in which the French and, more particularly, French merchants were the primary target, the earliest collection of satires in the Netherlands was that of the Gelrian poet Petrus Montanus ('s-Heerenberg, 1467/8–1507), published at Zwolle in 1501.[3] There are

---

[2] Philip Ford, "George Buchanan and the 'Satyra in Carolum Lotharingum Cardinalem'," in *Acta Conventus Neo-Latini Sanctandreani . . .* , ed. I. D. McFarlane (Binghamton, N.Y., 1986), 43–50.

[3] Our Petrus Montanus is not to be confused with his namesake, the Venetian humanist Pietro del Monte, who lived in the first half of the Quattrocento (1400/04–1457). On him, see J. Haller, *Piero da Monte. Ein Gelehrter und päpstlicher Beamter des 15. Jahrhunderts. Seine Briefsammlung* (Rome,

six of them, and this number clearly points to Persius as the preferred model. This pattern of six is then corroborated by my analysis of structure, wording, and style.

The remainder of my Brussels paper furnished a rapid sketch of Montanus's life, and dealt especially with the essential role which Gerardus Geldenhouwer (1482–1542)—also known as Noviomagus after his native town Nijmegen—played in the various editions of Montanus's satires; it also dealt with Geldenhouwer's own imitation of Montanus. By way of conclusion I stated that the satires of both Montanus and Geldenhouwer deserved closer scrutiny, not only with a view to establishing their relationship with classical models, especially Persius, but also so that we might see how the ideas of Italian humanists influenced their views on poetry in general and on satire in particular.[4]

Now, Italian humanism penetrated the Low Countries as a major cultural influence only in the second half of the fifteenth century. More and more scholars, clergymen, politicians, and students went to Italy and returned as enthusiastic adepts of the new learning. The first and foremost of these was Rudolphus Agricola (1444–1485), whom Erasmus rightly considered to be the man who brought the first "breeze" of humanism to the Low Countries (Allen, I, p. 2): "Rodolphus Agricola primus omnium aurulam quandam melioris litteraturae nobis invexit ex Italia."

On the other hand Italian humanists who failed to make a living in their homeland crossed the Alps and were active in France, Germany and the Low Countries, for instance Francesco Florio, Fausto Andrelini, Girolamo Balbi and Cornelio Vitelli in Paris; Stefano Surigono, Lodovico Bruni, Francesco da Crema, and Antonio Gratiadei at Louvain University.

Agricola, who in the second half of the fifteenth century was one of the few foreigners in Italy to reach a level of competence in Latin prose and poetry that astonished Italians, felt himself to be a cultural exile back in his homeland, no longer able to put together a decent verse or even a prose sentence.[5] He was convinced,

---

1941), and D. Quaglioni, *Pietro del Monte a Roma. La tradizione del "Repertorium Utriusque Iuris" (ca. 1453). Genesi e diffusione della letteratura giuridico-politica in età umanistica* (Rome, 1984).

[4] G. Tournoy, "The Beginnings of Neo-Latin Satire in the Low Countries," in *La Satire humaniste. Actes du colloque international des 31 mars, 1er et 2 avril 1993.* Edités par Rudolf de Smet (Louvain, 1994), 95–109.

[5] Cp. his letter to Alexander Hegius of September 20, 1480 in *R. Agricolae . . . Lucubrationes aliquot . . . caeteraque . . . omnia . . . opuscula . . . per Alardum Amstelredamum emendata* (Cologne, 1539), 187. A similar state of mind is expressed in an elegy by the German poet Jakob Locher Philomusus (1471–1528):

> Est exstincta mei penitus scintilla furoris
> Quo placui Latiis Felsineisque viris.
> Terram mutavi Latiam caelumque disertum,
> Eloquii sub quo flumina larga fluunt.
> . . .
> Inter Teutonicos cogor versare colonos
> Atque deas cantu sollicitare novem.

See Georg Ellinger, *Geschichte der neulateinischen Literatur Deutschlands im sechzehnten Jahrhundert*, 3

however, that the day would come when the Germans would outdo the Italians in eloquence and when Germany would be more Latin than Latium.[6]

And indeed humanist forces did strengthen rapidly. Moreover it is interesting to observe how, as a result, German attitudes towards Italy then swiftly changed, so mirroring, in fact, the shift in attitude of every generation of Italian humanists to their predecessors. This is well illustrated by the exchange of letters between Erasmus and his somewhat older friend, Cornelius Aurelius or Cornelis Gerard (born in Gouda, ca. 1460–1531), during the year 1489 (Allen, epp. 20–29). Aurelius evinces an almost blind veneration towards the Italian poet Hieronymus Balbus, whom he considers a second Ovid (ep. 25), whilst Erasmus's appraisal is more carefully balanced, even if he too has the greatest admiration for Lorenzo Valla, Francesco Filelfo, Enea Silvio Piccolomini, and others (ep. 23). A few decades later the Spanish humanist Juan Luis Vives, who lived at Bruges, would be much more severe in his judgment of Italian humanists, when giving a general appraisal of them in the third book of his *De tradendis disciplinis* or when discussing their art of letter writing in his *De conscribendis epistolis*, which starts with Petrarch.[7]

However, a fundamental point of difference with Italy remains. Even if in their youthful enthusiasm an Erasmus and many others looked up to Italian humanists and tried for one reason or another to work within the same spirit, nonetheless their moral and religious interests prevailed. The main "raison d'être" for them, if not the only one, of the study of the *humanae litterae* remained its importance for the *sacrae litterae*. Yet it may be observed that this attitude is also evident in some Italian humanists: for example, the Florentine poet Ugolino Verino (1438–1516), who as a youth wrote a few erotic elegies in his *Flametta* but who stressed in the dedicatory letter to Savonarola, which prefaced his poem *De christianae religionis ac vitae monasticae felicitate*, that the prime function of poetry is to sing the praise of God and his saints.[8]

Whilst this attitude is rather exceptional for Italy, it is normal for Transalpine humanism. Erasmus, for instance, announces in a letter to the Ghent Carmelite Arnoldus Bostius, datable probably to April 1498 (Allen, ep. 75), that he forsakes the world, deplores the sins of his youth, and wants to dedicate himself to the Holy Scriptures. Later, at the end of the year 1504, he will write to John Colet that he intends to concern himself with the Scriptures and to dedicate the rest of his life to them (Allen, ep. 181). He concludes his *Ciceronianus* also by saying that the ultimate

---

vols. (Berlin and Leipzig, 1929–1933), 1:429–430; and Harry C. Schnur (ed.), *Lateinische Gedichte deutscher Humanisten. Lateinisch und deutsch* (Stuttgart, 1978²), 244–245.

[6] Letter to R. Langius, in *R. Agricolae . . . Lucubrationes aliquot . . .* , 178–179: "Unum hoc tibi affirmo . . . summamque in spem adducor, fore aliquando, ut priscam insolenti Italiae et prope-modum occupatam bene dicendi gloriam extorqueamus, vindicemusque nos et ab ignominia, qua nos barbaros indoctosque et elingues, et si quid est in his incultius, esse nos iactitant, futuramque tam doctam atque literatam Germaniam nostram, ut non Latinius vel ipsum sit Latium."

[7] *J. L. Vivis Valentini Opera omnia*, ed. G. Majansius, 8 vols. (Valencia, 1782–1790), 6 (1785), 340–344 and 2 (1782), 313.

[8] Alfonso Lazzari, *Ugolino e Michele Verino. Studii biografici e critici. Contributi alla storia dell'umanesimo in Firenze* (Torino, 1897), 192–196.

goal of erudition, philosophy, and eloquence lies in the understanding and glorification of Christ.[9]

A similar state of mind is apparent in the letter addressed by Arnoldus Bostius at the beginning of the year 1499 to Cornelius Aurelius:[10] "Most modern poets," he writes, "charm our wanton ears, but are not in the least profitable to the mind. Your chaste and sacred poems, however, are lectures from the gospel" ("Poetae moderni plurimi aures sane prurientes delectant, verum nihil spiritui conferunt. Tua autem sancta et casta poemata lectiones sunt evangelicae").

No wonder then that classical satire, and Persius in particular, was read, studied, and imitated by quite a few humanists of the first generation in the Low Countries.

With regard to Persius, it has been observed that this satirist was preferred to Horace or Juvenal by the Fathers of the Church St. Augustine and St. Jerome, and hence by a host of subsequent writers from the end of Antiquity onwards. Not only the many *sententiae* in his satires, but above all the moral value of his ideas, inspired by Stoicism, made Persius—like Seneca—more than acceptable in a medieval world which was dominated by Christianity and which always had, therefore, an ambiguous attitude to pagan writers.

It has also been generally accepted for a long time that Horace was known during the Middle Ages almost exclusively for his *Sermones* and his *Epistolae*, whilst the Renaissance was more fascinated by his lyric poetry. Dante placed Horace, the satirist, in limbo, immediately after Homer but before Ovid and Lucan; Persius is also situated there, in close association with Vergil himself and some other writers.[11] Modern scholarship is inclined to a more carefully balanced appraisal,[12] but it cannot

---

[9] *Ciceronianus*, ed. P. Mesnard, in *Opera Omnia Desiderii Erasmi Roterodami*, I.2 (Amsterdam, 1971), 709: "Huc discuntur disciplinae, huc philosophia, huc eloquentia, ut Christum intelligamus, ut Christi gloriam celebremus."

[10] C. Molhuysen, "Cornelius Aurelius," *Nederlandsch Archief voor Kerkgeschiedenis*, n.s. 2 (1903), 23. On Cornelius Aurelius, see now Peter G. Bietenholz and Thomas B. Deutscher (eds.), *Contemporaries of Erasmus. A Biographical Register of the Renaissance and the Reformation*, 3 vols. (Toronto, Buffalo, London, 1985–1987), 2:88–89 (henceforth cited here as *CE*), and Karin Tilmans, *Aurelius en de Divisiekroniek van 1517. Historiografie en humanisme in Holland in de tijd van Erasmus* (Hilversum, 1988).

[11] Dante, *Inferno*, IV, 88–90:
> quelli è Omero poeta sovrano,
> l'altro è Orazio satiro che vène,
> Ovidio è il terzo e l'ultimo Lucano.

Dante, *Purgatorio*, XXII, 100–103:
> «Costoro e Persio e io e altri assai»,
> rispuose il duca mio «siam con quel greco
> che le Musa lattar più ch'altro mai
> nel primo cinghio del carcere cieco».

[12] See W. Ludwig (ed.), *Horace: l'oeuvre et les imitations: un siècle d'interprétation* (Genève, 1993), especially (1) K. Friis Jensen, "The Medieval Horace and His Lyrics," 257–298, and (2) W. Ludwig, "Horazrezeption in der Renaissance oder die Renaissance des Horaz," 305–371.

be doubted that Horace, and Persius even more so, were known and appreciated in the first place as "poetae ethici." In their works the combination of explicit or implicit criticism with moral intent proved to be a formula of success—one which reached a peak in the fifteenth century, as can be deduced from the impressive quantity of manuscripts, commentaries, and editions produced in that period.[13] Of course, the rapid spread of the printing press throughout Europe considerably contributed to this success. The first editions of Juvenal and Persius appeared at Rome *circa* 1469, whilst Horace, significantly, did not appear in print until a couple of years later (Venice 1471/72). In the more than eighty editions of Horace appearing before the end of the century it is not always easy to discern special interest in him as a satirist, since most of these are editions of the complete works. On the other hand, Juvenal and Persius were each published more than sixty times before 1500, more than a quarter of these being joint editions. During the sixteenth century Persius went through more than two hundred editions.

At this point let us consider how and when and where the Low Countries come into the picture.

First we shall have a quick glance at the material available—that is, at the editions of classical satires produced in the Low Countries. Then we shall deal with their reception by the local humanists; this will involve not only digging up quotations from, and allusions to, the satirists in such humanists' works but also looking at these humanists' activities in the field of editing and/or writing commentaries upon these texts. Finally, but most importantly, we shall examine their direct or indirect imitation of their satirical predecessors.

(1) In the first century of the printing press, editions of Latin satirists in the Low Countries are scarce. As I mentioned above, separate editions of Horace's satires are not numerous: in the whole of Europe, only seven before 1500;[14] and in the Low Countries, one single edition of Horace's *Sermones* published at Deventer 1490, followed by a few more during the first decades of the sixteenth century. Although

---

[13] See for Persius: Dorothy M. Robathan and F. Edward Cranz, "A. Persius Flaccus," in F. E. Cranz and P. O. Kristeller (eds.), *Catalogus translationum et commentariorum: Mediaeval and Renaissance Latin Translations and Commentaries. Annotated Lists and Guides*, III (Washington D.C., 1976), 201–312 (henceforth cited as *CTC*). Still valuable for having listed the printed editions is Morris H. Morgan, *A Bibliography of Persius* (Cambridge, Mass., 1909). For the manuscripts of the text and commentaries of Persius, see Paola Scarcia Piacentini, "Saggio di un censimento dei manoscritti contenenti il testo di Persio e gli scoli e commenti al testo," *Studi su Persio e la scoliastica persiana*, 3/1 (Rome, 1973), 5–125 and "Corrigenda e addenda al censimento dei manoscritti. Note bibliografiche. Indici. Concordantiae siglorum," *ibid.*, 3/2 (Rome, 1975), 131–192. For Horace we look forward to the impressive study by Antonio Iurilli, *Le edizioni di Quinto Orazio Flacco dal XV al XVIII secolo* (Florence, Olschki, 1995, in press). For Juvenal, see Eva M. Sanford, "Juvenalis, Decimus Junius," in P. O. Kristeller (ed.), *CTC* 1 (1960), 175–238 and 3 (1976), 432–445.

[14] M. Flodr, *Incunabula classicorum. Wiegendrucke der griechischen und römischen Literatur* (Amsterdam, 1973), 185–193.

over one hundred editions of Juvenal and Persius were published before 1500, only two saw the light of day in the Low Countries. These two satirists were published together by John of Westphalia in 1475 at Louvain, where they were probably commented upon in a university course. In addition, Persius alone was brought out at Antwerp *circa* 1490 by Gerard Leeu (Morgan, no. 34). Juvenal was too obscene, and at first only a collection of single lines, collected by Johannes Murmellius of Roermond (1480–1517), a pupil of Alexander Hegius, was published at Deventer by Albert Pafraet (NK I, 1242). This edition was followed a few years later by a few individual, innocent satires: for instance, satires 8 and 13, issued at Deventer in 1523 (NK I, 1243–1244);[15] or the three satires selected by Timannus Kemenerus, issued at Zwolle in 1519 "ab omni spurcitia vacuae" (NK I, 1245). Only from 1529 onwards were a few complete editions of Juvenal's *satyrae* published at Antwerp (NK II, 3287). Persius was the most successful of the three: his work went through six editions in the period 1500–1540 (NK, I, 1697–1701 and II, 3695).

Even if these statistics do have their importance, they provide only a very incomplete part of the picture. In addition to manuscripts of ancient satirists, which were avidly read and studied,[16] humanists of the Low Countries also had direct access to other editions of Horace, Juvenal, and Persius issued in Italy. They also knew Italian satirists, such as Francesco Filelfo, whose satires were published at Milan in 1476. Furthermore, they were on the whole extremely well informed on what was being published at Paris, Cologne, Strasbourg, or Leipzig.

(2) Perhaps the very first evaluation of the Roman satirists made in the Low Countries comes from Rudolphus Agricola in his brilliant treatise *De inventione dialectica*, finished on August 15, 1479 (as he stated when writing from Dillingen to Dietrich von Pleningen), but not printed until 1515. In the third book (and especially in the second chapter discussing the handling of emotions) Agricola observes that the three Roman satirists have the same goals and treat the same theme: the correction of life and manners and the castigation of vice. Each of them, however, has his own style. Horace prefers to achieve these goals through laughter. Persius is more severe and almost adopts the mask of a philosopher. Juvenal is more indignant and infuriated.[17]

---

[15] It is hardly coincidental that Johannes Murmellius published his *Juvenalis tres satirae* [7, 8, and 13] at Cologne in 1510. See D. Reichling, *Johannes Murmellius. Sein Leben und seine Werke. Nebst einem ausführlichen bibliographischen Verzeichniß sämmtlicher Schriften und einer Auswahl von Gedichten* (Freiburg i. B. 1880 = Nieuwkoop, 1963), 148.

[16] See for instance A. Derolez, "*Pan et Circenses*. The Reading of Juvenal in the School of the Ghent Hieronymites in the Fifteenth Century," in *De captu lectoris. Wirkungen des Buches im 15. und 16. Jahrhundert dargestellt an ausgewählten Handschriften und Drucken*, eds. W. Milde and W. Schuder (Berlin and New York, 1988), 105–115.

[17] L. Mundt (ed.), *Rudolf Agricola, De inventione dialectica libri tres—Drei Bücher über die Inventio dialectica*. Auf der Grundlage der Edition von Alardus von Amsterdam (1539) kritisch herausgegeben, übersetzt und kommentiert von L. M. (Tübingen, 1992), 440: "In satyra videmus, idem tribus illis, qui adhuc extant, Horatio, Persio et Iuvenali, institutum esse, eandemque rem tractari. Ea est, ut mores vitamque emendent et reprehendant vitia. Suum tamen quisque secutus est

Possibly more partisan is Agricola's fellow countryman, Fridericus Maurus or Moorman (†1482), who, whilst lamenting in one of his poems the neglect of classical poetry, included the satirist Horace among the most prestigious classical poets.[18] Moreover, the *iunctura* "satura ... acerba" that he uses in order to do this is a direct verbal echo of Horace's own *sat.* 2,1,1:

> ... Iam nulla poemata florent,
> Nusquam Vergilius et nusquam lusor amorum
> Naso legi dignus, satura nec Flaccus acerba.

In the generation after Agricola, Roman satirists would leave their mark upon the minds and the works of Dutch humanists. Erasmus included the three satirists in the series of Latin poets that he prized as models, as he indicated in his letter of 15 May 1489 (Allen, ep. 20) to Aurelius Cornelius, and he regularly quoted them in his works. This same Aurelius was also familiar with Persius when composing his *Marias*, a series of elegies in honour of the Virgin Mary, which were inspired by Baptista Mantuanus's *Parthenice* and which he finished in 1497. Together with the first part of his *Marias* Aurelius sent an introductory letter to Jacobus Faber of Deventer (1473–after 1517), in which he explained the reasons which had compelled him to write this work by paraphrasing the choliambic verses of Persius. These pious verses, as he puts it, were intended to serve as an antidote to neutralize the magpie poetesses who had found their way into the Deventer classrooms.[19]

The same attitude still marks the small poem accompanying the edition of the satires by Gerardus Geldenhouwer, printed by Dirk Martens at Louvain in 1515:[20]

---

colorem. Horatius ridentis speciem et 'ingenuo' (ut ipse ait) 'culpam defigere ludo' affectavit. Persius severiorem et prope philosophi personam accepit. Docendo itaque reprehendit, et reprehendendo docet. Iuvenalis indignantis et irati plerunque praefert speciem. Quare erectior paulo et profluentior carminis compositio magis decuerit eum, sicut et sal amarior plerunque et solutior orationis libertas."

[18] P. Schoonbeeg, "Friderici Mauri carmina. Edition with commentary," in F. Akkerman, G. C. Huisman, A. J. Vanderjagt (eds.), *Wessel Gansfort (1419–1489) and Northern Humanism* (Leiden, New York, Cologne, 1993), 329–386, esp. 342.

[19] "Igitur, cum ... didicissem poetridas (ut Persius ait) picas cum Devotorum Fratrum domus Florentie dispendio tum animarum periculo Daventriensis oppidi scholis advolasse et iam incipere labra simplicium prolui—ne dicam pollui—caballino, inflammatus zelo domus Dei ... tandem id operis, cuius modo partem habes, conscribere cepi." Published by J. IJsewijn, "Erasmus ex poeta theologus, sive de litterarum instauratarum apud Hollandos incunabulis," in *Scrinium Erasmianum*, ed. J. Coppens, 2 vols. (Leiden, 1969), 1:375–389 (p. 385).

[20] I quote from the original edition: *Cornelii Graphei Alustensis Carmen pastorale ... Gerardi Noviomagi Satyrae octo ad Verae Religionis cultores* (Louvain, Martens, 1515), fol. F.iii[r]:

> Nunc age, nunc veterum lasciva poemata vatum
> Linque, puer, quae sunt certa venena tibi,
> Et lege facundi nova carmina Noviomagi
> Namque tibi haec casta et munda Camena venit.

This text was reproduced with an error ("Ei" instead of "Et") by J. Prinsen, *Collectanea van*

"Come on now, child," writes the Louvain professor of Latin Hadrianus Barlandus, "leave now the lascivious verses of the ancient poets; they are a sure poison for you. Read now the new poems of the eloquent Noviomagus, for this Muse comes to you chaste and morally pure."

Persius's prologue also inspired Joannes Murmellius of Roermond (1480–1517) when Murmellius was composing the hendecasyllables that introduced his four books of *Elegiae morales* (1507). The author states that he wants his poems to be the frequent reading matter of students, in order to show them the way to an honest life (vv. 3–17):[21]

<blockquote>

    Qui late tua labra proluisti
5   Sacro Castalii liquore fontis.
    Hos, quaeso, tenues, amice versus
    . . . .   (quos)
10   Effudi, revide pioque limae
    Usu sordibus omnibus repurga,
    Ne mox in miseros liber cucullos
    Diruptus piper obtegat crocumve,
15   Sed crebris manibus scholasticorum
    Versetur magis et viam probatae
    Iucundo doceat canore vitae.

</blockquote>

In the first elegy of his third book he ranges between the poets that he considers to be immortalized by fame—Horace, Persius, and Juvenal (3, 1, 39–44):[22]

<blockquote>

Mulcebit doctas numerosus Horatius aures,
    in medio virtus aurea donec erit.
Persius in libro semper memorabitur uno,
    Lucanum tenebris tempora nulla dabunt.
Immensas mordax laudes Iuvenalis habebit,
    In toto quamvis algeat orbe fides.

</blockquote>

On the other hand, Juvenal is left out in one of Murmellius's epigrams, in which the author presents a venal schoolmaster promising learning in exchange for riches (vv. 11–12 and 15–16):[23]

Gerardus Geldenhauer Noviomagus, gevolgd door de herdruk van eenige zijner werken (Amsterdam, 1901), 175, and hence also with same editorial punctuation and textual error in the third line by Etienne Daxhelet, *Adrien Barlandus, humaniste belge 1486–1538. Sa vie—son oeuvre—sa personnalité* (Louvain, 1938), 222.

[21] A. Bömer, *Des Münsterischen Humanisten Johannes Murmellius Elegiarum moralium libri quattuor* (Münster, 1893), 3–4.

[22] Bömer, *Des Münsterischen Humanisten Johannes Murmellius Elegiarum*, 75.

[23] This collection of epigrams was published at Cologne in 1510. See A. Bömer, *Des Münsterischen Humanisten Johannes Murmellius De magistri et discipulorum officiis Epigrammatum liber* (Münster, 1892), 24–25, *epigr.* 11: "Philosophi sunt pecuniarum contemptores . . ."

> Ex odis Flacci varios componere versus,
>   Ex satiris mores vosque docebo pios.
>   . . . .
>
> Persius obscurus vulgo fortasse videtur,
>   Marte meo illustri lumine clarus erit.

In his *Scoparius*, the "broom" with which he wants to sweep away medieval barbarism, Murmellius not only cites a few verses from Juvenal's fourteenth satire but even from Francesco Filelfo's satires, which he may have read either in the first edition of Milan 1476 or in a later edition (Venice, 1502 or Paris, 1508).[24] Most impressive of all is the long list of classical and Neo-Latin authors, accompanied by the names of their various commentators, which Murmellius judges useful for his students. I will single out here the satirists. For Horace he mentions the commentaries not only of Porphyrio and Acron "eius simia" but also of Christophorus Landinus and Antonius Mancinellus. For Juvenal he recommends the commentaries of Angelus Sabinus, Domitius Calderinus, Georgius Merula, Georgius Valla, Joannes Britannicus, and Antonius Mancinellus. For Persius there is Cornutus, Bartholomaeus Fontius, Joannes Britannicus, Curius Lancilotus, and finally himself.

Murmellius did indeed publish a commentary on Persius at Deventer in 1516, along with a new edition of his text, in which he wanted to correct the many errors of his predecessors and to help his readers towards a correct understanding of Persius. This edition was very successful, for it was printed at least twenty times. From 1522 onwards it was accompanied by Hermann van den Busche's commentary on Persius's prologue and first satire.[25]

More influential still were no doubt the many editions and commentaries by the humanist printer Jodocus Badius of Ghent (1461 ca.–1535).[26] Badius, after establishing himself at Paris, became one of the most important links between Italy and the Low Countries. In his *Sylvae morales* (Lyons, 1492), he already included a commentary on part of Persius's second satire. This was followed by a complete commentary on Persius in his edition of Lyons 1499, which was partly based on what Badius had taught at Valence and at Lyons, as he stated in his introductory letter to Levinus Maurus and Guilhelmus Dives. It was accompanied by Joannes Britannicus's commentary and, more importantly, by the lectures of Filippo Beroaldo and Angelo Poliziano. This first edition went through sixteen more reprints, before it was revised and considerably enlarged by its author in 1523. Whilst still at Lyons Badius published in 1498 a full-scale commentary on Juvenal, which went through sixteen editions before 1550. The first edition of Horace's satires accompanied by Badius's commentary also appeared at Lyons in March 1499. It was soon reprinted a few times

---

[24] A. Bömer, *Ausgewählte Werke des Münsterischen Humanisten Johannes Murmellius* (Münster, 1895), 18 (Juvenal) and 74 (Filelfo).

[25] Reichling, *Johannes Murmellius*, 104–105 and 159–161. Hermann Joseph Liessem, *Hermann van dem Busche. Sein Leben und seine Schriften* (Cologne 1884–1908 = Nieuwkoop, 1965), 2:70–71.

[26] See Philippe Renouard, *Bibliographie de Josse Bade Ascensius*, 3 vols. (Paris, 1908) and *Imprimeurs et libraires parisiens du XVIe siècle*, II (Paris, 1964), passim; *CTC*, 1:230–231 and 3:273–275.

in quick succession along with Horace's *Epistles*, as well as more than twenty times in Horace's *Opera*.[27]

Furthermore, this list of quotations, allusions, editions, and commentaries could easily be extended. Commentaries, such as the one on Juvenal by the Cologne professor Arnold van Luyden of Tongeren (ca. 1470–1540), may still be extant, and the unexplored deposits of some libraries may have more than one surprise in store.[28]

(3) By far the most interesting point to be raised, however, is the attitude towards classical satire and towards Italian humanism of the two early authors who wrote a few satires of their own, Petrus Montanus and Gerard Geldenhouwer. However, before dealing with these in detail, it might be helpful first to give an overall picture of Latin satire in the Low Countries.

The first collection of satires in the Low Countries was by Petrus Montanus (1467/68–1507) who originated from 's-Heerenberg. Consisting of six poems, it was published at Zwolle in 1501 and was soon followed in 1506 and 1507 by two other editions of Montanus's satires containing two and three more poems respectively. A final satire by Montanus was published at Strasbourg in 1529, appended to the *Coena de herbarum virtutibus* of the Italian humanist Battista Fiera. There is no doubt that Montanus is much indebted to Persius, whom he considered the best Roman satirist and so *par excellence* the model to be followed. Montanus in his turn was much admired by Gerard Geldenhouwer, who was responsible for seeing through the press all the editions of Montanus's satires, except the first.

Geldenhouwer likewise composed eight satires of his own, a few before 1507,[29] and as many as the first six perhaps before 1512, as Martinus Dorpius seems to indicate in his letter of January 24, 1512, praising to the skies the satires which Geldenhouwer wanted him to judge.[30] As might be expected, the name of Geldenhouwer's venerated master Montanus appears in half of the satires, and quite a few of Montanus's verses reappear, unaltered or slightly altered, in Geldenhouwer's satires. As for the ancient satirists, Persius is still the most conspicuous model,[31] but the stronger influence of Horace is undeniable, not only in single words or *iuncturae*, but

---

[27] The 1499 edition, kept at Besançon, inc. 573, is not mentioned by Renouard. But see Olga Trtnik-Rossettini, *Les Influences anciennes et italiennes sur la satire en France au XVIe siècle* (Florence, 1958), 12. For the other editions, see Renouard, 2:499–517.

[28] *CTC*, 3:443. See, for instance, Albert Derolez, "Pan et Circenses. The Reading of Juvenal in the School of the Ghent Hieronymites in the Fifteenth Century," in *De captu lectoris. Wirkungen des Buches im 15. und 16. Jahrhundert dargestellt an ausgewaehlten Handschriften und Drucken*, eds. Wolfgang Milde and Werner Schuder (Berlin/New York, 1988), 105–115.

[29] In *sat.* V, 57 Geldenhouwer presents Montanus, who died in 1507, as still alive: "Is vivitque sibi et Musis, pia numina cernit."

[30] Prinsen, *Collectanea*, 151–152.

[31] For instance in the first satire: 3: "Quis leget haec?" (Pers. 1, 2); 8–9: "blanda . . . cauda" (Pers. 4, 15); 38–41: "Sed quid opus molles mordaci offendere versu / Auriculas? Vide sis, ne limine pellat egentem / Te comptus iuvenis. Serpentes pinge, recedo. / Hic tamen infodiam" (Pers, 1, 107–109; 113–114 and 120); 63: "obstipo capite" (Pers. 1, 80); 86: "tincta veneno" (Pers. 3, 37), and so on.

also in the style and in the choice of themes. Geldenhouwer's sixth satire, for instance, describes his journey from Sneek in Frisia by the Zuiderzee ("Flevum austrinum" or "Mare austrinum," now the IJssel Lake) via Staveren, Enkhuizen, Amsterdam, and Utrecht to his native town Nijmegen. From the first verse "Egressum Sneca me excepit Stavria" it is obvious that Geldenhouwer has found his inspiration in Horace's journey to Brundisium. Horace's fifth satire of the first book had in fact begun: "Egressum magna me accepit Aricia Roma."

The influence of Horace becomes even more marked in the course of the sixteenth century. Lambertus Hortensius of Montfoort (1500–1574), who spent most of his lifetime as a teacher at Naarden and is mainly known for his historical work, also wrote some satires. In them he denounced the moral corruption of the world in which he lived. Eight of them were published at Utrecht in 1552, with a dedication to Dirk van Zuylen van de Haer, bailiff of Utrecht (d. 1580) and future father-in-law of Janus Dousa. In the copy kept at the University Library of Utrecht, many more satires were added, copied directly from the autograph manuscript. These satires are clearly meant to be imitations of Horace, and so are the two by Janus Dousa (1545–1604) published in his first collection of poetry at Antwerp in 1569.[32]

For the beginning of the seventeenth century, only two more names are relevant: the Ghent humanist Johannes van Havre or Havraeus (1551–1625) and the Antwerper Petrus Scholirius (1582–1635). Both came from very wealthy families and went to live in Italy for several years; both were active for a while in local Flemish politics, and both produced elegant, light-hearted satires in a Horatian manner, refraining from personal attacks. Witness the poet Caspar Gevartius (1593–1666), secretary to the town of Antwerp, who looked after the final edition of Havraeus's three satires and who wrote in his dedicatory letter to Nicolas Rockox:[33] "has satyras, sed innoxias, in corruptos saeculi sui mores effudit." Similarly, in Scholirius's first Sermo, Apollo allows the poets to speak freely but requires them to be discreet when dealing with monarchs.[34]

---

[32] Epigrammatum lib. II, Satyrae II, Elegorum lib. I, Silvarum lib. II. The first part of this collection, viz. the two books of epigrams, has been edited with introduction and notes by Chris L. Heesakkers (Leiden, 1976). These satires, directed against Spanish politics in the Low Countries and especially against the duke of Alva, present a curious mixture of political and religious topics.

[33] Arx virtutis sive de vera animi tranquillitate satyrae tres, auctore Ioanne Van Havre Wallaei toparcha, Nob. et consulari viro Gandensi (Antwerp, 1627), 6.

[34] Petri Scholirii . . . Sermonum familiarium libri III, perpetuis et hactenus desideratis commentariis illustrati opera et studio Alberti Le Roy Antverpiensis . . . (Hermopoli [=Antwerp], 1683), I, 111–117:

> Ludite securi, cum libertate, poetae.
> Eruncate imis, prisca virtute, medullis
> Infelix lolium : regum super atria, Tempe.
> Distinguendam tamen sunt tempora : moribus istis
> Gratia debetur, calor et palpatio major
> Quam quorundam antiquis : Promiscua ludite, vates,
> De reliquis caute, de Principe relligiose.

With these two poets, Havraeus and Scholirius, the long line of Latin verse satire, in the form conceived by Lucilius and Horace, seems virtually to have come to an end in the Low Countries.

In the meantime, however, a new and vigorous variety of satire had began to blossom. In 1581 Justus Lipsius, then professor at Leiden University, published his *Satyra Menippea: Somnium: Lusus in nostri aevi criticos,* in which he ridiculed the way philologists of his own time maltreated classical texts. The genre immediately enjoyed a tremendous success, and Lipsius was soon imitated throughout Europe. In the Low Countries the Bruges humanist Andreas Hoius or Van Hoye (1551–1635), professor of Greek at Douai University from 1593 onwards, supplemented Lipsius's *Somnium* with his own *Apologia pro criticis,* in which he closely followed his model in style and wording. Hoius, moreover, wrote a *Somnium* of his own, the *De Gallicanis Capetiae stirpis regibus satyra sive Somnium.* It is a political satire directed against the French monarchy in defence of the Spanish policy in the Low Countries.[35] Other imitators included the better known Daniel Heinsius (1580–1635), author of no less than three Menippean satires, Petrus Cunaeus (1586–1638) with his *Sardi venales* (1612), and Lipsius's successor at Louvain Erycius Puteanus (1574–1646) with his *Comus* (1608).

The limited space available here does not permit me to pursue further this line of investigation, which would lead us too far away from our subject, and which has recently been thoroughly explored by Dr. Ingrid De Smet.[36] Nor may I look in detail at the interesting theoretical debate concerning the true name and nature of satire, to which several scholars of the Low Countries contributed, by either supporting or opposing the theories of scholars such as Julius Caesar Scaliger in his *Poetice*[37] or Isaac Casaubon. Nonetheless, I should at least mention the following: Daniel Heinsius and his *De satyra Horatiana liber* (1612), in which he strongly defended the Greek origin of satire; Petrus Cunaeus with his public lectures on Horace and Juvenal;[38] and Gerardus Ioannes Vossius, who tried to reconcile the

---

[35] Both were published together with Hoius's poetical paraphrase of *Ezechiel propheta* (Douai, Ioannes Bogardus, 1598). See now Dirk Sacré, "Andreas Hoius en Justus Lipsius (met een onbekende brief aan Lipsius)," *Handelingen van de Koninklijke Zuidnederlandse Maatschappij voor Taal-en Letterkunde en Geschiedenis* 47 (1993) [1995], 269–292 (289–290).

[36] Ingrid A. R. De Smet, *Menippean Satire and the Republic of Letters* (Genève: Droz, 1996). See also by the same author, "The Legacy of the Gourd Re-examined: The Fortune of Seneca's *Apocolocyntosis* and Its Influence on Humanist Satire," in *La Satire humaniste,* ed. Rudolf De Smet (Louvain, 1994), 49–75; and Anthony Grafton, "Petronius and Neo-Latin Satire: the Reception of the *Cena Trimalchionis,*" *Journal of the Warburg and Courtauld Institutes* 53 (1990), 237–249.

[37] J. C. Scaliger, *Poetices libri septem.* Faksimile-Neudruck der Ausgabe von Lyon 1561 mit einer Einleitung von August Buck (Stuttgart and Bad Cannstatt, 1964), I, 12 (pp. 19–20); III, 98 (pp. 149–150); VI, 6 (p. 322) and VI, 7 (pp. 334–338). See now also Iulius Caesar Scaliger, *Poetices libri septem. Sieben Bücher über die Dichtkunst,* Band I: Buch 1 und 2. Herausgegeben, übersetzt, eingeleitet und erläutert von Luc Deitz (Stuttgart and Bad Cannstatt, 1994), 186–191 (I, 12).

[38] *Petri Cunaei orationes argumenti varii* (Leipzig, 1693), 203ff.: "Oratio XI, habita cum Horatium publice praelecturus esset"; "Oratio XII, habita cum Juvenalis explicationem ordiretur."

theories of Scaliger and Casaubon in his *De artis poeticae natura ac constitutione liber* (Amsterdam, 1647).

Modern scholarship claims that Isaac Casaubon's long and methodical treatise, the *De satyrica Graecorum poesi, et Romanorum satira libri duo* (Paris, 1605),[39] originally conceived as an introduction to his Persius edition, was at the basis of the modern conception of classical satire. However, Casaubon's authoritative interpretation, clearly separating the two different forms of Roman satire from the Greek satyr play, did not appear out of the blue. The definition of satire advocated more than a century earlier by Giorgio Merula in the preface to his edition of Juvenal (Venice, 1478), which was to be expanded and refined by Angelo Poliziano in his *Praelectio in Persium* (1482/83), was already quite close to the position now generally accepted by critics. Jürgen Brummack even sustains: "Klar und richtig unterscheidet er [= Poliziano] Satyrspiel, menippeische und lucilische Satire ... Er ist in dieser Darstellung von Casaubonus (1605) nicht übertroffen worden."[40]

Poliziano's *Praelectio in Persium* was published for the first time in his *Opera Omnia* of Venice, July 1498. Almost immediately Jodocus Badius grasped its value and included it in his first edition of Persius, which he had printed on January 27, 1499 by Nicholas Wolf at Lyons and a year later at Paris. One of these two editions, most probably the Parisian one, was known in the Low Countries from the very beginning of the sixteenth century. It came into the hands of Petrus Montanus and Gerardus Geldenhouwer, who eagerly absorbed its contents before ventilating their own ideas on the nature of satire and their own judgment on the classical and contemporary practitioners of the genre. Geldenhouwer even used the last paragraph of Poliziano's *Praelectio in Persium* to serve as an introduction to his edition of Montanus's satires 10–12 (Zwolle, 1507).

Furthermore, of great significance is the series of topics discussed in the letters of Geldenhouwer and Montanus which introduce the second edition of Petrus Montanus's satires. In the first letter, addressed by Geldenhouwer to Montanus, Geldenhouwer describes a meeting with a young Gelrian, who can probably be identified as Gerardus Listrius (of Rhenen near Utrecht, 1485/90–after 1522), a humanist who is mainly known for his commentary on Erasmus's *Laus Stultitiae*, published at Basel in 1515.[41] Listrius is presented in the letter as a former student of Petrus Montanus, asking Geldenhouwer's advice on two problems which are intimately connected: first, whether it is proper to read pagan poetry; second, whether it is worthwhile to read religious works. Geldenhouwer does not seem very eager to answer and at first dismisses these questions, saying that the humanist Carmelite Baptista Mantuanus (1447–1516) has already discussed all this. Mantuanus indeed enjoyed enormous popularity

---

[39] Reprinted with an introduction by Peter S. Medine (New York, 1973).

[40] Angelo Poliziano, *Commento inedito alle satire di Persio*, a cura di Lucia Cesarini Martinelli e Roberto Ricciardi (Firenze, 1985), XXVII–XXXVIII and XLIX–LV. J. Brummack, "Zu Begriff und Theorie der Satire," *Deutsche Vierteljahresschrift für Literaturwissenschaft und Geistesgeschichte* 45 (1971) (= Sonderheft Forschungsreferate), *275–*377 (*294).

[41] See *CE* 2:335–336, and B. J. Spruyt, "Listrius *lutherizans*: His *Epistola theologica adversus Dominicanos Suollenses* (1520)," *Sixteenth Century Journal* 22 (1991): 727–751.

at that time, especially in Northern Europe, and several of his works had already been printed at Deventer. The work Geldenhouwer was referring to was of course Mantuanus's poem *Contra poetas impudice loquentes*, first printed in 1489, which ran through more than forty editions in the course of the next twenty years.[42]

However, on having second thoughts Geldenhouwer returns to the problem, which has been haunting him too. Why is it, he asks himself, that we give more attention to pagan than to Christian poetry? Has it to do with the attraction of forbidden fruit? Or have the ancient poets simply more authority and majesty? He then compares ancient and modern representatives of the different genres: with the exception, perhaps, of Vergil, whose counterpart is that other Mantuan, Baptista, he does not consider the modern poets inferior to the ancients. He finds Tibullus no more gifted than either Rudolphus Agricola or the Westphalian Herman van den Busche (Hermannus Buschius) or the naturalized French poet Fausto Andrelini, not to speak of Italians such as Antonio Panormita or Antonio Sabellico. Likewise, Leonardo Bruni, the supposed author of the *Poliscena*,[43] or even Johannes Reuchlin[44] may be placed on the same level as Terence. Indeed, how far, he asks himself, is the master of the famous Deventer school, Alexander Hegius, inferior to Catullus?

In the field of satire Geldenhouwer is somewhat more prudent. Even if he is convinced that modern authors may do as well as Persius, Juvenal, or Horace, it is obvious that he does not know the unpublished satires by Gregorio Correr, Lorenzo Lippi, and others. The only Latin satirist from Italy he seems to have read is Francesco Filelfo (1398–1481), who indeed published the largest corpus of satires in the fifteenth century, a hundred satires of a hundred hexameters each, making a total of ten thousand hexameters, divided into ten books: *Satyrarum hecatostichon decem decades.* Geldenhouwer could have read them in manuscript; more probably, he read them in the first edition of Milan 1476 or in the second, Venetian edition of 1502. In his letter, he maintains that he told Gerardus that Filelfo's satires are considered by quite a few people to be superficial and spiritless. At this point the young Gerardus is said by Geldenhouwer to have interrupted, putting forward the name of his former master Petrus Montanus, who in his judgment was the equal of Persius, Juvenal, or Horace. Since Geldenhouwer represents himself to Montanus as having been ignorant of Montanus's satires at the time, Gerardus is also said by Geldenhouwer to have furnished him with a copy of the first edition, and he, Geldenhouwer, has avidly read them over and over again. Geldenhouwer extols the merits of Montanus's satires with a Horatian quotation: "Omne enim punctum in eis ... tulisti," but he urges Montanus to correct the typographical errors, promising personally to see a revised edition through the press. Interestingly enough, he uses the term "characterisare" to

---

[42] Edmondo Coccia, *Le edizioni delle opere del Mantovano* (Rome, 1960), 115–116 and 139 lists the separate editions, to which the *Opera Omnia* have to be added.

[43] Heinz-Werner Nörenberg, "Leonardo [Brunis] *Poliscena* und ihre Stellung in der Tradition der römischen Komödie," *Humanistica Lovaniensia* 24 (1975): 1–28; G. Nonni, "Contributi allo studio della commedia umanistica: la *Poliscena*," *Atti e Memorie (dell') Arcadia* III.6 (1975–1976), 393–451.

[44] Reuchlin (1455–1522) is the author of two comedies: *Sergius* (1495) and *Henno* (1497).

indicate the process of printing, exactly the same term being used in the first edition of Juvenal and Persius printed at Louvain in 1475 by Johannes de Westfalia: "Presens satyrarum opus insigne Juvenalis et Persii . . . arte quadam caracterisandi modernissima feliciter consummatum."

In his long written reply, Petrus Montanus expounds his own views on satire. He begins by expressing gratitude for Geldenhouwer's judgment on his satires, even if it is coloured by benevolence and sympathy and therefore untrustworthy. He adds that it is also possible of course that he, Montanus, is blinded by self-love: "nisi et ipse quoque cecutiam amore meo mei, qui philautia Graece dicitur." This sentence is an implicit reference to Poliziano's *Praelectio in Persium*, which stated:[45] "Est enim cuique a natura ipsa ingenitus insitusque amor caecus sui, quem Graeci uno vocabulo φιλαυτίαν vocitarunt." Then Montanus embarks upon the difficult discussion of the laws of the genre, before passing in review satirists both ancient and modern.

For Montanus satire is a very specific genre, peculiar to Latin literature. It proceeds by way of dialogue, but a dialogue without real discussion ("tacitis personis"). It is full of allusions, titillations, associations, metaphors and is written in a concise and unrefined style. The satirist must combine severity with witty expression, erudition with moral chastisement. He must be able to treat a wide range of topics in a varied form of linguistic expression. His moral indignation is given expression through arresting turns of phrase, abrupt interruptions, and transitions. Above all, Montanus prizes hidden stings, or remarks aiming at several goals at once, not detectable by the average reader. He concludes that if he himself has taken all these rules into account, he may without presumption call himself the most distinguished of the satirists.

Then Montanus comes to the comparison of modern with ancient satirists. For Lucilius he depends mainly on Horace's portrayal of the inventor of the genre in the fourth of his first book of satires; but he modifies the Horatian view somewhat by including a paraphrase of Quintilian's judgment of Lucilius (*inst.* 10, 1, 94) and by adding that Lucilius is even better than Horace in portraying people ("prosopopeia"). On the other hand he calls Horace purer and terser than Lucilius, again following Quintilian (*ibid.*), but for him the structure ("dispositio") of Horace's satires falls short of perfection from time to time.

Even more elaborate is Montanus's evaluation of Persius and Juvenal, which reserves the highest admiration for the former. Montanus stresses Persius's constant emulation of Horace. He also quotes Quintilian, and St. Jerome, who called Persius a very fluent satirist (*epist.* 127, 6), and he agrees with Filippo Beroaldo in not finding Persius too harsh. Indeed, for Montanus Persius outdoes Horace and Juvenal in the exquisite choice of topics to treat. For that reason and for his literary craftmanship he rightly deserves the praise of Johannes Britannicus and many others, who consider him superior to other satirists. Some are inclined to give the place of honour to Juvenal, but for Montanus Juvenal is so unequal in his performance, so varied in his

---

[45] Angelo Poliziano, *Commento inedito alle satire di Persio*, a cura di Lucia Cesarini Martinelli e Roberto Ricciardi (Firenze, 1985), 3 (ll. 8–10).

stylistic levels, that it looks as if not all the satires were written by the same man. Moreover, grammatical errors disfigure them all too often.

Montanus skips the entire Middle Ages. His knowledge of modern Latin satire is limited, exactly as Geldenhouwer's is, to Francesco Filelfo. Montanus is less cautious than Geldenhouwer about speaking his mind. He finds Filelfo a sordid and scurrilous poet, spiritless and soporific,[46] who can be called a versifier rather than a poet. Filelfo teaches vices rather than castigates them, and he neither knows nor observes the laws of the genre, except for the *humilitas* of the style.[47] To soften this judgment somewhat, Montanus extols Filelfo's skills in prose composition. In this respect, he says, Filelfo can be compared to Cicero, who had no poetical talent either. Vergil on the other hand was not gifted for prose, but he is the Homer amongst Latin poets.

This passage inevitably recalls some of Filelfo's own verses in the ninth book of his *De iocis et seriis*, where he admits being inferior to Vergil in poetry and to Cicero in prose but proudly claims to be superior to Vergil in prose and to Cicero in verse.[48] Quite remarkable also is the fact that Montanus then seizes the opportunity to sing the praises of two Christian authors who were conversant with both prose and poetry, Lactantius and Cyprian.

In the review of ancient and modern satirists, Montanus reserves the last place for himself, just as Hieronymus, Sigebert of Gembloux or Trithemius had done in their literary histories. He is aware of the fact that by doing so he manoeuvres himself into a difficult position: he cannot praise himself without being considered arrogant, but on the other hand it is wicked to blame oneself. Therefore Montanus limits himself to stressing the variety and elegance of his own work.

Perhaps he is not so sure of himself as he pretends to be. He even finds it necessary to mention by name a few famous friends and rising stars in the sky of humanism, such as Joannes Murmellius, Hermannus Buschius, and Franciscus Craneveldius, who have all been so kind as to recommend his satires in an epigram or a letter.

Any roughness one may discern, says Montanus, is inherent in the genre, but it is also due in part to the philosophical topics that he treats. He has tried to compress into his satires the full richness of Plato, which he has been able to discover thanks to

---

[46] A few years later Vives will characterize Filelfo in the third book of his *De Tradendis Disciplinis* in very comparable terms: "Eius tamen lectio est molesta, quod motu omni et quasi vita caret." See his *Opera Omnia*, ed. G. Majansius, (Valencia 1785), 6:340.

[47] This part of his letter has been published by J. IJsewijn, "La fortuna del Filelfo nei Paesi Bassi," in *Francesco Filelfo nel quinto centenario della morte*. Medioevo e Umanesimo, vol. 58 (Padova, 1986), 529–550 (p. 542). Montanus's judgment has been repeated by Levinus Crucius in his *Threnodia in temeraria criticorum quorundam iudicia* (1548), vv. 51–52. See J. IJsewijn, "La fortuna," 550, and M.-J. Desmet-Goethals, *Levinus Crucius en zijn Threnodia (1548). Bijdrage tot de studie van het humanisme in de Nederlanden* (Brussels, 1985), 111–114.

[48] See Carlo de' Rosmini, *Vita di Francesco Filelfo da Tolentino*, 3 vols. (Milano, 1808), 3:149:

> Quod si Virgilius superat me carminis ullis
> Laudibus, orator ille ego sum melior.
> Sin Tulli eloquio praestat facundia nostro,
> Versibus ille meis cedit ubique minor.

Marsilio Ficino's *Theologia Platonica de immortalitate animorum*. If Montanus had no manuscript at his disposal, he can only have read this voluminous work, consisting of eighteen books, either in the first edition (Florence 1482) or more probably in the second edition (Venice, 1491), where it was appended to Ficino's Latin translation of Plato's *Opera Omnia*.[49] Montanus must have been very interested in the fundamental effort made by Ficino to reconcile Platonism with Christianity. His sixth satire, no doubt the most extensive and elaborate one, is no less than a verse paraphrase of Ficino's proof of the immortality of the individual soul, followed by a description of the pleasures of heaven and the horrors of hell. His tenth satire, entitled *De expetenda iusta morte*, is heavily annotated by Geldenhouwer, to whom it is dedicated. It draws heavily on classical and Christian writers such as Augustine, Jerome, Ambrose, Cyprian, but also on Plato and on Giovanni Pico della Mirandola's *Conclusiones*, *De ente et uno*, and *Oratio* or *De dignitate hominis*. Italian poets of whom Montanus is especially fond are Baptista Mantuanus and Fausto Andrelini. Indeed, in the second satire Mantuanus acts as a "monitor," inciting Montanus to write satires; in that same satire Marsilio Ficino and Pico della Mirandola are also mentioned. In his short eighth satire *De poetis*, Montanus condemns the bad poets, who do not deserve the name of "poets," being only "versificatores," and he glorifies Hermannus Buschius and Andrelini, whose poetical talents have even merited royal remuneration. Montanus's preferences for Andrelini are shared by a number of other humanists in the Low Countries.[50] Adrianus Barlandus for instance finds the quality of his verses equal to that of Persius's. According to Murmellius his glory will be eternal.[51] For Montanus's enthusiastic follower Geldenhouwer no poems are sweeter than Fausto Andrelini's *Livia* or Filippo Beroaldo's *Osculum Panthiae*; but immediately afterwards he recalls Pico della Mirandola's warning that all erotic poems should be thrown into the flames.[52]

In conclusion, Latin satire was never a very popular genre. Just as in Italy and elsewhere in Europe, so also in the Low Countries Latin verse satire was practised by only a handful of writers. We have seen that initially Persius was unmistakably the most conspicuous model. He was soon succeeded by Horace, but gradually the interest shifted from verse satire to Menippean satire, Justus Lipsius being the undisputed authority and model in that genre. We have shown how the Italian humanists exerted their influence, and how, furthermore, literary as well as more philosophical

---

[49] P. O. Kristeller, *Supplementum Ficinianum*, 2 vols. (Florence, 1937), 1:LX–LXI. See the reprint in Marsilio Ficino, *Opera omnia*, con una lettera introduttiva di P. O. Kristeller e una premessa di Mario Sancipriano (Turin, 1983), 78–414. A modern edition is available, with French translation, by Raymond Marcel, *Théologie platonicienne*, 3 vols. (Paris, 1964–1970).

[50] They have no doubt been influenced by Jodocus Badius, who in his letter introducing his edition of *Persii familiare commentum* (Lyons, 1499) stated: "... aut Faustum praecipuum Galliarum specimen ac litteraturae praesidium, regium dico illum musicum ac vatem clarissimum, Parrhisios tot annos erudientem." See Badius 3:147.

[51] See Godelieve Tournoy-Thoen, *Publi Fausti Andrelini Amores sive Livia. Met een bio-bibliografie van de auteur* (Brussels, 1982), 71–72.

[52] See Prinsen, *Collectanea*, 167–168 and Godelieve Tournoy-Thoen, op. cit.

currents were absorbed by writers of the Low Countries.

From antiquity onwards a great variety of themes, often of perennial interest, were treated by satirists, criticism of human vice being one of the recurrent topics. Only satirists in an independent social position and backed by friends in high circles, such as a Lucilius for instance, could afford to attack living persons. Other satirists, from Horace onwards, wisely refrained from this, either by treating touchy subjects in more general terms or by directing their shafts against deceased persons. Even so, every single one of them seems to have suffered hostile reactions to their works or at least strongly to have feared retaliation. According to Geldenhouwer (*sat.* 1, 3–4), Petrus Montanus's satires were thrown into the flames. Geldenhouwer himself declared in his introductory letter to Conrad Vecerius that his only purpose was to expose vice, not to harm anyone's good name. If he had done so, he was prepared to recant ("palinodiam canere").[53] I have already mentioned Apollo's advice to Petrus Scholirius. Moreover, in the field of Menippean satire Lipsius and Puteanus for instance had also to face more resentment from their contemporaries than they had expected.

This constant fear induced satirists to make continuous use of all kinds of stylistic devices to cloak the true meaning of their verses. By doing so they made sure that they were fully understood only by an inner circle living in the same social, political, and cultural context. The difficulty for us of reconstructing this context sometimes makes it impossible to understand exactly what or whom the satirists are aiming at. No wonder then that in the field of Neo-Latin satire much remains to be done. Nowadays we have to read the texts in old, rare, and sometimes unique editions and manuscripts. Thus we are in urgent need of good critical editions of each and every satirist. Essential also, and in the particular case of satire more than for other types of Neo-Latin text, is a full commentary, explaining classical allusions in style or wording as well as obscure or cloaked references to contemporary persons, and to political, social, or religious situations of the period.

In my opinion, only a team consisting of a trained classical scholar and a historian, joining forces with a medievalist and a philosopher, will ever be able to carry such an undertaking to a successful conclusion. I sincerely hope to see such a team constituted in the near future.

---

[53] See Prinsen, *Collectanea*, 155 and 153. For Conrad Vecerius, see now J. IJsewijn and G. Tournoy, "Litterae ad Craneveldium Balduinianae. A Preliminary Edition. Part 1. Letters 1–30 (March 1520–February 1521)," *Humanistica Lovaniensia* 41 (1992), 1–85 (35–38, Ep. 10).

Appendix

The severe restrictions concerning the length of the contributions in this volume allow me to present here only the first of a series of very interesting pieces introducing the editions of Petrus Montanus's satires, without any further commentary. I used the copy of the 1506 edition kept at the University Library at Marburg, and—for the passages crossed out (indicated by my italics)—that of the Houghton Library, Harvard.

fol. a.2ʳ Gerardus Noviomagus *cenobita Asperensis* Petro Montano S. D. P.

Interrogavit me iampridem, *dum in insula dive virginis Marie moram traherem*, vir praestantissime, Gerardus Gelriensis adulescens mehercle preter morum integritatem literarum quoque studiosus et doctus teque preceptore prestantissimo non indignus quondam discipulus, an allophylorum poetarum carmina deceat, an quoque opereprecium sit *religiosum* lectitare. Tum ego: "Baptista Mantuanus, vates haud ignobilis, hanc tuam questionem satis superque discussit et absolvit. Sed nescio, dixi, cur nos *religiosi* maiorem operam ethnicorum quam orthodoxorum poetarum carminibus impendimus. An quod magis vetita cupiamus, licet honesta magis iuvent, an quod veteribus sit maior et auctoritas et maiestas, etsi quandoque neotericis prestantior sit eruditio? Sed ut verum fateamur, quid Tibullus, princeps elegiaci carminis, habet quod deest Agricole et Buschio aut Fausto denegatur? Aut in quibus in eo genere carminis deficiunt Antonius Sabellicus, Panhormita et plerique alii? Nonne eque cum Tibullo culti, enodes, politi et celeres sunt?

"Sit Virgilius extra aleam, nisi velimus eius maiestati aut opponere aut potius adiicere alterum Mantuanum, Baptistam. Quid Persius, quid Iuvenalis, quid denique Horatius utilitatis, quid honeste ut ita dicam voluptatis, quid decoris, quid elegantie, quid denique divinitatis habent quod Philelfum preterit aut alium quemvis mihi incognitum, si Philelfus, ut multis visum est, nimis situm veternosum ducit? Quid prohibet Ioannem Capnionem, si malimus quam Leonardum, Terentio comparari? Quanto demum Catullo Alexander Hegius est inferior?"

Hec quum dixissem, "Demiror," inquit Gerardus, "cur preceptoris mei Petri Montani non memineris, quum is satyras tot acuminibus, titillationibus, sensiculis urbanitatibusque satyricis oppletas ediderit quot vel Persius vel Iuvenalis vel Horatius reliquerit?" Statimque satyras tuas mihi dono dedit, quas ut verum fateor quum non modo legissem, verum etiam lectitavissem, ipse expertus sum ea que Gerardus dixerat in laudem earum non modo vera esse sed et verissima. Omne enim punctum in eis, nisi quis velit esse lividulus, sine ulla refragatione tulisti. Verum, vir doctissime, in his satyris chalcographorum incuria quedam sunt perperam characterisata, que te castigare repurgareque etiam atque etiam rogo. Quod si ut spero feceris, rem quum Gerardo mihique tuisque conterraneis et discipulis, tum non modo Gelrie nostre sed et toti Germanie, noveris te fecisse gratissimam. Ego enim ut iustioribus characteribus imprimantur curabo. Vale, decus Gelrie, imo Germanie nostre.

E regali abbatia insula dive virginis Marie, XIII kalendas Iulias, anno a resurrectione christiana MCCCCCV.

B, fol. a.2ᵛ Petrus Montanus Gerardo Noviomago cenobite *Asperensi* S. D. P.

Etsi antehac, quod sciam, te vidi nunquam, attamen per benevolentiam et familiaritatem tuam officiosissimam, dum tuum lectitarem epistolium, visus sum coram audire Noviomagum. Illic enim aliquot annos egi et quales ingenio homines et moribus hoc coelum educet non ignoro: faciles quidem et affabiles et familiares, illis presertim quos diligunt et amant. Hoc coeli influvium tu redoles meque charum habes antea quam cognoris aut videris, cuius tibi gratias habeo immortales. Iudicium tuum de satyris nostris utinam esset non minus verum quam honorificum. Ego enim, conscientia testante, potius amorem in me ac benevolentiam interpretor quam iudicium. Iamdiu didici amorem cecum esse. Quamobrem tibi, amicissimo homini, minus credo de me iudicanti, nisi et ipse quoque cecutiam amore meo mei, qui philautia Graece dicitur. Amabilis quidem insania, que omne preclarum facinus velut umbra corpus sequitur et omnem dulcis virtutis honorem sua fatuitate inficit. Quicquid tamen de me sentis aut alios sentire appetis, id omne tibi debeo licet repugnet conscientia et pudor invitus toleret. Quod enim ceteros fallis, dum me predicas, ne tua quidem laudum tuarum ornamenta mihi invides, ut Achilles quoque arma sua Patroclo concessit. Quod vero falleris ipse meique nervi delectant te, ut nervosus puer Alceum, id mihi indicat ne vicia quidem mea non bella videri tibi. Utrunque amoris est et quidem vehementis. Quamobrem si ut facis me amas, dubitare non potes quin ego vehementer te redamem. Amor enim nullo magis nec emitur nec pensatur quam seipso. Sed nihil expectes ut te sicut mutuo amo ita vicissim laudem, ne inter duos scopulos et quasdam ingratitudinis et irrisionis Symplegadas navigans pericliter. Si enim laudes eadem mensura non remetiar, ingratitudinis arguar. At si eadem mensura referam, qui id potero, nisi tuas tibi homini facundissimo voces regeram? Tum ego nudus ut illa Aesopi cornicula incessero. Symplegadum concursus evitasse videor; nunc adhuc mihi Syrtis evincenda restat. Si tuas tibi voces non refundam nec regeram, more informis cornicule me alienis plumis coloratum illudendum exponam. Nihil securum, nihil tutum, undique turbines et estus instant. Contrahamus ergo tumida tempestatibus vela, sinus obliquemus, nihil refert quam lenti, quam angusti, dum saltem salvi portus intremus. Sed satis ambagibus balbutitum est.

Interrogasti preterea rem sane difficilem nec tutam iudicatu, quum quisque suo vivat stomacho. An huius scilicet tempestatis poete ullo modo antiquitati veniant comparandi? Iustam comparationem non temere quispiam fecerit, nisi cui comparanda penitissime dispecta sint et cognita. Id videmus, ipsos summos artifices fere non posse de sua arte iudicare. Omnes enim usu magis quam arte discunt. Revolve omnes nostre etatis egregios et pictores et sculptores. Quotusquisque est qui interrogatus respondere poterit: "Id artem, illud ingenium, hoc summam excogitationem redolet." Expertus loquor. Vides ergo quam sit res ardua aut bene iudicare aut bene comparare. Adde quod omnis comparatio sit invidiosa et vendicativa. Huic tamen questioni scripsisti nuper me satisfecisse tibi, quia paucis forte contentus es. Quam enim nuper ad te dedi epistulam, in ea magis visus sum mihi lusisse ambagibus quam aliquid dixisse. Verebar enim ne cui literas meas osten-/deres qui iudicia mea cum comparationibus deferret. Anxia nanque, ut dixi, res est comparatio et odiosa, omneque iudicium supinum et suspectum.

Reliquum est quod ad me attinere videtur, quem cum garrula antiquitate amplo et firmo ore comparas, licet is non sim qui memet ignorem. Sed agis tu sane pro altitudine et benignitate animi tui et summo erga me amore tuo, qui omnes quos amas similis tui existimas. Non potest non esse magni faciendus, qui alium non visum, solo virtutis odore, tanti ducit. Sed ego profecto non sum quem tanti estimes, nec me hunc, ut antea dixi, profiteor, at ne cogito quidem. Id tamen pro virili mea, etsi non enitar, conabor saltem, ut aliqua pensitatione videar fuisse dignus. Qui enim id in raris et magnis quod potuit voluit, dignus certe fuerit qui meliora potuisset. Quod ad me dico, id est ad meam professionem attinere videtur; satyricorum etiam in trutinam contulisti carmina et me pensum rogasti, ut ergo dicam quod mihi literatori licet cecutienti lippientibus videatur oculis.

Peculiare quiddam est et insigne privum (ut taceam de ceteris in singulis satyrarum scriptoribus, ut paulo mox dicam) quod omnes pene grammatici aut incuria aut inconsyderatione aut dissimulatione aut negligentia aut ignorantia quadam preterierunt, quum sit res scitu dignissima. Satyra genus est scriptionis rarissimum, quod solorum est Latinorum, dialogicos procedens sed tacitis personis, constans multa varietate, schematum obliquitatibus, allusione, sincopatione, titillationibus, reciprocis et apostrophicis sermonibus brevibusque quamobrem aliquantulum obscuris enigmatibus, allegoriis, translationibus, dicendi genere non forensi, id est non delicato et venusto. Quod et ipse Flaccus precepisse videtur:

> Silvis deducti caveant me iudice Fauni
> Ne velut innati triviis ac pene forenses
> Aut multum teneris iuvenentur versibus umquam.

Nihil minus satyrum meo iudicio decet quam delicata et luxurians venustas, que omnino irato et plerunque excandescenti animo repugnat. Non abnuerim tamen elegantiam et ornatum et exactam puritatem, licet paulo horridiora verba et novitate inflationis assumpta, que sua tantum auctoritate nituntur ipsis satyris sint congrua. Nec satyro demum acerbitas, sales, castigatio et morum eruditio nec sensiculorum crebra deerit memoria. Copia quoque rerum, varietas et cognitio non trivialis decet absolutum, qualem adhuc non vidi, satyrum. Omnia vehementie signa ubi res postulat ostendet. Nunc acerbus, alias acutus, mox salsus, tum acer, nonunquam ardens et velut stricto ense fulminans. Perite fiunt in satyris satyrici saltus et scisse narrationes, per quas animus poete perturbatus et ira excandescens exprimitur; qui crebro exestuans nusquam fere consistit. Quamobrem satyra imperitis hiare videtur, et esse penitus dissoluta creditur propter interloquutionem creberrimam. Quod si id loquendi genus cuneis impertinentibus committeretur, nihil esset absurdius auribus eruditorum praesertim. Cavendum est ne fiat personarum nimia confusio, varietatem fieri nihil prohibet. Gravis et aliquantulum dura dispositio satyram decet. Sed omnis nimietas vitii loco ducitur. Plurimum maiestatis et occulte eruditionis afferunt ille sagite que una iaculatione binos feriunt. In qua re magnus artifex est Iuvenalis. Maior autem in suis declamationibus Quintilianus, quare arbitror paucos esse qui eius oratoris acutissimi vi-/res intelligant. Nihil denique magis exornat satyricam urbanitatem quam illi latentes aculei quos vulgaris lector non deprehendit sed eum suspensum relinquunt, ut aliud credat, aliud auguret, aliud legat, aliud fere intelligat. Numerum quandoque mutari, sed cum arte, non invenustum est, personarum quoque varietas quaedam magnam vim habet. Quale est: "Quis palpitat illic?/ Quis rumpit sere metuenda silentia noctis?" Et iterum: "Quid furis o certo male fidum pectus amore?/ Quid non insimulet qui utcunque vagatur adulter?"

In satyris exactis longe plus debet posse intelligi quam dicitur. Quod facile deprehendet quisquis in re de qua loquimur in satyris aut expertus aut doctus est. Quod si quis numerum metrorum rebus accommodaverit—in qua re neminem praeter Homerum satis diligentem fuisse videmus—mirum quantum spiritus versibus adderetur. Sed res est immensi laboris, immoderate anxietatis, meditationis non satis existimabilis.

Hec sunt que mihi satyricam legem concernere videntur, que te volo scire me non ignorare, ne me scribentem et pugnantes andabatas pares existimes. Qui enim ea non satis intellexerit, huic scriptionis generi credendus est penitus inutilis. Utinam ego has huius carminis leges observaverim. Tum profecto dicerem absque ulla arrogantia me non tantum socium sed et omnium satyricorum principem.

Ut nihil amplius fit in quo ego tibi non satisfecerim: audi quam desyderas iamdudum comparationem. Lucillius, quantum ex censoribus eius et scriptis (hoc est frustis que adhuc negligenti supersunt seculo) coniicere licet, satis emuncte fuit naris, salis abundi, leporis decentis, acerbitatis et vehementie supra modum, varie eruditionis et libertatis quante non ullus poetarum. Tanta enim fuit amicorum potentia suffultus et tanto virtutis amore ardebat quanto non alius temere quispiam fuit poetarum. Facilis tamen et extemporalis nimium fuisse videtur, ita ut in lutulentiam Flacco visus sit declinasse. Fabius tamen aliter ac Horatius de eo sentit. Horatius tersior est Lucillio et multo absolutior; brevitate, interlocutione, ironia, vafricie, ceteros superat fortiterque persuadet. Non est tamen usquequaque castus in dispositione. In prosopopeia effingenda nemo Horatium vincit praeter Lucillium. Lucillius enim in eo negotio mirus opifex fuit. At ea figura non parum decoris satyre confert. Persius multum vere glorie, autore Fabio, quamvis uno libro meruit. Sermonis acerbitate, stili equalitate, allegoria, translatione, vehementia veroque satyrarum dicendi charactere alios infra se videt, etsi Horatium in omnibus pene emulatus est. Qui eum durum nimis in satyris autumant non cum Beroaldo aut mecum sentiunt. Omnis enim in eo duritas aut scabricies aut obscuritas ex rerum ignoratione nobis oritur. Divus Hieronymus eum dissertissimum satyricum appellat. Mira nanque in eo eruditio, plurimum venustatis, non parum demum felicitatis. Enormia radit vicia. Communia, exigua et levia epigrammaticis relinquit, quare mihi Persius magis quam aut Horatius aut Iuvenalis delectum videtur fecisse materie, utpote de indiscretis hominum votis, de falsa relligione, de sapientia, de virtutis pulchritudine, de ignavia, de acidis, de avaricia, de vera animi libertate, de summo bono metam vite constituendam, non ex tempore vivendum. Quo quidem materie delectu et vero in satyris dicendi genere meruit a Ioanne Britannico et plerisque aliis, omnibus eiusdem operis auctoribus preferri. Sunt tamen qui malint Iuvenalem propter carminis venustatem, alii id ipsum in Iuvenale reprehendunt, Horatium praecipientem / respicientes. Iuvenalis (taceo suavitatem carminis) obliquitate sermonis, sale, allusione, bifida criminis iaculatione, apostrophica urbanitate alios relinquit. Petulco diversionis saltu pleraque dicit satyricus, que in eo venusta, in alio feda rerum consequentia esset. Abrumpit, salit, exultat, apostrophat modestus rursum procedit, humi serpit, se componit, quandoque etiam cum maiestate incedens exurgit. Nihil horum est quod eum dedeceat. In his Iuvenalis multum se commendat. Orat enim facundissime. Non est tamen sibi similis per omnia, ut saepe mihi visum sit non eundem hominem illas Iuvenalis satyras composuisse, tam diversa in eis compositio, tam inequalis eruditio, tam diversum in eis relucet ingenium. Quanquam quid prohibet hominis ingenium tempore, loco, conditione, affectione variari. In grammatica non est usquequaque perfectus. Multum enim, sed forte per incuriam, errat. Est alioquin vates egregius.

Ad nostros venio. Philelfus sordidus est et scurrilis et qui vicia magis doceat quam castiget. In tota compositione languidus est et somniculosus, nec exurgit quandoque sed temere iacet. Neque eorum habet quicquam que ad satyram requiruntur, excepto uno humilitatis charactere. Leges autem ceteras huius carminis aut ignorasse aut effingere non potuisse videtur. Versificator est magis quam poeta. Parcat mihi, imo veritati veniam tribuat, homo christianus, cuius animus forsan est in celis, in quibus rudis sub sydere mundus lusus est et stulticia. Nihil superos offendit veritas, imo verum tacuisse vitii loco ducunt. Et sicuti verum libenter in terris audiverunt, ita facile sinunt vel de se verum dici in terris. In Philelfo videre licet illud Platonis esse verissimum: "pauci unum utrumque nemo." Clarus est Philelfus oratione pedestri sed natura eum versu destituit. Sic et Cicero soluta oratione fuit praestantissimus, contra versu ineptissimus et pene indocto similis. E diverso Virgilius libero dicendi genere non fuit pili faciendus, at carmine fuit clarissimus et poetarum Latinorum Homerus est. Duos tamen magnum decus inter christianos scriptores deprehendimus, qui utrumque perbelle valuissent si excoluissent scribendi genus utrumque, Lactantium dico et Cyprianum. Uterque enim et versu et oratione pedestri claret.

Ego tandem resto. Sed quid, etsi memet non ignorem, de me dicere tuto possim, ut preteream notam stulticie et impietatis? Quum omnis de sese predicatio arrogantia videtur—et omnis arrogantia fatua est et odiosa—tum illa ingenii et eruditionis insulsissima et molestissima. Rursus impii est seipsum vituperare. Id unum tamen dicam, quod nemo qui meum opus saltem olfecerit denegabit, nec varietatem nec elegantem compositionem nec artem in eo desyderari. Paulo forte durior et horridior videor. Id non mihi sed scribendi generi et congeste in meas lucubraciunculas philosophie imputabitur. In id enim meum opusculum tam plenos ex Platone haustus contuli, ut quicquid ille et interpres eius Marsilius tot voluminibus explicarunt— audacter dico—velle videor cursim et strictim, non tamen frustulatim sed integrum, licet non omne in meum qualecunque opusculum congessisse. Nihil tamen in hoc mihi vendico, neque quid magni de me profiteor, neque me ut miretur turba laboro. Sat mihi est me esse hominum paucorum piscem—philosophandum enim paucis Ennius precipit—quandoquidem paucis, inquit Cicero, iudicibus philosophia contenta est, multitudinem consulto ipsa fugiens eique ipsi et suspecta et invisa.

Buschius alter, ut recte sentientibus persuasum est, Martialis—tam enim apertus, laetus, floridus et ornatus est—me omnia satyrici carminis ornamenta habere predicat. Cuius est videre quod / subscribitur in meum opus epigramma.

Murmellius, item non infima pars vatum, tale de meis carminibus dedit iudicium quale est honorificentissimum; quod epigrammati prefato adiicio.

Drolshagius, vir non illitteratus, honestissimum meis satyris subscripsit elogium. Franciscus Craneveldius, iuvenis facundie et eruditionis precellentis, non nihil me commendat. Ioannem Vestphalum non vereor praedictis addere. Horum et tuo sincero iudicio ausim aliquid, nescio quid, profiteri aut saltem iactare.

Iterum dico non debes expectare ut te sicut mutuo amo etiam vicissim laudem. Animus estimandus est, nihil res ipsa. Sin autem animo gratiarum agendarum (quando me voce imparem agnosco) contentus esse potes, impellimur certe ad te, supra etiam quam valemus, sed longe tamen infra quam cupimus efferendum. Tu tamen interea, *si precibus tue spontis tantisper fieri poteris*, cura ut promissis respondeas et imprimatur hoc meum opusculum, iam satis superque revisum et castigatum. In quodvis pignus quemlibet etiam provoco, si in una uspiam littera menda deprehendatur; excepto quod in orthographia, ut est res anceps omnium maxime, que sunt partes grammatices, aliam et aliam opinionem, alias et alias rationes, alia et alia exemplaria sequar. Vale, xiiii kalendas Martias. Amerfordia, anno a natali christiano supra millesimum quingentesimo sexto.

Seminarium Philologiae Humanisticae, Leuven, Belgium

Seminars

Introduction*

FOKKE AKKERMAN

At the IANLS congress in Copenhagen (1991) Prof. Chris Heesakkers from Leiden, together with four colleagues, held a seminar on Dutch humanism *after* Erasmus. It was at this occasion that the idea occurred to us to try our hand at producing a counterpart and to give a seminar on Dutch humanism *before* Erasmus. We know, of course, that from the beginning of the fifteenth century, or even earlier, humanism and Neo-Latin made a first beginning at scattered places in the Netherlands, or, to use a more suitable term for our purpose, in the Low Countries (see IJsewijn 1975). In this seminar, however, we shall limit ourselves to the northeastern region of these lands and to the period from 1469 onwards[1] till approximately the beginning of Erasmus's activities and fame. In those times the region was called Frisia, and it covered the lands to the north and east of the river IJssel, on the banks of which were situated the prosperous cities of Kampen, Zwolle and Deventer. They were famous for their schools as early as the fourteenth century and for their printing presses in the second half of the fifteenth century. But here we will focus our attention on the town and province of Groningen, which, though in constant and close contact with the IJssel cities, were still located a hundred kilometres to the north and separated from them by tracts of wet moorland passable only with difficulty. The town of Groningen was then a semi-independent city-state, politically powerful in its region and economically prosperous. Another location, too, must be connected with early humanism in the region: this is the rich monastery of Aduard (Adwert), now a village eight kilometres from Groningen. The monastery is important because it was there that during the abbacy of Hendrik van Rees (abbot from 1449 till 1485), regular meetings of scholars took place, among whom, heterogeneous in their interests as

---

* For the correction of my English I am indebted to Prof. A. J. Vanderjagt. The literature used in the three papers of this seminar has been compiled in one list on pages 101–103; see also the bibliographies in *Rodolphus Agricola Phrisius* 1988 and *Wessel Ganfsort and Northern Humanism* 1993.

[1] The first Neo-Latin letters written by Rudolph Agricola and Rudolph von Langen date from 1469. The first poems are perhaps a little earlier. See the contributions by Adrie van der Laan and Pieter Schoonbeeg.

they were, several men were present who can be called humanists without restriction; soon these humanist activities were taking place also in the city of Groningen. The interesting thing is that these people formed a group in which they stimulated each other and kept contact even when living far from each other. The two most famous names in this group are those of Rudolph Agricola (1444–1485) and Wessel Gansfort (ca. 1419–1489), two personalities who have been at the centre of attention at two congresses held at Groningen in 1985 and 1989.

So much for the general background.[2] In what follows three different topics from the cultural scene of early humanism in Groningen will be briefly treated.

University of Groningen

---

[2] For the general background, see Akkerman 1994 and several articles in *Rodolphus Agricola Phrisius* 1988.

Bibliography for the Seminar on Dutch Humanism

Agricola, Rodolphus. *Lucubrationes*. Cologne, 1539.

Akkerman, F. "Rudolf Agricola, een humanistenleven." In *Algemeen Nederlands Tijdschrift voor Wijsbegeerte*, 75.1 (1983), 25–43.

————. "De Neolatijnse epistolografie—Rudolf Agricola." In *Lampas. Tijdschrift voor Nederlandse classici*, 18.5 (1985), 319–335. [= Akkerman 1985a]

————. "Agricola als musicus." In *Rudolf Agricola 1444–1485. Programma Orgelconcert Martinikerk Groningen 28 oktober 1985*, 3–8. [= Akkerman 1985b]

————. "Agricola and Groningen." In *Rodolphus Agricola Phrisius* 1988, 3–20.

————. "Agricola und der Humanismus im friesischen Raum." In *Rudolf Agricola*. Ed. W. Kühlmann. Bern etc., 1994, 49–66.

Bakker, F. J. "Roeloff Huusman, secretarius der Stadt Groningen 1479/80–1484." In *Rodolphus Agricola Phrisius* 1988, 99–111.

Bertolot, L. *Studien zum italienishen und deutschen Humanismus*, ed. P. O. Kristeller, 2 vols. (Storia e Letterature 129–130). Rome, 1975.

Bezold, F. von. *Rudolf Agricola, ein deutscher Vertreter der italienischen Renaissance*. München, 1884.

Coloniensis, Bartholomaeus. *Sylva Carminum*. Deventer, 1491.

————. *Libellus elegiacus de septenis doloribus Mariae*. Deventer, 1514.

Crecelius, W. (ed.). "Epistulae Rudolfi Langii sex." In *Gymnasium zu Elberfeld, Bericht über die Schuljahre 1874/5 und 1875/6*. Elberfeld, 1876, 3–12.

————. (ed.). "De Antonii Liberi Susatensis vita et scriptis commentatiuncula." In *Festschrift zur Begrüssung der XXXIV. Versammlung deutscher Philologen . . . zu Trier*. Bonn, 1879, 139–150.

Gansfort, Wessel. *Carmen lyricum de nativitate Christi*. Zwolle, 1486–1488.

————. *Farrago Wesseli*. Zwolle, 1522.

————. *Opera quae inveniri potuerunt omnia*. Groningen, 1614 (repr. Nieuwkoop 1966: Monumenta Humanistica Belgica, vol. I).

Ihm, G. *Der Humanist Rudolf Agricola, sein Leben und seine Schriften*. Paderborn, 1893.

IJsewijn, J. "The Coming of Humanism to the Low Countries." In *Itinerarium Italicum. The Profile of the Italian Renaissance in the Mirror of Its European Transformation*. Eds. J. A. Oberman and Th. A. Brady. Leiden, 1975, 193–301.

————. "Die humanistische Biographie." In *Biographie und Autobiographie in der Renaissance*. Ed. A. Buck. Wolfenbütteler Abhandlungen zur Renaissanceforschung, vol. 4. Wiesbaden, 1983, 1–19.

Jolles, A. *Einfache Formen. Legende. Sage. Mythe. Rätsel. Spruch. Kasus. Memorabile. Märchen. Witz.* Tübingen, [1930]; [3]1965.

Kan, J. B. "Wesseli Groningensis, Rodolphi Agricolae, Erasmi Roterodami Vitae ex Codice Vindobonensi typis descriptae." In *Erasmiani Gymnasii Programma Litterarium.* Rotterdam, 1894, 4–9.

Kooiman, P. "The Letters of Rudolph Agricola to Jacobus Barbirianus." In *Rudolphus Agricola Phrisius* 1988, 136–146.

Kristeller, P. O. *Iter Italicum III.* London–Leiden, 1983.

Kühlmann, W. (ed.). *Rudolf Agricola 1444–1485. Protagonist des nordeuropäischen Humanismus; zum 550. Geburtstag.* Bern, 1994.

Lampen, W. "Twee gedichten van Bartholomaeus van Keulen op Alkmaars patroonheiligen." In *Haarlemsche Bijdragen. Bouwstoffen voor de Geschiedenis van het Bisdom Haarlem,* 52 (1935), 112–127.

Nauwelaerts, M. A. M. *Rudolphus Agricola.* Den Haag, 1963.

Novati, F. (ed.). *Epistolario di Coluccio Salutati.* 5 vols. Rome, 1891–1911.

Parmet, A. *Leben und gesammelte Gedichte des ersten münsterschen Humanisten.* Münster, 1869.

Phillips, M. M. "Erasmus and Biography." In *University of Toronto Quarterly,* 42 (1973), 185–201.

Prete, S. *Studies in Latin Poets of the Quattrocento.* University of Kansas Humanistic Studies, vol. 49. Lawrence, 1978.

Reichling, D. *Johannes Murmellius. Sein Leben und seine Werke. Nebst einem ausführlichen bibliographischen Verzeichniß sämtlicher Schriften und einer Auswahl von Gedichten.* Freiburg i.B., 1880 (repr. Nieuwkoop, 1963).

Rijkenberg, E. H. "De geschiedenis en de reliquie van het mirakel van het H. Bloed te Alkmaar." In *Bijdragen voor de Geschiedenis van het Bisdom Haarlem,* 21 (1896), 377–397.

Rodolphus Agricola Phrisius (1444–1485). Proceedings of the International Conference at the University of Groningen 28–30 October 1985. Eds. F. Akkerman and A. J. Vanderjagt. Brill's Studies in Intellectual History, vol. 6. Leiden, 1988.

Santing, C. "Theodericus Ulsenius, alter Agricola? The Popularity of Agricola with Early Dutch Humanists." In *Rodolphus Agricola Phrisius* 1988, 170–180.

Schoonbeeg, P. "Agricola alter Maro." In *Rodolphus Agricola Phrisius* 1988, 189–199.

———. "Bartholomaeus Coloniensis: Two Fables." In *Acta Conventus Neo-Latini Torontoniensis.* Eds. A. Dalzell, C. Fantazzi, and R. J. Schoeck. Medieval & Renaissance Texts & Studies, vol. 86. Binghamton, 1991, 631–644.

————. "Friderici Mauri Carmina." In *Wessel Gansfort (1419–1489) and Northern Humanism* 1993, 329–386.

Sonkowsky, R. P. "A Fifteenth-century Rhetorical Opusculum." In *Classical, Mediaeval and Renaissance Studies in Honor of B. L. Ullman.* Ed. Ch. Henderson Jr. Vol. II. Rome, 1964, 259–281.

Spitz, L. W. *The Religious Renaissance of the German Humanists.* Cambridge, Mass., 1963.

Straube, W. "Die Agricola-Biographie des Johannes von Plieningen." In *Rudolf Agricola.* Ed. W. Kühlmann. Bern, 1994, 11–48.

Tresling, T. P. *Vita et merita Rudolphi Agricolae.* Groningen, 1830.

Velden, J. M. van der. *Rodolphus Agricola (Roelof Huusman). Een Nederlandsch Humanist der vijftiende eeuw.* Leiden, [1911].

Voragine, Jacobus de. *Legenda Aurea.* Cologne, 1483.

Vormbaum, R. *Die evangelischen Schulordnungen des 16. Jahrhunderts.* Gütersloh, 1860.

Waterbolk, E. H. "Deux poèmes inconnus de Rodolphe Agricola?" *Humanistica Lovaniensia,* 21 (1972), 37–49.

Weiss, J. M. "The Six Lives of Rudolph Agricola: Forms and Functions of the Humanist Biography." *Humanistica Lovaniensia,* 30 (1981), 19–39.

Wessel Gansfort (1419–1489) and Northern Humanism. Eds. F. Akkerman, G. C. Huisman, and A. J. Vanderjagt. Brill's Studies in Intellectual History, vol. 40. Leiden, 1993.

Worstbrock, F. J. "Agricola, Rudolph." In *Die deutsche Literatur des Mittelalters. Verfasserlexikon.* Ed. K. Ruh. Berlin, 1978, I:84–93.

————. "Liber, Antonius." In *Die deutsche Literatur des Mittelalters. Verfasserlexikon.* Ed. K. Ruh. Berlin. 1985, V:747–751.

A New Life for Agricola
Some Observations on the Sources[1]

FOKKE AKKERMAN

Relatively much has been written on the life of Rudolph Agricola. The six humanistic *vitae* from the fifteenth and sixteenth centuries themselves provide us with abundant material. Two additional cases may have been lost. Next, there are the *laudatio* in Erasmus's adage "Quid cani et balneo" and the many scattered passages concerning the Frisian hero in his work and correspondence. I counted forty-eight such *testimonia* in all; these date from the earliest letters until the very last years of Erasmus's life. From Agricola's own correspondence fifty-four letters have come down to us, and his name occurs in the correspondence of others as well. In modern historiography full-scale monographs or at least whole chapters on Agricola's life have been written by Tresling (1830), Von Bezold (1884), Ihm (1893), Van der Velden (1911), Nauwelaerts (1963), Spitz (1963), Worstbrock (1978); several aspects of his life were also treated in our collection of papers of 1988, and a new book of essays on Agricola has now appeared under the editorship of Professor Kühlmann in Heidelberg (1994).

Most of the modern biographical work on Agricola is written in the common positivistic or neo-positivistic way. On the basis of a wide and thorough reading, the authors form for themselves an image of their object and his times and then compose their monographs, constantly referring to scattered passages in their sources in order to build up this image into a literary portrait. This procedure has resulted in fascinating stories, which are nevertheless coloured representations of some kind of reality. In the last decades more work has been done in the field of the literary study of various sources. More insight has been gained into the aims of the humanistic *vita* and into the differences of style and tone and genre of the various works. I only mention the studies by Margaret Mann Phillips on "Erasmus and Biography" (1973), by IJsewijn on "Die humanistische Biographie" (1983) and, with special attention to

---

[1] For the bibliography, see pages 101–103.

Agricola, by James Michael Weiss (1981). Weiss concentrated on the six Latin lives of Agricola and gave a valuable start in the direction of a new, modern description. The present contribution will do no more than make some observations that are in addition to the article of Weiss.

First a few remarks on the *vita* by Johann (and Dietrich) von Pleningen (ca. 1500), for which I make use of my own article in Dutch of 1983 and of the recent chapter by Werner Straube (1994). In several ways the *vita* by the von Pleningens is the finest of the six: a many-sided portrayal of Agricola's person and a careful construction of his course of life. Weiss has praised this piece and rightly so. Since we know that Johann and Dietrich von Pleningen were close friends of Agricola and that they lived together with him in Pavia and Ferrara and later in Heidelberg and Rome, one could well hope that this source would be historically the most reliable. But if by "historically reliable" is meant "satisfying our modern historical taste and curiosity," the qualification becomes somewhat doubtful. In their handling of the biographical facts the von Pleningen brothers were very selective. This selectivity originated from literary and rhetorical motives, and it resulted in the omission of several aspects which, according to our standards, are extremely important for the humanist's development and activity, or they manipulated the data in a direction which is not in accordance with historical truth. Too little—almost nothing—is said about the beginnings of humanism in the North and about Agricola's Aduard (Adwert) circle: there is not a word about his position as a secretary of the town of Groningen or about his contacts with the city of Antwerp and his hopes of getting a post there. Yet about all this they could have been very well informed by Agricola himself, orally or through their correspondence, which they included in their own codex. There is nothing about his presence at the University of Heidelberg, nor on the lectures he gave there, nor on the disputations he took part in, although these were all activities with which they must have been perfectly well acquainted.

Another feature in the von Pleningens' *vita* that has to be reckoned with is the use of sources or models which the author made in writing his text. I see at least three of them: several of the *Vitae Caesarum* by Suetonius, the life of Petrarch written by Agricola himself, and his letter, nr. 38, to Barbirianus, known as *De formando studio*. The letter and the *Vita Petrarchae* were, of course, well known to Johann von Pleningen, because he included them in the codex of Agricola's work, for which his Life of Agricola served as an introduction. I have counted more than twenty passages where von Pleningen used Agricola's *Vita Petrarchae* literally, quoting even essential humanistic topics, which can be considered as the elementary building stones of the humanist ideology.[2] Since Agricola depicted Petrarch as the ideal humanist and mixed much of his own life pattern into his description of Petrarch—as Bertalot (1928,[2] 1975) and Waterbolk (1972) have established—it is especially interesting to see how von Pleningen uses this life of Petrarch again as a model for his *Vita* of Agricola. A sort of telescopic continuity thus determines the humanist *vita*; it becomes to a certain

---

[2] There is a strong analogy in the building up of the late-classical and medieval saint's life and legend, an illuminating treatment of which is given by André Jolles 1965, 23–60.

degree a fixed typology of the ideal life of the new type of scholar, to which the humanist in real life could try to adapt himself.

In fact, the *vita* written by Johann von Pleningen is in the first place a *descriptio personae*, some points of reference for which are taken from classical textbooks of rhetoric and the *Vitae Caesarum* by Suetonius. This *descriptio* is carefully built up from full
descriptions of his *corpus*, *animus*, *mens*, and *ingenium*. Furthermore it is a *curriculum disciplinarum*, consciously marshalled in a clear order, from grammar in Groningen to
Hebrew in Heidelberg. First Agricola learned grammar in the town school of Groningen, next rhetoric and dialectics at the university of Erfurt, natural philosophy, ethics,
and mathematics in Louvain, theology in Cologne, Roman law in Pavia. Then there
is a sharp break: law is rejected and Latin literature comes in its place; next follows
Greek in Ferrara and finally Hebrew in Heidelberg at the court of bishop von
Dalberg, who for this purpose hired a learned Jew for him. Such is the frame of
Agricola's life as a permanent student, for which the *Vita Petrarchae* and *De formando
studio*[3] served as models. Von Pleningen derived elements from both sources. This
regular pattern is here and there at variance with historical reality; for example, it is
not very probable that Agricola studied theology at Cologne after he had taken the
degree of *magister artium* at Louvain. There is somewhat more reason to believe Geldenhouwer, who tells us that he went from Louvain to France for some time.

In the third place the *vita* is an *enumeratio operum*: the *De inventione dialectica*, for
example, is praised at three crucial places in the text as a lasting monument to the
author's learning and as a germ of rich fruit for coming generations. This assertion
was written down ca. 1500, when the work had not yet been printed. Most of the
other *opuscula* of Agricola are listed also, but not much is made of his poetry. Only
the *Jodocus* poem is mentioned.[4]

Von Pleningen persistently claims that he is not able to write a true *vita*. For this
reason he calls his piece of writing only an "index seu commentarii vitae," which in
due time has to be made into a true work of rhetorical literature by others more
competent than he himself is in his own eyes. Although in themselves these declara-
tions of incapacity ("Unfähigkeitsbeteuerungen") are very topical, the space von
Pleningen spends on this topos—no less than fifty-three lines in all—suggests that he
is sincere in his low opinion of his own literary abilities. Since he had during his
work the *Vita Petrarchae* of Agricola constantly before his eyes, it may well be that he
became painfully aware of his own shortcomings as a stylist. Not unjustly so, for
Agricola's *Vita Petrarchae* is a brilliant piece indeed. And, according to Agricola, von
Pleningen was a keen judge in literary matters. In a letter he praises his *vera aestimatio*
of the *studia politiora* (Ep. 27).

---

[3] Especially for the two branches of philosophy (physics and ethics) von Pleningen's text borrows something from *De formando studio* (Agricola 1539, 194). Theology as a crown upon secular
ethics too seems more in accordance with *De form. stud.* than with Agricola's *curriculum*, for as the
son of a parish priest, he had no chance of entering upon an ecclesiastical career.

[4] It may well be that most of Agricola's activity as a poet took place in the North; cf.
Schoonbeeg in this seminar.

Because the *vita* by Goswinus van Halen (ca. 1525) is much poorer in construction and style, Weiss has little appreciation for it. Goswinus less consciously planned and composed his *vita*, which is in the form of a letter to Melanchthon. His writing is rather plain, and it does not look at all like a piece of fictitious rhetoric. Furthermore, he wrote at a much later time and is obviously attracted by other aspects of Agricola's career than the topics chosen by von Pleningen. In practically every sentence his *vita* contains interesting and reliable information on Agricola's life. The scope of his *vita* is limited, but he really knows what he is writing about. Through him we know about Agricola's parents and his brothers and sister, his earliest youth, his position as secretary of the city of Groningen, his girlfriend Ana and the amorous songs he wrote for her, and his contacts with a learned nun in his father's monastery.

Goswinus's is also the *vita* that tells us most about Agricola as a poet (see note 5 below). He makes mistakes in the chronology, though these may have also been caused partly by negligent copying of his text. Goswinus is chatty and has not mastered the technique of suppressing, omitting, and selecting. However, thanks to Goswinus, though through other texts than his *vita* of Agricola,[5] we are informed about the Aduard circle and the scholars who participated in it and about Agricola's friendship with Wessel Gansfort. We hear that they often had dinner together and that Agricola sometimes drank too much, so that he, Goswinus, had to conduct him home and pull off his boots. We get the picture of a man who, thanks to his influential father and to his many-sided learning, held an important office in his hometown. The father, Hendrik Vries, was abbot of the rich monastery of Selwerd close to the city walls of Groningen. He was on good terms with the bishop of Münster and with the city-fathers of Groningen. Agricola as viewed by Goswinus was a lively figure, who had scored triumphs in Italy of which his biographer is very proud. In the eyes of Goswinus, a very pious man himself, Agricola stemmed from a somewhat worldly, almost frivolous family.[6]

A very different picture emerges from the *vita* by von Pleningen: this is that of the humanistic scholar, who on his own initiative and by his own talents undertakes the new studies, who succeeds splendidly in his attempts and passes his knowledge on to his pupils. It is pretty certain that Johann von Pleningen developed much of the ability shown in his writing of this *vita* as a result of lessons from Agricola himself. He calls him *praeceptor (noster)* fourteen times, and twenty times he refers to his learning in a variety of epithets.

With regard to the lives of Geldenhouwer (1536) and Melanchthon (1539) I shall be brief. Geldenhouwer hailed from Nijmegen and studied in Louvain. He honours Agricola as the brilliant student in Louvain, as the learned Netherlander and pious

---

[5] Through the letters by Goswinus to Albert Hardenberg in Gansfort 1614; *De Wessele Groningensi*, ed. Kan 1894, 4–5; the story told by Regnerus Praedinius, see *Rodolphus Agricola Phrisius* 1988, 327.

[6] The impression of frivolity is evoked by the story about the double fatherhood of Hendrik Vries and the ambiguous joke about the relationship between Agricola and the nun Wandelvaert in his father's convent. Furthermore, Goswinus expands on his own piety but does not breathe a word about the religious life of his hero.

Christian, three qualities closely bound up with the personal circumstances and convictions of Geldenhouwer himself. Some additional information is given on Agricola's years in Louvain: his superfast mastering of French, his reading and/or copying of Quintilian, the Plinys, and Cicero, his library, his composition of love songs, and his contacts with the town of Nijmegen. In his letter to Alardus and in his academic oration Melanchthon presents Agricola primarily as a scholar at the University of Heidelberg; he has him participate in discussions and disputations with academic scholars and shows him as a teacher of Greek and Latin. Furthermore, he praises his sweet morals and the decent manners of his social intercourse with the high circles of the university and the courts of the bishop and the prince elector of the Palatinate. Melanchthon obviously uses Agricola as an exemplar of correct behaviour for scholarly, academical, and political circles and as propaganda for academic training and erudition.

The letters by and to Agricola form the other important source for his life. They allow us direct access to his feelings and thoughts and to his relationships with the early partisans and supporters of the humanistic cause. Every bit of his correspondence is moulded into a stylized, rhetorical form by his humanist pen. I think we are now fully aware that these writings cannot be used as simple factual, objective sources. In the biography by Van der Velden (1911) lavish attention was paid to each of Agricola's works, but in the entire book not a word is spent on the humanist letter as a literary form. Agricola's letters appear in the footnotes only as source references. In fact, they are just as selective as the other sources. For a correct estimation every item has to be judged in the context of its tone, the special relation it has with the addressee, and the situation of the moment.[7]

I think we should very carefully work up to a new sketch of Agricola's life. To begin with, an assessment has to be made of each individual document or text, its meaning and purpose. Subsequently it would be useful to collect all statements on the same subject from the various sources. I once did this for the subject "music," and it immediately proved useful for insight into the many-sided musicality of Agricola. I found fourteen passages on this matter and so easily outstripped the superficial knowledge that is to be gained from the usual handbooks on musical history in which Agricola is often mentioned.[8] At our congress of 1985, I considered in the same way the source material for Agricola's position in and relationship to his native country. Then also I had the feeling that I had detected a more interesting and complex situation than is suggested in any modern biographical sketch.

Because the source material in the case of Agricola is comparatively rich, a meticulous scrutiny of the available texts can produce a more subtle picture of Agricola's life and work. I have a very simple example at hand to illustrate this, that is, the case of Agricola's parents. Johann von Pleningen says:

---

[7] See Akkerman 1985a.

[8] See Kooiman 1988; a collection of texts on Agricola's musicality in Akkerman 1985b.

Natus est itaque Rhodolphus Agricola [. . .] parentibus quidem ac maioribus modicis, ut sua uirtute atque industria aliquando redderetur insignior.

In this passage the virtual finality of *ut* smacks almost too much of classical rhetorical precepts.[9] Goswinus van Halen really knew who Agricola's parents were, though he could hardly have known them, because they both died in 1480, the same year that Goswinus came as a twelve-year-old boy to Groningen. Nevertheless, his reports are full of real facts, with only a few mistakes:[10]

In pago praenominato Baffeltlo erat quidam licentiatus ut uocant theologiae, parochus sed nondum in sacerdotem unctus, Henricus Huysman ex sua familia dictus. Hic ex quadam puella filium sustulit quem Rodolphum appellauit. Puella autem Zycka nominabatur, quae postea nupsit cuidam sarcinatori Zico nomine, qui ex ea genuit duos filios et unam filiam.

Henricus Fredericus cum aliquot annos in Baffeltlo curam pastoralem obiuisset, electus est in abbatem in monasterio cui Zelwaer nomen est haud procul a moenibus oppidi Groningae ad aquilonem situm. Eadem hora qua electus est in abbatem uenit ad se quidam ex Baffeltlo euangelium postulans: natus est tibi, noue abbas, ex tua Zycka filius. Cui respondit: bene habet; felici, inquit, auspicio hic dies mihi illuxit. Hodie bis pater effectus sum; Deus bene uertat.

The investigation of all the relevant source material from the archives by Folkert Bakker (1988) has confirmed, even strengthened the impression derived from this written literary document: the father as well as the mother and the stepfather Sicco Schroeder (*sartor*) of Agricola did not belong to the highest elite of the landed gentry of the province but stemmed from prominent families, with landed property of their own and, in the case of his father, with a highly esteemed ecclesiastical function. So Geldenhouwer was fully correct, when he said: *Agricolarum familia apud Frisios inter honoratiores semper habita est.* This does not detract from the possibility that he could have fabricated this out of his rhetorical imagination. Weiss declares this statement "a blatant falsehood," which it surely is not. Weiss also criticizes the words *incomparabilis heros*, but I think that this term is quite in accordance with the humanist mood that wanted to transfer the title *heros* from the military caste to the realms of learning and intellectual life.

Melanchthon stresses the modest financial means of Agricola's parents:

Natus est Rodolphius Agricola in Frisia, in rure quodam non procul ab urbe Groninga, honestis parentibus, quorum facultates, ut sunt ibi, mediocres fuerunt, et unde liberis ad studia sumpta liberaliter suppeditare poterant.

---

[9] Cf. *Rhetorica ad Herennium* 3,7,13 *genus*—*in laude: quibus maioribus natus sit; si bono genere, parem aut excelsiorem fuisse; si humili genere, ipsum in suis, non in maiorum uirtutibus habuisse praesidium.*

[10] Mistakes are the name of the father (in the archival records he is always called Hendrik Vries), and a number of dates. The statement that he was a priest in Baflo, while not yet having been ordained, may also be false.

Nec tantum prudentia fuit, sed etiam quaedam animi celsitudo et mira discendi
auiditas, quod in Italiam, cum patrimonium haberet mediocre, profectus est, ut
melius doctrinae genus quaereret.

Apparently, those means were still sufficient to pay for the studies of the children.
Melanchthon is a propagandist for and a stimulator of education, and so he not only
makes an example out of Agricola to the students of the university but also of his
parents to their parents. Besides, "the modest means" are not a lie. Agricola's studies
were paid for from an ecclesiastical benefice, that is, half the yield of one farm in
Baflo. Compared to the means of some of his closest German companions in Pavia
and Ferrara, this money must have been rather modest. In Ferrara Agricola was in the
service of the duke Ercole d'Este and was paid for his time. The bishop of Augsburg,
Johann von Werdenberg, and the bishop of Worms, Johann von Dalberg, and also
Count Maurice of Spiegelberg had him in their service and provided for his living as
well.

Agricola's own statement ... *hominibus infime classis, inter quos me numero* ... can
only be explained by comparing his social status with that of his companions from
southern Germany (the letter from which the statement is taken [Ep. 8] is addressed
to Dietrich von Pleningen) and of his mighty and rich patrons. We should not forget
that he was their tutor, their *praeceptor*. I take it that they paid him for this.

In this way the words of Johann von Pleningen, *de parentibus ac maioribus modicis*,
can also be accounted for, not only socially and financially but perhaps still more so
intellectually. For Johann von Pleningen Agricola is the modern brilliant humanist.
Indeed, his father was licentiate in theology—though there are no records to confirm
this—but in comparison with the very different intellectual heights the son had
reached, his parents could certainly be regarded as modest people. From these considerations it can be concluded that not one of the sources sins against historical truth
but that each adapts its statements to the context and purposes for which it was
written.

In *De inuentione dialectica* Agricola himself used a metaphor of a father and his son,
who have different aims in mind when the father sends his son to study. The specific
chapter is on the philosophical notion of *finis*. Thus Agricola says: the purpose of
building (*aedificatio*) is a house, but the purpose of the builder is his wages, and the
purpose of the client, who has commissioned the building, is to live in the house or
to give or to sell it to someone else. And then the next metaphor runs as follows:

Istud etiam praetereundum non uidetur, posse unius plures esse fines, ut alius
sit operis, alius operantis, alius iubentis. [. . .] Sic studiorum proprius est finis
eruditio: at eius qui studet, potest etiam quidem finis esse eruditio, sed fortasse
est uel gloriae, uel lucri spes. At patris qui sumptum studenti praebet, amor,
incrementaque filii. Amici quoque qui suasit, ut aliquando opera fortasse et
eruditione studentis utatur. (*De inv. dial.* I,15)

The end of study is erudition, and in the view of the student it can also be the pure,
disinterested erudition that is the aim of the true humanist, as is said explicitly in *De
formando studio*. For others, perhaps, it is also the hope of fame or profit. The motive

of the father is the love and development of his son. And the motive of the friend who has advised him to study might be to profit through the help and erudition of the student. It is almost impossible that in writing down this metaphor Agricola did not have in mind his own studies, his own father, and his own rich friends and patrons. In that case this fine image harmonises perfectly well with what other sources have to report on the father of Agricola.

University of Groningen

Scribe quod innuptae possint memorare puellae[1]

PIETER SCHOONBEEG[*]

I have not placed this line from Murmellius at the head of my paper for the sole purpose of attracting attention.[2] It reflects one of the differences, but a conspicuous one, between the poetry of Italian humanists and that of the group whose works will be discussed in this paper.

Now these Northern humanists were forever in raptures about Italy and were constantly saying or implying or wishing that Apollo and the Muses or, if need be, they themselves would import the newly blossoming *studia humanitatis* from Italy to the Low Countries and Germany. Agricola, for example, writes to his friend, the Münster prelate Rudolf von Langen, "Unum tibi affirmo ... fore aliquando ut priscam insolenti Italiae et propemodum occupatam bene dicendi gloriam extorqueamus," that is, "I assure you of one thing, that a time will come that we will wrest the ancient and almost exclusive glory of eloquence from the hands of proud Italy" (Agricola 1539, 178). Rudolf von Langen raves about Lorenzo Valla and about a book that appears "ex eius officina depromptum" (Crecelius 1876, 7; the remark refers to the *Elegantiolae* by Agostino Dati). When Agricola returned from Italy Frederick Mormann described him in the following words: "uates Frisius ex finibus Italis/ ducens Aonidum choros," that is, the Frisian poet returning from Italy with the Muses in his wake. And not only that: he returns "honustus/ grandi fasce uoluminum optimorum," bowed down by an enormous load of excellent books (Schoonbeeg 1993, XVII, 3–4; XVIII, 23–24).

On the other hand no tones are dark enough to depict the remoteness of their native regions and the condition of learning, especially of the Latin language, in those parts. Agricola never ceases to lament that his native country is the "ultimus terrarum

---

[*] Pieter Schoonbeeg died tragically at the age of 47 following an accident in October 1997. IANLS mourns the untimely death of a member whose scholarly interests lay mainly with early Neo-Latin poetry of the Agricola circle in the Northern Netherlands and the poems of Frederick Mormann (Fridericus Maurus).

[1] For the bibliography, see pages 101–103.

[2] *Elegiae morales* I,1,21 in Reichling 1963, 168.

angulus," an out-of-the-way corner of the world, and when he returned to Groningen in 1480 he criticised, according to a letter he wrote to a friend, the lack of interest in the "litterae politiores."[3] Frederick Mormann speaks of a people situated "horrida et ultima sub Arcto," in the extreme North, that up till that moment uttered with gnashing teeth a barbarous dialect (Schoonbeeg 1993, XVIII, 30–32).

Rudolph von Langen wonders in one of his poems why the city of Cologne, a daughter of Rome at that, does not show the "vates et poetae humanitatisque professores," that is, the representatives of humanism, any respect (Parmet 1869, LVIII). In a letter to a young *aficionado* of the new cultural movement he warns him of the danger of getting stuck "in dialecticis" and admonishes him not to spend too much time and energy on the "modi significandi." Von Langen implies that these two aspects of traditional learning still dominate the educational field at home and that they are both hopelessly old-fashioned. The addressee of his letter had better read some books "de virtutibus," for example, by Aristotle. But not in the old translation that was still widely spread in the Low Countries and Germany; that was "sententiarum involucris plena, barbara, inlatina." No, he should use the new and faithful translation (by Leonardo Bruni) that was "fidelis, elegans et plana" (Crecelius 1876, 11–12).

Both Antonius Liber and a younger member of this set, Bartholomaeus of Cologne, wrote poems with the significant title, "In osores studiorum humanitatis," almost a *topos* in Northern humanism (Schoonbeeg 1993, 340; Barth. Coloniensis 1505, fol. [A V]r–v). The former directs the arrows of his wrath against those who despise rhetoric and poetry, the latter, more generally, derides the "garrula barbaries" that, according to his (wishful) thinking, will succeed nevermore in ousting the learned followers of the Muses from double-topped Mount Parnassus. In other epigrams he fulminates against those that simply are not able to speak a decent Latin: Zoilus, the personification of his laughingstock, talks with torrential rapidity when speaking his native tongue. When speaking Latin, however, the words trickle slowly from his lips like the viscous water of the Dead Sea or the pitch from the trees on Mount Ida (Barth. Coloniensis, *ibid.* fol. [A V]v).

The picture of the territory where this early humanism flourished, that results from all these complementary remarks, is extremely sombre and not sensibly different from that painted by Tacitus, more than 1300 years earlier: lying at the end of the world, perhaps not quite "ultima Thule," but, still, on the shore of the Ocean, is a country populated by a people shrouded in the clouds of a barbarous ignorance. This Northern barbarism is a stock *topos* of these early Northern humanists, but they and their new appreciation of poetry encountered massive resistance, as amply illustrated by Prof. IJsewijn in his article on "The Coming of Humanism to the Low Countries" (1975, 211–213). Education in the schools continued for the larger part during numerous decades in the same way as it had always done, notwithstanding the example and inspiration of men like Agricola and, later on, Erasmus. They themselves never taught in the schools, but men like Alexander Hegius, Antonius Liber, Frederick Mormann, and Bartholomaeus of Cologne disseminated their ideas, at first as

---

[3] Agricola, epp. 53 and 22. Cf. *Rodolphus Agricola Phrisius* 1988, 323 and 325.

lonely champions. (Alexander Hegius, by the way, will henceforth not be mentioned anymore in this discussion of the poetry by members of the Aduard [Adwert] Academy. His poems, as regards their Latinity, hold something like an in-between position between medieval and Neo-Latin poetry.) Not only geographically, but also, and especially, intellectually, these parts are separated by an unbridgeable abyss from Italy. Those happy few who have been able to see in person the force and vigour and vitality of the "renatae litterae" in the light of the Italian sun (and their influence on contemporary letters) may try to transplant these to their native regions, but they will have to reckon with an enormous resistance from their backward countrymen, in the words of Rudolf von Langen, "qui per dies et noctes arti nostre dicendi detrahunt remque inanem esse atque longe fugiendam censent," who are disparaging day and night our art of speaking and consider it a futile business that ought to be shunned (Crecelius 1876, 12). And Mormann, in one of his poems, complains of the fact that "arescunt studia,/ ... Pegasides Musae fleuisse uidentur amare/ quod sine amore iacent," liberal studies languish, the Pegasean Muses are seen to have been weeping bitterly because they are neglected, not loved any more (Schoonbeeg 1993, XIII, 3 and 8–9). Italy is their great example, the cynosure of their hopes and wishes.

But what in fact did these men, as humanist poets, actually bring back with them from Italy, and how did they use it? In order to examine the differences between the Neo-Latin poetry from the *milieu* of the "Aduard Academy" and that of the Italian Quattrocento, I will give a brief survey of the contents of this poetry. Four members of this group have left a substantial quantity of poetry: Agricola, Rudolf von Langen, Frederick Mormann, and Bartholomaeus of Cologne. Of men like Antonius Liber and Paulus Pelantinus only a couple of lines have been transmitted, and Moritz von Spiegelberg is said to have written poetry, but none of it has reached us.[4]

Agricola wrote about a thousand lines of poetry, nearly half of which consists of religious poetry. These are solemn, formal hymns addressed to saints that were fashionable at the time (St. Anne, for example), or for whom humanists had a special ve-

---

[4] The greater part of Agricola's poems has been published in Agricola 1539. The ode on St. Catherine of Alexandria has been partially printed in Van der Velden 1911, 218–219. Two other poems that are not in the Alardus edition have been published by Waterbolk 1972. For two poems that possibly can be attributed to Agricola, see Schoonbeeg 1988, 190 and note 6. Von Langen's poems have been published in Parmet 1869. For Mormann's poetry, see Schoonbeeg 1993. There is no modern edition of the complete poetical works of Bartholomaeus Coloniensis. His *Sylva Carminum* was published at Deventer in 1491, his *Libellus elegiacus de septenis doloribus Mariae* also at Deventer in 1514. For his poem on a Holy Blood Miracle, see Rijkenberg 1896; poems on St. Lawrence and St. Matthias are printed in Lampen 1935. The two fables have been published in Schoonbeeg 1991. There is no edition of his eclogue; see Kristeller 1983, 156ª and 611ª. Only a few poems by Antonius Liber are known: an epigram accompanying the edition of Titus Livius de Frulovisiis's *De Orthographia* (Cologne 1479); a poem in praise of the city of Cologne in Jacobus de Voragine 1483, fol. CCCCLVIr; a panegyrical poem dedicated to Wessel Gansfort on the latter's return from Italy in Gansfort 1522, fol. 4v and poem X in Schoonbeeg 1993, 340. Paulus Pelantinus wrote an *epitaphium* and an *epicedium* on Wessel Gansfort, printed in Gansfort 1614, ***2r–3v. Also by his hand is a *Carmen lyricum de nativitate Christi* (Zwolle 1486–1488).

neration (St. Catherine of Alexandria, patroness of the arts), or to whom Agricola himself was especially devoted for personal reasons (St. Judocus). The hymns to St. Anne and to St. Judocus contain personal elements in that they are a kind of *ex voto* poems, written on the occasion of deliverance from illnesses; he also wrote a "hymnus ad omnes sanctos." There is a great variety of occasional poems: professions of everlasting friendship to a Burgundian court official, to an otherwise unknown abbot Caspar, and to a certain Cribellius Mediolanensis, probably called Crivelli in the vernacular, who promised Agricola his copy of Pliny. There is an ode in the Horatian manner and spirit addressed to Rudolf von Langen, a poem in praise of Pavia, where he spent some time as a student, a poem as a covering letter for a gift of some fruit to Lucas Crassus, "doctor utriusque iuris," some lines that describe a picture of Christ's Ascension, a long and moving *epicedium* followed by an epitaph on the death of his friend Count Moritz von Spiegelberg, and a number of epigrams and other epitaphs.

Religious poems also constitute a large part of Rudolf von Langen's poetry. But contrary to Agricola he did not only write highly stylized and literary hymns addressed to saints. Some of these poems have a more emotional, popular character: perhaps one should say that they are more in accordance with medieval traditions; others bear relation to everyday religious practice. His nonreligious poetry consists of the usual occasional poems, professions of friendship, propemptica, epicedia, epitaphs, moralistic epigrams, etc., but also, and here von Langen differs from Agricola, poems that refer to important contemporary events: the siege laid by Charles the Bold to the city of Neuss in the archbishopric of Cologne and several other battles are mentioned, the ever-present Ottoman menace, and also, for example, the publication of a trilingual Bible by Adolphus Rusch.

Until quite recently only two poems by Frederick Mormann were known, both written in connection with Agricola's return to Groningen. A couple of years ago some more poems of this, up to that time, rather obscure member of the Aduard Academy came to light in a manuscript of the Bavarian State Library in Munich. In the way of religious poetry Mormann did not write formal hymns to saints as did Agricola, von Langen (occasionally) and Bartholomaeus of Cologne of whom I shall speak later on. There are two poems with religious overtones, one in connection with an epidemic, the other a kind of lament on the increasing depravity of mankind, and there is a hymn on Christ's Nativity. In his other poetry one comes across a poem on the occasion of Agricola's departure abroad, there are two urgent requests directed to a certain Wilhelmus to come home, and in two other cases he asks the poems he is writing to go abroad and greet two of his friends (a procedure, incidentally, for which there are classical precedents). In other poems Mormann is very much concerned with the "cause" of humanism, a preoccupation that occurs once in a while in von Langen's poetry but is totally absent from Agricola's poems. Then there is a poem in connection with the death of Charles the Bold and the subsequent release from imprisonment of Duke Adolphus of Guelders, a sign of his interest in contemporary affairs that is almost completely lacking in Agricola's poetry.

The larger part, if not all, of the poetry by Bartholomaeus of Cologne seems to have been written for the classroom. He was a teacher and his poems are unmistakable products of his job. His poems, or rather the language he uses, form a textbook of mythological, geographical, and astronomical knowledge and give examples of epic and pastoral usage, of epigrams in the manner of Martial, and of the vocabulary of comedy (the latter, by the way in a prose dialogue). His poems appear to be designed, *ut ita dicam*, to teach his pupils what phraseology to use in the various poetic *genres*. He wrote satirical and laudatory poems, two rather long fables that are in fact also satirical poems, and one eclogue, the only example of this *genre* in all the poetry of this group.

His religious poetry consists of a "Libellus elegiacus de septenis doloribus Mariae," a poem in connection with a Holy Blood miracle and two hymns to tutelary saints of the city where he was teaching. Although these last three poems were all related to the city where he was living and one could easily imagine them to have been written by order of the municipal or ecclesiastical authorities, even these have, oddly enough, the same textbook quality as his other poetry.

Summarizing this early Northern Neo-Latin poetry in more general terms one could say that as regards its form there are of course the usual large amounts of hexameters and elegiac distichs (which were also a feature of Neo-Latin poetry in the Italy of the first half of the Quattrocento but likewise constituted of course a relatively large part of classical Latin poetry) (Prete 1978, 3). But there were also, right from the beginning, poems written in the lyrical metres, for example, hendecasyllables, minor Asclepiads, Sapphic and Alcaic stanzas, and other combinations that occur in Horace and, for example, in the lyrical parts of Boethius's *De consolatione philosophiae*. In the content of this poetry there is nothing out of the ordinary; out of the ordinary things are what are so conspicuously missing.

Agricola was sufficiently aware of Petrarch's importance to write a biography of this champion of humanism. Petrarch was his example and model but apparently only up to a certain point. Like Petrarch, Agricola wrote Latin letters, treatises, poems. But Agricola never attempted, as far as we know, to write a larger epic poem or to compose eclogues, nor did anyone else in this circle, although the latter *genre* was much cultivated by the Italian poets of the Quattrocento. Not only Petrarch, the great example, wrote eclogues, but so did Tito Vespasiano Strozzi, who probably moved in the same circles as Agricola did at the Este court in Ferrara. Other writers of eclogues were Baptista Mantuanus, who was immensely popular in the Low Countries (but not very much so in his native country) and whose work found its way very early to the printing presses of precisely those regions where our poets lived or worked or stemmed from, and, for example, Enea Silvio Piccolomini, who perhaps more than anyone else acted as an intermediary between Southern and Northern humanism. The only eclogue written in this group is the one already mentioned by Bartholomaeus of Cologne and this, like the rest of his poetry, is another didactic vehicle, in this case for the usage of the bucolic and "georgic," so to speak, *genre*.

The elegiac distich as a metrical form was used by the poets of the Aduard Academy for widely diverging purposes but not for love poetry as it had been by, for example, Pontano, Enea Silvio, and Strozzi, nor for erotic, or rather salacious, poetry as it had been by Panormita. Agricola is said by some of his biographers to have written poems in the vernacular and in some other modern languages, including "carmina amatoria," but none of them have come down to us. The absence of this "genre," Neo-Latin love poetry, is surprising, not only when considering what there was in this area in Italy (and of which some of our poets must have been aware) but the more so when one takes into account the vernacular background of these Northern poets, in which erotic poetry abounded.

Drama, comedy and tragedy, is totally absent from the work of the poets in question, even from the work of a schoolmaster like Bartholomaeus of Cologne. In Italy Latin drama, both in Latin and in translation, began to be performed again during the second half of the fifteenth century; in the same period there was a new start in the writing of original Neo-Latin drama, in imitation of Terence, intended to be actually put on the stage. The imitation and the revival of Latin drama in the *milieu* of Northern humanism dates from the turn of the century.

On the other hand one could easily get the impression, from my summary of the contents of these poems, that there is an enormous amount of religious poetry. This is certainly true, although the earliest printed anthologies of Neo-Latin poetry, dating from the sixteenth century for the most part, and our modern anthologies, do not give very many religious poems. I for one should hesitate to conclude from this fact that Italian Neo-Latin poets wrote less religious poetry than their fellow-humanists from the North: there may have been a change in taste, even between the Quattrocento and the sixteenth century, and the influence of the Council of Trent may have made the composers of the early anthologies shrink back from publishing simply what they found in this field of poetry.

Some of the poets from the *milieu* of the Aduard Academy had first-hand knowledge of Italy and of Italian humanism: they lived and studied and worked there for some time. It is highly improbable that they, or at any rate a man like Agricola, who lived at the court of Ferrara, did not know, or were at least not aware of the fact, that drama and eclogues and love poetry were being written by the foremost representatives of Neo-Latin poetry in the country they allegedly admired so much. The reasons for the selective imitation of their Italian models or for the selective handling of their undoubtedly Italian inspiration to write poetry probably lay in the regional background and education and sensibility which they had in common and in the influence of the Modern Devotion.

That, at least, seems an obvious explanation. I am not quite sure that this is the whole answer, and I am not satisfied, where poetry is concerned, with the traditional explanations. Of course, Italian humanism and this type and phase of Northern humanism had widely differing backgrounds. Italian humanism flourished in the cities and their universities and at the courts of secular and spiritual princes, while in the North the only centres of learning were the monasteries, and the only universities, those of Cologne and Louvain, did not, at first, exactly welcome humanism.

Another traditional explanation, in its way as true and as valid as the first one, is that in Italy attempts to restore Latin found support in larger social circles while it coincided with a kind of national and patriotic longing for the glorious past of the Roman Empire, when Rome was mistress of the world, at a time when large parts of Italy nominally belonged to the "heilige römische Reich deutscher Nation" and foreign princes dominated great parts of a country that was a patchwork of larger and smaller states. Moreover, in Italy Latin and the various vernacular dialects could be regarded as the different faces of one and the same language, which made the attempt to revive classical Latin more easily comprehensible and accessible to a larger group of the population. In the North, however, any effort to restore Latin to its pristine glory was only understandable to the very few that had any Latin at all and was laudable only in the eyes of that part of them that was sensible to the beauties of classical Latin.

But even then the differences between Italian Neo-Latin poetry and that of the "members" of the Aduard Academy do not result as a matter of course from these diverging backgrounds and these differing aims and motives for the restoring of classical Latin. It is not at all clear why Agricola and the other members of this group should not write Latin love poetry. They were not all clergymen (and even then they could have pointed to illustrious medieval predecessors), and only one of them lived in a monastery (and that only part of his life); they were men of the world. It is not at all clear why it should all be—and now I can refer to the title of this paper: "Scribe quod innuptae possint memorare puellae"—why it should all be so highly moralistic.

The obvious answer is, seemingly: here, then, we see the influence of the Modern Devotion, the Brethren of the Common Life and of the Windesheim Congregation. But Agricola, like his great example Petrarch, wrote amatory poems in the vernacular, and the vernacular literature of the Low Countries abounded in erotic songs and stories. The influence of the Modern Devotion in the Low Countries, however, was certainly not restricted to the Latin poetry of this very select group of highly educated and erudite men. Why were no eclogues written in this *milieu*, except the one by Bartholomaeus of Cologne, which is almost a parody of an eclogue? Petrarch wrote eclogues, and the eclogues of Baptista Mantuanus were enormously popular in the Low Countries. The Modern Devotion could not be an obstacle in this matter, for eclogues can always be interpreted allegorically if necessary.

Why did they not write any drama? Petrarch, it is true, hardly wrote any drama, but one of the first products of (proto-)Renaissance Latin was Mussato's *Ecerinis*.[5] Latin drama was written in Italy, Latin drama was written in Germany, in an atmosphere more or less akin (but, after all, apparently less so) to that of the humanism we have been speaking of: Jacob Wimpheling produced his *Stylpho* in 1480. Moreover, Agricola's friend and patron, Johannes von Dalberg, bishop of Worms, had one of Reuchlin's Latin plays put on the stage, at his own court, in one of the last years of the fifteenth century. Besides, medieval Dutch literature had known drama, spiritual and secular, and in the second half of the fifteenth century the so-called Rederijkerskamers flourished in the Low Countries. These were literary societies, performing, amongst other things, plays, that found their members in the upper-middle classes of the Low Countries, precisely that part of the population that had been educated in the schools of the Brethren of the Common Life.

These are questions to which no ready answers can be given. One could imagine

---

[5] Professor IJsewijn kindly drew my attention to the fact that Petrarch, too, wrote drama, a comedy entitled *Philologia*, of which only one line has come down to us.

that these poets, given the resistance they were to meet, resolved to abstain from the more frivolous aspects of Italian Neo-Latin poetry. But then eclogues do not have to be frivolous, and perfectly innocent drama can be written. Besides, in the eyes of the more conservative *milieux* of the Low Countries nearly all Latin poetry, but especially poetry in the "new" manner, was suspect anyway.

On the other hand, one is, at times, sensible of an impression that this group of poets regarded itself as a very select and exclusive club, open only to the initiated: that it tried to keep at a distance the "profanum vulgus" and the literary forms and topics that it considered profane, profane perhaps because they also occurred in vernacular literature: that there was a kind of *esprit de corps* that laid down the rules for what one could and could not do in the field of Latin poetry: one should only write what was fit to be read also by young, unmarried girls. These poets, as a group, took pride in their rules and, like a newly founded religious order, guarded them jealously, at least for the generation of Agricola's and the next.

Be all this as it may, Petrarch served as a model for Italian humanists and, up to a point, for Agricola. Agricola held, in the eyes of other members of this group, a somewhat similar position, and whither Agricola failed to lead, the lesser men of this set did not follow.

University of Groningen

Antonius Liber and
Northern Humanist Epistolography[1]

ADRIE VAN DER LAAN

I n this paper I will discuss the *Familiarium epistolarum compendium* of the Northern
humanist Antonius Liber. After having presented a few biographical facts, I will
discuss the purpose, contents, and sources of his book. The second part of my paper
will then deal with the letters of Liber himself and those of his friend Rudolph von
Langen. I shall comment upon their contents, style, and Latinity.

It was in the year 1475 or 1476 that Johann Koelhoff the Elder printed in Cologne a *Familiarium epistolarum compendium* which had been composed by Antonius
Liber of Soest in Westphalia, Germany (Hain 10072=5229). This Liber is not a very
well known humanist, and the information that we have about him is scarce. The
date of his birth is unknown. No evidence remains of his matriculation at any university, but his own letters tell us that he studied at the University of Pavia before the
year 1469. These studies, or at least part of them, were paid for by the monks of the
monastery of Aduard (Adwert),[2] the famous monastery which, when Hendrik van
Rees was abbot there (1449–1485), witnessed the rise of the first group of humanists
in the Low Countries. Its most famous members were Wessel Gansfort and Rudolph
Agricola. Our Antonius Liber also participated in the humanist meetings at Aduard,
probably in the late sixties and early seventies. In these years he was a teacher at St.
Martin's School in Groningen, verger of St. Martin's Church, and *notarius* of the same
city.[3] Later on Liber moved to Kampen, where he was *notarius* in 1482, when Agricola visited him there (Agr. *Ep.* 29). In the same city he also performed the task of
secretarius from 1485 until 1499.[4] Finally, we know that he was a teacher at the Latin
schools in Amsterdam and Alkmaar; here he died around 1507.

Liber was not a gifted scholar like Agricola. His talents were more moderate but

---

[1] For the bibliography, see pages 101–103.
[2] Goswinus Halensis in a letter of 1528 to Albert Hardenberg; see Gansfort 1614, fol. **5r.
[3] Santing 1988, 177; Worstbrock 1985, 747; Bakker 1988, 106.
[4] Santing 1988, 177.

perhaps equally important. He was one of those who paved the way for the acceptance in the late fifteenth century (and eventual victory from the beginning of the sixteenth century onwards) of the humanist curriculum in the Latin Schools of the northern parts of the Low Countries. He devoted himself primarily to the restoration of classical Latin. Besides the *Compendium*, he wrote a grammar called *Aurora grammatice*, edited Tito Livio Frulovisi's book on orthography, and wrote a commentary on a hymn of Prudentius. There also survive four poems from his hand, one of which, significantly entitled *In osores studiorum humanitatis*, was only recently discovered in a Munich manuscript.[5]

Liber's *Familiarium epistolarum compendium* was published probably before December 1476. He composed it in Cologne, where he had gone for some business (perhaps on the orders of the city of Groningen, since he was in its service as a notary, and because in a letter written in Cologne to his wife Berta in Groningen, Liber mentions that he has to prolong his stay in the German town for reasons of town interest: *publice . . . utilitatis quedam . . . negotia* [fol. M9r]). As he tells us himself in the dedicatory letter addressed to Arnold von Hildesheim, who was at that time the principal of St. Martin's School in Groningen, he composed the book for the following reason:

> Optauisti, dum abs te discederem, Arnolde fidissime, ut Colonie inter tot tantasque bibliothecas constitutus aliquot familiarium epistolarum tibi colligerem. Quibus et uisis et perlectis scholares tui spretis barbarorum insciciis tersum forte nitidumque scribendi stilum amplecterentur. (fol. a2r)

Liber intended his book to present samples of classical style; he composed the *Compendium* "pro communium studencium profectu futurorumque rethorum ac oratorum eruditione" (loc. cit.). Of course, this idea of using letters for purposes of education was by no means a new one. Very widespread were Gasparino Barzizza's *Epistolae ad exercitationem accommodatae*. Closer to Groningen, Charles Menneken (Viruli), the head of the College of the Lily at the University of Louvain, composed a collection of over three hundred model letters, written by himself, for the students of the College. These letters were to provide the students with phrases they could use in their own correspondence. Consequently, each letter bore a heading indicating its subject. Books such as these show that the humanists did not abolish the medieval form of the *ars dictaminis*, they merely adjusted the contents to their own (stylistic) preferences. They continued the tradition of using the letter (authentic or written by themselves for the occasion) as a means of education. For example, Cicero's *Ad Familiares* feature in the school curriculum of many a sixteenth-century school in Germany.[6]

Liber's *Compendium* contains 348 letters by twenty different authors. From antiquity we find Cicero, Seneca, Jerome, Symmachus, Sidonius, and the letters attributed to the Greek tyrant of Akragas, Phalaris (in the Latin translation by Francesco Griffolini); from the Middle Ages, Bernard of Clairvaux, Thomas Aquinas and Thomas a Kempis; and from the humanist period, Coluccio Salutati (he is called

[5] Bayerische Staatsbibliothek, clm. 528, fol. 200v. See Schoonbeeg 1993, poem X.
[6] Vormbaum 1860, *passim*.

Veneto by Liber), Gasparino and Guineforte Barzizza, Leonardo Bruni, Poggio Bracciolini, Enea Silvio Piccolomini, Antonio Beccadelli, and Francesco Filelfo. The book
concludes with letters written by three members of the humanist circle at Aduard,
viz. Rudolph Agricola, Rudolph von Langen, and Antonius Liber himself. The
authors were not inserted into the book in chronological or alphabetical order; there
seems to be no pre-meditated sequence. Only occasionally can we detect the reason
why Liber put certain letters of one author in the order that he did. Those of Seneca,
Symmachus, and Sidonius are arranged in the traditional order that is still preserved
in the modern editions. The letters of Filelfo, Agricola, and von Langen are in
chronological order, and those of Antonio Beccadelli are arranged according to
addressee. However, in most instances there seems to have been no premeditated
principle of arrangement. Most likely, Liber inserted the authors and their letters into
his book in the order that he took them from the shelves of the library (or libraries)
in Cologne.

The letters of Francesco Filelfo support this supposition. By collating the texts, I
have been able to trace the source that Liber used for this section of his book. It was
the *editio princeps* of part of Filelfo's letters (16 books) that appeared in 1473 in Venice. The order in this edition is identical to the one in the *Compendium*, while Liber
left out those letters that he considered too lengthy to fit into his collection.

Which authors did Liber appreciate most? When looking at the number of pages
attributed to each author, we can see that Cicero, Beccadelli, Guineforte Barzizza,
Piccolomini, and Salutati occupy the highest number of folia. Of these, Cicero and
Piccolomini are no surprise at all, since they feature prominently in any humanist
anthology. Salutati's contribution is remarkable for the fact that it consists of only
one, but very lengthy, letter. It concerns his letter to Lodovico Alidosi.[7] It recommends the *studia humanitatis* as the road to eloquence, and consequently wisdom, and
gives detailed information on how to write a Latin speech. In Liber's book, it is divided into twelve chapters, each with its own heading indicating the contents. Very
striking is the presence of letters by Guineforte Barzizza; this son of Gasparino did
not gain much attention from his contemporaries nor, for that matter, from modern
scholars. Besides, very few editions of his letters came off the press; there is no modern edition, and the most recent one with a fair amount of his personal letters was
edited by Furietti in 1723. Liber must have used a manuscript as his source, since no
printed edition was available by 1476.

The letters in the *Compendium* deal with a variety of themes. They have not been
arranged according to topic. A favourite subject is that of the letter itself in connection with friendship; this does not come as a surprise, since the letter was, from
Cicero onwards, defined as a conversation between absent friends. Another important
theme is humanism (education, *studia humanitatis*). Obviously Liber used his book to
propagate the humanist cause in the classroom, unlike, for example, Viruli, in whose
letters this topic is almost completely absent. The letters of Seneca, Jerome, Bernard
of Clairvaux, Aquinas and a Kempis are different from the others, since they were

---

[7] Novati 1891–1911, 3:598–614.

clearly primarily selected for their religious or moral content: they deal only with ethics and matters of faith.

I have spent only a limited amount of time trying to discover the sources that Liber used. So far, I have detected two of them. I already mentioned one: the first printed edition (Venice 1473) of the letters of Filelfo. The second concerns a curious section of the *Compendium*.[8] After having inserted the letters of the authors mentioned above, but before including his own letters and those of Agricola and von Langen, Liber added a paragraph containing twelve anonymous letters. He claims to have picked them *ex diuersis hinc inde autoribus summa cum diligentia*. It took me quite some time and effort to discover their identity. Filelfo was the author of the last two letters in this section, and Liber copied them from the Venice edition. The remaining ten can be found in several manuscripts, nearly always anonymous. Besides, eleven *incunabula* (GW 8123–8133) contain the text of these letters as an appendix to the *Elegantiolae* of Agostino Dati from Siena (a text to which we shall turn our attention in a moment). The ten letters are part of a manual on the art of writing letters of petition and consolation composed by Gasparino Barzizza.[9] Liber omitted the theoretical parts of this manual and included ten of the twelve model letters it contained. Collation of the texts in manuscripts and *incunabula* proves that he used the *editio princeps* of the *Elegantiolae*, printed by Ulrich Zell in Cologne around 1470, as his source for these letters (GW 8123). However, Liber cannot generally have used printed editions only as sources for the *Compendium*, since the letters of several authors in his book had not been printed by 1476 (e.g., the letters of Poggio, Bruni, and Guineforte Barzizza). A lot of work will still have to be done on this subject.

The letters of the *sodales* from Aduard conclude the *Compendium*. By adding these letters here, Liber clearly wanted to take a stand: he declared himself and his friends part of the humanist movement. The contents of his and Rudolph von Langen's letters underline this. Von Langen's contribution consists of six letters, five of which were written to Antonius Liber in February and March of the year 1469, when von Langen was staying at the monastery of Aduard, and Liber was in Groningen.[10] One reply of Liber is also in the *Compendium*, besides his dedicatory letter to Von Hildesheim and five other letters. Together with the poems that are studied by Pieter Schoonbeeg, this correspondence is the oldest witness to the existence of the humanist circle at Aduard. It offers us a good picture of what these men were occupied with, what interested them, how their environment reacted to their ideas (though concerning this last item, one has to be careful not to put blind faith in the testimonies of the two biased enthusiasts: most humanists tended to exaggerate the resistance they encountered from the topical *barbari* in their surroundings). The correspondence shows that Liber and von Langen encouraged each other in their humanist studies: they fulminate against the barbaric climate in Groningen (Agricola, as we know, was to do the same thing during the years that he was *secretarius* of the city of Groningen

---

[8] For a detailed analysis, see my article in *Humanistica Lovaniensia*, 44 (1995): 137–67.

[9] As an appendix to his *De compositione*; see Sonkowsky 1964, 2:260 and 2:262–63.

[10] Edited by Crecelius (1876).

in the 1480s), discuss classical texts (or humanist translations) they have read or would like to read, send writings to be scrutinized for errors, and defend themselves against those that criticize their Latinity.

In a letter to Liber dated February 27th, 1469, von Langen mentions one humanist text in particular that he (and Liber) thought very highly of: the already mentioned *Elegantiolae* of Agostino Dati. Von Langen writes to Liber:

> ... te precor, ut cumprimum poteris mittas ad nos illud, quod nostris ex cartulis nobis deest. Capiemus, mihi crede, ex re ea paucula litterarum dulces fructus ibitque mihi cartula hec mea irremota comes. Tanti enim eius rei dignitatem facio, quanti unquam alicuius tante breuitatis feci. O Vallanam facundiam! O eius uiri ingenium immortalitate dignissimum! Qui Latinam a barbaris linguam miserabiliter oppressam releuasti, fouisti, suum ei imperium apud Romanos reddidisti. (fol. M4r)

The letter makes it clear that Liber possessed a copy of the *Elegantiolae* in Groningen. Most likely this was a manuscript, since according to the Gesamtkatalog the first printed edition probably appeared in 1470 (the one mentioned above printed by Zell in Cologne). Von Langen writes that he has transcribed it almost until the end but that he still lacks the part where the calendar is explained. He does not know its author but suspects that it comes from the "studio" of Valla. Strictly speaking, this is not correct, since Dati was a pupil of Filelfo. However, as its title indicates, the booklet could justifiably be characterized as an abridged edition of Valla's *Elegantiae linguae Latinae*. It deals with the same topics in the same way. Dati discusses the vocabulary and syntax of classical Latin, giving many examples from classical authors. This was just the kind of manual that the Northern pioneers of humanism needed to mould their own classical Latin style. The letters of von Langen (and, to a lesser extent, those of Liber, too) testify to the fact that their author used the *Elegantiolae* to improve the quality of his own Latin (judged by classical standards, that is). The letter that von Langen wrote to Liber on the 21st of March, 1469, shows this most clearly. First, he fulminates against the ignoramuses who had dared to criticize him and Liber, while themselves being incapable of understanding and appreciating the beautiful Latin, and consequently the thoughts, of the Fathers of the Church. Von Langen then turns to the fact that Liber had written to him that somebody had condemned the expression *pro uirili mea* that von Langen had used in one of his letters to Liber. Von Langen indignantly replies that this expression was used by the best Latin authors and then writes:

> Videat ille Latine lingue censor quos dixi ueteres: plura inueniet, quibus forte priscos male usos et ignorantie damnabit. Quid dicet, cum leget: Et id genus monstra, In presentiarum, Est locus in carcere quod Tullianum appellant, Est tibi cognomen [sic] Scipioni, Mille militum occisum est. (fol. M6r)

All the expressions used here by von Langen to prove his point can be found verbatim (or nearly so) in Dati as examples of idiomatic Latin. The only exception is *In presentiarum*, which is not treated by Dati as a separate item but is simply part of his own vocabulary. Moreover, von Langen actually corrects Dati by stating that Scipio is a *cognomen* (which it is). Dati refers to it as a *nomen* (GW 8037, fol. 29r: *est mihi nomen Scipioni; Scipioni cognomen Africano fuit*).

By quoting these examples in order to strengthen his case, von Langen, like Dati, shows himself to be not only an admirer but also a dedicated follower of Valla. In his turn an adherent of Quintilian (*Inst.* 1,6,3), Valla reestablished the view that usage (*consuetudo*) must be considered the main criterion (though not the only one, and never unconditionally) for establishing the validity of any Latin expression. Von Langen agrees. In reply to his critic, he defends himself by stating that

> qui uelim sciat sic me loquentem nulla linguam Latinam iniuria affecisse, sed optimos eius duces principesque sic loquentes imitatum esse. Qui si errauerint, longe cum eis errare malo quam cum eo ipso qui mea notauit uera sentire. (fol. M6r)

He then explicitly names Cicero and Quintilian as excellent authorities on the Latin language.

Unfortunately, it is impossible to say to what extent the style of von Langen and Liber was influenced by Dati's manual, since these letters are the oldest of their writings to survive. What can be seen is that both authors by no means fully comply with all the instructions given by Dati. Their most fundamental deviation concerns word order; when the subject of a sentence is explicitly stated, Dati prefers the sequence object-subject-verb to the more commonly used order subject-object-verb. Generally, both von Langen and Liber prefer the latter. There are numerous other instances in which both Northern humanists do not comply with Dati's preferences. However, we have to keep in mind (as Dati warns the reader at the beginning of his treatise) that there are no fixed rules of eloquence and elegance; very often, deviating from the prescriptions may result in something beautiful. Ultimately, it is for the *auditorum aures* to judge.

The *Compendium* contains six letters written by Rudolph von Langen. They all have a considerable length and deal mainly with the *studia humanitatis*. The sentences are mostly quite long and sometimes complicated; there are many subordinate clauses, even two of the fourth degree. As often in the case of letters written by Northern humanists, they contrast sharply with the apparent ease that characterizes the epistolary style of many Italian humanists (like, for example, Poggio and Filelfo). The opening sentence of von Langen's first letter to Liber illustrates this:

> Haberem meo quidem iuditio, quo te, humanis studiis deditissime, accusarem, quia, ut mihi tui cupidissimo discedens promiseras, non reuertisti, ni uia, que te inter et me est, plurimo limo lubrica ut est, detentus esses. (fol. M3r)

A conspicuous feature of von Langen's style is his frequent use of hyperbaton (*traiectio, transgressio*). An extreme use of this figure of style can obstruct a correct understanding of what the author is trying to say. In von Langen's case, such excesses are not to be found: one does not find any examples of obscurity due to an excessive use of hyperbaton. It is obvious, however, that he did not want his prose to be plain and simple as far as word-order (an important topic for humanists) was concerned. Another phenomenon of word-order in classical prose is the *clausula*. Inspired by T. O.

Tunberg's research of *clausulae* in the prose of Lorenzo Valla, I have tried to apply his method to the letters of von Langen. Unfortunately, the results showed that no statistically reliable answer could be given to the question: "Did von Langen try to create rhythmical patterns based on quantity at sentence-endings in his letters?" The total number of *clausulae* that could be put to the test was too small to produce statistically significant results. Consequently, it was also not possible to draw a definite conclusion concerning von Langen's preference for either *clausulae* or *cursus*. Of course, all this applies *a fortiori* to the letters of Liber, being even shorter than those of von Langen.

The vocabulary of von Langen's letters is classical. There are only a few nonclassical words to be found (*conducere* meaning "to accompany"; the noun *cubatus* for "bed"; and the noun *eneruatrix*, derived from the classical verb *eneruare* meaning "to weaken"). Besides this, von Langen apparently did not have a fully correct knowledge of the *ablatiuus absolutus*. Twice, he uses it when he should have used a *participium coniunctum*. One example is:

> ... meliora sciens probansque deteriora sequor presertim ad harum rerum doctos me scribente, ex quorum grege te sane unum esse perspectum mihi habeo. (fol. M5r)

The only other error von Langen makes is confusing the *indicatiuus futuri* with the *coniunctiuus praesentis*, but this mistake can be found even in the writings of prominent Italian humanists. The letters also testify to their author's broad knowledge of the heritage of classical literature. We find references to the classical Greek authors Plato, Aristotle, and Plutarch; to the classical Latin authors Plautus, Terence, Cicero, Virgil, Ovid, Valerius Maximus, Seneca, Quintilian, Curtius Rufus, Juvenal, Gellius; to the Christian Latin authors Jerome, Augustine, Ambrose, Lactantius, Cyprian; and to the humanists Valla, Dati, Piccolomini, and Bruni. Von Langen did not know Greek; he read the Greek authors through Latin translations.

Of the seven letters that Liber himself contributed to his book,[11] only three have a reasonable length. These are a reply to a letter by von Langen dating from 1469; a letter to his wife Berta in Groningen that he wrote during his stay in Cologne, telling her that he has to postpone his return; and his letter of dedication to von Hildesheim. The other four letters are short ones. Liber's style resembles that of his friend. However, many more nonclassical words and expressions can be found in Liber's letters: the adverbs *totaliter, digniter;* the adverbial expression *ad placitum*; the nouns *campestris, scholaris, beanus, demeritum*; the adjective *sospitus*; the verbs *rotare* (meaning "to babble") and *perspicere* (meaning "to take care of"); and the expression *certiorem reddere*. Furthermore, he writes *non magis* instead of *non iam*. Liber also makes one syntactical mistake in that he uses the subject of a sentence as the object of a *participium coniunctum* in the same sentence:

> ... aperienti mihi eas [*sc.* epistolas] summa cum alacritate tantam spirabant

---

[11] Edited by Crecelius (1879).

elegantiam, ut, sicut dici solet, comico sale ac lepore totaliter consperse mihi
uise sint. (fol. M8v)

As far as Liber's knowledge of the classical tradition is concerned, solely on the basis
of his letters, one could not conclude that it was very extensive: he refers only to
Cicero, Jerome, and Piccolomini. Fortunately (for him), his other works and the letters of von Langen prove otherwise.

What I have presented here were some results concerning the first part of my
thesis. Its second part deals with the Latinity of Rudolph Agricola's letters. I hope
that the results will help us in deepening our insights into a brand of Northern humanism before Erasmus, of which the correspondence between Rudolph von Langen
and Antonius Liber, presented to us by Liber's *Familiarium epistolarum compendium*, is
one of the oldest witnesses to survive.

Groningen, Netherlands

El Humanismo italiano y sus relaciones con el Humanismo hispano*

JENARO COSTAS

Miembros:
J. F. Alcina Rovira, Tarragona
L. Carrasco Reija, Madrid
M. Conde Salazar, Madrid
M. A. Díaz Gito, Cádiz
J. González Vázquez, Cádiz
J. M. Maestre Maestre, Cádiz
J. Pascual Barea, Cádiz
M. V. Pérez Custodio, Cádiz

E. Del Pino González, Cádiz
B. Pozuelo Calero, Cádiz
S. Ramos Maldonado, Cádiz
M. C. Ramos Santana, Cádiz
E. Rodríguez Peregrina, Granada
J. Salvadó Recasens, Tarragona
A. Serrano Cueto, Cádiz
M. Trascasas Casares, Madrid

Redactor: J. F. Alcina Rovira

En este seminario se intentará añadir algún nuevo dato a los sabidos hasta ahora sobre el tema, empezando por la presentación de algunos puntos referidos a las estancias de los humanistas españoles en Italia y su relación con los escritores italianos contemporáneos, y siguiendo con el análisis de la influencia literaria ejercida por la obra de los humanistas italianos en los españoles, tanto en la poesía como en la prosa. La mayor parte del material procede del desbroce de trabajos anteriores o tesis en curso de los miembros inscritos en este seminario sintetizando lo relativo al tema de las relaciones hispano-italianas. Evidentemente, con estos planteamientos no se pretende ofrecer una visión de conjunto ni un estado global de la cuestión. Solamente se intenta dar a conocer algunos trabajos y proporcionar unas acotaciones al tema ordenadas de la forma más clara que hemos podido.

El trabajo se estructurará en los siguientes apartados:

I. Estancias de los humanistas españoles en Italia: relación con los escritores italianos contemporáneos.

II. Influencia literaria de los humanistas italianos en los españoles.

    II.1. El libro y su difusión.

    II.2. Influencias literarias.

        II.2.1. Poesía.

        II.2.2. Prosa.

    II.3. Las ideas.

I. Estancias de los humanistas españoles en Italia: relación con los escritores italianos contemporáneos

Los españoles, como el resto de los europeos, sabían que en Italia se encontraba la cuna de la cultura en el Renacimiento y allí encaminaron sus pasos para formarse y ampliar estudios. Esta relación es conocida en líneas generales, pero sólo la lectura paciente de todas la obras conservadas hará posible conocer en detalle la vinculación: sabemos, por ejemplo, que *Hieronimus Plutinus, iurisconsultus Calaber, uir liberalibus studiis consumatissimus* estuvo en España y que tuvo relación con Martín Ivarra gracias a que éste nos lo dice en su *De prosodia*, según ha puesto de relieve Joan Salvadó Recasens.[1]

I.1. Castilla

Joaquín Pascual[2] ofrece numerosas noticias relativas a Italia, adonde se dirigían de hecho muchos de los bachilleres andaluces que hasta casi mediados del s. XVI habían de salir de su tierra para poder continuar sus estudios. En Siena estudió el sevillano Juan Partenio Tovar, que luego ocupó en Valencia la cátedra de Oratoria y Poética del Estudio hasta 1514, sobresaliendo como orador y poeta latino laureado. En el Colegio de los Españoles de Bolonia estudiaron Antonio de Lebrija y Rodrigo de Santaella, los primeros poetas latinos de altura y principales difusores de las nuevas ideas y gustos literarios del Renacimiento italiano en Sevilla, contribuyendo además, mediante sus obras de carácter técnico al aprendizaje del latín en España durante todo el siglo XVI.

Tras regresar de Italia, Antonio de Lebrija enseñó varios años en Sevilla, erigiéndose en maestro de un grupo de entusiastas partidarios de la poesía latina humanista, como Antonio Carrión, Pedro Núñez Delgado y Cristóbal Núñez. La influencia de la poesía latina del Renacimiento italiano es particularmente evidente en su *Salutatio ad patriam*, inspirada en un poema de Petrarca, así como en otras poesías, cuya edición crítica prepara J. M. Maestre Maestre.

En su introducción de *Maese Rodrigo de Santaella y Antonio Carrión, Poesías (Sevilla, 1504)*[3] estudia más detenidamente Joaquín Pascual la vida y obra de Santaella, quien

---

[1] J. Salvadó Recasens, *Martí Ivarra. Obra poètica* (Barcelona: Curial, en prensa).

[2] Cf. J. Pascual Barea, "Aproximación a la poesía latina del Renacimiento en Sevilla," *Excerpta Philologica* I.2 (1991): 567–599.

[3] Cf. J. Pascual Barea, *Maese Rodrigo de Santaella y Antonio Carrión, Poesías (Sevilla, 1504)* (Sevilla: Universidades de Sevilla y Cádiz, 1991), libro que incluye la edición crítica y traducción anotada de las *Odae* del arcediano y de todas las poesías conservadas de Carrión.

tras doctorarse en Artes y Teología al cabo de ocho años en el Colegio de los Españoles de Bolonia, viajó a Venecia antes de instalarse en Roma al servicio del cardenal Jacobo. De sus discursos en la curia de Sixto IV, de quien fue "familiar, camarero y continuo comensal," nos ha llegado la *Elegantissima oratio* que pronunció el viernes santo de 1477. A la Biblioteca Vaticana fue a parar el manuscrito de su *Dialogus contra impugnatorem caelibatus et castitatis presbyterorum ad Sixtum IV directus,* en respuesta a un escrito de Leonardo Leto, y a la Biblioteca Ambrosiana su *Oratio habita in die Parasceues coram Innocentium VIII,* pronunciado en 1490. Durante varios años fue visitador general de Sicilia a las órdenes de los Reyes Católicos saliendo ileso de un intento de envenenamiento por parte de sus enemigos. Como canónigo magistral, desarrolló en Sevilla una intensa actividad reformadora encaminada al reavivamiento cultural y espiritual de su pueblo de acuerdo con las directrices renovadoras y tolerantes del humanismo cristiano, contribuyendo a la difusión de las letras a través de la fundación del Colegio de Santa María de Jesús, luego Universidad de Sevilla, y de numerosos libros, como su célebre *Vocabularium,* fruto de su "siciliano peregrinaje," su *Arte de bien morir,* dedicado a la mujer de Fernando de Acuña, virrey de Sicilia, o las *Odae,* en las que recuerda sus viajes por el Tirreno. Atento a la actualidad de su tiempo, mantuvo una viva polémica con el marino genovés Cristóbal Colón, refutándole en el prólogo de su traducción del Libro de Marco Polo, impresa en mayo de 1503, que las tierras recién descubiertas correspondieran a las Indias descritas por Marco Polo, adelantándose por unos meses en anunciar el Descubrimiento de un Nuevo Mundo a Amerigo Vespuche, que injustamente dio nombre al Continente, asunto que Joaquín Pascual trata más detenidamente en otro artículo.[4]

Junto a estos sevillanos formados en Italia, también algunos humanistas italianos que ejercieron su magisterio en Sevilla contribuyeron a difundir los nuevos gustos poéticos del Renacimiento. El poeta siciliano Lucio Flaminio, que había sido alumno de Pomponio Leto, llegó a explicar públicamente en Sevilla diez lecciones diarias. Fue maestro de Pedro Núñez Delgado y se relacionó con Lebrija y Carrión.

El maestro Antonio Carrión, además de los poemas latinos que publicó en el libro de las *Odae* de Santaella y en los preliminares de otras obras, editó en 1506 con extensas anotaciones los *Disticha moralia* del italiano Miguel Verino.

La obra incluye unos poemas laudatorios de su compañero Pedro Núñez Delgado (1478–1535), discípulo del siciliano Lucio Flaminio, quien heredó en 1514 la cátedra de Gramática abandonada por su maestro Antonio de Lebrija, cuyas obras explicó, junto a las de autores antiguos y del Renacimiento italiano como Lorenzo Valla o Bautista Mantuano, cuyas *Parthenices* editó en 1515. En la edición póstuma de sus poemas en 1537 conocemos que también eran considerados autores modélicos Petrarca, Poliziano y Pedro Mártir de Anghiera. Estos poemas incluyen referencias entre otros, a Flaminio y Franco Leardo, los maestrescuelas Jerónimo Pinelo, de origen

---

[4] Cf. J. Pascual Barea, "Las primeras alusiones al Descubrimiento en la poesía latina de Sevilla," en J. Gil Fernández-J.M. Maestre Maestre (eds.), *Humanismo latino y Descubrimiento* (Sevilla: Universidad de Cádiz-Universidad de Sevilla, 1992), 167–179.

veneciano y el obispo de Valva Cristóbal de los Ríos, el obispo de Scalas, Baltasar del Río, etc.

Tras residir varios años en Roma, donde publicó en 1513 su discurso contra los turcos pronunciado en el V Concilio Lateranense, y donde fue camarero del papa León X y gobernador de Roma con Clemente VII, el obispo titular de Scalas y arcediano de Niebla Baltasar del Río organizó en Sevilla desde 1531 varias justas literarias, las primeras conocidas en España con composiciones latinas, promoviendo entre los jóvenes la pronunciación del latín al modo italiano. Apoyaba sus tesis el banquero genovés afincado en Sevilla Franco Leardo, de cuya figura y poemas latinos trata la comunicación de Joaquín Pascual Barea en el presente Congreso.

Amigo de ambos, así como de Fernando Colón, hijo del célebre Almirante genovés, fue el cronista Pedro Mejía (1497–1551), cuya *Silva de varia lección* fue traducida al italiano por Mambrino Roseo da Fabrino y publicada al menos treinta veces desde 1544.

Ya en la segunda mitad del siglo XVI, las estrechas relaciones con Italia vuelven a plasmarse de forma clara en la obra de Juan de Mal Lara, comentador de los emblemas del italiano Andrea Alciato, y autor de varios poemas para ilustrar varios cuadros de Tiziano, y en alabanza del autor del *Vocabulario de las dos lenguas toscana y castellana*.

El canónigo sevillano Gonzalo Ponce de León (1530?–1600?) vivió en Roma buena parte de su vida, donde editó varias obras y fue gran amigo del cardenal César Baronio, para cuyos *Annales* compuso dos poemas latinos laudatorios.

En 1586, el racionero sevillano Juan Bautista de Aguilar, doctor en Teología, compuso en Roma su *Epigrammatum libellus in dedicationem obelisci*, dedicado al papa Sixto V. En un *Carmen heroicum*, de medio millar de versos, cerebra la conquista a los sublevados de la ciudad de Maestricht por el duque de Parma, Alejandro Farnesio, a quien va dedicado.

El maestro Francisco de Medina se formó durante varios años en Italia, siguiendo el modelo de la poesía italiana tanto en la teoría como en la práctica de sus poemas latinos y castellanos, entre los que figura la traducción de un poema de Sannazaro. Esta poesía italianizante que propugna la escuela poética sevillana liderada por Herrera y que tiene como primer modelo a Garcilaso triunfa definitivamente en el último tercio de siglo XVI.

Joan Salvadó Recasens[5] ha estudiado la vinculación con Italia de la interesante figura de Juan Partenio Tovar, humanista que hemos de situar a caballo entre la Corona de Castilla y la de Aragón, dado que, aunque sevillano de nacimiento, fue uno de los primeros humanistas que contrató la Universidad de Valencia: cabe recordar que fue allí donde dio clases al célebre Luis Vives.

Tovar estudió en Siena, donde fue alumno del famoso jurista Mariano Sozzini de Siena (1401–1467), profesor de leyes en Siena y Padua. En Siena escribió Tovar, a los veinte años, algunas de sus églogas. Algunos de los epigramas de su *Epigrammaton libellus* están dedicados a personajes italianos. Por ejemplo el que dedica a Nicolas

---

[5] Cf. J. Salvadó Recasens, "Juan Partenio Tovar: maestro de Vives en Valencia," *Studia Philologica Valentina* I (1996): 111–124.

Burgense Patricio de Sena, que no es otro que Niccolò Borghesi da Siena (1432–1500), gran coleccionista de manuscritos clásicos y profesor de poesía y elocuencia en la Universidad de Siena. Encontramos también epigramas a los poetas "Silvio i Cantalicio": Cantalicio es probablemente Giambattista Cantalicio (c. 1450–1514), humanista relacionado con los Borgia; Silvio pudiera ser Eneas Silvio Piccolomini, que fue poeta latino además de novelista. A finales del siglo XV Tovar daba clases de gramática en Roma.

Por lo que a la producción de humanistas italianos sobre temas granadinos se refiere, Mª Dolores Rincón[6] ha tenido ocasión de poner de manifiesto que C. Verardi, autor de la *Historia Baetica* esta incuestionablemente conectado con el círculo de españoles en Roma: allí, entre otros, encontramos a Alonso de Palencia, autor de la *Guerra de Granada* y Diego Guillén de Avila, que escribe en 1499 un *Panegírico de la Reina Isabel de Castilla*. Un buen exponente de este contacto entre el humanismo español y el italiano es la conexión del propio César Borja con el círculo de Pomponio Leto, en relación, a su vez, con Rafael Riario, mecenas de Verardi y conocido por sus grandes simpatías hacia los Reyes Católicos. Otros personajes españoles claves de la época, igualmente conectados con el humanismo italiano, fueron Bernardino de Carvajal, embajador de los Reyes Católicos ante el Papa y autor del *Sermo in conmemoratione Victoriae Bacensis Civitatis* pronunciado en Roma a principios de 1490, y Pedro Bosca que fue el encargado de pronunciar en Roma el discurso por la toma de Granada, al igual que ya lo había hecho antes con motivo de la de Málaga.

I.2. Corona de Aragón

La vinculación de España con Italia durante el Renacimiento es tanto más fecunda en el caso de Aragón frente al de Castilla, dadas las relaciones históricas de la corona aragonesa con las tierras italianas durante el referido período.

Poco a poco vamos conociendo mejor la cultura latina del siglo XV catalán gracias a los esfuerzos de Mariàngela Vilallonga,[7] que no ha podido finalmente asistir a este seminario como proyectaba. De todas maneras tenemos graves lagunas en lo que se refiere a Valencia y Mallorca. Se trata de un mundo en el que predomina una cultura gótica, caballeresca y en lengua vulgar, en el que despunta lo que J. H. Lawrance[8] ha

---

[6] M. D. Rincón González, *Historia Baetica de Carlo Verardi. Drama humanístico sobre la toma de Granada* (Granada: Universidad de Granada, 1992).

[7] Jeroni Pau, *Obres*, ed. Mariàngela Vilallonga, 2 vols. (Barcelona: Curial, 1986); *id. Dos opuscles de Pere Miquel Carbonell* (Barcelona, 1988); *id.* (fijación del texto latino)-E. Duran, Antonio Beccadelli el Panormita, *Dels fets e dits del gran rey Alfonso. Versió catalana del segle XV de Jordi de Centelles* (Barcelona, 1990); *id.*, *La literatura llatina a Catalunya al segle XV* (Barcelona: Curial, 1993).

[8] J. H. Lawrance, "On Fifteenth-Century Spanish Vernacular Humanism," en I. Michael and R. Cardwell eds., *Medieval and Renaissance Studies in Honour of Robert Brian Tate* (Oxford, 1986), 63–79; en general una síntesis actualizada de la discusión en torno al llamado "Humanismo castellano del siglo XV" puede verse en, N. G. Round, "Fifteenth-Century Cultural Change" en su introducción a *Libro llamado Fedron. Plato's Phaedo translated by Pero Diaz de Toledo* (London–Madrid: Tamesis, 1993), 62–76.

llamado un humanismo vernáculo, basado en traducciones. Pero también hay un humanismo latino minoritario, como el de Pere Miquel Carbonell i Jeroni Pau, un humanismo que cada día nos depara nuevas sorpresas.

José María Maestre Maestre ha dedicado varios capítulos de su monografía sobre los humanistas alcañizanos[9] a estudiar la estrecha vinculación del Alcañiz quiñentista con Italia, vinculación esta tanto más lógica si recordamos, como ya dijimos, el preponderante papel de la Corona de Aragón en tierras italianas durante el Renacimiento.

Especial relevancia cobran las relaciones de los alcañizanos con el Colegio Vives, fundado por el coterráneo Andrés Vives y Altafulla sólo para alumnos de su ciudad natal: en la *Introducción*[10] hace J. M. Maestre Maestre una breve historia del Colegio desde 1524, año en que el médico papal concibió la idea de fundar la institución, hasta su desaparición en el s. XVIII; en el capítulo dedicado a Domingo Andrés[11] ofrece un elenco de los alumnos alcañizanos de los que se tiene constancia que pasaron por la citada institución, entre los que descuellan tanto Domingo Andrés como Pedro Ruiz de Moros.[12]

Menos importancia tienen, empero, las relaciones de Alcañiz con el Colegio de San Clemente de los Españoles de Bolonia:[13] totalmente documentados está el paso por el mismo de Juan Sobrarias, que nos ha dejado poemas dedicados tanto al santo patrón del Colegio como a la muerte del poeta Serafino Aquilano.[14]

Y dignos de destacar son, por último, los estudios de Bernardino Gómez Miedes en Roma a mediados del siglo XVI,[15] así como un posterior viaje del mismo a la Ciudad Eterna de 1574 a 1576. Estas estancias están en íntima relación con las propias obras del autor: el humanista nos dice que fue en Roma donde comenzó sus *Commentariorum de sale libri V* (pp. 233–237) y que fue en el viaje de regreso de la Ciudad Eterna de 1576 cuando, ante el peligro de que la nave naufragara en medio de una terrible tormenta, se vio obligado a tirar por la borda de la nave y a perder para siempre su tratado *De apibus uel de republica* (pp. 240–243); y no debemos olvidar que fue este mismo viaje el que aprovechó el luego prelado de Albarracín para inventar el milagro del baúl perdido y luego recuperado (pp. 239–244), narrado con detalle, aunque con determinadas divergencias, tanto en los *Commentariorum de sale libri V* como en la famosa *Epistula ad Gregorium XIII*.

---

[9] Cf. J. M. Maestre Maestre, *El humanismo alcañizano del siglo XVI. Textos y estudios de latín renacentista* (Cádiz, Servicio de Publicaciones de la Universidad de Cádiz—Instituto de Estudios Turolenses [C.S.I.C.]—Excmo. Ayuntamiento de Alcañiz, 1990). La obra es un estudio de conjunto del Alcañiz del Siglo de Oro, al mismo tiempo que una antología de textos que ilustran características literarias y sociológicas del referido foco cultural y abren nuevas líneas de investigación en el campo del latín renacentista.

[10] Cf. J. M. Maestre Maestre, *El humanismo alcañizano* . . . , LXXXVII–XCIII.

[11] Cf. Maestre Maestre, *El humanismo alcañizano* . . . , 341–345.

[12] Cf. para mayor información, Maestre Maestre, *El humanismo alcañizano* . . . , 72–73.

[13] Cf. Maestre Maestre, *El humanismo alcañizano* . . . , LXXXVI–LXXXVII.

[14] Cf. Maestre Maestre, *El humanismo alcañizano* . . . , 6–8.

[15] Cf. Maestre Maestre, *El humanismo alcañizano* . . . , 233–234.

Como era de esperar las estancias en tierras italianas de los humanistas alcañizanos han tenido el esperado reflejo en sus obras literarias. Así en los poemas latinos conservados de los *Poecilistichon siue uariorum libri V* de Domingo Andrés, estudiados y editados, con traducción al castellano, por José María Maestre Maestre,[16] dejan clara la relación del humanista alcañizano con Italia, que cabe situar entre 1550 y 1557. Gracias a los versos del propio Andrés, conocemos con detalle las peripecias de su viaje por mar y tierra a Italia y su posterior incorporación como soldado por falta de medios económicos a las tropas españolas de Siena (*carm.* II,24), la expectación de Lucca ante el asedio de esta última ciudad (*carm.* III,35), la derrota de Piero Strozzi en 1554 (*carm.* III,41) o las inundaciones que asolaron Italia en 1557 (*carm.* III,99).

La Musa del poeta nos dibuja también el ambiente cultural y literario italiano de aquél tiempo: sin olvidarnos de otros célebres personajes, como el jurista Antonio Scappo (*carm.* III,11) o los hermanos Carlos y Lelio Ruino y Pirro Malvezzi, participantes en los juegos y certámenes ecuestres de Bolonia (*carm.* II,25 y 26), en las *Poesías Varias* encontramos también alusiones a la polémica obra historiográfica de Paulo Jovio (*carm.* III,13) o a los *Symbolicarum quaestionum libri V* de Aquiles Bocchi (*carm.* III,27 y 28), cuya condición de caballero y poeta alaba también Andrés (*carm.* III,10).

Las relaciones con Bolonia, bien claras tanto por el hecho de que Scappo y Bocchi eran naturales de la misma, como por los referidos epigramas sobre los juegos ecuestres, obligan a pensar que en esta ciudad continuó Andrés los estudios universitarios comenzados en el *Studi General* de Valencia hacia 1545. Esta hipótesis, y, más concretamente, la posibilidad de que Domingo Andrés estudió en el Colegio Vives, cobra mucha más fuerza a la luz del poema III,68, que nos demuestra la amistad del poeta alcañizano con Miguel Rabbastén, alumno del citado colegio.

La estancia en Italia se deja sentir también, como ya anticipamos, en los *Commentariorum de sale libri V* del alcañizano Bernardino Gómez Miedes, cuya edición crítica y traducción al castellano ultima Sandra Ramos Maldonado.[17]

En el año 1579 se publica en Valencia por segunda vez la citada obra, ahora corregida y aumentada por el propio autor frente a los otrora cuatro libros que conoció su primera aparición pública también valenciana siete años antes y frente a los cuatro libros de la tercera edición realizada en Alemania en el 1605 por el médico francofurtés Petrus Uffenbach. Más de veinticinco años tardó en escribir y perfeccionar su obra este incansable viajero que recorrió media Europa recopilando todos aquellos datos que le sirvieran para su proyecto sobre la sal. Pero a pesar del reconocido amor a su patria, su educación parisina entre los más eminentes filósofos y humanistas

---

[16] Cf. J. M. Maestre Maestre, *"Poesías varias" del alcañizano Domingo Andrés* (Teruel: Instituto de Estudios Turolenses [C.S.I.C.], 1987). Sobre la influencia de los poetas italianos en determinados poemas de Domingo Andrés, cf. J. M. Maestre Maestre, "El mundo clásico como fuente indirecta en Domingo Andrés," *Habis* 21 (1990): 153–164.

[17] Cf. S. Ramos Maldonado, *Los "Commentariorum de sale libri V" del humanista alcañizano Bernardino Gómez Miedes. Introducción, edición crítica, traducción anotada e índices*, Tesis Doctoral dirigida por Juan Gil Fernández y José María Maestre Maestre (Universidad de Cádiz, 1995).

franceses de la época (noticia hasta ahora obviada por sus biógrafos), será Roma, no obstante, el lugar elegido como marco idóneo para realizar el "diálogo de la sal" entre Metrófilo (que representa el papel del autor) y el barcelonés Juan Quintana, paciente receptor de las enseñanzas de su amigo desarrolladas a lo largo de todo un día en la Roma del pontificado de Julio III.

No hay que pasar por alto además que en la elección del lugar dialógico influyeron sus diez años de estancia en Roma que Sandra Ramos Maldonado ha podido situar aproximadamente entre el 1548 y 1558, retrotrayendo, por tanto, unos años antes, al final del pontificado de Paulo III, su llegada a esta ciudad, que los bibliógrafos anteriores situaban en torno al 1552.

En los *Commentariorum de sale libri V* sobresalen por encima de todas las demás ciudades las referencias a Roma: arte, cultura, costumbres, religión, lengua … Los *Commentarios sobre la sal* constituyen, por tanto, para el lector, pero sobre todo, para el lector italiano, un documento de primerísima mano para conocer datos históricos, literarios y religiosos y costumbres de la Italia de la mitad del siglo XVI. Así, como ejemplo anecdótico e ilustrativo, el punto de arranque de toda la obra será el conflicto iniciado en una cena por Quintana debido a que violó una costumbre italiana que prohibía rociar con sal el plato del convidado, acusación que, junto a muchísimas otras, dará lugar a la encendida defensa de la sal (en todas sus acepciones, tanto propias como figuradas) por parte de Metrófilo/Miedes. Esta presencia e influencia romana, manifiesta a lo largo de los *Comentarios sobre la sal* alcanza no obstante su máxima expresión en el libro V, donde a partir del proverbio *Salem ne aliis porrigitis Romae qui uersatus non fuerit*, Bernardino Gómez Miedes principia todo un panegírico a una ciudad que define así (V,24,2): *urbem Romam, illustrissimum orbis terrarum monimentum, editissimam quandam prae se ferre sapientiae sedem perennemque esse disciplinae fontem, e quo uerissima apertissimaque rerum cognitio in uniuersas mundi partes diducatur.*

A Italia dirigió también sus pasos Juan de Verzosa (1523–1574), cuyos *Epistolarum libri IIII* va a sacar a la luz en una edición moderna Eduardo del Pino González.[18] De las ciento cincuenta epístolas que componen la colección, setenta y cinco—la mitad—están dedicadas a personajes italianos de la época. Y esto sin nombrar a los muchos que son citados dentro de cada composición. Las otras setenta y cinco epístolas están mayoritariamente dedicadas a españoles. La distribución de los destinatarios italianos es de la siguiente manera: hay diecinueve en el libro I, veinticinco en el libro II, otros tantos en el libro III y sólo seis en el libro IV, si bien ello se debe a que este libro tiene menos composiciones que los demás.

Los destinatarios de las *Epístolas* de Verzosa suelen ser personajes relevantes del

---

[18] Cf. E. Del Pino González, *Los "Epistolarum Libri IIII" de Juan de Verzosa: estudio introductorio, edición crítica, traducción anotada e indices,* Tesis Doctoral dirigida por Juan Gil Fernández y J.M. Maestre Maestre (Universidad de Cádiz, 1998). La colección epistolar en verso fue publicada en Palermo (1575) por Luis de Torres, sobrino del entonces arzobispo de Monreal del mismo nombre. López de Toro hizo una nueva edición del texto (*Las Epístolas de Juan de Verzosa* [Madrid, 1945]). Pero las deficiencias de la misma (abundantes errores en el texto latino y en la traducción, algunas carencias en la documentación histórica, ausencia de estudio métrico y de aparato de fuentes) han llevado a plantear una nueva edición.

momento, eclesiásticos y diplomáticos en general, tanto de la corte romana como de las diversas partes de Italia. Muchos de ellos destacan a la vez por su labor literaria. Es el caso de Trifón Bencio, que escribió en latín y en vulgar; de los hermanos Vulpi, de Novo Como; de Carlos Gualteruzzi, que publicó en Bolonia (1525) unas *Cento novelle antiche* y escribió unas *Lettere* (publicadas en Pesaro en 1834); o del bresciano Lorenzo Gámbara, cuyos *Poemata* fueron publicados en Roma (1555) y sus *Epistolae* en Nápoles (en el mismo año que las de Verzosa). Encontramos también a Juan Tonsi, a Juan Bautista Amaltei o el mantuano Hipólito Capilupi, que escribieron poesía latina y toscana. Marco Antonio Bobba fue también poeta latino y dedicó a Verzosa una epístola en verso que se publicó en 1575 junto con el epistolario verzosiano. Y no sólo encontramos poetas. Bernardino Cirillo escribió una historia de su tiempo, que se publicó en Roma en 1570 y el genovés Huberto Folieta también desarrolló una labor historiográfica. Juan Francisco Peranda dejó como fruto de su actividad diplomática una colección epistolar en prosa (publicada en Venecia, 1601), que se reeditó numerosas veces en el siglo XVII y pasó por ser colección modélica para la enseñanza del género.

Junto a los literatos, aparecen también profesores como Silvio Antoniani, que en 1565 era profesor de literatura de la Sapienza romana; o protectores de los humanistas, como la culta Hersilia Cortés, que publicó en Roma (1573) las obras de su tío el cardenal Gregorio (anteponiéndoles una dedicatoria en latín) y que escribió también poesía en vulgar (como se ve en la *Raccolta per donne romane*); o como Santiago Boncompagni a cuya familia pertenecía el futuro Gregorio XIII. No faltan tampoco cultos coleccionistas como Jerónimo Garimberto y Fulvio Orsini, eruditos como Francisco Vianelli y un helenista, el veronés Juan Bautista Gabio.

A través del epistolario, Verzosa aparece como uno más dentro de los círculos humanistas. Así, por ejemplo, a través de una epístola dedicada al poeta Francisco de Figueroa, sabemos que conoce al círculo de sieneses interesados en prestigiar literariamente a la lengua toscana. Cabe citar al arzobispo de Siena Francisco Bandini y a Niccolo Piccolomini del Mandolo, escritor en latín y en toscano. También a Claudio Tolomei, que escribió versos toscanos tratando de adaptar la métrica latina de la cantidad silábica, y a Fabio Benevoglienti, que fue traductor del latín al toscano y a quien Verzosa dedica otra epístola de la colección.

Verzosa muestra conocer también a los integrantes de la "Academia Vaticana." Además de dirigir una epístola al propio fundador de la Academia, San Carlos Borromeo, escribe otras tantas a Silvio Antoniani, Francisco Alciati, Carlos Visconti, Tolomeo Galli, Curcio Gonzaga y Guido Ferreri. Claudio Tolomei fundó también la "Academia della Nuova Poesia," que pretendía fomentar la adaptación de los metros latinos. Pues bien, Verzosa no sólo le escribe a él, sino también al conocido Aníbal Caro, integrante a su vez de dicha Academia.

Aunque la mayor parte de las Epístolas de Verzosa—que son literarias—no fuesen realmente enviadas, son un buen testimonio del conocimiento que Verzosa tenía de sus destinatarios. Por ejemplo, Verzosa alaba la labor de crítica textual sobre textos latinos antiguos de Gabriel Faerni. Sin embargo, las ediciones *emendatae* de Terencio y Cicerón, que hizo el poeta de Fano, aparecieron publicadas después de su muerte. Con lo cual, Verzosa conocía estas obras mucho antes de ser publicadas, coincidiendo con la gran fama de buen editor que tenía Faerni entre otros como Pedro Victorio, Leonardo Malaespina y Mateo Toscano.

Por otra parte, Faerni había sido llamado a Roma en 1561 para participar en la imprenta que publicaría las nuevas ediciones de los Padres de la Iglesia. La imprenta había sido auspiciada por Pío IV y Carlos Borromeo, contando también con el trabajo del conocido impresor veneciano Paulo Manucio, de Juan Bautista Amaltei y de Guillermo Sirletti. Todos ellos están también presentes en el epistolario verzosiano.

Por citar otros ejemplos, Verzosa conoce, antes de la publicación, los planes de Aníbal Ruscellai, diplomático florentino, de editar las obras de su tío Juan de la Casa. Y de la misma manera, anima a Pirro Bocchi (no debe llevar a confusión la identificación que hace López de Toro de este personaje boloñés con otro Pirro Bocchi florentino totalmente distinto) a continuar los *Historiae patriae ab urbe condita libri XIII* de su padre Aquiles, cosa que hizo Aníbal con un *liber XIV*.

En definitiva, las relaciones de España con Italia durante el Renacimiento son intensas. La propia realidad histórica de esa vinculación se deja ver muchas veces en el terreno literario: así, como recientemente ha estudiado Manuel Antonio Díaz Gito,[19] el poeta e historiador español Juan Cristóbal Calvete de Estrella (principios de siglo XVI–1573), un autor que jamás puso su pie en Córcega, escribió una obra, con trescientos setenta y tres hexámetros, que tiene como telón de fondo la citada isla.

II. Influencia literaria de los humanistas italianos en los españoles

II.1. El libro y su difusión

En el capítulo de influencias italianas interesa conocer, como tarea prioritaria, las ediciones de humanistas italianos que se hacen en España. Es de todos conocido que lo que se imprime en España refleja sólo parcialmente lo que realmente se leía. En cuanto a textos clásicos y humanísticos, una parte importante de las bibliotecas se nutre de libros importados de Venecia, Lyon o Basilea. A pesar de todo, el hecho de que un autor humanístico se imprima en la península es, por lo menos, índice de una línea de interés y sólo por ello justifica un estudio para el que J. F. Alcina nos ofrece los siguientes datos sobre poesía humanística.

Las ediciones de poetas neolatinos italianos están ligadas principalmente a la escuela como buena parte del humanismo desde fines del XV. Intentan sustituir otros textos y son reflejo y resultado de los intereses de los nuevos círculos. Por ejemplo el *Distichorum liber* de Michele Verino pretende sustituir a los *Disticha Catonis* y otros *libri minores* medievales y aparecen muchísimas ediciones desde la de Burgos de 1489.

---

[19] Cf. M. A. Díaz Gito, *El poema Corsica de Juan Cristóbal Calvete de Estrella (y otros dos poemas latinos), Un elogio del Secretario Real de Felipe II, D. Mateo Vázquez de Lecca,* Tesis de Licenciatura realizada bajo la dirección del Dr. D. José María Maestre Maestre (Universidad de Cádiz, 1990). En efecto, a pesar de lo que en buena lógica cabría esperar, no es la isla de Córcega el asunto principal de este poema, sino la figura del secretario real de Felipe II, Mateo Vázquez, a quien se le hace vincular por nacimiento con una antigua familia nobilísima arraigada en Córcega. De este modo, el autor aprovecha para dedicar parte de su poema a tratar el tema de la isla desde el punto de vista mitológico-legendario e histórico hasta llegar al cabo a la supuesta familia Lecca.

Entre estas ediciones de Verino merece señalarse la edición de Zaragoza de 1535 que ofrece como apéndice una colección de *Disticha* del italiano afincado en Francia Publio Fausto Andrelini que a lo que sé es la única edición hispana de un texto de ese autor. Una función docente debió tener también la rara edición barcelonesa del *De diuinis laudibus* de Pontano, impresa por Luschner en 1498. Era un texto destinado a un alumno excepcional, el príncipe Juan de Aragón, y quizá la temática religiosa y la categoría del destinatario justificaría la edición.

En la misma línea de uso escolar hay que colocar las ediciones de las *Silvae* de Poliziano: la primera aparece en Alcalá en 1515 y después vuelven a editarse en Salamanca en 1554 y 1596 con anotación de Francisco Sánchez de las Brozas. Es un texto de lectura escolar y sabemos que lo explicaba en clase Hernán Núñez Pinciano, Antonio de Nebrija, responsable de la edición de 1515, y naturalmente también el Brocense.

Las colecciones poéticas de profesores italianos afincados en España tienen un carácter más literario como la de Lucio Flaminio Sículo, *Libellus carminum* (en su *Miscelánea*, Salamanca, *c*. 1503), Lucio Marineo Sículo, *Carminum libri duo* en apéndice a sus *Epistolarum familiarium libri* (Valladolid, Brocar, 1514), Antonio Geraldini, *Carmen Bucolicum*, Salamanca, *c*. 1505, Pedro Mártir de Anglería, *Poemata* que se incluye en sus *Opera*, Sevilla, Cromberger, 1511 (hay otra edición de su poesía en Valencia, Vignaus, 1520). Son muestra de la capacidad poética en los nuevos géneros humanísticos de sus autores, aunque algunos no dejen de llevar notas escolares.

Uno de los fenómenos más notables del humanismo cristiano más o menos erasmista de la Península es la difusión que hace de Baptista Mantuano, que es sin duda, después de Verino, el poeta neolatino italiano más veces impreso en España: sus *Parthenice septem* se publicaron por primera vez en Sevilla en 1515 al cuidado del profesor de gramática Pedro Núñez Delgado. Después se edita en los círculos erasmistas de Alcalá, primero en 1523, en una edición prologada por el bachiller Fernando de Briviesca que alaba al Mantuano por ser más amplio que otros poetas cristianos de la Antigüedad y por sus relaciones con España, empezando con el linaje del *Noster Mantuanus* "noster inquam quia ab hispania oriundus est. habuit enim auum Antonium et eum bethicum qui cum Alfonso Siciliae rege ad Neapolim nauigans a Ianuensibus captus est ex quo natus est Petrus cognomento Espagnolus <*sic*> nostri Baptistae pater" [f. a1 V]. Esta edición, variando la dedicatoria, se reeditará en Alcalá en 1536. Por otra parte tenemos dos ediciones de Barcelona de parte de este texto: una de 1520, *Parthenice secunda que et Catharinaria inscribitur*, ed. A. Vaurentinus-J. Ascensius, Barcelona, Amorós, 1520?, otra de 1525 con el título de *Parthenice Mariana* (Barcelona, Durandus Salvaniach). Además se editó en Alcalá el *Liber fastorum* del carmelita en dos ediciones, una de 1520 por Brocar y otra de 1527 por Eguía.

Paralelo al éxito de Baptista Mantuano hay que colocar la curiosa edición de textos poéticos italianos encabezados por Sannazaro que se publica en Alcalá en 1534. En el mismo volumen se edita el *De partu Virginis* con la versificación del *Evangelio* de Arator como dos contrapuntos de un ideal del humanismo cristiano renacentista, como subraya el título *Sannazarii Opuscula . . . Quibus additi sunt libri duo de gestis Apostolorum neutra in parte inferiores.* Cierra el libro un epigrama recomendando la lectura de Arator del profesor complutense Ramiro de Daroca. El volumen incluye también textos de carácter más laico como las "Eclogae" de Sannazaro, una pieza de Casandra Marchesi "Ecloga Herpyllis Pharmaceutria" y el famoso poemita de Pietro Bembo "Benacus." Quizá la sorprendente mezcla de poemas eróticos y poemas religiosos se justifique por la voluntad de ofrecer variedad formal y el carácter religioso o de religiosidad probada de sus autores.

Por último, tenemos el caso singular de poesía latina editada con una clara función encomiástica y política: las ediciones del poema de Marcelino Verardi *Fernandus Seruatus* de Salamanca, s.i., *c.* 1494 (reeditada en Valladolid, P. Giraldi-M. de Planes, *c.* 1497) y la pequeña colección poética que encabeza *Marcellini Verardi Caesenatis Elegia*, Salamanca, 1499 y que incluye la "... Bernardini. Ricii. Mamertini de obitu Principis Iohannis Monodia" y otros textos a la muerte del príncipe don Juan.

Joaquín Luis Navarro López[20] ha estudiado el *Supplementum ad Aeneidos librum XII*, del humanista laudense Mafeo Veggio y su llegada a España. Dicho *Supplementum*, compuesto hacia 1428, publicado por primera vez hacia 1469 y editado desde 1471 hasta 1820 en unión de los *Opera omnia* de Virgilio, fue denominado ya en la edición veneciana de 1471 "*Aeneidos Liber XIII.*" Tal denominación inauguró una larga y exitosa serie de ediciones del poema vegiano por toda Europa junto con la epopeya virgiliana. España no constituyó ninguna excepción a tan entusiasta acogida, pues en fecha tan temprana como 1513 y 1516 vieron la luz en Zaragoza sendas ediciones de los *Opera omnia* virgilianos, a cargo del humanista alcañizano J. Sobrarias, en las que también se incluía el "*Aeneidos Liber XIII*" de M. Veggio.

Con relación a su contenido, señala J. L. Navarro que las dos fuentes primordiales que emplea M. Veggio son Virgilio y Ovidio: el primero por existir en la propia *Eneida* toda una serie de alusiones al futuro glorioso que aguarda a Eneas; el segundo por narrar en las *Metamorfosis* la culminación del ciclo mítico de Eneas con la apoteosis del héroe, siendo el interés por relatar al modo épico dicha apoteosis la razón de ser primordial de la obra de M. Veggio. Con relación a su estructura, J. L. Navarro indica que su aparente desequilibrio (508 vs. dedicados a la acción que tiene lugar durante los tres primeros días, 122 vs. dedicados al desenlace de la acción durante los tres años siguientes) no es en absoluto fortuito, sino que responde de lleno a la intención de M. Veggio de ir preparando al lector mediante un esquema dramático *in crescendo* para el triunfo supremo del héroe troyano. Con relación a su lengua señala J.L.N. que, como era de suponer, desde un principio, aproximadamente el 90% de los calcos textuales y contextuales detectados en el texto provienen de Virgilio y Ovidio (datos del todo coherentes con lo expuesto con anterioridad), y que, a su vez, los calcos procedentes del mantuano se polarizan casi al ciento por ciento en la *Eneida*, como era de esperar. Con relación a su métrica, J.L.N. indica que, aun sin ser idénticos los porcentajes técnicos de los hexámetros del mantuano y los del laudense, la más somera comparación entre ambos apunta de forma taxativamente indudable hacia Virgilio—y en concreto hacia la *Eneida*—también como modelo de Veggio.

---

[20] Cf. J.L. Navarro López, *El libro XIII de la "Eneida" compuesto por Mafeo Veggio*, Tesis de Licenciatura realizada bajo la dirección de José María Maestre Maestre (Universidad de Cádiz, 1989).

Finalmente, destaca J.L.N. que la octava edición de la versión castellana de la *Eneida* realizada por el humanista toledano Gregorio Hernández de Velasco y aparecida en Toledo en 1574, incluye también, como desde 1471 era norma en las ediciones latinas, la primera traducción castellana del así titulado "Libro tredécimo de Mapheo: el qual se dice Suplemento de la Eneyda de Virgilio."

En su trabajo *La obra poética del humanista Fernando de Arce: Adagios y Fábulas* Antonio Serrano Cueto[21] ha hecho un estudio de los materiales que ponían en circulación las colecciones de fábulas latinas del siglo XVI. Ello permite delimitar el ámbito en que Fernando de Arce pudo tener acceso a las fuentes de sus fábulas. Así se ve la importancia de las ediciones italianas en la difusión del género en España.

El trabajo de A.S.C. hasta la fecha ha sido un acercamiento al estado de fábulas latinas en el siglo XVI español, para cuya tarea es imprescindible contar con la labor de traducción y edición llevada a cabo por humanistas como Rinuccio, Valla, Accursio, Manucio, Faerno y otros.

Las colecciones de Rinuccio Aretino y Lorenzo Valla gozaron de enorme difusión en el Renacimiento europeo. La traducción latina de un centenar de fábulas esópicas griegas realizada por Rinuccio sirvió de modelo para numerosos editores, que, como Bono Accursio, buscaban un texto latino que adjuntar al texto griego transmitido por M. Planudes. A su vez, la escasa colección de Valla, de sólo treinta y tres piezas, circuló como libro de texto en las escuelas y universidades españolas hasta mediado el siglo XVI.

Espacio aparte merece la edición bilingüe realizada en 1505 por Aldo Manucio. Este libro, que llegó a desplazar las colecciones de Rinuccio y Accursio, tuvo amplia difusión por España.

Ahora bien, la influencia de estas colecciones en los humanistas españoles no sólo se concreta en la entrada de las mismas en el mercado editorial español. Como era de esperar, los lectores españoles las leen, las asimilan y las utilizan como modelos para sus propias traducciones o composiciones. Cabe destacar, entre ellos, a Fernando de Arce, Diego Girón y Simón Abril.

Rastrear esta influencia en toda su dimensión es tarea ardua. En primer lugar, por las escasas ediciones conservadas; en segundo lugar, porque las influencias e interrelaciones en el mundo de la literatura conforman un panorama demasiado intrincado. Así, por ejemplo, Arce pudo recibir influencia de la traducción aldina, pero no directamente, sino puenteada por los *Adagia* de Erasmo.[22]

II.2. *Influencias literarias*
II.2.1. Poesía

La poesia latina de los humanistas hispanos, como la del resto de Europa, hunde

---

[21] Cf. A. Serrano Cueto, *La obra poética del humanista Fernando de Arce: Adagios y Fábulas*, Tesis Doctoral realizada bajo la dirección de Juan Gil Fernández y José María Maestre Maestre (Universidad de Cádiz, 1993).

[22] Cf. A. Serrano Cueto, "La fábula grecolatina en los *Adagia* de Erasmo y su influencia en el humanista Fernando de Arce," *Myrtia* 7 (1992): 49–80.

sus raíces en la literatura latina clásica, pero en ocasiones el modelo inmediato es un contemporáneo italiano.

En muchos casos, la influencia arranca de un poeta italiano que escribe en vernáculo. Así J.F.A. dio a conocer en su día una pequeña colección de poemas amorosos del licenciado Francisco Pacheco en la que observaba la influencia de Petrarca;[23] Bartolomé Pozuelo, que ha editado y traducido los poemas,[24] ha destacado que se trata de un petrarquismo al servicio del ideario neoplatónico, un sistema que entra en España de la mano de tratados como los *Dialoghi di Amore* de León Hebreo o *Il Cortigiano* de Baltasar Castiglione.

En otros casos, el autor italiano imitado ha escrito en latín y no siempre resulta fácil su localización. Así José María Maestre Maestre[25] ha apuntado la posibilidad de quel el poema *De S. Heliseo carmelita* de Juan Baptista Mantuano pudo ser la fuente en la que se inspiró Serón para escribir el *excursus* sobre los profetas que encontramos en los vv. 101–122 del poema lírico a Carlos Muñoz. El mismo autor demuestra en otro artículo[26] que algunos de los poemas latinos de Domingo Andrés sobre la batalla de Lepanto, como III,102 o III,105 no se inspiraron directamente en los autores clásicos, sino que esa inspiración estuvo mediatizada por la influencia de determinadas composiciones sobre el mismo tema que aparecen en la colección que publicó en Venecia, al año siguiente del triunfo cristiano, Pedro Gherardi con el título de *In foedus et uictoriam contra Turcas iuxta sinum Corinthiacum Non. Octob. MDLXXI partam poemata uaria*.

La influencia de los italianos se constata también, como era de suponer, no sólo en el nivel literario sino también en el filológico, que, en cierta manera, establece los cimientos del anterior: las poéticas y retóricas italianas fueron leídas y releídas por los estudiosos españoles. Así lo demuestra, por ejemplo, el trabajo de María Violeta Pérez Custodio sobre la influencia de los *Poeticorum libri tres* de Jerónimo Vida, publicados en 1527, en los *Rhetoricorum libri quattuor* de Arias Montano, salidos a la luz en 1569.[27]

La referida investigación persigue un doble objetivo:

---

[23] Cf. J. F. Alcina Rovira, "Aproximación a la poesía latina del Canónigo Francisco Pacheco," *Boletín de la Real Academia de Buenas Letras de Barcelona* 36 (1975-1976): 255–262; id., "Humanismo y petrarquismo," en *Nebrija y la introducción del Renacimiento italiano en España. Actas de la III Academia literaria renacentista* (Salamanca, 1983), 145–156; "Petrarquismo latino en España, II: Hernán Ruiz de Villegas y la imitación de M. Marullo," *Nova Tellus* 4 (1986): 53–61.

[24] B. Pozuelo Calero, *El licenciado Francisco Pacheco. Sermones sobre la instauración de la libertad del espíritu y lírica amorosa* (Cádiz: Universidad de Cádiz-Universidad de Sevilla, 1993), 57–58 y 206–259.

[25] Cf. J. M. Maestre Maestre, "Notas de crítica textual y hermenéutica a la obra poética latina de Antonio Serón. IV: el poema lírico a Carlos Muñoz," *Humanistica Lovaniensia* 39 (1990): 219–245.

[26] Cf. Maestre Maestre, "El mundo clásico," 153–164.

[27] Cf. M. V. Pérez Custodio, "Las relaciones poética-retórica en la teoría literaria renacentista: Jerónimo Vida y Arias Montano," en J.M. Maestre Maestre-J. Pascual Barea (coordinadores), *Humanismo y Pervivencia del Mundo Clásico* (Cádiz: Servicio de Publicaciones de la Universidad de Cádiz-Instituto de Estudios Turolenses [C.S.I.C.], 1993), I.2: 759–774.

a. La constatación de la influencia concreta en fondo y forma que la obra del italiano ejerció sobre la del hispano. Esta influencia, si bien ya fue apuntada por Camilo Hectóreo y más modernamente por Menéndez Pelayo, no se había concretado con el cotejo de los textos de forma documental.

b. Una vez demostrado lo anterior, su aplicación a la polémica sobre la pérdida de perfiles que en el Renacimiento sufre la poética por influencia de la retórica.

Respecto al primer objetivo Pérez Custodio anticipa que las obras comparadas ofrecen una inmediata similitud: ambas están escritas en hexámetros, vehículo formal con claros antecedentes para una poética (baste recordar la horaciana) pero no así para una retórica, cuyas raíces clásicas se hunden en las obras de Cicerón y Quintiliano escritas en prosa. De otra parte, la obra de Jerónimo Vida fue un *best-seller* en la época y figuraba en la biblioteca de Arias Montano, como sabemos por un recuento de libros realizado por el propio humanista. A partir de aquí cobra cuerpo la hipótesis de que el hispano conocía muy de cerca la obra del cremonés, cuyo impacto se hace visible a lo largo de los casi cinco mil versos montanianos, siendo la más evidente muestra de dicha influencia el molde métrico en que el poeta de Fregenal enfundó su tratado retórico.

Los pasajes en que se aprecia, tanto en fondo como en forma, la dependencia de Arias Montano respecto a Vida son numerosos. Unos cuantos nos servirán ahora de botón de muestra:

• en lo relativo a las partes del discurso, ambos elaboran un misma teoría sobre el exordio (que debe tener un tono ascendente, tal como recomienda el orden natural), observándose en el hispano el gusto por insertar en esos hexámetros determinados clichés que ya se encuentran presentes en los pasajes en cuestión del italiano. Así sucede en

> Progressu, *potius* grauis atque modestus in ipsis
> *Principiis*, prudens paulatim surgit opusque
>
> (A.M. III,280–281)

donde se reproduce la secuencia *Principiis potius* presente en J. Vida II,37:

> Principiis potius semper maiora sequantur.

• en la doctrina sobre la *narratio* coinciden en puntos tan señalados como la consideración de la técnica de *in medias res*, la alteración del orden en los poetas arrebatados por el *furor diuinus*, la necesidad de la verosimilitud (*fides*) y la restricción del relato de portentos sólo a aquellos lugares donde intervengan seres divinos.

• en lo tocante a la capacidad compositiva, ambos poetas convergen en la recomendación de la tranquilidad espiritual y la huida de las pasiones:

> Vitam agitant uates, *procul* est sceleratus *habendi*
> Hinc *amor, insanae spes* longe atque impia uota
>
> (J.V. I,492–493)

> [. . .] *procul* omnis amor, odium *procul* omne

*Spes*que metusque atque omnis *opum uesana* cupido

(A.M. IV,80–81)

• La coincidencia en el tratamiento de determinadas figuras literarias queda resaltada por el hecho de que ambos autores escojan precisamente los mismos ejemplos. Por ejemplo, para la alegoría A. Montano usa el virgiliano

Claudite iam riuos, pueri; sat prata biberunt

verso que aparece inserto en el pasaje donde Vida habla de ese mismo *schema rhetoricum*:

Prata bibunt ridentque satis surgentibus agri.

• multitud de pasajes coincidentes, en fin, relativos a la acomodación del lenguaje al personaje y la adecuación de *uerba* y *res*, la alabanza final inserta en ambas obras, etc.

El cotejo de contextos donde el extremeño revela su exhaustivo conocimiento de la obra de Vida queda fuera de duda. Pero al igual que llaman la atención las semejanzas, se debe reparar en dos importantes diferencias: la extremada longitud de la *Rhetorica* montaniana (4994 versos) frente a la más moderada *Poetica* vidiana (1758 versos) y la inclusión de numerosas alusiones a amigos y maestros en la primera frente a su omisión en la segunda.

Estas dos discrepancias podrían salvarse si suponemos con Pérez Custodio que en un determinado momento—posiblemente en su viaje a Italia—el poeta hispano tuvo acceso a la primera redacción de la obra italiana (difundida hacia 1517 de forma muy restringida), pues en esta primera versión se alcanzaban los cuatro mil versos y se contenían múltiples referencias a contemporáneos.

Asumida, pues, la importante dependencia entre A. Montano y Vida, es hora de pasar al segundo objetivo. ¿Tanto se parecen ambas obras que puedan servir de sostén a la teoría de que la poética pierde en el siglo XVI su entidad a favor de la retórica? La conclusión de la investigadora es que no. Las obras coinciden en aquello que de común pueden tener ambas disciplinas, pero desde el enfoque propio de cada una de ellas. Siguiendo la línea de Howell, Pérez Custodio entiende que la retórica montaniana, como cabía esperar dentro de la tradición clásica, es un tratado de cómo lograr la creación no mimética (es decir, la que se basa en pruebas y argumentaciones) mientras la poética de Vida se centra en la creación mimética (a saber, la que se realiza mediante la ficción), aunque, como es un lugar común desde Aristóteles, ambas formas de creación comparten parcelas. Una de las innovaciones coincidentes en ambos tipos de artes en el siglo XVI será la introducción de alusiones a contenidos ajenos a la materia (excursos encomiásticos, propagandísticos, anécdotas, etc.). En este panorama de vasos comunicantes no se debe pasar por alto la importancia de tratados griegos como los de Demetrio y Longino, cuya influencia en la teoría literaria renacentista parece ser muy fuerte, y donde los pasajes ejemplificatorios de prosa y verso aparecen entremezclados.

Pero la influencia de los italianos no siempre es de índole estrictamente filológica, como ha puesto de relieve Joaquín Luis Navarro López en su edición de las setenta y dos odas latinas de los *Humanae salutis monumenta* de Benito Arias Montano,[28] cuya *editio princeps* vio la luz en Amberes en 1571.

En efecto, con excepción de la primera y de la septuagésima segunda, todas las odas van acompañadas de un grabado con motivos simbólicos, alusivo al contenido de la oda, que a su vez va precedido y seguido de un epigrama con lema y de una *subscriptio* relativos al contenido del grabado. Lógicamente a cualquier lector culto le vendrá de inmediato a la mente el género compositivo inaugurado hacia 1531 con la publicación en Augsburg de una obra destinada sin lugar a dudas a hacer época, a saber, el *Emblematum libellus* de Andrea Alciato. Por tanto, es paso obligado proceder a la colación de los *Monumenta* montanianos con los *emblemata* neolatinos.

Si bien no es posible por razones de espacio desarrollar *in extenso* la comparación entre ambos, señalemos tan sólo que los emblemata están constituidos por tres elementos (*lemma, symbolum, epigramma*) frente a los cuatro que componen las piezas de los Monumenta (*epigramma, tabula, subscriptio, carmen*) según el siguiente esquema:

- el *lemma* emblemático está representado por el *epigramma* y la *subscriptio*;

- el *symbolum* emblemático, como es obvio, por la *tabula*;

- el *epigramma* emblemático por el *carmen*.

En definitiva, aunque los catálogos de libros de emblemas europeos y españoles incluyen normalmente esta obra, Joaquín Luis Navarro ha precisado que los *Monumenta* de Arias Montano suponen un ulterior desarrollo mediante el enriquecimiento de sus componentes del género emblemático, sin el cual no sólo no serían comprensibles sino que con total seguridad no habrían sido lo que son.

II.2.2. Prosa

Como era de esperar, la prosa de los humanistas hispanos está repleta de imitaciones de los autores italianos. El influjo se manifiesta en ocasiones en las obras de otros humanistas italianos afincados en España. Así lo ha puesto de manifiesto Carmen Ramos Santana en su edición del *Liber de Parcis* de Lucio Marineo Sículo.[29]

Este siciliano juega un papel fundamental en las relaciones del Humanismo español y el italiano, ya que fue un humanista italiano cuya obra ejerció gran influencia en el Humanismo español, y un humanista español, en tanto que afincado en España, que aquí recibió el influjo de otros humanistas italianos. Marineo se afinca definitivamente en España en 1484. Tras doce años de profesor de poética y oratoria en la Universidad de Salamanca, se une a la Corte de los Reyes Católicos donde fue cronista real, capellán de Corte y profesor de los sacerdotes y hombres y mujeres vinculados

---

[28] Cf. J. L. Navarro López, *Los "Humanae Salutis Monumenta" de Benito Arias Montano. Introducción, edición crítica, traducción anotada e índices,* Tesis Doctoral realizada bajo la dirección de los Drs. Juan Gil y J. M. Maestre Maestre (Universidad de Cádiz, 1990).

[29] C. Ramos Santana, *La "Repetitio de verbo fero" y el "Liber de Parcis" de Lucio Marineo Sículo. Introducción, edición crítica, traducción anotada e índices,* Tesis de Licenciatura realizada bajo la dirección de J. M. Maestre Maestre (Universidad de Cádiz, 1992).

a la Corte, así como de jóvenes nobles. Tan numerosas obligaciones no le impidieron ser autor de una prolífica obra que abarca varios géneros, destacando su producción historiográfica, ni mantener fluidas relaciones con las personalidades intelectuales y políticas más importantes del momento, algunas de los cuales se convirtieron voluntariamente en sus alumnos al solicitarle consejos para su formación intelectual y humanística, como queda reflejado en sus *Epistolarum familiarum libri decem et septem* (Valladolid, 1514). Por tanto, el campo de influencia de Marineo como transmisor del Humanismo latino en España fue amplísimo, sumándose así a la pléyade de humanistas italianos que contribuyeron a dicha tarea.

Pero Marineo, una vez afincado en España, no quedó exento de recibir la influencia de otros humanistas italianos. Un ejemplo de ello lo constituye su *Liber de Parcis* publicado, junto al Epistolario, la *Repetitio de uerbo fero* y otras obras, en Valladolid en 1514. Es éste un tratado sobre las Parcas que además de un análisis del origen, los nombres y las funciones de estas diosas, contiene un estudio sobre la divinidad, la omnipotencia divina, el libre albedrío, los términos *fatum* y *fortuna*, y la influencia de la naturaleza, el destino y la fortuna en la vida del hombre. Años antes, en 1485, Giorgio Valla había publicado en Venecia su *In Ciceronis librum de Fato commentarium*, una edición con comentario de la obra de Cicerón. Marineo en el prefacio del *Liber de Parcis,* al exponer que el método empleado para la composición de su obra ha sido la recopilación de opiniones de diversos autores sobre el tema en cuestión, declara haber seguido más escrupulosa y profusamente el libro de Valla. En efecto, el siciliano tomó como fuente la obra de Valla hasta tal extremo que, de una parte, copió literalmente numerosos fragmentos de la misma y, de otra, basó muchas de sus ideas y argumentos en lo que Valla había expuesto. Como resultado, de los trece capítulos en los que temáticamente se puede dividir el *Liber,* cuatro y parte de un quinto reproducen palabras textuales de Valla; otros tres repiten sus ideas. La obra del siciliano es, por tanto, deudora del comentario que su compatriota compuso años antes.

La lectura de los italianos resulta indispensable para poder captar los entresijos que en muchas ocasiones encontramos detrás de determinados escritos, como los prólogos. Así José María Maestre Maestre ha demostrado en un artículo[30] que el montaje, que encontramos hacia el final del prólogo-dedicatoria de la *Minerua* del Brocense, de que el propio Nebrija, agonizando en Brozas en casa de su hijo Marcelo, le había nombrado a él poco menos que heredero de la profesión de gramático, así como el *Barbatos Perotos* que el Brocense engarza con habilidad allí mismo en dos versos de Virgilio (*Aen.* 4,625–626), ya antes utilizados por el propio Nebrija,[31] no se entienden bien sino a la luz del prólogo y comienzo de los *Cornucopiae siue linguae Latinae commentarii* de Nicolás Peroto.

La influencia de los italianos se deja sentir en cualquiera de los géneros literarios

---

[30] Cf. J. M. Maestre Maestre, " 'Barbatos Perotos': los tópicos del prólogo-dedicatoria de la Minerua," *Actas del Simposio Internacional IV Centenario de la Publicación de la Minerua del Brocense (1587–1987),* 203–232.

[31] Cf. J. M. Maestre Maestre, "El Brocense contra Nebrija: nuevos datos sobre el prólogo-dedicatoria de la Minerva," *Alor Novisimo* 16–18 (1988–1989): 22–32.

que abordemos. En un artículo Joaquín Pascual[32] ha estudiado, por ejemplo, cómo se desarrolló en España el cultivo de la inscripción sepulcral renacentista a partir de la influencia del Renacimiento italiano, desde la primera tumba renacentista de la ciudad, realizada por Miguel Florentín, la del cardenal Mendoza en 1502, quien trajo a su tierra el gusto por las letras y el arte antiguos que admiró en Roma, o los epitafios de algunos españoles enterrados en Roma por esas fechas, pasando por la influencia de los *epitaphia Romae inuenta et ab antiquis marmoribus transcripta* editados por Lucio Flaminio, maestro de Delgado, que los compone a comienzos de siglo.

Por último nos referiremos a la producción panegirista sobre los Reyes Católicos a cargo de humanistas italianos como Ugolino Verino (*Panegyricon ad Ferdinandum regem et Isabellam reginam Hispaniarum de Saracenae Baetidos gloriosa expugnatione*, de 1492) y Paolo Pompilio (*De triumpho granatensi panegyris*, también de 1492), que parecen haber ejercido una influencia notable sobre los panegíricos de los Reyes escritos por humanistas españoles como Juan Sobrarias y Guillén de Avila, entre otros.

En estrecha relación, asimismo, con estos autores de panegíricos está el importante papel desempeñado por los tantas veces citados humanistas italiano afincados en la España de los Reyes Católicos como Pedro Mártir de Anglería, Marineo Sículo o los hermanos Geraldini. Además del importante cometido que todos ellos desempeñan como preceptistas de lengua latina en la corte real, sirven de enlace con Italia, adonde envían noticias sobre los principales acontecimientos del momento, difundiendo la imagen de España por tierras italianas. En concreto, nos consta que Pomponio Leto, humanista muy vinculado al círculo de los españoles presentes en Italia, recibe noticias sobre la Guerra de Granada de Pedro Mártir y anima a Paolo Pompilio a escribir su Panegírico. Este importante papel de los humanistas italianos en España está siendo también objeto de estudio por parte de investigadores como la Dra. Rodríguez Peregrina, que lleva a cabo y dirige diversos trabajos sobre la obra de Pedro Mártir.

II.3. Las ideas

El campo de las traducciones de autores clásicos en España depende también en muchos casos de los modelos italianos. Leticia Carrasco estudia las traducciones de las *Metamorfosis* de Ovidio resaltando las dependencias, desde la primera que tenemos por Jorge de Bustamante (en prosa) que depende probablemente de la primera traducción italiana de Ioanni de Bonsignore (también en prosa), como se puede sospechar por las semejanzas desde los primeros versos:

> Prima che fusse mare, terra o cielo era un volto di natura in tuttol mondo e quelli del mondo el chiamaron Chaos e fu una grossa e non compartita compositione e era uno disconcio peso . . . (Bonsignore)

Antes que fuessen criados mar, tierra, ayre, ni cielos era un bulto de natura al

---

[32] Cf. J. Pascual Barea, "El epitafio latino renacentista en España," en Maestre Maestre-Pascual Barea (coordinadores), *Humanismo y Pervivencia del Mundo Clásico*, 727–748.

qual llamaron Chaos por ser en si una gruessa y no compartida composición y una massa o globo y desconcertado peso . . . (Bustamante)

A partir de mediados del siglo XVI todas las traducciones completas de las *Metamorfosis*, primero en Italia y después en España se hacen en verso. En esta moda son fundamentales las traducciones en verso de Ludovico Dolce (1553) y Iovanni Andrea dell'Anguillara (1561). Ya la traducción castellana de Antonio Pérez Sigler (1580) utiliza, según confiesa él mismo, el libro de Anguillara para las alegorías que acompañan a cada uno de los quince libros. También la traducción parcial de Felipe Mey (1586) tiene en cuenta los modelos italianos y sus formas de traducir como indica el propio traductor en el prólogo: ". . . quanto a la traducción no he guardado siempre una misma orden, porque el primero y segundo libro, que fueron trabajos casi del principio de mi mocedad, me desvié algunas veces del texto latino, imitando en parte a Ludovico Dolce, y en parse al Anguillara, (que han arromançado este libro en su lengua) y encaxando a bueltas dello de mi cosecha lo que me dictava la loçanía del ingenio juvenil amigo de novedades. En los demás libros he alargado menos la rienda . . ."

Mercedes Trascasas ha pretendido localizar el mayor número posible de traducciones, si no de todas las obras de clásicos griegos, sí de aquellas que nos parezcan más relevantes durante los siglos XV y XVI, en función de los siguientes objetivos: a.) Averiguar la causa que motiva el interés por esas obras entre los humanistas españoles e italianos; b.) Comprobar si se ha mantenido el texto y el espíritu original de la obra o han cambiado al pasarla a otra lengua; c.) Ver si hay interferencias entre los traductores españoles y entre los traductores italianos.

Se ha empezado por una de las obras más traducida tanto en España como Italia, a juzgar por la información de R. R. Bolgar y de T. S. Beardsley.[33] Se trata de las *Vidas Paralelas* de Plutarco. El móvil de esta elección ha sido simplemente el hecho de que la obra tuviera varias traducciones realizadas por humanistas españoles y por italianos.

Al hablar de Plutarco en España, y, en concreto de las *Vidas Paralelas*, hay que mencionar, aunque sólo sea de pasada a don Juan Fernández de Heredia, que fue el primero que en Occidente se interesó por trasladar las biografías de Plutarco a otra lengua al encargarlas traducir al aragonés (¿1379/1384?), como indica A. Pérez Jiménez.[34] La suerte de esta edición y su grado de influencia en España durante el siglo XV no la conocemos, según señala el propio Pérez Jiménez, aunque el nombre y la obra de Plutarco se incorporara a la conciencia cultural española del siglo XV. Sin embargo, fueron precisamente estas *Vidas* aragonesas las que sirvieron de modelo a

---

[33] Cf. R. R. Bolgar, *The Classical Heritage and Its Beneficiaries* (Cambridge, 1964), Appendix II, 521–523; T. S. Beardsley, Jr., *Hispano-Classical Translations, Printed between 1482–1699* (Pittsburgh–Louvain, 1970), 3, 5, 6, 8.

[34] A. Pérez Jiménez, "Plutarco y el humanismo español del renacimiento," en *Estudio sobre Plutarco: Obra y tradición (Actas del I symposion español sobre Plutarco. Fuengirola 1988)* (Málaga, 1990), 230–231.

una versión italiana anónima llevada a cabo entre 1395 y 1397, según A. Gómez Moreno.[35]

En el siglo XV contamos con el humanista español Alonso Fernández de Palencia que traduce las *Vidas* de Plutarco al castellano. Éste comienza el prólogo de su traducción con una dedicatoria al ilustre y muy magnífico señor don Rodrigo Ponce de León; y, a continuación, indica que se trata de una translación de las *Vidas* de Plutarco de latín en romance.[36] Efectivamente, Alonso de Palencia hizo esta versión castellana de las *Vidas Paralelas* a partir de la edición latina realizada en 1478 por Lapo Florentino, Leonardo Justiniano, Guarino, Antonio Tudertino, etc...., como él mismo manifiesta al comimienzo de la traducción de los distintos personajes: "Plutarco, dice, muy noble filósofo escribió la vida de Teseo en griego. Trasladóla en latín Lapo Florentino muy enseñado. Después el cronista Alonso de Palencia la tradujo en Romance Castellano." A continuación se refiere a Plutarco y a su obra, a quien destaca como excelente filósofo más que como historiador; y a sus *Vidas* como la más digna relación de notables hazañas de valerosos personajes contadas en un estilo maravilloso. Publicada en Sevilla en 1491, el único mérito que se le atribuye a esta traducción, según Pérez Jiménez, es el de haber colocado a España en primera línea después de Italia, de traducciones de las *Vidas* de latín a lengua vulgar.[37] Sin olvidar su influencia en las obras de carácter biográfico, sobre todo, como en la de *Los claros varones de España* de Hernando del Pulgar, entre otros, como el propio Pérez Jiménez reconoce.

Otro traductor de las *Vidas* de Plutarco es el humanista Francisco de Enzinas, buen conocedor de griego y latín. En 1547 se le atribuye la obra bajo el título *Las Vidas de dos ilustres varones, Cimón Griego y Lúcullo Romano*. En 1551, un año antes de su muerte, traduce las *Vidas* de Plutarco, que dedica a Carlos V. El título reza así: *El Primer Volumen de las Vidas de Ilustres y Excelentes Barones Griegos y Romanos pareadas, escritas primero en Lengua Griega por el grave Philósofo y verdadero historiador Plutarco de Cheronea y al presente traducidas en estilo castellano por Francisco d'Enzinas*. Al referirse a Plutarco dice que ningún otro autor profano de ninguna otra lengua puede

---

[35] A. Gómez Moreno, *España y la Italia de los humanistas* (Madrid, 1994), 95. En Italia, los humanistas se ocuparon especialmente de Luciano, Plutarco e Isócrates. En Plutarco se inspiraron las biografías humanísticas en tiempo de Petrarca, basadas sobre el concepto fundamental de que el hombre es actor de la historia. En 1482, B. Jaconello de Riete tradujo las *Vidas* completas de Plutarco, según informa Bolgar (Appendix II, 523). En 1537, se publicó en Venecia, sin nombre de autor *La seconda parte delle Vite di Plutarco de greco in latino y de latino in volgare tradotte*. En 1555, M. Lodovico Domenichi traduce a la lengua toscana *La prima parte delle Vite di Plutarcho*, que considera de gran utilidad. En 1563, M. Francesco Sansovino traduce la parte segunda *delle Vite de gli huomini illustri greci, et romani di Plutarcho Cheroneo*. En 1567, se publica en Venecia la traducción de Plutarco bajo el título *Vite di Plutarco Cheroneo de gli huomini illustri greci e romani. Nuovamente tradotte per M. Lodovico Domenichi et altri, et diligentemente confrontate co'testi greci per M. Lionardo Ghini*. De la traducción de Domenechi hemos encontrado varias ediciones (1570, 1587, 1620).

[36] En este período no hay ni ediciones griegas de Plutarco impresas en España ni tampoco traducciones latinas a diferencia de lo que ocurría en Italia donde las *Vidas* traducidas al latín eran tan populares.

[37] A. Pérez Jiménez, "Plutarco y el humanismo," 233.

compararse con la historia de Plutarco y a su estilo lo califica de ápero, duro, grave y dificultoso.

Bajo el mismo título se publica en 1562 en Colonia una traducción de Juan Castro de Salinas, que, según algunos, es plagio de la traducción de Encinas.[38] En esta edición se alude, entre otras cosas, al provecho que puede sacar el lector con su lectura y al goce de aquellos que no pueden leerla en su lengua natural y en latín.

Finalmente en 1576 aparece un breve compendio traducido por el muy R. P. Fray Tomás de Spinosa de los Monteros, publicado en París por Francisco de Prado bajo el título de *Heroicos hechos y vidas de varones Ilustres asy Griegos como Romanos*. El librito está dedicado al ilustre señor Don Diego de Zúñiga.

Matilde Conde Salazar compara las ideas pedagógicas en los tratados humanísticos de España e Italia y llega a la conclusión que los tratados españoles dan más importancia a la lengua materna, basándose en afirmaciones de Vives y la existencia de los conocidos textos de Nebrija sobre la lengua castellana.

En el campo de la teoría historiográfica el profesor Jenaro Costas compara los tratados italianos de Pontano (*Actius*, c. 1499) y Robortello (*De historica facultate*, 1548), con los de los españoles Fox Morcillo *De historiae institutione* (1557),[39] las secciones que dedica Vives a la historia en *De ratione dicendi* (1533) y *De disciplinis* (1531), y el "Memorial" de Juan Páez de Castro (c. 1555).[40] Es casi seguro que todos conociesen el diálogo de Pontano, que Fox Morcillo tuviese acceso a la obra de Vives, ya que ambos están vinculados al círculo filosófico y humanístico de Lovaina, mientras que Páez y Robortello fueron los dos estudiantes en Bolonia. Excepto Páez, todos encuadran la historia dentro de la retórica. Morcillo estructura las labores del historiador según el esquema tradicional de: *inventio, dispositio* y *elocutio*. Pontano, por su parte, toma el punto de arranque de la definición de Quintiliano (X,1,31): *historia est proxima poesi et quodammodo carmen solutum*. Vives y Morcillo dan un paso más y se esfuerzan por encajar el relato histórico entre los tipos de la *narratio*, como hace la *Rhet. ad Herennium* (1,8,13), en función de la verosimilitud. Vives, inspirado en R. Agrícola, añade un matiz, al resaltar el criterio de finalidad en la *narratio*, distinguiendo la que sirve para enseñar o explicar (historia), de la que sirve para persuadir y para entretener. Los historiadores que pueden servir como modelo varían. Los

---

[38] En uno de los ejemplares de este primer volumen de la traducción de Encinas, una nota, escrita a mano por un tal Don Pedro, dice que este mismo tomo se publicó en Colonia en el año 1562 a nombre de Juan Castro de Salinas, que sin duda fue plagio de éste o del impresor contra Francisco de Encinas. Y añade, además, la nota que Nicolás Antonio padeció engaño en cuanto a esto por no poner en su biblioteca más que la obra de Juan Castro y no la de Francisco de Encinas. A. Pérez Jiménez, en su artículo anteriormente citado, p. 236, opina que las seis primeras vidas son claramente de Francisco de Enzinas; las dos últimas dice que se atribuyen a Gracián de Alderete, y, Lasso de la Vega ha demostrado que son un calco de la traducción francesa hecha por Jorge de Selve y publicada en París en 1543.

[39] Para las citas de los teóricos renacentistas nos serviremos de la edición de sus obras en *Artis Historicae Penus*, I (Basileae, 1579).

[40] Publicado por Eustasio Esteban, "De las cosas necesarias para escribir historia," *La Ciudad de Dios*, no. 28 (1892), 601–610 y no. 29 (1892), 27–37.

historiae principes de Pontano son como para Quintiliano, Salustio y Livio. Según Páez, entre los griegos Herodoto fue el primero y Tucídides el segundo, en tanto que de los romanos, "aún en tiempo de Tullio no había historia públicada que mereciese ese nombre." En opinión de Morcillo, Jenofonte es de los griegos *omnium praestantissimus*, y los latinos son *minus culti atque elegantes*. Por lo demás, los modelos antiguos son aceptados aunque también son criticados en ocasiones, y se valoran detenidamente los conocimientos del historiador.

El tratamiento de Pontano es eminentemente literario desde su mismo comienzo: su hilo conductor son los conflictos bélicos y la explotación narrativa de cuanto los rodea. Esa atención minuciosa a las batallas ya se encuentra en la retorica de Jorge de Trebisonda y es recogida en parte también por Morcillo. Pero Vives, haciendo gala de su pacifismo, se opone frontalmente a las descripciones bélicas. En este corpus de tratadistas se podrían establecer dos grupos de afinidades generales: de un lado Pontano, Vives y Morcillo, y del otro Robortello y Páez, que coinciden en algunos puntos como la valoración de los conocimientos anticuarios, arqueológicos y etnográficos del historiador o la necesidad de callarse algunas cosas "que no aumentan la dignidad de la historia" (Robortello) o "porque muchas verdades no hacen al propósito de la historia" (Páez).

La posición de algunos humanistas italianos (Baltasar de Castiglione, Maquiavelo, y Gentili) y españoles (Alfonso de Valdés, Francisco de Vitoria, Luis Vives, Ginés de Sepúlveda) en la valoración ético-política de la guerra es analizada por M. José López de Ayala. La mayoría de los pensadores españoles mantienen unos criterios más ligados a la abstracción del Derecho natural, condenando la guerra como contraria a él. Sin embargo, a partir de la muerte de Erasmo, quien es la figura ideológica principal de Europa y que había condenado la guerra, ésta se acepta mayoritariamente por los pensadores españoles, aunque igualmente justificándola con respecto al Derecho natural. En cambio los italianos se presentan en todo momento como más pragmáticos y con mayor consideración hacia la realidad política y estatal, aceptando la guerra y subordinándola a éstas. Unos y otros se inspiran en los pensadores antiguos, y destaca además la influencia de S. Agustín.

Communications

Humanism in Alberti's Art Theory and the Human Body in the European Academies of Art

LISE BEK

In the following I shall present some new observations on Leon Battista Alberti's treatise on painting, the *De Pictura*, written in 1434, and followed the next year by an Italian version.[1] The latter was no doubt meant by the author to function as a kind of manual to the practising artist in his endeavour to fulfil the demands for an art in the new humanistic spirit. Whether it was read or not by the painters of his day, its impact upon their work was evidently considerable.

The Latin edition, for its part, was equally intended as a handbook, namely, for the humanistically educated public of this new art. But at the same time the ideas inaugurated by Alberti were widely diffused among the humanists, so as to become influential upon the score of treatises on the arts and sciences appearing over the centuries to come.

It was in this area of artistic and scientific theory, all permeated by Albertian thought, that the rules and precepts for the future academies of art were rooted. One might say, in fact, that although Alberti's ideal of the painter was moulded upon the Ciceronian one of the Roman republican free citizen, the *De Pictura* contains, in essence, the concept of painting that would serve the purposes of the crowned heads of enlightened absolutism. That was due not so much to its humanist character in form and style as to its rationalism in content.

In tracing the humanism in the Albertian text I shall, therefore, leave aside its literal and literary borrowings from ancient writers, thoroughly investigated by other scholars,[2] and concentrate upon two sources of inspiration, more substantial to the formation of the new Albertian concept of the art of painting as a true humanistic discipline. Thus attention will be drawn to the works of Aristotle, and to the *De*

---

[1] L. B. Alberti, *De Pictura & Della Pittura (1434/35)*, in *Opere volgari*, vol. 1, ed. C. Grayson (Bari, 1973).

[2] Cf. among others C. Grayson, *L. B. Alberti On Painting and On Sculpture. The Latin Texts of De Pictura and De Statua* (London, 1974).

Architectura by Vitruvius. Both authors are mentioned by name a couple of times in his text but are present in it more extensively.

My argument for singling out just those two writers among the many referred to by Alberti will gain support, it is hoped, from my preoccupation with the cultural analyses undertaken by Michel Foucault, especially in his works on the prison and on the clinical body,[3] as well as with the many recent studies based upon his work on the spatial and bodily concepts of the new world of the Renaissance and Modernity.[4]

By manipulating the Vitruvian and Aristotelian subject matter, Alberti succeeds in bringing about, in fact, the geometrisation not only of the pictorial representation but also of the phenomenon of sight in general, which might be seen as the equivalent in terms of vision to the rationality characteristic of humanistic thinking.

In this way, it seems to me, Alberti manages, far more than through his response to the humanists' mode of writing, to incorporate his art of painting into the realm of Renaissance mentality and to set up for it standards, valid even in the century of a René Descartes and beyond. It was in the Paris of Descartes and of Louis XIV, by the way, that the first royal academy was established. But as it provided the model for all later academies, from Madrid and London to Copenhagen, it will suffice here as the example.[5]

The treatment here will fall into two main parts. They will each concern Alberti's dependence on Vitruvius and Aristotle, as contributors to his innovative views on pictorial space and on the painted figure respectively, in both cases with a side view to the possible Albertian afterthoughts in other types of humanistic treatises and academic practice as well. Then follows, as the concluding part, some remarks on the Albertian influence upon the theory of art adhered to by the artists attached to the Parisian academy.

1. Alberti Reversing Vitruvius

As a starting point, a brief summary of the contents of the *De Pictura* would be in place.

Of its three books the first, entitled *Rudimenta*, lays out the scientific, optical, and geometrical foundation upon which to structure the picture as an intersection of the pyramid of vision and hence to calculate the central perspective construction of its spatial setting. Then follows, in Book II, on the *Ars*, an explanation of the three main categories of the picture, first *circumscriptio*, or the drawing of outlines, and next, *compositio*, the correct bringing together of the various elements outlined in a totality of form and content. It is in this connection, consequently, that Alberti introduces his idea of the *historia* as the key concept of the new kind of painting he is advocating.

[3] M. Foucault, *Surveiller et punir. Naissance de la prison* (Paris, 1987) as well as *Naissance de la clinique. Une archeologie du regard médical* (Paris, 1963).

[4] Cf. M. Feher, *Fragments for a History of the Human Body* (New York, 1989); *The Body Imaged. The Human Form and Visual Culture since the Renaissance*, ed. K. Adler and M. Pointon (Cambridge: 1993); and further T. Weimarck, *Akademi och anatomi* (Stockholm/Stehag, 1996).

[5] N. Pevsner, *Academies of Art. Past and Present* (New York, 1973).

Finally there is the *receptio luminis*, or treatment of light and colour. We will return later on to the first two issues of this tripartite division, generated, as may be discerned, from the disposition required for the well-ordered speech in classical rhetorics. The third book, on the *Artifex*, will be of minor importance here, except for the Vitruvian paraphrase to be commented upon next.

As regards Vitruvius, Alberti does not hesitate, in various instances, to oppose his Roman architect predecessor openly, in order to emphasize the novelty of his own views. In two places, however, in the middle of the first book, in § 12 and at the beginning of the third book, in § 52, he brings in, yet without reference to his source, precisely the only two passages in which Vitruvius is dealing with the matter of perspective.[6] In Book I chapter 2 he notices the rendering of depth in the painted prospect of the future building, the so-called *scenographia*. The other passage, to be found in the introduction to Book VII, is a description of how the illusion of plasticity is obtained in the painted set-pieces of the theatre. It is done by making the elements seem to protrude or recede although depicted on a flat surface.

The similarity of the corresponding Albertian phrases notwithstanding, the Renaissance writer is turning upside down the argumentation of his predecessor, referring in the latter case to his own intersection of the pyramid of vision. To Alberti, in other words, the plastically rendered elements were to be depicted as if located behind the picture plane, in the fictitious space created there by means of the perspective construction, not to spring out illusionistically into the beholder's own spatial reality.

In the former passage Vitruvius states that in the *scenographia* all lines have to correspond precisely to the point from which the beholder will be looking at the prospect (Fig. 1). In Alberti's reversion, however, it is said that, at first, the picture has to be made according to the pyramidal intersection, all lines converging in the apex of the perspective construction, or central point situated on the horizon line of the picture (Figs. 2–3). Afterwards, then, the beholder is obliged to step forwards and backwards in front of the painting until the correct viewing point, just opposite to that, is found. The difference between what Erwin Panofsky has termed the "subjective" perspective of Antiquity, based on Euclidean optics, and the "objective" one of the Renaissance, constructed upon Euclidean geometry, could hardly be demonstrated more clearly.[7]

In the first case the image of vision is conditioned by the beholder, in so far as its only fixed point will be his eye, the apex of the cone of sight embracing the things seen, be they real or painted. The objective perspective, for its part, is that conceived by Alberti himself and his artist companions, as constituted through the central perspective construction, relying on the Aristotelian physiology of sight as directed along straight lines. To this model, the world seen, whether in reality or in the picture, will inevitably present itself to the beholder as another world separated from his by the

---

[6] Vitruvius, *De Architectura libri decem*, ed. K. Fensterbuch (Darmstadt, 1976), I:2 and VI Intr.

[7] E. Panofsky, "Perspektive als 'symbolische Form'" in *Aufsätze zu Grundfragen der Kunstwissenschaft* (Berlin, 1964), 99–167.

intersection of the pyramid of vision. So the two pyramids, that of vision and that of perspective, stand in a reciprocal relation to one another, each on its side of their common basis. It follows from this that the things seen definitely become objects of vision as opposed to the subject-beholder.

It is this objective world of fiction, diminished in size, and formally reduced to naked geometry, that sets the stage for Alberti's pictorial composition. Its structural principle consists in a stereometric coordinate system emerging from the juxtaposition of the vertical grid dissecting the picture plane, a provision for the exact location of the surfaces drawn up on it,[8] with the horizontal one made up by the perspectival chessboard floor.

In principle, an identical way of proceeding reappears in the many writings on the perspective problem, from that of a Piero della Francesca, a Leonardo da Vinci, or an Albrecht Dürer,[9] right up to René Descartes.[10] Through this repeated re-utilization, it is true, Alberti's rather simple manner of construction was increasingly refined and its role as a painter's tool subsequently submitted to that of a subtle mathematical and philosophical instrument.

For Alberti, however, the construction was intended as a veritable cage of terminal points and lines to contain the painted figures, not as a restraining enclosure but on the contrary as an aid to their distribution, appropriate for the role they are supposed to play. Thus, to the painter, they functioned more like chess pawns, if one may say so, as compared to the flat, doll-like figures in medieval painting, these being rather more symbolical than representational in the way they act.

In the later treatises on the sister arts, a similar geometric spatiation is seen to be patterned out for the performance of dance and theatre, and even for the new polyphonic interplay of voices and instruments in music the same geometrical order of space is presupposed.[11] As a matter of fact, in his text, Alberti himself makes references to these three arts and especially to that of the theatre. He wants his figures to be virtually the proper actors of the play, not unlike the characters of the Aristotelian drama.

---

[8] The gridded partition of the picture plane was in normal use for the transposition of small-sized sketches to panel or wall. But Alberti, in his treatise, defines it as a veritable veil or net strapped upon a frame to be placed by the painter between him and the object or motive he intended to depict from nature (cf. *De Pictura* . . . , § 31). The same way of using it is seen in A. Dürer, *Unterweysung der Messung mit dem Zirkel und Richtscheyt in linien Ebenen und gantzem Corporen* (Nürnberg, 1525, repr. 1538).

[9] Piero della Francesca, *De prospectiua pingendi*, 2 vols., ed. G. Nicco Fasola (Florence, 1942); Leonardo da Vinci, *Treatise on Painting*, 2 vols., ed. A. Philip McMahon, introduction by L. H. Heydenrich (Princeton, 1956); Dürer, op. cit.

[10] R. Descartes, *Discours de la méthode* (Paris, 1637, repr. 1942).

[11] For the correspondence in the development of art and music cf. *i.a.* R. Wittkower, *Architectural Principles in the Age of Humanism* (London, 1967). It might be noticed, furthermore, that at a later date the foremost designer of festival settings in Jacobean England, Inigo Jones, regarded the masques set up by him as nothing else but Albertian *historiae*: cf. J. Peacock, "Inigo Jones as a Figurative Artist," in *Renaissance Bodies. The Human Figure in English Culture c. 1540–1660*, ed. L. Gent and N. Llewellyn (London, 1990), 154–179.

2. Alberti, the Aristotelian

In treating now what pertains to *compositio*, as he says, comprising paragraphs 35–45, Alberti lets himself be guided by Aristotle in what concerns the movements of the figures as well as their dramatic interrelation.[12] In composing his picture, Alberti argues, the painter has to follow the same order of sequence as when one is writing a text combining syllables into words, words into sentences, and these into meanings. Likewise, in pictorial composition, one must proceed from the interrelation of the surfaces outlined to that of the members, built up as they are from surfaces, and further to the modeling of the bodies and insertion of the figures into the *historia*. The composition or formal constitution of the picture is, in other words, the vehicle of the meaning embodied in the *historia*, the latter being understood by Alberti as a selected moment of dramatic or otherwise significant action, chosen by the painter as his genuine invention, from the stock of subject-matter to be found in biblical, mythological, historical, or literary accounts (Fig. 4). It was for such a purpose that Alberti would have the painter form his figures as individual characters in the Aristotelian manner, capable of expressing various moods and dispositions of mind, instead of merely symbolizing them.

But just as man, as stated by Aristotle, has only the physical movements of the body and its members through which to express such feelings, so the painter has no other way of depicting them either. Here, the author takes the opportunity to stress the difference between the living body, self-sustained and moving by itself as well as disposed to be affected by feelings, and the dead one, although an equal genius is required to represent the lifelessness of the latter. This is perhaps not only a characterization of the painter's skill but also an allusion to his interest in anatomical studies.

Alberti at first instructs his painter how to proportion the members correctly to each other. Proportioning, to be true, plays a major part also in the Albertian rationalization of pictorial space through the perspective construction, and may thus be seen as a means of bringing about the same rationality in the figure, making its members commensurable and hence mutually corresponding in size, as he points out.[13]

In his choice of the head as the member module, however, he is again in opposition to Vitruvius, who uses the length of the foot, which has since the beginning of time been a suitable architect's measurement. Alberti, for his part, prefers the head, not for practical reasons but because of its dignity. Similarly, the proportioning of the body as a whole was, to him, an aesthetic device to make it fit into the overall geometric pattern of the composition, fully as much as a functional one.

Alberti's partition of the body of his figure into its members and these again into an orderly and clear-cut pattern of sharply defined surfaces is quite in line with the incipient interest in anatomical dissection as a means of exploring the microcosm of

---

[12] For the inspiration Alberti received from Aristotle, see, for example, Grayson, *Alberti*. It should be noted, however, that Alberti's knowledge of the *Poetics* is derived indirectly *via* Horace.

[13] Cf. also R. Wittkower, "Brunelleschi and 'Proportion in Perspective,'" in *Journal of the Warburg and Courtauld Institutes*, 16 (1953), 275–291.

man by imposing upon the human body a cartographic code.[14] As is witnessed through both his drawn and written work, Leonardo da Vinci went far beyond Alberti in this matter.[15] And again in his graphical display of the inner organs of the opened-up body, their functional fitness is uncompromisingly subordinated to the perfection of geometry (Fig. 5).

Like the Albertian figure, the dead body to be anatomized was cut up into sections, too, but only to be rearranged according to a new system of order, as self-contained scientific objects of observation. Before that, however, the body had to be inscribed into another kind of order, that of geometry, by fixing it through nails and cords into a coordinate system of points and lines, arranged similarly to the Albertian grids, either upon the horizontal table of dissection or on the vertical plane of the wall, in front of which the corpse was hung up.[16]

Next in Alberti's explanation of composition follows his advice to the painter, when composing his figure, not only to render its outward appearance such as he sees it but also to build up the body from inside starting with the bones and the skeleton, and then clothing it successively with muscles, sinews, flesh, and skin: in the same way as when painting a draped figure it is necessary to commence with the nude.

Here, one is inevitably reminded of later academy practice of drawing after the live model. But there is even more resemblance between Alberti's way of forming the nude figure from inside outwards by dressing up its bones and the undressing process of dissection.

As his third item Alberti takes up the body in its actual functioning. In this respect he draws directly on the Aristotelian enumeration of seven kinds of movement possible when dislocating the body from one place to another.

It is worth noticing that in his description of how the body reacts when at rest or in activity, its tendency to balance itself symmetrically around its vertical axis is repeatedly stressed, and the figure is constantly compared to a mechanical weight-pulling system. Thus the body, when standing upright, is likened to a column with its foot, shaft, and capital, whereas the carrying of a burden turns it into a pair of balances (Fig. 6). In a similar manner, in the studio halls of the art academies, the living model was to be posed upon the turnable podium before the acutely watching eyes of the student-painters.

It may be more surprising, perhaps, to see the Albertian devices for the poses and movements of the painted figure reappear, together with his coordinate system of perspective, in the educational precepts for exercising the body in military training,

---

[14] Cf. L. Bargan, *Nature's Work of Art: The Human Body as Image of the World* (New Haven/London, 1975); K. G. Roberts and J. D. W. Tomlinson, *The Fabric of the Body: European Traditions of Anatomical Illustration* (Oxford, 1992); and J. Sawday, "The Fate of Marsyas: Dissecting the Renaissance Body," in *Renaissance Bodies,* (above n. 11), 111–135.

[15] Cf. G. Favo, "Anatomie und Physiologie," and C. F. Biaggi, "Anatomie und Kunst," both in *Leonardo da Vinci. Das Lebensbild eines Genies* (Wiesbaden, 1955), as well as D. L. Hodges, *Renaissance Fictions of Anatomy* (Amherst, 1985).

[16] For the placing of the body to be dissected, see also T. Weimarck, *Nya borddansen. En essä om det bildskapande bordet* (Stockholm/Stehag, 1992).

horse-riding, or fencing.[17] With particular emphasis they stressed uprightness in posture as a token of nobility and the aptitude to balance oneself appropriately in relation to the opposed axes of a vertical element, on the one hand, and the horizon, on the other.

His sexual differentiation of movements in his figures, although it had its parallels in contemporary treatises on conduct, was also to await its perfection till the instruction books on the artful dances of the sixteenth century.[18]

Furthermore, as a foreshadowing of the kinship, perhaps even compatibility, concerning the artistic and anatomical preoccupation with the human body that would become institutionalized in time, the pose with which Alberti finishes his description is revealing. Here the stretch is noted that pervades the total figure, from heel to fingertip, when depicted standing on tiptoe and reaching its arm as high up in the air as possible. In exactly that way the executed criminals to be dissected in the anatomical theatres might also be suspended, not rarely, by one arm, next to miming the forceful and, as the author says, gay-looking upwards movement of the Albertian figure.

So far Alberti on the composition of his *historia* as a rationally thought-out representation of figures in action inserted in a coherent spatial setting of geometric perspective (Fig. 7).

3. The Academies' Learnings from Alberti

Now right from the founding of the French academy,[19] the lessons taught by Alberti were at work as a guiding line, though not, however, as taken directly from his treatise, but transmitted by numerous followers and imitators. So, the academic theory embodied in the *Remarques sur la peinture* by Nicholas Poussin, on the movements of the human body in action,[20] as well as the guiding drawings by Charles le Brun for the depiction of facial expressions of various states of mind,[21] bear the Albertian stamp. Likewise, in Roger de Piles's Cartesian evaluation of the artists in his "balance des peintres,"[22] it was their qualifications in the Albertian categories of design, perspective, composition, expression, and so on, which were weighed.

As a matter of fact, up to the reforms of the academies in the previous century, the subjects on the teaching schedule remained essentially the same as those that constitute the humanistic *historia* as defined by Alberti: the rules of perspective, the drawing of the human body after antique statues as well as after the living model posing in attitudes not unlike those described by Alberti himself, and above all the acqui-

---

[17] For treatises on horse-riding and fencing, see, for example, Salvatore Fabris, *De lo schermo overo scienza d'arme* (Copenhagen, 1606).

[18] Cf. S. Fermor, "Movement and Gender in Sixteenth Century Italian Painting," in *The Body Imaged*, op. cit. (above n. 4), 129–145.

[19] Cf. Pevsner, op. cit. (above n. 5).

[20] Nicolas Poussin, *Lettres et propos sur l'art. Textes réunis et présentés par A. Blunt*, ed. A. Blunt (Paris, 1964).

[21] Charles le Brun, *A Method to Learn to Design the Passions* (1734, repr. Los Angeles, 1980).

[22] R. de Piles, *Balance des Peintres* (1709).

sition of an intimate knowledge of what was, most significantly, designated "the painter's anatomy." In this way, young art students were thought to be equipped to cope with the great royal commissions of historical compositions, the topic soon to become the highest ranking in the academic hierarchy of genres.[23]

What Alberti had intended in his *De Pictura* was not, we may suspect, to turn painting into a courtly art but to make it a humanistic discipline. And he did so less by the scholarly rhetorical dressing up of his style than by forming a new concept of painting as a rational exercise, based on the exact sciences of geometricised space and the anatomical body. His was the concept of the new world as organized by conscious man in definite space. Owing to this, he became one of the pioneers not only of Renaissance art theory but also of the rationality instrumental to the arts and sciences of the Enlightenment.

Aarhus University

---

[23] On the academies, see *Academies of Art between Renaissance and Romanticism, Leids Kunsthistorisch Jaarboek V–VI, 1986–1987* (Gravenhage, 1989).

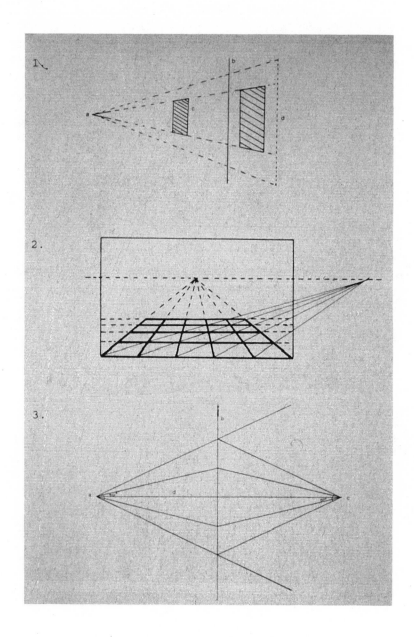

Top: Reconstruction, based on Vitruvius, of the rendering of depth
in ancient art according to the optics of Euclid.
Middle and bottom: Schematic indication of the way in which the Albertian
picture plane is seen, as an intersection of the pyramid of vision as well as
the basis of the reciprocal pyramid of perspective enclosing the pictorial space.

6. *Sandro Botticelli: altertavle, 1490-91, Firenze, Uffizierne.*

Sandro Botticelli, *The Annunciation of the Virgin Mary,*
in which the religious topic is turned into an Albertian *historia,* the
representation of a dramatic moment of action.
About 1472, Florence, The Uffizi. Courtesy Alinari/Art Resources, New York.

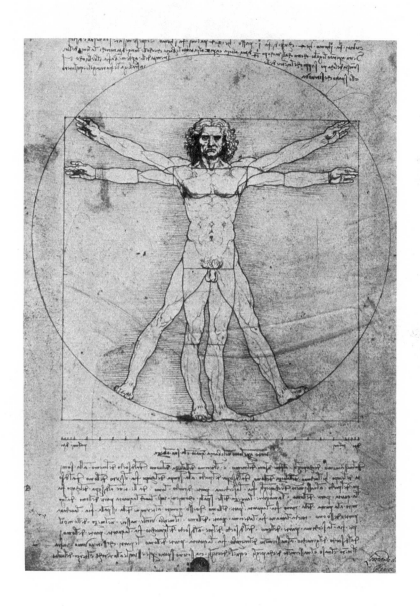

Leonardo da Vinci, *The Vitruvian Man.* c.1490, Venezia, Accademia.
Courtesy Alinari/Art Resources, New York.

Andrea Mantegna, *The Martyrdom of St. Sebastian*, the Albertian
figure-column. 1480. Courtesy Alinari/Art Resources, New York.

Sandro Botticelli, *Primavera*, a Neo-Platonic theme depicted as a composition in the Albertian sense with figures posed and grouped to display the human bodies in a variety of movements and interactions. About 1475, Florence, The Uffizi. Courtesy Alinari/Art Resources, New York.

Sofocle nel Rinascimento europeo:
Una fortuna troppo sconosciuta

ELIA BORZA

Il Cinquecento fu senz'altro il secolo durante il quale gli umanisti riscoprirono largamente Sofocle, per merito incontestabile dell'invenzione della stampa. Questa opinione, però, non è condivisa dagli studiosi del nostro secolo, secondo cui Sofocle conobbe pochissime edizioni e traduzioni durante il Cinquecento.[1] Le cifre più ottimistiche sono quelle di Randolph Hirsch, che nel 1964 ha contato 48 edizioni e traduzioni.[2]

Dal 1502, quando fu pubblicata da Aldo Manuzio la *princeps* delle sette tragedie di Sofocle, fino al 1600, quando fu stampato per la quarta volta l'*Aiace* latino di Giuseppe Scaligero, ci risultano invece non meno di 89 edizioni, traduzioni e commenti di Sofocle.[3] Una bella differenza rispetto alle stime dell'Hirsch! Se poi ci si spinge fino al 1621, il numero sale a 102. Dopo il 1600 si ebbero anche alcune ristampe di opere uscite nel corso del Cinquecento (per esempio l'*Aiace* latino dello Scaligero) e furono pubblicate per la prima volta traduzioni di autori che avevano già compiuto una traduzione prima del 1600 (per esempio Girolamo Giustiniano tradusse l'*Edipo Re* nel 1590, poi l'*Aiace* nel 1603 e l'*Edipo a Colono* nel 1610).

Dopo le "statistiche," che non sono il nostro scopo primario, poniamoci ora

---

[1] Si veda, per esempio: René Sturel, "Essai sur les traductions du théâtre grec en français avant 1550," *Revue d'Histoire Littéraire de la France* 20 (1913): 269; Marie Delcourt, *Essai sur les traductions des tragiques grecs et latins en France depuis la Renaissance* (Bruxelles, 1925), 4; J. T. Sheppard, *Aeschylus and Sophocles* (New York, 1927), 107–109; Raymond Lebègue, *La tragédie religieuse en France* (Paris, 1929), 465; R. C. Knight, *Racine et la Grèce* (Paris, 1950), 54.

[2] Randolph Hirsch, "The Printing Tradition of Aeschylus, Euripides, Sophocles and Aristophanes," *Gutenberg-Jahrbuch* (1964), 138–146.

[3] Nei dettagli: in Francia si ebbero 31 edizioni; in Italia 27, in Germania 21; negli antichi Paesi Bassi (Belgio e Olanda) 10, di cui 7 ad Anversa. Le edizioni del testo greco (completo o non) furono 28, più 11 accompagnate dalla traduzione latina. Si contano inoltre 34 traduzioni latine delle sette tragedie (34 + 11 = 45 traduzioni latine). Le traduzioni italiane furono ben 16; quelle francesi appena 3.

questa domanda: chi furono gli studiosi di Sofocle? Il suo primo editore o stampatore fu Aldo Manuzio: l'edizione principe di Sofocle uscì a Venezia nell'agosto del 1502.[4] Non si conosce con esattezza il suo curatore, ma pensiamo, come Deno John Geanakoplos nel suo *Greek Scholars in Venice*,[5] che Marco Musuro ebbe un ruolo importante nella sua realizzazione.

Nel 1518 Giano Lascaris pubblicò gli scoli antichi tratti dal codice *Laurenziano* del secolo X.[6] Amico e collaboratore di Aldo Manuzio sin dai primi anni del Cinquecento, il Lascaris partecipò al Collegio Greco di Roma fondato dal papa umanista Leone X. Lorenzo il Magnifico lo aveva inviato in Grecia alla ricerca di manoscritti per la sua biblioteca.

All'incirca quindici anni dopo, nel 1534, uscì l'edizione con il commento latino di Joachim Camerarius.[7] Nel 1567 la sua traduzione latina dell'*Aiace* venne pubblicata da Henri Estienne.[8]

Anche Pier Vettori studiò le tragedie di Sofocle: nel 1547, a Firenze, usciva per la sua cura la seconda edizione giuntina delle tragedie e degli scoli antichi di Sofocle (la prima, del '22, a cura di Antonio Francino il Vecchio, era una pessima copia dell'aldina). Nel 1553, a Parigi, Adrien Turnèbe pubblicò per la prima volta gli scoli di Demetrio Triclinio.

La prima traduzione latina delle sette tragedie di Sofocle fu quella di Giovanni Gabia Veronese, stampata a Venezia nel 1543 da Giovanni Battista di Borgofranco. Prima, però, c'erano state traduzioni di singole tragedie, come, ad esempio, nel 1533, quella di Jean Lonicer (*Aiace*),[9] e nel 1541 quella di Gentien Hervet (*Antigone*).[10] Nel 1549 Veit Winsheim pubblicò un'altra versione completa di Sofocle,[11] che conobbe un rilevante successo: fu riedita infatti tre volte: nel 1551, nel 1597 e nel 1603 (le sole *Trachinie* furono ristampate a Strasburgo nel 1584).[12] Non dobbiamo dimenticare la traduzione dell'*Elettra* di Coriolano Martirano, uscita nel 1556 a Napoli presso il Simonetta, con alcune tragedie di Eschilo e di Euripide.[13] L'ultima traduzione latina del XVI secolo fu quella dell'*Aiace* ad opera di Giuseppe Scaligero: edita per la prima volta a Parigi (J. Bienné) nel 1573, fu ristampata ben otto volte (1587, 1591, 1600, 1608, 1609, 1610, 1615 e 1621).

---

[4] *Sophoclis tragoediae septem cum commentariis*, Venetiis, in aedibus Aldi, 1502.

[5] Deno John Geanakoplos, *Greek Scholars in Venice. Studies in the Dissemination of Greek Learning from Byzantium to Western Europe* (Cambridge, Mass., 1962), 120–121, 131.

[6] *Commentarii in septem tragoedias* (Roma, 1518).

[7] Hagenau, ex officina Seceriana, 1534.

[8] *Tragoediae selectae Aeschylii, Sophoclis, Euripidis* (Genève: Henri Estienne, 1567). Per Sofocle, abbiamo: la traduzione in versi dell'*Aiace*, dell'*Elettra* e dell'*Antigone* (George Rataller); la traduzione in prosa dell'*Aiace* (Joachim Camerarius), dell'*Antigone* e dell'*Elettra* (François Portus).

[9] Bâle: Herwagen, 1533.

[10] Lyon: Etienne Dolet, 1541.

[11] Frankfurt: Pierre Brubach, 1549.

[12] *Sophoclis Trachiniae*, ed. Veit Winsheim (Strasbourg: Anton Bertram, 1584). Secondo Randolph Hirsch (146), in questa edizione ci sarebbe anche una traduzione tedesca.

[13] Il volume fu ristampato nel 1563.

La prima "traduzione" in una lingua volgare fu spagnola: la *Vengança de Agamenon* di Hernan Perez de Oliva, uscita a Burgos nel 1531.[14] Ma si tratta piuttosto di un adattamento delle *Coefore* di Eschilo e dell'*Elettra* di Sofocle che di una vera e propria traduzione; un esempio, se mai, della fortuna europea del tragico greco, che già aveva ispirato la *Sofonisba* del Trissino (1524)[15] e la *Rosmunda* del Rucellai (1525).[16]

In effetti, la prima traduzione volgare delle tragedie di Sofocle deve considerarsi quella italiana dell'*Antigone* curata dal fiorentino Luigi Alamanni che meritò tra il 1532 e il 1533 due edizioni, una a Lione e l'altra a Venezia (fu ristampata anche nel '42).[17] Nel 1537 vide la luce la prima traduzione francese, quella dell'*Elettra* curata da Lazare de Baïf, anch'egli membro del Collegio Greco di Leone X, e quindi legato all'Italia.[18] Al 1565 risale la prima traduzione italiana dell'*Edipo Re*, opera di Giovanni Andrea Dell'Anguillara.[19] Nel 1573 fu la volta dell'*Antigone* nella traduzione francese del figlio di Lazare de Baïf, Jean-Antoine.[20] Quindi, nel 1585, Orsatto Giustiniani tradusse in italiano l'*Edipo Re*, che fu poi rappresentato nel Teatro Olimpico di Vicenza nella serata inaugurale.[21] Tre anni dopo (1588), e sempre in italiano, fu pubblicata la traduzione dell'*Elettra* di Erasmo Degli Signori di Valvasone;[22] nel 1589, quella dell'*Edipo Re* di Pietro Angelio Bargeo;[23] quindi quelle di Girolamo Giustiniano, dell'*Edipo Re* nel 1590 (e nel 1610), dell'*Aiace* nel 1603 e dell'*Edipo a Colono* nel 1611.[24]

Quanto ai tipografi, la fortuna editoriale di Sofocle nel Cinquecento è legata in Italia ai nomi dei Manuzio e dei Giunta. Importante la ristampa nel 1547 della giuntina del '22 sottoposta al "lifting" del noto filologo Pier Vettori.

In Francia fu Henri Estienne a pubblicare molte edizioni, traduzioni e commenti di Sofocle. Suo è invece il commento pubblicato nel 1568 e ristampato nel 1603.[25]

---

[14] *La vengança de Agamenon. Tragedia que hizo Hernan Perez de Oliva, maestro, cuyo argomento es de Sophocles Poeta griego* (Burgos: Juan de Junta, 1531).

[15] "Composta probabilmente a Roma nel 1514–1515, presentata a Leone X nel 1518 e subito divulgata manoscritta, pubblicata infine a Roma nel luglio 1524 ed ancora ristampata nel settembre" (Renzo Cremante, "Nota introduttiva," in *Teatro del Cinquecento*, in *La letteratura italiana. Storia e testi*, vol.28/1 [Milano–Napoli, 1988], 3).

[16] "L'*editio princeps* della *Rosmunda* fu pubblicata a Siena il 27 aprile 1525, a poche settimane soltanto di distanza dalla morte dell'autore" (Cremante, 177). Ma "è verosimile che la *Rosmunda* fosse già compiuta agli inizi del 1516 (mentre nessuna testimonianza certa sembra avvalorare l'ipotesi di una rappresentazione)": Cremante, 165.

[17] Luigi Alamanni, *Opere Toscane* (Lyon: Sébastien Gryphe, 1533; Venezia: Pietro Nicolini da Sabio, 1533).

[18] *Electre de Sophocle* (Paris: Roffet, 1537).

[19] Venezia: Domenico Farri, 1565.

[20] Il volume non ha luogo di stampa.

[21] Venezia: Francesco Ziletti, 1585.

[22] Venezia: I Guerra fratelli, 1588.

[23] Firenze: Bartolomeo Sermartelli, 1589.

[24] *Edipo il Re* (Venezia: Sebastiano Combi, 1590); *Aiace* (Venezia: Lucio Spineda, 1603); *Edipo Re* (Venezia: Sebastiano Combi, 1610); *Edipo a Colono* (Venezia: Antonio Pinelli, 1611).

[25] *Henrici Stephani annotationes in Sophoclem et Euripidem quibus variae lectiones examinantur et pro*

Nei Paesi Bassi fu Christophe Plantin a stampare nel '79 l'edizione sofoclea di Guillaume Canter.[26] Il suo successore Rapheleng pubblicò inoltre un'edizione greca integrale nel 1593[27] e la traduzione latina dell'*Aiace* dello Scaligero nel 1615. In Svizzera, infine, lo stampatore di Sofocle fu Jean Oporin di Basilea.[28]

Passiamo ora al materiale manoscritto quattro e cinquecentesco, senza entrare nel lunghissimo discorso dei codici greci che riportano il testo delle tragedie di Sofocle.

I 47 codici da me individuati si possono classificare in tre categorie: alla prima appartengono i manoscritti che possiamo definire le "brutte copie" di edizioni stampate nel XVI secolo; alla seconda i codici inediti, o pubblicati dopo il XVI secolo (la maggior parte nel secolo scorso); alla terza categoria i commenti sofoclei del Quattro e del Cinquecento.

Nel primo gruppo (le cosidette "brutte copie") troviamo i nomi di Luigi Alamanni (*Antigone*),[29] Pietro Angelio Bargeo (*Edipo Re*),[30] Lazare e Jean-Antoine de Baïf (*Elettra* e *Antigone*),[31] e Florent Chrestien (*Filottete* greco-latino del 1586).[32]

Nella seconda categoria abbiamo traduzioni in latino, in italiano e in francese. Le traduzioni latine sono opera di Giovanni Manadori (*Edipo a Colono* autografo datato a 1594),[33] Filippo Melantone (*Versio Sophoclis*),[34] Alessandro Pazzi de' Medici (*Elettra* e *Edipo Re*),[35] Alessandro Sardi (*Aiace* e *Elettra*)[36] e di altri. C'è anche un manoscritto della Bibliothèque Nationale di Parigi, che contiene due traduzioni latine autografe (*Aiace* e *Elettra*) di Adrien Turnèbe.[37] Entrambe sono datate, l'*Aiace* 1551, l'*Elettra* 1556. Non dimentichiamoci poi di Marco Musuro e dei suoi corsi sofoclei: nel 1508 tradusse l'*Elettra* e possediamo tuttora gli appunti di un suo allievo, Jean Cuno.[38] La traduzione latina dell'*Aiace* conservata nel *Marciano latino* XIV.54, attribuita

---

mordosis emendatae substituuntur. Eiusdem tractatus de orthographia quorundam vocabulorum Sophocli cum caeteris tragicis communium. Eiusdem dissertatio de sophoclea imitatione Homeri (Genève: Henri Estienne, 1568); Sophoclis tragoediae VII. Graece edidit cum scholiis graecis et latina interpretatione (Paris: Paul Estienne, 1603).

[26] Antwerpen: Christophe Plantin, 1579.

[27] *Sophoclis tragoediae septem*, ed. Guillaume Canter (Leiden, 1593).

[28] *Commentatio explicationum omnium tragoediarum Sophoclis*, ed. Joachim Camerarius (Bâle: Jean Oporin, 1556); *Sophoclis tragoediae VII. Latine*, ed. Thomas Naogeorgos [Kirchmeyer] (Bâle: Jean Oporin, 1558).

[29] Firenze, Bibl. Nazionale Centrale, *Magliabechianus* II. VIII. 27; Firenze, Bibl. Laurenziana, *Antinori* 161 (214).

[30] Firenze, Bibl. Naz. Centrale, II. I. 154.

[31] Venezia, Bibl. Marciana, *Marciano Fr.* Z.24 (=235); Paris, Bibliothèque Nationale (non ancora identificato).

[32] Hamburg, Staats- und Universitätsbibliothek, *Cod. Philol.* 17.

[33] Firenze, Bibl. Naz. Centrale, *Magliab.* VII. 859.

[34] Zwickau, Ratsschulbibliothek, QQ 38, 1–11.

[35] Ravenna, Bibl. Classense, 372 (con correzioni autografe); Firenze, Bibl. Naz. Centrale, II. IV. 8 (*Magliab.* VII. 950 bis).

[36] Modena, Bibl. Estense, *Ital.* 219 (α.W.6.3).

[37] Paris, Bibliothèque Nationale, *Lat.* 13042.

[38] Marburg, Staatsbibliothek, *Lat. oct.* 374.

al grammatico padovano Pietro da Montagnana, potrebbe essere invece del professore di greco del Petrarca, Leonzio Pilato (ma questa bellissima ipotesi è ancora da accertare).[39] La traduzione è sopravvissuta anche in un codice modenese che contiene le opere di Pietro Angelio Bargeo.[40]

I traduttori francesi che ritroviamo nella seconda categoria sono due: Calvy de la Fontaine, autore della primissima traduzione francese in versi dell'*Antigone* (1542);[41] e Nicolas de Herberay des Essarts, traduttore di numerose opere spagnole, tra le quali l'*Agamennone* di Hernan Perez de Oliva.[42] I traduttori italiani sono tre: Alberto Parma (*Antigone* e *Elettra*),[43] Alessandro Pazzi de' Medici (*Edipo Re*)[44] e Bernardo Segni (*Edipo Re* del 1551).[45]

La terza categoria, quella dei commenti, contiene altri nomi illustri. Ad esempio, quello di Giovanni Tortelli, autore di un commento lessicale, conservato a Basilea, all'*Aiace* e all'*Elettra*.[46] Appunti di un altro allievo del Musuro, purtroppo anonimo, relativi a tutte le tragedie, si conservano nel codice *Vaticano latino* 11483.

Per concludere, i primi editori e traduttori di Sofocle furono, tra Quattro e Cinquecento, italiani e greci: il Musuro, il Lascaris, Aldo Manuzio, il Vettori. Seguono poi i francesi (Lazare de Baïf, Simon de Colines[47]), i tedeschi (Lonicer, Camerarius) e gli spagnoli (Hernan Perez de Oliva), che devono comunque la loro cultura, la loro perizia in greco (e in latino) a qualche umanista greco o italiano.[48] Lo stesso Aldo Manuzio doveva la sua conoscenza del greco a Guarino Veronese, che imparò a sua volta il greco da Manuele Crisolora. Guarino ebbe anche come alunno Demetrio Calcondila,[49] che lavorò poi insieme ad Aldo. Anche Giano Lascaris, alunno del Calcondila e maestro di Marco Musuro, fu in contatto con Aldo. Il Musuro fu il maestro di Lazare de Baïf e fu in contatto anche con il grande Erasmo da Rotterdam e con papa Leone X. Lo stesso Lascaris fu il maestro di Frosino Bonini. E Frosino Bonini insegnò il greco a Luigi Alamanni, il quale, insieme ad altri suoi illustri "coetanei" (Giovanni Rucellai, Alessandro Pazzi de' Medici, Pier Vettori, Donato

---

[39] Cf. Antonietta Porro, "La versione latina dell'*Ecuba* euripidea attribuita a Pietro da Montagnana," in *Dotti bizantini e libri greci nell'Italia del secolo XV. Atti del Convegno internazionale. Trento 22–23 ottobre 1990*, eds. Mariarosa Cortesi e Enrico V. Maltese (Napoli, 1992), 343–361.

[40] Modena, Bibl. Estense, *Lat.* 1077 (α.J.5.16).

[41] Soissons, Bibliothèque Communale, MS. 189 B.

[42] Berlin, Deutsche Staatsbibliothek, *Philipps* 1938.

[43] Bibl. Apostolica Vaticana, *Barber. lat.* 3734 e 3735.

[44] Firenze, Bibl. Naz. Centrale, II. IV. 7 (*Magliab. VII. 972*); Bibl. Apostolica Vaticana, *Barber. lat.* 4002.

[45] Firenze, Bibl. Naz. Centrale, II. I. 98 (autografo); *Magliab. VII. 317*.

[46] Bâle, Universitätsbibliothek, F VIII 3, fols. 278r–309v. Cf. Mariarosa Cortesi, "Il 'Vocabularium' greco di Giovanni Tortelli," *Italia Medioevale e Umanistica* 22 (1979): 449–483.

[47] Edizione greca completa edita a Parigi nel 1528.

[48] La nostra fonte principale, anche se dobbiamo ammettere che vi sono degli errori, è stato: Mario Emilio Cosenza, *Biographical and Bibliographical Dictionary of the Italian Humanists and of the World of Classical Scholarship in Italy, 1300–1800*, 6 vols. (Boston, 1962–1967).

[49] Il Calcondila fu anche il maestro di Gian Giorgio Trissino, di Leone X e di Niccolò Leonico Tomeo.

Giannotti), fu discepolo anche di Francesco Cattani da Diacceto il Vecchio, che aveva a sua volta avuto come maestro Oliviero Arduini, alunno di Marsilio Ficino. E il Ficino era stato maestro anche del Diacceto.

Alla luce dei 150 titoli circa, tra manoscritti e stampe, da noi individuati, la fortuna di Sofocle nel Rinascimento europeo va completamente ridisegnata. Si è avuta comunque la prova della preferenza che la cultura umanistica (al contrario di Aristofane nelle *Rane*,[50] che fa di Eschilo il primo dei tragici e di Sofocle il suo supplente) accordò a Sofocle rispetto a Eschilo, poeta dal linguaggio troppo oscuro e dal testo troppo trasandato, che contò nel corso del Cinquecento soltanto 21 stampe.[51]

Come appendice al nostro discorso vorrei avanzare alcune ipotesi che ci sono state suggerite nel corso del dibattito seguito alla lettura della nostra comunicazione e che sono ancora tutte da verificare.[52] Ad esempio, quanto influì la riscoperta della *Poetica* di Aristotele sulla fortuna di Sofocle? Non fu certo un caso che la serata inaugurale del Teatro Olimpico di Vicenza, nel 1585, proponesse l'*Edipo Re*, qualificata da Aristotele come la tragedia per eccellenza. Non è neanche un caso che uno dei maggiori studiosi di Aristotele del Cinquecento fosse proprio il Vettori. Si dovrebbe poi indagare sulle tragedie italiane del XVI secolo, come la *Sofonisba* del Trissino, l'*Orbecche* del Giraldi, o ancora la *Tullia* di Lodovico Martelli e la *Rosmunda* di Giovanni Rucellai, tutte ispirate al modello sofocleo. Un'altra domanda che ci dovremmo porre è se ci furono, nel corso del secolo, altre rappresentazioni teatrali delle tragedie sofoclee, oltre che a Vicenza. Infine, se come sembra ci fu un vero e proprio "culto" di Sofocle nel Rinascimento europeo, è arrivato il momento di addurne le prove.

Université Catholique de Louvain,
Louvain-la-Neuve

---

[50] Aristofane, *Le Rane*, 1515–1519.

[51] Cf. Monique Mund-Dopchie, *La survie d'Eschyle à la Renaissance* (Louvain, 1984).

[52] Vorrei ringraziare qui i proff. Michele Cataudella, Lucia Gualdo Rosa e Josef IJsewijn per i loro apprezzati interventi.

Übersetzungen aus den lateinischen Klassikern im italienischen und spanischen Humanismus

LETICIA CARRASCO REIJA

Eines der wichtigsten Charakteristika der Renaissance in Europa war die Rückkehr zu den Texten der Klassischen Antike. Da jedoch nicht jedermann imstande war, die Klassiker in der originalen Sprache zu lesen, fingen die Humanisten an, diese Texte zu übersetzen, um die griechische und römische Kultur zu verbreiten. Der anonyme Autor der ersten spanischen Übersetzung von Äsop erklärt in seinem Vorwort: "por que al su superhabundante discreción y muy begnívola nobleza reciba [la obra] auctoridad y sea distribuida alos vulgares y personas non doctas y letradas, como de muy piadoso padre alos fijos."

Obwohl in der Renaissance die Anzahl der Übersetzungen aus dem Lateinischen ziemlich groß war, schrieben die italienische Humanisten ihre Werke am liebsten lateinisch oder italienisch oder sie übersetzten griechische Werke ins Lateinische. Die italienische Produktion im Bereich der Übersetzungen war in dieser Zeit geringer als in Ländern wie Frankreich, Spanien, England oder Deutschland.[1]

Man kann die italienischen und spanischen Übersetzungen in folgende drei Gruppen einteilen: erstens in direkte, zweitens in indirekte und drittens in gemischte Übersetzungen. Das hier gewählte Kriterium für die Einteilung ist der vom Autor als Vorlage für seine Übersetzung benützte Text. Man könnte denken, daß es sich bei Übersetzungen lateinischer Texte ins Spanische und Italienische immer um Übersetzungen aus dem Lateinischen handelt. Dies ist jedoch nicht immer der Fall.

Die erste Gruppe von Übersetzungen enthält Übersetzungen, deren Übersetzer den gewählten lateinischen Autor in der Ursprache las und übersetzte. Das heißt, die Übersetzung ist Lateinisch-Spanisch oder Lateinisch-Italienisch. Der Übersetzer wählte jedoch auch oft als Vorlage für seine Übersetzung einen bereits in eine andere

---

[1] Vgl. G. Highet, *The Classical Tradition: Greek and Roman Influences on Western Literature* (New York, 1949); R. R. Bolgar, *The Classical Heritage and Its Beneficiaries* (Cambridge, 1977); M. E. Cosenza, *Biographical and Bibliographical Dictionary of the Italian Humanist: The World of Classical Scholarship in Italy, 1300–1800* (Boston, 1962).

moderne Sprache übersetzten klassischen Text. Spanische Übersetzer griffen dabei meist zu italienischen oder französischen Übersetzungen. Dieser Fall wird hier als indirekte Übersetzung bezeichnet. Im Fall der gemischten Übersetzungsart schließlich benützt der Übersetzer den originalen lateinischen Text als Vorlage, zieht gelegentlich jedoch auch eine italienische oder französische Übersetzung hinzu.

Die erste Übersetzungsart findet sich öfter in Italien als in Spanien.[2] Man muß darauf hinweisen, daß der italienische Humanismus sich mit der philologischen Aufgabe des Übersetzens bereits seit dem 15. Jahrhundert befaßt hatte. Die italienischen Humanisten, meistens unterstützt durch Mäzene, betrieben mit Eifer die Suche von griechischen und lateinischen Handschriften vor allem in europäischen Klöstern. Diese Handschriften oder Kopien von ihnen wurden in Bibliotheken gesammelt, wo sie für die Philologen leicht zugänglich waren. So war es für die italienische Übersetzer leichter, die klassichen Texte selbst zur Hand zu haben. Aber auch in Spanien wurden direkte Übersetzungen von den lateinischen Urtexten gemacht.

Erstens befanden sich damals viele Spanier in Italien. In den bedeutendsten politischen Städten wie Neapel, Rom, Mailand, Genua, Venedig und Siena hatten sich zahlreiche Spanier niedergelassen, hauptsächlich Militärs. In den ersten Jahrzenten des 16. Jahrhunderts bildeten die Spanier ein Sechstel der römischen Einwohner. Berühmte spanische Humanisten wie Nebrija oder Sepúlveda sind in Italien zur Schule gegangen. Am Hof der Borgias wohnte der Dichter Juan Sobrarias von Alcañiz und in Rom Alonso de Palencia und Juan de Mena. Diese und andere Autoren hatten große Bedeutung für die Verbreitung der italienischen Kultur in Spanien. Zweitens wurden auch italienische Humanisten in hohen spanischen Kreisen aufgenommen. Bevor Lucio Marineo Siculo am Hof der Katholischen Könige ankam, war er schon zwölf Jahre lang Lehrer an der Universidad de Salamanca gewesen. Andere Humanisten wie Pedro Mártir de Anglería oder Alejandro Giraldino haben am Anfang des 16. Jahrhunderts die italienische Kultur in Spanien verbreitet. Daneben waren für die spanischen Übersetzer italienische Drucker, Buchhändler und Händler wichtig. Während des 16. Jahrhunderts ließen sich viele italienische Drucker in Städten wie Barcelona, Zaragoza oder Sevilla nieder. Italienische Buchhändler vertrieben in Spanien in Italien gedruckte Bücher. Solche wurden auch durch Spanier, die sich in Italien aufhielten, erworben. Die spanische Botschaft in Venedig spielte dabei eine wichtige Rolle, speziell der Sekretär des spanischen Botschafters Cristóbal de Salazar. Er hat 400 griechische und lateinische Bücher an den spanischen Hof gesandt.[3]

Spanische Übersetzer verfügten so über italienische Ausgaben und Übersetzungen lateinischer Klassiker. Trotzdem litten die Übersetzer am Anfang des 16. Jahrhunderts

---

[2] Vgl. R. Sabbadini, "Del tradurre i classici antichi in Italia," in *Atene e Roma* 19–20 (luglio–agosto 1900), 201–216; F. Maggini, *I primi volgarizzamenti dei classici latini* (Florencia, 1952); Gianfranco Folena, "Volgarizzare e tradurre: idea e terminologia della traduzione dal medio evo italiano e romanzo all'Umanesimo Europeo," in: *La Traduzione: Saggi e Studi* (Trieste, 1973); C. Dionisotti, "Traduzione classica e volgarizzamenti," in: *Geografia e storia della letteratura italiana* (Turin, 1972), 156–210.

[3] Vgl. O. Arróniz, *La influencia italiana en el nacimiento de la comedia española* (Madrid, 1969), 13–22.

unter einem erheblichen Mangel an Hilfsmitteln. Es gab anonym kompilierte Glossare. Auch stellten manche Übersetzer selbst welche her. Aber das war nicht das einzige Problem: fast alle spanischen Übersetzer entschuldigen sich im Vorwort für ihre möglicherweise fehlerhaften Übersetzungen, da sie der Meinung waren, daß die spanische Sprache nicht so reich wie das Latein war. Aus diesem Grunde sei es für sie oft unmöglich gewesen die Texte richtig zu interpretieren. So erklärt Juan de Encina folgendes im Vorwort zu seiner Übersetzung der Eklogen von Vergil: "Muchas dificultades hallo enla traducción de aquesta obra por el gran defeto de vocablos que ay en la lengua castellana en comparación de la latina, de donde se causa en muchos lugares no poder les dar la propia significación."[4]

Wegen dieser Schwierigkeiten[5] entstanden oft die Übersetzungen, die hier als indirekt bezeichnet worden sind. Unter diesen sind die Übersetzungen aus den griechischen Klassikern Sonderfälle. Sie waren meist zuerst ins Lateinische übersetzt worden, und nachher vom Latein in eine der modernen Sprachen.

Im Folgenden soll ein nach Gattungen geordneter Überblick über die Renaissanceübersetzungen der wichtigsten Werke der lateinischen Literatur ins Italienische und Spanische im Zeitalter der Renaissance gegeben werden.[6]

1. Epik

Im Laufe des 15. Jahrhunderts erscheinen die ersten Paraphrasen in Prosa, wie die Übersetzung der Aeneis von Enrique de Villena. In der ersten Hälfte des 16. Jahrhunderts finden wir bereits Versionen von italienischen Autoren in Gedichtform, wie die von Cambiatore von 1532 oder die von Ludovico Dolce von 1560. Im Laufe dieser Jahre gibt es auch viele Teilübersetzungen. So übersetzte Hippolito de'Medici das zweite Buch 1539, Piccolomini das vierte Buch 1540. Letzteres ist das am häufigsten übersetzte Buch in Italien. In Spanien erscheint 1555 eine Übersetzung von Hernández de Velasco, in der die Gespräche in Ottaverime und die Erzählung in freien Versen übersetzt sind. Diese Übersetzung stand sehr lange Zeit in gutem Ruf. 1581 kommt eine der berühmtesten Übersetzungen der Aeneis heraus, und zwar die Version von Annibale Caro, bei der der gekünstelte Stil des Übersetzers besonders erwähnenswert ist. In Spanien erscheint am Ende des Jahrhunderts eine Prosaüber-

---

[4] Vgl. Juan del Encina, *Cancionero de todas las obras*, ed. Emilio Cotarelo y Mori (Madrid, 1928), 30.

[5] Über die Schwierigkeiten beim Übersetzen vom Lateinischen ins Spanische vgl. Théodore S. Beardsley, "La traduction des auteurs classiques," in: *L'Humanisme dans les lettres espagnoles*, XIX Colloque International d'Etudes Humanistes (Tours, 1976), 51–64, und P. Russel, *Traducción y traductores en la Península Ibérica, 1400–1550* (Bellaterra, 1985).

[6] Vgl. zu den spanischen Übersetzungen insgesammt Théodore S. Beardsley, Hispano-Classical Translations Printed between 1482 and 1699 (Pittsburgh, 1970); M. Rodríguez Pantoja, "Traducciones y Traductores," in: *Los Humanistas Españoles y el Humanismo Europeo. IV Simposio de Filología Clásica* (Murcia, 1990), 91–124; P. O. Kristeller and F. E. Cranz (eds.) *Catalogus Translationum et Commentariorum. Medieval and Renaissance Latin Translations and Commentaries. Annotated Lists and Guides* (Washington, 1960ff.); M. Menéndez Pelayo, *Bibliografía Hispano-Latina Clásica* (Santander, 1951); J. A. Pellicer y Safocarda, *Ensayo de una Biblioteca de Traductores Españoles* (Madrid, 1778).

setzung der Aeneis von Diego López, die später von Autoren wie Antonio de Ayala oder Fray Antonio de Moya benützt wurde. Auf Übersetzungen der Metamorphosen von Ovid wird später noch eingegangen werden.

2. Historiographie

Historiographische Werke wurden von den spanischen Humanisten oft übersetzt. Die älteste gedruckte spanische Version der *Commentarii* Caesars ist die von Diego López de Toledo von 1498. Er war Sekretär der Katholischen Könige. Später, 1566, erschien in Spanien eine Aphorismensammlung, die prinzipiell aus den *Commentarii* stammte. Die wichtigsten Übersetzongen in Italien waren die von Urtica della Porta Genovese von 1512, die von Popoleschi von 1518 und die von Baidelli von 1557.

In der Mitte des 15. Jahrhunderts übersetzte Vasco de Guzmán Sallust ins Spanische, und zwar auf Wunsch seines Vetters Fernán Pérez de Guzmán, und vor der Jahrhundertwende erschien eine neue Übersetzung von Francisco Vidal de Noya (1493). Im Laufe des 16. Jahrhunderts haben Ortica della Porta Genovese (1518), Lalio Carani (1550) und P. Spinola (1564) Sallust übersetzt.

Livius wurde schon früh übersetzt. Man sagt, daß Boccaccio eine italienische Version von den Büchern erstellte, die damals bekannt waren. Später ist Livius in Italien von Luca Bonacorsi (1472), Ruggiero Ferrari (1476) und Nardi (1540) übersetzt worden. López de Ayala, Grosskanzler von Kastilien, übersetzte ihn ins Spanische mit Hilfe einer französischen Übersetzung von Bersuire. Er benützte aber auch den lateinischen Text. 1520 veröffentlichte Pedro de la Vega "La primera, tercera y quarta [décadas] enteras según en latín se hallan y las otras onze según la abreviación de Lucio Floro"; 1550 erschien die Livius-Übersetzung von Francisco de Enzinas.

Die spanischen Humanisten interessierten sich für Tacitus erst am Ende des 16. Jahrhunderts. Angeblich hat Pedro Simón Abril das Werk des Tacitus ins Spanische übersetzt, aber diese Übersetzung wurde nie gedruckt. Die erste bekannte Übersetzung ins Italienische ist die Übersetzung des *Agricola* von G. M. Manelli (1585). Die erste spanische Tacitus-Übersetzung ist die von Baltasar Alamos y Barrientos (1614). In Italien übersetzte Politi das ganze Werk ins Italienische (1616).

3. Philosophie

Die Dialoge von Cicero waren in Spanien und in Italien sehr berühmt vor allem *De amicitia* und *De senectute*. Die Übersetzung von *De amacitia*, die sich in der Bibliothek des Marquis von Santillana befand, und die spanische Übersetzung von *De senectute* durch Alfonso de Cartagena wurden gegen Mitte des 15. Jahrhunderts erstellt. Die erste italienische Übersetzung aus Cicero ist die von Galeoto da Bologna (1472). Unter den zahlreichen Übersetzungen ins Italienische ist vor allem die Übersetzung von Ludovico Dolce (1547) zu nennen. Alfonso de Cartagena, der an der römischen Philosophie sehr interessiert war, übersetzte auch Senecas' Werke *De providentia*, *De vita beata* und *De clementia*.

4. Theater

Plautus ist einer der am häufigsten übersetzten Autoren. Die Hofdichter von Ferrara übersetzten seine Komödien schon 1486. Später wurden andere italienische

Versionen veröffentlicht wie die von Pandolfo Colonnutio und die von Berrardo Ferrarese (1530). Außerdem liebte man auch, Komödien zu modernisieren und zu bearbeiten. Das Werk von Plautus wurde auch in Spanien mehrfach übersetzt. Francisco López de Villalobos übersetzte den *Amphitryon*, als er in Salamanca studierte, und gab ihn 1515 heraus. Fernán Pérez de la Oliva übersetzte die gleiche Komödie in einer freieren Form. Juan de Timoneda veröffentlicht 1559 *Amphitryon*, *Menaechmi* und eine Komödie genannt *Cornelia*. Das letze Werk ist original, die beiden ersten Komödien sind mehr bearbeitet als übersetzt, jedoch überschrieben mit "traduzida por Juan de Timoneda."[7] 1555 veröffentlichte Juan de Verzosa schliesslich seine spanische Version der *Menaechmi* und des *Miles Gloriosus*.

Das Werk des Terenz hatte in Spanien nicht so viel Glück. Man mußte bis 1577 warten, um eine vollständige Übersetzung seiner Komödien—durch Pedro Simón Abril—zu finden.

5. Redekunst

Andrés Laguna übersetzte 1557 die Reden gegen Catilina ins Spanische. Die Verteidigungsreden *Pro Marcello* und *Pio Ligario* sind von Martín Laso de Oropesa 1578 übersetzt worden. Pedro Simón Abril veröffentlichte 1574 einige der Verrinen. Diese Werke waren schon ins Italienische übersetzt worden, und zwar von Tramezzino (1554) und von Padova (1549).

6. Andere Werke

Die Briefe von Cicero an seine Freunde waren in Italien berühmter als in Spanien. Die erste italienische Übersetzung von Fausto ist aus dem Jahr 1544. In Spanien erscheint die Übersetzung von Pedro Simón Abril erst im Jahr 1572.

1481 veröffentlichte Bernardo Pulci eine italienische Version der *Bucolica* von Vergil. Juan del Enzina schreibt 1496 die *Bucolica* ins Spanische um. Diese wurden auch 1574 von Juan de Idiáquez und 1618 von Cristóbal Mesa übersetzt, zusammen mit einer Version der *Georgica*. Damals waren die italienische Übersetzungen von Mario Nigreschi und Bernardo Daniello bereits vorhanden.

Tiraboschi informiert uns in seiner *Geschichte der Italienischen Literatur* darüber, daß in Italien die Zahl der Übersetzungen von Horaz sehr knapp sei. Tatsächlich gibt es nicht viele vollständige Übersetzungen wegen der Schwierigkeit dieses Dichters. Es gibt jedoch in jeder Sprache viele Teilübersetzungen. Manchmal handelt es sich nur um ein einziges Gedicht. In Italien erscheint 1595 eine komplette Horaz-Übersetzung von Giovanni Giorgini. Einige Jahre später, 1599, erschien die komplette spanische Übersetzung von Juan de Viedma. Zu erwähnen ist hier auch die ausgezeichnete Übersetzung von zwanzig Oden, die Fray Luis de León 1631 herausgab.

Übersetzungen der Satiren des Persius gab es nur wenige. In Italien finden wir die Übersetzung von Sergio Vallone 1576, in Spanien die von Diego López 1609.

---

[7] Gemäss J. P. W. Crawford, "Notes on the Amphitrion and Los Menennos of Juan de Timoneda," *Modern Language Notes* 9 (1914), 250–251, stammt der Amphitrion aus einer Übersetzung von López de Villalobos.

Die *Metamorphosen* des Apuleius wurden von Boiardo Ende des 15. Jahrhunderts ins Italienische übersetzt, von Diego López Cortegana 1514 ins Spanische.

Das Verhältnis zwischen Spanien und Italien im Bereich der Übersetzung lateinischer Klassiker soll nun an Ovids *Metamorphosen* näher illustriert werden, da sie eines der in der Renaissance am meisten übersetzten Werke sind, und zwar sowohl in Italien als auch in Spanien. Die erste bekannte Übersetzung der *Metamorphosen* ist die des italienischen Humanisten Giovanni de Bonsignore. Es handelt sich um eine Prosaübersetzung mit Allegoresen nach jeder Episode. Es folgt die Übersetzung des Spaniers Jorge de Bustamante, die auch in Prosa geschrieben ist, jedoch ohne zusätzliche Allegoresen. Aus dem vom Autor selbst geschriebenen Vorwort ergibt sich, daß er in Santander geboren war und in Alcalá de Henares studiert hatte, und obwohl er uns keine Nachricht von seinen Beziehungen zum italienischen Humanismus gibt, informiert er doch darüber, daß er noch andere Übersetzungen von Ovid in verschiedene moderne Sprachen kannte: "toscanos, franceses, bohemios y otras muchas naciones (. . .) cada una en sus propias y vulgares lenguas tienen traduzido este libro."[8] Aus diesen Worten und aus dem Vergleich seiner Übersetzung und der Übersetzung von Bonsignore ist zu vermuten, dass der spanische Humanist die italienische Übersetzung gekannt hat. Man vergleiche die ersten Verse der *Metamorphosen* bei Bonsignore: "Prima che fusse mare, terra o cielo era un volto di natura in tuttol mondo e quelli del mondo el chiamaron Chaos e fue una grossa e non compartita compositione e era uno disconcio peso. . . ."[9] und bei Bustamante: "Antes que fuessen criados mar, tierra, ayre, ni cielos era un bulto de natura al qual llamaron Chaos por ser en si una gruessa y no compartida composición y una massa o globo y desconcertado peso. . . ."[10]

Von der Mitte des 16. Jahrhunderts an werden alle italienischen und spanischen Übersetzungen der *Metamorphosen* in Versen gemacht. Seit langer Zeit hatte in Italien der elfsilbige Vers, die Ottaverime und der reimlose Vers Erfolge erzielt. In Spanien führt Juan Boscán um die Mitte des Jahrhunderts diese neuen Versmaße in die spanische Lyrik ein. In dieser Epoche stärkten sich die Beziehungen zwischen den spanischen und italienischen Humanisten erheblich. Fast alle spanischen Renaissancedichter haben in Italien studiert, sind dorthin gereist oder haben dort ein Amt verwaltet. Boscán selbst studierte mit Marineo Sículo und verblieb einige Zeit in Venedig; auch Hurtado de Mendoza studierte in Italien und wurde Botschafter in Venedig und Rom; Dichter wie Hernando de Acuña oder Gutierre de Cetina nahmen an Feldzüge in Italien teil.

In dieser zweiten Hälfte des 16. Jahrhunderts erschienen die zwei vollständigen italienischen Übersetzungen der *Metamorphosen*, die den größten Einfluß auf die spanischen Übersetzungen ausübten. Es handelt sich dabei um die Übersetzung von

---

[8] Jorge de Bustamante, *Las Transformaciones de Ovidio en lengua española, repartidas en quince libros* (Salamanca, 1580. Biblioteca Nacional de Madrid, r/29240).

[9] Bonsignore, *Il Metamorphoseos di Ovidio* (Venecia, 1517. Biblioteca Nacional de Madrid, r/22289).

[10] Cf. n. 8.

Ludovico Dolce 1553 und die von Giovanni Andrea del'Anguillara 1561. Beide Dichter besuchten häufig die Hofkreise der Epoche auf der Suche nach Mäzenen. Anguillara verblieb einige Jahre in Lyon, wo er seine Übersetzung der *Metamorphosen* unter der Patronage König Heinrichs IV. von Frankreich und von Caterina von Medici veröffentlichte. Was ihre eigenen Werke betrifft, so werden er und Dolce als schmeichlerische Dichter von mangelhafter Qualität betrachtet. Ihre Übersetzungen waren jedoch sehr berühmt und wurden oft herausgegeben. In beiden Fällen sind es Übersetzungen in Ottaverimen, in denen die Autoren den Urtext meistens nicht genau wiedergeben, sondern aus Streben nach ästhetischer Perfektion ihm eine eigene Form zu geben suchen. Diese Tendenz wird auch von einigen spanischen Übersetzern der Epoche wie Felipe Mey ausgeübt, der im Vorwort seiner Übersetzung schreibt: " . . . con haver en Italia muchas traducciones deste libro (porque yo he visto quatro o cinco diferentes) ha prevalecido, hablando generalmente, la de Juan Andrea del Anguilara, con ir tan agena a la letra, que lo que añade es otro tanto o más que el mismo Metamorfoseos."[11]

Die erste vollständige spanische Versübersetzung der *Metamorphosen* ist die von Antonio Pérez Sigler von 1580. Der Autor erklärt im Vorwort als Zweck seiner Übersetzung die weitere Verbreitung des lateinischen Klassikers. Er sei von Freunden und Herren dazu ermuntert worden, Ovid zu übersetzen: ". . . comunicasse estas fabulas a muchos y a muy curiosos ingenios que por estar en la lengua latina (puesto que en algunos libros españoles hallaron algunas apuntadas) les era oculto el origen dellas."[12] Dieser Übersetzer übersetzt nicht in dem freien Stil der italienischen Übersetzungen, sondern versucht, den lateinischen Urtext möglichst genau wiederzugeben "sin me apartar un punto." Trotzdem benützt er die Übersetzung von Anguillara, wie er uns selbst mitteilt, für die Allegoresen, die in jedes der fünfzehn Bücher eingefügt sind.

Sechs Jahre später, 1586, erscheint die zweite Übersetzung der *Metamorphosen*. Obwohl es sich in diesem Fall nicht um eine vollständige Übersetzung handelt (nur die ersten sieben Bücher sind übersetzt), ist die Übersetzung von Felipe Mey einer der wichtigsten Übersetzungen des Jahrhunderts. Die poetische Übersetzung von Mey wurde in zwei verschiedenen Epochen seines Lebens geschrieben. In seiner Jugendzeit übersetzte er die zwei ersten Bücher und einige Jahre später, als er im Dienste des Erzbischofs Antonio Agustín stand, übersetzte er weiter bis zum siebten Buch. Es gibt einen deutlichen Unterschied zwischen beiden Teilstücken. Der Übersetzter selbst erklärt seinen Lesern im Vorwort der Ausgabe von 1586: ". . . quanto a la traducción no he guardado siempre una misma orden, porque el primero y segundo libro, que fueron trabajos casi del principio de mi mocedad, me desvie algunas veces del texto latino; imitando en parte a Ludovico Dolce, y en parte a Anguillara, (que han arromançado este libro en su lengua) y encaxando a bueltas dello de mi

---

[11] Felipe Mey, *Del/Metamorfoseos/de Ovidio en Otava Rima/Traduzido/por Felipe Mey/Siete Libros/* . . . (Tarragona, 1586. Biblioteca Nacional de Madrid, r/12941).

[12] Antonio Pérez Sigler, *Las Transformaciones de Ovidio* (Salamanca, 1580. Biblioteca Nacional de Madrid, r/8246).

cosecha lo que me dictava la loçania del ingenio juvenil amigo de novedades. En los demas libros he alargado menos la rienda. Alguna vez me haure desmandado de corto, callando alguna cosa de poca importancia o por respeto a la honestidad, o de nuestra religión. . . ."[13]

Diese Erklärung von Felipe Mey fasst die beiden Tendenzen zusammen, die die spanische Dichtung im Laufe des 16. Jahrhunderts prägten: in einer ersten Epoche setzte sich unter den spanischen Humanisten die italienische Tendenz durch; in der zweiten Epoche schloß sich die italienische Tendenz mit der nationalen Tendenz zusammen. Die spanische Dichtung gewann so ihre Eigenart.

Schliesslich noch einige Worte über die poetische Übersetzung der *Metamorphosen*, die als die beste Renaissanceübersetzung bezeichnet worden ist. Gemeint ist die Übersetzung, die Sánchez de Viana 1589 herausgab. Dieser Arzt von Valladolid schrieb seine Übersetzung in Ottaverimen, als er im Dienste von Hernando Vera, der Verwaltungsrat für Indien war, stand; und widmet ihm auch diese Arbeit. Obwohl wir auch in diesem Fall den Einfluß der italienischen Übersetzungen bemerken können, bemüht sich Sánchez de Viana offensichtlich, sich an den Urtext von Ovid zuhalten.

Es muß hier darauf verzichtet werden, die zahlreichen anderen italienischen und spanischen Voll- und Teilübersetzungen der *Metamorphosen* zu würdigen, die aus diesem Werk eines der populärsten der Renaissance machten.

Universidad Nacional de Educación a Distancia, Madrid

---

[13] Cf. n. 11.

L'Édition du Cornu Copiae de Niccolò Perotti

JEAN-LOUIS CHARLET

En février 1477, N. Perotti quitte dans des conditions difficiles son gouverne-ment pontifical à Pérouse et se retire à Sassoferrato, ou plus exactement dans sa villa *Curifugia*.[1] Il reprend alors les fiches lexicographiques qu'il a accumulées depuis au moins 20 ans (avant la rédaction des *Rudimenta grammatices* à Viterbe en 1468) pour rédiger son grand œuvre, le *Cornu copiae*. Dans la mesure où Perotti y parle de Calderini comme de quelqu'un de vivant, le *Cornu copiae*, ou du moins ce qui nous en est parvenu (première partie?) a dû être rédigé en 1477–1478, puisque Calderini est mort prématurément en juin 1478. Sous prétexte de commentaire à Martial (*Liber de spectaculis* et livre 1 des *Epigrammata* dans le *Cornu copiae* qui nous a été transmis), et en suivant le texte du poète latin, Perotti rédige en fait une manière de diction-naire étymologique, analogique et encyclopédique du latin.[2] Cette œuvre, d'une ampleur monstrueuse, sera la source des dictionnaires latins humanistes: Calepino, R. Estienne et, plus tard, directement ou indirectement, Forcellini-Facciolati.

Perotti a fait copier le texte de son ouvrage par son secrétaire (peut-être son neveu Pirro), mais il a lui-même introduit dans les marges ou entre les lignes des annota-tions, corrections ou ajouts. Ce manuscrit, l'actuel Urbinas latinus 301,[3] fut dédié au

---

[1] Sur la vie de Perotti, voir G. Mercati, *Per la cronologia della vita e degli scritti di Niccolò Perotti, arcivescovo*, Studi e Testi 44 (Roma, 1925; réimpression 1973). Sur son œuvre, J. L. Charlet, "Un humaniste trop peu connu, Niccolò Perotti: prolégomènes à une nouvelle édition du *Cornu copiae*," *REL* 65 (1987 [1989]): 210–227; et "État présent des études sur N. Perotti," *Umanesimo fanese nel '400*, Quaderno di "Nuovi studi fanesi" (Fano, 1993), 69–112. Sur la villa Curifugia, "*Curifugia*, la villa *Sans-souci*: Niccolò Perotti ("locataire") de Pline le Jeune (*Corn. c.* 18,11 = *Ald.* c. 731–732)," à paraître dans *Studi Umanistici Piceni* 15 (1995), 37–44.

[2] Sur ce point, voir la thèse que M. Furno a préparée sous ma direction, en cours de publi-cation: *L'amour du mot: méthode et culture d'un humaniste à travers le* Cornu copiae *de Niccolò Perotti* (Genève, 1995).

[3] Sur ce manuscrit, voir Mercati, *Per la cronologia*, p. 119–126; L. Michelini Tocci, "Agapito bibliotecario dotto," *Collectanea Vaticana in honorem A.M. Card. Albareda* II, Studi e Testi 220 (Vaticano, 1962), 270–271 et A. Marucchi, "Codici di Niccolò Perotti nella biblioteca Vaticana,"

duc d'Urbino Federico de Montefeltre, avec la probable arrière-pensée d'obtenir de ce mécène l'argent nécessaire à la publication d'un tel ouvrage.

Perotti mourut en 1480, Federico en 1482, et le *Cornu copiae* resta à l'état manuscrit dans la bibliothèque d'Urbino. En juillet 1484, le pape Sixte IV envoie à Urbino le préfet de la Vaticane Bartolomeo Manfredi, muni d'un bref pour le comte Ottaviano Ubaldini, tuteur de Guidubaldo, dans lequel il demandait une copie du *liber Cornu Copie* conservé dans la bibliothèque ducale.[4] La Vaticane ne reçut jamais la copie demandée, mais, le 14 mai 1489, le *Cornu copiae* est imprimé à Venise chez Paganino de' Paganini (H. 12697), par les soins de L. Odasi, précepteur de Guidubaldo.

Dans la dédicace à son élève, Odasi définit rapidement ce qu'est le *Cornu copiae* et affirme que Perotti n'a pas eu le temps d'achever son travail et, notamment, qu'il n'a pas eu le temps de le corriger: *Quin etiam hoc opus eodem ut opinor casu pluribus in locis mendosum nec recognoscere satis nec castigare potuit. Quod ego proximis mensibus iussu et auspicio tuo diligentissime lectitaui et, quoad per me fieri potuit, emendatissimum reddidi.* Odasi a donc volontairement corrigé le texte de Perotti. En quelques rares cas il a, à juste titre, corrigé des fautes de copie. Mais, le plus souvent, il a arbitrairement modifié le texte de Perotti, en fonction de l'idée qu'il se faisait du "bon latin": emploi des modes, des démonstratifs . . . Par ailleurs, il a fait des fautes de lecture et omis certains passages, parfois par oubli d'un ajout marginal de Perotti,[5] le plus souvent par saut du même au même. Pour la première épigramme, qui représente environ 10% de l'ensemble, les omissions représentent près de 1% du texte. J'ai aussi attiré l'attention sur certaine modification dans la présentation du texte: dans un passage de l'épigramme 3, Perotti lui-même avait ajouté dans la marge de gauche une citation d'Augustin sur le goût de sa mère Monique pour le vin pur sous forme d'un calligramme représentant un verre.[6] Odasi, suivi par ses successeurs, a fait imprimer le texte en supprimant le calligramme. Enfin, j'ai pu établir, à partir de deux fautes caractéristiques, que l'*editio princeps* repose en réalité sur une copie de l'Urbinas, et non sur l'Urbinas lui-même.[7] Guidubaldo n'a pas dû vouloir laisser partir son manuscrit et Odasi a dû en faire (ou en faire faire) une copie pour l'emmener à Venise.

Toutes les éditions imprimées jusqu'en 1536, sauf pour un bifolio vagant oublié par Odasi, mal retranscrit par Polydore Virgile (une centaine d'erreurs ou changements) pour l'édition de G. Tacuino (Venise 1496, H. 12704) et repris sous une forme corrigée par les éditeurs successifs, remontent directement ou indirectement à celle d'Odasi. C'est dire que, pour retrouver le texte de Perotti, il faut reprendre l'Urbinas lat. 301. C'est ce que j'ai décidé de faire quand, sur la sollicitation de mon

---

Humanistica Lovaniensia 34A (*Roma humanistica*, Mélanges J. Ruysschaert) (Leuven, 1985), 99–125 (ici, p. 110–111).

[4] Mercati, *Per la cronologia*, p. 126.

[5] C'est le cas pour la plus longue omission que j'ai jusqu'à présent constatée (t. 3, paragraphe 147, plus de quatre lignes, composés d'*œno*-).

[6] *Epigr.* 3, 370. Voir "Papyrus, parchemin et papier dans le *Cornu copiae* de Niccolò Perotti," *Studi Umanistici Piceni* 13 (1993): 49–57 (ici, p. 53 n. 2).

[7] *État présent*, p. 109, n. 135.

ami S. Prete, j'ai entrepris, d'abord avec M. Furno, puis seul, et maintenant avec une équipe internationale, l'édition critique du *Cornu copiae*.

Le recours au manuscrit permet en outre de noter dans l'apparat ce qui a été corrigé ou ajouté par Perotti. Ces modifications sont parfois très révélatrices de la personnalité de Perotti, par exemple, dans l'*Épigramme* 3 (paragraphe 189), l'étymologie de *Nicolaus*, prénom de l'auteur. Le texte corrigé (et imprimé) dit: *Et Nicolaus uictor populi, quod nomen conuenire nobis aduersus Sentinatium nostrorum popellum nuper aperte demonstrauimus.* Mais la première version était: *Et Nicolaus uictor populus seu uictor populi.* Perotti n'a gardé que la seconde étymologie, en l'appliquant à ses propres démêlés avec ses concitoyens! Dans d'autres cas, les modifications peuvent porter sur des points de controverses, notamment avec Calderini (e.g., *scriblita* en 1,3); dans des disputes où l'on s'accuse mutuellement de plagiat, il n'est pas indifférent de savoir si le texte de Perotti appartient à la première rédaction ou s'il a été rajouté.

L'édition scientifique doit donc reposer sur le manuscrit (U). Mais elle ne peut ignorer les éditions imprimées, car l'influence culturelle du *Cornu copiae*, considérable pendant au moins un demi-siècle, s'est exercée par les livres imprimés et non par le manuscrit. Une étude de ces éditions m'en a fait sélectionner trois:[8] la *princeps*, déjà citée, source de toutes les autres (o); celle préparée par Polydore Virgile, pour les raisons déjà mentionnées (v) et une Aldine, pour la correction des citations grecques et en raison du très grand rayonnement de cette édition. Il n'est d'ailleurs pas impossible (mais je ne suis pas encore en état de le démontrer) qu'Alde Manuce, pour sa première édition (juillet 1499), ait pu remonter à la copie utilisée pour l'*editio princeps* d'Odasi[9]; l'Aldine comporte toutefois des interpolations.[10] En accord avec S. Prete, nous avons choisi la dernière Aldine (1526/1527 = a), parce qu'elle est la première à avoir un index fort commode des mots grecs. L'apparat critique donne donc les variantes de ces trois éditions, à l'exclusion des *orthographica* non significatifs.

Quels principes d'édition avons-nous adoptés? Pour les *orthographica*, j'ai tenu au respect de la volonté et des habitudes de Perotti, même quand il s'éloigne des normes classiques. C'est le texte de Perotti dans sa verdeur primitive qui est imprimé. Ainsi, le nom de Pline est orthographié *Plynius* car Perotti le rattache étymologiquement au verbe grec πλύνω lauo (2,430). Le verbe *definio* est presque toujours orthographié *diffinio*, comme chez Valla qui considère ce mot comme composé de *dis* et *finio* (*Adn. Rh.*). On trouve encore *syncerus*, comme chez Valla (*eleg.* 6,37), parce que le mot est considéré comme formé de σύν et *cera*. ... Perotti distingue habituellement la conjonction *qum* (exceptionnellement *quum*), qui vient de *qui*, de la préposition *cum*.[11] L'enclitique *que* est presque toujours détaché du mot précédent, comme son équiva-

---

[8] Voir "Observations sur certaines éditions du *Cornu copiae*," *Res Publica Litterarum* 11 (= *Studi Umanistici Piceni* 8 [1988]), 83–96.

[9] *État présent*, p. 109, n. 135.

[10] Par exemple, *epigr.* 3,259, une citation grecque de Lucien a été ajoutée.

[11] *Epigr.* 3,10: "*Qum*, quod ueteres *quom* scribebant, est que aliquando aduerbium temporis et significat quando"; 3,13: "*Cum* uere praepositio primogenia est nec á *qui* deducitur, ideo que non per *q* sed per *c* scribitur."

lent grec τε. J'ai aussi rétabli, à partir du deuxième volume,[12] le système d'accentuation de certains mots invariables.

Le cas le plus difficile est celui des citations grecques. Malgré son activité de traducteur, Perotti n'est pas un très bon helléniste. Il y a sur le manuscrit, de sa main, un certain nombre de fautes d'accentuation, voire d'orthographe. Il est difficile de déterminer s'il s'agit de fautes involontaires à corriger, ou de graphies intentionnelles à conserver comme témoin du grec de Perotti. En outre, certaines formes sont byzantines ou l'orthographe correspond à la prononciation du grec moderne (celle de Bessarion, et donc de Perotti).

Pour la commodité du lecteur moderne, nous avons normalisé la ponctuation (selon les habitudes françaises) et les majuscules, en conservant toutefois des majuscules qui peuvent sembler aberrantes, mais qui sont voulues par Perotti: initiales des citations, mots à mettre en relief (*Rex, Poeta*). . . .

Le texte, épigramme par épigramme, est numéroté en paragraphes, pour faciliter la lecture et les références, alors que le manuscrit ignore les alinéas et ne connaît d'autre division que celle en épigrammes. Enfin, pour respecter l'intention de Perotti qui, sur le manuscrit, a repris en marge d'une part les mots lemmes et d'autre part les noms d'auteurs ou de personnages historiques cités, j'ai proposé de faire ressortir ces mots en gras. La difficulté est que, pour les passages qu'il a lui-même ajoutés, Perotti n'a pas toujours reporté en marge les lemmes et les auteurs. J'ai proposé de normaliser en gras tous les noms d'auteurs cités, ce qui répond manifestement à l'intention de Perotti. Mais je n'ai pas estimé possible de le faire pour les lemmes car, sur ce point, l'usage de Perotti manque de rigueur et de constance.

Enfin, l'édition comporte un apparat des sources. *Hic labor!* Un tel apparat est fondamental dans ce type de compilation. Il permet d'apprécier la culture de l'auteur, d'établir des comparaisons et de mesurer son degré d'originalité, et aussi de déterminer ses méthodes de travail et donc le fonctionnement du livre. Comme la source privilégiée d'un compilateur est souvent le compilateur précédent, qui n'est généralement pas nommé (sauf pour être contredit!), beaucoup de citations sont indirectes, parfois au troisième, voire au quatrième degré. Pour Perotti, ces sources immédiates, mais rarement citées, sont Varron (*De lingua latina*), les grammairiens, commentateurs ou lexicographes de l'Antiquité tardive: Aulu-Gelle, Nonius, Festus abrégé par Paul Diacre, Servius, Macrobe, Donat, Priscien. Mais, sans le dire, Perotti utilise aussi les lexicographes médiévaux (Papias, Vguccione, Balbi) et deux grandes œuvres humanistes: les *Elegantiae* de L. Valla et le *De orthographia* de G. Tortelli.[13] Pour respecter la complexité des sources, j'ai mis au point un système qui permet d'indiquer au lecteur si la citation est fidèle ou non ou s'il s'agit d'une variante, et si elle est indirecte.

Trois *indices* facilitent la consultation du livre: celui des mots grecs; celui des lemmes latins, avec des renvois à l'orthographe classique dans les cas les plus difficiles.

---

[12] Voir t. 2, 1991, introduction, p. 3.

[13] Dont je viens de publier, avec la collaboration de M. Furno, *L'Index des lemmes* (Aix-en-Provence, 1994). Cet instrument de travail est une conséquence directe de l'édition du *Cornu copiae*.

Enfin, l'index des sources, avec un système qui permet de déterminer si la citation est directe ou non, correcte ou non, mal attribuée; explicite ou non (depuis le deuxième volume); en grec ou en traduction latine (depuis le troisième volume).

L'édition est publiée à Sassoferrato, par l'Istituto Internazionale di Studi Piceni: le tome 1 (*epigr.* 1) en 1989; le second (*epigr.* 2) en 1991; le troisième (*epigr.* 3) en 1993, soit environ 43% de l'ensemble. Depuis la mort de S. Prete en juin 1991, j'assume la coordination scientifique de cette édition internationale. Le quatrième volume (*epigr.* 4, 5 et 6), préparé par Marianne Pade et Johann Ramminger, vient d'être achevé et sera disponible en octobre 1994. Je prépare le cinquième (*epigr.* 7 à 20) avec Pernille Harsting (édition prévue en juin 1995); Fabio Stok, le sixième (édition prévue en juin 1996); et le septième et dernier, préparé par des collègues de Salerne et les collaborateurs des volumes précédents, est prévu pour juin 1997. Ces sept volumes constitueront l'édition scientifique du *Cornu copiae*, la première depuis 1536. Mais nous prévoyons déjà d'en faire une seconde revue et corrigée: d'abord, parce que nous avons progressivement affiné notre méthode; ensuite, parce que l'identification de toutes les sources antiques, médiévales et humanistes (en particulier cachées) d'un tel ouvrage ne peut pas se faire complètement du premier coup[14] et certains problèmes, comme celui des citations non identifiées qui a suscité des controverses,[15] devront être repris quand nous aurons un corpus complet ... c'est-à-dire quand la première édition sera finie: vérifications dans les œuvres apocryphes, inédites ou imprimées dans de rares incunables. ... Cette seconde édition envisagée ne compterait que quatre (gros) volumes: trois tomes de texte et un tome d'index, ce qui rendrait la consultation plus aisée.

Université de Provence

---

[14] Chaque année, depuis 1989, je publie une liste d'*Addenda et corrigenda*.

[15] Bibliographie de la question dans *État présent*, p. 91–93 et notes correspondantes.

Italian Humanism in the Court of King Robert of Anjou

PAUL M. CLOGAN

From 1309 to 1343 King Robert of Anjou, son of Charles II of the Angevin dynasty, governed from Naples one of the most prominent kingdoms in Europe, including extensive territories in northern Italy and southern France and for a time the regions of Athens and Thebes. As Angevin king and leader of the Guelf party in Italy, Robert was regarded as the most powerful Italian prince of his day. Petrarch and Boccaccio praised him as a patron of the arts, jurisprudence, and literature, though Dante described him as a *re da sermone*. Petrarch chose to undertake his three-day examination for the poet-laureateship at the court of King Robert, and the young Boccaccio probably found the sophisticated, academic, artistic, and trilingual spirit of the Neapolitan Angevin court more inspiring than the city of Florence. Robert was influential in attracting several of the leading scholars of the time to Naples which was then known for its remarkable libraries. At the king's request, Paolo di Perugia served as the royal librarian, and Dionigi da Borgo San Sepolcro, who had recently published his commentary on Valerius Maximus, came to Naples in 1337.

Among the works commissioned by King Robert while Boccaccio was at his court was an illuminated copy of the second redaction of the *Histoire ancienne jusqu'à César*, probably in 1340, British Library MS Royal 20 D.I. This redaction of the *romans d'antiquité* which includes a prose version of the *Roman de Thèbes* reveals the perpetuation of the Angevin dynasty as well as interest in the ideal moral conduct of rulers in Robert's court. The purpose of this article is to show that the odd combination of epic structure and romance material which has puzzled critics for a long time had already been achieved in the tradition of the *roman antique* and in particular the *Roman de Thèbes*.

Boccaccio's *Teseida* provided an ironic alternative to Dante's Christian appropriation of classical poetry. Composed during his youthful sojourn in King Robert's court and finished in Florence (1339–1341), while Petrarch was composing his Latin epic at Vaucluse, the *Teseida* represents Boccaccio's desire to revive classical epic after two centuries of romance. He composed the *Teseida* in an elaborate epic style and divided it into twelve books, with approximately the same number of lines as the *Aeneid*. His work reveals his enthusiasm for the classical epic tradition, conventions, and epic style, an enthusiasm he shared with his contemporaries. He compiled his poem from various sources,[1] including an annotated manuscript of the *Thebaid*, Lactantius Placidus' commentary, and some version of the *Roman de Thèbes*. As many of the manuscripts of the *Thebaid* contained Latin verse arguments or summaries of each book, so the *Teseida* has verse arguments for each book, which is subdivided into chapters, as well as prose glosses to the text which were added by Boccaccio. These self-exegetical glosses provide explanatory and interpretative notes and remain anonymous as in the tradition of glossed manuscripts of classical Latin epics. Yet they are in keeping with Boccaccio's strong desire to imitate the formal structure and epic style of classical Latin epic models in the vernacular. Inspired by Dante's challenge in *De vulgari eloquentia* (II.2) that in Italy no poet had imitated the *Aeneid* in the vernacular, Boccaccio responds in *Teseida* 12.84 that he is the first to write an epic or the first to sing of arms in the vernacular. Boccaccio's claim has caused considerable discussion among *Teseida* critics.[2] Although he aspired to be the first to sing of arms in the vernacular, the heterogeneous structure of the *Teseida* and the transformation of classical epic into medieval romance created a "tension" or "contradiction" between epic form and romance material.[3] His intention as suggested in the title of the autograph manuscript seems to have been twofold: to retell the classical story of Theseus and the fall of the city of Thebes (Books 1–2) and to narrate the nuptials of Emilia or the long love story of Palamon and Arcita for the hand of Emilia, the young Amazon princess (Books 3–12). Teseo is not the center of interest after Book 2. At the beginning of Book 3 Boccaccio announces his plan to change his narration from that of the Theban war to the love rivalry of two Theban knights. Whether Boccaccio invented the central action of Books 3–12 remains questionable. Although the story of the rivalry of Palamon and Arcita for the love of Emilia has not been

---

[1] See Natalino Sapegno, *Il Trecento* ("Storia letteraria d'Italia" [rev. ed.; Milan, 1938]), 312–319, 396, n. 30. On Boccaccio's classical sources, see Antonio Enzo Quaglio, "Tra Fonti e testo del Filacolo," *Giornale storico della letteratura italiana* 139 (1962): 321–369, 513–540. On the sources of the *Teseida*, see Alberto Limentani, "Boccaccio traduttore di Stazio," *Rassegna italiana di letteratura* 64 (1960): 231–242; Limentani's edition of the *Teseida* in *Tutte le Opere* (Milan, 1964–) vol. 2; Limentani, "Tendenze della prosa del Boccaccio ai margini della *Teseida*," *Giornale storico della letteratura italiana* 135 (1958): 524–551; Giuseppe Velli, "L'Apoteosi di Arcita: Ideologia e coscienza storica nel *Teseida*," *Studi e problemi di critica testuale* 5 (1972): 33–66; Piero Boitani, *Chaucer and Boccaccio*, Medium Aevum Monographs, New Series 8 (Oxford, 1977), 61–71; Robert Hollander, "The Validity of Boccaccio's Self-Exegesis in His *Teseida*," *Medievalia et Humanistica*, New Series 8 (1977): 163–183; and Bruno Porcelli, "Il *Teseida* del Boccaccio fra la *Tebaide* e *The Knight's Tale*," *Studi e problemi di critica testuale* 32 (1986): 57–80.

[2] See Alberto Limentani, in *Tutte le opere di Giovanni Boccaccio* (see n. 1), 2:233; Carlo Muscetta, *Giovanni Boccaccio*, Letteratura Italiana Laterza 8 (Bari, 1972), 78; Piero Boitani, *Chaucer and Boccaccio* (Oxford, 1977), 10; and Giuseppe Anceschi, *Boiardo: Orlando innamorato* (Milan, 1978) 1:viii.

[3] Salvatore Battaglia, *Le Epoche della letteratura italiana* (Naples, 1965), 342.

found in a history of Thebes or Greece, Greek, Byzantine, and French sources have been suggested by critics who have noted the odd combination of classical epic form and chivalric romance material in the *Teseida*.[4] But this odd combination of epic structure and medieval romance which has puzzled both Boccaccio and Chaucer critics for a long time had already been achieved, as I shall show, in the tradition of the *romans antiques* and in particular in the *Roman de Thèbes*.

The revival of ancient learning in the twelfth century led to the inception of the *roman antique* and the birth of this new genre with its many offsprings.[5] The epic stories of Thebes, Enéas, Troy, and Alexandre and the heroes associated with them are adapted to the wider romance context and clothed with the ornaments of chivalry. The stories are related in a manner in which the conflict between Christian and pagan virtues, and the difference between historical and classical elements become indistinct. Each of these poems celebrates a direct relationship with an ancient book endowed with magical authority, and the poet views himself as a translator of the treasury of the book. Unlike hagiographic and epic writers who are loyal to their original sources, the romancers view the world of experience as a book which is both the source and the site of the understanding of history perceived and expressed. The bookishness of the *roman antique* draws attention to the book as a significant source and symbol and vests the romance with dignity. The *translatio* of the romancer employs analogy concerning the ancient book and bestows a new dignity on the role of the narrator who becomes the sole mediator between a contemporary audience and ancient material. The authority of the narrator in the *roman antique* is that of the clerkly narrator figure who possesses and expresses clerkly virtues. His clerkliness or learnedness is evident in the conscious use of the *translatio studii* topos, especially in the prologue, and his authority is determined by his use of it. The voice of the clerkly narrator, unlike the affective voice of the epic narrator, engages in a process of distancing which is linked to the learning and culture he brings to his text. And his attitude toward his text digresses markedly from that of the epic narrator.

The true *roman antique* is formed by the existence of a Latin book for the

---

[4] See, mainly, Gustav Koerting, *Boccaccio's Leben und Werke* (Leipzig, 1880); Vincenzo Crescini, *Contributo agli studi sul Boccaccio, con documenti inediti* (Turin, 1887); Crescini, *Kritischer Jahresbericht über die Fortschritte der romanischen Philologie* 3 (1897): 395; Crescini, *Atti del Reale istituto veneto* 60 (1900–1901): 449–457; Paolo Savj-Lopez, "Sulle Fonti della *Teseide*," *Giornale storico della letteratura italiana* 36 (1900): 57–78; Savj-Lopez, *Storie tebane in Italia* (Bergamo, 1905); Salvatore Impellizzeri, *Il "Digenis Akritas," l'epopea di Bisanzio* (Florence, 1940); and Henry Kahane and Renée Kahane, "Akritas and Arcita: A Byzantine Source of Boccaccio's *Teseida*," *Speculum* 20 (1945): 415–425.

[5] On the source of the genesis of the *roman antique*, see Edmond Faral, *Recherches sur les sources latines des contes et des romans courtois du moyen âge* (Paris, 1913), 399. On the revival of classical learning, see Charles Homer Haskins, *The Renaissance of the Twelfth Century* (Cambridge, Mass., 1927); *L'Humanisme médiéval . . .* [Colloque de Strasbourg] (Paris, 1964); *Entretiens sur la Renaissance du 12ᵉ siècle* (Paris, 1968); Renate Blumenfeld-Kosinski, "Old French Narrative Genres: Towards the Definition of the *Roman Antique*," *Romance Philology* 34 (1980): 143–159; and Barbara Nolan, "Ovid's *Heroides* Contextualized: Foolish Love and Legitimate Marriage in the *Roman d'Eneas*," *Mediævalia* 13 (1987): 157–187.

inception of the *translatio studii*, and the book has to be recognized as the work of an *auctor* in the curriculum. The dignity of the book of the Latin curriculum author imparts remarkable authority to the *roman antique*, establishing a traditional genre with its unique system and poetic function. The three Old French narrative texts—*Roman de Thèbes, Roman d'Enéas*, and *Roman de Troie*—traditionally referred to as *romans d'antiquité*, represent a distinct genre initiated in the mid-twelfth century in Northern France and, combined with the romance tradition, markedly influenced the development of Old French and Middle English narrative.[6] These twelfth-century versions of classical legend follow the general direction of ancient legendary history but elude classical tragedy and highlight the theme of love and friendship.[7] In adapting the classical narrative to the twelfth-century audience, the clerkly narrator affectively altered the meaning of the past, mediated the distance between the two, and generated a dynamic genre in the development of romance.

One of the distinctive characteristics of the *roman antique* is the emphasis on the narrator's clerkly authority, which is closely related to the twelfth-century renaissance and the idea, as expressed by Bernard of Chartres, that imitation of the ancients was the foundation for culture. The revival of classical learning enhanced the position of the clerk who as narrator mediated and recovered the past. His learnedness is seen in his use of the *translatio studii* topos,[8] suggesting the continuity of ancient learning in the context of a later society. The ancients' authority and intellectual culture serve as the background for a new kind of writing, and the learning of the past is renewed in the clerkly work. The poet assumes the role of the clerkly narrator figure whose learning and culture regarding the ancient book generate an enormous difference between the poet and the narrator in his poetry and help distance the narrator's voice in the text.[9]

The *romans d'antiquité* were granted the status of history as they assumed historical and political relevance for the Anglo-Normans and were associated with the institution of the Norman-Angevin dynasty in England and later with the fratricidal and parricidal rebellions of the sons of Henry II.[10] Noble families tried to legitimize

---

[6] See, for example, Marie de France, *Guigemar* in Jean Rychner's CFMA edition of the *Lais* (Paris, 1973).

[7] See Jean-Charles Payen, "Structure et sens du Roman de Thèbes," *Moyen Age* 76 (1970): 493–513; Raymond Cormier, "The Present State of Studies on the *Roman de Eneas*," *Cultura Neolatina* 31 (1971): 7–39; and Cormier, "The Problem of Anachronism: Recent Scholarship on the French Medieval Romances of Antiquity," *Philological Quarterly* 53 (1974): 145–157.

[8] On *translatio studii*, see Michelle A. Freeman, *The Poetics of* Translatio Studii *and* Conjoincture: Chrétien de Troyes' Cligés. French Forum Monographs, XII (Lexington, Kentucky, 1979); E. R. Curtius, *European Literature and the Latin Middle Ages*, trans. W. R. Trask (Princeton, 1973) 29; and Etienne Gilson, *Les Idées et les Lettres* (Paris, 1930), *s.v.* "L'humanisme médiéval."

[9] See Blumenfeld-Kosinski, "Old French Narrative Genres" (see n. 5), 145–147.

[10] On the political, social and economic world of Henry II and his sons, see W. L. Warren, *Henry II* (Berkeley, 1973); on the government of Henry's continental domains, see Prosper Boissonnade, "L'ascension, le déclin et la chute d'un grand état féodal du centreouest: les Taillefer et les Lusignans, comtes de la Marche et d'Angoulême et leurs relations avec les Capétiens et les Plantagenets (1137–1314)," *Bulletins et Mémoires de la Société Archéologique et Historique de la Charente*

their status by relying upon primogeniture and laying claim to property and, in particular, land to safeguard and preserve its transmission to family descendants.[11] Lineage, inheritance, and rectitude were important concerns to the Anglo-Normans as they "projected themselves into the past and identified themselves with the pre-Norman history of England," claiming descent from the Celts and Anglo-Saxons.[12] The rise of the new Norman-Angevin dynasty at this time and place is largely due to contemporary political and historical concerns as well as to Angevin ideology. The idea of *translatio imperii* furnished the new French-speaking dynasty with a fitting "historical" legitimization.[13] The rise of the vernacular as a recognized literary form at this time and place is attributable in large measure to the *roman antique* poets who adapted the learned traditions of Latin (*translatio studii*) and contemporary political and historical pursuits (*translatio imperii*) to Old French, generating the genre of romance as a new narrative form. The literary conjoining of these two topoi in mid-twelfth-century Old French narrative for the purpose of "legitimizing political power" sanctioned the genre of the *roman antique* and created new opportunities for poetic

---

(1935): 1–258; Boissonnade, "Administrateurs laïques et ecclésiastiques anglo-normands en Poitou à l'epoque d'Henri II Plantagenet (1152–1189)," *Bulletin de la Société des Antiquaires de l'Ouest*, 3rd series, 5 (1919): 156–190; Jacques Boussard, *Le Comté d'Anjou sous Henri Plantegenet et ses Fils (1151–1204)* (Paris, 1938); Boussard, *Le Gouvernement d'Henri II Plantegenet* (Paris, 1956); Boussard, "La vie en Anjou aux Xe et XIIe siècles," *Le Moyen Age*, 4th series, 5 (1950): 29–68; Boussard, "Trois actes d'Henri Plantagenet relatifs à ses possessions françaises," *Bibliothèque de l'Ecole des Chartes* 118 (1960): 51–57.

[11] On the Normans and Normandy, see John Le Patourel, *The Norman Empire* (Oxford, 1976) and "The Plantagenet Dominions," *History* 1 (1965): 289–308; Ralph H. C. Davis, *The Normans and Their Myth* (London, 1976); David C. Douglas, *The Norman Achievement 1050–1100* (Berkeley, 1969) and *The Norman Fate, 1100–1154* (Berkeley, 1976); and Amy Kelly, *Eleanor of Aquitaine and the Four Kings* (London, 1952).

[12] Davis, *The Normans* (see n. 11), 131. On the historiographical combination of English and Norman history, see William of Malmesbury's *Gesta Regum* (1125) and Geffrey Gaimar's *Estoire des Engleis* (1135–1140) as cited by Davis, *The Normans* (see n. 11), 131. On the literary significance of lineage and rectitude in twelfth-century society, see R. Howard Bloch, *Etymologies and Genealogies: A Literary Anthropology of the French Middle Ages* (Chicago, 1983), 64–91; Gabielle M. Spiegel, "Genealogy: Form and Function in Medieval Historical Narrative," *History and Theory* 22 (1983): 43–53; and Lee W. Patterson, *Negotiating the Past: The Historical Understanding of Medieval Literature* (Madison, 1987), 157–195. On lineage and inheritance in Anglo-Norman Romance, see Susan Crane, *Insular Romance: Politics, Faith, and Culture in Anglo-Norman and Middle English Literature* (Berkeley, 1986), 13–91.

[13] See Robert Folz, *The Concept of Empire in Western Europe*, trans. S. A. Ogilvie (London, 1969), who cites a letter to Frederick Barbarossa in which Henry II accepts the former's *imperium*. On *translatio imperii*, see Werner Goez, *Translatio Imperii* (Tübingen, 1958); Charles T. Davis, *Dante and the Idea of Rome* (Oxford, 1957); C. Stephen Jaeger, *The Origins of Courtliness* (Philadelphia, 1985), 263–264; H. Grundmann, "Sacerdotium, Regnum, Studium," *Archiv für Kulturgeschichte* 34 (1952): 5–21; P. A. van den Baar, *Die kirchliche Lehre der Translatio Imperii Romani: bis zur Mitte des 13. Jahrhunderts. Analecta Gregoriana*, vol. 78 (Rome, 1956); Giovanna Angeli, *L'Eneas e i primi romanzi volgari* (Milan, 1971), who shows the Angevin provenance of *Eneas*; and Blumenfeld-Kosinski, "Old French Narrative Genres" (see n. 5), 157–158.

narrative.[14] The aim of the *roman antique* poets was to express values that were central to the Norman-Angevin dynasty: the pursuit of inheritance, triumphant leadership, and the just war. When we place *Thèbes* in the conceptual framework of the *roman antique* and in the context of the Norman-Angevin enterprise from which it emerged, its poetic purpose becomes clear.

One of the earliest negotiations of a medieval author of romance regarding the historical understanding of the relation of ancient and medieval elements in his work occurs in the prologue to *Thèbes*. The poet perceives his role and authority as that of the clerkly narrator figure.

> Qui sages est nel doit celer,
> ainz doit por ce son senz moutrer
> que quant il ert du siecle alez
> touz jors en soit mes ramenbrez.
> Se danz Omers et danz Platons
> et Virgiles et Quicerons
> leur sapience celissant,
> ja n'en fust mes parlé avant.
> Pour ce n'en veul mon senz tesir,
> ma sapience retenir,
> ainz me delite a raconter
> chose digne por ramenbrer.
> Or s'en tesent de cest mestier,
> se ne sont clerc ou chevalier,
> car ausi pueent escouter
> conme li asnes a harper.
>
> (1–16)

That wisdom should not be hidden is the author's justification for writing poetry. The poet's duty obliges him to share his knowledge with his audience for the sake of immortality: "He who is wise should not hide it, / Because ... / He may not then be remembered for it always." The poet-narrator associates his role with that of four great ancient authors, Homer, Plato, Virgil, and Cicero, who would not be remembered today if they had hidden their knowledge and not made known their wisdom. The *translatio* of wisdom proceeds from ancient Greece and Rome to twelfth-century France, the home of the *Thèbes* poet and the region in northwestern Europe that was then under Norman-Angevin rule. He takes great delight in recounting something worth remembering and identifies his audience as "clerc ou chevalier," the learned

---

[14] See Blumenfeld-Kosinski, "Old French Narrative Genres" (see n. 5), 148. On the theory of Old French narrative genres and history, see H. R. Jauss, "Theorie der Gattungen und Literatur des Mittelalters," *Grundriss der romanischen Literaturen des Mittelalters*, I (Heidelberg, 1972), 1:106–138, p. 130; H. U. Gumbrecht, "Literary Translation and Its Social Conditioning in the Middle Ages: Four Spanish Romances of the 13th Century," *Yale French Studies* 51 (1974): 205–222; and Paul Zumthor, *Essai de poétique médiévale* (Paris, 1972).

or noble. All the others may go on their way, "For they can listen only / As the ass to the harper." This prologue suggests that the poet is distancing himself from his material. The standard justification for writing poetry, that wisdom should not be hidden or the possession of knowledge makes it a duty to impart it, connects wisdom ethos to poetry and situates poetic creation in rewriting a classical pre-text.

The essential elements of the *translatio studii* topos appear in this prologue as the poet identifies himself, not by name, but by his craft and as a learned witness to a text.[15] The intense focus on the authority of the clerkly narrator, one of the distinctive characteristics of the *roman antique*, clearly identifies him as the successor of the ancients in the process of authorization. Yet the author of *Thèbes* does not identify himself by name, unlike Benoit de Sainte-Maure who names himself in the *Roman de Troie*, nor does he refer to Statius, his immediate source,[16] in the *exordium* of the ancients in the prologue where he mentioned two Greek and two Roman authors. This omission is complicated by the poet's three allusions to Statius later in his narrative (MS C 2739, 7463, 8905) when the Old French poet deviates from the text of the *Thebaid* to appropriate and manipulate new material or to alter and modify the classical pre-text for a specific purpose. The poet's curious inconsistency in his allusions to Statius, his immediate source and *auctor*, is more than a medieval preference for ancient and Latin over contemporary and vernacular sources of historical information. Like Guido who does not mention Benoit's *Roman de Troie*, the *Thèbes* poet appropriates the *auctoritas* of Statius in the act of poetic creation. In addition to serving as literary model, Statius is invoked to authenticate and validate radical changes to the classical pre-text and new material reflecting contemporary political, social, and economic concerns. As an *auctor* whose name appeared on several curriculum lists established by normative selections, Statius was recognized as "a treasury of worldly wisdom and general philosophy."[17] The *Thèbes* poet, whose clerkly profession was to imitate an *auctor*, appropriates new material into the Theban narrative in the process of *translatio studii* and *translatio imperii*, creating and poeticizing truth under the allusion to the *auctor* figure who serves to validate it.

This process of poetic creation is characteristic of the *romans antiques* and in particular of *Thèbes* and marks its contribution to romance literature. The new genre represents mid-twelfth-century political and historical forces involved in the pursuit of an inheritance in the emergence of the Norman-Angevin dynasty. The clerkly narrator figure in *Thèbes*, who expresses his dependence on and independence of the *auctor* figure, links the past with the present, conjoins the wisdom of the ancients with contemporary poetic truth, and legitimatizes mid-twelfth-century political and historical endeavors. The pursuit of an inheritance which was of great importance and concern to Louis VII, Eleanor of Aquitaine, Henry II, and his fratricidal and parri-

---

[15] Karl D. Uitti, *Story, Myth, and Celebration in Old French Narrative Poetry, 1050–1200* (Princeton, 1973), 151.

[16] L. G. Donovan, *Recherches sur le "Roman de Thèbes"* (Paris, 1975), 17–29.

[17] See Curtius, *European Literature and the Latin Middle Ages*, 49–50, 58–60; and Blumenfeld-Kosinski, "Old French Narrative Genres" (see n. 5), 153–156.

cidal sons has its literary representation in the fraternal strife of Eteocles and
Polynices, the cursed sons of Oedipus, for the throne of the kingdom of Thebes. The
moral purpose of the clerkly narrator figure in *Thèbes*, seen in his recovering the past
and renewing the present through the process of *translatio imperii*, is to represent the
dangers and dire consequences of civil war in the Norman-Angevin kingdom.[18]

This literary and political intention of the *Thèbes* poet has its origin in the dual
purpose of Statius and is expressed in terms congenial to the *chansons de geste* yet
developed in a manner to appeal to the sophisticated interests of a clerkly or knightly
public. The fraternal strife of the Theban brothers, Eteocles and Polynices, was predetermined according to the humanistic thought of Bernardus Silvestris[19] by the
incestuous parricide of their father Oedipus. Cursed as both the sons and brothers of
Oedipus, they are doomed from the beginning to a life of discord and desolation
without any hope of relief or salvation. The Theban tragedy marks the horrible crime
in the world without God.[20] The Old French poet treats this Statian theme of
crime, sin, and discord as a *consolatio philosophiae* in accordance with mid-twelfth-century humanistic thought.[21]

A few examples will suffice here. In the *Thebaid* (2. 249–305) Statius described the
wedding banquet of the daughters of Adrastus, Argia and Deipyle, to Polynices and
Tydeus, ominously. Exiled from Thebes and with bitterness and hatred in his heart,
Polynices journeys to Argos through a storm of supernatural magnitude. He takes
refuge in the forecourt of the palace of Adrastus, king of Argos, and there encounters
and fights Tydeus, an exile from Calydon. Adrastus, a peaceful man but without male
heir and the antithesis of Oedipus, intervenes and recognizes in the two warriors the
fulfillment of the oracle regarding the future marriage of his two daughters. Statius
narrates the scene which is prescient of the future with dark allusion to the myth of
Linus and Coroebus and to grief and torment as the two innocent Argive princesses,
the embodiment of virtue and duty, are drawn with their father into the fate of
Thebes by their marriage. The Old French poet develops the episode (519–1100) as
a *consolatio philosophiae*, without allusion to the myth of Linus and Coroebus or to

---

[18] On the influence of Eleanor of Aquitaine on the development of twelfth-century vernacular
literature, see Rita Lejeune, "Le rôle littéraire d'Aliénor d'Aquitaine et de sa famille," *Cultura
Neolatina* 14 (1954): 5–57; Lejeune, "Le rôle littéraire de la famille d'Aliénor d'Aquitaine," *Cahiers
de civilisation médiévale* 1 (1958): 319–337. On the influence of Henry II as patron of Anglo-
Norman historiography, see Charles Homer Haskins, "Henry II as a Patron of Literature," in
Essays in Medieval History Presented to T. F. Tout (Manchester, 1925), 71–77; A. L. Poole, *From
Domesday Book to Magna Carta, 1087–1216*, The Oxford History of England (2nd ed.; Oxford,
1955), 161; and Jean-Guy Gouttebroze, "Henry II Plantagenet: patron des historiographes anglo-
normands de langue d'oïl," in *La Littérature angevine médiévale: Actes du colloque du samedi 22 mars
1980*, ed. Georges Cesbron (Maulévrier, 1981), 91–105; and Blumenfeld-Kosinski, "Old French
Narrative Genres" (see n. 5), 158.

[19] See Bernardus Silvestris, *De Mundi Universitate*, ed. C. S. Barach and J. Wrobel (Innsbruck,
1876), 16.

[20] See Paul Renucci, *Dante, disciple et juge du monde gréco-latin* (Paris, 1954), 247.

[21] See Alfred Adler, "The *Roman de Thèbes*, a *Consolatio Philosophiae*," *Romanische Forschungen*
72 (1960): 257–276; and Curtius, *European Literature and the Latin Middle Ages*, 173–179.

foreboding feelings of grief and emptiness. After the Theban brothers have formulated
a new law decreeing that each would reign and have the land on alternate years while
the other would be in exile, and thus they would reign equally and the assembled
barons decide that the eldest son should reign the first year and the younger son the
second year, Polynice leaves Thebes weeping, journeys to the king of Greece, rides
through the terrible tempest, and encounters the good-humored Thideus who asks
for only six feet of shelter in the porch of Adraste. In the great duel Polynice wears
the hide of a fierce lion that Oedipus gave him and Thideus wears the hide of a wild
boar that used to devastate the country. Adraste intervenes and recognizes the lineage
and high nobility of the valiant knights and makes them pledge to be friends and
companions for life. In the banquet scene (887–1018) Adraste proposes to give them
his daughters in marriage as well as his land. Thideus gracefully accepts the king's
generous proposal and defers to his companion Polynice first choice allowing him to
choose the elder as if more pleasing, though the other was no less pleasing. The scene
is full of courtesy, courtliness, and beauty. Much attention is given to the rich
description of the dress and appearance of the two knights, Adraste, the lavish palace,
and the beauty of the two princesses whose laughter and kisses are worth more than
London or Poitiers. The king extends the lavish celebrations for fifteen days because
he wishes to bind his sons-in-law with his men. The *translatio* of this ominous scene
in *Thebaid* to joyful celebration without any dark allusions in *Thèbes* is a *consolatio philosophiae*, the representation of mid-twelfth-century humanistic views of courtly
beauty and grace above tragic reality and in accordance with the political intentions
of the poet.

Near the end of Book 8 of the *Thebaid* Statius narrates the death of Tydeus, em-
poisoned by the animal lust for blood and the impulses of war, and his final bestial act
of drinking the gory brains of Melanippus. Statius dwells on the indignation of the
Greeks aroused by Tydeus' bestiality, and Eteocles refuses to release the hero's corpse
for burial and allows it to be treated savagely. In his *translatio* of the death of Thideus
(6509–7240), the Old French poet develops the Boethian theme of *consolatio philosophiae*. He first describes in great detail the armor of Etheocles (6509–6550), his
noble and wondrous horse Blanchenue (6551–6571), and his ten distinguished companions (6597–6680). Thideus, who is mortally wounded by the strong bow of Melanippus, a foot soldier who loses his head, does not commit the bestial act. Instead
Polynice praises his companion and brother-in-law who had promised to help him
regain his land (6749–6809), and Adraste in his speech (7191–7224) turns grief into
consolation by proposing to send Thideus' infant son to Thideus' father who had only
one heir to inherit his domain: "Et fera lui mout grant confort" (7206). The Old
French poet notes that the child is named Diomède, and he will represent his father
well and perform many courageous deeds and acts of chivalry and will be one of the
great Trojan heroes (7229–7240). There is consolation in the death of Thideus, for
his son will restore his father's spirit.

When we relocate *Thèbes* in the conceptual framework of the *roman antique* and in
the context of the Angevin legacy from which it probably emerged, it can be viewed
as expressing the political and social values of other medieval versions of classical
stories. The political importance of the Theban myth and the romancer's interest in

an authentic representation of antiquity in rewriting the classical pre-text probably contribute to the *Thèbes'* great influence on Boccaccio. The redaction of *Thèbes* in the deluxe copy of the *Histoire ancienne jusqu'à César* commissioned by King Robert of Anjou reflects his concern with the perpetuation of the Angevin dynasty and the question of legitimate political marriage and the practice of princely virtue.

Wayland, Massachusetts

Descrivere la terra: le fonti classiche nel
Liber de situ Iapygiae
di Antonio De Ferrariis Galateo

DOMENICO DEFILIPPIS

Nel 1510 moriva a Bruges Giovanni Adorno, autore di una precoce descrizione "umanistica" della costa pugliese, elaborata già nel 1471, ma sottoposta a continua revisione negli anni successivi. Qualche anno prima, nel 1507, l'umanista salentino Antonio De Ferrariis Galateo, che aveva tentato un'analoga impresa, rendeva noti i risultati della sua attenta e puntuale indagine corografica sulla Iapigia, la parte estrema della Puglia, che Biondo Flavio non aveva inserito nella sua monumentale illustrazione dell'Italia, arrestandosi ai territori del Gargano e delle Tremiti, probabilmente per mancanza di informatori. La diversa tipologia dei due testi non ne rende improponibile e azzardato l'accostamento: sebbene il resoconto di Giovanni Adorno sia inserito nel più ampio e articolato percorso descrittivo del suo *Itinerario in Terra Santa* e il *De situ Iapygiae* del Galateo costituisca invece una organica monografia sul Salento, ambedue gli scritti rappresentano, alle soglie dell'età moderna, il più maturo approccio con la realtà geografica pugliese condotto seguendo gli innovativi schemi introdotti dalla nuova cultura.[1]

---

[1] Cf., per Biondo Flavio e la sua *Italia illustrata*, la "voce" curata da Riccardo Fubini per il *Dizionario Biografico degli Italiani*, vol. 10 (Roma, 1968), 539–559; Rita Cappelletto, "*Italia illustrata* di Biondo Flavio," in *Letteratura Italiana,* ed. A. Asor Rosa. *Le Opere*, vol. 1, (Torino: Einaudi, 1992), 681–712; O. Clavuot, *Biondos "Italia illustrata." Summa oder Neuschoepfung? Ueber die Arbeitsmethoden eines Humanisten*, Tübingen 1990; e, in questi *Acta*, Angelo Mazzocco, "The Spread of Italian Humanism in Europe: The Case of Biondo Flavio"; per G. Adorno, l'*Itinéraire d'Anselme Adorno en Terre Sainte (1470–1471)*, eds. J. Heers et G. de Groër. Sources d'Histoire Médiévale publiées par l'Institut de Recherce et d'Histoire des Textes (Paris, 1978); per A. De Ferrariis Galateo, la "voce" curata da Claudio Griggio nel *Dizionario critico della Letteratura Italiana* (Torino: UTET, 1986²), 116–122, e la scheda bio-bibliografica di Francesco Tateo in "Antonio Galateo, *Epistolae*," in *Puglia Neo-Latina*, eds. F. Tateo, M. de Nichilo, P. Sisto (Bari: Cacucci, 1994), 19–29. Per i rapporti tra il *De situ Iapygiae*, la *Geographia* di Strabone e l'*Italia illustrata* cf. Domenico

Giovanni Adorno, nella premessa all'*Itinerario*,[2] giustificava la sua scrittura col ricorso al noto *topos* d'età classica che esaltava l'immagine dell'uomo, cittadino del mondo, impegnato in una incessante azione di conoscenza finalizzata allo smantellamento delle pericolose, perché ingannatrici, strutture epistemologiche innalzate dalla ignoranza diffusa, che ostacolavano l'affermazione di una visione irenica dell'umana convivenza. Il Galateo, a sua volta, mostrava di aderire al canone straboniano, che tendeva a riqualificare in un'ottica totalizzante, quella del filosofo, il lavoro e gli *officia* del geografo, e confezionava il *De situ* mediando, come già aveva fatto il Biondo, le esigenze di una moderna informazione, attenta alla contemporaneità e alla corretta valutazione del dato documentario, con quelle di uno scrupoloso censimento e recupero delle fonti antiche e medievali. E se il punto di massima divergenza tra Galateo e Adorno si registra proprio nell'uso dei classici, perché Adorno si limitava quasi sempre a riportare solo le proprie impressioni di viaggio ovvero quanto gli era stato riferito sul posto, il maggior distacco tra Biondo e Galateo si coglie, invece, nel diverso impatto con la realtà del tempo: alla *curiositas* tutta erudita dello storico forlivese si affiancava e infine prevaleva nel *De situ* la vigile attenzione per l'*ethos* degli abitanti—un vezzo riconducibile sicuramente alla prassi investigativa del geografo-filosofo Strabone e alla professione di medico esercitata dal Galateo—e, soprattutto, il puntiglioso resoconto delle condizioni degli apparati difensivi dei singoli centri, un interesse che è prioritario anche per Giovanni Adorno.

Se Biondo Flavio con la composizione dell'*Italia illustrata* si proponeva infatti di sanare la grave frattura tra un passato ormai remoto e un presente che, recando i segni dello sconvolgimento portato dalle invasioni barbariche, non offriva una agevole lettura della topografia e della toponomastica del territorio a chi avesse cercato di rintracciarvi i luoghi antichi ricordati dagli *auctores*, Galateo e Adorno avvertivano, oltre a ciò, la necessità di fornire un contributo inedito e attendibile alla conoscenza del sistema difensivo della Puglia, interpretando le legittime aspettative dei destinatari dei loro lavori.

Giovanni Adorno, per desiderio del padre Anselmo, uomo di fiducia di Giovanni III re di Scozia, dal quale era stato incaricato di numerose missioni diplomatiche, dedicò nel 1471 l'*Itinerario* al sovrano scozzese in un momento in cui il timore in Occidente per l'avanzata dei Turchi, che appena l'anno prima, nel 1470, si erano impossessati dell'isola di Negroponte, andava crescendo e avrebbe raggiunto il momento di massima *escalation* nel 1480 in seguito all'occupazione di Otranto, in Puglia appunto, pericolosa testa di ponte per un'ulteriore penetrazione turca in Italia e in Europa. Il Galateo, che invece visse dal privilegiato osservatorio salentino i tragici fatti otrantini, rispondeva con la stesura del *De situ* alla pressante sollecitazione rivoltagli da un autorevole esponente della nuova classe dirigente napoletana, Giovanni Battista Spinelli, avvocato affermato e di successo, diplomatico di provata esperienza al tempo degli Aragonesi e portavoce degli interessi dell'antica nobiltà regnicola.

Defilippis, "L'edizione basileense e la tradizione manoscritta del *De situ Iapygiae* di A. De Ferrariis Galateo," *Quaderni* dell'Istituto Nazionale di Studi sul Rinascimento meridionale 1 (1984): 25–50.

[2] *Itinéraire* 26.

Motivazioni di ordine strategico e ragioni di tipo più squisitamente politico trovavano però nel *De situ* una risposta del tutto inaspettata: non un'arida e asettica scrittura tecnica, come tante ne sarebbero state prodotte tra Cinque e Seicento, né un'illustrazione scarna e stringata delle località della Iapigia con puntuali cenni a quanto di curioso, di insolito o di caratteristico esse potessero offrire all'occasionale visitatore, come avveniva, per la Puglia, nell'*Itinerario* del "forestiero" Giovanni Adorno, ma un'opera dalla struttura complessa, che programmaticamente ambiva a gareggiare con i modelli antichi, e segnatamente con la *Geografia* di Strabone, che si avvaleva di un lessico geografico estremamente rispettoso della terminologia adottata da Mela, Solino, Plinio e dallo Strabone latino curato da Guarino Veronese e Gregorio Tifernate;[3] un'opera, insomma, dal sicuro taglio letterario che si imponeva per l'accuratezza espositiva, lo stile raffinato e la novità dei contenuti.

L'impostazione del *De situ* è di sicura matrice straboniana, sebbene l'esordio, privo di una qualsivoglia premessa che, come accade nella *Geographia*,[4] introduca la materia affrontata e ne spieghi la scelta, entri immediatamente nel vivo dell'esposizione. L'apertura solenne dal tono asciutto e pregnante: "Quae nunc Italia dicitur ab Alpibus ortum habens," denuncia immediatamente l'appartenenza dell'opera a un ben definito genere letterario e la sicura preferenza dell'autore per il "breviloquio," sorretta, per ammissione dello stesso Galateo, dall'indiscussa autorità di Galeno,[5] sicché una semplice frase risulta molto più efficace di una più complessa introduzione retoricamente strutturata. La essenziale descrizione dei confini settentrionali della Penisola ricalca il parallelo passo della *Geografia* di Strabone: "Post infimas Alpium radices eius, quam aetate nostra Italiam vocant, initium est;"[6] ma l'umanista accoglie subito dopo la testimonianza di Mela sui mari che la bagnano e sullo sviluppo della dorsale appenninica che la attraversa: "Supero et Infero mari abluitur inque ortum hibernum et meridie porrecta, perpetuis Apoenini iugis duabus peninsulis, seu, ut Graeci dicunt, cheronensis finitur, quae quasi vertices sunt seu coni bifidae arboris."[7] Così Galateo, e Pomponio Mela "... se media perpetuo iugo Appennini montis attollens inter Hadriaticum et Tuscum, sive, ut aliter eadem appellantur, inter Superum mare et Inferum, excurrit diu solida. Verum ubi longe abit, in duo cornua finditur ...";[8] quindi usa probabilmente una citazione sallustiana riportata da Servio nel commento ad *Eneide* 3. 400, per definire le due penisole che chiudono l'Italia: se infatti i "vertices ... seu coni bifidae arboris" sembrano rinviare allo straboniano "reliqua Italia angusta quidem et oblonga in duas excurrit vertices,"[9] piuttosto che ai "per sinus lunatos duo cornua emittens" di Plinio[10] o ancora ai "cornua" di Mela, "duabus

---

[3] Strabo, *Geographia*, trad. Guarinus Veronensis et Gregorius Tiphernas (Roma: C. Sweynheim et A. Pannartz, 1469).

[4] *Geographia* 1. 1–23.

[5] Antonii Galatei *Liber de situ Iapygiae* (Basilea: P. Perna, 1558), 9.

[6] *Geographia* 5. 1. 1: si cita, qui e in seguito, la trad. latina cit., utilizzata dal Galateo.

[7] *De situ* 9.

[8] Pomponii Melae *De chorographia* 2. 58.

[9] *Geographia* 5. 1. 3.

[10] *Nat. Hist.* 3. 5. 43.

peninsulis" pare invece di origine serviana: "Omnis Italia coacta in angustias finditur in duo promuntoria, Bruttium et Sallentum." "Finitur" può infine leggersi come una ricercata *variatio* in luogo del ricorrente "finditur," e l'immagine dell'albero bifido pare risolvere in modo assai originale sia la difficoltà avvertita da Strabone di poter efficacemente assimilare la forma della penisola italiana ad una figura geometrica,[11] sia la poco felice similitudine proposta da Plinio tra l'aspetto dell'Italia e la foglia di quercia.[12]

Questo veloce saggio ricognitivo evidenzia la molteplicità dei riferimenti tematici e lessicali agli *auctores* della scrittura galateana, una ricchezza che non impedisce di rintracciare, al di là del pesante affastellamento di citazioni, il collaudato schema d'impianto straboniano. La serrata sequenza descrittiva dei confini dell'Italia, il ricordo del passato splendore magno-greco del Mezzogiorno totalmente azzerato dai recenti conflitti religiosi tra Greci e Latini e dall'espansione dell'Islam verso Occidente, il nostalgico rimpianto per la cultura greca diffusasi nelle colonie italiane, culla della civiltà e del diritto, la lucida spiegazione dell'origine e della progressiva estensione all'intera Penisola del nome Italia, e infine la accurata segnalazione delle distanze intercorrenti tra il promontorio Iapigio e i punti di riferimento nautici più noti del Mediterraneo—sia pur aggiornate dall'umanista che ne rilevò le misure sulle moderne carte di navigazione—,[13] recuperano il percorso narrativo del capitolo 2. 1–3 del libro V e dei capitoli 1.1 e 3. 5 del libro VI della *Geografia* di Strabone, coagulando attorno a questo filo conduttore una svariata serie di testimonianze classiche e di osservazioni personali.

Dopo un'ampia parte introduttiva in cui indagava il senso del lavoro del geografo (libro I) e discuteva le opinioni di Eratostene ed Ipparco (libro II), Strabone delineava una prima ripartizione del mondo per fasce climatiche. Galateo dopo aver definito le coordinate geografiche dell'Italia e delle due penisole estreme, fornendo della Iapigia le distanze tra le varie località che ne segnavano il perimetro costiero—il contesto dipende da Strabone e da Plinio, ma, al solito, i valori delle misurazioni sono corrette dall'umanista—,[14] richiamandosi anch'egli a quel tipo di suddivisione tracciava un puntiglioso elenco delle località comprese nel quarto clima. Questa porzione della terra, che includeva la Iapigia, Napoli e la parte meridionale dell'Italia, veniva giudicata, col sostegno dell'autorevole opinione di Avicenna, Apono, Alberto Magno, Aristotele e Galeno, la zona più temperata in assoluto, nella quale gli uomini vantavano un'indole e dei costumi superiori, tali da consentire loro di primeggiare su tutti gli altri abitanti del pianeta che occupavano invece aree meno favorevoli all'insediamento umano.[15] La sintetica descrizione di Strabone, attenta a definire più i limiti di ciascuna zona, che i siti in essa contenuti, non rispondeva all'esigenza avvertita dall'umanista di dimostrare come la civiltà avesse avuto origine e si fosse inizialmente

---

[11] *Geographia* 5. 1. 2.
[12] *Nat. Hist.* 3. 5. 43.
[13] *De situ* 9–15.
[14] *De situ* 12–15; *Geographia* 6. 1. 11; 6. 3. 1; *Nat. Hist.* 3. 11. 99–100.
[15] *De situ* 15–19.

diffusa proprio nei paesi del quarto clima, dall'Assiria, la Media e la Mesopotamia, alla Grecia, la Magna Grecia, le isole Egee e dell'Asia Minore, e perciò Galateo privilegiava, per la sua rassegna, la *Geografia* di Tolomeo e utilizzava, forse, le tavole che corredavano la più recente edizione a quel tempo disponibile della monumentale opera, quella stampata a Roma per i tipi di Pietro da Torre nel 1490: con le grafie peculiari dei toponimi presenti in questa stampa sembra infatti concordare il lungo elenco di località redatto dal Galateo, che, procedendo da Oriente verso Occidente, segnala, regione dopo regione, prima i centri della costa e poi quelli dell'interno.[16]

E' ancora l'inserimento di un passo di Strabone, quello che introduce nel libro VI la illustrazione del sito della Iapigia, a segnare la sensibile cesura tra la prima sezione di carattere più generale, fin qui indagata, del *De situ* e la seconda, nella quale l'umanista esaminava i peculiari aspetti insediativi della penisola salentina sotto il profilo socio-politico ed economico, oltre che storico e topografico.

> Terra deinceps Iapygia non sine admiratione commoda oppido est. Nam cum in superno tergo aspera videatur, ubi aratris panditur altioris fertilitatis glebas invenies, cumque aquarum indiga est nihilominus leta suppeditat pascua et arboribus referta spectatur. Haec etiam omnis regio aliquando copiosa admodum mortalium multitudine floruit et tredecim urbes habuit. Nunc autem excepto Tarento atque Brundusio cetera exigua sunt oppidula, adeo absumptae sunt vires. Salentinos Cretensium fuisse coloniam memoriae proditum est.[17]

La citazione vale come testimonianza e come momento di provocazione. La liquidatoria dichiarazione di inconsistenza della realtà urbana della Iapigia, "exigua sunt oppidula," cui Strabone faceva seguire un cenno velocissimo ad alcuni borghi, ricordandone appena i nomi e qualche notizia storica (*ad Barin, seu Baretum, ut nunc vocatur, ut autem antea Beretem, Leuca, Hydruntem* ovvero *Hydrontem, Rhodiae, Lupiae, Salepia, Thyreae* ovvero *Uriam* o *Veretum*) avrebbe potuto costituire, insieme con le stringate informazioni pliniane, appena più ricche per la toponomastica, ma più avare di notizie storiche,[18] un ostacolo insormontabile e un sicuro deterrente per chi si fosse proposto di ripercorrere un itinerario apparentemente privo di attrattive e di interesse. E' invece su questo punto nodale che si gioca la sfida tra antico e moderno, sul ribaltamento, cioè, di una visione in negativo, sulla rivalutazione di una regione emarginata, posta "in extremo angulo Italiae." E il Galateo, adottando un accorgimento già sperimentato dal Biondo, ricorreva ad un duplice espediente: si affidava agli *auctores*, fossero essi poeti come Virgilio, Lucano, Ovidio, o storici, come Livio, o geografi, come Tolomeo, Mela, Solino, o naturalisti, come Galeno, Ippocrate, o

---

[16] *De situ* 16–18: per la grafia "galateana" dei toponimi occorre tuttavia tener conto della copia di dedica del *De situ* (cod. 22 del Fondo S. Martino, Aggiunti, della Biblioteca Nazionale di Napoli) più fedele all'*usus* dell'autore di quanto non lo sia la stampa. Cf. D. Defilippis, "L'edizione . . . ," e Adolf E. Nordenskiöld, *Facsimile-Atlas to the Early History of Cartography with Reproduction of the Most important Maps Printed in the XV and XVI Centuries* (New York: Dover Publications, 1973).

[17] *Geographia* 6. 3. 5.

[18] *Nat. Hist.* 3. 11. 99–103.

filosofi, come Avicenna e Averroé oltre che Aristotele e Platone, o oratori, come
Cicerone, per tentare il recupero di una completa documentazione, corretta e attendibile, sulla antica nobiltà degli insediamenti e si avvaleva della sua personale testimonianza per vantare il rinnovato prestigio di cui godeva allora la Iapigia.[19] Sotto
la sua penna gli "exigua oppidula" si trasformano inaspettatamente in cittadine indus-
triose, ben fortificate, economicamente ricche e pronte a recepire *in toto* le nuove
istanze culturali provenienti dalla Capitale del Viceregno. Il radicale mutamento è
reso possibile dalla diversa sensibilità dello scrittore che, da umanista, è animato da
una incondizionata ammirazione per l'antico, sicché si trova ad operare in una prospettiva opposta a quella da cui muoveva Strabone.

> Hoc autem tempore, praeter Tarentum Regiumque et Neapolim, omnes in
> barbaros transisse mores obvenit ... Sed terrae ambitum tractanti et quae hoc
> tempore sint, et nonnulla superioris aetatis dicenda sunt, praesertim cum gloria
> nobilitata fuerint.[20]

affermava Strabone privilegiando la contemporaneità nell'ottica pragmatica del coro-
grafo che scrive per il principe. A lui polemicamente il Galateo obiettava:

> Non placet in hoc Strabonis sententia: ait enim se tantum ea loca scribere, quae
> suo tempore clara erant et nota, scire vero quae occubuerunt nullam esse ait
> utilitatem. Ego eorum, qui aliqua memorata digna gesserunt, etsi vita functi
> sunt, male habere cognitionem, quam eorum, qui nunc illustres habentur.[21]

E' infatti proprio la ripresa di un interrotto dialogo con l'antico, reso possibile dal
ritrovamento e dalla conoscenza dei classici, così come da un'esplorazione del territorio condotta con gusto archeologico, che consente di annullare gli effetti della cor-
rosiva decadenza dell'età di mezzo e di riappropriarsi di una memoria storica che si

---

[19] Cf. D. Defilippis, "L'edizione ..." Per tali ragioni il Galateo accoglie inaspettatamente nel
De situ anche la testimonianza di un geografo dell'età di mezzo, Guidone: cf. Ravennatis Anonymi
Cosmographia et Guidonis *Geographica*, eds. M. Pinder et G. Parthey (Aalen, 1962). La decisione di
utilizzare una fonte non sempre attendibile e certo non umanisticamente formata, sebbene nel-
l'accattivante *Prologo* Guidone non mancasse di citare Catone l'Uticense, Lucano e Cicerone, oltre
che Mosé e le Sacre Scritture per dimostrare la necessità dell'impegno nella vita civile e giustificare
la validità della sua opera scritta a beneficio dell'intera società umana, dovette certamente maturare
nell' incertezza di poter rintracciare nella *Geographia* una guida altrettanto completa ai restanti
luoghi della Iapigia così come era avvenuto per Taranto e di Brindisi; nel geografo medievale,
invece, Galateo vedeva registrata una mappa degli insediamenti abitativi assai simile a quella della
sua età e perciò si serviva di questo pur scarno materiale documentario per tracciare le linee
direttrici della sua descrizione, che, procedendo secondo l'ordine di Strabone da Taranto a Brindisi
e non viceversa, come accadeva in Guidone, terminava a Nardò: "Neritum longe finis chartaeque
viaeque" (*De situ* 123), concludeva il Galateo imitando la chiusa oraziana della nota satira (1. 5) in
cui si narra del tormentato tragitto da Roma a Brindisi, e desiderando forse in tal modo avvertire
il lettore di essersi voluto cimentare a completare, a suo modo, il gustoso *reportage* del poeta latino
sulla Puglia, arrestatosi proprio alle soglie della Iapigia.
[20] *Geographia* 6. 1. 2.
[21] *De situ* 20.

credeva ineluttabilmente dispersa. Il Galateo agiva nella convinzione che per arginare quel progressivo imbarbarimento di costumi notato già da Strabone ("in barbaros transisse mores obvenit") e ormai estesosi all'Italia intera, si dovesse rivalutare la antichissima matrice greca della regione, da cui traeva origine quel peculiare *ethos* dei suoi abitanti, incredibilmente sopravvissuto alle devastatrici azioni del tempo e del fato. Il percorso descrittivo si intrecciava allora inevitabilmente con quello etico, e la riabilitazione del sito della Iapigia diventava per l'umanista il pretesto per intraprendere un nuovo viaggio, per accingersi, emulo del mitico Giasone e del moderno Colombo, alla scoperta di un "Nuovo Mondo" della civile convivenza, fondato sull'adesione a quei ritrovati valori morali che l'età contemporanea pareva aver smarrito del tutto, complice la devastante e perniciosa azione della avarizia e della lussuria.[22]

> ... tu avivi determinato avere ne lo viagio uno compagno, me volente e desiderante tale camino ... Adunca concessia de cosa che multe accasioni mi teneno, niuna n'è più potente che la pagura del mare ... Tu speri vedere più certamente quelle cose le quali la mia penna da quinci che quelle da quindi l'occhio tuo te mostrarà.

Con queste parole Francesco Petrarca nel suo *Itinerarium*, ora citato da un volgarizzamento meridionale del XV secolo che ne attesta il successo nel Mezzogiorno ben prima dell'apparizione della stampa del testo originale in latino del 1501, prometteva al suo mancato compagno di viaggio in Terra Santa di dedicargli una breve guida ai luoghi che avrebbe incontrato lungo in cammino, sì da rendergli più tollerabile la sua assenza. E dichiarava ancora:

> Adunque primamente racconterò quelle cose le quali alla salute dell'anima, da poi ‹quelle› che a la notizia de le cose e ad ornamento dello ingegno, ultimamente quelle che la memoria de li essempii e a destare l'animo pairano e mesuro longo viagio con breve stile. La prima sollicitudine ... è a lo postutto de religioso e fidele animo, l'altra è d'animo fervente e studioso, la terza è da militare a grande animo.[23]

Sono, questi indicati, gli elementi costitutivi che, variamente combinati tra loro, sorreggono la scrittura petrarchesca e, ad eccezione del primo, sono essi i medesimi su cui si struttura il *De situ*. Al senso di religiosità cristiana, che inevitabilmente si insinua ovunque in un racconto di viaggio in Terra Santa, il Galateo sostituisce una reverente attenzione, quasi sacrale, per quella religiosità laica su cui si fonda la convivenza umana nella sua accezione più alta, la quale trova a sua volta piena attuazione nell'applicazione di un codice etico circoscritto e definito già in antico dalla filosofia greca e sperimentato già con successo nelle città e nelle colonie greche.

---

[22] *De situ* 35.

[23] Cf. l'"Introduzione" al *Volgarizzamento meridionale anonimo* di Francesco Petrarca, *Itinerarium breve de Ianua usque ad Ierusalem et Terram Sanctam*, ed. A. Paolella (Bologna: Commissione per i testi di lingua, 1993): le citazioni sono a pp. 4–9 *passim*.

Il viaggio a Gerusalemme, alle radici della cristianità e alla riscoperta del Cristo, si muta, nel caso del *De situ*, in un affascinate percorso a ritroso nel tempo, alla ricerca di quella identità culturale che recupera all'uomo la sua dignità primigenia e lo libera dalla barbarie; la funzione catartica, che si attuava mediante il lungo e pericoloso viaggio verso Gerusalemme, viene demandata, in questo caso, ad un tortuoso peregrinare per i luoghi della Iapigia, per giungere, poco per volta, a riappropriarsi di una *civilitas* tenacemente abbarbicata ai muti resti di un mondo ritenuto scomparso, che invece vive nell'*ethos* di un popolo che ancora crede negli eterni valori della fedeltà e dell'onestà e ancora sa apprezzare e praticare la virtù.

Quel messaggio, che nell'*Itinerarium* del Petrarca si fa più forte quando l'autore giunge a descrivere i luoghi in cui visse e operò il Cristo, sommessamente si snoda, nel *De situ*, tra le pieghe del discorso geografico, che, come avviene nell'*Itinerarium*, a tratti si fa riflessione etica: è questo l'elemento di novità che segna lo scarto tra il *De situ* e i suoi rintracciati modelli archetipici, da quello antico di Strabone alla recente prova di Biondo Flavio. La più scaltrita pratica con i classici consente al Galateo di dispiegare un repertorio erudito di citazioni decisamente più nutrito e interessante di quello, invero assai limitato e circoscritto, esibito dal Petrarca, il quale pur rivela pienamente la sua formazione preumanistica quando con procedimento assimilabile a quello galateano descrive quei siti di cui ha conoscenza diretta, come avviene per Genova.[24]

Ma è soprattutto l'insospettabile apparentamento tematico di talune considerazioni che permette di individuare il sottile *fil-rouge* che lega i due testi. L'*Itinerarium* si apre con un'annotazione sulla instabilità e imprevedibilità della fortuna, un classico *topos*, che tuttavia ricorre all'inizio del *De situ* in un contesto straboniano, come si è detto, nel quale la trattazione di quel tema era assolutamente assente. E se l'accostamento tra fortuna e volontà divina serve al Petrarca per biasimare l'incontentabilità dell'animo umano e per esortare a nutrire maggior fiducia nella provvidenzialità degli accadimenti, nel *De situ* l'immagine della fortuna che si coniuga con quella dell'inesorabile decadenza della civiltà greca costituisce l'avvio di quel percorso iniziatico che rivelerà la sconfitta dell'azione negativa svolta dalla stessa fortuna: questa infatti risulterà vinta in un caso dalla rinnovata fede in Dio, nell'altro dalla progressiva riscoperta di quella ineguagliabile e immortale forma di *civilitas* che pareva irrimediabilmente messa in discussione dal gioco del fato.[25] La serie di riscontri non si limita tuttavia a questa pur significativa assonanza iniziale: Petrarca, di fronte a quel che resta di Luni, non può trattenere un moto di condanna per la libidine che è causa della rovina di uomini grandi e potenti e di ricche e prosperose città e nazioni, e così Galateo censura i "maxima vitia, avaritia atque luxuria" al ricordo della passata grandezza di Taranto e, più in generale, dei grandi imperi dell'antichità, dal Medio e Persiano e Macedone a quello Romano, per giungere infine alla constatazione della misera disfatta della cristianità che si consuma ai suoi giorni.[26] Altro obiettivo polemico comune è il

---

[24] *Itinerarium* 4.
[25] *Itinerarium* 1; *De situ* 11.
[26] *Itinerarium* 6. 2–3; *De situ* 35–36.

volgo rozzo e ignorante, afflitto da un incurabile male, la credulità che genera la superstizione, la quale a sua volta determina tra gli uomini un diffuso stato di assoggettamento intellettuale e di malessere sociale.[27] Petrarca e Galateo introducono infine entrambi un lungo *excursus* per testimoniare la stretta correlazione esistente tra *natura loci* e *complexiones* degli abitanti; anche in questo caso la questione, ampiamente dibattuta nei testi di medicina e di storia naturale, viene rivisitata dai due autori in un'ottica assai simile, che privilegia la nota etica, tesa a demonizzare l' *immanitas* che inequivocabilmente connota i popoli di regioni impervie e non temperate.[28]

L'importante ruolo politico ricoperto dal dedicatario del *De situ* sollecitava tuttavia il Galateo, impegnato in quegli anni con la stesura del *De educatione* (1505) e dell'*Esposizione del "Pater Noster"* (1509)[29] in una dura azione di denuncia contro l'affermarsi di una brutale e rozza forma di ragion di stato sostenuta dai conquistatori e che pareva sconvolgere le aspettative ireniche e di riforma religiosa diffuse nei più sensibili circoli umanistici d'Europa, a moltiplicare le pause di riflessione e ad indirizzarne le tematiche con un preciso proposito, quello di enunciare un esemplare codice comportamentale, quasi una rinnovata *institutio principis*, aderendo al quale i nuovi governanti potessero favorire l'auspicato avvento di una nuova età dell'oro. E' in questa prospettiva che vanno lette le osservazioni sulla follia umana, pronta ad attribuire a delle bestie feroci, invece che miti "ut erat decentius et naturae magis consentaneum," il dominio del mondo animale, immagine riflessa del mondo degli uomini; oppure la decisa confutazione delle accuse mosse dagli Stoici e dagli Epicurei nei confronti di una natura giudicata "noverca" verso gli uomini e oltremodo generosa, invece, con le altre specie animali: la polemica è alimentata dalla tesi sostenuta da Plinio ad apertura del libro VII della *Naturalis Historia*; ovvero, ancora, la articolata discussione sui diversi modelli di governo e sulle loro rispettive degenerazioni, che, condotta sulla scorta delle osservazioni aristoteliche contenute nella *Politica*, mostrava di privilegiare l'instaurazione di un regime che non favorisse né gli interessi economici delle classi meno abbienti (democrazia), né quelli dei benestanti (oligarchia), ma riuscisse ad armonizzare le esigenze e a salvaguardare i diritti di tutti gli strati sociali, in una visione che si ispirava alle note teorie platoniche sulla repubblica, e tendesse a realizzare quell'idea di *politia*, felicemente sperimentata in antico ad Atene e a Taranto e, nell'età moderna, in alcune, sebbene poche, città d'Italia.[30]

Con la pregnante immagine dell'antica e mitica grandezza di Taranto, elevata a simbolo della più alta affermazione della civiltà ellenica in Italia, iniziava il lungo viaggio per le terre del Salento, che si concludeva, altrettanto significativamente, zoomando sulla città futura, Nardò. Sotto la guida di un barone educato a Napoli dal Pontano, il marchese Belisario Acquaviva, l'importante centro salentino si avviava a

---

[27] *Itinerarium* 8. 4.21–23; *De situ* 116–117.

[28] *Itinerarium* 12. 8; *De situ* 15. 19–20, 23–24.

[29] Cf. Antonio De Ferrariis, dit Galateo, *De educatione (1505)*, ed. C. Vecce et P. Tordeur (Leuven: Peeters Press, 1993); Antonio Iurilli, "Coordinate cronologiche dell' *Esposizione del 'Pater Noster'* di Antonio Galateo," *Giornale storico della Letteratura Italiana* 159 (1982): 536–550.

[30] *De situ* 23–24, 26–30, 34–36.

prefigurare, infatti, l'ideale città dell'età del Viceregno, governata, com'era, da un principe illuminato, sede di una scuola di alti studi dedita sia al recupero della tradizione letteraria greca, sia alla perfetta educazione etica e militare della futura classe dirigente, immersa in un ecosistema naturale perfettamente equilibrato e dotata finanche di salutari terme che, insieme con l'Accademia del Lauro, voluta dall'Acquaviva, contribuivano a ricreare perfettamente un clima antico; laddove la riproposta dell'antico non è sinonimo di nostalgico e sterile ritorno al passato, ma indispensabile elemento propulsore per la realizzazione della perfetta città moderna.[31]

Università de Bari

---

[31] *De situ* 122–123.

Les Relations entre humanistes
lombards et lyonnais au XVIème siècle:
Gaudenzio Merula et Sébastien Gryphe

COLETTE DEMAIZIERE

On connaît bien l'importance et la diversité des liens entre la France et l'Italie au XVIème siècle: relations belliqueuses, certes, mais aussi relations d'affaires et immense influence artistique des poètes, peintres et sculpteurs italiens sur la Renaissance française. La ville de Lyon conserve encore dans le bel ensemble Renaissance du "Vieux Lyon" de riches demeures de banquiers italiens du temps de François Ier.

La découverte, due en partie au hasard, à la bibliothèque municipale de Lyon, d'un ouvrage de Gaudenzio Merula consacré aux Gaulois cisalpins et imprimé, à Lyon, chez Sébastien Gryphe, en 1538, a éveillé notre curiosité: pourquoi cet auteur qui, s'il n'est milanais d'origine, est du moins un grand laudateur de Milan, a-t-il choisi de se faire publier chez un imprimeur lyonnais? Pour tenter de répondre à cette question, il nous faudra évoquer d'abord les relations entre Lyon et l'Italie, puis les deux protagonistes: Gryphe et Merula ainsi que l'ouvrage considéré avant de formuler des hypothèses de réponse.

Sur un plan général, rappelons seulement que le roi de France Louis XII, qui revendiquait le Milanais comme héritage de sa grand-mère Valentine Visconti, a fait son entrée solennelle à Milan en 1499 et que François Ier entrera à son tour dans Milan en 1524. Dès la fin du XVème siècle, Lyon est devenu l'un des grands centres européens de l'imprimerie et de la librairie. Ses échanges avec Milan sont très importants. Vers 1530, Lyon est une ville moyenne, marchande et cosmopolite, plus libre que Paris car elle n'a pas de faculté de théologie. De nombreux étrangers y résident, exerçant leur commerce, en particulier dans les métiers du livre. Lyon est un carrefour par sa position géographique, frontalière à l'époque, et presque aux confins des différentes entités politiques. La colonie italienne y est ancienne et considérable et Enea Balmas[1] rappelé que les banquiers italiens y constituent une vraie puissance

---

[1] Enea Balmas, "Librai italiani a Lion," in Atti del Congresso internazionale *Il Rinascimento a*

financière. L'édition est un domaine de très grande activité et on estime qu'entre 1550 et 1560, 5 à 600 personnes travaillent à Lyon dans les métiers du livre. Les quatre grandes foires annuelles permettent une bonne ouverture au marché européen qui s'étend à Francfort, Anvers, Bâle, Genève et l'Italie du nord jusqu'à Venise. Ainsi, un ouvrage en latin (langue de communication internationale) édité à Lyon, sera assuré d'une excellente diffusion. Autour de l'activité commerciale du livre, se multiplient les échanges intellectuels qu'illustre bien un texte au parcours très significatif: le *De natura hominis* de Nemesius d'Emèse, traduit du grec en latin au moyen âge puis à nouveau par l'humaniste de Plaisance Giorgio Valla et publié à Lyon chez S. Gryphe en 1538 par Gaudenzio Merula qui l'a découvert dans la bibliothèque de Giorgio Merula à Milan.[2]

Sébastien Gryphe, né en Souabe, est arrivé à Lyon vers 1515. En 1532, il reçoit ses "lettres de naturalité" de François Ier et développe un atelier d'imprimerie très important. Il travaille beaucoup pour l'Italie. Loué pour la beauté de ses caractères et la correction de ses éditions, il est au premier rang des imprimeurs lyonnais et joue le rôle d'un intermédiaire prudent entre les divers courants de l'humanisme et de la Réforme. Ugo Rozzo[3] insiste sur son ouverture idéologique et sur l'abondance de la production de son atelier.

Gaudenzio Merula est un auteur médiocre et peu connu. Notre source principale est faite de deux publications d'Attilio Butti, "Vita e scritti di Gaudenzio Merula," in *Archivio Storico* Lombardo, série III, vol. XII, 1899, pp. 125-167, 333-392. Merula est piémontais d'origine car il est né dans les environs de Novare mais comme il a vécu un certain temps à Vigevano dans le duché de Milan et qu'il voue son ouvrage à l'exaltation de la cité de Milan, on peut, à bon droit, estimer qu'il appartient intellectuellement au milieu humaniste de Lombardie. Son village natal est Borgolavezzaro et il est peut-être apparenté à Giorgio Merula dont il parle une fois comme de "consanguineus meus." En 1524, Gaudenzio Merula se trouve à Milan où on le signale encore en 1537, 1538 et 1543, après quoi il partage son temps entre son village natal et la ville de Novare dont il est fait citoyen. Il aurait alors enseigné à Novare, Abbiategrasso et Vigevano. En 1550, il est mis en congé de son enseignement pour restriction économique. On le retrouve à Turin puis à Novare en 1554. Soupçonné de luthéranisme car il répète volontiers les accusations des hérétiques contre le clergé, il est amnistié par le cardinal Moroni mais subit ensuite un procès à Milan pour "hérésie." Son juge, qui est aussi son ami, Bonaventura Castiglioni l'absout mais peu après Merula tombe malade et meurt en 4 jours, le 22 mars 1555.

Lione (Macerata, 1985). Pubblicazioni della Facolta di Lettere e Filosofia, Universita degli studi di Macerata.

[2] Nemesius, évêque d'Emèse (IVème–Vème siècle) a laissé un ouvrage en grec qui eut, au moyen âge, deux traductions latines d'Alfano da Salerno et de Burgundio da Pisa: *De natura hominis*. Il fut traduit à nouveau en latin par l'humaniste Giorgio Valla en 1535 puis par Nicasius Ellebodius en 1565 (Anvers, Plantin). Cf. L. Sozzi, "La dignitas hominis chez les auteurs lyonnais du XVIème siècle," in *L'humanisme lyonnais au XVIème siècle* (Presses univ. de Grenoble, 1974), 295–338.

[3] Ugo Rozzo, "La cultura italiana nelle edizioni lionesi di Sébastien Gryphe (1531–1541)," in *La Bibliofilia*, anno XC, 1988, pp. 161–195.

L'ouvrage que nous présentons est le *De Gallorum cisalpinorum antiquitate ac origine*, Lyon, S. Gryphe, 1538. Cette date pose un problème, en effet, l'ouvrage est suivi d'une *Querela apologetica*, datée de 1537, qui répond à des critiques faites au *De Gallorum* ... ce qui supposerait une première diffusion avant 1537. Y a-t-il eu une première diffusion limitée ou une erreur de date pour l'édition ou la défense? L'ouvrage (in 8°) comprend 230 pages: 213 + 17 pour l'*Apologia*. Il est composé en 3 livres. Le livre I (11 chapitres) commence par une adresse au Mécène: Hippolyto Mayno Augustae Bacienorum comiti, qui est Ippolito Maino, comte de Bassignana, qualifié de "Mecoenas optime." On ne sait pas grand chose de lui puisque Merula, au ch. 5 du 1er livre, consacré aux familles célèbres des Insubres, se contente de dire (p. 44): "Maynorum gloriam satius est hoc loco tacere quam de illis pauca dicere." Notons simplement que ce Mécène est jeune car, a deux reprises, Merula parle de lui comme d'un "adulescens." Le thème central de l'ouvrage est défini dès la dédicace où Merula déclare vouloir montrer "les origines des Gaulois c'est-à-dire les nôtres." Il se veut donc absolument gaulois cisalpin, ni descendant des Romains ni des Lombards germaniques et, d'ailleurs, parlant du peuple du Milanais, il n'écrit jamais les Lombards mais les Insubres.

Selon une mode littéraire très répandue à l'époque, l'ouvrage est mis en scène en une sorte de dialogue assorti d'un défi narratif. Des hommes cultivés se sont échappés de la ville vers les délices de la campagne. Ils ont quitté Padoue et Bologne et tous, Bonaventure et Nicolas Castilion, Benedictus Jovius, Baptista Landulphus, Blasius Phyletus, Hortensius Appianus, Annibal Cruceius et Petrus Franciscus Busca attendent, près d'une fraîche fontaine, l'arrivée d'André Alciat, leur Socrate. C'est Landulphe qui demande à Nicolas Castilion d'exposer l'antiquité de la Gaule cisalpine que les auteurs grecs et latins n'ont pas traitée. Quelques détails continueront la fiction de cette réunion littéraire: arrivée d'un messager, changement d'interlocuteur[4] ou de lieu, le lendemain, mais celui qui s'exprime en réalité est bien Gaudenzio Merula.

L'ensemble du livre I entremêle, non sans un certain désordre, les commentaires de type géographique: division des Gaules, présentation des peuples et des familles célèbres des Insubres. A la limite du district de Novare, se trouve Burgum Lavizariuim (Borgolavezzaro) où sont les derniers membres de la famille des Merula. Entre le Tessin, l'Adda, le Pô et les Alpes, c'est le pays des Insubres (Insubria). Milan, fondée par Bellovèse, roi des Celtes, presque en même temps que Rome, est la métropole de toute la Gaule cisalpine et le marché de toute l'Europe. Suit un éloge de Milan dont l'auteur vante la clémence du ciel, la fertilité du sol et les richesses. Elle eut à subir les invasions barbares: Attila, les Goths, les Vandales et les Lombards. Didier, vaincu par Charlemagne, ayant été le dernier roi des Lombards, Merula raisonne comme si les Lombards disparaissaient politiquement et, si l'on peut dire, "ethnologiquement," de telle sorte que, au-delà dans le temps, il se veut descendant des Gaulois cisalpins comme s'il n'avait absolument rien à faire des Lombards germaniques alors qu'il y a forcément eu, au moins, un mélange de populations.

---

[4] Dans la suite de la discussion, interviendront Ottone, Giacomo Maieto, Bernardo Feliciano, Gualteri Corbetta et Adriano Crivelli.

Le livre II reprend la description de la Gaule cisalpine mais est consacré, cette fois, à la Cispadane: entre le Pô, l'Apennin et le Rubicon. Il compte 19 chapitres qui présentent des peuples, passent en revue les diverses régions des Alpes, les fleuves et les lacs. Tout le dernier chapitre est une longue digression sur les institutions à propos du privilège de couronner les empereurs.

Le livre III mêle des réflexions sur l'étymologie de certains noms: Celtes, Gaulois, Galates, Insubre "quasi subimbres" puis, le chap. 3 dans un grand désordre, passe à Noé/Janus, qui donna son nom au Janicule. Comme après la mort de Janus, son successeur est Comerus Gallus, l'Italie prend le nom de Gallia "et encore maintenant cette partie, notre Gaule, conserve ce nom." Le chap. 5 conduit son auteur à une sorte de "réappropriation" des Lombards: "erant Longobardi maiores nostri Germani: imo ut Corn. Tacitus attestatur, nobilissimi Germanorum qui, trucidatis Romanis et Gotthis Italiam omnem tenuerunt." Ce passage est immédiatement suivi d'un couplet antisémite; puis l'auteur revient aux Lombards dont il souligne le caractère belliqueux et cruel avant de traiter (chap. 6) des moeurs des Gaulois cisalpins, plus grands par la taille que les Italiens mais plus petits que les Gaulois transalpins et les Germains. Suit une énumération (chap. 7) de toutes les ressources de la Gaule cisalpine: produits agricoles et richesses du sous-sol. Le chap. 10 est fait de spéculations linguistiques sur l'idiome ancien des Gaulois, les deux Gaules ayant eu un idiome semblable mais différent du reste de l'Italie. A partir de là (chap. 11 à 17), tout le texte est consacré à la gloire de la ville de Milan, à l'exaltation de ses origines et à la démonstration de sa supériorité sur Rome, Florence et Venise. De longs récits guerriers étoffent ce chapitre et mettent tous en valeur le grand courage des Gaulois dont l'un des plus hauts faits d'armes a été la prise de Rome sous la conduite de Brennus. Merula montre comment, dans les batailles, les Gaulois cisalpins et particulièrement les Insubres, ont pris part à l'histoire de l'Italie et de Rome, en s'impliquant aussi dans sa politique, par exemple à la mort de César en prenant le parti de Brutus contre Antoine. Le chap. 12 est consacré aux origines de Milan, plus nobles que celles de Rome car c'est un roi celte Bellovèse qui fonda Milan tandis que Rome fut fondée par des bergers. Le chap. 13 vante le site de Milan sous un ciel tempéré, dans une zone fertile et bien irriguée, ce qui expliquerait le nom de la cité: Mediolanum comme "inter amnes media," de même que la région de Mésopotamie. Revenant, au chap. 15, sur la noblesse des fondateurs de Milan, il écrit que les Romains peuvent, certes, dire "nous avons été troyens" mais que les Romains actuels ne sont plus à la hauteur et il l'exprime avec des mots très durs: "perobscura videbitur eorum successio, vilis, abjecta. Nihil ergo haec haereditas existimanda est," et, plus loin, "scio enim Romanos tantum fuisse bellaces olim et praeclari, quantum hac aetate sunt imbelles et inglorii." L'attaque contre Rome se poursuit au chap. 16 qui s'achève sur un discours moralisant concernant la loyauté des peuples. Enfin, le chap. 17 raconte un combat naval entre Vénitiens et Milanais devant Crémone. Le récit en est très détaillé, agrémenté de discours des chefs comme César en a placés dans ses *Commentaires* et s'achève sur un morceau de bravoure, qui ne manque pas d'un certain souffle, pour montrer que la victoire des Milanais a résulté de la qualité de la stratégie et du moral des troupes.

L'ouvrage se termine sur ce passage glorieux et il est suivi d'une *Querela apologetica*, datée de juillet 1537. Merula dit sa déception: il croyait avoir été utile à ses contemporains et à la postérité mais il a éveillé l'hostilité. Il semble, d'après sa réponse, qu'il ait été critiqué essentiellement sur deux points: son style et sa façon de raconter l'histoire ou de présenter la topographie. Il répond sous la forme d'un dialogue entre Zoilus[5] et Merula. Zoilus lui dit qu'il a perdu son temps car Ptolémée, Strabon et Pline ont fait mieux que lui en topographie, Tite-Live, Salluste et Tacite en histoire. Il n'en disconvient pas mais fait observer que ces historiens ne pouvaient décrire la prise de Tunis par Charles Quint ou la captivité de Louis Sforza en France. Quant à la topographie des villes, elle a beaucoup changé depuis Ptolémée. Comme Zoilus estime qu'il n'a rien dit sur l'origine des Gaulois transalpins, Merula, qui ne veut rien ajouter à leur sujet, se lance dans un développement sur les Francs saliens et leurs lois, leur établissement en Gaule et la lignée de Charlemagne, vainqueur de Didier, roi des Lombards. Il en profite pour rappeler que c'est Pépin, succédant à Charles le chauve, qui établit que Milan serait appelée capitale de l'Italie car elle était la métropole de la Gaule citérieure. Il ne perd jamais de vue son but essentiel, qui est la gloire de Milan![6]

Le contenu de ces critiques révèle bien que ce sont surtout des querelles d'intellectuels jaloux, qui ne méritaient guère une quelconque censure. Il nous reste donc à nous demander pourquoi Gaudenzio Merula, qui n'est jamais allé à Lyon, semble-t-il, a jugé bon de se faire éditer chez Sébastien Gryphe.

Qu'il y ait eu à ce choix des raisons commerciales, c'est indéniable. Milan est une grande ville marchande mais, dans le domaine du marché du livre et de tout ce qui s'y rattache, Lyon est bien supérieur. Une meilleure diffusion est certainement assurée à partir de Lyon.

Peut-il y avoir des raisons religieuses? Ugo Rozzo, qui a étudié la place de la culture italienne dans les éditions lyonnaises de Sébastien Gryphe, a observé que Gryphe avait édité une certaine littérature italienne engagée au plan religieux et des oeuvres de nombreux auteurs liés, de diverses manières, aux dissensions en matière de religion. En 1534, Ortensio Lando, qui a quitté Bologne et l'ordre des ermites auquel il appartenait, arrive à Lyon. Or son arrivée coïncide presque avec celle d'Etienne Dolet qui sera un collaborateur de S. Gryphe. Lando et Dolet ont pu se connaître à Padoue où tous deux se trouvaient en 1527 et Lando va, lui aussi, travailler chez Gryphe comme correcteur et conseil en 1534–1535. Dans ses *Forcianae quaestiones*, publiées à Naples en 1535, Lando met en scène des discussions qui se seraient déroulées dans une villa près de Lucques et, parmi les interlocuteurs, nous retrouvons

---

[5] Zoilus est un grammairien d'Alexandrie, détracteur d'Homère. Déjà chez Ovide et Martial, on disait "un zoïle" pour désigner un critique systématique ou de mauvaise foi et qui s'en prenait à quelqu'un dont le talent était bien supérieur au sien. La rancoeur de Merula s'exprime à travers le choix d'un tel interlocuteur dans cette *querela apologetica*.

[6] Cet éloge dithyrambique et exclusif de Milan avait dû froisser les gens de Novare, qui avaient honoré Merula. En effet, Sozzi ("La dignitas hominis," note 38) nous apprend que dans une lettre autographe adressée à Gryphe par Giovan Battista Plozio, humaniste et juriste de Novare, celui-ci envoie à Gryphe, de la part de Merula, un éloge de la ville de Novare, destiné à être inséré dans une nouvelle édition du *De Gallorum*.

Gaudenzio Merula et Etienne Dolet. Merula était pour Lando un ami de Novare et Lando figure dans le *De Gallorum* ... comme Hortensius Appianus. A cette époque, Merula, s'il est parfois soupçonné de sympathies pour la Réforme en raison des propos critiques qu'il tient au sujet du clergé, ne s'affiche cependant pas comme un partisan déterminé. On lui a reproché la poursuite de sa correspondance avec Sébastien Münster, le célèbre cosmographe, ancien franciscain passé à la Réforme. D'autre part, dans l'oeuvre de Merula, un seul ouvrage fut condamné, c'est le *Liber memorabillum*, qui eut une première édition à Venise en 1550 puis fut condamné par l'Index, "nisi repurgetur" et publié à Lyon en 1556 chez M. Bonhomme. Ugo Rozzo pense que la condamnation est due aux pages traitant d'astrologie et de démonologie. Deux ans avant cette édition, dans une lettre de 1554 adressée à Jean Calvin, Merula l'informait de sa "conversion."[7] En 1538, il n'appartient certainement pas encore à la religion réformée et le *De Gallorum* ... ne comporte aucune allusion aux thèmes de la Réforme si ce ne sont quelques allusions critiques à la Rome actuelle. D'autre part, S. Gryphe, qui garda toujours d'excellentes relations avec le cardinal Sadolet et qui fut inhumé à St-Nizier, est, en sa conscience, resté fidèle à la religion catholique mais c'est un esprit ouvert et tolérant. Il est donc tout à fait possible que, éclairé par Lando sur l'atmosphère qui régnait dans les ateliers de S. Gryphe, désireux de voir son ouvrage édité sans difficultés et bien diffusé, Merula ait fait le choix de l'imprimerie lyonnaise.

Il y a encore une troisième raison, aussi importante et peut-être plus déterminante que les deux premières, c'est le sujet même du livre: le thème gaulois. Faut-il aller jusqu'à dire que Merula était du "parti français"? Butti rapporte que, dans sa chronique, sous la rubrique 1524, Merula a écrit: "tunc temporis ego cum Gallis eram," interprété par Ceruti[8] comme l'affirmation d'une sympathie politique en faveur de la France. Cette conclusion semble hâtive si l'on considère que, par ailleurs, dans le *De Gallorum* ... on trouve une référence très louangeuse à Charles Quint "invictissimus et felicissimus" qui, par sa victoire de Tunis, "tantam gloriam assecutus est ut proxime nunc ad deos accedat." Encore faudrait-il aussi s'accorder sur le sens de *cum*: il pouvait se trouver *avec* les Français à Milan sans être forcément de leurs partisans. En revanche, ce qui apparaît sans conteste c'est qu'il est du "parti gaulois" et donc qu'il adhère totalement à la "Celtomanie" ou "Celtophilie" de l'époque. Claude-Gilbert Dubois[9] a bien montré que remonter à Noé par les "vieux Gaulois" c'était, en partie, s'affranchir des racines gréco-latines et que l'unité, recherchée jusque là du côté de la civilisation romaine ou de la chrétienté, conduit, à cause des antagonismes politiques des états europeens et de l'éclatement de la religion chrétienne, à un repli de chaque nation sur elle-même pour y trouver sa propre grandeur. En France, se développe un mythe nationaliste du Gaulois et sa résistance à l'envahisseur romain symbolise aussi

---

[7] Rappelons que Merula est mort en 1555 et que c'est, selon Rozzo, un an avant sa mort qu'il envoie cette fameuse lettre à Calvin (Rozzo, "La cultura italiana," p. 181).

[8] Ceruti, *Biblioth. Hist. Ital.* (Milano, 1876).

[9] Claude-Gilbert Dubois, *Celtes et Gaulois au XVIème siècle. Le développement littéraire d'un mythe nationaliste* (Paris, 1972), pp. 28, 55, 110 et suiv.

la volonté de se libérer de Rome, capitale de l'Empire romain et aussi ville des papes. C'est la "primauté de la gent gallique" de Guillaume Postel ou le mythe du "bon Gaulois" cher au parti protestant, cf. *Franco-Gallia* de François Hotman, Genève 1573. A cela s'ajoute le fait que, dès le début du siècle (1519), au moment où François Ier et Charles Quint s'affrontent pour l'élection à l'Empire, se développe aussi en Europe une sorte de pangermanisme, inspiré de la *Germanie* de Tacite. De là, une réaction d'écrivains qui s'appuient sur Annius de Viterbe et qui opposent un peuple gaulois cultivé à la "barbarie" des Germains. Gaudenzio Merula est dans cette ligne lorsqu'il préfère ostensiblement les Gaulois aux Lombards et qu'il veut élever Milan au-dessus de Rome.

Il n'est pas né à Milan, il a fréquenté Novare et Turin mais, s'il a une "petite patrie" natale, Borgolavezzaro, il a aussi une plus grande patrie, qui est le pays des Insubres (seul nom qu'il veuille lui donner avec celui de Gallia cisalpina). Toute sa conviction, dans l'ouvrage de 1538, plaide en faveur de ses ancêtres, les Gaulois (cis-alpins) et de la ville-phare: Milan. Il était sans doute plus facile et plus opportun de publier cela chez les Gaulois, c'est-à-dire en France qu'à Venise ou à Milan.

Université Jean Moulin Lyon III

The Pope's Favorite Humanist in the Land of Reformation: On the Reception of the Works of Giannozzo Manetti in Sixteenth-Century Germany and France

CHRISTOPH DRÖGE[*]

When confronted with a title referring to the northwest–European echo of the writings of the fifteenth-century Florentine statesman, orator, and humanist Giannozzo Manetti (1396–1459), one might easily expect one of those "very short books" of the kind of "the influence of Zen Buddhism on Elizabethan drama." And, though at some times during my studies on Manetti in general, when I felt that he must have been known north of the Alps, I feared my instinct had led me astray and that the answer lay in the short sentence "there is none." Nevertheless, I found the "book" to be somewhat longer than that.

We are in Italy, and here Manetti, one of the major figures of early Florentine "umanesimo civico," needs no long introduction. Contemporaries praised his legendary eloquence, Vespasiano da Bisticci lauded his immense learning, and the Medicis so much feared his prestige and influence that Cosimo il Vecchio drove him into exile. Pope Nicholas V welcomed him to Rome, where he enjoyed favor and protection, until Alfonso the Magnanimous of Aragon, whom Manetti had vividly combatted during his diplomatic missions in the thirties and forties, lured him to Naples. Here he wrote the largest part of his philosophical treatises, and here he died, mourned by kings and praised by poets such as il Panormita. His works include Ciceronian-style Orationes,[1] among which are the famous funeral speech for Leonardo

---

[*] Auctorem hunc de humanitatis quoque studiis optime meritem duobus fere mensibus post conventum Barensem peractum iam praematura morte abreptum esse vehementer dolet Societas Internationalis Studiis Neolatinis Provehendis.

[1] See H. W. Wittschier, *Giannozzo Manetti: Das Corpus der Orationes* (Cologne/Graz, 1968).

Bruni[2] and the congratulatory address to Pope Nicholas V on his election, an only recently edited *Dialogus consolatorius de morte filii*,[3] an unedited *Symposium* on the relationship between man and the animal kingdom,[4] biographies of Socrates, Seneca,[5] Dante, Petrarch, Boccaccio and of his friend Pope Nicholas V, as well as the treatise *De dignitate et excellentia hominis*,[6] together with Pico della Mirandola's *Oratio* called *De hominis dignitate*,[7] the most significant Renaissance treatise on this noble subject.[8] Manetti also drew particular fame from his Hebrew studies, being the first Florentine humanist to master the Holy Tongue and to study Jewish commentaries on the Bible. Basing himself on this knowledge which he acquired from Florentine Jews, he began retranslating the Bible from the Hebrew original into Neo-Latin, an enterprise of which only a new translation of the Book of Psalms was completed, as well as a *Liber Apologeticus* for this same translation[9] insisting on the legitimacy of correcting Jerome's *Vulgata*. An unedited and fragmentary *Adversus Iudaeos et Gentes* was probably intended to sum up Manetti's theological ideas. After his death, the ensuing rise of Neo-Platonist humanism in Florence and the whole of Italy, for which Manetti's personal blend of Studia Humanitatis and religious quest helped pave the way, considerably eclipsed the impact of his writings.

Among the outstanding personal characteristics attributed to Manetti one may count his deep piety, his firm belief in the truth of the Christian revelation, which he took for "non fede ma certezza." He is said to have believed that he would have to give account of each minute of his life on the day of judgment, that he depised idleness, believed in the worth of human labor and the legitimacy of its material reward, abstained from excessive eating and drinking,[10] yet refrained from asceticism, cherished his wife, and praised the blessings of marriage—even the joys of sexual intercourse!—in his *De dignitate et excellentia hominis*. Add to this his scientific attitude to the Scriptures, his reevaluation of Hebrew studies and of critical examination of long-hallowed traditions, and you might find yourself tempted to see in Manetti a Protestant or even a Puritan *ante rem*, something like a Connecticut Yankee at the

---

[2] "Oratio funebris in solemni Leonardi Aretini . . . laureatione," Wittschier, *Giannozzo Manetti: Das corpus*, 70–78.

[3] A. de Petris (ed.), *Giannozzo Manetti: Dialogus Consolatorius de morte filii* (Rome, 1983).

[4] See Ch. Dröge: "Giannozzo Manetti und Marsilio Ficino: Das Symposium im Humanismus," in J. Müller-Hofstede (ed.), *Florenz in der Frührenaissance. Festschrift für Paul Oskar Kristeller zum 85. Geburtstag* (forthcoming).

[5] A. de Petris, *Giannozzo Manetti: Vita Socratis et Senecae* (Firenze, 1979).

[6] Modern editions: E. R. Leonard (ed.), *Giannozzo Manetti: De dignitate et excellentia hominis* (Padova, 1975); A. Buck (ed.), *Von der Würde und Erhabenheit des Menschen* (ed. with a German translation) (Hamburg, 1990).

[7] E. Garin (ed.), *Giovanni Pico della Mirandola: De Hominis Dignitate* (Firenze, 1942), 101–165.

[8] Cf. Ch. Dröge, *Giannozzo Manetti als Denker und Hebraist* (Frankfurt/Bern, 1987).

[9] A. de Petris (ed.), *Giannozzo Manetti. Apologeticus* (Roma, 1981). Cf. Ch. Dröge, *Giannozzo Manetti als Denker . . .* , 50ff.

[10] On the above-mentioned characteristics, see A. Greco (ed.), *Vespasiano da Bisticci: Le Vite* (Florence, 1976), 2 vols., "Vita di Messer Giannozzo Manetti," I, 485–538; "Commentario alla Vita di Messer Giannozzo Manetti," II, 513–627.

Court of King Alfonso, the writings of whom Luther, Zwingli, Calvin or John Knox ought to have enthusiastically claimed as an early prefiguration of their dearest tenets.

Yet, this extreme is as far from the truth as its opposite, the absence of any echo. Let us remember that Manetti was firmly rooted in his belief in the sanctity of the Roman Church, that he in fact was among the few humanists who knew and valued medieval scholastic thought, who quoted (in *Adversus Iudaeos et Gentes*[11]) Anselm of Canterbury and Thomas Aquinas, and that his relationship with the pope was one of deep loyalty, and, in the case of Tommaso Parentucelli, later Nicholas V, of cordial friendship. And I have already pointed out elsewhere that there is good reason to believe that Manetti took up Hebrew studies not so much for religious but for "agonistic" reasons, to keep up with the at his time famous Venetian humanist Marco Lippomanno, known to have mastered Hebrew as early as the twenties of the fifteenth century. The retranslation of the Book of Psalms was written not against the will of Rome, but—for a large part—in the Papal Palace. Yet his religious profile seems to fit surprisingly well into forms that developed in the context of Protestantism. Was he therefore more of a dissenter than he himself knew? Or did Rome so considerably shift its position between 1450 and 1550? Was therefore the Reform, as many especially Protestant historians have repeatedly claimed, in more than one respect the spiritual heir of Italian humanism? With these questions in mind, let us now examine the tangible evidence of the presence of Manetti's writings in the lands of Reformation.

Manetti's literary profile is characterized by four outstanding features: his Hebrew studies, his translation of the Book of Psalms, his treatise on human dignity, and his outstanding role as a humanist orator.

The reception of Manetti's Hebrew studies, which has—ever since Cassuto's[12] and Garofalo's[13] discoveries and Trinkaus's brilliant analysis in his book *In Our Image and Likeness*[14]—considerably fashioned Manetti's image for contemporary scholarship, appears rather weak. That Manetti knew Hebrew was generally known by way of anecdotes referring to disputations with Jews as transmitted by Naldo Naldi, a rather mediocre Neo-Platonic poet of Ficino's circle who wrote a biography of Manetti which circulated rather widely in Italy but was not printed until the eighteenth century, when Muratori included it in his *Rerum Italicarum Scriptores*. Through Naldi, Pico della Mirandola most certainly knew of Manetti, and so perhaps did

---

[11] See Ch. Dröge, "Die Idee der *dignitas hominis* in Manettis Protesti di Giustizia," *Wolfenbütteler Renaissance-Mitteilungen* 12 (1988): 144–147.

[12] U. Cassuto, *I manoscritti palatini ebraici della Biblioteca Apostolica Vaticana e la loro Storia* (Città del Vaticano, 1939).

[13] S. Garofalo, "Gli umanisti del secolo XV e la Bibbia," *Biblica* 27 (1946): 338–375.

[14] Ch. Trinkaus, "Studia humanitatis and Studia divinitatis: The Christian Renaissance in Italy," especially "The Beginnings of Hebrew Studies: Bruni vs. Manetti," in *In Our Image and Likeness. Humanity and Divinity in Italian Humanist Thought*. 2 vols. (London, 1970), II, 553ff., and 578ff. See also my article, "Quia morem Hieronymi in transferendo cognovi. Le début des études hébraiques chez les humanistes florentins," in I. Zinguer (ed.), *L'Hébreu à la Renaissance* (Leiden, 1992).

Reuchlin, who visited Florence in 1490, though there is to my knowledge no proof for this acquaintance. Manetti owned a large collection of Hebrew books, which around 1550 were bought, together with most of Manetti's library, by the Fugger family of Augsburg. But by the time these reached Germany, Hebrew studies of humanists such as Reuchlin, Sebastian Münster, or Konrad Pellikan already, as Thomas Willi pointed out in his profound article on Hebrew studies in Basel,[15] had advanced much beyond the state reached by Manetti, and there was not much the South German Hebraist of the 1550s could still learn from him. Yet it is noteworthy how far especially Sebastian Münster's method and his theoretical conclusions paralleled those of Manetti: he too maintained the necessity of correcting Jerome's *Vulgata* and the legitimacy of putting previous translations to a critical examination, and he learned Hebrew from a highly educated Jewish contemporary, Elias Levita, just as Manetti derived his rabbinical learning from Immanuel ben Abraham of San Miniato. The reformed "Zeitgeist" of Basel seems to have typologically "reproduced" the phenomenon of Hebrew studies "alla maniera di Messer Giannozzo Manetti Fiorentino"—even if Münster or Brunfels and their likes never read a line by Giannozzo's hand.

Very much the same is to be said about the translation of the book of Psalms. It is noteworthy how far Manetti, by translating Alfonso's favorite biblical book—the reading of which the Middle Ages had confined to clerics and kings because of the intimacy of its dialogue between God and man—prefigured the Reformation's predilection for the Psalms, which to Luther were the Bible in a nutshell. Yet, though a large number of manuscripts of Manetti's Psalms did in fact exist in the Fugger Library after 1550, we find no parallel here to Erasmus's discovery of Valla's *Collatio Novi Testamenti* and his publication of these under the title of *Adnotationes*, a circumstance which linked early humanist New Testament scholarship to Reformation-age Bible studies. We may deduce that even if someone did in fact read Manetti's translations in the sixteenth century in Augsburg, they no longer would appear interesting to him in view of the high level of Hebrew studies already achieved at the time. Last but not least, Manetti's translation of the Psalms was disregarded precisely because of its language: Manetti translated from Hebrew into *our* language, into Neo-Latin, whereas in the sixteenth century it was the new translations from Hebrew into vernacular that made the real impact. In 1524, Psalm 130, "Mima'amakim kraticha Adonay, Adonay Shim'ah beKoli" simply sounded more exciting when sung to Luther's emotional lines "Aus tiefer Not schrei ich zu dir / Herr Gott erhör mein Rufen" than in Manetti's calm, decorous ("invocavi" for Jerome's "clamavi"!) and Ciceronically elegant "De profundis invocavi te domine, domine exaudi vocem meam. . . ."—even if "kraticha" does mean "I called thee," and not "I yell to thee."

So let us now turn our attention to Manetti's treatise *On Human Dignity*. Here we are confronted with the first tangible evidence of a transalpine reception of a work by Manetti, since in 1532 the Basel printer Cratander issued an edition of Manetti's

---

[15] Th. Willi, "Der Beitrag des Hebräischen zum Werden der Reformation in Basel," *Theologische Zeitschrift* (Basel) 35 (1979): 139–154.

treatise. This edition, dedicated to the Austrian chancellor Nikolaus Rabenhaupt, was edited from a manuscript owned by the Swabian-born German humanist Johannes Alexander Brassicanus (1500–1539), son of the humanist Johannes Brassicanus and an eminent scholar of Greek, who sojourned for a long time in Vienna and who in 1522 took over Reuchlin's chair at the University of Ingolstadt. Brassicanus is well documented among the leading figures of German humanism: thus, Johannes Choler mentions him in a letter to Erasmus in 1531,[16] Amerbach does likewise in a letter of 1528[17] to Beatus Rhenanus, to whom Brassicanus was seemingly linked by a close friendship,[18] and one of his closest interlocutors, to whom he owed much of his professional advancement, was the eminent scholar and diplomat Johannes Cuspinian (1473–1529).[19]

This edition of Manetti's treatise features a short introduction by Brassicanus, in which he stresses above all Manetti's Greek scholarship and the fact that he learned from Chrysoloras, the father of West European Greek studies: "Fuit is Ianocius ex peruetusta nobilique familia, uir egregie nobilis, adhaec insigniter eruditus: quippe unus ex iis qui e Manuelis Chrysolore ludo tanquam e Pythagore secretiore schola probe formatus exierit."[20]

Of this edition there is at least one mention in humanist correspondence. In a letter written in Basel on the 27th of May 1532 Bonifatius Amerbach sent to his close friend Andrea Alciato, the great reformer of Renaissance juridical studies nowadays best known as the alleged *pater et princeps* of the Emblem genre, a list of the latest publications by the Cratander press, among which is "et Janotii cuiusdam Florentini de dignitate hominis quattuor libros."[21] This "cuiusdam" does not exactly create the impression of a wide German-Swiss "fama" of Manetti, yet now we know that Alciato knew of Manetti, and, having taught at Bourges University until 1533, it is not impossible that he could have contributed to his reception in France, and even mentioned him before his unruly pupil Jean Calvin.

But, be it through Alciato or others, Manetti's treatise was indeed known in France. In 1558, the Breton rhetorician Pierre Boaistuau of Nantes, author of a widely read *Theatre du Monde*, published a *Bref discours de l'excellence et dignité de l'homme*, a work which he had first written in Latin and then translated into French and dedicated to "Messieurs Iacques & Alexandre de Betoun, Gentilshommes Escossais frères." In this book, which was printed seven times from 1558 to 1619, he

---

[16] J. Förstemann/O. Günther (eds.), *Briefe an Desiderius Erasmus von Rotterdam* (Leipzig, 1904), 185.

[17] A. Hartman (ed.), *Die Amerbachkorrespondenz* (Basel, 1942–), 4: letter of 24 September 1528.

[18] Cf. the letter of 23 December 1520 by Brassicanus in A. Horawitz/K. Hartfelder (eds.), *Briefwechsel des Beatus Rhenanus* (Hildesheim, 1966), 261.

[19] H. Ankwicz von Kleehoven, *Johann Cuspinians Briefwechsel* (Munich, 1933), 128ff.

[20] CLARISSIMI VI/ RI IANOCII DE MANE/ ctis, Equitis ac Iuresconsulti Floren/ tini, ad inclytum Arragonum/ Regem ALFONSUM,/ de dignitate & excel=/lentia hominis Li/ bri IIII.// Ex bibliotheca IO. ALEXANDRI / BRASSICANI Iuresconsulti,/ recent. in lucem aediti./ BASILEAE/ M.D.XXXII. (page 3).

[21] Hartmann, *Die Amerbachkorrespondenz*, 138.

mentions Manetti and Bartolomeo Facio: "Joinct aussi qu'il y a quelques autheurs modernes et autres, qui se sont exercez en semblables sujets comme Janotius, Bartolomeus Facius. . . ,"[22] and some passages even prove a close acquaintance with Manetti's text. The recent editor seems unaware of the Basel printed edition of Manetti's treatise, and many older commentators of Boaistuau's treatise were unable to identify "Janotius"—a difficulty we shall return to. The history of Manetti's echo in France—where Manettian manuscripts of early date are comparatively rare—has yet to be written. We may, however, on the basis of Boaistuau's sources and manner of writing and of Lionello Sozzi's studies on the idea of the "dignitas hominis" in France,[23] assume that a certain echo of Manettian thought seems to have existed in the milieu of mildly heterodox intellectuals of Neo-Platonic leanings, dedicated to a rather cryptic, often esoteric style in texts referring to the relationship between man and the universe: the intellectual climate that in Lyon produced, for example, Maurice Scève.

How did Manetti's treatise on human dignity, how did his oeuvre in general cross the Alps? Of the manuscripts of De dignitate et excellentia surviving to this day, none can be proven to have been available north of the Alps before 1550. Brassicanus's manuscript, the archetype for the Basel edition, is lost, and all suggestions as to its provenience remain speculative: Elisabeth Leonard, the modern editor of this treatise, has suggested an Hungarian origin,[24] basing herself on Brassicanus's Viennese contacts with Magyar exiles pointed out by Bietenholz in his valuable study of the Basel press,[25] but one could just as well think of Reuchlin and the Ingolstadt chair as a link between Florence and Brassicanus. There is however a third possibility, and this one leads us to the fourth "pillar" upon which Manetti's fame rests: his Orationes.

Already in the 1920s the German Reformation historian Paul Joachimsen pointed out the wide interest Florentine civic humanism had engendered in southwestern Germany, where patricians like Nikolaus von Wyle or Johann Brassicanus the Elder, the father of "our" Brassicanus, showed a considerable predilection for Leonardo Bruni. Among the books owned by Brassicanus the younger, the Austrian National Library still possesses a collection of Bruni's paraphrases of Platonic dialogues.[26] Now, a brief survey of the manuscript tradition of Bruni in Germany and elsewhere shows that most frequently Bruni's works were bound together with Manetti's funeral speech for the great Aretino,[27] a speech that because of its richness in biographical information was widely used as a kind of "Vita." I therefore tend to believe that it

---

[22] M. Simonin (ed.), Bref Discours de l'Excellence et Dignité de l'Homme (Geneva, 1982), 42.

[23] Lionello Sozzi, La "dignité de l'homme" à la Renaissance (Torino, 1982), 4 and 29; see also idem, "La dignitas hominis dans la littérature française de la Renaissance," in A. H. T. Levi (ed.), Humanism in France at the End of the Middle Ages and in the Early Renaissance (Manchester/New York, 1970), 176–198, especially 178.

[24] Leonard, Giannozzo Manetti: De dignitate, xi.

[25] Peter Bietenholz, Der italienische Humanismus und die Blütezeit des Buchdrucks in Basel. Die Baseler Drucke italienischer Autoren von 1530 bis zum Ende des 16. Jahrhunderts, in E. Bonjour and W. Kaegi (eds.), Baseler Beiträge zur Geschichtswissenschaft (Basel/Stuttgart, 1959), 122–123.

[26] Cod. vindob. lat. 2384, cf. Kristeller, Iter Italicum, 62.

[27] For example, in MS St. Peter Pap. 38 of the Badische Landesbibliothek, Karlsruhe.

was this *oratio* that attracted attention to Manetti, that through this attention given to Bruni's biographer, other works by Manetti slowly penetrated north, eventually preparing the way for the *one and only* printed edition of a book by our Giannozzo, whose name, frequently misunderstood because of the un-Latin, "volgare" diminutive "-ozzo" which it preserves, appears in such a variety of forms ("Janoctius," "Janotius," even "Jamritius") that to this day it can happen that mentions of Manetti in humanist correspondence do not appear in the indexes of modern editions.[28] We may therefore expect many more traces of "Janoctius quisdam," of "Jamritius Florentius" or of other onomastic masks of Manetti than I have found up to now. Let me just cite two more examples: the Brussels manuscript 11466–8 of the Bibliothèque Royale Albert I, written, according to Van der Gheyn, in the sixteenth century north of the Alps, contains, among notes on Bruni and texts by Petrarch, a note on Petrarch extracted from Manetti's *De illustribus longaevis*, a work, unedited to this day, dedicated to Luis de Guzman, of which today only three manuscripts—two Palatina and one Barberini—exist. On the other hand, the University Library of Greifswald in northeastern Germany owns a large manuscript compilation of Stoic writings, probably bound together by a Polish owner in the sixteenth century, which features Manetti's *Vita Senecae*.[29] The Stoic revival promoted by Justus Lipsius at the end of the sixteenth century apparently drew some attention to Giannozzo's biography of the great Stoic philosopher!

It is in the context of this Neo-Stoic trend that we can also situate the first printings of Manettian works after Brassicanus's edition of the *De dignitate*. Manetti's library, sold by the Fuggers to the Electors of the Palatinate, remained in Heidelberg until that town fell victim to Catholic troops during the Thirty Years' War, and the Bibliotheca Palatina was donated by the conquerors to the Papal Library in Rome. During their stay in Heidelberg, Manetti's books were used and examined around the beginning of the seventeenth century by the great Protestant humanist scholar Johann Gruter, a pupil of Justus Lipsius. As he was using Manettian books for his editions of Seneca and others, his attention was drawn to their owner and his works. Most likely as a result of this attention, Gruter's Hanau printer produced two editions of Manettian speeches in 1611, namely, the congratulatory speech on the wedding of Alfonso's son Ferrante and the *Oratio de laudibus pacis*. Two years later, an edition of Manetti's congratulatory address on the coronation of Emperor Frederick III was printed in Frankfurt from a lost manuscript owned by Melchior Haiminsfeld. It was not until 1650 that a Padua editor, Thomasini, produced Manetti's *Vita Petrarchae*, and in 1717 again a German editor, Struwe in Strasburg, reprinted the speech for Frederick III. Only Muratori's editions after 1731 changed this exclusively German-Swiss Protestant printing history of Manetti, yet it may be amusing to note that of the four doctoral dissertations published in the twentieth century on Manetti, three were German, and the first modern vernacular language the *De dignitate et excellentia hominis* was integrally translated into was equally German.

---

[28] E.g., in the *Amerbachkorrespondenz*, op. cit.
[29] MS lat. 629.

What made the Germans like Manetti so much? Was he really something of a "proto-Protestant," or was it merely that he once addressed a speech to a German emperor? I believe it was neither of the two exclusively, but more the fact that his main treatise was banned by the Catholic inquisition, first in Spain in 1583 and then in 1590 in all Catholic states. Thereby, a shadow had fallen on the totality of his writings in his home country. The only Florentine copy of Brassicanus's Basel edition carries the seal: "proibito donec emendetur. . . ." But why was the *De dignitate* put on the *Index librorum prohibitorum*? Up to now, only speculations have been raised.

Manetti's view of the dignity of man includes one of the most daring tenets Renaissance humanism ever uttered on the relationship of God and Man: the idea of man partaking in the divine essence by means of his own creative power, the power to act, to understand, to build, to work and thereby to change the face of the world for the better. Manetti's idea of man as a creator has nothing of the esoteric doctrines of the later Renaissance: his proof of man's divine power is no Paracelsian *homunculus* hidden in a dark attic, no alchemistic procedure. Rather, Manetti's proof of man's divine essence lies in the cities man builds, the discoveries he makes, the machines he constructs: "Nostrae denique sunt omnia machinamenta que admirabilis et pene incredibilis humani vel divini potius ingenii acies et acrimonia singulari quadam ac precipua solertia moliri fabricarique constituit."[30] Did the Spanish Inquisition sense the power of these words that foreshadow not so much the age of Luther's Reform as that of Voltaire and Benjamin Franklin? Or did the Inquisitors simply state that Manetti once dared call the arguments of Pope Innocent III, the earlier dean Lotharius, on human misery "childish"? We do not know what occurred during the secret discussions of the Inquisitors, but one thing is sure: by *excluding* Manetti from their own Catholic world, by exiling his works from Tuscany's radiant skies and from the sunny shores of the Arno, they drove Pope Nicholas V's close friend, the pious Giannozzo, into the century-long exclusive intellectual property of the Protestant world, which itself, one must say in this case, did not exactly "increase the talents it received."

But Giannozzo Manetti is just one example, a small example of the power of ideological narrow-mindedness to impoverish a nation's cultural heritage. Italian humanism created many beginnings, beginnings in thought, in artistic creation, in technical invention, that in the following centuries Italy itself could not, for the most various reasons, contain within its bounds, and which, when returning home after a "foreign" metamorphosis, seemed strange and at times even frightening to the Italians themselves. Humanist bible scholarship, understood differently under a different sky, can produce a new religious movement, a reform of the Church, and the belief in the divine spark present in the artist's and sculptor's creative instinct can, once applied to the inventor and the engineer, transform an entire planet. Whether in this way, Italian humanism is to be regarded as the revered mother of our modern world or as a wizard's helper, is a question I leave to you to ponder.

Köln

---

[30] Leonard, *Giannozzo Manetti: De dignitate*, 78.

George Herbert's Memoriae Matris Sacrum
and Petrarch's Sonnets

PHILIP C. DUST

pplying R. J. Schoeck's prolegomenic *Intertextuality and Renaissance Texts*[1] to the tradition of Petrarch's sonnet form as it emerges in George Herbert's *Memoriae Matris Sacrum*, I have found that Herbert adapts several Petrarchan *topoi* to important motifs of his poems. Schoeck makes his point about the text as a woven amalgam of previous texts using especially Petrarch's own "Ascent of Mont Ventoux" (*Fam.* IV.1) which echoes "Pliny, Livy, Ovid, Cicero, Virgil, and Seneca, as well as the Bible and St. Augustine (and Augustine quoting Scripture and Seneca)."[2] Herbert's own indebtedness to Augustine, a copy of whose works Petrarch carried always with him, is well known.[3]

If Petrarch's intertextual weaving of previous authors into his own work is significant for the Renaissance as a period in which polyphanic literary texts develop, his own influence on future Renaissance texts is huge. Leonard Forster has summed up that influence, which countless scholars have traced, in his classic little masterpiece *The Icy Fire*.[4] As Herbert remembers the genteel virtues of his mother in his poems, Forster's emphasis on the "political Petrarchism of the Virgin Queen," Elizabeth, is echoed.[5] In the context of his personal love and devotion to his mother, Herbert portrays her as a type of an Elizabeth who had consciously used Petrarchism as a model for controlling her courtiers and governing England as an orderly state.

While the practice of writing funerary Latin verse had been commonplace in English universities, as J. W. Binns points out in his *Intellectual Culture in Elizabethan and Jacobean England*, and Herbert had engaged in the writing of such verse with his poems on the deaths of Prince Henry, Queen Anne, and Lord Bacon, his poems on

---

[1] Bamberg: H. Kaiser-Verlag, 1984.
[2] Schoeck, 46–51.
[3] Schoeck, 46. Herbert mentions the works of Augustine in his will.
[4] Cambridge: Cambridge Univ. Press, 1969.
[5] Forster, 122–147.

the death of his mother, precisely because of their use of Petrarchan *topoi*, transcend his own and most such verse.[6] Binns cites Wills' *Poematum liber* (1573) for generic types of funerary verse.[7] The only one of them Herbert actually uses is in Poem 13, which he titles an *Epitaphium*; in his hands a full expression not only of a poem "related in a book" but an expression of virginity as a sublime Petrarchan quality. The real model of poetic theory in the genres, as Binns observes, was to be Julius Caesar Scaliger in his *Poetici libri septem* (Lyons, 1561), who "helped adapt ancient generic patterns to Christian Renaissance use."[8]

But we cannot neglect the effect of the vernacular tradition of Petrarch's sonnets on Latin poetry. Although, as Theodor Mommsen comments, there was no such interaction between Petrarch's own Latin and Italian poetry, there was between his vernacular and the Latin poetry of the Renaissance.[9] Forster cites many, not the least of which are Joannes Secundus in Belgium and Mathias Sarbiewski in Poland.[10] As the first wrote as a love poet and the second as a religious, I argue that Herbert wrote both from filial love and intense religious faith.

Although Robert Durling's translation of the Sonnets does not make the division between those sonnets written during Laura's life and those after her death, Anna Maria Armi's does.[11] Armi's distinction preserves the deep sense that Petrarch had of the mortality and immortality of the perfect lady and her ultimate triumph in heaven. This sense Herbert has about his mother, and he uses Petrarch's *topoi*, especially of sonnets written after Laura's death, to express his own assertion of his mother's triumph.

The late sixteenth and early seventeenth centuries provided at least three editions of Petrarch's sonnets which would have been readily available to Herbert: *Il Petrarca, con nuove spositioni* (Venetia: Giorgio Angelieri, 1586); *Il Petrarca, nuovamente ridotto alla vera lettione* (Venetia: Domenico Imberti, 1600); and *Il Petrarca nuovamente ristampato e diligentemente corretto* (Venetia: Niccolo Misserini, 1610).

Specific *topoi* in Petrarch's sonnets and Herbert's poems are those of Fate, gardens, rivers, the soul, and cosmic apotheosis, especially that of the virgin-mother. Forster has commented at length on the last two.[12] The last, while it is Petrarch's ultimate consolation in religious devotion to the Virgin, is not Herbert's final expression of devotion to his mother. Rather, Herbert by way of postscript expresses a kind of nihilistic grief only to find fulfillment in silence that Petrarch expresses, as Fred

---

[6] Leeds: Francis Cairns, 1990. The poem to Henry and the one to Anne were published in 1619; the one to Bacon in 1626. The poems to his mother were appended to John Donne's *Sermon of Commemoration of the Lady Danvers*, given and printed in 1627.

[7] Binns, 60.

[8] Binns, 73–74.

[9] *Petrarch: Sonnets and Songs*, trans. Anna Maria Armi (New York: Pantheon, 1946).

[10] Forster, 46, 47, and *passim*.

[11] Armi; the first are sonnets 1–258; the second, sonnets 259–356. In the Petrarch MS, there is simply a blank page separating the sonnets. I follow Armi's distinction based on the sense of the poems.

[12] Forster, 9, 21, 25 and 122–147.

Nichols has observed, in the *Liber sine nomine*.[13] "This one time I write, to be forever still." (*Semel/scribo perpetuo ut sileam* [ll.7–8].)

As Herbert addresses his mother (Poem 11) it is clear that a fatal attraction exists between them in her passing and in his misery over that death. Their union is expressed by a reference to the sisters of Fate:

> The Fates haven't cut your thread alone now,
> But by your death I am unraveled too.

> Non tibi nunc soli filum abrupere sorores,
>   Dissutus videor funere & ipse tuo.

> (ll.11–12)[14]

So Petrarch's fate is inextricably mixed with Laura's death in Sonnet 296:

> Envious Fates, you soon broke the spindle that was spinning a soft, bright thread around my bonds.[15]

> Invide Parche, sí repente il fuso
> Troncaste, ch' attorcea soave et chiaro
> Stame al mio laccio[16]

> (ll.5–7)

Herbert's and Petrarch's sorrows are bound fast to their loves, the one to his mother, the other to Laura.

Poems 4 and 5 of Herbert's collection make ample use of gardens to express his grief. In number 4, the image of the garden fades into the image of the stars. In number 5, the image of the garden becomes an image of death.

While Herbert's mother lived, the gardens were life. Now they are no more. The poet says,

> Now, you gardens, wither, gardens
> That made your mistress happy.
> You have adorned the coffin, you cannot now
> Stay fresh.

> Horti, deliciae *Dominae*, marcescite tandem;

---

[13] "Petrarch's *Liber sine nomine* and the Limits of Language," in *Acta Conventus Neo-Latini Hafniensis*, ed. Rhoda Schur, Ann Moss, Philip Dust, *et al.* (Binghamton, N.Y.: Medieval & Renaissance Texts & Studies, 1994), 741–750.

[14] All quotes from Herbert's Latin poetry and translations from them are taken from *The Latin Poetry of George Herbert*, ed. and trans. Mark McCloskey and Paul R. Murphy (Athens, Ohio: Ohio University Press, 1965).

[15] All translations from Petrarch's sonnets are taken from *Petrarch's Lyric Poems*, trans. and ed. Robert M. Durling (Cambridge, Mass: Harvard University Press, 1976).

[16] All texts of Petrarch's poems are taken from *Francesco Petrarca: Canzoniere*, ed. Gianfranco Contini (Alpignano: Alberto Tallone, 1974). Line numbers are Durling's.

> Ornâstis capulum, nec superesse licet.
>
> (5.1–2)

And he continues further in the vein of Petrarch:

> And so I call you resting places,
> Not gardens now, while her
> No longer here, each flower bed
> Brings back!
>
> Quare haud vos hortos, sed coemeteria dico,
>   Dum torus absentem quisque reponit heram.
>
> (5.9–10)

So in Petrarch's Sonnet 301, the valleys, filled with buds, fish, flowers, and grass become symbols of death.

> O valley full of my laments, rivers often rising by my weeping, be as of the forest, wandering birds, and fishes that these banks rein in, air warmed and cleared by my sighs, sweet path become so bitter, hill that pleased and now displeases me.
>
> Valle che de' lamenti miei se' piena,
> Fiume che spesso del mio pianger cresci,
> Fere selvestre, vaghi augelli et pesci,
> Che l'una et l' altra verda riva affrena,
>   Aria de' miei sospir' calda et serena,
> Dolce sentier che sí amaro rïesci,
> Colle che mi piacesti, or mi rincresci
>
> (ll.1–7)

In Sonnet 303 Petrarch again describes the garden now lost because of Laura's death:

> flowers, leaves, grass, shadows, caves, waves, gentle breezes, closed valleys, high hills, and open slopes
>
> Fior', frondi, herbe, ombre, antri, onde, aure soavi,
> Valli chiuse, alti colli et piaggie apriche
>
> (ll.5–6)

and he concludes,

> my days were so bright, now they are as dark as Death who causes it.
>
> I dí miei fur sí chiari, or son sí foschi,
> Come Morte che 'l fa
>
> (ll.12–13)

Both poets recall the myth of the primal garden Eden, lost to the ravages of death. Herbert goes so far as to reject a merely worldly Edenic happiness for the heavenly happiness promised by God in its stead:

Rather than a humble garden,
My mother, dewy with those pleasures
That do not end, an Eden tills
Which the big breathing of the North Wind
Cannot enter. O heaven to me
My mother's name, the glory of it,
And what I owe it.

Mater perpetuis vuida gaudijs,
    Horto pro tenui colit
Edenem Boreae flatibus inuium,
    Quin caeli mihi sunt mei,
Materni decus, & debita nominis

(4.2–6)

Petrarch too accepts the dissolution of the earthly garden in Sonnnet 280 where he
first laments the passing of earlier pastoral bliss:

nor have I ever seen a valley with so many hidden, trusty places for
sighing; nor do I believe that Love ever had, in Cyprus or on any
other shore, such sweet nests.

Né già mai vidi valle aver sí spessi
Luoghi da sospirar reposti et fidi;
Né credo già ch' Amore in Cipro avessi,
O in altra riva, sí soavi nidi

(ll.5–8)

But then he is consoled by Laura in the heavenly bliss of an eternal Eden, heaven:

But you, born in a happy hour, who call me from Heaven; by the
memory of your untimely death you beg me to scorn the world and its
sweet hooks.

Ma tu, ben nata che dal ciel mi chiami,
Per la memoria di tua morte acerba
Preghi ch' i' sprezzi 'l mondo e i suoi dolci hami.

(ll.12–14)

Both poets find hope in the depths of sorrow with the thought of immortality, the
conquest of death, if not of its sorrow.

Water, symbol of both death and life, is a *topos* for each poet singing of his native
rivers. Herbert's collection opens with the image of the fountain into which are
poured his tears and the hyperbolic statement that the Thames is dry compared with
those tears (Poem 1). The tears fade into the liquid ink of his writing pen "to make
a river dark with grieving."

In flumen moerore nigrum si funderer ardens

(1.5)

The poet returns to the river motif in the next-to-last poem of the collection (Poem 18), where he at first urges the Thames to rise up against heaven and then, recanting, says it should not approach his mother there, but better "In darkness you should flow by us who weep."

> Καὶ πρέπον ὧδε παρὰ δακρυόεσσι ῥέειν.
> (18.6)

So Petrarch involves the Tiber, Arno, and Po as vehicles for his sighs over the fate of his motherland, Italy (Sonnet 128). In Sonnet 208, the Rhone is addressed and urged to

> Kiss her foot or her lovely white hand; tell her (let your kiss be heard as words): "The spirit is ready, but the flesh is weary."

echoing Matthew 26:41.

> Basciale 'l piede, o la man bella et bianca;
> Dille, e 'l basciar sie 'nvece di parole:
> Lo spirto è pronto, ma la carne è stanca.
> (ll.12–14)

Platonic soul-body psychology is accepted by both Herbert and Petrarch as a philosophical foundation for their poetic expression of a dichotomous sorrow and joy. For Herbert (Poem 14), his own soul has been one with his mother's life. At her death, therefore, he feels he is left as a lifeless body.

> The soul's weak wall alone, the spirit's
> Blind urn, my friend, seek at this grave

> Ψυχῆς ἀσθενὲς ἕρκος, ἀμαυρὸν πνεύματος ἄγγος,
> Τῷδε παρὰ τύμβῳ δίζεο, φίλε, μόνον.
> (14.1–2)

Such is the text of Petrarch in Sonnet 94:

> When through my eyes to my deepest heart comes the image that masters me, every other departs, and the powers that the soul distribute leave the members an almost immobile weight.

> Quando giugne per gli occhi al cor profondo
> L'imagin donna, ogni altra indi si parte,
> Et le vertú che l'anima comparte
> Lascian le membra, quasi immobil pondo
> (ll.1–4)

Much has been made by Julia Conaway Bondanella of Petrarch's Sonnet 323 in which the poet is pictured standing at a window through which are presented allegorical figures.[17] Herbert writes in Greek (Poem 14):

---

[17] "Petrarch as Visionary: The Import of Canzone 323," in *Francis Petrarch, Six Centuries Later:*

The mind sheds its light,
Flashing through heaven now, as through a window
That once through her beloved body flashed.

ἀλλὰ νόος·
Ὃς διὰ σωματίου πρότερον καὶ νῦν δὶ Ὀλύμπου
Ἀστράπτων, θυρίδων ὡς δία, νεῖμε σέλας.
(14.6–8)

The cosmic apotheosis of the soul-mind appearing in the image of the window as a revelation of it to physical mortals is too important in both poets to be underestimated. Both are trying to express an immortality, an eternity of being, while both are acutely conscious of their bodily attachment to the physical world. Further, both are also seeking a poetic means to express the loss of physical being in those to whom they are so devoted.

As the allegorical figures pass before Petrarch at the window, so do events from his mother's life, and qualities of her stewardship pass before Herbert's window throughout his poems. Herbert uses the laurel in this context (Poem 9) where he says:

(For how can there be laurels for me,
How nectar, unless with you
I pass the day in song)

(nam quae mihi laurus,
Quod nectar, nisi cum te celebrare diem?)
(9.15–16)

Bondanella describes Petrarch's laurel in Sonnet 323: "The plant traditionally immune to lightning, the laurel, is without warning uprooted by a flash from the heavens."[18] For both poets, death is that lightning-flash. But for both, the window reveals immortality.

Herbert's *Epitaphium* (Poem 13) at once proclaims his mother as a "Modest virgin, faithful wife, / Strict mother"

Virgo pudens, vxor fida, seuera parens
(13.2)

The apparent oxymoron derives from the place of the Virgin Mary, both virgin and mother. Petrarch's Sonnet 366, "Vergine bella," incorporates that important religious tradition as a magnificent conclusion of all his sonnets. Like the Virgin Mother, Herbert's mother has been "the fiery contention of lord and commoner alike / The first her divinity attracting, / Her holiness the second."

A Symposium, ed. Aldo Scaglione. North Carolina Studies in the Romance Languages and Literatures: Symposium 3 (Chapel Hill: Dept. of Romance Languages, University of North Carolina, 1975): 105–127.
[18] Bondanella, 121–122.

> Magnatúmque inopúmque aequum certamen & ardor:
> Nobilitate illos, hos pietate rapit.
>
> (13.3–4)

This "holiness" or, better, "piety" is found in Petrarch's description of the Virgin as a "solid shield of afflicted people":

> O saldo scudo de l'afflicte genti
>
> (1.17)

Petrarch says of the Virgin:

> you have gathered into yourself three sweet names: mother, daughter, and bridge, O glorious Virgin
>
> Tre dolci et cari nomi ài in te raccolti,
> Madre, figliuola et sposa:
> Vergine glorïosa
>
> (11.45–47)

Paradoxically enough, it was Mary's humility as the handmaid of the Lord, the *ancilla Domini*, which raised her to heavenly glory. As Herbert says of his mother:

> Proud
> And meek at once, she unlinked
> Regions linked: she took her joy
> In earth's possessions, and in the stars'.
>
> Sic excelsa humilísque simul loca dissita iunxit,
> Quicquid habet tellus, quicquid & astra, fruens.
>
> (13.5–6)

So Petrarch's virgin is one "who lightens this life and adorns the other":

> Ch' allumi questa vita et l'altra adorni
>
> (1.29)

And as was the case with Herbert's mother, she achieves heaven through her humility, she "who through true and highest humility mounted to Heaven."

> che per vera et altissima umilitate salisti al ciel
>
> (11.41–42)

Herbert's Latin "excelsa humilisque" echoes perfectly Petrarch's Italian "altissima umilitate."

Herbert was deeply impressed with Petrarch's figuring of Laura as a mother in Sonnet 285. There Petrarch says,

> Never did a pitying mother to her dear son
> or a loving wife to her beloved husband
> give so many sighs . . .

as she gives to me, who seeing from her eternal home my heavy
exile, often returns to me with her usual affection and with her
brow adorned with double pity,
now that of a mother, now that of a lover.

> Né mai pietosa madre al caro figlio
> Né donna accesa al suo sposo dilecto
> Die' con tanti sospir'. . . .
>   Come a me quella che 'l mio grave exiglio
> Mirando dal suo eterno alto ricetto,
> Spesso a me torna co l'usato affecto,
> Et di doppia pietate ornata il ciglio:
>   Or di madre, or d'amante
>
> (11.1–9)

The whole of Herbert's *Memoriae Matris Sacrum* is founded on this conceit of a
mother who is enshrined in heaven and who pities her son still in earthly exile. Poem
3 concludes with the poet offering himself the kind of consolation Petrarch's Laura
offered to Petrarch in this metaphysical conceit:

> Multiply your rays of light
> That I may wind and twist
> My hand in them, and, my mother staying
> Where she is, climb up to her.

> Fac radios saltem ingemines, vt dextra tortos
>   Implicet, & matrem, matre manente, petam.
>
> (3.9–10)

The divine image of the silk scarf let down from heaven in Herbert's English "The
Pearl" (ll.37–40) is here evoked in Latin.

Herbert's constant theme about this mother, as is Petrarch's about Laura, is that
death has released the women from the imperfections of life in this world and raised
them to cosmic splendor in heavenly beatitude. In contrast with the happiness the
women have attained, both poets are left shattered and grieving, the most vital part
of their beings having been taken from them. In Herbert's poetry this gives rise to
mixed feelings of sorrow over death and consolation over belief in immortality.
Likewise it had been Petrarch's constant theme of lament and rapture over Laura's
death. As for Herbert, his mother has become for him a figure of love, so Petrarch's
love, Laura, had become for him a mother-figure. And both love and mother are
eternized in the ecstatic figure of the Virgin Mary.

Northern Illinois University

Scaenica Faceta: *The Choral Odes of Johannes Reuchlin's* Scaenica Progymnasmata *(1497)*

GLENN EHRSTINE

For almost five centuries now, arbiters of German literature have been united in their praise of Johannes Reuchlin's *Scaenica Progymnasmata* of 1497, more commonly known by the name of *Henno*.[1] Authorities from Sebastian Brant and Johann Christoph Gottsched to Stefan Rhein agree that Reuchlin's farce was the first successful Terentian comedy brought forth by German Humanism.[2] Beyond this *opinio communis*, however, agreement becomes rare indeed. Little consensus exists, for example, on the work's possible source, with researchers alternately pleading for the influence of the French farce *Maître Pathelin* or the Italian *commedia dell'arte*.[3] Similar

---

[1] The most recent edition of the play chooses the latter title: Johannes Reuchlin, *Henno*, ed. and trans. Harry C. Schnur (Stuttgart: Reclam, 1970). Schnur bases his Latin text largely upon the play's 1511 edition, which appeared in the Tübingen press of Thomas Anshelm. He also draws upon the earlier edition of Hugo Holstein, *Johann Reuchlins Komödien. Ein Beitrag zur Geschichte des lateinischen Schuldramas* (Halle: Verlag der Buchhandlung des Waisenhauses, 1888), 11–34.

[2] Stefan Rhein, "Johannes Reuchlin," *Deutsche Dichter der Frühen Neuzeit (1450–1600). Ihr Leben und Werk*, ed. Stephan Füssel (Berlin: Erich Schmidt, 1993), 149.

[3] Most scholars, in agreement with Ludwig Geiger's monumental Reuchlin biography, assume Reuchlin drew upon the French farce *Maître Pathelin*, which he may have encountered during legal studies in Poitiers in 1480–1481. However, Hans Rupprich and others point to evidence that Reuchlin based his characters on figures from the Italian *commedia dell'arte*. Considering that Philip Melanchthon refers to *Henno* as a "fabula Gallica," the argument for a French source seems much more convincing, yet there is no reason why Reuchlin could not have altered the French characters according to stock Italian figures, as Max Brod has suggested. Most recently, Otto Brunken has surveyed the scholarship and concluded that the Italian influence predominates. Ludwig Geiger, *Johann Reuchlin. Sein Leben und seine Werke* (Leipzig: Duncker and Humblot, 1871), 82–91; Hans Rupprich, "Johannes Reuchlin und seine Bedeutung im europäischen Humanismus," in *Johannes Reuchlin 1455–1522. Festgabe seiner Vaterstadt Pforzheim zur 500. Wiederkehr seines Geburtstages*, ed. Manfred Krebs (Pforzheim: Selbstverlag der Stadt, 1955), 20; "Declamatio de Capnione Phorcensi," *Philippi Melanchthonis Opera quæ supersunt omnia*, Corpus Reformatorum XI (Halle: C. A. Schwetske et filius, 1843), 1004; Max Brod, *Johannes Reuchlin und*

speculation abounds as to the source of the play's four choral odes, as such choruses were common to the Greek dramatic tradition but not the Latin.[4] While such questions deserve their due, the quibbling over *Henno*'s possible models has unfortunately obstructed the more crucial task of examining the play itself. Only recently have Jane O. Newman and James A. Parente, Jr. rectified this situation by drawing attention, respectively, to the text's important performative and political aspects. Yet even these two scholars reach diametrically opposed conclusions on the role of the play's choral odes.[5] Clearly, no assumption on these interludes is valid without thorough investigation both of their origin and of their relationship to corresponding acts. Upon closer textual analysis, it becomes evident that the choruses do not, as often assumed, serve moral edification but rather valorize and ironize the poetic ideal of Reuchlin and his humanist audience. Indeed, as they contain *Henno*'s earliest recorded verses, they are a crucial key in understanding Reuchlin's work.

The play's plot is as follows. The peasant Henno has discovered his wife's hidden savings and gives the money to Dromo, his clever servant, so that he might buy him cloth for a new coat from the merchant Danista. Dromo, however, keeps the funds for himself and, at the same time, receives cloth from Danista on Henno's credit, which he sells for even more money. When both Henno and Danista want their money or merchandise, Dromo denies having received anything. Forced to defend himself in court, he plays dumb on the advice of the lawyer Petrucius, answering "ble" to all questions. The judge, believing him an idiot, sets him free, after which he escapes Petrucius's demands for payment with "ble" as well. Having proven his wit, he reconciles with Henno and finally marries his daughter.

Located respectively at the close of the first four acts, the odes appear inappropriate in terms of both content and verse. While two choruses respectively praise the honest poverty of Henno's family and bemoan the mendacity of the courtroom, the remaining pair ignores other moral dilemmas, in particular the deceitful success of Dromo. Moreover, Reuchlin, who composed the acts in quantitative

---

sein Kampf. Eine historische Monographie (Stuttgart: W. Kohlhammer, 1965), 135. Otto Brunken, "Johannes Reuchlin (1455–1522): Scenica Progymnasmata: Hoc est: Ludicra Preexercitamenta. Basel 1498," in *Handbuch zur Kinder- und Jugendliteratur. Vom Beginn des Buchdrucks bis 1570*, ed. Theodor Brüggemann (Stuttgart: J. B. Metzler, 1987), 339–342.

[4] Heinz Otto Burger, Eckehard Catholy, Otto Brunken, and Johannes Bolte have suggested, respectively, that Reuchlin drew on Seneca, Aristophanes, the *commedia dell'arte*, or his own desire to surpass Plautus and Terence, whose plays contain no choruses. Heinz Otto Burger, *Renaissance, Humanismus, Reformation. Deutsche Literatur im europäischen Kontext* (Bad Homburg: Verlag Gehlen, 1969), 278; Eckehard Catholy, *Das deutsche Lustspiel. I: Vom Mittelalter bis zum Ende der Barockzeit*, Sprache und Literatur 47 (Stuttgart: W. Kohlhammer, 1969), 202, n. 230; Brunken, "Reuchlin, Scenica Progymnasmata," *Handbuch der Kinder- und Jugendliteratur*, 342; Gulielmus Gnapheus, *Acolastus*, ed. Johannes Bolte (Berlin: Speyer & Peters, 1891), ix.

[5] Jane O. Newman, "Textuality Versus Performativity in Neo-Latin Drama: Johannes Reuchlin's *Henno*," *Theatre Journal* 38 (1986): 262, 266–267, 268; James A. Parente, Jr., "Empowering Readers: Humanism, Politics, and Money in Early Modern German Drama," in *The Harvest of Humanism in Central Europe. Essays in Honor of Lewis W. Spitz*, ed. Manfred P. Fleischer (St. Louis: Concordia, 1992), 270, 272.

iambic trimeter, wrote the odes in rhymed, stressed Latin, customarily an abomination for his humanist contemporaries. Thus the nineteenth-century scholar Hugo Holstein saw it necessary to defend the play against these apparent deficiencies.[6] His defense of the choruses themselves, however, merely entailed briefly demonstrating the relationship to their respective acts;[7] his remarks, in fact, do little more than paraphrase Reuchlin's own annotations to the play, contained in the Wimpheling manuscript of the play in the university library of Uppsala.[8] More recent comments on these interludes also remain quite cursory, summarily attributing to them some degree of moral commentary.[9] Indeed, the only new insight into the choruses is that not they, but rather those of Jakob Locher's *Historia de rege Franciae*, are the first choruses set to music in the history of German theater.[10] To date, all scholarship has ignored the most obvious starting point for an investigation of the odes: their relationship to the chorus of Reuchlin's previous play *Sergius vel Capitis Caput*.

The link between *Henno* and *Sergius* lies, superficially, in Reuchlin's recycling of the refrain from the earlier play's sole chorus for the third ode of *Scænica Progymnasmata*: *Musis, poetis et sacro Phoebo referte gratias*. Their interdependence, however, runs deeper, as their circumstances of composition reveal. Reuchlin composed both plays among friends and members of the Heidelberg *Sodalitas litteraria Rhenana*, where he had fled from Stuttgart after the death of the Württemberg Duke Eberhard im Bart. The new duke, Eberhard the Younger, stood under the influence of Conrad Holzinger, an Augustinian monk who was hostile to Reuchlin.[11] To avenge himself for his forced flight,[12] Reuchlin first wrote *Sergius*, whose stark diatribe lambasted Holzinger and other opponents of humanism, in addition to ridiculing the veneration of relics. However, the leader of the Heidelberg circle, Bishop Johann von Dalberg, advised against a performance, citing the power of a Franciscan at the Palatinate court who might take offense at the play's mockery of monks. As a replacement, Reuchlin created *Henno*, which young students performed in the palace of the bishop on 31

---

[6] "Zwar möchte man den Chören den rechten Rhythmus und die innige Verbindung mit der Handlung absprechen, aber selbst wenn man diesen Mangel anerkennen müßte, so sind doch die Vorzüge des Stückes so hervorstehend, daß sie ... den Verfasser mit Recht an die Spitze der dramatischen Literatur der Neuzeit stellen." Holstein, *Johann Reuchlins Komödien*, 34.

[7] Holstein, *Johann Reuchlins Komödien*, 144–145.

[8] Compare Holstein's remarks on pp. 144–145 with his own edition of Reuchlin's commentary: Holstein, *Johann Reuchlins Komödien*, 97–106. The notes on lines 144–152, 229–236, 278–295 and 356–373 treat the choral odes.

[9] Brod, *Johannes Reuchlin und sein Kampf*, 138, 141, 142, 143; Schnur, ed., *Henno*, 55–56; Brunken, "Reuchlin, Scenica Progymnasmata," *Handbuch zur Kinder- und Jugendliteratur*, 334; Rhein, "Johannes Reuchlin," *Deutsche Dichter der Frühen Neuzeit*, 147–148, 149.

[10] Bernhard Coppel, "Jakob Locher und seine in Freiburg aufgeführten Dramen," in *Acta Conventus Neo-Latini Amstelodamensis. Proceedings of the Second International Congress of Neo-Latin Studies*, ed. P. Tuynman, G. C. Kuiper and E. Keßler (Munich: Wilhelm Fink, 1979), 263.

[11] For this and the following, see Geiger, *Johann Reuchlin*, 39–49, 79–82.

[12] Unfortunately, historical evidence is scanty; Brod, for example, sees no direct connection to Holzinger in the play: Brod, *Johannes Reuchlin und sein Kampf*, 129. Rhein is also cautious on this point: Rhein, "Johannes Reuchlin," *Deutsche Dichter der Frühen Neuzeit*, 149.

January 1497. The new material appears innocuous, yet it would seem strange indeed if Reuchlin were to have completely abandoned his efforts to skewer his foes with pointed pen.

By adapting *Sergius*'s closing ode, Reuchlin retained a now muted invective against Holzinger or others who would undermine the *studia humanitatis*. In *Sergius*, the original seven strophes are silent on such enemies, praising instead literature and the divine mission of poets. The ode thus functioned as an encomium of the self-styled *vates* at the expense of the corrupt clerics in the play itself. As *Henno* was otherwise devoid of villainous scholastics, Reuchlin altered the chorus to introduce them here, keeping the refrain but otherwise creating three original strophes. In the new verses, the theme of poets' heavenly gifts disappears, replaced by an attack on their illiterate adversaries. Moreover, the appearance of this harangue after the third act is by no means arbitrary, for it is in this act that men of letters gain special significance. Danista, upon recognizing Dromo's deceit, deems him a *vir trilitterus*, the adjective coined by Reuchlin in variation of Plautus's *trium litterarum homo* for *fur*, or "thief."[13] The revised ode follows quickly upon this charge and takes up the topic of letters again, now applied to ignorant scholastics: *Hinc hostis est audaculus, qui nescit ullas litteras.*[14] In other words, Dromo is a thief, a three-letter man, but those who have no letters whatsoever (i.e., uneducated theologians) are even worse than thieves: they are the enemies of true poetry. Given the ultimate origin of the ode in the context of *Sergius*, it is not difficult to associate this critique with Conrad Holzinger, though it could just as easily apply to any member of the Heidelberg university who opposed Reuchlin's efforts to teach Hebrew there.[15]

Displaced by this invective, the original praise of humanist poets in *Sergius*'s chorus spreads to the additional choral odes that Reuchlin created specifically for *Henno*. It is here that Reuchlin steps forward as pedagogue, seeking new recruits for classical studies and fostering better latinity.[16] Yet as Parente has noted, the promotion of ancient letters had potent political overtones, since through them, humanists justified their claims to sociopolitical hegemony in the Holy Roman Empire.[17] Reuchlin's odes were an integral part of this appeal.[18] The aggrandizement of humanist studies is the common element of all choruses, even where it does not explicitly appear. The second chorus devotes itself solely to this laudation of poetry, whereas the first and fourth integrate their appeal in a discussion of the preceding act. Thus, in chorus four, Reuchlin condemns the rampant corruption of the courtroom illustrated by the lawyer Petrucius's complicity in Dromo's deception. In contrast, those who avoid the courts and follow the muses will achieve peace and eternal fame. The first chorus speaks ostensibly only of poverty, yet this entreaty must be seen in the context of the

---

[13] Holstein, *Johann Reuchlins Komödien*, 104. See also Schnur, ed., *Henno*, 55.

[14] "Henno," *Johann Reuchlins Komödien*, ed. Holstein, 23, lines 286–287.

[15] Geiger, *Johann Reuchlin*, 45.

[16] See here especially Brunken, "Reuchlin, Scenica Progymnasmata," *Handbuch zur Kinder- und Jugendliteratur*, 331–339.

[17] Parente, "Empowering Readers," 280.

[18] Parente, "Empowering Readers," 270–271.

impoverished students who made up Reuchlin's intended audience. In his 1512 commentary on Reuchlin's play, Jacob Spiegel emphasized in his discussion of this section that poverty begets wisdom and that the poor study more ardently.[19] Similar in their respective situations to Stylpho and Vincentius in Jacob Wimpheling's *Stylpho* (1480),[20] young students may have often found it much more lucrative to pursue well-endowed benefices requiring little classical learning than to indulge in humanist studies that, without a patron, might lead to a financially uncertain future. Thus the first chorus encourages would-be scholars to remain steadfast in their pursuit of learning for learning's sake and to wear their impoverishment as a badge. This does not negate the applicability of the first chorus as a moral maxim; however, it is the only chorus with such didacticism. When one compares this to the recurring exaltation of the *studia humanitatis* in all other choruses, it becomes clear that their function was not so much to provide moral commentary on the action of the play[21] as to address the young audience as potential collaborators in the humanist project, inspiring their interest in classical letters and polemicizing against those who found fault with the new learning.

Henno, of course, shared this self-serving valorization with other humanist school dramas. However, by confining it to the choral odes, Reuchlin was free to devote himself in the acts to a more studied imitation of the Palliata. This represented a great improvement over earlier efforts such as *Stylpho* or Johannes Kerckmeister's *Codrus* (1485),[22] both of which attempted to emulate Roman New Comedy while simultaneously addressing the contemporary concerns of their humanist audience. *Sergius*, too, suffers from the same weakness, sacrificing dramatic tension for unstructured attacks on adversaries of the new learning. In *Henno*, however, Reuchlin tightens the play's coherence by limiting humanist self-praise to the choruses alone.

Reuchlin further contributed to the success of his appeal by keeping the choruses in the same light, humorous tone as the rest of the work. This becomes apparent, above all, in a certain self-ironization. Thus the attack on advocates and judges in the fourth chorus, indeed the whole portrayal of the lawyer Petrucius, is a gentle poke at Reuchlin's own profession.[23] Then, again, there is the term *trilitterus*, used to char-

---

[19] " . . . pauperes, qui urgente rerum inopia student ardentissime, nec ullis uoluptatum illecebris emolliuntur, sed per ardua quaeque prorumpunt. . . . Hinc grecis in ore frequens est uerbum, Paupertas sapientiam sortita est." *Ioannis Reuchlin Phorcensis scaenica progymnasmata, hoc est ludicra praeexercitamenta, cum explanatione Iacobi Spiegel Selestani* (Tübingen: in aedibus Thoma Anselmi, 1512), Gii[v]. For more on Spiegel's commentary, see Steven Rowan and Gerhild Scholz Williams, "Jacob Spiegel on Gianfrancesco Pico and Reuchlin: Poetry, Scholarship and Politics in Germany in 1512," *Bibliothèque d'Humanisme et Renaissance* 44 (1982): 301–305.

[20] Jakob Wimpheling, *Stylpho*, ed. and trans. Harry C. Schnur (Stuttgart: Reclam, 1971).

[21] Cf. Brunken, "Reuchlin, Scenica Progymnasmata," *Handbuch zur Kinder- und Jugendliteratur*, 334.

[22] Johannes Kerckmeister, *Codrus. Ein neulateinisches Drama aus dem Jahre 1485*, ed. Lothar Mundt (Berlin: Walter de Gruyter, 1969).

[23] However, the critique has its serious aspects, too, as Reuchlin viewed the legal profession at times with critical scepticism. See Geiger, *Johann Reuchlin*, 62–64.

acterize Dromo. Reuchlin created this neologism especially for the play, and Dromo's and Danista's stage debate as to its proper meaning invites us to probe its significance more deeply. We have already observed that, through its connection to the following chorus, *trilitterus* enters into the realm of learning and distinguishes the literate from the illiterate. Moreover, when one considers that Reuchlin's contemporaries celebrated him, in the words of Conrad Celtis, as the *trium linguarum interpres*[24] and that the original inspiration for the new word came from Plautus's *trium litterarum homo,* it is highly likely that Reuchlin here coyly referred to himself and his mastery of Latin, Greek, and Hebrew. This does not mean that Reuchlin wished to identify himself with the character of the clever servant, but it does demonstrate that he retained enough distance from humanist pursuits to ironize his own abilities. The irony, however, does not undermine the overarching exaltation of the poetic craft. It is, rather, a conscious yet impish acknowledgement of the imperative of classical imitation.

This exploration of the relationship between the choruses and *Henno* as a whole, however, still leaves the question of the ode's meter unanswered. The first and most likely solution is, in a manner, almost prosaic: The verses, set to music, submitted to the demands of the melody, rather than vice versa. This is borne out not only by the testimony of Spiegel's commentary[25] but also by the research of R. v. Liliencron, who has demonstrated that the simplistic interaction between text and music in *Henno*'s choral odes represents the earliest stage of this genre in the sixteenth century, a far cry from the sophisticated Sapphic strophes and intricate melodies of later plays.[26] Nevertheless, it still remains surprising that a humanist of Reuchlin's stature would compose in the often vilified stressed meter of medieval Latin. Thus I would like to suggest another, somewhat speculative aspect to at least the third ode's qualitative verse: its suitability as an ironic vehicle to lampoon unlettered men in the very "barbaric" verse they practiced. In performance, the young singers could have easily exaggerated the verses's accentuation while simultaneously decrying the artlessness of those who regularly employed such meter. Yet whatever Reuchlin's motivation in employing such rhythm, it is important to note that, as in his ironization of the humanist ideal, he again took liberties with classical models.

From a hermeneutic perspective, however, matters of meter are secondary. *Henno*'s choral odes derive their special significance from their central position in the play's origin and its appeal for humanist studies. They also participate in the comedy of the

---

[24] Taken from Conrad Celtis's ode to Reuchlin in Geiger, ed., *Johann Reuchlins Briefwechsel*, 68. Adam Werner, rector of the Heidelberg university, spoke similarly of Reuchlin in his verses that accompanied the play's didascalia in the printed editions: *Cui dea . . . dat Pallas linguis posse sonare tribus.* "Henno," ed. Holstein, 34, lines 15–16.

[25] Commenting on Reuchlin's assertion that all of *Henno* was composed in iambic trimeter, Spiegel noted: "Preter choros qui concentu ac melodia coguntur uariis esse pedibus." *Scaenica progymnasmata . . . cum explanatione Iacobi Spiegel*, Aiii^v.

[26] R. v. Liliencron, "Die Chorgesänge des lateinisch-deutschen Schuldramas im XVI. Jahrhundert," *Vierteljahresschrift für Musikwissenschaft* 6 (1890): 314–316. Cf. Otto Francke, *Terenz und die lateinische Schulcomoedie in Deutschland* (Weimar: H. Böhlau, 1877), 116.

work, playing upon the knowledge and expectations of its humanist audience. The ironic distance maintained by Reuchlin in the odes is yet another of the liberties taken with his classical model recently emphasized by Jane Newman, who underscores above all *Henno*'s debt to popular carnival and farcical elements.[27] However, contrary to Newman's conclusion that such liberties threatened the predominancy of humanist literary studies, *Henno*'s choruses demonstrate that Reuchlin's license with his model did not necessarily undermine its validity. The valorization of classical studies remains intact despite any irony; their glorification, rather, served to empower humanists in their efforts to obtain positions of influence at court.[28] If a conspiracy amongst humanists to stress the play's classical elements did indeed exist, as Newman would suggest,[29] then it resided in the exploitation of antiquity to warrant their aspirations to positions of political and social influence. The canon of Roman literary culture certainly possessed a stronger appeal for their noble patrons than *Henno*'s indebtedness to popular farces and carnival culture, and it is no surprise that Reuchlin, Spiegel, and others emphasized the play's classical elements at the expense of its popular forebears. Nonetheless, it would be a mistake to overlook Reuchlin's playfulness with the humanist ideal. This unique combination of classical imitation with ironic distance, which allowed Reuchlin to transcend the narrow scope of school drama that had fettered his predecessors, is perhaps best summed up in the closing verses of *Henno*'s second ode: *diligamus ergo nos / vates caelitus sacros, / quorum ludos scaenicos / ostendimus facete.*

The University of Iowa

---

[27] Newman, "Textuality vs. Performativity," 267–272.

[28] Parente, "Empowering Readers," 266–267.

[29] Newman, "Textuality vs. Performativity," 272–273.

The Mythologiae *of*
Natale Conti and the Pléiade

PHILIP FORD

L ittle is known, beyond the list of his publications, of the life of Natale Conti,[1] yet his *Mythologiae* has long been considered one of the most influential works of Renaissance mythography, opening a window onto the way in which writers throughout Europe understood and exploited the myths of the Greco-Roman world. Jean Seznec's discussion of Conti's contribution to sixteenth-century mythography was without doubt of the utmost importance in establishing his reputation amongst scholars working on the Renaissance,[2] and even before that, his work was an important source for art historians, intellectual historians, and literary critics.

Despite all this, nobody has devoted any full-length study to his writings, while what has been said about the influence of the *Mythologiae* is in certain respects misleading, as I discovered when I started work on this paper. As a result of these discoveries, my conclusions will be somewhat different from what was originally intended.

Of central significance for any assessment of Conti's influence on the French Renaissance is the date of the *editio princeps* of the *Mythologiae*. For Seznec, as for Franck L. Schoell before him, there was no question but that the work dated from 1551:

> Editions of Conti's *Mythology* succeeded one another at very short intervals: it appeared three times in Venice, in 1551, 1568, and 1581; four times in Frankfort, in 1581, 1584, 1585, and 1596; three times in Paris, in 1583, 1588, and 1605. . . .[3]

---

[1] For an excellent summary of what is known, see the *Dizionario biografico degli italiani* (Rome, 1960–), vol. 28, 454–457.

[2] See J. Seznec, *The Survival of the Pagan Gods: The Mythological Tradition and Its Place in Renaissance Humanism and Art* (repr. Princeton, 1972), first published in French in 1940 as *La Survivance des dieux antiques*.

[3] Seznec, *Survival*, p. 279. See also Franck L. Schoell, *Études sur l'humanisme continental en*

Yet over the years, doubt has been expressed about the existence of the 1551 edition, for example, by R. Ricciardi in the *Dizionario biografico degli italiani*.[4] Perhaps more tellingly, the 1551 edition does not figure in the *Index Aureliensis* of books printed in the sixteenth century.[5] One work by Conti was published, however, by the Aldine presses in that year, the *De venatione*. Domenico Bassi, writing in 1937, says of it:

> E' un poemetto in quattro canti, edito la prima volta a Venezia, da Aldo *iunior*, nel 1551, a sè, e non, come dicono alcuni biografi, colla 'Mitologia.' In calce a questa fu pubblicato la prima volta nel 1581.[6]

What seems to have happened is that, because the two works were printed together in Venice in 1581, it was assumed that this had also occurred in 1551, giving rise to the myth of the mid-century edition of the *Mythologiae*.

However, internal evidence at the end of the 1567/8 Venice edition of the *Mythologiae*, published by Comin da Trino, supports the hypothesis that this was in fact the first edition of the work.[7] On fol. 307[r] of this edition, Conti acknowledges his gratitude to two men in particular, without whose support, he says, he would never have published the *Mythologiae*:

> Deinde gratias agere debent [studiosi homines] nonnullis viris illustribus, inter quos principem locum obtinet vir clarissimus & optimus Renaldus FERRE-RIVS Praesidens Parlamenti Parisiensis, omnibus quidem egregiis animi dotibus ornatissimus; & Valerius Faenzus Quaesitor prauitatis haereticae apud Venetos prudentissimus; quorum autoritas plurimum me impulit, vt ista ipsa ederem ad omnium commoditatem, quae mihi per vniuersum prope vitae meae cursum ad facilitatem meorum studiorum mihi comparaueram. Fateor illud ingenue, quod nisi me tantorum virorum autoritas commouisset, nunquam eram ista in lucem emissurus . . .

Angleterre à la fin de la Renaissance, Bibliothèque de la Revue de littérature comparée, 29 (Paris, 1926), 27.

[4] Ricciardi writes, *Dizionario* (above, n.1), 455: "Lo Schoell e il Guillon ne citano una prima edizione del 1551, il Tiraboschi una del 1561–64; se realmente vi furono, queste edizioni possono presumibilmente considerarsi abbozzi di quella veneta del 1568."

[5] *Index Aureliensis: Catalogus librorum sedecimo saeculo impressorum* (Baden-Baden, 1962–); see vol. 9 (1991), 416–420 for the entry on Conti.

[6] D. Bassi, "Un' opera mitologica del secolo XVI," Reale Istituto Lombardo di Scienze e Lettere, Milano, *Rendiconti*, 70 (1937): 9–20, p. 10.

[7] NATALIS COMITIS | MYTHOLOGIAE, | SIVE EXPLICATIONVM FABVLARVM | *LIBRI DECEM.* | IN QUIBVS OMNIA PROPE | Naturalis & Moralis philosophiae dogmata sub anti- | quorum fabulis contenta fuisse | Demonstratur. | *CVM LOCVPLETISSIMIS INDI-CIBVS | eorum scriptorum, qui in his libris citantur, rerumque | notabilium, & multorum nominum | ad fabulas pertinentium | explicationibus.* | OPVS NON TANTVM HVMANARVM, | sed etiam sacrarum literarum & Philosophiae studiosis | perutile, ac prope necessarium. | CVM PRIVI-LEGIO. | [Device] | VENETIIS | M D LXVII. | This edition, which some title pages attribute to 1567 and others to 1568, is available in a facsimile version, by Garland Publishing Inc. (New York and London, 1976).

A brief biographical consideration of these two men will serve to pinpoint the period of their acquaintance with Conti. Arnaud du Ferrier (born between 1508 and 1511, died 1585) was educated in France and Italy as a lawyer (he received his LL.D. at Bologna in 1533). He became *président aux enquêtes* in the Paris Parlement in February 1555 and showed himself to be on the side of the moderates in his dealings with French Protestants. In 1562, he was sent as French ambassador to the Council of Trent, strongly supporting Gallican interests there, and in the following year, he took up an appointment as French ambassador in Venice, where he remained until June 1567. It is clearly during this period that he made the acquaintance of Conti, who appears to have lived all his life in Venice, and more than likely that it was he who encouraged Conti to dedicate his work to Charles IX of France.[8]

Valerio Faenzi was a very different person. He was a Dominican friar from Verona and a member, in the Thomist section, of the Accademia veneziana, which published one of his books, the *De montium origine . . . dialogus* (Venice, 1561). He was appointed Inquisitor in Venice on 4 April 1566 by Pope Pius V and was succeeded by Aurelio Schellino on 12 July 1569.[9] He seems to have carried out his duties with enthusiasm, gaining the approbation of the papal nuncio, Giovanni Antonio Facchinetti, who recommended him for the bishopric of Chioggia in April 1569.[10] It is interesting to note that Facchinetti's opinion of du Ferrier, on the other hand, at least on theological matters, was far from enthusiastic: du Ferrier was suspected by Facchinetti of being a Protestant, and on three successive Sundays he had him followed from sunrise to sunset to see if he attended mass. He did not.[11]

Conti's statement that "if I had not been roused by the encouragement of such great men, I should never have published this work" clearly rules out the possibility of a 1551 *editio princeps* and establishes the 1567/8 edition as the only real contender. This, of course, would partly explain why Seznec was forced to admit that "we cannot, however, prove any specific borrowing by Ronsard from Conti" since only that part of Ronsard's poetry written after 1568 would be susceptible to influence from the *Mythologiae*.

However, Conti does appear at first sight to share with the Pléiade a similar attitude towards mythology, and this has no doubt to a large extent led to the assumption that at least some of his interpretations influenced them. Like Jean Dorat, he

---

[8] For details concerning the life of du Ferrier, see the article by Y. Destianges in the *Dictionnaire de biographie française* (Paris, 1933–), vol. 11, p. 1393.

[9] See Bartolomeo Cecchetti, *La republica di Venezia e la corte di Roma nei rapporti della religione*, 2 vols. (Venice, 1874), 2:10. For further details, see the *Nunziature di Venezia*, edited by Aldo Stella, vol. 8 (March 1566–March 1569) (Rome, 1963).

[10] See *Nunziature di Venezia*, edited by Aldo Stella, vol. 9 (26 March 1569–21 May 1571) (Rome, 1972): ". . . le posso ben affermare ch'egli non manca d'ogni sollecitudine alle cose di S. Offitio et che da molti qui si crede che S. S.tà sia per consolarlo di questa chiesa" (Facchinetti to Michele Bonelli, 27 April 1569). In fact, he did not receive this post.

[11] Facchinetti writes of him: "Dell' ambasciatore di Francia, egli qui è più tosto in opinione di luterano che di cattolico et da un suo di casa si è inteso che egli va di rado a messa," *Nunziature di Venezia*, vol. 8, p. 76.

believed that ancient myths were simply a veil to protect from the masses divinely revealed truths and that the multiplicity of gods in the ancient world reflects the inability of the masses to conceive of God properly:

> Atque id eo magis; quod uniuersa philosophiae praecepta sub his ipsis fabulis antiquitus continebantur: quippe cum non ita multis annis ante Aristotelis, & Platonis, & caeterorum philosophorum tempora, omnia philosophiae dogmata non aperte, sed obscure sub quibusdam integumentis traderentur. Graeci enim cum occultam philosophandi rationem ab Aegyptiis in patriam adduxissent, ne res admirabiles in uulgus ederentur, quod illis male perceptis ab religione, & ab omni probitate plerunque id facile desciscat; & ipsi per fabulas philosophari clam coeperunt. (fol. 4ʳ)

> Non sunt igitur Dii illi antiquorum, sed fabulae illae partim naturae res occultas habent, partim mores informant, partim sunt inania vulgi figmenta, vt dicebamus. (fol. 9ᵛ)

This last statement points to the two principal forms of allegorical exegesis favoured by Conti in his *Mythologiae*: the physical explanation and the ethical or moral explanation. Although he further develops his ideas on the subject in book I, chapter II, "De fabularum utilitate," he is only really elaborating on this basic division when he establishes nine categories of myth, of which the first contains the "naturae secreta" and the other eight various moral lessons.[12] Although Conti mentions other types of explanation in discussing individual fables, for example, the euhemeristic or historical method of exegesis much used by Boccaccio in the *Genealogiae deorum gentilium libri*, he does not personally endorse this approach, as may be seen from part of his discussion of Hercules' labours, introduced by the somewhat sceptical words: "Fuerunt tamen nonnulli qui res ab Hercule gestas ad historiam *retorserint* . . ." (fol. 210ᵛ, my emphasis). Moreover, unlike Dorat, he clearly believes that some fables have no moral or educational value whatsoever ("inania vulgi figmenta").

In order, however, to compare the methodologies of Conti and Dorat, I propose to consider the ways in which the two humanists deal with one myth, the Sirens, and to consider Dorat's treatment of that myth in the notes based on his lectures which are preserved in the Bibliotheca Ambrosiana in Milan.[13] Conti discusses the Sirens in chapter 13 of Book VII (fols. 224ʳ–226ᵛ) and also provides an etymological explanation of their names in his "Nominum . . . explicatio," fol. 339ᵛ: "Sirenes a dicendo εἴρω dico. vel a σύρειν trahere." At the beginning of the chapter, he briefly

---

[12] See fol. 5ʳ, where the various kinds of myth are described and illustrated. According to Conti, the moral myths are designed either to warn people against undesirable things (*fortunae inconstantia, impurae opiniones, res turpes, auaritiae sordes, temeritas, flagitia*) or to encourage them to good things (*strenuitas, virtutes*).

[13] MS number A 184. See on this subject two articles by Geneviève Demerson, "Dorat, commentateur d'Homère," in *Études seiziémistes offertes à M. le professeur V.-L. Saulnier*, Travaux d'Humanisme et Renaissance, 177 (Geneva, 1980), 223–234; and "Qui peuvent être les Lestrygons?" *Vita Latina*, 70 (1978): 36–42.

describes what the Sirens were famous for, who their parents were (the river Achelous and the muse Terpsichore, or, according to some, Melpomene, Sterope, or Calliope), and their various deeds before they took up their career as wreckers. He also discusses their location, their appearance (birds, with human faces), their individual names, and their musical talents (one sang, the second played the flute, the third the lyre). Alluding to the etymological explanation of "Siren," he writes:

> Mirabilis profecto esse dicebatur harum Sirenum suauitas cantus, quando vel in apertam pernitiem homines *trahebant*, efficiebantque vt sui ipsorum obliti in manifestam caedem se *trahi* paterentur. (fol. 224ʳ, my italics)

He goes on to cite what pseudo-Orpheus says about them in his *Argonautica*, as well as Apollonius of Rhodes and Homer.

His allegorical explanations for the Sirens fall into the physical and moral categories which we would expect from Conti's opening remarks. He quotes an explanation attributed to Archippus, *De piscibus* V, according to which

> loca quaedam marina in angustias quasdam praeruptis montibus contracta fuisse, in quas illisi fluctus sonum cum suauitate & harmonia emittentes nauigantes allicerent ad visendum, quo cum appulissent vndarum impetu delati absorbebantur. (fol. 225ᵛ)

Other explanations are that they were seashore prostitutes who attracted sailors by their singing, rapacious birds from India, or, following Horace, *Satires* II.3.14–15, that they represented slothfulness.[14] However, Conti's preferred explanation is a moral one, that they stand for "voluptates, & earum titillationes" (fol. 226ʳ). He goes on to develop this idea, supporting his argument by an etymological analysis of the names attributed to individual Sirens, for example:

> quid enim est Pisinoe? an non vis menti facile suadens? πείθειν enim suadere, νόος [*sic*] mens est. at vero Aglaope suauis est aspectu, Telxiope vel solo aspectu delectat, cum θέλγειν delectare significet. (*ibidem*)

To avoid their snares, it is necessary to bind oneself to the mast of reason, like Odysseus. The final explanation offered by Conti is that the Sirens represent flattering and sycophantic counsellors who lead their prince into wrongdoing:

> Haec vna causa est cur tam frequenter mutati sint principes regionum Italiae, neque idem regulus fuerit diutius eiusdem regionis: cum nihil neque firmius sit, neque stabilius eo regno, quod a sapiente principe gubernetur. (fol. 226ᵛ)

Dorat starts his discussion by mentioning the notion that the Sirens are birds with human faces, or else dangerous reefs, but immediately dismisses two of the explanations offered by Conti:

---

[14] "Vitanda est improba Siren / desidia . . ."

Neque uero per has ut plurimi existimant sunt intelligendae meretrices aut
uoluptates quae unumquemque perdere consueuerunt. (fol. 11ʳ)

He cites Cicero, *De finibus* V.8.49, who sees the Sirens as attracting people to their
destruction through their promises of knowledge. They represent

> . . . scientias illecebrarum plenas atque suaui quodam eloquio rerumque iucunda
> nouitate et mirabilium narratione exornatas quibus ita parum cauti homines
> detinentur ut totam uitam in illis consumere uelint. (*ibidem*)

Although it is reasonable, when young, to devote some time to such studies, which
include "poesis, historia, oratoria facultas, naturae inuestigatio, et rerum quae oblecta-
tionem animo adferunt contemplatio quales denique mathematicae. . . ," you should,
like Odysseus, eventually pass them by, "ad patriam id est beatitudinem ueram
aspirantes." The mast for Dorat is "certus animi scopus et propositum" from which
the wise man cannot be deflected. Like Conti, Dorat derives the Sirens' name from
either εἴρω or σύρειν, but unlike Conti he discusses the idea that the three Sirens
plus Calypso stand for the four subjects of the *quadrivium*. He also suggests that
Odysseus' being bound to the mast by his companions represents the philosopher/
teacher who will only impart his knowledge if compelled to do so by his pupils, and
he cites mythical and historical parallels in support of this (Proteus, Silenus, and
Epicurus). Finally, Dorat offers the explanation that the Sirens may have been a group
of prophetesses who lived around the same time as the Sibyls.

It is clear that, despite the elements which they have in common, the emphasis of
treatment in these two exegeses is very different. As usual, Dorat eschews the more
obvious moral explanations—that the Sirens represent prostitutes or sexual pleasure—
and sees their allurements in terms of the temptation of knowledge which, however,
diverts people from what should be their true quest, the return to the heavenly
homeland. Nevertheless, what the two versions share is a thorough and systematic
discussion of the ancient sources and the reliance on etymology in order to pierce the
veil of the myth to reach its inner meaning. If we compare these two versions with
the treatment in the *De deis gentium varia et multiplex historia* of 1548, we notice that
Giraldi does not set out to treat his subject so exhaustively and is often content to
refer his readers to primary sources without bothering to cite them *in extenso*.

It would appear, therefore, that it is this comprehensiveness of treatment on the
part of Conti, coupled with the absence, until recent years, of detailed information
about Dorat's approach to exegesis, that has contributed to the notion that the
Pléiade were influenced by the *Mythologiae*. Indeed, as Seznec indicates, sixteenth-
century commentaries on Ronsard, such as that of Marc-Antoine Muret, cite the
Mythologiae as shedding light on Ronsard's poetry, but this must clearly be as an
afterthought.[15] Thus, commenting on the word "Sereine" in *Les Amours*, 16, "Je

---

[15] For a useful modern edition of Muret's commentaries on *Les Amours*, see *Commentaires au
premier livre des "Amours" de Ronsard*, edited by Jacques Chomarat, Marie-Madeleine Fragonard,
and Gisèle Mathieu-Castellani, Travaux d'Humanisme et Renaissance, 207 (Geneva, 1985).

veulx darder par l'univers ma peine" (L. IV.19–20),[16] Muret writes in 1553:

Les Sereines furent filles du fleuue Aceloïs [sic], & d'vne des Muses (les vns disent de Calliope, les autres de Terpsichore) qui auoient le haut du corps en façon d' oyseaux, & le bas en forme de pucelles: ou comme les autres disent, le haut en forme de pucelles, & le bas en forme de poissons. Elles se tenoient en vne Isle de la mer Sicilienne, qui se nommoit l'isle fleurie, & chantoient merueilleusement bien, tellement qu'elles allechoient les Nautonniers par la douceur de leurs chants, & les tiroient en des destroits de mer, où ils perissoient. Mais Vlysse qui auoit esté aduerty de cela par la Nymphe Circe, lors qu'il y voulut passer, estoupa de cire les oreilles de tous ses compagnons, & se fit lier estroitement au mast de la nauire: & par ainsi euita le danger. Homere le raconte au 12. de l'*Odyssée*. Je parlerai quelque fois des Sereines plus amplement sur le cinquiesme des *Odes*, en l'Ode aux trois princesses Angloises.

Only in the 1622 edition do we find the additional reference to Conti: "Voyez le 1. chap. du 9. liure de la Mythologie."[17] In general, Ronsard uses the myth of the Sirens in a positive way, more in line with Dorat's interpretation than with that of Conti. For example, in the ode referred to in Muret's commentary (L. III.41–49), written in 1551, the three daughters of Edward Seymour, Anne, Margaret, and Jane, are said to surpass even the Sirens in that the content of their song is inspired by Christianity, while in 1567, in "Les Sereines representées au canal du jardin de Monseigneur d'Orleans à Fonteine-Bleau" (L. XIII.231–39), Ronsard uses them to prophesy a happy future for Charles IX and his family. Compare:

> Si veux je encor pour l' avenir
> (Des destins prophetes nous sommes)
> T' ouvrir ce qui ne peut venir
> Desoubz l' entendement des hommes.
>
> (L. XIII.237.29–32)

In conclusion, therefore, we are forced to admit that it is unlikely that the *Mythologiae* had any real direct influence on the writings of the Pléiade. Du Bellay was dead before the 1568 edition, Ronsard, at the age of 44, had already amassed a considerable knowledge of mythology, and Dorat was undoubtedly responsible for much of their learning. Moreover, although Ronsard and du Bellay were not averse to exploiting moral allegorizations of myths, Ronsard in particular had a more syncretist approach to religion than Conti and would frequently opt for myths with strong

---

[16] References to Ronsard are to the *Œuvres complètes*, edited by Paul Laumonier, revised and completed by Isidore Silver and Raymond Lebègue, 20 vols. (Paris, 1914–1975), abbreviated as L, and followed by volume number, page number, and line number.

[17] See vol. I, p. 9 of the 1623 edition of Ronsard's works. A facsimile of *Le Premier Livre des Amours* is printed in *Commentaire* . . . , edited by Chomarat et al., which also has a list of variants. Similarly, a reference to Conti concerning the Gorgons was added to the commentary on *Amours* 8, "Lors que mon œil . . ." (L. IV.12) in 1597, as was a reference concerning Bellerophon in *Amours* 15, "Ha! qu'à bon droit . . ." (L. IV.18). See Chomarat et al., p. 5, p. 2, and p. 4.

Neo-Platonic elements in order to add a more mystical dimension to his poetry. However, Conti's real contribution to Pléiade poetics was as a reference book for later readers of their works, as evidenced by the references to the *Mythologiae* in the late sixteenth-century commentaries. While no doubt drawing on the same sources that the Pléiade had used, his detailed treatment of the myths provided an unparalleled fount of information on the Greco-Roman world.

Clare College, Cambridge

Renaissance *Fasti* *Commentaries* and *Antiquarianism*

ANGELA FRITSEN

The *Fasti*, Ovid's six-book poem on the festivals and rites of the Roman calendar for January–June, has never lacked a readership, however small. There are periods in history, however, when it particularly flourished. We find one such period of renewed interest in the poem in humanist Italy, as witnessed by a composite edition of commentaries on the *Fasti* which appeared in Venice on June 12, 1497 and prevailed in numerous reprints for the next quarter of a century.[1] This standard edition combined the work of Paolo Marsi of Pescina (*editio princeps*, Venice: Baptista de Tortis, 1482) and Antonio Costanzi of Fano (*editio princeps*, Rome: Eucharius Silber, 1489). A distinctively Italian project of the late *quattrocento*, the *Fasti* commentaries were produced by men with strong antiquarian interests. It is the link between the *Fasti* and these particular humanists which will be examined. Whatever Ovid's original thematic intention, the *Fasti* gained fresh meaning through a new audience and in a new age.

It is my contention that the *Fasti* was a central text for disciples of Roman antiquarianism; Costanzi already alerts us to this in his commentary's preface. After a programmatic defense of reading the *Fasti* for its salutary moral benefits, he continues with:

> Add to this the fact that many of the most magnificent temples and buildings of Rome, once the display of Roman majesty, of which either only the ruins of the foundations remain or no traces are visible at all to today's earnest explorer, appear nearly whole and undestroyed in this work of Ovid's, so that the zealous can easily see and contemplate those things which are barely discernible to their eyes.[2]

---

[1] Reprints appeared in 1502, 1508, 1510, 1512, 1520, and 1527.

[2] *Accedit ad haec quod pleraque urbis templa magnificentissima et aedificia olim Romanam ostentantia maiestatem, e quibus hac aetate fundamentorum tantum reliquiae manent aut certe nulla vestigia vel diligenter*

The *Fasti* both fosters and provides the opportunity to test one's antiquarian knowledge of Rome. For Costanzi the *Romanae antiquitates* are not only those proper to Rome, however, but also those found in his native town of Fano.[3] Thus in order to narrow our discussion the following remarks will focus on the commentary by his colleague Paolo Marsi, professor of rhetoric at Rome 1480–1484,[4] and on the influence on Marsi of Pomponio Leto, founder of the Roman Academy. It is in this circle that we find the specifically Roman origin and context for studying the *Fasti* during the Renaissance.

Requisite from the outset is a definition of the term antiquarianism as it pertains to members of the Roman Academy and, consequently, to my analysis. It is helpful to make two distinctions. In the narrow sense, antiquarianism signifies the enthusiasm for the tangible, physical remains of antiquity, for ruins, coins, and inscriptions, for example. Representative of this understanding or approach is the book by Roberto Weiss, *The Renaissance Discovery of Classical Antiquity*.[5] In a broader sense, antiquarianism means the study of Roman civilization as a whole, as reflected in its rites, customs, and institutions. Both perspectives are evident in the Renaissance commentaries on the *Fasti*. Indeed, for the humanists antiquarianism meant precisely the reconstitution of both artifacts and institutions; the two studies were complementary and co-existent.[6] Thus the interest in archeological remains helped Renaissance intellectuals better understand the society which they were trying to reconstruct.

Antiquarianism was the particular domain of study of the Roman Academy, embodied by its leader, the famed and somewhat eccentric university professor Pomponio Leto, who gave walking tours of the sites of ancient Rome, gardened according to the precepts of Columella, and visited the early Christian catacombs along the Via Appia.[7] The colophon of Marai's 1482 commentary on the *Fasti* associates his work with the Academy milieu by giving the date of publication as "in the fourth year from the reinstatement of the *sodalitas*, when Cardinal Domenico della Rovere

---

explorantibus sese offerunt, in eodem opere paene integra et inviolata monstrantur, ut eius modi rerum studiosis quae cernere minime possunt ea facile et videre et contemplari liceat.

[3] See Roberto Weiss, "L'Arco di Augusto a Fano nel Rinascimento," *Italia medioevale e umanistica* 8 (1965): 351–358.

[4] For his biography, see Arnaldo della Torre, *Paolo Marso da Pescina. Contributo alla Storia dell' Accademia Pomponiana* (Rocca S. Casciano: L. Cappelli, 1903).

[5] 2nd ed. London, 1988.

[6] Paradigmatic are Flavio Biondo's *Roma instaurata* (1446) and *Roma triumphans* (1459), which in their complementary nature reflect the two halves of the Varronian ideal. In his *Antiquitates rerum humanarum et divinarum* Varro had incorporated detailed descriptions of monuments, for example, with accounts of customs and rites. See Angelo Mazzocco, "Biondo Flavio and the Antiquarian Tradition," in *Acta Conventus Neo-Latini Bononiensis*, ed. Richard J. Schoeck (Binghamton, N.Y.: Medieval & Renaissance Texts & Studies, 1985), 125, and for a discussion of the twofold nature of Renaissance antiquarianism, "Linee di sviluppo dell'antiquaria del Rinascimento," in *Poesia e Poetica delle Rovine di Roma. Momenti e Problemi*, ed. Vincenzo di Caprio. Quaderni di Studi Romani, ser. 1, no. 47 (Rome, 1987), 55.

[7] Information on Pomponio Leto and his activities has been variously collected, but see della Torre (as in n. 4) and Vladimiro Zabughin, *Giulio Pomponio Leto*, 2 vols. (Roma: La vita letteraria, 1909–1912).

was its protector and Pomponio Leto, Publio Astreo, and Paolo Marso were censors."[8] This is a clear reference to the Roman Academy, which had in fact been suppressed in 1468 by Paul II on charges of heresy, paganism, and republicanism; it was reestablished ten years later, in 1478, under Sixtus IV, whose brother was Domenico della Rovere. Thus Marsi was a member of the so-called second Roman Academy, and in 1482 he and Leto shared an organizational role, that of "censor," which incidentally is the kind of classical epithet typically used by the Academy's antiquarian enthusiasts.

Thus the Renaissance reception of Ovid's *Fasti* can be placed within the historical framework of the Roman Academy. It is Leto himself who directly influenced and encouraged the academic pursuits of Paolo Marsi and other members of the Roman Academy. Leto's legacy with regard to the *Fasti* becomes apparent in the preface of Marsi's commentary. There we read:

> Many years before me Pomponio, the most devoted interpreter of antiquity and all Latinity, wrote a few things on the *Fasti*. I followed afterwards, running over the entire gamut of Ovid's work, leaving nothing unconsidered or undiscussed.[9]

Two Pomponian manuscripts on the *Fasti* are extant: *Vat. lat.* 3263 and *Vat. lat.* 3264. The former, written in Leto's hand, contains extensive notes and is the major codex. It is upon this manuscript, no. 3263, that I will base my subsequent analysis. The *terminus post quem* for its composition has been fixed at 1488.[10] Therefore, it dates to the last period of Leto's career and suggests his lifelong commitment to the *Fasti*. Indeed, Arnaldo della Torre suggests that Leto was already teaching Ovid's *Fasti* when Marsi first began attending his lectures in Rome, after 1457.[11] However, the post-1488 notes are not what Marsi refers to in his preface, since his own commentary is earlier. Marsi remarks that Leto had written "a few things" on the *Fasti*, and, in fact, it is a scattering of remarks in Leto's hand that appear in the *de luxe* manuscript *Vat. lat.* 3264. This manuscript dates to the period between 1469 and 1471,[12] following Leto's release from prison during the Academy's suppression, and it was produced for a wealthy private pupil of his, Fabio Mazzatosta. Mazzatosta was a member of the second Roman Academy, as we know from the classical version of his name, "Fabius Ambustus," scratched on the catacomb walls of Ss. Marcellino e Pietro

---

[8] . . . *Pau[li] Marsi Piscin[natis] Poe[tae] Romani fideliss[ime] Fast[orum] Interpretationem Baptista Tortius a Neocastro Venettis imprimendam curavit anno salutis MCCCCLXXXII et a constituta sodalitate an[no] IIII D[omenico] R[uverio] car[dinali] divi Clemen[tis], Protectore Pont[ifice] Firman[o] et Nestore Malvis[io] Praefectis Pomponio Laeto P[ublio] Astreo et Paolo Marso Censorib[us] IX. Cal. Ianuar.*

[9] *Scripserat in Fastos pluribus ante me annis pauca tamen fidelissimus antiquitatis et totius latinitatis interpres Pomponius noster; postea nos secuti provinciam omnem percurrimus, nihil intactum nihilque indiscussum relinquentes.*

[10] Zabughin (vol. 2), 153.

[11] Della Torre, 21.

[12] Zabughin (vol. 2), 25.

on the via Labicana during a visit by Leto and his group.[13] Clearly then, if Leto prepared notes for Mazzatosta, he thought the *Fasti* important not only for his students in general but, more specifically, for members of the Roman Academy. It was in this circle, led by Leto, that the *Fasti* was studied.

Leto's influence on Marsi's thought can be traced in Leto's extensive notes from after 1488. The similarity of purpose in the work of the two humanists reflects their common interest in Roman topography and ruins, antiquarianism in the "narrow" sense. For instance, at *F.* 5.294 Leto glosses "Publiciumque" as follows:

> The Publician road is on the Quirinal, facing west. Better said, it is northwest. At the lower end there is the temple of Apollo and Clatra, at the upper end there was the Capitol in antiquity. . . .[14]

The single word in Ovid prompts Leto to make a topographical and archeological excursus. That Leto would include his archeological discovery and identification of a Roman temple not only in his topographical works, where one would expect it, but also in his *Fasti* notes demonstrates his antiquarian interest in the *Fasti*. But let us consider his comment for method as well, for subsequent comparison with Marsi's approach. The so-called temple of Apollo and Clatra appears in Leto's regionary catalogue of Rome[15] and (with an alternate spelling) in the record of his walking tour of the ancient sites of the city.[16] The classical monument is in fact one of Leto's own invention, suggested to him through an imaginative error; there is after all no known goddess *Clatra*. De Rossi has suggested that Leto found the fragment of an inscription on the Quirinal, which contained (in some form) the words *fores clatratae*, known from actual epigraphical collections. Leto might have turned the *fores clatratae*, or latticed gates of a temple of Apollo, into a goddess affiliated with Apollo.[17]

Marsi inherited from Leto this interest in tangible Roman ruins and their inclusion and discussion within the context of Ovid's *Fasti*. The avid search for Roman ruins and artifacts is apparent at *F.* 1.521, "care nepos Palla," where Marsi remarks: "yet I never saw any tomb of Pallas at Rome, nor could I identify ceremonies in honor of the dead or anything else from the traditional rites."[18] Clearly Marsi remembers the report by William of Malmesbury, that in the eleventh century a farmer digging in

---

[13] G. Lumbroso, "Gli accademici alle catacombe," *Archivio della società romana di storia patria* 12 (1890): 216.

[14] *Clivus PUBLICIVS in Quirinali colle est occasum versus. Melius inter occasum et boream. Ex parte inferiore habet templum Apollinis et Clatrae, ex superiore Capitolinum vetus. . . .*

[15] See Giovanni Battista de Rossi, "Note di topografia romana raccolte dalla bocca di Pomponio Leto e testo pomponiano della *Notitia Regionum Urbis Romae*," *Studi e documenti di storia e diritto* 3 (Rome, 1882): 76.

[16] *Excerpta a Pomponio dum inter ambulandum cuidam domino ultramontano reliquias ac ruinas urbis ostenderet*, in *Codice topografico della città di Roma*, ed. Roberto Valentini and Giuseppe Zucchetti, vol. 4 (Roma: Tipografia del Senato, 1953), 428.

[17] De Rossi, "Note di topografia romana," 72.

[18] *Ego tamen neque sepulchrum Romae Pallantis ullum vidi, neque parentalia neque aliud ex consuetis sacris cognoscere quicquam potui.*

his fields found the colossal body of Pallas, glowing with an aureole.[19] Legend or hearsay spurred the Roman antiquarians to look for the lost remains of antiquity, what they could no longer see as well as what they did see. The discovery of a burial site would, in this case in particular, instruct them about Roman society.

Frequently, the antiquarians stumbled upon actual finds. For instance, in his commentary Marsi also excitedly reports the recent unearthing of a Roman monument. At *F*. 1.582 on the legend of Hercules Victor, so named because he had slain Cacus, and his divinity had consequently been recognized by Evander, Marsi reports:

> Who would believe, now that so many ages have passed since that altar was famous, that in my time, while I was teaching in Rome, the marble quarriers found the Ara Maxima in a far corner of the foro Boario, and they dug up the bronze statue of Hercules, along with various inscriptions. These were all immediately taken to the Capitoline and placed in the Palazzo dei Conservatori, so that everyone could see them.[20]

The colossal bronze statue of Hercules, which Pliny reports (*Nat.* 34.33) was draped in regalia at every triumph, was found during the demolition of the remains of a round temple of Hercules, confused here by Marsi with the Ara Maxima which lay in the vicinity. The excavation caused a stir, as the report by Marsi attests; one imagines that the Academy members were present at the archeological site in the foro Boario or, as the news traveled, that they rushed over in person.[21]

Leto's habitual amblings around Rome and his archeological searches evidently inspired Marsi. For instance, a topic taken up by both the teacher and student is the location of the Viminal hill. Marsi reports having found inscriptions in this area with the indication "in alta semita," the principal street which ran northeast along the Quirinal to the porta Collina.[22] Indeed, this kind of topographical exploration is reminiscent of Leto's discovery of inscriptions alluding to *fores clatratae* on the Quirinal. But Leto's influence on Marsi is traceable in his methodology, as well as in his antiquarian interest in the artifacts of ancient Rome: they are both *using* epigraphy. Leto

---

[19] See Arturo Graf, *Roma nella memoria e nelle immaginazioni del Medio Evo*, vol. 1 (Torino, 1882), 93.

[20] *Verum quis crederet tot iam elapsis saeculis ab eo tempore quo celebris erat illa ara, illis diebus quo haec Romae profitebar, in ultimo angulo fori Boarii ab his qui marmora inquirebant reperta est ara Maxima, et effossa aerea Herculis statua, cum multis circa eam epigrammatibus, quae omnia delata mox fuere in Capitolium et in atrio dominorum Conservatorum collocata, atque omnibus visenda patent?*

[21] In fact, Marsi's commentary is evidence for the date of the statue's discovery, which scholars could not pinpoint beyond the pontificate of Sixtus IV, 1471–1484 (see, for example, A. Michaelis, "Storia della collezione Capitolina di antichità fino all'inaugurazione del Museo [1734]," in *Römische Mitteilungen* 6 [1891]: 15; cf. Phyllis Pray Bober and Ruth Rubinstein, *Renaissance Artists and Antique Sculpture: A Handbook of Sources* [London: Harvey Miller, 1986], 164). Marsi's testimony enables us to fix the discovery between 1480, when he was hired as professor of rhetoric at Rome, and December 1482, the publication of the commentary.

[22] . . . *ut constet illum esse Viminalem, invenimus nuper plures tabulas et publicas scriptas quin gentis iam antea annis cum inscriptione "in alta semita" in colle Viminali et regione caballorum* . . . (*F*. 1.259).

and Marsi have looked beyond literary sources to archeological remains as a means of historical evidence. While *auctores* still continued to provide the antiquarians with a basis for their research, so that even recently discovered works were plumbed for information, the tide was changing enough that, to quote Anthony Grafton, "the humanists gradually learned to take a serious interest in three-dimensional remains as well as literary texts."[23] Thus in his *Fasti* comments, Leto often cites evidence found, as he says, "in marmore" (*sic* at 5.721, 723, and 725). At *F.* 3.667 he quotes the proximity of Bovillae to Rome and adds *Ego a sinistra parte viae Appiae vidi marmur in quo scriptum erat S.P.Q:Bovillanus.* Epigraphy has become an instrument of research for the scholars of the Roman Academy.

This reliance on things visible also manifests itself in other ways. For instance, in his notes Leto has written in capitals alongside "farra" (*F.* 1.693) QVOMODO FAR TORRETVR, and in his explanation of the method of grinding and toasting spelt, he refers to what he has seen on his journeys in Russia, between June 1472 and the spring of 1473: *vidi ego interfuique et gustavi*, he says. Personal, empirical observation becomes proof, it becomes a tool for historical evidence, in support of what Ovid says in the *Fasti*.

Marsi applies this type of methodology much more often and, generally, to a further extreme than Leto does. To cite but one example, in his exegesis of the rites of the dea Muta (*F.* 2.571), Marsi recounts from his trip to Spain in 1468 and to Greece and Asia Minor in 1469.[24] The Mute Goddess was said to have silenced the lips of calumniators, but as to how the ritual precisely worked, Marsi says,

> The poet has not revealed. Still, let us interpret his words according to the secret rite, which is easy enough for me, since I have seen it in many places in just the way Ovid reported. In Euboea there was a certain holy man both Greek by birth and learned in Greek letters. The winter I spent in Chalcis I sometimes left ship to go see him. In the meantime he wanted me to show him something of our literature. I once found him with a book whose title was *On Arcane Magic* by some Thessalian. Among the rites therein he turned to this one written in Greek, which he wanted to try out because there were some slanderers who would not stop vilifying him. Wonderful to say: he suppressed their slander. The same thing happened in my presence when I was in Seville and later on in Rhodes.[25]

---

[23] "The Ancient City Restored: Archaeology, Ecclesiastical History, and Egyptology," in *Rome Reborn: The Vatican Library and Renaissance Culture*, ed. Anthony Grafton (Washington: Library of Congress, 1993), 88.

[24] Rossella Bianchi, "Il commento a Lucano e il 'Natalis' di Paolo Marsi," in *Miscellanea Augusto Campana*, vol. 1, ed. Rino Avesani, Giuseppe Billanovich, et al., Medioevo e umanesimo, vol. 44 (Padova: Antenore, 1981), 97–98.

[25] *Poeta tamen id non aperit. Nos tamen sua verba cum mysterio interpretemur, quod facillimum est nobis qui vidimus id idem fieri pluribus in locis eoque modo quo a poeta refertur. Praeterea religiosus quidam in Euboea erat qui, ut genere Graecus, ita et Graecis litteris eruditus. Ad quem aliquando cum per hiberna in Chalcide essemus e triremi confugiebam. Volebat enim interdum ut aliquid nostrarum litterarum aperirem. Hunc semel repperi librum tenentem cuius inscriptio erat de arcanis Veneficiis cuiusdam Thessali. Inter cetera*

Marsi's eyewitness account verifies the authenticity and efficacy of this ritual spell in the *Fasti*. Marsi's method is to work his way backwards: he can apply his own experience to the reading in Ovid; he tests Ovid. Because this happened to him, Marsi, Ovid must be telling the truth. Moreover, in watching a ceremony, he also imitates Ovid, who often claims knowledge of a rite through personal participation. For instance, at the festival of the Palilia Ovid says "I myself jumped through the flames placed three in a row" (*certe ego transsilui positas ter in ordine flammas*, F. 4.727).

The reliance on personal experience, that is, on one's own sensory perception, can be compared in the two humanists, Marsi and Leto. At F. 2.110–11, Marsi glosses *dura penna*, in the passage on the swan that pierced by an arrow sings his melodious dying note, as follows:

> This is because swans when they are old have a stiff little feather on their forehead, as though they had been pierced; Pomponio noticed this in the far confines of Germany and I did in Ionia. . . . Thus Ovid does not say "dura penna" without reason; I am only amazed that others have not observed this.[26]

Of course, Marsi has made an amusing mistake. He has understood "penna" in its literal definition. It is a bird's feather instead of the arrow that the feather represents, through metonymy, because it makes up the arrow's quill. This leads him to strain at a plausible scientific explanation about the nature of old swans. The precedent can be found in Leto's own note to the passage in question:

> Old swans have a narrow bristly feather in the down on their forehead. Some write that the swan's brain is injured by this feather [and] they conclude that the swan then sings most sweetly, when he is about to die. I myself have heard the song of the swan in the Scythian marshes.[27]

Clearly, this empirical method of observation is not really scientific. In the end, Leto still employs inductive rather than deductive reasoning. Summoning personal experience as proof simply allows the humanist to impose his own reading—or misreading—on Ovid's text.

While the above example demonstrates that Leto's methodology as well as antiquarian interest influenced his students, I would like to close by repeating my assertion that textual work on Ovid's *Fasti* was a cultural phenomenon particular to Leto and his followers. Marsi in his comment on the swan referred to Leto's trip to

---

Graece scriptum hoc sacrum adverti, quod ille eo tempore voluit experiri cum essent aliquot maledici, qui eum conviciis lacessere non desinebant. Mirum quidem dictum est; compescuit illorum maledicentiam. Idem accidit et me praesente in Hispali et postea Rhodi.

[26] *quia in senecta pennam quandam habent duriusculam frontem [sic] natam velut traiectam, quod observavit Pomponius in extrema Germania et ego in Ionia. Seniores enim cygni illam traiectam habent, ceteri non. Poeta igitur non sine ratione hoc dixit, sed miror ab aliis non fuisse observatum.*

[27] *Cygnis senescentibus penna exigua dura in pluma frontis innascitur. Sunt qui scribu[n]t ea penna cerebrum oloris ledi s[u]avissime canere existimant eum tunc moriturum. Audivi ego canentis cygnos in paludibus Scytharum. Incolae ignorabant an ille esset moriturus qui canebat. Suavis est concentus dum illi canunt et cum unus canit videntur esse plures.*

Germany, which occurred between the spring of 1479 and that of 1483, possibly in the winter of 1482–1483;[28] and his own trip to Greece and Asia Minor. Marsi's trip was, as a matter of fact, earlier. He accompanied his patron, the Venetian ambassador Nicola Canal, to the East in 1469. Marsi and Leto obviously shared interesting information concerning their respective journeys. This suggests again an ongoing study of the *Fasti* by Leto and his circle over the years and in different places but always within the purview of the Roman Academy. Moreover, since Marsi's commentary was published at the end of 1482, during Leto's period abroad, he obviously used his mentor as his authority and stamp of approval.

Yale University

---

[28] The precise chronology of Leto's journeys is uncertain, since his *Commentarioli* are lost. See Leto's biography by Josef Delz and A. J. Dunston in *Catalogus Translationum et Commentariorum*, vol. 3 (Washington: Catholic University of America Press, 1976), 380.

Juan Luis Vives'
De Europea dissidiis et bello Turcico:
Its Place in the 1526 Ensemble

EDWARD V. GEORGE

B etween 1514 and 1523, Juan Luis Vives experimented liberally with various literary genres such as fictitious narrative, dialogue, allegorical monologue, and historical declamation. However, from late 1523 to 1538 such creative undertakings are virtually absent, except for the dialogue *De Europae dissidiis et bello Turcico*. It first appeared in print as part of an ensemble volume with the similar name *De Europae dissidiis et re publica* (Bruges: de Croock, 1526). My purpose is to show that the interactions among the works in the ensemble are important to an interpretation of the *De dissidiis*. To avoid confusion I will call the dialogue the *De dissidiis* and the book in which it appears "the 1526 ensemble," or simply "the ensemble."[1]

The *De dissidiis* occurs in the underworld. The mythical judge Minos, the prophet Tiresias, the Roman Republican hero Scipio Africanus, and two recently deceased representative Europeans, Polypragmon ("Busy with Affairs") and Basilius Colax ("Royal Flatterer"), discuss the crowds of dead souls arriving at the River Styx from slaughters in European wars. Polypragmon reports on recent military and political follies committed by monarchs, popes, and armies. Vives's contempt for the earthly warriors' foolish, self-centered avarice is unmistakable in the comments of Minos and Tiresias on these events. When the speakers ponder what is to be done, Scipio, in the longest and most shocking speech of the dialogue, proposes that European unity be galvanized around an aggressive campaign of conquest against the Turkish empire. He even cites among the incentives for such a campaign the chance offered to the Christian monarchs to satiate their greed for territory and glory on a lavish scale. Tiresias rejoins in a more pious vein, counseling trust in the Lord, peace among the Christian kings, and a defensive alliance that will save Christian Europe from the Turks; but

---

[1] Unless otherwise noted, I cite Vives's works by volume and page number from Juan Luis Vives, *Opera Omnia* (Valencia: Montfort, 1782ff.), abbreviated as *VOO*.

even he holds out the possibility of a lucrative campaign of eastern conquest as merely a lesser evil in the event that it should occur.

Michael Zappala has argued convincingly that the differences between Tiresias and Scipio can best be understood by treating the *De dissidiis* as a Lucianic "open" dialogue; that is, an inquiry with theoretically uncertain outcome, and not a "closed" dialogue, which would be a pure and simple work of advocacy for a single ideological position masquerading as an open exchange.[2] However, Zappala goes on to suggest that Tiresias and Scipio offer "contradictory solutions to the Turkish problem" (828). After surveying the 1526 ensemble, which as a whole do not enter into Zappala's discussion, I will offer a somewhat different description of the situation.

The contents of the 1526 ensemble are presented in the following table:

Vives, *De Europae dissidiis et re publica*: Contents

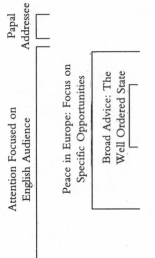

1. Letter to Adrian VI, the new pope, on disturbances in Europe. (Oct. 12, 1522. *VOO* 5: 164–174.)
2. Letter to Henry VIII, on the capture of King Francis I of France. (Mar. 12, 1525. *VOO* 6: 449–452.)
3. Second Letter to Henry VIII, on war and peace. (Oct. 8, 1525. *VOO* 5: 175–186.)
4. *De Europae dissidiis et bello Turcico*. Undedicated. (Oct. 1526. *VOO* 6: 452–481.)
5. Letter to Cardinal Wolsey, dedicating Isocratean translations. (Dec. 15, 1523. *VOO* 5: 1–5.) Translations of Isocrates' *Areopagiticus* and *Nicocles*: reflections on good citizens and good monarchs. (*VOO* 5: 6–61.)
6. Letter to John Longland, Bishop of Lincoln and member of the King's Council, urging the wisdom and nobility of making the first move toward peace. (July 8, 1524. *VOO* 5: 461–464.)

Vives himself regarded the entire 1526 ensemble as a single work despite the variety of origin among its parts.[3] The evidence is in a December 1526 letter to Francis

---

[2] Michael Zappala, "Vives' *De Europae Dissidiis et Bello Turcico*, the Quattrocento Dialogue and 'Open' Discourse," in *Acta Conventus Neo-Latini Torontonensis*, ed. Alexander Dalzell et al., Medieval & Renaissance Texts & Studies, vol. 86 (Binghamton, N.Y.: Medieval & Renaissance Texts & Studies, 1991), 823–830, cf. 825.

[3] The apparent dramatic date of the dialogue is August 1526. Cf. *VOO* 6: 463. Polypragmon has just arrived in the wake of the Ottoman devastation inflicted on Hungary in that month and regrets he could not have lived to see the story unfold further. Cf. also Fr. Calero in Juan Luis Vives, *De Europae dissidiis et republica. Sobre las dissensiones de Europa, y sobre el estado*, translation and notes by Francisco Calero and Maria José Echarte (Valencia: Ajuntament de València, 1992), 64 n. 40.

Cranevelt, when Vives observes: "Nuper libellum 'De dissidijs Europae' edidj: non dubito, quin sit istuc perlatus. . . . Est opus conveniens huic statui temporum."[4] Vives then summarizes for Cranevelt the roles played by various powers in the conflict over Italy and alludes to the August Turkish victory at Mohacs and the death of the Hungarian ruler. Vives's concluding comment is: "Vide, quaeso, ubi? Velut in harena, spectante communi hoste laeto atque applausuro, utercunque vincat, & incitaturo ad saevitiam!" A loose translation would be: "Look, I ask you: where are they? In an arena, while their common enemy enjoys himself in the stands, poised to cheer no matter who wins, and ready to urge the contenders on to savagery!"[5] Vives indeed here echoes the main purpose found in the 1526 ensemble, namely, the promotion of European unity.

The *De dissidiis*, which focuses on this purpose, follows all the other 1526 ensemble items chronologically, is written specifically for the occasion of the volume's appearance, and covers most broadly the themes of the ensemble. In compiling his *opus*, then, Vives penned the flamboyantly original *De dissidiis* in the final stages, while referring to the ideas found in his other selections.

The observer who peruses the 1526 ensemble will note that *consultatio*, or offering of advice, is one objective which is present in every case, explicitly in the epistles and implicitly in the Isocratean speeches, and, as we will see shortly, the *De dissidiis*. The first letter is directed to the Dutch Pope Adrian, who bears universal responsibility for Europe's welfare, temporal as well as spiritual. The perspective sketched in this first letter echoes Vives's own pan-European concerns[6] before he focuses on the series of English correspondents which follows.

Vives commends the new pope's character and his superiority to the men of old— *veteres illi*, further unspecified—who regard war as the path to virtue, vigor, and glory. How the Turk must enjoy the sight of European carnage! How barbarously we Christians deal with one another, adds Vives, trampling on our spiritually fraternal relationship (168–171). Vives then passes from European war to the restoration of peace in the Church: here, he advises, the only hope is to call a council and resort to

---

[4] *Literae virorum eruditorum ad Franciscum Craneveldium 1522–1528*, ed., notes, and commentary, Henry de Vocht (Louvain: Libraire Universitaire, 1928), 566–569, Ep. no. 217, Vives to Cranevelt.

[5] *Literae ad Craneveldium* (cited above, n. 4), 568. On Vives's concern with quarreling among Europe's monarchs in 1526, see also his letter to Cranevelt of June 10 (ibid., 508, Ep. no. 193): "atqui iam hoc nec Deo, nec hominibus probatur, interturbari pacem orbis per eos, a quibus in primis decebat procuratam et conseruatam. Vide quo deduxerunt rem opes immodicae! Dicunt coniurare multos aduersus Carolum," etc. Cf. also *De dissidiis*, 481: "de communi salute consultent, ne, dum contentius pergunt certare, victorem fessum, victum et fractum absumat communis hostis recens, integer, validus."

[6] Calero in *Sobre las dissensiones* (cited above, n. 3), 13 n. 5 identifies the war between Charles V and Francis I and the uproar caused by Luther. Cf. also Antonio Fontán, "La politica Europea en la perspectiva de Vives," in *Erasmus in Hispania: Vives in Belgio. Acta Colloquii Brugensis 23–26 IX 1985*, ed. Jozef IJsewijn and Angel Losada (Leuven: Peeters, 1986), 28–72, with a discussion (38–40) of the letter to Adrian.

reasonable dialogue. Themes that will mark the *De dissidiis* occur here: royal squabbling and other uproars in Europe, the consequent delight of the Turks, the need for Christian concord. Tiresias in the *De dissidiis*, like Vives here questioning the *veteres illi*, takes issue with the ancient authorities whom Basilius Colax cites on the subject of the excellence of warfare (*VOO* 6: 472). The spirit of confidence in reason which animates the epistles of the ensemble provides a marked contrast to the skepticism of Tiresias in the *De dissidiis*, who fears that monarchs' passions have rendered good advice useless.

The next item in the ensemble, the first letter to Henry, comes during a period of closeness between Vives and the monarch[7] and reacts to a specific historical event: the capture of Francis I of France at the battle of Pavia. Vives urges that Henry and Charles V seize this lucky chance by exercising mercy toward the defeated, thus winning over the erstwhile French enemy and demonstrating the victors' divine virtues.[8]

In the second letter to Henry, coming in "a time of peace," Vives announces that he will preach his usual gospel of peace. The grounds of the discussion are much broader than those of the previous letter; here, before offering specific advice, Vives sketches the needs of a well-run monarchy. The prince, the soul of the commonwealth and the model for his citizens,[9] should listen to good advice, no matter how unpalatable. *Edoceri reprehendi*: to be instructed is to be chastised (*VOO* 5: 176). If the king fosters his subjects' welfare and virtue, the populace so guided will rule itself and will require only caution rather than censure (180).

But good order is possible only in peacetime; hence Vives launches into a traditional litany of the blessings of peace and the curses of war.[10] His last word is a specific recommendation: a pact with Charles V, to ensure that this flower of peace does not prove a fruitless fantasy.

The *De dissidiis*, which we will discuss last, comes next. The Isocratean translations which follow the *De dissidiis* include a dedication to Cardinal Wolsey, whose goodwill toward Vives was uncertain in 1526, a time when Wolsey had reason to favor the French king over the Emperor Charles. Vives had been serving at Oxford with the benefit of funds provided by Wolsey when these translations were originally presented in October 1523, and so their reappearance here would serve to recall the historic connection between the powerful prelate and his renowned scholarly dependent. I associate the Isocratean pieces with the second letter to Henry: like it, they range broadly across matters affecting the healthy conduct of the commonwealth, dealing in the *Areopagiticus* with the qualities of the good citizen who upholds the worthy constitution, and in the *Nicocles* with the loyalty owed by subjects to the good monarch.

---

[7] Cf. Vives, *Sobre las dissensiones* (cited above, n. 3), 27 n. 1.

[8] *VOO* 6: 451; cf. Vives, *Sobre las dissensiones*, 29 n. 4, and the letter to Adrian, *VOO* 5: 169.

[9] Therefore he should think of himself as in a crowded theater under the gaze of all (*VOO* 5: 175; cf. the letter to Adrian, *VOO* 5: 166 for another drama metaphor).

[10] It is you through whom we are safe, Vives tells the king: it is noteworthy that by the use of the first person, "tuti sumus" (183), Vives this time includes himself under Henry's direction, while in the letter to Adrian he had regarded himself as a subject of the Emperor Charles.

The last item, the letter to Longland, concentrates on a specific historical point, like the epistle to Adrian and the first letter to Henry. Vives notes that he hears embassies for peace are abroad, and he writes to promote the process. In one striking moment he pushes his audience to a higher ethical standard than anywhere else in the 1526 ensemble. Challenging the truism that it is a disgrace to be the first to offer peace to an enemy, he resorts to the New World for an example, citing unspecified peoples in the Caribbean, among whom the person adopting this course is held in the highest honor. He makes the logical *a minore ad maiorem* argument: those Caribbeans shame us, the victims of our own lusts, who presume to call ourselves Christians; why can we not follow their example (*VOO* 5: 462)? Here we see an instance of the dissolution of polarities Zappala points out in the *De dissidiis*.[11] The Turk, cautions Vives, will be the only beneficiary of our mutual violence.[12]

A reading of these other pieces in the 1526 ensemble suggests some adjustment to our view of the *De dissidiis*. First: there should be one qualification to the "openness" of the dialogue discussed by Zappala, with its accompanying elimination of polarities such as Europe/Asia or Christian/Turk. Zappala observes that in the *De dissidiis* Vives "defuses the antithesis Turks/Europeans, for example, by pointing the finger at his own Europe."[13] However, Vives aims his finger rather carefully. Close examination of the *De dissidiis* shows that the English escape the sharp and specifically targeted criticism leveled at the French, Spanish, popes, and Italians. It is true that the English do not completely avoid castigation.[14] But the characterization of French and Spanish monarchs and popes is much more severe and personal: there is no anti-English remark to rival the criticisms of Francis's self-defeating lust for war (462), Charles's reliance on bribery (460), the pope's arrogance in presuming to give and take away kingdoms (465), the split of Naples like a cache of loot between Ferdinand of Aragon and Louis XII of France (458), and the hideous reputation of the Spanish soldiers (462–463). Alongside these reproaches, the gentle handling of England is conspicuous. And it is not that there was no relevant English misbehavior to allude to. In the historical record, we find atrocities and conflicts to which the English were party and which in the *De dissidiis* are ignored: the unsuccessful Anglo-Spanish campaign in 1512 to take Aquitaine from the French king; Wolsey's subsidies to Swiss and imperial armies against the French king; the Earl of Surrey's 1522 expedition into Picardy;

---

[11] Zappala, "Vives' *De Europae Dissidiis et Bello Turcico*," 826–827.

[12] More copiously than anywhere else in the ensemble, Vives persistently uses the first person plural in this letter: *Our* actual needs, he declares, are so modest; *we* are hypocrites, like the Hebrews worshiping gold; *we* talk like God's children and act like his enemies. The device is a shield, protecting Vives from the need to criticize delinquent statesmen by name.

[13] Zappala, "Vives' *De Europae Dissidiis et Bello Turcico*," 826.

[14] In brief allusions they are, like others, found susceptible to intergroup hate (*VOO* 6.454); they side with the Burgundians against the French in the closing stages of the Hundred Years' War (456; cf. Vives, *Sobre las dissensiones,* 55 n. 12); Henry VIII is enticed into war along with Ferdinand of Aragon by Pope Leo X; and in extremely brief language using an evasive passive voice, "Scotorum Rex Jacobus in acie ab Anglis caesus est" (459; see further below). Britain and the Emperor Charles align against Francis of France and the Scots in 1521 (461).

and the abortive march on Paris by the Duke of Suffolk and 11,000 troops in 1523.[15] The mild and quick allusion to the bloody defeat of the Scots at the battle of Flodden in 1513, with the deaths of James IV and thousands of others, is characteristic: Polypragmon merely says, "Scotorum Rex Jacobus in acie ab Anglis caesus est."

In fact, Henry earns a rare compliment. When Tiresias focuses on the desirability of a rapprochement between Charles and Francis (*iuvenes duo*, 480), he expresses confidence that Henry (*tertium illum*) will not stand in the way of a firm connection between them, especially since Henry did what he could in sending aid, although late, to Hungary, despite the great distance from his realm; for Henry thereby showed that he appreciated the gravity of a struggle for a Christian prince's domain. Vives's treatment of the English is explainable if we assume that they are the principal audience he envisions and that he is at pains to avoid alienating them: both the remainder of the 1526 ensemble and the position of Vives himself in 1526, still hoping for stable support from an English source, urge this assumption. The *De dissidiis* may indeed be an "open" dialogue, as Zappala observes, but it nonetheless discriminates finely in choosing its targets. Vives's caution *edoceri reprehendi* in the second letter to Henry, cited above, is quite out of harmony with his own practice in sparing the English in the *De dissidiis*.

The second observation we can make is on the relationship between Tiresias's and Scipio's apparently conflicting remarks in the *De dissidiis*. One priority dominates the 1526 ensemble as a whole: reconciliation among Europe's monarchs, whether for civilized living, the healing of religious rifts in Christianity, or the protection of Europe from the Turks. The epistles in the ensemble are examples of *consultatio*, or the rendering of advice: in view of Vives's characterization of the ensemble as a unity in the letter to Cranevelt quoted above, it is logical to regard the *De dissidiis* also as a more audacious form of *consultatio*. For the dialogue's characters are meant to speak persuasively to the community of influential European statesmen. At this point Vives's own 1523 treatise *De consultatione* is worth examining for clues to the *De dissidiis*, all the more so as we know that Turkish and other international tensions were on his mind when he wrote that earlier work.[16] In the *De dissidiis* Tiresias refers repeatedly to the fear that emotions have gripped the players in European politics so firmly that no reasonable appeal will find a hearing (464, 480, 481). In a rather desperate strategy, Vives places alongside Tiresias a persuasive voice of another kind in the person of Scipio. Scipio is one who can claim the ear of the kings: he knows war, he knows war against easterners, he shares the royal appetite for aggrandizement and glory. Here Vives's strategy corresponds to his remarks in the *De*

---

[15] John Guy, *Tudor England* (Oxford: Oxford University Press, 1988), 84, 105–107.

[16] Twice in the *De consultatione* Vives uses hypothetical examples echoing the politics and conflicts addressed in the *De dissidiis*. What if the French were to occupy a city? He poses several questions which should be answered before a bellicose response. He then imagines a case in which the Sultan threatens to attack Europe unless Cyprus is ceded to him. Vives suggests that a fight for Cyprus might be desirable for the very purpose of precipitating the promised European attack; for then our weapons would be pointed against the Turk instead of each other (*VOO* 2: 256–257).

consultatione about the importance of the *persona* of the adviser as a source of persuasion (*VOO* 2: 238–239); and here Scipio is a qualified adviser. His is a direct appeal to the very *affectus*, emotions, which Tiresias says block out receptivity to counsel. Vives has additional pertinent remarks in the *De consultatione* on the arousal of *affectus*:

> Affectus non sunt in hoc genere [i.e., in consultatione] ... concitandi et perturbandi, propterea quod alienum id videtur a gravitate et probitate, quae in consultationibus exigitur. Vellicantur tamen nonnunquam, idque vel ex rebus ipsis per amplificationem, si ostendantur esse graviores, atrociores, maiores, meliores, honorificentiores, utiliores, iucundiores, tutiores quam primum intuenti videantur, praesertim accommodatis his ad aliquem affectum quo maxime teneatur, vel proximum ei, ut atrocitas atque indignitas iracundo proponatur, *iniuria vel contemptus superbo, alienum bonum invido, honor ambitioso, divitiae avaro,* ambiguum dictum suspicaci, periculum meticuloso, labor segni.
>
> (*VOO* 2: 254: emphasis mine.)

Just previously Vives has prescribed: "praecipua bona sunt in pietate, deinde quae pluribus prosunt, iisque bonis, praeferenda illis quae paucioribus, et diuturna momentaneis aut temporariis, et solida speciosis tantum, et pura bona quam ex bonis et malis temperata" (*VOO* 2: 251). He speaks not of ruling out the distasteful course of action but of preference when preference is possible. In other words, he is implicitly capable of advising the embrace of a lesser evil when necessary. European unity is so urgent a priority that Vives, by voicing in the *De dissidiis* some despicable alternatives for the sake of the immediate practical aim, interrupts the stream of appeals to reason found in the epistles of the 1526 ensemble. Even Tiresias could be described as engaging in *vellicare*, unobtrusively stirring up the baser emotions that might interest the kings in getting along with each other. Scipio speaks the language of a greedy monarch, while Tiresias takes the high road and puts Christ first. The two messages are contiguous, not expressive of a real dilemma. Tiresias's *vellicatio* briefly exposes the link between them. Scipio's recommendation is a dark corollary to Tiresias's repeatedly expressed fears that the emotionally blinded kings or their counselors will not listen to rational advice.

It is, then, no surprise that the dialogue climaxes in a painful but nonetheless definite conclusion: the circumstances call for a war against the Turks. The gentle rhetorical handling of the English audience, indeed the very existence of the book, would have no meaning apart from an intention to communicate specific advice which the writer hopes will be heeded; and advice there is. Fight the Turks. The message is divided between two messengers. To Scipio it falls to advocate the unpleasant but unavoidable call to arms, in terms that appeal frankly to the European rulers' baser instincts. Tiresias takes up the commentary with pious, velvet-gloved insistence that with Christ we have everything, without him, nothing. But the ostensibly humane prophet complements, rather than contradicting, the mailed-fist advice of Scipio. His irenic words are not inconsistent with Scipio's call to arms. Not for the first time or for the last in the Western tradition do pacific postures serve as masks for violent intentions.

In Vives's stance revealed by the 1526 ensemble as a whole, the main problem is not the choice between a defensive alliance and an offensive alliance: the main problem is achieving European unity, whether or not it leads to an aggressive war against the Turks. Under cover of the mimetic genre of the *De dissidiis*, Vives the persuader frames an appeal to the European monarchs on the grounds of their own materialistic principles. Zappala calls Tiresias's and Scipio's proposals "contradictory solutions to the Turkish problem" (828); but even he admits that they are not totally contradictory. Where the discourse of all the other compositions in the 1526 ensemble presumes rational and teachable audiences, the *De dissidiis* makes a different set of assumptions, though in pursuit of the same goal of European unity. It presents a range of alternatives for pursuing this unity at all costs. It enunciates high Christian ideals; but it also provides for the possibility that the last chance for rational discourse may indeed have been swept away by corrupt passions, as Tiresias fears. In that case Scipio's recitation of the lesser evils becomes pertinent. The *De dissidiis* is the only item in the 1526 ensemble that is neither directed at nor dedicated to anyone in particular. Thus Vives not surprisingly avoids commenting directly on just how this enigmatic piece is to be taken. He veils himself behind the personae of the *De dissidiis* to produce a bold, even desperate, rhetorical capstone to the *De Europae dissidiis et re publica*.[17]

Texas Tech University

---

[17] I wish to acknowledge the helpful comments of Prof. Walther Ludwig and other attendees of the IANLS session where this paper was read. The National Endowment for the Humanities, the Program for Cooperation between Spain's Ministry of Culture and United States Universities, and the Texas Tech University Faculty Development Leave program provided funds and leisure that facilitated my research. I thank Gilbert Tournoy, Jozef IJsewijn, and Marc van der Poel for useful discussions of this paper.

Towards a New World Senatus Doctorum: The Liminary Verse of the Magnalia Christi Americana

GILBERT L. GIGLIOTTI

I n the "General Introduction" of his 1702 *Magnalia Christi Americana*, subtitled *The Ecclesiastical History of New England from Its First Planting in the Year of Our Lord 1698*, the Puritan minister and author Cotton Mather (1663–1728) proclaims: "Whether New England may Live any where else or no, it must Live in our History."[1] Accordingly, over the course of the seven books of Plutarchan biographies that comprise this self-styled epic of the American Puritan church, Mather, both for his immediate audience and for posterity, consciously aims at creating imaginatively a New England that, perhaps, never existed in fact.[2]

As part of this rhetorical creation of America, and in an effort to depict a community of American scholars in the tradition of the Renaissance humanists, Mather opens the *Magnalia* with a series of Neo-Latin and English commendatory poems composed by New England divines such as Nicholas Noyes of Salem, John Danforth of Dorchester, and Henry Selijns of New York, as well as Benjamin Tompson, teacher at the Roxbury Latin School.[3] By all but inventing, in his text, this literary circle of American "humanists," since no such practice of liminary verse had previously existed in the Massachusetts Bay Colony, Mather introduces a decidedly Renaissance dimension to his pious history of New England congregationalism. For,

---

[1] Cotton Mather, *Magnalia Christi Americana* (Cambridge: Belknap Press, 1977), 94. This edition will be the source of all quotations except where noted.

[2] Sacvan Bercovitch, *The Rites of Assent* (New York: Routledge, 1993), 136–137.

[3] Noyes and Tompson contributed prefatory poems in both Latin and English. Timothy Woodbridge, minister of Hartford, and Grindal Rawson, pastor of Mendon, each contributed an English poem.

unlike conventional dedications,[4] the tradition of commendatory verses was "mainly a Renaissance invention spread among circles of humanist scholars."[5] And it is within this humanist context that Mather offers these poems to his readers.[6]

Clearly, Mather's initiation of the Anglo-American practice of composing and publishing commendatory verses owes much to the steady advancement of life in the colonies. By the end of the seventeenth century, as Thomas Ryan writes:

> Some, at least, of the Puritans had attained sufficient leisure time to reach back into the world they had left behind in Europe and interest themselves once again in the literature, science, philosophy, and theology of their time.[7]

Nevertheless, such a conspicuously literary, that is, humanist,[8] facet as liminary verse may seem incongruous with the preferred didacticism of the Puritan plain style, which David Leverenz has described as the "straightforward language of collective dependence."[9] In "Antiquities," Book I of the *Magnalia*, however, Mather decries any such potential conflict when he underscores the historical significance and temporal coincidence "at the Conclusion of the Fifteenth, and the beginning of the Sixteenth Century" of the "Three most memorable things which have been born a very great Aspect upon Human Affairs . . . : the Resurrection of Literature . . . the opening of America . . . [and] the Reformation of Religion."[10] The simultaneity of the Renaissance, the European discovery of America, and the Reformation only proves to Mather their intimate relationship and interconnectedness. America, he goes on to write, since it formerly was "beyond the Bounds wherein the Church of God had thro' all former Ages been circumscribed," consequently had been deprived, in Mather's words, of "the Two Benefits, Literature and Religion."[11] As Mather's own

---

[4] An eleven-page "Attestation" by John Higginson (1616–1708), pastor of the Church at Salem, precedes the poems.

[5] Franklin B. Williams, *Index of Dedications and Commendatory Verses in English Books before 1641* (London, 1962), xi. Cf. J. W. Binns, *Intellectual Culture in Elizabethan and Jacobean England: The Latin Writings of the Age* (Leeds: Francis Cairns, 1990), 165 and I. D. McFarlane, *Renaissance Latin Poetry* (New York: Barnes and Noble, 1986), 17.

[6] Gustaaf Van Cromphout, "Cotton Mather: The Puritan Historian as Renaissance Humanist," *American Literature* 49 (1977): 327–337. Van Cromphout argues that Mather is "the most impressive exemplar of the humanist tradition in American Puritanism" and that through the baroque style of the *Magnalia*, his *magnum opus*, he tried, as a true humanist historian, to "bridge the gap between history and rhetoric, between history and literary art." He failed to mention his adoption of the humanist tradition of liminary verse.

[7] Thomas Ryan, "Poetry of John Danforth," *PAAS* 78 (1968): 137.

[8] Cf. Paul Oskar Kristeller, *Renaissance Thought* (New York: Harper Torchbooks, 1961), 10: "Renaissance Humanism was not as such a philosophical tendency or system, but rather a cultural and educational program which emphasized and developed an important but limited area of studies . . . that . . . might roughly be described as literature."

[9] David Leverenz, *The Language of Puritan Feeling* (New Brunswick: Rutgers University Press, 1980), 6.

[10] Mather, *Magnalia Christi Americana*, 118.

[11] Mather, *Magnalia Christi Americana*, 118.

baroque and densely allusive prose style—what he himself termed his "massy style"—illustrates: religion and literature go hand-in-hand.[12] In fact, in Mather's works, Sacvan Bercovitch argues that:

> The plethora of learned citations ... in Hebrew, Greek, and Latin, present themselves as choice moments of truth, fragmentary revelations of God's will, reordered in accordance with the nature of the Holy Commonwealth.[13]

Further, according to the title of John Danforth's liminary couplet, Cotton Mather is the *antistes politus*, the "refined high priest," of both *literae sacrae*, "scripture," as well as *literatura*, "the classics." Thus, as conceived and presented in the *Magnalia*, the New World now is reaping both "benefits," literature and religion, to which the liminary verse clearly attests.

The five Neo-Latin poems—Selijns's seventy-one-line "*In Jesu Christi Magnalia Americana*," two ogdoasticha based upon four anagrams by Noyes, an anagrammatic couplet by Danforth, and a six-line "*Celebratio*" by Tompson—serve a dual function within the text. first, they fit J. W. Binns's general description of the traditional liminary verses of Renaissance texts:

> The poems are formal encomia praising the moral, intellectual and stylistic qualities of the work. They are also prime occasions for short displays of highly concentrated manneristic literary brilliance—consciously artful flourishes and preludes to the work in question.[14]

Secondly, while "most dedicatory poems" only "evince some awareness of what the book to which they are attached is all about,"[15] the Neo-Latin liminary verses of the *Magnalia* function even more integrally. They both capture Mather's own mannerist style and emphasize the three key issues of the history as a whole: (1) the advancement and future prospects of faith and learning in the New World; (2) the tradition of faith personified both by the text and by Cotton Mather himself; and, most significantly, (3) the sacred meaning of the myth that is "America."

Henry Selijns's seventy-one-line *In Jesu Christi Magnalia Americana*, the longest of the Neo-Latin verses, most closely approximates the epic scope and patriotic element of Mather's ecclesiastical history. Selijns (1636–1701), for instance, employs a traditional Greco-Roman theme, *translatio studii et artium*, the westward progression (and improvement) of learning and the arts, within a genre to be more fully developed during the late colonial and early national periods: the "Rising Glory of America" poem.[16]

---

[12] Cf. Leo Kaiser, "On the Latin Verse Passages in Cotton Mather's *Magnalia Christi Americana*," *Early American Literature* 10 (1975/6): 301–306.

[13] Bercovitch, *Rites*, 138.

[14] Binns, *Intellectual Culture*, 171. Liminary verse customarily "employ[s] all kinds of manneristic devices" and "frequently ... take its title from the number of its lines."

[15] Binns, *Intellectual Culture*, 171.

[16] Paul Lauter, *The Heath Anthology of American Literature*, vol. 1 (Lexington: D. C. Heath, 1994), 1021. The genre takes its name from the 1771 collaboration of Philip Freneau and Hugh

The poem, in its depiction of the transplanting of Christianity and Learning to the shores of the New World with the advent of Puritanism, commences with a description of America as the European explorers found it (line 12):

Nullus erat, nisi brutus homo: Sine lege, Deoque.

No more, however. Quoting Aeneas, when he first sees the bloodied ghost of Hector (*Aeneid* 2.274), *Quantum mutatus ab illo est* (line 19), Selijns characterizes the transformation of America in the most primordial of images: *E tenebris Lux est* (line 28), that is, the light of Faith (lines 28–32), Learning (lines 39–42), and, most significantly, Peace (line 51). And these powerful forces, which, according to the poem, began converting the natives, founded Harvard College, and established a general peace throughout the colony, respectively, have transformed the New World as a direct result of their escaping from a decadent Europe mired in war and religious controversy (lines 54–58):

Mars nulli cedit. Nihil exitialius armis.
Testis adest. Europa docet lacrymabile Bellum,
Hispani Belgae, Germani, & quotquot in Orbe
Sunt Veteri, Rigidisq; plagis vexantur & armis.
Quas Sectas vetus Orbis habet, quae dogmata Carnis?

Thus, America is a haven from the horrors of the past and the sole hope for the future.

At the poem's conclusion, however, Selijns leaves the "Rising Glory of America" and, in very traditional encomiastic language, returns to the more immediate occasion of his poem—the *Magnalia* and its author (lines 69–71):

Vive Liber, totique Orbi Miracula monstres,
Quae sunt extra Orbem. Cottone, in saecula vive;
Et dum Mundus erit, vivat tua Fama per Orbem.

The four remaining Neo-Latin liminary poems, while still reflecting the primary themes of the *Magnalia* as a whole, as the verses of Selijns had done, shift the primary focus to Mather, its author, instead. The two hexametric ogdoasticha of Nicholas Noyes (1647–1717) and the elegiac couplet of John Danforth (1660–1730), for example, demonstrate the intricate explication that made typology, in general, so central to Puritan thought and the anagram, in particular, so popular with Puritan writers. Frequently, anagrams, that is, "the transposition of the letters of a word or phrase to form a new word or phrase,"[17] "were used alongside hymns, sermons, and ballads

---

Henry Brackenridge, "A Poem on the Rising Glory of America," which "explored the myth of the westward course of empire and arts from the old world to the new world."

[17] J. A. Cuddon, *The Penguin Dictionary of Literary Terms and Literary Theory* (New York: Penguin, 1992), 38.

to provide some sense of order in the Puritan world."[18] For since God created everything, everything, in turn—a death, a storm, a name—no matter how seemingly negligible, reflected God. To make sense of any particular, one needed only to examine it closely enough. The anagrammatic poems, therefore, simply reflect in microcosm what Mather had writ large in the *Magnalia*. As Mather aimed at conveying his understanding of how God worked through the lives of notable Puritans, both Noyes and Danforth utilize the anagram to observe and comprehend the place and significance of Mather himself in God's plan.

Cotton Mather, through the intense scrutiny of his name, thus becomes both the chronicler and physical manifestation of the ancestral *mores*, *fides*, and *cultus* (line 5). In Noyes's second poem, for instance, Mather not only *unctat demort'os* . . . , "embalms" the deceased Puritan fathers through his biographies (and that, of course, is not without a great deal of poetic license[19]) but so embodies the forefathers that *fit praesentes praeterita aetas* (line 2). In fact, the very name of Cotton Mather, both before and after anagrammatizing, reflects his centrality within New England Puritan history (line 8):

Nomen praesagit, nec non Anagrammata, vates.

As the grandson and namesake of the two pillars of the first generation in Massachusetts, John Cotton and Richard Mather, respectively, he is heir to their fame, but, as Noyes's various anagrams suggest, Mather also symbolizes, indeed personifies, the sanctity and learning of the ancestors: *EST DUO SANCTORUM, NATUS ES DOCTORUM*, and *SENATUS DOCTORUM*.

Similarly, in Danforth's anagram and elegiac couplet, Mather[20] is characterized not merely as soldier of Christ but as an entire cohort. The emphasis upon Mather's moral strength and power reflects not only the imposing size of Mather's *Magnalia* but also his lifelong work ethic that would produce over 400 separate publications (including sermons, religious tracts, educational manuals, scientific papers, a medical treatise, and a massive unpublished biblical commentary). Such a biographical slant to the couplet, of course, reflects the Plutarchan nature of the *Magnalia* but also is quite

---

[18] Jeffrey Walker, "Anagrams and Acrostics: Puritan Poetic Wit," in *Puritan Poets and Poetics: Seventeenth-Century American Poetry in Theory and Practice*, ed. Peter White (University Park, Pa.: Pennsylvania State University Press, 1985), 256.

[19] Cf. the "translator's note" concerning Noyes' anagrams on Mather in the 1853 Hartford edition of the *Magnalia* (1.20):

The first of the foregoing specimens . . . will compare favorably with its class. . . . Little can be said in praise of his other anagrams. The third is very unfortunate, for the first word is not Latin and the second cannot without a most unjustifiable exercising of poetic license be forced into hexameter verse.

[20] The rendering of Mather's name in Latin as both *Cottonus Maderus* and *Cottonus Matherus* illustrates not only the fluidity of orthography and, most probably, pronunciation in America in the late seventeenth and early eighteenth centuries but also the leeway allowed for the demonstration of the liminal poet's wit.

consistent with the rest of Danforth's own poetic output.[21] For, in general, Danforth's poems, the bulk of which are funeral elegies, aim at "mak[ing] sense of the individual life."[22] Mather's life, as succinctly summed up by Danforth, makes sense only by recognizing his truly remarkable production in the service of God. If we are soldiers, he stresses, then Mather is an army!

Mather's impressive energy on God's behalf is likewise the subject of both *Celeberrimi Cottoni Matheri Celebratio* and its English companion poem by Benjamin Tompson (1642–1714). The poet humorously develops the image of his former pupil as "Necromancer," who "raises his Countries Father's Ashes Urn'd," and who, "by his more Familiar Arts,/ Unseals our Hero's Tombs, and gives them Air" (lines 1–5). Often taken by critics as a "gentle" satire of Mather's keen interest in demonic possession and his post facto defense of the Salem witch trials in his 1693 *The Wonders of the Invisible World*,[23] the poems, in fact, owe their central conceit, biography as necromancy, to Mather himself.[24]

At the beginning of his 1697 *Pietas in Patriam, The Life of His Excellency Sir William Phips*, Mather describes the procedure by which a chemist, having extracted the essential "salt" of a plant and:

> keeping the Salt in a Glass Hermetically sealed, . . . can by applying a Soft Fire to the Glass, make the Vegetable rise by little and little out of its Ashes.[25]

He continues by suggesting that while the biographer can:

> without any criminal Necromancy, call up the shape of any Dead Ancestor from the Dust . . . there is some Resemblance of these Curiosities, which is performed, when we do in a Book, as in a Glass, reserve the History of our Departed Friends. . . .

The basic process of biography, then, is bringing the dead back to life.

Tompson's poem, however, unlike Noyes's ogdoastichon *Unctas demort'os*, underscores not the results of "resurrecting" or "embalming" the dead (i.e., fame for the author and historical perspective for the reader), as much the effort and skill necessary for such an undertaking. In the *Celebratio*, after all, it is Mather who "has recalled" the *Patrios Manes* (line 1), and it is *Arte* (line 4), "by the skill," of the author that they have been sent from heaven (line 3). Indeed, it is the act of Mather's writing, the textual realization of the epic image of New England which Mather presents in the *Magnalia*, that Tompson celebrates. As Bercovitch suggests:

---

[21] Ryan, "Poetry of John Danforth," 129–193. John Danforth composed twenty-four poems.

[22] Robert Daly, "The Danforths: Puritan Poets in the Woods of Arcadia," in White, ed., *Puritan Poets and Poetics*, 155.

[23] Peter White, *Benjamin Tompson, Colonial Bard* (University Park, Pa.: Pennsylvania State University Press, 1980), 163.

[24] Peter White, "Cannibals and Turks: Benjamin Tompson's Image of the Native American," in White, ed., *Puritan Poets and Poetics*, 200. Tompson himself had pursued alchemy, among other arts and sciences, after his graduation from Harvard in 1662.

[25] Mather, *Magnalia Christi Americana*, 276.

. . . by and large, in the *Magnalia*, it is the visionary element that predominates. In the epic world where his New England "live," Mather felt free to collapse tradition, invention, dream, and reality into metaphors that made the errand impervious to history.[26]

Thus, while Henry Selijns's poem most obviously approximates the epic sweep of the *Magnalia*, it is Tompson's verses that reflect a more complete understanding of the truly epic nature of Mather's work. Mather's New England, as a work of rhetorical creation, "transcends all material boundaries . . . [and] becomes, as with Milton's Eden, the focal point for a cosmic war that will decisively alter human history."[27] In other words, the art of Mather, the necromancer, reconstitutes the past into a vital and potent myth of the future.

From the time of its publication, critics frequently have read the *Magnalia* and its "massy style" as Mather's self-justifying jeremiad, his attempt both to harangue his lazy contemporaries back into the Calvinist fold[28] and to project an image of cultural sophistication aimed at assuring the world of the tradition and future of the errand into the American wilderness.[29] However, as Sacvan Bercovitch has argued, a far more sophisticated dynamic is at work in Mather's writings as a whole. Less interested in either New England's irrevocable past or its degenerate present than in the portrait of America as the "inevitable future,"[30] Mather ". . . centered the image of America where it really always belonged, in the symbolic imagination."[31] Unwilling to settle for anything less than a perfect America, Mather rhetorically creates his own; as Mather himself writes: "Whether New England may Live any where else or no, it must Live in our History."[32]

The Neo-Latin liminary verse of the *Magnalia* consequently can be seen to parallel and illuminate, in microcosm, Mather's creation of this mythic America. As a preface to his work, he begets a previously nonexistent humanist circle through an "individual act of will and vision,"[33] and, consequently, an "assembly of the learned," a *SENATUS DOCTORUM*, springs anagrammatically, as it were, from the mind of Cotton Mather. This assembly, in turn, simultaneously wilderness prophets and lovers of literature, Puritans and humanists, comes to embody the very epic task which Mather had embraced: the unification of disparate textual traditions through the establishment of a rhetorical and mythic America. In the end, therefore, it is his own

---

[26] Bercovitch, *Rites*, 141.

[27] Sacvan Bercovitch, "New England Epic: Cotton Mather's *Magnalia Christi Americana*," *ELH* 33 (1966): 342.

[28] Leverenz, *Language of Puritan Feeling*, 223.

[29] John Canup, *Out of the Wilderness: The Emergence of an American Identity in Colonial New England* (Middletown, Conn.: Wesleyan University Press, 1990), 6.

[30] Sacvan Bercovitch, *The Puritan Origins of the American Self* (New Haven: Yale University Press, 1975), 133.

[31] Bercovitch, *Puritan*, 132.

[32] Mather, *Magnalia Christi Americana*, 94.

[33] Bercovitch, *Puritan*, 132.

monumental myth-making rather than his grandfather's *Realpolitik* that is reflected in his adaptation of *Aeneid* 1.33 on the title page:

Tantae molis erat pro Christo condere gentem.

For Puritan New England ceased to exist long ago, but Mather's powerful myth of "America" continues to live.

Central Connecticut State University

L'eredità umanistica nella lirica meridionale del secolo XVI: spunti su Ludovico Paterno

RAFFAELE GIRARDI

I veloci spunti qui proposti sull'esperienza lirica paterniana vanno considerati come uno dei numerosi, possibili luoghi di verifica di un problema critico più generale, che si pone—credo—quando ci s'interroghi circa la reale funzione svolta nell' esperienza lirica meridionale dalla tradizione classica e dal più recente passato umanistico.

Ci corre il dubbio che a lungo il giudizio su quell'esperienza abbia subito una ingiustificata limitazione e in qualche caso una dannosa deformazione, galvanizzato com'era dalla necessità di dare al Petrarca e al Bembo tutto ciò che a loro competeva nella genesi propriamente italiana di un grande e duraturo modello linguistico-poetico: una "grammatica del dominio," si è detto,[1] che dava un fondamento anche ideologico all'aristocratico esercizio della scrittura petrarchistica. Una prassi lirica, insomma—per dirla nei modi usati dal Quondam proprio per il Paterno—destinata ad "esaurire" i "nuclei tematici e strutturali del codice Petrarca-Bembo . . . tramite lo svolgimento di tutte le loro possibilità lessicali e formali." Quella pratica di massa della poesia si sarebbe così tradotta, inopinatamente, "nel raddoppio progressivo . . . delle strutture fondamentali della scrittura lirica tradizionale," ossia in "vera e propria scrittura automatica."[2]

1. Diciamo subito che, se questi giudizi hanno un senso nel caso dell'ambizioso progetto messo in atto dal Paterno con la megaraccolta *Il Nuovo Petrarca*,[3] con molta più difficoltà si attagliano ad altri, non meno significativi, momenti della complessa

---

[1] Cf. Giancarlo Mazzacurati, "Pietro Bembo: la grammatica del dominio," *Lavoro critico* 7–8 (1976): 195–235. Ma dello stesso studioso si veda ora il più complesso e suggestivo piano d'analisi offerto in *Il rinascimento dei moderni. La crisi culturale del XVI secolo e la negazione delle origini* (Bologna: Il Mulino, 1985), 65–147.

[2] Cf. Giulio Ferroni e Amedeo Quondam, *La "locuzione artificiosa." Teoria ed esperienza della lirica a Napoli nell'età del Manierismo* (Roma: Bulzoni, 1973), 340.

[3] Venezia: Valvassori, 1560.

esperienza lirica paterniana. Si prenda l'esempio della ricchissima silloge *Le nuove fiamme*,[4] un'opera in cinque libri, a ciascuno dei quali corrisponde una partizione di genere lirico: I: sonetti e canzoni pastorali; II: stanze; III: elegie; IV: egloghe; V: nenie e tumuli. La raccolta, già nel frontespizio, dà per la verità conferma di un' ambizione capace di smaltire con grande rapidità e disinvoltura ogni residuo imbarazzo legato al controverso esordio del primo titolo paterniano, *Il Nuovo Petrarca*, già sottoposto a un cambiamento *in extremis* (probabilmente coatto), perché ritenuto, non senza ragione, eccessivamente pretenzioso: un "titolo insolente e vano," secondo il severo avviso del curatore ai lettori della nuova edizione, recante il nuovo titolo *Mirzia*.[5]

In realtà, sotto il velo della mera questione di deontologia e di costume editoriale, è proprio quella tenacia progettuale del Paterno che c'interessa. In particolare importa verificare se il complesso processo di riconversione classicistica indubbiamente in atto nelle *Nuove fiamme* configuri in sede critica semplicemente un problema di fonti, che in nulla modifichi lo schema di giudizio incentrato sul "sistema della ripetizione,"[6] valido, come si sa, per il Paterno e in linea di massima per tutti gli altri rappresentanti del manierismo napoletano; o se invece lo stesso rapporto con la poesia antica, arricchito—nei modi ecletticamente 'sperimentali' che si cercherà di dilucidare— dall'esperienza del Quattrocento umanistico, in specie napoletano, non sia esso l'originale contrassegno di un'esperienza poetica di rottura, consapevolmente incline ad uno strenuo esercizio di almeno provvisoria autonomia rispetto al modello dominante del petrarchismo/bembismo; e se inoltre non provengano proprio da un tale intenso riannodamento di legami con la classicità gli elementi propri di una vistosa dissoluzione strutturale di quel sistema codificato.

2. Le *Nuove fiamme*, a parte il persistente motivo della morte, dea dissolutrice, connesso ai simulacri di un perduto amore (Mirzia), sono innanzitutto un ambizioso viaggio oltre i confini dell'autobiografia erotico-sentimentale di stampo petrarchesco: un viaggio rivolto a perlustrare nuovi orizzonti tematico-espressivi, fra mito classico e nuove forme di mimesi arcadica. E' la ricerca di un nuovo linguaggio e di un più complesso mito della poesia, che sembra recuperare tutta intera l'immagine classica del poeta-vate, padrone a suo modo dei saperi, piegati alla funzione universale della rappresentazione artistica.

Forme e misure di questa rinnovata ricerca del mito non stupisce che riescano ad acclimatarsi, nel loro tono e senso peculiare, con un forte recupero di realismo del linguaggio e dell'espressione poetica: è forse questo il tratto più interessante del diffuso sperimentalismo paterniano. In ciascuno dei generi usati nelle *Nuove fiamme* affiora una sorta di incontinente desiderio di commistione, che è decisa inclinazione a quel "vario canto," che nella *Nenia* I (*Nuove fiamme* 5. 50) è tale per colpa della "Fortuna iniqua," la Fortuna d'amore, che "è varia anch'essa," ma che in realtà

---

[4] Venezia: Valvassori, 1561; poi Lione: Rovillio, 1568, da cui si cita.
[5] Napoli: Scotto, 1564.
[6] Cf. Ferroni-Quondam, *La "locuzione artificiosa,"* 211–233 (Quondam).

designa una più complessiva e coinvolgente vocazione di questa scrittura al sincretismo degli stili. E' insomma una poesia che si affida ad una sperimentazione ininterrotta, da protrarre fino a compulsare, attraverso una grande moltitudine di "generi," la forza evocativa di una *inventio* nuova, entro il quadro di un mito "diverso," che torna alla classicità come a una sorgente di valori ideologici ed espressivi capaci di rinnovare il gusto della "maraviglia" proprio per effetto della distanza storica e di una più intensa funzione mimetica.

"Negli andamenti umani—spiegava il Gliandini già nella presentazione ai lettori della seconda *Mirzia*—le cose che ci sono presenti assai meno ci *sono* di maraviglia che le lontane," con esplicito riferimento alla "lontananza" storica della letteratura greca e latina. Così come, nello spirito moderno, è "sconveniente per i begli ingegni restar sempre nel cerchio del Petrarca."

Si tratta in realtà, non solo per il Paterno, di una strategia di recupero, intesa paradossalmente a restituire attualità e forza sublimante al processo della mimesi e modellizzazione letteraria: il referente ultimo e l'oggetto stesso di tale processo va identificato nei rapporti di solidarietà all'interno dell'aristocrazia napoletana. Essa è dunque anche una restituzione di energia "civile" al messaggio poetico, che recupera in pieno e assume come tramite fondamentale, ovvero come segno di un'indispensabile continuità, i passati fulgori della tradizione umanistica "aragonese."

Si prenda nelle *Nuove fiamme* il *Lamento di Damone* (libro I), un'elegia amorosa in terza rima, che rinnova finanche nella voga del *versus intercalaris* il suggestivo esperimento metrico della *Mirtia* di Leon Battista Alberti, facendo sentire l'eco di antiche modulazioni liriche risalenti a Mosco e a Teocrito, attraverso la fondamentale mediazione della poesia neolatina. Il *Lamento* paterniano di sicuro non ignora l'esperimento metrico in volgare del Sannazaro, *Se mai per meraviglia alzando il viso*, definito dalla didascalia dei codici una "Lamentazione sopra il corpo del Redentor del mondo a' mortali."[7] Ma è con la lirica latina degli ultimi grandi napoletani che essa soprattutto intende misurarsi.

Parlando di elegia, a rigore, si dovrebbe navigare in territorio di generi non propriamente lirici, stando al dettato della poetica minturniana, che addirittura vuole l'elegia assimilata all'epica.

Resta il fatto, nel *Lamento* paterniano, di una parola dai toni dolorosi, che con le sue formule iterative rinnova il pianto per il "perduto intelletto" e per l'"estinto . . . core," vittime di un'antica pena d'amore: un canto insomma già fedele alla costante funzione conativa, direbbe Jacobson, di larga parte del messaggio poetico di stampo classico-elegiaco, anche in ambito umanistico. A quest'ultimo occorre subito far riferimento, visto il rilievo che va conferito a una delle sicure fonti del Paterno: l'egloga pontaniana *Meliseus*.

Del canto in morte di Ariadna, che adombra una pena storica (il dolore del Pontano per la moglie estinta), si perde, nel lamento paterniano, l'impostazione dialogica, ma non il tenue sfondo arcadico,[8] che anzi il Paterno arricchisce di toni ed emblemi,

---

[7] Cf. Jacopo Sannazaro, *Sonetti e canzoni*, in *Opere volgari*, ed. A. Mauro (Bari: Laterza, 1961), 210–211.

[8] Sintonie evidenti sono da riscontrare fra le prime due terzine del lamento paterniano e i vv.

grazie, come si vedrà, anche ad una forte presenza della lezione sannazariana; e nemmeno si perde la chiara intenzione mimetico-rievocativa che dà un carattere all' intero epicedio. Ma è alla bucolica sannazariana che bisogna ricorrere per un più corposo riscontro di matrici. Prendiamo la terzina che apre il *Lamento* paterniano:

> Poscia ch'avolti in tenebroso horrore
> son già tutti d'Arcadia i sacri boschi,
> piangete, o Ninfe, e con voi pianga Amore.

Essa ospita già in terza posizione un verso-ritornello, e fa eco, con parziale ricalco, all'esordio del solitario Ergasto nell'egloga XI del Sannazaro (*Poi che 'l soave stile e 'l dolce canto / sperar non lice più per questo bosco, / ricominciate, o Muse, il vostro pianto*),[9] che si distende anch'essa scandita con regolarità da un endecasillabo intercalare (anche in Sannazaro è il v. 3 della terzina d'apertura). Anche ai vv. 4–12 del Sannazaro i simboli naturali di un paesaggio emblematicamente sintonizzato col clima doloroso dell'epicedio si ripropongono assolutamente simili a quelli del Damone paterniano (vv. 4–15), che li riorganizza in un soliloquio d'andamento anaforico, insistente sull'invito alla partecipazione dolorosa (*Piangete . . . / Piangete . . .*). Ma poi tutta una sequenza ottativa del lamento di Ergasto, da *Piangete, valli abandonate sole* (v. 16) al ritornello del v. 21, si ricicla nel pianto di Damone ai vv. 13–27, offrendo il riuso di varie parole-rima.

Ancor più nell'esperimento del canto nuziale, canto d'occasione naturalmente, e ad alto tasso di ritualità, sembra esplicarsi la funzione eminentemente conativa di questa parola poetica. Parlo dell' *Epithalamio nelle nozze del Serenissimo Re Filippo d'Austria et Maria Regina d'Inghilterra*, che in regime metrico di già piena libertà strutturale, sfiorata appena dall'esigua disciplina del *versus intercalaris*, affida al flusso disinvolto e persino incontinente dei suoi centonovanta endecasillabi sciolti l'esigua ma a suo modo fascinosa suggestione topica della melodia votiva, tutta consumata nella trasfigurazione mitica del nobile vincolo coniugale:

> Almo figliuol d'Urania, ch'i bei crini
> cinto di fior d'amaraco odorato
> fai sempre risonar di voci allegre
> il colle d'Helicona e i cavi sassi
> aonii e thespi, o ben nato Himeneo,
> se mai per lingua di leggiadra Ninfa
> movesti 'l passo al suon de le mie voci,
> lascia Hippocrene e a le nozze hor vola
> grandi e reali; e tede et pini alluma,
> e prendi il luteo socco, et vien danzando,

---

44 e 79–82 dell'egloga "Meliseus," in Ioannis Ioviani Pontani *Carmina. Ecloghe–Elegie–Liriche*, ed. J. Oeschger (Bari: Laterza, 1948); ma poi anche in ordine sparso, come fra i vv. 46–47 del lamento e i pontaniani vv. 140–142.

[9] *Arcadia* 11.1–3, in Sannazaro, ed. Mauro cit., 106.

hor che ti chiaman le tre Grazie, il ciglio
di frondi coronate et di viole.

Nel respiro dilatato di questa parola augurale, così sovente basata su costruzioni e
movimenti di periodo di accentuato andamento classico, ardui nel loro restare entro
le paratie strutturali del metro volgare, si distendono i suoni e ritmi di una sottile e
suadente apologia dell'eros coniugale, che richiama impudica alla memoria del colto
uditorio nobiliare la sua fonte catulliana, uno dei cosiddetti *carmina docta*, ossia *Collis
o Heliconiei*, cui deve davvero molto. Gli deve innanzitutto una capacità di modulazione espressivo-canora e finanche un impasto lessicale decisamente non petrar-
cheschi: lo si riscontra fin dalla prima dozzina di versi or ora citati, da raffrontare con
le due strofe d'apertura del carme catulliano,[10] soprattutto per la danza rituale alla
quale Imeneo in entrambi i componimenti è invitato.

Eppure, l'esortazione al piacere, che aleggia sulla scena dell'epitalamio paterniano,
il caldo e un po' azzardato invito a quel *bel desio non mai provato innanzi* che lei *colma
e riempie* (vv. 34–35), a dispetto della fonte, ha da restare entro i confini di una mori-
gerata passione, che pur consumata fra *vergini verbene* e *maschi incensi* (v. 32), faccia
risaltare il decoro di un *licito amore* e *santo e onesto* (v. 33), prestigioso simulacro di una
felicità pubblica da esibire come forma ideale.

Si tiene lontano insomma, il Paterno, almeno in questo, dalla sensualità liberata e
impudica che è di Catullo e sarà poi del Pontano. In compenso, non ha freni nel rappresentare quell'immagine di felicità privata e coniugale come espressione simbolica,
promessa di un bene collettivo tutto da sognare: un'età dell'oro (v. 208ff.) tempo-
ralmente rovesciata, pensata finalmente non già come oggetto di rimpianto, relegato
in un nostalgico e remoto passato, ma come proiezione ottimistica su un futuro
governato dalle magnifiche sorti e progressive delle grandi monarchie europee.

Ma si diceva del Pontano. Al pontaniano *De amore coniugali*, che è certo presente
al Paterno, occorrerà senz'altro far riferimento in virtù di una sorta di accattivante
triangolarità che a più riprese s'istituisce in alcune suggestive riprese del comune
archetipo catulliano.

Si prenda, nell'*Epitalamio* delle *Nuove fiamme*, il riferimento al rito preparatorio
delle Ninfe Amadriadi in onore del simbolico arrivo di Imeneo:

Vieni, Himene Himeneo, vieni Himeneo

. . .

L'Hamadriade Ninfe han già tenuti
in ben rosato odor quattro et sei giorni
fioriti rami di novella mirto
per ornarti la fronte: o Dio giocondo
padre di gioia e di allegrezza eterna,
non più tardar: vedi che come 'l fiore

---

[10] "Collis o Heliconiei / cultor, Uraniae genus, / qui rapis teneram ad virum / virginem, o
Hymenaee Hymen, / O Hymen Hymenaee, // Cinge tempora floribus / suave olentis amaraci,
/ flammeum cape laetus, huc / huc veni niveo gerens / luteum pede soccum" (*Carmina* 63. 1–10).

>   del purpureo hiacinto assai più vago
>   appar fra gli altri, così ancor fra l'altre
>   questa scesa dal ciel. . . .

(vv. 39, 42–50)

Così la fonte catulliana:

>   Namque Iunia Manlio
>   . . .
>   floridis velut enitens
>   myrtus Asia ramulis,
>   quos Amadryades deae
>   ludicrum sibi rosido
>   nutriunt humore

(vv. 16, 21–25)

e più avanti:

>   Talis in vario solet
>   divitis domini hortulo
>   stare flos hyacinthinus.

(vv. 100–102)

Ma l'attenzione al testo pontaniano è indubitabile e, come si può vedere, il processo di contaminazione si fa complesso e per molti versi inestricabile. Così recita il Pontano nell'*Epithalamium in nuptiis Aureliae filiae*,[11] dunque in un contesto psicologico e sentimentale anch'esso particolare, ben diverso da quello del Paterno e di Catullo:

>   Laetus ut ad thalamos carmina pangit Hymen,
>   pulcher Hymen, Hymenaeus, Hymen, cui filia vatis
>   se colit, et thalamos nupta pudica parat;
>   qualis roscidulo florens hyacinthus in horto
>   puniceo primae certat honore rosae,
>   hunc Dryades coluere, hunc et coluere Napeae,
>   Nais et assidua fessa rigavit aqua.
>   Myrtus honos Veneris, myrto laetantur amantes.

(vv. 40–47)

Chi cerchi nel lessico e negli stilemi paterniani i segni di un rapporto in questo caso privilegiato con l'immaginario "naturale" del Pontano, colga pure in quel *purpureo giacinto assai più vago* (v. 48) del Paterno l'insistita rilettura del *purpureus hyacintus* che figura nel pontaniano *Epithalamium in nuptiis Eugeniae filiae* (v. 7).[12]

Ma più avanti, con le immagini congiunte del mondo, che senza Imeneo è visto come una vite priva di sostegno, e della giovane sposa tolta al seno della madre,

---

[11] Ed. cit., 176–180.
[12] Ed. cit., 180–185.

l'archetipo catulliano sembra tornare ad imporsi. Questi i versi paterniani:

> Vieni, Himene Himeneo, vieni Himeneo,
> vieni, che 'l mondo senza te sarebbe
> qual vite che non habbia o palo o tronco
> od olmo, a cui si appoggi: o dio possente
> a tor del sen de la pietosa madre
> la cara figlia et al suo sposo darla.

(vv. 52–57)

Così invece la fonte, che volge in positivo, come similitudine della gestualità erotica, l'immagine e l'azione della sinuosa vite:

> Tuus . . . vir
>
> . . .
>
> Lenta sed velut adsitas
> vitis implicat arbores,
> implicabitur in tuum
> complexum. . . .

(vv. 101–102, 106–109)

avendo già proposto, poco prima, in autonoma strofetta, lo spunto del giovane sposo che sottrae la vergine al seno materno:

> Tu fero iuveni in manus
> floridam ipse puellam
> dedis a gremio suae
> matris, o Hymenaee Hymen.

(vv. 56–59)

Ma ancora una volta la corrispondente soluzione del Pontano torna a interferire con qualche titolo di merito in più, limitatamente a quest'ultima immagine:

> Quam raptam matrisque sinu colloque parentis
> coniugis ad cari limina ducit Hymen.

(vv. 81–82)

grazie soprattutto a quel *raptam matrisque sinu*, più aderente alla soluzione paterniana.

3. La corposa sezione di *Egloghe* delle *Nuove fiamme* (libro IV) non fa che confermare questa strenua inclinazione a distanziare quanto più possibile il linguaggio di questo immaginario mitico-realistico dai confini del sistema espressivo petrarchesco. Nell'intento sperimentale che governa questa singolare oscillazione della scrittura fra referente mitologico e realismo—e parlo della cifra forse più originale di tutta la poesia delle *Nuove fiamme*—c'è spazio non solo per una *performance* metrica sempre più ricca e spericolata, ma anche per un complesso intreccio di soluzioni retorico-espressive e di scelte tematiche, che conducono infine ad una evidente frantumazione il sistema tradizionale del petrarchismo ereditato, ancora operante per la verità nei risultati espressivi del Paterno elegiaco, quello del terzo libro delle *Nuove fiamme*.

Nella congerie degli stili e dei generi che quest'ultima sezione esibisce (nella partizione per registri: il "marittimo," l'"amoroso," il "lugubre" e l'"illustre") ritorna la sperimentale inclinazione a trasmutare in nuove atmosfere e scenari mitici la sostanza realistica—o meglio naturalistica—di una poesia totalizzante, esaustiva, che tesaurizza e poi dilapida senza residui intere tradizioni tematiche e registri di genere, sovente cercando su territori di confine del linguaggio petrarchesco, ma ancor più spesso in repertori lessicali extra-lirici e comunque rigorosamente estranei al cantore di Laura, gli strumenti idonei ad una nuova grammatica dell'immaginario collettivo.

Si prenda ad esempio la prima egloga paterniana, *Pharmaceutria*, il racconto dialogico di una pena d'amore consumata fra preghiere pagane e incantesimi erotici (di sannazariana memoria),[13] consumati sullo sfondo di una Mergellina mitica e magica. L'assillo del "vario canto" è già tutto in evidenza nella struttura polimetrica di questo microdramma "piscatorio." Nella prima parte in terzine a rima incatenata il *versus intercalaris* ritma in chiave magico-rituale la formula d'auspicio dell'amante Erminia: *Ardete, o versi, ardete il mio nemico.* A questa prima parte si attacca una canzone a cinque strofe eterometriche senza congedo, che poi ricede il campo ad una serie conclusiva di terzine anch'esse a rima incatenata.

Oppure si prenda *Eufemo*, la seconda egloga, una gara fra pescatori, Leodoco ed Ofelte, giudice Eufemo, sulla falsariga anch'essa di un abbozzo sannazariano.[14] E' una tenzone viva, spigliata, dai toni di dialogo a tratti oltraggiosi: l'espressione di un realismo per altro commisto alle suggestioni di un Olimpo minore, esoterico e sconosciuto, dove ancora una volta è il sincretismo mitico-realistico che pervade l'intera rappresentazione e costituisce, soprattutto nel lessico (decisamente non petrarchesco), il carattere più proprio dell'*inventio* paterniana.

Nella quinta egloga "marittima," *Nisa,* l'inclinazione elegiaca ha modo di liberarsi in un'effusione di canto questa volta non condizionato da obblighi di rima e di regolari partizioni strofiche, dilagando nell'ormai prediletta modulazione del racconto lirico per frammenti, per rapidi baleni d'immagini, come nella sapida chiusura del lamento di Egone per la perdita della sua Nisa:

> Sì poi da Capri alcun nocchier, vegnendo,
> rauco griderà su da l'alta poppa
> a suoi compagni:—Oh, dal sinistro corno
> chinate al destro la gonfiata vela,
> lascinsi intatti gl'infamati scogli
> per la morte d'Egon!—Queste parole
> sonava Egone. Intanto le veloci
> stelle a l'occaso havean piegato i raggi,
> e l'Aurora discinta e sonnacchiosa

---

[13] Cf. Jacopo Sannazaro, *Egloghe–Elegie–Odi–Epigrammi*, ed. G. Castello (Milano: Signorelli, 1928), egl. 5.

[14] Sannazaro, egl. 6.

le marine irrigava e le campagne
col pianto suo versato a goccia a goccia.

(vv. 40–50)

in cui l'urgenza del libero e quasi prosastico flusso narrativo rompe le paratie metriche, offrendo l'esempio di una scrittura poetica che a mezzo Cinquecento già naviga verso territori di dissoluzione delle strutture e delle misure tradizionali.

Sono occasioni, queste (e mi riferisco ora all'intero percorso delle *Nuove fiamme*), nelle quali il bagaglio lessicale paterniano, per sottrazione di materiali a una grande congerie di registri speciali (al repertorio botanico in primo luogo, ma in copiosa misura anche a quello zoologico, tecnico-agricolo e marinaresco), continua a crescere su se stesso, facendo proliferare ormai a dismisura la distanza di questo linguaggio lirico dal lessico petrarchistico, a conferma del fatto che matura in questa esperienza di scrittura un profondo bisogno di strumenti altri della comunicazione poetica, capaci di liberare la soggettività creativa e comunicativa della letteratura napoletana dal cerchio angusto di un ordine immutabile, proprio come proclamava il Gliandini ai lettori della seconda *Mirzia*.

4. Altro capitolo da aprire, se qui ce ne fosse lo spazio, sarebbe quello sui *Tumuli* paterniani, che altri contributi offrono a chi intenda ricostruire in tutte le sue articolazioni (tematiche, retoriche, metriche) la fondamentale matrice classico-umanistica del lavoro poetico condotto per le *Nuove fiamme*.

Si consenta invece, per rapidamente colcludere, solo un accenno alle *Nenie*, una sezione che almeno nel titolo sembrerebbe indicare un ritorno questa volta esplicito all'alveo di un genere che il Pontano aveva interpretato sulla scorta di un suggestivo, affabile e vezzoso lirismo da interno domestico. Essa in realtà prende la strada di un nostalgico e doloroso (e forse anche ripetitivo) racconto d'amore, sorretto dall'ormai familiare libertà espressiva dell'endecasillabo sciolto: un racconto imperniato sull' ossessivo ricordo della morte di quella "pianta gentile," che già tante lacrime (e tante parole in rima) aveva fatto scorrere sullo scrittoio del "nuovo Petrarca."

Eppure, quel racconto ora conosce momenti di particolare finezza elegiaca, come nel delicato finale della quinta nenia, che conclude il canto doloroso di un amante per una mimetica Tirrenia. E', mi pare, uno dei più suggestivi frammenti, fra quanti se ne conoscono, nell'ambito della letteratura napoletana, dedicati all'invocatissimo Sebeto:

Qui non si vede et ode
altro che l'onda piana
del bel Sebeto, il cui tranquillo umore,
rotto di pietra in pietra,
quasi notturna cetra,
a profondo dormir incanta il core.
Vien, Sonno, e fa che 'l tuo figliuol riprenda
le sue forme e t'intenda.
Poi, con la bianca e bella mano ignuda

> tosto la moglie tua gli occhi ti chiuda.
> (vv. 93–102)

A queste parentesi di stupito languore il nuovo vate di Partenope affida i suoi sogni più veri e più ambiziosi, che parlano al nobile uditorio napoletano come dal fondo di una coscienza sapientemente narcotizzata: già compromessa comunque dal sottile ma visibilissimo disegno di un'apologia della felicità presente, che, come si deduce dalla terzina conclusiva del componimento *La Trasformatione* (*Nuove fiamme*, p. 476 sgg.), non ha bisogno di mimesi, e del resto non è bene che rischi l'equivoco dei mezzi termini:

> ... La presente aventurosa etate,
> se ben (com'altri tien) non passi e vinca
> l'età passate, almen bella pareggia.

Università di Bari

Italian Influences on Early Humanist
Educational Theory at Cracow (1495–1530)

JACQUELINE GLOMSKI

B y the time the humanist movement reached Poland at the end of the fifteenth
century, it had acquired the marks of the various cultures through which it had
passed. It was not by chance that the two men who were largely responsible for
planting the seed of humanism on Polish soil, Philip Buonaccorsi Callimachus and
Conrad Celtis, were representatives of the two major strains of humanism, the Italian
and the German, which would initially influence the Polish version. Later on, in the
early sixteenth century, French, Dutch, and Swiss elements would also have an effect
on the development of the young movement. Cracow was to become a base for
communication with humanists from the west and for the dissemination of humanist
pedagogy to the south.

Humanism had gained a foothold in Cracow thanks to the energies of Buonaccorsi
and Celtis.[1] Buonaccorsi had fled Rome because of involvement in a conspiracy to
assassinate Pope Paul II, and was granted refuge by Gregory of Sanok, the bishop of
Lwów, in 1470. Buonaccorsi eventually became a foreign policy advisor to the kings
Kazimierz Jagiellończyk and Jan Olbracht and remained in Cracow until his death.
He wrote humanistic erotic poetry, historical biography, and political treatises. Celtis,
the renowned wandering German humanist, arrived at Cracow in the spring of 1489
and stayed until 1491. Celtis, together with Buonaccorsi, founded the *Sodalitas
Litteraria Vistulana*, an organization whose members met to discuss classical literature
and to read from their own poetry. Celtis also made an effort to transplant humanist
learning onto Polish soil through his unofficial lectures in the students' residences at
Cracow.

Buonaccorsi's and Celtis's eventual successors were a group of scholars who took

---

[1] For a summary in English of Callimachus's and Celtis's activities in Poland, see Harold B.
Segel, *Renaissance Culture in Poland* (Ithaca, N.Y., 1989), 36–106. The standard work on Celtis in
English is Lewis Spitz, *Conrad Celtis: The German Arch-Humanist* (Cambridge, 1957); in Polish,
Antonina Jelicz, *Konrad Celtis: Na tle wczesnego renesansu w Polsce* (Warsaw, 1956).

on the responsibility of keeping humanism alive in Cracow in the face of attacks by conservative elements. These young humanists, many of German origin, conducted lectures at the students' residences, published texts, handbooks, and treatises for teachers and learners of classical Latin, and generally worked towards the integration of the humanist curriculum and humanist teaching methods into university and school education in the Polish kingdom, as well as in German and Hungarian territories. At this time, direct cultural contact between Poland and Italy was not as strong, in spite of the marriage of Sigismund I to Bona Sforza in 1518, as it would become at mid-century, when young Polish noblemen began to travel in large numbers to Italy to be educated. Yet the influence of Italian humanism can be detected in the pedagogical writings of early humanists who either taught or studied at Cracow, even though these scholars had never visited Italy.

The efforts of this generation to cultivate humanist pedagogy were manifested in the association of three men, Rudolf Agricola Junior, Valentine Eck, and Leonard Cox, who were resident together in Cracow from 1518 to 1521. It was in Cracow in 1518 that Leonard Cox probably first met Rudolf Agricola Junior and Valentine Eck, who had both already been there together for some seven years. Rudolf Agricola Junior,[2] originally from Wasserburg on Lake Constance, had reached Cracow *via* Leipzig in the summer of 1510. After receiving his Baccalaureate in the autumn of 1511, he began to lecture privately on the classics and immediately gathered a coterie of students around him, among whom was Valentine Eck, also from the Lake Constance region. Eck,[3] too, had come to Cracow by way of Leipzig, arriving in the Polish city in 1511. Leonard Cox,[4] born in Monmouth, Wales, had left Britain for the continent about 1513 to study in Paris and Tübingen. He matriculated at Cracow in September 1518 and in December of that year delivered a speech in praise of the university, entitled *De laudibus celeberrimae Cracoviensis Academiae.*

---

[2] For information on Rudolf Agricola the Younger, see Gustav Bauch, *Deutsche Scholaren in Krakau in der Zeit der Renaissance 1460–1520* (Breslau, 1901), 68–69; Bauch, *Rudolf Agricola Junior* (Breslau, 1892); C. Morawski, *Histoire de l'Université de Cracovie. Moyen Age et Renaissance.* 3 vols. (Paris, 1900), 3: 107–110; Henryk Barycz, *Historja Uniwersytetu Jagiellońskiego w epoce humanizmu* (Cracow, 1935), 31–37.

[3] On Eck, see Gustav Bauch, "Valentin Eck und Georg Werner. Zwei Lebensbilder aus der Zeit der Besitzergreifung Ungarns durch die Habsburger," *Ungarische Revue* 14 (1894): 40–57; Walenty Eck, "Dialog o rządzeniu rzecząpospolitą," translated and edited by Stefan Kazikowski, *Studia i materiały z dziejów nauki polskiej* Series A, no. 13 (1975): 3–19.

[4] On Cox, see Henryk Barycz, "Znaczenie Uniwersytetu Krakowskiego w początkach rozwoju erazmianizmu w Polece," *Zeszyty naukowe Uniwersytetu Jagiellońskiego. Prace historyczne* 33 (1971): 23–38; Andrew Breeze, "Leonard Cox, a Welsh Humanist in Poland and Hungary," *The National Library of Wales Journal* 25 (Winter, 1988): 399–409; S. F. Ryle, "An English Humanist in Eastern Europe: Leonard Cox (c. 1495–c. 1550)," *Studi Umanistici Piceni* 12 (1992): 223–231; Henryk Zins, "Leonard Coxe and the Erasmian Circles in Poland," *Annales Universitatis Mariae Curie-Skłodowska Sectio F* (1973): 153–179; Henryk Zins, "Angielski humanista Leonard Coxe i polscy erasmianczycy," *Roczniki humanistyczne* 20 (1972): 63–82; and Henryk Zins, "A British Humanist and the University of Krakow at the Beginning of the Sixteenth Century: A Chapter in Anglo-Polish Relations in the Age of the Renaissance," *Renaissance Studies* 8 (March 1994): 13–39.

Leonard Cox and Valentine Eck were to develop a close working relationship which would last at least ten years,[5] but Agricola died at an early age. In 1517 Eck took up the post of headmaster at the town school of Bardejov, in what is now Slovakia, then the kingdom of Hungary. In 1520, Cox followed Eck to Slovakia and became headmaster of the town school in Levoča, located to the southwest of Bardejov. Both Eck and Cox returned to Cracow sporadically. In 1514 Agricola left Cracow for Vienna, but he returned at the end of 1517. In 1518 Agricola was awarded, through the efforts of his patrons, the chair of poetry at Cracow. Unfortunately the German humanist was never properly paid. In 1520 he stated his intentions to leave Cracow for Leipzig or Wittenberg,[6] but before he could do so he became fatally ill, dying in March 1521.

Influences of fifteenth-century Italian humanism appear in the three pedagogical genres practised by these early Cracovian humanists: textual editions, handbooks, and treatises. Rudolf Agricola prepared editions of ancient and humanist authors for the use of students, and his publication record reflects a mission to educate young humanists in the proper composition of Latin prose and poetry. His editions of Beroaldo's *Modus epistolandi* and Mancinelli's *Opusculum de componendis versibus* appeared at Cracow during the years 1512 and 1513. Valentine Eck's *De versificandi arte opusculum*, a handbook on the composition of poetry, grew out of an informal course which he gave during the winter of 1514–1515[7] and showed the influence of the Italian grammarians Tortelli, Politian, Perotti, Niger, and Ferretus. Leonard Cox's most important contribution to humanist pedagogy was his treatise *Libellus de erudienda iuventute*, published at Cracow in 1526, which encompassed his views on schooling and which was a continuation of the traditions established in fifteenth-century Italy by Vergerio, Battista Guarini, Aeneas Silvius, and Maffeo Vegio.

Rudolf Agricola Junior was the first of the group to reach Cracow, and his work was the first to exhibit the influence of the Italians. He edited handbooks for the teaching of Latin verse and prose composition, classical and pseudo-classical texts for reading, and philosophical and theological treatises. Agricola seems to have been more interested in the Italian writers earlier on in his career, as all the editions of their texts which he produced at Cracow appeared before 1514. These works include Cleophilus Phanensis, *Coetus poetarum*, 1511; Beroaldo, *Modus epistolandi*, 1512; Maffeo Vegio, *Philalethes*, 1512; Mancinelli, *Opusculum de componendis versibus* and *Opusculum de poetica virtute*, 1513; and Beroaldo, *An orator sit philosopho et medico ante ponendus*, 1513.

---

[5] See A. Breeze and J. Glomski, "An Early British Treatise upon Education: Leonard Cox's *De erudienda iuventute* (1526)," *Humanistica Lovaniensia* 40 (1991): 160.

[6] Expressed in his correspondence to the humanist Joachim Vadianus, as reported by Morawski, 118.

[7] As Eck himself states in the introduction to *De versificandi arte opusculum* (Cracow, 1521), A2[v].

Agricola evidently printed his edition of Beroaldo's *Modus epistolandi*[8] as an accompaniment to his extramural classes on Latin composition. In his introduction to the work, Agricola stated that his intention in publishing Beroaldo's treatise was not to create a crib for lazy pupils but to facilitate the students' acquisition of an elegant Latin prose style in imitation of Cicero and other classical authors.[9] Agricola's student, Valentine Eck, added an appendix to the work, a selection from Jacob Wimpfeling's *Elegantiae minores*, attesting a simultaneous influence of both Italian and transalpine humanism. Agricola's publication of Beroaldo's handbook on letter-writing supplemented Franciscus Niger's *Ars de epistolis*, which had already been printed twice in Cracow, in 1503 and 1508,[10] and which had been employed in official lectures at the university since 1493.[11]

With his printing of Mancinelli's *Opusculum de componendis versibus*[12] and *Opusculum de poetica virtute*,[13] Agricola was the first to make two of this Italian grammarian's popular handbooks on versification readily available to Cracow academics. The publication of these works also temporarily filled the need for a printed manual on versification until Eck's *De versificandi arte* went to press in 1515. Mancinelli's *Opusculum de componendis versibus*, also known as *Versilogus*, was a short handbook on versification which quickly guided the pupils through the rules of quantity and the principles of the metric foot. Agricola attached Mancinelli's *Opusculum de poetica virtute* to the handbook presumably as a propaganda tactic, for this work was a defense of poetry, containing, among other topics, a selection of quotations from classical authors pertaining to the goodness of poetry and humanistic study. Certainly, it was also employed to help the pupils memorize verses from the classics.

Valentine Eck wrote *De versificandi arte opusculum* at the request of his students to whom he had been lecturing at the German students' hostel in the winter of 1514–1515. *De versificandi arte*, a fifty-five page handbook, was initially printed in Cracow in 1515 and then reprinted in 1521 and 1539. *De versificandi arte opusculum* was composed in a simple outline style which took the learner through the four elements of poetry: letters, syllables, feet, metres. The section on syllables contained twenty-three rules for determining the length of a syllable. The chapters on feet and metres contained elaborate charts listing each type to be learned together with its origin or definition. Eck also included sections on the "rules of poetic art," where he gave general suggestions on writing poetry well and on scansion and the structure of verse. The

---

[8] *Modus epistolandi* was first printed in *Margarita philosophica nova* (Strasbourg, 1508). (I thank my colleague Jill Kraye and also Judith Rice Henderson, University of Saskatchewan, for their assistance in establishing the *editio princeps* of this work.)

[9] Bauch, "Valentin Eck und Georg Werner," 42.

[10] Lidia Winniczuk, "The Latin Manuals of Epistolography in Poland in the Fifteenth and Sixteenth Centuries," in *Acta Conventus Neo-Latini Sanctandreani. Proceedings of the Fifth International Congress of Neo-Latin Studies*, ed. I. D. McFarlane (Binghamton, N.Y.: Medieval & Renaissance Texts & Studies, 1985), 557.

[11] W. Wisłocki, *Liber Diligentiarum Facultatis Artisticae Universitatis Cracoviensis. Pars I (1487–1563)*. Archiwum do dziejów literatury i oświaty w Polsce, vol. 4 (Cracow, 1886), 369.

[12] Antonius Mancinellus, *Versilogus* (*editio princeps*, Venice, 1492).

[13] Antonius Mancinellus, *De poetica virtute* (*editio princeps*, Rome, c. 1492).

section on structure was based on the odes of Horace and was illustrated with detailed charts using notes and numbers. Every rule or point formulated by Eck was followed by copious examples from over two dozen classical or Renaissance authors, major as well as minor figures.

Eck's handbook is considered the culmination of the tradition of humanistic poetics taught at the University of Cracow, begun by Conrad Celtis in 1489–1491.[14] Although Eck did not mention his source for *De versificandi arte,* stating only that he had collected examples from his teachers,[15] it is generally accepted that he relied mostly on the handbooks of the former Cracovians Laurentius Corvinus and Heinrich Bebel and also on that of the Parisian, Jean Despauter. Still, the influence of the fifteenth-century Italian grammarians can be clearly seen. For his section on letters, Eck borrowed from Tortelli,[16] Politian,[17] and Perotti;[18] for his section on feet, from Niger;[19] and for his section on the structure of verse, from Ferretus.[20] Eck, moreover, cited Mancinelli in his section on syllabic length,[21] and his presentation of Horatian verse forms was descended from those of Ferretus and Perotti.[22] Although the scheme of Eck's work is one found in antiquity,[23] the general layout and organization of Eck's handbook probably owed much to Niger, who had his *Grammatica* arranged in five main sections: De syllabarum quantitatibus, De syllabarum accentibus et modis punctandi, De metrica oratione et carminum qualitatibus, De genere et specie metri carminum varietate, De poemate et poesi et de poetarum officio. Like Eck, Niger stated brief rules and then provided an example.

Although Eck's handbook was largely a compilation, his work shows a definite development in humanist pedagogical methods and also probably reveals Eck's own talent for teaching. Eck's handbook must have had great value for both the teachers and students of his time, since his presentation of the grammatical and poetic rules was much more concise and clear than those of his predecessors, including the handbooks of the Italians.[24] His handling of Horatian metre, for example, was more precise than that of Perotti and Ferretus, and his work was much richer in metric

---

[14] Sergiusz Chądzyński and Cyprian Mielczarski, "Seminarium Zakładu Badań Kopernikańskich," *Kwartalnik historii nauki i techniki* 26 (1981): 734.

[15] *De versificandi arte opusculum,* A2ᵛ.

[16] Ioannes Tortellius, *Commentariorum grammaticorum de orthographia dictionum e graecis tractarum opus (editio princeps,* Treviso, 1477).

[17] Angelus Politianus, *Miscellaneorum centuriae primae,* in *Omnia opera (editio princeps,* Venice, 1498).

[18] Nicolaus Perottus, *Rudimenta grammatices (editio princeps,* Rome, 1473).

[19] Franciscus Niger, *Grammatica . . . cum metrica arte eiusdem (editio princeps,* Venice, 1480).

[20] Nicolaus Ferretus, *Opera (Liber tertius de arte poetica) (editio princeps,* Venice, 1507). For details on Eck's debt to the Italian grammarians, see Cyprian Mielczarski, "Podręcznik 'De arte versificandi' Walentego Ecka na tle humanistycznej teorii wersyfikacji" (Master's Thesis, University of Warsaw, Department of Classical Philology, n.d.), 21–52, 57–58.

[21] Mielczarski, 37.

[22] Mielczarski, 50–51.

[23] Mielczarski, 22.

[24] See Mielczarski, 57–58. I am here stating my agreement with Mielczarski's observations on the importance of Eck's contribution to the tradition of the humanist *ars versificandi.*

exempla taken from ancient and contemporary humanist poetry.[25] Eck's importance for humanist pedagogy in east central Europe lies in that he was presenting, with the exception of Mancinelli's *Opusculum de componendis versibus,* the Italians' work on versification for the first time in print at Cracow. Eck's printing of musical notation and of charts with numbers to represent the length and the placement of feet in a metrical verse formalized humanist teaching methods.

In *Libellus de erudienda iuventute,*[26] Leonard Cox stated his purpose as assisting teachers in motivating their students step by step towards proficiency in Latin. At the very beginning of his essay, Cox acknowledged his debt to Vergerio,[27] Battista Guarini,[28] Maffeo Vegio,[29] and Aeneas Silvius.[30] Since Cox was using the same sources as the Italians—Pseudo-Plutarch, Quintilian, and Jerome—, it is difficult to know whether his comments come directly from those authorities or were filtered through the Italians. This is especially so when Cox repeats an anecdote used by one of the Italian writers, as with the example of Trajan and his tutor Plutarch, mentioned by Aeneas Silvius,[31] or that of Alexander the Great and Leonides, found in Battista Guarini.[32] In spite of a commonality of sources, it is still possible to trace the presence of the fifteenth-century Italian pedagogical writers in Cox's treatise.

Of all the Italian handbooks, *De erudienda iuventute* resembled in structure and content most closely that of Battista Guarini. Cox's *De erudienda iuventute* was divided into two sections. The first consisted of a discussion of the nature of education, and the second was a prescription for the humanist curriculum, containing recommendations for both the learning of Latin grammar and the study of the "auctores." Similarly, the first part of Battista's *De ordine docendi et studendi* was taken up with reflections on the ideal schoolmaster, the relationship between the schoolmaster and the pupils, and the creation of a favorable atmosphere for learning; while the second section dealt with the teaching of Latin and Greek in a two-step process, "methodicen" and "historicen." Cox, however, did not imitate Guarini's third section, a sort of postscript with a listing of ideal conditions to promote good study.

The similarities between the structure and content of Cox's treatise and Battista

---

[25] Mielczarski, 52.

[26] For the text of this treatise with an introduction and notes, see Breeze and Glomski, as cited in note 5.

[27] Pier Paolo Vergerio, *De ingenuis moribus et liberalibus studiis adulescentiae* (*editio princeps,* Venice, c. 1492). I quote from the edition by A. Gnesotto, in *Atti e Memorie Accademia di Padova* 34, no. 2 (no. 2, 1918): 75–156.

[28] Battista Guarini, *De ordine docendi et studendi* (*editio princeps,* Ferrara, 1474). I quote from the edition by Luigi Piacente (Bari, 1975).

[29] Maffeo Vegio, *De educatione liberorum et eorum claris moribus* (*editio princeps,* Milan, 1491). The first three books of this treatise were edited by Sister Maria Walburg Fanning, as vol. 1 of the series, Studies in Medieval and Renaissance Latin (Washington, D.C., 1933).

[30] Aeneas Silvius, *De educatione liberorum* (*editio princeps,* Cologne, c. 1470). I quote from the edition by Joel Stanislaus Nelson (Washington, D.C., 1940).

[31] Aeneas Silvius, *De educatione liberorum,* 99.

[32] Battista Guarini, *De ordine docendi,* 38.

Guarini's *De ordine docendi et studendi* may have grown out of similarities in their contexts. Cox addressed the question of educating boys who would be attending a town school, while Battista's treatise described a program of study in the tradition of the gymnasium curriculum established by his father, Guarino. Neither author showed concern for the customs of the nobility, as did Vergerio or Aeneas Silvius. Moreover, the aim of Maffeo Vegio's *De educatione liberorum* was the rearing of children in general, with school education referred to as a subset of the main topic.

In his remarks on the nature of education, Cox expressed three major concerns which echoed those of the Italian humanists. The first was the influence of the teacher upon the impressionable young boy. All the humanists were concerned about the effect a dishonorable teacher might have on the pupils. Along with Cox, Aeneas Silvius, Vergerio, and Battista, all remarked on the difficulty of erasing an error or vice once learned.[33] Cox's second major concern was the boys' motivation to learn. Cox believed the teacher's praise should be sufficient encouragement, but like Vergerio,[34] he thought that with some pupils the schoolmasters might simply have to resort to corporal punishment.[35] Cox was in agreement with all four Italian humanists when he stated that the teachers should be loved by their pupils rather than feared by them. Cox's third consideration, that the aim of education is to teach children to fear God and respect their elders, was a theme which colored humanist pedagogical writings to the extent that it may be considered a commonplace.

The influence of the Italian pedagogical writers remains concentrated in Cox's philosophical considerations. When it comes to practical matters, such as prescriptions for the curriculum and for the conducting of lessons, the presence of the Italians in *De erudienda iuventute* is less noticeable. Cox's handling of grammar instruction and his strong argument for including Greek in the curriculum shared a certain affinity with Battista's views,[36] and Cox's choices of authors—Vergil, Terence, Cicero, and Ovid—for the most part coincided with those of the Italians. But, for his approach to the teaching and reading of texts, Cox succumbed to northern influences and relied on Erasmus.

The educational publications of Rudolf Agricola Junior, Valentine Eck, and Leonard Cox represent not only three different genres but, more importantly, three different methods of assimilating the work of the fifteenth-century Italians into early Polish humanist pedagogy. Rudolf Agricola's output of editions of complete texts hinted at a need for quick publications to fill a lack in available handbooks. Valentine Eck's manual of Latin verse composition integrated the work of the earlier Italians

---

[33] Aeneas Silvius, *De educatione liberorum*, 100; Vergerio, *De ingenuis moribus*, 128; Battista Guarini, *De ordine docendi*, 40. Cox employed the same quotation from Horace as Guarini: "Quo semel est imbuta recens servabit odorem testa diu" (Horace, *Epistles* 1.2.69–70). See Breeze and Glomski (note 5 above), 128.

[34] Vergerio, *De ingenuis moribus*, 101–102.

[35] Aeneas Silvius and Maffeo Vegio were opposed to the use of corporal punishment. See J. S. Nelson's introduction to Aeneas Silvius (as cited in note 30), 57. Battista was also against the beating of students (*De ordine docendi*, 40).

[36] For Battista's views on the study of Greek, see *De ordine docendi*, 54–58.

with that of the northern humanists in order to present the most correct theories of classical Latin versification. Finally, Leonard Cox took the educational philosophies of the Italians into consideration when fashioning a program of instruction in the Latin language. Through their efforts, Agricola, Eck, and Cox brought the ideas of the preceding generation of Italian humanists into print at Cracow and thus strengthened the position of humanist pedagogy there.

The Warburg Institute

Little Italy on the Rhône: A Look at Lyons, Mainly from an Emblematic Point of View

MONIKA GRÜNBERG-DRÖGE

Although in the sixteenth century Lyons was built not so much on the Rhône as on its confluent the Saône (which flows into the Rhône just about south of the old city), it is nevertheless the latter which, then as now, represented the main waterway linking France with the Mediterranean in general and with Italy in particular. The Rhône bridges—obviously fewer then than today—had for a long time already permitted military, economic, and cultural contacts between these two countries. Lyons by all means was—especially between the late fifteenth and the end of the sixteenth centuries—one of the most Italianate French towns. A large Italian community of merchants, manufacturers, and bankers was firmly established in the city, its fate closely linked to the Lyonese fairs (in favour of whose reinstatement—in 1494, after a ten years' abolition period—it had discreetly lobbied at the eve of the outbreak of the so-called Italian wars); this community was actively contributing, for its own benefit and that of its host homeland, to the prosperity of the capital of the Gauls.[1]

In this period of economic renaissance in Lyons—partly at least under Italian auspices—an atmosphere propitious to arts and letters, some of which found their origin in humanist and related circles in Italy and were only too readily imported from there to France, was soon able to develop. Artists and poets freshly come (or, for that matter, freshly fled) from the peninsula frequently found asylum in the houses of the rich and influential Italians of Lyons, who were taking part in all the aspects of

---

[1] Cf. J. Mathorez, "Notes sur les Italiens en France du XIIIe siècle jusqu'au règne de Charles VIII," *Bulletin italien*, four articles in vols. 39–40 (1917–1918); Lucien Romier, "Lyon et le cosmopolitisme au début de la Renaissance française," *Bibliothèque d'Humanisme et Renaissance* 11 (1949): 28–42; James B. Wadsworth, *Lyons 1473–1503: The Beginnings of Cosmopolitanism* (Cambridge, Mass., 1962); Albert Baur, ch. I, "Les débuts de la Renaissance à Lyon" et passim, in *Maurice Scève et la Renaissance Lyonnaise—étude d'histoire littéraire* (Paris, 1906; rpt. Genève, 1969).

economic, political, social, and cultural life. It was under the latter's protection that these refugees first mixed with the local cultural life. But the French also were great promoters of Italian arts and letters, which many had become acquainted with in the wake of the Italian wars even more than through the peaceful exchanges of the markets and fairs. The flourishing printing industry of Lyons—in which however the Italians played only a comparatively minor role—also largely contributed to the distribution in France and abroad of works of Italian authorship or character and of intellectual currents of Italian origin such as Humanism, Neo-Platonism, or Petrarchism.[2]

In Lyons the Italian intellectuals found two courses of action open to them: either to present to the curious public and to the imitation-ready writers among their French hosts the literary traditions imported unchanged from their homeland—as did, for example, the Florentine poet Luigi Alamanni, the protégé of the French court;[3] or else to become fully immersed in the local customs and interests of their country of adoption, a course of action perhaps best represented by the cultural activities of the polyglot polygrapher Gabriele Symeoni,[4] another Florentine who for many years flourished in Lyons, where he dedicated a large number of his works to local authorities of both Italian and French descent. The fact that most of these dedications could be composed (when not in Latin) in Italian, a language almost as current in Lyons as French was,[5] manifests the degree of Italianization of French cultural life in the period in question. Not only the court but also the burghers, the better-off merchants, the craftsmen or the artists could read, possibly even write, and certainly converse in Italian, then almost a second official idiom next to the definitely official

---

[2] On the Italians among the printers of Lyons (e.g., Vincenzo de Portonariis of Trino, the Gabiano family of Piedmont, and especially the Giuntas of Florence), cf. Natalie Zemon Davis, "Le monde de l'imprimerie humaniste: Lyon," in *Histoire de l'édition française*, tome I: *Le livre conquérant (Du moyen âge au milieu du XVIIe siècle)* (Paris, 1982), or Enea Balmas, "Librai italiani a Lione" and Riccardo Scrivano, "Libri e autori italiani a Lione nel XVI secolo," both in *Il Rinascimento a Lione*, 2 vols. (Roma, 1988), 1:60–82 and 2: 925–036, respectively. On the contribution of printing to the spread of humanism in Lyons, cf. Romier, 37f., and H. J. Martin, "Le rôle de l'imprimerie lyonnaise dans le premier humanisme français," in *L'Humanisme français au début de la Renaissance* (Paris, 1973), 81–91.

[3] Alamanni intermittently dwelt in Lyons from 1522 to the end of his life in 1556 and undertook several diplomatic missions for the French kings. His poetry—composed in Italian and for the most part inspired by classical models, among them the *Greek Anthology*—included works composed or published in France and dedicated to French dignitaries (cf. his *Opere toscane* [Lyons, 1532–1533], dedicated to Francis I).

[4] Born in Florence 1509, died in Turin 1575; he was intermittently active (as diplomat and military man as well as poet) in France, especially in Lyons, from 1528 to 1560. On this figure, see T. Renucci, *Un aventurier des lettres au XVIe siècle: Gabriel Symeoni* (Paris, 1943); C. Coulardot, "Un humaniste florentin à Lyon au XVIe siècle," *Revue de l'Université de Lyon* (1933), and also Claude Albert Mayer, "Gabriele Simeoni et le premier sonnet français," *Studi francesi* 18 (1974): 213–223.

[5] As demonstrated by Jean Lemaire de Belges's *Traicté intitulé la Concorde des deux langages*, published in 1513.

Latin, to which French was raised as an alternative only in 1539 with the decree of Villers-Cotterêts.

Among the early representatives of such Lyonese admirers and for that matter distributors of modern Italianate cultural trends in France the comparatively, and in our opinion unjustly, unknown figure of the courtier and mainly vernacular author Pierre Sala is not unworthy of mention.[6] He is best known (if at all) for his Arthurian novels, his romanced historical compilations, and his pre-emblematic productions, which latter are currently increasingly valued. Yet Pierre Sala also knew Latin[7] and gathered some short historical notes on the history of his hometown, praising its antiquity and Roman origins.[8] Humanistic epigraphy was in fact a comparatively new Italian import to French civilization, and the Lombards—whose culture was most accessible to the French due to their long-time hold on Milan—were particularly active in documenting therewith the valorous antiquity of their respective hometowns.[9] In Lyons however the fashion of "antiquarianism" only really starts with Sala and the better renowned polygrapher and medical doctor Symphorien Champier.[10] Sala's own contribution to the topic is contained in a unique manuscript of the Bibliothèque Nationale of Paris entitled *Antiquitez de Lyon*,[11] in which heterogeneous materials are gathered pell-mell, regardless of subject or even of language. Among several investigations of the antiquity of Sala's own hometown and the burial customs of the ancients in general,[12] there also are several epigraphic records of ancient Roman inscriptions from Lyons or its surroundings. Some are from monuments apparently surviving on Sala's own land; others come from as far away as the "boundaries of Hercules" in La Coruña, and even from Rome:[13] the latter inscrip-

---

[6] Born in Lyons before 1457, died there around 1529. On this figure and for further relevant bibliography, see my article "Pierre Sala—antiquaire, humaniste et homme de lettres lyonnais du XVIe siècle," *Travaux de l'Institut d'Histoire de l'Art de Lyon* 16 (1993; *Aspects du XVIe siècle à Lyon*): 4–33; for Sala's acquaintance with Italy and Italian see pp. 8–9, nn. 19, 22 et passim.

[7] Cf. his verse translation of *Le régime contre la pestilence*, on occasion of the visit of Francis I to Lyons in 1522, from a Latin original composed by Basel doctors around 1520.

[8] Incidentally, it was his half-brother Jehan who, the year of Pierre's death, saw to the remission of the recently discovered Claudian tables to the city municipality; cf. *Corpus Inscriptionum Latinarum* (= *CIL*; Berlin, 1862–), XIII, no. 1668.

[9] Cf. Giorgio Merula, Benedetto Giovio, or Andrea Alciati, whose epigraphic collections were well known in France via either printed or manuscript distribution.

[10] Cf. *CIL* XIII, xli, 248ff., especially 256–258. On Champier (e.g., *CIL* XIII, 257), who was born in 1471 and died around 1537/9 and is the author of a large number of medical and philosophical works, cf. M. P. Allut, *Étude biographique et bibliographique sur Symphorien Champier* (Lyon, 1859), and numerous recent contributions: e.g., in the acts of the conference (held at Lyons in May 1972) *L'Humanisme lyonnais au XVIe siècle* (Grenoble, 1974).

[11] MS fr. 5447.

[12] "De anticalia Lugduni," *Antiquitez . . . ,* fols. 38–45; fols. 52–62 concerning the great fire of Lyons of 50 B.C.; "Anciennes pompes funeralles," *Antiquitez . . . ,* fols. 8v–24v.

[13] From Lyons and surroundings come the inscriptions recorded as *CIL* XIII, nos. 1674, 1686, 1695, 1709, 1895, 1916, 1918, 1921, 2104 (the latter from Sala's house, the "Anticaille" on the hill of Fourvière), 2178, 2188, 2209, 2231 (the latter from his land in Vaise); *CIL* XII, no. 1904.

tions Sala certainly never saw but rather must have copied from a not yet identified manuscript source. It is not clear why he collected these particular inscriptions but the fact in itself documents the readiness of this Lyonese to glean epigraphic memorabilia from both manuscripts and his actual surroundings, in keeping with the fashion introduced by the Italians. It is also to be noted that for Sala epigraphy was significantly compatible with his vernacular "emblems," as the setting of the latter in placards shaped in the form of "tabulae ansariae" clearly demonstrates.[14]

Regarding epigraphy Sala was certainly not original: many other humanists all across Europe were busy collecting—or for that matter faking—Roman lapidary inscriptions in an effort to document the best of the ancient history and customs of their homelands through original vestiges.[15] Sala was merely among the earliest to do so in France in general[16] and in Lyons in particular. His bias for antiquarianism was subsequently shared by a large number of his Lyonese compatriots: among these are the above-named Symphorien Champier,[17] as well as Claude Bellièvre,[18] Guillaume du Choul,[19] and the previously mentioned Florentine Gabriele Symeoni. Whereas, however, Champier had already left Lyons by the time he composed his major works on the city's glorious past, Symeoni—at several occasions a more or less

From La Coruña: *CIL* II, nos. 2559 or 5639 respectively. From Rome: *CIL* VI v, nos. 13★ (idem XI 337★), 8703, 9693, 12652, 18324, also Burmann, *Anthologia latina* IV, no. 146.

[14] Cf. Grünberg-Dröge, "Sala," p. 29 and fig. 7.

[15] Cf. R. E. Asher, "Myth, Legend and History in Renaissance France," *Studi francesi* 13 (1969): 409–419, especially 413f. (rpt. in his *National Myths in Renaissance France: Francus, Samothes and the Druids* [Edinburgh, 1993]).

[16] See, however, the role played in this respect by Jean Lemaire de Belges's *Illustrations de Gaule et Singularitez de Troie*, first published 1509; cf. Franco Simone, "Une entreprise oubliée des humanistes français—De la prise de conscience historique du renouveau culturel à la naissance de la première histoire littéraire," *Humanism in France at the End of the Middle Ages and in the Early Renaissance*, ed. A. H. T. Levi (Manchester, 1970); idem, "Historiographie et mythographie dans la culture française du XVIe siècle: analyse d'un texte oublié," in *L'Humanisme lyonnais au XVIe siècle*, 125–148, and "La composition des *Illustrations de Gaule* de Jean Lemaire de Belges," ibid., 233–244.

[17] Cf. his *Petit traicté de la noblesse et ancienneté de la ville de Lyon* (Paris, n.d.), *L'origine et antiquité de la cité de Lion . . .* (translated into French by Guillaume Ramèze), and *L'Antiquité de la cité de Lyon ensemble la rebeine ou rebellion du populaire contre les conseillers de la cité en 1529 et la hiérarchie de l'église métropolitaine* (ed. Guigue, Lyons 1884).

[18] Son of a rich Lyonese family, born 1487, died 1557. He acted as city official in his hometown between 1523 and 1528 and was—in his capacity as collector of antiquities—responsible for the purchase of the Claudian tables by the Lyons municipality. His works (unpublished in his lifetime and only printed in bibliophile editions of the nineteenth and twentieth centuries) include the *Lugdunum priscum* and *Souvenirs de voyages en Italie et en Orient, notes historiques. . . .*

[19] Born 1500, died after 1555; he acted as king's counsellor. He composed a *Discours de la religion des anciens Romains* (Lyons, 1547; rpt. 1556, etc.), a *Discours sur la Castrametation et discipline militaire des Romains . . . Des Bains et antiques exercitations grecques et romaines . . . De la religion des anciens Romains* (Lyons, 1555; rpt. 1556, etc.; also translated into Latin, Italian, and Spanish), and an *Épître consolatoire envoyée à Mme de Cevrières* (on the great fire of Lyons; Lyons, 1555).

long-term resident of the city—did not hesitate to contribute his own research to the knowledge or embellishment of his host-town and its worthy traditions, in keeping with the antiquarian fashion of the natives: thus he translated into Italian several works of the Lyonese historian Guillaume du Choul,[20] who in the meantime had become his friend; he also published some works of his own in a similar vein, showing more passion than discretion for epigraphy and Latin sources,[21] and he even composed a treatise on the origin and antiquities of Lyons, still in manuscript at his death in Turin in 1575. Symeoni also engaged in the study of the more modern customs fashionable in the city (such as the then much admired devices or *imprese*[22]) and proposed to increase its charm with new, though classically oriented confections, such as his para-emblematic version of Ovid's *Metamorphoses* (composed of *ottava rima* units illustrating a pre-prepared comprehensive picture cycle[23]) self-avowedly intended to provide themes for the decoration of Diane de Poitiers' garden walls.[24] Many of Symeoni's works found great acclaim and even more so in eventual French translations, which his Lyonese publishers had no difficulty in providing.[25]

In the period between the first decennia and the middle of the sixteenth century, which witnessed the explosive phase of Lyons' (mainly French) writing and publishing, the city saw the birth and decline of two literary currents. One was the Neo-Latin school of poetry better known under the name of "sodalitium Lugdunense," centered around the thinker and publisher Étienne Dolet.[26] The other—with which

---

[20] Cf. *Discorso della religione antica de' Romani* (Lyons, 1558, etc.), *Discorso sopra la castrametatione e disciplina militare de' Romani; con i bagni ed esercizj antichi de' Greci e de' Romani* (Lyons, 1555, etc).

[21] *Illustrazioni di* (or: *Discorso degli) epitaffi e medaglie antiche* (Lyons, 1558, 1560), or the dual-language (Italian and French) *Présage du triomphe des Gaulois* (Lyons, 1555) on an antique ring found in the city.

[22] *Imprese eroiche e morali* (or: *Sentenziose imprese* [Lyons, 1559, etc.]). The French translation, entitled *Devises et emblèmes héroiques et morales* (frequently appended to Paolo Giovio's *Dialogo delle imprese militari e amorose*), appeared together with an independent Latin and another Spanish version, the same year as the Italian original (repeated in 1561, etc.).

[23] *La vita et metamorphoseo d'Ovidio, figurato & abbreviato in forma d'Epigrammi da M. Gabriele Symeoni* (Lyons, 1559). On this edition and those related to it, cf. Alison Saunders, "The Sixteenth-century French Emblem Book: Writers and Printers," *Studi francesi* 92 (1987): 173–190, esp. 181 n. 47.

[24] See the *Metamorfoseo* . . . , dedication, p. 5.

[25] I.e., the above-mentioned and much appreciated *Illustrazioni di epitaffi e medaglie antiche*; see also the *Dialogo pio e speculativo* (translated into French by Chappuis under the title of *Description de la Limagne d'Auvergne* [Lyons, 1561]). Symeoni occasionally also translated his own works, thus his *Commentarii sopra la tetrarchia* . . . (Venice, 1546)—part of which became *Epitome du duché de Ferrare* (Paris, 1553)—or his *Interprétation grecque, latine, toscane et française du Monstre, ou énigme d'Italie* (Lyons, 1555).

[26] Born in Orleans in 1509, died as martyr of his evangelical faith in Lyons in 1546. A renowned Lyons printer from 1538 onwards and originally famous as a Latinist, he increasingly devoted his efforts to the promotion of the French vernacular. On this figure, as well as on the "sodalitium Lugdunense," see among others V.-L. Saulnier, *Maurice Scève* (Paris, 1948–1949; rpt. Geneva, 1981), ch. VI: "L'heure de Dolet," or H. Weber, "La pensée d'Étienne Dolet et le combat humaniste," *L'Humanisme à Lyon*, 339–358.

the cultural Renaissance in Lyons is frequently directly associated—was the so-called Lyons school of poetry ("l'école lyonnaise"), a French vernacular Petrarchist and Neo-Platonist literary stream, the best known representative of which is Maurice Scève, who, in the wake of the newly arisen cult around Petrarch,[27] had "discovered" and identified the poet's muse Laura's grave at Avignon.[28] Both schools shared more than is generally assumed; many of the members of the one also participated in the other group, or at least knew each other and stood in more or less close literary or personal contact to one another. Thus the members and associates of the loosely knit "sodalitium" all met in the house of Guillaume Scève,[29] the brother of the leader of the French poetic school of Lyons and himself a friend of the above-mentioned Gabriele Symeoni's.[30] Maurice Scève himself participated in both schools: an antiquarian in love with inscriptions, even if of a more modern vein,[31] he contributed Neo-Latin poetry to the "sodalitium,"[32] showed himself particularly receptive of both Neo-Latin and vernacular Italian influences, and enriched French literary history with his emblematically structured, Petrarchan-influenced love canzoniere *Délie, objet de la plus haulte vertu*.[33] This work is systematically, though only partly illustrated[34]—a unique occurrence in both the author's as well as his publisher's careers[35]—and documents the high favour "picture poetry" (*picta poesis*)

---

[27] Cf. Franco Simone, "Note sulla fortuna del Petrarca in Francia nella prima metà del cinquecento," *Giornale storico della letteratura italiana* 127 (1950): 1–59, and 128 (1951): 1–40. Petrarch's stay in Avignon (on papal territory, though) and Laura's role as his muse were beginning to be increasingly valued as basically French contributions to this Italian poet's work.

[28] On this episode, see Saulnier, *Maurice Scève*, ch. II: "Les origines et le tombeau de Laure." On Scève's role in this affair (reported by the Lyonese editor De Tournes) see the Italian sonnet supposedly found in Laura's grave and given to Petrarch himself, yet currently attributed to our Lyonese poet; cf. Maurice Scève, *Œuvres complètes*, ed. Pascal Quignard (Paris, 1974), p. 374.

[29] On the long but little-documented tradition of such informal symposia in Lyons, see Eugène Vial, "La légende de l'Académie de Fourvière," *Bibliothèque d'Humanisme et Renaissance* 8 (1946): 253–266, or Grünberg-Dröge, "Sala," 13–17.

[30] Cf. Scève's sonnet "En grace du Seigneur G. Symeon, auteur et amy, Maurice Sceve sur le Monstre oblique et droit d'Italie," placed as introduction to Symeoni's *Interprétation . . . du Monstre, ou énigme d'Italie*. Scève must have become acquainted with Symeoni through his in-law Du Choul; cf. Saulnier, "Un opuscule inconnu de Gabriel Symeoni," *Bibliothèque d'Humanisme et Renaissance* 10 (1948): 179–184.

[31] Cf. Scève's contributions to the triumphal entry of Henri II to Lyons in 1548—in which were equally involved the emblem writer Barthélémy Aneau, the emblem illustrator Bernard Salomon and Pierre Sala's younger half-brother, the previously mentioned city-captain Jehan Sala—that were published in the *Magnificence de la superbe et triumphante entrée . . .* (Lyons, 1548; cf. his *Œuvres complètes*, ed. Quignard, 511–568).

[32] Cf. Scève, *Œuvres complètes*, ed. Quignard, 349–351, 361–362, and 415–416.

[33] Lyons, 1544, rpt. (with a new set of illustrations) 1564. Cf. the critical edition of Ian D. McFarlane (Cambridge, 1966) or the facsimile reprint, Continental Emblem Books, no. 22, with an introduction by Dudley Wilson (Menston, 1972).

[34] There are only 50 woodcuts to 449 "dizains" in the *Délie*, each nine "dizains" basically introduced by a picture. Cf. McFarlane, 16–22, or Dorothy Gabe Coleman, *An Illustrated Love "Canzoniere": The Délie of Maurice Scève* (Geneva, 1981).

[35] Neither Scève, not for that matter either Sulpice Sabon or Antoine Constantin (who in

enjoyed in Lyons towards the middle of the sixteenth century.

Whereas Sala (with his manuscript *Énigmes* [or: *emblèmes et devises d'amour* ...]) had been a vernacular precursor of the emblematic genre, and Scève (with his partly illustrated *Délie*) or Symeoni (with his *Imprese* ... and especially his *Metamorfoseo d'Ovidio figurato* ...) count among the authors of emblematic or para-emblematic productions, the man generally credited with the very invention of this most successful genre that the emblems proved to be in the sixteenth and following centuries was another Italian, the Milanese jurist Andrea Alciato (or, as some would have it, Alciati[36]), whose fortunes were at the time closely linked, if not to the city of Lyons itself,[37] at least to its close geographical and political surroundings. After having taught law at the University of Avignon on papal territory, Alciato was hired by the French king[38] to take the chair of jurisprudence in Bourges, the comparatively new university sponsored by the French court[39] and catering to the Lyonese intelligentsia. Alciato, whose juristic reputation lay with his profoundly learned humanistic interpretation and evaluation of Roman law, occupied this position between 1529 and 1533, the very period during which the first edition of the little book of illustrated epigrams (of basically humanistic inspiration and execution) on which his future fame was to be established first appeared in print.[40] After an intermediary, almost incidental set of publications in Augsburg (1531–1534, at the press of Heinrich Steyner) and in Paris (1534–1544, published by Chrestien Wechel with the blessing of the author), and with the exception of an isolated unique Venetian edition of *inedita* (1546, published by the sons of Aldus Manutius), it was in Lyons that the fortunes of Alciato's *Emblemata* and of the emblem genre as a whole really soared: of the some 125 sixteenth-century editions of Alciato's emblems, well around 50, that is, some 40 percent (the highest percentage pertaining to any single location), are Lyons-based.[41] It is in Lyons that the several above-mentioned strands of Alciato's

---

1543 and again in 1544 and 1545 published "à l'enseigne du rocher" works by Scève's friend Clément Marot) seem to have ever been involved in the publication of another emblem book.

[36] Born at Alzate? in 1492, died at Pavia in 1550. On this figure, see Henri Green, *Andrea Alciati and His Book of Emblems: A Biographical and Bibliographical Study* (London, 1872; rpt. New York, n.d.) and more recently Roberto Abbondanza, "Andrea Alciato [Alciati]," *Dizionario biografico degli italiani*, 2:69–77.

[37] He only seems to have traveled through the town on his way to and from Bourges; cf. Gian Luigi Barni, *Le lettere di Andrea Alciato giureconsulto* (Florence, 1953), 89 et passim.

[38] On the circumstances of this nomination—in which François cardinal of Touron (1489–1562, archbishop of Lyons after 1551), the king's counsellor and great connoisseur of Italian arts and letters, played a particularly important role—see my contribution "The *De singulari certamine liber* in the Context of Its Time," in Denis Drysdall, ed., *Alciato, the Man and His Time*, currently in press.

[39] Cf. Du Chasseint, "De l'université de Bourges," *Revue du Berry* (1866), and Raymond Raynal, *Histoire du Berry* (Bourges, 1846; rpt. Paris, 1972).

[40] In Augsburg, 1531, at the press of Heinrich Steyner. The date of composition of the individual epigrams contained therein has not been conclusively determined.

[41] The sixteenth-century Parisian editions of Alciato's emblems amount to about 30% of the total, the Antwerp ones to about 12%, Augsburg and Leiden each 5%, Frankfurt 4%, Basel 3%.

emblems, together with some new and hitherto unknown pieces, were put together and ordered into semantic groups in 1548/9[42] by an admirer and earlier Bourges student of Alciato's, Barthélémy Aneau,[43] who also eventually provided many of the emblems with fitting reference as to the rhetorical figures of speech they are assumed to exemplify, and with short commentaries called *epimythia*.[44]

Two Lyonese publishing houses in particular competed for the favour of the emblem-reading public: the De Tournes (father and son) and the partners Guillaume Rouille and Macé Bonhomme. Whereas the first chose to address themselves to the learned public via the more extensive Latin *Commentariola* of another Alciato scholar, the German Sebastian Stockhamer, first published in 1556,[45] the latter association preferred to appeal to the more general public with an extensive, in fact comprehensive illustrative cycle, and also attempted to capture the attention of even the non-Latin readers by means of vernacular translations. This was in itself no utterly new attempt: Chrestien Wechel, the acknowledged Parisian editor of Alciato's *Emblemata*, had already contributed a French translation by Jehan Lefevre in 1536 and a German one by Wolfgang Hunger in 1542. In Lyons, however, new translations came into being: a Spanish translation by Bernardino Daza was established in 1548,[46] a new French one provided in 1549 by Barthélémy Aneau himself, and the same year an Italian one by the somewhat elusive Giovanni Marquale also appeared.[47] No other Italian translation of Alciato's emblems was made in the course of the sixteenth century; only in the seventeenth century did several authors such as Giulio Cesare Capaccio,[48] Paolo Emilio Cadamosto,[49] or Aurelio Amalteo[50] provide more or less complete translations of the Alciatine epigrams, but none of these enjoyed the same success of distribution as Marquale's. The latter's all

---

[42] This reordering first occurred anonymously in 1548 (cf. Green, item 31, pp. 150f.) in 1549 (cf. Green, item 38, pp. 158ff.), a slightly altered order from Aneau's acknowledged contribution.

[43] Born in Bourges during the first years of the sixteenth century, he was killed by students in Lyons in 1561. He studied law in Bourges and taught rhetoric at the Collège de la Trinité in Lyons, whose principal he eventually became, besides acting as corrector for Macé Bonhomme's printing business. Himself a member of the "école Lyonnaise," he composed works of a satirical, pedagogical, or encomiastic vein. He also provided a French translation, the *Emblèmes d'Alciat* (Lyons, 1549).

[44] First published in 1549; cf. Green, item no. 39, pp. 162–163 et passim, and Denis Drysdall, "The Pleasant and the Profitable: Alciati's Emblems and Barthélémy Aneau," *New Zealand Journal of French Studies* 7 (1986): 5–22.

[45] Cf. Green, item 56, pp. 177f.

[46] This translation may have already existed in either 1540 or 1542; it was not actually published before 1549.

[47] Reedited and enlarged in 1551. Barely anything is known of the translator Marquale.

[48] *Il Principe . . . tratto da gli Emblemi dell'Alciato, con . . . avvertimento politici e morali . . .* (Venice, 1620); cf. Green, item no. 151, pp. 251–253.

[49] *Emblemi di Andrea Alciato . . . del Latino nel Vulgare Italiano ridotti . . .* (Padova, 1626); cf. Green, item 155, pp. 256–257.

[50] See the manuscript *Emblemi dell'Alciato* of around 1670–1680, conserved at Keir Library; cf. Green, item 166, pp. 266–269.

in all rather hasty and not very accurate nor for that matter very poetically qualitative translation, which in 1549 covered only 136 emblems, and went up to no more than 181 (of the 221 available) in 1551, was dedicated to the Doge Francesco Donato of Venice,[51] in other words, to an Italian of Italy, although the translation was made for a printer of Lyons in France, and a more appropriate dedication should have concerned a local dignitary. This was no unique case, however,[52] and probably documented Marquale's connections more than it did those of his editors Rouille or Bonhomme. What this information amounts to is that around the middle of the six-teenth century, with the author of the emblems still alive, Lyons was providing the nonscholarly Italian comfortable access to a fashionable genre of increasing favour by means of a translation meant as an object of re-importation to the very homeland of the author of the genre.[53] In other words, although the original contents of the emblems *and* the Latin language selected as their appropriate means of expression had been of the best Italian humanist stock, it was at least some of the Lyons editions, and in our particular case Marquale's translation into the mother tongue of the author, that conquered the book market of Alciato's very homeland, which had nothing of its own to offer in order to satisfy the public's demand for this genre. For a number of years Lyons thus practically controlled the emblem-book market and even contri-buted to the expansion of an originally Italian humanistic product back to its Italian cradle.[54] Thus the Lyonese printers showed themselves worthy of the trust put in them by their Italian models. Occasionally they even managed to surpass their mas-ters, surely to the latter's satisfaction: as indeed the publishing policy of our Alciato, especially with respect to his juridical treatises[55]—to him of much greater impor-tance than his *Emblemata*—no doubt demonstrates.

Emblematic and para-emblematic literature developed massively in the sixteenth century: Alciato's work was not only enlarged, translated and commented upon,[56]

---

[51] Seventy-ninth doge of Venice, born in 1473, died in 1558, doge between the 24th of November 1545 and the 23rd of May 1553. He also was the dedicatee of Symeoni's above-mentioned *Tetrarchia* . . . (Venice, 1548).

[52] Compare the dedication of Aneau's French translation of the Alciatine emblems of 1549 to the Scots nobleman James Hamilton, Earl of Arran; on this figure cf. Green, pp. 159–160.

[53] For the educated Italians however, Latin was—more than any Italian dialect—the very language of learning and of literature (cf. Green, p. 165).

[54] Indeed Lyonese publishers frequently produced for export: compare their publishing policy of Spanish books—including emblem books—intended for the Iberian Peninsula and the New World book market.

[55] The publishing houses of Jacopo Giunta and of Sebastian Gryphius of Lyons were par-ticularly favoured by the jurist Alciato, although works of his were also printed there by Vincenzo de Portonariis, Guillaume Rouille, Jean Bérion, the brothers Frellon, Antoine Vincent, and Théobalde Payen. Although Alciato also dealt with various Basel publishers, most of whom he had been introduced to by Bonifatius Amerbach, and also authorised publications made by Chrestien Wechel of Paris, or by his Milanese compatriot Minuzio, he never employed the Bourges university press.

[56] Sixteenth-century commentaries were provided by the above-mentioned Barthélémy Aneau in 1549 (apparently reused by Feyerabend in 1567) and Sebastian Stockhamer in 1556; also by

it was also emulated by—first and foremost—a number of French and especially Lyonese authors or such who had printing and other connections to Lyons, as were: Barthélémy Aneau,[57] Pierre Cousteau,[58] Maurice Scève, Guillaume Guéroult,[59] the Toulousain Guillaume de La Perrière[60] and—later in the century—the first female author of the first religious emblem cycle ever, Georgette de Montenay.[61] These authors elaborated in either Latin or French upon the Alciatine model, which

---

Claude Mignault (Minos) in 1571 and by Francisco Sanchez (Sanctius) in 1573. Sixteenth-century translations of Alciato's emblems other than the ones previously mentioned are Jeremias Held's (into German, 1567), Mignault's (into French, 1583), and Geoffrey Whitney's (into English, 1586).

[57] Besides his already-mentioned work on Alciato's emblems, Aneau also composed an Ovid-inspired book of emblems called *Picta poesis. Ut pictura poesis erit* (Lyons, 1552; translated by himself into French the same year under the title of *L'Imagination poétique*), a para-emblematic work, the *Décades de la description . . . des animaux . . .* (Lyons, 1549), and a translation of the third *Livre* [. . .] *de la Métamorphose d'Ovide*, introduced by the emblem-theoretical *Préparation de voie à la lecture et intelligence de la Métamorphose d'Ovide et de tous poëtes fabuleux* (Lyons, 1556).

[58] Barely anything is known of the life of this jurist, whose other works are *Adversariorum ex pandectis . . . liber prior* (Lyons, 1554) and his *De pace carmen* (Lyons, 1559). His emblem book, *Pegma cum narrationibus philosophicis* (Lyons, 1555), was translated into French by Lanteaume de Romieu under the title *Le Pegme avec les narrations philosophiques* (published in 1555 without the philosophical commentaries and again in 1560 containing those).

[59] Born in Rouen in 1507, died in Lyon in 1564. A Protestant author of libertine tendencies, the in-law of Lyons publishers, he also composed a number of French translations of the Psalms. To his more directly emblematic productions belong *Le premier livre des emblèmes* (Lyons, 1550; reedited by De Vaux de Lancey, Rouen, 1937), and the *Second livre de la description des animaux, contenant le blason des oiseaux* (Lyons, 1550). On this figure, see Daniela Boccassini, *La parola riscritta. Guillaume Guéroult, poeta e traduttore nella Francia della Riforma* (Firenze, 1985).

[60] Born in Toulouse in 1499, died there in 1553. He was a juridically schooled priest of Neo-Platonic inclinations, also active as local historian and college director. His more directly emblematic works are the *Théâtre des bons engins* (Paris, 1539/40; facsimile rpt. Gainesville, Florida, 1964, and London, 1973), the French and Latin *Morosophie . . . contenant cent emblèmes moraux* (published posthumously in Lyons, 1553) and the unillustrated *Cent considérations d'amour* (Lyons, 1543; rpt. 1548), and *Considérations des quatre mondes* (Lyons and Toulouse, 1552). On this figure, cf. Greta Dexter, "Guillaume de La Perrière," *Bibliothèque d'Humanisme et Renaissance* 16 (1955): 56–73, eadem, "La 'Morosophie' de La Perrière," *Les Lettres Romanes* 30 (1976): 64–75, and Irene Schwendemann, *Probleme humanistischer Moralistik in den emblematischen Werken des Guillaume de La Perrière* (Munich, 1966).

[61] For her biography, see Elisabeth Labrousse, "Georgette de Montenay et ses Emblèmes chrestiens (1571)," *Bulletin de la Société d'Histoire du Protestantisme Français* 134 (1988): 730–734. She was probably born in Normandy around 1540 and apparently died in 1607. Her only known work is the evangelically inspired *Emblèmes ou devises chrestiens* (Lyons, 1571; rpt. 1584 etc., and edited in facsimile London, 1973, and Paris, 1989), which only counts as the first religious emblem cycle if we disregard such para-emblematic productions as La Perrière's unillustrated *Considérations des quatre mondes*. On this figure, cf. Paulette Choné, *Emblèmes et pensée symbolique en Lorraine (1525–1633)* (Paris, 1991), book III, ch. I, 2, pp. 568–626, and Régine Reynolds-Cornell, *Witnessing an Era: Georgette de Montenay and the "Emblèmes ou devises chrestiennes"* (Birmingham, Ala., 1987).

they, however, mingled with indigenous sources of no less interest. Their contributions reiterated the humanist model taught by the master: reference to law, to classical pagan mythology, to scholarly commentaries, to rhetorics, quotations from antique sources and schoolbook texts, as well as numerous back-references to, or elaborations on, the original emblems of Alciato himself. In other words, the first generation of French emblematists—in fact, of emblematists as a whole—was mainly composed of Lyonese of origin or by choice,[62] reacting, out of some inner preparation, to the original model proposed by an Italian at some time in economic exile, that is, on the payroll of the French university of Bourges. Yet by elaborating on the model, they widened it to extents possibly way beyond the scope of the original product: thus Aneau, for example, both in his edition of Alciato's *Emblemata* and in his own *Picta Poesis*, so largely inspired as it was by Ovid's *Metamorphoses*, employed his master's invention for practising rhetoric with his students of the Collège de la Trinité of Lyons, just as many teachers subsequently used these very emblems as a means of teaching their young pupils not only morals but also Latin. The jurist Cousteau, on the other hand, used his emblems (published under the title of *Pegma*) to discuss another of the master's objectives, namely law. The emblems of Guillaume de La Perrière, thought to be the first imitation of Alciato in France, reunite—both in his early *Théâtre des bons engins* and in his posthumously published *Morosophie*—the teachings of the master with autochthonic models of a nonhumanistic type.[63] Maurice Scève, of whom we already spoke in connection with the "sodalitium Lugdunense" and with the Neo-Platonizing, Petrarchizing "Lyons school of poetry," accordingly transformed the loosely structured emblematic genre as used by Alciato into a thematically stringent structural component of his Petrarcan love *canzoniere*. Finally Guéroult's first—and only—emblem book, *Le premier livre d'emblèmes*, rejoins the *editio princeps* of Alciato's *Emblematum liber* in its loosely configured, unsystematic mixture of multiple genres. Of the Lyons-oriented French emblematists, only Georgette de Montenay—who, however, published much too late in the century as to be counted among the first generation of Alciato's followers—broke with the Italian's model (not without however acknowledging her debt to him[64]) in order to produce a nonepigrammatic, nonhumanistic, definitely non–Catholic and certainly non-Latin book of "Emblèmes chrétiens."[65] All and each of these developments and transformations document the strong independent creative hold the Lyonese had on the imported idea of the emblematic genre.

Köln

---

[62] Exceptions to this rule are, for example, the Parisian Gilles Corrozet, Jean Mercier of Bourges, Jean Jacques Boissard of Metz, or the theologian Théodore de Bèze, active in Geneva.

[63] Thus the sayings, proverbs, *sententiae*, paraphrases of classical and medieval sources, fables, anecdotes, references to current events, religious tales etc., used there; cf. Alison Saunders, *The Sixteenth Century French Emblem Book: A Useful and Decorative Genre* (Geneva/Paris, 1988).

[64] Cf. in the dedication of her *Emblémes . . .* to Jeanne d'Albret, ll. 113–115.

[65] This affirmation, however, need be somewhat mitigated in view of the evidence of the frequently Latin lemmas; also the huitain serving as subscription in fact represents but one of the French versions of the classical epigram.

Sannazaro nella letteratura olandese

ANTONIUS J. E. HARMSEN

C hi cercasse il nome del Sannazaro nei cataloghi delle grandi biblioteche troverebbe, fra le altre, un'edizione olandese del 1730. Anche prima di questa data alcuni poeti olandesi hanno mostrato un certo interesse per Jacopo Sannazaro o Actius Syncerus Sannazarius (1458–1530), il poeta napoletano che ha arricchito la letteratura bucolica con la variante dell'ecloga piscatoria. Accanto alle *Eclogae piscatoriae*, che sono del resto imitazioni fedeli di Virgilio, Sannazaro scrisse il poema epico *De partu Virginis*, due libri di elegie, tre libri di epigrammi, rime volgari e l'*Arcadia*, un romanzo pastorale nel quale si alternano parti in prosa e versi.[1]

La commistione di cristianesimo e cultura antica nel *De partu Virginis* avrà forse attratto gli umanisti olandesi, ma nei loro circoli prevalentemente protestanti assai poco è stato prodotto ad imitazione di quel lavoro.[2] Anzi, gli scarsi accenni al poema contengono un giudizio negativo, perché la mitologia pagana e il culto cristiano vi si mescolano in modo intollerabile.[3] Gli epigrammi e le elegie si prestavano meglio all'imitazione, ma ancora di più le *Eclogae piscatoriae*, che senza difficoltà potevano essere trasposte nell'Olanda ricca di acque. Anche la letteratura arcadica è un terreno attraente per i poeti olandesi. Le peculiarità che rendevano la vita e l'opera del Sannazaro interessanti sono le vive descrizioni della zona intorno a Napoli, la perfetta imitazione della letteratura classica ed il fatto che egli giaccia sepolto in prossimità della tomba di Virgilio, in Santa Maria del Parto, una chiesa da lui stesso costruita. Una caratteristica che si nota inoltre nella sua opera e ben si presta all'imitazione è

---

[1] Un ringraziamento a Dick van der Mark e Silvia Naldini. Su Sannazaro si veda W. J. Kennedy, *Jacopo Sannazaro and the Uses of Pastoral* (Hannover, 1983); C. Kidwell, *Sannazaro and Arcadia* (London, 1993).

[2] In Germania la produzione è invece notevole: cf. Walther Ludwig, "Vom Jordan zur Donau. Die Rezeption Sannazaros durch Joachim Münsinger von Frundeck," *Humanistica Lovaniensia* 62 (1993): 252–258. Sull'influsso del *De partu Virginis* su Münsinger von Frundeck (ca. 1540).

[3] W. A. P. Smit, *Kalliope in de Nederlanden. Het renaissancisisch-klassicistische epos van 1550 tot 1850* (Assen, 1975) 1: 143 e 187.

l'intreccio degli eventi naturali con i sentimenti dei suoi personaggi.

Divulgazione dell'opera del Sannazaro nei Paesi Bassi

Nell'ambito di un ristretto circolo di intellettuali il nome del Sannazaro è sempre stato noto in Olanda. Questo, Sannazaro lo deve, se non altro, al fatto di essere menzionato nel *Ciceronianus* di Erasmo; in verità, in quella sede, gli viene inferto un duro colpo ("A che vale l'invocazione alle Muse e a Febo nel *De partu Virginis?*"),[4] ma Erasmo cita anche le *Eclogae piscatoriae* come esempio di imitazione creativa. Assai presto Giano Secondo (1511–1536) imitava Sannazaro, per esempio nei suoi *Basia*.[5]

Che Sannazaro godesse in Olanda di una certa notorietà si può dedurre dal notevole numero di esemplari delle sue opere che si trovavano nelle biblioteche olandesi del seicento e del settecento. Benchè più numerose siano le tracce di libri di Petrarca, Ariosto, Boccaccio, Castiglione e Aretino, la diffusione del Sannazaro si può ben paragonare a quella di altri autori italiani, come Tasso, Dante e Marino. Si tratta sia delle opere latine che di quelle italiane, in edizioni stampate in Italia, Francia e Paesi Bassi. Nei cataloghi dei grandi librai in Olanda e in almeno 48 cataloghi di aste di biblioteche di privati si trovano uno o più esemplari di opere del Sannazaro.[6] Molti tra coloro che ne possedevano copie, si sono anche attivamente occupati del poeta napoletano. Uno di loro, Petrus Francius, possedeva anche un ritratto dipinto del poeta.

Poesia neolatina fino al 1650

Sannazaro ha esercitato un'influenza varia sulla poesia neolatina in Olanda. Ci sono poeti che lo menzionano soltanto, poeti che ne imitano i testi e poeti che lo seguono sul sentiero del rinnovamento dell'egloga virgiliana. Una poesia in morte del Sanna-

---

[4] Erasmo, *Ciceronianus*, in *Opera omnia* 1, 2 (Amsterdam, 1971), 700. *LB* 1, 1020.

[5] Nei commenti alla poesia di Janus Secundus la connessione tra i suoi *Basia* e gli epigrammi amorosi fu proposta alla fine del Settecento. Letteratura recente su questo argomento: J. P. Guépin, *De kunst van Janus Secundus* (Amsterdam, 1991).

[6] Un ringraziamento a E. Hofland, Leiden. Si tratta dei cataloghi di aste del periodo 1610–1780, di Bonaventura Vulcanius (1610), Adrianus Pauw (1654), Daniel Heinsius (1656), Gerardus Joannes Vossius (1656), Johannes van Vliet (1666), Jacobus Golius (1668), Henricus van der Hem (1674), Johannes Thysius (1677), Willem Momma (1680), Jacobus Lydius (1680), Nicolaus Heinsius (1682), Theodorus Hillensbergh (1683), Jacob Oisel (1687), Nicolaus Heinsius (1683), Gulielmus Goesius (1687), Lucas Schacht (1689), Arnoldus Biscop (1698), Cornelis Nicolai (1698), Bartholomeus Cromhout (1703), Joan Six (1706), Petrus Francius (1705), Marcus Meiboom (1705), Janus Broukhusius (1708), Gustav Carlson (1711), Thomas Nicolaas van der Mark (1712), Gysbertus Eding (1721), Johannes Theodorus Schalbruch (1723), Cornelis van Arkel (1725), David van Hoogstraten (1725), Henricus Hadrianus van der Mark (1727), Everhardus Rouse (1728), Alexander Cunningham (1730), Pieter Vlaming (1734), Hermannus van der Wall (1734), Gosuinus Uilenbroek (1741), Willem van der Muelen (1741), Gisbertus opten Noorth (1742), Raymond Bakker (1760), Hendrick de Witte Thierens (1763), Abraham de Brauw (1763), Jacobus der Kinderen (1764), Pieter van Damme (1764), Jacques Philippe d'Orville (1764), Jacobus Callebout (1765), Pietro Antonio Locatelli (1765), Pietro Antonio Bolongaro Crevenna (1776), Rijklof Michaël van Goens (1776) e Petrus Burmannus Secundus (1779). Cf. inoltre i cataloghi dei librai Laurensz, de Janssoons van Waesberge, Elzevier, J. Janssonius, Blaeu e Pierre Gosse.

zaro fu scritta da Nicolaus Grudius (1504–1570), che celebra la familiarità del Sannazaro con Apollo e le Muse, e segnala il fatto che egli ha trovato la sua ultima dimora nei pressi del sepolcro di Virgilio.[7] Il poeta fiammingo Jacobus Sluperius (De Sluyper) (1532–1582) è il primo a cimentarsi, sull'esempio del Sannazaro, nel genere dell'ecloga. Ne scrive un gran numero, tra cui due ecloghe venatorie, "Tityrus" e "Callirhoe," e una nautica "Damastor."[8] Questo tipo di esercizi viene proseguito da Ugo Grozio, autore dell'ecloga "Myrtilus, sive idyllium nauticum, ad Danielem Heinsium" (1602).[9] Janus Dousa Pater (1545–1604) conosceva a memoria varie poesie del Sannazaro e rielaborò alcuni dei suoi epigrammi.[10] Due ecloghe piscatorie figurano nell'opera di Petrus Stratenus: *Venus Zeelanda et alia ejus poëmata* (1641).[11] Frequenti sono le allusioni al Sannazaro nella poesia neolatina di Nicolaus Heinsius (1620–1681). Un esempio si trova nella sua elegia *Pausilypus*, dove la natura gli fa avvertire la presenza del poeta delle ecloghe.[12]

Gerardus Joannes Vossius riprende quasi letteralmente nelle sue *Institutiones poeticae* (1647) il giudizio negativo di Erasmo sul *De partu Virginis*.[13]

Poesia in lingua olandese fino al 1700

Il primo accenno a Sannazaro nella letteratura olandese si trova nella lettera in rima manoscritta di Jan van Hout del 1578.[14] Questi menziona Sannazaro come uno dei poeti italiani degni di imitazione, assieme a Boccaccio, Dante, Bembo, Aretino ed Ariosto. Uno dei più antichi documenti importanti che dimostrano la conoscenza della produzione letteraria italiana nell'ambito della letteratura olandese è la "Rijmbrief uit Florence" (*Lettera in versi da Firenze*), scritta nel 1600 da P. C. Hooft. Questi fa notare che Napoli, per la precisione Pozzuoli, può vantare di albergare sia il sepolcro di Virgilio che quello del Sannazaro.[15] Karel van Mander cita nel suo *Schilderboek* (1604) un ampio brano dall'*Arcadia* sui dipinti del tempio di Pales e ricorda il

---

[7] *Actio Syncero Sannazario nobili Neapolitano, poëtae primario,* in Nicolaus Grudius, Hadrianus Marius e Joannes Secundus, *Poemata* (Leiden: Ludovicus Elzevirius, 1612), 143.

[8] Apparve nei *Poemata* stampati ad Anversa nel 1575 da Joannes Bellerus.

[9] In Daniel Heinsius, *Emendationes et notae in Theocriti Idyllia bucolica* (Leiden: Commelianus, 1603). Edizione moderna: *The Poetry of Hugo Grotius. Original Poetry 1602–1603,* ed. A. Eyffinger (Assen, 1988), 303–317.

[10] Ianus Douza a Noortwyck, *Epigrammatum libri II,* ed. Chr. L. Heesakkers (Leiden, 1976), 24; Chr. L. Heesakkers, *Praecidanea Dousana* (Amsterdam, 1976), 113 e 133–134.

[11] Petrus Stratenus, *Venus Zeelanda et alia ejus poëmata,* ed. C. Boyus (l'Aja: Theodorus Maire, 1641), 169 e 184.

[12] Pubblicato in Actius Syncerus Sannazarius, *Opera Latina,* ed. J. Broukhusius (Amsterdam: Henricus Wetstenius, 1689), fols. 11r–12r.

[13] G. J. Vossius, *Poeticarum institutionum libri tres* (Amsterdam: L. Elzevirius, 1647), § 3.4.12, p. 15.

[14] Archivio comunale di Leida. Il testo è datato da T. Schoonheim, "Jan van Houts Tot Cuenraet de Rechtere," *Tijdschrift voor Nederlandse taal- en letterkunde* 106 (1990): 281–286.

[15] P. C. Hooft, "Aen de camer In Liefd' Bloeyende," in *Lyrische poëzie,* ed. P. Tuynman e G. P. van der Stroom (Amsterdam, 1994), 1: 30, v. 165; cf. 37, v. 147. Nelle edizioni a stampa del diciassettesimo secolo Sannazaro non appare, ma il suo nome è presente nelle versioni manoscritte.

passo dell'*Arcadia*, in cui Sannazaro descrive un vaso dipinto dal Mantegna, sul quale è rappresentata una ninfa che allatta un piccolo satiro.[16]

Compaiono anche ecloghe piscatorie nella poesia in lingua olandese. Una influenza diretta del Sannazaro su di esse non è esclusa, ma difficile da dimostrare. Roemer Visscher (1547–1620) scrisse "Een visschers praetjen" (*Una conversazione piscatoria*), forse per rendere omaggio al proprio nome (Visscher vuol dire "pescatore"), ma in ogni modo questa poesia rientra nel genere.[17] Nella raccolta di poesie *De Zeeuwsche nachtegael* (1623) si trova un dialogo d'amore di Jacob Hobius tra un pescatore ed una fanciulla.[18]

Il genere della poesia pastorale viene promosso dall'apparire della traduzione in prosa del Vondel delle *Ecloghe* di Virgilio nel 1646.[19] Nel 1648 vengono pubblicati i carmi latini del Sannazaro da Schulperoort ad Amsterdam in un'edizione modesta e piena di errori.[20] Poco dopo appaiono alcune traduzioni olandesi e rielaborazioni degli epigrammi e della seconda ecloga. Uno dei più noti epigrammi del Sannazaro è "De mirabili urbe Venetiis."[21] In occasione della pace di Münster questo epigramma viene adattato ad Amsterdam da Jan Six (1648): mentre Sannazaro chiama Roma opera degli uomini, ma Venezia opera degli dei, il Six chiama Venezia e Roma opera degli uomini, in contrapposizione alla divina Amsterdam.[22] Oltre a questa rielaborazione esistono di quell'epigramma ben tre traduzioni in olandese, quella del Goddaeus del 1656, quella del Van den Bos del 1661 e quella del Vlaming del 1730.[23] La seconda ecloga piscatoria del Sannazaro, "Galatea," viene integralmente tradotta da Jeremias de Decker (1654).[24] Questi presenta una tipica traduzione letterale, fedele all'originale che prova ad uguagliare in bellezza attraverso l'uso di figure retoriche, secondo il gusto barocco del tempo. Egli traduce inoltre l'epigramma "Ad Vesbiam," nel quale il poeta allo stesso tempo piange come il Nilo e brucia come l'Etna. L'epigramma 2.130 di De Decker, dal titolo in lingua italiana

---

[16] In K. van Mander, *Den grondt der edel vry schilder-const*, ed. H. Miedema (Utrecht, 1973), 1: 143–147, 164–165; 2: 483–484, 497–498. Cf. *Arcadia*, Prosa XI; O. Kurz, "Sannazaro and Mantegna," in *Studi in onore di Riccardo Filangieri* (Napoli, 1959), 2: 277–283.

[17] Roemer Visscher, *Brabbeling. By hem selven oversien, en meer als de helft vermeerdert* (Amsterdam: Willem Jansz., 1614), 170–173.

[18] J. Hobius, "Visscher-praetie. Tsamensprekers Steven ende Martijntje Visschers-kinderen," in *Zeeusche nachtegael* (Middelburg: J. P. vande Venne, 1623), fols. D3r–D4v.

[19] Amsterdam: Weduwe A. de Wees, 1646; versione in prosa Amsterdam: Weduwe A. de Wees, 1660.

[20] A. S. Sannazarius, *Opera omnia* (Amsterdam: Joannes Schulperoort, 1648).

[21] A. S. Sannazarius, *Epigrammata* 1.26.

[22] *Olyf-krans der vreede* (Amsterdam: Tymen Houthaak voor Gerrit van Goedesberg), 326. Cf. Jan Six, *Gedichten*, ed. A. E. Jacobs (Assen, 1991), 1: 456; 2: 485. Anche nel suo "Schetse van Venecie, opgedraagen aan Jan van Aalst, Jan Druivestein, Pieter Sluijer, Jan van Uffelen, en Abraham Heirmans, kooplieden aldaar" Jan Six nomina Sannazaro.

[23] Conradus Goddaeus, *Nieuwe gedichten* (Harderwijk: Iohan Tol, 1656). Prefazione, 24. Per Lambert van den Bos e Pieter Vlaming si veda qui sotto.

[24] "Galatea, of visschers-klachte. Vyt het Latijn van Zannazarius," in Jeremias de Decker, *Gedichten* (Amsterdam: Jacob Colom, 1656), 157–160.

"Nilo negli occhi, Aetna nel cuore," tratta lo stesso tema. Un ulteriore riferimento al poeta italiano è presente nelle note al "Lof der geldsucht" (*Lode dell'avarizia*), in cui viene citato l'epigramma 3.8, "In Leonem X. Pont. Max."—uno degli epigrammi antipapali.

Un tesoro di dati sulla cultura italiana si trova nella guida di Lambert van de Bos: *Wegh-wyser door Italien* (*Guida d'Italia*) (1661). Egli cita nella descrizione di Venezia l'epigramma sulla città in latino, propone a fianco la sua traduzione in olandese, e menziona, nella descrizione di Napoli, il sepolcro di Virgilio e la casa del Sannazaro.[25]

Il pastore protestante dell'Aja, Joannes Vollenhove, la cui raccolta di poesie viene pubblicata nel 1686, ha tradotto gli epigrammi del Sannazaro su Annibale, Didone e Catone.[26]

L'Edizione di Broukhusius

L'edizione del Sannazaro di Schulperoort (Amsterdam 1648) era priva di annotazioni, ma nel 1689 apparve ad Amsterdam un'edizione con commento di mano di Joan van Broekhuizen o Janus Broukhusius (1649–1707).[27] Questi vi inserì la prefazione di Paulus Manutius, la vita del Sannazaro di Paolo Giovio e l'elegia *Pausilypus* di Nicolaus Heinsius. Incluse anche gli epigrammi antipapali che erano stati censurati nelle edizioni precedenti. Nel suo commento indicò luoghi paralleli dei poeti antichi e inserì particolari poco noti, tratti dalla storia e dalla vita del Sannazaro. Talvolta fece anche dei commenti ironici sulla poesia amorosa, come nell'*Elegia* 1, 10 che mise in relazione con *Arcadia* 7: "Familiare est poëtis, etiam iis qui nunquam amaverunt, amorem aliquem sibi fingere, unde scriptionis petant argumentum."[28]

Di questa edizione il Van Broekhuizen conservò un esemplare fornito di pagine bianche nel quale continuò ad apporre annotazioni pensando ad una nuova edizione. Questo esemplare fu acquistato dopo la sua morte da David van Hoogstraten, che aveva l'intenzione di pubblicare nuovamente il lavoro; dopo la morte di Van Hoogstraten l'esemplare fu comprato ad un'asta da Pieter Vlaming ed infine passò alla Biblioteca Universitaria di Leida.[29] Il Vlaming completò le annotazioni, e così ebbe origine la seconda stampa dell'edizione del Van Broekhuizen, pubblicata nel 1728 molto arricchita e senz'altro più bella. Anche l'esemplare con note manoscritte dell'edizione del 1689 di Petrus Burmannus Secundus (1713–1778) si trova nella Biblioteca Universitaria di Leida.[30] Il Burmannus preparava una quarta edizione olandese che non è mai stata pubblicata.

---

[25] Lambert van den Bosch, *Wegh-wyser door Italien* (Dordrecht: Abraham Andriesz, 1661).

[26] Joannes Vollenhove, *Poëzy* (Amsterdam: Hendrik Boom e Wed. Dirk Boom, 1686) 618 = Ep. 1. 54; 640 = Ep. 1.28; 649 = Ep. 2.52.

[27] J. A. Worp, "Joan van Broekhuizen." *Tijdschrift voor Nederlandsche taal- en letterkunde* 10 (1891): 40–113; A. S. Sannazarius, *Opera* (Amsterdam: Henricus Wetstenius, 1689); A. S. Sannazarius, *Opera* (Amsterdam: Vidua G. onder de Linden, 1728).

[28] Ed. 1689, 182.

[29] Biblioteca Universitaria Leiden, 765 C 15.

[30] Biblioteca Universitaria Leiden, 765 F 18.

Il commento vergato dal Van Broekhuizen e dal Vlaming contiene molte note a nomi propri e nomi geografici, per le quali vengono utilizzate le numerose monografie e enciclopedie sull'Italia che si trovavano allora nelle biblioteche olandesi, come, ad esempio, la *Vita di Cesare Borgia* di Tomaso Tomasi; il *Liber de immanitate* di Giovanni Pontano; le *Neapolitanae historiae* di Giulio Cesare Capaccio; la *Biblioteca Napoletana* di Nicolò Toppi; e la *Bibliotheca Sicula sive de scriptoribus Siculis* di Antonino Mongitore.

Il commento del Burmannus, che dunque è rimasto inedito, è di natura diversa. Questi non si interessa tanto ai particolari biografici, quanto alle tecniche letterarie, all'imitazione dei luoghi classici, e alla determinazione del testo corretto del Sannazaro. Registra soprattutto passi paralleli di Properzio e Catullo. Il Burmannus indica per primo i versi ripresi da Giano Secondo,[31] migliora il testo della ecloga *Pausilypus* dello Heinsius, e aggiunge: "Has immutationes descripsi ex exemplari poematum N. Heinsii, qui sua manu haec eo, quo adposui, modo, emendaverat. Exemplar autem illud possidet cognatus meus Carolus Crucius, et mecum id communicavit."

La raccolta di poesie latine del Van Broekhuizen fu pubblicata nel 1711 da Franciscus Halma ad Amsterdam.[32] Si trovano in essa otto ecloghe, la quarta delle quali è un dialogo tra navigatori. La raccolta è preceduta da un'elegia di David van Hoogstraten, "In obitum Jani Broukhusii," dove questi viene lodato per il suo lavoro sul Sannazaro.

Nella sua edizione di Properzio[33] Van Broekhuizen cita varie volte il Sannazaro, per spiegare il testo di Properzio o per segnalare parallelismi interessanti. Anche Giano Secondo viene citato con lo stesso fine; molto più spesso, tuttavia, vengono citati gli autori latini a cui si fa riferimento (Virgilio, Tibullo, Orazio ed Ovidio).

Poesia neolatina dopo il 1650

Petrus Francius (1645–1704) fu a partire dal 1674 professore di storia e di retorica all'università di Amsterdam. Era un oratore egregio e scriveva versi sciolti in latino e in olandese. Nella sua poesia appaiono spesso accenni al Sannazaro, come si nota anche nella lunga elegia del 1675, *Vitae privatae commoda*.[34] In essa il Francius racconta come egli venga condotto in un viaggio di piacere attraverso l'Italia, e in diversi luoghi goda dei ricordi dell'antichità, tra gli altri a Posillipo, dove pensa a Virgilio e a Sannazaro. Con piacere vorrebbe riposare sotto gli alberi che anche a Sannazaro offrirono la loro ombra; lo stesso motivo appare in Nicolaus Heinsius nella sua ecloga "Pausilypus." Il Francius scrisse sei ecloghe, e in esse troviamo una delle scarse tracce del *De partu Virginis* in una canzone pastorale dove Tityro e Licidas

---

[31] Commento all'epigramma 1.61, "Ad amicam," p. 130, con riferimento all'*Epistola* 2.1 "Ad Aegidium Buslidium" di Janus Secundus.

[32] Janus Broukhusius, *Poematum libri sedecim*, ed. David Hoogstratanus (Amsterdam: Franciscus Halma, 1711).

[33] Propertius, *Carmina*, ed. J. Broukhusius (Amsterdam: Wetstenii, 1702).

[34] *Vitae privatae commoda ad v.d. Henricum Solingium Trajectinum, medicum ac philosophum insignem* (Amsterdam: Daniel Elzevier, 1675).

cantano la nascita di Cristo. Il poeta si cimenta anche in un'ecloga piscatoria: un lamento d'amore del pescatore Dameta.

Da giovane il Francius si recò in Inghilterra, Francia ed Italia, e a Napoli colse, presso il sepolcro di Virgilio, delle foglie d'alloro, che in seguito distribuì ai suoi amici letterati. Come ringraziamento Pieter Verhoek (1633–1702) scrisse il poema in lingua olandese: "Papier voor laurier. Aen den Heere Petrus Francius, toen hy my eenige Laurierbladen, by hem over 't graf van Virgiel geplukt, vereerde." ("Carta per lauro. Al Signor Petrus Francius, che mi fece omaggio di alcune foglie d'alloro, da lui raccolte sul sepolcro di Virgilio").[35] L'edizione è illustrata da una stampa del "Sepolcro di Virgilio" e della "Grotta di Posillipo." Il poeta esprime rammarico per non aver potuto visitare personalmente il sepolcro di Virgilio; se ciò fosse avvenuto avrebbe potuto soffermarsi anche presso quello del Sannazaro.

Dedicata al Francius è la raccolta di poesie *Galatea* di Hadrianus Relandus (1676–1718).[36] Non vi sono vere e proprie ecloghe piscatorie, ma in particolare nell'*Elegia* 11 è presente il tema dell'amante che si lamenta sulla riva per la sua Galatea assente. Nel 1809 comparve una ristampa di questa raccolta completa di note esplicative a cura del nipote di Burmanno, Petrus Bosscha (1789–1871), in cui vengono indicati una decina di passi paralleli nell'opera del Sannazaro. Anche le imitazioni del Sannazaro nelle poesie latine di Janus Secundus sono indicate da Petrus Bosscha, che probabilmente utilizzò per questo le note marginali non pubblicate di suo zio.[37]

Gerardus Nicolaus Heerkens (1726–1801) di Groningen trascorse alcuni anni in Italia; descrisse la sua esperienza in una lunga poesia didattica, *Italicorum libri tres*. In una poesia liminare di J. H. Hoefft Sannazaro viene menzionato insieme a Petrarca, Dante, Ariosto e Tasso tra i più celebri poeti italiani.[38]

La traduzione dell'Arcadia del 1730

L'influsso dell'opera volgare del Sannazaro sulla produzione letteraria olandese è difficilmente dimostrabile. Gli elementi della poesia del Sannazaro sono assorbiti nella grande corrente del cosiddetto petrarchismo. Solo il lirico cattolico Joannes Stalpart van der Wiele (1579–1630) rielabora la lirica in italiano del Sannazaro, quantunque non utilizzi un'edizione delle *Rime* bensì la raccolta di madrigali di Luca Marenzio (1553–1599).[39] Una traduzione dell'*Arcadia* fu pubblicata solo nel Settecento: mentre in Francia erano apparse traduzioni già nel 1544 e in Spagna nel 1547, in Olanda bisogna attendere il 1730. Pieter Vlaming tradusse l'*Arcadia*[40] e aggiunse una

---

[35] In Pieter Verhoek, *Poëzy. Nevens zyn treurspel van Karel den Stouten, Hertogh van Bourgondie* (Amsterdam: Willem Barents, 1726), 141–145.

[36] Hadrianus Relandus, *Galatea. Lusus poeticus* (Franeker: M. vander Veen, 1735).

[37] Johannes Secundus, *Opera omnia. Emendatius et cum notis adhuc ineditis P. Burmanni Secundi*, ed. P. Bosscha (Leiden, 1821).

[38] G. N. Heerkens, *Italicorum libri tres* (Groningen: Vidua Henrici Vecheri, 1793), XIII.

[39] Joannes Stalpart van der Wiele, *Madrigalia*, ed. M. C. A. van der Heiden (Zwolle, 1960), 114, 132 e 136.

[40] M. S. J. Cox-Andrau, *De dichter Pieter Vlaming (1686–1734). Een studie over zijn werk met een levensbeschrijving* (Bussum, 1976), 129–187.

nuova Vita del Sannazaro ed una storia della casa di Aragona.[41] In appendice alla Vita presenta un elenco di 44 autori da lui utilizzati. Il testo è appesantito da passi circostanziati sui contemporanei del Sannazaro, il Pontano soprattutto. Il libro contiene alcune belle stampe, basate su disegni che Jacques Philippe d'Orville, professore universitario di lingue antiche ad Amsterdam, aveva fatto fare a Napoli. Come argomento per motivare la stima del Sannazaro viene narrata la storia dell'epigramma su Venezia, che al poeta fruttò tante centinaia di scudi d'oro quanti erano i versi in esso contenuti e che fece sì che il suo ritratto fosse conservato nel palazzo del doge fino a quando non andò perduto in un incendio. Questo epigramma è inserito nella Vita sia nell'originale latino, che nella traduzione olandese.

Poesia in lingua olandese dopo il 1700

Jan Baptista Wellekens (1658–1726)[42] è il maggiore rappresentante della poesia pastorale ed è anche l'autore di una dissertazione sul poema pastorale, "Verhandeling van het herdersdicht."[43] Come pittore ha viaggiato a lungo attraverso l'Italia, dove ha conosciuto la poesia bucolica degli imitatori del Sannazaro, che poco dopo si sarebbero radunati nella Accademia degli Arcadi. Si conservano due ecloghe piscatorie di sua mano e una canzone del cacciatore i cui protagonisti sono un cacciatore, un uccellatore e un coro di cacciatori. Ciò che lo attrae in questo genere di poesia è soprattutto l'ingenuità, che diventa carattere precipuo della sua poetica.

Anche Katharina Johanna de With scrisse delle ecloghe piscatorie olandesi originali. Tradusse due drammi pastorali italiani: De getrouwe herderin di Francesco Contarini e Fillis van Scirus di Guidubaldo Bonarelli della Rovere. Poiché non conosceva a fondo la lingua latina fece tradurre le due ultime ecloghe piscatorie del Sannazaro in olandese dal pastore protestante Alberti da Krommenie,[44] e sul modello di queste scrisse nove canti piscatori (1719–1727). Alcuni di essi sono poesie di compleanno, ed ella si cimenta nell'ambito di questo genere facendo parlare accanto ai pescatori anche dei pastori.[45]

Per quanto riguarda il contenuto delle ecloghe piscatorie si fecero nuovi

---

[41] Arcadia van Sannazarius. Benevens eene korte geschiedens van den huize van Arragon, en het leven des dichters door Pieter Vlaming. Met aenteekeningen en figuuren (Amsterdam: A. Wor e Erven G. onder de Linden, 1730).

[42] Sul Wellekens cf. R. Pennink, Silvander (Jan Baptista Wellekens) 1658–1726 (Haarlem, 1957).

[43] Jan Baptista Wellekens, Verhandeling van het herdersdicht, ed. J. D. P. Warners (Utrecht, 1965); si veda anche J. L. P. Blommendaal, De zachte toon der herdersfluit. De pastorale poëtica van Jan Baptista Wellekens (Utrecht, 1987).

[44] Si veda la sua poesia di ringraziamento nella Fillis van Scirus [. . .] nevens eenige andere gedichten van dezelve, bestaende in herderszangen, visscherszangen, enz (Amsterdam: A. Wor e Erven G. onder de Linden, 1728), 278–279. Altre traduzioni da G. Blok (Epigr. 2,33 in Straboos wereldbeschryvinge, Amsterdam, 1693), D. van Hoogstraten (Epigr. 1: 17, 22, 26, 69 e 70, 2: 7 e 56, in Gedichten, Amsterdam, 1697) e M. de Roever (Salices e Ecl. Pisc. 1–3, in Dichtlievende verlustiging, Leiden, 1762).

[45] Es.: "Lyda. Visschers- en herderszang. Ter geboortevieringe van jongkvrouwe Maria Mein," (1717) in De getrouwe herderin (Rotterdam: Arnold Willis, 1719), 80–85.

esperimenti nel diciottesimo secolo. Così nacque un tipo di poesia di compleanno volutamente comica. Il canto del pescatore "Meewis" di Cornelis Boon van Engelant, "Visscherszang op het verjaergetyde van den Heere Jacob Braet, Schout der Stede en Landen van Vlaerdingen," contiene una descrizione ironica di un inutile viaggio del Meewis per celebrare il compleanno di Golveling; una tempesta rende impossibile il viaggio, ma la prospettiva di un pomeriggio tranquillo a casa col suo amico Grondenier l'attira di più. Mangeranno e brinderanno alla salute di Golveling e di sua moglie Watergont.[46]

Anche nella poesia epitalamica si usavano canti pastorali variandoli con ecloghe piscatorie, senza sentire ancora un legame col Sannazaro. Esponente tipico di questa corrente è Pieter Langendijk (1683–1756), noto specialmente come poeta ufficiale della camera di retorica di Haarlem "Trouw moet blijken" (*Fedeltà deve manifestarsi*) e come autore di commedie. Scrisse ecloghe pastorali, ecloghe piscatorie e campestri, e soprattutto epitalami.

Conclusione

La poesia del Sannazaro ha trovato una piccola cerchia di ammiratori nei Paesi Bassi, in particolare tra i poeti neolatini. Sovente ci si esercita, in Olanda, nel genere da lui inaugurato delle ecloghe piscatorie, sia da parte di poeti neolatini, che di poeti in lingua olandese. Soltanto in alcuni casi (Jeremias de Decker e Katharina Joanna de With), però, si può dimostrare un influsso diretto delle *Eclogae piscatoriae*. La lirica volgare del poeta ha dato i suoi frutti praticamente soltanto all'inizio del diciottesimo secolo ed in seguito a questo rifiorire dell'interesse comparve nel 1730 una traduzione completa dell'*Arcadia*. Nella seconda metà del diciassettesimo secolo l'interesse per il Sannazaro è limitato agli accademici.

Una sola volta il Sannazaro si è pronunciato su un olandese, esprimendo un giudizio sfavorevole. Uno dei suoi epigrammi satireggia il contegno irresoluto di Papa Adriano VI: quando Solimano I minaccia Roma, il Papa si nasconde in Vaticano.[47] Per quanto è possibile giudicare, queste rime sferzanti non hanno influenzato in alcun modo il giudizio degli Olandesi sul Sannazaro.

Universiteit Leiden

---

[46] In Cornelis Boon van Engelant, *Gedichten* (Delft: Reinier Boitet, 1730), 110–114.

[47] *Epigrammaton liber* 3.4: "In Adrianum Pontificem Maximum." ("Classe virisque potens domitoque Oriente superbus / Barbarus in Latias dux quatit arma domos. / In Vaticano noster latet: hunc tamen alto, / Christe, vides coelo (proh dolor) et pateris?")

Paolo Giovio's Descriptio Hyberniae:
Humanist Chorography or Political Manifesto?

ERIC HAYWOOD

The *Descriptio Britanniae, Scotiae, Hyberniae et Orchadum* of Paolo Giovio (1483–1552) was published in Venice (by Michele Tramezino) in 1548, but it appears to have been completed, as it were, in 1543, for the latest event referred to in the work is the wedding of Henry VIII to Catherine Parr, which took place that year. Curiously there is no reference to the death of Henry (a central figure in the work), which occurred in 1547.[1]

My subject is Giovio's description of Ireland. Despite the existence of some full-length descriptions of the country (Gerald of Wales's *Topographia hibernica*, some chapters in Ranulph Higden's *Polychronicon*, which are essentially a summary of Gerald, and a section in Polydore Vergil's *Anglica historia*),[2] or indeed *because* of these works, the view of Ireland in Giovio's day had changed little since the days of Strabo.

---

[1] There is also a modern edition of the *Descriptio* in Pauli Iovii, *Opera. IX: Dialogi et descriptiones*, ed. E. Travi and M. Penco (Rome: Istituto Poligrafico e Zecca dello Stato, 1984). All quotes are taken from this edition. On Giovio see F. Chabod, "Paolo Giovio," in his *Scritti sul Rinascimento* (Turin: Einaudi, 1967), 241–267; B. Croce, "La grandiosa aneddotica storica di Paolo Giovio," in his *Poeti e scrittori del pieno e del tardo Rinascimento* (Bari: Laterza, 1958), 2:27–55; id., "Intorno a Paolo Giovio," in his *Conversazioni critiche* (Bari: Laterza, 1932), 3:296–308; G. Ferrero, "Giovio, Paolo," in *Dizionario critico della letteratura italiana*, ed. V. Branca (Turin: UTET, 1974), 2:219–221; T. F. Mayer, "Reginald Pole in Paolo Giovio's *Descriptio*: A Strategy for Reconversion," *The Sixteenth Century Journal* 16 (1985): 431–450 (the title of my article and some of its ideas were suggested by and are a reply to the views of Mayer; see his article for a more detailed bibliography); *Paolo Giovio. Il Rinascimento e la memoria. Atti del convegno, Como, 3–5/6/1983* (Como: Società Storica Comense, 1985).

[2] Giraldi Cambrensis, *Topographia hibernica et expugnatio hibernica*, ed. J. F. Dimock (Wiesbaden: Kraus Reprint, 1964). Ranulph Higden, *Polychronicon*, ed. C. Babington (London: Longman etc., 1865), 1:328–382. Polydori Vergilii, *Anglicae historiae libri vigintiseptem* (Basel: Thomas Guarinus, 1570): the passage on Ireland occurs in the section on Henry II, bk. XIII, pp. 220–223. For the editions of Vergil's history, see Denys Hay, *Polydore Vergil* (Oxford: Clarendon, 1952).

To be sure, Ireland was now a Christian country, but it was considered to be only superficially so and continued to be seen as a land on the edge of the known and inhabitable world and *therefore* a land peopled by savages. Indeed some saw it as the very paradigm of savagery: in the 1534 edition of Peter Martyr's *History of the Indies* the reader is told not to be surprised if the island of Hispaniola is inhabited by savages, "che ancora nell'isola Hibernia . . . si sa trovarsi uomini infiniti salvatichi."[3] And on the whole Ireland remained a country not worth knowing about: Strabo had used the very example of Ireland to illustrate his theory that there "would be no advantage in knowing countries on the edge of the world and their inhabitants" (*Geog.* 2.5.8), and the same view was echoed some fifteen centuries later by Pius II in his *De Europa*, when he hurried away from Ireland, "quoniam nihil dignum gestum accepimus."[4] The only reason why the country may have been worth knowing about was to prove that it was a land of savages waiting to be conquered—which is the opinion of both Gerald of Wales and Polydore Vergil. Because Ireland was on the edge of the world, it was also seen, by some, as a land of miracles and mysteries: "Ibernia fabulosa," as Ariosto was to call it (*Orlando furioso*, 10.92.1). Thus Gerald of Wales also aimed in the *Topography* to recount the mysteries of the West, just as others had recounted those of the East, and in Fazio degli Uberti's *Dittamondo* Ibernia, despite its apparent savagery, becomes a kind of earthly paradise.[5] All in all, though, Ireland was little known in Italy. And by the end of the sixteenth century no new information to speak of had become available: Porcacchi simply copied Vergil, Botero and Anania Gerald of Wales. And even though the Irish may now be defenders of the Faith against the cruelties of Calvin and Zwingli (in Botero's words), they continue to be savages. It is not surprising then that Tasso, who was influenced by Anania, should speak of "la divisa dal mondo ultima Irlanda" (*Gerusalemme liberata* 1.44.8).[6]

Giovio's *Descriptio Hyberniae* has much in common with other (earlier and later) descriptions of Ireland, focusing as it does on the "mores" of the Irish (their character, habits and politics), the country's "situs" (where it is, what it's like, etc.) and

---

[3] Pietro Martire, *Sommario dell'istoria dell'Indie occidentali*, in Giovanni Battista Ramusio, *Navigazioni e viaggi*, ed. M. Milanesi (Turin: Einaudi, 1985), 5:195.

[4] Strabo, *Geography*, with trans. by H. L. Jones (London: Heinemann, 1960), 1:443–447. For Strabo's views on Ireland, see also *Geog.* 2.1.13 (ibid., 271) and 4.5.4 (op. cit. [London: Heinemann, 1923], 2:259–261). Aeneae Sylvii Piccolominei, *In Europam*, in his *Opera quae extant omnia* (Basel: Henricpetrinus, [1551]), chap. XLVI ("De Scotia & mirandis apud Orcades arboribus, suos fructus in aves mutantibus. Item de Hibernia").

[5] "Ut sicut orientalium regionum prodigia, diligenti auctorum opera, in publicae notitiae lucem dudum prodiere, sic et occidentalia, hactenus quidem abdita fere et incognita, nostro tandem labore his vel occiduis temporibus inveniant editorem" (*Topographia*, cit., 74). Fazio degli Uberti, *Il dittamondo e le rime*, ed. G. Corsi (Bari: Laterza, 1952), 1:328–331.

[6] Thomaso Porcacchi, *L'isole più famose del mondo* (Venice: Simon Galignani, 1604), 12–15. Giovanni Botero, *Le relationi universali* (Venice: Alessandro Vecchi, 1618) 1.2.3:51–52. Giovanni Lorenzo d'Anania, *L'universale fabrica del mondo overo cosmografia* (Venice: San Vito, 1576). For Anania's influence on Tasso see B. Basile, "Sogni di terre lontane," in his *Poëta melancholicus* (Pisa: Pacini, 1984), 325–368.

its miracles, yet in parts the *Descriptio* has a very distinctive air. Giovio knows a lot about Irish exports, particularly to Italy, and about the navigability of Ireland's waterways (information he had obviously gleaned from merchants), he is very well informed about Irish modes of warfare, especially about a type of soldiery native to Ireland (the galloglasses), and he pays a good deal of attention to the figure of one particular Irishman: the man he calls Conatus Honel.

Conn Bacach O'Neill was a Gaelic lord and Ulster chieftain, the leader of the Gaelic chiefs opposed to the English Crown. He had successfully resisted the English forces, though in the end he had been persuaded to surrender to Henry VIII, who re-granted him his lands and created him earl of Tyrone. This happened in 1541–1542. Despite his surrender, however, he was to continue being a thorn in the side of the English and the focus of opposition to the Crown, and when Elizabeth came to the throne in 1558 he was still one of the monarchy's greatest concerns.[7] Giovio mentions him as an effective warrior and a just leader, successful in fighting off the English but ultimately induced to make peace with Henry VIII. This, however, is referred to early on in the *Descriptio*, and by the end of the work the focus is on Conn's large and disciplined forces, on how well he treats them, on the fighting skills of the Irish, and on their magnanimity in the face of death.

All in all, Giovio's depiction of the Irish is a positive one. In that sense it is quite unlike anything that had gone before—in particular quite unlike Vergil's depiction, which cannot therefore, contrary to what some may believe, have been one of Giovio's sources. Where Vergil's Irish are civil only if they live under the English but are otherwise faceless and nameless "sylvestres," Giovio's are simple and uncorrupted, good Christians with a love of justice and a hatred of tyranny, whose only blemishes are their shameless women and the ease with which men swop wives for concubines. Giovio too gave Ireland what she had never had before: a name, and that name, as we have seen, is Conn O'Neill.

Giovio's treatment of Ireland, then, is clearly a case of continuation and transformation. But in this process, what part, if any, can be attributed to humanism? Opinions are divided as to whether the *Descriptio* is a typical humanist work and Giovio a typical humanist. Looking at the question purely from the Irish angle, it was not possible, strictly speaking, to be a humanist, since there existed no classical model, no classical description of Ireland. And there was so little to be found on Ireland in classical authors, that it was not possible to do for Ireland what, say, Biondo had done, and Leandro Alberti was doing for Italy (i.e., collating, interpreting, and updating the knowledge of the ancients).[8] There were of course classical models for other countries, such as Strabo's or Tacitus's (*Germania*), and Giovio may well have been

---

[7] On Conn O'Neill, see Nicholas Canny, *From Reformation to Restoration: Ireland 1534-1660* (Dublin: Helicon, 1987); Steven G. Ellis, *Tudor Ireland. Crown, Community and the Conflict of Cultures 1470–1603* (London: Longman, 1985); *A New History of Ireland. III: Early Modern Ireland*, ed. T. W. Moody, F. X. Martin, and F. J. Byrne (Oxford: Clarendon, 1976).

[8] Flavio Biondo, *De Italia illustrata* (Venice: Venetum de Vitalibus, 1503); Leandro Alberti, *Descrittione di tutta Italia* (Bologna: Anselmo Giaccarelli, 1550).

inspired by these, especially Tacitus, whom he quotes a fair bit in the *Descriptio* and probably strove to imitate. Following Tacitus, possibly, Giovio shows greater impartiality than other describers of Ireland and a greater sensibility to the "mentalité" of the people: his portrait of the Irish is ethnographically more coherent and less subject to climatic "partis-pris." Certainly Giovio was very much the humanist in making history begin with Rome (the British Isles have no history to speak of before the Roman invasion), in putting Rome at the centre of his universe, and in choosing to follow a classical model of the world (his starting point—for what was meant to be a description of the whole world—is the British Isles not, as he admits, because of Britain's role in opening up the seas beyond, but because Ptolemy had declared it to be "ad occidentem solem prima terrarum"). Giovio thus deliberately turns his back on the New World, to gaze firmly in the direction of Italy, "quondam gentium omnium [victrix]."[9]

But though its author may be a humanist, is the *Descriptio* a (humanist) chorography? It is, in the sense which Giovio could have read about in the introduction to his copy of Ptolemy: it is a "pictura" not a "figuratio," as geography was meant to be, it depicts the "quale" not the "quantum," the part ("aurem aut oculum") not the whole ("caput").[10] Yet in many ways one could say that what Giovio did was not all that different from what Gerald of Wales or Ranulph Higden had done. For sure Gerald's instinct to read the world, and especially the miracles of the world, as signs from God is not to be found in Giovio, but the miracles are still there, where in what are probably more typical humanist works—those of Pius II and Vergil—they had been explicitly played down or left out.[11] Moreover, Giovio's unsystematic

---

[9] *Descriptio*, cit., 90.

[10] "Finis chorographiae est partem totius sigillatim animadvertere, ut si quis aurem tamen aut oculum pingat. Geographiae vero totum inspicere iuxta proportionem, ut si integrum quis caput designaret.... Versatur autem chorographia quam maxime circa quale magis quam circa quantum eorum quae describuntur.... Unde chorographia pictura eget, nullusque eam recte componet nisi homo pictor. Geographia autem non idem expostulat, nam poterit quis per puras lineas nudasque denotationes loca figere ac figurationes generales inscribere" (Claudii Ptolemei, *Geographiae opus* [Argentine: Ioannis Schottus, 1513], 5).

[11] "Sunt et aves hic multae, quae bernacae vocantur; quas mirum in modum, contra naturam, natura producit; ... Ex lignis namque abietinis, per aequora devolutis, primo quasi gummi nascuntur. Dehinc tanquam ab alga ligno cohaerente, conchilibus testis ad liberiorem formationem inclusae, per rostra dependent; et sic quousque processu temporis, firmam plumarum vestituram indutae, vel in aquas decidunt, vel in aeris libertatem volatu se transferunt. Ex succo ligneo marinoque, occulta nimis admirandaque seminii ratione, alimenta simul incrementaque suscipiunt.... Resipisce, infelix Judaee, resipisce vel sero. Primam hominis generationem ex limo sine mare et femina, secundamque ex mare sine femina, ob legis venerationem diffiteri non audes.... Quartam vero, in qua sola salus est, ex femina scilicet sine mare, obstinata malitia in propriam perniciem detestaris. Erubesce, miser, erubesce; et saltem ad naturam recurre. Quae ad argumenta fidei, ad instructionem nostram, nova quotidie animalia sine omni mare vel femina procreat et producit" (*Topographia*, cit., 47–49). "In eo [Boando] supra Armacanam stagnum haud peramplum admirabilis naturae celebratur, in quo si pertica ex acrifolii planta in vado defigatur, et post aliquot menses revellatur, extremam partem, quae limo inhaeserit, in ferrum conversam, secundam vero, quam

approach, with its backward and forward movement and its lack of any clear ordering principle, is not all that different from either Gerald's or Higden's. And was Giovio, one may ask, who was writing about Ireland from the enclosed world of his "studio" (although he may have had better informants), doing anything very different from what Higden had done, writing from the enclosed world of his monastery? It is difficult therefore to fit the *Descriptio* into the humanist and chorographical strait-jacket.

But it might be more fruitful to approach the question from a slightly different angle, and ask ourselves what the purpose of the *Descriptio* was, what it was written for. On this score one can detect in Giovio a certain degree of ambiguity—which is also to be found, it seems to me, in his humanist contemporaries and predecessors. Chorography, according to Giovio (and he does use the term, in a letter to Lelio Torelli), is an essential tool of the historian, offering a mirror for the proper under-standing of events.[12] Yet, if the *Descriptio* is chorography in that sense, its links with history are very tenuous indeed: although dealing with historical events, it does so in an imprecise manner, containing elements which are historically irrelevant (such as, for instance, the miracles) and also inaccurate (showing Henry VIII, for instance, as being still alive and the matrimonial/divorce question as unresolved). In the dedi-cation, moreover, Giovio presents the work as light relief from history: "sepositis his-toriis," he now turns his mind, he says, "molliore stilo ad iucundissimum scribendi genus," which is more "ocio languentibus" than "studiosis."[13] It has thus, in effect, little to do with history. For his part Polydore Vergil is equally ambivalent regarding the use of chorography. He presents his description of Ireland as a *digression* from the main theme of his work (which is the *history* of England), and he casts it in a mould which is essentially a-historical, i.e., which lacks any sense of the dynamic of history, for he includes it in the section dealing with Henry II's invasion of Ireland, in order however to shed light on the Ireland of Henry VIII. By thus undermining the very notion of historical change, Vergil seems to undermine the very notion of history

---

profluentis continue abluerit, in cotem duratam spectantibus ostendet; miraculo quoque proximum videtur ex putri ligno, naufragiorumque reliquiis, quae illisae litoribus perpetuis Oceani fluctibus agitentur, concipi enascique et demum evolare inde aves, quae in usu mensarum sint, et nostris anatibus assimilentur" (*Descriptio*, cit., 121). "Audiveramus nos olim arborem esse in Scotia, quae supra ripam fluminis enata fructus produceret anetarum formam habentes & eos quidem, cum maturitati proximi essent, sponte sua decidere alios in terram alios in aquam, & in terram deiectos putrescere, in aquam vero demersos mox animatos enare sub aquis & in aere plumis pennisque evolare. De qua re cum audivimus investigaremus, didicimus miracula semper remotius fugere famosamque arborem non in Scotia sed apud Orcades insulas inveniri. Illud tamen nobis in Scotia miraculum repraesentatum est, nam pauperes pene nudos ad templa mendicantes, acceptis lapidibus eleemosynae gratia datis, laetos abijsse conspeximus; id genus lapidis sive sulphurea sive alia pingui materia praeditum pro ligno, quo regio nuda est, comburitur" (Piccolominei, *In Europam*, cit.). "Miracula autem Hyberniae, quae vulgo praedicantur, quoniam eo remotius fugere solent quo diligentius inquirantur, repetere supervacaneum duximus, arbitrantes nos satis de ea insula hic apposite dixisse" (Vergilii, *Anglica historia*, cit., 223).

[12] Quoted in Chabod, cit., 264.

[13] *Descriptio*, cit., 89.

itself, or at least the possibility of a symbiotic link between history and chorography. This ambiguity regarding the function of chorography is not confined to Giovio and Vergil. We also find it, it seems to me, in Biondo, say, and Leandro Alberti. The reason for it is probably that within the humanist scheme of things, the humanist concept of history, there is no real place for chorography. Chorography pertains to history, but it is separate from history. It deals with things of which it is not clear whether they precede history, as it were, or follow in its wake: must we know what Ireland is like in order to understand her history, or are we curious to know what Ireland is like because she *has* a history? Moreover it deals with things of which history has no need, or indeed which historians have reason to fear, for if the nature of a people is given and unchanging, can there really be any history? And if historical events follow the same pattern wherever they take place, is there really any point in knowing about where they take place? That is why Giovio has to dismiss his work as "light relief"—from history.

But if it was light relief, was it light relief with a serious intent? Was it, as has been suggested, political propaganda? If it were, there would certainly have been nothing new in using descriptions of Ireland for political purposes. Both Gerald of Wales and Polydore Vergil had done so, Gerald to justify Henry II's invasion of the island, Vergil to shore up the legitimacy of the Tudor monarchy and its claim to Ireland. The *Descriptio*, it has been argued, is anti-Henrician, pro-Catholic propaganda. There is no doubt that the problem of Henry VIII looms large in the *Descriptio Britanniae*, and that it was central to Giovio's preoccupations (as we know from his Histories and Letters). As a result of Henry's divorce and his Church reforms, Ireland had acquired a political and strategic significance in Europe which it had never had before. It had become a possible bulwark against the Reformation, and an ally for the papal and imperial cause. It is well known that agents of Henry VIII's Continental enemies were in secret contact with the Irish, seeking to enlist their support in the fight against the schismatic king. In this context it undoubtedly had become imperative to know more about Ireland, and about one Irishman in particular: Henry's leading antagonist, Conn O'Neill. At the time Giovio was writing the *Descriptio*, Henry's enemies were pinning their hopes on Conn, the leader of the Irish rebels. In 1542, just one year before what I have called the completion-date of the *Descriptio*, the first Jesuits had come on a mission to Ireland, bearing a personal message from Pope Paul III to Conn. At that time Conn showed no interest in meeting the Jesuits, since he had just surrendered to the king, but in years to come he was to prove that his loyalty to the Crown was less than whole-hearted. Those were the years too in which the English problem was much agitated in Italy, as elsewhere on the Continent. We need only think of Bandello's "novelliere," in which Henry's cruelty is the focus of several stories (e.g., 2.34 and 3.42), or of William Thomas's *Il pellegrino inglese*, published in 1552, which seeks to defend Henry against the accusation, amongst others, of having "per forza conquistato il Reame d'Irlanda, ne 'l quale non ha titolo, né giuridittione, né che fare."[14] In that context, it is indeed very tempting

---

[14] *Il pellegrino inglese, ne 'l quale si difende l'innocente & la sincera vita de 'l pio & religioso re*

and plausible to view the *Descriptio* as grist to the mill of those who sought, if not to overthrow Henry (since he was now dead), then to attack and delegitimize the schismatic Crown of England (now resting on the very Protestant head of Edward VI), and to portray the Irish as safe and credible allies in that struggle. And might it not specifically have been intended, one may ask, as a foil to the "official" portrait of the Irish painted by the Tudor historiographer Polydore Vergil?

If that is what it was, however, it should be noted that nowhere in the *Descriptio* does Giovio explicitly state that to be his aim. Moreover, nowhere in his *Historiae*, as far as I am aware, is the probability of such a scenario ever discussed—indeed I believe that nowhere in the *Historiae* is there ever any discussion about Ireland. It is also debatable to what extent the *Descriptio* is an anti-Henrician tract. Whereas in his other writings Giovio can be quite ruthless in his criticisms of Henry, in the *Descriptio*, it seems to me, he presents him not so much as an evil figure, but rather as a tragic one: a king who is surrounded by evil counsellors and has been struck by madness, but a king who is basically good and, what is more, has enormous power and great wealth.[15] If that is so, the *Descriptio* could be seen as quite the opposite to anti-English propaganda. While ostensibly taking the side of Catholic Ireland, it could have been a veiled warning to those who pinned their hopes on the Irish not to underestimate the strength of the English Crown, whose position was unlikely to be undermined by the effective but perhaps primitive forces of Conn O'Neill.

If the *Descriptio* does not fit either the chorography or the propaganda mould perfectly, perhaps it could be seen in another light. In the introduction Giovio states that his description of the British Isles is but a first step in the description of the whole world. This means that the work is in fact an embryonic cosmography. Perhaps it was intended to rival the *Cosmographia* (*De Asia* and *De Europa*) of Pius II, which had been enjoying a fair degree of editorial success and in 1544 had been translated into Italian.[16] It is clear that Giovio had read Pius, although he never actually quotes him, and he probably felt that Pius's information needed updating, especially the "nihil dignum gestum" concerning Ireland. The *Descriptio* might thus have been intended as a kind of "flier" for a forthcoming, updated cosmography. But why publish a work which was itself not up to date? Perhaps Giovio, who had most likely been nurturing his plan for some time, was anxious to ward off another challenge, for the Protestant Sebastian Münster had just published the first version of what was soon to become a European best-seller, his own *Cosmographia*. It was in

---

d'Inghilterra Henrico ottavo, bugiardamente calonniato da Clemente VII & da gl'altri adulatori de la Sedia Antichristiana (s.l.: 1542, no pp. nos.).

[15] Compare the favourable picture of Henry in the *Descriptio Britanniae* (for instance: "Has tantas opes et copias imperio obtinet Henricus, cui natura fortunaque supra regium nomen incomparabilis formae, et maxime praestantis ingenii accumulata dona contulerunt" [op. cit., 104]) with, e.g., letter 249 of 21 February 1547 to Pier Luigi Farnese, where Henry is called "cruento e impio tiranno d'Inghilterra" (Pauli Iovii, *Opera. II: Lettere. II (1544–1552)*, ed. G. G. Ferrero [Rome: Istituto Poligrafico dello Stato, 1958], 69).

[16] Including the Italian translation (Venice: Vincenzo Vangris), the *Cosmographia* had already been through approximately ten editions, in Italy, France, and Germany.

German, but in 1550 it was to come out in the language of the European intelligentsia, Latin. It could well be that Giovio, who was always well informed on what was happening in Europe, had been told in 1548 of the impending publication of this Latin version, and thus hoped to stake his own ground. Perhaps, if he was able to read German, he also intended to highlight the deficiences and bias of Münster, whose Irish were "grob, onhöfflich und fast ruch" and over whom "der künig von Engelland ist herr."[17] If Giovio did not succeed in sabotaging Münster's plans, at least his efforts were not entirely in vain. Indeed by the 1550s Münster's original (German) description of Ireland was giving way to a plagiarism (with some additions) of the *Descriptio*. What is more, Münster (and one may wonder whether this was not intentional, Protestant "counter-sabotage" on his part) had decided to dispatch Conn O'Neill, the hero of Giovio and the papal cause, who was to live until 1559, to a premature death![18]

This strange metamorphosis brings us back to the theme of the conference, and bearing that in mind, we may now summarise. We have seen that: (1) Giovio's *Descriptio* does not transform radically the way of writing about Ireland, but it does transform the image of Ireland (in Italy); that transformation, though, was not destined to last long, and by the end of the century things were to continue very much as they had before. (2) In the *Descriptio* Giovio responds to the transformations occurring in the world about him (the world of politics and the publishing world) but with only a degree of success. (3) This, apart from bad timing, may have been due to the enduring power of certain humanist instincts, which did not allow for the intrusion of chorography into the field of history, and which tended to look backwards for their models—to times when the centre of the universe was still in Rome and the Mediterranean.

University College Dublin

---

[17] S. Münster, *Cosmographia* (Basel: Henricpetrinus, 1545), xxxix. The description of Ireland in the Basle: Henricpetrinus, 1544 edition is the same, but I have not been able to consult the Frankfurt: Egenolff, 1537 edition listed in the National Union catalogue.

[18] "Hultoniae, Hyberniae regioni potiori, nostro aevo Connatius Honel praefuit clarus bello, qui equitum 4000 peditum 12000 in aciem contra Havardum Anglum eduxit, in amicitiam Anglorum deinde traductus, pacem cum eis coluit. Quo mortuo, cum Thomas Giraldinus Hyberniae praefectus parentem ab Anglo necatum audijsset, anno 1534 seditionem excitavit, armavit supra 40000 peditum & equitum ad res magno Hybernorum periculo & damno, conditionibus quibusdam demum sopita fuit" (S. Münster, *Cosmographia universalis* [Basel: Henricpetrinus, 1558], 44). In the 1550s editions of the *Cosmographia* (German, Latin, Italian, French?) this paragraph about Conn O'Neill has been added to the original description of Ireland. In the 1560s and later editions, the original description has been replaced by a full-fledged plagiarism of Giovio's *Descriptio*.

Producing Concordances to Scottish Neo-Latin Texts: An Exercise in Computerized Neo-Latin Lexicography

ALISTAIR INGLIS-TAYLOR

When I joined the Scottish Neo-Latin Dictionary Project, under Roger Green's direction, at St. Andrews, in March 1994, about two years' work had been dedicated to the project already, first by Deborah Ford and, more recently, by Philip Burton. An exhaustive list or biographical bibliography of Scottish Neo-Latin authors and their works printed before A.D. 1700 had been compiled and revised, research undertaken into suitable software packages for processing texts of those works, and selected example texts scanned into machine-readable format.

Having assembled the biographical bibliography of Scottish Neo-Latin authors in print, our strategy was to enable computerized contextual recording of every lexical type within the corpus, in each of its occurrences, by creating lemmatized concordances for the works identified. The first stage in this process is to transfer all the works identified into machine-readable format. This will be done, where possible, using a Hewlett-Packard Scanjet machine. However, the print of texts published before about A.D. 1800 is not suitable for scanning, and texts with no subsequent editions must be keyed-in by hand. Recent texts may be subject to copyright restrictions. All texts will be prepared in accordance with a Standard Generalized Mark-up Language (SGML) definition, showing information on texts which will not be relevant to text-processing software but is important for human beings, such as the author's name, chapter or line numbers, and letters of the addressee's name. To denote that information is for human consumption only. It is formatted as COCOA references—placed between angle brackets—and may then be ignored by our text-processing software.

The texts prepared in accordance with SGML can then be broken down into alphabetical lists of words sorted under their main lemma (for example, verbs under present indicative active first-person singular, adjectives and substantives under nominative singular, etc.). This presents all words in a readily digestible format and enables easy recognition of neologisms.

Two principal software tools have been identified to carry out this processing: the

Oxford Concordance Program is produced by Oxford University Computing Service, and LEMLAT is produced by the Istituta Linguistica Computazionale in Pisa. First of all, the raw text is broken down into an alphabetical list of the words that it contains by the Oxford Concordance Program in 'wordlist' mode. The SGML annotation is discarded. Figures 1 and 2 show raw text input to and wordlist output from the Oxford Concordance Program. The frequency of words within a text is shown in the right-hand column of the Oxford Concordance Program output in Figure 2.

The output is fed to LEMLAT, which lemmatizes the words in the list, identifying the lemma or headword from which each is derived, through analysis and comparison with its massive database. For example 'haec' is recognized as a form of the lemma 'hic.' An example of LEMLAT output is shown at Figure 3. Words containing uppercase letters are not lemmatized by LEMLAT. It will be noticed that LEMLAT makes no decision on the level of headword or lemma to be used in the lexicographical process. For example, in the output in Figure 3, 'coctis' is shown as a form of the intermediate lemma 'coctus' as well as of the ultimate lemma 'coquo.' Also LEMLAT cannot distinguish between homographs: 'arce' in Figure 3 is shown as either the imperative singular of the verb 'arceo' or the ablative singular of the substantive 'arx.' The user must return to the context in the original raw text to eliminate the inapplicable lemma. In this case, from line 7 of Figure 1, we are able to see that 'arce' is a form of the lemma 'arx.'

Finally the edited output from LEMLAT can be included as headwords in the control file for a second run of the Oxford Concordance Program, this time in 'concordance' mode. Figure 4 shows the product. Words processed by LEMLAT and included in the control file's headwords list are grouped under their lemma: 'harum,' 'haec,' and 'hoc,' for example, all appear under 'hic.' Different forms of words not processed by LEMLAT, such as 'Sancti' and 'Sanctae' in Figure 1, which include uppercase letters, will be placed in separate lists. Each token is displayed with line references and context from the text. The size of the raw text used initially may be limited by the ceiling on headword numbers available in the Oxford Concordance Program at this stage. With the current limit of 300 headwords, an optimum raw text size is around 750 words in an average piece of Neo-Latin prose.

Unfortunately this is not a perfect world, and so the output from the Oxford Concordance Program is not compatible with LEMLAT, and LEMLAT's output is not suitable for the Oxford Concordance Program. The change to the Oxford Concordance Program output is trivial, but the output from LEMLAT needs more manipulation. My chief interest in the project concerns the development of software applications to carry out this manipulation. The new applications will edit the various files into formats suitable for subsequent stages of processing. In addition, if time allows, they may, in cases where lexical forms have been assigned to intermediate and ultimate lemmas, be able to offer elimination of either alternative. A headword policy for the dictionary project will have to be formulated by this stage. Homographs can be recognized and flagged by the St. Andrews bespoke applications, but human intervention will always be required to select the relevant lemma from the context.

For portability, the applications are being written in the programming language 'C,' to run on UNIX operating systems. Minimal adjustment will be required, therefore, to make them compatible for PCs running DOS. The versions of the Oxford Concordance Program and LEMLAT that we have also run on UNIX or DOS for PCs. The chief virtue of the system is that it will be suitable for potential Latin dictionary compilers throughout the world. All the output is in Latin, and so the only English one has to read is the error messages, and, of course, the prompts for input and output file names. Development of the ancillaries is well under way, and should be completed this year.

Another benefit of computer processing is the ease of compilation and printing once a lexicon has been selected. There are, of course, tasks which cannot be performed with the aid of computers. Much time must be spent by traditional methods in identifying novelty and development of usage, as D. R. Howlett has emphasized in his article "The Use of Traditional and Computer Techniques in Compiling and Printing a Dictionary of Medieval Latin from British Sources."[1]

My report would be incomplete if I did not draw attention to some of the difficulties which we have faced and still have to face in developing our dictionary. Funding will probably always be elusive for Latin projects, and so we are grateful to the British Academy for the support they have provided. However, since projects are generally funded on a year-to-year basis, continuity is an additional hurdle. Every time funding is renewed, a new researcher is appointed, and he or she must spend several weeks familiarising him or herself with the nature of the project and the work achieved so far. This slows down progress substantially. Although it is often not possible to secure permanent funding for research, there are ways in which continuity can be improved. A lesson worth learning from the world of commerce is the value of documentation. Careful recording of work and progress helps to avoid duplication and eliminate wasted effort when new staff join a project.

Another problem we have faced is the state of the texts to be used. We cannot scan very old texts, and so we seek, where possible, newer editions of the texts which interest us. We are then at the mercy of the text editors. Their interpretations and the decisions they have made on standardisation of spelling and punctuation anticipate any orthographical policies we may develop for the treatment of the texts we are using.

Use of the original texts brings problems of its own. We have seen already that they may not be scanned, with the result that much effort must be expended keying them in by hand. It is wasteful for Latin specialists to carry out this work, and so we consider employing clerical support to perform the task. However, distinguishing the archaic 's' from 'f' is problematic, and unfamiliarity with the language may result in an unusually high number of typographical errors. The typist will have to become accustomed to the SGML definition too. More general problems with texts occur because LEMLAT, reasonably enough, assumes that any word beginning with an

---

[1] In *The Possibilities and Limits of the Computer in Producing and Publishing Dictionaries. Proceedings of the European Science Foundation Workshop, Pisa, 1981*, edd. A Zampolli and A. Cappelli. Linguistica Computazionale, III (1983), 153–159.

uppercase letter is a name and makes no attempt to lemmatize it. (The attempt to formulate rules for the lemmatization of names of all the nationalities likely to appear in the Latin corpus would be prohibitively expensive and liable to produce numerous possibilities for any given form.) Consequently, older texts, which pre-date the convention for starting Latin sentences with a lowercase letter, need to be adjusted before they can be processed. Also there is the difficulty that for some texts, we know of only one or a few inaccessible copies.

The news is not all bad, however. The project to develop computer applications at St. Andrews is progressing well, and, when it has been completed, it should benefit substantially anyone wishing to proceed on another country's corpus of printed Neo-Latin. The machine-readable texts which we produce as an intermediate stage may also have relevance to those undertaking statistical textual analysis and lexicon comparisons. This work is already arousing interest in universities, both among Latin specialists and among modern linguists and historians at locations across the world.

Figure 1. Raw Text Input

\<A Alesius\>
\<T Edinburgh\>

EDINBURGI REGIAE SCOTORUM URBIS DESCRIPTIO,
PER ALEXANDRUM ALESIUM, SCOTUM, SACRAE THEOLOGIAE DOC-
    TOREM.
ab occidente urbis assurgit mons, et alta rupes,
atque arx in rupe, sub qua undique est profunda vallis, nisi
ea parte qua respicit urbem; quare arx est inexpugnabilis   5
nisi ex urbe, nec quisquam ad eam scandere posset etiam
scalis, tam praeceps et dura est petra, in qua
vultures nidificant. harum avium nidos depredantur juvenes
audaciores, ex arce in sportis demissi. haec arx vocatur
castrum puellarum, clauditque urbem ab occidente. caeterum   10
ad orientem urbis est augustissimum monasterium Sanctae
Crucis, habens annexum palatium regis et amoenissimos
hortos, quos claudit lacus ad fundum montis cathedrae
Arthuri. in hoc monte inveniuntur praetiosi lapides, clara
die radiantes, adamantes praecipue. in urbe sunt duae magnae   15
viae ab arce puellarum usque ad monasterium et regium
palatium, lapidibus quadris stratae, praesterim regia via.
est suburbium ad occidentem, dimidio milario longum,
vocaturque via Sancti Cuthberti. sunt in urbe multa
monasteria et templa, praesertim Franciscani, Dominicastri,   20
ecclesia Mariae de campo, collegium sacerdotum, et aliud
collegium Trinitatis, hospitale S. Thomae. urbs ipsa non
est constructa ex coctis, sed naturalibus . . . lapidibus.

Figure 2. Output from Oxford Concordance Program: First Run

ab	3
ad	5
adamantes	1
ALESIUM	1
ALEXANDRUM	1
aliud	1
alta	1
amoenissimos	1
annexum	1
arce	2
Arthuri	1
arx	3
assurgit	1
atque	1
audaciores	1
augustissimum	1
avium	1
caeterum	1
campo	1
castrum	1
cathedrae	1
clara	1
claudit	1
clauditque	1
coctis	1

Figure 3. Output from LEMLAT: Edited

ab	a
ab	ab
ad	ad
adamantes	adamas
adamantes	adamans
adamantes	adamo
aliud	alius
alta	altus
alta	alo
amoenissimos	amoenissimus
amoenissimos	amoenus
annexum	adnecto
annexum	adnectus
arce	arceo
arce	arx

assurgit	assurgo
atque	atque
audaciores	audacior
audaciores	audax
augustissimum	augustissimus
augustissimum	augustus
caeterum	caeterus
. . . .	
coctis	coctus
coctis	coquo

Figure 4. Output from Oxford Concordance Program: Second Run

habeo 1
12 Crucis, habens annexum palatium regis et amoenissimos

hic 3
8 nidificant. harum avium nidos depredantur juvenes
9 ex arce in sportis demissi. haec arx vocatur
14 in hoc monte inveniuntur praetiosi lapides, clara

hortus 1
13 hortos, quos claudit lacus ad fundum montis

hospitalis 1
22 collegium Trinitatis, hospitale S. Thomae. urbs ipsa

. . . .

sacerdos 1
21 ecclesia Mariae de campo, collegium sacerdotum,

Sanctae 1
11 urbis est augustissimum monasterium Sanctae

Sancti 1
19 vocaturque via Sancti Cuthberti. sunt in urbe multa

Roehampton Institute, London

L'opera di Orazio
fra editoria e scuole umanistiche

ANTONIO IURILLI

Non è facile districarsi fra gli esordi dell'editoria oraziana, a lungo segnati da incerte attribuzioni, da inquietanti fantasmi e da singolari episodi di bibliomania,[1] spesso prodotti dal bisogno di antedatare un inizio editoriale considerato eccessivamente tardo per un classico, nonostante la precoce presenza, non priva di maliziosi sottintesi, di uno dei più ambigui documenti dell'epicureismo oraziano (l'ode *Diffugere nives* . . .) in appendice al testo capitale dell'etica stoica romana, il *De officiis* di Cicerone, stampato a Magonza nel 1465 da Fust e Schöffer.[2]

In effetti, decisamente tarda appare la ormai certa *editio princeps* del *corpus* oraziano (un modesto *in-quarto* uscito a Venezia fra il 1471 e il 1472 dai torchi dell'anonimo stampatore della traduzione filelfiana del *De officiis vitae solitariae* di San Basilio),[3] la quale sembra manifestare tutti i limiti di una ricezione sulla quale continuava forse a pesare l'indifferenza, se non ostilità, delle antiche scuole monastiche ed episcopali, a loro volta eredi, nonostante l'effimero affermarsi di un'*aetas horatiana* promossa dal Circolo Palatino all'interno della cultura carolingia, del sostanziale sfavore di cui aveva sofferto Orazio presso le scuole di età imperiale.

E' peraltro appena il caso di accennare al mediocre interesse esegetico manifestato dal primo Umanesimo all'opera di Orazio, che fa tutt'uno con la sua ancillarità nell'insegnamento: un discorso che, tuttavia, sta meritando una diversa attenzione.[4] Di

---

[1] Se ne veda un interessante esempio in George D. Painter "A Horatian Ghost," in *Studies in Fifteenth-century Printing* (London, 1984), 65–69.

[2] Cf. Hain 1142, 1144.

[3] Cf. Hain 8866.

[4] Sull'interesse degli umanisti all'opera oraziana ancora utili sono i contributi di Gaetano Curcio, *Orazio studiato in Italia dal sec. XIII al XVIII* (Catania, 1913), 39–122; Roberto Valentini, *Come Orazio fu giudicato nell'Umanesimo* (Pavia, 1915). Ma significativi incrementi sono venuti da alcune relazioni svolte al Convegno oraziano di Licenza (aprile 1993), i cui Atti sono in corso di pubblicazione presso l'Istituto Poligrafico e Zecca dello Stato, Roma.

fatto, il relativo disinteresse della proto-editoria per l'opera oraziana sembra risentire dalla limitata domanda della scuola e della modesta considerazione di cui godevano i primi commenti umanistici al *corpus* oraziano.

Ignorati, per esempio, appaiono da un incunabolo romano apparso tra il 1474 e il 1475 maestri come Martino Filetico e Antonio Calcillo, che pure avevano letto Orazio nello *Studium Urbis* fra gli anni '60 e '70.[5] A propiziare e a curare quell'edizione erano stati, del resto, Francesco Elio Marchese, un retore estraneo all'ambiente universitario, ma amico di Pomponio Leto quel tanto che gli consentì di constatare le lacerazioni consumatesi nel mondo accademico romano fra gli ex-ascritti all'Accademia bessarionea, e Angelo Sabino il quale, lettore di retorica presso lo *Studium Urbis*, proprio a causa di quei contrasti aveva perduto l'insegnamento universitario.[6]

Il progetto editoriale mirava, anzi, con non poco coraggio, a rimuovere proprio la mediazione scolastica e ad offrire un testo fruibile col solo apporto della tradizione vetero-esegetica dello pseudo-Acrone e di Porfirione: una scelta orgogliosamente rivendicata dallo *sponsor* dell'impresa, Giovanni Alvise Toscani, avvocato concistoriale in grado di dialogare con l'ambiente universitario, ma soprattutto con la Curia, della quale tentava di assecondare i gusti.

A parte la precoce novità editoriale di un classico affiancato da due commenti, la prima stampa romana di Orazio a noi nota si accredita come significativo riflesso editoriale del mutato atteggiamento che la cultura umanistica, sulla scia del Petrarca, andava assumendo verso l'opera del Venosino, privilegiandone decisamente la componente lirica in opposizione a quella satirico-gnomica e a quella stilistico-prescrittiva prevalenti in età medievale e ancora viva nell'editoria d'oltralpe, la quale non a caso accoglie per la prima volta Orazio in una antologia di *moralia* pubblicata a Strasburgo nel 1472, mentre a Caen, alcuni anni dopo, l'unico incunabolo di area normanna

---

[5] *Carmina, Carmen Saeculare, Epodon, Ars Poetica (Comm. Acronis et Porphyrionis)*, [Roma: Bartholomaeus Guldinbeck o Wendelinus de Wila], 1474–1475 c.: cf. Paola Casciano, Giovanni Castoldi, Maria Pia Critelli e altri, *Indice delle edizioni romane a stampa (1467–1500)*, in appendice a *Scrittura, biblioteche e stampa a Roma nel Quattrocento. Aspetti e problemi* (Città del Vaticano, 1980) = IERS 351. Sui commenti universitari del Filetico, educatore dei figli di Alessandro Sforza, signore di Pesaro, cf. Giovanni Mercati, "Tre dettati universitari dell'umanistica Martino Filetico sopra Persio, Giovenale ed Orazio," in *Classical and Medieval Studies in Honor of Edward Kennard Rand* (New York, 1938), 221–230, ora in Id., *Opere minori* (Città del Vaticano, 1984), 13–24; D. M. Robathan, "A Postscript on Martino Filetico," *Medievalia et Humanistica* 8 (1954): 56–61. Sull'attività intellettuale e sulle polemiche universitarie del Filetico, cf. Carlo Dionisotti, "*Lavinia venit litora*. Polemica virgiliana di M. Filetico," *Italia Medievale e Umanistica* 1 (1958): 283–315: 303–304. Sul Calcillo, nativo di Sessa Aurunca, pontaniano e amico del Panormita, noto soprattutto per l'attività di grammatico e di lessicografo (fu forse l'ispiratore del *De proprietate verborum* di Iuniano Maio), cf. Roberto Ricciardi, "Angelo Poliziano, Giuniano Maio, Antonio Calcillo," *Rinascimento* 8 (1968): 277–309: 287–289.

[6] Sul ruolo svolto dal Marchese e dal Sabino nell'ambito dell'editoria romana del Quattrocento cf. Concetta Bianca, "Il soggiorno romano di Francesco Elio Marchese," in *Letteratura fra centro e periferia. Studi in memoria di Pasquale Alberto De Lisio*, eds. Gioacchino Paparelli e Sebastiano Martelli (Napoli, 1987), 221–248.

(una tipica edizione "interlineare," destinata a ricevere nelle linee bianche le note degli scolari) era riservata alle sole *Epistole*.[7]

La scelta editoriale del Marchese e del Sabino era invece decisamente caduta su Orazio lirico. In quegli stessi anni il Perotti, che era amico del Sabino, inaugurava un fortunato filone di studi metrici offrendo ai tipografi un agile manualetto destinato a corredare moltissime edizioni oraziane del Cinquecento, e riproponendo alle scuole umanistiche la fortuna medievale di Orazio, maturata proprio nell'ambito della tradizione metrico-prosodica latina.

Credo che in questa stessa prospettiva sia possibile spiegare la genesi di un precoce quanto eccentrico Orazio ferrarese, uscito nel 1474, che esclude dal *corpus* oraziano proprio le *Satire* e l'*Ars Poetica*.[8]

L'iniziativa si colloca agli esordi della tipografia ferrarese, peraltro scarsamente incoraggiati da Borso, e non sembra voler aspirare al grande mercato editoriale, nonostante il ruolo ormai acquisito da Ferrara di crocevia degli scambi librari. Agostino Carnerio, figlio di Bernardo, prototipografo del Ducato, concepisce anzi il suo Orazio dimidiato proprio in funzione del consumo locale e probabilmente ispirato da una precisa domanda sia della scuola che della corte, non insensibile, certo, alle suggestioni della lirica oraziana, visto che al suo interno maturarono in tempi di poco successivi alcune fra le prime versioni musicate di Orazio.

Nella vicina Mantova Vittorino da Feltre, il quale fin dal 1433 si era procurato una copia del commento pseudo-acroniano ai *Carmina* che Ambrogio Traversari, di passaggio per Mantova, trascrisse, dicendola irreperibile a Firenze (mentre nella stessa Ferrara persino un teologo, ma colto bibliofilo, Battista Panetti, ne possedeva un esemplare),[9] aveva frattanto inserito la lirica oraziana nel canone pedagogico dei suoi allievi col dichiarato proposito di affinarne il gusto poetico. E proprio accogliendo gli umori critico-letterari del circolo ferrarese, Angelo Decembrio, che in Spagna aveva copiato l'intero commento dello Pseudo-Acrone, riconosceva in quegli stessi anni, nell'ambito del suo canone di scrittori greci e latini, particolare prestigio all'Orazio lirico, lamentandone la immeritata subalternità agli epici e agli elegiaci.[10]

A confermare le tendenze filo-oraziane di un clima culturale almeno geograficamente omogeneo, a Verona Battista Guarini inseriva Orazio subito dopo Virgilio nel canone dei poeti latini utili all'insegnamento.[11] E non mi sembra privo di significato

---

[7] Cf. rispettivamente *Pharetra doctorum et philosophorum* . . . (Strassburg: Johann Mentelin, [1472, non ante]): Hain-Copinger 12908; *Horatii Epistolarum libri duo* (Cadomi: Jacobus Durand et Aegidius Quijove, 6 VI 1480): Hain 8913.

[8] *Horatii Epistolae–Horatii Carmina [I–IV]–Epodon liber–Carmen saeculare* (Ferrara: Agostino Carneri, 1474): Hain 8900.

[9] Cf. Remigio Sabbadini, *Le scoperte dei codici ne' secoli XIV e XV*, ed. E. Garin (Firenze, 1967), 94, 132, 188.

[10] Angeli Decembrii *De Politia literaria* (Basileae, 1562), 27: "Subinde omnia Horatii opera tenenda sunt. Non eamdem habere videntur Camoenarum dulcedinem aetate nostra elegiis et heroicis tantum assueta, licet priscis forte temporibus et lyricorum genera summe delectarent."

[11] Cf. Baptistae Guarini *De ordine docendi ac studendi* [Ferrara: Andrea Belfort, 1474] (ma la data dell'opera accreditata dalla tradizione ms. è 1459), ora nell'ediz. critica, con traduzione e note di

il fatto che il primo episodio di penetrazione umanistica dell'opera oraziana nella cultura ungherese maturi attraverso la mediazione di quel Giano Pannonio, poeta magiaro divenuto vescovo di Pécs, che aveva studiato alla scuola ferrarese di Guarino.

Su Orazio lirico aveva intanto svolto numerosi corsi universitari lungo tutti gli anni '60 a Firenze anche Cristoforo Landino, esordendo nel 1461 con un corso sui *Carmina* cui seguì la lettura dell'*Ars Poetica* come sussidio al corso sull'oratoria e sulla poetica svolto nel 1464–1465: una emblematica scelta di indirizzo, peraltro sintonica con le simpatie per Orazio lirico manifestate in quegli anni dallo stesso Lorenzo, una scelta che interrompeva il lungo silenzio dello Studio sul poeta (nonostante il magistero di "classicisti" come Filelfo, Marsuppini, Manetti), e dalla quale scaturì il suo fortunatissimo commento al *corpus* raziano, un commento di impianto retorico-critico, piuttosto che filologico o filosofico-morale, condotto all'insegna di complesse ragioni culturali e di poetica attive nella cultura umanistica e destinate a trasferirsi in quella rinascimentale come modello per la sterminata letteratura critica sulla precettistica poetica. L'impegno medievale di valorizzare la gnomica dell'"Orazio satiro" cedeva quindi, nella lettura landiniana al bisogno di indagare "sapientiam huius poetae in rebus ipsis inveniendis et mirificum consilium atque artificium in singulis disponendis atque ornandis." Il *corpus* lirico si caricava di fini pedagogici "ad iuvenile ingenium excitandum et ad linguam expoliendam atque ornandam," proprio sulla scia del nuovo canone di autori per la scuola che il magistero del Guarini aveva imposto. L'Orazio lirico e precettore di stile poetico diveniva anzi la premessa imprescindibile per leggere e spiegare la lirica dei "moderni," Petrarca in testa.[12]

Era dunque fatale che l'editoria incunabolistica riconoscesse al commento landiniano un primato tradottosi in almeno ventuno fra riedizioni e ristampe (più di una all'anno), a partire dalla sontuosa *princeps* di Antonio Miscomini del 1482,[13] dedicata, con accorta scelta politica, a Guidubaldo da Montefeltro, figlio appena decenne di Federico: un raffinatissimo *in-folio*, che il Gesner avrebbe definito "inter principes Horatii editiones," tirato anche in pergamena, e impreziosito in alcuni esemplari da iniziali in oro e azzurro, decorazioni a bianchi girari su due lati e splendide miniature: un simbolo, indubbiamente, della matura editoria fiorentina negli anni dell'apogeo laurenziano, la quale proponeva a stampa un Orazio commentato dal più prestigioso maestro dello Studio della città ad oltre dieci anni dall'uscita della *princeps* veneziana, e quando ormai il mercato era saturato dalle numerose edizioni veneziane e milanesi, puntando proprio sulla qualità e sulla carica innovativa del commento, che sanciva l'avvenuta assimilazione della poetica oraziana nel sistema retorico-stilistico dell'Uma-

---

Luigi Piacente (Bari, 1975): "Horatius praeter optimam poeticae artis cognitionem, sermonis proprietatem, mea sententia suppeditabit, nec quemque facile invenies in rerum epithetis Vergilio magis adhaerentem; adde quod aliorum satyrorum intellectum multa nobis accomodat" (70–71).

[12] Sul commento landiniano ad Orazio cf. Roberto Cardini, *La critica del Landino* (Firenze, 1973).

[13] *Christophori Landini florentini in Quinti Horatii Flacci libros omnes ad illustrissimum Guidonem Feltrium magni Federici ducis filium interpretationes* . . . (Florentiae, impressum per Antonium Miscominum, [5 VIII]1482): Hain-Copinger-Reichling 8881.

nesimo. La stampa poi in apertura dell'*Ode* del Poliziano ad Orazio, parallela all'epistola del Ficino inserita nel proemio del commento landiniano a Dante, che allude a un Orazio rinnovato dall'interpretazione del maestro "come un serpente che cambia squame a primavera," era infine l'omaggio reso all'astro nascente dello Studio fiorentino e il riconoscimento, in parte forzato, di una sorta di continuità "neoplatonica," che si presumeva di leggere, per esempio, nell'accentuazione dell'identità Orazio=Orfeo, o nella insistita immagine del poeta liberato dai ceppi della barbarie medievale, nonostante le riserve più volte manifestate dal Poliziano sul metodo esegetico applicato proprio a Orazio dal suo antico maestro.

L'edizione del commento landiniano additava indubbiamente nuove possibili intese fra editoria e accademia, ma imponeva un difficile termine di confronto. Se le maggiori tipografie veneziane lo reiteravano ossessivamente per tutto lo scorcio del secolo contando su una committenza scolastica sufficientemente sicura, altre officine meno prestigiose, ma proprio per questo bisognose di diversificare il prodotto, avevano frattanto tentato nuove vie accogliendo l'iniziativa di alcuni umanisti locali tendente a rivitalizzare, attraverso il restauro filologico, la tradizione vetero-esegetica dello pseudo-Acrone e di Porfirione, spesso in funzione scopertamente antilandiniana.

E' quello che accade nella stessa Venezia con Ludovico de Strazzarolis, revisore degli scolii pseudo-acroniani, e col bergamasco Raffaele Regio, professore di *humanae litterae* a Padova e a Venezia, restauratore del commento porfirioneo a Orazio. Entrambi i lavori filologici approdano ad una edizione prodotta nel 1481 da Michele Manzolo, che vanta due primati: quello di essere la prima edizione completa e datata di Orazio coi due commenti antichi, e quello di presentare per la prima volta i commenti sinotticamente stampati col testo.[14]

Anche nella Milano sforzesca, dove alcuni anni prima un colto filologo, collaboratore e finanziatore della protostampa lombarda, Bonino Mombrizio, amico di Pier Candido Decembrio, aveva favorito un vero e proprio *exploit* di edizioni oraziane, si consuma nel 1486 (cioè quattro anni dopo l'esordio editoriale del commento landiniano, che non a caso non avrà edizioni milanesi), l'ennesimo episodio di rilancio editoriale dei due antichi commenti a Orazio in funzione antilandiniana. Il pugliese Alessandro Minuziano, assurto non senza l'appoggio dell'*entourage* ducale al ruolo di discusso professore di eloquenza nelle Scuole Palatine, ma soprattutto attivo nell'editoria prima come *sponsor*, poi come tipografo-editore, finanzia, proprio negli anni di maggiore fortuna del commento landiniano, un Orazio corredato dai due antichi commenti manifestando esplicita la volontà di opporre al maestro fiorentino, come "antidoto," lo pseudo-Acrone e soprattutto un Porfirione che egli vantava di aver emendato sulla scorta di un manoscritto in suo possesso. La personale avversione al Landino, consegnata alla *nuncupatoria* premessa alla sua edizione di Orazio, e giocata sulla triviale omofonia "comentum/conatum," raggiunge, anzi, toni di inconsueta veemenza.[15]

---

[14] *Quinti Horatii Flacci Opera cum commentariis Acronis per Lodovicum de Strazarolis Tarvisanum recogniti praecedente Porphyrionis in Horatii opera commentum per Raphael Regium castigato* [Venezia: Michele Manzolo, 13 VIII 1481, non ante]: Hain-Copinger 8878.

[15] *Quinti Horatii Flacci Opera, comm. Acron et Porphyrion*, [Precede:] Alexander Minutianus,

A parte le intemperanze verbali di un troppo disinvolto maestro che, incurante di un'accusa di plagio mossagli da Aulo Giano Parrasio proprio per un corso oraziano, avrebbe in seguito millantato a più riprese meriti filologici e editoriali nei confronti di un Orazio "ita emendatus, ut eius interpretes non multum desideres"[16] l'editoria italiana appare negli ultimi anni del secolo decisamente stimolata dalla scuola a produrre edizioni a commento plurimo che offrissero insieme i frutti dell'antica e della moderna esegesi oraziana: si trattava naturalmente di edizioni decisamente prive di velleità estetiche, anzi modellate sul tradizionale *in folio* da banco e sulla classica pagina bicolonnare che dispone il testo al centro e i commenti ai lati.

E sempre a Venezia usciva per le cure dell'umanista pesarese Giovanni Francesco Superchio nel 1490 dall'officina del mantovano Giorgio Arrivabene il primo Orazio che vedeva affiancati i due commenti antichi a quello del Landino.[17] Qualche anno più tardi vi si sarebbe aggiunto il commento di Antonio Mancinelli, maturato nello Studio romano e dedicato a quel Pomponio Leto che vent'anni prima non aveva favorito la fortuna editoriale dei commenti del Filetico e del Calcillo, ma che ora accoglieva favorevolmente un'esegesi attenta sia all'*artificium* stilistico che al contenuto filosofico, e aliena ormai dal pregiudizio gnomico-pedagogico di ascendenza medievale.[18]

Non potendo ancora contare su una consistente tradizione esegetica, l'editoria germanica si mostra attenta alle prime proposte di sistemazione filologica del *corpus* oraziano. Da questa sensibilità sembra infatti mossa, al volgere del secolo, l'iniziativa tipografica più alta di area germanica, frutto della collaborazione fra un raffinato tipografo di Strasburgo, Johan Grüninger, esponente di spicco della grande scuola silografica alsaziana di fine secolo, e Jacob Locher, poeta laureato e professore a Friburgo: si tratta di una iniziativa che sostituisce alla dovizia esegetica tipicamente italiana, una più accurata sistemazione testuale perseguita attraverso la *recensio* di soli codici tedeschi: insomma, una monumentale edizione nazionale di Orazio, stampata in eleganti caratteri gotici con l'esplicita intenzione di offrire un prodotto di livello alla colta borghesia germanica, al cui mondo e alla cui etica vengono peraltro ricondotti sentenze, costumi, ambienti e figure della Roma oraziana rappresentati nelle centosette splendide silografie dell'antica scuola renana che adornano il libro.[19]

Epistola Bartholomaeo Calco (Milano: Antonio Zarotto, ed. Alessandro Minuziano, [11 III] 1486): Hain-Reichling 8880.

[16] Cf. *Quinti Horatii Flacci Odarum libri quatuor. Epod. Carmen saeculare . . .* (Milano: Alessandro Minuziano, 30 XI 1502): cf. Herbert Mayow Adams, *Catalogue of Books Printed on the Continent of Europe 1501–1600 in Cambridge Libraries* (Cambridge, 1967), 855. In testa al fol. 1r si legge: *Horatius ita emendatus, ut eius interpretes non multum desideres Lector candidissime.*

[17] *Quinti Horatii Flacci Opera*, comm. Acronis et Porphyrionis, Christophori Landini. Praemittitur *tabula postillarum, Johannis Francisci Philomusi epistola, eiusdem carmen ad principem Iohannem Sfortiam* (Venezia: Giorgio Arrivabene, 4 II 1490–1491): Hain-Copinger 8887.

[18] *Quinti Horatii Flacci Opera* [comm. Acron, Porphyrion, Christophorus Landinus, Antonius Mancinellus] (Venezia: Filippo Pinzi, ed. Bernardino Resina, 28 II 1492–1493): Hain-Copinger 8888.

[19] *Quinti Horatii Flacci Opera cum quibusdam annotationibus imaginibusque pulcherrimis aptisque ad*

Anche Aldo Manuzio indirizzava il suo Orazio, all'inizio del nuovo secolo, ad un colto borghese veneziano, Marino Sanudo, emblematico esponente di un nuovo pubblico che si affacciava (o si voleva che si affacciasse) al mercato del libro, assicurandogli un'amena e disimpegnata lettura che l'indaffarato camerlengo avrebbe potuto gustare dovunque grazie ad alcune innovazioni editoriali: l'ottavo come formato, l'italico come carattere, il testo come protagonista assoluto della pagina: insomma, l'enchiridio.[20]

Ma quell'Orazio, che usciva solo un mese dopo il celebre Virgilio "da mano," che aveva segnato una svolta nella storia del libro e della lettura dei classici, e che già recava una dura diffida ai contraffattori lionesi, voleva in realtà andare ben oltre il pur auspicato successo editoriale legato all'innovazione tipografica. La specifica competenza metrico-filologica di Aldo sulla poesia oraziana, documentata da quell'aureo *De metris horatianis*, destinato a imporsi lungo tutto il Cinquecento nel canone esegetico del Venosino, lo induceva infatti a caldeggiare un'edizione dei classici non imbrigliata dai commenti, eppure testualmente plausibile presso quegli umanisti veneziani, rappresentati soprattutto dal Sabellico (col quale non a caso Aldo intrattenne rapporti meno che tiepidi), che ancora guardavano alla stampa come ad una pericolosa corruttrice di testi. Lo stesso carattere italico, apprezzato anche per la capacità di conservare nel procedimento tipografico la preziosa manualità del manoscritto, era una calcolata provocazione verso chi, come alcuni umanisti, disprezzava della stampa proprio la sua "serialità."[21]

A manifestare intanto, all'inizio del nuovo secolo, l'attenuarsi del primato esegetico italiano, era intervenuto il lavoro editoriale di Josse Bade, il cui proposito di confezionare un prodotto scolasticamente spendibile si manifesta nel commento parigino del 1503 alle *Satire* e alle *Epistole*, un commento da lui stesso definito *familiaris* e con dichiarata modestia subordinato a quello *exactissimus* del Mancinelli.[22] In realtà, il filologo fiammingo, che aveva apprezzato Orazio attraverso l'insegnamento di Battista Guarini a Ferrara e l'esercizio filologico di Filippo Beroaldo a Mantova, lavorava sul testo offerto dall'edizione veneziana di Filippo Pinzi del 1492 con modeste

---

odarum conceptus et sententias (Strasbourg: Johan Reinhard Grüninger, Jacob Locher ed., 12 III 1498): Hain-Copinger 8898.

[20] *Horatius* (Venetiis, apud Aldum Romanum, [maggio] 1501): cf. Antoine Augustin Renouard, *Annali delle edizioni Aldine. Con notizie sulla famiglia dei Giunti e repertorio delle loro edizioni fino al 1550 . . .* (Bologna, 1953), 27–28.

[21] Cf. soprattutto Martin Lowry, *The World of Aldus Manutius. Business and Scholarship in Renaissance Venice* (Oxford, 1979), [trad. ital.: *Il mondo di Aldo Manuzio. Affari e cultura nella Venezia del Rinascimento*, ed. Paolo Pavanini (Roma, 1984)]; *Aldo Manuzio editore. Dediche, prefazioni, note ai testi*, introd. di Carlo Dionisotti, testo latino con traduzione e note di Giuseppe Orlandi (Milano, 1975).

[22] *Quinti Horatii Flacci Opera cum exactissima Antonii Mancinelli et familiari Jodoci Badii Ascensii explanatione* (Parisiis: Johannes Petit, ed. Jodocus Badius Ascensius, venundantur in vico divi Iacobi a Dionysio Roce, 18 V–22 IX 1503): cf. Philippe Renouard, *Bibliographie des impressions et des oeuvres de Josse Badius Ascensius, imprimeur et humaniste, 1462–1535* (Paris, 1908; reprint, New York, 1967).

pretese ermeneutiche, che non ne impedirono tuttavia un consistente successo, favorito certo dalle relazioni che seppe tessere con tipografi/editori del calibro di Johann Trechsel e Jean Petit e dal cenacolo di umanisti che seppe costruire intorno a sé: un successo continuatosi lungo tutto il '500 attraverso almeno quaranta fra riedizioni e ristampe.

Ma ancor più indicativo di una sostanziale perdita di peso delle scuole umanistiche italiane, appare qualche decennio dopo l'intervento del filologo francese Marc-Antoine Muret nel restauro che Paolo Manuzio intraprende a metà Cinquecento dell'ormai vetusto Orazio del padre: una serie di proposte di *emendationes* che sarebbero poi confluite negli otto libri di *Variae lectiones* che il Muret pubblicò a Parigi nel 1578.

Questo dimostrava che il mercato editoriale poteva ormai essere movimentato solo con l'offerta di testi filologicamente sempre più affinati. Tale intuizione sembra aver indotto in quegli anni Cristophe Plantin ad accogliere nelle sue officine di Anversa e di Leida un vero e proprio *staff* di filologi chiamato ad attuare un ampio progetto di revisione testuale del *corpus* oraziano. Smantellato l'apparato esegetico di scuola italiana e francese (eccetto il commento metrico di Aldo), Plantin immette sul mercato i nuovi commenti di Teodoro Poelman e di Lieven van der Beken (Torrentius); il prezioso *index* di Thomas Treter; i commenti all'*Ars poetica* di Giovanni Sambuco e dell'olandese Peter Nannius; ma soprattutto il commento di Jacques van Cruick che, recuperando il famoso *Blandinianus vetustissimus*, delinea nel *Commentator Cruquianus* una nuova, per quanto spesso controversa, *recensio* della tradizione manoscritta.[23]

Un tentativo altrettanto poderoso e controverso di sconvolgere la tradizione ermeneutica oraziana avrebbe compiuto, dopo le "deviazioni" (per così dire) moralistiche e parodistiche del Seicento, un secolo e mezzo dopo Richard Bentley nel suo Orazio, spesso (troppo spesso per i suoi detrattori) assoggettato a disinvolte *emendationes ope ingenii*: un estremo frutto, indubbiamente, di una stagione filologica partita proprio dalle sistemazioni, spesso velleitarie, dei filologi cinquecenteschi. Era comunque il preludio ad una nuova prospettiva filologica che avrebbe impegnato numerosi studiosi a partire dalla stagione lachmaniana, grazie ai quali il *corpus* oraziano, insieme a numerosi altri testi di autori classici, latini e greci, conseguì quella forma che solo la filologia novecentesca avrebbe saputo restaurare con ben più maturo metodo.

Università di Bari

---

[23] Cf. rispettivamente: *Quintus Horatius Flaccus Theodori Pulmanni studio curaque emendatus. Aldi Manutii de metris horatianis* (Antuerpiae, ex officina Christophori Plantini, 9 II 1564); *Quintus Horatius Flaccus cum erudito Laevini Torrentii commentario nunc primum in lucem edito. Item Petri Nannii Alcmariani in Artem Poeticam* (Antuerpiae, ex officina Plantiniana, apud Ioannem Moretum, 1608); *Quinti Horatii Flacci Poemata omnia quibus respondet index Thomae Treteri nuper excusus* (Antuerpiae, ex officina Christophori Plantini, 1576); *Ars Poetica Horatii Flacci et in eam paraphrasis et* παρεκβολαι *sive commentariolum Ioannis Sambuci tirnaviensis pannonii* (Antuerpiae, ex officina Christophori Plantini, 1564); *Quintus Horatius Flaccus ex antiquissimis undecim librorum mss. et schedis aliquot emendatus et plurimis locis cum commentariis antiquis expurgatus et editus, opera Jacobi Cruquii Messenii. Eiusdem in eundem enarrationes, observationes et variae lectiones cum aliis quibusdam et indice locupletissimo* (Antuerpiae, ex officina Christophori Plantini, 1578).

L'humaniste allemand
Johannes Caesarius (ca. 1468–1550)

COLETTE JEUDY

D epuis l'excellente notice que lui a consacrée Friedrich August Eckstein en 1876,[1] l'humaniste allemand Johannes Caesarius n'a guère suscité l'intérêt des chercheurs. Seuls certains aspects de sa vie et de son œuvre ont été étudiés avec plus de précision, comme ses relations avec Erasme[2] ou le contenu et l'influence de sa *Dialectica* ou encore ses éditions de l'*Histoire naturelle* de Pline.[3] Mais il nous manque une recension complète de ses œuvres, éditions et commentaires et nous ne savons guère par exemple comment il a appris, puis enseigné le grec. Originaire de Jülich aux Pays-Bas, il a en fait une place à part dans l'humanisme rhénan, par sa formation complétée en France et en Italie, par son enseignement privé, hors des cadres de l'université, auprès des familles princières, et par ses nombreux déplacements. Latiniste et helléniste accompli, il fut aussi médecin et s'intéressa aussi bien aux textes médicaux qu'à la grammaire, à la rhétorique et à la dialectique. Passionné par l'étude des textes antiques et contemporains autant que par l'enseignement du grec et du latin, il a été profondément marqué par l'humanisme italien.

Johannes Caesarius est né à Jülich vers 1468 et mort près de Cologne, le 19 décembre 1550, dans la communauté des Frères de la Vie commune à Weydenbach. Les débuts de sa formation sont mal connus et rien ne prouve qu'il ait été l'élève d'Alexander Hegius à Deventer, où il enseigna lui-même plus tard. Le 9 novembre 1491, il est immatriculé comme *pauper* à la faculté des arts de l'université de Cologne.

---

[1] *Allgemeine deutsche Biographie* (Leipzig, 1876), 3: 689–691; cf. aussi *Neue deutsche Biographie* (Berlin, 1957), 3: 90–91 [Heinrich Grimm]; W. Pökel, *Philologisches Schriftsteller-Lexikon* (Leipzig, 1882; repr. Darmstadt, 1966), 38.

[2] Ilse Guenther, "Johannes Caesarius," in *Contemporaries of Erasmus*, ed. Peter G. Bietenholz et Thomas B. Deutscher (Toronto/Buffalo/London, 1985), 1: 238–239.

[3] Charles G. Nauert, Jr., "Caius Plinius Secundus," in *Catalogus translationum et commentariorum: Mediaeval and Renaissance Latin Translations and Commentaries*, ed. F. Edward Cranz et Paul Oskar Kristeller (Washington, D.C., 1980), 4: 363–367.

Il poursuivit ses études à Paris auprès de l'humaniste français Jacques Lefèvre d'Etaples, qui lui apprit entre autres la philosophie aristotélicienne. Bachelier en 1496, maître-ès-arts en 1498, il enseigna en 1508 à Deventer, où il fut aussi correcteur de l'imprimeur Richard Pafraet. En décembre 1508, il partit pour Rome avec le jeune comte Hermann de Neuenahr, dont il était précepteur, lors d'une mission pour confirmer l'élection de l'archevêque Philipp von Dhaun. A cette occasion, il passa en 1509 un certain temps à Bologne, où il approfondit sa connaissance de la langue grecque au point d'être considéré comme le fondateur des études grecques dans la région du bas Rhin et en Westphalie. A son retour, en 1510, il commença à enseigner le grec et le latin à Cologne, mais à titre privé. Comme il n'avait pas de poste officiel, il put voyager et professer à différents endroits tout en gardant Cologne comme base. Il put ainsi retourner en Italie, à l'université de Sienne, où il obtint son doctorat en médecine le 12 octobre 1513.[4] En 1518–1519 il était à Münster à cause de la peste, en 1527 à Leipzig auprès de Melchior Lotter et l'hiver suivant à Königstein et à Stolberg dans la famille des comtes de Stolberg. En 1529, il retourna à Mayence, où il était déjà présent en 1524. Mais il passa l'essentiel de son temps à Cologne, où son enseignement était très renommé. Parmi ses élèves, on peut citer: Heinrich Glareanus, qui lui dédia en 1515 son panégyrique de l'empereur Maximilien 1er, Peter Mosellanus, qui lui dédia sa traduction du *Plutos* d'Aristophane, Agrippa von Nettesheim, Gerhard Listrius et le Suisse Heinrich Bullinger. Très apprécié des familles nobles, il fut aussi précepteur de plusieurs jeunes comtes auxquels il dédia certaines de ses œuvres et auxquels il était très attaché, comme le prouvent les lettres de dédicace: les comtes de Solm, Wied, Isenburg, Stolberg et Neunahr. Ces deux dernières familles assurèrent sa subsistance à la fin de sa vie. En 1548 il entra dans la communauté des Frères de la Vie commune à Weydenbach, près de Cologne, où il mourut le 19 décembre 1550.

Pendant sa longue vie, il fut en étroite relation et en active correspondance avec bon nombre d'humanistes de son époque, particulièrement avec Erasme depuis 1515. Ce dernier lui dédia sa traduction de la grammaire grecque de Théodore Gaza.[5] Caesarius se lia d'amitié avec plusieurs réformateurs, dont Spalatinus, Johann Lange d'Erfurt, Melanchthon et Heinrich Bullinger, dont il étudia attentivement les écrits exégétiques à la fin de sa vie. Fervent défenseur de Johann Reuchlin aux côtés d'Erasme, il témoigna par la suite sa sympathie aux réformateurs, tout en restant dans l'église traditionnelle. Une étude approfondie de sa correspondance, dont une partie est encore inédite, permettrait peut-être d'en savoir plus sur l'évolution de son attitude face à la Réforme.

Il était nécessaire de retracer brièvement sa vie pour mieux comprendre l'œuvre qu'il nous a laissée.[6] Voici comment le qualifie son disciple Heinrich Glareanus en

---

[4] Document conservé aux archives archiépiscopales de Sienne, cf. Gustav C. Knod, *Deutsche Studenten in Bologna* (Strasbourg, 1899), 83 n° 571.

[5] *Opus epistolarum Des. Erasmi Roterodami*, ed. P. S. Allen, 12 vols. (Oxford, 1906–1958), 2: 264–266 (*Ep.* 428) et 3: 214–215 (*Ep.* 771).

[6] Dans les catalogues de bibliothèques, il y a encore parfois confusion avec l'humaniste italien

lui dédiant en 1515 à Bâle son Panégyrique de l'empereur Maximilien 1er: "physicus, mathematicus, medicinae doctor, graecaeque latinaeque linguae apprime doctus."[7] Certes il est d'abord enseignant et pédagogue, mais depuis son séjour à Sienne, il est aussi médecin et a pratiqué occasionnellement la médecine. D'où son intérêt pour les auteurs médicaux classiques et contemporains, pour lesquels il a établi une édition souvent commentée. Dans son œuvre, éditions de textes et manuels personnels sont indissociables comme deux volets de son enseignement. Aussi l'*Index Aureliensis*[8] nous donne-t-il un aperçu complètement tronqué de l'activité littéraire de Caesarius en ne relevant que les œuvres considérées comme personnelles (*Dialectica, Rhetorica, Compendiaria artis grammaticae*) sans faire de renvois aux éditions d'auteurs. Malgré sa brièveté, la notice du répertoire intitulé *L'Europe des humanistes*[9] sera un utile complèment, mettant bien en lumière cet aspect important de la production des humanistes. Pour être complet il faudrait aussi examiner les impressions successives d'un même ouvrage car elles comportent souvent des modifications et des additions de Caesarius lui-même, et elles sont le reflet d'un enseignement vivant et d'une étude des textes constamment renouvelée. Essayons au moins, pour le moment, de dresser une liste de ses différentes œuvres en suivant l'ordre chronologique et en passant plus rapidement, faute de temps, sur celles qui sont mieux connues par des travaux récents.

Ses premières éditions découlent de l'enseignement qu'il a suivi à Paris auprès de Lefèvre d'Etaples. Dès 1500, il fit imprimer par Jakob van Breda à Deventer l'introduction de Lefèvre d'Etaples à l'*Ethique* d'Aristote, intitulée *Ars moralis philosophiae* ou *Epitome in moralem philosophiam*.[10] En 1504 suivit le *Fundamentum logicae* ou *Introductio in terminorum cognitionem in libros Logicorum Aristotelis* de Josse Clichthove,[11] qui expliquait la philosophie aristotélicienne à Paris en même temps que l'humaniste français. Ce manuel fut d'abord imprimé à Deventer par Richard Pafraet avec une *declaratio* de Johannes Caesarius, qui avait été utilisé comme correcteur. Il fut réimprimé en 1534 à Paris par Christian Wechel,[12] avec un commentaire de Caesarius intercalé

Giovanni Paolo Cesario de Cosenza (Janus Caesarius Consentinus), né dans la première moitié du 16ᵉ siècle et mort probablement à Rome après 1570. Cf. *Dizionario biografico degli Italiani* (Roma, 1980), 24: 211–213 [M. Vigilante]; E. Giordano, "Giano Cesario," in *La cultura umanistica nell'Italia meridionale*, ed. P. A. De Lisio (Napoli, 1981), 123–136.

[7] Ed. Basileae, par J. Parcum, 1554. Cf. Fritz Büsser, "Glareanus, Heinrich," in *Contemporaries of Erasmus* (Toronto, 1986), 2: 105–108.

[8] *Index Aureliensis. Catalogus librorum sedecimo saeculo impressorum*. Prima pars. Tomus VI (Aureliae Aquensis: 1976), 142–151.

[9] *L'Europe des humanistes* (XIVᵉ–XVIᵉ siècles). Répertoire établi par Jean-François Maillard, Judith Kecskeméti et Monique Portalier avec la collaboration de Thérèse Redier (Paris, 1995).

[10] Cf. le titre de l'exemplaire acquis par la British Library: *Short-Title Catalogue of Books Printed in the Netherlands and Belgium and of Dutch and Flemish Books Printed in Other Countries from 1470 to 1600 now in the British Museum* (London, 1965), 124.

[11] Cf. *Index Aureliensis* I, 9 (Aureliae Aquensis, 1991), 121 n°. 141.769.

[12] Avec une lettre de dédicace à Servatius Aedicollius (Huyslberch) originaire de Cologne. Cf. Gabriella Mezzanotte, "Una nuova testimonianza della fortuna petrarchesca nei Paesi Bassi," *Humanistica Lovaniensia* 29 (1980), 166–171.

après chaque définition de terme aristotélicien donnée par Clichthove. Vers 1507, Caesarius fit paraître à Cologne un autre commentaire de Lefèvre d'Etaples, l'*Introductio in arithmeticam Boecii.*

C'est aussi par Richard Pafraet à Deventer qu'il fit imprimer en 1506 les *Epîtres* d'Horace. Particulièrement renommé pour ses éditions d'auteurs classiques en collaboration avec Alexander Hegius, Pafraet avait déjà publié en 1488 et 1490 l'*Ars poetica* d'Horace.[13] Caesarius choisit les *Epîtres* pour leur contenu moral, comme l'exprime clairement le titre même de l'édition, à mettre sans doute en parallèle avec celui de Lefèvre d'Etaples pour l'*Ethique* d'Aristote: *Institutio moralis philosophiae metrica.* Chaque épître est précédée d'un *argumentum* analysant brièvement son contenu. Une deuxième édition suivit à Cologne en 1523 par l'imprimeur Johann Soter, dédiée à Anton et Salentin von Isenburg, dont Caesarius était alors précepteur.[14]

Dès 1507, il participa à l'impression de la *Consolatio philosophiae* de Boèce par Albrecht Pafraet à Deventer. Mais c'est seulement en 1535 qu'il en donna une nouvelle édition améliorée, accompagnée du commentaire de Johannes Murmellius et de celui de Rudolf Agricola partiellement.[15] Dans une présentation claire et élégante, sortie des presses d'Eucharius Cervicornus à Cologne, le texte de Boèce alterne avec les commentaires, en plus petits caractères et indiqués en marge par les abréviations "JOHAN. MUR." et "RODOL. AGRICO." Les vers cités par Murmellius dans son commentaire sont encore dans une typographie différente et les mots commentés sont repris en marge. Seul le commentaire de Murmellius recouvre les cinq livres de la *Consolatio*, celui d'Agricola s'arrête à la fin du premier livre. Selon la nouvelle orientation donnée en Allemagne dès 1514–1516 à la diffusion de la *Consolation* de Boèce, les commentaires de Murmellius et de Rudolf Agricola ont remplacé le commentaire sans grand intérêt du Pseudo Thomas d'Aquin, associé précédemment au commentaire plus humaniste et plus littéraire de Josse Bade.[16] Nous avons conservé au moins six exemplaires de cette édition de Caesarius.

C'est encore à Cologne dans l'imprimerie de Cervicornus que parut en 1520 le manuel de dialectique qui lui assura une grande renommée à travers l'Europe.[17] Plus de soixante-dix éditions se sont succédé jusqu'à la fin du XVIᵉ siècle. Les centres les plus importants sont, dans l'ordre décroissant, Cologne, Lyon, Venise, Mayence, Cracovie, Paris (six éditions imprimées entre 1530 et 1539) et Leipzig. Suivant l'exemple de son maître Lefèvre d'Etaples, il divisa sa *Dialectique* en dix traités, qui

---

[13] Cf. Miroslav Flodr, *Incunabula classicorum. Wiegendrucke der griechischen und römischen Literatur* (Amsterdam, 1973), 192.

[14] Cf. Konrad Wiedemann, "Anton and Salentin von Isenburg," in *Contemporaries of Erasmus* (Toronto, 1986), 2: 228.

[15] Cf. *Index Aureliensis* I, 4 (Aureliae Aquensis, 1970), 438 nᵒ. 121.097.

[16] Cf. Pierre Courcelle, *La Consolation de Philosophie dans la tradition littéraire. Antécédents et postérité de Boèce* (Paris, 1967), 322–332.

[17] *Index Aureliensis* I, 6 (Aureliae Aquensis, 1976), 142–151; Wilhelm Risse, *Bibliographia logica. Verzeichnis der Druckschriften zur Logik* (Hildesheim, 1965) 1: 243 et passim. Liste complétée par Peter Mack dans son Ph.D. du Warburg Institute, University of London: "Rudolf Agricola and Renaissance Dialectic," 1983, 312–314.

respectent fidèlement l'*Organon* d'Aristote. La liste des autorités qu'il invoque est impressionnante et elle change au cours des différentes éditions. On relève le nom de plusieurs humanistes: Giorgio Trapezuntio, Hegius, Rudolf Agricola, Lorenzo Valla, Giorgio Valla, Erasme, Linacrius, Lefèvre d'Etaples, Clichthove, mais aussi à la fin, celui du célèbre logicien de l'université de Paris au XIVe siècle: Jean Buridan. Son manuel est cependant assez traditionnel et utilise beaucoup Cicéron, Boèce et Marius Victorinus, comme le montrent l'analyse détaillée de Cesare Vasoli[18] et les travaux récents de Peter Mack.[19] Caesarius améliore à plusieurs reprises ce manuel dont l'étude fut vivement recommandée par Melanchthon en même temps que celle de Rudolf Agricola.

En 1524 Caesarius confia toujours au même imprimeur son édition complète de la *Naturalis Historia* de Pline l'Ancien, d'abord en un volume in-folio, puis en format octavo avec division en sept parties, chacune précédée d'un bref résumé du contenu des cinq livres qu'elle renferme. Dédiée au comte Hermann de Neunahr, son élève et mécène, devenu le plus célèbre des chanoines humanistes de Cologne,[20] l'édition est accompagnée, surtout dans les vingt premiers livres, de scolies marginales abondantes et prétend améliorer considérablement le texte de Pline en corrigeant les conjectures et les erreurs introduites depuis les *Castigationes* d'Ermolao Barbaro. Elle s'inscrit dans tout le mouvement humaniste de controverses philologiques qui s'est développé autour de l'*Histoire naturelle* de Pline.[21] Bien que réputée à Cologne, l'édition de Caesarius fut vite dépassée. Ses commentaires séparés du livre II en 1536 et surtout des livres IX et XXXII en 1534 méritent plus d'attention.

En 1525 il rassembla pour ses trois élèves, les comtes Heinrich, Philipp et Eberhard de Stolberg-Werniguerode,[22] trois petits traités de grammaire antique. Ce recueil fut imprimé par Peter Quentell à Cologne sous le titre: "Compendiaria artis grammaticae institutio per Johannem Caesarium nuper congesta, autoribus cum primis Aspero iuniore, Aelio Donato et Phoca, cum epitome de constructione partium orationis."[23] Après une longue lettre de dédicace vient d'abord le petit traité du pseudo Asper,[24] de structure antique, avec ses quatre chapitres *De arte*, *De littera*, *De syllaba*, *De pedibus* précédant les parties du discours. De nombreuses divisions à visée

---

[18] Cesare Vasoli, "Ricerche sulle *Dialettiche* del Cinquecento," *Rivista critica di storia della filosofia* 20 (1965), 132–150 et 451.

[19] P. Mack, "Valla's Dialectic in the North. 2: Further Commentaries," *Vivarium* 30,2 (1992), 268–270; *Renaissance Argument. Valla and Agricola in the Traditions of Rhetorik and Dialectic* (Leiden/ New York/Köln, 1993), 292–300 et passim.

[20] Cf. Justus Hashagen, "Hauptrichtungen des rheinischen Humanismus," *Annalen des Historischen Vereins für den Niederrhein* 106 (1922), 30–31.

[21] Cf. Charles G. Nauert Jr., "Caius Plinius Secundus" (*supra* n. 3), 297–422.

[22] Article entitled "Heinrich von Stolberg," in *Allgemeine deutsche Biographie* (Leipzig, 1893), 36: 335–339 [Jacobs].

[23] *Index Aureliensis* I, 6 (Aureliae Aquensis, 1976), 142 n°. 128.885, 143 n°. 128.887 et 128.892.

[24] Ed. Heinrich Keil, in *Grammatici latini* 5 (Leipzig, 1868), 547–554. A ne pas confondre avec *Asper minor*, grammaire irlandaise du VIIe s.

pédagogique en facilitent la lecture et Caesarius a parfois intercalé quelques scolies annoncées par un pied de mouche et imprimées différemment.[25] Après suit le livre II de l'*Ars maior* de Donat sur les huit parties du discours dans une présentation analogue. Enfin l'*Ars* de Phocas,[26] grammairien à Rome au début du Ve siècle, sur le nom et le verbe. Caesarius est particulièrement élogieux envers Phocas, peut-être à cause de son nom et de son intérêt pour les mots grecs. Il a mis beaucoup de soin à la correction du texte, à sa présentation et à sa division en chapitres. Il a ajouté plus de quatre-vingt-dix scolies, certaines assez longues, qui révèlent bien la personnalité de leur auteur. A côté de Priscien et de Diomède, il invoque beaucoup de poètes classiques, mais aussi Pline, Celse, Quintus Serenus Sammonicus et le *De arboribus* de Columelle. En appendice figurent quelques chapitres sur les supins et sur les règles de syntaxe, extraites des *Rudimenta grammatices* de Niccolò Perotti.[27] Ce recueil grammatical fut réimprimé à Leipzig en 1527, à Deventer en 1529 et à Freiburg-im-Breisgau en 1533 avec quelques modifications et davantage de scolies pour Phocas.

En juillet 1526 il dédia de nouveau au comte Heinrich von Stolberg une édition de la grammaire de Diomède, suivie de l'*Ars maior* de Donat dans sa totalité, qu'il fit imprimer à Haguenau par Johann Soter. En 1527 Josse Bade fit sortir à Paris une nouvelle édition pourvue en tête de six pages d'annotations émanant à la fois de lui-même (elles sont indiquées par l'abréviation "Ascen.") et de Caesarius (abrégé "Ces.").[28] Elles sont beaucoup plus abondantes pour Donat que pour Diomède et renvoient successivement aux textes des deux grammairiens et à la pagination en reprenant les lemmes. Eckstein reproche à Caesarius d'avoir suivi pour Diomède les remaniements d'Hermann von dem Busche sans recourir aux manuscrits et l'accuse d'être plus un interpolateur qu'un éditeur. En fait, même encore actuellement, nous manquons d'une véritable édition critique et celle de Caesarius fut imprimée plusieurs fois en 1533, en 1536 et à Leipzig en 1541, sans doute parce que le texte de Diomède était rare en Allemagne.

En 1527 et 1528, Caesarius consacra son activité aux œuvres médicales aussi bien antiques que contemporaines. Il fit d'abord imprimer à Cologne par Eucharius Cervicornus deux traités d'anatomie italiens de la fin du siècle précédent: l'*Anatomice siue Historia corporis humani* d'Alessandro Benedetti (ca. 1450–1512) et le *De humanae faciei, corporis partibus* de Giorgio della Valle (ca. 1430–1499). Célèbre surtout pour le journal qu'il écrivit pendant la campagne des Vénitiens contre le roi de France

---

[25] La première édition par Lorenzo Astemio à Fani en 1503 était sans commentaire ni scolies.

[26] Ed. Keil, in *Grammatici latini* 5, 410–439. L'*Ars* fut imprimée pour la première fois à Milan en 1473 par Zaroto, sans commentaire ni scolies. Cf. Colette Jeudy, "L'*Ars de nomine et verbo* de Phocas: manuscrits et commentaires médiévaux," *Viator* 5 (1974), 61–156.

[27] Comme les scolies de Phocas, les extraits de Perotti mériteraient une étude approfondie. Sur la diffusion des *Rudimenta Grammatices* en Allemagne, cf. Keith Percival, "The Influence of Perotti's Rudimenta in the Cinquecento," in *Protrepticon* (Mélanges G. Secchi Tarugi) (Milano, 1989), 91–100; Jean-Louis Charlet, "Préoccupations pédagogiques dans les *Rudimenta Grammatices* de Niccolò Perotti," in *L'Educazione e la formazione intellettuale nell'età dell'Umanesimo* (Milano, 1992), 206–215.

[28] Philippe Renouard, *Imprimeurs et libraires parisiens du XVIe siècle* (Paris, 1969), 2: 241 n°. 590.

Charles VIII en 1495, Benedetti est aussi le fondateur de l'école d'anatomie de Padoue. Ses leçons étaient suivies par un large public, dont Ermolao Barbaro et l'empereur Maximilien 1er, auquel il dédia l'*Anatomice*. Décrivant essentiellement les lésions anatomiques provoquées par les différentes maladies, il développa les connaissances anatomo-pathologiques et souhaitait étendre la pratique de l'autopsie, alors limitée aux cadavres des condamnés. L'*Historia corporis humani*, la plus importante de ses œuvres, fut largement diffusée de son vivant en Italie et hors d'Italie et longtemps après sa mort. Imprimée dès 1493 à Venise, elle fut réimprimée plusieurs fois à Venise, à Paris et à Strasbourg. Caesarius en donna la première édition allemande avec quelques brèves scolies et avec l'opuscule de Giorgio della Valle sur le même sujet, en complément.[29]

En 1528 l'humaniste allemand se tourna vers les auteurs médiévaux antiques et fit imprimer à Haguenau par Johann Setzer les huit livres du *De re medica* de Celse. Deux opuscules accompagnent cette grande œuvre: le *De medicina praecepta saluberrima*, poème de Quintus Serenus Sammonicus, et le *De ponderibus et mensuris* de Remius Favinus. Comme il l'avait déjà fait pour la grammaire, il dédia ces trois traités aux trois frères de la famille von Stolberg: Celse à Ludwig, Quintus Serenus à Heinrich et le *De ponderibus et mensuris* à Albrecht. L'édition est pourvue de scolies abondantes, portant essentiellement sur l'explication des mots et renvoyant aussi bien aux auteurs classiques qu'aux contemporains. Réimprimée par Johann Soter à Solingen en 1538, l'édition de Caesarius servit souvent de base aux éditions suivantes.[30] Séparés de Celse, les deux opuscules ont été repris plusieurs fois, notamment par Simon Coline à Paris en 1533.

Etroitement liée à la dialectique, comme le voulait Aristote, la *Rhetorica* de Caesarius, sortie en 1534 à Cologne des presses de Johann von Aich, ne connut pas le même succès que sa *Dialectica*. Mais elle fut quand même réimprimée une bonne douzaine de fois,[31] notamment à Leipzig, où il avait enseigné, et à Paris. Dédié à deux de ses élèves Anton von Schauenburg et Johann von Wied, ce manuel divisé en sept *tractatus* est bien construit et bien écrit. Il est assez traditionnel et suit surtout Cicéron, Quintilien et Aristote. Dans la liste d'auteurs préliminaire, figurent aussi des contemporains, Melanchthon, pour lequel il avait une grande admiration, Giorgio Trapezunzio et Francesco Maturanzo.[32]

La même année 1534, Caesarius fit imprimer à Strasbourg, par Jakob Cammerlander, deux recueils de textes scientifiques. Le premier rassemble la traduction latine par Laurentius Lippius Collensis en 1478, de l'*Halieutika* d'Oppianos, poème didactique sur la pêche, puis les livres 9 et 32 de l'*Histoire naturelle* de Pline, consacrés aux animaux aquatiques. Il s'achève par le *De piscibus Romanis*, petit traité composé

[29] *Index Aureliensis* I, 3 (Aureliae Aquensis, 1968), 531–532 n°. 116.597; M. Crespi, "Benedetti, Alessandro," in *Dizionario biografico degli Italiani* (Roma, 1966), 8: 244–247.

[30] *Index Aureliensis* I, 7 (Aureliae Aquensis, 1982), 274 n°. 135.093 et 275 n°. 135.097; Ludwig Choulant, *Handbuch der Bücherkunde für die ältere Medicin* (Leipzig, 1841), 169.

[31] *Index Aureliensis* I, 6 (Aureliae Aquensis, 1976), 143–148.

[32] Voir les études de C. Vasoli et P. Mack, citées *supra* nn. 18 et 19.

en 1524 sur le même sujet par l'humaniste de Côme, Paolo Giovio. La traduction latine d'Oppianos est précédée de la *Vita Oppiani* du traducteur et accompagnée de ses arguments en vers. Pour les livres 9 et 32 de Pline, Caesarius a ajouté un abondant commentaire marginal, considérablement enrichi par rapport aux notes de l'édition complète de l'*Histoire naturelle* de 1524. Il a intercalé aussi quelques scolies dans le texte de Paolo Giovio.[33] Cet ensemble, qui se complète heureusement, montre bien l'intérêt pour le vocabulaire concernant les poissons qui pose effectivement de nombreux problèmes de morphologie et de sémantique.

Le deuxième recueil est consacré à la médecine et réunit l'*Isagoge Johannitii in artem parvam Galeni*[34] et les deux petites œuvres laissées par un médecin de l'école de Salerne, Copho: l'*Ars medendi*, compendium de thérapie générale, et l'*Anatome porci*, qui permettait de mieux comprendre l'anatomie humaine à travers la dissection du porc.[35]

En 1536 Caesarius reprit partiellement son travail sur l'*Histoire naturelle* de Pline pour rééditer le livre II. Il n'est pas étonnant qu'il ait tenté d'approfondir la cosmologie plinienne. Il a ajouté les *Castigationes primae et secundae* d'Ermolao Barbaro ainsi que quelques annotations personnelles plus brèves et des remarques sur le style de Pline. A part quelques petits changements, cette réédition n'apporte que peu de modification ou d'enrichissement dans le commentaire.[36]

La même année, il fit imprimer à Cologne par Gottfried Hittorp, dans l'officine d'Eucharius Cervicornus, les sept livres des *Histoires* d'Orose contre les païens: *Adversus paganos*. La version définitive de cette histoire universelle fut composée à Carthage en 416–417. C'est un des ouvrages les plus répandus dans les bibliothèques médiévales et l'*editio princeps*, datée de 1471, a été suivie de beaucoup d'autres à la fin du XVe et au cours du XVIe siècle.[37] Caesarius a dédié la sienne à un membre de la famille des comtes de Wittgenstein, Georg a Seina, et il dit avoir collationné plusieurs manuscrits, qu'il ne décrit pas malheureusement. Le texte d'Orose est précédé de la *Vita Orosii* de Gennade de Marseille.

En 1537 il revint à la médecine avec le *Compendium* ou *Collectorium fere totius medicinae* de Niccolò Bertuccio[38] sorti des presses de Melchior von Neuss à Cologne. Niccolò Bertuccio, mort à Bologne en 1347, était titulaire de la chaire d'anatomie de l'université. Son traité systématique sur les différentes maladies, leurs symptômes, leur

---

[33] Joseph Benzing, *Die Drucke Jakobs Cammerlanders zu Strassburg 1531–1548* (Wien/Zürich, 1963), 25 n°. 85; Jean Ritter, *Bibliographie strasbourgeoise* (Baden-Baden, 1985), 2: 348 n°. 25.

[34] Cf. Danièle Jacquart, "A l'aube de la Renaissance médicale des XIe–XIIe siècles: l'*Isagoge Johannitii* et son traducteur," *Bibliothèque de l'Ecole des Chartes* 144 (1986), 209–240.

[35] J. Benzing, *Drucke Jacobs* (*supra* n. 33), 18 n°. 51; J. Ritter, *Bibliographie* (*supra* n. 33), 2: 347 n°. 20.

[36] Cf. C. G. Nauert, Jr., "Caius Plinius Secundus" (*supra* n. 3), 365–366.

[37] Ed. Karl Zangemeister, *Corpus scriptorum ecclesiasticorum latinorum*, vol. 5 (Wien, 1882; repr. Leipzig, 1889); *Orose. Histoires (Contre les Païens)* éd. et trans. Marie-Pierre Arnaud-Lindet (Paris, 1990). Elles ne mentionnent pas l'édition de Caesarius.

[38] M. Crespi, "Bertuccio, Nicola," in *Dizionario biografico degli Italiani* (Roma, 1967), 9: 651; George Sarton, *Introduction to the History of Science* (Baltimore, 1947), 3: 847–848.

prognostic et leur traitement, avait été imprimé deux fois à Lyon, en 1509 et 1518. Caesarius affirme en avoir considérablement amélioré le texte et son édition, la première en Allemagne, eut beaucoup de succès. Nous en conservons au moins treize exemplaires.[39]

Cette présentation rapide et certainement incomplète de l'activité littéraire de Johannes Caesarius montre bien la nécessité de consacrer bientôt une bonne monographie à cet humaniste allemand que Justus Hashagen, à la suite de Krafft, considérait comme la personnalité la plus éminente de l'humanisme rhénan.[40]

CNRS / Institut de recherche et d'histoire des textes

---

[39] *Index Aureliensis* I, 4 (Aureliae Aquensis, 1970), 123 n°. 118.112.

[40] "Die hervorragendste Erscheinung des rheinischen Humanismus," J. Hashagen, "Hauptrichtungen" (*supra* n. 20), 37. Caesarius est aussi l'auteur d'un poème saphique en l'honneur de Georgius Sibutus, qui figure en tête de l'édition de l'*Ars memorativa* de ce dernier. Cf. *infra*, la communication du professeur Johann Ramminger.

The Impact of the
Italian Poetic Tradition in Lithuania

RASA JURGELĖNAITĖ

A fter the Grand Duchy of Lithuania was Christianized in the late fourteenth
through the early fifteenth centuries, political and cultural relations between
Lithuania and Italy, as well as with other West European countries, became more and
more intensive. Thanks to these relations, Renaissance ideas first reached Lithuania.
The Latin language began to establish its position as a language of science and lit-
erature, and even as an official language of correspondence of the court side by side
with the old Byelorussian. In the late fifteenth century, as in most other European
countries, a theory of the Roman origin of the Lithuanian nobility appears in the
Lithuanian annals.[1] One of the most prominent humanists of the time, Michalo
Lituanus (1490–1560), proposed to declare Latin an official language of the Grand
Duchy of Lithuania, on the ground that ". . . idioma Ruthenorum alienum sit a nobis
Lituanis, hoc est, Italianis, Italico sanguine oriundis."[2]

The first elementary schools based on the teaching of Latin were opened in the
Grand Duchy of Lithuania in the late fourteenth century.[3] In 1447, noblemen of the
Grand Duchy were granted permission to travel to foreign countries without restriction, and this was signified by the increasing number of students from Lithuania in the
universities of Europe.[4] Young men from the Grand Duchy of Lithuania from the late
fourteenth till the early sixteenth centuries would most frequently continue their
studies in the nearest higher school—the University of Cracow, established in 1364.
Though in the late fifteenth and early sixteenth centuries humanistic ideas found
intensive manifestation in the cultural life of Cracow University, teaching standards

---

[1] Mečislovas Jučas, *Lietuvos metraščiai* (Vilnius, 1968), 57.

[2] Michalo Lituanus, *De moribus tartarorum, lituanorum et moschorum* (Basileae, 1615), 23.

[3] Saulius Sužiedėlis, "Švietimas Didžiojoje Lietuvos Kunigaikštijoje," *Lietuvių enciklopedija*, vol.
15 (Vilnius, 1990), 744–745.

[4] Adolfas Šapoka, "Kur senovėje lietuviai mokslo ieškojo," in Vaclovas Biržiška, ed., *Lietuvos
studentai užsienio universitetuose XIV–XVIII amžiais* (Chicago, 1987), 23.

did not satisfy students from Lithuania.[5] Therefore, very often young men from Lithuania continued their studies in the universities of Leipzig, Leiden, Heidelberg, Munich, Geneva, Basel, Ingolstadt, and others.[6] However, the universities of Italy were an especially important and desirable part of their academic pilgrimage. According to the latest research, which is far from complete yet, from the late fourteenth till the late seventeenth centuries, there were matriculated in the universities of Italy sixty-nine students in the University of Padua, eleven in Bologna, thirteen in Rome, and three in Siena.[7]

Almost all the humanists who made a contribution to Latin poetry written in the Grand Duchy of Lithuania either studied in Italy at some point in their careers or sojourned there, sometimes for substantial periods of time, as academic travelers, members of church entourages, or diplomats. The humanism that developed in the Grand Duchy of Lithuania, as well as in the whole Commonwealth of Poland and Lithuania (declared in 1569), was nourished from the same sources as the western European movement and shared the same sense of cosmopolitanism and universality.

During the sixteenth and early seventeenth centuries in the Grand Duchy of Lithuania there were two significant centres where Latin humanistic poetry was created. The first were the literary circles surrounding the court of the grand duke of Lithuania in Vilnius. In the late fifteenth and early sixteenth centuries at the court of the grand duke Alexander (1492–1506), there was already established a humanistic Latin milieu. The Lithuanian connection with the West, and particularly with Italy, was strengthened by the presence of the court of the Milanese princess Bona Sforza (1494–1557), who became queen of Poland in 1518. Her son, grand duke of Lithuania Sigismundus Augustus (1520–1572), moved to Vilnius in 1544 and later on, already as king of Poland, he spent more time there than in Cracow. Sigismundus Augustus was the owner of a great collection of works of art and a valuable library, and the court at that time was frequented by numerous painters, architects, and musicians from Italy. Scientific disputations and recitations of poetry, mostly written in Latin, as well as luxurious festivities in honor of significant dates or deeds of the members of the grand duke's family or his retinue, took place in the palace at Vilnius.[8] Humanist circles, the most prominent of which was at the court of the grand duke Sigismundus Augustus, were created out of the humanists' sense of membership in an elite community of like-minded people who had a common Latin tongue that blunted national differences.

Later on, when the Jesuit Academy was established in Vilnius in 1579, a solid foundation for a poetical school of high standards was laid there. The Academy had the traditional structure of a humanistic school, a philological education—the *studia*

---

[5] Marcelinas Ročka, "Lietuvių studentai Krokuvos universitete ir humanizmo pradžia Lietuvoje," *Literatūra* 9 (Vilnius, 1966): 68.

[6] Šapoka, op. cit., 24–30.

[7] Vaclovas Biržiška, *Lietuvos studentai užsienio universitetuose XIV–XVIII amžiais* (Chicago, 1987), 163, 166, 170–173.

[8] Jurgis Jurginis, Vytautas Merkys, Adolfas Tautavičius, *Vilniaus miesto istorija* (Vilnius, 1968), 116–117.

humaniora consisted of classes in grammar, poetics, and rhetoric, and were based on the studies of ancient, mainly Latin, texts.[9] New aesthetic ideas and changes in literary fashion reached Vilnius very fast and were at once presented in the courses by the professors of the Academy. Professors of the Academy as well as students wrote and published verses in Latin, mostly occasional poetry. So it is evident that both centres where humanistic Latin literature was created were located in the capital of the Grand Duchy of Lithuania—the city of Vilnius—the place where the society of the multinational Grand Duchy had opened itself to the world.

Travelling through Italy as well as through the whole of Europe, the humanists from the Grand Duchy bought and ordered books. The most copious collection of books, containing writings in classical Greek and Latin, as well as books of contemporary European humanists, was in the court of Sigismundus Augustus in Vilnius Castle. In the late sixteenth century there were about 4,000 volumes in the collection, which later on were donated to a newly-established Vilnius Academy.[10] The families of the most prominent noblemen of the Grand Duchy: Radivilus, Chodkevicius, Sapieha, Pac, collected books in their palaces as well. The young nobleman Ioannes Sapieha expressed his passion for Italian culture by signing his books in Italy as "Giovanni Sapieha."[11] Though the catalogs of all these libraries are not available now, it is possible to maintain that in almost all personal libraries there were the most famous books of Italian humanists, such as *Il Principe* by Niccolò Machiavelli, *Oratio de hominis dignitate* by Giovanni Pico della Mirandola, *De viris illustribus* and *De remediis utriusque Fortunae* by Francesco Petrarch, *Il Cortegiano* by Baldassare Castiglione, etc. We can clearly see the influence of this entire genre of tractates on the publicistic writings of the humanists of the Grand Duchy of Lithuania, disputing questions of politics and religion, as well in the verse poems written by them.

As regards works of poetry, the most popular at the time after the verses of Francesco Petrarch were the books of verses by Giovanni Pontano. For instance, a manuscript of the reminiscences of one clergyman from the Grand Duchy, where he describes his pilgrimage through the holy places, churches, and monasteries of Italy, includes a large list of books he had brought from Italy. It contains mostly works by the Fathers of the Church, a few books by classical Greek and Latin authors, and a volume of verses by Giovanni Pontano.[12]

Turning our attention to the Latin poetry written in the Grand Duchy of Lithuania, we should indicate that rare indeed was the humanist for whom poetry was more than a welcome respite from concerns of church and state, politics and diplomacy, science and learning. One of the most prominent humanistic figures, who

[9] Levas Vladimirovas, "400 metų kultūros, švietimo ir mokslo tarnyboje," *Kultūros kryžkelėje* (Vilnius, 1970), 8.

[10] Ludwik Piechnik, *Pochątki Academii Wileńskiej 1570–1599* (Rzym, 1984), 206–214.

[11] Levas Vladimirovas, *Knygos istorija: Senovė. Viduramžiai. Renesansas. XVI–XVII amžiai* (Vilnius, 1979), 508.

[12] *Catalogus librorum spiritualium tam in lingua latina quam italica.* VUB RS F3-1095.

spent about twenty years living in the Grand Duchy of Lithuania, was the Spaniard Petrus Roysius Maureus (or Pedro Ruiz de Moros, 1505–1571). After his studies in the universities of Bologna, Padua, Venice, Florence, and Rome, the doctor of law Petrus Roysius became a professor at Cracow University. A few years later he moved to the Grand Duchy of Lithuania where he became legal adviser to the grand duke Sigismundus Augustus and took part in the writing of the Second Statute of Lithuania (1566). He took up his duties as priest of the church of the small town of Kražiai, and later on, as priest of the church of St. John in Vilnius, was one of the teachers in the school of this church.[13] In spite of his numerous duties, Petrus Roysius became famous as a poet who wrote mostly satires and epigrams taunting the vices, failings, and weaknesses of noblemen and peasants. His verses, written in the form of *faceciae*, which was popular in Italy during the fifteenth and sixteenth centuries and later spread throughout the whole of Europe, were undoubtedly influenced by the book of Poggio Bracciolini, *Liber facetiarum* (1470), reprinted in Cracow in 1592.[14]

In 1523 there was published in Cracow the 1,072-line *De statura, feritate ac venatione bisontis carmen*, written by Nicolaus Hussovianus (Mikołaj z Hussowa or Mikołaj Hussowczyk, between 1475 and 1533 or shortly thereafter), who was born in the territory of the Grand Duchy of Lithuania. Hussovianus came to Rome as a member of the retinue of bishop Erasmus Vitelius Ciołek (1474–1522) and stayed there till 1523. Bishop Ciołek was dispatched by the king of Poland and the grand duke of Lithuania Alexander as his envoy to the Vatican, where he moved in papal circles. Pope Leo X was so fascinated with Ciołek's stories about the Polish-Lithuanian woods and with his descriptions of the bison of the eastern forests that Ciołek determined to satisfy the pope's curiosity by having the hide of a bison brought from Lithuania to Rome, where it would be stuffed and exhibited. At the same time he commissioned Hussovianus to write a poem about the bison, a poem that would also describe the nature of the Grand Duchy of Lithuania. However, nothing of the plan was realized save Hussovianus's poem, because of the death of Pope Leo X in 1521.[15] Two years later the poem was printed with a dedication to Queen Bona Sforza as a token of gratitude for her patronage. With his poem, Nicolaus Hussovianus tried to emulate writings in this vein by Italian poets, such as Ercole Strozzi, who wrote *Venatio ad divam Lucretiam Ferrariae ducem* (1513) about the hunting of the king of France Charles VIII, and Guido Postumo Silvestri, who composed *Elegia ad Petrum Pactium* (1524) about the hunting exploits of Pope Leo himself. Hussovianus was also acquainted with a poem by Adriano da Corneto, *Ad Ascanium cardinalem s. Viti Venatio* (1505), and we can notice a lot of resemblances in the closing passages of both poems.[16] Nevertheless, the poem is not only about hunting bison in the forest of the Grand Duchy

---

[13] Marcelinas Ročka, "Lietuviškoji Petro Roizijaus poezijos tematika ir jo kultūrinė veikla Lietuvoje," *Literatūra* 8 (Vilnius, 1965): 130.

[14] A copy of the book is preserved in the library of the Vilnius Academy.

[15] Harold B. Segel, *Renaissance Culture in Poland. The Rise of Humanism, 1470–1543* (Ithaca and London, 1989), 139–140.

[16] Benediktas Kazlauskas, "Mikalojus Husovianas ir jo 'Giesmė apie stumbrą,' " Mikalojus Husovianas, *Giesmė apie stumbrą* (Vilnius, 1977), 12.

of Lithuania, but in a broader sense about the author's native land. One of the longest digressions in the poem is an extended panegyric to the grand duke of Lithuania Vytautas (1401–1430), who initiated bison-hunting as a way of preparing young men for combat. Writing proudly about the past greatness of the Grand Duchy of Lithuania, Hussovianus portrays Vytautas as a wise, stern but just ruler, who loves peace but understands the need to prepare for war. Such a portrait of Vytautas the Great, undoubtedly influenced by the ideas of Machiavelli, Pico della Mirandola, and Petrarch, also appears in another prominent poem of the time, the 3,300 hexameter-line *Radivilias*, composed by Ioannes Radvanus, a poet from the court of the duke Sigismundus Augustus, and printed in Vilnius in 1588.

After the Vilnius Academy was established in 1579, in spite of the strict rules of the traditional Jesuit humanistic school, oriented mostly to classical Latin literature, many students from the Grand Duchy of Lithuania and other countries became acquainted with the writings of Italian humanists. In manuscript courses of rhetoric read in the Vilnius Academy in the seventeenth century, among the works of Aristotle, Cicero, and Quintilian, one can find the names of the professor of rhetoric and philosophy in Rome, Marcus Muretus (1526–1585), the professor of rhetoric, philosophy, and theology in Genoa, Julius Nigronius (1553–1627), the professor of rhetoric in Rome, Petrus Perpinianus (1530–1566), and others.[17] They were recommended by the professors as wonderful examples of perfect style. In the library of the Vilnius Academy were numerous books by Italian rhetoricians, such as *Libri tres de imitatione; Orationes; Epistolaeque* by the professor of rhetoric, Bartholomeo Ricci, and *De elegantiis linguae Latinae* by Lorenzo Valla (Basileae, 1543). The book by Aldus Manutius, *Elegantiae linguae latinae*, was reprinted in Vilnius in 1598.[18]

Professors taught their students to write epigrams, epitaphs, and elegies taking as examples the verses of Francesco Petrarca, Giovanni Pontano, Emanuel Tesauro, and Aloisius Giuglari.[19] In the library of the Vilnius Academy there are preserved two books of verses by Giovanni Pontano from the sixteenth century, published in Venice in 1533 and in Basel in 1556. On the basis of the material of my research I would be bold enough to maintain that students of the Vilnius Academy were acquainted with the verses of Pontano and used them as models for imitation as well. For instance, in the funeral verses written by the students one could find the same *loci communes* and even the same composition of the verses as in *Tumulorum libri* by Pontano.

The most prominent cultural mediator between Italy and the Grand Duchy of Lithuania was Matthias Casimirus Sarbievius (or Maciej Kazimierz Sarbiewski, 1595–1640). He spent three years studying theology in Rome in 1622–1625, where he became well-known as a poet and was called "Horatius Sarmaticus," and where he

---

[17] Eugenija Ulčinaitė, *Teoria retoryczna w Polsce i na Litwie w XVII wieku: Próba rekonstrukcji schematu retorycznego* (Wrocław, 1984), 150.

[18] Kazimiera Čepienė, Irena Petrauskienė, *Vilniaus akademijos spaustuvės leidiniai 1576–1805: Bibliografija* (Vilnius, 1979), 20.

[19] Eugenija Ulčinaitė, "Renesanso ir Baroko poezija," *Dainos pasauliui, saulei ir sau: Lietuvos XVI–XVII amžiaus poezijos antologija* (Vilnius, 1993), 11–12.

began to write the main part of his poetics, *De acuto et arguto*, which he read during his lectures on poetics at Vilnius Academy, where he was a close friend of the Italian scholars Famianus Strada, Hieronymus Petrucci, Alexander Donati, and others. The first book of his poetry, printed in 1625 in Cologne,[20] for the most part consists of verses dedicated to his friends and patrons, Italian churchmen and noblemen. Sarbievius was crowned with laurels by Pope Urban VIII himself as some time before, Petrarch had been by Pope Benedict XII.

Summarizing this brief survey we should point out that the first more or less profound knowledge of Italian poetry as well as Italian culture by humanists of the Grand Duchy of Lithuania was founded on personal experience and contacts made during their frequent travels to Italy from the late fifteenth century onwards. Aesthetic and philosophical ideas of Italian humanists such as Machiavelli, Pico della Mirandola, Petrarch, and others found their expression in the first Latin poems written in the Grand Duchy. From the late sixteenth century rhetorical and poetical ideas of contemporary Italian professors began to be constantly presented and taught in the courses of poetics and rhetoric at the newly established Vilnius Academy. Verses of Italian poets were used as instances and models for imitation by the students, and this fact played no small part in the process of creating a poetical school at Vilnius Academy.

Vilnius, Lithuania

---

[20] *Matthias Casimiri Sarbievii . . . Lyricorum libri tres* (Coloniae Agrippinae, 1625).

Ascensius, Landino, and Virgil: Continuity and Transformation in Renaissance Commentary

CRAIG KALLENDORF

A ny study of the commentary in Renaissance Latin literature must inevitably consider the work of Jodocus Badius Ascensius (1462–1535), for this Flemish scholar-printer prepared commentaries to some 110 different texts by more than seventy authors at the same time as he was supervising the printing of more than 750 different editions.[1] Ascensius's commentary on Virgil is of unusual interest because of its acknowledged debt to the earlier work of the Florentine humanist Cristoforo Landino.[2] In this essay I shall try to identify both the principal points of continuity between the two commentaries and the chief differences between them, as a case study in how Italian humanism shaped the development of Virgilian studies across the Alps.

Like commentators for hundreds of years before him, Ascensius begins with an *accessus*, an introduction which provides a "means of approaching" the text.[3] As part

---

[1] The basic source on Ascensius's life and works remains Philippe Renouard, *Bibliographie des impressions et des oeuvres de Josse Badius Ascensius, imprimeur et humaniste, 1462–1535* (1908; repr. New York: Burt Franklin, 1967). The statistics are from Fred Schreiber, "The French Scholar-Printer of the Renaissance," a lecture given at Columbia University on July 16 and 17, 1991. As August Buck has observed, it is striking how many humanist commentaries like this one remain largely unstudied ("Die Ethik im humanistischen Studienprogramm," in *Ethik im Humanismus*, ed. Walter Rüegg and Dieter Wuttke. Beiträge zur Humanismusforschung, vol. 5 [Boppard: Boldt, 1979], 39–40).

[2] I have studied Ascensius's commentary in *Publii Virgilii Maronis poetae Mantuani universum poema* . . . (Venice: Ioannes Maria Bonellus, 1558), where he acknowledges his debt to Landino on fol. 139v, at *Aen.* 1.267–285; fol. 141r, on *Aen.* 1.286–296; fol. 151r, on *Aen.* 1.532; fol. 164r, on *Aen.* 2.122; etc. Further references to this commentary will appear in the text.

[3] On the *accessus ad auctores*, see Konrad von Hirsau, *Dialogus super auctores*, ed. R. B. C. Huygens (Leiden: Brill, 1970); and A. J. Minnis, *Medieval Theory of Authorship: Scholastic Literary Attitudes in the Later Middle Ages*, 2nd ed. (Philadelphia: University of Pennsylvania Press, 1998), 72–92.

of this *accessus*, Ascensius defines the "intentio auctoris," which is "ut et reipublicae et sibi quam plurimum per huius operis editionem prosit," for "constituisse videtur simul et iucunda et idonea dicere vitae." To benefit the state, Virgil endowed Aeneas with wisdom, courage, justice, temperance, and all the other virtues as well, then set him up to be imitated by Augustus. Indeed, since he knew that the Romans would not accept a work of literature which did not offer something to the understanding of morality and the preservation of the state, Virgil used the sixth book of the *Aeneid* to establish punishment for the guilty and rewards for the just, to show that service to the state also brings glory to the individual—an intention he shares with every good author ("haec communis est omnibus bona et bene scribentibus intentio": fols. 123v–124r).

Structuring the moral tone of this passage is an explicit reliance on the *Ars poetica* of Horace, whose analysis of the utility and delight of poetry (line 333) had exercised a continuous impact on criticism since antiquity and which Ascensius himself had commented upon around 1500.[4] As he wrote in his notes on Book 4 of the *Aeneid*, "cum ergo in toto opere, tum hic poeta et delectat et prodest plurimum, nam simul et iucunda et idonea dicere vitae instituit" (fol. 202v, on *Aen.* 4.1–29). The pleasurable things, to be sure, are described with great frequency and power, but Ascensius's real concern, as he admits in his commentary on Virgil's description of the Elysian fields, is with the things which profit (fols. 258r–v, on *Aen.* 6.656–671).

This particular approach is found in Landino as well. Landino lectured on the *Ars poetica* at the Florentine *Studio* in 1464–1465,[5] and his commentary on Horace was published in 1482; indeed, in the preface to this commentary, Landino declares Horace and Virgil (along with Dante) to be the poets most worthy of study. Later on in the same preface, Landino asserts that Horace practiced what he preached by developing the theory from the *Ars poetica* in his own poetry, which contains "omnia bene vivendi praecepta." That is, Horace's poetry condemns fear, sloth, impiety, indolence, and the other vices at the same time as it praises justice, courage, respect for parents, and the other virtues.[6] Since Landino believed that all his favorite poets conveyed essentially the same message, he repeats this passage almost verbatim in his commentary on Virgil.[7]

As this last passage suggests, humanist literary criticism regularly conflated Horace's profit-and-delight dictum with another critical approach. Bernard Weinberg has observed that Ascensius read the *Ars poetica* "as if it were part of the classical-medieval

---

[4] Bernard Weinberg, *A History of Literary Criticism in the Italian Renaissance*, 2 vols. (Chicago: University of Chicago Press, 1961), 1:71–88.

[5] The fullest information on Landino's lecture cycle is provided by Arthur Field, "Cristoforo Landino's First Lectures on Dante," *Renaissance Quarterly* 39 (1986): 21, which is based in part on Roberto Cardini, *La critica del Landino* (Florence: Sansoni, 1973), 16–17, 334–341.

[6] "Christophori Landini Florentini in Q. Horatii Flacci libros omnes ad illustrissimum Guidonem Feltrium Magni Federici ducis filium interpretationes incipiunt feliciter," in Cristoforo Landino, *Scritti critici e teorici*, ed. Roberto Cardini, 2 vols. (Rome: Bulzoni, 1974), 1:198, 202.

[7] "Christophori Landini Florentini in P. Vergilii interpretationes prohemium ad Petrum Medicem Magni Laurentii filium feliciter incipit," in *Scritti critici*, ed. Cardini, 1:215.

rhetorical tradition."[8] By this, he means that Ascensius finds explanations for Horace's ideas about decorum, the rhetorical categories of invention, disposition, and style, and so forth, in the works of Cicero and Quintilian. This is fine as far as it goes, and it colors the commentary to Virgil as well (cf. fol. 136r, on *Aen.* 1.198–207). However, I would add that Ascensius draws heavily as well on another part of the rhetorical tradition: the association between epic poetry and epideictic, the rhetoric of praise and blame.

According to Aristotle, whose scheme was passed on to the Roman rhetoricians and then to later ages as well, oratory could be divided into three kinds: deliberative, judicial (or forensic), and epideictic. The third kind, epideictic, relies on praise and blame as its distinctive elements and directs these elements toward attaining virtue and vice.[9] As O. B. Hardison, Jr. and Brian Vickers have shown, the principles of epideictic rhetoric became entangled with the principles of literary criticism in late antiquity, so that the praise of virtue and condemnation of vice came to be seen as a legitimate goal of poetry and criticism as well as speechmaking.[10] Thus when Coluccio Salutati, the fourteenth-century chancellor of Florence and fervent admirer of the classics, read line 333 of Horace's *Ars poetica*, he immediately interpreted it as part of the praise-and-blame tradition: "Principaliter igitur utilitati vituperatio correspondet, delectationi laus. . . ."[11]

This approach to poetry affects Ascensius's reading of the *Aeneid* from the very first line, for when Virgil "sings" the deeds of famous men, he praises them by singing, so that "laudo" is to be understood in place of "cano" (fol. 125r, on *Aen.* 1.1). What is to be praised is the virtue of Aeneas, by which men might be instructed in how to live well (fol. 126v, on *Aen.* 1.8–11). From this point on, Ascensius finds a great many opportunities to highlight the virtuous activities of Virgil's hero and the moral lessons of his story. When Aeneas and his men arrive in Carthage, for example, the Trojan leader does not think of resting his weary body but climbs a rock to see whether anything around him threatens the safety of his crew, which is praiseworthy action (fol. 135r, on *Aen.* 1.180–197). And when Aeneas and his men arrive outside the gates of Dis, Virgil arranges for him to learn the punishments of the evildoers confined inside in order to deter the readers of the *Aeneid* from wrongdoing (fol. 255r, on *Aen.* 6.259–279).

To be sure, there are times when Ascensius must exercise a good deal of critical ingenuity in order to praise what Aeneas does. For example, he takes great care to exculpate Aeneas from any charge of treason or cowardice in his flight from Troy:

Docet quomodo ab Hectore excitatus sit, et ad fugam faciendam admonitus, in qua re ingeniosus poeta, miro utitur artificio, nam sic Aeneam a proditione

---

[8] *A History of Literary Criticism*, 1:84.

[9] Aristotle, *Rhetoric* 1358a–b, 1366a.

[10] O. B. Hardison, Jr., *The Enduring Monument: A Study of the Idea of Praise in Renaissance Literary Theory and Practice* (1962; repr. Westport, Conn.: Greenwood Press, 1973); and Brian Vickers, "Epideictic and Epic in the Renaissance," *New Literary History* 14 (1982–83): 497–537.

[11] *De laboribus Herculis*, ed. B. L. Ullman, 2 vols. (Zurich: Thesaurus Mundi, 1951), 1:68.

purgat, ut et fugam illi gloriosam facit. Purgatur quidam a proditione, quod cum ceteris, eadem fraude deceptus, somno indulgebat, et si quaeratur cur non etiam cum ceteris perierit, respondet, quia ab Hectore admonitus, ex[s]urrexit et virtute, qua plurimum potuit, praecipue ducente deo, per tela, per hostes, evasit. Fugam autem, inclytam facit, quia solus ad hoc a diis electus est, ut deos et sacra per fugam servet.... (fol. 169r, on *Aen.* 2.268–295)

Similarly Aeneas is to be praised for the dalliance at Carthage, since he did not love in a base and vulgar manner, but he was loved ("amatus est"), and not by someone who had cast aside her honor but by someone who was pursued by Venus and deceived by Cupid (fol. 202v, on *Aen.* 4.11; cf. fol. 156v, on *Aen.* 1.705–722). Even the final scene in which the enraged Aeneas slays Turnus after he surrenders and begs for mercy ends up redounding to Aeneas's credit: the entire book recounts the praises of Aeneas, so that this final victory must mark the final attainment of heroic glory (fol. 351r, on the arguments printed at the beginning of *Aen.* 12; cf. fol. 367r, on *Aen.* 12.930–952).[12]

In short, a significant part of Ascensius's critical effort is devoted to identifying the virtues of Aeneas and to establishing the rewards that come to virtuous heroes like him. This is one of the most distinctive features of Landino's commentary, and it is highlighted immediately in the proem:

> Qua obsecro ille acrimonia, quo verborum fulmine metum, ignaviam, luxuriam, incontinentiam, impietatem, perfidiam ac omnia iniustitiae genera reliquaque *vitia insectatur vexatque? Quibus contra laudibus,* quibus praemiis invictam animi magnitudinem, et pro patria, pro parentibus, pro cognatis amicisque consideratam periculorum susceptionem, religionem in Deum, pietatem in maiores, caritatem in omnes prosequitur! ... Ita locum concludam, ut *universam huius scriptoris poesim laudem esse virtutis* atque omnia ad illam referri sine dubitatione affirmem.[13] (emphasis mine)

Like the Horatian emphasis on utility with which it is compatible, this reading of epic poetry through the filter of epideictic rhetoric passed unchanged from Landino's commentary into Ascensius's.

It is worth noting here, moreover, that Ascensius and Landino had a common source for this approach. Ascensius's normal procedure is to break Virgil's text into manageable sections, then to construe each section under the rubric "ordo est" along with a discussion of whatever he undertakes to explain. This discussion is based overwhelmingly, as he openly acknowledges, on the late fourth-century commentator Tiberius Claudius Donatus. Even more than Ascensius, Donatus is single-minded in his adherence to the praise-and-blame approach to the *Aeneid.* Virgil's "materiae

---

[12] For Ascensius, the moral content of a passage could even determine whether it deserved to remain in the text. For example, when Aeneas told Dido about becoming so angry at Helen that he considered killing her (*Aen.* 2.559ff.), Ascensius used its inappropriate moral content to resolve the debates over the textual authenticity of the passage by banishing it from further consideration.

[13] "In P. Vergilii interpretationes prohemium," 1:215–216.

genus," as Donatus notes at the beginning of his commentary, is "laudativum," so that Virgil's goal is to show Aeneas as "vacuus omni culpa et magno praeconio praeferendus."[14] Donatus took every possible occasion to praise Aeneas's virtues: he is a good leader (on *Aen.* 1.159–179), pious toward the gods (on *Aen.* 1.379), chaste (on *Aen.* 1.310–320), handsome and brave (on *Aen.* 1.594–595), and so forth. Donatus also exercises his critical ingenuity to highlight what he sees as Virgil's ex-culpation of Aeneas: Aeneas is blameless for fleeing Troy because it had been destined to fall (on *Aen.* 1.1), and he emerges from Carthage with his good name intact. Donatus even outlines a defense that Aeneas could have presented had there been time in the story for it (on *Aen.* 4.271). It is easy to hear echoes of this approach in Ascensius's commentary: indeed, his dependence on Donatus is so great that when a *lacuna* in his source prevents him from his normal borrowings, Ascensius feels com-pelled to acknowledge the fact (e.g., on *Aen.* 4.388–436, 6.1–39, etc.).[15]

While such a heavy level of borrowing may be due to a scholarly laziness of sorts, this is not the only explanation. For one thing, as Rita Copeland has pointed out, "commentaries themselves become texts to be appropriated by later exegetes and to be incorporated in later commentaries," so that in fact Ascensius's appropriation of Donatus reflects a common maneuver among commentators who, after all, feel little inclined to reinvent the proverbial wheel when a body of notes already exists for their text.[16] What is more, as a good humanist, Ascensius believed not only that the literature of antiquity occupied a privileged place in the culture of his day but that the interpretation of this literature should be grounded as much as possible in the culture in which it had been produced.[17] The humanists never found a commentary from the Augustan Age, of course, but they felt particularly fortunate to have re-covered a commentary like Donatus's that was not too much later than the poem itself. Thus when Ascensius worked through the *Aeneid* as a guide to moral life, he could be confident that this interpretation was authorized by a great critic who was speaking to him across the centuries from the very culture in which Virgil himself had lived and worked.[18] And finally, it is not an accident that the first fifteenth-

---

[14] Citations from Donatus are to *Interpretationes Vergilianae*, ed. Henricus Georgii (Leipzig: Teubner, 1905–1906), and will be placed in the text. In opposition to most modern scholars, Marisa Squillante Saccone has recently argued that Donatus captures a number of readings that are worth retaining (*Le Interpretationes Vergilianae di Tiberio Donato* [Naples: Società Editrice Napole-tana, 1985], 119).

[15] Modern texts are still based on the same manuscripts that became available in the fifteenth century, and there are still a good number of *lacunae*. See Peter K. Marshall, "Tiberius Claudius Donatus in the Fifteenth Century," in *Tria Lustra: Essays and Notes Presented to John Pinsent. . .*, ed. H. D. Jocelyn and H. Hurt. Liverpool Classical Papers, vol. 3 (Liverpool: Liverpool Classical Monthly, 1993), 325–328.

[16] *Rhetoric, Hermeneutics, and Translation: Academic Traditions and Vernacular Texts*. Cambridge Studies in Medieval Literature (Cambridge: Cambridge University Press, 1991), 65.

[17] Eugenio Garin, *Italian Humanism: Philosophy and Civic Life in the Renaissance*, trans. Peter Munz (Oxford: Basil Blackwell, 1965), 1–17.

[18] Relying on the ancient critics (e.g., Suetonius, *Augustus* 89.2), modern scholars continue to stress the connection between poetic production and moral ideals in Augustan Rome.

century scholar to have worked through Donatus's commentary systematically was Landino, who prepared an epitome that was printed at least twenty times by the turn of the century.[19] In other words, Ascensius's reliance on Donatus is due in part to his reliance on Landino, who had pointed him toward the same source.

A final point of contact between Ascensius and Landino was that both scholars approached Virgil's poetry as an example of *theologia poetica*, poetry which contained prophetic wisdom from early Greece and Egypt. As Landino explains it,

> Neque enim alius est magnus verusque poeta quam theologus, quod non solum Aristotelis tanti philosophi auctoritas testimoniumque ostendit, sed ipsorum quoque scripta apertissime docent. Duplex enim theologia est: altera quam priscam vocant, cuius divinus ille vir Mercurius cognomine Trimegistus primus fontem aperuit, altera nostra est, quae non modo verior comprobatur, sed ita verissima, ut neque addi quicquam nec imminui inde possit.[20]

That is, ancient poets like Orpheus, Linus, and Musaeus—and Virgil—could see some, though not all, of the truths of Christianity, so that for Landino, *Eclogue* 4 could be referred to the coming of Christ and *Aeneid* 6 could be illuminated by reference to Job, the Psalms, and the gospel of John.[21]

Ascensius also advocated the search for parallels between Scripture and Virgil, a practice he refers to as "confirming the secular through the sacred" ("prophana sacris confirmare": fol. 258v, on *Aen.* 6.656–671). For example, the Roman custom of *devotio*, in which heroes like the Decii willingly sacrificed their lives for their country, is easy to transfer to a Christian value matrix, where the saints willingly sacrifice their lives for their faith (fol. 157r, on *Aen.* 1.712).[22] The entire sixth book of the *Aeneid* presents "multa Christiano non indigna" (fol. 237r, on the arguments preceding *Aen.* 6): the eternal punishment of the guilty, the purgation of those souls only slightly defiled, the type and order of punishments meted out to sinners, and so forth. First we find the infants who died without baptism, then those who are in purgatory because of a venial sin or because they have not yet finished doing penance, then those who

---

[19] Vladimiro Zabughin, *Vergilio nel Rinascimento italiano da Dante a Torquato Tasso*, 2 vols. (Bologna: Zanichelli, 1921), 1:189, argued that Donatus's commentary had little impact among the humanists, but as Roberto Cardini has pointed out (*Scritti critici*, 2:292–294), subsequent research has revealed that the commentary was at least known to a number of prominent Quattrocento humanists, among whom were Angelo Poliziano, Battista Guarino, Poggio Bracciolini, Niccolò Niccoli, and Giovanni Pontano.

[20] "In P. Vergilii interpretationes prohemium," 1:230, with Cardini's commentary, 2:303–306. The literature on *theologia poetica* is substantial, but a useful orientation may be found in Charles Trinkaus, *In Our Image and Likeness: Humanity and Divinity in Italian Humanist Thought*, 2 vols. (Chicago: University of Chicago Press, 1970), esp. 2:683–721; and Stanley Meltzoff, *Botticelli, Signorelli and Savonarola: Theologia Poetica and Painting from Boccaccio to Poliziano*. Biblioteca di "Lettere Italiane," vol. 32 (Florence: Leo S. Olschki, 1987).

[21] On *Eclogue* 4, see Zabughin, *Vergilio*, 1:195–196; for the references in the commentary on *Aeneid* 6, see *Vergilius cum quinque commentariis* (Venice: n.p., 1492), fols. 230v, 231v, and 249v–250r.

[22] See Livy, 8.9, 10.28.

brought an everlasting death to their body or their soul; one and the same fire torments them all, yet they suffer in accordance with the gravity of their sin (fol. 251v, on *Aen.* 6.424–439). Paradise, by contrast, is inhabited first by those who died for what they believed in, then by priests and prophets, then by those whose learning and actions benefited others (fol. 258v, on *Aen.* 6.656–671).[23]

Thus there are four principal points of contact between Ascensius and Landino. First, both commentators analyze Virgil's poetry in Horatian terms, as literature designed to produce utility and pleasure in the reader. Second, both commentators, however, were primarily interested in the utility to be gained by reading Virgil, for both viewed ancient epic through the filter of epideictic rhetoric, through which virtue was praised and vice condemned. Third, both scholars drew heavily from Donatus, whose commentary on Virgil provided a model from antiquity for their own interpretive inclinations. And finally, both Ascensius and Landino approached Virgil's poetry as an example of *theologia poetica*—that is, as pagan literature which foreshadowed the moral truths of Christianity.

There are a couple of areas, however, in which the critical practice of Ascensius diverges from that of Landino. For one thing, there is a pronounced Neoplatonic flavor to Landino's commentary which is not carried over into Ascensius's. This is a striking difference, for much of Landino's importance as a critic of the *Aeneid* arises from his being the first humanist to work out a detailed critique of the poem in which all the major points from the first six books are subordinated to an overarching Neoplatonic scheme. This scheme rests on an analysis of the virtues that establishes a hierarchy of moral good:

> Divinus enim Plato, cum virtutes de vita et moribus easdem quas ceteri posuisset, ita ad postremum illas diversis sive ordinibus sive generibus distinguit, ut alia quadam ratione ab iis illas coli ostendat, qui coetus ac civitates adamant, alia ab iis, qui omnem mortalitatem dediscere cupientes et humanarum rerum odio moti ad sola divina cognoscenda eriguntur, alia postremo ab iis, qui ab omni iam contagione expiati in solis divinis versantur. Primas igitur "civilis" dixit, secundas "purgatorias" ac tertias "animi iam purgati."[24]

For Landino, interpreting the *Aeneid* meant showing how Aeneas passed in turn through each of these stages, purifying his soul and moving at last toward the *summum bonum.*

We can only speculate about why Ascensius chose to suppress most of Landino's Neoplatonism. For one thing, I suspect that a northern European scholar was less attracted to this approach than a Florentine who was working alongside Ficino at the

---

[23] A fuller development of the relationship between *theologia poetica* and humanist criticism of Virgil may be found in my "From Virgil to Vida: The *Poeta Theologus* in Italian Renaissance Commentary," in press in *Journal of the History of Ideas.*

[24] *Disputationes Camaldulenses*, ed. Peter Lohe (Florence: Sansoni, 1980), 153. Landino's allegorical interpretation of Virgil is discussed in my *In Praise of Aeneas: Virgil and Epideictic Rhetoric in the Early Italian Renaissance* (Hanover and London: University Press of New England, 1989), 129–165, with earlier treatments referenced in the notes.

time when the so-called Platonic Academy was dominating Tuscan intellectual life.[25] More important, perhaps, is a difference in the target audience for the commentaries. Both commentators, of course, hoped that their work would guide their readers to a better understanding of the text. Ascensius's commentary, however, is clearly aimed at a younger student, for there is noticeably more help with difficult vocabulary and much more attention to basic grammar and syntax.[26] A younger student who was still struggling to find the subject of one of Virgil's sentences could hardly be expected, for example, to integrate the Harpies into the subtleties of Neoplatonic allegory, so Ascensius downplayed this part of Landino's commentary.

Nevertheless, Ascensius's commentary can only be understood as an extension of and reaction to Landino's. Thus when Landino's work passed out of fashion, Ascensius's replaced it as the commentary of choice for publishers throughout Europe, as part of the process by which Italian humanism transformed the intellectual life of the Renaissance.

Texas A&M University

---

[25] The best recent treatment of this subject is Arthur Field, *The Origins of the Platonic Academy of Florence* (Princeton: Princeton University Press, 1988).

[26] Paul Gerhard Schmidt, "Iodocus Basius Ascensius als Kommentator," in *Der Kommentator in der Renaissance*, ed. August Buck and Otto Herding. Deutsche Forschungsgemeinschaft, Kommission für Humanismusforschung, vol. 1 (Boppard: Boldt, 1975), 63–71.

"Ne suffreth nat that men yow doon offence":
The Griselda Figure in
Boccaccio, Petrarch, and Chaucer

JOAN LARSEN KLEIN

Most men who have read about Griselda have seen in her obedience and patience virtues which they believed human wives could not emulate. Petrarch, a misogynist himself, did not believe her story not only because it was about a woman, but also because the woman was a poor "little peasant woman" ("rusticana hec muliercula").[1] He preferred to call her story a "tale," deriving from it a moral which applied only to men, "viris," not "hominibus." That man, Petrarch says, deserves "to number among the men overflowing with constancy whoever would suffer without a murmur for his God what this little peasant woman suffered for her mortal husband" (*Letters of Old Age*, II, 668). Petrarch bases his moral application on a text of James the Apostle which James also directed towards men, his "beloved brethren": God, said James, "cannot be tempted by evil," and "He himself tempts no man"[2] ("ipse neminem temptet").[3]

But Petrarch had some warrant for an exemplary interpretation of Boccaccio's story. Boccaccio claimed in the "Conclusione" that his stories, read rightly, were both useful and honest, able to yield utility and fruit.[4] In his "Proemio," Boccaccio likewise claimed that his female readers could pick useful counsel from his stories, "utile consiglio potranno pigliare" (5), and for this reason, perhaps, called his stories

---

[1] Petrarch, *Letters of Old Age*, trans. Aldo S. Bernardo, Saul Levin, and Reta A. Bernardo (Baltimore: The Johns Hopkins University Press, 1992), II, 668; J. Burke Severs, *The Literary Relationships of Chaucer's Clerkes Tale* (New Haven: Yale University Press, 1942), 288.

[2] Trans. Robert Dudley French, rpt. in *The Canterbury Tales*, ed. V. A. Kolve and Glending Olson (New York: Norton, 1989), 388.

[3] James 1:14. James addresses his epistle only to his "beloved brethren," not to women. The Latin is from Petrarch *ap.* Severs, 288.

[4] *Decameron*, a cura di Vittore Branca (Firenze: Accademia della Crusca, 1976), 719.

as well as "novelle," fables, parables, or histories, "favole, o parabole o istorie" (4).

Boccaccio invites his readers, in other words, to see his stories at least as exemplary and at most as analogical or allegorical. Nor was Petrarch the only reader who took him at his word. Modern critics, following Boccaccio in the *Genealogia Deorum Gentilium*, persist in seeing the Griselda story as something like allegory, wherein truth is veiled by "a fair and fitting garment of fiction" and Griselda herself becomes a "figura Christi," a "Christ archetype."[5] Boccaccio, however, insists he wrote his stories to and about women, indeed most gracious women, "graziosissime donne" (9). It seems to me hard on women, consequently, to be told by some modern critics that arguably the best woman in the *Decameron* allegorically represents not a woman at all, but rather the Son of God.

Some years ago Vittore Branca in *Boccaccio Medievale* identified Griselda with the Virgin Mary, not Christ, " 'umile ed alta più che creatura.' "[6] This identification seems more in keeping with Boccaccio's ostensibly female audience and perhaps with what may be Griselda's analogues, Beatrice and Laura. Boccaccio's language also echoes descriptions of other Biblical figures, as Priscilla Martin has suggested, among them Rebecca and the Samaritan woman.[7] Although Griselda is likely, as Marga Cottino-Jones also suggests, an "embodiment of love on a sacrificial level" (296), I would note that Griselda allows her children to be sacrificed out of love for her husband, as Mary, perhaps, underwent the sacrifice of Christ, and that Griselda is rewarded by the restoration of her children, as Mary was, perhaps, by Christ's resurrection and her assumption. Boccaccio cultivates a further identification of Griselda with Mary when Dioneo evokes images reminiscent of the Annunciation and the Nativity and when he apprehends in her a divine spirit: "anche nelle povere case piovono dal cielo de' divini spiriti" (712).

But it is easier to think that Griselda typifies Mary or even Christ than it is to think, as Petrarch did, that Gualtieri typifies God. Petrarch circumvented this difficulty by scrapping many of Gualtieri's more unsavory attributes, to quote David Wallace, by passing over "without comment," "Walter's tyrannical proclivities" (190). It is hard to believe, moreover, that Boccaccio intended his readers to remember the text from James which Petrarch used to authorize his interpretation of the Griselda story, because nothing in James's epistle has anything to do with relations

---

[5] Marga Cottino-Jones, "Fabula vs. Figura: Another Interpretation of the Griselda Story," *Italica* 50 (1973): 38–52, rpt. in *The Decameron*, trans. Mark Musa and Peter Bondanella (New York: Norton, 1977), 295–297. See also David Wallace, "'Whan She Translated Was': A Chaucerian Critique of the Petrarchan Academy," in *Literary Practice and Social Change in Britain, 1380–1530*, ed. Lee Patterson (Berkeley: University of California Press, 1990), 186, 197–198.

[6] *Boccaccio Medievale e Nuovi Studi sul Decameron*, 5th ed. (Firenze: G. C. Sansoni, 1981), 97. See also Griselda's attitude towards her husband's subjects: "similmente verso i subditi del marito era tanto graziosa e tanto benigna" (706).

[7] Priscilla Martin, in *Chaucer's Women: Nuns, Wives, and Amazons* (Iowa City, 1990), 144–145, sees Griselda as a "saint and martyr and imitation of Christ" and her marriage "as an election to a martyrdom of willing suffering and humiliation."

between husbands and wives or even ruler and ruled, all which lie at the heart of Boccaccio's story. If Boccaccio expected his readers to remember any Biblical text, it was more likely one far closer to the Griselda story, one more important in the Middle Ages to marriage and the church, one, indeed, which Boccaccio alludes to in his "Introduzione" when he has Elissa agree that men are women's head (Ephesians 5:22–23): "Wives, be subject to your husbands as to your Lord: for the husband is the head of the wife as Christ is the head of the Church." ("Mulieres viris suis subditae sint, sicut Domino: Quoniam vir caput est mulieris: sicut Christus caput est ecclesiae."[8] Boccaccio: "Disse allora Elissa:—Veramente gli uomini sono delle femine capo," 20.) This is the command upon which marriage was based in the Middle Ages and afterwards and which was incorporated in the marriage ceremony itself. If we read the Griselda story in the light of Paul's charge, the story may not seem quite so outrageous. For Griselda is the living embodiment of Paul's charge to wives. She obeys Gualtieri without question as her lord and head, "dominus et caput," and she addresses him as one would address the Lord, "Signor mio." If we likewise read the relationship between Griselda and Gualtieri as analogous to that between the Church and Christ, then Griselda becomes emblematic of the Church, and her love for Gualtieri follows the first of Christ's great commandments (Matt. 22:37–40): "Love the Lord your God with all your heart, and with all your soul, and with all your mind." ("Diliges Dominum Deum tuum. . . .") Boccaccio may further wish his readers to identify Griselda at least in some measure with the seven young Florentine women who had congregated before their journey in that Florentine church dedicated to the Virgin, Santa Maria Novella, and who returned to it at the end of their journey. Boccaccio may also intend us to consider the young women of the *brigata* like Griselda in yet another way. Though Petrarch and the second reader of his story did not believe that women could act with the love, faith, patience, and constancy that Griselda displayed,[9] Panfilo insists that the young women in the *brigata* remained honest, chaste, and in harmony throughout their journey, despite the examples set by licentious women in the stories, by the temptations to concupiscence the stories represented, and by the food, drink, songs, and music they all enjoyed: "(cose tutte da incitare le deboli menti a cose meno oneste), niuno atto, niuna parolla, niuna cosa né dalla vostra parte né dalla nostra ci ho conosciuta da biasimare; continua onestà, continua concordia, continua fraternal dimestichezza me ci è paruta vedere e sentire" (713). That their behavior was also contrary to Boccaccio's descriptions of Florentines vitiated by the plague seems further to associate the young women in the *brigata* with Griselda—and thus suggests that at least some women are capable of approaching her example.

But Boccaccio and Petrarch manipulate the perspectives from which they view the

---

[8] *Biblia sacra juxta vulgatae exemplaria. . .* , ed. Louis Claude Fillion, 5th ed. (Paris: Letouzey et Ane, 1901).

[9] *Letters of Old Age*, II, 670. Although Petrarch qualifies his misogny by listing a few good wives (Porcia, Hypsicratea, Alcestis) who gave their lives for their husbands, none, like Griselda, were asked to sacrifice their children at their husband's whim.

Gualtieri/Valterius figure very differently, and this contributes to their radically diverse assessment of him. Petrarch, of course, believed the story a fiction or fable[10] and saw it as an exemplum of the right relationship of man to God. Although we do not know how Boccaccio regarded the "truth" of his story, both Dioneo, its narrator, and the *brigata* react to it as if it were fact. As a consequence, they, like the characters within the story, condemn Gualtieri's abuse of Griselda. Dioneo goes so far as to insist that Gualtieri's treatment of his wife is a mad bestiality, "una matta bestialità," the example of which no man ought to follow and the success of which is a sin: "la quale io non consiglio alcun che segua, per ciò che gran peccato fu che a costui ben n'avenisse" (703). Far from counseling all men to follow the example of Griselda, as Petrarch does, Dioneo wishes that Gualtieri had met with a wife who found herself another lover after she was thrown out of her husband's house in her shift, a lover who might at least have given her a nice-looking dress ("quando, fuor di casa, l'avesse fuori in camiscia cacciata, s'avesse sì a un altro fatto scuotere il pilliccione, che riuscita ne fosse una bella roba," 712). The young women echo Dioneo's condemnation, though not his obscenity, by reviling Gualtieri and praising Griselda: "assai le donne, chi d'una parte e chi d'altra tirando, chi biasimando una cosa, un'altra intorno a essa lodandone" (713).[11] I am suggesting that Boccaccio limits the perspective from which the actions of Gualtieri may be judged to Gualtieri's subjects within the story and to its narrator and hearers outside of it, in other words, to ordinary humans who cannot see beyond efficient to final causes and who do not pretend to teleological insight. In this, they are unlike Gualtieri, who claims to work towards a foreseen end, an "antiveduto fine" (711), or Petrarch, who claims to understand the meaning of these events and God's purposes therein. The reaction of Dioneo, the *brigata*, and the subjects of Gualtieri, furthermore, is also Boccaccio's, enunciated in the first words of the *Decameron* itself: It is human nature to have compassion upon the afflicted: "Humana cosa è aver compassione degli afflitti" ("Proemio," 3).

Nonetheless, Boccaccio also places the *brigata* and the stories they tell in the context of the plague that ravaged Florence, an event, he suggests, which must be understood teleologically if it is to be understood at all, an event which he assumes was visited upon Florence either through the operation of the stars or by the just anger of God—as a punishment for sin and the correction of sinners: "la quale, per operazion de' corpi superiori o per le nostre inique opere da giusta ira di Dio a nostra correzione mandata sopra i mortali" ("Introduzione," 9). The description of the plague which follows Boccaccio's declaration, however, underscores its arbitrary nature—in that it struck down the good and the bad alike, indiscriminately savaging men, women, and children. The ravages of the plague, furthermore, resemble Gual-

---

[10] "Whoever asks me whether it is true, that is, whether I have written a history or just a tale ("an historiam scripserim an fabulam," Severs, 292), I shall reply with the words of Crispus, 'let the responsibility fall on the author', namely my Giovanni," *Letters of Old Age*, II, 656.

[11] The reaction of Dioneo and the *brigata* is also close to what Gualtieri's "subditi" said about the supposed murders of her children: "il biasimavan forte e reputavanlo crudele uomo e alla donna avevan grandissima compassione," 707.

tieri's treatment of Griselda, for her children are torn from her, she believes, to be killed, their bodies left to be devoured by carrion birds and wild animals or allowed to putrefy like the unburied corpses in plague-ridden Florence. When her daughter is returned to her, there is even a suggestion—which Shakespeare picks up in *The Winter's Tale*—that she is being returned only to be violated once again through an incestuous "marriage" with her father. Dioneo's story, finally, is the last and so, as Petrarch says, the most important story in the *Decameron*. It may be, therefore, that Boccaccio intends his readers to understand Dioneo's story analogically, to see in it the complaint of the suffering members of Christ's Church in plague-ridden Florence against a God who appears to treat them even more cruelly than Gualtieri treated Griselda.[12] Certainly, as he describes the plague in the "Introduzione," Boccaccio speaks as bitterly against what he calls the cruelty of heaven ("la crudeltà del cielo," 16) as Dioneo does the "matta bestialità" of Gualtieri.[13]

Petrarch may not have connected the Griselda story in the *Decameron* with Boccaccio's description of the plague, and thus could not see in it a terrorized protest, like Job's, against the fury of God. On the contrary, Petrarch suggests that the Griselda story might soothe away the dark recollections of the plague, for the "sweet" story charmed him, he said; it gave him pleasure and delight: ("ita michi placuit . . . tam dulcis ystoria delectaret, cum et michi semper ante multos annos audita placuisset," 291). Because Petrarch detached Boccaccio's story from its context, it may have been easier for him to see in it a moral exemplum designed to instruct men, if not women, in their duties towards God. Petrarch, however, also suppressed the angry protests of the *brigata* against Gualtieri along with their sympathetic support of Griselda—unless Petrarch intended the reactions of the first readers of his translation (reported in the *Letters of Old Age*) to replace Boccaccio's frame. These suppressions, together with his introduction of the framing device which initiates a new, masculine point of view, change the emphasis of the Griselda story from Boccaccio's, which was upon Gualtieri's cruelty, to Petrarch's own, which is upon Griselda's patience and obedience.

But Petrarch makes another point about audience which has a further impact on his interpretation of the story. He insists that Boccaccio was writing in the Italian vernacular for readers very different from the more cultivated men who would read the story's Latin translation. Boccaccio's readers might have actually enjoyed his lewd stories in the vernacular. They were men "who seemed likely to read such things," because, said Petrarch (astoundingly, given his stance as moral arbitrator), "variety in morals excuses variety in style" (*Letters of Old Age*, II, 655). Although it is not clear for whom he thought Boccaccio wrote his *Decameron*, Petrarch appears not to have

---

[12] In "Nominalism and the Dynamics of the *Clerk's Tale*: *Homo Viator* as Woman," forthcoming (113), Elizabeth D. Kirk discusses Walter's cruelty in relation to the problem of evil and links both to the Book of Job: "How can the suffering in the world be reconciled with the goodness of God?"

[13] Although Wallace (190) says Walter "might be seen as God's agent" or "as a tyrant, be compared to the Black Death," he sees in this story mainly a protest against tyrants, perhaps the Duke of Athens.

believed they were women, for he uses masculine, not feminine, pronouns throughout to describe them: "et eorum qui lecturi talia videbantur" (290, l. 16). He seems
to have thought, too, that Boccaccio's readers were men neither learned nor cultured
enough to appreciate the new piece which Petrarch called pious and grave ("quaedam
pia et gravia") and which he had translated into the language of humanists, "his
words" ("meis verbis explicui," 291, l. 44). Petrarch makes this point again when he
insists that his first readers were men of "excellent parts," "wide attainments," and
"ability," his friends, members of his own academy.[14] Given such a rarefied male
ambience, it is no wonder that Petrarch was convinced that only a few men like
himself and no living woman (handicapped by ignorance and her sex) could imitate
Griselda's "steadfastness" ("que michi vix imitabilis videtur," 288, l. 71). In fact,
when Petrarch speaks of Griselda's virtue, he suggests that her character has been
perfected by, perhaps could only be perfected by, masculine, not feminine, characteristics. It is the "vigor of manhood and the wisdom of age" that lie in her breast
(trans. French, 380; "sed virilis senilisque animus virgineo latebat in pectore," 260,
ll. 8–9). As a result, only "steadfast men" ("constantibus viris"), says Petrarch, could
endure for God what Griselda was fabled to endure for a mortal husband.[15] Petrarch
identifies himself not only with Griselda when he imbues her with the "vigor of
manhood" and the "wisdom of age," but also, somehow, with Gualtieri when he says
that Valterius looked at Griselda not with lust, but "with the sober thoughts of an
older man" (trans. French, 380)—although Boccaccio and Petrarch, too, for that matter explicitly says that Gualteri is a young man, "un giovane" (703).

It seems right to suggest, following Wallace (191–207), that the Clerk's tale is a
critique of Petrarch's version of the Griselda story. Chaucer returns the Griselda story
from what the Clerk calls Petrarch's Latin "Heigh style"[16] to yet another vernacular.
At the same time, he removes Petrarch's translation from the rarefied plane of
universalized moral exempla to a localized historical moment even more particular
than the temporal setting in which Dioneo placed it.[17] (Not only is Petrarch dead,
said the Clerk; so is Walter, Grisilde, and "eek hire pacience," [1177]; her son, now
married, reigns in his father's stead.) But the Clerk goes beyond Boccaccio and
Petrarch in other ways too. Where Boccaccio seems to have focused on Gualtieri's
cruelty and Petrarch on Griselda's faith, patience, and obedience, the Clerk seems to
focus upon the person of Grisilda and her sufferings as a woman and a wife. More-

---

[14] See Wallace, "When She Translated Was," 161–163 and *passim*. For Petrarch's sense of
himself and his friends as superior to less "cultivated" men and nearly all women, see Wallace,
179–184.

[15] "Abunde ego constantibus viris ascripserim, quisquis is fuerit, qui pro Deo suo sine mur-
mure paciatur quod pro suo mortali coniuge rusticana hec muliercula passa est." Severs, 288.

[16] "The Clerk's Tale," 41, 1148, in *The Riverside Chaucer*, 3rd ed., ed. Larry D. Benson
(Boston: Houghton Mifflin, 1987).

[17] Robin Kirkpatrick, in "The Griselda Story in Boccaccio, Petrarch and Chaucer," *Chaucer
and the Italian Trecento*, ed. Piero Boitani (Cambridge: Cambridge University Press, 1983), 231–
248, 240, emphasizes Petrarch's intent to focus on "the general patterns that govern humanity."

over, where Petrarch imagined that Griselda's virtue was due to her manly constancy
and venerable wisdom, the Clerk insists that Grisilde's virtue lies in her perfected
"wommanhede" (239). Indeed, the Clerk insists that Grisilde's virtues, her truth and
humility, are virtues particular to women—not to men, not even Job (932)!

> Thogh clerkes preise wommen but a lite,
> Ther kan no man in humblesse him acquite
> As womman kan, ne kan been half so trewe
> As wommen been. . . .   (935–938)

Just as women's virtues are their own, so too, implies the Clerk, are their sufferings.
For the Clerk widens Dioneo's single-minded attack on Gualtieri to include other
husbands who, stubborn in "sturdinesse" (698–705), deliberately exacerbate the sufferings of their wives: "But as for me, I seye that yvele it sit/To assaye a wyf whan
that it is no nede,/And putten hire in angwyssh and in drede" (460–462). But the
Clerk also incorporates new elements in the Griselda story, elements which further
delineate her pain and suffering. Only in the Clerk's version of the story, for instance,
is Grisilde expressly made to understand that her daughter will be haled out to murder on her account: "For this nyght shaltow dyen for my sake" (560), she says. When
Grisilde comes to realize that Walter blames her for her daughter's "death," however,
she ceases to think of Walter as her daughter's father. Instead, she consigns her
daughter's soul to that more kindly father, Christ, who died for "us," she says, as her
daughter will die for her (556–560).

    When Walter tells Grisilde that she must also give her son up to death, and
Grisilde speaks of her pains at his birth, the Clerk expands Petrarch's bare "laborem"
(Severs, 274, 16–17) to describe not only the pains of childbirth, but also, I think, the
nausea of morning sickness: "first siknesse, and after, wo and peyne" (651). It is even
possible that Chaucer (and perhaps the Clerk as well) means his audience to think
that Walter designs his "temptation" of Grisilde first to destroy her perception of
herself (and even her being) as a mother, for he orders his sergeant, she believes, to
murder her children, and second to destroy her perception of herself (and even her
being) as a wife, for he pretends to divorce her and marry another younger and
prettier than she.[18]

    In the period, however, women had little identity other than as daughters, wives,
mothers, and, of course, widows. Because she is a true wife, the Clerk says, Grisilde
vows to Walter that she will live as a "wydwe clene" (836). Unlike Walter, the Clerk
adds, Grisilde vows she will never marry again, never take "another man to hous-
bonde or to make" (l. 840). Unlike Petrarch, however, the Clerk has Grisilde indict
Walter in a complaint that evokes further pity,[19] for she contrasts his new, har-

---

[18] This might remind us of Satan, who tempts men and women and destroys marriages, not
God, who "tempts no man," as both Petrarch and the Clerk emphasize when they quote James
the Apostle.

[19] See Kirkpatrick (240–242), who discusses at length the function of "pitee" in the Clerk's
Tale.

dened, unfeeling attitude towards her with that tenderness he showed to her on their wedding day (857):

> O goode God! How gentil and how kynde
> Ye semed by youre speche and youre visage
> The day that maked was oure mariage!
>   (852–854)

At the same time, Grisilde suggests that she accepted Walter as her husband on account of his kindness, not his wealth and power or lordship.

But from the beginning Walter's conception of marriage was very different from Grisilde's. When Walter's man first urged him to marry, he did so in terms of an oxymoron, urging Walter to bow his neck "under that blisful yok/Of soveraynetee" (113–114).[20] Walter, however, rejects both the ideas of bliss and sovereignty when he insists that marriage will take away his freedom and press him into "servage" (147).

Walter's grievance, notwithstanding, is identical to that of all the married men on the pilgrimage—the Host, for instance, and the Merchant, who views his two-month-old marriage as a "snare" and himself as the victim of his wife's "hye malice," "crueltee," and "cursednesse" (1222–1238). Like Walter, in other words, the husbands on the pilgrimage also invert the relationship between man and wife which the Clerk describes so graphically in his tale. As they do, they come to see themselves occupying the position that Grisilde did, living like her in "sorwe and care" (1228), suffering like her under the dominion of a ruthless mate. They do not interpret the Clerk's story, as Boccaccio may have wished his readers to interpret his tale, to mean that husbands should treat their wives with more love and compassion than Walter did. They assume instead that only men are capable of being like Griselda—as both Petrarch and the Clerk, of course, also alleged when they applied the epistle of James to themselves and all men: "for that every wight in *his* degree/Sholde be constant in adversitee/As was Grisilde" (1145–1147, emphasis mine).

The Clerk, however, alters the moral Petrarch applied to the Griselda story, for the Clerk applies it mainly to the evils of the married state, as his diatribe against the wife of Bath suggests, not more largely to all human adversity, as Petrarch did.[21] Even so, the Clerk continues however narrowly to align himself with Petrarch rather than Boccaccio, painting the Wife of Bath as a Valterius/Walter figure—like a "greet camaille" (1196), a "tygre yond in Inde" (1199), and himself, indeed all poor married men, weaker even than Grisilde, weeping, wailing, and cowering "as doth a quaille" (1206).

There is evidence, however, that Chaucer composed the Clerk's tale with Dioneo's story as well as Petrarch's translation in mind. The Clerk insists, for example, that the introduction which Petrarch added to Boccaccio's story is "a thyng imper-

---

[20] Petrarch's word was nothing like "blisful"; he spoke of a "lawful yoke" ("collumque non liberum modo sed imperiosum legiptimo subicias iugo," Severs, 256).

[21] "Probat tamen et sepe nos multis ac gravibus flagellis exerceri sinit." Severs, 288.

tinent" (54) and describes "deyntevous vitaille" (265) at the wedding feast—a reference to food which Boccaccio, but not Petrarch, mentions.[22] We remember that Boccaccio in his "Proemio" counseled women to pick out the useful counsel his stories provide in order to know what actions to avoid and what to follow ("in quanto potranno cognoscere quello che sia da fuggire, e che sia similmente da segui- tare," 3) and that Dioneo would have preferred Griselda to behave in ways that the Wife of Bath might have applauded and may have emulated. Although Chaucer's celibate Clerk identified himself and other men with Griselda and even composed his "song" against the Wife of Bath for the sole benefit of the "lordinges" on the pil- grimage, it may be that Chaucer, following Boccaccio and Dioneo both, may have wished to direct his female readers (and the Host's and Merchant's neglected wives?) to take the Clerk's words in his song as servicable advice to women, to "suffreth nat that men yow doon offence" (1197). Certainly the facts of the Griselda story do more than hint at the undercurrent of domestic violence in the period which social his- torians are only now beginning to investigate. More like Boccaccio than Petrarch, Chaucer might also have wished to elicit pity for all those wives whose husbands threatened them with poverty and divorce, and their children with incest and murder.

University of Illinois

---

[22] Kirkpatrick, p. 244, although she does not see any direct indebtendess to Boccaccio, does note that Chaucer returns "to the simple oppositions that Boccaccio creates in his tale," and that the Clerk "unconsciously" echoes the disgust against Walter of "Boccaccio's narrator, Dioneo." I would argue that the Clerk, who is Chaucer's creation, can't "unconsciously" echo anyone, but that Chaucer could and perhaps intentionally did echo Boccaccio. See Janet Levarie Smarr, "Mercury in the Garden: Mythographical Methods in the *Merchant's Tale* and *Decameron* 7.9," in *The Mythographic Art: Classical Fable and the Rise of the Vernacular in Early France and England*, ed. Jane Chance (Gainesville: University of Florida Press, 1990), 199–214, who argues for similarly close connections between *Decameron* 7.9 and the *Merchant's Tale*.

Die Korrespondenz der
Olympia Fulvia Morata (1526–1555)
als Dokument italo-deutscher Begegnungen

RAINER KÖSSLING

In den Matrikelbüchern der 1409 gegründeten Universität Leipzig finden sich seit den frühen Zeiten am Rande oder Fuße der Kolumnen Vermerke, die den Namen einzelner Inskribierter hinzugefügt sind.[1] Während ein Teil davon diszi-plinarische Vergehen und die dafür verhängten Strafen festhielt, wiesen nicht wenige auf später erworbene Verdienste der betreffenden Studenten oder Magister hin.

Zu dem für das WS 1513 eingeschriebenen "dns Eobanus de Franckenberck magister Erfordensis" heißt es "Eobanus Hessus poeta"; "Hermannus Buschius Mona-steriensis," Hermann von dem Busche, immatrikuliert im SS 1503, fand als "decus nostrae academiae" lobende Erwähnung; und "Ulricus Huttenus de Buchen," zu einer Gebühr von 10 Groschen zum WS 1507 inscribiert, erfuhr als "Poeta et orator eloquentissimus, qui obiit anno etc. XXIII" rühmendes Gedenken.

Zum Selbstverständnis einer Universitas magistrorum et scholarium gehörte es schon damals, daß neben dem hohen wissenschaftlichen Ansehen der Lehrenden auch die bedeutenden Leistungen ihrer ehemaligen Studenten das Renommee der Alma mater prägten. Aus dem Rahmen solcher Glossen fällt nun nach Umfang wie Inhalt jene, die dem für das SS 1532 in die Matrikel eingetragenen "Andreas Grundler Sweinfordensis" zuteil wurde: "Andreas Grundel vel Grundler, medicinae doctor exi-mius, maritus Olympiae Moratae feminae in utraque lingua doctissimae, cuius extant monumenta. Haec una cum marito doctore Sveinfordiae toto tempore obsidionis, quae duravit ultra annum et trimestre, mansit, nam ibi maritus medicum agebat. Post excidium urbis utrique Heitelbergae. Mortuus 1554."[2]

Dieser Eintrag stammt von einer Hand des 16. Jahrhunderts, und dem Schreiber

---

[1] *Die Matrikel der Universität Leipzig* Bd. 1–3, Hg. von G. Erler (Leipzig 1895), (= *Codex diplomaticus Saxoniae regiae*. Bd. 16–18), hier Bd. 1.

[2] Wie Anm. 1, 607.

lag allem Anschein nach die Erstausgabe von Olympia Moratas Schriften (1558) vor; denn im Gegensatz zu der Bezeichnung "opera" der späteren Editionen enthielt allein ihr Titel das Wort "monumenta." Sieht man einmal davon ab, daß Grundler nicht 1554, sondern ein Jahr später starb, so fällt auf, daß die sehr ausführlich gehaltene Notiz großenteils Aussagen über die mulier bilinguis Olympia Morata enthält. Der "medicinae doctor eximius" wurde hier offenbar vor allem als Ehegatte einer über die Maßen gelehrten Frau der Erwähnung wert befunden, ja die Begegnung mit seinem Namen scheint dem Schreiber einen nicht unwillkommenen Anlaß geboten zu haben, sein Wissen über die Morata zu notieren.

Olympia Fulvia Morata wurde 1526 in Ferrara geboren. Ihr Vater Fulvio Pellegrino Morato hatte sich als Gelehrter und Pädagoge Ansehen erworben, stand mit Männern wie dem Dichter-Gelehrten Calcagnini auf freundschaftlichem Fuß und war zeitweilig am Hof d'Este Prinzenerzieher. Seine älteste Tochter Olympia befähigte er bereits in ihrem frühen Alter zu einer sicheren Beherrschung der lateinischen Sprache in Schrift und Wort und machte sie mit bedeutenden Werke der antik-römischen Literatur bekannt. Im Alter von 14 Jahren wurde sie zur Studiengefährtin der 1531 geborenen Prinzessin Anna bestimmt und am ferraresischen Hof aufgenommen. Dort blieb sie bis zum Tode ihres Vaters im Jahre 1548. 1549 oder 1550 heiratete sie den in Ferrara weilenden deutschen Arzt Andreas Grundler.[3] Mit ihm und in Begleitung ihres jüngeren Bruders Emilio begab sie sich 1550 nach Deutschland. In seiner Vaterstadt Schweinfurt übernahm Grundler das Amt des Stadtarztes, hier in Franken lebte das Paar, bis die Stadt infolge militärischer Auseinandersetzungen des Markgräfler Krieges am 13. Juni 1554 zerstört wurde. Ihrer Habe beraubt und zur Flucht getrieben, gelangte die Morata mit Mann und Bruder schließlich nach Heidelberg. Durch Fürsprache der kurfürstlichen Schwester begünstigt, erhielt Grundler hier am 12. Juli desselben Jahres eine Professur für Medizin. Seine Gattin, vom Kurfürsten Friedrich II. von der Pfalz hierzu eingeladen, erteilte Privatunterricht in Griechisch. Die Gesundheit der jungen Frau war jedoch—nicht zuletzt durch die Folgen der Stadtbelagerung, – vernichtung und Flucht—schwer angegriffen. Am 29. Oktober 1555 starb Olympia Morata an Tuberkulose. Wenige Wochen später raffte wohl die Pest ihren Mann und ihren Bruder Emilio dahin.

"Cuius extant monumenta" hieß es in der Leipziger Matrikel. Die schriftliche Hinterlassenschaft der Morata ist nur lückenhaft überliefert. Sie wurde, die Relikte der Korrespondenz eingeschlossen, von einem Freund der Familie Morato, dem italienischen Gelehrten und Glaubensflüchtling Celio Secondo Curione (1503–1569), gesammelt und zuerst 1558, in vermehrter Auflage 1562 bei Pietro Perna in Basel veröffentlicht; eine nochmals erweiterte Edition erschien nach Curiones Tod 1570 ebenfalls bei Perna, ein Nachdruck davon 1580.[4] Das Opus umfaßt griechische und

---

[3] G. Weiss, "Dr. Andreas Grundler (ca. 1506–1555)," *Mainfränkisches Jahrbuch für Geschichte und Kunst* 34 (1982): 1–32.

[4] Im folgenden wird zitiert nach Carettis Ausgabe: Olimpia Morata. Epistolario (1540–1555). Con uno studio introduttivo di L. Caretti (Ferrara 1940, [R. Deputazione di storia patria per l'Emilia e la Romagna. Sezione di Ferrara]).

lateinische Dichtung und Prosa. Nach Inhalt, Gehalt sowie mit der Rezeption literarischer und poetischer Formen der Antike stehen die Texte in renaissance-humanistischer Gelehrtentradition. Hinsichtlich der sprachlichen Gestaltung und äußeren Form gilt dies gleichfalls für die tradierten Teile der Korrespondenz. 52 von der Morata geschriebene und 15 an sie gerichtete Briefe sind auf uns gekommen. Mit ihnen besitzen wir das wichtigste Quellenmaterial für die Biographie der gelehrten Frau, Zeugnisse ihrer geistigen Kultur und ihrer Glaubenshaltung sowie Dokumente der persönlichen Verbindungen, die sie anstrebte oder unterhielt.

Bereits in seinen äußeren Umrissen manifestiert der Lebenslauf der Morata von ihrer Jugend bis zu ihrem Ableben eine tiefgehende persönliche italienisch-deutsche Begegnung. Doch das Zeugnis der Korrespondenz und besonders die Beachtung des von dieser erfaßten Personenkreises lassen dieses Bild italo-deutscher Beziehungen punktuell differenzierter erscheinen. Für zwei Abschnitte ihres Lebens soll dies im folgenden zu zeigen versucht werden: 1. für die Zeit ihrer Studien am Hofe von Ferrara (1540–1548) und 2. für die Jahre in Deutschland (1550–1554).

Geistig-kulturelles Leben fand seit Generationen am Hofe von Ferrara intensive Pflege. Die Herzöge legten nicht zuletzt auf die gediegene und umfassende Bildung ihrer Kinder hohen Wert und übertrugen sie namhaften Gelehrten. Unter ihnen befand sich Pellegrino Morato. Fürstin Renata, die Tochter des Königs Ludwig XII. von Frankreich und Gattin Ercoles II., war eine hochgebildete Frau. Mit der Erziehung ihrer Töchter Anna, Lucrezia und Eleonora betraute sie auch zwei Deutsche, die damals in Ferrara weilten: die Brüder Kilian und Johann Sinapius (Senf) aus Schweinfurt. Ausschlaggebend für diese Wahl mochte wohl ihre Gelehrsamkeit gewesen sein, nicht zuletzt gewiß auch ihre calvinistische Glaubenshaltung, in der sich die Fürstin mit ihnen verbunden wußte.

Unter den frühen, in Ferrara verfaßten Briefen der Morata haben zwei, leider undatiert überlieferte, zum Adressaten Kilian Sinapius (1506–1563), der von Hause aus Jurist war und am 16. Juli 1544 in Ferrara zum Doktor promoviert wurde.[5] Wie aus den Schreiben, von denen das eine lateinisch, das andere griechisch abgefaßt ist, hervorgeht, führte er die Schülerinnen in die Anfangsgründe des Griechischen ein. Offenbar hatte er die Morata brieflich und mit Nachdruck ermuntert, in der Pflege der humanistischen Studien nicht nachzulassen (". . . me vehementer ad studia politioris humanitatis hortari visus sis;" Caretti S. 57), und sie antwortete darauf mit dem emphatischen Bekenntnis, in ihnen das beste und vortrefflichste Geschenk Gottes an die Menschheit zu erkennen: "Nam istis studiis nihil hominum generi a Deo immortali datum esse melius neque praestantius, semper in animum induxi meum." In ihrem Lehrer erblickte Olympia Morata zudem ein Vorbild an—wie sie schrieb—Sinnesart, Tüchtigkeit und Gelehrsamkeit ("τὸν τρόπον καὶ τὴν ἀρετὴν καὶ τὴν μάθησιν" [Caretti S. 58]). Als Probe ihrer Sprachbeherrschung sandte sie ihm einen kleinen griechischen Aufsatz über den legendären Römer Mucius Scaevola. Unverkennbar spiegelt sich in der Wertschätzung der Humaniora, in dem Streben nach

---

[5] G. Pardi, *Titoli dottorali conferiti dallo studio di Ferrara nei sec. XV e XVI* (Lucca 1900).

sprachlicher Kultur, das aus diesen beiden kurzen Briefen spricht, auch das pädagogisch prägende Wirken des Lehrers wider.

Fünf Briefe aus dieser Zeit entstammen der Korrespondenz mit Johann Sinapius (1505–1561).[6] Dieser war als Schüler bedeutender deutscher Repräsentanten des Renaissancehumanismus in seiner geistigen Haltung geprägt worden und hatte 1529 die Professur für griechische Sprache und Literatur in Heidelberg übernommen. Für die Verteidigung und Förderung humanistischer Studien trat er wiederholt nachdrücklich ein, unter anderem mit einer Rede, *Adversus ignaviam et sordes eorum, qui literas humaniores negligunt aut contemnunt, eo quod non sint de pane lucrando*, die er in Heidelberg 1530 vortrug.[7] Indessen mochte er wohl selbst an der Eignung gräzistischer Studien als materielle Lebensgrundlage jedenfalls in Deutschland Zweifel hegen, denn schon 1531 legte er sein Lehramt nieder und übersiedelte nach Italien, um sich—eingedenk der Erfahrung "Dat Galenus opes"—dem Studium der Medizin zu widmen, und zwar in Ferrara. Dort wurde er am 23. Juni 1535 zum Doctor medicinae promoviert, im Oktober zum Professor berufen, dann von Renata als Hofarzt bestallt und zudem mit der Erziehung der Prinzessinen beauftragt. 1538 heiratete er die ebenfalls lateinisch gebildete Hofdame Francoise Boussiron de Grand-Ry, die in den Morata-Briefen unter der Namensform Bucinoria Erwähnung finden sollte.

Sinapius' pädagogische Tätigkeit wird vor allem in einer Aufführung von Terenz' *Adelphoe* faßbar. Er hatte mit den Kindern der Fürsten die Komödie auf lateinisch einstudiert, die Aufführung fand am 22. April 1543 in Anwesenheit und zu Ehren Papst Pauls III. und erhielt selbstverständlich großen Beifall.

Am akademischen Leben in Ferrara nahmen die Sinapii lebhaft teil: Johann fungierte von 1533 bis 1548 nicht weniger denn vierzehnmal als Zeuge bei Promotionen. Sowohl zu italienischen Humanisten als auch zu deutschen Landsleuten unterhielten sie enge Kontakte. Zu den ersteren gehörte Lilio Gregorio Giraldo, zu den letzteren Valentin Carchesius, vor allem aber Andreas Grundler, die beide im Begriff standen, dort ihr Medizinstudium abzuschließen. Von der geistigen Verbundenheit, die zwischen den deutschen und italienischen Gelehrten bestand, hat Giraldi ein literarisches Zeugnis gegeben: In dem zweiten seiner Dialoge *De poetis nostrorum temporum* legte er nämlich die Würdigung der zeitgenössischen deutschen und französischen Dichter seinem Arzt "Andreas Gruntherus"—Grundler—in den Mund.[8] Am Schluß dieser Ausführungen, an exponierter Stelle mithin, erwähnt Grundler Johann Sinapius als einen Mann, der nach dem Ausweis früherer Arbeiten durchaus den Poetae zuzurechnen wäre, hätte er nicht anderen Studien den Vorrang eingeräumt: "Fuisset et Ioannes Sinapius, meus propinquus, inter poetas iure conlocandus, qui et suo ingenio multos versus edidit et ex Graecis multos transtulit: ut est ex Luciano Podagra, ni illum philosophiae et medicinae studia a mansuetioribus Musis avocas-

---

[6] H. Holstein, "Johannes Sinapius, ein deutscher Humanist (1505–1561)" in *Neunzehnter Jahresbericht über das Königliche Gymnasium zu Wilhelmshaven. Ostern 1901* (Wilhelmshaven 1901).

[7] Sie erschien im Druck "Haganoae in officina Ioan. Secerii" 1530 (UB Leipzig: Phil 502).

[8] Lilius Gregorius Gyraldus, *De poetis nostrorum temporum*, Hg. von K. Wotke (Berlin 1894, = Lateinische Literaturdenkmäler des XV. und XVI. Jahrhunderts, 10).

sent."⁹ Die Ehrung Grundlers kulminiert schließlich in dessen Krönung mit dem Lorbeer und der Erhebung in den ordo poetarum. Olympia Morata verlieren wir nicht aus dem Blick. Ihr widmet in dem zitierten Dialog der Gelehrte Antimachus, rühmende Worte: Da ihre Begabung das beim weiblichen Geschlecht übliche Maß übertreffe und sie in den griechischen und lateinischen Wissenschaften vorzüglich gebildet sei, erscheine sie ihren Zuhörern als ein Wunderkind; jüngst habe sie Grundler geheiratet: "... Olympia Morata, puella supra sexum ingeniosa, nam non contenta vernaculo sermone, Latinas et Graecas litteras apprime erudita, miraculum fere omnibus, qui eam audiunt esse videtur. Haec his diebus nupsit Grunthero huic nostro...."¹⁰ Das heißt, die persönlichen Beziehungen zwischen deutschen und italienischen Humanisten waren so eng, daß ihnen Giraldi diese Würdigung gab. Die Handlung des Dialogs ist in das Jahr 1548 gelegt. Damals brach, vom Treiben der Gegenreformation in Ferrara abgestoßen und um die Stelle des Leibarztes beim Würzburger Bischof zu übernehmen, Johann Sinapius mit Ehefrau und Tochter nach Deutschland auf. Die oben erwähnten Briefe der Morata an ihn enthielten gute Ratschläge für die Erhaltung der Gesundheit und Alltägliches. Zwei sind ihm nach Deutschland gesandt worden. Die junge Frau gemahnt ihn darin an die Erfüllung eines Anliegens, das sie ihm mit auf die Reise gegeben hatte: Er möchte sie dem König sowie dem Fugger empfehlen, beiden Persönlichkeiten Gedichte von ihr überreichen und auf diese Weise "nostrum negotium" (Caretti S. 63) unterstützen. In dem Bewußtsein ihrer dichterischen Begabung und ihrer Kunstfertigkeit hatte sie—der Gepflogenheit zeitgenössischer Poeten folgend—Gedichte aus ihrer Feder den beiden Mächtigen zugeeignet in der Hoffnung, dafür eine Gunst zu erlangen; und diese Erwartung war hochgespannt, denn die Morata beabsichtigte, von ihrer Erfüllung die weitere Gestaltung ihrer beider Pläne abhängig zu machen: "Nihil enim certi de rebus nostris statuere possumus, ni prius quid ille responderit intelleximus. Quapropter si nos omni cura, sollicitudine, metu liberatos velis, te vehementer etiam atque etiam rogo, ut negotium nostrum ita suscipias et tractes apud regem et Fuggerum illisque nos ita commendes, ut tuam commendationem non fuisse vulgarem mox intelligamus.... Commendo tibi perquam diligenter mea carmina" (Caretti S. 63f.). Gelegenheit zur Erfüllung des Wunsches mochte sich Sinapius von seinem Aufenthalt in Augsburg versprochen haben; dort machte er am 18. Mai 1548 Station, während in der Stadt der Reichstag gehalten wurde. Im Briefwechsel der Morata ist von dem Anliegen nicht wieder die Rede, ein Erfolg war der Fürsprache—wenn es überhaupt dazu kam—wohl nicht beschieden. Gleichwohl bemerkenswert ist in unserem Zusammenhang der Versuch, vorausschauend einträgliche Verbindungen in Deutschland zu suchen und auf diesem Weg zur Zukunftsplanung der Grundlers beizutragen.

1550 reist Grundler mit Gattin und Schwager nach Deutschland. Zunächst aus Österreich, wo man einige Zeit verweilte, dann aus Deutschland begann die Morata sogleich, Freunden aus Italien Nachricht über ihre Reise und Ankunft zu geben.

---

⁹ Wie Anm. 8, 70.
¹⁰ Wie Anm. 8, 94.

Briefe gingen an Gregorio Giraldi, an die Freundin Lavinia della Rovere-Orsini, vor allem an Celio Secondo Curione.[11] Daneben führte die junge Frau im Auftrag ihres Mannes die Korrespondenz mit ihren Gastgebern aus Schwaz und Augsburg, dem königlichen Rat Georg Hörmann und seinem Sohn Anton. Durch deren Vermittlung war Grundler eine Professur für Medizin in Linz in Aussicht gestellt worden. Grundler lehnte jedoch ab. Die Gründe für diese auf den ersten Blick kaum verständliche Entscheidung deuten sich in Briefen an. Es war die Besorgnis, in Linz nicht offen und unbehelligt dem reformierten Glauben gemäß leben zu können: "... modo illic nos Christianos aperte profiteri liceat et sacris pontificum non uti" (Caretti S. 83) heißt es diesbezüglich in einem Brief an Georg Hörmann.

Die geistige und emotionale Verbundenheit mit den deutschen Freunden und Bekannten aus Ferrara hatte weiterhin Bestand: Die brieflichen Verbindungen erhielt weitgehend die Morata aufrecht: zu Johann Sinapius und seiner Familie; diese Kontakte blieben eng, zeitweilig nahm die Morata die Tochter Theodora Sinapius zu sich, um ihr Unterricht zu erteilen; zu Kilian Sinapius; zu Lorenz Schleenried, der ihnen Bücher aus Ferrara nachsandte und den sie um Nachricht über die Verhältnisse in Ferrara bat; zu Valentin Carchesius, dem sie zu seiner Promotion am 24. Dezember 1551 gratulierte und den sie um die Übermittlung eines Briefes an ihre Mutter ersuchte.

Zugleich unterhielt sie in Schweinfurt die Verbindung zu einem Kreis religiös gleichgesinnter Männer, unter ihnen befand sich der ihr aus Ferrara bekannte Schulmeister Johannes Cremer und der Pfarrer Johann Lindemann, ein Verwandter Martin Luthers. Vermittelt durch Curio, entstanden Kontakte zu dem Basler Korrektor und humanistischen Gelehrten Basilius Johannes Herold sowie zu den prominenten Buchdruckern Isengrin, Oporin, Herwagen, Froben und Bischoff. In einem Brief—der freilich nun schon am 1. Dezember 1554 aus Heidelberg gesandt wurde—läßt sie diesen ihren Dank für die Übersendung von Büchern übermitteln, "... qui nos tot luculentis scriptoribus donarunt" (Caretti S. 114).

Nicht eigentlich ein Zeugnis italienisch-deutscher Begegnungen ist der Brief eines uns ansonst nicht bekannten Hieronmus Angenosius: Dieser bedankte sich für den Griechischunterricht den ihm in Heidelberg durch die Morata erteilt hatte. Der Brief bildet zugleich einen Beweis dafür, daß die Gattin des Medizinprofessors Grunthler in Heidelberg privatim Griechisch lehrte. Einzelheiten wissen wir darüber leider nicht.[12]

Seit ihrer Ankunft dieseits der Alpen verrieten die Briefe eine zunehmend engere Hinwendung der Morata zu den studia divina. Bibellektüre wird hierzu ebenso gehört haben wie die Beschäftigung mit den Schriften des deutschen Reformators Martin Luther. Nicht zuletzt darum scheint ihr auch die Beförderung reformatorischer Bestrebungen in Italien ein Herzensanliegen geblieben zu sein. Zwei Versuche

---

[11] M. Kutter, *Celio Secondo Curione. Sein Leben und sein Werk (1503–1569)* (Basler Beiträge zur Geschichtswissenschaft, 54) (Basel 1955).

[12] Vgl. N. Holzberg, "Olympia Morata und die Anfänge des Griechischen an der Universität Heidelberg," *Heidelberger Jahrbücher* 31 (1987): 77–93.

unternahm sie mit dem Ziel, Luthers Lehre ihren Landsleuten zu vermitteln: In einem Schreiben vom 26. Mai 1553 bat sie den streitbaren Lutheraner Johannes Flacius Illyricus, er möchte, da sie selbst des Deutschen nicht hinlänglich mächtig sei, zu diesem Zweck eine deutsche Schrift Luthers in das Italienische übersetzen oder persönlich eine Darstellung reformatorischer Positionen auf italienisch zu verfassen: "Si autem libellum aliquem Lutheri germanice scriptum, in quo eorum publicos errores coarguit, in italicum converteres . . . aut tu de eadem hac re aliquid italice componeres, . . ." (Caretti S. 88). Zugleich verwies sie, um nicht ausführlicher werden zu müssen, auf ein Schreiben Johann Cremers an Flacius; mit dem Deutschen verband sie das Bestreben, der Reformation Lutherischer Prägung auch jenseits der Alpen Heimatrecht zu schaffen.

Mit einem anderen Versuch wandte sie sich an den Juristen Petrus Paulus Vergerius. Er war der Reformation verbunden, hatte der Morata seine Schriften zugesandt, und dies nahm sie zum Anlaß für die Bitte, er möchte von Luthers Großen Katechismus, dessen lateinische Fassung von Vincentius Obsopoeus 1529 in Hagenau erschienen war, eine italienische Version anfertigen; sie könne von großem Nutzen sein, ". . . quanto emolumento nostris Italis (praesertim iuventuti) futurum id sit, ex ipso libro, si diligenter pervolveris, cognosces" (Caretti S. 120). Der Erfolg blieb beiden Ansinnen versagt.

Es ist eine bunte Vielfalt von Begegnungen und Verbindungen zwischen italienischen sowie deutschen und in einem Falle auch schweizerischen Gelehrten, die sich in Olympia Moratas Korrespondenz widerspiegelt. Diese gründete im wesentlichen auf der Gemeinsamkeit renaissance-humanistischer Bildung und—mehr oder weniger ausgeprägt—auf reformatorischer Glaubenshaltung. Möglicherweise hatte der deutsche Dichter Goethe auch diese Kontakte im Blick, als er unter dem 30. Januar 1828 in seinem Tagebuch notierte: "Las in den Briefen der Olympia Fulvia Morata, und es ging mir über den eigentlichen, damaligen, protestantischen Zustand ein ganz neues Licht auf. Meine Bemerkungen denke niederzuschreiben."[13]

Universität Leipzig

---

[13] J. W. von Goethe, *Briefe und Tagebücher*, Hg. von H. G. Gräf (Leipzig o. J.), 2:670.

Neulateinische "mimetische" Gedichte

MARION LAUSBERG

V or einigen Jahren hat Winfried Albert unter dem etwas mißverständlichen
Titel *Das mimetische Gedicht* einen bestimmten Gedichttyp der Antike behandelt, als dessen Entdecker er Wilamowitz bezeichnet.[1] Ich möchte im folgenden
einige Beispiele für diesen Gedichttyp aus der neulateinischen Literatur vorstellen.
Die Auswahl des Materials beruht nicht auf systematischer Suche; dementsprechend
bescheiden ist meine Zielsetzung: Ich möchte insbesondere auf das Verhältnis zu antiken Vorbildern eingehen und zeigen, daß der Gedichttyp in seiner besonderen Struktur und seinen sprachlichen Formen nicht erst in der neueren Forschung, sondern in
den Imitatio antiker Modelle faktisch schon in der Renaissance erkannt und rezipiert
worden ist.

Mein erstes Beispiel soll zugleich erläutern, was hier trotz der terminologischen
Bedenken im Anschluß an Albert als 'mimetisches Gedicht' bezeichnet werden soll.
Mitten in dem Brief, den Castiglione seine Frau Hippolyte an sich schreiben läßt und
in dem sie über seine Abwesenheit klagt, findet sich der Vers V.67:[2]

> Quid queror? en tua mi scribenti epistola venit

> ("Was klage ich? Siehe, während ich schreibe, ist ein Brief von Dir
> gekommen.")

Während des Schreibens ist durch die Ankunft eines Briefes eine Situationsver-
änderung eingetreten, auf die die Schreiberin hinweist und auf die sie dann reagiert.
Albert definiert folgendermaßen: "Ein mimetisches Gedicht besteht in einer poetisch
gestalteten zusammenhängenden Rede, die eine als Sprecher auftretende Person in
einer Szenerie äußert und in der sie auf Vorgänge oder Geschehnisse Bezug nimmt,

---

[1] W. Albert, *Das mimetische Gedicht in der Antike* (Frankfurt a.M., 1988). Vgl. meine Rezension
in: *Gnomon* 66 (1994), 176–179.

[2] Ed. W. Ludwig, "Castiglione, la moglie e Ovidio," in: *Medioevo e rinascimento* 5, n.s. 2
(1991), 81–98; ders., "Castiglione, seine Frau Hippolyta und Ovid," in: *Die Frau in der Renaissance*,
hrsg. P. G. Schmidt (Wiesbaden 1994), 99–156.

die sich während des Sprechens in der Szenerie ereignen und eine Szenerieveränderung bewirken."[3]

Die ganze Briefelegie Castigliones steht natürlich in der Nachfolge der Heroinenbriefe Ovids, und in einem dieser Briefe findet sich eine Situationsänderung, die, wie der wörtliche Anklang zeigt, das Vorbild für Castiglione gewesen ist; Walther Ludwig hat in seiner ausführlichen Interpretation des Gedichts darauf hingewiesen: Ov. *Epist. heroid.* 9,143:

> Sed quid ego haec refero? scribenti nuntia venit
> fama.

Castiglione übernimmt die sprachliche Form, mit der hier die Sprecherin auf die Szenerieveränderung hinweist, das Partizip Präsens *scribenti* im Dativ und das Verbum *venit* im Perfekt, eingeleitet durch eine Frage. Die Situationsänderung gibt dem Dichter die Möglichkeit, eine veränderte psychische Stimmung in das Gedicht mit einzubeziehen. Die Zweifel der Frau daran, ob der Mann an sie überhaupt noch denkt, werden etwas beschwichtigt. Im Unterschied zu Ovid ist es bei neulateinischen Dichtern eine Situations- und Stimmungsveränderung zum Besseren hin, wie Walther Ludwig ausführt, im Unterschied zu der generell gedrückten Stimmung der ovidischen Heroiden. Die Anlehnung in Gesamtstruktur und Wortlaut ist mit einer kreativen Umformung der antiken elegischen und Heroidentradition verbunden.

Die Stellung des Situationswechsels in der Struktur der Gedichte, die dichterische Funktion und die sprachlichen Signale, mit denen dem Leser diese Szenerieveränderung mitgeteilt werden, wie z.B. der Erzählung, der Prophezeiung oder der Anweisungsserie, das sind Gesichtspunkte, die Albert in seiner Dissertation kaum berücksichtigt, die aber für eine Interpretation solcher Gedichte m.E. wohl wichtiger wären als die Art der Szenerieveränderung (z.B. unwillkürliche physische Veränderungen am Sprecher, Handbewegungen, Ortsveränderungen), die Albert zur Grundlage einer differenzierten Typologie macht und der er fast ausschließlich seine Aufmerksamkeit widmet. Ich werde im folgenden im wesentlichen nach den von mir genannten Kriterien vorgehen.

Andersartig als bei den angeführten Briefen ist die Funktion der Szenerieveränderung, wenn sie nicht innerhalb des Gedichtes, sondern an dessen Schluß steht. Hierzu gehört der Typ der Gebetserhörung,[4] wie er in der Antike in Ovids Exildichtung *Ep. ex Pont.* 2,8 vorliegt, einem Gebet an ein Bild der kaiserlichen Familie. An dessen Ende glaubt der Sprecher eine weniger finstere Miene auf den Gesichtern zu erkennen; die Hoffnung auf ein günstigeres Schicksal des verbannten Dichters erhält so das letzte Wort in der Elegie.

Ein neulateinisches Beispiel für einen solchen hoffnungsvollen Abschluß eines Gebets findet sich in einer an Maria gerichtete Ode des Jacob Balde *Lyr.* 2,42. Der Sprecher bemerkt ein Zeichen, einen Ton seiner Leier aus dem nahen Winkel, und

---

[3] Albert, 24.
[4] Vgl. hierzu Albert, 233f.

glaubt, dies als Indiz für die Erhörung seines Gebets deuten zu können.[5] Es handelt sich um ein Gebet um Befreiung aus einem Fieber; Gedichte in eigener Krankheit sind, auf der Basis von Tibull 1,3, ein beliebtes Thema der neulateinischen Dichtung.[6] Die Tibullelegie endet zwar ebenfalls in einer hoffnungsvollen Stimmung, aber diese wird nicht in mimetischer Gestaltung aufgrund eines während des Sprechens bemerkten Zeichens geäußert, sondern nur als ersehnte Zukunftsvision dargeboten.[7] Beim Neulateiner Molza bleibt die düstere Stimmung erhalten: der Sprecher glaubt schon die Ruder des Charon zu hören.[8] Für Balde dürfte die poetische Gestaltung einer Gebetserhörung ein besonders passender Ausdruck seiner christlichen Zuversicht gewesen sein. Die Form findet sich bei ihm allerdings auch in einer—im christlichen Sinne nicht als eigentliches Gebet zu verstehenden—Bitte an den personifizierten Schlaf *Lyr.* 2,36. Das Gebet steht in der Tradition der Silve des Statius an den Schlaf (5,4), die in der Neuzeit vielfach nachgeahmt worden ist. Balde gibt dieser Tradition durch den Abschluß mit einer Erhörung der Bitte einen neuen und besonders wirkungsvollen Abschluß: Auf einmal befällt den Sprecher Trägheit und er wird so müde, daß er nicht einmal mehr vom Stuhl ins Bett zu gehen vermag.[9] Mimetisch gestaltete erfolgreiche Anrufung des Schlafs für einen anderen findet sich im Neulateinischen aber auch schon in den *Naeniae* des Giovanni Pontano (*Naenia prima*):[10]

```
 1    Somne, veni ...
15    Venisti, bone somne, boni pater alme soporis,
         qui curas hominum corporaque aegra levas.
```

---

[5] Jacob Balde, *Carmina lyrica*, ed. P. Benno Müller (Regensburg 1884; Nachdr. Hildesheim 1977); Jacob Balde S.J., *Opera Poetica omnia*, Bd. I, Neudruck der Ausgabe München 1729, hrsg. W. Kühlmann und H. Wiegand (Frankfurt a.M. 1990), *Lyr.* 2,41,13ff. *Quid in propinquo concinit angulo? / An sponte motae sunt citharae fides? / ... Amplector omen.*

[6] Vgl. W. Ludwig, "Petrus Lotichius Secundus and the Roman Elegists: Prolegomena to a Study of Neo-Latin Elegy," in: W. Ludwig, *Litterae Neolatinae* (München 1989) (zuerst 1976), 202–217, hier 216 Anm. 66; W. Kühlmann, "Selbstverständigung im Leiden. Zur Bewältigung von Krankheitserfahrungen im versgebundenen Schrifttum der Frühen Neuzeit," in: *Acta Conventus Neo-Latini Hafniensis* (Binghamton, N.Y. 1994), 547–555.

[7] Vergleichbar ist auch Ps.-Tib. 3,10, ein Gebet an Phoebus in der Krankheit der Geliebten des Cerinthus, in dem der Sprecher nach der Bitte an den Gott sich tröstend an Cerinthus wendet: V. 15: *pone metum, Cerinthe, deus non laedit amantes.* Die Zuversicht beruht hier aber nicht auf einem während des Sprechens empfangenen Zeichen.

[8] Francesco Maria Molza, in: *Renaissance Latin Verse. An Anthology*, ed. A. Perosa und J. Sparrow (London, 1979), S.265ff., V.92 ff.: *iam vocat in nigros mors tenebrosa lacus, / increpitatque moras Lethaeae portitor undae, / et remi auditus per loca senta fragor.*

[9] V. 53ff.: *Pro vota! / cuius damnor inertiae? / Totus labasco; vix lubet hiscere; / Piget moveri. Sella lectus / Esto: puer citharam repone.* Bei M. Wehrli, *Jacob Balde, Dichtungen, lateinisch und deutsch* (Köln/Olten 1963), S.43 ist durch die Fehlübersetzung von *cuius damnor inertiae* die gesamte Gedichtstruktur verunklärt: "O der Gelübde! Was für ein müßig Spiel!"

[10] *Poeti Latini del quattrocento*, ed. F. Arnaldi, L. Gualdo Rosa und L. Monti Sabia (Milano/Napoli, 1964), S.490. Mimetisches Sprechen findet sich auch in weiteren *Naeniae*.

Als Abfolge von Gebet und Gebetserhörung gestaltet Iacopo Sannazaro ein Gedicht zur Geburt eines Kindes, *Eleg.* 1,4.[11] Die ersten zehn Verse bitten die Geburtsgöttin Lucina um Hilfe und Epiphanie; in Vers 11 wird dann ihre Anwesenheit festgestellt:

> Lucis adest dea magna; metum jam comprime, Garlon:
> non frustra est lacrimis illa vocata tuis.

Nach der Aufforderung, die Göttin zu verehren, erfolgt einige Verse später der Hinweis auf die nunmehr stattfindende und dann schon erfolgte Geburt (V.18f.):

> iam parit adventu tacta puella deae:
> iam puerum est enixa.

Die Schlußverse sind dem soeben geborenen Knaben gewidmet, als Rühmung und Segenswünsche. Hier steht die Gebetserhörung also nicht am Schluß, sondern während des Sprechens finden mehrere Stufen eines Vorgangs statt, die der Sprecher mit seinen Worten feststellt und kommentierend begleitet. Der Leser wird unmittelbar in das Geschehen hineinversetzt, er erlebt die Geburt beim Lesen des Gedichts mit. Dieses Hineinnehmen in einen längeren Vorgang ist ein in der Antike besonders geläufiger Typ des mimetischen Gedichts, insbesondere bei der Schilderung von Festverläufen. Catulls mimetisch gestaltetes Hochzeitsgedicht 61 ist auch in seiner mimetischen Struktur im Neulateinischen z.B. von Pontano und Petrus Lotichius Secundus[12] aufgegriffen worden, worauf hier nur kurz hingewiesen werden kann; die Gedichte verdienten gerade unter diesem Gesichtspunkt eine eigene Betrachtung.

Speziell auf eine Geburt ist der Darstellungstyp jedoch in der Antike offenbar zumindest noch nicht so deutlich angewendet worden. Daß es überhaupt nicht so einfach war, ein passendes antikes Modell für ein Gedicht auf eine Geburt zu finden, zeigt Pontanos Gedicht auf die Geburt seines Sohnes *De amore coniugali* 1,10; hier liegt eher der Typ des Gedichtes für spätere Geburtsfeiern, bes. Tib. 2,2, zugrunde. Hauptmuster für die angeführte Elegie des Sannazaro war offenbar Vergils 4. Ekloge, die den motivischen Rahmen bildet. Hier findet sich gegen Anfang eine Bitte an Lucina (V. 10 *casta fave Lucina*), und nach der im Futur gehaltenen Prophezeiung richtet sich die Anrede an den Knaben; die Aufforderung an ihn, die Mutter anzulachen, hat Sannazaro am Schluß seines Gedichtes aufgegriffen. Daß der Knabe, der bei der Bitte an Lucina noch mit dem Präsenspartizip *nascenti puero* (V.8) versehen worden war, nun offenbar als schon geboren zu betrachten ist, gibt dem Gedicht

---

[11] *Iacobi Sannazarii opera omnia Latine scripta* (Venedig 1535).

[12] Pontano, *De amore coniugali* 1,3, in: *Poeti Latini* (a.o.), S.448ff. (auf seine eigene Hochzeit). Lotichius, *Eleg.* 4,3 und 6,42 (*Petri Lotichii Secundi Solitariensis Poemata quae exstant omnia*, ed. C. T. Kretzschmar [Dresden 1773]). Vgl. auch das Trauergedicht *Eleg.* 3,7 und dazu Ludwig, "Petrus Lotichius," 213 Anm. 51.

einen zumindest latent mimetischen Charakter,[13] den Sannazaro ausgebaut und ausgestaltet hat.

Hineinversetzen in eine Szenerie, in der sich die Situation mehrfach ändert, das tut Ioannes Secundus in seiner Elegie 2,9,[14] in der er den Schlaf bittet, sein Mädchen, das neben ihm liegt, zu verlassen. Im weiteren Verlauf des Redens stellt der Sprecher dann zunächst fest, daß der Schlaf dabei ist, wegzugehen, mit einem Verbum im Präsens:

> Somnus abit, sensi, leviori pectus amatum
> iam gravat illa mihi pondere, somnus abit.

Noch später dann bemerkt er, daß sie verschiedene Dinge tut, die beweisen, daß sie nicht mehr schläft: an ihren Haaren nestelt, sich die Augen reibt und ihn küßt.

> In niveo lapsos formavit pollice crineis,
>   lumina permulsit semireclusa manu,
> et mihi basiolum strinxit trepidante labello.

Der Liebende und die schlafende, dann aufwachende Geliebte, diese Grundsituation findet sich in der antiken Liebeselegie in Properz 1,3; doch ist diese Elegie Erzählung einer vergangenen Begebenheit, nicht mimetisches Sprechen in der Gegenwart. Daß Secundus an dieses Gedicht gedacht hat, zeigt aber der wörtliche Anklang an Prop. 1,3,23:

> et modo gaudebam lapsos formare capillos

in dem angeführten Vers

> in niveo lapsos formavit pollice crineis.

Was bei Properz der Liebende an der schlafenden Geliebten tut, hat Secundus umgeformt zu einem Zeichen ihres eigenen Aufwachens. Bei Properz kommt weiterhin der Liebhaber erst zu Besuch zu der schlafenden Geliebten, sie liegen nicht miteinander im Bett; eine solche Situation der glücklichen Liebe ist in der antiken, vorwiegend klagenden Liebeselegie ohnehin die Ausnahme. Bei Properz findet sie sich bezeichnenderweise nur im erzählenden Rückblick auf eine solche Nacht 2,15, nicht als beglückende Gegenwart. Der Unterschied der Sprechweisen, Erzählung oder mimetisch-gegenwärtiges Sprechen, ist hier durchaus Indiz einer unterschiedlichen Darstellung der Liebe. Das Motiv des Aufweckens aus dem Schlaf, dort umgekehrt

---

[13] F. Dornseiff, "Verschmähtes zu Vergil, Horaz und Properz," in: *Berichte über die Verhandlungen der Sächs. Ges. d. Wiss. Leipzig*, phil.-hist. Kl. 97, 6 (Berlin 1951), 45 bestreitet, daß in *Ecl.* 4 "während des Gedichts die Zeit weitergeht"; das zu erwartende Kind könne schon vor seiner Geburt mit *parve puer* angeredet werden; vgl. Albert, *Das mimetische Gedicht*, 6; W. Kraus, *Vergils vierte Ekloge. Ein kritisches Hypomnema*, ANRW II 31.1 (Berlin/New York 1980), 604–645, hier 609 und 633.

[14] Joannes Secundus, *Opera nunc primum in lucem edita*. Facsimile edition (Utrecht 1541; Nieuwkoop 1969).

vor der Frau zum Mann, kann dabei durchaus aus eben dieser Properzelegie angeregt sein.[15]

Weniger selbständig als in den angeführten neulateinischen Gedichten ist das mimetische Sprechen der Antike aufgegriffen bei einem Dichter nicht des ersten Ranges, Faustus Andrelinus (*Amores* 2,11). Nachdem vom Warten auf eine Antwort der Geliebten die Rede gewesen war, glaubt er gegen Schluß des Gedichts die Tür knarren zu hören als günstiges Zeichen. Dies bleibt relativ eng am Lied des Alphesiboeus in der 8. Ekloge Vergils, in dem ein Flammenzeichen und das Bellen des Hundes am Schluß das Kommen des Daphnis anzeigen.[16]

Etwas näher eingehen möchte ich abschließend noch auf die Elegie des Petrus Lotichius Secundus an den Mond (1,5), die wieder einem bedeutenden Autor gehört. Fraiman hat in ihrer Dissertation eine Reihe wörtlicher Anklänge an antike Stellen registriert,[17] doch bleibt sie bei solchen Detailbemerkungen stehen. Auf die Beziehung der Gesamtstruktur zu antiken Vorbildern geht sie nicht ein. Der Sprecher befindet sich auf einer Reise bei Nacht. Zu Beginn bemerkt er, daß weder Mond noch Sterne sich zeigen, und er richtet an den Mond die Bitte, ihm den Weg zu erleuchten. Später dann stellt er fest, daß jetzt die kleineren Sterne sich zeigen, und noch später, daß der Mond nunmehr aus den Wolken hervorgetreten ist. Am Schluß weist er dann auf das Nahen des Lichts und das Kommen des Morgensterns hin; so finden Nacht und Weg ein Ende. Durch das mimetische Sprechen wird der Leser auch hier in die Situation mit hineingenommen und erlebt ihre verschiedenen Stadien mit; mit dem abschließenden Tagesanbruch finden Grundsituation und Gedicht ihre Abrundung. Sprechen bei Nacht, deren Zeit während des Sprechens vergeht und an deren Ende der Tag anbricht, diese Situation hat ihre Entsprechung in Ovids Paraklausithyron, in der der wartende Liebhaber den Türwächter um Einlaß bittet und in einem Refrainvers vom Fortschreiten der Zeit spricht: *tempora noctis eunt*. Daß Lotichius gerade an Ovid *Am*. 1,6 gedacht hat, darauf weisen auch einige wörtliche Anklänge an aufeinanderfolgenden Versanfängen:

Ovid	Lotichius
33 non ego	11 non ego
43 at memini	25 at memini
49 fallimur an	31 fallor an
51 fallimur	35 fallor

---

[15] Prop. 2,15,7f.: *illa meos somno lapsos patefecit ocellos / ore suo et dixit 'Sicine, lente, iaces?'*

[16] *Publi Fausti Andrelini Amores sive Livia*, ed. G. Tournoy-Thoen (Brüssel 1982) (Verhandlingen von de koninklijke Academie voor wetenschappen, letteren en schone Kunsten van Belgie, Klasse der letteren 44, 100), S. 364ff., V. 41f.: *Sed quid concusso crepuerunt cardine postes? / An bona festinus nuncius acta refert?* Das Zeichen, das hier das Nahen der Geliebten anzeigt, ist an Ov. *Am*. 1,6,49: *Fallimur, an verso sonuerunt cardine postes?* angelehnt (Verweis auf diese Stelle in der genannten Ausgabe), eine Stelle, die ihrerseits eine Reminiszenz an Verg. *Ecl*. 8 ist.

[17] K. A. O'Rourke Fraiman, "Petrus Lotichius Secundus, Elegiarum liber primus," ed. with an introduction, translation, and commentary (diss., Columbia Univ. 1973).

Wie der Sprecher bei Lotichius V. 11 versichert, daß er kein Verbrechen vorhat, so der Sprecher bei Ovid, daß er ungefährlich sei (V. 33). Mit den Worten *at memini* leitet Lotichius die Erinnerung an eine umgekehrte Situation ein, wo der Mond gerade nicht dem Wunsch des Sprechers gemäß schien; so weisen auch bei Ovid die Worte *at memini* auf eine umgekehrte Situation hin, wo der Wächter nicht wie jetzt vielleicht schlief, wo aber gerade sein Wachen dem Sprecher unerwünscht war. Die Situation, auf die der Sprecher bei Lotichius Bezug nimmt, ist gerade die des Paraklausithyron, also die des ovidischen Vorbilds (V. 25f.):

> at memini caecae cum fretus munere noctis
> nuper amans foribus serta daturus eram.

Mit den angeführten Versen wird also das Gedicht des Lotichius als ein Gegenstück zu einem Paraklausithyron gekennzeichnet. Damit ist wohl nicht nur speziell auf Ovids Elegie 1,6 verwiesen, sondern allgemein auf die Thematik der römischen Liebeselegie. Diese Elegie des Lotichius ist, wie auch die anderen des 1. Buches,[18] keine Liebeselegie, und im kontrastierenden Bezug wird die thematische Andersartigkeit geradezu programmatisch bewußt gemacht. Die Imitatio antiker Vorbilder verbindet sich hier wie auch sonst bei Lotichius mit thematischer Eigenständigkeit.[19] Auch das formale Darstellungsmittel des mimetischen Sprechens hat er zu eigenen Zwecken frei gestaltet. Hier zeichnet es eindrucksvoll den Weg durch das Dunkel zum Licht, dem wohl auch symbolische Bedeutung zukommen soll.

Eine Bemerkung verdienen auch die sprachlichen Zeichen, mit denen Lotichius (und andere neulateinische Autoren) die Szenerieveränderung markieren. Es sind dies in der Elegie 1,5 Verben im Präsens, unterstützt durch hinweisendes *en* (42) und *ecce* (115), sowie vor allem das *iam* (42.63). Solches *iam* findet sich in antiken mimetischen Gedichten etwa bei Tibull (2,1,87 *iam nox iungit equos*) und Ovid (*Am.* 1,6,66 *iamque pruinosos molitur Lucifer axes*; 3,2, 43.65.77; zu *en* vgl. 3,2,75). Eine andere, bei Ovid mehrfach vorkommende Junktur (*Am.* 3,6,85; *Trist.* 1,2,34; Albert 211), *dum loquor*, benutzt Lotichius in einem der Epithalamien (*Eleg.* 6,42,93 *dum loquor, en*). Die in Eleg. 1,5,31 im Unterschied zu Ov. *Am.* 1,6,49 nicht in mimetischem Sinne genutzte Wendung *fallor an* ist im Epithalamium Eleg. 4,3 von Lotichius als mimetisches Signal eingesetzt (97 *Fallor? an . . . tympana . . . dedere sonum?*).

Der Sprecher von Ovids Paraklausithyron hat keinen Erfolg, und wenn hier am Schluß der Morgenstern aufgeht, so war sein Warten vergeblich. Vergeblich sind auch die Bitten an Aurora in einer anderen Elegie Ovids (*Am.* 1,13), noch nicht aufzugehen, weil die Liebenden noch beieinander bleiben möchten, und vergeblich ist

---

[18] Vgl. dazu Ludwig, "Petrus Lotichius," 211; Fraiman 84.

[19] Grundsätzlich wichtig hierzu P. L. Schmidt, *"unde utriusque poetae elegans artificium admirari licebit.* Zur Ovid-Rezeption (*Am.* 2,6) des Petrus Lotichius Secundus (*El.* 2,7), in: *Der altsprachliche Unterricht* 23, 6 (1980), 54–71. Zur Anrede speziell an den Mond ist noch zu vergleichen Ov. *Am.* 1,13 mit der Anrede an Aurora (die V. 44 mit Luna verglichen wird) sowie die Anrede an die Mondgöttin in Theokrits Pharmakeutria. Einfluß der Pharmakeutria auf ein anderes Gedicht des Lotichius vermutet G. Ellinger, *Geschichte der neulateinischen Literatur Deutschlands im sechzehnten Jahrhundert II* (Berlin/Leipzig 1929), 381.

die Bitte an den Fluß in dem mimetischen Gedicht *Am.* 3,6; er schwillt sogar noch an (V. 85), statt seine Fluten zu beruhigen. Positiven Ausgang hat dagegen die Werbung im mimetischen Circusgedicht *Am.* 3,2 sowie Vergils 8. Ekloge mit der Rückkehr des Daphnis. Aber generell ist doch auffällig, daß insgesamt die mimetischen Gedichte der neulateinischen Autoren anscheinend eher als die antiken zu einem zuversichtlichen positiven Ausgang tendieren. Den Hintergrund bildet wohl das produktive Mißverständnis von Horazens Elegientheorie *voti sententia compos* (*Ars* 76), auf dessen Bedeutung für die neulateinische Elegie generell und auch speziell für den mimetisch dargestellten Stimmungswechsel in Castigliones Gedicht Walther Ludwig hingewiesen hat.[20]

Erst eine umfassendere Durchsicht des neulateinischen Materials wird genauere Aufschlüsse über die Art und Weise der Übernahme und Umformung antiker mimetischer Gedichte in der Neuzeit bringen können und etwa Fragen danach, was etwa nicht imitiert wurde, oder ob innerhalb der neulateinischen Dichtung bestimmte Entwicklungen und Bezugnahmen auszumachen sind, beantworten lassen. Die volkssprachliche Dichtung der Epoche wäre weiterhin miteinzubeziehen; dabei können neulateinische Gedichte ihrerseits als Vorbild gewirkt haben. Für ein mimetisch gestaltetes Epithalamium auf die eigene Hochzeit, wie es im Englischen Spenser dichtet, bietet nicht der ebenfalls stark einwirkende antike Autor Catull mit seinem 61. Gedicht auf die Hochzeit eines anderen, sondern der Neulateiner Pontano ein Vorbild. Der künstlerische Höhepunkt, den Spenser in Weiterführung und Vertiefung der Tradition des mimetischen Sprechens verwirklicht hat,[21] dürfte wohl in der neulateinischen Dichtung nicht erreicht worden sein. Dennoch vermögen die angeführten Beispiele wenigstens vorläufig zu zeigen, wie die Dichter der Renaissance und des Barock einen bestimmten Gedichttyp erkannt und in sehr eigenständiger Weise aufgegriffen haben.

Universität Augsburg

---

[20] "Petrus Lotichius" 205f.; "Castiglione" (1994), 123.

[21] Zur Bedeutung des Zeitablaufs in Spensers Gedicht, vgl. W. Clemen, *Spensers Epithalamion*, (Sitzungsber. d. Bayerischen Ak. d. Wiss., phil.-hist. Kl., 1964, 8), (München 1964), bes. 17ff.

Idee sulla guerra e la pace
negli umanisti italiani e spagnoli del secolo XVI

MARIA JOSÉ LÓPEZ AYALA Y GENOVÉS

L'idea della guerra, vale a dire il modo in cui si è diffusa e articolata in certe epoche e società, costituisce di per sé una questione di enorme importanza storica.[1] Il periodo da noi preso in considerazione, nella storiografia spagnola e italiana, inizia nel 1453 con due assedi: in Europa occidentale, la conquista di Bordeaux che mise fine alla Guerra dei Cento Anni, in Europa orientale, la caduta di Costantinopoli che segnò definitivamente la supremazia dei Turchi in Grecia e nei Balcani.

Nella stessa linea di assestamento di basi nazionali solide, a partire dal 1482, tre anni dopo il matrimonio tra Isabella e Ferdinando che riunì le corone di Castiglia ed Aragona, si intrapresero, per un periodo di dieci anni, una serie di campagne militari che riuscirono infine ad espellere i Musulmani dal Regno di Granada, dove godevano di ampi diritti dal secolo XIII. La situazione a sud delle Alpi era radicalmente diversa.[2] L'anno 1453 fu una data cruciale anche per la conclusione della lunga guerra tra Milano e Venezia, che produsse—con la pace di Lodi—un patto di non aggressione tra i principali stati dell'Italia: Firenze, Roma ed il Regno di Napoli.

La prassi delle guerre come momento importante di un processo di autodefinizione territoriale, all'interno di frontiere più o meno tradizionali e di lingue approssimativamente nazionali, cominciò ad imporsi in tutta l'Europa.

In questo periodo notevole fu l'influenza di Sant'Agostino e di Erasmo. La dottrina agostiniana contiene le tre condizioni fondamentali per la guerra, quelle che saranno invocate nel corso della storia della teoria della guerra giusta: l'autorità del principe, una causa giusta ed un'intenzione retta. Come vedremo, questa conclusione può essere applicata in gran parte al secolo XVI. Erasmo godé in Spagna di una grande popolarità, mentre non fu così in Italia, e nessuno può dubitare del suo odio

---

[1] José A. Fernández Santamaría, *El Estado, la guerra y la paz. El pensamiento político Español en el Renacimiento 1516–1559* (Madrid: Akal, 1988); John Rigby Hale, *Guerra y Sociedad en la Europa del Renacimiento 1450–1620* (Madrid: Ministerio de Defensa, 1990).

[2] Frederick L. Taylor, *Art of War in Italy 1494–1529* (Cambridge, 1921).

genuino contro la guerra, come lo esprime nel suo *De pacis quaerimonia*.

Nel Rinascimento si deve distinguere tra le guerre civili o internazionali e le rivolte locali, variabili nella loro intensità.[3] La guerra riguardava la società e per gli uomini di Stato la pace globale era un mito.[4] Le interpretazioni generalizzate sull'inevitabilità della guerra, data l'ambizione dei governanti e la natura dell'uomo come animale politico, condussero a formulare teorie del tipo di quelle di Luigi Porto: "la pace porta ricchezze, la ricchezza orgoglio, l'orgoglio ira, l'ira la guerra, la guerra povertà, la povertà rassegnazione, la rassegnazione pace, la pace ricchezza," e così all'infinito.[5]

Riassumendo, le idee sulla guerra, la sua origine, la sua pratica e i suoi effetti hanno una straordinaria importanza poiché si trovano alla base del pensiero politico. Allo stesso tempo, molto importante fu il concetto di pace, una pace che, malgrado i sospetti, era considerata dalla quasi totalità degli scrittori come qualcosa di positivo, accessibile, prolungabile e soprattutto come una fase importante e vantaggiosa della vita nazionale. La pace non è un concetto statico, ma un principio dinamico che, come il "bene" agostiniano, scompare periodicamente. La guerra può essere superata solo dall'azione dello Stato.

Che conclusioni si possono trarre dall'analisi dei maggiori umanisti che scrivono sulla guerra ed elogiano la pace? Questo sarà l'obiettivo del nostro lavoro, che comprenderà soltanto la prima metà del secolo XVI, data l'estensione dell'argomento. In primo luogo converrà ricordare che gli umanisti, uomini di grande personalità e fine sensibilità, si sentirono indifesi di fronte ad un evento che risultava evidente, ma che era impossibile capire nella sua autentica natura. Ma fino a che punto detestavano questi autori la violenza? Il secolo XVI fu un periodo di crisi. Un'ingrediente fondamentale di questa crisi fu la guerra, che acquisì un'importanza cruciale proprio perché restava valido lo schema agostiniano per il quale uomo, stato e guerra sono in profonda interrelazione.

Numerosi furono pertanto i letterati sia spagnoli che italiani che si soffermarono a riflettere sulla guerra, ovviamente partendo da diverse concezioni filosofiche, teologiche e giuridiche. In ambito spagnolo, da un punto di vista cronologico e tematico il trinitario Alonso de Castrillo[6] precede gli apologisti dell'impero. Il suo *Tractado de Republica* rappresenta un approccio alla crisi *legislativa* castigliana, assolutamente estraneo all'ideologia imperiale e invece influenzato dalle idee del costituzionalismo medievale. L'opera costituisce, sul terreno del pensiero politico, un monumento isolato all'interno degli avvenimenti che portarono a quella che è stata chiamata la prima rivoluzione moderna. L'argomento della cittadinanza, affrontato nel *Tractado*, scompare dalla letteratura politica castigliana posteriore al Castrillo. Bisognerà arrivare a

---

[3] John Rigby Hale, *Renaissance War Studies* (London, 1983).

[4] John Rigby Hale, "Capitoli sulla guerra," in *New Cambridge Modern History*, vols. 1–3 (Cambridge, 1957, 1958, 1968).

[5] Manuel Fernández Álvarez, *La sociedad española en el Renacimiento* (Madrid: Cátedra, 1974).

[6] Alonso de Castrillo, *Tractado de Republica* (Madrid: Instituto de Estudios Políticos, 1958).

Ginés de Sepúlveda, ed al declino dell'era erasmiana, per osservare una simile enfasi sull'argomento.

A partire dall'inizio del XVI secolo l'ordine monarchico fu in Spagna pienamente accettato. Da allora il pensiero politico o abbracciò l'idea della monarchia in una versione imperialista, temperata appena dal quasi-misticismo dell'umanesimo cristiano di Alfonso de Valdés, oppure la negò soltanto nella parte ecumenica, accettandone tutte le altre implicazioni, come nel caso di Francisco de Vitoria. Soltanto quando l'influenza di Erasmo sarà del tutto tramontata, un certo contrasto rinascerà con l'"imperialismo" di Ginés de Sepúlveda. Invano dobbiamo cercare in Alfonso de Valdés, nato a Cuenca forse nel 1490, il pensatore desideroso di penetrare nei segreti della politica o l'uomo di affari; al contrario troviamo il moralista che cerca rimedio ai mali dell'ingiustizia sociale e all'anarchia provocata dall'inettitudine politica. Le opere che reclamano l'attenzione sono il *Diálogo de las cosas ocurridas en Roma* e il *Diálogo de Mercurio y Carón*.[7] Nella prima, sulla guerra tra Carlo V e Clemente VII, il Valdés rivela le sue idee circa la concordia e la discordia. Tutta la tematica della seconda opera ruota invece attorno a tre punti basilari, che ricordano in qualche modo il triplo ruolo di Valdés come umanista, uomo di affari e devoto servitore dell'imperatore, e avvocato difensore della riforma cattolica. Come negli scritti di Luis Vives, il significato del messaggio del *Diálogo de las cosas ocurridas en Roma* è indubbio: qualsiasi tentativo di riforma politica deve essere preceduto e seguito dalla pace; un governante che è occupato nella guerra può difficilmente dedicare attenzione al popolo; innanzi tutto il principe deve imparare a governare; il popolo sarà poi il riflesso fedele del suo carattere e del suo comportamento. Ma la radicalizzazione del pensiero del Valdés ha un altro importante corollario, come vedremo quando analizzeremo il pensiero di Francisco de Vitoria, poiché lo schema politico creato dalla scuola di Salamanca richiedeva una netta separazione tra le sfere di interesse dell'ordine naturale e di quello soprannaturale. Valdés presenta una separazione soltanto apparente tra Chiesa e Stato, in quanto non traccia una linea rigorosa tra il ruolo secolare dello Stato e la missione spirituale della Chiesa, e concepisce l'idea imperiale come lo strumento più conveniente, dato che la guerra non solo è in contraddizione con la dottrina cristiana, ma si scontra anche con i principi naturali. Il Valdés non è un pacifista, anzi sostiene con estrema chiarezza la possibilità che un principe si senta costretto a fare la guerra. Forse uno degli aspetti più interessanti della sua teoria sulla guerra giusta consiste proprio nel fatto che i suoi assiomi fondamentali possono essere interpretati in diversi modi.

I problemi politici posti dalla annessione del Nuovo Mondo alla corona castigliana provocarono la nascita di una filosofia politica, di cui il massimo rappresentante è Francisco de Vitoria della scuola salmantina, nato a Vitoria tra il 1483 e il 1486 e

---

[7] Alfonso de Valdés, *Diálogo de las cosas acaecidas en Roma*, ed. R. Navarro Durán (Madrid, 1994); Marcel Bataillon, "Alfonso de Valdés autor del 'Diálogo de Mercurio y Carón'," in *Omaggio offerto a Menéndez Pidal* (Madrid, 1925), 1: 403–415.

autore delle opere: *De Indis* e *De iure belli Hispanorum in barbaros*.[8] In primo luogo dobbiamo considerare che l'universalismo politico non era una sopravvivenza obsoleta del passato circoscritta alla Spagna, e d'altra parte, non solo il pensiero di Vitoria e della scuola spagnola, ma tutto il contributo alla filosofia politica dell'epoca di Erasmo—l'umanesimo cristiano e l'empirismo machiavellico—soffrono di mancanza di originalità o di insufficienza ideologica. Il pensiero politico spagnolo a partire dal Vitoria fino a Francisco Suárez trova il suo fondamento nella ragione e nella fede, principi che gli autori spagnoli vedevano rappresentati rispettivamente nell'Antico e nel Nuovo Testamento. Vitoria cercò di trovare i mezzi che rendessero possibile preservare l'unità dell'Europa cristiana, tenendo conto delle condizioni che precorrono la nuova era: religioni diverse, conquista di territori, ambizioni dei governanti, ecc. Sia in Europa che in America queste condizioni avevano qualcosa in comune: la guerra. Il fenomeno coinvolgeva l'uomo come essere etico. L'argomento della guerra ha una grande importanza nel pensiero politico di Vitoria ed è molto lontano da quello del Vives, per il quale la guerra è sinonimo di discordia irrimediabile. La concordia, che è la pace tra gli uomini, non può esistere per molto tempo senza la guerra e la guerra, che è parte integrante della vita dell'uomo in società, può essere capita adeguatamente solo sulla base della legge della natura. La guerra crea lo stato e lo stato sancisce ed istituzionalizza la guerra. I teologi spagnoli affermavano che l'alternativa alla guerra giusta era il caos e l'anarchia.

Francisco de Vitoria è affascinato dal potenziale di virtù contenuto nel mestiere e nella persona del principe cristiano. Tutti i pericoli che la teoria della guerra giusta comporta, sono considerati e analizzati dal Vitoria che, in questo modo, verso la metà del secolo, rendeva considerevolmente più moderata la posizione tradizionale sulla guerra.

Dato che il problema della guerra occupa un ruolo importante nelle teorie politiche dei pensatori spagnoli, in nessun altro autore possiamo trovare così ben espressa la interrelazione tra la politica e la concordia-discordia come in Luis Vives (1490), il quale fissò le regole della pacificazione dell'Europa contrastando gli egoismi e le cupidigie delle nazioni, e fu uno dei più notevoli rappresentanti della letteratura del diritto di guerra, durante il secolo XVI. Vives per proprio temperamento odiava profondamente la guerra, tanto da essere riconosciuto come il campione della pace e della concordia tra i principi cristiani della sua epoca.

Alfonso de Valdés e Luis Vives sostengono punti di vista diversi sul ruolo e i doveri dei monarchi in generale e dell'imperatore in particolare. Nel pensiero politico di Vives l'argomento che senza dubbio occupa un posto preminente è la concordia, considerata come una cosa necessaria per il mondo, mentre la discordia è vista come l'ostacolo che si oppone alla riforma, testimonianza dell'opera negativa dell'uomo che rifiuta di collaborare. Ammette che lo stato e la guerra vanno ineludibilmente assieme. Lo stato dipende dalla dialettica concordia-discordia.[9] Di conseguenza la

---

[8] Francisco de Vitoria, *De Indis – De iure belli Hispanorum in barbaros*, ed. V. Beltrán de Heredia (Madrid, 1939).

[9] Cf. le sue *Obras Completas*, ed. L. Riber (Madrid, 1947).

guerra si trova alla base di tutte le concezioni contemporanee dello stato e coinvolge l'uomo come essere etico.

Luis Vives e Francisco de Vitoria concordano nell'affermàre che tutti gli uomini sono responsabili della guerra, in questo modo viene anche implicato lo stato. Vives non è un rivoluzionario e non propone l'insurrezione come mezzo per risolvere i problemi; nella sua filosofia politica, basata su una accettazione dello stato come istituzione auspicabile, anche se temporaneamente, appare sempre la sua inquietudine per la guerra e la pace. Per lui la guerra non solo sovverte la giustizia e la libertà nella comunità, ma dato che trasforma il re in un tiranno, suscita i dissensi interni e la guerra civile.

La guerra, che per i neoscolastici era un mezzo per preservare lo stato, per Vives minaccia di affondare le zattere che offrono protezione all'uomo, anche se questi ha la speranza di recuperare l'integrità della "respublica Christiana." La filosofia giuridica del Vives si accentra sui problemi del suo tempo con l'obiettivo di persuadere princ001 e governanti a condurre una politica di pace. Presentiva la necessità dell'esistenza di una "società internazionale," cioè di una comunità di nazioni organizzate giuridicamente. Ebbe una "concezione pacifista della pace,"[10] diametralmente opposta a quella espressa dalla nefasta formula "si vis pacem para bellum," che tante stragi ha causato all'umanità. Vives è stato un difensore non intransigente dei dogmi della Chiesa e della dottrina sociale; un deciso individualista, polemico contro le posizioni collettive a favore della violenza. Rappresenta nell'Europa del Rinascimento l'esponente più alto della cultura umanistica. I suoi libri sono un appello alla concordia, senza la quale né le virtù individuali, né lo sforzo collettivo produrrebbero alcun risultato.

Grazie alla scoperta dell'America abbiamo il magnifico propagandista delle cause degli indiani, Bartolomé de las Casas,[11] e l'opera erudita del suo oppositore, Ginés de Sepúlveda,[12] nato verso il 1490 ed esponente di una fase dell'umanesimo spagnolo di influenza italiana, estranea alla corrente parallela dell'umanesimo erasmiano. Questo autore, che conobbe tre re, riunisce in sé un'insieme di idee politiche inseparabili da altri pensatori già esaminati: la dottrina della guerra giusta, il diritto naturale, lo "ius gentium" e la schiavitù civile o naturale. Analizza la teoria della guerra giusta e questa è il mezzo scelto dall'umanista per salvaguardare e preservare la gerarchia dell'ordine naturale decretato da Dio. Nel Democrates primus espone la sua posizione sulla guerra, fondata sulla legge naturale. La guerra giusta, che non sarà mai necessaria, sarà malgrado tutto un mezzo per ottenere una pace giusta. Ed è proprio questo l'unico fine lecito di una guerra che si considera giusta: permettere agli uomini di vivere in pace, giustamente e virtuosamente, dato che la pace è ciò che preserva la società umana. Nel De Regno, la Cohortatio ad Carolum, il Democrates alter, la Apologia

---

[10] Carlos Riba y García, *Luis Vives y el pacifismo* (Zaragoza: Universidad de Zaragoza, 1933–1934).

[11] Bartolomé de Las Casas, *Historia de Indias* (México: Fondo de Cultura Económica, 1951).

[12] Angel Losada, "Juan Ginés de Sepúlveda. Estudio Bibliográfico," *Revista Bibliográfica y documental* 3–4 (1947): 315–393; Juan Beneyto, *Ginés de Sepúlveda, humanista y soldado* (Madrid, 1944).

pro libro de iustis belli causis e nelle *Proposiciones*, allo stesso tempo che si fa difensore della guerra giusta, con la quale vuole rifiutare le offese ed evitare che le nazioni cadano nella schiavitù, afferma che la guerra non deve mai essere desiderata per se stessa e, se è necessaria, deve essere condotta da uomini buoni, perché possa essere un mezzo per ottenere la pace. Questa giustificazione della guerra, che permette all'uomo di respingere la violenza con la violenza, quando non esiste altra possibilità per recuperare i beni rubati, esige che il governante abbia esaurito tutte le soluzioni pacifiche, in modo da privare il malvagio della capacità di fare il male e assicurare all'uomo una vita pacifica e tranquilla.

Fin qui il panorama che ci offre la storiografia spagnola. Passeremo ora ad esaminare i rappresentanti della storiografia italiana del secolo XVI per i quali l'influenza della Spagna è stata notevole.

Dai diversi Stati italiani che configurano l'Italia del XV e XVI secolo, sorgono voci che nascono da una "coscienza italiana" e opere che proclamano e difendono la libertà di una Italia il cui dominio si contendono Francia e Spagna. Agli albori del XVI secolo inizia in Italia una reazione contro "l'antico" come modello e norma. Il conflitto tra le due mentalità, quella che continua a credere nel "rinnovamento" e quella che non vuole altro che "prototipi," trova la sua massima espressione in Machiavelli e Guicciardini, quest'ultimo con lo sguardo rivolto solo verso la realtà presente. Entrambi descrivendo le forze determinanti della politica e della storia, mirano in realtà a giustificare o la concezione democratica o quella aristocratica. Divennero i fondatori della scienza politica considerata come un risorgere della saggezza politica del mondo antico.

L'influenza degli umanisti e uomini di stato è comunque più evidente. Matteo Palmieri (1406–1475), pur essendo un difensore della pace e della prosperità, cerca un cambiamento nella milizia, difendendo quella comunale: nel suo *Libro della vita civile* critica la milizia mercenaria, auspicando l'arruolamento dei cittadini. Francesco Patrizi (1412–1494), nel *De institutione rei publicae,* consiglia il servizio militare obbligatorio per tutti i giovani. Entrambi deplorano la mollezza dei loro tempi e la mancanza di spirito eroico, considerando l'interesse mercantilistico come causa dell'indifferenza politica dell'epoca.

Baldassare Castiglione (1478–1529) è un uomo di armi e di corte, cui Clemente VII affidò la Nunziatura in Spagna (1525). Considerato come il miglior trattato di educazione sociale del tempo, nel suo *Cortegiano*[13] il Castiglione si assunse il compito di elaborare l'ideale del nuovo uomo di corte al servizio del principe. Il "cortigiano" deve essere di alto lignaggio ed abile nell'uso e esercizio delle armi senza presunzione e senza trascurare la letteratura.

Machiavelli (1469–1527)[14] conobbe la maggior parte dei politici del suo tempo, tranne Ferdinando il Cattolico. Malgrado ciò, ebbe una profonda conoscenza di

---

[13] Baldassarre de Castiglione, *Il libro del Cortegiano*, ed. A. González Palencia (Madrid: CSIC, 1942).

[14] Felix Gilbert, *Machiavelli e il suo tempo* (Bologna: Il Mulino, 1964); Gennaro Sasso, *Niccolò Machiavelli* (Bologna: Il Mulino, 1980).

questo periodo spagnolo e creò una serie di miti politici. Interprete fedele della realtà politica cui aspirava l'uomo del Rinascimento, il Machiavelli è l'uomo che va contro lo spirito del suo tempo, il critico implacabile di un periodo di cui percepisce chiaramente le debolezze;[15] traccia pertanto una linea di demarcazione netta tra se stesso e i suoi predecessori "idealisti," che avevano cercato di adattare e subordinare la teoria politica a schemi teologici o metafisici. L'intero pensiero politico di Machiavelli tende inevitabilmente a indagare la funzione del potere militare nella vita politica; ad ogni occasione insiste infatti sulla guerra e sulla grande importanza di una buona disciplina militare. Le critiche negative sono rivolte al sistema militare e alla condotta della guerra in Italia durante il Quattrocento, determinati da prevalenti interessi finanziari. Machiavelli come teorico della guerra, benché si occupi di particolari organizzazioni e di tattica militare, in realtà trascende questi argomenti e discute delle condizioni politiche e delle loro relazioni rispetto a una buona organizzazione militare.

Un'analisi delle teorie politiche di Machiavelli non si può quindi limitare all'*Arte della Guerra*, opera esclusivamente dedicata a problemi militari. Anche negli scritti politici e storici, *Il Principe*, i *Discorsi* e le *Istorie Fiorentine*,[16] la guerra e l'organizzazione militare hanno una parte importante sotto forma di suggerimenti. Le osservazioni di carattere militare sono tuttavia di natura essenzialmente negativa e rappresentano la critica alle istituzioni militari del tempo. L'*Arte della Guerra*, il grande manuale di arte militare su cui è principalmente basata la fama di Machiavelli come teorico della guerra, offre una esposizione sistematica, e anche largamente tecnica, delle idee militari e tratta un programma positivo di riforma militare.

Machiavelli stese del resto il *memorandum*, in base al quale fu promulgata l'ordinanza del 1506, la legge che stabiliva il servizio militare obbligatorio per tutti gli uomini dai 18 ai 30 anni. Egli indagò a fondo le relazioni tra il potere politico e quello militare. Le sue esperienze personali lo portarono a un esame oggettivo della crisi militare dell'epoca in cui viveva, divenendo così il primo teorico militare dell'Europa moderna. E' un errore valutare le teorie militari di Machiavelli dal punto di vista della loro utilità immediata, perché esse in realtà produssero una nuova impostazione dei problemi della guerra, delle esigenze e dell'organizzazione militare.

Francesco Guicciardini[17] iniziò la sua carriera politica negli anni 1511–1512, quando fu designato ambasciatore di Firenze alla corte di Ferdinando il Cattolico. Ammiratore del re di Spagna fu anche un grande difensore del regime monarchico. Le sue teorie generali sulla politica e sullo stato le espose nei *Ricordi politici e civili*.[18] La sua straordinaria capacità politica risulta patente nelle due opere storiche, le *Storie fiorentine*, dove dà prova dei legami esistenti tra le istituzioni politiche e le istituzioni

[15] Nino Borsellino, *Niccolò Machiavelli* (Roma–Bari: Laterza, 1989).

[16] Cf. *Tutte le opere storiche e letterarie di Niccolò Machiavelli*, ed. Mazzoni e M. Casella (Firenze, 1929).

[17] Federico Chabod, *Escritos sobre el Renacimiento* (México: Fondo de Cultura Económica, 1990), 193–204; Marcel Gagneux, *Présence et influence de l'Espagne dans la culture italienne de la Renaissance* (París: Université de la Sorbonne Nouvelle, 1978), 53–112.

[18] Francesco Guicciardini, *Ricordi politici e civili*, ed. R. Spongano (Firenze, 1951), 78.

militari, e la *Storia d'Italia*,[19] dove condanna fermamente la politica di neutralità perseguita da Firenze. Nella *Relazione sulla Spagna*, scritta al termine della sua missione diplomatica, parla dell'armata spagnola, che considera come un adattamento della tattica svizzera a quella italiana. La corte spagnola, grazie al suo realismo, arricchì il pensiero del Guicciardini. Nel *Discorso di Logrogno* sostiene che le buone istituzioni sono inutili senza una organizzazione efficace dello stato; è per questo motivo che condanna il mercenarismo e sottolinea il vantaggio di un esercito nazionale.

Guicciardini è uno storico che di fronte ai fatti assume due posizioni: nelle prime *Storie* è mosso da una fortissima volontà d'azione; nella *Storia* invece si mantiene distante, osservando le cose così come sono successe e studiando le motivazioni delle azioni. Questo autore, che definisce l'arte della politica interna ed estera, separa la morale dalla politica e scrive che la natura della guerra—giusta o ingiusta—non ha nessun peso sul suo risultato, si distingue per i contributi che apporta, a partire dalla descrizione minuziosa degli avvenimenti interni di una città o dalla considerazione della ripercussione nella storia della penisola dei fatti accaduti in altri paesi.

Concludendo, diremo che una concezione religiosa della guerra, il servizio militare limitato alla classe dei cavalieri e un codice morale-legale, questi sono i fattori che determinarono le forme dell'organizzazione militare come i sistemi di guerra nel Medioevo. Il carattere temporaneo del servizio militare rendeva difficile una stretta disciplina. Poiché l'organizzazione militare era un prodotto tipico dell'intero sistema sociale del Medioevo, ogni cambiamento fondamentale si ripercuoteva inevitabilmente nel campo militare. Nel Rinascimento mutamenti nella composizione dell'esercito e nella tecnica militare finirono per trasformare anche lo spirito dell'organizzazione militare.[20] Come risultato di una situazione per cui la guerra non era più intrapresa come un dovere religioso, lo scopo del servizio militare divenne il guadagno. Sorse il problema morale se fosse una colpa seguire una professione che comportava uccisione di altre persone. Le menti più elevate discussero la possibilità di abolire la piaga della guerra e della milizia. La composizione e il carattere dell'organizzazione militare, il suo posto e la sua importanza nell'ordine sociale, erano divenuti problemi da riesaminare.[21]

UNED. Madrid

[19] Francesco Guicciardini, *Storia d'Italia*, ed. C. Panigada (Bari, 1939), 3: 332–338.

[20] Piero Pieri, "L'evoluzione dell'arte militare nei secoli XV, XVI e XVII e la guerra del secolo XVIII," in *Nuove Questioni di Storia Moderna* (Milano, 1966), 2: 1123–1179.

[21] Piero Pieri, "La scienza militare italiana nel rinascimento," *Rivista Storica Italiana* 50 (1933): 262–281.

Lucian and Paradox in the Early Quattrocento

DAVID MARSH

T he paradoxical encomium began as the counterpart of classical encomium, an important genre of epideictic rhetoric which grew out of speeches given at funerals and festivals.[1] In the second century A.D., the Greek satirist Lucian composed a short paradoxical encomium titled *The Fly*. He also exploited the rhetoric of paradox in four other works which were popular in the Renaissance. Lucian's parodies of Socratic inquiry in *The Parasite* and *The Professor of Public Speaking*, his travesty of tragic style in *Gout*, and his ironic narration in the *True Story* provided important models for the three principal subjects of sixteenth-century satirical eulogy: animals, diseases, and vices.[2] But the origins of Renaissance paradoxical writing date from the early Quattrocento, when Guarino of Verona translated Lucian's *The Fly* and *The Parasite* between 1403 and 1418.

A summary of these two works will provide the background to Quattrocento paradoxical literature. Lucian's *The Fly* begins with a pseudo-scientific description of the fly and proceeds to celebrate her social and intellectual skills. The fly's courage is sung by none other than Homer, who (in *Iliad* 17.520) compares his bravest heroes to flies. Lucian traces the origin of flies to an ancient myth about a human maiden named Muia ("Fly" in Greek), who fell in love with the youth Endymion and was changed into a fly by her jealous rival Selene, the goddess of the moon. And Lucian adds that history records two celebrated women named Muia. "But although I still have much to say on this topic," the author concludes, "I shall stop now lest I am accused of making an elephant out of a fly, as the proverb says."

The humor of *The Fly* lies in its anthropocentric distortion. Lucian praises the fly using encomiastic arguments more often applied to great men, including allusions to Homer and Plato, and a mythological lineage. By declaring flies superior to bees, moreover, Lucian's mock encomium reverses two of the standard themes of classical

---

[1] Theodore C. Burgess, "Epideictic Rhetoric," *University of Chicago Studies in Classical Philology* 3 (1902): 89–261.

[2] C.-A. Mayer, *Lucien de Samosate et la Renaissance française* (Geneva, 1984); Annette Tomarken, *The Smile of Truth: The French Satirical Eulogy and Its Antecedents* (Princeton, 1990).

eulogy, namely, the generosity of the individual and the harmony of society. Compared to bees, flies in fact appear both parasitic and antisocial.

Like *The Fly*, Lucian's *The Parasite* exploits paradoxical rhetoric, in this case to parody Platonic dialogue.[3] The discussion takes place between Simon, an accomplished parasite or sponger, and Tychiades, a sort of Lucianic "straight man." Simon says that "sponging" is a noble art (*techné*), which he defines as a system of knowledge intended to attain pleasure. Using hedonism as his touchstone, Simon declares all other ways of life inferior, for the simple reason that the parasite alone is truly happy. Rich people worry about their wealth, and philosophers are clearly wretched. In wartime, the parasite, being well-fed, makes a fine soldier; while in peacetime, he is sociable and athletic.

Although Lucian's *The Fly* and *The Parasite* differ greatly in their length and style, they share two features which were to influence the paradoxical encomium of the Renaissance. First, they employ comparison (Latin *comparatio*, or Greek *súnchrisis*), as ancient rhetoricians recommend in epideictic rhetoric.[4] The fly is superior to the bee, and the parasite superior to the philosopher. Second, in praising their subjects, both encomia consider hedonistic criteria certain proof of superiority. The fly partakes of kingly feasts, and the parasite is invited to the most sumptuous banquets. These two Lucianic features will become a hallmark of Renaissance paradoxical rhetoric.

The early Quattrocento witnessed the rebirth of epideictic rhetoric, a genre that has recently been studied by O'Malley and McManamon.[5] Less well known are the paradoxical writings of Quattrocento humanists, such as Leonardo Bruni's 1407 *Oratio Heliogabali ad meretrices*. Inspired by *Scriptores Historiae Augustae* 26.3, which describes the emperor Heliogabalus addressing the prostitutes of Rome in a quasi-military oration, Bruni recreated this discourse in an ironic spirit. The climax of the speech, a sexual emancipation proclamation for all Roman women, was inspired by Plato, whose works Bruni had been translating into Latin:

> As for our women, I myself shall determine whether I have less power in
> Rome than a certain philosopher in his imaginary republic . . . I am pleased to
> enact a law, which will make all women common property.[6]

In mocking the sexual communism of Plato's *Republic*, this preposterous decree both echoes Lucian's *True Story* 2.17 and *Philosophies for Sale* 17 and exorcises a doctrine

---

[3] W. H. Tackaberry, *Lucian's Relation to Plato and the Post-Aristotelian Philosophers* (Toronto, 1930), 69–71; Tomarken, *The Smile of Truth*, 8–12.

[4] Burgess, "Epideictic Rhetoric," 125–126.

[5] John O'Malley, *Praise and Blame in Renaissance Rome: Rhetoric, Doctrine, and Reform in the Sacred Orators of the Papal Court, c. 1450–1521* (Durham, 1979); John McManamon, *Funeral Oratory and the Cultural Ideals of Italian Humanism* (Chapel Hill, 1989).

[6] University of Chicago Library, MS. 32, fol. 22: "Sed de mulieribus nostris ipse uidero, experiarque profecto an minus mihi Romae liceat, quam philosopho nescio cui in sua quadam ciuitate, quam ipse finxerat, licuerit. Etenim mihi cordi est . . . legem ferre, per quam mulieres omnes fiant communes."

which Quattrocento humanists found particularly troubling.[7] The *Oratio Heliogabali* also anticipates the hedonistic license of Lorenzo Valla's *De voluptate*, as Bruni was well aware when he defended the piece in a letter to Niccolò Niccoli of 7 January 1408.

Two paradoxical encomia of the early Quattrocento are Latin eulogies of animals written by Leon Battista Alberti. The first, *Canis*, dating from 1438, is a funeral oration for the author's deceased dog. The second, *Musca*, is an imaginative reworking of Lucian's *The Fly*, which Alberti composed in 1441 after reading the piece in the Latin version by Guarino of Verona.[8]

Significantly, these mock encomia follow close upon two encomiastic biographies which Alberti composed between 1432 and 1438. The first is the *Vita S. Potiti* (ca. 1432–1434), the biography of an obscure second-century martyr, which Alberti undertook—reluctantly, it seems—at the request of his superior Biagio Molin, patriarch of Grado.[9] The second, Alberti's *Vita*, is an autobiography written (like Caesar's *Commentaries*) in the third person and modeled after the Greek biographies of Plutarch and Diogenes Laertius.[10] In composing the *Vita S. Potiti*, Alberti clearly sensed the difficulty of praising the saint's fanatical devotion and violent martyrdom, for the work is laden with irony and scarcely moves the reader to admiration. In writing his own life, as in casting his self-portrait medallions, Alberti found a classicizing style the most effective means of revealing his personal aspirations. Thus, for Alberti, encomiastic writing was an ambiguous mixture of positive and negative elements. In the positive manner of his autobiography, he could generously lavish praise on an individual's ancestry, education, achievements, and witty sayings. But in the negative manner of his *Vita S. Potiti*, Alberti the hired encomiast demonstrates that the rhetorical task of writing laudations could be applied indifferently. It is no accident that in his dinner piece *Defunctus*, written before 1434, Alberti caricatures a bishop's funeral oration as mindless babbling.

The proem of Alberti's *Canis* evokes Pliny the Younger's *Panegyric of Trajan* by stressing the Roman tradition of the public *laudatio*. Of course, since funeral orations in Alberti's day generally accompanied a requiem, the irony of his discourse also plays on the incongruity of a dog celebrated in the solemn context of Christian ritual. Alberti further praises eulogists whose speeches inspire the living, especially the young, to emulate their illustrious forebears; accordingly, his eulogy proper begins with an account of the deceased's ancestry. Alberti says that his dog was born to prominent parents who were descended from the most distinguished canines of antiquity. Then, describing his dog's character, Alberti stresses the principal canine virtues of loyalty and bravery in a passage largely derived from Pliny's *Natural History*

---

[7] James Hankins, *Plato in the Italian Renaissance* (Leiden, 1990), 149–153.

[8] For *Canis*, see L. B. Alberti, *Apologhi ed elogi*, ed. Rosario Contarino (Genoa, 1984); for *Musca*, Alberti, *Opuscoli inediti: Musca, Vita S. Potiti*, ed. Cecil Grayson (Florence, 1954).

[9] Alberti, *Opuscoli inediti*, 31–32.

[10] Riccardo Fubini and Anna Menci Gallorini, "L'autobiografia di Leon Battista Alberti: Studio e edizione," *Rinascimento* 12 (1972): 21–78.

and Plutarch's *On the Cleverness of Animals*. A more recent source was provided by the Greek *Encomium of the Dog* by the Byzantine scholar Theodore Gaza, which lists further instances of canine fidelity and fortitude.[11]

After these historical examples, Alberti praises his deceased pet's valor and prudence in wartime and his cultivation of the arts and learning in peacetime—a balanced account of virtues borrowed from Lucian's *The Fly*. He further recounts how his dog abandoned his former pursuits and devoted himself to study when he saw how his master searched for wisdom. At once, like Socrates welcoming the fair Alcibiades, Alberti embraced this handsome canine, whose outward beauty matched the excellence of his soul. Indeed, the nobility of his dog's countenance could only have been faithfully rendered by the skill of Zeuxis, the ancient Greek painter who once painted Helen of Troy by combining the features of five beautiful maidens.[12]

The implied parallel between Alberti and Socrates shifts the encomium from biography to autobiography, and the next few pages of *Canis* present distinct echoes of Alberti's *Vita*. Thus, Alberti's dog possessed a quick mind, combining the memory of a Hortensius and the versatility of a Cato. He was an exemplar of personal virtues, shunning wealth and pleasures. He lived simply, with little care for clothing or luxurious sleeping quarters. To his friends, he was a loyal guardian of secrets; but to his enemies he proved, like Hercules, a zealous avenger of wrongs. He pursued the study of the most difficult subjects and strove to achieve the highest fame and glory—even cultivating music by singing to the moon!

Alberti's dog accompanied him daily to the gymnasium and befriended any dogs who seemed philosophical. There is hardly any need to enumerate all his virtues: it suffices to recall the devotion he inspired in others, and the grief which his death has occasioned. In his peroration (a paradoxical *comparatio*), Alberti compares his dog to great men of antiquity, contrasting their imperfections to his pet's freedom from vice. Compared to his virtuous dog, Aristotle was greedy, Plato wanton, Cicero ambitious, and Sulla cruel; Caesar was a tyrant, Cato a womanizer, and Crassus a moneygrubber. Who could fail to mourn such a paragon among dogs? In his final moments, this dog (treacherously poisoned) sought out his master and kissed him tearfully. Farewell, my dog, Alberti concludes, and be immortal, as your virtue deserves.

Around 1438, Guarino of Verona sent his version of Lucian's *The Fly* to Scipione Mainenti, bishop of Modena. Soon thereafter, Alberti read a copy of this work and decided to compose his own encomium of the fly, which he simply titled *Musca* and dedicated to the young Florentine humanist Cristoforo Landino (1424–1498). Alberti's *Musca* elaborates Lucian's encomium first by comparing the fly to the bee, whose merits have been falsely exaggerated, presumably in Virgil's *Fourth Georgic*. If bees claim Io as their ancestor, flies boast descent from the centaurs. The fly's foremost excellence lies in her military virtues. Flies attack in phalanxlike squadrons, camp only where their safety is certain, and (like the ancient Spartans) rouse

---

[11] Migne, *Patrologia graeca*, 161: 985–998.

[12] For Zeuxis, see Cicero, *De inventione* 1.1–3; Pliny, *Natural History* 35.64; and Alberti's 1435 treatise *On Painting*.

themselves to combat with martial music. The fly's wartime valor is matched by her peacetime virtues. Unlike bees and other winged creatures, the fly is neither destructive nor rapacious, preferring public banquets and shunning civil strife. The fly abounds in virtues like piety: witness her constant presence on sacrificial altars. The fly's keen eyesight and infinite curiosity, moreover, make her a tireless researcher. Yet although the fly witnesses many shameful deeds, it never becomes a malicious informant.

As for intellectual virtues, Alberti praises the fly's musical expertise and her knowledge of mathematics and geography. Since Pythagoras founded these sciences, Alberti suggests that the Pythagoreans learned music from flies—based on the outlandish derivation of Greek *musica* from Latin *musca*—and he speculates that Pythagoras sacrificed not to the Muses (*musis*) but to flies (*muscis*). If the fly's learning arouses the hostility of the ignorant masses, her untiring inquisitiveness in fact rivals that of philosophers like Plato and Pliny the Elder. Yet the fly is the object of numerous calumnies and often falls prey to the deadly spider. "I would say more," Alberti concludes in a variation on Lucian's abrupt ending, "but I am prevented by a thick crowd of flies."

A third example of Albertian paradoxical encomium is found in Book 2 of *Momus*, a prose satire completed around 1450.[13] Having returned from his temporary exile on earth, Momus attends a celestial banquet, during which he attempts to regain favor with the gods by entertaining them with stories of human life. In a survey of professions indebted to Horace and Lucian, Momus finds fault with all man's estates but one—the life of the vagabond (*erro*). First, Momus says, he tried a military career but soon tired of it because its glory and bloodshed served no ideal of justice. Next, he thought to become a king but found that governing in fact is a form of servitude. Momus also considered commerce, until he realized that the desire for wealth engenders more cares than contentment. At last, he resolved to become a vagabond. While recapitulating the satirical *topoi* of careers, Alberti's eulogy of the vagabond also inaugurates the Western tradition of picaresque literature. As Edmond Cros has observed, Alberti's Momus is the ancestor of the Spanish *pícaro* and is mirrored in the scoundrel-hero Guzmán de Alfarache in the novel of Mateo Alemán (1599–1604).[14]

A final work featuring paradoxical encomium is the *Disputatio inter terram solem et aurum* composed in 1452 by the curial humanist Maffeo Vegio (1407–1458).[15] It consists of a three-part debate in which the elements Earth, Sun, and Gold praise themselves, with the Creator himself as judge of which is the best. In the first speech, the Earth vaunts her superiority by describing at length the wondrous beauty and harmony of nature, including a lengthy encomium of bees, the subject of Virgil's *Fourth Georgic*. The second speech is delivered by the Sun, who is curiously brief. Stepping forward with placid confidence, the Sun lists various aspects of his per-

---

[13] Leon Battista Alberti, *Momo o del principe*, ed. Rino Consolo (Genoa, 1986), 114–128.

[14] Edmond Cros, *Protée et le gueux: Recherches sur les origines et la nature du récit picaresque dans Guzmán de Alfarache* (Paris, 1967), 239.

[15] Maphaeus Vegius, *Disputatio inter Solem, Terram, et Aurum* (Paris, 1511).

fection, claiming in essence to represent the splendor and majesty of the universe.

Having the final say in the contest, the third speaker, Gold, begins by refuting his opponents' arguments, belittling both the Earth and the Sun. The Earth errs in claiming as her own the accomplishments of mankind, which are only achieved by Gold's devotees; and the Sun cannot glory in terrestrial wonders. Self-praise soon yields to paradoxical encomium, and Gold praises himself as the foundation of society and the driving force behind all the professions and arts and even religion.[16] To be sure, Gold observes, there are philosophers who claim to despise me, but they lie through their teeth. Without gold, who would become a teacher, a logician, a musician, an orator, or a poet? Gold now paints a series of vivid satirical portraits of the most prestigious professions: lawyers, courtiers, and priests. The anticlerical satire is particularly virulent. If there were no gold, would priests perform sacred rites, or prelates act so zealously?

Gold also claims to inspire men of lesser professions, such as farmers, merchants, and soldiers. The mention of warfare leads Gold to admit that not all his effects are positive. "Not all glitters that comes of Gold." But Gold uses this confession as proof of greater sincerity than its rivals. Does not Earth produce harmful things like flies, wasps, hornets, mosquitoes, bedbugs, fleas, scorpions, crocodiles, and countless serpents?[17] Do not the Sun's rays sometimes cause great drought and damage? Gold too has both good and bad effects on mankind. As for the bad, Gold confesses to being "the source of all ills" that mortals devise against each other—an echo of St. Paul's "root of all evil" (1 Tim. 6:10) that Gold recasts in asserting his power over mankind.

Gold describes how the human passion for wealth occasions treachery and violence and concludes that money is the ultimate test of character. A fool seen with Gold is instantly admired and praised, but a sage deserted by Gold faces universal scorn. Rulers blessed by Gold will be loved by their subjects and feared by their enemies. With an apology for giving possible offense, Gold now begins a provocative peroration which combines the risqué passages in Bruni and Valla with the anticlerical polemics of Poggio and other humanists. Gold claims to be the ideal matchmaker. He can make a senile dodderer seem an attractive match and can melt the coldest woman's heart. Gold can take even the most ignorant and make him rector of an abbey. If the Sun can claim such metamorphic power, says Gold, let him speak now! But Gold's speech has already won general approval, and the Sun concedes defeat by contracting his rays and fading into gloom.

Rutgers University

---

[16] Vegio's Gold declares himself the source of all things good and bad: see Vegio 1511, fol. x[v] ("fons ego et origo sum horum bonorum") and xii ("scio equidem originem me esse omnium malorum"). Wealth is declared the cause of source of all things good and bad in Aristophanes, *Plutus* 182–183. Vegio may have known the passage in Bruni's translation (ca. 1440): see Leonardo Bruni, *Versione del Pluto di Aristofane (vv. 1–269)*, ed. Maria and Enzo Cecchini (Florence, 1965), 12: "Solissima enim omnium tu [Wealth] es causa . . . bonorumque et malorum."

[17] In Alberti's *Momus* (ed. Consolo, p. 22), the protagonist maliciously fills the world with *bedbugs*, maggots, drones, *hornets*, and dung-beetles.

Andreas Velleius's
Commentarius de scribenda historia Danica (1578)
and Its European Background

LARS BOJE MORTENSEN

Theory and practice of history are rare partners in real life. Occasionally weddings take place, but the ceremony seems to be more important than what it initiates—a shared life thereafter. Those practising historians who do embellish their accounts with fashionable philosophical catchwords mostly annoy their colleagues and are frequently ignored by the professional philosophers of history. Such a gap in communication between historians and philosophers began to show as early as the sixteenth century, when history emerged as an academic discipline in its own right.

In the present paper I want to discuss a text which stands at the crossroads between the theory and practice of history, a 40-page treatise—*Commentarius de scribenda historia Danica*—written by the Danish humanist Andreas Velleius (Anders Sørensen Vedel, 1542–1616) in 1578. Very briefly I will present the specific background for the work, then I will attempt to characterise some major treatises on history before Velleius, and finally I will elucidate the treatise against the international background and *vice versa*.

Velleius's *Commentarius*

Velleius did not publish his *Commentarius* in printed form, but he submitted it at least twice to members of the Danish government, first in the Latin version in 1578 and then in a slightly rewritten Danish version three years later.[1] The *Commentarius*

---

[1] Velleius's commentary is best put into its historical context by H. Ilsøe, "Svaning, Vedel, Huitfeldt og Krag. Omkring spørgsmålet om den første historiografudnævnelse," in *Tradition og kritik. Festskrift til S. Ellehøj* (København, 1984), 235–258. The two versions are discussed by L. B. Mortensen, "Den latinske version af Anders Sørensen Vedels historiografiske programskrift (Gks 2437 4o)," in *Latin og nationalsprog i Norden*, eds. M. Alenius, B. Bergh, I. Boserup, K. Friis-Jensen, and M. Skafte-Jensen. *Renæssancestudier* vol. 5 (København, 1991), 34–44.

is best understood as a sort of application. It is clearly structured in three chapters:

I. Caussæ impulsiuæ, cur de scribenda historia Danica cogitet magistratus
1. Officium magistratus.
2. Exempla eorum qui pariter historici et gubernatores reipublicæ extiterunt.
3. Dignitas et amplitudo rerum gestarum a Danis.
4. Aliorum regnorum exempla.
5. Res Danicæ mala fide ab exteris relatæ.
6. Amor patriæ.
7. Vtilitas historiæ Danicæ.
8. Laus redundans in regiam maiestatem ex scriptione historiæ nostræ.
9. Occasio scribendi opportuna.

II. Methodus qua scribi debeat historia Danica.
1. Forma et idea vniuersi operis comprenda.
2. Chorographia Daniæ.
3. Tractatus de moribus et origine gentis Danicæ.
4. Fundamentum historiæ Danicæ certum.
5. Chronologia certa.
6. Res relligionis annotandæ.
7. Narratio historiæ de quibus rebus maxime suscipietur.
8. Res gestæ in exteris regnis a nostris peculiariter scribendæ.

III. Idoneus scriptor historiæ Danicæ.
1. Historia nostra debet scribi ab vno et pluribus.
2. Historicus noster doctrina et natura atque vsu rerum sit instructus.
3. Historicus sit liber affectibus.
4. Historicus quando suum debeat interponere iudicium.
5. Historicus noster debet esse studiosus antiquitatis et omnium historiarum.
6. Linguarum cognitio necessaria historico.
7. Sumtus præbendi historico necessarii.

First Velleius tries to convince the king (Frederik II, 1559–1588) and the Privy Council that a new full history of Denmark is badly needed; next he outlines plans for research and writing; and finally he discusses how the historian must be properly equipped for the task, mentally as well as financially. Naturally he denies that he has hatched this plan for his own good, but in fact he had for some years been moving himself into a position from which he could claim to be the official historian of the realm. As a court preacher he knew the right people, and he was drilling his pen in

---

A full text of both versions is to be included in a critical edition of Vedel's minor historiographical writings, now in preparation.

On Velleius in English there is L. B. Mortensen, "Anders Sørensen Vedel. The Latin Writings of a Vernacular Humanist," in *A History of Nordic Neo-Latin Literature*, ed. M. Skafte Jensen (Odense, 1995), 267–280, and K. Skovgaard-Petersen, "Carion's Chronicle in Sixteenth-Century Danish Historiography," forthcoming in *Symbolae Osloenses* 73 (1998).

both Latin and Danish, in theology as well as history. He had offered a Lutheran adaptation in Danish verse of Platina's (1421–1481) papal chronicle—with a title that left nothing unsaid: *Antichristus Romanus*. And he had translated the great Medieval Latin history of Denmark from around 1200, Saxo Grammaticus's *Gesta Danorum*.

The government did to some extent care about history. For some time another man, Hans Svaning, had been working as a loosely attached propagandist and historian, and from 1580 one can consider Velleius his successor, even if he did not inherit the research notes and the full ecclesiastical prebend before Svaning's death in 1584. The Danish version of the *Commentarius* from 1581, and also some even later notes in the still unpublished autograph manuscript of the Latin version, suggest that Velleius was not content; he had cut a vague deal with the government, but he had certainly not been given free access to royal archives nor had he been granted the virtual research institute with translators, copyists, and so on that he had asked for in his *Commentarius*. From the eventual failure of Velleius's project it is clear that the king and the Privy Council were in no doubt about the substance of the deal: they considered all Velleius's material on Danish history government property, and in 1595 he had to pass it all on to a newly appointed successor—and that was quite a pile of notes, copies of medieval texts, and so forth, but not really any proper historical writing.

But let us return to happier times when Velleius was an up-and-coming man. In 1578 he opened the second chapter of his *Commentarius* with these words:

> Scripserunt de ratione instituendæ historiæ, tum veterum, tum recentiorum plurimi commentarios sanè doctos et elegantes. Verùm in illis omnibus hoc ego semper desideraui, quod vniuersæ tantùm historiæ methodum ac rationem in genere tractarunt; quum non eam tantùm solam scire atque nosse debeat bonus historicus, sed maximoperè etiam necessarium sit peculiarem aliquam tenere rationem, qua singularum monarchiarum et priuatorum imperiorum atque illustrium vrbium sint scribendæ historiæ.

> Many ancient as well as modern authors have written quite learned and elegant treatises on the systematic establishment of history. But I have always considered them to be deficient in one respect, i.e., they have only discussed method and system for comprehensive historical writing in general. But such knowledge is not sufficient for the good historian; first of all one needs some specific system when one is to write a history of single kingdoms, separate nations, and eminent cities.

Let us probe into this disavowal. Velleius is in fact saying that he is familiar with a number of theoretical treatises but that they did not help him solve his problems. I would like to argue that Velleius is here overplaying a good hand: he is actually drawing rather heavily on a number of standard problems and questions formulated in theoretical literature current in his day. The *Commentarius* is throughout a fine work of Velleius's own making, but there is no denying that many questions and some of the answers were gleaned from contemporary theoretical literature. On the other hand I also want to concede to him that he did hold some rather good cards.

Because he is discussing a specific task—the composition of a history of Denmark—his *Commentarius* in many ways reflects a truer picture of sixteenth-century historiographical problems than does much of the purely theoretical literature.[2] So he is to a large degree right: a man who was worried about his access to Old Norse literature as an historical source—it was only being rediscovered around this time, and no Danes mastered the language—must have felt rather sidetracked by endless discussions on which kinds of speeches the historian should include in his narrative.

Theoretical Treatises before Velleius

In the above quotation Velleius mentions both ancient and modern writers, but even if the classical passages in Lucian, Cicero, Polybius, and others loomed large in sixteenth-century minds, Velleius no doubt had his main attention on the modern authors, indeed the very recent ones. The theoretical literature boomed only after ca. 1540. It has been suggested that the discovery of Aristotle's *Poetics* was partly responsible for the new development: it elicited numerous commentaries and treatises on the art of poetry, which in turn provoked the question whether history was also an art in its own right.[3] But one should hardly accept the theorists' perspective *prima facie*: Historical research and writing had already taken some important new turns in the fifteenth and early sixteenth centuries, and the theoretical literature was more a symptom of the growing independence of history as an art and a science than the inspiration for it.[4]

The major treatises composed in the decades before Velleius's were of Italian, Spanish, and French origin.[5] But minor items such as C. Pezelius, *Oratio de argumento*

---

[2] Other internal memoranda of this sort no doubt existed in the sixteenth century, but I am only aware of one (to which Prof. Jenaro Costas Rodriguez kindly drew my attention), written around 1555 by a little known court historiographer of Charles V, Juan Páez de Castro: "De las cosas necesarias para escribir historia," ed. E. Esteban, *La Ciudad de Dios* 28 and 29 (1892): 601–610 and 27–37. A few striking similarities between Velleius and Páez are explicable in terms of a common humanistic background and of similar tasks.

[3] G. Cotroneo, *I trattatisti dell' "ars historica"* (Napoli, 1971), 121–168.

[4] On the basis of Italian material the case of the primacy of practice over theory is eloquently put by E. Cochrane, *Historians and Historiography in the Italian Renaissance* (Chicago and London, 1981), esp. pp. 479–487.

[5] As guides and shortcuts through a large literature I have had indispensable help especially from the many illuminating works by Kelley, and from the anthologies by Wolf and Kessler (see below for full citations of these works), but also from the studies by Cotroneo and Cochrane mentioned above: D. R. Kelley, "*Historia integra*: Francois Baudouin and His Conception of History," *Journal of the History of Ideas* 25 (1964): 35–57; id., *Foundations of Modern Historical Scholarship. Language, Law, and History in the French Renaissance* (New York, 1970); id., "The Theory of History," in *The Cambridge History of Renaissance Philosophy*, ed. C. B. Schmitt (Cambridge, 1988), 746–761; id. (ed.), *Versions of History from Antiquity to the Enlightenment* (New Haven and London, 1991); E. Kessler (ed.), *Theoretiker humanistischer Geschichtsschreibung*, (München, 1971); J. Wolf (ed.), *Artis historicae penus. Octodecim scriptorum tam veterum quàm recentiorum monumentis*, 2 vols. (Basel, 1579). I have also used J. H. Franklin, *Jean Bodin and the Sixteenth-century Revolution in the Methodology of Law and History* (New York and London, 1963); R. Landfester, *Historia magistra vitae. Untersuchungen zur humanistischen Geschichtstheorie des 14. bis 16. Jahrhunderts*, Travaux d'huma-

historiarum et fructu ex earum lectione petendo (Wittenberg, 1568)[6] or T. Blundeville, *The True Order and Method of Wryting and Reading Hystories* (London, 1574)[7] show that Germanic-speaking countries did draw on the discussions so powerfully launched by the Italians, Spaniards, and French. Velleius was certainly not an isolated phenomenon north of the Alps.

When I first began to look at these treatises, I thought it would be easy to classify them into three groups. First are those which gave prescriptions for writing history. Fox Morzillo's *De historiæ institutione liber* (Antwerp, 1557),[8] Viperani's *De scribenda historia* (Antwerp, 1569),[9] and Foglietta's *De ratione scribendae historiae* (Rome, 1574)[10] should count as straightforward instances. They deal with matters such as what reading and other background the historian must have, what types of causes one can ascribe to events, how to deal with simultaneous actions in the narrative, and so on. The second group would include those which prescribed the proper reading of history, and here one could easily list Chytræus, *De lectione historiarum recte instituenda* (Rostock, 1563),[11] Aconcio's *Delle osservationi et avvertimenti che aver si debbono nel legger delle historie* (written ca. 1564),[12] and Pezelius's *Oratio*. Here one is taken through various lessons taught by historical works, or one is simply offered an annotated bibliography of major historians through the ages. The third group would consist of the more demanding and historically important pieces, such as the three celebrated ones: Patrizi's *Della historia diece dialoghi* (Venice, 1560),[13] Baudouin's *De institutione historiæ universæ et eius cum iurisprudentia coniunctione* (Paris, 1561),[14] and Bodin's *Methodus ad facilem historiarum cognitionem* (Paris, 1566).[15] The heading for those could read something like "Philosophical reasoning about the nature of the past, the historian's access to it, and the status of history within the sciences." Bodin's revolutionary repudiation of the four world empires as a fundamental structure of the past is one such piece of reasoning, his thoughts about types and values of sources another. Similarly Baudouin's emphasis on legal and institutional history breaks new ground for the method of history and its place among the sciences.

Gradually I realized why no one had suggested this classification before. First of all

---

nisme et renaissance 123 (Genève, 1972); and G. Spini, "Historiography: The Art of History in the Italian Counter-Reformation," in E. Cochrane (ed.), *The Late Italian Renaissance 1525–1630* (New York, 1970), 91–133 [first ed. of the article appeared in Italian in 1948].

[6] Wolf, vol. 2, pp. 603–617.

[7] Ed. H. G. Dick, *The Huntington Library Quarterly* 3 (1939/40): 149–170.

[8] Wolf, vol. 1, pp. 743–837.

[9] Kessler; also in Wolf.

[10] Kessler; also in Wolf.

[11] Wolf, vol. 2, pp. 452–565.

[12] Kessler.

[13] Kessler; Latin transl. in Wolf.

[14] Wolf, vol. 1, pp. 593–742. This treatise served as a major source for Velleius, as can be documented in the forthcoming edition (see note 1).

[15] Wolf, vol. 1, pp. 1–396.

because there are too many overlaps. Viperani, for instance, discusses philosophically what history is, Bodin includes a fine reading list of historical works, Atanagi's *Ragionamento della istoria* (Venice, 1559)[16] deals with a bit of everything, and so on. My apprehension grew when I read the preface of Wolf's anthology. Having argued how important history is, he gives the following *raison d'être* for the anthology (vol. I, 5v): praise is due, he says, not only to historians "but especially to those who have thrown light on the ancient authors' works and have opened a way for our understanding of their histories."

The entire theoretical literature is seen simply as a series of commentaries on ancient historians! On second thoughts, this makes some sense. The overwhelming majority of examples and quotations in the treatises come from ancient authorities such as Thucydides, Polybius, Cicero, Sallust, Livy, and Tacitus. Classical references are so ubiquitous, in fact, that discussions on historical causes, descriptions of battles, the truth of historical narrative, and so forth can be read as interpretations of the classical tradition rather than suggestions, plans and methodology for contemporary historians. For Wolf these were not alternatives because the ancient historians were indisputable models.

My neat tripartition does not fare particularly well. But I leave it there for the reader, at least as a possible frame for understanding various functions of the treatises.

How Typical Is Velleius?

Let me move on to firmer ground and give a few tastes of Velleius's Commentarius and its background. A standard topic among the theorists was, Is the historian to express his own judgement? By this they mean moralising on events as well as explicitly favouring one reliable source instead of another. Velleius also raises the question, and in line with many of the theorists he answers in the affirmative.[17] But Velleius's wording reflects that of Bodin, who was of the opposite conviction.[18] Bodin wants dubious cases to be left to the reader to decide, and dislikes interventions on the part of the author. He expresses preference for historians like Xenophon, Thucydides, Suetonius, Caesar, Guiccardini, and Sleidan.[19] History, he says, should be like a tablet in a public place, an image used also by Velleius when referring to "certain authors" who think that the historian should keep his private opinion to himself. Bodin does, however, add the reservation that personal judgements are a lesser evil when they come from men of military and political experience as opposed to armchair historians.[20] Likewise, another rebel against the authority of the ancients, Patrizi, criticises historians' penchant for philosophising on the side.[21] Velleius's argument against these modern authorities is that if an intelligent and upright man has

---

[16] Kessler.

[17] Cf. Velleius 3,4 with Atanagi (ed. Kessler), 82; Viperani (ed. Kessler), 45–49; Fox Morzillo (ed. Wolf), 775. Cotroneo, *I trattatisti*, pp. 395–396 summarizes the debate.

[18] As pointed out by Ilsøe, "Svaning, Vedel," 241.

[19] Bodin (ed. Wolf), 46.

[20] Bodin (ed. Wolf), 45.

[21] Patrizi 59r–v (ed. Kessler).

been chosen to write the history, he should be allowed now and then to draw the readers' attention to good and bad. One may also see here Velleius's recognition of the Melanchthonian view that divine lessons can be extracted from all history, and that these should be pointed out by the historian.

In chapter 2,4 of the *Commentarius*, Velleius discusses the beginnings of Danish history:

> Constituendum est postea certum historiæ exordium seu fundamentum, a quo deinde vniuersæ historiæ tela exstruenda atque pertexenda est. Id vt firmum habeatur maximopere annitendum censeo, ne nobis vsu veniat, quod iis accidit, qui ab ipso Troiæ excidio, nescio quas fabulas, instar spolia quædam adhuc fumo incendii istius recenti foetentia, nauseantibus conantur obtrudere lectoribus.

> Next we have to establish a firm beginning or foundation for the narrative from which the web of the entire history can be extracted and woven to the end. We must be very careful, I think, to find something solid and not to fall into the habit of those who go back to the fall of Troy or some such nonsense and try to throw to their disgusted readers spoils still fresh with stench from the smoke of that fire.

It was a common enough trend in humanistic historiography to criticise mythical origins; at the beginning of the sixteenth century Paolo Emilio had doubted the Trojan origin of the French and Polydore Vergil that of the English; but such voices were not universally popular among the French and the English, and the Trojan ghost kept coming down from the attic.[22] Significantly such a recurrent issue in contemporary historical writing did not concern the theorists, apart from one: Bodin. He devoted the entire chapter nine (out of ten) to the question of peoples and their origins. His methodological comments and his skepticism towards Trojan and other myths are likely to have influenced Velleius as much as did other historians of similar conviction.

A fundamental question for the Renaissance historian, indeed for any historian is, What is history about? As expounded by Kelley it was exactly in the fifteenth and especially sixteenth centuries that the first battles against drum-and-trumpet history were fought with success. Baudouin and others began talking about "historia perfecta," "historia integra," "historia consummata," and so on.[23] According to Baudouin not only Eurocentrism had to be overcome by including national histories from all over the globe, but the very subject of history should be expanded from wars and politics to legal and institutional history. Baudouin's Protestant inclinations also led him to the opinion that sacred and secular affairs ought to be viewed as two sides of one process—a point we shall return to. We may smile at these dreams of complete or perfect history, knowing, as we do, that history is not complete without

---

[22] J. W. Binns, *Intellectual Culture in Elizabethan and Jacobean England. The Latin Writings of the Age* (Leeds, 1990), 178–179, 182–186.

[23] Kelley, "*Historia integra*," 51.

ideological history, economic history, history of women, history of private life, and so on. On the other hand, we should perhaps restrain ourselves a little when talking about the "histoire totale" that some of us are supposedly writing today. Who can guess which subjects will have been historicized in a century or so?[24]

Velleius took also took a stand in this matter. In chapter 2,7 he says:

> Cruentorum bellorum commemorationi non plus tribuendum est quàm ipsis bellorum gerendorum occasionibus, consiliis et euentis. Non enim describenda bella, minimè bella vt ad ea inflammentur animi principum, sed potius vt aliorum infaustis edocti exemplis caueant prudenter et maturè, ne temerariis bellorum ansis implicentur.

> In the narrative one should pay less attention to cruel wars than to the occasions, plans, and results of warfare. Wars should certainly not be described in a way that instigates the minds of princes, but rather—by pointing to other people's miserable experience—one that makes them prudent and cautious not to get involved in risky military adventures.

For the first part of this statement Velleius is on the firmest possible ground. The *locus classicus* is Polybius 3,31 where he explains the reasons for the Second Punic War. No one will be able to learn from history, he says, if we do not focus on the background and the results of the war rather than just describing the battles. Renaissance scholars knew this by heart, as they knew the similar words of Cicero, *De Oratore* 2,63: the historian should consider *consilia, acta, eventus* and not forget to explain the *causae*. The echo of these passages in the theoretical treatises is enormous, but Velleius's wording seems to come closest to that of Chytræus and Baudouin.[25] What is remarkable about the passage is Velleius's almost pacifist tone, something for which he had little support among theorists or historians. Wars are cruel, and their exemplary value in history should only be negative. Viperani does ask the question why warfare, which in itself is abominable, fills the pages of historiography. But he excuses the habit of classical (and modern) historians in two ways: the extreme conditions of war offer the best illustration of virtues and of the wheel of fortune. Moreover, he says, nothing is more frequent among men than fighting. Atanagi also explicitly accepts the dominance of military affairs and advises the historian to ascend to poetic heights when describing battles.[26] There may be specific reasons for Velleius's open-hearted disgust with warfare; he was a bookworm steeped in Lutheran theology, and he was writing for a comparatively peaceful king who generally favoured diplomacy over warfare. Velleius's argument would hardly have been accepted by Frederik II's more

---

[24] Cf. Kelley, *Versions of History*, 501.

[25] Chytræus c2r (in the Rostock, 1563 ed.); Baudouin p. 618 (ed. Wolf); cf. Fox Morzillo (ed. Wolf), 771 and 778; Viperani (ed. Kessler), 31–32; and in general Landfester, *Historia magistra,* 108–129.

[26] Viperani (ed. Kessler), 16–17; Atanagi (ed. Kessler), 82; an outspoken pacifist attitude is found also in the chapter on history by Vives, in the third book of *De ratione dicendi* (*Opera*, Basel, 1555, vol. 1, p. 139).

martial successor, Christian IV. Velleius may also be appealing to the Privy Council which was generally more hesitant to engage in armed conflict than the king.

However that may be, the feeling that history was more than kings and wars was growing dramatically in the sixteenth century, and in this respect Velleius was typical of the new trends.

In this vein our author argues that religious affairs must be presented as an integrated part of history (ch. 2,6). Here in particular he gives away his Lutheran pedigree. None of the Italian *artes historiae* finds this a subject worthy of discussion.[27] The Lutheran combination of sacred and civil history was no doubt influenced by the Melanchthonian Carion's *Chronicle*, and Sleidan became its pioneer in practice.[28] If he needed it, Velleius could confirm his views in Baudouin and Chytræus, but it was actually a rather straightforward choice. The reformation in Denmark had come about only four decades before Velleius wrote, and the new order was to be understood as God's grace shining on the Danes. The sacred and civil worked together as never before—but it was all so fresh that it needed to be said again and again; in fact Velleius had already made the point repeatedly in sermons and other publications.[29]

I have now come to my final point, which is even more fundamental than the question of the proper subject of history, namely, why bother to write history? The reflex answer by the theorists, including Velleius, would be: "history teaches by example," or in Ciceronian Latin "historia magistra vitae."[30] It enhances our wisdom and skills, and we are able, individually or as a group, to conduct ourselves in a morally better way. But we should hardly accept this as a sufficient reason for the wealth of historical literature produced by the humanists. All possible human virtues and vices were already covered by the collection of historical examples by Valerius Maximus and in similar literature.[31] There must be more to it than that.

Again Velleius's *Commentarius* is interesting. The entire first chapter attempts to persuade the Danish government that it would benefit from a new full history of Denmark. The exemplary argument is not an important one there. It does emerge in paragraph three but not very strongly: previous deeds by the Danes are so glorious that they should not be forgotten. But Velleius obviously felt that other arguments would impress the king and the Privy Council more. Among those we find (see the synopsis above): the administration must have some record of the past in order to promote faith and strengthen the authority of the laws (1.1). This argument is supported by a long list of rulers from Moses to Alfonso I of Naples who wrote or commissioned historical works (1.2). Another point is that if we do not write about ourselves, others will either ignore us or lie about us. When people abroad hear the

---

[27] In practice also, sacred history was ignored by Italian humanist historians, see Cochrane, *Historians*, 445–478.

[28] Kelley, "The Theory," 751.

[29] See Skovgaard-Petersen, "Carion's Chronicle" and Mortensen, "The Latin Writings."

[30] For Velleius' own exemplary thinking, see K. Friis-Jensen, *Vedels Saxo og den danske adel* (København, 1993).

[31] Cochrane, *Historians*, 486.

name Denmark or Danish, they pull a face as if it was some part of the new world (1.4). Linked to this argument is an even stronger one: without a reliable record of the past, territorial claims cannot be upheld (1.7). And what about those mapmakers who depict the Orkneys, Shetland, and Greenland as if they did not belong to Norway and thus were not subject to the Danish crown? (2.2). Finally Velleius adds, of course, that a new history will render the king's name immortal. So history serves national identity and glory.

All this may seem a sad fall from humanist ideals of history teaching moral lessons by example, but I would like to contend that in comparison to the purely theoretical treatises Velleius's *Commentarius*—on account of its peculiar blend of theory and practice—in fact brings us much closer to the real reasons for writing history in the Renaissance.

Bergen

Humanists and the Invention of Literary History

ANN MOSS

D id the humanists invent literary history? They are often credited with inventing an historical consciousness of the past perceived as radically other, a
different world in which things were done differently. Nevertheless, as their Neo-
Latin literary productions demonstrate with particular force, humanists grounded their
corporate enterprise on a belief that the past and the present could speak with one
voice. Humanistic Latin was painstakingly reconstructed from the verbal documents
of a past civilization in order to revive ancient patterns of communication, resurrect
the body of a long dead culture, and reactivate the values which had energized its
moral life. From very selective examples, this paper attempts to show that it was in
the ambiguous territory lying between the past as passed and the past as potential
present that the humanists invented literary history.

Poets, as was generally known, were not historians. Art, not chronology, determined the ordering of their material; and fiction, not fact, was their proper subject.[1]
So when Poliziano sets out to enumerate divinely inspired poets in his poem called
Nutricia written in 1486, it is on the muse of poetry he calls, rather than on the muse
of history. Indeed, he sets the origins of poetical composition in an imagined pre-
history, a dream-time of myth when Jupiter tuned the spheres to melodies heard by
men, a primitive world of versified oracles, healing-songs and magic-songs, in which
harmonious language was the instrument whereby the savage were civilized, and
learnt moral rule and social law from the "arcanae leges" regulating the rhythms of
poetry.[2] Poliziano's Platonizing myth of cultural development slips into history as he
embarks on his praise of poets. Historical development, however, is not his theme.

---

[1] Cf. Vida, *De arte poetica* (1527) II. 59–61: "Nec, quacunque viam suadet res gesta, sequuntur.
Plerumque a mediis, arrepto tempore, fari Incipiunt, ubi facta vident iam carmine digna;" and,
well before that among the Latins, Macrobius, *Saturnalia* V. ii. 9. The essentially fictive nature of
poetry was even more of a commonplace, e.g., Landino in his commentary on Horace (1494
edition, fol. CLXV v): "manifestum est species poetarum fictas esse oportere, nam nos delectare
volunt."

[2] See Ange Politien, *Les Silves*, ed. and trans. P. Galand (Paris, 1987).

The origins, works, life, and death of a whole galaxy of Greek and Latin poets are rehearsed in eruditely periphrastic language which eschews mere fact, and in an order of appearance which juxtaposes like and unlike, disciple and rival, in a sequence deliberately at odds with chronology.[3] Poliziano's poets are not historically distanced from us and from each other. They are arrayed synchronically so as to immerse the reader in the revived language and culture of ancient poetic production, a language of verbal memory by which the student is summoned to recognize pastiche, allusions, and quotations signaling the presence of particular poets, and a culture of imitation and emulation in which the modern writer is invited to participate.

Poliziano was not only a poet but a textual critic, and it was representatives of that side of his activity, editors rather than poets, who needed to historicize authors and their works in order to argue the validity of emendations, conjectures, and interpretative readings. Late fifteenth-century editors often included a biography of their author, usually compiled from information contained within the author's own works and reproducing none of the lore which had accumulated round the major classical writers in the Middle Ages. The medieval period had had its lists of authors and their works, generally as part of encyclopedias with other ends in view, or as exemplary figures in catalogues of people worthy of praise or makers undone by death. But the notion of a history of ancient literature as such, contained within a defined period of time, covering all authors and making chronological relationships between them, only materializes with the advent of a work like the *De poetis latinis* of Poliziano's own pupil, Petro Ricci (Petrus Crinitus), published at Florence in 1505. This is a succession of short, matter-of-fact lives of the Latin poets, ending with Sidonius Apollinaris.

Ricci is anxious to establish chronological relationships, noting, for example, that Ovid was born in the same year as Tibullus and died in the same year as Livy. However, Ricci writes as a rhetorician and a grammarian every bit as much as an historian. Possibilities for turning the historical evidence into a rhetorical defence of poetry against its moralizing detractors are grasped with enthusiasm, with Ovid as a prime example.[4] Ricci chooses to go soberly through his facts, from which, nevertheless, there emerges a praiseworthy Ovid of honourable estate and blameless life. His works are listed with brief comments formulated in the limited, stylized vocabulary available to the humanist grammarian. Ovid's literary virtues are thus judged to be "numerous and varied passages of learned reference" and "extraordinary craftmanship in expression." Matters of erudition and varieties of well-turned phrases and figures were the stock-in-trade of the contemporary school grammarian, who could find material for this sort of exposition in almost any text. However, the vocabulary of the grammatical commentary or *enarratio* was a blunt instrument for making critical

---

[3] The basic plan of Poliziano's catalogue may be derived from Quintilian's list of Greek and Latin authors in *Institutio oratoria* X. i, which is not a history of literature but a survey of stylistic qualities of authors loosely arranged by genre; Poliziano's ordering approximates to Quintilian's sequence of Greek poets, but with the Latins interleaved, not listed separately.

[4] The section on Ovid is pp. 458–462 of Petrus Crinitus, *De honesta disciplina libri XXV. De poetis latinis libri V* (Basel, 1532).

distinctions between poets, even after they had been carefully distinguished in historical sequence.

Forty years later, Lilio Gregorio Giraldi approached literary history on a much broader front in every way in his *Historiae poetarum tam graecorum quam latinorum dialogi decem*, published at Basel in 1545.[5] Unlike Ricci's history, which is essentially a list predetermined by chronology, and unlike Poliziano's poetically structured myth of poetic culture, Giraldi combined linear historical narrative and a more artistic *dispositio* in a demonstration dialogue.[6] It starts from a ground plan, a spatial configuration rather than a temporal sequence, in the form of an imaginary hieroglyphic picture of poetry, surrounded by imaginary miniature portraits of all the poets.[7] Development is to be by way of an allegorical interpretation of the central picture and successive identifications of all the portraits. The mode of discourse is that of revelation, and this exactly mirrors the initial disclosures about the image of poetry itself (mostly to be found in Book I). Giraldi later continues with explanations of the different forms which poetry takes (tragedy and comedy in Books VI to VIII, lyric and epigram in Books IX and X), after giving us in Books II to V an essentially chronological enumeration of poets from Orpheus and the mythical Greeks through classical Greece and Rome to the early medieval period. While most of the entries for individual poets inevitably turn out to be brief lives and lists of works, the icon of poetry displayed at the threshold of the investigation remains a dominant and unifying memory throughout the subsequent fragmentation of the primordial image into differences of time and kind.

Poetry for Giraldi is allegorical language, the only communication we have with the divine, "which cannot be understood or explained by any other system, that is unless its meaning is shown to us wrapped and veiled in mystic signs."[8] Giraldi consciously amalgamates all aspects of a long tradition of allegorical interpretation, taking in Neo-Platonism, the medieval tradition, and allegorical exegesis of the Bible. Once poetry is identified in this way as a system of allegorical signifiers, there is a tendency for it to be dehistoricized. The referents of allegorical interpretation of the more mystical variety favoured by Giraldi are extra-textual and extra-temporal. Historically contextualized authors and particularities of style, language, and genre are effaced if all texts are read as if written in one and the same code. However, this move towards abolishing distinctions of time and kind is checked by Giraldi's formation as a

---

[5] For more information on the *Dialogi,* see M. Mund-Dopchie, "Lilio Gregorio Gyraldi et sa contribution à l'histoire des tragiques grecs au XVIe siècle," *Humanistica Lovaniensia* 34A (1985): 137–149.

[6] In the preface to the first dialogue Giraldi tells how the book grew out of discussions between himself and two friends on the subject of poetry and poets, conducted over a reading of Poliziano s *Nutricia.*

[7] The origin of this way of proceeding by imaginary portraits may be the lost *Imagines* of Varro, which Giraldi names as an ancient forerunner of his literary history, along with several other, mainly Greek, authorities. It is a display of empty erudition: no histories of literature survive from the ancient world, and Giraldi is working from citations in other authors.

[8] L. G. Giraldus, *Historiae poetarum tam graecorum quam latinorum dialogi decem* (Basel, 1545), 11.

humanist sensitive to historical change and linguistic difference. He explores theories which look for the origins of poetic writing in the invention of script, in the relationship between poetry and music, and in the etymology of various ancient synonyms for poets. On the strictly biographical side of his enterprise Giraldi differs little in manner or approach from Ricci, adding factual information where he can. His critical vocabulary remains largely within the bland idiom which grammarians used to characterize diction and style. A more idiosyncratic feature of his book is the inordinate space allotted to traces of poets whose works are no longer extant. Here a rift between the past as passed and the past as potential present begins to show. Giraldi's historian's sense of what had been the literary culture of the ancient world reveals the narrowly unhistorical view of humanist grammarians claiming to restore a linguistic Golden Age on such fragmentary evidence.

Not that Giraldi disparaged their initiative or the results they had so far obtained. His *Dialogi duo de poetis nostrorum temporum* (Florence, 1551) is a list of modern poets, with critical judgements, starting more or less with the major humanists, Pontano, Marullo, and Sannazaro, and extending across Europe. Inevitably there is a vast preponderance of Italians. There is certainly a heavy bias in favour of Latin poetry. Although vernacular poets are mentioned, not always dishonourably, any poet who can write decent Latin and descends to the vernacular has fallen irretrievably from grace. The work has a comprehensive geographical spread, but historical considerations play a very secondary role to Giraldi's rather rudimentary exercises in comparative criticism. He aligns his modern poets, not to make of them a collective history of modern literature but to judge them against each other according to received standards of stylistic elegance derived from their classical prototypes. However, these judgements are phrased in exactly the same catch-all idiom of the grammarians in the previous treatises. Once grammatical commentary is taken out of the margins of an actual text, its weapons for critical analysis seem merely to beat the air.

Giraldi's survey of modern poetry goes some way towards producing a canon, but one much weighted in favour of the Italian humanists. As an Italian himself, he speaks from within a cultural hegemony which can easily equate built-in bias with historical fact. Nevertheless, the history of the sixteenth century is in part a history of national rivalries, and this was to colour and develop the emerging discipline of literary history. Outside the Italian peninsula catalogues of authors can take on a much more competitive edge. They are often used as proof of national superiority either with respect to the ancients or to the culturally dominant Italians. To take but one example, Symphorien Champier, who played a leading part in the transmission of Italian Neo-Platonism into France, published various panegyrics of French culture. Champier stages a Franco-Italian dispute in letters exchanged between himself and Italian correspondents, first in his *De triplici disciplina* (Lyon, 1508), in which his Italian friend supplies a list of notable Italian authors, and then in a *Duellum epistolare* (Lyon and Venice, 1519), in which Champier returns to the attack with a survey of the major figures in the contemporary cultural scene in France, all of them models of "facilitas," "candor," "gravitas," and the other virtues of humanist style. All the writers mentioned as representative of their respective national traditions are writers of Latin. Once vernacular literature was involved in this debate, it becomes too com-

plex for us to follow here. Suffice it to say that it is not until the latter end of the sixteenth century that the hold of Latin humanistic criteria becomes sufficiently relaxed
for French antiquarians to feel able to construct a literary history out of the curiosities
remaining from their own long dead vernacular writers lying well outside the
humanist canon.[9]

In the middle of the sixteenth century, such an extension of literary history would
have run counter to the perception that any review of past literary achievements had
a normative function in respect to standards set for present writers, particularly poets.
This amalgam of historical information and prescriptive criticism, still somewhat
loosely meshed in Giraldi, was to be much more rigorously weighed and mixed in a
work which transported the humanist genre of literary history north across the Alps.
Julius Caesar Scaliger, an Italian settled in France since 1525, included a historical
survey of Latin poetry in Book VI (Hypercriticus) of his *Poetices libri septem* (Lyon,
1561). The reader is no longer invited to a leisurely tutorial, as in the dialogues of
Giraldi. Scaliger lectures us in a forceful display of rhetorical arguments replete with
technical vocabulary. Furthermore, Scaliger dismisses the interpretative mode in
which Giraldi had unwrapped the objects of his investigation. Scaliger has little time
for poetry as sacred medium and ecstatic language. In his historical schema, poetry
was at its most crude and uncultivated in the primitive, mythical stages of its development, and it reached excellence only when poets acquired a precise, rational
understanding of their art.[10]

Scaliger begins his historical survey with a division of Latin poetry into five stages.
These are not like the four ages of the world, degenerating progressively from the
Creation to the present, from Golden Age to Iron; nor are they like the four ages of
man, growing from infancy to maturity and then falling into an inevitable decline.
Latin literature went from meagre beginnings through the growth period from Ennius to Plautus, to sturdy strength in Terence, Catullus, Tibullus, and Horace, and
brilliant splendour in Virgil. Then gradually its bloom faded from Martial to Statius,
until a decrepit old age set in, ending with Ausonius. But, unlike mortal men, culture
can come to life again, as it has since the time of Petrarch, and now Latin poets go
from strength to strength and may yet rival the best of the ancients, apart from Virgil.
The assumption made by Scaliger, that the literature of the past has lessons which can
be learnt and repeated in the present, leads him to ascribe to literary history a pattern

---

[9] The chief documents are Claude Fauchet's *Recueil de l'origine de la langue et poésie françoise*
(1581) and Etienne Pasquier's sixth (later seventh) book of his *Recherches de la France* (1596).
Instruments de travail were provided at the same period in the form of two vernacular bibliographies, both called *Bibliothèque françoise*, both published in 1584, by François de La Croix du
Maine at Paris and by Antoine Du Verdier at Lyon.

[10] For the more theoretical aspects of Scaliger's poetics, see R. M. Ferraro, *Giudizi critici e
criteri estetici nei "Poetices libri septem" (1561) di Giulio Cesare Scaligero rispetto alla teoria litteraria del
Rinascimento* (Chapel Hill, 1971); also, *La statue et l'empreinte. La poétique de J.-C. Scaliger*, eds. C.
Balavoine and P. Laurens (Paris, 1986), which includes an article comparing Scaliger and Giraldi
(A. Stegmann, "Le *De poetis* de L. G. Giraldi [1555] et l'*Hypercriticus* de Jules-César Scaliger": 35–
48); and *Acta Scaligeriana*, eds. J. IJsewijn et al. (Agen, 1986).

of recurrence which no other history has. His *Hypercriticus,* therefore, unites historical perspective with present purpose, and signals this by adopting an order of exposition which is poetical, rather than historical, starting with a prologue on Plautus and Terence, leaping forward *in medias res* to the earlier *recentiores,* who take us from Petrarch and Marullo in no very chronological order to Pontano, Sannazaro, and Fracastoro, and then back over the unspeakable Middle Ages to the poets of the Roman decline, moving thence backwards in time and upwards in quality towards speechless adoration at the altar of Virgil.

Despite the historical format, the fractured chronology and the absence of any biographical details signal that this is not an attempt to excavate and understand the past. It is an abstracted lesson for the present reader and writer, with the analysis of literary texts firmly located within the province of the humanist rhetorician, not the humanist historian. In contrast with Giraldi, Scaliger lists only authors whose work survives for our scrutiny and is not the least interested in inferior writers or in the vernaculars, ruled out of account by his stated conviction that excellence comparable with that of the ancients can only be achieved in their language. The best of the moderns (Vida, Pontano, Sannazaro, Fracastoro) "could do better." But "could do better" is precisely the point of Scaliger's schoolmasterly cavils. His historical periodization of cyclical literary development and decline locates his contemporaries at a point where they may see their efforts rewarded with greater successes to come, provided they learn from him to be critics as well as poets.

Scaliger's partial and partisan coverage of recent poetry and Giraldi's more inclusive survey of "poets of our time," published ten years previously, are very limited and controlled universes selectively constructed out of the mass of works available both in print and in printed bibliographies.[11] Emergent literary history is an exercise in quality control inextricably implicated in the establishment of standards and canons. It also, despite Scaliger's concentration on texts, tends to reflect and in turn promote the preoccupation with the lives of authors consequent on the humanists' interest in the historical contextualization of literary works. The best known manifestation of this kind of literary history was by an exact contemporary of Giraldi, Paolo Giovio, whose *Elogia virorum literis illustrium* became best known in the splendid edition from Basel in 1577.[12] The basis of Giovio's work is not texts, as it was for Scaliger, but pictures, as had been the case in Giraldi's history of ancient poets. But Giovio's gallery has none of the revelatory mystique attendant on Giraldi's interpretative paradigm for unveiling images located only in a museum of the mind. Giovio's museum was a material entity, built on the shores of Lake Como and housing his collection of portraits of famous men. In the 1577 edition of his book we are invited to browse through a randomly arranged sequence of engraved portraits, mainly portraits of the great men of letters of the age of the humanists. Our eyes are

---

[11] Notably the recently published works of Konrad Gesner, the *Bibliotheca universalis* (Zurich, 1545) and the *Pandectae* (Zurich, 1548).

[12] The 1577 edition accompanied its miniature biographies with engraved portraits, lacking in the earlier editions of 1546 and 1557.

entirely fixed on their physical attributes, our minds are invited to dwell on their life and works recounted as inseparable parts of a single narrative history in the information provided on each of Giovio's exhibits. So, in a single sentence on page 73, and without further comment, we read of Poliziano's deformed morals, noble countenance, enormous nose, bad sight, sharp mind, his self-conceit in respect of his own work and his contempt for that of others. Death overtook him as he tried to assuage the morbid fever of his passion for a noble youth by frenzedly singing poetry. And so Poliziano passes into literary history.

What is conspicuously lacking in this picture gallery is a sense of literary history as a discipline of inquiry. By 1623, when Francis Bacon published his *De augmentis scientiarum*, he is able to take for granted the existence of *Historia literaria* as a specific division of history in general. But what Bacon finds wanting is a serious and coherent programme for contextualizing documents of a literary kind within the historical circumstances of their production. His own programme gives short shrift to lives of authors and does not waste time apportioning praise and blame "more criticorum." With authors left for dead, and critics sidelined, a truly historical inquiry into past events and causes in the Republic of Letters will show the way, so Bacon optimistically asserts, to a new, possibly different, but certainly best of all possible literary polities in time to come.[13]

Durham

---

[13] Francis Bacon, *De augmentis scientiarum*, II. iv, in his *Works*, eds. J. Spedding, R. L. Ellis, D. D. Heath, 14 vols. (London, 1857–1874), I: 502–504.

Humanist Values in Thomas More's
Life of Giovanni Pico della Mirandola

CLARE M. MURPHY

I t is fitting that what was perhaps the earliest published work of England's greatest humanist is an English translation of Gianfrancesco Pico's Latin biography of his uncle Giovanni, first published in 1498, just over three years after Pico's death. Particularly in his *Oration on the Dignity of Man*, Giovanni Pico seems to rank as the seminal Renaissance humanist. Very early in his valuable little book *Humanism in the Renaissance*, Sem Dresden writes, for example, "... it is certainly true that this oration is considered to be *the* manifesto of the Renaissance and of humanism."[1]

Dedication

More's parents had known the parents of Edward and Joyce Lee, grandchildren of a Lord Mayor of London, and apparently the More and Lee children had played together.[2] As a New Year's gift, probably in 1505, More dedicated his biography of Pico to their daughter Joyce, a nun of the Poor Clares. He opens his dedicatory letter with a reference to one of the dearest of humanist values, friendship. The beginning of the year, writes More to his "right entirely beloved sister in Christ," has for a long time been an occasion for friends to exchange gifts, "as the witness of their love and friendship ..." (CW 1, 51).[3]

In his title More refers to Giovanni Pico——"John Picus"——as "an excellent cunning man in all sciences, and virtuous of living" (CW 1, 49). In his *Oration* Pico exhorts his readers: "Let us disdain the things of the earth, let us hold in contempt the

---

[1] London: Weidenfeld and Nicolson, 1968, 11. Translated from the Dutch by Margaret King.

[2] E. E. Reynolds, *The Field Is Won: The Life and Death of St. Thomas More* (Milwaukee: Bruce Publishing Company, 1966), 44.

[3] Quotations from *The Complete Works of St. Thomas More* (Yale Univ. Press, 1963–1997) are cited in my text as "CW (volume) and (page)." *English Poems, Life of Pico, The Last Things*, ed. Anthony S. G. Edwards, Katherine Gardiner Rodgers, and Clarence H. Miller, 1997. Spelling and punctuation modernized.

things of the sky, and finally, leaving behind us all that is of the world, let us soar beyond the earthly realm to that realm nearest the most exalted Godhead."[4] In a similar vein, More writes to Joyce: "I . . . have sent you such a present as may bear witness of my tender love and zeal to the happy continuance and gracious increase of virtue in your soul: and whereas the gifts of other folk declare that they wish their friends to be worldly fortunate mine testifies that I desire to have you godly prosperous" (CW 1, 51).

Pico's Early Life

Some four years after the presentation of this edifying gift to an enclosed nun, More's fellow humanist and future martyr, John Fisher, was to preach the funeral sermon for Henry VII. The bishop, however, refuses to praise the late king's "mighty power," "riches incomparable," or "buildings most goodly," for "all be but *fumus et umbra*, a smoke that soon vanishes, and a shadow soon passing away."[5] Something of the same spirit seems to have permeated Pico's young lay translator. Where Gianfrancesco stresses his uncle's collateral descent from a nephew of the Emperor Constantine, More mentions this fact, but leaves out details of the pedigree and instead adds a didactic passage on the irrelevance of noble ancestry. Already skilled in the niceties of *sprezzatura*, More concludes that the important matter is Pico's own dazzling learning and virtue, which alas, his own "rude learning be far unable sufficiently to express" (CW 1, 53). In 1730, Edward Jessup published in London *The Lives of Picus and Pascal.* Jessup made a somewhat different assessment of More's powers, pointing out that Pico's memory had for 200 years subsisted "like fire under embers" through "the vast and penetrating capacity of an author so universally renown'd as Sir Thomas More."[6]

More very early gives a description of Pico's "person" in a manner which considerably resembles that to be used by Erasmus in his letter of July 23, 1519, to Ulrich von Hutten, which became the earliest biography of More.[7] If anything, however, More's physical description of Pico is briefer than that of More by Erasmus, as if to pass over quickly this less important aspect.

Renaissance humanists did not know that they were Renaissance humanists; they did know, however, that one could study "humanity," and this is the study that More says young Pico was set to "under the rule and governance of his mother" (CW 1, 55). In his fourteenth year young Giovanni was sent to Bologna to study canon law "by the commandment of his mother (which longed very sore to have

---

[4] Joannes Picus Mirandulanus, *Opera Omnia* (Torino: Bottega d'Erasmo, 1971), 316: "*Dedignemur terrestria, coelestia contemnamus, & quicquid mundi est denique posthabentes, ultra mundanam curiam eminentissimae diuinitati proximam aduolemus.*"

[5] John E. B. Mayor, ed., *The English Works of John Fisher*, Part I (London: Early English Text Society, 1876, rpt. 1935), 269–270. Spelling and punctuation modernized.

[6] *The Lives of Picus and Pascal* (J. Hooke, 1730), b2, recto and verso.

[7] R. A. B. Mynors, trans., and Peter G. Bietenholz, annot., *The Correspondence of Erasmus: Letters 993 to 1121.* Collected Works of Erasmus, Volume 7 (Toronto: Univ. of Toronto Press, 1987), 17. Subsequent references to this letter will be given in the text as CWE 7.

him priest)" (CW 1, 55). Twice within two paragraphs More mentions that it is Pico's mother, the nobly born Julia, who is responsible for his education, as it was later to be Lady Alice who presided over the "school" which More was to establish in his own household. And did More think of Julia in his Epigram 143, "To Candidus: How to Choose a Wife": "Happy is the woman whose education permits her to derive from the best of ancient works the principles which confer a blessing on life. . . . If she is well instructed herself, then some day she will teach your little grandsons, at an early age, to read" (CW 3/II, 187)?[8]

During his two years at Bologna, More tells us, Pico compiled "a sum upon all the decretals," a branch of canon law, but then left that study, finding it dry; thenceforth he "gave himself whole to speculation and philosophy, as well human as divine" (CW 1, 56). How closely More must have identified here with Pico, even though their pursuits of study were somewhat reversed. At the same age that Pico went to Bologna, More went to Oxford, there to pursue the humanist studies he so loved. Two years later he, too, changed the course of his pursuits—against his will, however. Following not "the commandment of his mother" but rather the orders of his father, More was taken from *studia humanitatis* at Oxford and sent to the London Inns of Court for the more "practical" study of English common law, the profession of his father, the future Judge John More. Unlike Pico he could not give "himself wholly to speculation and philosophy," yet he never renounced these studies; and his first recorded public lectures were not as a lawyer, but as a philosopher "as well human as divine," expounding St. Augustine's *City of God* to London audiences.

Pico the Humanist

More spends some time describing Pico's journey to Rome, his attempts to debate his 900 theses, his vanity, as well as the jealousy of the powerful who blocked him until his activities were approved by Pope Alexander VI. How could More know that he himself in more mature years, less vain but also distrusted, would take on the powerful theologians of Louvain or professors at Oxford, and indeed Joyce Lee's own brother Edward, in defense of his best friend Erasmus and of humanist learning? These letters constitute in themselves an entire volume in the Yale edition, Volume 15, *In Defense of Humanism,* edited by Daniel Kinney, 1986.

The maliciousness of his detractors drove Pico more and more toward the spiritual, and he was converted from a life "somewhat fallen into wantonness" (CW 1, 59). He burned five books written in his youth and "from thenceforth he gave himself day and night most fervently to the studies of Scripture, in which he wrote many noble books" (CW 1, 60). How could More know that thirty years later at his trial, he would point out that he "did not wish to answer anything else . . . about the said statute, except that I, being dead to the world, thought not at all of such things but only of the Passion of Jesus Christ"?[9] The fruit of this meditation is *De tristitia*

---

[8] *Latin Poems,* ed. Clarence H. Miller et al. (New Haven and London: Yale Univ. Press, 1984).

[9] Nicholas Harpsfield, *The life and death of S' Thomas Moore* . . . (London: Early English Text

Christi, but More's lifelong study of Scripture can be appreciated by any reader who glances at Germain Marc'hadour's five-volume *The Bible in the Works of St. Thomas More.*[10] Indeed, More's knowledge of Scripture and its commentators did not endear him to Henry VIII when this knowledge led him to answers other than those wished for in "the King's Great Matter" of his divorce from Catherine of Aragon.

Not surprisingly, More devotes considerable space to Pico's universal learning. Here a reader finds the seeds of More's attitudes toward *studia humanitatis,* liberal education in the sense that it is the education which *liberates* the mind from the tyranny of received opinion, and of public opinion. Pico was so learned in all sciences "that which of them soever you had considered in him, you would have thought that he had taken that one for his only study." Most remarkably, "he came thereto by himself with the strength of his own wit, for the love of God and profit of His Church, without masters, so that we may say of him, that Epicurus the philosopher said of himself, that he was his own master" (CW 1, 62).

This pun on being one's own master, not only teacher but also overseer, expresses a concept that was to become central to More's "school." In his 1518 letter to his children's tutor William Gonnell, More writes that "the reward of wisdom is too solid to be lost with riches or to perish with beauty, since it depends on the inner knowledge of what is right, not on the talk of men, than which nothing is more foolish or mischievous."[11] This concept of being one's own master seems to have indeed prevailed in the More "school." In his 1524 Colloquy, "The Abbot and the Learned Lady" (*Erudita puella*), Erasmus casts Margaret More Roper as Magdalia, a charming and brilliant young wife for whose wits the dull monk Antronius is no match. She is delighted that her husband is so different from Antronius, for she says "learning endears him more to me and me to him." The monk has already upbraided her learning, claiming "the public agrees with me, because it's a rare and exceptional thing for a woman to know Latin." To this she replies, "Why cite the public, the worst possible authority on conduct? Why tell me of custom, the mistress of every vice? Accustom yourself to the best...."[12]

Varia

More outlines in Pico some personal practices or attributes that were also, or were to become, his own: "Every day at certain hours he gave himself to prayer" (CW 1, 64). And Erasmus writes of More: "He has his fixed hours at which he says his prayers, and they are not conventional but come from the heart" (CWE 7, 24). In a practice that may seem masochistic in the light of current spirituality, yet was revered

---

Society, 1932), Appendix II, "The Paris News Letter," ed. Elsie Vaughan Hitchcock, 260: *"je ne voullu respondre autre chose ... dudit statut, sinon que moy estant mort au monde, je ne pensois point en telles choses, mais seullement en la passion de Jhesus Crist...."*

[10] Nieuwkoop: De Graaf, 1969–1972.

[11] *St. Thomas More: Selected Letters,* ed. Elizabeth Frances Rogers (New Haven: Yale Univ. Press, 1961, 1967), 104.

[12] *Colloquies,* volume 39 of *The Collected Works of Erasmus,* trans. Craig R. Thompson (Toronto: Univ. of Toronto Press, 1997), 504 and 503.

in the past, More writes that Pico "many days (and namely those days which represent unto us the passion and death that Christ suffered for our sake) beat and scourged his own flesh in remembrance of that great benefit and for cleansing of his old offenses" (CW 1, 64–65). More, too, wore a hairshirt and used a whip on himself. These penances seemed not to affect the dispositions of their practitioners, however; More praises in Pico an attribute of his own: Pico "was of cheer always merry and of so benign nature that he was never troubled with anger" (CW 1, 65). "Merry" was a particularly favored word of More: they would all be merry in heaven, he assured his family from the Tower.

A paragraph of the biography is entitled "Of his liberality and contempt of riches" (CW 1, 67–68). Erasmus writes thus of More: "From any love of filthy lucre he is absolutely free" (CWE 7, 22). More titles the following paragraph "Of his loving mind and virtuous behaviour to his friends" (CW 1, 68), while Erasmus says of More: "Friendship he seems born and designed for; no one is more openhearted in making friends or more tenacious in keeping them" (CWE 7, 18).

Final Days

More writes that Pico "eschewed dignities," despised worldly glory, and "set more by devotion than cunning" (CW 1, 66–67). Indeed, the spirit of More's 1534 Tower prayers and meditations seems to have been nourished thirty years earlier in his involvement with the life of the converted Pico. Does More himself not pray to "eschew dignity" and "despise worldly glory" when he writes in "A Godly meditation"

> Give me thy grace, good Lord,
> To set the world at nought . . .

and

> Not to long to hear of any worldly things
> But that the hearing of worldly fantasies
> may be to me displeasant . . . (CW 13, 226)?[13]

More quotes Pico as saying to a man more learned than good: "If we had evermore before our eyes the painful death of Christ which he suffered for the love of us, and then if we would again think upon our death, we should well beware of sin" (CW 1, 69). More in the Tower writes in "A Devout Prayer": "Good Lord, give me the grace in all my fear and agony to have recourse to that great fear and wonderful agony, that thou my sweet savior had at the Mount of Olivet before thy most bitter passion" (CW 13, 229), and in "A Godly meditation": "to have continually in mind the passion that Christ / suffered for me" (CW 13, 227).

§ § §

---

[13] *Treatise on the Passion, Treatise on the Blessed Body, Instructions and Prayers*, ed. Garry E. Haupt, 1976. Spelling and punctuation modernized.

Pico died at the age of 31, the victim of a fever that carried him off in three days. It would be strange indeed if More did not take seriously the death of a young man so near his own age, and did not himself meditate on death while writing of Pico's. Such meditation may have been the stimulus for More's unfinished *The Last Things* of a dozen years later. Of that projected treatise on death, judgment, hell, and heaven, he completed only the section on death. His sister's son Albertus tried to comfort the dying Pico by pointing out that death is the end of the body's ailments, but Pico replied that what pleased him most about death is that it brings the end to sin, "as he trusted the shortness of his life should leave him no space to sin and offend" (CW 1, 72). This somewhat uncommon way of looking at death is not repeated by More. His "Godly meditation" does, however, reflect a sense of using the time left in life to rid himself of sin and thus "to buy the time again that I before have lost," to cut off idle conversation and unnecessary recreation, and to consider the loss of everything and anything "right nought for the winning of Christ" (CW 13, 227).

Speculations

How many deaths More had seen in the roughly thirty years between the time he translated Gianfrancesco's *Vita Pici* and faced his own we can merely guess. Did he choose Antony as the elder of the two interlocutors of *A Dialogue of Comfort Against Tribulation* only because that name suggests the archetypal hermit, St. Antony of the Desert? Or did he perhaps remember that he had written of Pico: "the executor of his movable goods he made one Antony, his brother" (CW 1, 72)? Did More remember that he had described the vision of Pico in purgatory that Savonarola claimed to have had (CW 1, 73), remember it when he wrote in "A Godly meditation" that he would gladly suffer his purgatory on earth (CW 13, 226)? Did he recall that he concluded his biography of Pico as he had begun it, by a pious addition? More asks his readers to pray for Pico in his purgatory so that when he quits it for heaven Pico might pray for us to be in the next life "partners of that unspeakable joy" (CW 1, 75), all together "merry in God"?

§ § §

Seeing the translator as a betrayer is a frequent trope. Does it function here? Gianfrancesco Pico and his friend Pietro Cardinal Bembo exchanged several letters on the subject of *imitatio*. Literary imitation was to Bembo the total commitment to a text, to a style, to a way of thinking. The imitator becomes part of the personality of the one imitated. The two are commuted and transferred into one another.[14] Perhaps more fruitful than the concept *traduttore, traditore* in reflecting upon More's

---

[14] Giorgio Santangelo, ed., *Le epistole "De imitatione" di Giovanfrancesco Pico della Mirandola e di Pietro Bembo* (Florence: Olschki, 1954), 56–57. An English translation of the Pico-Bembo correspondence on the subject of imitation can be found in Izora Scott, *Controversies over the Imitation of Cicero* (New York: Columbia Univ. Press, 1910), Vol. 2, 1–18.

translation of *Vita Pici* would be calling to mind the high art that translation was in sixteenth-century England. Did the translator More, like Bembo's imitator, *become* his text? Was the personality of Giovanni Pico della Mirandola commuted and transferred into that of Thomas More? And was the personality of More commuted and transferred into that of his subject? Did he create as well as describe the uncle of Gianfrancesco Pico?

MOREANUM
Université Catholique de l'Ouest

Les Jardins de l'éloquence

COLETTE NATIVEL

L es *Vacationes autumnales, siue de perfecta oratoris actione & pronuntiatione libri III* du
Père Louis de Cressolles, parues à Paris en 1620, furent admirées, au même titre
que son *Theatrum veterum*, par le monde savant contemporain.[1] L'ouvrage, qui ne fut
jamais réédité, a pourtant retenu l'attention des chercheurs et il serait présomptueux,
après les travaux de Marc Fumaroli et de Christian Mouchel[2] en particulier, de pré-
tendre apporter de nouveaux éléments à l'analyse de la rhétorique de Cressolles.

Mon point de vue est autre. Il s'agira d'étudier la mise en oeuvre des concepts de
la rhétorique antique dans la "description d'un très beau jardin"—c'est le titre du premier chapitre du livre III—dont on peut se demander quelle est la fonction dans un
tel traité.

Cressolles présente ainsi son traité. Quatre jeunes élèves ou anciens élèves des
jésuites en vacances exposent leurs vues sur l'action et la prononciation: Iuventus, un
étudiant en rhétorique et Victor, un étudiant en philosophie, rendent visitent à leur
ami Honoré, bachelier en droit. Un bachelier en théologie, Théodore, déjà rompu
à la pratique de l'éloquence, les rejoint ensuite. Les *Vacationes* différeraient donc peu
des dialogues cicéroniens, si l'auteur ne procédait à une double variation sur le
schéma connu. Outre qu'il étudie celle des *partes dicendi* la moins développée par les
anciens, il transforme et amplifie la mise en scène au point que les *Vacationes* tiennent
plus de la narration que du dialogue de jardin traditionnel. De fait, un bon tiers du
livre est consacré à tout autre chose qu'au débat annoncé; les doctes exposés s'insèrent
dans un véritable récit qui s'ouvre sur ces mots dignes des meilleurs contes: *Duo
fuerunt lectissimi Adolescentes, quos in patriae suae Lyceo . . . Musae gremio suo aluerant.
Ambo nobiles & honesta familia nati, quique vigilias, curas, cogitationes in studio sapientiae*

---

[1] Sur Cressoles (1568–1634), secrétaire du général des jésuites Muzio Vitelleschi à partir de
1619: P. de Ribadeneyra (S. J.), *Bibliotheca scriptorum Societatis Jesu*, Rome, 1676; Leone Allatius
Apes Urbanae . . . (Rome, 1633); Adrien Baillet, *Jugemens des savans . . .* (Amsterdam, 1725).

[2] M. Fumaroli, *L'âge de l'éloquence*, Genève, 1980, pp. 299–324; C. Mouchel, *Cicéron et
Sénèque dans la rhétorique de la Renaissance*, Marburg, 1990, pp. 297–315. Cf. aussi Philippe Salazar,
*Les théories de la voix au XVII*ᵉ *siècle*, thèse (Paris IV, avril 1992), à paraître.

defigerent . . . Nec parentes ulla ratione dubitabant, fore illos aliquando familiae decora, patriae lumina . . . (p. 1). Après une première digression sur l'intérêt des vacances et une brève présentation de la demeure d'Honoré, vient la longue description de la bibliothèque dont chaque section est ornée des effigies des représentants majeurs de chaque domaine du savoir, Saint Thomas pour la théologie, Aristote pour la médecine et la philosophie, pour la poésie et la rhétorique Démosthène et Cicéron. Le commentaire de ces images est l'occasion de dire les *uirtutes* de ces maîtres. Puis l'explication de la présence, insolite en ces lieux, d'un miroir qui appartient "non seulement au monde immonde de Vénus (*mundo immundo*), mais aussi au chaste matériel des orateurs et des philosophes" (p. 85), amène l'exposé sur l'action du second livre. Celui-ci se clôt sur une nouvelle digression, le repas des jeunes gens s'accompagnant d'une dissertation sur les repas érudits. Le livre III enfin, consacré à la prononciation, commence par la dernière digression, la description des jardins.

Cressolles justifie ainsi cette forme narrative. Il s'agit d'une *dissertatio iuuenilis* qu'il faut rendre plaisante. Et il compare son traité à une fable à épisodes qui serait composée d'une *paraskeué*, suivie d'un *parodos*.[3] À cette volonté, bien conforme à la pédagogie jésuite, d'agrémenter son enseignement, s'ajoute un souci de composition. La cohérence de l'ouvrage est plus grande qu'il n'y paraît.

Les quatre digressions se font écho: à l'exposé sur les vacances et l'*otium* répond celui sur les repas d'érudits. Mais surtout Cressolles établit une correspondance entre les deux lieux principaux du débat—la bibliothèque et le jardin—par la bouche d'un des personnages qui compare la bibliothèque, lieu de la *memoria*, au "jardin des amours" et au "très agréable bois sacré des Grâces" (p. 49: *Amorum hortum, & amoenissimum Gratiarum lucum*). Si la bibliothèque est un jardin, le jardin est un lieu de mémoire. La fonction des citations dans sa description le montre. Non seulement elles rappellent au souvenir les jardins du passé, référents qui permettent d'en apprécier les beautés, mais encore elles se substituent à la parole défaillante des spectateurs saisis d'étonnement. C'est ainsi que Victor s'écrit (p. 455): "Je manque vraiment de mots pour exprimer ce que je ressens"—et il y supplée par une citation des *Dictiones* d'Ennode, puis une autre des *Mythologiae* de Fulgence à quoi s'enchaîne un extrait des *Lettres* de Cyprien—et la louange qu'il fait de la fontaine quand il reprend, en quelque sorte, la parole s'achève sur une ultime citation de Martial. L'éloge se dit dans un centon de citations qui invite à lire ces jardins comme un livre.

Le jardin était le cadre habituel des dialogues cicéroniens. On en retrouve ici maint élément; le lecteur des *Jardins romains* de Pierre Grimal[4] les reconnaîtra sans qu'il soit besoin de les relever. Et c'est bien sous l'égide de l'Arpinate que se déroule la promenade. La place qu'il occupe dans les *Vacationes* est prépondérante. Il a été présenté dans la description de la bibliothèque (p. 77) comme "la divinité de la langue et du talent" (*linguae & ingenii . . . diuinitas*). Son effigie montrait "son éloquence couronnée, illuminée par la lumière et le prodige de la flamme" (*Coronata*

---

[3] *Ad Lectorem*, p. [1]. Étant donné le peu d'espace imparti, on a le plus souvent choisi de donner soit le texte latin, soit sa traduction.

[4] Pierre Grimal, *Les jardins romains* (Paris, 1974).

eiusdem eloquentia, luce & flaminis prodigio illuminata). Et l'un des devisants ajoutait (p. 82), saluant en lui "la fleur de toutes les grâces," "j'aurais voulu qu'on n'eût pas peint ici seulement une flamme, mais même une fontaine, source du fleuve d'or de l'éloquence."[5] À l'entrée du jardin, par un nouveau jeu de miroir, son souvenir s'offre au visiteur à travers la statue de Minerve qui l'accueille. On sait l'admiration qu'il éprouvait pour la statue de Phidias, avec quelle ardeur il en cherchait les répliques pour orner ses jardins. "Au lieu," écrit Cressolles (p. 453), "de statues de Priape, Vertumne ou Vénus qui étaient d'ordinaire vénérées dans les jardins des Anciens comme des divinités gardiennes des lieux, il y avait, sculptée en marbre de Paros, la chaste et sage vierge Minerve." Mais loin d'être la guerrière du sculpteur athénien, cette Minerve incarne l'éloquence pacifique et pacifiante chère à l'Arpinate et illustre ses formules célèbres du *Brutus* 12, 45, *cedant arma togae*, ou du *De oratore* 1, 30, *pacis est comes eloquentia*. Le texte continue ainsi (p. 454): "son visage était lumineux, ses yeux brillants, elle était pudiquement voilée, telle à peu près que Cicéron la vit, guide de la réflexion, inspiratrice d'actions divines. Au lieu de l'égide, de la tête singulière de la Gorgone, elle tenait de sa gauche un livre dont la couverture de face était dorée et, de dos, mauve et ponctuée de petites étoiles dorées. Il n'y avait pas de casque sur la tête auguste de la plus humaine des déesses, mais une petite couronne de laurier agrémentée de perles d'olivier voilait ses boucles convenablement enlacées dans des anneaux: les muses voyaient ainsi en elle une amie pacifique." Ces étoiles qui illuminent le livre de la déesse ont déjà été évoquées plus haut (p. 81), dans la bibliothèque, à propos de l'image de Cicéron encore qui, "nouveau Jupiter"..., "s'est fait le démiurge du *logos* et a introduit dans le discours une composition et une structure admirables, pour le dire d'un mot, cosmique. Là, comme feraient des étoiles, les figures, avec leur incroyable éclat, illuminent tout: là on ne trouve pas une seule Vénus, mais toutes..."[6] La beauté toute de décence et de sagesse de la déesse inspiratrice du grand orateur, comme elle doit présider à l'art oratoire, imprègne ces lieux et métamorphose de sa présence le jardin des *Vacationes*. Lieu emblématique de la rhétorique, il n'est plus seulement le cadre agréable qu'il était dans les dialogues cicéroniens; son parcours constitue une sorte d'itinéraire initiatique que suivent les jeunes gens et qui les conduit d'émerveillement en émerveillement. Telles les effigies des maîtres anciens qui dans la bibliothèque disaient leurs *virtutes*, les ornements du jardin, convient le lecteur, comme ses visiteurs, à une véritable herméneutique.

Ainsi, une citation du *De re rustica* de Varron, bien naturelle ici, prend, dans la bouche de Théodore, un double sens et illustre cette analogie entre l'art des jardins et la rhétorique: *Omnis fructus docti Varonis opinione, quinto denique gradu peruenit ad perfectum, hic quaecumque in oculos incidunt, omnibus suis numeris absoluta sunt & perfecta*

---

[5] Traduction d'Alain Michel, p. 272, in: "Aspects de l'humanisme jésuite" (cahier préparé par Marc Fumaroli), in: *Revue des sciences humaines* 158 (1975): 246–293.

[6] Traduction d'A. Michel, "Aspects," pp. 272–273. Cf. aussi p. 574, trad. C. Mouchel, *Cicéron et Sénèque*, p. 313: "Quand je considère ces maîtres de la véritable éloquence..., quand je vois leur discours orné et rehaussé de sages pensées et de paroles graves, je crois voir le ciel revêtu et illuminé d'astres innombrables, où resplendit Mercure, le neveu de l'éloquent Atlas, où scintille non pas une Vénus, mais une infinité."

(p. 456). Comment ne pas rapprocher ces cinq étapes des cinq *partes dicendi*, la dernière, l'action, venant parachever les quatre autres? À cette métamorphose du *topos* littéraire succède un nouvel avatar. Il fallait un décor royal pour deviser de l'art royal qu'est la rhétorique, aussi Cressolles choisit-il de transporter dans l'espace imaginaire de sa fiction un lieu réel, les jardins royaux de Saint-Germain-en-Laye. Il nous donne cette clef: *Similia quaedam sunt in hortis regiis prope Lutetiam Parisiorum, ad oppidum Sancti Germani* (p. 459).

Saint-Germain comportait alors deux châteaux. Près de l'ancien château des Capétiens embelli par François 1er, Henri II avait fait édifier par Philibert de l'Orme une nouvelle demeure. Agrandi par Étienne du Pérac à la fin des guerres de religion, ce Château Neuf fut entouré de jardins dessinés par Claude Mollet et ornés de fontaines par l'hydraulicien Thomas Francini.[7] Une série de gravures d'Abraham Bosse et plusieurs textes nous donnent, malgré quelques contradictions, une idée de leur ordonnance entre la fin du XVIe siècle et celle du XVIIe et permettent d'apprécier les différents états de leur décoration. Les *Antiquités et recherches des villes, places et châteaux les plus remarquables de toute la France* d'André Duchesne, dans leur édition de Paris, 1614, décrivent ce que put voir Cressolles.

Les jardins s'étageaient en trois terrasses le long de la falaise qui surplombe la Seine. Ils étaient renommés pour leurs pièces d'eau et surtout les nymphées dont étaient creusés les murs de soutènement de la deuxième et de la troisième terrasse et qui contenaient d'étonnantes machines hydrauliques. Sous la première, détruite par un éboulement et reconstruite selon un autre dessin en 1662, se trouvait la grotte de la demoiselle, un automate qui jouait de l'orgue hydraulique, puis la grotte de Persée et Andromède. Les automates y représentaient le combat du héros contre le monstre. Venait ensuite la grotte de Neptune: le dieu émergeait de l'eau sur son char entouré d'un cortège de tritons, puis disparaissait dans les flots. Enfin, il y avait la grotte des maréchaux qui battaient le fer sur une enclume. Sous la troisième terrasse, on voyait la grotte d'Orphée et une grotte sèche, c'est-à-dire sans jets d'eau, la grotte des flambeaux. Tous les témoins évoquent le raffinement des mosaïques de coquillages qui pavaient les murs, la musique des eaux qui imitait le chant des oiseaux.

Si le jardin des *Vacationes* emprunte ses beautés à ceux de Saint-Germain—même décoration "à la française" avec parterres de broderie et fontaines, mêmes grottes marquetées de coquillages et peuplées d'automates—, une série de petites modifications transforme le décor initial et apporte une sorte de réponse visuelle aux grands problèmes de la rhétorique—celui des effets auxquels doit tendre le discours, ceux de la *varietas* et de l'*aptum*, celui des rôles respectifs de l'*ars* et de la *natura*—et ces pages sont à lire comme des prolégomènes au chapitre suivant *Vtrum eloquentia naturae vi an potius artificio nitatur*.

La rhétorique de ces jardins privilégie l'effet. Le *stupor* qu'ils suscitent chez les jeunes visiteurs est répété à l'envi: *Introgressi adolescentes subito admiratione cohorruerunt, in ea loci amoenitate, quae opinionem omnem superabat* (p. 453). Victor s'écrit (p. 455):

---

[7] Francini (1571–1651) appelé de Toscane par Henri IV, obtint de Louis XIII la charge d'intendant des eaux et fontaines. Il conçut les parcs de Fontainebleau et du Luxembourg.

mens haeret & fluctuatur, & animus mihi per oculos eripitur hanc intuenti optimitatem, hanc texturam Gratiarum, & elegantiarum pandecta. Proh quanta, & quam bella & insatiabilis omnium species atque varietas! Vt omnes sensus humanissima & liquida voluptate complentur! Ce *stupor* naît, comme dans l'éloquence cicéronienne, de l'abondance et de la *varietas: Erat autem ita elegans & artificiosa omnis hortis descriptio, vt cum magna esset rerum & opificii varietas quam te cumque in partem dedisses, nova quaedam inauditae seges delectationis occurreret* (p. 454). Le pavement des grottes associe des coquillages "d'une très grande variété de formes et de couleurs" (*summa varietate formae & coloris*), on y voit "la fleur de tous les genres" (*flos ibi omnium generum*) (p. 457). Invité à passer de la topographie à la topique oratoire, le lecteur est renvoyé à la méthode de Cressolles. La beauté des mosaïques de la grotte procède de la même esthétique de la citation et de la juxtaposition qui a guidé sa démarche: *Cura fuit non tam a nobis monita expromere quam super iis rebus exquirere antiquorum sapientiam, quorum gemmis opus hoc tessellatum secimus, & laboriose vermiculatum. Quidam forte inculcata nimium testimonia ad eamdem rem illustrandam illuminandamque reprehendent: alii non aequo animo accipient ea diuerticula, quae ad nonnullam delectationem ipsa varietate efficiendam aucupati sumus: erunt & qui centones male sartos & conciliatos nominabunt* (p. [2]).

Mais cette variété suppose des choix. Comme dans un beau discours, elle doit être réglée par les lois de la mesure et de l'*aptum*. Les ornements sont accumulés, mais cet *ornatus* n'est pas gratuit. La recherche de la beauté est associée à l'utilité comme le voulait Cicéron après les Stoïciens. Ainsi, "l'onde limpide [de la fontaine] se répandait en flots abondants non seulement pour l'agrément, mais aussi pour des besoins particuliers" (*non modo ad voluptatem, sed ad singulares quoque vtilitates . . .*) (p. 454). Les grottes ne sont pas purement ornementales, elles mettent en scène les merveilles de l'éloquence—et de l'éloquence seule. Car Cressolles en omet certaines qui existaient alors, celle en particulier d'Orphée: ses jardins, même s'ils en partagent la douceur, ne sont pas le *locus amoenus* de la poésie, mais ceux de l'éloquence qui se sert des mythes comme d'illustrations allégoriques, sans en faire sa matière. Et le jeune Victor souligne (p. 455) que leurs beautés font oublier celles des jardins mythiques chantés par les poètes: *Haec vbertas omnigena florum & herbarum, in Midae rosetis & Adonidis hortis non fuit: Haec poma Iunonis digna gameliis, Alcinoi copiam Hesperidumque pometum longe anteeunt.* Si le lecteur ne manque pas de songer aux *ekphraseis* des romans grecs, aux jardins d'Armide ou à ceux de l'*Astrée*, il est vivement ramené à l'objet du débat par Honoré qui souligne l'analogie entre ce décor et l'éloquence: *nunquam laetius quam hodierna die, in hac laeta & picturata commendatione vestra locus hic effloruit, ita mihi videor, non rosas aut uiolas, aut minuta huiusmodi quaepiam & quotidiana, sed diuinum quoddam genus orationis omnium gratiarum flosculis & corollis redundans olere* (p. 456).

Cette *varietas* suppose enfin une concentration des effets. Cressolles réunit en un seul édifice plusieurs des ornements dispersés dans les grottes de Saint-Germain et imagine une spectaculaire scénographie qui leur donne plus d'efficace. À l'extérieur du nymphée, il place les maréchaux dont l'activité évoque "une ville bien organisée." Au contraire, l'intérieur avec Neptune et son cortège, puis le triomphe de Persée sur le monstre, semble d'abord le domaine du mythe, mais la paix des hommes revient avec le spectacle de la jeune fille à l'orgue. J'apporterai une nuance à la lecture que

Marc Fumaroli fit de ces scènes.[8] Il remarque très justement que "les machines du nymphée, le char de Neptune, le vol de Persée et l'orgue hydraulique, symbolisent les trois styles, le sublime, le moyen et le simple dans la version 'douce' chère à Cressolles," mais il se fonde sur les trois dernières seulement. Si on leur ajoute celle qui se trouve à l'extérieur, on constate que les scènes de paix—la cité laborieuse et la jeune musicienne—encadrent deux spectacles plus grands ou violents. On pourrait donc voir dans la machine des maréchaux l'évocation du style simple, dans celle de la demoiselle une représentation du style moyen et dans les deux scènes centrales deux versions du sublime, le sublime de la simplicité dans celle de Neptune, celui de la véhémence dans celle de Persée. Si tout en ces lieux est conçu "pour la beauté et la douceur" (*ad pulchritudinem amoenitatemque*) (p. 456), si la paix du jardin en fait le théâtre privilégié de la parole pacifique, cette douceur n'interdit pas la véhémence quand elle est nécessaire. De même, l'action sera adaptée au mode. C'est ce que montrent les mouvements des automates doués d'une éloquence muette: le monstre effraie par "son oeil flamboyant" (*flammantibus oculis*), "son aspect terrible et horrifiant" (*horrifica specie & immani*) (p. 459), tandis que la jeune fille "remuant un peu la tête, semblait comme saisir de l'oreille . . . l'incroyable suavité des sonorités" (*modice caput mouens, aure veluti captare videbatur incredibilem illam sonorum suauitatem. . . .*) (p. 459).

Cressolles, ce n'est pas étonnant dans un traité sur l'action et la prononciation, ne néglige pas les sens, et l'oeil d'abord. Il se plaît à décrire la brillance du marbre, les mosaïques de nacre qui "vibraient d'un éclat doux et argenté" (*dulci quodam & argenteo splendore*) (p. 458). L'ouïe se satisfait aussi de la musique harmonieuse de l'orgue, du chant des oiseaux, qu'il soit réel ou feint (p. 459). Mais il ne s'agit pas de s'en tenir à cette vaine volupté qu'est le plaisir des sens et que les sophistes cherchaient à apporter à leurs auditeurs. Cressolles la blâme: . . . *cum vellent mirabiliter omnia dicere, & blanditiis elegantissimae voluptatis perfundere animos audientium & suauitudine complere, . . . inducebant . . .* "*pictae tectoria linguae*," *& mollissimam pronunciationem* (p. 473). Refusant ces fards efféminés, la bonne prononciation, la prononciation virile obéit aux lois de la bienséance. Sans négliger la *voluptas aurium* qui lui fait proscrire les sonorités "grossières et campagnardes" (*agrestem & subrusticum . . . sonum*) (p. 473), elle demeure naturelle. Son brillant, son charme, elle ne les cherche pas dans les séductions d'une fadeur douceâtre, mais dans l'assentiment avec la nature et l'adaptation aux circonstances. Elle évite enfin la satiété. Et le maître des lieux ne montrera pas à ses amis toutes les merveilles du jardin.

La dernière question à envisager, celle des apports de la nature et de l'art à la création, était au centre de la réflexion rhétorique des anciens. On connaît les pages du *De oratore* ou de *L'institution oratoire* que Cicéron et Quintilien lui ont consacrées et qui aboutissaient à cette position modérée que si talent et art conspirent à la perfection de l'oeuvre, celle-ci ne peut rien sans celle-là. Si le jeune Victor met en évidence la seule féconde abondance de la nature (p. 455), le sage Théodore souligne ensuite (p. 456) le concours de "la rare et remarquable fécondité de la nature et de la

---

[8] "Aspects . . ." (n. 5), p. 273.

très admirable et louable mise en oeuvre de l'art" (*naturae foecunditatem, artisque industriam plane admirabilem & praedicandam*). Il loue ces beautés "si nombreuses, si grandes" qui, "qu'elles soient le fruit du génie (*genio*) de la nature ou qu'elles aient été achevées par l'ingéniosité (*ingenio*) des hommes, écrasent de leur supériorité tout ce qui aurait pu séduire l'esprit humain" (p. 456). La dialectique entre ces deux facteurs est subtilement évoquée. La description des grottes montre une nature artiste: "Il y avait d'abord des lépas, des patelles et de nombreuses espèces de tellines, des coquilles transparentes que l'admirable travail de la nature avait variées (*discriminata summo naturae opificio*) en y traçant des bandes et des petites lignes et qui étaient d'un raffinement remarquable; puis des pétoncles de très belle taille dont la forme procurait le plus vif plaisir au spectateur: des cannelures et des nervures faisaient un peu saillie sur les côtés et, comme si elles avaient été mesurées à la règle et au compas, grâce à quelque incroyable mécanique de la nature (*incredibili quadam naturae machinatione*), fuyaient jusqu'aux bordures plissées, tandis que des lignes également espacées les traversaient obliquement" (p. 457); mais le rôle des doctes mains des artisans est aussitôt rappelé: "l'art d'une main savante (*doctae manus artificio*) [les] avaient réunis en un tout dans la mosaïque." L'art qui transforme la nature, qui taille les bosquets en molosses, en Alcide ou en centaures (p. 454), doit donner l'illusion d'une seconde nature, la représentation sembler elle-même naturelle. Ainsi les grottes artificielles ont été conçues *ad imaginem specus natiui arte reddendam* (p. 457), leur décoration mêle des éléments naturels—les coquillages—et factices—les machines hydrauliques—mais toujours elle tend à recréer une autre nature. Comme le miroir de la bibliothèque reflétait l'orateur en représentation, ce jardin est à la fois la nature et la représentation de la nature.

Ces pages, exemple de l'*exquisitus flos orationis* cher à Cressolles, doivent leur beauté aux principes mêmes qui y sont suggérés. Rien de trop ici malgré la théâtralité de la description. Ces jardins, loin d'être un ornement stérile, mettent en oeuvre les principes rhétoriques et esthétiques de Cressolles. *Vt rhetorica horti.*

L'éloquence de Cressolles, telle jadis celle de Cicéron, cherche une voie moyenne entre les excès de l'asianisme et de l'atticisme. Si elle a le goût du ton juste, de la mesure, de la bienséance, en un mot, de l'harmonie, elle ne refuse pas l'ornementation, le mouvement et l'abondance. Il ne s'agit pas de cette "abondance stérile" que blâme Boileau au chapitre 1 de l'*Art poétique*, mais d'une abondance maîtrisée qui se traduit dans le choix de la variété. L'*imitatio naturae* conduit Cressolles à cette synthèse: la nature artiste est servie par l'art qui l'imite dans son choix de la diversité.

Ainsi, le *stupor* que produit un beau spectacle ou un beau discours ne naît pas tant de leur douceur ou de leur véhémence, que du sentiment presque indéfinissable de leur nécessité—soit de la grâce que promeut la rhétorique de Cressolles.

Paris, France

De ineditis operibus iis, quae quidem Latine Dominicus quidam Cyllenius Graecus in Italia decimo sexto conscripserit saeculo[1]

KARL AUGUST NEUHAUSEN

A. *Exordium ac partitio*

Consideranti diu, quemadmodum quam iustissime quaestionibus hoc in Barensi conventu Neo-Latino tractandis satisfacere possem,[2] nulla mihi res est aptior .visa, quam si humanistae cuiusdam memoriam repeterem illius nostra quidem aetate parum cogniti sive prorsus iacentis in oblivione, sed eiusdem in Italiae praesertim regionibus ita morati, ut Bessarionis fortasse similiumve Graecorum secutus exempla scilicet utriusque veteris linguae peritus suis ipsius quoque operibus ostenderet Latino sermone confectis, quantum humanismus tum per propriam sui velut patriam propagatus valeret in antiquarum omni litterarum et continuanda simul hereditate et transformanda posterisque tradenda.

 Est igitur mihi propositum nunc ab oblivione vindicare Dominicum eundem Cyllenium, qui quattuor abhinc fere saeculis ipse semet in Graecia natum esse cognomine suo testatus cum in aliis urbibus Italicis tum Florentiae floruit, sed cuius cuncta Latine scripta paene funditus adhuc esse videantur oblitterata. Quattuor enim exstare codices manu scriptos eorum operum, quae quidem hucusque non edita composuisset Dominicus Cyllenius Graecus, in utroque primo iam *Itineris Italici* sui grandis volumine[3] dudum confirmavit ipse Paulus O. Kristeller, quem laetamur nonagenarium mox esse feliciter evasurum.[4] Divisa autem est illa quadriga tamquam Cyllenia

---

[1] Adnotationibus aliquot exceptis praelectionis huiusce tenor universus ad anni 1994 mensem Augustum accommodatus manet.

[2] Respicienda nempe naviter ubique est haec propria congressus omnis inscriptio: *The Impact of Italian Humanism: Continuations and Transformations.*

[3] Vol. I (1961) pp. 46 et 292; vol. II (1967) pp. 74 et 406.

[4] Natum eundem in Germania constat esse die 22° m. Maii a. 1905°. Liber ad eundem honorandum is, cuius miscellanea statuendum est ei compluribus esse iam annis ante dedicata in

nondum mandata typographis in duas partes, quarum una ad militarem pertinet mundum, altera multo maior ad rem publicam ac philosophiae theologiaeque quasdam gravissimas quaestiones.

Iam vero plura quidem ad auctoris ignoti fere Cyllenii nomen aut vitam mores libros spectantia eademque certiora forsitan illis, quae Kristeller nobiscum singula communicavit, interea neque in lucem apparet esse protracta nec divulgata—excepta tantum aliquatenus ea relatione, quam Anconae biennio ante publice protuli, cum humanista Cyriacus ibidem ortus idemque excellens antiquorum conditor studiorum sollemniter sescentenarius celebraretur;[5] namque hanc equidem inscripsi commentationem in Actis illius Anconitani conventus postea demum prodituris *Dominicus quidam Cyllenius Graecus quonam in opere quatenus sit Cyriacum Anconitanum imitatus Mercurii dei cultorem vel maxime egregium.*[6]

B. *Tractatio*

Itaque ut inter Cyriacana nuper natalicia selectas unius dumtaxat codicis manu scripti particulas aliquot Mercuriales investigavi, sic hoc in generali quodam congressu Cyllenii nostri potius omnia, quae quidem manserint, Latine scripta quattuor eaque singulis custodita codicibus sub uno velut aspectu censeo collocanda.

(I) Bipertitae divisionis operum Cyllenii caput prius

Principium ergo sumendum est ab ea duplici classe, cuius codex manu scriptus alter idemque in bibliotheca Civitatis Vaticanae conservatus inscribitur *Dominici Cyllenii Greci de castrametatione Romanorum Grecorum Hebreorum Cyri regis Persarum Turcarum atque recentiorum libellus.*[7] Verumenimvero—ut fateri festinem verum—me mehercule pacis amantissimo vix ne excogitari quidem potest minus quisquam idoneus, qui castris in metandis sit occupatus aut omnino de militari disserat re qualibet bellicosaque. Quae cum ita sint, enitar tamen, ut augeantur saltem atque emendentur illa, quae Kristeller iam obtulit eruta, quo commodius queat sublevari, cuiuscumque interest maxime cum in castrenses incumbere rationes a Cyllenio quondam exhibitas tum omnem hunc libellum aliquando perinde atque cetera eiusdem auctoris inedita prelo subicienda curare.

---

universitate Bonnensi, quod nondum imprimi potuit, nemo est quin ferat aegerrime.

[5] Nam cum a. 1392° eum Anconae lucem ferant aspexisse, sescentis post annis eadem in urbe complures dies (m. Febr. a. 1992°) quam maximis ille cum istius civitatis tum litterarum rei publicae honoribus est affectus. Verumtamen eiusdem Cyriacani conventus Acta quinque demum annis post in vulgus sunt hoc edita titulo: "Ciriaco d'Ancona e la cultura antiquaria dell'umanesimo. Atti del Convegno internazionale nel VI centenario della nascita a cura di Gianfranco Paci e Sergio Sconocchia, Reggio Emilia, Edizioni Diabasis 1997."

[6] Op. cit., pp. 253–268. Accedit, ut earum vicissim commentationum, quibus quidem in Cyriaci textus inquirere Latinos proprie mihi foret destinatum, postrema sit ipsa quoque interim publicata: "Die vergessene 'göttliche Kunst der Totenerweckung': Cyriacus von Ancona als Begründer der Erforschung der Antike in der Frührenaissance," in: *Atlas-Bonner Beiträge zur Renaissanceforschung*, I (Coloniae 1996), 51–68.

[7] Cf. Kristeller, *Iter Italicum*, vol. II p. 406.

Ac primum quidem totum istius de castrorum metatione opusculi codicem statuamus necesse est constare ex foliis fere septuaginta, quorum longe plurima (fol. 9–66) consentaneum est rem illam potissimum explicandam comprehensam habere; praemissus autem est iisdem libelli in XXI capita distributi et brevis titulus et index, quorum uterque paginarum caret numeris, atque introductio fusior (fol. 3–8), cuius initio desunt duo videlicet folia. Deinde, antequam castrorum ipsa metatio qualis Cyllenia sit adumbretur, animadvertere nos oportet, quando codex ille sit exaratus. Eundem enim anno 1656° non ab auctore libelli—priore quippe saeculo vixit,—sed aliena manu descriptum esse duobus internis comprobatur indiciis.[8] Ac nomen quoque auctoris aeque atque in ceteris eiusdem operibus Latinis explanari non potest, nisi codicis textus ipse consulitur. Nam solis duabus paginis illis, quibus singulae leguntur inscriptiones, Dominici Cyllenii Graeci nomen occurrit, quasi vero tria haec istius nominis elementa vel ipsa prae se ferant, quid sibi velint quantamque vim eadem habere sint existimanda.

Quapropter hic commemorasse sufficiat ex uno *Graeci* cognomine perspici posse Cyllenium nostrum nescio qua Graeca nimirum ortum familia decimo sexto mediante fere saeculo vel sua sponte vel alterius instar Aeneae profugum in Italiam pervenisse. *Cyllenii* vero nominis notionem duplici via rationeque inita debere nos arbitror interpretari. Etenim ab altera parte, quoniam Mercurius Iovis filius Cylleneo vertice in lucem editus idemque inde ab Anconitani Cyriaci temporibus humanistarum tamquam deus elatus ad summum ascenderit dignitatis gradum, nonnullos tunc homines constat e Graeciae finibus ad Italicas profectos regiones singulos exstitisse, qui gentilicio suo nomine deposito quasi quidam reduces Mercurii *Cyllenii* sibi nomen imponere maluerunt; ita factum est, ut Kristeller in *Itineris Italici* quodam indice personarum[9] enumeraret deinceps Cyllenios quinque,[10] quorum nomina hoc ornata splendore divino redolere manifestum est origines Graecas. Unde praeterea colligitur Cyllenii nomen a Dominico heroe nostro Graeco etiam ea mente usurpatum esse, ut gentilicii nominis cuiusque in -*ius* desinentis consuetudinem vere Romanam suum in usum convertisse videretur. Iisdem itaque adductus causis (ne neglegatur altera rei pars enucleandae) suo Cyllenius ficto nomini gentilicio praeposuit tale nomen, quale tralaticii vice praenominis fungeretur. Enimvero noster idem Cyllenius Graecus, cum *Dominicus* familiariter vellet vocari, praenomen hoc ad Cyriacum imprimis Cyllenii dei illius cultorem eximium videtur accommodavisse, praesertim quia reliqui quattuor Cyllenii humanistae, quos Kristeller citavit, alia singuli praetulere praenomina.

Quibus quidem cognitis rebus vix licet coniectare plura nos de Cyllenii nostri nomine, vitae curriculo moribusque comperturos fuisse, nisi duo folia codicis illius desideraremus amissa. Quantum autem momenti eidem huic Dominici Cyllenii de metatione castrorum libello iam aequales eius duxerint tribuendum, vel inde potest

---

[8] Reperitur utique numerus anni "1656" praemissus et indici capitum XXI, quae complectitur tractatus, et eiusdem ipsius exordio.

[9] Vol. II p. 649.

[10] Antecedente enim eo Cyllenio, qui nullo praeditus exhibetur alio nomine, alphabetico scilicet ordine illic inter se excipiunt *Antaeus, Bernardinus, Dominicus, Nicolaus, Raphael Cyllenius*.

percipi, quod aliud Latinum Graeci illius auctoris opus nullum videtur habitum esse dignum, quod in exterum et in Italicum quidem sermonem eadem aetate iam transferretur; nam de titulo versionis huiusce Mediolani conservatae, sed (clausis nempe parumper Ambrosianae bibliothecae foribus iisdemque nondum apertis[11]) a memet adhuc quidem non collatae Kristeller[12] rursus nos facit certiores: *Degli alloggiamenti del campo secondo i Romani, Greci, Ebrei, Persiani, Turchi e moderni, al duca di Albucherche.* At Latinus ipse Cyllenii tractatus non duodeviginti modo—ut ille contendit—, sed unum et viginti continet capita; nam vicesimo capite Cyllenius agit de castra egrediendi ratione generaliter apud recentiores obvia gentes, postremo navat operam soli Turcarum regis rationi castra metandi. Quamquam maxima certe pars opusculi dedicata Romanorum est castrensibus rebus antiquis; simulatque enim in universam castrorum et materiam inquisivit et formam, duodecim idem impendit capita toti cum Caesaris tum omnium ordini Romanorum, quo constituto tum castra militum dirigi consuevissent; verum singula tantum capita Cyllenius consumenda rebatur in Graecorum, Hebraeorum Cyrique regis Persarum ea, quam appellavit, *castrametatione.*

Ex hoc igitur conspectu quamvis succincto facillime quemque spero posse concludere Cyllenium nostrum non Frontini modo semet aliorumque veterum scriptorum, quos sciret esse versatos in militaribus rebus, sectatorem aut archaeologicis quaestionibus unice deditum voluisse praestare, sed id quoque esse molitum, ut illa, quae castris antiquis usui fuisse videretur, ad suum ipsius usque aetatem continuata nonnullis offerret contemporaneis transformanda.

Nec vero Cyllenius haecce sibi consequenda proponere destitit, cum anno 1564º *Ad illustrissimum Comitem Ioannem Anguisolam Comi gubernatorem iustissimum* misit id opusculum,[13] cuius inscriptio triplicem quandam speciem gerere perhibetur; frontispicio codicis enim Raimondi cuiusdam manu scripti promittitur *Dominici Cillenii Greci Novocomensis de militari ordine Romanorum ceterarum rerum,* exordio libelli sequentis adnuntiatur *Dominici Cyllenii Greci Comensis de Romanorum exercitus ordine Greco ac recentiori libellus* (sic!), at auctor ipse contra denique eundem usus hisce verbis perorat: *Hactenus de militari ordine Romanorum atque aliarum gentium satis dictum sit.* Quocirca quindecim iis titulis, qui sunt praemissi capitibus singulis, significatur Cyllenium Romanorum utique ordini militari longe plurimum spatii tribuisse; sed singula quoque capitula concessit cum Graecorum armis phalangique Macedonicae tum recentiori militum ordini.

Atque hac in disputatione militari legenda confiteor haud mediocri mihi fuisse solacio, quod statim sensi Cyllenium non tam gerendi cuiusvis belli quam prohibendi potius evitandique cogitationes suas litteris mandavisse. Namque ut primum relicta Florentia se contulit Comum ita quidem, ut Novocomensis seu simpliciter Comensis afficeretur agnomine, eiusdem urbis principi illi dedicatoriam epistulam recepturo salutem plurimam dixit, cum exorsus est asseverare sibi iam dudum exploratum fuisse

---

[11] Eadem querella pertinet etiam ad opus infra (cum adn. 14) citandum.

[12] *Iter Italicum,* vol. I p. 302.

[13] Kristeller, *Iter Italicum,* vol. I p. 46; aliquanto plura mecum litteris comiter missis communicavit Comensis urbis *Biblioteca Comunale.*

omnium animantium genus praecipue divinum pacis numen optare; quapropter, quod asseruisset ipse Cicero nihil gloriosius esse quam tyrannum occidere,[14] summam sibi laudem illum peperisse atque etiam immortalitatem adeptum esse, quia sublato tyranno pacem omnibus comparavisset.

(II) Bipertitae divisionis operum Cyllenii caput posterius

Eo magis igitur doleo ad rei publicae iam philosophiaeque fines transgressurus iisdem mihi de causis, quibus illud de castrametatione opusculum Italice conversum inspicere sim ipse prohibitus, ne hoc quidem contigisse, ut Ambrosianum illo plane graviorem adirem codicem manu scriptum, quo contineri fertur Cyllenii nostri liber quidam inscriptus *De re publica, ad Achademicos Affidatos Papiae*.[15] Requirendum enim id quidem fore praecipue iudico nobis, num Cyllenius Ciceronis sit secutus doctrinam sex scilicet illius de re publica libris id temporis nondum recuperatis; amplius autem illis vocibus ad Cyllenii de re publica sententiam referendis prodere Kristeller supersedit.

Restat hic ergo (paulisper adversante Fortuna), ut ineditus perlustretur is dialogus, qui non secus quam militaris ille liber uterque mihi suppetit copiatus, iisdem vero duobus opusculis longe vi momentoque antecellere censendus est. Etenim hoc ipsum opus singulare biennio ante, dum Cyriacana sollemnia peraguntur Anconae,[16] ea tantum mente primus arcessivi tenebris quibus latuerat ereptum, ut auctor Cyllenius Cyriaci illius priscorum humanistarum facile principis praesentaretur imitator. Nunc autem opportunitatem mihi nancto danda est opera, ut totum idem opus pateat accuratius perquirendum. Itaque est primum necesse statui, qualis sit titulus istius operis[17] quadringentis triginta duobus abhinc annis manu scripti tandemque nobis in medio ponendi: *Dominici Cyllenii Graeci de libera hominis voluntate, beatorum, Angelorum, ac Dei*; deest enim addita *dei* nomen in *Itineris Italici* volumine, quo primo describitur hoc ipsum de libero arbitrio opus a Cyllenio tum prolatum. Dicatum autem idem erat Florentiae quidem exaratum, sed iam pridem Pisis conservatum Kalendis Novembribus a. 1562[i] *Cosmo Medici excellentissimo Florentiarum ac Senarum Duci*.[18]

Quibus praemonitis haud mirum est Florentinas has Cyllenii Graeci de libera cum hominum tum Dei voluntate, quippe quae quaestio vere philosophica ab utroque illo militari tractatu minoris profecto putando tam aperte abhorreret, forma quoque aliquanto pulchriore dari foras ornamentisque tamquam splendidioribus vestitas debuisse prodire. Ita factum est, ut Cyllenius, quae sibi proposuerat explicanda, non tam perpetuae cuiusdam orationis filo semet ipsum duceret par esse contexere quam dramatici instar dialogi decerneret porrigenda; namque induta philosophi persona finxit sermonem esse quondam inter duos peregrinos eosdemque praestantes viros insti-

---

[14] Satis est (ut alia omittam) conferre Cic. off. II 19.

[15] Kristeller, *Iter Italicum*, vol. I p. 292.

[16] Cf. supra (cum adn. 4).

[17] Kristeller, *Iter Italicum*, vol. II p. 74.

[18] Haec omnia quidem ex praemissa dedicatoria perspiciuntur epistula (fol. 1ʳ et 6ʳ); sequitur eam ipse dialogus, cuius libri sex complent folia LXXII (7ʳ–78ᵛ) eademque a me continenter una cum prioribus reliquis iam transcripta.

tutum omnemque hunc dialogum quasi coram legentibus habitum coegit sex in libros distributum, ita quidem ut amborum universa collocutio dispertiretur tres in dies, quibus singulis auctor binos ait libros respondere.

Delineato tali tenore atque ordine conficti illius colloquii non nimis est difficile cognitu, quaenam potissimum exemplaria dialogorum litteris mandatorum Cyllenius noster sibi sumpserit aemulanda; cum enim suum de voluntate hominis libera sermonem comminisceretur, eundem auctorem Latinum, ut animum erigeret opusque ad altius fastigium videretur attolli, in promptu est cum alios Ciceronis tum sex *De re publica* libros coniunxisse cum uno, quem librum ab illo constat editum esse *De fato*.

Atqui idem Cyllenius, etsi rem ipsam quoque fati simillimam tractare constituit, neque in urbis Romae qualibet villa aut inter consulares viros sermonem illum suum successisse simulavit neque ipsum se eidem interfuisse colloquio. Immo vero sedem eam, ubi collocutionis scaena fuisset olim, ab Italia reliquaque Europa avocatam collocavit humanista Graecus in paulo remotiore illa quidem, sed non minus illustri regione Aegyptia prope ripas Nili fluminis sita; personas autem duas ipsas, quae participes dialogi tum exstitisse dicuntur, loquentes induxit et deum eminentem Mercurium (sive Hermetem Trismegistum[19]) consule vel optimo quoque non inferiorem et Philonem philosophum Academicum eundemque eximium ipsius Ciceronis magistrum.

Quantis igitur qualibusque ex fontibus et Graecarum veterum et Latinarum hauserit litterarum, Cyllenius arguit ipse iam sermonis exordio, cum Philonem utpote eruditissimum fingit hac perpolita usum sententia se huic applicavisse Mercurio (fol. 7):

> *Ea quidem sciendi cupiditas, o facunde Mercuri, quae Pythagoram Aegyptum petere, ad*
> *Persas proficisci, Cretam, Lacedaemona navigare, ad Olimpicum Certamen descendere,*
> *ac in illam Italiae partem, tunc maiorem Graeciam appellatam pergere coepit, quae*
> *Platonem omnium mortalium sapientissimum multas orbis partes lustrare, ut Aegyptum,*
> *Nili fluminis inexplicabiles ripas, vastissimos campos, flexuosos et obliquos fossarum*
> *ambitus Aegyptiorum Seniorum uti discipulum ac in Italiam transgredi compulit, me*
> *hodie tantum itineris emensum ad tua limina traxit, veterem quidem amicum cum studio*
> *visendi, tum quandam olim inceptam quaestionem nec perfectam causam dirimendi.*

Aristotelis summi fretum auctoritate (principio quippe Metaphysicorum[20] cunctos etiam homines natura scire proclamantis appetere) neque Horatii simul immemorem, cuius poetae praeclari hymnus Mercurio singulariter oblatus invocandi iisdem fere verbis inchoatur,[21] Philonem quoque hic tam efficaciter introductum exordiri cum Mercurio deo colloqui quis nostrum est, quin interposita nulla dubitatione percipiat? At vero Larisaeum eundem Philonem—atque adeo Cyllenium auctorem ipsum quo-

---

[19] De huius rediviva renascentiae temporibus figura nuperrime disputavi: "Hermes/Merkur im frühen Renaissance-Humanismus: Das neue Bild eines prominenten antiken Gottes in der 'Africa' und im übrigen lateinischen Werk Petrarcas," *Mittellateinisches Jahrbuch* 28,2 (1993), 59–102.

[20] Arist. Met. A 980ª.

[21] Hor. carm. I 10,1: *Mercuri, facunde nepos Atlantis.*

que e Graecia oriundum—deinde non utriusque liquet illius viri quamvis insignis pressisse vestigia, sed monumenta magis aliorsum pertinentia coagmentavisse,[22] cum varias Pythagorae per orbem terrarum peregrinationes cum iis copularet itineribus, quae quidem Plato praecipue cum in Italiam fecisset tum in Aegyptum.

Etenim Aegyptiacus is Mercurius, quem a Philone Graeco Cyllenius narrat ut veteris amicitiae foedere coniunctum denuo tum esse visitatum atque in caelum laudibus elatum, non tam ille facundus Horatii custos aut Pythagoreorum recognoscendus est deus quidam quam Termaximus idem Mercurius sive Hermes Trismegistus, cuius mentionem iam Plato quoque iniecerat, verum cuius imaginem longe vel illustrissimam Florentiae centum iam annis, priusquam Cyllenius primo praeclaram hanc ingressus est urbem, ingeniosissime Marsilius Ficinus animo conceperat iisdem videlicet testimoniis nixus, quae Cyllenius ex antiquorum videtur auctorum libris depromp-sisse, ut dei nova quaedam emergeret Cyllenii figura Mercurii.[23] Namque postquam Florentinus ipse Ficinus tam pertinaciter est opinatus Trismegistum suum Mercurium vel Pythagora vel Platone saeculis aliquot antiquiorem in Aegypto veteres iam et paganorum Graecorum obvolutas et Christianorum simul patrum revelatas pronun-tiavisse doctrinas, dilucide quidem haec oculis subiecta conceptio Mercurialis sed abstrusa tamen quindecim fere decennia totum per litterarum orbem pervagata tot tantorumque hominum animos quamvis doctorum occupavit, ut plus etiam ceteris omnibus veterum auctorum praeceptis memoriae proditis tunc valere videretur, donec I. Casaubonus admodum firmis philologorum rationibus fultus evicit ipsam Hermeticam illam informationem, quam priscis temporibus exortam Ficinus sibi persuaserat esse divinam, radicitus esse tollendam. Defunctam autem esse eandem ne nostra quidem aetate celeberrimus ipse mode probavit Umbertus Eco, cum superstites Trismegisti illius Mercurius Casaubonique personas quasi quosdam principes in media posuit ea fabula romanensi, cuius titulum accepimus a pendiculo quodam traxisse nomen suum.

At Dominicus contra Cyllenius noster quinque fere decenniis, antequam Casau-bonus Ficinianas Mercurii illius fictiones funditus evertit, Cosmo Florentiae Sena-rumque duci suos de libero arbitrio libro dedicavit, cum nec desiit Ficini depictio Mercurialis vigere et ipsa Florentia totius arx renascentiae maximeque egregii cuius-que humanistae domicilium florere perrexit. Itaque satis esse causae videtur, cur miremur omnium humanistarum, qui inde iam a Petrarcae temporibus exstitissent, nullius ne mentionem quidem fecisse Cyllenium Graecum. Etsi enim reputandum est Petri Pomponatii Mantuani a. 1525° mortui libros quinque De fato, de libero arbitrio et de praedestinatione [24] exaratos quinque fere post illum Cyllenii dialogum conscriptum annis (a. 1567°) factos esse publici iuris, hoc saltem profecto conici potest atque adeo

---

[22] Tacendis hic ceteris fontibus, qui quidem Mercurium concernant ad Nili plagas residentem, commemoretur unus Valerius Max. 8,7, ext. 3.

[23] Fusius hac omni de re compluries ipse disserui: cf. adn. 18.

[24] De hoc opere eiusque auctore quaestiones instituit novissime J. Wonde: *Subjekt und Unsterblichkeit bei Pietro Pomponazzi*, Stutgardiae et Lipsiae 1994 (= *Beiträge zur Altertumskunde*, vol. 48).

postulandum videtur a Cyllenio si non in ipso dialogo at certe intra prooemium et Laurentium Vallam, cuius dialogus *De libero arbitrio* inscriptus iam pridem foras esset datus, et Martinum Lutherum[25] eiusque adversarium Erasmum et utriusque aequalem Philippum Melanchthonem aliosve commemoratos esse, qui iisdem de rebus illo priores disputavissent.

Cyllenius autem, siquidem erat ei ipsi quoque persuasum Ficinianam illam imaginem Hermeticam esse veram, Mercurium suum cum Academico Philone non sua ipsius aetate, sed antiquis exeuntibus saeculis voluit esse sermocinatum. Itaque postquam ipse iam in praefatione neminem nominavit nisi Platonem, Aristotelem Ciceronemque, qui principes singuli praeter ceteros paganos sapientiae duces floruissent, Cyllenius id est sedulo consecutus, ut soli fere veteres Christianae religionis praeceptores suo quisque nomine laudarentur; namque exceptis iterum et Aristotele et Cicerone, quorum auctoritate noster Cyllenius ut humanista identidem nititur, idem cum Philonem Platonicae sectae philosophum tum divinum etiam Mercurium nullas citare sinit litteras praeter Veteris Novique Testamenti locos necnon posteriorum trium Ecclesiasticorum scripta complura et ea quidem Augustini, Dionysii Areopagitae Damascenique Ioannis.[26]

Ex his igitur auctoribus solis a Cyllenio nominatis illud simul potest colligi, quibusnam compulsus causis Mercurii Philonisque sermonem Cyllenius finxerit esse habitum antiquitatis aetate labentis. Atque hoc denique cognito temporis *termino, post quem* colloquium illud institutum esse simuletur, facillime a quoque patet eam quoque quaestionem solutum iri, quae reprehensionis ansam iis datura sit certe, quoscumque fugerit, qualis sit omnino ea via ratioque, quam Cyllenius adhibuerit hoc in opusculo componendo.

Celavit enim idem Cyllenius neque omnino silere non potuit litteras illas, quibus ipsis ei nullas perspicuum est maiori plerumque fuisse emolumento. Nam plurima Cyllenius eorum, quae sex suis *De libera hominis voluntate, beatorum, Angelorum, ac Dei* libris commendabat, petivit a lectione continua duorum auctorum, quarum uterque medio iam aevo maximam adeptus est gloriam; ita fit, ut in Cyllenii dialogo ubique soleant inveniri posse vestigia partim Petri Lombardi *Sententiarum* quattuor librorum, partim *Summae Theologiae* ipius Aquinatis Thomae.[27] Iam vero Cyllenius ut Graecus sollerter effecit, ut ea, quae quidem e Latinis esset illis operibus uberrimis mutuatus, mutatis mutandis suis ipsius scopis adaptata praeberet. Hermes igitur Graecorum

---

[25] De utroque hoc scriptore scilicet inter nostrum huncce conventum iam locutus est J. Lindhardt: "Martin Luther and Laurentius Valla on Free Will."

[26] Locos omnes, quos ex huiusce triumviratus operibus contiguis a Cyllenio reppererat excerptos, diligenter digessit in ordinem Chr. Bräunl Bonnensis; cui quidem adulescenti totius philologiae studiosissimo (ne mihimet ipsi videar arrogavisse, quod alteri debeat tribui) gratias ago maximas, praesertim quia promisit idem ille nunc promovendus, cum aliquando plus esset otii nactus, rem a se susceptum iri planius illustrandam.

[27] Non ego nescius, si cuncta fere contulissem, quae quidem ex utriusque huius auctoris summi libris intellexi Cyllenium deprompsisse, pluribus mihi paginis opus fore quam concedi liceret aut aequum esset, illorum opera declarare Cyllenii secretos quidem penitus, sed gravissimos fontes malui quam eorundem singulas ad amussim expedire sententias.

idemque Romanorum Mercurius ceteris deis olim perinde gratissimus atque hominibus antiquis tot talesque interea vicissitudines passus adeo denique est transformatus,
ut renatarum etiam litterarum temporibus in ipsa urbe Florentia praeco vel maxime
existimaretur idoneus, qui Catholicorum imprimis genuina propagaret placita, quorum fundamenta princeps theologorum iecerat ipse Thomas Aquinas.

C. *Peroratio*

En ergo Christiana tali Mercurii illius *Iove sati* perpetrata metamorphosi specimen
quoddam videtur exhibuisse Dominicus Cyllenius Graecus ipsius rei, cui generaliter
enodandae studemus hac in sede Barensi viribus cunctis; namque in eruendo, quibusnam modis continuo per humanismi tramites Italicos evenire potuerit, ut nova qualibet specie resuscitata quaevis vetus figura prodiret in scaenam, cum meae relationis
tum omnis congressus nostri vertitur cardo. Nec vero dubium est, quin, si scrutatus
augustiora forte quaecumque nostrum in iter Italicum cadentia detexissem, quibus
Cyllenii textus absconditiores (iique ex aliis ipsius Italiae scriniis huc primum advecti)
paululo praeponderarentur, eadem equidem lumina praesertim aut etiam totius humanismi columina fuerim libens antepositurus.

Universitas Bonnensi

Navagero's Lusus *and the Pastoral Tradition*

FRED J. NICHOLS

One of the most distinctive contributions made to the literary tradition of the pastoral is that of the Venetian aristocrat and humanist Andrea Navagero. This particular accomplishment was the invention of a form which afterwards came to be called the *lusus pastoralis*, which might be translated as "pastoral diversion." The basic idea was simply to create a miniature pastoral text, to fix in time some aspect of the bucolic world in what has been more recently termed a pastoral epigram. The aim of this article will be to take a look at how he did this, to see what its consequences were for the Renaissance practice of pastoral, and to speculate about why his example had such an impact upon poets who came immediately after him.

Navagero's poetry is more remarkable for its quality than for its quantity. The collection of poems published in Venice in 1530,[1] after the poet's death the year before, entitled simply *Lusus*, contains only forty-four poems, not all of them pastorals. There are six pastoral poems of more or less conventional length, if we take, as Navagero and his age did, Virgil's *Eclogues* as a norm. These six poems range from fifty-three to one hundred four lines, and certainly have their place in the pastoral tradition being part of the background to the pastorals of John Milton, for instance.[2] But the collection also includes more than twenty short poems which have pastoral themes in terms of character or setting. Judging by the frequency with which certain of these poems or their general poetic strategy were imitated, they made a very strong impression on poets in the century or so following Navagero and it is on these short texts that I will focus my attention.

---

[1] *Andreae Naugerii Patricii Veneti Orationes Duae, Carminaque Nonnulla* (Venice: Tacuini, 1530). I have used the edition, with English translation, by Alice E. Wilson, *Andreae Navagero Lusus* (Nieuwkoop: De Graaf, 1973).

[2] Amaryllis is the absent beloved in Navagero's eclogue "Iolas," and the name appears again in Milton's "Lycidas" (line 69). It is frequently used in the Neo-Latin pastoral tradition. See my article " 'Lycidas,' 'Epitaphium Damonis,' The Empty Dream, and the Failed Song," in *Acta Conventus Neo-Latini Lovaniensis*, ed., J. IJsewijn and E. Kessler (Leuven: Leuven University Press/ Munich: Fink, 1973), 445–446.

It is clear where Navagero got the idea for creating very brief pastoral poems, as short as four or six lines. The *Greek Anthology* has epigrams which have to do with pastoral figures, in particular in Book Six, which contains dedicatory epigrams. These are short poems, varying from two to ten lines, in which a character, usually identified by name, dedicates some object or objects to a god, in return for some past or potential favor. In this sixth book of the *Greek Anthology* seven poems are concerned with offerings made by shepherds.[3]

In surveying Navagero with the Greek text in mind, one is struck by the fact that his collected poetry begins with a cluster of pastoral dedicatory poems. It should be noted that the order of the poems in the 1530 edition, an order followed by all subsequent editions, may not be one devised by Navagero himself, who died rather suddenly at the age of forty-six. His poetic works seem to have been edited by his friend and fellow poet Girolamo Pracastoro.[4] But in any case the order was devised by someone sensitive to the novelty of what Navagero had done with the tradition.

This initial cluster of seventeen short poems has its own structure. First there are eight dedicatory poems, beginning with an invocation to Ceres to bless the Crops which have just been planted. The ninth poem, which invites the wayfarer into the cool shade of a spring, is not a dedicatory poem and is one to which I will return. It is followed by another group of eight dedicatory poems. The last of them is not on a pastoral subject. It is concerned with Euphro, weary of the poverty that has been her lot as a follower of Pallas Athena, earning her living as a weaver of cloth and baskets. She offers the tools of her trade to the goddess in her shrine before abandoning her to follow a quite different goddess, Venus.

While the poem is not a pastoral it is embedded in a pastoral context, since it is followed by a poem, longish for an epigram (sixteen lines), about a handsome Arcadian shepherd boy who wastes away when he is spurned by the girl he is courting. After his death however, he is carried off by Venus to her Idalian grove, where he is rewarded with the love of one of Venus's attendant nymphs. Euphro's offering poem, although not a pastoral, does serve as a transition piece, introducing us to the next part of the collection, where love, physical desire, becomes a more central concern. The latter part of the collection contains among other things seven poems in which the poet, speaking in his own person, complains of his unrequited passion for a young lady named Ryella, as well as a few other poems in which the inconstant first-person voice expresses his desire for other women. Navagero thus

---

[3] W. R. Paton, ed., *The Greek Anthology*, 5 vols. (Cambridge: Harvard University Press/ London: Heinemann, 1958-63). Book Six is in the first volume. Paton lists seven poems in it as offerings by shepherds (297), but poems 78, 79, and 80 also have pastoral connotations. The exact extent of Navagero's use of the *Greek Anthology* has been traced by James Hutton, *The Greek Anthology in Italy to the Year 1800* (Ithaca: Cornell University Press, 1935), 189–192, as well as by Wilson, *Lusus*, 13, 84.

[4] Wilson (*Lusus*, 18) here follows William Roscoe, who suggested that Fracastoro was responsible for the order of the poems in the first edition.

takes his place in the tradition of Catullan erotic verse which Walther Ludwig has examined in his essay "Catullus Renatus."[5]

I want to look more closely at Euphro's poem because this is perhaps the place where Navagero follows the *Greek Anthology* most closely, and therefore where differences of tone and strategy are more significant. There are other texts among the sixteen dedicatory poems which have a thematic relationship to epigrams in the *Greek Anthology*. They usually concern a shepherd dedicating some part of a wild animal he has killed, but these poems never follow the Greek very closely for more than a phrase or a line.

The anonymous Greek text about Bitto is clear and straightforward:

> Κερκίδα τὴν φιλοεργὸν ᾿Αθηναίῃ θέτο Βιττὼ
> ἄνθεμα, λιμηρῆς ἄρμενον ἐργασίης,
> πάντας ἀποστύξασα γυνὴ τότε τοὺς ἐν ἐρίθοις
> μόχθους καὶ στυγερὰς φροντίδας ἱστοπόνων·
> εἶπε δ᾿ ᾿Αθηαίῃ· "Τῶν Κύπριδος ἄψομαι ἔργων,
> τὴν Πάριδος κατὰ σοῦ ψῆφον ἐνεγκαμένη·"

Bitto dedicated to Athena her industrious loomcomb, the implement of her scanty livelihood, for then she conceived a hatred for all toil among workfolk, and for the weaver's wretched cares. To Athena she said, "I will take to the works of Cypris, voting like Paris against thee."[6]

The first word of the poem is the comb, the dedicated object, not offered, as is more usual in the sixth book of the *Anthology*, because of anything Bitto has received or might receive. Here the comb is the instrument of a profession she has come to detest, and so it is being abandoned along with the goddess. The conclusion is amusing with its reference to the judgment of Paris. Bitto too is rejecting Athena for Aphrodite, following a somewhat problematic precedent. Since Bitto's concern is with earning a living, we might suppose that the way in which she will attach herself to the work of Aphrodite is by taking up prostitution, presumably more lucrative than weaving.

Navagero's version of this poem, to begin with, is longer, as are almost all Neo-Latin texts written in emulation or competition with ancient models:

> Iam telas, calathosque, omnesque perosa labores,
> Quos vitae quaestus pauperioris habet:
> Palladio radium cum templo appenderet Euphro:
> Iamque sequi Venerem constituisset: ait.
> Hactenus o mihi culta vale dea: et haec tua multi
> Instrumenta tibi plena laboris habe.

---

[5] Walther Ludwig, *Litterae neolatinae: Schriften zur neulateinischen Literatur* (Munich: Fink, 1989), 162–194.

[6] *Greek Anthology* 1:322–323.

> Iam tua perpessam dudum mala, lenis habebit:
> Adiungetque suo me Cytherea choro.
> Nec mirum, quam praetulerit phryx arbiter: a me
> Si praelata tibi nunc quoque Cypris erit.[7]

It is here the distaff, not a comb, which is being offered, and Euphro has more to do, and to dislike, than Bitto; she also makes baskets. But especially she has more to say, and this accounts for the greater length of Navagero's poem. This expansion means that certain notions can be reiterated. The idea of time enters into the Latin text; the prominence of the word *iam*, which has no equivalent in the Greek, is striking. Equally striking are the words which follow Euphro's complaint about the length of time she has suffered *mala*, evils:. "Lenis habebit:/ Adiungetque suo me Cytherea choro." She is going to become one of the nymphs attending on Venus, like the nymph who falls in love with the Arcadian shepherd in the poem that follows this one in Navagero's collection. And Venus acquires an adjective; she is now *lenis*, gentle. It is harder to see an implication of prostitution here, and the pastoral poems among which this text is located create a sense of context which also works against this idea. Navagero has softened and shaded the sharp and harsh world of the *Greek Anthology*. The concluding reference to the judgment of Paris does not have the bite and snap of the Greek original.

What is also striking is how un-Virgilian this short text is, and it is Virgil who provides the standard pastoral model for poets of Navagero's time and place. His friend Fracastoro makes Navagero the central figure of his own dialogue on poetry, which he also names after him, *Naugerius, sive de poetica*.[8] At the beginning of that dialogue Navagero before the discussion begins pulls out his portable Virgil, which he always carries with him, and begins to recite from the *Eclogues*:

> Naugerius . . . e sinu correpto pugillari Maronis, quem numquam dimittere consueverat, tanto impetu, sed et tanta harmonia legere cepit (erat enim, ut scis, mirae suavitatis in legendo) ut nobis videretur et ille quasi furens effectus, et nos nihil umquam suavius audisse. Qui, cum Bucolica fere dimidia eo furore legisset, postremo exclamans libellum a se projecit.[9]

Having read with great effect almost half of the *Eclogues*, the impassioned poet throws the book from him. Shortly after, another of the interlocutors in the dialogue, also a friend of the poet, Giambattista della Torre, explains that the spirit of Virgil himself inhabits the pleasant country setting, a classic *locus amoenus*, where the discussion is taking place: "Nunc vero arbitror, Virgilii Manes, qui loca haec incolunt vexare Naugerium."[10] It is the spirit of Virgil that has taken possession of the poet while he reads the words of his Roman predecessor.

---

[7] Wilson, *Lusus*, 32–33.

[8] Quotations from the *Naugerius* are from *Andreae Naugerii . . . Opera Omnia* (Venice: Remondini, 1754), which reprints the 1718 edition of Navagero edited by G. Antonio Volpi.

[9] *Naugerius*, 206.

[10] *Naugerius*, 2067.

This depiction of our poet by one who knew him well shows us a man literally possessed by Virgil, and yet the mind is teased by the image of the poet throwing the book away from him in the middle of the reading of it. Is there what Harold Bloom has called "an anxiety of influence"[11] at work here? Fracastoro has Navagero insert himself into the Virgilian context but not all the pastorals that Navagero wrote are Virgilian pastorals.

Navagero, as previously mentioned, did write six pastorale of standard eclogue length, which do insert themselves in varying ways into the Virgilian tradition, often using names drawn from Virgil as was already the custom in Neo-Latin pastoral. The eclogue entitled "Damon" honors Pope Julius II much as Virgil honors the emperor Augustus. By putting a stop to a military incursion which threatens the very existence of country life, Julus, as the warlike pope is called here, makes possible the preservation of country life and the renewal of pastoral song. One amusing detail is the fact that these classical shepherds who worship the pagan deities perform *sacra*, sacred rites, for Julius as though the pope were himself a pagan deity.

Another poem responding to a Virgilian text is the longest of Navagero's poems. It celebrates the birth of a son to another of Navagero's friends, the Venetian general Bartolommeo d'Alviano. This poem is at one level clearly a response to the most famous of Virgil's eclogues, the fourth or "Messianic," although it is a response structured differently from its Virgilian model. It enumerates beings such as the Muses, the Graces, and the Fates, who come to bestow gifts on the boy, and it recounts the career of a general destined to bring peace through his victories. Closer to Virgil in some ways, and full of verbal and structural echoes of the Roman poet, is Navagero's eclogue "Iolas," in which the unhappy shepherd Iolas withdraws into a cavern to lament the absence of his Amaryllis. While the poem is full of Virgilian locutions and themes—for instance, carving a text in the bark of a tree—there is a wistfulness and melancholy in Navagero's text which is not quite like anything in the *Eclogues*. Thus in his longer pastoral poems Navagero situates himself in a tradition of Neo-Latin responses to Virgil in which his predecessors are such figures as Pontano and Castiglione, both of whom are alluded to in these eclogues.[12] But even here his imitation of Virgil is far from a slavish one.

Let us look again now at the initial cluster of seventeen poems, which I have been arguing, represent a non-Virgilian approach to the pastoral, rooted in the example of the dedication poems in the *Greek Anthology*. To see them that way one must understand the term pastoral in the broad sense of concern with figures from country life and country landscapes. It is possible to distinguish, in terms of Virgilian precedent, between two kinds of rural poems, the pastoral and the Georgia, the former being concerned with shepherds and the latter concerned with farmers of various kinds,

---

[11] Harold Bloom, *The Anxiety of Influence: A Theory of Poetizer* (Near Yorks Oxford University Press, 1973).

[12] See W. Leonard Grant, *Neo-Latin Literature and the Pastoral* (Chapel Hill: University of North Carolina Press, 1965), 333. Examples of eclogues responding to the Virgilian tradition in revisionary ways are Pontano's "Lepidina" and Castiglione's "Alcon."

including vine-growers. It is interesting that in the first decades of the sixteenth century, Neo-Latin poets thoroughly conflated these two traditions. An extreme example going even beyond the agricultural are Sannazaro's *Piscatory Epilogues*, which apply the strategy of Virgilian pastoral to the lives of fisherman in the Bay of Naples. Many other examples could be given, but what lies behind this conflation seems to be a more basic opposition between the city and people who work outside the city, whether they be shepherds or farmers, hunters or even fishermen. It is not surprising, then, that those who have traced verbal echoes of Virgil in Navagero's pastoral poems have found reminiscences of phrases from the *Geodesics* as well as from the *Eclogues*.[13]

I would argue that the chief originality of the non-Virgilian approach to the pastoral practiced in these poems is the privileging of moments of time. Each of the dedicatory poems focuses on the moment of consecration, the point in time in which the poem situates itself. From this present instant there is a turn to the past or the future, to that which the offering is given in thanks for, either something which happened in the past or something which it is hoped will happen in the future. There can be no sustained discourse in these poems and the sense of isolated individual moments is reinforced by the fact that characters are not often carried over from one poem to another.

The opening poem, addressed to Ceres, illustrates how this works. The planting of the crops has just been finished and the poem is located at the subsequent moment of celebration addressed to the goddess. Indeed this text is the verbal part of that celebration, its expression in formal language. The song presents two possible futures. One is that the crops will be blighted by weather or pests; the point of the offering is to avert this. The other is that the fields will be fruitful, and the song is confident that this will be so: "Sic erit." But the focus is on the present moment of dancing and of offerings, and of a prayer to the goddess which is the poem itself.

Other poems follow this basic pattern—projecting from the present focus into the past or future—with some variations. A hunter with the pastoral name of Iolas has killed a stag and offers its horns to Pan. A vine-grower makes an offering to Bacchus so that the vineyard will flourish. An aspect of the projection into the past or the future is the reminiscence of past offerings (the hunter has often hung up the skins of the beasts he has killed as offerings to Pan) or the promise of more offerings in the future. After the successful harvest there will be more offerings to Ceres. A lover may make an offering to Venus in the hope of poessessing his beloved or he may (in this case the character Thyrsis is carried over from one poem to the next) make an offering after he has possessed his beloved. In one case the offering is not to a paean deity but to the beloved herself, in effect a bribe to get her to slip out of the house at night into the hazel trees to get the gifts her suitor has bought in the city. And there are two poems where the offerings are not addressed to a deity but are simply left in remembrance of a faithful dog slain by a wild beast. Here it is the text itself that performs the function of remembrance.

---

[13] See the notes and commentary in Wilson, *Lusus*, 84–94.

What there is no place for here is anything like sustained narrative. An eclogue of conventional length does provide scope for story telling, although a Virgilian eclogue is just as likely to imply a story as it is to tell it. But longer eclogues, and this is true of Navagero's as well as Virgil's, do express a mood or a condition which extends over an expanse of time. They do situate themselves in a specific temporal space, but the length of time that reading them or reciting them takes leaves us with the sense of a continuum. The pastoral epigram by its briefness, its focus on one moment, gives us a sharp sense of how passing the moment is. One factor in the sense of melancholy which is a particular quality of Navagero's pastorals is the way they remind us of the fleetingness of the moment. That moment passes away, but it is the test which remains.

I want finally to look at one other poem in the collection adapted from the *Greek Anthology*, the ninth in the sequence, the one at the center of the opening group of seventeen poems under discussion:

> Et gelidus fans est: et nulls salubrior unda
>   Et molli circum gramine terra viret:
> Et ramis arcent soles frondentibus alni:
>   Et levis in nullo gratior aura loco est:
> Et medio Titan nunc ardentissimus axe est:
>   Exustusque gravi sidere fervet ager.
> Siste viator iter: nimio iam torridus aestu es:
>   Iam nequeunt lassi longius ire pedes.
> Accubitu langorem, aestum aura, umbraque virenti,
>   Perspicuo poteris fonte levare sitim.[14]

The poem is the description of a cool and inviting spring addressed to a *viator*, a way-farer—the only time the word is used in Navagero's poetry. The word occurs frequently in ancient and Neo-Latin epitaphs where the wayfarer is invited to read the inscription on a tomb and so becomes a figure of the reader. If the word has that sense in this different context (the sense that it has, for instance, in the *De Tumulis* of Giovanni Pontano) then this text invites the reader into the world it creates, as I once argued many years ago.[15] I have said that this is not a dedicatory poem. It is not, but there is a sense in which it definitely is an offering. If the *viator* is the reader, in this poem the text explicitly offers itself to the reader. The cool shady spring is not a place we can stay in—we are after all *viatores*—but it is a place where we can rest in the time that it takes to read, or recite, the poem.

Here, we are far from the process of Virgilian pastoral. And the example of Navagero was one which impressed the poets who came after him. His younger contem-

---

[14] Wilson, 24–25. This poem's indebtedness to an anonymous poem in the *Greek Anthology* (9:374), 3:204, has been noted by Hutton (191) and Wilson (84). Here too Navagero expands upon his shorter model and develops a fairly straightforward description of a spring into a more resonant invitation.

[15] In my *Anthology of Neo-Latin Poetry* (New Haven: Yale University Press, 1979), 56–57.

porary and acquaintance Marcantonio Flaminio has in the third book of his *Carmina* a collection of *Lusus Pastorales*, twenty-nine pastoral epigrams, which, although most of them are not dedication poems, have been thought to have a relationship to Navagero.[16] His own individual contribution to this tradition is his fourth book, a cycle of twenty-two pastoral poems recounting the unhappy love of Hyella and Iolas. Here the narrative impulse, closely related to that of a sonnet sequence, reasserts itself, and there is a curious mixing of subgenres because the muse the poet invokes to insure him to tell this sad country love story is the Muse of Catullus.

And Navagero had echoes outside of Latin poetry. I will simply mention here the best known, the *Divers Jeux Rustiques* of the French poet Joachim Du Bellay.[17] (Note that *jeux rustiques* is a translation of *lusus pastorales*.) This collection contains adaptations of twelve of Navagero's pastorals transposed into the French countryside, and one of them, "D'un vanneur de blé aux vents," has become a standard French anthology piece. Like Navagero, Du Bellay is a poet of melancholy temperament possessed by a sense of the loss that comes with time. He clearly found Navagero a congenial model.

The Renaissance, in Latin and the vernacular, was the period of the greatest flowering and development of the pastoral since ancient times. While he is largely unknown today, Navagero, while acknowledging the Virgilian eclogue tradition at the same time he is exploring possibilities outside of it, stands as one of the most important renovators in Latin of the tradition of classical pastoral.

Graduate Center, City University of New York

---

[16] Commentators have accepted that Navagero's *Lusus* preceded those of Flaminio, who was fifteen years younger. Wilson (17) notes that Navagero's short pastorals were perhaps written early in the poet's career, which place them in the first decade of the sixteenth century at the latest.

Carol Maddison, in her biography, *Marcantonio Flaminio, Poet, Humanist and Reformer* (London s Routledge, 1965), dates the earliest of Flaminio's *Lusus* to 1521 and describes them as "modelled on Navagero's" (29).

[17] Du Bellay's use of Navagero has been documented by Henri Chamard in the notes to his edition of the *Divers Jeux Rustiques*. See Du Bellay's *Oeuvres poétiques* (Paris: Nizet, 1987), 5:13n. Navagero's influence on other French poets, such as Mellin de Saint-Gelais and Desportes, has been noted by Ernesto Lamma, "Andrea Navagero Poeta," *La Rassegna Nazionale* 160 (1908): 292.

Mito e natura nel
De hortis Hesperidum
di Giovanni Pontano

ISABELLA NUOVO

La rilettura del *De hortis Hesperidum*, il poemetto georgico dedicato dal Pontano negli ultimi anni della sua vita alla coltivazione del cedro, la pianta esotica venuta dall'Oriente ad adornare le campagne d'Italia e di Napoli in particolare, ha offerto un campo di osservazione assai interessante per esplorare le specificità di un testo che, rappresentando quasi il testamento spirituale dell'umanista napoletano, non può non racchiudere la cifra di plurimi messaggi. Anche le coordinate cronologiche entro cui si dispiegano l'avvio della stesura dell'operetta e la sua definitiva conclusione e revisione, cioè gli anni 1499–1503, si connotano emblematicamente come il periodo storico più traumatico per il Regno di Napoli, che vive in quello scorcio di secolo l'irrimediabile caduta della dinastia aragonese, l'irreversibile dominio degli Spagnoli e la lenta diaspora dell'Accademia napoletana, avviata proprio dalla morte del Pontano, che in quel tragico 1503 concludeva la sua vicenda esistenziale quasi a suggellare la fine di un'epoca storica.

Inaspettatamente dedicata al condottiero Francesco Gonzaga, vincitore della battaglia di Fornovo (1495), l'operetta, la cui esile impalcatura storica non dà pienamente ragione di quella scelta, sembrerebbe limitarsi ad offrire l'estrema estenuazione della ben più robusta ispirazione naturalistica pontaniana nella maniera del poema georgico di tradizione virgiliana. Ma proprio ricucendo la rarefatta filigrana dei drammatici avvenimenti storico-politici con i *topoi* letterari–quello del giardino delle Esperidi e il mito dell'età dell'oro–, e con il candore dei temi familiari–la villa di Antignano e il rimpianto del perduto amore coniugale–si può tentare di far riaffiorare quello spessore ideologico intenzionalmente dissimulato dall'autore in una operazione letteraria che proprio alla luce dei suoi ultimi impegni culturali non può ridursi alle pur sapienti nozioni agricole in essa sciorinate o alle mitologiche finezze che l'alimentano o al rasserenante effetto georgico che la pervade. E' pur vero che in questa suggestiva scrittura della vecchiaia Pontano, abbandonandosi a toni poetici più leggeri, sembra diffrangersi dalle ponderose strategie compositive abitualmente praticate, ma è anche vero che il concepimento del poema, la celebrazione dell'albero del cedro, attingendo nostalgicamente al ricordo di una vicina realtà geografica, paesaggistica e familiare, non ancora decantatasi nell'archivio della memoria, diventava attraverso l'esibita eternità della pianta la consapevole proiezione di un esemplare simbolo di vita ideale e il consuntivo della sua intera progettualità poetica.

Scavando pazientemente nelle pieghe del lussureggiante racconto del mito inventato dal Pontano, secondo cui il cedro deriverebbe dalla trasformazione di Adone mutato in pianta da Venere perché rimanesse eterno il ricordo del suo amore, si rintracciano non solo i molteplici fili tematici che costituiscono l'ordito sul quale l'esuberante *inventio* del Pontano tesse con straordinaria tecnica musiva la trama narrativa, ma anche le latenti resistenze che si oppongono all'ardito tentativo di rinnovare e rilegittimare i moderni strumenti di progettazione artistica. Intanto una prima spia della disposizione psicologica e della tensione ideologica che animava l'umanista napoletano durante la composizione del *De hortis* ci è offerta proprio da un comprensibile mutamento di registro tra l'euforica celebrazione di Francesco Gonzaga, signore di Mantova, eroico vincitore dei Francesi, che pervade la dedica, e i versi encomiastici distribuiti nel corso dell'opera (1. 46–52; 2. 23–33, 534–576) e la cupa atmosfera che si addensa invece successivamente, nella fase della revisione, quando l'amaro disinganno per il tradimento perpetrato dai Francesi è ormai avvertito in tutta la sua ineluttabile tragicità (1. 329–330).

Pontano aveva entusiasticamente esortato il signore di Mantova a dedicare, dopo le fatiche della guerra, un po' del suo tempo alla lettura di un'opera sulla coltivazione del cedro e a seguire l'esempio di Marte, che non disdegnò gli "hortensia dona." Sebbene in seguito agli ultimi avvenimenti storici quella dedica sarebbe potuta apparire ormai inattuale, tuttavia al Pontano premeva, come ha già ben messo in rilievo Francesco Tateo in un suo saggio, non perdere l'opportunità di stabilire una suggestiva corrispondenza con il poema virgiliano delle *Georgiche*, creando un evidente parallelo tra Ottaviano e il mecenate Francesco Gonzaga. Questi infatti "nel fallimento della monarchia aragonese figura come l'auspicato vendicatore dell'Italia virgiliana contro l'invasione dei nuovi Galli." (F. Tateo, "Le origini cittadine nella storiografia del Mezzogiorno," in *I miti della storiografia umanistica* [Roma: Bulzoni, 1990], 71).

Ma il meccanismo dell'allusione letteraria innescato da Pontano va ben oltre la più scontata cooperazione interpretativa del lettore. Il poeta si compiace delle sue variazioni, lavora sulle differenze, indicando anche in tal modo la sua disposizione verso i modelli. Indagare perciò le stratificazioni citazionali accumulate nel testo non significa soltanto accedere al laboratorio del Pontano *artifex* appropriandosi dei suoi strumenti lessicali, ma soprattutto familiarizzare con una precisa concezione della tecnica poetica musiva, che fa del suo modello un *exemplar* o una "matrice generativa," elaborando così un complesso sistema di rapporti interni e realizzando una nuova atmosfera poetica. L'analisi del rapporto tra Pontano e i suoi *auctores* latini, specie Virgilio, conferma che egli attinge da un ampio ventaglio di possibilità allusive e indifferentemente dai due livelli di imitazione. Ma per entrambi questi poli della memoria poetica, quel che più conta è che nel procedimento allusivo si genera, com'è noto, una sorta di tensione tra la parola scritta e lo sfondo culturale evocato, si crea cioè una intensa carica emozionale che investe i termini reali di tanti significati nuovi. Ovviamente quanto più profonda è la collaborazione del lettore e la sua collusione col testo, tanto più si cattura la chiave del sistema e si raggiunge attraverso l'agnizione memoriale il concepimento poetico, fertile di innesti, di trapianti, di spessore letterario. Se passiamo a considerare infatti il segreto della suggestione che Ovidio esercita su Pontano, ci accorgiamo che esso risiede essenzialmente nel tripudio della fantasia rappresentato dalle *Metamorfosi*. La mitologia ovidiana è seducentemente dinamica e in questa attività mitopoietica l'estrema mobilità dei corpi e della psiche si converte in straordinari giochi di forme. L'attrazione per l'appariscente componente figurativa opera efficacemente sull'immaginario dell'umanista, che mutua dall'opera ovidiana le scene dai contorni più corposi e più facilmente proiettabili in plastiche sequenze di immagini. Il mito centrale del *De hortis Hesperidum* è ovviamente di ovidiana memoria: Venere e Adone sono ancora insieme nel dramma consumato dalla morte precoce di lui, mutato in pianta per volontà della dea. Le frequenti spie lessicali, variamente disseminate nel poema, concorrono a definire un ritratto che si ricompone lentamente nella mente del lettore. Lo stesso Adone pontaniano è un eroe ovidiano, più che un personaggio virgiliano: Virgilio aveva presentato Adone come pastore (*Ecl.* 10. 18) in sintonia con Teocrito, ricordando che anche Adone "oves ad flumina pavit"; Pontano invece ne fa un cacciatore, secondo una tipica stilizzazione alessandrina comune alle *Metamorfosi* ovidiane.

La favola pontaniana di Adone si ispira dunque ad Ovidio, operando però un'audace contaminazione dei due distinti episodi di Adone e di Dafne. L'umanista spregiudicato attinge liberamente ora all'uno, ora all'altro, variando sapientemente, ma anche a volte ricalcando palesemente. La metamorfosi ovidiana di Adone (*Met.* 10. 708ss.) che si esauriva in un unico e compatto quadro, si è sdoppiato in Pontano in due diversi brani: il capitolo "De conversione Adonis in citrum" (1. 68–101), che descrive il pianto di Venere e il momento culminante della metamorfosi, e il capitolo "De ratione decoris hortensis" (1. 386–451), in cui si narra l'antefatto e Adone viene presentato in abbigliamento da caccia; segue poi il drammatico momento del ferimento. E' noto che nelle *Metamorfosi* Adone viene ucciso da un cinghiale durante una battuta di caccia: Venere, straziata, versa sul sangue dell'amato del nettare che, fermentando, si muta in fiore, l'anemone dalla breve vita ("anemos" = vento). Nel *De hortis* Venere cosparge il corpo di Adone di ambrosia e lo immerge nell'onda Idalia (1. 77–78), forse su reminiscenza ovidiana dell'apoteosi di Enea (*Met.* 14. 600–608). Nella riscrittura pontaniana dunque Adone, nato secondo il mito dall'albero mirra, si trasforma anch'egli in albero, il cedro, che però, al contrario dell'anemone, è destinato all'eternità.

L'impianto del racconto pontaniano, tuttavia, utilizza anche la metamorfosi ovidiana di Dafne (*Met.* 1. 549ss.). Nell'opera antica la ninfa, inseguita da Apollo, invoca la trasformazione in albero per sottrarsi alla presa del dio; assistiamo così all'agghiacciante mutamento che si compie dalla testa in giù: i piedi si radicano nel suolo e il capo si trasforma in chioma; Apollo tenta di imprimere baci almeno sul tronco, che però contorcendosi si nega; infine il dio pronuncia solennemente all'indirizzo della splendida pianta un augurio di vita perenne e di perenne rigoglio. Solo in quel momento Dafne-Alloro accoglie le parole addolorate di Apollo e scuotendo la chioma sembra quasi voler esprimere il suo estremo consenso. Nel *De hortis Hesperidum* la situazione si rovescia: la Venere pontaniana attua la trasformazione di Adone, morto, come suggello del suo eterno amore; la stessa costruzione della sequenza è invertita: è la chioma di Adone che progressivamente si irrigidisce nelle radici del cedro, e la metamorfosi si compie dalla testa in su (1. 82–83). Anche Venere bacia il legno, che però non si sottrae; anche Venere preannunzia un destino di vita eterna al cedro. E la pianta dà segni della sua nuova sensibilità lasciando cadere una pioggia di fiori.

La riscrittura del mito da parte del Pontano aderiva così perfettamente alla prassi degli *auctores* latini, con i quali ambiva identificarsi e competere. L'invenzione, in questo caso, non rientra integralmente nella sfera delle opzioni del suo fare poetico, vi rientra invece l'originalità nella ricomposizione di antiche tessere che ridisegnano un nuovo quadro. D'altra parte una delle caratteristiche del discorso mitico è proprio quello di non approdare mai ad una forma definitiva; la sua esistenza si rinnova e si arricchisce proprio attraverso l'apporto delle varianti.

Ma la sostituzione del cedro all'anemone nella creazione pontaniana obbediva anche ad una complessa riflessione teorica sul fine della poesia, quale l'umanista era andato lungamente articolando nell'*Actius*, e rispecchiava parallelamente l'esplicita simpatia dell'autore per il filone eziologico-alessandrino. La nobilitazione della campagna napoletana e il gioco dell'anti-destino, leggibili nella moderna favola del cedro, si fondevano esemplarmente proponendosi con estrema evidenza come la trascrizione poetica di un preciso progetto teorico e ideologico. La celebrazione di un tipico paesaggio naturale, nel cui panorama rientrano trionfalmente gli agrumi, rilanciava, in chiave mitica, il primato della terra campana che, nonostante le recenti ferite e i guasti devastanti provocati dalle barbare invasioni straniere, conservava quasi per volere divino la smagliante bellezza di una natura inviolabile e incorruttibile. Il gioco dell'anti-destino dal canto suo, operante in molti racconti mitici, è l'espediente per stravolgere l'ordine naturale delle cose, annullando i processi degenerativi e perseguendo una antica utopia umana: l'immortalità.. Ma per Pontano il gioco dell'anti-destino si avvaleva del cedro quale chiara metafora della sola eternità umanamente raggiungibile, quella garantita dal "sublime" della poesia. Il motivo metaforico è così suggestivo per la sensibilità pontaniana e così aderente alla sua percezione della sensualità della natura da tradursi non solo in termini di riscrittura mitica, ma anche di vera e propria scrittura. Eppure la emozionante solennità della natura, sia che venga avvertita come nei poemi astrologici nella grandiosità della sua forza cosmica, sia che venga più serenamente colta nella diretta partecipazione alla vita degli uomini, come nel poema didascalico, diventava alla fine un pretesto per la celebrazione dell'uomo e delle sue infinite potenzialità.

L'accostamento del cedro alla simbolica pianta dell'alloro non si esaurisce però nella pur coinvolgente lettura intertestuale, bensì rivela una più profonda direzione interpretativa. All'alloro, che simboleggia la poesia apollinea, si affianca il cedro, che rimanda alla nuova poesia, che Pontano andava sperimentando nel riposato ozio di Antignano. Troppo note sono le sue teorie sull'arte e le posizioni di poetica riassumibili nella nota formulazione della poesia come "admiratio" per accennarvi ancora in questa sede, ma certamente non si può negare che la turgida scrittura del *De hortis* e la meraviglia destata dai giardini di cedro si impongono come l'inequivocabile esemplificazione di quelle spinte progettuali. La bellezza come decoro, tesa ad eliminare dalla natura ogni traccia di selvatichezza, l'insistenza sugli elementi più sensuali che connotano la pianta del cedro: l'inebriante profumo, il colore smagliante, producono, attraverso la palpitante forza figurativa della descrizione, una vera sensazione di *voluptas*. E questa a sua volta si amplifica nel capitolo "De opere topiario" dedicato all'arte di adornare il giardino col solo fine di realizzare la gioia dei sensi. Qui l'arte-artificio si identifica *in toto* con la bellezza di una natura perfettamente agghindata, finendo col fare del perfetto giardino una coperta ricamata, un arazzo, e si candida anche all'eternità attraverso la stirpe del cedro, che trionfa sulla legge di natura, quella della caducità.

Per siglare lo stupore derivante da questo inserto descrittivo Pontano vi aggiungeva un fine quadro mitologico: il *topos* del canto delle Parche, che sancisce la perenne vita del cedro tessendo in senso contrario gli stami della vita di Adone e ribaltando la trama del destino. Nel canto delle Parche il motivo dell'eternità diventa sempre più insistente, fino a rappresentare il tema dominante del poema. Il quadro conclusivo delle Parche ci riporta questa volta a Catullo, al *carme* 64, e puntualmente in questa sezione si infittiscono le concordanze lessicali e tematiche con l'elegiaco latino. Anche il tenue accenno alla coperta ricamata (1. 525), rievoca l'*ekfrasis* del drappo nuziale dell'epitalamio di Teti e Peleo e un'analoga sensazione di atemporalità o di sospensione in un tempo mitico.

L'inesauribile vena creativa, rimpolpata dal gioco allusivo del mito, persegue, nel *De hortis*, un ideale di magnificenza, e questo processo di traduzione in termini poetici e favolosi di un profondo e attuale ideale umano va colto tenendo presente il sottile metodo allegorizzante proprio dell'arte umanistica. Attraverso dunque la *voluptas*, la sensazione di meraviglia e l'aspirazione all'eternità espressi dal cedro si attuava la sutura tra il poemetto georgico e la più pensosa trattatistica del Pontano. D'altra parte gli *Orti* pontaniani si inserivano tempestivamente nel panorama che dell'idea del giardino si andava sempre più affermando nella produzione letteraria umanistica. L'eternità del cedro, al di là della *fabula* classica diventa un connotato topico dell'età dell'oro. Rosario Assunto in *Il paesaggio e l'estetica* individuava nel giardino il paesaggio assoluto in cui la bipolarità arte/natura, idea/realtà si armonizzano. Un paesaggio culturale inventato dall'uomo in cui ancora una volta la bellezza è decoro, è ornato, è *ars addita naturae*. La vita armoniosa del cedro, nel testo del Pontano, il profumo raffinato del suo frutto, privo di ogni selvatichezza e supportato dalla cura amorevole e costante dell'uomo, sono quasi simbolo del recuperato connubio uomo-cosmo-natura, che si nutre sì della cifra mitica di un *topos*, quale quello dell'età aurea, ma in un'ottica tutta umanistica di conciliazione tra arte e natura e di elogio dell'industria umana.

Dissociatisi dalle *fabulae* pagane, spesso di ascendenza ovidiana, all'interno della cornice aurea del giardino, gli *Orti* pontaniani si rivelano vicini al giardino di Venere delle *Stanze* del Poliziano. Tuttavia in quest'ultimo i pomi dorati smarriscono ogni rapporto con la realtà per offrirsi come il prezioso prodotto di arte e parola, il simbolo di un mondo immaginario non contaminato dal contingente; Pontano tenta invece di ridipingere in moduli classici una realtà affettuosamente vicina e familiare, per cui il richiamo alla classicità più che in una lontananza temporale favolosa, si traduce nel *De hortis* anche nella dimensione storica del presente.

E questa storia e questo presente rivendicano i propri diritti pur nello spazio

privilegiato del giardino/Eden. Il motivo della dedica al Gonzaga rimanda indiscuti-
bilmente ad una dimensione storica, addirittura militare, che la *pax naturae* e gli ozi
degli orti avrebbero dovuto compensare. Ma la pace e gli ozi sono possibili entro la
prospettiva della guerra: la felicità edenica deve essere tutelata da una superiore virtù
militare. In Pontano non trovava spazio la polemica anticortigiana e anticittadina,
piuttosto egli fa suo il concetto virgiliano della *pax* come risultato di interventi militari tesi ad assicurare l'autodifesa del Regno. E a questa prospettiva si affiancava quella
della *pax naturae* che in Virgilio coagulava nell' *Ecloga* IV i temi più diffusi dell'età
dell'oro, fino a giungere alla celebre formulazione escatologica del mito. Pontano
invece contribuì alla sua mondanizzazione, sensibile com'era all'idea di una fusione
tra la pace edenica dell'età aurea e la lasciva atmosfera del regno di Venere. La sintesi
avveniva infatti nel *De hortis,* in cui la favola di Venere e Adone si innesta sul mito
classico dei pomi delle Esperidi e si nutre del filone georgico. Il giardino pontaniano,
tuttavia, conserva ed esalta tutti i tratti del paradiso terrestre, ma sostituisce al *topos*
della produzione spontanea, la fattiva operosità dell'uomo, che quasi gareggia con la
natura. Il giardino di cedri, nella sua fioritura e nel suo rigoglio, ricorre senza imbarazzo al serbatoio lessicale dell' *Ecloga* IV: da notare il riuso di un epiteto prezioso,
Assyrius, che in Pontano come in Virgilio allude alla universalità dell'età aurea, la
quale consente la diffusione di piante propriamente orientali, come l'amomo ovvero
il cedro, anche in altri contesti geoclimatici. Né manca il canto d'auspicio delle
Parche; persino l'elemento erotico concorre a completare il quadro di una perfetta
estasi della natura: si confronti *De hortis* 2. 239 "ament et saxa," parole pronunciate
da Amore in occasione delle nozze della madre Venere, che legittimano nello scenario dell'età dell'oro il trionfo della suprema legge dell'amore.

Ma se in Virgilio questi elementi sono rigidamente separati dalla serie antitetica
degli attrezzi agricoli (falci, rastrelli) e dalla *nautica pinus*, ovvero la navigazione,
proprie dell'età del ferro, al contrario in Pontano dal connubio di tecnica e natura
l'esito "età aurea" viene decisamente potenziato. L'elogio dell'industria poi si colloca
sul solco del primato dell'uomo-*artifex*, indiscussa conquista dell'Umanesimo. Nel *De
hortis* si dissolve la percezione conflittuale del rapporto età ferrea-aurea propria
dell'*Ecloga* IV e lo stato aureo non è più in contrasto con l'industria e il lavoro, che
anzi ne diventano indispensabili presupposti. Pontano inserisce anche lo scambio delle
merci nell'inserto sulle lodi dell'industria umana, confermando il ribaltamento che la
concezione ha subito per effetto dell'ottica umanistica. Anzi egli sviluppa un lungo
brano, dal v. 346 al v. 363 del libro I, in cui allude ad una inedita rotta di navigazione che dal mare occidentale, circumnavigando l'Africa, giunge ai lidi indiani, dove
si può gustare la singolare dolcezza del cedro. La suggestione dell'impresa condotta
proprio in quegli anni (1499) da Vasco de Gama era troppo forte per non trovare
un'eco nei versi pontaniani; e ancora nel libro II l'umanista napoletano, inorgoglito
da quei viaggi d'esplorazione, dichiara a Francesco Gonzaga: "Io reco a te i cedri dai
campi degli Etiopi e dalla costa dei Garamanti." L'Africa, esplorata da tempo, ma
ancora ricca di misterioso fascino, ben si prestava a fornire lo sfondo geografico più
opportuno perché la favola di Adone/cedro sfumasse i suoi contorni nell'evanescenza
di un mito prezioso.

Senza dubbio più assimilabili al modello virgiliano sono le frequenti e palmari corrispondenze con il poema didascalico riecheggiate dal Pontano anche nella sapiente architettura dei proemi e dei finali. In Virgilio l'accenno alle terre esotiche confluisce poi nell'ampio brano sulle lodi dell'Italia, che nasce dal confronto tra terre o civiltà diverse, in particolare l'Occidente e l'Oriente. In Pontano non casualmente il finale del poema accorpava le lodi dell'Italia con l'impresa trionfale di Francesco Gonzaga, dinanzi al quale si inchinano le varie regioni e, nella chiusa, in un tripudio di toponomastica locale, l'intera Campania viene passata in rassegna fino all'apoteosi di Antignana, allietata ora anche dalla fulgente presenza dei cedri.

L'amore del Pontano per la villa di Antignano e le cure da lui dedicate in compagnia della moglie Adriana ai suoi agrumeti rivivono in un'atmosfera fortemente intimistica in un brano del *De hortis* in cui la vivacità della diretta esperienza naturalistica si coniugava allo struggente rimpianto per la perdita della compagna alla quale pure invidiava il più fortunato destino, che le aveva risparmiato di assistere tragicamente impotente alle luttuose vicende familiari e alle drammatiche sorti del Regno di Napoli. Nel motivo topico della raccolta dei fiori in comune, Pontano ripristinava il suo legame con Adriana, ovviamente a livello memoriale ed evocativo, ed esortando la consorte a raccogliere ancora i fiori del cedro in sua compagnia, come erano soliti fare in passato, caricava quella pianta di una estrema simbologia e ne faceva non solo la trasparente metafora dell'eternatrice operazione poetica, ma anche la gelosa depositaria di quel complice raccordo tra passato e presente, cui il poeta affidava la perennità dei suoi ricordi.

Nota di riferimento bibliografico

Per il testo dell'operetta pontaniana si rimanda a Iohannis Ioviani Pontani *Carmina*, ed. B. Soldati (Firenze, 1902), 1: 229–261; sempre valida per un primo approccio con la poesia pontaniana l'"Introduzione" di Francesco Arnaldi a *Poeti latini del Quattrocento*, eds. F. Arnaldi, L. Gualdo Rosa, L. Monti Sabia (Milano–Napoli: Ricciardi, 1964), XLIX–LXVI (alle pp. 780–783 due brani del *De hortis Hesperidum*. [1. 128–145; 1.311–335] con traduzione di L. Monti Sabia). Fondamentale rimane il contributo di Francesco Tateo, "Natura e civiltà del *De hortis Hesperidum*," in *Astrologia e moralità in Giovanni Pontano* (Bari: Adriatica, 1960), 103–118, ma dello stesso autore cf.: *I miti della storiografia umanistica* (Roma: Bulzoni, 1990); "I miti partenopei nella letteratura umanistica," in *Da Malebolge alla Senna. Studi letterari in onore di G. Santangelo* (Palermo: Palumbo, 1994), 785–796; *Umanesimo etico di G. Pontano* (Lecce: Milella, 1972); "Virgilio nella cultura umanistica del Mezzogiorno d'Italia," in *Atti del Convegno virgiliano di Brindisi nel bimillenario della morte* (Perugia, 1983), 137–155. Per gli aspetti filologici e il problema della datazione del *De hortis* cf. Mauro de Nichilo, "Lo sconosciuto apografo avellinese del *De hortis Hesperidum* di G. Pontano," *Filologia e Critica* 2 (1977): 217–246. Per una bibliografia essenziale sul Pontano e le interpretazioni critiche più recenti cf. Francesco Arnaldi–Liliana Monti Sabia, "Giovanni Pontano," in *Dizionario critico della Letteratura italiana*, ed. V. Branca (Torino: UTET, 1986²), 3: 503–508; Rodger Friedman, "A Bibliographical Introduction to the Study of Neapolitan Renaissance Literature," *Lettere Italiane* 44 (1992), 106–125; Silvia Sbordone, *Saggio di bibliografia delle opere e della vita di G. Pontano*. Quaderni dell'Accademia Pontaniana no. 3 (Napoli, 1982); Liliana Monti Sabia, "La trasfigurazione di Virgilio nella poesia del Pontano," in *Atti del Convegno virgiliano*, 47–63; Giovanni Parenti, *Poeta Proteus alter. Forma e storia di tre libri di Pontano* (Firenze: Olschki, 1985); Francesco D'Episcopo, "Il Virgilio di Pontano," in *Rinascimento meridionale e altri studi in onore di Mario Santoro* (Napoli: S.E.N., 1987), 39–48; Giacomo Ferraù, *Pontano critico* (Messina: Centro di Studi Umanistici, 1983); Donatella Coppini, "*Carmina* di G. Pontano," in *Letteratura Italiana*, ed. A. Asor Rosa, *Le Opere*, vol. 1 (Torino: Einaudi, 1992), 713–741. Sulla centralità del mito nella produzione umanistica e sulla questione della "riscrittura" cf. *Il mito nel Rinascimento*. Atti del III Convegno Internazionale di Studi Umanistici, ed. L. Rotondi Secchi Tarugi (Milano: Nuovi Orizzonti, 1993); Maurizio Bettini, "Le riscritture del mito," in *Lo spazio letterario di Roma antica*, vol. 1 (Roma: Salerno Editrice, 1989), 15–35; Gian Biagio Conte-Alessandro Barchiesi, "Imitazione e arte allusiva. Modi e funzioni dell'intertestualità," in *Lo spazio letterario*, 81–114; Vincenzo Fera, "Problemi e percorsi della ricezione umanistica," in *Lo spazio letterario*, 513–543. Il *topos* dell'età dell'oro è trattato con particolare attenzione da Gustavo Costa, *La leggenda dei secoli d'oro nella letteratura italiana* (Bari: Laterza, 1972). Al ruolo svolto dal giardino/Eden nella produzione umanistica hanno dedicato pagine fondamentali Rosario Assunto, *Il paesaggio e l'estetica*, 2 vols. (Napoli: Giannini, 1973); Gianni Venturi, *Le scene dell'Eden. Teatro, arte, giardini nella letteratura italiana* (Ferrara, 1979); Id., "*Picta poësis*: ricerche sulla poesia e giardino dalle origini al Seicento," in *Storia d'Italia. Annali*, vol. 5 (Torino: Einaudi, 1982), 665ss.; Lise Bek, "*Ut ars natura–ut natura ars*. Le ville di Plinio e il concetto del giardino nel Rinascimento," *Analecta Romana Instituti Danici* 7 (1971): 109–156.

Università di Bari

L'umanesimo gesuitico nella Polonia del Cinque e Seicento tra Occidente e Oriente

JAN OKOŃ

L'oggetto di questo intervento è molto semplice, anche se un po' generico: una prima parte dedicata all'umanesimo gesuitico nella Polonia del Cinque e Seicento—aggiungendo specificatamente per il caso polacco il Seicento—e una seconda parte riguardante l'analisi comparativa delle affinità e diversità fra l'umanesimo gesuitico sviluppatosi nell'Europa occidentale e quello sviluppatosi nell'Europa orientale.

1. Per poter chiarire la prima parte, si deve premettere che in polacco il termine "gesuitico," in senso stretto, vulgato, ha sempre avuto nel corso dei secoli una valenza negativa. In Polonia infatti la letteratura antigesuitica abbonda, e tra le opere più citate c'è il pamphlet *Monita privata* (1614), libello apocrifo ispirato da un esame di teologia andato male. Ma il suo autore, Gerolamo Zahorowski, allievo dei gesuiti, revocò in seguito tali "consigli segreti," si riconciliò con l'ordine e ne ottenne il perdono. Il libello tuttavia, per lo scandalo che suscitò, divenne famoso nei paesi occidentali e per due secoli fu tradotto in francese, tedesco, italiano, inglese, e poi anche in russo (conobbe nel complesso più di 40 edizioni!).[1]

Secondo il parere di chi vi parla, anche per quanto concerne il modo di intendere il concetto di "umanesimo gesuitico" si dovrebbe risalire agli inizi, per liberare il medesimo dai significati aggiunti nei secoli successivi.

Sappiamo tutti che dapprincipio, nel Cinquecento, la parola "umanesimo" non esisteva, benché fossero attivi e operosi gli umanisti. Il primo a introdurre, nel 1808, il termine *Humanismus* fu il maestro bavarese Fr. I. Niethammer, amico di Hegel. Rifacendosi alla consuetudine rinascimentale, Niethammer usò il termine "Humanis-

---

[1] Prima edizione: Hieronim Zahorowski, *Monita privata Societatis Iesu*, Turnacii 1612 (luogo e data falsi; Cracoviae 1614?).

mus" per definire una generica formazione classica, con particolare riferimento alla poesia o, in senso più ampio, alla letteratura antica.[2]

Se dunque si risale a tali significati originali, si viene ricondotti alla formazione umanistica, a quella *eruditio* classica così caratteristica dei gesuiti da essere insegnata nelle loro scuole, secondo l'esempio dei Fratelli della Vita Comune, e il modello educativo di Johann Sturm. L'istruzione poi, cioè l'*eruditio*, ovvero la conoscenza in genere, non era fine a se stessa, bensì costituiva un mezzo volto unicamente al raggiungimento della vita etica, ovvero della *pietas christiana*, cui doveva condurre l'educazione dei giovani.

L'accettazione del mondo antico, del suo patrimonio intellettuale e culturale, era condizionata dalla sua capacità "didattica" (ossia parenetica). Questo era il modo di pensare dei gesuiti, ma la pensavano in modo simile anche i protestanti, e perfino Erasmo da Rotterdam. Tra costoro si può dire che i gesuiti fossero i più aperti, anche se si deve aggiungere che erano anche i più solerti nell'attività missionaria (conformemente al motto *Ad M.D.G.=Ad Maiorem Dei Gloriam*).

E ancora un'osservazione. Oggetto dell'intervento non è propriamente la pedagogia, sebbene esso sia stato inserito proprio in questa sezione e riguardi l'attività delle scuole gesuitiche. Scopo del presente lavoro è precisamente quello di illustrare l'attività dei gesuiti analizzando l'organizzazione dei loro teatri scolastici, formati sul modello delle scuole umanistiche e sulle idee di J. Sturm. Non sarebbe forse errato ricercare la fonte di tale concezione—quella del teatro scolastico come esercizio, ma anche come divertimento—in epoca ancora precedente, nei manuali di Erasmo da Rotterdam, come il *De pueris statim ac liberaliter instituendis*. E se concordiamo su questo, si dovrebbe citare anche la teoria e la pratica delle scuole italiane, su cui si basò Erasmo. Bisognerebbe anche menzionare famosi pedagoghi italiani, quali Gasparino Barzizza, Pier Paolo Vergerio, Maffeo Vegio e Francesco Filelfo. Tutti costoro, già nel Quattrocento, si richiamavano ai principi della pedagogia antica e, proponendosi lo sviluppo armonioso dei fanciulli, ne curavano la crescita sia fisica che mentale e morale. Si trattava di un umanesimo pratico, coltivato anche dallo stesso Erasmo che più volte, nella sua casa di Basilea, accolse i discepoli quasi fossero suoi familiari. Nel caso dei gesuiti, la differenza eclatante consisterebbe nella dimensione del fenomeno, nell' opposizione dialettica tra il programma unificato degli studi e i "fruitori," oltre misura differenziati, per non dire "di massa."

Semplificando, proveremo ad aggiungere che punto di riferimento per l'umanesimo dei gesuiti, ordine istituito nel 1540, non deve essere necessariamente l'Umanesimo italiano—e dunque con il 1527 come data limite—ma piuttosto l'anno 1528, quando Erasmo scrisse il dialogo *Ciceronianus* (Basel, Io. Froben), ulteriore colpo inferto agli umanisti italiani e al loro concetto di umanesimo, che non teneva conto della contemporaneità, non solo cristiana. Non sarebbe forse neppure erroneo parlare di un'autentica concomitanza di fatti. Loro comune denominatore sarebbe la diffusione delle idee erasmiane. Nel 1527, mentre le truppe spagnole saccheggiavano

---

[2] Cf. Vito R. Giustiniani, "Homo, Humanus and the Meanings of 'Humanism'," *Journal of the History of Ideas* 46 (1985): 167–195.

Roma, papale e umanistica, nella stessa Spagna comparve la traduzione (una delle diciassette eseguite nel Cinquecento) dell'*Enchiridion militis christiani* (traduzione italiana: 1538).

In entrambe le sue opere, e cioè nell'*Enchiridion militis christiani* e nel dialogo *Ciceronianus*, Erasmo espresse la sua idea di *humanitas* (dell'umanesimo cristiano rinascimentale) in rapporto con l'eredità dell'antico. E' superfluo ricordare che il problema, definito tramite l'opposizione *ciceronianus—christianus*, risaliva ai tempi di san Gerolamo, e che Erasmo avrebbe potuto trovarne una soluzione vicina alla propria in Lorenzo Valla, i cui *Elegantiarum libri* uscirono nel 1471. Si deve invece sottolineare la grande sensibilità, con la quale difende il patrimonio intellettuale dell'antichità e il diritto di avvalersene, soprattutto nella poesia, quando in *Enchiridion* afferma: ". . . in litteris Poetarum et Philosophorum gentilium, modo modice ac per aetatem quis eas attingat, et quasi in transcursu arripiat, non autem immoretur, et veluti ad scopulos Sirenaeos consenescat."[3]

Non era trascurabile per gli umanisti questa allusione finale: lo studio umanistico infatti dovrebbe essere soltanto un mezzo e non lo scopo. Erasmo raccomandava inoltre (come per la lettura della Bibbia) un'interpretazione allegorica della poesia di Omero e di Virgilio. Non troviamo invece nei suoi scritti l'atteggiamento estasiato, se non addirittura trionfalistico del Rinascimento verso gli autori antichi. Del resto, prese decisamente posizione: "Obscenos autem Poetas, suaserim omnino non attingere, aut certe non introspicere penitius. . . ."[4]

Era già un indizio dell'opposizione all'antichità, atteggiamento presente durante tutto il Cinquecento, come del resto in seguito. E' interessante come nel campo del teatro appunto con l'opposizione all'antichità si spieghi la messa in scena dei drammi umanistici: questi infatti sostituivano gli "originali" antichi. Un esempio precoce proveniente dalla Polonia è il *Iudicium Paridis*, dramma latino dell'umanista tedesco Jacob Locher, ispirato al mito molto noto, rappresentato al Wawel nel 1522 dagli studenti dell'Accademia di Cracovia, al cospetto del re Sigismondo I e della regina Bona Sforza. Il capo del gruppo, Stanisław di Łowicz, nella prefazione al testo scrisse: "Hoc ingenui pueri aule Hierusalem incolae ludere proponunt, quoniam illis dignum est, iocos Plautinos Menechmosque ac Davos [!], Terentianosque Eunuchos plebi relinquendo."[5]

Ancora alla metà del Cinquecento si dichiararono contrari alle immorali commedie antiche scrittori polacchi assai noti, come Mikołaj Rej (nel rifacimento ispirato allo *Zodiacus vitae* di Palingenio intitolato *Wizerunk własny żywota człowieka poczciwego—Il ritratto fedele della vita di un uomo onesto*, 1558) o come Marcin Bielski (nella moralistica *Komedyja Justyna i Konstancyjej—La commedia di Giustino e di Costanza*, 1557). Nell'ambito delle edizioni "purgate" di Terenzio note in tutta Europa, si può citare l'edizione uscita nel 1590 a Poznań dell'*Andria* ("ad usum publicarum scholarum ab

---

[3] Desiderii Erasmi Roterodami, *Opera omnia*, cura et imp. P. Vander, vol. 5 (Lugduni Batavorum, 1704), col. 8.

[4] Desiderii Erasmi Roterodami, *Opera omnia*, col. 8.

[5] Iacobus Locher, *Iudicium Paridis* (Cracoviae, apud Florianum [Unglerum], 1522), fol. Av.

omnibus obscoenitatibus expurgata"). Altrettanto noto è il *Terentius christianus* di Cornelius Schoneus (umanista olandese e luterano di Gand), autore di commedie ispirate a temi biblici, scritte però avvalendosi della fraseologia e del vocabolario di Terenzio. Ancora verso la fine del Cinquecento si affrontò su tali testi l'insegnamento del latino nel ginnasio luterano di Danzica, mentre copie dello Schoneus si trovavano nelle biblioteche gesuitiche, così come gli *Adagia* di Erasmo da Rotterdam. Le motivazioni di questa opposizione all'antichità sono da ricondursi a ragioni morali ed educative. Era l'opposizione della civiltà dei tempi nuovi verso l'antichità greco-romana. Aggiungeremo però che costituiva un esiguo contrappeso nei confronti del più diffuso consenso verso l'antichità.

Passiamo quindi rapidamente ad illustrare i fatti che sono all'origine di tale consenso. Terenzio veniva letto all'Accademia di Cracovia per lo meno dal 1480 (un suo codice d'altronde si trovava già nel 1110 nella Biblioteca del Capitolo di Cracovia, presso il Wawel). Nell'arco di cinquantacinque anni, dal 1489 al 1544, gli *Acta rectoralia* annotano 44 letture di Terenzio, condotte da 32 magistri. Si leggeva anche Plauto, ma solo sette volte negli anni 1509–1542 (è curioso che gli inventari delle biblioteche private indichino che si preferiva leggere più Plauto che Terenzio). Solo sporadicamente, dal 1490, all'Accademia di Cracovia si lesse Seneca.[6] Nel 1513 l'editore della *Troas* (Vienna, Hier. Wietor e Jo. Singrenius), il poeta neolatino Paulus Crosnensis, raccomandava anch'egli nella sua introduzione in versi: "Seuera vatis volue poemata."[7]

Appunto: *volve*, e cioè "leggi," ma non "rappresenta"! Sappiamo, a dire il vero, che perfino i gesuiti rappresentarono nel Cinquecento Plauto (*Aulularia, Captivi, Curculio* e *Menaechmi*: in Europa per lo meno 11 spettacoli, in Polonia solo 2 o 3), sporadicamente Terenzio (*Adelphi*: 3 rappresentazioni nei collegi tedeschi) e Seneca (*Thyestes*: Olomouc, 1573).[8] E che ancora negli anni 1618, 1643 e 1644 recitarono Plauto gli studenti di Cracovia (*Mostellaria* e *Aulularia*).[9] Quasi sempre nel Cinquecento i drammi antichi venivano piuttosto letti che recitati: erano oggetto di letture scolastiche o accademiche. Per principio poi li si leggeva non come drammi, ma piuttosto come testi di filosofia popolare, a scopo edificante, quasi in risposta alle aspettative di Erasmo, e quindi *ridolti*, perfino dal punto di vista editoriale, a una raccolta di sentenze. Appunto sull'onda di tale tendenza conobbero un enorme successo gli *Adagia* di Erasmo.

2. E tuttavia in Polonia siamo testimoni di un vero e proprio *shock* (se non addirittura scandalo) suscitato dalle scuole dei gesuiti, e sempre a causa del teatro. Ciò si

---

[6] Lidia Winniczuk, *Terencjusz w Polsce* (Warszawa, 1934), 1–24; Andrzej Kruczyński, "Dramat antyczny w Polsce w okresie Odrodzenia," in Julian Lewański, *Dramat i teatr średniowiecza i renesansu w Polsce* (Warszawa, 1981), 192–193.

[7] Lucius Annaeus Seneca, *Troas*, ed. P. Crosnensis (Viennae: H. Wietor, J. Singrenius, 1513), fol. a₁r.

[8] Jan Poplatek, *Studia z dziejów jezuickiego teatru szkolnego w Polsce* (Wrocław, 1957), 192–193.

[9] Karolina Targosz, "Teatr Szkół Nowodworskich w Krakowie w XVII wieku," *Pamiętnik Teatralny* (1976): 1–2 (97–98), 30–31.

verifica nonostante i lunghi decenni di preparativi spesi ad accogliere l'antichità e il teatro antico, e nonostante gli indubbi meriti della Accademia di Cracovia in questo campo.

I dati d'archivio indicano che, malgrado le continue limitazioni da parte delle autorità dell'ordine, il numero delle rappresentazioni teatrali presso i gesuiti polacchi crebbe e che esse divennero la manifestazione dell'attività delle scuole stesse.[10] Un esempio, uno tra i tanti. Nella Poznań del 1573 i giovani del collegio recitarono, nella collegiata patrizia della città, il dialogo *La nascita di Gesù e i pastori*. La calca fu tale che gli spettatori si sedettero addirittura sugli altari; tra loro, del resto, si trovavano anche appartenenti ad altre fedi religiose. La cosa (il disordine organizzativo) scandalizzò i preti diocesani, che espressero le loro rimostranze contro i gesuiti, e ottennero dal vescovo che fossero proibite le rappresentazioni all'interno della chiesa.[11] In altri casi sappiamo che gli spettatori convergevano da tutta la regione per assistere agli spettacoli dei gesuiti, percorrendo parecchi chilometri, pur di non rinunciare all'irresistibile richiamo; arrivavano i cattolici, ma anche i protestanti e gli ortodossi. Non a caso nell'anno 1705, in occasione di un soggiorno a Wilno (agli inizi della grande guerra nordica del 1700–1721), lo stesso zar Pietro I si fece invitare alle recite organizzate in occasione della fine dell'anno scolastico. I gesuiti allestirono qualcosa di eccezionale e di adeguato ("actus ad rem et mentem eius vernacula lingua instructus"); leggiamo nella cronaca del collegio: "Adfuit cum filio [ossia con il figlio maggiore, Aleksej Piotrowicz, nato nel 1690], ducibus et ministris ... intentus rei seriem audivit perstititque, quoadusque promotorum ad altiores classes nomina legi desiissent."[12]

Nella laconica annotazione, la parte più interessante consiste in quel che è stato sottaciuto: in questo caso, infatti, il silenzio indica che Pietro I (il quale nonostante l'avversione ufficiale verso i gesuiti ne tollerava però tacitamente l'attività pedagogica in Russia) dopo lo spettacolo non si congratulò né con i gesuiti né con gli allievi-attori. Non meno interessante è il fatto che, sebbene impegnato in guerra, lo zar non seppe rinunciare alla tentazione di assistere a questo spettacolo, in quanto manifestazione di vita pubblica e forma di cultura (aggiungeremo: di cultura occidentale).

Torniamo tuttavia al contrasto cui si accennava prima. L'Accademia di Cracovia, paventando di perdere il monopolio che esercitava sull'insegnamento, diede il via ai libelli antigesuitici, ad esempio l'*Equitis Poloni in Iesuitas actio prima*, del 1590 c. Il suo autore constatava, suo malgrado, che i gesuiti "hanno aperto numerosi collegi, cui accorre da ogni dove la gioventù; la maggior parte dei nobili terrieri, e i più ragguardevoli tra questi, ambisce a far studiare presso costoro i propri figli, in quanto vanno famosi per la grande scienza ... e hanno un qualche speciale metodo di inseg-

---

[10] Jan Okoń, *Dramat i teatr szkolny. Sceny jezuickie XVII wieku* (Wrocław, 1970), 70–79; Id., "Jezuicka scena religijna w Polsce XVII w.," in *Dramat i teatr religijny w Polsce*, ed. I. Sławińska, W. Kaczmarek (Lublin, 1991), 79–86.

[11] Poplatek, *Studia*, 120.

[12] *Historia Collegii Vilnensis Societatis Jesu anno 1705*, Archivum Romanum Societatis Jesu, Lith. 45, fol. 120rv.

namento." E ancora: "con grande sfarzo e pompa organizzano rappresentazioni di commedie e di tragedie; da esse si aspettano il massimo della gloria e del vantaggio, con questa unica arte attirano a sé numerosi allievi."

Nelle pagine successive l'autore si scandalizza che i gesuiti abbiano introdotto nelle loro chiese gli organi, e che con questo "sfoggio di esteriorità" attirino "le donne volubili e i giovani," mentre soltanto "gli uomini seri ed avveduti" sono rimasti fedeli alla chiesa della Vergine Maria.[13] Uno dei professori di Cracovia, paventando l'apertura di un loro collegio, ancora nel 1628 rimproverava ai gesuiti di aver mandato nella città un rettore "con parecchie casse ... di declamazioni, versi ... tragedie, intermezzi."[14] Altrove leggiamo che venivano inviati da Roma dei testi teatrali.[15]

3. Ma perchè era tanto pericoloso questo teatro per coloro che contendevano il controllo dell'attività didattica? E come era in generale tale teatro?

Qui, nell'ambito della IANLS, una risposta parziale si è avuta ventiquattro anni orsono, al I Congresso di Leuven. La relazione intitolata *Remarks about the Jesuit Schooldrama in Poland* fu presentata allora dalla prof.ssa Lidia Winniczuk,[16] allieva di Gustaw Przychocki, autore di una monografia su Plauto (1925). L'intervento presentò il complesso degli studi e delle ricerche sulla ricezione dell'antichità in Polonia, realizzate nel corso di un paio di decenni, o meglio, di un paio di generazioni, in quanto bisogna qui ricordare anche il filologo danese Adolf Stender-Petersen, le cui orme ha seguito la Winniczuk, in particolare occupandosi di un codice del Collegio di Poznań scritto fra il 1599 e il 1627. Ecco i risultati delle sue ricerche: i gesuiti non mettevano direttamente in scena i testi teatrali antichi, né le commedie di Plauto o di Terenzio, né le tragedie di Seneca, ma conoscevano questi autori così bene da inserire delle loro frasi in contesti e in rappresentazioni nuove. Si trattava di interventi non soltanto stilistici, ma addirittura intertestuali, cui, in poesia, corrisponde l'opera di Matthia Casimirus Sarbiewski (1595–1640), l'*Orazio Sarmata*, molto noto in Europa. Iniziative di questo genere, fino a poco tempo fa poco considerate perfino dai filologi, in quanto indicavano un allontanamento dalle convenzioni classiche (per definizione autentiche), oggi sono apprezzate per le loro implicazioni sociali e, al contempo, come segno del nuovo metodo di apprendimento del latino: ricopiando intere frasi e locuzioni.[17] Questo metodo si affermò per forza di inerzia, in seguito forse ai lunghi decenni di edizioni "purgate," caratterizzate unicamente dalla citazione di sentenze, o alla diffusione di compilazioni mnemotecniche contenenti *adagi*—non solo quelli di Erasmo.

---

[13] *Equitis Poloni in Iesuitas actio prima* (s.l. et a.; Cracoviae, ca. 1590). Cf. *Literatura antyjezuicka w Polsce 1578–1625. Antologia*, ed. J. Tazbir (Warszawa, 1963), 53–58.

[14] Cf. Henryk Barycz, *Historia Szkół Nowodworskich od założenia do reformy H. Kołłątaja (1588–1777)* (Kraków, 1939–1947), 90.

[15] Poplatek, *Studia*, 195.

[16] Lidia Winniczuk, "Some Observations on Jesuit Schooldrama in Poland," in *Acta Conventus Neo-Latini Lovaniensis*, ed. J. IJsewijn and E. Kessler (Leuven–München, 1973), 721–725.

[17] Jerzy Axer, "Tradycja klasyczna w polskojęzycznej poezji renesansowej a mechanizmy odbioru tej poezji," *Pamiętnik Literacki* 75 (1984): 207–216.

Ma quali furono i frutti di tale metodo? Esemplare è il caso di Giovanni Crisostomo Pasek (ca. 1636–1701), il più famoso scrittore di memorie del XVII secolo, ex
alunno del collegio di seconda, se non di terza categoria, di Rawa. Costui ormai alla
fine della sua vita, scrivendo le sue memorie, dopo quarant'anni trascorsi prima come
uomo d'armi e poi come agricoltore, era in grado di citare, quasi senza commettere
errori, una quantità innumerevole di frasi e sentenze latine, al punto che le sue
memorie furono considerate, nei manuali marxisti di storia della letteratura polacca,
come uno spaventoso esempio di cattivo gusto.

Nel campo della poesia, ivi compresa la poesia drammatica, il nuovo modo di
affrontare i testi della tradizione antica rese meno rigide le usanze stilistiche: la mede-
sima opera poteva attingere sia da Seneca, che da Terenzio, da Orazio e Ovidio, da
Omero e dalla Bibbia, e perfino da Erasmo. Non si trattava soltanto dell'*imitatio* rinascimentale: le ricerche più recenti rivelano che tutto un sistema di allusioni letterarie
è presente nei testi gesuitici. In essi si trovano riferimenti alla realtà politica, pedagogica e religiosa.

Pur attenendosi, in sostanza, allo stile dei classici, i gesuiti potevano d'altronde, a
fini espressivi, rinunciare alle convenzioni e parlare direttamente al pubblico, come
dimostrano ad esempio nei testi in prosa.[18] Ancora un altro fenomeno è la diffusione
(in luogo dello stile senechiano) dello stile epico. Appreso dall'*Eneide* di Virgilio (che
i gesuiti leggono fino alla metà del XVIII secolo), esso contribuì a creare la nuova
forma dei drammi, più marcatamente epica, in cui predomina la *fabula*: per questi
drammi, quindi, il tipo più opportuno di rappresentazione era quello in cui si cam-
biavano di continuo le scenografie e le decorazioni pittoriche, proprio per evidenziare
l'importanza della trama, considerata elemento primario dei nuovi drammi. Il pubblico infatti esigeva che gli spettacoli ricorressero a sempre maggiori attrattive. Tra le
altre manifestazioni citeremo una nuova variante del genere delle *pastorales sacrae* (*eclogae*), diffuse come dialoghi recitati in occasione del Natale e la cui specificità stilistica
risale alle *Bucoliche* di Virgilio.

4. Dunque, un atteggiamento del tutto nuovo nei confronti dell'antichità. Non la tradizionale lettura dei maestri, o addirittura il tradizionalismo che in essa si esprimeva
nei metodi didattici, immutati dal XV secolo, e negli atteggiamenti, bensì un modo
di rendere più accattivante lo studio, e una focalizzazione dei suoi scopi, della sua applicazione pratica, non solo nel teatro, ma anche nella vita. E' questo nuovo modo di
considerare la tradizione che influisce sulla forma e sul contenuto del testo poetico,
rinnovandone anche lo stile.

Si tratta di umanesimo ancora rinascimentale, o ormai di manierismo, se non di
barocco?

Tentando di rispondere, ritorniamo ancora una volta a Erasmo da Rotterdam, e
segnatamente al dialogo *Ciceronianus*. L'autentica imitazione di Cicerone, dice Erasmo, consiste nell'imitare lo spirito delle sue azioni, e non il solo stile o le parole, in

---

[18] Katarzyna Kotońska, "Uwagi o stylu polskiej tragedii jezuickiej XVI i początku XVII
wieku," in *Jezuici a kultura polska*, ed. L. Grzebień, S. Obirek (Kraków, 1993), 143–156.

qualche modo astraendo dal contesto delle opere. Occorre inoltre tener conto del fatto che Cicerone era un erudito e che era padrone della scienza del suo tempo. Un oratore contemporaneo dovrebbe, analogamente, conoscere altrettanto bene il mondo che lo circonda. Solo che la nuova realtà è completamente diversa, differente da quella dell'antichità. Tutto infatti è cambiato: la religione e le leggi, le consuetudini e il modo di vestire. Il mondo dell'antichità è scomparso totalmente, con i suoi cerimoniali e con il suo vocabolario. Il mondo nuovo, invece è quello del cristianesimo, caratterizzato da nuove regole di vita e da concezioni, ignote a Cicerone, quali il digiuno, l'espiazione dei peccati, la preghiera, la carità, la fede, la speranza e così via. Bisogna perciò parlare di questo mondo, in una lingua che Cicerone non conosceva.[19]

Questo problema rientra, ormai, nel campo della filosofia della lingua e fa riferimento alle leggi del suo sviluppo. Costituisce un postulato sempre valido per i vari periodi e le varie civiltà. I gesuiti, a quanto pare, condividevano questo atteggiamento, e lo misero in pratica. Lo comprova perfino l'esempio costituito dallo spettacolo allestito in vernacula lingua per Pietro I. Uniformandosi alla tradizione, conservarono al contempo il retaggio umanistico dell'antichità sotto forma di letture scolastiche, fisse e immutate fino alla metà del XVIII sec. Da questo punto di vista i gesuiti divennero a loro volta gradualmente dei tradizionalisti. Grazie a ciò, tuttavia, sempre nuove generazioni fecero l'esperienza dell'incontro diretto con l'antichità, esperienza sempre uguale a causa dell'uniformità dei testi.

5. Ancora qualche parola sull'opposizione "Oriente-Occidente." Nel secolo XVII, contemporaneamente alla diffusione dei collegi gesuiti, nei territori dell'antica Polonia, delle odierne Bielorussia, Ucraina, Russia, Lituania o Lettonia, gradualmente ridiventava attuale la conoscenza dell'antichità, e si andava concretizzando la sua nuova forma. Non soltanto veniva plasmandosi il modo di pensare degli allievi—appunto secondo il modello umanistico—, ma essi man mano si inserivano nel mondo della cultura mediterranea, cresciuto sulla civiltà antica. I contenuti racchiusi nel concetto di Umanesimo hanno di certo subìto dei cambiamenti; tuttavia sono rimaste le componenti immutabili della cultura antica, le sue convenzioni, espresse, innanzitutto, dalle opere letterarie. E' un fatto che esse abbiano parlato in modo diverso ai loro differenti "fruitori." Si sono imbattute poi in una barriera ancor più invalicabile. La barriera dell'ortodossia, del cristianesimo che per principio non ammetteva la cultura laica, e tanto più la cultura pagana dell'antichità. E se poi quest'ultima fece la sua comparsa in territorio ortodosso, all'epoca di Pietro I, e ancor prima in enclavi come l'Accademia Mohilana di Kiev, ciò avvenne per il tramite dei collegi gesuitici (dai quali l'Accademia di Kiev attingeva sia i programmi che i discepoli). Soltanto nel confronto con l'Est ortodosso si rivela nella giusta luce l'attività volta all'integrazione culturale dell'ordine dei Gesuiti, basata su due principi in evoluzione e tuttavia allo stesso tempo immutabili: la cristianità della Roma papale e la lingua scritta degli antichi Romani.

Kraków

---

[19] Desiderii Erasmi Roterodami, *Opera omnia*, vol. 1 (1703), coll. 992–996.

Presenze e assenze di umanisti italiani nella biblioteca di Samuel Pufendorf

FIAMMETTA PALLADINI

L'oggetto della nostra ricerca richiede una piccola precisazione metodologica. Poiché la designazione "umanista italiano" è per sua natura generica e può essere estesa *ad libitum* a comprendere tutti gli scrittori nati in Italia nel Quattrocento e nel Cinquecento, si tenga presente che si userà qui la qualifica di umanista italiano solo per quegli autori che, nati in Italia, operarono prevalentemente in Italia e si occuparono di "studia humanitatis." Escludiamo quindi dal campo della nostra considerazione la teologia, la filosofia che non sia filosofia morale, la giurisprudenza, le scienze naturali; mentre includiamo, oltre che la grammatica e la retorica, la storia e la filosofia morale e politica. Quanto al luogo della nostra ricerca, vale a dire la biblioteca di Samuel Pufendorf, poiché non è qui il caso di affrontare il discorso complessivo sulla configurazione e la natura della biblioteca privata del noto giusnaturalista tedesco,[1] ci si contenterà di dare su di essa solo alcuni pochi punti di riferimento.

Poco meno di tre anni dopo la morte del nostro autore (cioè nel settembre 1697), la vedova mise in vendita all'asta la biblioteca del defunto marito,[2] a Berlino, dove questi era morto e dove ella era restata ad abitare. Per questa vendita ella fece compilare e stampare un catalogo, in cui, come spesso avveniva, non figura il nome del defunto possessore dei libri.[3] Questo catalogo, rarissimo,[4] è l'unica testimonianza

---

[1] Questo verrà fatto da chi scrive nella Introduzione all'edizione da lei curata del catalogo d'asta, che verrà pubblicata presumibilmente nel 1996.

[2] E' quanto ci risulta dalla lettera di Catharina Elisabeth von Palthen vedova von Pufendorf a Christian Thomasius del 29.4.1697 in *Briefe Samuel Pufendorfs an Christian Thomasius (1687–1693)*, ed. E. Gigas (München–Leipzig, 1897; repr. Scriptor, 1980), 75–78.

[3] *Catalogus Bibliothecae Illustris, selectissimis varii Generis atque Idiomatis Libris refertae, cuius Auctio consueta Lege habebitur Berolini die 20. Septembr. et seqq. In Aedibus Koenigianis in Platea, cui S. Georgius nomen dedit, vulgo St. Georgen-Straße, singulis diebus ab hora secunda pomeridiana* (1697).

Per l'abitudine di non mettere il nome del proprietario dei libri nel catalogo d'asta, così come per gli altri dati statistici su cui si fondano le affermazioni che si fanno più sotto nel testo, cf. H. D. Gebauer, *Bücherauktionen in Deutschland im 17. Jahrhundert* (Bonn, 1981).

[4] Si conservano solo tre copie, una a Hannover, Niedersächsischelandesbibliothek: (6) an TA

che possediamo della biblioteca di Pufendorf, perché i libri andarono dispersi in quell'asta, né a chi parla è riuscito, malgrado gli sforzi fatti, di rintracciarne il percorso e l'attuale esistenza.[5]

Si trattava di una biblioteca che, paragonata a quelle dell'epoca, possiamo definire medio-piccola: 1663 volumi, comprendenti 1905 opere identificabili, che tuttavia, considerando la trentina di volumi collettanei di cui non si elenca il contenuto, se non genericamente (*Scripta quaedam, Ein Band allerhand Streitschriften, Disputationes variae*), si può ragionevolmente fare arrivare a circa 2000. Se non era una grande biblioteca, dunque, era però una biblioteca sceltissima, non nel senso della specializzazione—che, anzi, si tratta di una tipica biblioteca polyhistorica seicentesca, che spazia dalla teologia alla letteratura, dalla medicina alla storia, dalle relazioni di viaggio alla matematica, dal diritto alla filologia—, quanto piuttosto nel senso della qualità delle edizioni possedute. Era, inoltre, una biblioteca molto attuale (le edizioni contemporanee al loro possessore costituiscono più dei due terzi del totale) e che puntava molto sulla maneggevolezza dei libri (due terzi dei libri è costituita dai piccoli formati in 12° e in 8°). Bastino questi pochi cenni per dare un'idea dell'ambiente in cui avviene la nostra ricerca.

Ora chi, scorrendo il rarissimo catalogo, ordinato solo per formato, sperasse di trovarvi molti dei nomi dei più famosi pre-umanisti e umanisti italiani del Tre-Quattrocento, quelli, ad esempio (per citare alla rinfusa i nomi che vengono in mente per primi), di Petrarca, Bruni, Bracciolini, Vergerio, Traversari, Filelfo, Barbaro, o ancora, Guarino, Valla, Biondo, Alberti, Landino, Poliziano, Platina, Pontano, resterebbe deluso. Degli autori nominati egli incontrerebbe solo Petrarca (ma non l'umanista, bensì il poeta del *Canzoniere*: 12° 257),[6] il Platina delle *Vite dei Pontefici* (12° 23),[7] il Collenuccio e il Pontano delle *Res Neapolitanae* (8° 506)[8] e la prima edizione—seicentesca—dello *Hodoeporicon* di Traversari (4° 143).[9] Se poi, sfozandosi un poco, cercasse di trovare altri nomi di umanisti italiani del '400 che non rientrino tra quelli, ovvii, citati sopra, egli potrebbe ancora scoprire quel singolare commento a Marziale, il cui indice costituisce un vero e proprio lessico latino, che è il *Cornucopiae*

6621; una a Kopenhagen, Kongelige Bibliothek: Danske Afd. 51.235 8°; e un'altra a San Pietroburgo, Saltykov-Shchedrin State Public Library: 16.134.8.89.

[5] Ad eccezione di un libro acquistato da un privato in antiquariato ad Hannover nel 1983, sulla cui pagina di risguardo l'antico possessore annotò di aver comprato il volume nell'asta dei libri di Pufendorf. A questo *unicum* vanno aggiunti alcuni volumi collettanei, simili ad alcuni della biblioteca pufendorfiana, che erano posseduti dalla Staatsbibliothek di Berlin prima della seconda guerra mondiale.

[6] *Il Petrarca. Nuovamente ridotto alla vera lettione. Con un Discorso sopra la qualità del suo amore del sig. Pietro Cresci* (Venezia, 1592).

[7] Bartolomeo Platina, *De vitis ac gestis Summorum Pontificum* (1645).

[8] *Res Neapolitanae, id est: Historiae Pandulphi Collenutii et Johannis Joviani Pontani conscriptae* (Dordrecht, 1618).

[9] *Beati Ambrosii . . . Camaldulensis Hodoeporicon. A Nicolao Bartholini Bargensi . . . publicae luci assertum* (Firenze, [1680]).

di Niccolò Perotti (f° 136)[10] e nulla più.

Già più fortunato sarebbe se si spostasse verso la fine del secolo, in traccia di autori che si collocano tra Quattro e Cinquecento. Egli troverebbe, infatti, non solo le *Lectiones antiquae* di Celio Rodigino (f° 17)[11] e quel fortunatissimo *best-seller* che furono i *Dies geniales* di Alessandro D'Alessandro (8° 442),[12] ma addirittura gli *Opera omnia* di Bembo,[13] l'unico umanista italiano (se si prescinde dal caso, probabilmente diverso, di Olimpia Fulvia Morati, su cui torneremo più avanti) ad essere rappresentato nella biblioteca di Pufendorf dalla sua opera completa. Questa tendenza all'incremento delle presenze di umanisti italiani si rafforza quanto più ci si addentra nel Cinquecento. Appartengono a questo secolo, infatti, non solo opere classiche di filologia umanistica italiana come il *Thesaurus Ciceronianus* di Nizolio (f° 75),[14] manuali di mitologia come quello di Natale Conti (8° 80),[15] grammatiche latine come quella del gesuita romano Orazio Torsellini (12° 309.2),[16] opere di antiquaria e di storia del diritto romano come le *Antiquitates Romanae* di Paolo Manuzio (8° 332),[17] ma anche una rara satira umanistica di Gerolamo Rorario (4° 217),[18] i *Poemata* di Marco Gerolamo Vida (12° 227),[19] opere di filosofia morale e politica come *La civil conversazione* di Stefano Guazzo (8° 312),[20] il *Galateo* di Monsignor Della Casa (12° 236.2), e gli *Arcana politica* (12° 39) di Gerolamo Cardano,[21] nonchè opere di storia. In quest'ultimo campo—oltre alla massiccia presenza delle opere di Machiavelli e di Guicciardini, sulle quali non possiamo intrattenerci qui, dal momento che la loro importanza e il loro significato va ben al di là di quelli riassumibili sotto l'etichetta di "umanesimo italiano"—c'è da segnalare il *De republica Venetorum* di Gaspare Contarini (12° 51.2),[22] l'*Historia sui temporis* di Giovio (f° 89)[23] e il manuale sugli storici romani di Pietro Angelio da Barga (12° 294).[24]

Chi si fermasse, dunque, alla prima lettura del catalogo, dovrebbe concluderne che il secolo per eccellenza dell'Umanesimo italiano, il Quattrocento, ha lasciato tracce ben flebili nella biblioteca di Pufendorf, la quale riflette piuttosto l'Umanesimo del

---

[10] Nell'edizione aldina, Venezia, 1513.

[11] Basel, 1517.

[12] Frankfurt, 1591.

[13] Strasbourg, 1652.

[14] *Nizolius sive Thesaurus Ciceronianus . . . Nunc a Jacobo Cellario* (Basel, 1583).

[15] Natale Conti, *Mythologiae sive explicationis fabularum libri decem* (Frankfurt, 1596).

[16] Orazio Torsellini, *De particulis latinae orationis* (Köln, 1611).

[17] Venezia, 1559.

[18] Gerolamo Rorario, *Murium in Campegianis hortis degentium, adversus N. Bestii, Vicarii Pontificii, edictum, oratio pro seipsis* (Augsburg, [1663]).

[19] Antwerp, 1558.

[20] Venezia, 1616.

[21] Leiden, 1635. Del medesimo autore Pufendorf possedeva anche il *De propria vita liber. Ex bibliotheca G. Naudaei* (Amsterdam, 1654).

[22] Leiden, 1626.

[23] Paris, 1553–1560.

[24] Pietro Angelio da Barga, *Quo ordine Scriptorum Historiae Romanae monimenta legenda sint libellus* (Sorø, 1642).

XVI secolo (e, in quest'ambito, molto più l'Umanesimo tedesco e il tardo Umanesimo dei Paesi Bassi, che non quello italiano).

Tuttavia, chi si limitasse a percorrere i nomi che compaiono nel catalogo sbaglierebbe, giacché gli sfuggirebbe, in tal modo, quello che è, a nostro avviso, il vero lascito della filologia umanistica italiana nella biblioteca di Pufendorf. Si tratta dell'opera di traduzione ed edizione di testi per cui gli umanisti italiani furono e sono giustamente famosi e che non può risultare alla lettura di un catalogo che si limita a citare il nome dell'autore, il titolo abbreviato, il luogo e la data di stampa di ciascuna opera elencata. Sicché, quando ci troviamo, ad esempio, di fronte ad un titolo come: *Vitruvii de Architectura libri X*, Amsteld. [16]49. cum fig. (f° 97), sarà solo l'autopsia della bella edizione elzeviriana che ci farà scoprire, con qualche sorpresa, che in essa, oltre all'opera di Vitruvio e al commento cinquecentesco di Daniele Barbaro, sono contenuti pure il *De sculptura* di Pomponio Gaurico e il *De pictura* di Leon Battista Alberti, che, quindi, non è del tutto assente dalla biblioteca di Pufendorf, come a prima vista credevamo. Lo stesso avviene per Poliziano, che è presente come traduttore di Erodiano (8° 82),[25] per Traversari, traduttore di Diogene Laerzio (4° 200.1),[26] per Guarini, traduttore di Strabone (12° 297),[27] per Ermolao Barbaro, traduttore della *Retorica* di Aristotele (8° 345),[28] ma soprattutto per Valla, che non solo compare come traduttore di Erodoto in ben tre (12° 332, 8° 273, f° 102.1)[29] delle cinque edizioni dello storico greco possedute da Pufendorf, e come traduttore di Tucidide (f° 102.2),[30] ma anche come autore della famosa *De falso credita et ementita Constantini donatione*, che si nasconde, per così dire, nella raccolta *De iurisdictione, autoritate et praeeminentia imperiali ac potestate ecclesiastica*, curata dal giurista sassone Simon Schard e pubblicata a Basilea nel 1566 (f° 38), nella quale raccolta, sia detto per inciso, è compreso anche il *De monarchia* di Dante, un altro autore, a prima vista, assente nella biblioteca di Pufendorf.

Prestando quindi attenzione ai traduttori, agli editori e ai commentatori dei classici posseduti da Pufendorf troveremo molti altri nomi di umanisti italiani del Quattrocento e del Cinquecento: quello di Giorgio Merula, commentatore degli *Scriptores de re rustica* (8° 111),[31] quello di Antonio Bonfini, traduttore di Philostratus, *Sophistarum vitae* (4° 200.2),[32] quelli di Ambrogio Leone, traduttore di Actuarius, *De urinis*

---

[25] Herodianus, *Historiarum libri octo, cum notis et animadversionibus J.H. Böcleri* (Strasbourg, 1662).

[26] L'edizione, certamente parigina, inizio XVI sec., non può essere determinata con maggiore precisione.

[27] Strabo, *De situ orbis libri XVII* (Amsterdam, 1652).

[28] Aristoteles, *De arte dicendi libri tres* (Paris, 1549).

[29] Si tratta, nell'ordine, delle seguenti edizioni: Herodotus, *Historiae lib. IX et De vita Homeri libellus . . . utraque ab Henr. Stephano recognita* (Frankfurt, 1594); idem (Basel, 1559); idem (Genève, 1566).

[30] Thucydides, *De bello Peloponnesiaco libri octo . . . ex interpretatione Laurentii Vallae ab Henrico Stephano recognita* (Genève, 1564).

[31] Nell'edizione aldina, Venezia, 1514.

[32] [Strasbourg], 1516.

e di Celio Calcagnini, traduttore di Aristotele, *De coloribus,* entrambi nella silloge *De urinis,* pubblicata a Utrecht nel 1670 (8° 503); di nuovo Natale Conti, questa volta come traduttore di Athenaeus, *Dipnosophistae* (8° 424),[33] Ferdinando Balami, traduttore del *De ossibus* di Galeno (12° 427).[34] Ma c'è soprattutto un nome che non va dimenticato nella biblioteca di Pufendorf, ed è quello dei Manuzio. Nessuno che conosca l'importanza della tipografia veneziana di Aldo[35] e di suo figlio Paolo nella storia delle edizioni umanistiche e, più in generale, nella storia dell'editoria, se ne stupirà più di tanto, ma è comunque notevole che Pufendorf, che possedeva una biblioteca polihistorica da lavoro, con una netta preferenza per le edizioni più recenti e nessuna propensione per il collezionismo di edizioni antiche e rare, se fece un'eccezione, la fece per alcune edizioni di Aldo, di cui possedeva la prima edizione dell'Erodoto greco (f° 114),[36] l'edizione del 1513 del *Cornucopiae* di Perotti e l'edizione degli *Scriptores de re rustica* del 1514 a cura del Merula, delle quali abbiamo parlato sopra, e una piccola aldina di Virgilio non altrimenti identificabile (8° 460.1). Ma è soprattutto l'attività di Paolo come commentatore delle epistole di Cicerone, che è documentata nella biblioteca pufendorfiana: oltre all'edizione delle *Familiares* con note di Paolo del 1562 (8° 300), Pufendorf possedeva un'edizione del 1579 del suo commento alle *Familiares* (f° 113) e una del 1580 del suo commento alle *Epistolae ad Atticum* (8° 266). D'altronde, Pufendorf doveva avere un'alta opinione dei "ciceroniani" italiani se, oltre a questi commenti ciceroniani di Paolo Manuzio e al lessico del Nizolio già menzionato, possedeva ben due edizioni del *De officiis* con commenti di umanisti italiani: il commento dell'allievo di Pomponio Leto, Pietro Marso, nell'edizione Venezia 1492 (f° 32.2) (ed è questo, significativamente, uno dei soli tre incunaboli posseduti da Pufendorf), e i commenti di Francesco Maturanzio e di Celio Calcagnini nell'edizione parigina del 1562 (4° 90).

Ritorniamo un momento ai due umanisti italiani di cui Pufendorf possedeva gli *Opera omnia:* Pietro Bembo e Olimpia Fulvia Morati. E' sempre molto difficile indovinare perché proprio un certo autore e un certo libro siano rappresentati in una biblioteca. Vi possono anche essere motivi estrinseci, come l'accessibilità di un certa edizione per un certo compratore (ed è questo sicuramente il caso dell'edizione strasburghese del 1652 dell'opera di Bembo); resta il fatto, tuttavia, che se qualcuno si dà la pena di possedere gli *Opera omnia* di un autore nella sua biblioteca, vuol dire che attribuisce una certa importanza a quell'autore. Ora, perché proprio Bembo e la Morati? Io credo, data l'importanza che Pufendorf accordava agli "storici domestici," come diceva lui,[37] di ogni nazione, che la ragione del suo interesse per il Bembo sia da ricercare nel fatto che questi fosse anche storico di Venezia; anche se, forse, non va sottovalutata nemmeno la sua qualità di teorico della lingua italiana, che per il

---

[33] Lyon, 1556.

[34] Galenus, *De ossibus Graece et latine. Accedunt Vesalii, Sylvii, Heneri, Eustachi ad Galeni doctrinam Exercitationes. Ex bibliotheca Joannis van Horne* (Leiden, 1665).

[35] Su Aldo cf. di Carlo Dionisotti, "Aldo Manuzio umanista," *Lettere italiane* 12 (1960): 375–400, e la "Introduzione," in *Aldo Manuzio editore: dediche, prefazioni, note ai testi* (Milano, 1975).

[36] Venezia, 1502.

[37] Cf. l'introduzione alla *Einleitung zu der Historie* (1682).

Pufendorf, che possedeva tesauri, grammatiche e dizionari italiani, nonché manuali per scrivere lettere in bello stile italiano, non doveva essere indifferente.

Diverso è il caso dell'opera di Olimpia Fulvia Morati, che, pur essendo una fine poetessa neolatina e soprattutto neogreca, ed essendo nata come umanista alla scuola di suo padre, Pellegrino Fulvio Morati, nell'ambiente dell'Umanesimo ferrarese, si sviluppò poi nel senso della religiosità riformata passando alla storia piuttosto che come umanista, come protagonista della diaspora protestante italiana, come interlocutrice di altri protestanti italiani famosi, quale fu, ad esempio, Celio Secondo Curione, e, infine—a causa delle pene sofferte nelle sue peregrinazioni, della sua morte precoce, della sua *pietas* e della fedeltà alle sue convinzioni religiose—come "martire" protestante. Ora, a mio avviso, Pufendorf acquistò l'edizione curata da Curione per Perna[38] delle opere di Olimpia più come documento della storia del protestantesimo, più come epistolario erudito (nella raccolta hanno infatti un posto importante le lettere della e alla Morati) che non per i suoi poemi greci e le sue opere letterarie.

Quali sono le conclusioni che possiamo trarre da questa ispezione mirata della biblioteca di Pufendorf? Che trattandosi di una biblioteca messa insieme, nella seconda metà del Seicento, da un protestante, professionalmente attivo come filosofo morale e politico e come storico, che badava molto più all'attualità dell'informazione che non alla rarità dei suoi acquisti, più alla qualità dell'edizione che al suo aspetto esteriore, che prediligeva i formati piccoli e maneggevoli ai grossi volumi in folio, la presenza in essa degli umanisti italiani non è poi così irrilevante come potrebbe apparire a prima vista. Soprattutto se si considera che il Pufendorf era certamente molto più legato all'Umanesimo protestante tedesco-olandese che non a quello italiano, molto più interessato agli autori della ragion di stato di Cinque-seicento che non alla trattatistica dei Castiglione e dei Landino.

CNR ROMA–BERLIN

---

[38] Basel, 1580.

Le Banquier génois Franco Leardo, un poète latin de Séville dans la première moitié du XVIème siècle

JOACHIM PASCUAL BAREA

Franco Leardo est connu comme le principal armateur particulier de l'expédition du vénitien Sébastien Caboto aux îles Moluques en 1526. Mais on a oublié qu'il fut un poète latin, ami de Jean Louis Vives et des humanistes et écrivains de Séville de la première moitié du XVIème siècle, notamment de Balthazar del Río, Pierre Núñez Delgado et Pierre Mexia, qui le considéraient comme un grand poète, ce que ne confirment pas tout à fait les quatre-vingts vers des six poèmes conservés du génois. Nous le verrons.

La présence de banquiers de Gênes à Séville, déjà constatée pendant la période musulmane, bénéficia des privilèges des rois de Castille et devint plus importante encore lors des voyages sur l'Atlantique entrepris sous le règne d'Isabelle la Catholique. Il y avait même un quartier de Séville dit de Gênes, dont la plupart des habitants venaient d'Italie et notamment de Gênes. Dans ce quartier, Leardo possédait à vie en 1509 une maison très proche de la chapelle du Collège de sainte Marie de Jésus qui devint l'Université de Séville.

Il était probablement déjà l'ami de Pierre Núñez Delgado, né en 1478, qui fut le successeur de son maître Antoine de Lebrida à la chaire de latin de l'école de saint Michel en 1514. Leardo, qui devait avoir à peu près le même âge que Delgado, lui écrivit un poème, aujourd'hui perdu, à propos du rhume et de la toux qui le gênaient depuis quinze jours, l'obligeant à garder le lit. Delgado répondit à son jeune ami, qu'il considérait comme un écrivain et poète extraordinaire, par un autre poème sur un remède imaginaire contre la toux.

Les expéditions maritimes vers l'Asie par la route de l'Ouest que Christophe Colomb avait cherchée en vain étaient devenues une entreprise réalisable grâce à la découverte d'un détroit au sud du Nouveau Continent par le portugais Magellan et à la première circumnavigation du monde accomplie en 1522 par l'espagnol El Cano. Deux années plus tard, Franco Leardo s'engagea avec d'autres armateurs à financer une expédition aux iles Moluques commandée par le marin vénitien Sébastien Caboto. Mis à part l'Empereur Charles Quint qui avait signé le contrat le 4 mars 1525, Franco Leardo en fut le principal investisseur particulier avec Sylvestre de Brine et il fut aussi un des députés pour toutes les affaires concernant la flotte.

Après quelques problèmes entre le capitaine Caboto et les armateurs qui venaient de tous les pays de l'Europe, sauf la France et le Portugal, le 3 avril 1526, deux cent cinquante hommes partirent finalement vers l'Asie par le détroit de Magellan sur trois nefs et une caravelle. Cependant, lors d'une escale sur la côte de Pernambouc, ils apprirent les formidables dangers de ce détroit, mais aussi qu'ils arriveraient dans un pays très riche en d'argent s'ils remontaient le fleuve de la Plata qui pouvait peut-être offrir un accès plus facile vers l'Asie. Ils prirent donc cette route où ils entendirent des autochtones parler des richesses du Roi Blanc qui était en réalité le Roi Inca du Pérou. Pendant deux années, ils essayèrent en vain d'atteindre ce royaume et beaucoup de marins furent tués dans des combats avec les autochtones. A Séville, Leardo et les autres armateurs refusèrent en 1529 de secourir Caboto et le Roi de l'Espagne renonça au commerce avec les Moluques qu'il céda au Portugal. Au retour de Caboto à Séville, les accusations et réclamations des armateurs qui avaient perdu leur argent se succédèrent contre lui. Leardo même fut en procès avec le Vénitien et d'autres marins dès 1531 et pendant six années.

Cette catastrophe commerciale ne signifia pourtant pas pour Leardo la banqueroute ni la fin de son goût pour la poésie latine. Entre l'Épiphanie de 1532 et de 1534, il écrivit quatre poèmes qu'il récita lors des joutes littéraires organisées par Balthazar del Río, archidiacre et évêque de Scalas, dans sa chapelle de la cathédrale de Séville, et qui sont les premières Joutes connues en Espagne avec des poèmes et discours en latin.

L'évêque de Scalas, qui avait traduit en italien le récit de la victoire de Cisneros à Oran en 1509, s'était habitué à la prononciation italienne du latin lors de ses années passées à Rome. Il avait été camérier du pape Léon X à qui il avait adressé en 1513 un discours contre les turcs. Il avait été nommé gouverneur de la ville éternelle par le pape Clément VII. Il prétendait donc que les enfants espagnols apprissent à prononcer le latin à l'italienne. Leardo l'encouragea à le faire dans un poème, dans lequel il attribue à la période arabe les sons particuliers de l'espagnol et où il soutient que tout le monde devrait prononcer le latin comme en Italie, car c'est en Italie que cette langue est née.

Dans les joutes suivantes, Leardo offrit à l'évêque, comme cadeau de Noël, un poème qui, d'après lui, rendrait son nom éternel. Les deux poèmes suivants devaient être un éloge en six distiques de saint Paul et de sainte Catherine. Dans le premier, il emploie un distique de plus, mais renonce à l'éloge, car il considère impossible de le faire avec dignité et préfère de taire plutôt que d'en dire trop peu. Dans le poème à sainte Catherine, il commence l'éloge, mais, au dernier vers, l'interrompt brusquement pour dire que le nombre limité de vers du poème l'empêche d'en dire davantage.

Le premier de ces quatre poèmes avait été récité lors de la joute présidée par l'archevêque de Séville Alphonse Manrique, inquisiteur érasmiste, en 1532, alors que la direction effective de la justice inquisitoriale était déjà aux mains des ennemis de ses idées humanistes et tolérantes. Leardo connaissait donc très bien la position officielle de l'Espagne sur la religion et les persécutions récentes contre les groupes les plus proches des idées d'Erasme. Il savait donc qu'il valait mieux ne plus cultiver des amitiés qui pouvaient devenir nuisibles. Il avait entretenu jadis une correspondence en latin avec l'humaniste valencien exilé, Jean Louis Vives. N'ayant reçu aucune lettre du génois pendant longtemps, avant sa mort en 1540, Vives écrivit une lettre à son cher ami Franco Leardo. Il espérait que leur amitié persisterait, malgré des temps de silence dus à leurs obligations ou au manque de sujet sur quoi écrire. Vives mentionne aussi dans sa lettre un frère de Leardo, probablement Jean ou Jean Pierre, qui, après la mort de Franco, tint ouverte la banque des Leardo à Séville jusqu'à 1553.

Les deux derniers poèmes de Leardo que nous connaissons sont adressés aux lecteurs de deux livres de ses amis, Núñez Delgado et Pierre Mexía, ce qui montre l'excellente réputation de Léardo auprès de ces érudits. Dans le poème écrit pour l'édition des poèmes latins de Delgado en 1537, il recommande aux jeunes élèves de lire sans peur ces pièces dont les vers difficiles ont été expliqués dans des "gloses par Christophe Núñez, qu'il encourage à publier le livre avec fierté sans prêter l'oreille aux critiques envieuses."

Dans le poème écrit pour la première édition de la *Silva de varia lección*, publiée à Séville en 1540, il explique au lecteur habitué à trouver les livres importants écrits en latin que Mexía aurait pu le faire aussi, s'il l'avait voulu, puisqu'il est considéré comme un savant, mais qu'il a préféré être utile à la majorité qui ne comprend pas le latin. L'amitié de Leardo avec le cosmographe royal s'explique par leur intérêt commun pour la cartographie et la littérature et par une communauté d'idées et d'amis. Comme Leardo, Mexía avait participé aux joutes de l'évêque de Scalas dont l'amitié lui avait été particulièrement utile pour connaître des livres difficiles à trouver. Tous deux avaient aussi entretenu une correspondence en latin avec Louis Vives.

Outre ses relations avérées avec Mexía, Núñez Delgado, Christophe Núñez et Balthazar del Río, le génois devait connaître aussi d'autres humanistes et poètes latins de Séville dont la plupart étaient liés à l'École de saint Michel et qui ont tous été loués ou mentionnés par Delgado. Parmi eux, il a pu connaître les prédécesseurs de Delgado à la chaire de latin, Jean de Trespuentes et Antoine de Lebrija; les écolâtres Jérôme Pinelo, fils d'un banquier vénitien, et Christophe de los Ríos; le professeur et poète latin Antoine Carrión; les maîtres de Mal Lara et d'Arias Montano, Pierre Fernández et Jean de Quirós qui ont loué aussi Mexía dans des poèmes latins; Diego de Cortegana qui traduisit Érasme, *etc.* Ils appartiennent tous à la deuxième génération des poètes latins de Séville, qui succéda à la génération représentée par Lebrija, Santaella et le sicilien Lucius Flaminius, qui ont exercé une particulière influence sur Núñez Delgado.

Cette deuxième génération a connu la période d'apogée de l'humanisme chrétien réformateur que Santaella avait représenté à Séville. Mexia était un admirateur d'Érasme, dont la dernière lettre envoyée en Espagne, aux vêpres de Noël de 1533, est adressée à lui et à son frère. L'archevêque de Séville Alphonse Manrique et le pape Léon X, qui avait nommé Balthazar del Río évêque de Scalas en 1515, estimaient aussi Erasme. Leardo avait été leur allié, ainsi que celui de Vives. Comme Christophe Núñez et comme Pierre Benoît de Basiñana, un autre armateur génois qui avait été son associé lors de l'expédition de Caboto et qui, le 13 décembre 1546, donna à son cousin les oeuvres complètes d'Erasme, il connaissait probablement les livres du hollandais.

Le dernier fait que nous connaissons sur Leardo qui devait être alors sexagénaire est qu'il tenait ouverte sa banque à Séville en 1545, sans doute peu avant sa mort, car en 1550 la banque des Leardo apparaît pour la première fois sous le nom de Pierre Jean, probablement son frère, qui l'avait jadis mis en relations avec Vives.

Bien que le petit nombre des vers conservés de Leardo ne nous permettent pas de tirer des conclusions définitives, l'analyse de ces quarante distiques élégiaques et leur comparaison avec ceux d'autres poètes latins sévillans contemporains, comme Santaella, Carrión, Trespuentes ou son ami Núñez Delgado, permettent pourtant d'évaluer à peu près sa connaissance de la langue, de la métrique et de la rhétorique latine et d'établir la liste des auteurs qu'il connaissait et imitait le plus souvent.

Des seize combinaisons possibles de dactyles et spondées dans les quatre premiers pieds de l'hexamètre, les deux plus usitées sont les mêmes chez Leardo et Virgile; les quatre suivantes aussi, bien que dans un ordre différent. Dans les hexamètres de Leardo, la fréquence des spondées est plus grande que celle des dactyles, ce qui prouve que son style est beaucoup plus proche de celui de Virgile que de celui d'Ovide, et cela dans une mesure inhabituelle dans la poésie latine de la Renaissance. À la différence aussi d'autres poètes contemporains, il emploie très fréquemment l'élision dans ses hexamètres (52,5 fois pour 100 vers), un peu plus que Virgile dans l'Énéide (43,69 fois pour 100 vers).

Comme chez la plupart des poètes de la Renaissance, il n'y a pas dans ses poèmes de vers exceptionnels, tels que le vers spondaïque, le vers hypermètre ou le vers avec hiatus. La coupe de l'hexamètre est toujours penthémimère, à l'exception de deux vers (II, 1 et 5) avec triple A (trihémimère plus trochaïque plus hephthémimère), qui sont les deux types d'hexamètres les plus usités dans la poésie latine classique. Il observe, comme tous les poètes de la Renaissance, les restrictions relatives à l'emploi de monosyllabes à la fin du vers ou devant la coupe penthémimère de l'hexamètre ainsi qu'à la fin du premier hémistiche du pentamètre. Il sait aussi que le mot final du pentamètre doit être dissyllabe, comme dans les *Amours* d'Ovide et la seule exception dans ses vers est un tétrasyllabe (I,26; *barbaries*), qui est aussi admis et préférable de loin à un trisyllabe.

Même s'il n'était pas un poète extraordinaire, il connaissait bien les règles les plus importantes de la métrique des poètes latins anciens, notamment de Virgile dont il avait profondément assimilé le style, et il avait surtout de l'esprit pour exprimer dans ses vers tout ce qu'il voulait dire avec grâce et originalité. Outre la métrique, l'influence de Virgile se manifeste dans des expressions empruntées à l'*Énéide*, particulièrement quand il décrit la joute de l'évêque de Scalas avec des mots employés par Virgile dans les jeux en l'honneur d'Anchise (I,15: *promisso munere*). Cependant les distiques élégiaques, et les sulets de ces poèmes, entraînent un nombre plus élevé d'expressions d'Ovide *(barbara lingua, cetera turba, causa timoris, candide lector)*, ainsi que de Martial *(desine mirari)* et d'autres poètes.

Quant à l'emploi des figures, on constate fréquemment la métonymie habituelle des noms de dieux pour éviter des mots banals, particulièrement dans le deuxième poème: Mars, Lares, Cérès, Phoebus désignent la guerre, le foyer, les céréales, et l'inspiration poétique. Les oies sont appelées "oiseaux de Junon," et il y a d'autres mentions poétiques au vin Falerne, à la Muse de Piérie, etc. Il y a aussi des comparaisons et des métaphores de guerre (l'évêque de Scalas doit vaincre en capitaine les partisans de la prononciation du latin à l'espagnole) et marines (les difficultés des poètes pour dire en douze vers les louanges de saint Paul ressemblent à celles des marins qui traversaient l'Océan dans de petits navires); un pentamètre construit avec deux phrases tout à fait parallèles *(quod dedit hic munus, quod parat iste datum)*; une construction de trois membres avec allitération en t *(studio, rationibus, arte)*; deux jeux étymologiques entre *Latium* et *Latinum* empruntés à Virgile, et d'autres procédés qui révèlent une formation littéraire acceptable.

Mais il n'est pas difficile de trouver aussi dans les poèmes de Leardo des gaucheries dans la métrique, le style et la langue qui ne sont pas dignes du tout des éloges qu'il reçoit de Núñez Delgado, qui l'appelle "l'honneur sublime des poètes" *(vatum sublimis honos)*, et telles qu'on en trouve rarement dans les vers d'autres poètes latins de la Renaissance en Espagne.

Dans les deux premiers poèmes adressés à l'évêque de Scalas, il emploie trop de vocatifs (quatre fois *praesul*, qu'on trouve aussi dans le poème suivant, et une fois *pastor*), apparemment comme un procédé pour achever plus facilement le vers. A la fin du premier hémistiche d'un pentamètre (I,22), on trouve le mot *perge*, qui a la voyelle finale brève, ce qui n'est pas généralement admis. Il n'est pas admis non plus, et on ne le voit que très rarement dans les vers d'autres poètes, de faire commencer un pentamètre par un monosyllabe annulé *(qui innumeri)*.

Dans le deuxième distique du premier poème, il emploie la périphrase d'obligation "faire à quelqu'un" construite avec un infinitif, *propriis abscedere terris fecit* au lieu de *propriis terris expulit*, sous l'influence sans doute des périphrases verbales propres aux langues romanes, particulièrement de l'espagnol ou l'italien *(fare qualcuno)*. Dans ce même vers, l'expression normale pour *externas terras quaerere*, "chercher des terres étrangères," *buscar tierras extrañas*, aurait été en latin *externas terras petere*, par exemple.

La phrase du treizième vers, *pueros pueris committere tentas*, "tu essaies de faire s'affronter les enfants," se dirait en latin tout simplement *committis pueros pueris* ou *committis pueros inter se* et semble être influencé par l'italien *tentare* (essayer de). Au vers quatorze de ce poème, *dare principium*, au lieu d'*incipere*, semble construit à partir de l'italien *dare principio* (commencer).

Dans le deuxième poème, il emploie, probablement *metri causa, aues*, comme en espagnol *aves*, au lieu du mot *alites*, qu'on aurait attendu en latin.

Le troisième vers du troisième poème, *totos pisces numerare*, montre un emploi propre des langues romanes, *tutt i pesci*, de *tutos* au lieu de *omnes*, qui n'est même pas justifié par le désir de variété. Dans le quatrième distique de ce poème, la construction correcte de *longos recessus mente parant* aurait été *mentem parant longis recessibus*.

Dans le quatrième poème, le quatrième distique montre une double construction de *nec potuit* trop embrouillée: dans la première, impersonnelle, *nec potuit*—"il n'a pas été possible"—a pour sujet une proposition infinitive, "que les formidables cadeaux et les menaces la dissuadent de'"; dans la seconde, personnelle, "la fille savante" est le sujet de ce même *potuit*, qui dans ce cas signifie simplement "peut."

Dans le cinquième poème, le troisième vers comporte deux conjonctions copulatives *(et, -que)*, dont la deuxième ne sert qu'à éviter l'élision. Au dixième vers, on lit *pendere invida verba nihil* au lieu de la forme correcte du génitif *nihili*.

Et pour finir, dans le dernier poème, au lieu d'*intelligere*, Leardo écrit *capere latina verba* avec l'acception insolite de "comprendre les mots latins," comme en italien *capire le parole latine.*

Pour conclure, le banquier génois semble connaître la versification latine mieux que la langue latine même. Franco Leardo ne fut certainement pas un bon poète latin; il ne fut pas un banquier fortuné non plus. Mais sa personnalité et ses poèmes latins servent très bien à illustrer quelques aspects des rapports entre l'humanisme italien et l'humanisme espagnol, qui furent particulièrement riches à Séville.

Bibliographie

Bataillon, Marcel: *Érasme et l'Espagne,* Paris, 1937.

Carande, Ramón: *Carlos V y sus banqueros. La vida económica en Castilla (1516–1556),* 2ème ed., Madrid, 1965.

Gil, Juan: "Los armadores de Sebastián Caboto: un inglés entre italianos," *Anuario de Estudios Americanos* XLV (Séville, 1988), 3–63.

Montoto, Santiago: *Justas poéticas sevillanas del siglo XVI (1531–1542). Reimpresas por primera vez del ejemplar único, con un estudio preliminar,* Valence, 1955 (*cf.* Biblioteca Nacional de Madrid, R-6086).

Medina, José Toribio: *El veneciano Sebastián Caboto, al servicio de España, y especialmente de su proyectado viaje a las Molucas por el Estrecho de Magallanes y al reconocimiento de la costa del continente hasta la gobernación de Pedrarias Dávila,* 2 vols., Santiago de Chile, 1908.

Núñez Delgado, Pedro: *Epigrammata,* Séville, 1537 (*cf.* Thèse de Doctorat de Francisco Vera, avec étude préliminaire, édition critique, traduction, annotations et index, Universidad de Cádiz, 1990).

Pascual, Joaquín: "Aproximación a la poesía latina del Renacimiento en Sevilla," *Excerpta Philologica* I.1 (Cadix, 1991), 567–599.

Santaella, Maese Rodrigo de Carrión, Antonio: *Poesías (Sevilla, 1504). Introducción, edición crítica, traducción, notas e índices de Joaquín Pascual,* Universidad de Sevilla, Séville, 1991.

Vivis Valentini, Joannis Ludovici: *Opera Omnia,* ed. Gregorius Mayansius, Valence, 1782–1790 (rééd. Londres, 1964), vol. VII, p. 218.

Appendix Franci Leardi Genvensis Carmina

I

AD AMPLISSIMVM DOMINVM D. BALTHASAREM DEL RIO
EPISCOPVM SCALENSEM
FRANCVS LEARDVS GENVENSIS

Corrupit Latiam quondam yens barbara linguam,
    Venit ad Hispanos cum furibunda Lares.
Illam dira fames propriis abscedere terris
    Fecit et externas quaerere Marte diu.
5   Hinc reor et fama est haec regna Hispana colentes
    Quaedam subdure verba latina loqui.
Tu, praesul, Latti tactus sermonis amore,
    Hic cupis ut Latio verba latina sonent.
Et licet id curas studio, rationibus, arte,
10   Vsibus Hispanus nititur ipse suis.
Vtrinque arguitur; cedis non ipse, Latini
    Sermonis Latium certior esse caput.
At solers pueros pueris committere tentas,
    Principium votis dant pia bella tuis.
15   Ingenia exacuis promisso munere, praesul,
    Per te victores praemia grata ferunt.
Eia agite ! o iuuenes, vobis has quaerite palmas,
    Quas meliora dabunt carmina, prosa, sonus.
O tua quam prosunt populis spectacula, pastor !
20   O quam sunt sacro praeside digna dari !
Euadent docti, discent proferre latine.
    Macte animo, perge; nam cito compos eris.
Prima breui veniet grates habitura Scalensi
    Hispalis, hinc dabitis caetera turba manus.
25   Sic tibi par veniet, ducibus quae gloria venit:
    A duce gens pulsa est, praesule barbaries.

II

AD REVERENDVM AC MAGNIFICVM DOMINVM D. BALTHASAREM
DEL RIO
EPISCOPVM SCALENSEM
FRANCI LEARDI GENVENSIS EPIGRAMMA

Hoc Domini natale tibi, doctissime praesul,
    Non Iunonis aues phasiacasque dabo.
Nec mihi sunt pingues turdi nec vina Falerna,
    In varios orbes non mihi torta Ceres.

5   Haec alii peritura dabunt, ego carmina tantum,
           Quamuis Pieria non bene culta manu.
       Omnia sed dederit, praesul, vel carmine paruo
           Qui tibi dat nomen esse perenne tuum.

III

AD EVNDEM DOMINVM EPISCOPVM SCALENSEM IDEM FRANCVS
QVOD DVODECIM VERSIBVS VELIT DIVVM PAVLVM LAVDARI POSSE

       Bis sex in numeris Pauli pertexere laudes
           Qui vult Maeonides sit licet atque Maro,
       Nititur hic totos pisces numerare profundi,
           Omne pecus campi, sydera cuncta poli.
5   Deficiunt vates tanto sub pondere laudum,
           Et duros aditus copia tanta facit.
       Dum tamen hoc pelagus subeunt longosque recessus
           Mente parant, portum parua carina negat.
       Digne igitur praesul, nauem da vatibus altam
10   Quo valeant cursu commodiore vehi.
       Tunc dextro Phoebo tanti miracula diui
           Cantibus et iusto carmine ad astra ferent.
       Nanque ego de Paulo satius reor esse silendum,
           Quam sub praescripto carmine pauca loqui.

IV

IN LAVDEM DIVAE CATHARINAE
FRANCI LEARDI GENVENSIS
EPIGRAMMA

       Bis sex versiculis Catharinae includere laudes
           Est humeris, fateor, sarcina dura meis.
       Sed veniens placidus, da, Phoebe, in carmina vires,
           Te breuibus numeris multa fauente canam.
5   Haec princeps Christum teneris induta sub annis,
           Spreuit pro vero numina falsa Deo.
       Nec velli hinc potuit pergrandia dona minasque
           Nec vinci argutis docta puella viris.
       Carceris haud metuit tenebras, chalybemque rotarum,
10   Iussa libens gladio colla secanda dedit.
       Virgo manu angelica tumulata est vertice Synae,
           Atque ibi. . . . Sed numerus dicere plura vetat.

V
FRANCI LEARDI GENVENSIS
ET AD IVVENES ET AD CHRISTOPHORVM NVÑEZ CARMEN

Nunc legite, o iuuenes, venerandi insigne poetae
    Hoc opus, ingeniis pabula lauta nouis.
Mitius et vestris blandumque aspectibus offert
    Sese, nulla modo causa timoris adest.
5   Christophorus Nuñez dedit huic glossaria; duri
    Quicquid habet, calamo laeuigat ille suo.
Gratia pro inuento referenda est aequa duobus,
    Quod dedit hic munus, quod parat iste datum.
Ede, ergo, audenti lenitum fronte libellum,
10   Christophore, et pendas inuida verba nihil.
Nam genus est hominum, quod, cum nil utile possit
    Prodere, cunctorum carpere scripta iuuat.

VI
FRANCVS LEARDVS
AD LATINVM LECTOREM

Desine mirari materna hoc edere lingua,
    Petrum Messiam, candide lector, opus.
Ille quidem poterat latiis componere verbis,
    Vt qui inter doctos est numerandus eques.
5   Sed voluit librum multis prodesse, vel illis,
    Qui innumeri capiunt verba latina minus.
Hos reor atque alios nunquam legisse pigebit,
    Vtrique inuenient plurima digna legi.

Notes d'édition

I	16	*forte:* ferent
II	2	fasiacas S
III	2	Meonides S
IV	12	ibi. sed S
VI	2	Messian *ed. princeps*

Universidad de Cádiz

Pangrammatischer Manierismus in der akademischen lateinischen Dichtung Finnlands des 17. Jahrhunderts

REIJO PITKÄRANTA

Das Wort 'Manierismus' hat seine Wurzeln in der kunstgeschichtlichen Terminologie der Renaissance.[1] Etymologisch hängt es mit dem altfranzösischen Substantiv 'manière' (seit 1120), d. h. 'Art und Weise,' zusammen,[2] das seinerseits auf das lateinische *manuarius* 'zu den Händen gehörig' und *manus* 'Hand' zurückgeht.[3] Das Substantiv *maniera* erhielt im Italienischen u. a. die Bedeutung 'Anmut,' 'Eleganz,' 'individuelle künstlerische Eigenart.'[4] Giorgio Vasari (1511–1574) beschrieb den Mangel an *bella maniera* zugleich als künstlerischen Mangel.[5] Die Bezeichnung Manierismus (*manierismo*) wurde erstmals von Luigi Lanzi benutzt, der sie in seinem 1795–1796 erschienenen Buch abwertend auf die italienische Malerei nach Raffael bezog.[6] Heute versteht man unter diesem Begriff einen gewollt übertreibenden und gekünstelten Stil im Übergang zwischen Renaissance und Barock.[7] Jene

---

[1] Werner Weisbach, "Der Manierismus," in *Zeitschrift für bildende Kunst* 30 (Leipzig, 1919): 161-183; Georg Weise, *Il manierismo. Bilancio critico del problema stilistico e culturale* (Accademia toscana di scienze e lettere "La Colombaria," Studi 20. Firenze, 1971); G. Boehm, "Manierismus," in: *Historisches Wörterbuch der Philosophie*, hrsg. von Joachim Ritter und Karlfried Gründer, Band 5 (Basel, 1980), 724ff. (mit Literatur).

[2] Walther von Wartburg, *Französisches etymologisches Wörterbuch* (Basel, 1969) 6:1, 280ff.

[3] Das Adjektiv *manuarius* erscheint bei Suetonius (frg. 7) in der Verbindung *ad molas manuarias* 'Handmühle;' Gellius (2. Jh.) berichtet (16,7,3) von Laberius, einem Mimendichter des 1. Jh.s vor Chr., er habe gern neue Wörter geschaffen, z. B. *manuarius* 'mit der Hand geschickt,' 'Dieb,' s. *Thesaurus Linguae Latinae* VIII 335, 26ff.; vgl. von Wartburg, a. a. O. 282.

[4] Salvatore Battaglia, *Grande dizionario della lingua italiana*, 9 (Torino, 1975), 676ff.

[5] Giorgio Vasari, *Le vite de' piu eccellenti pittori, scultori ed architetti*, hrsg. Milanesi (Firenze, 1878–1885), 2:106; vgl. Boehm, a. a. O. 724.

[6] Luigi Lanzi, *Storia pittorica della Italia* I (Bassano, 1795–1796), 210: *Il metodo quanto è vantaggioso all'artista, che così moltiplica i suoi guadagni, altrettanto è nocivo all'arte, che per tal via urta necessariamente nel manierismo, o sia alterazione dal vero.*

[7] Weisbach, 161; *Duden Deutsches Universalwörterbuch* (Mannheim/Wien/Zürich, 1989), 986; *Brockhaus-Enzyklopädie*, Bd. 14 (Mannheim, 1991), 145.

Zeit des Manierismus wurde später als eine Phase künstlerischen Niedergangs bewertet.[8] Die Stilrichtung war durch eine Auflösung und Verzerrung der Formen, durch groteske Ornamentik, überlange Proportionen und starke Kontraste gekennzeichnet. Der Manierismus bildet also einen diametralen Gegensatz zur klassischen Stilform, die im Anschluß an antike Vorbilder Klarheit und Strenge der Gliederung, Geradlinigkeit und die Gesetzmäßigkeit der Verhältnisse betont.[9]

Der Begriff 'Manierismus' erweiterte sein Gebrauchsgebiet nach dem Zweiten Weltkrieg, als Ernst Robert Curtius ihn in die Literaturwissenschaft einführte.[10] Es handelt sich um eine gekünstelte Schreibweise mit Neigung zum Anormalen und Spielerischen: während der Klassiker die Dinge in natürlicher und dem Gegenstand angemessener Form sagt, bevorzugt der Manierist das Künstliche und Verkünstelte vor dem Natürlichen. Eine Erscheinungsform dieser Spielerei ist die Ausdrucksweise, die Curtius den 'pangrammatischen Manierismus' nennt.[11] Sie besteht darin, dass möglichst viele aufeinanderfolgende Wörter mit demselben Buchstaben beginnen. Was das Lateinische betrifft, begegnet schon bei Naevius ein Vers, der aus solch einer gehäuften Alliteration besteht (com. 113): *libera lingua loquemur ludis Liberalibus.* Donatus (Keil IV, 398, 20f.) hatte der Figur den Namen παρόμοιον gegeben, und auch Isidorus (orig. 1,36,14) gebraucht diesen Terminus. Als Beispiel dafür erwähnen beide Autoren den berühmten Vers des Ennius (ann. 109): *O Tite, tute, Tati, tibi tanta, tyranne, tulisti.* Diese Schmuckform wurde in ciceronischer Zeit verpönt, und diese Einschätzung teilt Isidorus. Er schätzt mehr den vergilianischen Stil, in dem die alliterierenden Worte nicht durch den ganzen Vers laufen, z. B. (Aen. 3, 183): *sola mihi tales casus Cassandra canebat.*[12]

Die pangrammatische Künstelei wucherte in der Spätantike und im Mittelalter. Aelius Spartianus erzählt, daß Geta, der Bruder Caracallas, Gastmähler veranstaltete, bei denen die Namen der einzelnen Gerichte alliterierten: während er an einem Tage sich mit *anser, apruna* und *anas* beköstigen liess, war die Tafel an einem anderen Tage mit *pullus, perdix, pavus, porcellus, piscis* und *perna* gedeckt.[13] Im Mittelalter wird dieses Buchstabenspiel sehr oft gebraucht. Berühmt ist das Gedicht des Mönches Hucbald von St. Amand: die Ecloga de calvis, die er an Karl den Kahlen richtete, besteht aus 146 Hexametern, in denen jedes Wort—zu Ehren des Königs—mit einem c beginnt: '*Carmina, clarisonae, calvis cantate, Camenae!*'[14] Die volkssprachlichen

---

[8] Boehm, 724.

[9] Boehm, 724; *Duden*, 986.

[10] Ernst Robert Curtius, *Europäische Literatur und lateinisches Mittelalter* (Bern, 1948; 10. Auflage, Bern/München, 1984), 277ff.

[11] Curtius (1984), 287.

[12] Vgl. Eduard Wölfflin, *Ausgewählte Schriften* (Leipzig, 1903), 239; J. B. Hofmann–Anton Szantyr, *Lateinische Syntax und Stilistik* (Handbuch der Altertumswissenschaft II.2.2., München, 1965), 700ff.

[13] Spartianus, Geta 5,7: *habebat etiam istam consuetudinem, ut convivia et maxime prandia per singulas litteras iuberet scientibus servis, velut in quo erat anser, apruna, anas, item pullus, perdix, pavus, porcellus, piscis, perna et quae in eam litteram genera edulium caderent, et item phasianus, farrata, ficus et talia.*

[14] Text: J.-P. Migne, *Patrologia Latina* 132 (Parisiis, 1880), 1042–1046; vgl. Max Manitius, *Geschichte der lateinischen Literatur des Mittelalters* I (Handbuch der Klassischen Altertumswissenschaft IX:2, München, 1911), 588ff.

Dichter des 16. Jahrhunderts bieten Beispiele für diese Spielerei. So richtet etwa Pierre Ronsard (gest. 1585) an die himmlische Maria, die Mutter Jesu, eine poetische Litanei mit den Worten: "*Marie, mère merveilleuse / Marguerite mundifiée / Mère miséricordieuse,*" usw.[15]

Diese Art des Manierismus zeigt sich auch etwa in der akademischen lateinischen Dichtung Finnlands des 17. Jahrhunderts. Es sei erwähnt, dass Finnland zu jener Zeit ein Grossfürstentum Schwedens war. Gustav II. Adolf hatte Schweden zur führenden Macht in Nordeuropa und zur europäischen Grossmacht erhoben.[16] Diese politische Situation führte u. a. zur Gründung der ersten Universität Finnlands in Turku im Jahre 1640,[17] und im Kreis dieser Akademie wurde in der Folgezeit eine beträchtliche Menge von verschiedenartiger gelehrter Literatur herausgegeben.[18] Neben den lateinischen Dissertationen, die die Studenten zur Erlangung der Magistergrades zu verfassen hatten,[19] bestand das akademische Schrifttum aus *orationes*, wie man die öffentlichen Reden nannte, sowie aus Dedikations- und Gratulationsgedichten verschiedener Art.[20]

Im Jahre 1653 veröffentlichte ein schwedischer Stipendiat namens Jacob Eurenius an der Universität Turku eine metrische Rede über das Paradies.[21] Das Gedicht besteht aus 386 Hexametern, in denen jedes Wort mit p anfängt. Auf dem Titelblatt der Arbeit steht: *Pneumate pacifero, Praecelso praeside, puro / Proclamat patriam Paradisum primiparentum / poenas peccati, patientis promeritumque.* Der Autor will also unter der Leitung des dreieinigen Gottes das Paradies als Heimat der ersten Menschen, die Strafe für den Sündenfall und das Verdienst des Heilands behandeln. Dasselbe Thema wird in einem anderen pangrammatischen Gedicht berührt: es handelt sich um eine metrische Rede namens *De Salvatoris Jesu Christi benefactis*, die im Jahre 1656 in Turku herausgegeben wurde. Der Autor war Petrus Gyllenius, ein schwedischer Student, der mit Hilfe eines königlichen Stipendiums an der Universität Turku stu-

---

[15] Jean-Claude Margolin, "Alliteration," in: *Historisches Wörterbuch der Rhetorik*, hrsg. von Gert Ueding, Band 1 (Tübingen, 1992), 410f.

[16] Vgl. etwa Sten Lindroth, *Svensk lärdomshistoria. Stormaktstiden* (Södertälje, 1975), passim.

[17] Ivar A. Heikel, *Helsingin yliopisto 1640-1940* (Helsinki, 1940), 6ff.; Matti Klinge (et al.), *Kuninkaallinen Turun akatemia 1640-1808* (Helsinki, 1987), 60ff.

[18] Die akademische Literatur der Universität Turku wurde schon 1719 in einer Bibliographie behandelt: A. A. Stiernman, *Aboa Literata* (Holmiae, 1790; repr. Helsinki, 1990); vgl. Reijo Pitkäranta, *Neulateinische Wörter und Neologismen in den Dissertationen Finnlands des 17. Jahrhunderts* (Helsinki, 1992), 14f.

[19] Vgl. Jorma Vallinkoski, *Turun akatemian väitöskirjat 1642–1828. Die Dissertationen der alten Universität Turku (Academia Aboensis) 1642–1828*, I–II (Helsinki, 1962–1966; 1967–1969).

[20] Ivar A. Heikel, *Filologins studium vid Åbo universitet* (Helsingfors, 1894), 151ff.; Klinge, 95ff.; 442ff.; vgl. Toini Melander, *Personskrifter hänförande sig till Finland 1562–1713. Bibliografisk förteckning 1–5* (Helsinki, 1951–1959); Iiro Kajanto, *Humanism in a Christian Society II. Classical Moral Philosophy and Oratory in Finland 1640–1713* (Helsinki, 1990).

[21] Jacobus Eurenius, *Oratio metrica de peramoeno Paradiso, primorum patria, prolapsisque primaevis poenave peccati propitiique paciferi promerito* (Aboae 1653); vgl. Stiernman, 50; Heikel (1894), 160; Klinge, 451. Zu Eurenius s. Vilhelm Lagus, *Album studiosorum Academiae Aboensis MDCXL–MDCCCXXVII*, I (Helsingfors, 1891), 48; Vallinkoski II, 132.

dierte.[22] Sein Kunstwerk umfasst ganze 724 Hexameter, deren alle Wörter mit s anlauten. Es ist ein Gesang zum Lobe des Heilands in Anerkennung seiner Verdienste um die ganze Menschheit, besonders aber um das schwedische Volk. Die Rede beginnt mit den Begrüssungsworten, gerichtet an Eskil Petraeus, den Bischof von Turku: (v. 1) *Salve Scripturae Sacrae supreme sacerdos.* Die beiden Reden schliessen sich zuerst an den Schöpfungsbericht und die darauf folgenden Ereignisse der Genesis an. Die Darstellungsweise der beiden Manieristen wird natürlich davon bestimmt, ob der Anfangsbuchstabe p oder s ist. So wird etwa die Erschaffung der Welt von Eurenius folgendermassen ausgedrückt (v. 26ff): *Principio patris primordia plana potentis / purpureusque polus permagnae planitiesque / praepropere primo productae pulvere pleno / Primitias penitus permistas principe palma / permutat plane; pol! perdurabile pondus/ pergraphicumque parat, praestingens plurima pulchra.* Die entsprechende Stelle lautet bei Gyllenius (v. 40ff.): *Scrutator sensus, Salvator singula sanans/ Sidera suspendit summis splendentia stellis / Suspendit Solem, sublimia sidera, stellas / Sphaerae supposuit sublimi singula signa /Saturnoque seni Solem, stellasque serenas/ Suspenditque salo sermone solum spatiosum,* usw. Im Anschluss an die Bibelstelle (Genesis 12) "Da brachte die Erde alle Arten von Pflanzen hervor," erwähnt Eurenius gut siebzig mit p anlautende Pflanzennamen, von denen die meisten bei Plinius vorkommen. Es gibt aber auch Unterschiede: während Plinius (nat. 19,124) für den Sumpfeppich die griechische Bezeichnung *heleoselinum* (gr. ἐλειοσέλινον) gebraucht, verwendet Eurenius dafür die neulateinische Zusammensetzung *paludiapium,* natürlich zur Erzielung der Alliteration.[23]

Der erste Mensch heisst bei Eurenius zuerst (v. 107) *perdomitor,* d. h. Bezähmer der Natur, dann (v. 115) *physiognomus* 'der Naturkenner,' da Adam gemäss der Bibel (Gen. 2,20) allen lebendigen Wesen ihre Namen gab. Dieses Substantiv fehlt sowohl in griechischen wie auch in lateinischen Wörterbüchern. Andere Bezeichnungen für Adam sind etwa (v. 120) *princeps* und (v. 121) *procus.* Für Gyllenius ist er etwa (v. 164) *socius* und (v. 165) *sponsus.* Auch der Name Evas wird auf verschiedene Weise umschrieben. Vor dem Sündenfall heisst sie bei Eurenius z. B. (v. 121) *pulchra puella* und (v. 177) *parens praelepida.* Gyllenius verwendet seinerseits die Umschreibungen (v. 166) *splendidula sponsa* und (v. 167) *sponsa sodalis.* Nach dem Sündenfall wird Eva unter anderem als (v. 213) *prolapsa puella,* (v. 193) *sponsa scelesta,* (v. 197) *squalida sponsa* oder einfach als (v. 199) *stolida* und (v. 201) *stupida* bezeichnet. Dann wird die Sintflut beschrieben (v. 242ff.).

Gemäss der Rede des Gyllenius stammt das schwedische Volk von Sem, dem ältesten Sohn Noahs ab.[24] Dies hängt damit zusammen, dass die Arche nach der Flut auf den Felsen des Skythenlands landete (v. 435): *Scytthica saxa scapham servaverunt scopulique.* Weil die Einwohner Schwedens ihrer Herkunft nach Skythen und dadurch Nachkommen Sems seien, sei ihre Heimat Schweden älter als die anderen Länder (v.

---

[22] Petrus M. Gyllenius, *Oratio metrica de salvatoris Jesu Christi benefactis* (Aboae, 1656); vgl. Stiernman, 48; Heikel (1894), 160. Zu Gyllenius s. Lagus I, 40; Vallinkoski II, 149.

[23] Vgl. *paludapium* seit 1632; s. R. E. Latham, *Revised Medieval Latin Word-List* (London, 1965), 329.

[24] Vgl. M. G. Schybergson, *Historiens studium vid Åbo Universitet* (Helsingfors, 1891), 2ff.; Lindroth, 235ff., 249ff.

455ff.): *Suecia Sardinia senior spatiosa salubris / Suecia Sicania senior stabilita sagittis / Suecia Samaria senior selecta sacellis.* In Schweden gebe es 73 Städte. Die Anzahl wird folgendermassen ausgedrückt (v. 493): *sexaginta sex, septem superaddita sunto.* Die Hauptstadt ist das immerschöne Stockholm, der Wohnsitz der Könige (v. 496): *sceptrigerum sedes Stockholmia splendida semper.*

Ein weiterer Pangrammatist war Daniel Sarcovius, ein finnischer Student, der gegen Ende des 17. Jahrhunderts an der Universität seiner Heimat Turku studierte und später als Professor für Logik und Physik an der Universität Dorpat tätig war.[25] Einer von seinen Lehrern in Turku war Martin Miltopaeus, Professor für römische Literatur. Als dieser im Jahre 1679 starb, verfasste Daniel Sarcovius zum Andenken an den Verstorbenen ein pangrammatisches Gedächtnisgedicht, das aus 155 Hexametern besteht.[26] Zur Ehre und Erinnerung an den Namen des Miltopaeus hat Sarcovius in seinen Versen nur solche Wörter gebraucht, die mit m beginnen. Der Titel der Schrift lautet: *Mnemosynon magno mecaenati miserorum / Martino Miltopaeo, magnoque magistro.* Als Beispiel für die Verskunst des Sarcovius sei die Beschreibung der Todesstunde von Miltopaeus vorgebracht (v.138f.): *Mox mutus, malas mordet, modiceque movendo / membra, malum mittit mundum, moriturque modeste.* Darauf folgt die Laudatio (v. 140f.): *mas meritis magnus, medicus, Maro, melliloquusque / mystaque multiscius maiorque meo monimento.*

In den vorliegenden Texten gibt es eine Anzahl von Neologismen, d. h. solche neulateinische Wörter, die in den existierenden lateinischen Lexika fehlen. Ich erwähne hier nun einige. Die Zusammensetzungen mit dem griechischen Vorderglied *pan-* oder *panto-* erinnern uns an die graecolateinische Terminologiewelle, die am Ende des 16. Jahrhunderts in dem neulateinischen Schrifttum in Mode kam. Hierher gehört etwa das Adjektiv (Eurenius v. 22) *pangentius* 'alle Völker betreffend:'[27] es erscheint als Epitheton Gottes im Vokativ *perpie pangentique Pater.* Ein Neologismus ist ferner das Substantiv *pansophia* 'das Alles-Wissen:' von der Sünde Adams und Evas wird gesagt (Eurenius v. 187): *parvi pendentes praescriptum pansophiamve.* Der Terminus ist in der Barockzeit geprägt und scheint zuerst in einem Sammelheft von Rosenkreuzerschriften im Jahre 1616 aufzutauchen.[28] Als Fachausdruck war die Pansophie der Name einer religiös-philosophischen Bewegung, die eine Zusammenfassung aller Wissenschaften zu einer Universalwissenschaft anstrebte.[29]—Ein weiteres Kompositum dieser Art ist (v. 220) *panurgus* in der Verbindung *proles . . . Panurgi* 'Gottes Sohn', d. h. Jesus. Es handelt sich um ein griechisches Adjektiv πανοῦργος, das Aristoteles in seiner Ethik (6,12) gebraucht hat, und zwar in der Bedeutung 'zu jedem Geschäft tüchtig,' 'gewandt' 'geschickt.' Ein entsprechender lateinischer Ausdruck ist etwa *omnicreans* 'allerschaffend' bei Augustinus (conf. 11,13). Auf Gott bezieht sich

---

[25] Stiernman, 106; Lagus I, 163; Vallinkoski II, 218.

[26] Daniel Sarcovius, *Mnemosynon magno mecaenati miserorum Martino Miltopaeo, magnoque magistro* (sine loco et anno); vgl. Melander, 288 (n° 762).

[27] Das Wort fehlt in den Wörterbüchern.

[28] Wilhelm Schmidt-Biggemann, "Pansophie," in: *Historisches Wörterbuch der Philosophie,* hrsg. von Joachim Ritter und Karlfried Gründer, Band 7 (Basel, 1989), 55ff.

[29] Vgl. *Duden,* 1116.

auch die Zusammensetzung (v. 279) *panta-gubernans* 'allbeherrschend.'

Andere Neuprägungen weisen das lateinische Präfix *per-* auf. Es liegt auf der Hand, dass *per-* in diesen Fällen vorwiegend nur wegen der Alliteration hinzugefügt wurde. Während der Naturforscher bei Cicero (nat. deor. 1,83) *speculator venatorque naturae* heisst, gebraucht Eurenius in seiner Rede für ihn die Bezeichnung (v. 64) *perspeculator*, vielleicht zum ersten Mal. Er hat auch solche hierher gehörende hapax legomena wie (v. 60) *perodorifer* 'sehr riechend,' (v. 108) *perdomitare* 'völlig bewältigen' und (v. 109) *perpenetrare* 'tief in etwas eindringen.'

Die vorliegenden Gedichte bieten ferner ein paar Ergänzungen zu der lateinischen Wörtergruppe auf *-cola*, in der das Schlussglied die Bedeutung 'Bewohner' hat.[30] Das im Plural gebrauchte Wort (v. 358) *pollicolae* (= *policolae*) bezieht sich auf die Engel, weil sie im Himmelsgewölbe (*polus*) wohnen. Die Stare hausen dagegen in Teichen: daher sind sie von Gyllenius (v. 78) als *sturni stagnicolae* gekennzeichnet. Der Verfolger dieser Stare sei (v. 79) *silvivagus sagittator*, d. h. der Jäger, der in den Wäldern herumschweife. Das Adjektiv ist nicht anderswo überliefert. In Schweden gebe es rauhe Wälder oder (v. 131) *sylvae scabrigerae*, wie Gyllenius es schön ausdrückt. Auch dieses Adjektiv scheint eine Neuschöpfung zu sein. Dasselbe gilt noch etwa für das Wort (v. 290) *Sarigena* 'der Nachkomme von Sara, Gattin Abrahams.' Auch (v. 82) *musophilus* 'musenliebend,' das Sarcovius einmal gebraucht, scheint ein Neologismus im Lateinischen zu sein.

Die hier dargebrachten Beispiele für den pangrammatischen Manierismus in der akademischen Dichtung Finnlands entsprechen kaum dem Stilideal der modernen Poesie, wie auch solche übermässige Alliterationen schon im klassischen Altertum verpönt wurden. Die Geschmacksverschiebung in Richtung der Stile des manieristischen Typs lässt sich bei den Autoren der sogenannten Silbernen Latinität beobachten, wobei der Manierismus als eine späte Version des Asianismus angesehen werden kann. Der pangrammatische Manierismus ist eine typische Erscheinungsform des Barocks, dessen Kunst, Musik und Literatur stark von der Rhetorik beeinflusst wurden.[31] Curtius spricht in diesem Zusammenhang von einer 'barbarisch-naiven Schmuckform.'[32] Wie dem es auch sei, wurden die akademischen Dichter des 17. Jahrhunderts mit ihrer pangrammatischen Künstelei vor allem vom Ideal des *doctus poeta* getragen. Mit ihren Kunstwerken wollten sie sich vor allem an ein gebildetes Publikum wenden, um bei ihnen Beifall und Ansehen für ihre sprachliche Virtuosität zu gewinnen.

Universität Helsinki

---

[30] Vgl. Pitkäranta, 51f.

[31] Vgl. Joachim Knape, "Barock," in: *Historisches Wörterbuch der Rhetorik*, hrsg. von Gert Ueding, Band 1 (Tübingen, 1992), 1285ff.; Gert Ueding, "Dichtung," a. a. O., Band 2 (Tübingen, 1994), 721ff.

[32] Curtius (1984), 287. [Zusatz von W. Ludwig: Zum Pangrammatismus im 16. Jahrhundert vgl. auch die Dichtungen von Christianus Pierius (= Christian von Nydeck, um 1530– nach 1583): *Paupertas poetarum, Praestigiis pertinacique Plutonis pugna parata, primitusque per pauperem Pierium poetam publicata* (Tübingen, 1566) und *Christus crucifixus, carmen cothornatum catastrophicumque* (Frankfurt am Main, 1576). Es handelt sich um hexametrische mit p bzw. c beginnende Gedichte; zum Verfasser s. O. Haug, *Pfarrerbuch Württembergisch Franken*, T. 2 (Stuttgart, 1981), 334.]

Caractère de l'historiographie de
Juan Ginés de Sepúlveda: l'histoire de Philippe II*

BARTOLOMÉ POZUELO CALERO

Toute recherche sur la littérature latine de la Renaissance doit tenir grand compte d'une question fondamentale: l'*imitatio*. C'est un présupposé sur lequel nous sommes, je suppose, tous d'accord. Mais l'*imitatio* peut s'exercer dans de nombreux domaines: style, formes littéraires, thèmes, *etc*. En ce qui concerne l'historiographie, je considère que, par rapport à l'imitation, il faut étudier, avant tout, trois aspects:

1. Les genres de l'historiographie: sont-ils les mêmes que ceux de l'Antiquité (*annales, historiae, commentarii*, monographies, *etc*.), ou y a-t-il des formes nouvelles?
2. Le style: y a-t-il un auteur ancien choisi comme modèle stylistique par l'auteur de la Renaissance?
3. Le caractère historiographique.

C'est sur cette dernière question que porte cette communication. Je me propose d'analyser le caractère historiographique de l'oeuvre de Juan Ginés de Sepúlveda (1490–1573), chroniqueur officiel de Charles Quint, et, après lui, de Philippe II.[1] Je vais limiter mon étude à la dernière des quatre grandes oeuvres historiques composées par Sepúlveda: le *De rebus gestis Philippi secundi*, qui comprend trois livres.

Avant tout, il faudrait rappeler *paucis uerbis* les caractères de l'historiographie romaine. Suivant le resumé de Wals,[2] on peut fondamentalement parler de quatre ten-

---

* Ce travail fait partie du projet de recherche PS93-0164 de la DGICYT, Ministerio de Educación y Ciencia, España.

[1] L'oeuvre fondamentale sur Sepúlveda continue à être A. Losada, *Juan Ginés de Sepúlveda a través de su «Epistolario» y nuevos documentos* (CSIC, Madrid 1973 = 1949). On peut trouver une abondante bibliographie dans le dernier livre publié sur l'historien: L. Rivero Garcia, *El latín del «De Orbe Novo» de Juan Ginés de Sepúlveda* (Univ. de Sevilla, 1993).

[2] P. G. Walsh, *Livy: His Historical Aims and Methods* (Cambridge 1970), p. 22 ss.

dances historiographiques: chaque auteur les réalisera différemment, selon ses buts et sa pensée. Ce sont les suivantes:

1. La tendance pragmatique, dérivée de Thucydide et Polybe. Elle pourrait être caractérisée comme suit:
   a) But: l'utilité pour l'homme d'État.
   b) Méthode: analyse de la vérité historique (par-dessus les considérations littéraires).

2. Tendance rhétorique (dérivée d'Hérodote et des sophistes).
   a) But: le charme littéraire.
   b) Méthode: prédilection pour le récit de scènes de conquête de villes, de morts d'hommes célèbres, de batailles, d'assemblées, *etc.*

3. Tendance tragique. C'est une spécialisation de la tendance rhétorique, mise en pratique par Duris de Samos et Philarque.
   a) But: provoquer chez le lecteur des passions telles que la pitié, l'horreur, *etc.*
   b) Méthode: construction soigneuse de scènes pathétiques, telles que la conquête de villes, par exemple, à l'aide de la structure de la tragédie.

4. Tendance moralisatrice, créée par Isocrate et développée par les stoïciens.
   a) But: inviter l'audience à la vertu et l'écarter du vice.
   b) Méthode: chercher des exemples historiques dans lesquels les vertueux sont récompensés par le succès, et les méchants sont punis.

À ces quatre tendances, on peut en ajouter une autre:

5. Tendance propagandiste, pratiquée par Jules César:
   a) But: la propagande politique.
   b) Méthode: 1) Offrir la version des faits de la partie qui écrit. 2) Manifester ses raisons et arguments. 3) Mettre en évidence le manque de raisons de la partie adverse.

Voici les tendances historiographiques qu'on rencontre dans la littérature romaine. Parmi les historiens, comme vous le savez, 1) Jules César met nettement en pratique la tendance propagandiste, 2) Salluste avant tout la tendance pragmatique, puis, la moralisatrice, 3) Tite Live la tendance moralisatrice, puis la pragmatique, la rhétorique et la tragique.

Quelles sont donc les tendances historiques mises en pratique par Sepúlveda? Après avoir étudié son *De rebus gestis Philippi secundi*, je peux dire que Sepúlveda ne pratique pas uniformément une tendance historique ou autre; mais que la tendance historique pratiquée dépend de la nature des faits qu'il raconte. Le contenu des deux premiers livres peut être résumé suivant ce schéma:

Livre I:
1) (1) Abdication de Carlos V et Philippe II.
2) (2–47) Guerres avec le Pape Paul IV et avec Henri IV de France (1556–1559; bataille de Saint-Quentin et Paix de Cateau-Cambrésis).

Livre II:
1) (1–16) Afrique: campagne contre le roi de Tlemcen, finie en désastre.
2) (17–28) Espagne: procès pour hérésie.
3) (29–32) Espagne: noces de Philippe II avec Isabelle de Valois.
4) (33–66) Afrique: campagne contre Tripoli: désastre de Djerba (Meninx).

On constate qu'il y a une différence fondamentale entre les livres I et II: le premier porte sur des conflits politiques et militaires entre l'Espagne d'un côté, et Rome et la France de l'autre; par contre, le livre II raconte essentiellement deux campagnes militaires contre les Africains qui finirent en désastre. Cela veut dire que la finalité des deux livres est tout à fait différente: celle du premier consiste à exposer aux lecteurs (latinistes) de toute l'Europe les raisons de la politique espagnole et à présenter Paul IV et Henri IV de France comme les responsables de la guerre. Quelle est la modalité historiographique pertinente à ce but? Évidemment la propagandiste, celle que cultiva César, dans le même but, à l'occasion de sa guerre contre Pompée. Elle est donc celle que met en pratique Sepúlveda dans ce premier livre.

La finalité du livre II sera bien différente, comme nous le verrons plus tard.

Mais nous voudrions d'abord souligner la façon dont les caractéristiques les plus notables de l'historiographie propagandiste apparaissent dans ce livre premier:

I) Le premier aspect à considérer est la présentation de la partie adverse. Pour le faire, je vous propose de lire le chapitre II de ce livre.[3]

Paulus quartus Pontifex Maximus patria Neapolitanus ex nobili Garrafarum familia in demortui Marcelli secundi locum affecta iam aetate successit.

Jusqu'ici, il n'y a rien de remarquable: c'est une présentation neutre. Mais poursuivons la lecture:

Is, ut erat rerum nouarum studiosus . . .

Voilà le premier trait caractéristique de la présentation des adversaires dans l'histoire propagandiste: l'attribution à ceux-ci de défauts de moralité. Notez que c'est la première chose dite sur Paul IV. Poursuivons:

. . . et ab Hispanis alienum animum gerebat propter iniurias quas sibi ab eis in se uel propinquis accepisse uidebatur, . . .

Voilà un second trait: l'auteur décrit des sentiments prêtés à l'adversaire. Remarquez l'emphase que l'allitération (*ab Hispanis alienum animum*) donne à l'expression; remarquez aussi que le premier mot est *Hispanis*. Notez, de même, le verbe *uidebatur*, qui fait allusion à la frivolité du Pape. Mais poursuivons:

---

[3] Je suis la seule édition faite jusqu'à présent: *Ioannis Genesii SEPVLVEDAE, Cordubensis, Opera, cum edita tum inedita, accurante Regia Historiae Academia,* I–IV (Madrid 1780). Une équipe interuniversitaire espagnole, financée par l'Ayuntamiento de Pozoblanco, ville natale de l'historien, est en train de faire une nouvelle édition et traduction des *opera omnia*.

... nihil habuit potius initio pontificatus quam ut Hispanos Regno Neapolitano depelleret, quod facile fore reputabat si ad Neapolitanorum ciuium suorum studium, quod sibi largiter pollicebatur, Gallorum regis Henrici amicitia bellique societas accederet, de cuius animo ab Hispanis auerso nihilo minus prolixe sibi promittebat.

Dans ce texte, on peut voir une troisième caractéristique concernant la présentation de l'adversaire: l'auteur fait ressortir l'erreur, la bêtise même, de la conduite de l'adversaire. Sepúlveda se conduit avec grande subtilité: il introduit la décision du Pape avec la formule ironique *nihil habuit potius ... quam*; elle est suivie de la présentation de son projet formulée d'une manière extrêmement concise: *Hispanos Regno Neapolitano depelleret*; ce brusque énoncé devait sembler, sans doute, étonnant, extravagant. En effet, le lecteur reçoit à peu près le message suivant: le Pape est un halluciné privé du sens du possible. Cette impression se confirme quand on lit l'argumentation politique prêtée au Pape: *quod facile fore* (notez l'allitération qui attire l'attention du lecteur sur ces paroles) *reputabat* (*reputabat* est plus fort que *putabat*: la décision a été longuement considérée) *si ad Neapolitanorum ciuium suorum studium*, (première condition pour le succès de sa politique: "l'adhésion au Pape des citoyens de Naples"), *quod sibi largiter pollicebatur ...*

Examinons le texte: le Pape considère qu'étant donné qu'il est napolitain, tout le Royaume de Naples appuiera son projet; notez aussi la superbe qui se cache derrière l'absolue certitude que le Pape a de l'adhésion de ses concitoyens à son projet; or ce n'est pas la superbe, mais l'humilité et la modestie qu'on attend d'un Pape: c'est ainsi que Sepúlveda, historien officiel, justifie que Philippe d'Espagne, un roi chrétien, fasse la guerre contre le Pape de la Chrétienté. Mais la guerre n'est que la première condition au succès du Pape; la seconde est ajoutée ensuite: *Gallorum regis Henrici amicitia bellique societas accederet, de cuius animo ab Hispanis auerso nihilo minus prolixe sibi promittebat.* L'expression bimembre *amicitia bellique societas* et le verbe d'addition *accederet* intensifient l'idée de difficulté. Finalement, on peut noter l'insistance sur la naïveté du Pape: *nihilo minus prolixe sibi promittebat.*

En définitive, dans ces textes, comme dans tout le livre premier, Sepúlveda met en pratique l'historiographie propagandiste en utilisant les mêmes procédés que César.[4]

Jusqu'ici nous avons analysé la présentation de l'adversaire, un des aspects les plus caractéristiques de l'historiographie propagandiste. Nous allons maintenant analyser trois autres aspects qui caractérisent eux aussi cette tendance historiographique.

1. L'auteur présente d'un ton élogieux les actions du héros. Voici un exemple dans lequel il fait ressortir la façon dont Philippe II essaie jusqu'à la fin d'éviter la guerre:

---

[4] A) Attribution à l'adversaire de défauts de moralité: Caes., *ciu.* 1,7,1: [à propos de Pompée] *A quibus [inimicis] deductum ac deprauatum Pompeium queritur [Caesar] inuidia atque obtrectatione laudis suae.* B) Sentiments intérieurs attribués à l'adversaire: Caes., *ciu.* 1,4,1 *Catonem ueteres inimicitiae Caesaris incitant et dolor repulsae.* C) L'auteur fait ressortir l'erreur de la conduite de l'adversaire: Caes., *ciu.* 1,4,2 *Lentulus ... se ... alterum fore Syllam inter suos gloriatur ad quem summa imperii redeat.*

Sepul. Phil. 1,14: . . . *cognito Henrici consilio [sc. Italiae inuadendae]. . . , **tamen, ut** **pacem quatenus posset retineret et publicae quieti quoquo modo consuleret** [notez l'expression bimembre], iniuriam dissimulanter tulit.*

Comparons avec ce fragment où César souligne également ses efforts pour éviter la guerre:

Caes., *ciu.* 1,2,2s.: *Atque haec Caesar ita administrabat ut condiciones pacis dimittendas non existimaret . . . Atque ea res saepe temptata etsi impetus eius consiliaque tardabat, tamen **omnibus rebus in eo perseuerandum putabat.***

2. Le deuxième consiste dans l'insertion de discours du héros dans lesquels il expose systématiquement ses raisons. Voici, par exemple, une lettre au discours indirect adressée par Philippe II aux Vénitiens:

Sepul. Phil. 1,16: . . . *cui [sc. Philippo] pace et concordia et iustitia nihil potius, nihil optabilius esset; itaque arma se inuitissimum sumere a Paulo Pontifice coactum esse, non ut cuipiam per iniuriam noceret, sed ut grauem iniuriam a se suisque clientibus propulsaret, et iniustis Pauli Pontificis conatibus obsisteret.*

C'est une technique elle aussi typique de César, comme le montre ce fragment d'un discours qu'il adresse au Sénat à la suite de son entrée à Rome, l'année 49:

Caes., *ciu.* 1,32,2s: *Coacto senatu, iniurias inimicorum commemorat. Docet se nullum extraordinarium honorem appetisse, sed exspectato legitimo tempore consulatus eo fuisse contentum quod omnibus ciuibus pateret. Latum ab X tribunis plebis contradicentibus inimicis, Catone uero acerrime repugnante et pristina consuetudine dicendi mora dies extrahente, ut sui ratio absentis haberetur . . .*

3. Le troisième aspect, finalement, consiste à présenter les faits historiques selon la vision de la partie défendue par l'auteur. Évidemment, c'est là le but fondamental qui inspire les oeuvres historiques de tendance propagandiste.

Si on ne lisait que ce premier livre de l'*Histoire de Philippe II*, on penserait assurément qu'elle n'est qu'une oeuvre de propagande. On est donc fort surpris quand on lit le second livre, où la tendance historiographique est bien différente. Comme on l'a vu, ce deuxième livre raconte deux campagnes espagnoles en Afrique qui ont fini, toutes deux, comme nous l'avons dit, en désastre. La finalité cherchée par Sepúlveda n'est pas du tout propagandiste; il ne se propose pas de persuader quiconque de l'opportunité ou non de ces campagnes; mais il ne se borne pas non plus à faire un récit neutre des faits. Loin de là, Sepúlveda, en racontant les faits, expose une thèse personnelle-comme le fait Salluste. On le sait, Salluste ne se contente pas de rapporter des événements historiques; il les raconte de manière que nous recevions un message, une thèse personnelle. Dans son *Catilina*, par exemple, on devine la thèse suivante: "la route qu'ont suivie les faits à l'occasion de la conspiration de Catilina a conduit Rome à la perte de bien des Romains de valeur; en conséquence, les hommes qui ont dirigé la politique, notamment Caton et Cicéron, ont commis une erreur que tous les Romains ont payée." Il s'agit d'une thèse qui est le produit d'une réflexion historique et qui est utile à l'homme d'État pour éviter les décisions qui mènent au désastre. C'est pour cela que nous appelons pragmatique cette modalité de l'histoire.

L'intention de Sepúlveda dans le livre II de l'*Histoire de Philippe II* est plus ou moins la même. Et la thèse qu'il transmet est la suivante: "les désastres militaires en Afrique se sont produits à cause de l'incompétence." Dans la campagne contre Tripoli, par exemple, dès le début, il fait ressortir que la situation est inquiétante:

> Sepul. *Phil.* 2,36: *Sed antequam classis et impositus exercitus Syracusis discederet, Italici milites, qui diutius nauibus contenti fuerant et angustius impositi et parum commodis commeatibus usi, ualetudine tentari coeperunt, inualescente latiusque serpente morbo, qui multos omnis generis absumpsit.*

Notre auteur présente l'épidémie comme le résultat des erreurs des chefs de la campagne; et ce n'est ni une, ni deux, mais trois erreurs qui en sont causes. Ces trois erreurs sont présentées en *polysindeton*: cela intensifie l'idée d'accumulation. Les événements sont donc narrés de façon à appuyer la thèse de l'historien. D'autre part, il faut remarquer que le ton de ce livre est différent de celui du livre premier. Dans le livre premier, un ton critique comme celui du texte que nous venons de lire serait inconcevable.

Le résultat de cette désastreuse campagne fut la perte presque totale de la flotte et de l'armée espagnole. Après avoir narré cette fin, Sepúlveda a cette réflexion absolument typique de l'histoire pragmatique:

> Sepul. *Phil.* 2,55: *Verumtamen hoc in bello et nauigatione multa, ut multorum sermo est* [notez: il se cache derrière "l'opinion de bien de gens"], *tam lente, tanta incuria et securitate, praeterque rei militaris rationem administrata sunt-quae pereuntibus occasionibus rem longissime traherent-, etc.*

En définitive, ce deuxième livre, comme nous l'avons constaté, a été écrit dans une perspective pragmatique. La narration de Sepúlveda montre que l'organisation des deux campagnes africaines a été mauvaise. Et la lecture de son l'oeuvre offre à l'homme d'État des clefs pour éviter la répétition de telles erreurs.

Je passe maintenant à une autre question: dans quelle mesure y a t-il des tendances historiographiques autres que la propagandiste (1er livre) et la pragmatique (deuxième livre)?

1. Les fragments inspirés par la tendance moralisatrice apparaissent souvent. C'est le cas, par exemple, du texte suivant, où, à propos de l'hostilité de Henri IV envers Philippe II, nous pouvons lire:

> Sepul. *Phil.* 1,21: . . . *nihil iam aliud quam de bello palam et aperte cum Philippo ex omni parte gerendo* [notez l'idée de démesure] *cogitabat, ne rei bene gerendae et magnarum rerum occasiones, quas ipse sibi fingebat, perire pateretur.* Ensuite, il ajoute la cause de cette soudaine hostilité: *Nam, Carolo patre de medio sublato, Philippi adolescentiam et rerum bellicarum insolentiam Henricus, qui earum magnum usum habebat, prae se contemnebat* [le mot *contemnere* est typique, déjà chez les historiens romains, pour faire allusion à la conduite orgueilleuse].

Naturellement, ce manque de scrupules a obtenu le châtiment mérité, quand le Français fut battu par l'Espagnol à Saint-Quentin. Mais il y a aussi des comportements marqués par l'*hubris* dans la partie espagnole, comme vous le pouvez voir dans le l'exemple suivant:

Sepul. *Phil.* 2,8: . . . *quorum [sc. Maurorum] multitudinem male armatam et bellorum insolentem facile contemnebant* . . . [notez, ici également, le verbe *contemnere*].

Ce cas de superbe obtient, lui aussi, le châtiment dû.

2. La tendance rhétorique, au contraire, est plus exceptionnelle dans les livres I et II. On en a un rare exemple dans le texte suivant, où l'auteur insère une référence, dépourvue de signification historique, à un soldat grec qui a préféré la mort à la reddition:

Sepul. *Phil.* 2,53: *Quo in loco nautici militis, natione Graeci, facinus non est silentio praetereundum, qui, ceteris, ne frustra temere diutius propugnarent, cedentibus deditionemque facientibus, ipse solus in puppe cum gladio et scuto permansit, nec, ullis suorum uocibus ne temere et inutiliter amplius repugnaret dehortantium, deterreri potuit quin urgentibus hostibus pertinaciter repugnaret, donec multorum concursu uulneribus confossus, egregie, sese ultus et multis uulneribus illatis, caderet, dum scilicet magno constanteque animo mortem honestissimam turpi seruituti longe praeferendam putat.*

Toutefois, cette tendance, la rhétorique, domine dans le livre troisième, le dernier de l'*Histoire de Philippe II.* L'argument de ce troisième livre n'est apte ni à la modalité propagandiste ni à la pragmatique; en conséquence, Sepúlveda fait des efforts pour donner charme et aménité à son récit. Mais le temps limité de cette exposé ne nous permet pas d'analyser ces textes.

3. Finalement, on peut trouver des scènes inspirées de la tendance tragique, surtout dans le livre troisième. C'est le cas du texte suivant, un *excursus* où nous lisons le récit de la terrible malchance qui a poursuivi un homme, Gonzalo Morillo, qui, après avoir été capturé deux fois par les Turcs, trouva la mort dans un naufrage qui eut lieu dans un port:

Sepul. *Phil.* 3,4: *Praeterea [sc. periit] qui in Neapolitana classe officio praeerat, quem inspectorem appellant, earumque sex pro ductore praeerat, Gonsalus Morillus meus conterraneus, cuius supra mentionem feci, uir fortis et industrius magis quam fortunatus: bis fuerat a Turcis bello captus et Byzantium in seruitutem deductus—primum ad Castellum Nouum, in ora Dalmatiae, nuper ad Meningem insulam—, bis a fratribus, uiris optimis et singulari pietate, non paruo pretio redemptus; qui cum in castra Neapolitana utroque tempore rediuisset, honori fuit a ductoribus habitus, et praefecturis uoluntate regis auctus. Quibus laboribus et periculis exhaustis, dum se putat meliori et laetiori fortunae fuisse reseruatum, uelut in alto tempestatibus ereptus, in portu miserabili naufragio periit. Tanta est rerum humanarum inconstantia, tam fallaces spes saepe fortuna mortalibus ostentat.*

On notera, dans le texte, les expressions qui intensifient le pathétique: à la ligne 3, l'antithèse entre les bonnes qualités de l'homme et sa malchance: *uir fortis et industrius magis quam fortunatus.* A la fin, le brusque contraste entre, d'une part, ses espoirs (*dum se putat meliori et laetiori* [notez la construction bimembre] *fortunae fuisse* [notez l'allitération] *reseruatum*), et, de l'autre, la fatalité qui l'entraîne. On remarquera la formidable référence à la force du destin (*uelut in alto tempestatibus ereptus*), d'un haut niveau littéraire, et l'emphase sur le pathétique (l'adjectif *miserabili*), la première position du syntagme *in portu*, "dans le port."

En conclusion, l'oeuvre de Sepúlveda n'est pas limitée à une seule des tendances historiques de l'Antiquité; nous avons vu que le livre premier répond avant tout à la tendance propagandiste, comme nous nous y attendions, étant donné que l'auteur est un chroniqueur officiel. Mais dans le deuxième livre qui raconte deux campagnes militaires désastreuses, Sepúlveda adopte le point de vue pragmatique. Et dans le troisième, il préfère le charme et l'aménité littéraires, de sorte qu'il pratique la tendance rhétorique.

Le récit du premier livre est froid; le deuxième, au contraire, est plus chaud et personnel, et, en conséquence, plus élevé, du point de vue littéraire. D'ailleurs, cette liberté exercée par Sepúlveda a, peut-être, contribué au fait que son oeuvre historique soit restée si longtemps inédite.

Universidad de Cádiz

Lampridio and the Poetic Sodalities
in Rome in the 1510s and 1520s

STELLA P. REVARD

Hailed by his contemporaries at his death in 1540 as the new Pindar, Benedetto Lampridio of Cremona is usually remembered as the first Italian poet who attempted to imitate Pindar's strophic verse in Latin and to achieve what Horace himself hoped for but despaired of accomplishing—true Pindaric imitation.[1] Yet Lampridio deserves to be remembered for another reason, however, as one of the poets of the literary sodalities in Rome under Leo X, a poet who undertook to commemorate his times and his contemporaries in Pindaric verse and thus preserved for us a view of Rome both during and after the age of Leo.

Born sometime before 1500 and educated by Marco Musuro in Padua, Lampridio probably came to Rome at the accession of Leo X in 1513. He was one of the teachers at the Collegio dei Greci, the school that Leo sponsored on the Quirinal in Angelo Colocci's villa and for which Leo at Pietro Bembo's behest brought to Rome both Musuro, Lampridio's old teacher, and Joannes Lascaris, the celebrated Greek scholar.[2] His interest in Pindaric imitation probably dates from this period, for he was clearly involved in Leo's other humanistic project, the development of a printing press in Rome that might rival Aldus's at Venice. The first book to come from the new press in 1515 was a copy of Pindar's odes, for which Lampridio wrote a commendatory epigram in Greek to Cornelio Benigno, who with Colocci and Chigi

---

[1] My thanks to Julia Gaisser and Phyllis Bober, co-chairs of an NEH seminar on Roman humanism in 1990, for which a first version of this paper was written. Jean Dorat described Lampridio as a poet who was to Cremona what Virgil was to Mantua, another Pindar: [epigram in *Carmina Illustrium Poetarum Italorum*, ed. J. M. Toscanus (Paris, 1576), 1:83r]. Paulo Giovio in his *Elogia Doctorum Virorum* (Antwerp, 1557) includes three commendatory epigrams on Lampridio (one by Marco Antonio Flaminio), as well as a brief life and assessment of his odes (pp. 219–220).

[2] See Vittorio Fanelli, "Il Ginnasio Greco di Leone X a Roma," *Studi Romani* 9 (1961): 379–393; also see Giovio, *Elogia Doctorum Virorum*, 219. Lampridio's affectionate ode to Lascaris may date from this period.

probably sponsored the project.[3] Lampridio was a member of Colocci's, Mellini's, and Goritz's literary circles, as his odes to poets and scholars of these literary groups testify, and maintained cordial relations with them after he left Rome in 1521 for Padua where he taught Greek.[4] Pierius Valerianus refers to Lampridio both in his prose and in his poetry, addressing one witty epigram to the philosophic sodality of poets in Padua, in which he names Lampridio as among the eight Muses and asks that he himself be admitted as a ninth.[5]

Lampridio's odes are of interest to us both as Pindaric imitations and as cultural and historical documents, addressed mostly to actual living persons, that tell us about the literary world in Rome, taking us from about 1513, the beginning of Leo's golden age, to the accessions of Adrian VI and Clement VII, to the sack of Rome in 1527, and finally to the reconstruction of Rome with Paul III. Lampridio writes to political figures—Henry VIII of England, Francesco Sforza II, Bishop Giberti of Verona, Leo X—as well as to humanists, poets, friends, and patrons.[6] Whether he writes in the triads that he developed for his new Pindaric verse or in more common verse forms, Lampridio attempts to bring a Pindaric stance to his poetry. Following the example of earlier Pindaric imitators such as Francesco Filelfo, he extends the range of Pindaric imitation, commemorating friends and associates in the Pindaric manner in order to assure that their names and accomplishments would survive for future ages.[7] Although circulated during his lifetime, Lampridio's poems were not printed until 1550, ten years after his death.[8]

---

[3] See Pindar, Odes (Rome, 1515). The Pindar was printed from a Vatican copy of the odes rather than the Ambrosian recension that Aldus had used for his Pindar, printed just two years earlier in Venice in 1513. Leo brought Zacharias Callierges, a former associate of Aldus, to Rome to oversee the printing press.

[4] Colocci refers to Lampridio in his letters, and Bembo sent his son to study with Lampridio. Lampridio wrote an ode on the son's death. See Federico Ubaldini, Vita Angeli Colotii episcopi Nucerini (Rome, 1673), ed. Vittorio Fanelli (Vatican City, 1969). Also see Vita di Mons. Angelo Colocci, ed. and trans. Vittorio Fanelli (Vatican City, 1969); Atti del convegno di studi su Angelo Colocci (Iesi, 1969); Francesco Piovan, "Lampridio, Bembo e Altri," Italia Medioevale e Umanistica 30 (1987): 179–197.

[5] "Ad Sodales Patavij philosophantes," Hexametri Odae et Epigrammata (Ferrara, 1550), 126v. Valerianus also addressed other poems to Lampridio, among them a humanistic poem on his loves and his studies. See Pierius Valerianus, "Eiusdem Pierii Valeriani Amicitia Romana"; "Ad Benedictum Lampridium de Mentis auocatione Daphnia rusticante" in Amorum Libri V (Venice, 1549), 89r–92v; 7r–8v. Also see Sadoleto's description of the poets in Rome at the time: Jacopo Sadoleto, "Epistola" (to Colocci) in Vat. Lat. 4103, 16–17.

[6] His other verse includes a few perfunctory amatory or mythological pieces—to Venus, to the fugitive Cupid, and to his mistress Neaera.

[7] Giovanni Battista Pio, the secretary of Giulio de' Medici, praises Pindar as a poet who honored men of his time: "Dedicatory Epistle," De Urbe Roma (Bologna, 1520).

[8] Benedictus Lampridius, Carmina (Venice, 1550). His verse was reprinted in the following anthologies: Carmina Illustrium Poetarum Italorum, ed. J. M. Toscanus (Paris, 1576), 1: 83v–152v; Delitiae CC. Italorum Poetarum, Huius Superiorisque Ævi Illustrium, ed. Ranutius Gherus (Frankfurt, 1608), I, 2: 1271–1384. I quote from and make page references to the 1550 edition. See Carol Maddison, Apollo and the Nine (Baltimore, 1960).

The brief epigram that Lampridio wrote for Leo X's *possesso* in 1513 sets the tone for his work.

> Olim habuit Cypris sua tempora: tempora Mauors
> Olim habuit; sua nunc tempora Pallas habet.
>   ("De Suis Temporibus," *Carmina Illustrium*
>   *Poetarum Italorum*, 1: 152v)

The epigram expresses well the hope of scholars and poets at Leo's accession that they were leaving behind both the ages of the luxury-loving venereal Alexander VI and the Mars-like Julius II and were entering an age of Minerva when they would thrive.[9] For them Leo, often referred to as the Augustus who followed Julius, would usher in a "pax romana." Despite Leo's best intentions to cultivate the arts, the age of gold was not to last. Lampridio wrote several odes for Leo. "In Diem Cosmi Medici" (17r–v) celebrates Leo's generosity to poets and the people of Rome alike, for it commemorates the Feast of San Cosimo, the patron saint of the Medici, for which Leo had mounted lavish spectacles during the opening years of his pontificate, and names the pope as Leo Maximus who has brought peace and security to Rome.[10] A second ode to Leo (24r–26v) clearly echoes both Pindar's *Olympia* 2, written for an ancient patron of the arts, Theron of Acragas, and Horace's ode for Augustus (2.2). "For whom should I take my lyre in hand," Lampridio asks, "whom should I celebrate more potently with Dircean verses?" Lampridio calls upon the Muses to praise his patron, who now holds the sway in Rome. The ode veers between praise of Leo as a Medici—the man who brought the Florentine sensibility to Rome—the great descendent of Cosimo, the founder of the Medici family, who fulfilled his family's "destiny" by becoming pope, and praise of Leo as the new Augustus who restores the ancient city of Rome to its former glory, both politically and culturally. It was Etruria, he says, that first moved support for studies, and Leo's father, Lorenzo de' Medici, who made Florence flower and its glory shine throughout the world. Now that Lorenzo's son has come to Rome, he is the Genius who pours the Florentine riches from his cornucopia. Moreover, the very king of heaven has given the scepter to the divine Leo to lead the race of Romulus and to raise Rome to its former glory. "O happy race of Aeneas," Lampridio exclaims, and "Florence, thrice and four times happy!" Yet amidst this celebration Lampridio does not ignore Leo's troubles and sorrow, the thwarting of his political ambitions with the deaths of his brother Giuliano and his nephew Lorenzo, as well as the continuing wars in Italy and the threat of Turkish power. The ode must have been written toward the end rather than the beginning of Leo's pontificate, probably in 1520. Yet Lampridio is celebratory throughout, binding the pope's brow with the victor's laurel, celebrating him as

---

[9] For descriptions of the *possesso*, see Ludwig Pastor, *The History of the Popes*, ed. and trans. Ralph Francis Kerr (London, 1950), 8: 183; Rodolfo Lanciani, *The Golden Days of the Renaissance in Rome* (London, 1906), 294; Domenico Gnoli, *La Roma di Leon X* (Milan, 1938), 176; also see William Roscoe, *The Life and Pontificate of Leo the Tenth* (Liverpool, 1805).

[10] For the description of Leo's celebrations for the saint's day, see Gnoli, 108–124.

Caesar as well as Olympic victor, and concluding with a Pindaric aphorism appropriate both to a victorious pope or a victorious athlete:

> Non quisquis spatijs sudat Olympicis,
> Veloces agitans equos,
> Pulchris iuncta refert tempora frondibus. (26v)

Lampridio's ode on Pietro Mellini's villa (27r–37v) is the longest and most elaborate of his Pindaric odes and celebrates Roman humanism in a different way. Principally, it is a tribute to Pietro Mellini, an important patron of the arts in Rome, that includes a celebration of both Pietro and his villa. In many ways a joyous poem that extols poetry's place in Roman life, it also laments Celso Mellini, Pietro's brother, a promising poet who had died recently, in 1519. It opens with celebration of the villa itself, a place so pleasing that the gods themselves—that is, the ancient Roman deities—would choose to dwell here. Lampridio compares it to the very garden of the Hesperides, where Nature is temperate and where no wintry blasts come, where spring flowers bloom and where autumn also brings her abundance in fruit. A place of all pleasure, it is also inhabited by Neaera, the poet's mistress or her mythological equivalent, and the poets—the race of Phoebus—come to sing sweet tunes to the lyre and to raise the praises of this house to heaven. With a profusion of mythic details Lampridio compliments the villa which—like many of the villas of the period—probably featured ancient Roman wall-paintings that depicted the very gods the myths concern.

As Lampridio had praised the Florentine ancestors of Leo, so he praises Mellini's Roman forebears. In this decade under Leo many of the ancient families such as the Mellini were proclaiming their Roman heritage—their "Romanitas."[11] In good Pindaric style Lampridio praises not only Pietro's ancient forebears but his more immediate kin, particularly his father Mario, the head of the family, whose marriage to Ginevra Cibo, the niece of Pope Innocent VIII, raised the Mellini fortunes even higher.[12] Yet no sooner does Lampridio allude to this illustrious marriage and to the birth of Ginevra's sons—Celso and Pietro—than he turns his notes to tragic.

> Eheu Camoenae quo rapitis, memor
> Luctum mens iterat, dolore soluor
> Rursum. truces eheu fuistis
> Parcae nimis, semper truces . . . (35r)

At this point Lampridio remembers—or more appropriately signals his failure up to

---

[11] The Mellini *gens* actually claimed to go back to the Roman Republic, their family having been alluded to by Cicero. Part of the famous quarrel between the Belgian humanist Christophe de Longueil (Longolius) and Celso Mellini involved Longueil's alleged insult to this ancient Roman heritage.

[12] On the Mellini family, see Gasparo Alveri, *Roma in ogni stato* (Rome, 1664), 44–57; Carlo Cecchelli, *Le Grandi Famiglie Romane* (Rome, 1946); Iacobus Laurus, *De Familia Millina* (Rome, 1636); Gnoli, 155, 162.

this point to remember—the death of Celso Mellini.[13] It is an artful and thoroughly Pindaric device. In narrating in the first part of the ode the myths of Venus and Adonis and of Hercules and Hylas, both of which feature the loss of a beloved young man, Lampridio calls Celso to mind, long before he ever alludes to him directly. As he told how Venus searched for Adonis, or Hercules for Hylas, it was truly the search for the dead Celso that was the subtext of these quests. The consolatory movement had already begun in the ode, moreover, as he told how Venus, inconsolable over Adonis's death, went to the garden of the Hesperides and, having dreamed of a wondrous tree with golden fruit, woke to be reunited to her lover transformed into this tree.[14]

It was Lampridio's intent all along to celebrate the two brothers together, both of whom were friends to poets and poets themselves. The villa where they entertained the societies of poets recalls them both, as it does the poetic performances that took place there, such events that Lampridio even manages to describe in Pindaric fashion as the equivalent of winning athletic victories. Like an Olympic victor Pietro has managed his chariot so well that he has twice passed the turning post. But Lampridio also remembers a sad occasion, how the news of Celso's death came to Pope Leo, who had honored Celso previously by conferring the poetic laurel.[15] Celso had given the first fruits of his wit to his country, but the harsh season has killed the early crocus—the flowering of Celso's genius, and Celso will not return with the other flowers of the spring. Once more, however, myth works in this poem in a consolatory fashion, for now Lampridio alludes to Castor and Pollux, perhaps recalling Pindar's description in *Nemea* 10 of Pollux praying to his father Zeus for his brother's life.[16] The absent Celso is the dead Castor, who has been transported to the stars but whose "manes" still dwell at the villa. Lampridio tells how Pietro, just like Pollux, calls out for Celso with a solitary voice. Mediating between classical and Christian consolation, Lampridio says that Celso yet lives in Pietro. Whoever has been faithful to the altars of the Muses cannot perish. The lyre will remember how he struck melodies—and Apollo will remember too. Whom—other than Celso—did Apollo love more? In alluding to the two famous brothers—symbols for the Roman Quirites—Lampridio also reminds us of the Mellini's Romanitas.

Returning now to a more hopeful note, Lampridio alludes to Pietro's marriage to Ersilia Caffarelli that held promise that a new Mario would be born to honor Pietro's father Mario.[17] Implicit also in this reference is the tacit recognition that the future

---

[13] Laments for Celso Mellini, written by his Roman friends, were gathered in a volume: *In Celsi Archelai Melini funere amicorum lacrimae* (Rome, [ca. 1520]).

[14] Lampridio follows Pontano's *De hortis hesperidum* in recounting this version of the Adonis myth.

[15] After Celso's death the pope had a bridge constructed at the site of Celso's drowning with verses commending the young poet. See Lanciani, 314, 317.

[16] See *Nemea* 10. 49–91.

[17] The marriage to Ersilia Caffarelli took place in February 1521 and was the second marriage for Pietro; his first wife had died earlier. Specified in the marriage contract was that the first son should be named Mario after Pietro's father. Mario Mellini died in 1523. See Alveri, 52–53. Lam-

child will also take the place of the dead brother. The ode concludes with several witty mythic comparisons—Pietro as he extends cups of wine to his guests is compared to Chiron, who welcomes Hercules, but also to Ulysses, who offers the Cyclops sweet drink. The merriment of the poets at the villa is also likened to Bacchic celebrations where all join in the dance to the accompaniment of the pipe, a fitting conclusion to Lampridio's longest and most elaborate Pindaric ode and his most expansive evocation of the poetic sodalities at Rome.

Lampridio's poems to poet-friends continue after he leaves Rome for Padua and take us into the pontificates of Adrian VI and Clement VII, marked by growing political stress and diminished patronage for poets and scholars alike. The light-hearted stanzas that Lampridio wrote to Balthasar Castiglione (16r–v) appear to belong to the happy days of the sodalities under Leo. He gently chastises Castiglione for neglecting the Muses and bids him bind his hair once more with Castalian garlands. A Tuscan beauty with a fair forehead and dark eyes and hair is waiting for him to touch the lyre, and Angelus—perhaps he refers to Angelo Colocci—calls on him to sing and is ready to fill his cup with wine. Come, Lampridio urges, do not contemn the Muses and lead the rites to Father Liber. When the Roman Ennius was about to sing of war, he steeped himself first in wine, and so did Homer when he sang either of wily Ulysses or of the funeral ceremonies at Troy.

The ode to Pietro Corsi (45r–47r), another poet of the Colocci circle, begins in the same mood, evoking a *locus amoenus* congenial to the Muses. But it also refers to disquieting political circumstances: rumors of what Spain or France is about to do. Far from the vulgar mob and the stir of political life, the poet takes the lyre in hand and asks the Pindaric question: "What young man should we praise? Who is deserving in his virtue to be lifted to high Olympus?" The young man Lampridio plans to praise is not an athlete or a prince but the young Florentine poet, Lorenzo Bartolini, to whom Lampridio had addressed two odes and whom Corsi also commended in his poem, "De civitate Castellana Faliscorum" (Rome, 1525).[18] With Bartolini at his side, says Lampridio, he could advance with Jove's favor to a Muses' Elysium. Once more Lampridio suggests that the villas and gardens in Rome are the very equivalent on earth to the blessed isles. Regretting his friend's absence, he tells Corsi that golden Phoebus delights in him. Come to us, says Lampridio, and join the company of goat-footed satyrs and nymphs, who are dedicated to both Phoebus and Bacchus.

More sombre is the pair of odes that Lampridio wrote in the early 1520s to Ercole Rangone (18r–v), the gifted musician whom Leo made cardinal in 1517, and to Antonio Tebaldeo (9v–10v), one of the two poets whose features are recognizable in Raphael's famous painting of Parnassus in the Stanza della Segnatura. The odes are

---

pridio's address to Hersilia in the poem suggests that she is now pregnant and expecting the new Marius. Hersilia, a noted Roman name, was the name of Romulus's wife; moreover, the allusion to a new Marius must also have called up associations of the noted ancient Roman general C. Marius.

[18] See *Carmina*: "Quis posset ulli fidere foemine" (39r–40r) and "Laurento Bartholino" (44v–45v), both of which allude to Bartolini's mistress Lesbia.

written to console poet-friends on the death of poets close to them—the ode to
Ercole Rangone condoling the death of Guido Postumo Silvestri in 1521, Rangone's
teacher and a poet much loved by Leo X, and the ode to Antonio Tebaldeo, the
death of Timoteo Bendedei in 1522, a poet from Tebaldeo's native Ferrara, prominent in Ercole I's circle and celebrated by Ariosto in *Orlando Furioso*. Both poets were
associated with Colocci, who wrote an epitaph on Bendedei's death (extant in the
Colocci papers). The odes are touching in that they are not addressed directly to the
dead poets, but to the friends that Lampridio condoles on their deaths. The ode to
Rangone opens abruptly, as though Lampridio had just heard of Postumo's death:
"Quid audio? qui Nuntij? eheu Posthumus / Obit Poeta maximus" (18r). In referring
to Postumo as the greatest of poets, Lampridio pays tribute not so much to Postumo's
stature as a poet, but to his unique place in Roman society. Postumo was one of the
habitués of Leo's hunting lodge, the Magliana, and wrote verse not only in honor of
Leo's favorite, Serapica, but also to celebrate Leo's spectacles and his love for
hunting.[19] Lampridio takes care to remark on Leo's delight in Postumo's verse: "illa
quum lepore mellitissimo / Condita uerba promeret" (18r). While expressing the
Christian view that death is unavoidable, the ode also regrets the void Postumo's
death leaves in Rome—who can take his place, who can sing the deeds he once
sang? Like his verses on Postumo, Lampridio's ode to Tebaldeo on Bendedei expresses affectionate concern for Tebaldeo as well as a shared grief for Timoteo,
Tebaldeo's mentor and friend. Lampridio opens the ode by calling attention to his
own special relationship to Tebaldeo, whom he calls an honest judge of his own
work. Lampridio may even be suggesting that Tebaldeo is to him what Bendedei was
to the Ferrarese poet—mentor and model. Like the previous poem, this poem expresses the sense that the death of one poet diminishes the others in his group. As he
sings the elegies for the passing of these two poets, Lampridio may even be marking
(with the death of Leo also in 1521) the passing of an era.

Elegiac tones dominate in the odes that follow. "Ad Furnium" (37v–38v)—like
the ode to Corsi—seems at first only a poetic epistle that expresses regret at Francesco
Maria Molza's absence and hope for his return.[20] Writing apparently after the accession of Clement VII, Lampridio alludes in this ode not to joyful poetic activities, but
to the devastation of plague and war. He hopes, however, that Jupiter will look once
more with favor on the walls of old Romulus; the lyre will sound again on the Jani-
culum, and peace will be at hand. Echoing Virgil's fourth eclogue, he predicts the
return of the age of Saturn when Rome will once more conquer the eastern empire
and a new Homer will be born. Yet his tone is timid, not confident, as it had been
in the earlier odes, where the golden age seemed a *fait accompli*.[21] Accordingly Lam-

---

[19] See Roscoe, 3: 318–323; Gnoli, 224–225, 256–257.

[20] Probably Furnius is Francesco Maria Molza whom Lampridio addresses by his poetic
cognomen Furnius, adopted to compliment his lady Furnia. But Giovanni Francesco Forni, also
from Modena, used the name Furnius and was in Rome in 1524. See Fanelli, 73n.

[21] Even as late as 1522 in his ode to Janus Ruffus (Giovanni Ruffo Teodoli, archbishop of
Cosenza), a confidant of Adrian VI, Lampridio could express hope that the golden age of Rome
was not past, now that "optimus Adrianus" had assumed the papacy.

pridio concludes with a modest wish—that he be permitted to live his brief space of life in the company of his friend.

It is tempting to read the long philosophic ode (47r–48v) to Lazaro Bonamico (1479–1552) with its extended opening reflections on the precariousness of human fate and its even more extended myth on the story of Deucalion and Pyrrha and the flood as a comment on the sack of Rome in 1527. Bonamico, who, like Lampridio, was a student of Musuro's, and taught at Padua, had been in Rome until shortly before the sack and had been in communication with humanists such as Colocci immediately afterwards. In expressing the hope that the Fates may permit the horses of the sun to run their course for him and his friend, Lampridio seems to be responding to recent reversals in fortune. Developing the myth of the flood in a Pindaric fashion, he offers through it reassurance that though the "end" of the world may appear at hand, yet human beings can survive even the worst of catastrophes. After Jupiter had covered the earth with water, Deucalion and Pyrrha at the advice of Themis cast stones over their shoulders in order to bring new souls to life. Rome, he seems to say, has experienced its "flood," but the Fates will decree a new beginning. He then urges his friend Lazaro to interpret the old oracles of the Greeks: "Speak the song, which your heart knows, a song worthy of Delian laurels" (48r). Lampridio has not lost his faith in the vatic power of the poet. As he alludes to the devastation of modern Rome, he may even be pointing to the epigram that Bonamico wrote on the ruin of ancient Rome: "What now remains of Rome but an empty name?"[22] He concludes the poem, however, by drawing a Christian moral. Once the Almighty Father condemned the whole race to the pit of hell, but now that very God who can move the earth with a nod can decree a new beginning. A new cycle is about to start, a happier time, if we can elude the rock in a still dangerous ocean.

Another ode written after the sack is a melancholy counterpart to the idyllic verses on Mellini's villa. The ode on the olive villa of Cardinal Lorenzo Pucci (12v–14r) begins with an invocation to the gods of the hills and to Pallas, whose tree, of course, was the olive. Recollecting fondly the Roman villa of the Florentine cardinal who so often welcomed poets when they wished to retire from Rome, Lampridio describes its idyllic setting and remembers his poet friends, among them Antonio Nerli and Paulo Bombasi. Bombasi, secretary to the cardinal, had tragically been killed by a mob during the sack when he was trying to follow the cardinal to safety.[23] The savage wolf has torn them with his tooth, Lampridio comments, for Jupiter tests those he loves with hardship. The final strophe of the poem is a lament over fallen Rome: O Rome, how changed you are! Where can we go for the society

---

[22] See Toscanus, 1: 241r.

[23] Both poets are named by Francesco Arsilli in De Poetis Urbanis [Coryciana, ed. Blosius Palladius (Rome, 1524)], as having belonged to the sodalities in Rome during this period. See Roscoe, The Life and Pontificate of Leo the Tenth, 3: 3–22. Nerli has a poem included in the Coryciana; Bombasi is mentioned in the Colocci papers. See Fanelli, ed., Vita di Mons. Angelo Colocci, n. 47, 163, 114–115. Bombasi was a teacher of Greek and Latin educated at Bologna, the son-in-law of Scipio Carteromachus (Scipione Forteguerri), a friend of Aldus Manutius and of Erasmus. Valerianus remembers his death in De Literatorum infelicitate (Venice, 1620), 1: 22.

of Thalia, now that the happy choruses are silent and Pan and his nymphs are gone and Pallas has left the grove she once loved so much? (13v–14r) At the beginning of Leo X's papacy, Lampridio had predicted the beginning of the age of Pallas Minerva. It would appear that the age of Pallas was now over.

Of the last poems that Lampridio wrote on Rome, one is an epistle (60v–66r) to the Roman official and diplomat, Latino Giovenale de' Manetti,[24] the other an ode (49r–51r) written to Bernardino Trebazio, a scholar, translator, and editor, who lived in Padua. In the final three strophes of the ode to Trebazio Lampridio turns his eyes to Rome and to the fields that have been devastated by war, regretting the state of letters in the *caput mundi* after the sack. The queen of cities has fallen—and how miserable is the shame of the Quirites, the degenerate race of Romulus, the children of Aeneas, who have permitted their sacred temples to be ground to dust!—Lampridio's final wish is that Julian wisdom and Peter-like will might chase the host from Italy and permit Rome to rise again. In the Giovenale poetic epistle, written after the accession of Paul III in 1534, his thoughts are more optimistic. He not only lauds the revival of Rome under the new pope but also recalls fondly the age of Leo when Bembo and Sadoleto and Musuro flourished. Lampridio's letter is a reaffirmation of humanistic values. He pays special tribute to the role of the Medici in inspiring Greek and Latin studies, and he reaffirms also the Pindaric ideals of celebrating in verse the achievement of deserving literary men of the age. In fact, the letter tacitly recommends to Paul III that he honor poets as Leo had. In a final hopeful note Lampridio looks to the young Roman to whom he writes to revive the traditions of those literary sodalities he had once so much enjoyed in his young manhood as a teacher and a scholar at the Collegio dei Greci in Rome under Leo X.

Southern Illinois University, Edwardsville

---

[24] On whom see especially Léon Dorez, *La Cour du Pape Paul III*, 2 vols. (Paris, 1932), 2: 115–141.

Presenza dell'elemento italiano nella stampa di libri spagnoli o di tematica spagnola in tipografie tedesche del XV secolo e degli inizi del XVI

MARIA DOLORES RINCÓN GONZÁLEZ

Innanzi tutto è necessario circoscrivere il tema in un tempo e in uno spazio preciso. Ci riferiremo alla zone dell'antica Germania, i cui confini adesso coincidono con nazioni diverse: parte dell'attuale Germania, l'Alsazia e l'Alto Reno, regioni che hanno mantenuto fra loro stretti contatti intellettuali e politici fino al XV secolo.

D'altra parte il nostro campo di lavoro comprende gli eventi spagnoli fino ai primi anni del XVI secolo. Eventi che ebbero eco in tutta Europa, anche se non tutti furono veramente importanti; in alcuni casi ebbero infatti una risonanza che non corrispondeva ai loro scarsi effetti. Gli eventi ai quali intendiamo riferirci sono: il successo della Guerra di Granata, l'attentato al Ferdinando il Cattolico a Barcellona, la scoperta dell'America e l'ascesa al trono imperiale di Carlo V. Tenendo in considerazione queste tre premesse di luogo, di tempo e di tema, abbiamo studiato il processo di elaborazione di alcune operazioni tipografiche per arrivare ad una serie di conclusioni che dimostrano ancora una volta gli stretti contatti esistenti tra le comunità internazionali degli umanisti dell'epoca.

Si sa che la politica spagnola difendeva in quegli anni i suoi interessi in Italia, la sua relazione con l'Impero ed i confini dei nuovi territori d'oltremare. Utilizzò, quindi, in forma più evidente in Italia che in altri luoghi mezzi di propaganda che divulgarono efficacemente quegli eventi per creare un'immagine dei re cattolici come *speculum principum*. In questo modo intendeva piegare il risultato della lotta tra la Spagna e la Francia per i territori italiani e per la successione dell'Impero a favore degli interessi spagnoli; al tempo stesso favoriva il compromesso finale del *Tratado de Tordesillas*, nel quale si fissavano i confini della giurisdizione fra spagnoli e portoghesi nelle *insulis in mari Indico nuper inventis*. Divulgare, quindi, quella serie di successi richiedeva un mezzo materiale veloce, come era la stampa, e senza frontiere, come allora era la lingua latina. Il primo fu offerto dalle tipografie tedesche, senza trascurare il ruolo iniziale della stampa romana, il secondo fu risolto dalla penna di alcuni umanisti italiani.

Per chiarire la prima di queste affermazioni dobbiamo soffermarci sulle stampe dei luoghi citati, perché ovviamente stimola la nostra attenzione verificare come di una cinquantina di edizioni prodotte tra il 1493 e il 1508 della famosa lettera di Colombo, solo tre furono realizzate in Spagna, o ancora come della commedia umanistica che tratta della conquista di Granata si ebbero sette edizioni di incunabili, di cui solo due in Spagna.[1] In entrambi i casi, quasi tutte le edizioni straniere videro la luce in Germania ed il loro testo fu scritto o tradotto in latino da un italiano. A volte, quando la tematica è diversa, le opere stampate nelle zone vicine all'Alta Renania provengono direttamente dalla Spagna o sono di autori spagnoli. Così succede con alcuni libri stampati a Strasburgo o a Selestat,[2] centri collegati al circolo degli umanisti sorto intorno all'École Latine di Selestat, dove troviamo personaggi, come Jakob Wimpfeling, che favorirono la pubblicazione di apologisti come Mota di Burgos, amico di Jakob Spigel, o di Vicente Ferrer, la cui opera fu stampata nella tipografia di Johann Grüninger[3] a Strasburgo e poi a Basilea, o di Alfonso di Spina, anch'egli originario della penisola iberica e la cui produzioni vide la luce nella tipografia del medesimo Jean Mentel.[4] Lo stesso carattere didattico che in alcuni casi presentano le pubblicazioni vicine al circolo di Selestat può giustificare l'edizione di Juan Luis Vives fatta da Lazar Schürer nel 1520.[5]

Ma i libri della tematica riferita all'inizio della nostra esposizione ci conducono d'altra parte al grande fulcro dell'umanesimo meridionale europeo, l'Italia e, in modo particolare, a Roma. Così possiamo tracciare un triangolo, Spagna-Roma-Germania, nel quale ogni angolo svolge un suo ruolo da una prospettiva e da interessi diversi che, attraverso il libro stampato e la lingua latina, contribuiscono alla diffusione degli eventi già citati. Le ragioni che produssero questo fenomeno furono varie e collegate tra di loro, nonostante in alcuni casi fossero accidentali.

Questi libri furono stampati nelle tipografie di Basilea, Strasburgo, Francoforte, ecc., perché da una parte esistevano interessi tedeschi collegati alla politica imperiale e a determinati generi letterari come il teatro; dall'altra gli Spagnoli avevano interesse a far conoscere a tutta l'Europa quegli eventi che creavano una immagine prestigiosa della monarchia spagnola. Cominciamo dai primi.

In quei luoghi del Centroeuropa, come in altre regioni, due temi di attualità suscitavano grande interesse fra gli umanisti: il problema turco e la questione imperiale relativa soprattutto alla successione. Gli Ottomani, allora padroni di Belgrado e Constantinopoli, rappresentavano una grave minaccia per i paesi più vicini e questa situazione suscitava un sentimento di pericolo fisico e culturale; da qui i frequenti

---

[1] Carlos Gilly, *Spanien und Basler Buchdruck bis 1600* (Basel-Frankfurt a. M., 1985), 247.

[2] Frank J. Ritter, *Histoire de l'Imprimerie alsacienne aux XVe et XVIe siècles* (Strasburg, 1955); Charles Schmidt, *Histoire littéraire de l'Alsace à fin du XVe et au commencement du XVIe siècle* (Paris, 1879; repr. 1966).

[3] Vicentius Ferreirus, *Sermones* (Strasburg, 1503).

[4] Alphonsus Spina, *Fortalitium fidei* (Strasburg, 1462).

[5] Juan Luis Vives, *Adversus pseudodialecticos, eiusdem Pompeius fugens* (Selestat, 1520).

proclami per indire crociate contro i Turchi, incentivati da numerose opere e compendi, fra cui fu facile includere il tema della Guerra di Granata, interpretato come un contrappeso all'avanzata turca. Nella mentalità del tempo, infatti, all'unità dei re cristiani si opponeva il blocco delle forze di religione islamica. D'altra parte, la politica di vincoli matrimoniali svolta dal re spagnolo aveva aumentato le simpatie per i sovrani di Spagna e permise Carlo V di diventare imperatore. La posizione politica di alcuni umanisti collaborò a quel progetto imperiale e in tal senso è molto eloquente la *Congratulatio* che Sebatian Brant dedicò a Ferdinando di Aragona, per i suoi successi a Granata ed oltremare, nel frontespizio dell'edizione di Basilea del 1494 dell'*Historia Baetica*. L'autore, facendo riferimento alla Germania, scrive:

> O patria, o foelix Germania, si tibi reges
> Aut fortuna pares aut deus ipse daret.
> Credo equidem cunctus nostris sub legibus orbis
> Iam dudum foret, et clymmata cuncta soli.[6]

Ma dobbiamo sottolineare anche altri interessi nel patrocinio di quelle edizioni. È abbastanza significativo che siano commedie umanistiche a trattare degli avvenimenti riferiti e che si interessino a queste opere autori come Jakob Locher, nel caso della *Historia Baetica*, la cui edizione di Basilea fu realizzata sotto la supervisione del suo maestro Sebastian Brant, o nel caso del *Fernandus Servatus*, dramma sull'incidente occorso al Cattolico a Barcellona nel 1492, che fu stampato nella tipografia di Matthias Schürer mentre vi lavorava Peter Schott. Per di più dobbiamo considerare che la copia manoscritta della commedia su Granata fu aggiunta dallo stesso Hartmann Schedel ad una raccolta di drammi umanistici; pertanto è necessario ammettere il ruolo importante che giocò il crescente interesse per determinati generi letterari, in particolare il teatro, cosa che almeno in parte spiega perché un evento senza speciali risultati, come fu quello di Barcellona del 1492, abbia meritato l'edizione di Matthias Schürer sotto la supervisione, quasi con certezza, del Beato Renano.[7] Già nel XVI secolo alcune di queste opere sono presenti all'interno delle grandi collezioni dovute alla passione degli uomini di cultura tedeschi per le grandi compilazioni, generalmente raggruppate sotto il titolo di *Scriptores Rerum Germanicarum, Hispanarum, ecc.*, come per esempio l'opera di Roberto Monacho *Bellum christianorum principum ... contra Saracenos*[8] che raccoglie l'*Historia Baetica* in consonanza con la suddetta *turke Frage*, o la *Hispania illustrata* di Andreas Schott.[9]

In Germania, dunque, c'erano interessi politici, ovvero di propaganda politica a favore della pretese spagnole verso l'Impero e verso l'Italia, ma c'erano anche interessi letterari e scientifici in rapporto con la scoperta dell'America che produssero una serie

---

[6] Sebastian Brant, "In Bethicum triumphum congratulatio," in *Historia Baetica* de Carlo Verardi (Basel, 1494).

[7] Robert Walter, *Beatus Rhenanus. Citoyen de Sélestat ami d'Erasme. Anthologie de sa correspondance* (Strasburg, 1986), 40, 176; Marcellino Verardi, *Fernandus Servatus* (Strasburg, 1513).

[8] *Bellum christianorum principum praecipue Gallorum contra Saracenos ...* auctore Roberto Monacho (Basilea, 1533).

[9] Andreas Schott, *Hispania illustrata* (Frankfurt, 1603).

di cosmografie, come quelli di Matthias Ringmann (Philesius), e Martin Waldse-müller (Hylacomylus), nel 1507 a Saint-Diè, in cui per la prima volta si dà il nome al nuovo continente.[10]

Tali potrebbero essere le cause che dalla prospettiva tedesca favorirono le edizioni di libri di tematica spagnola, senza dimenticare, peraltro, che gli uomini di cultura credevano di avere l'obbligo morale di pubblicare e divulgare libri utili, missione che aveva trovato nella stampa il suo alleato più fedele. Questo sentimento ha molte testi-monianze negli scritti dedicati alla scoperta della stampa, come, per esempio, il poema che S. Brant indirizzò al suo amico Johann Bergmann di Olpe, *De praestantia artis impressoriae a Germanis nuper inventae*.[11] Encomi di tale natura possono trovarsi per tutta l'Europa e certamente non mancano esempi nelle lettere di scrittori spagnoli, come Alonso di Herrera, Lázaro di Velasco o Diego di Valera, il quale scriveva:

> Gozen los lectores de nuestros dias y los que vinieren, de bien tamaño como es el arte dela emprenta, porque parece vna marauilla por dios reuelada para que hayan lumbre los ciegos dela ygnorancia, pues muchos primero andauan turbados enlas tinieblas por mengua de libros no instruydos enla doctrina delos costumbres dela virtud y mal enseñados enla muy sancta y sagrada scriptura . . . y pueden agora sin mucho trabajo con pocos gastos hauer tanta parte como ingenio de cada vno tomar pudiere. . . .[12]

Alcune delle opere citate non ebbero tuttavia un'edizione spagnola e furono divulgate in Spagna attraverso libri stampati a Roma, Strasburgo, Norimberga, Francoforte, Basilea, Selestat, ecc. Ne è un esempio molto eloquente la lettera latina di Colombo già ricordata. Questa situazione potrebbe sembrarci anche più contrad-dittoria, se consideriamo l'importanza propagandistica che quelle opere ebbero per la politica spagnola e la scarsità degli apporti della tipografia spagnola, scarsità giustificata da diverse cause che ha studiato opportunamente Carlos Gilly.[13]

D'altro canto alla fine del XV secolo la stampa spagnola non si era ancora evoluta tecnicamente e non aveva raggiunto lo sviluppo di quella dell'Alto Reno. Il primo tipografo che lavorò in Spagna, Johann Parix di Heidelberg, cominciò nel 1472 con il testo del Sinodo di Segovia.[14] Alcune città come Valenza, Barcellona, ecc., videro la nascita della stampa ad opera di individui venuti dalla Germania,[15] mentre in altre parti del paese la tipografia fu diretta da uno spagnolo, ma spesso con la collabora-zione di italiani e, come nel caso di Antonio Nebrija, la produzione fu vincolata anche all'attività dell'umanista. Ma, nonostante ciò, la stampa spagnola non decollò e per molto tempo ancora il manoscritto continuò a fare concorrenza ai libri stampati.

---

[10] *Cosmographiae introductio . . . Insuper quattuor Americi Vespucii navigationes* (Saint-Die, 1507).

[11] Sebastian Brant, *Varia Carmina* (Basel, 1482), fol. iv.

[12] Diego de Valera, *Crónica* (1482).

[13] Carlos Gilly, op. cit.

[14] Carlos Romero de Lecea, *El V centenario de la introducción de la imprenta en España. Segovia 1472* (Madrid, 1972).

[15] Dietrich Briesemeister, "Die deutschen Frühdrucker in Spanien," *Sonderdruck aus Gutenberg-Jahrbuch* (1993).

Molto spesso le edizioni spagnole derivano da quelle straniere, come ebbero modo di lamentarsi Juan de Vergara e Juan Luis Vives.

Per di più la nascente stampa fu ostacolata da gravissime difficoltà di tipo materiale, alle quali si unirono fenomeni paralleli come il ritardo in Spagna della *latinità umanistica* che causò la carenza di correttori di testi scritti soprattutto in latino. Altra grande difficoltà fu l'assenza di tipografi e ciò spiega la presenza dei tedeschi e degli italiani. Ma senza dubbio, uno dei più importanti ostacoli fu la ristrettezza dei mezzi economici e l'assenza di una borghesia mercantile interessata all'editoria, senza dimenticare problemi come la cattiva qualità della carta. Inoltre il lavoro editoriale era indirizzato soprattutto a coprire le esigenze dell'insegnamento, per cui gli umanisti avevano bisogno di ricorrere alle tipografie straniere se volevano pubblicare qualsiasi altro tipo di opera.[16]

Come abbiamo detto, il ritardo della latinità umanistica fu un altro fattore che ostacolò la divulgazione dei successi spagnoli. Il latino era uno strumento di comunicazione che superava le frontiere e facilitava, senza altre interpretazioni, la diffusione rapida e diretta di quello che si propagava; la rozzezza e l'imperizia, in questo senso, dei cronisti spagnoli rappresentava un grave ostacolo, che fu superato grazie alla penna di alcuni italiani; cosicché quando il testo che parlava di tali successi non fu scritto in latino, la sua eco fu limitata all'ambito spagnola, e ciò provocò negative conseguenze storiche: la conoscenza di testimonianze e cronache, come quella di Bernal Díaz del Castillo, avrebbe ostacolato la divulgazione della *Leyenda Negra Española*. Certamente ci furono anche storici spagnoli che scrissero in latino, ma più tardi furono costretti a tradurre le loro cronache in castiglano, come afferma Juan de Mariana: *por el poco conocimiento que de ordinario hoy tienen en España de la lengua latina aun los que en otras ciencias y profesiones se aventajan.*[17] Per cause simili dovette farlo anche José de Acosta.

Questa mancanza di perizia latina coincise con l'inizio di un nuovo sentimento nazionale che potenziava l'aspetto comunitario e dava maggior credito alla propia lengua, e con esso favoriva una tendenza generale ad usare la lingua volgare, sintomo di una nuova consapevolezza di comunità storica che difendeva le proprie peculiarità. L'uso della lingua volgare significava conservare la continuità con le generazioni anteriori e mantenere un profondo segno distintivo. Rende una buona testimonianza la comune espressione nei testi castigliani *nuetro español / mi español*, chiaramente esposto da Carlo V nel suo discorso a Roma. Il nuovo sentimento aveva anche aspetti extralinguistici, che furono potenziati dalla emozione provocata nella mentalità del tempo dalla scoperta dell'America. L'America era la grande novità che metteva in discussione i postulati dell'Antichità e li sostituiva, perché veniva ormai a mancare quella verità che fino ad allora era stata indiscussa. Citarli serviva soltanto ad avvalorare di più il nuovo, e così, come sosteneva José Antonio Maravall, il mito degli antichi si dissipò mentre i nuovi tempi li superavano.[18] Di qui l'orgoglio di sentirse superiori nella politica, nella tecnica, nel pensiero, perché si manifestava un universo nuovo non de-

---

[16] Luis Gil, *Panorama social del humanismo español (1500–1800)* (Madrid, 1981), 286.

[17] Juan de Mariana, "Historia General de España," *Biblioteca de Autores Españoles* (Madrid, 1950), LI.

[18] José Antonio Maravall, *Antiguos y modernos* (Madrid, 1986), 404ff.

scritto prima nella lingua latina.

Certamente quando Machiavelli parlava della Germania poteva citare Tacito ignorando l'opera di Enea Silvio Piccolomini, ma sulle *isole recentemente scoperte nel mare Indico* non si disponeva di fonti antiche, per cui quando ci si riferiva all'Antichità, si voleva far notare il parallelismo fra il mondo antico ed il mondo moderno, fra l'impero romano e l'impero spagnolo, fra il latino ed il castigliano ..., perché era anche evidente il concetto che definiva la lingua come la compagna del potere, concetto bene argomentato da Antonio di Nebrija nella sua grammatica. Ma questo sentimento di superamento dei classici non rimase circoscritto solo alla Spagna, qualcosa di simile sentirono altri scrittori; lo stesso Sebastian Brant, quando parlava della stupidità degli umani, si riferiva anche all'errore di Plinio.[19]

Nonostante tutto quello che abbiamo detto, la diplomazia spagnola della fine del XV secolo sviluppò alcuni elementi propagandistici, in cui giocò un ruolo veramente importante l'elemento italiano. Generalmente quei libri erano scritti o tradotti in latino, in entrambi i casi gli autori erano italiani vicini ai circoli ispanofili di Roma. A questo punto è interessante considerare un esempio abbastanza esplicativo del meccanismo utilizzato in tutto il processo di divulgazione che andava dalla corte spagnola, il luogo protagonista, a Roma, centro importantissimo della diplomazia dei re cattolici, per arrivare finalmente alle corti d'Europa attraverso tipografie romane oppure tedesche.

C'è un incunabolo francese della Bibliothèque Nationale di Parigi che traduce un compendio latino degli ultimi episodi della Guerra di Granata.[20] È interessante soffermarsi sulle informazioni fornite dal traduttore francese circa il processo compiuto per realizzare la versione latina e divulgare il contenuto del compendio. Riferisce infatti nella introduzione come giunsero le notizie a Roma e come lì i protonotari spagnoli, Bernardino López di Carvajal e Juan Ruíz di Medina, incaricarono venti segretari di scrivere il testo in latino, che poi venne inviato alle corti d'Europa. Si seguì un procedimento simile con la lettera colombina tradotta da L. di Cosco, la cui edizione romana del 1493 fu seguita, fra le altre, da quella di Basilea del 1494 che raccoglieva nello stesso volume la commedia di Carlo Verardi su Granata.[21]

La diplomazia spagnola a Roma ebbe mezzi adeguati per patrocinare la divulgazione per tutta Europa dei successi spagnoli in anni cruciali per la Spagna, perché erano in gioco i territori italiani, la questione dell'Impero e la determinazione dei confini territoriali fra portoghesi e spagnoli nel Nuovo Mondo dopo il ritorno di Colombo. Il lavoro degli agenti spagnoli alla corte del Papa fu molto attivo ed ottenne i risultati sperati di fronte agli interessi francesi.

Tutto questo succedeva in Italia, ma il lavoro degli scrittori italiani si svolse anche alla corte di Spagna attraverso uomini di lettere come Marineo Siculo o Pietro

---

[19] Sebastian Brant, *Narrenschiff* (Basel, 1494).

[20] Georges Hamel, "Un incunable français relatif à la prise de Grenade," *Revue Hispanique* 36 (1916): 159ff.

[21] Ma. Dolores Rincón González, "La toma de Granada y el descubrimiento de América en la edición de Basilea de 1494," in *V Congreso Internacional de Historia de América* (Granada, 1992) 2: 29ff.

Martire di Angleria. Tutti sanno che una parte piuttosto importante e vasta della storiografia spagnola del tempo fu scritta da italiani e con ragione si lamentava Sebastián Fox Morcillo dell'assenza di scrittori spagnoli che avessero redatto le loro cronache in latino, perché era indegno che altre nazioni conoscessero la storia della Spagna soltano attraverso autori stranieri come Joannes Vasaeus, Paolo Giovio, il Sabellico, il Riccio, il Volterrano, ecc.[22] Ciò spiega il fatto che Iohannes Basilius Herold di Basilea nella sua opera storica, fra trenta nomi di autori italiani menziona soltanto uno spagnolo, Pedro Mejía, scrittore di una cronaca imperiale, da lui consultato del resto nella traduzione italiana di Lodovico Dolce.[23]

Oltre al procedimento già esposto, che faceva partire da Roma le notizie elaborate nel mezzo adeguato, gli eventi spagnoli conobbero altre vie per arrivare in Germania, per cui è opportuno sottolineare le relazioni italo—tedesche, che vanno dai contatti di Erasmo con l'Italia allo stanziamento di tedeschi nelle città italiane, senza dimenticare quelli che rimasero per un po' di tempo attratti dallo splendore del suo umanesimo, oppure dalla fama delle sue università. Fra questi ultimi, poiché attinente al tema che trattiamo, dobbiamo ricordare Jakob Locher, molto interessato al teatro e autore di alcuni drammi su temi di attualità. Locher abitò a Roma nel 1493 e, quando ritornò al suo paese, è molto probabile che portasse con sé un esemplare della *Historia Baetica*, la cui edizione di Basilea era stata fatta sotto la supervisione del suo maestro Sebastian Brant. Probabilmente anche il medico umanista Hartmann Schedel mosso dallo stesso interesse fece una copia manoscritta di quella commedia nel 1495; Schedel raccolse, inoltre, documenti relativi a Granata e una serie di drammi umanistici. Nella stessa direzione, Nicolas Gerbel, dopo il suo soggiorno a Venezia ed il suo dottorato a Bologna, abitò a Strasburgo e fu collaboratore di Matthias Schürer, tipografo che lavorò più di tutti per la diffusione dell'umanesimo in quella città; nei primi anni della sua attività stampò undici opere, di cui sette di umanisti tedeschi ed italiani, fra cui Francesco Filelfo, Pomponio Leto, Marcellino Verardi, autore con Carlo Verardi della commedia sull'attentato del re a Barcellona, *Fernandus Servatus*. Anche Peter Schott dopo il soggiorno a Bologna ed in altri centri d'Italia abitò a Selestat e si lamentò della rozzezza di quella zona ricordandosi del tempo vissuto in Italia. In seguito, con l'arrivo di Sebastian Brant, in Alsazia si assistette ad un gran fiorire dell'Umanesimo.

Oltre a queste connessioni, forti furono i legami che crearono i tedeschi stabilitisi in Italia come tipografi, alcuni dei quali introdussero la stampa in diverse città: è il caso di Sixtus Riessinger di Gulz a Napoli, e poi a Roma. Berthold Rihing e Basilius di Argentaria lavorarono a Napoli, a Venezia Florentinus di Strasburgo, a Bologna Nicolas Gerbel. A Roma, da dove partirono quasi tutte le edizioni dei libri cui si è fatto riferimento, visse Eucharius Silber e nella sua tipografia furono stampati la maggioranza di quei testi ed altri pure di propaganda spagnola, benché di minore diffusione, come una serie di discorsi commemorativi dei successi spagnoli.

Universidad de Granada

---

[22] Sebastián Fox Morcillo, *De historiae institutione dialogus* (Basel, 1570) 2: 813.

[23] Joseph Basilius Herold, *De bello sacro continuata historia* (Basel, 1560).

Le Séjour d'Olivier de Magny à Rome
(mars 1555–octobre 1556)
et l'influence de l'Humanisme italien
sure ses Odes de 1559

FRANÇOIS ROUGET

Olivier de Magny, poète important de "La Pléiade" et trop négligé de la critique, avait comme bon nombre de ses condisciples fait le voyage de Rome. Peu après le départ de Joachim Du Bellay, il quitte Paris et accompagne en qualité de secrétaire Jean d'Avanson, Président du Conseil privé du Roi, nommé ambassadeur auprès du Vatican, afin de défendre les intérêts français auprès du Pape Jules III.

Magny y retrouve alors ses camarades qu'il recense dans ses *Souspirs*, publiés à son retour (en 1557), et il se met au service des cardinaux français et de d'Avanson. Il réalise ainsi des travaux d'écriture (lettres et documents juridiques) qui ne l'enchantent guère et qui l'inciteront à se plaindre. En cela, les *Souspirs* de Magny et les *Regrets* de Du Bellay participent d'une même expérience de l'échec.[1]

Pourtant, cela serait sans compter l'enthousiasme poétique et la curiosité dont font preuve les deux compères à Rome. Comme Du Bellay, Magny met à profit son séjour romain pour tisser des liens nouveaux avec des protecteurs potentiels, et surtout, il redécouvre la littérature italienne composée en latin.

C'est l'impact des lectures latines de Magny sur ses trois premiers livres des *Odes* que nous nous proposons de définir maintenant.

I. L'activité littéraire
On peut diviser l'activité littéraire de Magny pendant ses dix-huit mois de pré-

---

[1] Voir respectivement Magny, *Souspirs*, éd. D. Wilkin (Genève: Droz, 1978), XIII, CXXXVIII, et Du Bellay, *Regrets*, éd. M. Screech (Genève: Droz, 1966), XV, XLVIII, LXXXV–LXXXVI, et *passim*.

sence à Rome, et peut-être à Ferrare, en trois champs principaux.

D'une part, une activité de rédaction impersonnelle et immédiate, diplomatique et juridique importante, dont témoignent les archives des fonds français à la Bibliothèque Nationale de France et celles du Vatican. Cette écriture, qui se réduit à un effort mécanique de copie sous la dictée des cardinaux d'Armagnac et de Tournon, et de Jean d'Avanson, constituait le pain quotidien du poète. Du Bellay évoque en des termes saisissants cette fonction fastidieuse et ressentie comme dégradante.[2] Magny reste plus discret, d'autant qu'il a su tirer avantage de ce rôle de subalterne. Sur l'initiative de son protecteur d'Avanson, qui interviendra auprès du Roi en sa faveur, il obtiendra la charge de Contrôleur extraordinaire des Guerres à l'automne de 1556. Par ailleurs, habitué à servir sous la dictée de protecteurs multiples (déjà avant 1554, il avait copié la traduction de l'*Iliade* par Hugues Salel),[3] Magny ne semble pas avoir souffert autant que son compatriote Du Bellay, revenu lui de ses illusions.

La deuxième forme d'écriture à Rome, à laquelle Magny semble s'être joint, est la poésie satirique clandestine. Les pasquils ou pasquinades, ces pièces en vers latins, italiens et français, qui circulaient sous le manteau, prenaient pour cible les vices de la papauté. Caraffa, Del Monte, et d'autres, se voient ridiculisés férocement. Ces pièces, dispersées, figurent entre autres dans les fonds de la B. N. F.[4] Ainsi, dans le Fonds Dupuy (n°. 736), on trouve des pasquils français anonymes rédigés de 1554 à 1561, et d'autres signés de la main de Du Bellay. L'un, daté de janvier 1555, remanié par la suite, constituera le sonnet 113 des *Regrets*.[5] Et sur un autre feuillet, on observe la copie manuscrite du futur sonnet 86 du même recueil. Quant à Magny, il paraît s'être inspiré de pièces françaises et latines recensées dans la Collection Gaignières (B. N. F., Fonds fr. 25567) pour composer son ode satirique "Sur la mort de Jules Pape troisième" (*Odes*, II.9). On y retrouve, dans les premiers vers, les jeux de mots favoris sur le nom de Del Monte ("monté/feinte bonté/dévale") et tous les traits de la perversité légendaire de ce pape, mort fin mars 1555.

Enfin, la troisième dimension de l'activité littéraire de Magny à Rome, la plus personnelle mais aussi à la concrétisation la moins immédiate, concerne la production poétique proprement dite. Nous disons la moins immédiate parce qu'elle s'inscrit dans un effort d'innutrition et de refonte, et dans une chaîne de communication plus lente. Ce n'est qu'en 1557 et 1559 que Magny publiera les *Souspirs* et les cinq livres des *Odes* qu'il avait partiellement rédigés à Rome.

Magny alors écrit beaucoup, échange des vers avec Du Bellay; ils se consultent, se conseillent mutuellement, et il n'est pas étonnant de constater de multiples rapproche-

---

[2] Voir les *Regrets*, *passim*.

[3] Magny avait collaboré à la traduction française de l'*Iliade* pour les dix premiers livres, mais c'est lui aussi qui en éditera les livres XI et XII à la mort de Salel (*Les Unziesme et douzieme livres de l'Iliade d'Homère* . . . [Paris: V. Sertenas, 1554]).

[4] Voir aussi G. Dickinson, *Du Bellay in Rome* (Leiden: Brill, 1960), qui en recense quelques-unes aux pages 147–153.

[5] Voir à la B.N.F., Mss., Fonds fr., Dupuy, no. 736, fol. 236 r. Le vers 14 du sonnet des *Regrets* ("A Dagaut") s'adressait à l'origine à un destinataire anonyme: "Voilà mon bon Seigneur des nouvelles de Rome." Voir aussi *ibid.* (fol. 235v–236r), la copie manuscrite du sonnet 86.

ments entre les deux œuvres, notamment à propos de leurs sources néo-latines.[6]

II. L'influence néo-latine sur les *Odes* de 1559

Magny, lecteur curieux, fait feu de tout bois dans ses *Odes*. Il imite et traduit parfois le *Zodiacus Vitae* de Marcel Palingène; à l'occasion il le cite, comme dans l'ode "Au cardinal Georges d'Armaignac" (I.8). Mieux, c'est sans doute à cette époque qu'il avait conçu le dessein de traduire l'œuvre de Stellatus. Il en parle dans une ode "A Jean Du Thier" (I.9), mais cette traduction ne nous est pas parvenue.[7]

Outre les développements didactiques de Palingène, Magny a retenu dans ses odes le fonds iconographique puisé chez Alciat. Absent de ses œuvres antérieures, puis intégré dans les vers pour sa valeur morale, il devient dans le recueil de 1559 une vignette poétique à part entière, traitée pour elle-même. Dans l'ode "Du Temps et de l'Occasion" (II.8), Magny reprend l'emblème "In Occasionem" d'Alciat (*Embl.*, 1536, XVI) pour souligner sa portée didactique, cela au moyen des commentaires des scoliastes G. Corrozet, Le Fèvre et La Perrière. Rejetant la prosopopée ou le dialogisme, Magny met l'accent sur la description et sur la glose empruntée surtout à Le Fèvre. Alors que cette ode constituait en 1555 la deuxième partie d'une ode plus longue à Louise Labé (la première étant composée de l'ode "A Antoine Fumée" [II.6]), elle se voit séparée, isolée de son contexte, comme si l'auteur avait voulu redonner à l'emblème sa valeur morale et lui restituer toute sa dimension visuelle.[8]

III. La redécouverte des *Carmina quinque illustrium poetarum*

Nous voudrions clore ce survol de l'influence de la littérature néo-latine italienne avec la poésie, et en particulier avec les anthologies, parce que ce sont elles qui ont le plus contribué à façonner la poésie votive et rustique du troisième livre des *Odes* de Magny.

Si l'on connaît bien maintenant l'impact des anthologies poétiques italiennes renaissantes en langue vernaculaire, et notamment le rôle joué par les anthologies Giolito dans l'expansion et la connaissance des Italiens en France,[9] en revanche on s'est peu penché sur l'imitation des Néo-Latins réunis dans les anthologies.

L'une des plus importantes est celle des *Carmina quinque illustrium poetarum*, parue à Lyon en 1548, augmentée en 1549 à Florence ainsi qu'en 1552, et rééditée jusqu'en 1756! De plus, une version de cette anthologie paraîtra à Paris, chez Nicolas Le Riche (s.d.), sous le titre de *Doctissimorum nostra aetate italorum epigrammata*. C'est dire la fortune de ce florilège regroupant les œuvres de Bembo, Castiglione, Navagero, Flaminio, Cotta, et d'autres ensuite.

---

[6] À ce sujet, voir l'"Introduction" des *Souspirs*, éd. citée, p. 12–15.

[7] Sur ce point, voir mon article "Les sources et les imitations dans les trois premiers livres des *Odes* d'Olivier de Magny (1559)," *Bulletin de l'Histoire de la Renaissance* 56, 2 (1994): 396–397.

[8] *Bulletin de l'Histoire de la Renaissance* 56, 2 (1994): 397–398.

[9] Voir notamment l'excellente étude de M.-F. Piéjus, "Lecture et écriture selon des anthologies poétiques au XVIe siècle en Italie," in: *L'Écrivain face à son public en France et en Italie à la Renaissance*, Actes du Colloque International de Tours (1986), éd. C. A. Fiorato et J.-C. Margolin (Paris: Vrin, 1989), p. 337–358.

Ces textes étaient connus en France avant le séjour romain de Du Bellay et de Magny. Ronsard, dans son *Bocage* de 1554, avait déjà traduit ou adapté quelques-unes des pièces de Naugerius.[10] Mais c'est véritablement à Rome, où la vogue des Néo-Latins est à son apogée, que l'Angevin et le Quercynois les redécouvrent.[11]

Deux Italiens ont la faveur de nos poètes: Navagero et Flaminio. Les poésies latines du premier "étaient dans toutes les mains, quand Du Bellay fit le voyage d'Italie" (H. Chamard),[12] et elles ont laissé une trace certaine sur les pièces légères et badines de Magny. Bien que Jules Favre, son biographe, ne mentionne nulle part le nom de Navagero et son rôle dans la création poétique du poète français,[13] son influence n'est pas négligeable dans le livre III des *Odes*.

Comme Du Bellay, avec lequel il partage le choix des emprunts à Navagero,[14] Magny adapte plus qu'il ne traduit littéralement. Ainsi, la série des vœux à Pan (III.14), à Vénus (III.18), à Palès (III.15), imite respectivement les pièces "Lyconis vota Pani Deo," "Vota Veneri ad felicitandos amantium amores" et "Vota Telesonis Cereri, Baccho et Pali Deae." Mais, à l'occasion, Magny se libère de son modèle en pratiquant une technique littéraire qui lui est chère: la contamination. Ainsi, le "Vœu à Venus" (III.18) semble fusionner plusieurs passages de trois groupes de vœux de Navagero: "Vota Veneri...," déjà cités, et les "Vota Veneri, ut amantibus faveat" (poème auquel Magny emprunte le thème central) et "Ad Venerem, ut pertinacem Lalagem molliat," qui offre à notre poète l'idée de la promesse d'offrandes. La dernière strophe saphique de Navagero:

> Spargam odoratas violas, rosasque
> Ipse ego, votique reus secabo
> Grata torquate ante tuas columbae
> Guttura flammas.

se voit rendue par ce dernier sizain en français:

> Mais bien j'iray à ton honneur,
> Si par toy j'ay tant de bon heur,
> T'apporter des rozes nouvelles,
> Des œilletz freschement cueilliz,

---

[10] *Cf. Œuvres complètes*, éd. P. Laumonier (Paris: STFM, 1965), t. VI, pp. 14–18.

[11] *Cf.* entre autres, l'épître "A Monsieur d'Avanson" en tête des *Regrets*, où Du Bellay transpose Navagero (*Ex Philemone*, aux vv. 73 et suivants de l'épître, et dans le sonnet 52 des *Regrets*). Voir surtout les *Divers jeux rustiques* (1558) où l'Angevin adapte et traduit Navagero dans une série de pièces rustiques.

[12] Voir *Joachim Du Bellay (1522–1560)* (Lille, 1900; Genève: Slatkine Reprints, 1969), p. 407.

[13] *Cf. Olivier de Magny (1529?–1561), étude biographique et littéraire* (Paris: Garnier, 1885).

[14] Sur la vie et l'œuvre de Navagero (Naugerius), voir C. Maddison, *Apollo and the Nine: A History of the Ode* (London: Routledge and Kegan Paul, 1960), chap. 3, p. 98 et suiv., et ses *Lusus* dans *Carmina quinque illustrium poetarum* (Florence: L. Torrentium, 1549), p. 22 et *sqq.*; voir aussi les *Doctissimorum nostra aetate italorum epigrammata* (Paris: N. Le Riche, s.d.).

Des marguerites, et des lis
Avec un pair de Colombelles.

Autant Magny concentre en français et disperse librement les sources italiennes de Navagero dans ses poèmes, autant il suit fidèlement et dilue en français le latin de Flaminio. C'est d'ailleurs celui-ci que Magny imite avec le plus de bonheur et le plus de fréquence. C'est que le ton, la grâce et l'aisance "musicale" de l'Italien correspondaient parfaitement au tempérament du Français.[15]

Dans les *Odes* de 1559, Magny recourt à Flaminio à maintes reprises. Dans le livre I, l'ode "De la Santé" (I.8) est l'amplification d'une ode saphique de Flaminio, l'"Hymnus in bonam valetudinem," à laquelle s'ajoutent peut-être des réminiscences de Marot (premier imitateur de l'"Hymnus"), de Ronsard et de Du Bellay.[16] Mais ce qui distingue cette ode de Magny, c'est sa prolixité. À partir de sept strophes saphiques de Flaminio, on passe à douze quatrains hétérométriques chez Marot (le quatrain reproduisant le patron strophique latin) puis à 39 sizains d'octosyllabes chez Magny.[17] S'il traduit parfois le latin mot à mot, s'il suit fidèlement le texte d'origine, en revanche il ne peut contraindre son inspiration copieuse. La maladie du cardinal d'Armagnac (destinataire de l'ode) n'est qu'un prétexte à l'éloge et la source néo-latine une occasion pour disserter sur l'inconstance de la condition humaine. Au bout du compte, le canevas néo-latin disparaît sous une multitude de références mythologiques brodées à l'envi.

Mais parfois, Magny fait preuve de plus de mesure dans l'adaptation des vers de Flaminio. L'ode finale du livre I, "Aux Graces," provient directement de l'ode saphique "Ad Gratias" (*Carmina quinque...*, 1549, p. 134). Magny transpose le nom du destinataire: Farnese devient Marguerite. Et surtout il double le nombre de vers dans sa version: on passe ainsi de trois strophes saphiques à six quatrains isométriques. Par fidélité, l'invocation initiale (strophe 1), l'offrande (strophe 2) et la dédicace (strophe 3) se voient augmentées en proportion dans le texte français. Magny amplifie certes, mais parvient avec élégance à restituer les divers mouvements de la période oratoire latine et le glissement rhétorique qui part de la nomination, puis passe au don, pour finir sur l'éloge.

Avec une semblable réussite, Magny distribue une série de vœux dans le livre III. L'"Hymne de Bacchus" (III.12), bien que dominé par l'influence de Marulle, et les

---

[15] Sur M. A. Flaminio, on consultera, outre l'ouvrage cité de C. Maddison, la monographie qu'elle a consacrée à ce poète: *M. A. Flaminio, Poet, Humanist and Reformer* (Chapel Hill: Univ. of North Carolina Press, 1965). La critique souligne chez l'Italien son aisance et sa fidélité aux Anciens (p. 115). Voir aussi mon article cité, pp. 398–399. Et sur la vogue de Flaminio, voir Scévole de Sainte-Marthe, *Les Premières poésies* (Paris: F. Morel, 1569), "Complaintes pastorales traduites du latin de M. A. Flamin," p. 68 et *sqq.*

[16] Voir l'analyse de cette pièce dans notre article cité, p. 399.

[17] Voir aussi l'imitation que Scévole de Sainte-Marthe a faite de l'ode de Flaminio dans ses *Premières poésies* (1569), éd. citée, IV, fol. 112v–fol. 113v ("Chant de la santé": 13 sizains hétérométriques en 7-3-7-7-3-7/ffmf²f²m). Cette pièce fut aussi recensée dans sa traduction française de C. Marot (pour les 22 premiers vers) dans l'anthologie poétique de G. Corrozet, *Le Parnasse...* (Paris: Galiot et Corrozet, 1578) ("Santé," p. 118).

autres pièces bachiques (III.13 et 16) viennent tout droit des poèmes a-strophiques de Flaminio. Les six sizains de la première ode (III.13) amplifient par une richesse de détails descriptifs et comparatifs les 14 vers d'une pièce "Ad Bacchum."[18] La seconde, respectant la proportion des dix vers de Flaminio,[19] adapte en quatre quatrains la trame de l'ode latine et substitue au personnage de Pygmalion celui du "glouton Breton," ennemi encombrant de Magny et de Du Bellay[20] à Rome.

Outre cette série d'odes bachiques, Magny emprunte à Flaminio les registres familial et sentimental. Sur le modèle des pièces "Ad Joanum Antonium Flaminium patrem morientem" et "Ad Veturiam matrem, et Julium, et Faustum fratres mortuos,"[21] il compose les odes "A Michel de Magny, son pere mourant" (III.20) et "Sur le tombeau de Marguerite de Parra, sa mere" (III.21). Magny suit l'Italien pour le thème et le mouvement des vers, mais s'en écarte pour l'insertion de détails biographiques. La source latine fonctionne comme un déclencheur de l'expression lyrique, à partir d'une communauté de voix et d'émotions partagées.

Enfin, nous aimerions terminer cette étude comparée de Flaminio et de Magny en citant l'une des plus belles réussites poétiques de la source latine et de sa version en français. Nous faisons allusion à cette pièce en vers choliambiques et à refrain intitulée "Ad Agellum suum,"[22] et que Magny a rendue par "A sa demeure des champs" (III.19). Nous ne citons que le poème latin de Flaminio même si les deux pièces mériteraient d'être citées en totalité[23] tant elles parviennent, par le rythme et la musicalité intrinsèque au vers, à suggérer le bonheur rustique et la mélancolie:

> Formosa silva, vosque lucidi fontes,
> Et candidarum templa sancta Nympharum,
> Quam me beatum, quamque disputem acceptum,
> Si vivere, et mori in sinu queam uestro.
> Nunc me necessitas acerba longinquas
> Adire terras cogit, et peregrinis
> Corpusculum laboribus fatigare.
> At tu Diana, montis istius custos,
> Si saepe dulci fistula tuas laudes
> Cantavi, et aram floribus coronaui,
> Da cito Dea ad tuos redire secessus.
> Sed seu redibo, seu negauerint Parcae,
> Dum meminero mei, tui memor vivam,

---

[18] "Tu, qui centimanum potes gigantem" (*Carmina quinque* . . . , 1549, p. 151–152).

[19] "Ad Bacchum" ("Hanc vitem tibi dedico racemis"), *ibid.*, p. 148.

[20] *Cf.* Du Bellay, *Regrets*, sonnets 57 et 58.

[21] *Cf. Carmina quinque.* . . , 1549, p. 125–126.

[22] *Carmina quinque.* . . , 1549, p. 116: "Formosa silva, vosque lucidi fontes." Voir aussi d'autres pièces adressées au même lieu, p. 121–123.

[23] Pour le texte français de Magny, voir notre édition critique des *Trois premiers livres des Odes* (Genève: Droz, T.L.F. 459, 1995), p. 298–299.

Formosa silva, vosque lucidi fontes,
Et candidarum templa sancta Nympharum.

La pièce de Flaminio comporte quinze vers; celle de Magny quarante-deux. Les mêmes contours s'y dessinent. La vision du pays aimé, le vœu d'y mourir, la nécessité du départ, l'invocation et le vœu au retour, et le serment de fidélité au terroir, sont autant de mouvements qui ouvrent et referment ces pièces teintées de nostalgie. Si Flaminio trouve dans le contre-point des vers 1–4 et 12–15 une forme de balancement rhétorique et rythmique propre à rendre cette idée de va-et-vient vers la terre natale, Magny de son côté accentue les effets d'écho à la rime et de refrain pour conforter la circularité de la chanson et le repli souhaité dans le terroir du Quercy.

Si Carol Maddison note fort justement que l'ode "Ad Agellum suum" est une œuvre d'art maîtrisée, d'une grande beauté rythmique et conceptuelle, et l'un des chefs-d'œuvre de Flaminio dans la veine élégiaque,[24] on peut en dire autant de son imitateur et continuateur.

Magny aura trouvé en Flaminio l'âme sœur, tant recherchée. Comme d'autres couples de la littérature, Baudelaire-Poe, Nerval-Goethe, le duo Magny-Flaminio paraît exemplaire. Magny puise chez son modèle un exemple de beauté mais aussi les germes d'un lyrisme personnel à venir, à développer et à transmettre.

C'est paradoxalement en se tenant au plus près de sa source latine qu'il parvient à distinguer son poème, par la simplicité de l'expression, la grâce des images et la clarté des lignes.

Victoria College, Université de Toronto

---

[24] *Cf.* le commentaire de C. Maddison sur ce poème dans *M. A. Flaminio. . .* , pp. 69–70: "*Formosa silva* is one of Flaminio's masterpieces in the elegiac mood. . . . The language is simple, the outline is clean and the emotion is sincere."

The Celebrations for the Marriage of Sigismund I of Poland and Bona Sforza, Duchess of Bari

STEPHEN RYLE

The marriage in April 1518 of King Sigismund I, ruler of the Polish–Lithuanian confederacy, to Bona Sforza, granddaughter of Alfonso II, the Aragonese king of Naples, was certainly one of the most imaginative dynastic alliances in the entire pageant of European history. The union of two royal houses so distant in terms of geography, and yet both members of the cultural entity that constituted western Christendom, held out the hope of a splendid future for the Polish crown, combining the vigour of its Slav and Baltic heredity with the refinements of civilization embodied in the person of the young duchess. It was not a marriage contracted for the purpose of territorial aggrandisement: in the event Bona's claim to the Duchy of Bari proved to be a burden rather than an asset to the rulers of Poland during the succeeding two hundred years.[1] Rather it was the outcome of a combination of existing alliances, relationships, and common interests which had the effect of cementing the Polish kingdom even more firmly than it had been before into the western European sphere of influence, and of making it less likely that Poland would turn its back on the west and come under the domination of the ever-increasing power of Muscovy.

Sigismund's first wife, the Hungarian princess Barbara Zapolya, had died in October 1515 after giving birth to her second daughter. The king was already in his midforties, and there was now an increasingly urgent incentive for him to remarry in the hope of producing a male heir in order to maintain the political stability of eastern

---

[1] The most comprehensive biography of Bona Sforza is by W. Pociecha, *Królowa Bona*, 4 vols. (Poznań, 1949–1958). See also two articles in the collection entitled *La Regina Bona Sforza tra Puglia e Polonia. Atti del Convegno promosso dall'Associazione Culturale "Regina Bona Sforza" . . . Bari, Castello Svevo, 27 aprile 1980* (Wrocław, 1987): G. Pinto, "Bona Sforza duchessa di Bari e regina di Polonia," pp. 5–15, and G. Cioffari, "Bona Sforza. Aspetti religiosi ed umanitari della sua personalità," pp. 62–106.

Europe. Within a few months of Barbara's death the emperor Maximilian I had begun to urge Sigismund to look for a new bride. At first the king declared that the wound of his bereavement was too recent to allow him to contemplate the prospect of remarrying;[2] but eventually, after his forces had consolidated their positions on the eastern frontier, he yielded to the promptings of his advisers, and the search for a second wife began.

The earliest candidate to be considered was Eleanor of Austria, granddaughter of Maximilian and elder sister of Charles, the young king of Spain.[3] This idea was promoted by the emperor himself and was supported by Piotr Tomicki, the Polish vice-chancellor.[4] However, the anti-Hapsburg faction among the Polish aristocracy, led by Jan Łaski, the archbishop of Gniezno, proposed the daughter of Anna Radziwiłł, duchess of Mazovia. If Sigismund had agreed to this suggestion, the monarchy's ties with the Lithuanian nobility would have been strengthened; but such a decision would also have implied a turning-away from the policy of identifying Poland ever more closely with western Europe, and the king was firmly opposed to it.[5]

The name of Bona Sforza was added to the list of potential brides during the summer of 1516. Bona's father Gian Galeazzo Sforza had been ousted from the succession to the Duchy of Milan which was rightfully his by Ludovico il Moro, and after Gian Galeazzo's death in 1494 his widow Isabella of Aragon attempted to regain the title for Bona, her sole surviving child, by means of marriage-alliances. When these plans proved fruitless, the emperor, whose second wife Bianca Maria had been Gian Galeazzo's sister, persuaded Isabella to agree to the suggestion that Bona should be considered as an alternative candidate to fulfil the role of consort to the Polish king. The idea seems to have been proposed initially by one of Maximilian's most trusted councillors, Sigmund von Herberstein, who was later to gain a distinguished place in the annals of ethnography for his account of the way of life of the people of Muscovy.[6] Herberstein's proposal was eagerly seconded by Joannes Dantiscus, the Polish ambassador to the empire.[7] Dantiscus had virtually been adopted as his own envoy by Maximilian, who had sent him on three missions to Venice to negotiate

---

[2] *Acta Tomiciana: Epistole. Legationes. Responsa . . . Sigismundi . . . Primi, Regis Polonie . . .* , 17 vols., (Poznań, etc., 1852–1966) (hereafter *A.T.*), IV:37.

[3] For Eleanor of Austria, see P. G. Bietenholz and T. B. Deutscher (eds.) *Contemporaries of Erasmus. A Biographical Register of the Renaissance and Reformation*, 3 vols. (Toronto, 1985–1987) (hereafter *CEBR*), 1:426–427.

[4] *A.T.* IV:38. See also A. Le Glay, *Correspondance de l'empereur Maximilien I' et de Marguerite d'Autriche* (Paris, 1839), II:299–301. For Tomicki, see *CEBR* 3:327–329.

[5] *A.T.* IV:39, 48–49, 51–54. See also Pinto, "Bona Sforza duchessa di Bari e regina di Polonia" (above, n. 1), 9–10.

[6] For Herberstein, see *Neue Deutsche Biographie* (Berlin, 1953–) (hereafter *NDB*), 8:579–580. See also the letter written to Herberstein by Isabella of Aragon printed in the edition of Herberstein's 'Selbstbiographie' by T. G. von Karajan, *Fontes Rerum Austriacarum, Scriptores* I (Vienna, 1855), 111–112, and *A.T.* IV:223. Herberstein's *Rerum Moscovitarum Commentarii* were first printed at Vienna in 1549.

[7] For Dantiscus, see most recently J. IJsewijn and W. Bracke (eds.), *Joannes Dautiscus (1485–1548): Polish Ambassador and Humanist* (Brussels, 1996).

terms of peace and had bestowed on him a grant of nobility, a doctorate of Laws, and the poet's laurel, the first awarded to a "Sarmatian." Despite Tomicki's scorn at the suggestion of Bona's name,[8] Sigismund wrote to the members of his council in October 1516, outlining the merits of the two ladies and the advantages each might bring in the form of a dowry.[9] He stated that the emperor had offered to bring them together at Vienna or elsewhere so that Sigismund could examine them for himself and make his choice.[10] Tomicki even raised the possibility of a third candidate in the person of Mary Tudor, sister of the English king Henry VIII, who had recently been left a widow through the death of her husband of a few months, Louis XII of France.[11] She, however, promptly took her fate into her own hands by marrying Charles Brandon, duke of Suffolk.

During the early months of 1517 Sigismund made clear to the emperor his preference for Eleanor and expressed the hope that arrangements for the marriage could be finalised when the year's campaigning season was over.[12] But the emperor had failed to take into account either the anxieties of the Spanish and Burgundian nobles[13] or, it seems, the dynastic designs of Eleanor's brother Charles: the former were concerned that if Eleanor's brothers died without heirs, they might become subjects of a future king of Poland, and Charles was determined that his sister should marry the king of Portugal in the hope of achieving the dream of uniting the Iberian peninsula under a single monarch. When he became aware of these objections Sigismund wasted no more time in making up his mind. He would marry Bona Sforza, a decision made all the easier as a result of the arrival in Vilnius of a mission from Isabella that included Bona's former tutor, Crisostomo Colonna, bringing with him a portrait of Bona.[14]

The wedding preparations were set in hand straightaway, and Sigismund despatched an embassy to Bari. It arrived there on 5 November, only to find that Bona and her mother had left a few days earlier for Naples, where Isabella had arranged a splendid celebration. The bride eventually sailed with her retinue from Manfredonia at the end of December, landed at Fiume on the Istrian peninsula, and then made her way overland to Cracow, where she was received by the king on 15 April. The marriage was solemnized three days later.

Our knowledge concerning the celebrations associated with the wedding is derived principally from the extremely detailed account of the events written in Latin prose by Justus Ludovicus Decius and dedicated to Tomicki.[15] Such an auspicious

---

[8] *A.T.* IV:55–56.

[9] *A.T.* IV:46.

[10] *A.T.* IV:46.

[11] *A.T.* IV:50.

[12] *A.T.* IV:177–178, 178–180.

[13] Sigismund to Krzystof Szydlowiecki, *A.T.* IV:199.

[14] Ibid.: "praeterea venit cum nuncio secretarius matris ipsius virginis et imaginem eius attulit, que nobis bene placet."

[15] *Diarii et earum quae memoratu digna . . . nuptiis gesta . . . Descriptio* (Cracow, 1518), reprinted in *A.T.* IV:298–327. For Decius' career, see *CEBR* 1:380–382.

occasion was bound to attract representatives from a very wide range of communities, large and small, and among the distinguished guests or included in their retinues were many humanists whose presence added a literary lustre to the dazzling splendour of the festivities. It is difficult to think of any other occasion which would have brought together humanists from such a diverse geographical area, embracing as it did the nations of eastern and central Europe as well as Naples, Rome, and many other Italian city-states.

Eight poems written to celebrate the marriage are recorded, of which four have appeared in print. Six of the eight, including all the printed works, are mentioned by Decius in the preface to his account of the wedding:

> nam quis Andrea Cricio nepote tuo concentu moduloque auditus unquam dulcior? quis Hieronymo Balbo doctior? Laurentio Corvino quis venustior? Vrsino Gasparo quis facundior? Dantisco Joanne quis eleganti ubertate copiosior? Agricolaque quis gravior esse poterit? qui omnes Epithalamiis aut ceteris lucubrationibus suis perpetue memorie hec memoranda condonabunt.[16]

The first to compose his epithalamium was Andrzej Krzycki, Tomicki's nephew, whose poem consisted of 351 hexameters.[17] He was followed by Laurentius Corvinus, who composed a pair of poems, the first in 110 lines of elegiacs and the second, an invocation to Fama, in 51 hexameters.[18] The third surviving poem, by Caspar Ursinus Velius in 337 hexameters, appeared at the head of his collected edition of poetry in five books printed by Froben at Basel in March 1522. Velius probably participated in the celebrations as one of the attendants on Johannes Thurzo, the bishop of Wrocław. The last of the epithalamia to be published, and by some distance the longest, was that by Joannes Dantiscus. Dantiscus never issued it during his lifetime but made alterations and additions up to 1535 or even later. As preserved, it consists of 679 hexameters and has two alternative endings. It was first printed by Stanislaw Skimina in his edition of Dantiscus' poems, published in 1950.[19]

However, in addition to Decius' account and the four surviving epithalamia, we hear of four further poems that are no longer extant. Several sources besides Decius indicate that an epithalamium was composed by Rudolf Agricola the Younger,[20] and its apparent loss constitutes from certain points of view the most unfortunate gap in our knowledge about the celebrations. Agricola was the leading humanist based in Cracow at this period, and his poem, to judge from the recommendation expressed by Corvinus in the final couplet of his *Ad Famam*, would have provided at the very

---

[16] Decius, ibid.: *A.T.* IV:298.

[17] *Epithalamium Divi Sigismundi Regis et Inclitae Bonae Reginae Poloniae*, in *Andreae Cricii Carmina*, ed. C. Morawski (*Corpus antiquissimorum poetarum Poloniae latinorum*, 3 [Cracow, 1888]), 62–75. For Krzycki's career, see *CEBR* 2:275–278.

[18] For Laurentius Corvinus, see *NDB* 3:372. His poems on the marriage of Sigismund I and Bona Sforza are printed in *A.T.* IV:292–296.

[19] *Ioannis Dantisci Carmina*, ed. S. Skimina (*Corpus antiquissimorum poetarum Poloniae latinorum*, 7) (Cracow, 1950), 99–132.

[20] For Rudolf Agricola the Younger, see *NDB* 1:103.

least a verse counterpart to Decius' description of the arrival of the bride and her entourage and presumably much more besides. Corvinus ends his invocation to Fama with the following verses:

> Sed non ante redi, quam tu diffuderis omnes
> Per maris et terra tractus et splendida regis
> Facta Sigismundi et regali hymeneon honore
> Magna quoque edideris large convivia mense,
> Extulerisque Bonam Latia de sede profectam
> Laudibus egregiis nulli in bonitate secundam
> Reginam et magno passim memoraveris ore.
> Quo redimita modo? et quanto regina triumpho?
> Quo splendore potens Graccovinam ingressa sit urbem
> Rudolphi Agricole disces de carmine vatis.[21]

As it is we possess only Agricola's liminary verses prefacing Decius' account to mark his poetic contribution to the events:

> Connubii sacra regalis, magnumque paratum
> Et causam, ingressum, principiumque leges.
> Qualis erat splendor, quae magnificentia Regis
> SISMVNDI et populi quam numerosa cohors.
> Vsque etiam ad malum Decius bene scribit ab ovo,
> In re cui tali est indubitata fides.
> Huic sunt perque annos perspecta negocia multos,
> Regia non ullos plenius acta refert.
> Barbara si ponit quandoque vocabula, linguae
> Dissona Romanae, res quoque talis erat.
> Interdum licet eloquio rem scribere, doctis
> Displiceat quamvis nec suboletque, rudi
> Simplicitas veri eloquium non suaue requirit,
> Haec etenim nuda est, nec phalerata placet.[22]

Our only information about the second of the lost poems comes from Decius' preface. He refers to a composition by the Venetian humanist Girolamo Balbi (Hieronymus Balbus), who was present at the festivities in the role of Hungarian ambassador. Decius' account gives him special mention, and states that he was accompanied by twenty-six knights.[23] It is possible that Balbi's description of the wedding, if it was ever completed, was not a poem at all, but one of the *ceterae lucubrationes* referred to by Decius.

The third of the missing compositions, in this case definitely a poem, is the most intriguing of all, and probably the most serious loss as far as scholarship is concerned.

---

[21] Laurentius Corvinus, *Ad Famam* 42–51, *A.T.* IV:296.

[22] Decius, *Diarii . . . Descriptio*, 1518, a1v.

[23] *A.T.* IV:310.

Melchior von Watt, one of the brothers of the Swiss humanist and later leading reformer from Sankt Gallen better known by the Latin form of his name as Joachim Vadianus, wrote to Joachim from Cracow a week after the wedding, mentioning Krzycki's poem, which had already apparently reached Joachim in Vienna. He also stated that poems by Corvinus, Dantiscus, Agricola, and Ursinus were due to be published, as well as one written by Celius, "omnium doctissimus," who was full of praise and admiration for Joachim.[24] This Celius is none other than Celio Calcagnini, who together with Ludovico Ariosto was present at the proceedings among the company of over 350 attendants upon Cardinal Ippolito d'Este.[25] Calcagnini's epithalamium was not included in the edition of his Carmina published along with those of Giovanni Battista Pigna and the Latin poems of Ariosto at Venice in 1553. Perhaps he did not in the end compose one: if he did, its rediscovery would be of great interest.[26]

The remaining lost poem, which must have been the earliest of all the compositions to be written and printed, was by Vadianus himself,[27] who at that time held the chair of Rhetoric at the University of Vienna. He would undoubtedly have witnessed the arrival of the bride-to-be and her party in that city towards the end of February, and he may even have been the author of the "learned and lengthy" speech delivered by the Viennese academy and later printed, which is referred to by Decius.[28] During March Vadianus had an elegiac poem celebrating the wedding printed in Vienna, and another edition was produced in Cracow on 15 April, the day of Bona's arrival, by Hieronymus Vietor.[29] Possibly these were both unique copies which have failed to survive.

Of the four extant poetic contributions to the festivities the pair of poems by Laurentius Corvinus carries the least weight in terms of literary significance. His elegiac poem is divided into two halves of which the second consists of a retelling of the legend concerning the foundation of the city of Cracow; and his hexameter invocation to Fama serves essentially as an invitation to read Agricola's lost epithalamium.

Krzycki's is in many ways the most accomplished of the surviving poems. Both he and Dantiscus include extensive passages devoted to King Sigismund's military prowess. Although such a procedure can easily be justified in terms of the conventions of the genre as constituting an encomium of the bridegroom to match that of the bride, it tends to give both poems the character as much of *epyllion* as of *epithalamion*. This

---

[24] "Nuptiarum pompam celebrem admodum Corvinus, Dantiscus, Agricola, Ursinus et omnium doctissimus ille Celius carmine hominibus vulgabunt. Cricii versum, ut puto, legisti. Celius non satis laudare te potest unquam; usque adeo Vadianum suum et amat et admiratur." E. Arbenz (ed.), *Vadianische Briefsammlung* (St. Gallen, 1890–1913), I, no. 119, p. 215 (139).

[25] For Calcagnini, see *Dizionario Biografico degli Italiani* (Rome, 1960–), 16:492–498.

[26] Pociecha (above, n. 1) prints Calcagnini's effusive letter of thanks to his Polish host Jakub Staszkowski written at the end of November 1518. This mentions Krzycki's epithalamium but does not refer to one composed by Calcagnini himself: *Królowa Bona* I:275–277.

[27] For Vadianus, see *CEBR* 3:364–365.

[28] Decius, *A.T.* IV:302.

[29] K. Estreicher, *Bibliografia Polska* (Cracow, 1938), 32:187.

aspect is even more clearly marked in the case of Dantiscus' poem, owing to its larger scale. Each poem may be aptly illustrated by its passage describing the effect of Bona's portrait on Sigismund. Krzycki's runs as follows:

It cita in Hesperiam Cypris, cita Iuno sub Arcton,
Caesaris ante omnes Pallas tamen urget ad aulam
Officiumque suum satagit prior ipsa subire.
Quae dum iussa Iovis, dum munus perficit omne,
Pingitur interea facies divina puellae
Sfortines dextram Paphia ducente magistri
Et miscente charin, multumque cupidinis arti.
Namque et consiliis et rebus utrimque paratis
Mittitur ad terras Helices celer aureus ore
Nuntius et vatum Sirenis gloria regni,
Qui meruit tanti sponsor, qui pronubus esse
Coniugii, fido fretus fultusque patrono,
Praesule navigero vestri huius laude senatus.
Ille ubi pervenit, qua tristi Vilia fonte
Lapsa suae liquidis Vilnae coniungitur undis
Et simul exitium miseri testantur amoris,
Egregie mandata refert simulacraque pandit,
E quibus absconsus per lumina nigra Cupido
Provolat extemplo et cordis penetralia prendit.
Miratur princeps formam praeque omnibus effert
Saepeque nunc recipit, sola nunc parte recondit,
Quoque magis spectat, tacitum magis haurit amorem.
Sic ignara dei Dido cum tractat Iulum
Et vulnus venis et caecum carpserat ignem.
Denique cum sublime genus teque, inclite Caesar,
Tum raram meditans, sua magna incendia, formam
Dat victas rex iste manus, quas tota tremiscit
Sarmatiae fera gens vicinaque cuncta potestas.[30]

The equivalent passage in Dantiscus' epithalamium comes as the climax of a description of Bona's beauty, her gifts of personality, and her distinguished descent. The first five lines of this extract refer to Sigmund von Herberstein and the next six to Dantiscus himself, indicating the influence the two men exerted in bringing about the betrothal. The god Mars is addressing Sigismund:

Haec est, quam caesar tibi Maximilianus habendam
Despondit per legatum, qui nomen honesto
De saxo sumit, cuius tibi cognita virtus
Atque fide pectus constans, industria sollers

---

[30] Krzycki, *Epithalamium*, 180–207.

> Sedulitasque animi magnis in rebus agendis.
> Hanc tibi, qui primus cinxit sua tempora lauro
> Sarmata, describens Augusti suasit ab aula
> Non contemnendam, quo tempore nuntius iret
> Ad Venetos toties, quos aequoreis palus ambit
> Circumfusa vadis, cum magno ut foedus inirent
> Caesare, perpessus discrimina mille viarum.
> Haec est, attonitus cuius simulacra repente
> Picta videns, tacitum cepisti in pectore vulnus,
> Miratusque oculosque, genas et rubra labella,
> Duxisti gemitus.[31]

The epithalamium by Caspar Ursinus Velius perhaps gives the reader a more immediate sense of the actual events of the wedding than any of the other poems. One section in particular fills out a detail mentioned by Decius in a way that conveys a vivid picture of what was experienced by those present. In describing the entry of the royal procession into Cracow, Decius refers to Bona as "equo pulcherrimo vecta":[32] Velius' passage illustrates both the spirit of the young woman as she retains control of the nervous animal and the admiration she arouses in the populace:

> Subiectos spectat populos, blandumque tuetur
> Spumanti sublimis equo: qualem neque ducit
> Cornipedum domitor melius, giratque per auras
> Cyllaron. ipse suo gestit sub pondere et auro
> Instratus sonipes, subterque volubilis errat,
> Argutum excutiens caput: illa gubernat euntem
> Hinc atque hinc animosa, suisque involvit habenis
> Rursum laxatis indulgens libera frenis:
> Arbitria aspectatque ducem gaudetque marito
> Et regi par ire suo. Stupet omnis et astat
> Turba virum, ac matres tantam mirantur equi vim
> Virginis ire manu, et digitis parere sedentis.[33]

This type of description is not found in extant Latin poetry before Statius. It was developed in later antiquity by poets like Claudian and Sidonius Apollinaris. Here Velius may possibly be recalling the preliminaries to the combat of Superbia and Mens Humilis in Prudentius' *Psychomachia*.[34] In such a passage Neo-Latin poetry reveals the catholicity of its creative accomplishment and illustrates its ability on many occasions to stand comparison with the poetry of the ancient world.

University of Leeds

---

[31] Dantiscus, *Epithalamium Reginae Bonae*, ed. S. Skimina, XXIV:378–392.

[32] Decius, *A.T.* IV:305.

[33] Caspar Ursinus Velius, *Epithalamion . . . Sigismundi Regis Poloniae et inclytae Reginae Bonae*, 258–269 (1522 ed., c2).

[34] Prudentius, *Psych.* 190–200.

The Humanist Books of Bishop Richard Fox Given to Corpus Christi College in 1528

RICHARD J. SCHOECK

The library of Corpus Christi College, Oxford was praised, rather extravagantly, by Erasmus in a letter from Louvain to John Claymond, the first president of the college that had been founded in 1517, although it was years in the planning.[1] Erasmus's letter is dated 27 June 1519, and it is epistle 990; there Erasmus writes:

> Many parts of the world owe their renown to some famous monument. It was the vast Colossus gave Rhodes its fame, Caria owes it to the sepulchre of Mausolus, Memphis to the Pyramids, Cnidus to its statue of Venus, Thebes to its magical figure of Memnon. I foresee that in days to come this college, like some most holy temple sacred to all that is best in literature, will be reckoned all over the world to be one of the chief glories of Britain, and that more men will be drawn to Oxford by the spectacle of that library rich in the three tongues, where no good author is lacking, and no bad one finds a place, than

---

[1] It is not absolutely clear when Bishop Richard Fox began to plan for the foundation of a collegiate institution at Oxford, but I would date the thinking about it at the time of his serving with Bishop John Fisher in establishing St. John's College, Cambridge, as two of the executors of the estate of Lady Margaret Beaufort in 1509. Perhaps the concept began to take place even earlier, while Fox was chancellor of the University of Cambridge in 1500—certainly, one must look to his friendship with Erasmus, whom he probably met in 1499–1505 and whom he hosted in 1505. The long process of shaping the statutes of Corpus Christi College, Oxford was well under way in 1515–1516, for Fox had obtained a royal license to found a Benedictine house of studies in the spring of 1513, and he had begun to acquire property for the site of his college as early as 1511. See J. McConica, "The Rise of the Undergraduate College," in *The History of the University of Oxford*, vol. III, *The Collegiate University*, ed. J. McConica (Oxford, 1986), 17–18; Thomas Fowler, *The History of Corpus Christi College* (Oxford, 1893); J. G. Milne, *The Early History of Corpus Christi College Oxford* (Oxford, 1946); and *Letters of Richard Fox 1486–1527*, ed. P. S. and H. M. Allen (Oxford, 1929).

ever were attracted to Rome in olden days by the prospect of so many mar-vels.[2]

One might call this letter an example of the rhetoric of extravagant praise, and far from the library being rich in the three tongues, there was only Reuchlin's *De rudimentis hebraicis* of 1506 to mark more than a latent interest in Hebrew.[3]

Yet the library does possess a very special interest both as a superlatively repre-sentative collection of the humanistic thrust of the Renaissance and as the library used not only in the early part of the sixteenth century by Vives and Lupset, but later in the century by Jewel, Rainolds, and Hooker, three Corpus men who shared a passion for Greek, rhetoric, and patristic learning.[4] But little has been written of the forma-tion of the library, beyond the remarks of P. S. Allen and the article of J. R. Liddell, more than half a century ago.[5]

From a list of books made at the death of Fox in 1528 we learn that he gave handsomely to Corpus Christi College: more than twenty manuscripts and well over a hundred printed books, of which latter a third were Greek.[6] Where did these books come from and when were they purchased or collected by Fox? Further, how did they relate to the program of studies that Fox so vigorously detailed in his statutes for his beloved college?[7] These are the questions that I shall attempt to answer in this brief paper.

A nucleus may have been provided by the collection of Latin books that had been made by Fox's predecessor in the see of Durham, John Shirwood, an important figure in fifteenth-century English humanism, as Roberto Weiss and others have shown.[8]

---

[2] *Collected Works of Erasmus* (Toronto, 1974–; = *CWE*), 6:405–407 (letter no. 990).

[3] In his comment upon this letter in *CWE*, Peter G. Bietenholz observes that "the new college was not, however, strictly speaking trilingual, unless Hebrew were regarded as implicit in the study of divinity." That argument can be made with some force, and I think (as I have de-tailed elsewhere) that the founder's intention was that Hebrew be studied for the better under-standing of the Old Testament: certainly the pace of Hebrew studies began to pick up in the mid-1520s.

[4] See further R. J. Schoeck, "From Erasmus to Hooker: An Overview," in *Richard Hooker and the Construction of Christian Community*, ed. A. S. McGrade (Tempe, Ariz.: MRTS, 1997), 59–73.

[5] P. S. Allen, "Bishop Shirwood of Durham and His Library," *English Historical Review* 25 (1910): 445–456. J. R. Liddell, "The Library of Corpus Christi College, Oxford, in the Sixteenth Century," *The Library*, 4th ser., 18 (1938): 385–416.

[6] The books are listed by A. B. Emden, *A Biographical Register of the University of Oxford to A.D. 1500* (Oxford, 1957–1959; = *BROU*), 2: 717–719, in their original order; Liddell follows the 1589 Catalogue and then lists those books according to their original donors during the sixteenth century.

[7] See the translation of the statutes by G. R. M. Ward, *The Foundation Statutes of Bishop Fox for Corpus Christi College* (Oxford, 1843).

[8] Shirwood (d. 1494) proceeded M.A. in March 1450 and then went to Paris for further studies; from there he went on to Italy so that he might learn Greek, and after his stay in Rome, he returned to England with a collection of Greek authors—a notable thing in that decade of the 1450s. In 1460 he was appointed chancellor of Exeter, and in 1483 he became bishop of Durham. Shirwood is known to have written a *Liber de ludo arithmomachie* (Rome, 1482), and his interest in

P. S. Allen wrote directly to the first of the questions I put, although his answers now require some modification:

> The nucleus of the library with which Bishop Foxe endowed his college of Corpus Christi in Oxford is a collection of books made principally at Rome in the last quarter of the fifteenth century by John Shirwood, who was Foxe's predecessor in the see of Durham. As Shirwood bought his books he wrote his name in them, usually on the last leaf, with the time and place of purchase; and the dates which he thus contributes ... make it possible to amplify his biography considerably, whilst at the same time we get an interesting view of the books which an English bishop collected and read in the days when printing was just beginning to encourage the formation of private libraries.[9]

But Shirwood was no ordinary or representative English bishop. First, his patron was George Neville, brother of Warwick the kingmaker and first cousin to Edward IV; and Neville too was interested in, even a patron of Greek learning; and under Neville's patronage the fortunes of Shirwood himself prospered. By 1461 he was able to begin his collection of manuscripts, and after his return to Rome in 1476 he bought steadily. In January 1493 he fell ill and died in Rome; there his property was attached by crown warrant, and his Latin books were acquired by Fox. Shirwood's purchasing of books seems to have ended before 1488: therefore any books printed after that date must have been acquired by Fox himself.

In the list of books made in 1528 there is a large number of books printed from about 1471 to about 1486 (more than forty percent), and these books were doubtless the nucleus of which Allen has spoken. The early tastes of Fox can perhaps be judged from the list of books given to the Collegiate Church of Bishop Auckland, County Durham, in 1499,[10] which are overwhelmingly medieval: legal, scriptural, pastoral in nature. However, the caution should be voiced against seeing the 1499 and the 1528 lists in black and white terms. It is possible that in 1499 Fox recognized the changes in his own tastes and situation; for he was bishop of Durham from 1494 to 1501, then of Winchester after 1501, and his own library needs were not after 1499 what they had been while he was bishop of Exeter (1486–1492) and of Bath and Wells (1492–1494). There may well have been several motives for his gift of medieval books to Auckland. I am more interested in enquiring into the development of Bishop Fox's catholicity of taste in books and learning as revealed in the books bequeathed to Corpus in 1528—his catholicity and his intentions for endowing an institution.

There were opportunities for learning and broadening interests that have not been recorded, or have not been identified in the extant literature on Fox. I have in mind

---

mathematics would explain the number of books in Fox's library dealing with this subject, and perhaps much later Tunstall's work in mathematics. See Roberto Weiss, *Humanism in England during the Fifteenth Century*, 2d ed. (Oxford, 1957); and P. S. Allen, "Bishop Shirwood" (see n. 5).

[9] Allen, "Bishop Shirwood," 455.

[10] Given in Emden, *BROU*, 2: 719.

Fox's letter of September 1489 to Gunthorp, a respected fifteenth-century human-ist,—Fox being then forty-one—on the occasion of the visit of French ambassadors, among whose entourage was the leading French humanistic scholar Robert Gaguin, also a leading canonist and writer on theological topics of interest to Fox.[11] Evidence is lacking, but speculation surely is permitted on the possible significance of Fox's meeting with Gaguin. Perhaps that meeting is to be seen as background to Fox's wanting to acquire Shirwood's books, and then the actual acquisition of thirty-odd books in 1494 must have provided yet another kind of opportunity for learning.

I would add next the visit of Erasmus, who came to England for the first time in 1499 and perhaps carried with him the recommendations or introduction of Gaguin, with whom he had been associated in Paris in the 1490s. Erasmus and Fox "must have first met in 1500," Trapp writes, and I am in agreement. We must weigh even more the importance of the probability that Fox was Erasmus's host in London in 1505.[12] The opportunities for discussion of humanistic learning, of the importance of Greek (which was at the forefront of Erasmus's interests in the early years of the century), and perhaps even for the founding of new institutions of education and learning—these were rich and exciting possibilities for Erasmus and Fox. Erasmus later was involved with Colet in the planning of St. Paul's School and with Busleiden in the planning of the Collegium trilingue in Louvain; Fox was chancellor of Cambridge University in 1499–1500, and from 1507 to 1518 he was master of Pembroke College, Cambridge. These experiences would have given him his insights into the administration of a collegiate institution that bore fruit in his foundation of Corpus Christi College at the end of this period.[13]

Perhaps still more worthy of our reflection is the experience of functioning with Fisher and others as executors of the estate of Lady Margaret Beaufort, after her death in 1509, leading to the foundation of St. John's College, Cambridge, a foundation which had not been completely planned before her death.[14]

Fox had the opportunity as a member of the king's council and—as the crime writers put it—he had the means, as bishop of Winchester, that prize of the realm, and by this time too he had the motive or desire.

Let us then examine more closely the list of books given by Fox in 1528. If it be true to say, as Allen does, that the nucleus of the library is the collection of books

---

[11] For a brief biographical sketch of Gaguin, see *Contemporaries of Erasmus: A Biographical Register* . . . (Toronto, 1985–1987; = *CEBR*), 2:69–70. It is worth recording that a copy of Gaguin's *De rebus gestis francorum* of 1497—a work on which Thomas More wrote with some heated rhetoric—found its way into Fox's collection: Liddell #86, p. 406. On Gaguin and Fox, see *Letters of Fox*, ed. Allen, 12.

[12] J. B. Trapp, *CEBR* 2:46–49, p. 48, citing Epistles 185 & 186, which are dated "from the bishop's palace."

[13] On the career of Fox, see Trapp (cited in n. 12) and Emden, *BROU*, 2:715–719.

[14] On the foundation of St. John's College, Cambridge, see H. C. Porter, *Reformation and Reaction in Tudor Cambridge* (Cambridge, 1958), 11: "The foundation charter [of St. John's] was issued in April 1511." The story of the building of the college is told in T. Baker, *History of St John the Evangelist College, Cambridge*, ed. J. E. B. Mayor, 2 vols. (Cambridge, 1869), 1:61–74.

made principally at Rome in the last quarter of the fifteenth century—and that substantially is true—then we must refine that statement further. Nearly half of the books in the 1528 list were printed after the death of Shirwood: these must have been purchased by Fox himself. Of those books printed after 1494, the year of Shirwood's death, as traditionally given,[15] over half are Greek, and a third of these were books printed within half a dozen years of Shirwood's death; thus we may assume that they were purchased soon after the date of printing. Does this not throw light on the puzzling question of the Greek collection of Shirwood that was not purchased by Fox?[16] I think that we may conclude that Fox in fact preferred the printed texts which were at that time being issued from the Aldine press, and he did not think that Shirwood's Greek manuscripts were worth the taking, or worth the price.[17]

What is still more interesting is to compare the list of authors recommended for study in Fox's statutes for Corpus, written not later than 1516 for the foundation of his college. Prescribed Latin prose authors were Cicero (*Epistulae, Orationes, De Officiis*), Sallust, Valerius Maximus, and Suetonius. Copies of all these authors except Sallust were given by Fox to his college.[18] For an advanced Latin course, Pliny, Livy, Cicero (*De Oratore*), and Quintilian were the set books; and all these except Pliny are among the books given by Fox. Pliny was the lifework of Claymond, and there is much Pliny (notably Claymond's voluminous commentary on Pliny's *Natural History*) in his gifts to the college.[19] For Latin verse, Virgil, Ovid, Lucan, Juvenal, Terence, and Plautus were prescribed; but curiously Fox did not leave a Virgil to his college. Lectures were also to be given by the Reader in Humanity on the *Elegantiae* of Laurentius Valla and the *Noctes Atticae* of Aulus Gellius (copies of which were presented),[20] or the *Miscellanea* of Politian (of which no copy was presented, however).[21]

When we turn to the statutes' provisions for Greek, we find that the Reader in Greek was to lecture three days of the week on Theodore or some other approved grammarian, with the orations of Isocrates, Lucian, or Philostratus; and on the other days he was to lecture on Aristophanes, Theocritus, Euripides, Sophocles, Pindar,

---

[15] He died on 14 January 1493/4 in Rome, but Allen ("Bishop Shirwood," 452 and n. 45) argues persuasively for 1493 rather than 1494 (in the modern calendar).

[16] See Allen, "Bishop Shirwood," 455, for his posing of the question that he answers with the surmise that he overlooked them.

[17] See further Liddell, "The Library of Corpus Christi College, Oxford," 387.

[18] I have no explanation for Sallust's being missing from the collection of books given in 1528.

[19] Claymond was well known as a collector of books and manuscripts, and some 74 titles came to Corpus at his death in 1537 (Liddell, 401). These books and manuscripts included a number purchased from the executors at the death of Grocyn in 1519, and of the 74 titles cited about 16 had been the property of Grocyn. See also M. Vessey, "*Ad Memoriam Claymundi*: An English Humanist, His College, and His Books," published in these Bari *Acta*.

[20] On the importance of Valla to Erasmus, see R. J. Schoeck, *Erasmus of Europe: The Prince of Humanists*, 1501–1536 (Edinburgh, 1993), 44–46.

[21] On the donation of Gellius and Valla, see Liddell, "The Library of Corpus Christi College, Oxford," 388.

Hesiod, or other poets, with portions of Demosthenes, Thucydides, Aristotle, Theophrastus, or Plutarch; Homer, the Greek Anthology, Plato, and Greek patristic writers were reserved for holiday reading. This list of prescribed authors corresponds closely with the Greek books given by Fox, although there is no Sophocles among Fox's books.[22]

The Reader in Theology was to read and expound portions of Scripture daily at two o'clock, using the works of the Fathers rather than medieval theologians— however, Fox's bequest included Nicholas of Lyra and several commentaries on the *Sentences* of Peter Lombard, required by university statutes.

The close correspondence of Fox's prescriptions in his college statutes with the books purchased indicates a long-term program of building up the library, to which he obviously gave much thought. It would seem highly likely that Fox's concentrated book-buying program began soon after his acquisition of Shirwood's nucleus books: perhaps that was in fact a spur. But I would also urge that his meeting with Erasmus, together with his chancellorship of Cambridge in 1499–1500—strange coincidence that the two events should occur in the same year—followed by his mastership of Pembroke and his working with Fisher on the foundation of St. John's College, precipitated his thinking about his own foundation. The library occupied a central position, both in the physical plan of the college and in the provision for key texts in the educational scheme. In this we see the weight of emphasis upon Greek and upon the Church Fathers. Clearly by 1499 there had been a turning point in Fox's thinking, for the books given by him to Bishop Auckland all fall within the limits of the medieval apparatus of learning. At about this time, then, my thesis is, Fox immediately set about forming a collection of books that would not merely celebrate the New Learning (in the sense of the *studia humanitatis*, with central position accorded to Cicero) but would also provide the necessary tools for a college devoted to scholarship illuminated by Greek language, thought, and literature, and by the Church Fathers, rather than by medieval authors. Surely Erasmus was the inspiration.

The concept or ambition was reinforced by the immediate appointment of men like Vives, and the choice of John Claymond as the first president was an inspired one. Claymond was already president of Magdalen, but Fox—who seems to have been a Magdalen man himself and drew considerably from its resources in staffing his new college—apparently had his eye on Claymond long before the actual foundation of Corpus. The close friendship of Claymond and Fox can be dated as early as 1486, and letters between them are extant from as early as 1506. Claymond purchased a number of manuscripts, mainly Greek, from the library of William Grocyn, and these passed into the Corpus library during Claymond's lifetime. Claymond was notable as a scholar, with his great work being a commentary on the *Natural History* of Pliny: this four-volume work is in Basel, doubtless because it was apparently submitted to Froben for publication. Of the large number of manuscripts and books given by Claymond to the Corpus library, about twenty were Greek.

---

[22] Liddell declares that there was no Hesiod; but I find Hesiod in the 1501 codex, bound with Eusebius.

Returning to the building up of Fox's library, we find many books printed during the first decade of the sixteenth century: about a quarter of the total books in the library. What is notable among them is Fox's attention to the Aldine texts of the Greek and Latin classics, beginning with such authors as Euripides and Lucian, both printed in 1503 and both of whom Erasmus was editing or translating. The interest in Greek grows steadily: Demosthenes in 1504, the *Rhetores graeci* 1508, and the *Commentarii in rhetores* 1510,[23] and much of the Greek historians.

We can now, I think, take up the questions posed at the beginning of this paper, and offer at least provisional answers to them. Where did the books come from? We know that the nucleus was owing to Shirwood, but two-thirds came after Shirwood's death. After Fox's return to England with the future Henry VII in 1485, Fox made a number of trips to the Continent: his peace negotiations with France in 1513–1514, for example, and we must assume that he made connections with booksellers on the Continent who acted as agents for him upon his return to England. To be sure, there were such men as the Oxford bookseller in Oxford, whose record of sales in the year 1520 is so important.[24] But we know that humanistic manuscripts had been exported to England from Italy in the fifteenth century and that these manuscripts were often transcribed again in England.[25] More study needs to be made of Fox and the book trade.

What is amply clear is that the program of book collecting correlated very closely with the program of studies that Fox so explicitly and so vigorously detailed in his statutes for his beloved "bee-hive," as he repeatedly called his foundation in the statutes. It is this remarkably close correlation that makes the study of the humanistic books of Bishop Richard Fox so fascinating.[26]

Lawrence, Kansas

---

[23] In my paper on Corpus, "From Erasmus to Richard Hooker" (see n. 4), I have commented on the centrality of rhetoric in the Corpus program. It is no accident that John Jewel, John Rainolds, and Richard Hooker—all superb rhetoricians—were all Corpus men.

[24] See F. Madan, "The Daily Ledger of John Dorne, 1520," in *Collectanea*, 1st ser., Oxford Historical Society, 1885): 71–177. The ledger is MSS 131 CCC. I have not yet checked to see how many of the titles in Fox's bequest are duplicated in Dorne's ledger (or day-book, as it is more usually called). That should be done, for a number of reasons.

[25] On the book trade, see N. J. M. Kerling's study, "Caxton and the Trade in Printed Books," *The Book Collector*, 4 (1955): 190–199.

[26] In 1528–1529 Cuthbert Tunstall made a gift of books to Cambridge University that included Greek MSS and printed books: see Emden, *BROU*, 3:1915.

Two Trends of Historiography at the Court of King Christian IV (1588–1648): The Latin Histories of Denmark by Johannes Pontanus and Johannes Meursius *

KAREN SKOVGAARD-PETERSEN

In an essay published in 1990 Arnaldo Momigliano drew attention to a persistent distinction in Western historiography between two approaches, one erudite and learned with a lot of information, one aesthetic and rhetorical, concerned with politics and with an emphasis on moral utility. The same point is made by another authority in this field, Donald R. Kelley, who notes that the tension between the two trends becomes particularly acute in the Renaissance, both in theoretical discussions about history and in historical writing.[1]

During the 1630s two full-scale Latin histories of Denmark were published. They were both composed at the request of the Danish king Christian IV and the authors were both Dutch, belonging to the same learned Dutch humanistic *milieu*. But their histories of Denmark are remarkably different, and the difference corresponds to some extent to Momigliano's and Kelley's distinction.

The authors are Johannes Pontanus (1571–1639) and Johannes Meursius (1579–1639), who both enjoyed a solid reputation as classical scholars and historians.[2] Pon-

---

* The paper is a part of my larger research project, supported by the Carlsberg Foundation, on Pontanus's and Meursius's histories of Denmark.

[1] Arnaldo Momigliano: "The Rise of Antiquarian Research," in *The Classical Foundations of Modern Historiography*. Sather Classical Lectures 54 (Berkeley, Los Angeles, Oxford, 1990), 54–79. Donald R. Kelley: *Versions of History from Antiquity to the Enlightenment* (New Haven and London, 1991), 370–371, 439, 500.

[2] On Pontanus's life, see the substantial biography by H. F. Rørdam, "Den kongelige Historiograf, Dr. Johan Isaksen Pontanus," in *Historiske Samlinger og Studier III* (København, 1898),

tanus was engaged in 1618 by the Danish king as royal historiographer to write the history of Denmark from the earliest times. But in 1624, when the government had apparently become impatient, Meursius was hired to write the more recent history, from 1448 and onwards, and from then on they were both at work. Unlike Pontanus, Meursius actually moved to Denmark where he was employed as professor of history at the newly established academy for young noblemen in the Danish town of Sorø (on Zealand). But Pontanus had old connections with Denmark where he was born and had spent his childhood. He was able to read Danish.

Meursius was the first to publish the results of his efforts. In 1630 his history of the first three Danish kings of the Oldenborg line came out.[3] One year later Pontanus's account of the preceding period, from the beginning of Danish history to 1448, followed. With this the history of the country up to 1523 was now covered. But for reasons not entirely clear, both Pontanus and Meursius were now asked to continue, Meursius with the early history and Pontanus with the later period from 1448 onwards. Apparently, the ambition of the Danish government at this point was to produce two contemporary Latin histories of Denmark.

But this plan was only partly realized. Meursius managed to complete his version up to 1448, and this second part of his *History* was published in 1638, together with the first part.[4] He also embarked on the later history, after 1523, but never got farther than 1550, and this part of his work was not printed until the eighteenth century.[5] Pontanus left his version of the history from 1448 to 1588 in manuscript—which was also published in the next century.[6]

These are the somewhat complicated facts about the publication of the two contemporary Dutch histories of Denmark. Written at the same time for the same employer and dealing with the same material, these two Latin national histories present a fine field for studying the historiographical tension between learned research and entertaining narrative.[7]

1–24, 440–492. Meursius's life has not been the subject of any study on a larger scale since the early eighteenth century.

[3] *Ioannis Mevrsi Historiæ Danicæ Libri III. . . . Hafniæ, Apud Ioach. Moltkenivm Bibliopolam ibidem. Anno M. D. C. XXX.*

[4] In the edition from 1638 Meursius's *History* is printed together with his *Historia Belgica* (first ed. 1612): *Ioannis Mevrsii Historica; Danica pariter, & Belgica; uno Tomo comprehensa. . . . Amstelodami, apud Guilielmum & Ioannem Blaev, M D CXXXVIII.*

[5] In vol. IX (1746) of Meursius's *Opera Omnia* I–XII, ed. J. Lamius (Firenze, 1741–1763).

[6] In *Monumenta inedita rerum Germanicarum, præcipue Cimbricarum et Megapolensium*, ed. E. J. v. Westphalen, II (Leipzig, 1740), cols. 713–1230.

[7] On other aspects of the two histories of Denmark, see my "The Beginnings of Danish History in the *Rerum Danicarum Historia* (Amsterdam, 1631) of Johannes Pontanus (1571–1639)," in *Acta Conventus Neo-Latini Hafnienis. Proceedings of the Eighth International Congress of Neo-Latin Studies* (Binghamton, N.Y., 1994), 907–916. And my "Tacitus and Tacitism in Johannes Meursius' *Historia Danica* (1630-38)," *Symbolae Osloenses* 70 (1995): 212–240.

Meursius's Censure of Pontanus

I shall take as my point of departure a set of comments that Meursius made when reading Pontanus's *History of Denmark*.[8] They date from the 1630s and were probably made as part of Meursius's preparations for his own version of the early part of Danish history. Considering the size of Pontanus's work, these notes are few. Besides, they only deal with points of criticism—after all they are the product of a rival. Nevertheless, some of the comments throw an interesting light on the difference in the two men's ideas about the style of a Latin national history.

A considerable part of Meursius's comments deals with questions of correct Latin usage. Meursius reveals himself as a die-hard purist, disapproving of words and expressions which occur only once in classical texts:

> *potionatam*] Hoc vocabulo solus utitur Suetonius in Caligula cap. 1. [Suetonius is the only one who uses this word, *Caligula*, chap. 1.] (col. 1143).

Some of Pontanus's expressions are quite unacceptable to Meursius, and, as Pontanus's fellow countryman, he is able to explain their origin:

> *ad plenum*] Est idiotismus Belgicus. Latine dixisset *plene*. [This is a Dutch expression. In Latin it would be *plene*.] (col. 1143).[9]

> *caput ei ense deverberat*] Est idiotismus Belgicus. [This is a Dutch expression.] (col. 1143).[10]

In some cases the magisterial tone is even stronger:

> *quae supra aquas imminebant, stipitibus*] Stipes est masculini generis, non feminini. Inspice Grammaticam, Pontane. [Stipes is masculine, not feminine. Take a look in your grammar, Pontanus.] (col. 1144).

> *exigiturum*] Vapula Prisciane. Docent Grammatici dicendum esse exacturum. [Receive a flogging, Priscian. The grammarians teach us that it should be exacturum.] (col. 1143).

From these linguistic comments we get an idea of one aspect of the difference between the two works: Meursius pays more much more attention to literary elegance. But he also finds faults with Pontanus's choice of subject matter. I shall give an example.

One of the first Danish kings, from the very remote and legendary past, was Svibdagerus. Saxo Grammaticus, who wrote a history of Denmark (*Gesta Danorum*) in

---

[8] Printed together with Meursius's History in vol. IX of his *Opera Omnia* (see note 5), cols. 1141–1148. The text is also found, with some additions, in a MS. in the Royal Library in Copenhagen, Gl. kgl. S. 2428, 4. Besides, a copy of Pontanus's work with Meursius's notes (though not in his own hand) is extant in the University Library in Lund, according to O. Walde, *Storhetstidens litterära krigsbyten* (Uppsala and Stockholm, 1916–1920), II, 408, n. 1.

[9] The Flemish equivalent is "Ten volle." I am grateful to Prof. Jozef IJsewijn for this and the following Dutch translation.

[10] The Flemish equivalent is "het hoofd afslaan met een zwaard."

about 1200, has not very much to tell about him. But from his short account we learn that during Svibdagerus's reign a giant took care of the children of the previous king. Saxo then, in a small digression, describes the three different kinds of sooth-sayers in these days. And this piece of cultural history obviously inspired Pontanus. Having dealt with Svibdagerus's history in just eight lines, he then devotes one and a half folio pages to pointing out that Saxo's three types of fortune-tellers have their close parallels in classical antiquity. His aim is to demonstrate that these magicians were not exclusively Nordic, and he calls attention to a number of classical authors, such as Martianus Capella, Cicero, Cæsar, Ammianus Marcellinus, Tacitus, and Lucan (pp. 13–15).

But in Meursius's view, this demonstration was completely out of place. As he tersely puts it: "This whole chapter is philological rather than historical. And it has nothing to do with Svibdagerus."[11] By "philological" Meursius seems to mean that Pontanus here discusses interpretation of classical texts—and this was simply not appropriate in a work of history. Similarly he later on criticizes Pontanus's attempt to emend the text of Saxo: "He should not pose as 'critic' in a work of history"[12]— again, in a historical work matters of textual criticism should not be discussed.

Now, in Pontanus's work, thematic digressions like the one about the magicians are frequent. He describes in some detail how Maria of Aragon around AD 1000 had a man killed after having tried in vain to seduce him. His wife then, by ordeal of fire, proved his innocence to the emperor, Maria's husband (pp. 140–141). Another digression is concerned with the invention of gunpowder (pp. 507–508), and another with the invention of printing (p. 621), just to mention a few examples.

Meursius evidently disapproved of all these discussions and digressions. This is clear not only from his comment on the magicians but also from the fact that he himself in his own *History of Denmark* omits all such discussions. Even in passages where he obviously follows Pontanus's version closely, we can observe how he leaves out all material which is not part of the historical narrative of wars and politics. Ge-nerally speaking, he sticks to the subject matter of the classical historians Thucydides, Xenophon, Polybius, Sallust, Livy, and Tacitus.

His censure of Pontanus may be summed up by the concept of *decorum*. Pontanus's inclusion of "philological" subjects as well as his unclassical vocabulary were in Meur-sius's view inappropriate in a work of history. The same goes for another prominent feature of Pontanus's work, though Meursius does not comment upon it in his notes. Throughout Pontanus refers to his sources of information—primarily medieval his-torians but also a huge number of classical authors and contemporary historians. Actually he not only refers to other authors, he also quotes them, often at length. Some quotations take up several of his packed folio pages. And apart from literary texts, he also gives the words of documents, inscriptions, and songs. And he not only mixes his own discourse with all kinds of quotations, he also frequently transcribes a

---

[11] "Totum hoc caput potius Philologicum est, quam historicum; neque ad Svibdagerum per-tinet" (col. 1141).

[12] "Non recte in Historia Criticum agit" (col. 1143).

source without any indication. The result is a considerable stylistical diversity.

Meursius's own practice clearly indicates that all these quotations and references were at odds with his sense of *decorum*. In his work, not a single quotation is found. And only a few times does he mention any sources. He obviously endeavoured to obtain a totally homogeneous narrative—and he achieved it.

The Antiquarian Approach

Now I shall say no more about Meursius's censure of Pontanus; instead I shall turn to possible inspirations for Pontanus. It seems to me that his work is closely related to contemporary antiquarian studies. The term "antiquarian" is primarily used of systematic investigation of classical antiquity, but also of corresponding descriptions of the antiquities of contemporary European countries. Flavio Biondo's *Italia illustrata* (first ed. 1474) is, in Momigliano's words, "the forerunner of the systematic antiquarian handbooks," and he was "the founder of modern scientific research of the antiquities of all the countries of Europe."[13]

Among the important works of national antiquarianism to which Momigliano here refers was William Camden's *Britannia* (first ed. 1586). This work is, as typical of the antiquarian approach, primarily organized according to themes, not according to chronology. Though Pontanus's *History of Denmark* differs from it in this respect, it must be counted among his important souces of inspiration. He not only refers to Camden with respect, he also borrows material from him and takes up the same topics for discussion, such as the early migrations of the European peoples. Both Camden and Pontanus are fond of etymological deductions.

The antiquarian works deal with a variety of subjects. The past is not only described in terms of wars and heroic deeds. Ways of living, language, traditions, political and legal institutions play a significant part. Pontanus has placed information of this sort in his huge appendix "Chorographia Danica." Here he gives not only a geographical and topographical description of the various parts of Denmark but also—among other things—a survey of the structure of Danish society and a presentation of the most prominent men of learning in Denmark. This is a purely antiquarian piece, which takes up more than a fifth of the whole work. But even within the history itself, as we have already seen, his numerous digressions, such as the one about the use of ordeal of fire and the one about the magicians, makes it clear that history in his view consisted of more than wars and kings.

The spread of printing from 1500 and onwards must have been of decisive importance for antiquarian studies. A work like Pontanus's *History of Denmark* reveals the author's aquaintance with a vast range of texts—*and* his ability to extract new information from the constellation of those texts.

In his account of the Viking Age, for instance, Pontanus supplements the account of Saxo Grammaticus with English, French, and German medieval and later literature. The result is, of course, very different from the national tradition which went back

---

[13] Momigliano 1990 (see note 1), 70–71.

to Saxo. The merit of Pontanus's approach is that he succeeds in describing Danish history in its broader, Northern European, context.[14]

In short, it seems to me that Pontanus's *History of Denmark*—and the whole antiquarian trend of historical writing in the sixteenth and seventeenth centuries—is a good illustration of Elizabeth Eisenstein's thesis about the impact of printing. Using examples from other branches of learning, she argues that the advent of printing paved the way for a revolution of learning, by making the comparison of many texts possible—which is exactly what we can observe in Pontanus's work.[15]

Moralizing History

Now let us turn to Meursius's *History*. As I have already suggested, he has confined himself to the traditional subject matter of history. But he also focuses on other aspects of history than Pontanus. I shall illustrate this with Meursius's own version of the story of the legendary king Svibdagerus, which he found so poorly treated by Pontanus. Meursius tells the king's story almost as briefly as Pontanus. But instead of Pontanus's antiquarian digression on different sorts of magicians, he points to the moral lesson to be drawn. From Svibdagerus's fate, says Meursius, we see a general rule confirmed—that a king who has made his way to power by crime will lose it shortly afterwards.[16]

Moral lessons like this abound in Meursius's work. Throughout he points out how divine justice rules the world. Consider this judgement on Svibdagerus's predecessor, King Gram:

> He was a great king, in whom nothing can be censured except his matrimonial fickleness and his repudiation (of his wife). This behaviour is disgraceful and illegal also for kings, and God, who is both the author and the upholder of matrimony, will not leave it unpunished.[17]

We are here in the legendary past. Throughout the course of history, Meursius uses the same Christian values as the basis of his judgements. In this case, the king's matrimonial infidelity is censured. The same sin was committed by a Danish king, Chris-

---

[14] Another more ideological consequence of Pontanus's method is that the importance of Denmark at that time is demonstrated by his references and quotations from so many different authors who all tell of Danish raids and conquests.

[15] Elizabeth Eisenstein, *The Printing Press as an Agent of Change* I–II (London, New York, Melbourne, 1979).

[16] "Ille primus, cæso Gramo, trium borealium regnorum potens, cum Guthormo, Grami filio maiori, precibus uxoris suæ, Daniam mox tributariam, Sueciamque Asmundo suo concessisset, ac Norvagiam sibi solam retineret, ab Hadingo, filiorum Grami altero, patris cædem vindicare cupiente, ad Gothlandiam, prælio navali victus, interficitur: ac parata scelere regna, quum non diu tenuisset maxima cum ignominia, uti fere fieri solet, rursum amittit" (p. 3 in the 1638 ed.).

[17] "Princeps magnus, & in quo nil reprehendas, quam amoris conjugalis inconstantiam, & repudia: etiam regibus indecora, & illicita; neque a Deo, ut auctore matrimonii, ita quoque assertore, impunita, quanquam sæpe per libidinem usitata" (p. 3 in the 1638 ed.).

tian II, at a much later date—in the early sixteenth century—and he was similarly afflicted with divine punishment.

In fact, Meursius sometimes adds a moral lesson to a description of a course of events, in which he otherwise follows Pontanus—since in the latter's work the ethical aspect is not very prominent. The lessons to be learnt stand out clearly everywhere in Meursius's *History*. And this has to do with another significant feature, his lucid narrative. In several instances we can observe how he tries to point out connections which were not so clear in his source while omitting irrelevant details. He complies fully with the Ciceronian ideal of history writing: "In history there is nothing more pleasing than brevity, clear and correct."[18]

In most respects, then, Meursius displays a classicizing sense of *decorum*. It goes for his vocabulary, syntax, his exclusion of antiquarian material and quotations, and the scarcity of references to other authors. His emphasis on the didactic function of historiography is also rooted in antiquity, though he has given it a distinct Christian flavour throughout.

I cannot point to any specific contemporary model of Meursius, and I must confine myself to some tentative remarks. His classicizing style and his concentration on politics and wars link him with the older humanist historiography. So does his emphasis on the role of individual characters. It is manifested by his evaluations of the virtues and vices of each king at the end of his reign, a feature found also in, e.g., Polydore Vergil's *History of England* (first ed. 1534). This work was, along with Paulus Aemilius's *History of France* (first ed. 1539),[19] among the very influential Latin national histories of the early sixteenth century, and I think both of them may be be regarded as possible inspirations for Meursius. But again the Christian character of Meursius's moral reflections is a significant difference. God is a frequent actor in his narrative, a feature which—at least this is my impression—is especially prominent in the historiography influenced by Melanchthon.

The Role of the Classics

Finally, I shall briefly draw attention to another aspect of the fundamental difference between Pontanus's and Meursius's histories of Denmark. It is a somewhat paradoxical aspect of Meursius's classicizing style that he practically never mentions a classical name. In fact, he never refers to an author or to a figure or a event of classical history.[20] His solid classical training is apparent on every page but only through allusions, vocabulary, syntax, and choice of subject matter. In this respect he seems to be even more classicizing, or more of a purist, than any of his humanist predecessors—and the contrast with Pontanus is striking.

Pontanus displays his classical learning right on the surface, through his innu-

---

[18] "Nihil est enim in historia pura et inlustri brevitate dulcius" (Cicero, *Brutus*, chap. 262).

[19] The 1539 edition comprised books I–X. In 1516 or 1517 books I–IV had been published, and in 1519, books I–VI.

[20] The only exception is, as far as I can see, his observation that the birth of Christ took place during the reign of Augustus in Rome and Frode Fredegod in Denmark (p. 21 in the 1638 ed.).

merable references to classical authors and to figures and events of classical history. In addition, he often draws parallels between events of Danish history and phenomena of the classical world. Classicál antiquity is present everywhere in Pontanus's work. But, as Meursius pointed out, Pontanus has no scruples about introducing nonclassical words and expressions. He has abandoned the stylistic aspirations of the early humanists.

To put it briefly: Meursius imitates classical historiography, while Pontanus uses the information found in classical texts. This difference in their use of classical literature is related to a broader issue, the concept of authority, or in other words: how do they convince their readers of the truth of their narratives? Meursius's authority stems, broadly speaking, from the classicizing style—the traditional humanistic device of creating authority through *imitatio*. Pontanus, on the other hand, bases his authority on his constant display of knowledge of a vast number of sources, classical as well as nonclassical, and his explicit arguing for or against the points of view of other authors. Again, the sheer number of texts used by Pontanus forms the basis of a qualitative difference. But the crucial point in this case is of course that he informs the reader about all these sources—and, correspondingly, that Meursius only rarely refers to his sources (which, incidentally, were much fewer).

In these two contemporary Latin histories of Denmark, then, we may see an instance of the persistent tension between the entertaining and stylistically refined narrative on the one hand, and the antiquarian, erudite piece of research on the other; and with the benefit of hindsight we may describe this case as a clash between a conservative and classicizing kind of historical writing and a more modern one in which the use of as many sources as possible is an ideal and where information on a variety of subjects and documentation of the information prevails over literary elegance and moral judgements.

Bergen

Quelques notes sur la présence de Maffeo Vegio en Espagne*

JULIÁN SOLANA PUJALTE

L a présence de l'oeuvre de l'humaniste italien Maffeo Vegio en Espagne n'a pas été analysée, ni même envisagée jusqu'à présent. Dans cette étude nous essaierons d'apporter une série de renseignements, inconnus ou dispersés jusqu'ici, qui permettent une évaluation provisoire de cette présence. Nous diviserons notre travail en quatre parties: (a) éditions espagnoles de ses oeuvres, (b) traductions espagnoles, (c) diffusion dans nos bibliothèques, (d) jugements critiques et publications récentes.

1. Éditions

La première oeuvre de Maffeo Vegio publiée en Espagne fut son *Supplementum* à l'*Énéide* de Virgile. La première édition vit la lumière en 1513 à Zaragoza. Comme cela avait été habituel au XVᵉ siècle, elle parut dans la première édition espagnole des *Oeuvres Complètes* de Virgile, après le dernier livre de l'*Énéide*. L'imprimeur fut Georg Koch et l'éminent humaniste d'Alcañiz Juan Sobrarias s'occupa de l'édition.[1] Une deuxième édition de la même oeuvre parut sous les mêmes presses et sous le soin du même éditeur en 1516. D'après le très petit nombre d'exemplaires que l'on a conservé de ces deux éditions, on peut supposer que celles-ci n'eurent pas une diffusion importante.[2] J.L. Navarro López a édité et étudié récemment les deux éditions.[3]

Il faut attendre presque un siècle et demi pour connaître une autre édition espa-

---

* Ce travail est inclus dans le projet de recherche PS93–0164 de la DGICYT.

[1] À propos de Sobrarias, *cf.* J.M. Maestre, *El humanismo alcañizano del s. XVI. Textos y estudios de latín renacentista* (Cádiz, 1990), 3 ss. suivi d'une bibliographie et d'une étude de sa production. Sur les détails de l'édition cf. J.M. Sánchez, *Bibliografía Aragonesa del s. XVI (1501–1600)*, édition facsimilé de R. Moralejo y L. Tobar (Madrid, 1991), 111–113, qu'ignore, d'ailleurs, dans la description du volume, le *Supplementum* de Vegio. Sur G. Koch, *cf.* D. Briesemeister, "Die deutschen Früdrucker in Spanien," Sonderdruck aus *Gutenberg-Jahrbuch* (1993): 57.

[2] 1513: Madrid *BN*; Zaragoza *BU*; Pamplona *BP* (2). 1516: Madrid *BN* (2).

[3] *El libro XIII de la Eneida compuesto por Mafeo Vegio: las ediciones de Juan Sobrarias de 1513 y 1516*, mémoire de licence inédit (Cádiz, 1989).

gnole du *Supplementum*. Dans notre Bibliothèque Nationale, nous avons trouvé un imprimé[4] qui, peut-être à cause de ses caractéristiques, est passé inaperçu aux chercheurs. Il s'agit des *Publi Virgilii Maronis Opera argumentis et animadversionibus illustrata*, sans mention de lieu, d'imprimeur ni de date d'édition. Toutefois, d'après les données que la licence d'impression, les *errata* et la taxe nous apportent, on peut conclure que le livre fut imprimé à Madrid, entre Avril et Juillet de 1653, sous les presses de Gabriel de León. Le *Supplementum* occupe les ff. 228v–238r, après le livre XII de l'*Énéide* et son en-tête contient l'*erratum* suivant: *Maphaei V. Laudensis XXII (sic) librorum Aeneidos Supplementum*. Dans notre Bibliothèque Nationale on conserve aussi un exemplaire[5] très similaire au précédent, mais qui a perdu les premiers folios,[6] raison pour laquelle il n'est pas possible de connaître le lieu d'édition, ni la date, ni l'éditeur. Il n'est même pas possible de déduire ces données de la licence d'impression, comme dans l'exemplaire précédent. Cependant, l'imprimé est identique à celui-ci en ce qui concerne le texte et tous les détails d'impression jusqu'au f. 82r, où le livre III de l'*Énéide* commence. La similitude est telle que ce deuxième imprimé a le même *erratum* dont nous avons plus haut mentionné la présence à l'en-tête du *Supplementum*. Ici, cependant, il occupe les ff. 229v–240v. Il s'agit, évidemment, d'une autre édition de la même année ou d'une date immédiatement antérieure ou postérieure, imprimée aussi sous les presses de Gabriel de León.

La dernière édition de ce siècle du *Supplementum* est celle qui parut à Barcelona en 1676 dans l'imprimerie de Antonio Lacavalleria.[7] Comme d'habitude le *Supplementum* est imprimé après le livre XII de l'*Énéide* et il occupe les pages 433–453.[8]

Le XVIIIe siècle apporta deux autres éditions de cette même oeuvre. Elles présentent la particularité d'être les deux seules éditions bilingues du *Supplementum* éditées en Espagne. Le texte latin y est accompagné de la traduction castillane réalisée au XVIe siècle par Gregorio Hernández de Velasco, que nous analyserons plus loin. Toutes les deux parurent à Valencia dans les ateliers des frères Orga en 1777 et 1795.

Mais le *Supplementum* ne fut pas la seule oeuvre de Vegio éditée en Espagne. En 1554 un volume intitulé *Meditationes atque alia quamplurima tum divi Augustini tum aliorum sanctorum opuscula* parut à Alcalá de Henares sous les presses de Juan de Brocar. On y trouve, parmi les différentes oeuvres religieuses de S. Augustin et d'autres auteurs ecclésiastiques, la *Salutatio Beatae Monicae* de Maffeo Vegio (ff. 4v–7r).[9]

2. Traductions

La première version castillane complète de l'*Énéide* parut en 1555 à Toledo et Gre-

---

   [4] Cote 3/4414.

   [5] Cote 7/11443.

   [6] Tous ceux qui précèdent le commencement du texte des *Bucoliques*, première oeuvre éditée.

   [7] *Publii Vergilii Maronis Opera*, Barcinone, ex Typog. Antonii Lacavalleria, 6176 (*sic*, au lieu de 1676).

   [8] Madrid *BN* cote 3/48173.

   [9] *Cf.* L. Rafaelle, *op. cit.*, 84 (nn. 28) et 123. De cette pièce, nous ne connaissons que deux exemplaires: Lisboa *BN* cote R/9011; Madrid *BN* cote R/20861. *Cf.* J. Martín Abad, *La imprenta en Alcalá de Henares (1502–1600)* (Madrid, 1991), 637.

gorio Hernández de Velasco en fut l'auteur. Traduite en hendécasyllabes isolés (parties narratives) et en *octavas reales* (discours), elle fut très lue à l'époque et connut plusieurs éditions jusqu'à 1574 où *esta última impression reformada y limada con mucho estudio y cuydado, de tal manera que se puede dezir nueua traducción* parut aussi à Toledo. À la version de l'*Énéide*, s'ajoute celle des *Églogues* I et IV et le *libro tredécimo de Mapheo Vegio, poeta laudense, intitulado Supplemento de la Eneida de Virgilio*. La version de Hernández de Velasco connut trois nouvelles éditions tout au long du XVIe siècle.[10]

Au XVIIe siècle cette version fut remplacée par celle de Diego López, disciple de Sánchez de las Brozas, el Brocense. Rien que dans ce siècle cette version commentée connut douze éditions.[11] C'est pourquoi la version de Hernández de Velasco ne reparut qu'une seule fois tout au long de ce siècle.[12] Néanmoins, au XVIIIe siècle, peut-être sous l'influence de G. Mayans,[13] la version de Hernández de Velasco connut cinq nouvelles réimpressions.[14]

On peut assurer que la traduction castillane du *Supplementum* due à Hernández de Velasco et son édition suivante, parue avec celle de l'*Énéide* du même auteur, contribua de façon décisive à la diffusion de l'oeuvre de l'humaniste de Lodi en Espagne. Cette diffusion fut favorisée d'une part par son incontestable qualité littéraire, de l'autre, non seulement par la grande quantité des éditions existantes, mais aussi par sa présence continue dans les imprimeries et dans les librairies tout au long des XVIe, XVIIe et XVIIIe siècles.

La deuxième et dernière traduction castillane du *Supplementum* est celle que fit José Rafael Larrañaga, au XVIIIe siècle, dans le cadre de la traduction que l'auteur mexicain réalisa de l'oeuvre complète de Virgile.[15]

On a toujours pensé que les seules traductions castillanes de Vegio étaient celles que nous venons d'énumérer. Il fallut attendre 1988 pour savoir, grâce aux travaux de

---

[10] Toledo 1577 en casa de Diego de Ayala; Alcalá 1585 en casa de Juan Iñiguez de Lequerica; Zaragoza 1586 en casa de Lorenço y Diego de Robles Hermanos. A propos de Hernández de Velasco et sa traduction, *cf.* N. Antonio, *Biblioteca Hispana Nova siue Hispanorum scriptorum qui ab anno MD ad MDCLXXXIV floruere notitia . . .* (Madrid 1783–1788) s.u.; M. Menéndez Pelayo, *Bibliografía hispano-latina clásica* (Santander, 1952) vol. VIII, 366–372; M. Allué, y Morer, "Que a Virgilio nos diste castellano. Un traductor en verso de la Eneida," *Poesía Española* 96 (1960): 25–30; A. Blecua, "El entorno poético de Fray Luis," *Academia Literaria Renacentista* I (Salamanca, 1981) 83 et J. A. Izquierdo, *Diego López o el Virgilianismo español en la escuela del Brocense* (Cáceres, 1989) 51–52. Sur les éditions de cette oeuvre, *cf.* M. Menéndez Pelayo, *op. cit.*, 208–17; A. Palau y Dulcet, *Manual del librero hispanoamericano . . .* (Barcelona 1948–1977, 2e édition) vol. 27, 332 y 335 ss.

[11] *Cf.* A. Rodríguez Moñino, "Un traductor extremeño de Virgilio" dans *Curiosidades Bibliográficas* (Madrid, 1946) 135–146 et surtout J.A. Izquierdo, *op. cit.*, chap. IV: "La traducción de Diego López: análisis y difusión," 62–127.

[12] Lisboa 1614, por Vicente Aluarez.

[13] *Cf.* J. A. Izquierdo, *op. cit.*, 52.

[14] Madrid 1768, par Francisco Xavier García; Valencia 1776, par Benito Monfort; Valencia 1777, par Josef y Thomas de Orga; Valencia 1793, par Benito Monfort; Valencia 1795, par les frères de Orga.

[15] México, en la oficina de los herederos del Licd. D. Joseph de Jáuregui, 1787/8. Il m'a été impossible de le consulter. Je cite d'après les données de A. Palau y Dulcet, *op. cit.*, vol. 27, 333.

Jesús López[16] et de A. Calvo Kaneko,[17] que le manuscrit 9/753 de la Real Academia de la Historia à Madrid contenait une traduction castillane inédite d'un dialogue
intitulé *Luciani Palinurus*. Il ne s'agissait pas en réalité d'une oeuvre de Lucien, mais du
dialogue lucianesque de Maffeo Vegio *De miseria et felicitate*.

On sait que le dialogue de Vegio, composé probablement vers 1445, eut une diffusion considérable, non pas sous le titre que son auteur lui donna mais avec celui de
Palinurus. Ce dialogue a été souvent attribué à Lucien avec le même titre, aussi bien
dans le cas de manuscrits que dans celui d'imprimés de fin du XVᵉ siècle et début du
XVIᵉ siècle.[18]

On trouve la traduction mentionnée dans un manuscrit mélangé, une sorte de
cahier de notes du fameux humaniste de Córdoba, Juan Ginés de Sepúlveda.[19] Le
même manuscrit contient une autre traduction de Sepúlveda (l'homélie *Quod nemo
laeditur . . .* de saint Jean Chrysostome) et plusieurs annotations tirées de livres publiés
en 1553 et 1554.[20] L'analyse détaillée de la traduction de Vegio et surtout du genre
de corrections, suppressions et ajouts que celle-ci présente, nous a permis de conclure
qu'il s'agit non pas d'une simple transcription d'une traduction préexistante, mais
d'une traduction originale de Juan Ginés de Sepúlveda.[21]

L'intérêt de cette version est multiple. D'une part, elle apporte une donnée de plus
sur l'influence de Lucien en Espagne au XVIᵉ siècle.[22] D'autre part, et c'est cela qui

---

[16] *El diálogo en el Renacimiento español* (Madrid, 1988).

[17] "El diálogo satírico en el siglo XVI: Juan Ginés de Sepúlveda y la traducción del *Palinuro*"
(diss., University of Michigan, 1988).

[18] À propos de son attribution à Lucien au titre de *Palinurus*, *cf.* C. Barni, *op. cit.*, 154; C.
Thompson, *The Traslation of Lucian by Erasmus and St. Thomas More* (Ithaca, 1940) 4; G. Berger,
"Präliminaren zu einer kritischen Edition von Maffeo Vegios Supplement zur Äneis," *Acta
Conventus Neolatini Amstelodamensis* (München, 1979) 84, 89–90; Ch. Robinson, *Lucian and His
Influence in Europe* (London, 1979) 84; E. Mattioli, *Luciano e l'Umanesimo* (Napoli, 1980), 149–150;
A. Calvo Kaneko, *op. cit.*, 11–12. Sur la diffusion de ce dialogue à la Renaissance cf. G. Berger,
op. cit., *ibid.*, qui a comptabilisé au moins 34 mss. de cette oeuvre. On peut trouver une relation
des éditions parues avec ce titre et attribution chez E. P. Goldschmidt, "The First Edition of
Lucian of Samosata," *The Warburg and Courtauld Institutes* 14 (1951): 14; E. Mattioli, *op. cit.*, 149–
150 et A. Calvo Kaneko, *op. cit.*, 11–14.

[19] À propos de J.G. de Sepúlveda, vid. *De vita et scriptis Io. Genesii Sepulvedae cordubensis
commentarius*, in *Opera cum edita tum inedita* (Madrid, 1780) I–CII et le livre de A. Losada, *Juan
Ginés de Sepúlveda a través de su "Epistolario" y nuevos documentos*, (Madrid, 1949; reprint 1973). On
peut trouver des études d'ensemble dans *Juan Ginés de Sepúlveda y su Crónica Indiana*, ed. Seminario
Americanista de la Universidad de Valladolid (Valladolid, 1976); *El Cardenal Albornoz y el Colegio
de España*, ed. E. Verdera (Bolonia, 1979) et dans les *Actas del Congreso Internacional V Centenario
del Nacimiento del Doctor Juan Ginés de Sepúlveda* (Córdoba, 1993).

[20] Il s'agit des notes tirées des oeuvres de Francisco López de Gómara, Juan Arce de Otalora
y Pedro de Alcocer. *Cf.* J. Solana, "Un manuscrito semidesconocido de Juan Ginés de Sepúlveda,"
Cuadernos de Filología Clásica. Estudios Latinos 7 (1994): 187–215.

[21] *Cf.* J. Solana, *op. cit.*; "Errores de traducción y *limae labor* como criterios de autoría: a propósito de una versión castellana de Juan Ginés de Sepúlveda de un diálogo de Maffeo Vegio," *IV
Jornadas de Filología Latina* (Córdoba, 1993).

[22] Sur l'influence de Lucien en Espagne, *cf.* A. Vives Coll, *Luciano de Samosata en España
(1500–1700)* (Valladolid, 1959); M. Zappala, "Lucian in Italy and Spain (1400–1600)" (diss., Har-

nous concerne spécialement ici, cette version avance de vingt ans, à 1554, la première traduction de Vegio en castillan, qui n'est pas, comme on le croyait jusqu'à il n'y a pas longtemps, celle du *Aeneidos Supplementum* de H. de Vegio, mais celle de l'un de ses dialogues, celui *De miseria et felicitate* plus connu comme *Luciani Palinurus*. Nous devons préciser, toutefois, que les deux traductions ne sont pas analysables suivant les mêmes paramètres. Celle de Sepúlveda ne laisse pas d'être, d'après nous, un simple exercice littéraire dans lequel l'humaniste mesure ses propres forces dans le domaine de la langue vulgaire, un amusement savant, une expérience, si l'on veut. En aucune façon cet exercice ne semble destiné à dépasser le milieu privé.[23] Par contre, la raison d'être de la traduction de H. de Vegio est justement sa destination à l'imprimerie.

3. Diffusion en Bibliothèques Espagnoles

3.1. Manuscrits

Nous avons localisé seize manuscrits de Vegio dans nos bibliothèques,[24] la plupart d'entre eux présentent un incontestable intérêt. Le plus important, c'est, sans doute, le *Scorialensis* f. II.12, écrit vers la moitié du XVe siècle en Italie par Juan Vintimiglia, manuscrit qui contient, comme nous préciserons, une vaste sélection de l'oeuvre poétique de l'auteur (ff. 77r–113v).[25] De plus, c'est le seul manuscrit espagnol qui contient plus d'une oeuvre de l'auteur de Lodi. Nous citerons ensuite les oeuvres conservées avec la référence au ms. où elles se trouvent:

• *Aeneidos liber XIII*: Escorial *R. Mon.* f. II.12 (ff. 77r–86r) (Italie, s. XVe); T.III.2 (ff.

---

vard University, 1976); *Lucian of Samosata in the Two Hesperias. An Essay in Literary and Cultural Translation*, Scripta Humanistica vol. 65 (Potomac, 1990).

[23] Ces traductions apportent d'elles-mêmes une nouvelle vision de la personnalité littéraire de Sepúlveda, considéré avec raison comme le plus cicéronien de nos humanistes. Ses oeuvres sont écrites en un latin dont l'élégance a été mise en relief à l'unanimité. Il faut se rappeler qu'Erasmus fait mention de Sepúlveda dans son *Ciceronianus* (3691–3692, éd. A. Gambaro, Roma, 1965) mention qui sembla cependant, excessivement froide à l'humaniste de Pozoblanco (*Antapologia* IX, *Epistulae I, 13*). *Cf.* aussi entre autres les opinions dans ce même sens de García Matamoros: *Genus orationis habet fusum, tractum et cum lenitate quadam profluens, quale historia, auctore Cicerone, postulare videtur ... neminemque unum esse in his, qui de claris doctrina viris aetate nostra scripserunt, qui non Hispanorum primum Genesium Sepulvedam meminisset.* (*Pro adserenda Hispanorum eruditione* 122. Je cite d'après l'édition de J. López de Toro [Madrid, 1943]); Andreas Schott: *Ad stilum quod attinet, poetica leviter tinctus fuit, soluta oratione Ciceronem semper aemulatus* (*Ioannis Genesii Sepulvedae Opera* I, *Testimonia et elogia* p. 5); M. Menéndez Pelayo, *Bibliografía Hispano-latina clásica*, vol. III (Santander, 1950–1553), 251–262; A. Losada, *op. cit.*, 324–327 et J. M. Núñez González, "Bolonia y el ciceronianismo en España: Juan Ginés de Sepúlveda y Antonio Agustín," dans *Estudios sobre los orígenes de las Universidades españolas* (Valladolid, 1988), 206–220; *El ciceronianismo en España* (Valladolid, 1993), 54–61.

[24] J'ai utilisé G. Antolín, *Catálogo de los Códices Latinos de la Real Biblioteca del Escorial*, 5 vols. (Madrid, 1910–1923); P.O. Kristeller, *Iter Italicum* IV (II) (London-Leiden-New York-Kybenhaun-Köln, 1989) et L. Rubio, *Catálogo de los manuscritos clásicos latinos existentes en España* (Madrid, 1984).

[25] À propos de l'interêt de ce ms. pour l'édition du *Supplementum*, *cf. Das Aeneissupplement des Maffeo Vegio*, eingelitet, nach den Handschriften herausgegeben, übersetzt und mit einem Index versehen von B. Schneider (Weinheim, 1985), 30.

217v–227r) (s. XVᵉ); T.III.14 (ff. 225r–236r) (s. XVᵉ).

- *In rusticos liber*: Madrid *BN* 18246 (ff. 65r–70v) (s. XVᵉ); Escorial *R. Mon.* f. II.12 (ff. 91v–95v).
- *Astyanax*: Escorial *R. Mon.* f. II.12 (ff. 86v–91v).
- *Elegiarum libri III*: Escorial *R. Mon.* f. II.12 (ff. 95v–116r).
- *Versus*: Escorial f. II.12 (ff. 116r–118v).²⁶
- *Epigrammata*: Escorial *R. Mon.* f. II.12 (ff. 118v–121r)
- *Antoniados libri IV*: Escorial *R. Mon.* f. II.12 (ff. 121r–128v).
- *Psalmi poenitentiales ex Davide traducti*: Escorial *R. Mon.* f. II.12 (ff. 128v–132r).
- *Poésies religieuses*: Escorial *R. Mon.* f. II.12 (ff. 128v–132v).²⁷
- *Disceptatio inter terram, solem et aurum*: Madrid Archivo Hco. Universitario, UCompl, cod. 140 (s. XVᵉ–XVIᵉ); Sevilla BCapCol 5-6-28 (s. XVᵉ); Toledo Archivo y Biblioteca Capitulares cod. 27,8 (ff. 93r–107r) (s. XVᵉ).
- *De veritate et Philalethe*: Granada *BU* cod. B 108 (ff. 99r–118v) (Espagne, s. XVᵉ).
- *De rebus antiquis memorabilibus Basilicae S. Petri Rome*: Madrid *BN* 8575 (X211). Toledo Archivo y Biblioteca Capitulares cod.25, 50 (s. XVᵉI–XVIIᵉ).
- *De vita et obitu Caelestini V*: Madrid *BN* 9321 (Cc219) (s. XVIᵉ); Madrid *BN* 11105 (Jj191) (s. XVIᵉ).
- *De educatione liberorum*: Madrid *BN* 9207 (Bb66) (an. 1444); Madrid *BN* 8419 (X184) (an. 1444).
- *Liber de verborum significatione*: Madrid Archivo Histórico Universitario, UCompl, ms. 11 (*olim* 83) (Italie, s. XVᵉ).
- *Epistolae*: Valladolid *BU* cod. 325 (ff. 6 y 47) (Italie, s. XVᵉ) deux lettres dirigées à P. Cándido Decembrio. Il y en a une autre de Decembrio à Vegio.

3.2. Imprimés

Étant donné que nos fonds anciens sont catalogués d'une façon assez incomplète, exception faite des incunables,²⁸ les données que nous apportons ne peuvent qu'être provisoires.²⁹

Nous avons localisé des exemplaires de 29 éditions incunables: vingt-trois sont du *Supplementum*, quatre du *Luciani Palinurus*, une de deux de ses dialogues (*Dialogus Veritatis et Philalethes, Dialogus de felicitate et miseria*) inclus dans une très ancienne anthologie du genre³⁰ et la dernière du *Liber e iurisconsultorum scriptis excerptus*.

---

²⁶ Référence détaillé chez G. Antolín, *op. cit.*, vol. I, 165. *Cf.* L. Raffaelle, op. cit., 184, 202–203.

²⁷ Référence détaillée chez G. Antolín, *op. cit.*, vol. I, p. 166. *Cf.* L. Raffaelle, op. cit., 122–123.

²⁸ Biblioteca Nacional, *Catálogo General de Incunables en Bibliotecas Españolas*, 2 vol. (Madrid, 1990) coordinado y dirigido por F. García Craviotto; Biblioteca Nacional, *Catálogo General de Incunables en Bibliotecas Españolas. Adiciones y correcciones* (Madrid, 1991); J. Martín Abad, *Catálogo de incunables de la Biblioteca Nacional. Segundo apéndice* (Madrid, 1993).

²⁹ Cet exposé n'est pas le lieu approprié pour une description detaillée des imprimés végiens de nos bibliothèques. C'est un travail que je suis en train de faire et que j'espère achever bientôt. Je me limiterai à présenter quelques données intéressantes.

³⁰ *Dialogi decem variorum auctorum. . .* , s.l. [Coloniae], s.i. [Flores S. Agustini], 1473.

Nous avons localisé des exemplaires de quarante-six éditions différentes du XVIᵉ siècle: trente et une du *Supplementum*, quatre éditions d'autres oeuvres poétiques,[31] trois de ses dialogues[32] et une du *De traslatione corporis S. Monicae*,[33] *une autre du De perseverantia religionis*,[34] et une autre du *De educatione liberorum* accompagné du *Dialogus veritatis et Philalethes*.[35] Les cinq autres éditions correspondent aux traductions castillanes du Supplementum de H. de Vegio

Du XVIIᵉ siècle nous n'avons localisé que six éditions. L'une correspond à l'édition d'ensemble de ses oeuvres publiée à Lyon[36] et l'autre à la seule édition de ce siècle de la traduction de Hernández de Velasco.[37] Les quatre autres éditions correspondent au *Supplementum*, toujours édité après le livre XII de l'*Énéide*. Il convient de souligner que trois de ces éditions sont les éditions espagnoles décrites ci-dessus.

Du XVIIIᵉ siècle on ne conserve que des exemplaires des cinq éditions de la traduction de Hernández de Velasco.

4. Études

Je ne connais aucune étude publiée en Espagne sur Maffeo Vegio avant notre siècle. La seule chose que j'ai pu glaner c'est une petite référence du jésuite Juan Luis de la Cerda, dans son célèbre et monumental commentaire de l'oeuvre complète de Virgile (1617), où il loue formellement l'imitation de Vegio, mais critique l'idée que l'*Énéide* eût besoin d'une suite: "*Vide et Maphaeum Vegium in Supplemento Virgiliano, quod opus laude est dignum, si versus spectes, quia multi ad umbram Maronis et modulum, sed inscientissimum si mentem auctoris, qui insanissime putavit non finem Aeneidi impositum et Virgilium egere supplemento illo, cum nulla tam sit in circinum ducta periodus quam opus Virgilianum.*"[38]

Depuis moins d'une décennie, avec l'intérêt croissant pour le latin de l'humanisme, quelques travaux, qui font allusion à Vegio et que je ne citerai qu'au passage, ont paru en Espagne. Juan Luis Navarro a consacré sa thèse de licence, comme je l'ai déjà

---

[31] *Pindari Bellum Troianum ex Homero. M. Veggii Astyanax. Epigrammata quaedam*, s.l., s.i., s.d.; *Epigrammata ... In rusticos. Convivium deorum*, Mediolani, Ioannes de Castiliano, s.d. [1521]; *Meditationes atque alia quamplurima tum divi Augustini tum aliorum sanctorum opuscula*, Compluti, Juan de Brocar, 1554, ff. 4v–7r, qui contient une poèsie sur Ste. Mónica: *Salve lux matrum mater sanctissima salve*; *Carmen M. Vegii Laudensis et epitaphium in sepulcro S, Monicae*, Romae, 1586.

[32] Deux éditions du *De miseria et felicitate*, mais incluses dans les oeuvres de Lucien avec le titre de *Palinurus* (Bononiae, 1502, Alexander Lippus; Paris, 1505, Gaspardus Philippe) et une autre de cette même oeuvre avec son titre originel, accompagnée du *Inter inferiora ... disputatio* (Basilea, A. Cratander, 1518).

[33] Romae, 1586. Elle se trouve parmi les ff. du ms. 8435 de la BN de Madrid.

[34] Parisiis, B. Rembolt et I. Waterloes, 1511.

[35] Parrhisius, B. Rembolt et I. Waterloes, 1511.

[36] *Opuscula sacra et opera quae reperiri potuerunt omnia* dans *Maxima Bibliotheca veterum patrum et antiquorum scriptorum ecclesiasticorum*, t. 26, Lugduni, 1677.

[37] Lisboa, Vicente Alvarez, 1614.

[38] *P. Virgilii Maronis posteriores sex libri Aeneidos argumentis, explicationibus et notis illustrati auctore Ioanne Ludovico de la Cerda Toletano Societatis Iesu, in curia Philippi Regis Hispaniae Primario Eloquentiae Professore*, Lugduni, sumptibus Horatii Cardon., 1617, p. 755. Je remercie mon cher collègue J. A. Izquierdo, de l'Université de Valladolid, pour cette citation.

mentionné, aux éditions de Zaragoza du Supplementum; il a étudié les sources, la langue et la métrique de l'oeuvre, et l'a traduite. V. Cristobal a étudié dans un travail récent[39] le succès du *Supplementum* et son but, c'est-à-dire, d'après lui, imiter Virgilie et non pas compléter son oeuvre. Il a commenté quelques passages en analysant la présence de Virgile ou d'autres modèles, il a défendu quelques lectures et finalement a souligné l'aspect traditionnel de ses comparaisons. Le caractère strictement virgilien de quelques aspects de la versification du *Supplementum* (synalephe et clausule du vers) a été mis en relief par J. Solana,[40] face à la thèse non virgilienne de W. Duckworth[41] qui n'a pas été contestée nettement jusqu'à présent. Finalement J. Closa a mis en évidence ce que la *Traslatio Sanctae Monicae* de l'auteur de Lodi doit à la tradition classique et chrétienne.[42]

Conclusions

La seule oeuvre de Maffeo Vegio éditée et traduite en Espagne et qui en même temps soit présente aussi bien en imprimé qu'en mss. dans nos bibliothèques, c'est l'*Aeneidos Supplementum*. C'est dire que la connaissance de Vegio est indissolublement associée à sa condition de continuateur de l'épopée virgilienne. La traduction castillane de Hernández de Velasco fut sans doute l'instrument qui contribua le plus à sa diffusion, étant donné sa présence continue dans l'imprimerie pendant les XVIe, XVIIe et XVIIIe siècles, conséquence de son incontestable qualité littéraire.

D'après ce que nous savons, les dialogues de Vegio durent avoir aussi une certaine diffusion, même si elle ne fut pas comparable naturellement à celle du *Supplementum*. Nous déduisons cette affirmation des quatre mss. et neufs éditions localisés dans nos bibliothèques. Même s'il est difficile de le préciser, le dialogue peut-être le plus répandu, bien que cela soit un peu paradoxal, fut celui de *De miseria et felicitate*. Ce dialogue apparaît dans cinq de ces éditions parmi les oeuvres de Lucien, avec le titre de *Palinurus* et seulement dans trois parmi celles de Vegio La seule traduction castillane de ses dialogues, celle que Juan Ginés de Sepúlveda réalisa en 1554 en le croyant un *Luciani Palinurus*, paraît confirmer cette idée.

Le reste de son oeuvre semble avoir eu une diffusion beaucoup plus réduite.

Ces conclusions ont forcément un caractère provisoire. Une étude de la réception de Vegio dans la littérature, l'histoire de l'éducation, l'hagiographie ou l'archéologie chrétienne, qui reste hors de notre but actuel, devra compléter nécessairement cette première approche.

Universidad de Córdoba

---

[39] "Maffeo Vegio y su libro XIII de la Eneida," *Cuadernos de Filología Clásica. Estudios Latinos* 5 (1993): 189–210.

[40] "Los modelos métricos de *Aeneidos Supplementum de Maffeo Vegio*," dans *Actas del XI Simposio de la Sección Catalana de la S.E.E.C.* (Octubre, 1993); "El hexámetro del *Aeneidos liber XIII* de Maffeo Vegio y sus modelos clásicos (I)," sous presse.

[41] *Cf.* "Maphaeus Vegius and Vergil's *Aeneid*: A Metrical Momparison," *CPh* 64,1 (1969): 1–6.

[42] "Tradición clásica y cristiana en la *Traslatio S. Monicae* de Mafeo Veggio," dans *Actas del I Simposio de Latín Cristiano* (Salamanca, 1990), 223–228.

"Venere doma Marte." A proposito di uno sconosciuto corso universitario su Lucrezio di Pomponio Leto

GIUSEPPE SOLARO

N el 1971, nel secondo volume del *Catalogus Translationum et Commentariorum (Mediaeval and Renaissance Latin Translations and Commentaries)*, Wolfgang Bernard Fleischmann, affrontando il tema della fortuna del *De rerum natura* di Lucrezio in epoca umanistica, scriveva:

> In the early years of the *cinquecento*, lectures on Lucretius were given under private auspices by Erasmus' friend Egnatius (Giambattista Cipelli) at Venice. We know that Lambinus publicly lectured on Lucretius in Paris, at the Collège de France, in the early 1560s. During the same period, Francesco Vimercato's lectures at the same institution (published as *Aristotelis Meteorologicorum Commentarii*, 1556; and as *Principes de la Nature*, 1596) reflect Lucretius' views on physics and meteorology. Beyond these isolated instances, no record of the use of Lucretius in courses has survived from the fifteenth and sixteenth centuries.

Dopo aver delineato un simile quadro della quasi completa assenza di Lucrezio dalla programmazione dell'insegnamento accademico nei secoli XV e XVI, Fleischmann cercava quindi di spiegare le ragioni del fenomeno: "two reasons—osservava—may be suggested for the exclusion of Lucretius from the curricula of Renaissance schools: his unequivocal assertion of the soul's mortality, and what the age considered the archaic, rough and prose-like character of his style."[1]

Le due ragioni, che Fleischmann adduceva per spiegare l'esclusione del *De rerum natura* dai programmi dell'insegnamento pubblico in età umanistica, erano dunque una di ordine contenutistico (la negazione dell'immortalità dell'anima insieme con la negazione della provvidenza divina rendevano il poema lucreziano del tutto incompatibile

---

[1] Wolfgang B. Fleischmann, "Lucretius Carus, Titus," in *Catalogus Translationum et Commentariorum*, vol. 2 (Washington, D.C., 1971), 352.

con la dottrina cristiana, che dominava ancora in epoca umanistica) ed una di ordine stilistico (l'eloquio di Lucrezio doveva essere apparso agli umanisti troppo duro e quasi prosastico).

Ora, che il poema lucreziano abbia in ogni epoca suscitato delle perplessità e talora delle vere e proprie forme di avversione a causa della concezione epicurea del mondo, della divinità e dell'uomo, che lo alimenta e ispira, è un fatto a tutti ben noto. E in verità anche gli umanisti, i quali, sebbene operassero in un clima di riscoperta dei testi e dei valori della civiltà classica, non di rado continuarono a professare ossequio, per lo meno da un punto di vista formale, ai dettami del cristianesimo, furono ben consapevoli del fatto che la divulgazione di un'opera come il *De rerum natura* necessitasse per ragioni ideologiche della massima cautela e prudenza.

E' per questo, ad esempio, che Giovan Battista Pio (ca. 1460/64–ca. 1540/48), autore della prima moderna edizione commentata del *De rerum natura* (pubblicata a Bologna nel 1511 e ristampata poi a Parigi nel 1514), avverte la necessità di ricordare qua e là nel suo commento l'empietà, rispetto al dogma cattolico, dell'opera lucreziana, con frasi cautelative del tipo "... lucretianae opinioni tum discutiendae (quoniam est impia) tum excutiendae," oppure "a pietate nostrae theologiae haec acerbitas et irreligio procul explodatur," o ancora, additando il lettore, "ne tibi Lucretius insidiosis rugientis leonis crocodilitis, serris et corniculatis argumentis armatus officiat, aegida Minervae theologicae induamus."[2]

Quanto poi alla seconda motivazione addotta da Fleischmann, il fastidio degli umanisti per lo stile duro e prosastico di Lucrezio, anche in questo caso non mancano ben precise testimonianze. E però, quel che risulta attestato non è tanto la negazione delle capacità poetiche di Lucrezio, quanto piuttosto, una volta riconosciuta una certa asprezza e prosaicità dello stile del poema, il tentativo in certi casi davvero commovente di "salvarlo" esteticamente, facendo riferimento alle notevoli difficoltà che Lucrezio doveva aver incontrato nel mettere in versi una materia cosi inadatta alla poesia come la scienza della natura. Così, se è vero—come lo stesso Fleischmann ricordava poco dopo il brano testé citato—che il fiorentino Petrus Crinitus (Pietro Del Riccio Baldi, 1475–1507), nel capitolo del suo *De poetis Latinis* dedicato a Lucrezio (Florentiae 1505, lib. II, cap. XIX), si rende conto benissimo e stigmatizza il fatto che i "Lucreti versus" siano talora "duriores ... et quasi orationi solutae similes," è però anche vero che subito dopo giustifica Lucrezio, rilevando che quel modo di scrivere "fuit ... proprium illis temporibus" e che "ille enim stilus maxime tum placebat."

Ma il giudizio di Fleischmann va oggi rivisto non tanto per quel che attiene

---

[2] Cito queste frasi del Pio da Ezio Raimondi, "Il primo commento umanistico a Lucrezio," in *Tra latino e volgare. Per Carlo Dionisotti*, 2 vols. (Padova, 1974), 2: 663. Si è discusso molto, e con posizioni spesso contrastanti, intorno al problema dell'ortodossia cattolica di cui il Pio darebbe prova nel suo commento lucreziano. Su ciò cf.: Simone Fraisse, *Une conquête du rationalisme. L'influence de Lucrèce en France au seizième siècle* (Paris, 1962), 24 (*contra* Alberto Tenenti, *Belfagor* 18 [1963]: 736–737); Françoise Joukovsky, "Quelques sources épicuriennes au XVIe siècle," *Bibliothèque d'Humanisme et Renaissance* 31 (1969): 14 (*contra* Eugenio Garin, "Commenti lucreziani," *Rivista Critica di Storia della Filosofia* 28 [1973]: 84–85).

all'interpretazione che lo studioso dava dell'esclusione di Lucrezio dai programmi d'insegnamento in età umanistica, quanto più radicalmente per quel che riguarda l'affermazione stessa di una siffatta esclusione così diffusa e generalizzata. Oggi è possibile infatti addurre almeno due significativi casi che documentano l'impiego del *De rerum natura* in età umanistica in ambito universitario.

Il primo, cronologicamente parlando, dei due casi, collocabile nella seconda metà del secolo XV, rappresenta l'oggetto di questa mia comunicazione. Prima di parlarne, accennerò brevemente all'altro caso, databile nella prima metà del secolo XVI.

Nel 1611, a Lovanio, Erycius Puteanus (1574–1646) pubblicò per la prima volta, con il titolo di *Somnium sive Paralipomena Virgili* e *Somnium alterum, in librum secundum Lucretii praefatio*, due discorsi, conservati in altrettanti manoscritti, del noto umanista belga Petrus Nannius (P. Nanninck, 1496/1500–1557).[3] Il Nannius, noto ai filologi classici per aver scoperto il codice, oggi perduto, che tramandava la vita svetoniana di Orazio, il cosiddetto "Blandinianus antiquissimus," insegnò all'Università di Lovanio dal 1539 in avanti, tenendo corsi su autori come Cicerone, Livio, Orazio, Virgilio ed anche Lucrezio.

La *praefatio* pubblicata per la prima volta dal Puteanus, altro non è, infatti, che il discorso, con il quale il Nannius introdusse un corso di lezioni dedicato al secondo libro del *De rerum natura*, corso del quale non restano però purtroppo tracce ulteriori. Il testo è privo di una datazione esplicita, ma sulla base di alcuni riferimenti cronologici interni, è possibile datare sia la *praefatio* che, di conseguenza, anche le lezioni alle quali essa avviava nell'anno accademico 1542–1543.

De hoc satis. L'altro esempio che è oggi possibile addurre come documento dell'interesse per Lucrezio in età umanistica in ambito universitario pertiene ad un notissimo umanista italiano, il salernitano Pomponio Leto (1428–1498).

Nel 1884, uno studioso olandese, J. Woltjer, in un breve articolo dal titolo "De anno natali T. Lucretii poetae," apparso negli *Jahrbücher für klassische Philologie* (pp. 134–138), comunicò di aver scoperto quella che egli definiva "vita Lucretii a Pomponio Laeto enarrata," una biografia, cioè, di Lucrezio, composta da Pomponio Leto. Si trattava di un breve testo manoscritto, conservato, con la semplice intestazione "Pomponius Laetus," nei fogli di guardia di un incunabolo lucreziano posseduto dalla Biblioteca Universitaria di Utrecht (la segnatura odierna è Litt. Lat. X fol. 82 rar.), copia dell'edizione in folio del *De rerum natura* stampata a Verona da Paul Friedenperger nell'anno 1486 (Hain 10282).

La comunicazione del Woltjer, dispersa com'era in una nota in calce ad un articolo di differente argomento, finì col passare inosservata, almeno fino a quando, dieci anni dopo, ed esattamente il 23 giugno 1894, sul settimanale *The Academy* (pp. 519–520), lo studioso inglese John Masson diede notizia di un ritrovamento del tutto analogo a quello effettuato dal Woltjer. Masson aveva scoperto che nei fogli di guardia di un esemplare, posseduto dalla British Library di Londra e segnato IA 23564, di un'altra

---

[3] Su questo umanista, ed in particolare sulla sua *praefatio in Lucretium*, della quale mi accingo a dire, si veda Dirk Sacré, "Nannius's Somnia," in *La satire humaniste. Actes du Colloque international des 31 mars, 1er et 2 avril 1993*, ed. R. De Smet (Bruxelles, 1994), 77–93.

edizione umanistica del *De rerum natura* (Venezia 1495–Hain 10283), si trovava conservato un testo manoscritto, anch'esso concernente la biografia di Lucrezio, composto da un altro ben noto umanista italiano, allievo del Pontano, il lucano Girolamo Borgia (nato nel 1480 e morto non prima del 13 giugno 1550). Masson sosteneva che il Borgia (se non proprio già il suo maestro, il Pontano) si fosse imbattuto in un codice del *De rerum natura* corredato di una sintesi della vita lucreziana contenuta nel perduto *De poetis* di Svetonio, e che l'avesse quindi utilizzata per quel suo scritto su Lucrezio conservato nei fogli di guardia dell'incunabolo lucreziano della British Library.

A questo punto entrò in scena il Woltjer, il quale, in un articolo apparso su *Mnemosyne* nel 1895 ("Studia Lucretiana. II. De vita Lucretii," 222–233), richiamò l'attenzione degli studios) i proprio sulla scoperta fatta da lui in precedenza. In questo modo, adducendo cioè il caso del tutto analogo della vita lucreziana di Pomponio Leto, il Woltjer intendeva dimostrare, contro il Masson, che anche nel caso della vita borgiana di Lucrezio si aveva a che fare non con il ritrovamento di prezioso materiale risalente al mondo antico, ma con la personale e moderna elaborazione di un umanista, basata su testimonianze sulla vita di Lucrezio né rare né ignote, bensì del tutto note e individuabili mediante una attenta analisi testuale (in primis la famosa notizia su Lucrezio che si legge nel *Chronicon* di San Girolamo, alla 171ª Olimpiade).

Il Masson rimase molto infastidito dall'attacco, peraltro del tutto fondato, del Woltjer. Così, in una breve nota apparsa su *The Classical Review* nel 1896 (pp. 323–324), a proposito dell'intervento del Woltjer, in tono acremente polemico, osservò: "as to the curious matter which Dr. Woltjer found on the fly-leaf of a copy of the Verona edition ... it is almost needless to say that no parallel can be drawn between data such as these, derived from such a source, and information embodied in the preface to an edition of Lucretius containing the text of a noted scholar and student of MSS. like Pontanus, a preface which was written by his secretary (also a distinguished man of letters) and was apparently revised by Pontanus himself."[4]

Così scrivendo, però, il Masson mostrava di non essere affatto consapevole del significativo ruolo assolto dal Leto nel mondo umanistico, certamente non inferiore a quello svolto dal "segretario" del Pontano, come Masson chiamava il Borgia: errore di valutazione, nel quale lo studioso inglese non sarebbe certo incorso, se avesse conosciuto almeno il celebre e sentito epigramma che lo stesso Pontano, maestro del Borgia, dedicò al Leto, dopo la morte di quest'ultimo.[5]

Ma non è certo un confronto tra il Leto e il Borgia, quel che qui si vuole delineare. E' un fatto, però, che, mentre la vita lucreziana del Borgia ha goduto per decenni di una notevole attenzione da parte degli studiosi, nessuno mai dai tempi del

---

[4] John Masson, "New Data Presumably from Suetonius' Life of Lucretius," *The Classical Review* 10 (1896): 324.

[5] "Pomponi, tibi pro tumulo sit laurea silva,/ ossa maris rores myrteaque umbra tegant/ teque tegant artusque tuos violaeque rosaeque,/ ver alet, zephyros spiret et ipse cinis,/ stillet et ipse cinis quas et Parnasus et ipse/ Thespis et ipsa sues Pipla ministrat aqua" (Ioannis Ioviani Pontani *De tumulis* [1.16], ed. Liliana M. Sabia [Napoli, 1974], 87).

Woltjer si è preoccupato di verificare direttamente che cosa fosse esattamente il testo pomponiano che lo studioso olandese aveva riportato alla luce e reso noto solo in minima parte nei suoi articoli.

Vladimir Zabughin, il benemerito studioso russo autore negli anni 1909–1912 di una ben nota e consultatissima monografia, peraltro incompiuta, sulla vita e l'opera del Leto, nel raccogliere gli sporadici riferimenti a Lucrezio che sono rinvenibili nei commenti dell'umanista alle opere di altri autori della letteratura latina, segnalò tra gli altri esempi la sintomatica frase "Venus Martem domat et in eius gremio cubat Mars," che Pomponio annotò nel codice Vat. lat. 3279, contenente la *Tebaide* di Stazio, in margine ai versi 3.263–265 del poema (fol. 38r), facendola seguire dalla citazione di alcuni versi del proemio del *De rerum natura* di Lucrezio (1.31–34).[6]

"Sarebbe però ben deluso—metteva in guardia lo Zabughin—chi cercasse in questi squarci del poeta-filosofo una comprova del preteso epicureismo di Pomponio: questi riferisce al solito i versi meno filosofici dell'opera."[7] L'idea che lo Zabughin si era fatto dell'interesse del Leto per Lucrezio, il "poeta-filosofo," si basava però su una conoscenza molto parziale, in quanto era appunto limitata, come si è detto, ai soli fugaci cenni a Lucrezio che si possono cogliere qua e là nei manoscritti pomponiani che tramandano le note dell'umanista su altri autori della latinità, le cui opere il Leto lesse e commentò soprattutto nell'ambito dei corsi universitari che egli svolse come professore di retorica presso lo *Studium Urbis* nella seconda metà del Quattrocento.[8] Probabilmente, se fosse stato al corrente della scoperta del Woltjer, che dimostrava un preciso e diretto interesse del Leto per Lucrezio, ma che non viene affatto menzionata nella sua monografia su Pomponio, lo Zabughin avrebbe espresso un giudizio ben diverso.

Quella che il Woltjer chiamava "vita Lucretii a Pomponio Laeto enarrata," altro non è, infatti, che la lezione introduttiva ad un corso tenuto dall'umanista sul *De rerum natura* di Lucrezio, una lezione che si presenta non a caso come un vero e proprio *accessus ad auctorem*, in cui Pomponio intende avviare con una serie di notizie preliminari la lettura commentata del poema lucreziano.[9]

L'umanista prende le mosse da un passo di Varrone, che viene da lui adottato

---

[6] Cf. Vladimiro Zabughin, *Giulio Pomponio Leto. Saggio critico*, 2 vols. (Grottaferrata, 1910–1912), 2: 55 e n. 318. Ho avuto modo di verificare personalmente, completandone la trascrizione data dallo Zabughin, questa glossa pomponiana contenuta nel citato codice vaticano di Stazio.

[7] Zabughin, 2: 51. Sull'adesione all'epicureismo da parte di Pomponio e dei membri dell'Accademia da lui fondata, si veda in particolare Robert Bongiorno, "15th-Century Anti-Christian Epicureanism and the Roman Academy," *Agora* 2 (1973): 60–67.

[8] Sull'insegnamento universitario del Leto si vedano i dati e la bibliografia raccolti da Maria C. Dorati da Empoli, "I lettori dello Studio e i maestri di grammatica a Roma da Sisto IV ad Alessandro VI," *Rassegna degli Archivi di Stato* 40 (1980): 122 e nn. 1–8.

[9] Sulla tecnica dell'*accessus ad auctorem*, che ha, com'è noto, origini tardoantiche e medioevali e continua poi in età umanistica, cf. Silvia Rizzo, "Una prolusione del Poliziano e i commentatori greci di Aristotele," in *Studi in onore di Anthos Ardizzoni* (Roma, 1978), 761–768 e bibliografia alla n. 2.

come punto di riferimento per l'ordine da seguire in tutta la sua esposizione:[10] "M. Varro—esordisce infatti il Leto—Romanae linguae parens, tria observanda rebus omnibus tradit: origo, dignitas et ars" (rr. 2–3; cf. Varr. *Rust.* 2.1.1). Tuttavia, mentre Varrone, nel *De re rustica*, applicava questo schema (*oricgo, dignitas* e *ars*) alla trattazione di una vile materia, la pastorizia, Pomponio lo applica alla filosofia, la materia di cui gli preme parlare, dovendo egli preparare i suoi allievi allo studio di un'opera filosofica quale il *De rerum natura.*

In base allo schema prefissato, Pomponio affronta quindi anzitutto il tema delle origini della filosofia (rr. 5–11), ricollegando la sapienza a Dio e facendone così un dono della bontà divina, e passa poi a parlare della *dignitas*, cioè dell'importanza della filosofia (rr. 11–14), delineando un breve schizzo dei principali rappresentanti della disciplina filosofica nella Roma antica, tra i quali appunto Lucrezio, sulla cui biografia si intrattiene a lungo (rr. 17–51), citando le principali testimonianze antiche sul poeta (nell'ordine Varrone, Girolamo, Cicerone, Quintiliano, Ovidio). La trattazione del terzo punto, l'*ars*, e cioè il contenuto vero e proprio della scienza filosofica, viene invece rimandata dall'umanista a quella che egli stesso definisce, con espressione tecnica, l'"expositio operis," e cioè quella lettura commentata del poema lucreziano che l'umanista sta per intraprendere: "de arte dicere—egli infatti precisa—in praesentia necesse non est: in expositione operis pro facultate atque viribus ingenii nostri aperiemus" (rr. 51–53).

E' questo un passaggio testuale di primaria rilevanza, poiché ci consente di affermare con sicurezza che quel che si è letto fino a questo punto costituisce—come si è detto—il discorso propedeutico ad una lettura interpretata del *De rerum natura.* Dopo questa precisazione da parte dell'umanista segue infatti un commento dedicato al proemio dell'opera lucreziana, il famoso inno a Venere, ovvero quel luogo del poema, l'esordio appunto, da cui il Leto non poteva che incominciare la sua esposizione.

La figura di Venere viene analizzata con grande attenzione per le curiosità erudite, siano esse le varie etimologie del nome della dea o questioni inerenti alla mitologia o all'astrologia, e con costante riferimento alle fonti classiche: un modo di procedere, questo, che, grazie ai molti esempi già raccolti ed esaminati a suo tempo dallo Zabughin, sappiamo essere una costante dei molteplici commenti dedicati da Pomponio nelle sue lezioni universitarie agli autori antichi.

A dire il vero, sia in queste note strettamente legate al testo del *De rerum natura* che nella parte generale che le precede, il Leto evita di trattare problemi squisitamente filosofici e si rifugia nella sua erudizione minuta e in dotte divagazioni, insomma in un tipo di discussione che è più vicino alla concreta e terrena filologia che non alla astratta e sottile scienza filosofica. Dunque, anche dopo la "riscoperta" delle carte pomponiane di Utrecht, continua ad avere un suo valore il duro giudizio espresso a suo tempo dal Wilamowitz, secondo il quale "affatto ignaro di filosofia, a

---

[10] I righi in base ai quali viene qui di seguito citata la prolusione lucreziana del Leto sono quelli dell'edizione da me curata nel 1993 (Pomponio Leto, *Lucrezio*, ed. G. Solaro [Palermo, 1993]).

Roma Pomponio Leto era trasportato dal solo romanticismo nazionale."[11]

Ma—ci si deve chiedere—abbiamo a che fare con appunti personali del Leto o con *dictata* raccolti da allievi?

Tutto lascia propendere per la seconda ipotesi: anzitutto, da un punto di vista stilistico, il carattere chiaramente desultorio, "orale," della prosa latina, che è proprio di note prese a lezione ἀπὸ φωνῆς, non prive quindi di durezze grammaticali e sintattiche, oltre che di veri e propri errori di tipo auditivo (come la sostituzione del più facile *Fannius* al posto di *Amafanius* o *Amafinius*, nome di filosofo epicureo, nel rigo 17); in secondo luogo, la presenza di rinvii del Leto a momenti successivi dell' esposizione, che in certi casi non vengono rispettati (cf. r. 11 "de quo paulo post dicemus"); infine, il frequente uso, specie nella parte iniziale, del verbo *dicere* o di suoi sinonimi (r. 4, r. 5 [*disserere*], r. 11, r. 51).

Del resto, non saremmo certo di fronte all'unico caso di trasmissione di *dictata* pomponiani nei fogli di guardia di un'edizione a stampa di un autore antico. Un esempio del tutto analogo fu segnalato alla fine del secolo scorso da Pierre de Nolhac nel suo splendido volume su *La bibliothèque de Fulvio Orsini* (Paris, 1887, 207): si trattava di alcune pagine manoscritte·premesse ad un esemplare dell'edizione veneziana di Sallustio del 1481 (Hain 14211), attualmente conservato presso la Biblioteca Vaticana (Inc. Vat. II 111). Ebbene, queste pagine, come fu in seguito dimostrato dallo Zabughin, presentano i *dictata* relativi alla lezione introduttiva di un corso universitario dell'umanista dedicato a Sallustio, *praelectio* nella quale Pomponio tracciò un quadro articolato del genere storiografico e dei suoi principali rappresentanti nel mondo antico (così come accade per la filosofia nell'incunabolo lucreziano).[12]

Per la verità, le pagine manoscritte premesse all'incunabolo lucreziano di Utrecht molto probabilmente non sono *dictata* originali, ma la trascrizione di *dictata* contenuti originariamente in un manoscritto del *De rerum natura* e ricopiati poi sull'incunabolo. Alla fine dell'incunabolo si legge infatti una sottoscrizione, nella quale il protonotario apostolico Sebastiano Priuli ed il suo *adscripticius*, il parmense Francesco Cerreto, affermano di aver collazionato nel mese di ottobre dell'anno 1492 il testo lucreziano così come si presentava nell'incunabolo conservato oggi ad Utrecht con un non meglio precisato "codex Pomponianus": "castigatus fuit hic codex cum codice Pomponiano a R(everendo) P(atre) D(omino) Sebast. Priolo, protonotario apostolico ac S(anctissimi) D(omini) N(ostri) referendario et secretario, nec non a Francisco Cerreto Parmensi eiusdem ads(c)ripticio. Romae, mense Octobris 1492, anno primo pont. Alexandri VI."

Ora, nulla esclude, in teoria, che nella sottoscrizione *codex* debba intendersi in entrambi i casi non come "manoscritto" ma come *codex impressus*, cioè edizione a stampa, e che dunque i *dictata* pomponiani tramandati all'inizio dell'incunabolo di Utrecht (nella sottoscrizione citato come "hic codex") provengano da un altro testo

[11] Ulrich von Wilamowitz-Moellendorff, *Storia della filologia classica* (1927), trad. di Fausto Codino (Torino, 1967), 38.

[12] Cf. Zabughin, 2: 141–146.

a stampa, opportunamente annotato, del *De rerum natura*, che aveva in qualche modo a che fare con Pomponio Leto o con la sua scuola, tanto da poter essere definito "codex Pomponianus." Tuttavia, da una vasta e articolata documentazione sappiamo dell'esistenza di vari manoscritti lucreziani, in certi casi tuttora conservati, in altri perduti, che furono personalmente scritti ovvero maneggiati e/o posseduti da Pomponio e che circolarono negli ambienti umanistici, da uno dei quali deve con molta probabilità provenire, oltre che la gran quantità di varianti testuali e scolii che, grazie alla collazione di Priuli e Cerreto, circonda ancor oggi il testo dell'incunabolo di Utrecht, anche la lezione introduttiva a Lucrezio tramandata nei fogli di guardia.[13]

Ciò assodato, l'ottobre del 1492, data nella quale le note pomponiane furono trascritte da Priuli e Cerreto, può essere senz'altro considerato quale *terminus ante quem* per la datazione del corso lucreziano del Leto. Sulla base di un significativo indizio interno, è possibile però circoscrivere meglio l'arco di tempo nel quale collocare il corso. Infatti, a conclusione del suo commento al proemio lucreziano, Pomponio cita alla lettera un brano della *Vita Epicuri* di Diogene Laerzio (10.34), riportandolo nella traduzione latina di Ambrogio Traversari, che fu pubblicata a Roma intorno al 1472 (Hain 6196): una pubblicazione, questa, che fu curata da Elio Francesco Marchese, e che lo stesso Pomponio, il quale—com'è ben noto—con la lingua greca non ebbe mai molta domestichezza, aveva più volte sollecitato.[14] L'anno 1472 può dunque essere considerato quale *terminus post quem* per la datazione del corso.

Nel saggio sulla fortuna del *De rerum natura* che citavamo qui in principio, Wolfgang B. Fleischmann, a proposito della vita borgiana di Lucrezio, osservava: "This brief biography is probably concocted from scraps of information amplified by Borgia's imagination, but has been conjectured to derive either from Suetonius or from Pomponius Laetus."[15]

Ora, se tra Svetonio e la vita borgiana, com'è stato ormai ampiamente dimostrato dalla critica, non c'è in realtà alcun nesso diretto, invece, poiché la vita borgiana è databile con certezza nell'anno 1502, la possibilità di una dipendenza di questo studiatissimo testo dalla meno fortunata vita lucreziana del Leto può essere oggi tranquillamente considerata.[16]

Università di Bari

---

[13] Per maggiori dettagli sull'intricata questione relativa a quanti e quali furono esattamente i manoscritti del *De rerum natura* che è possibile mettere in relazione con il Leto, si veda l'introduzione alla mia edizione della vita pomponiana di Lucrezio (op. cit., 21–24).

[14] Su ciò cf. Eugenio Garin, "La prima traduzione latina di Diogene Laerzio," *Giornale Critico della Filosofia Italiana* 38 (1959): 283–284.

[15] Fleischmann, "Lucretius," 349.

[16] Per un'ipotesi di derivazione di un particolare brano della vita borgiana di Lucrezio da quella di Pomponio Leto, cf. Renata Fabbri, "La 'Vita Borgiana' di Lucrezio nel quadro delle biografie umanistiche," *Lettere Italiane* 36 (1984): 353–354.

Sur l'édition des poésies d'Horace
dédiée à Stefan Batory (1584)

JERZY STARNAWSKI

L'auteur de l'édition traitée fut un philoloque italien, Bernardo Partenio da Spilimbergo (mort en 1589), dont les oeuvres de jeunesse parurent dès la première moitie du XVIe siècle.[1] Quand il publait des oeuvres en latin, il les signait du nom de Parthenius ce qui le rapprochait de Virgile, appelé parfois Parthenias.

Le volume des poésies d'Horace est dédié au roi polonais, Stefan Batory, souverain utilisant constamment la langue latine, et se compose de deux parties différenciées non seulement par des pages de titre, mais aussi par une pagination particulière. La première partie intitulée Bernardini Parthenii Spilimbergii *In Q. Horatii Flacci Carmina atque Epodos Commentarii quibus poetae artificium, quia ad imitationem atque ad poeticae scribendum aperitur*. Venetiis 1584. Et sur la page de titre nous pouvons lire en bas: *Ad Stephanum Bathori Potentiss[imum] Poloniae Regem* etc. La deuxième partie est intitulée *Q. Horatii Flacci Sermonum libri IV seu Satyrarum libri II, Epistolarum libri II. Cum argumentis ad lectoris maiorem facilitatem*. Venetiis 1584.

Dans la lettre dédicatoire à Stefan Batory l'auteur rappelle que le roi perse n'avait jamais été salué sans cadeau. Cela l'encourage à offrir au roi polonais le fruit de son travail qu'il a désigne comme "munusculum." C'étaient les commentaires du texte d'Horace. Il affirme qu'il n'apportait aucune nouvelle confirmation; qu'il considère comme fruit de son travail l'appareil qui accompagne les chants d'Horace. Pourquoi un spécialiste vénitien d'Horace a-t-il offert au roi polonais son édition?

Il le justifie comme suit:

Id ego eo libentius feci, quod te litterarum, maximarumque artium studiis ab adolescentia delectatum atque ingeniis favere omnes praedicant. Quod nobis vel eo confirmatum est, quod claros ex Italia viros ingenti pecunia invitasti, facile declarans te nihil malle, quam ut optimae disciplinae in tuo regno efflores-

---

[1] Voir Gian-Giuseppe Lituti: *Notizie delle vite ed opere scritte da'letterati del Friuli* [...] V. 2 (Venezia, 1762), 111–113. Friuli est un autre nom du village de Partenio, Spilimberg.

cant. Hinc factum est, quam ob rem ex omnibus regionibus in Poloniam litteras migrare audiamus.... Idque agis, ut quibus ipse studiis fuisti institutus, iisdem cives tui erudiantur....[2]

Ayant rendu l'hommage à Stefan Batory comme mécène de la culture et la science, Parthenius s'adresse ensuite au monarque comme à un commandant vainqueur; il termine ses louanges en ces termes:

Quam ob rem quem tibi ex vetustissimis imperatoribus homines conferant, non reperiunt, profecto poetae, qui omnia admirabiliora faciunt, vix talia fingere potuissent.

L'éditeur énumère avec beaucoup de précision les événements de la guerre de Moscou, en rapportant les épisodes de la jeunesse du monarque, à cette époque-là le prince de Transylvanie. Il s'adresse au roi ainsi:

Dii boni, ut tibi illud, quod M. Tullius de Pompeio dixit, convenire videtur difficile esse dictu an hostes armati virtutem tuam pugnantes magis timuerint, an victi benignitatem magis adamarint.

Il se réfère à Cicéron, en particulier au discours *De imperio Cn. Pompei* dans lequel (c. 42) nous lisons:

. . . utrum hostes magis virtutem eius pugnantes timuerint, an mansuetudinem victi dilexerint.

La pensée cicéronienne a été paraphrasée.

En célébrant la sagesse du roi, l'auteur de la lettre énumère ces deux auteurs d'éloges: de la Pologne—Stanisław Reszka, secrétaire de Hosius vivant à Rome, de la Hongrie: Wolfgang Kovacs, chancelier de Transylvanie.

En ce qui concerne Stanisław Reszka, il est mentionné glorieusement dans la correspondance du grand Lipsius. L'éminent Torquato Tasso s'intéressait aussi à Hosius et l'a éternisé dans sa poésie.[3] La commentateur présente son oeuvre en raccourci en espérant que le roi polonais va récompenser son effort:

---

[2] Dans cet éloge de Stefan Batory Partenio se compare à Marc-Antoine Muret, plus célèbre que lui, qui dans sa lettre de 1578 à Paolo Sacranus écrit:

Stephanus, Poloniae Rex, qui et aliis regis virtutibus ornatissimus est et hoc supra caeteros omnes reges, qui multis ab hinc seculis vixerunt, eximium habet, quod et amat unice homines eruditos, et ipse omni elegantis doctrinae genere mirifice excultus est, miserat in Italiam unum e domesticis suis, qui quasi delectum quendam haberet, praestantium doctrina virorum eosque optimis admodum propriis conditionibus, in Poloniam invitaret, ad Academiam novam, quam Rex Cracoviae instituere parabat.

Cité selon: M. Antoni Mureti (. . .) *Epistolae* (. . .). *Editio ultima ab authore emendata et integro epistolarum* (. . .) *libro iam recens adaucta* (Coloniae Agrippinae, 1611), p. 111. Les letres de Muret ont déjà été publiées plusieurs fois.

[3] Voir Petrus Burmannus (ed.): *Sylloges epistolarum a viris illustribus scriptarum.* V. 1. 1727, s. 76, 78; 651–654; Justus Lipsius: *Opera omnia* . . . (Antverpiae, 1627), p. XLVII.

Cum in praesentia nihil habeam, quo meum animum Maiestati tuae declarare pro meritis tuis possim, non sum veritus meos istos *Commentarios*, quos in Horatium, poetarum elegantissimum, conscripsi, tibi dicare.... Fieri tamen posset, si Maiestati tuae liceret aut vacaret aliqua ex iis audire, ut non frustra susceptum laborem hunc fuisse statueres. Ibi enim via feliciter poetico more scribendi aperitur, latissimi campi ad imitationem patent. Quam rationem minus cognitam atque perspectam esse quam plurimis et iis praesertim, qui se iactant ac venditant, et versus praeclare scribere profitentur, docti intelligunt. Omne fere artificium, quo poeta usus est in suis lyricis scribendis, unde tantum laudis est consecutus, quodque ante omnia in excellentissimis scriptoribus quaerendum, investigadumque est, ostenditur.

L'adjectif *elegans* désignait à la fin du XVIᵉ et au début du XVIIᵉ s. un poète éminent et on l'employait souvent. On le trouve surtout dans la correspondance de l'époque entre les écrivains éminents. Environ quarante ans plut tôt Bernardinus Parthenius (Partenio) avait composé un traité sur la dignité de la langue latine, *Pro lingua Latina oratio* (1545). Il y parle d'Horace:

excellentissimi iudici et consilii optimi vates (...), cuius tam gravis est authoritas, ut nemo sit, nisi quispiam ridicule insanus, qui eius iudicium tot clarissimorum hominum sententia commendatum, publicoque signo omnium Latinorum iam pridem obsignatum audeat rescindere.

Conformément aux habitudes de l'époque de la Renaissance de munir les oeuvres éditées de poèmes publicataires, l'édition d'Horace de Parthenius contient le poème "Francisci Melchiori Opitegrini" (26 v.) dont plus de la moitié est consacrée à la Pologne (v. 13–26):

> Te septem colles nunc primum, et Romula tellus
> Agnoscunt nitido detractis corpore larvis.
> 15   Praecipue agnoscet dives Polonia regnis,
> Clara viris, clara ingeniis, et Marte superba.
> Illic Magnanimus te Rex, quem Moschica late
> Terra tremit cui regna alio sub sole resurgunt,
> Excipiet, sacra quem Maiestate verendum
> 20   In placida arridens mitis Clementia fronte
> Ad superos vehit. Augustum hic mirabere lapsum
> Coelo iterum, atque novum sydus splendescere terris.
> Tu vero nostris nunc tandem redditus auris
> Pulchrior, Elysiis sublatus ad aethera, Regis,
> 25   Quo maius nihil, aut melius fataere potentis
> Implicitus genibus, pronus dabis oscula plantis.

La préface adressée *nobilissimis atque illustribus Academicis Vicentinis* parle entre autres sujets du théâtre, dont se vante Vicenza. Horace est mentionné comme le chantre de Pindare (il était dans l'ode IV,2). Comme il écrivait sur Pindare, il convient d'écrire sur lui. Suit la vie d'Horace *ex Lilio Gregorio Gyraldo*,[4] puis les textes des odes et épodes d'Horace avec des commentaires nombreux, parfois de plusieurs pages, pour une ode courte. Toutes les oeuvres d'Horace sont intitulées brièvement. La partie contenant *Satyres* et *Épîtres* a un appareil différent, n'est pas munie de commentaires et chaque oeuvre est précédée uniquement d'un *argumentum*, selon la tradition des éditions des tragédies antiques. Certains *argumenta* sont très courts (une phrase): Par ex. l'*argumentum* qui précède la lettre I,6:

> Admirabilis Epistola, qua declaratur felicitatem esse molestiis et curis vacare.

Il en est de plus longs. Le plus long précède évidemment l'Épître aux *Pisons*:

> Cum tam multi in poeticam scripserint, supervacaneum esse arbitror velle aquam mari addere. In iis autem omnibus, qui in ea re laborarunt, ego, pro mea sententia, primas Vincentio Magio[5] defero ut qui huius libri exactam atque absolutam cognitionem tenere capiat, nulla fortasse alia ope indigeat. Cum ad Aristotelis exemplum se Horatius totum composuerit, quod nemo negarit, tam diligens praeceptorum illius philosophi fuit, ut nihil fere de suo contulisse Horatius videatur, conferet omnes locos poeta cum Aristotelis praeceptis ut videri possit Horatius nihil sibi tam proposuisse, quam totum Aristotelem exprimere. Sed in diversa ratione facit, ac via, nam modo reprehendit, modo irridet satyrice agens. Utrum vero liber de arte poetica an Epistola ad Pisones appellandum sit hoc, parum interest. In hoc egregiam operam navavit Magius summus philosophus, atque ea vidit in hoc opere, quod nemo unquam antea somniavit. Pro omnibus igitur, qui in hoc explicando infuderunt, magna gratia Magio habenda est. Legant hanc poetices studiosi, nihil absolutius sibi afferri potuisse statuent.

Parthenio exposait la parenté de la poétique d'Horace avec celle d'Aristote dans son oeuvre italienne écrite beacoup plus tôt *Della imitazione poetica* (1560). Les commentaires aux chants et épodes d'Horace, c'est dans la partie minimale des interprétations linguistiques, de courtes explicitations de sens. En voici quelques-unes, par exemple dans le commentaire à l'ode II,18 (*Non ebur, neque aureum* ...):

> *Non ebur*, significat se minus valere opibus, sed ingenio praestare, pulcherrimas autem assumit species, quae in divitiis ponuntur. Qui modus peculiaris est bonis poetis, de quo tam saepe admonuimus.

> *Ebur*, pro quacunque re pretiosa usurpatur, quamvis pro poculis, pro vasis, ac signis ex ebore confectis, poni solitum sit.

Dominent ici les explications renvoyant à d'autres extraits d'Horace, de nombreux

---

[4] Le fragment sur Horace est extrait de l'oeuvre *Historia poetarum tam Graecorum quam Latinorum, dialogi decem*, X[e] dialogue. Voir L. G. Giraldus: *Opera quae extant omnia*. V. 2 (Basileae, 1580), 359.

[5] Vicenzo Maggi, un philologue classique italien, prépara vers 1550 le commentaire de *La Poétique* d'Aristote.

auteurs grecs et romains. Le philologue dans l'oeuvre déjà mentionnée avait présenté en quelque sorte sa théorie comparatiste. Le commentaire élaboré 24 ans plus tard, fait aussi preuve de ses intérêts dans ce domaine. Tout le commentaire c'est une grande étude comparatiste. Conformément au traité de 1560 dans lequel l'humaniste italien avait souligné que ses affinités intellectuelles liaient Horace avec Virgile, dans son commentaire il analyse consciencieusement l'auteur des *Bucoliques, Géorgiques* et *Enéide*. Il n'en reste pas à Virgile. Il situe Horace dans le contexte plus large des auteurs antiques, il considère les auteurs humanistes comme la littérature critique du sujet, à laquelle il se réfère. La pierre fondamentale de ce problème est mise en lumière dans le traité *Della imitazione* (p. 25) où l'idée horacienne du *De arte poetica*:

> Publica materies privati iuris erit, si
> Non circa vilem, patulumque moraberis orbem (v. 131–132)

est liée à Triphon par la citation de sa pensée *le sentenze e le materie d'un altro intere nostre fare si possono*. Cela est frappant dès le début. Il n'est pas difficile de rapprocher l'ode I,1 (*Maecenas atavis . . .*) de la *Satyre* I,1 (*Qui fit Maecenas . . .*) ce que le commentateur fit (c. 1er v.). Mais la généralisation exprimée par:

> Maecenas varia esse hominum ingenia, variisque studiis eos delectari ostendit
> haec sententia a multis celebrata est

reçut l'illustration dans laquelle Homère trouva sa place:

> ἄλλος γάρ τ'ἄλλοισίν γε ἐπιτέρπεται ἔργοις (*Od.* 14, 228)

Ainsi que Archestratus Gelensis:

> . . . χαίρει γὰρ ὁ μὲν τούτοις ὁ δὲ ἐκείνοις

Et Pindare:

> Τερπὸν δ' ἐν ἀνθρώποις ἴσυν ἔσσεται οὐδέν(*Olimp.* 8, 53)

Et Virgile:

> . . . *trahit sua quemque voluptas* (*Ecl.* 2, 65)

Les allusions comparatistes sont très courtes chez Parthenius, elles ne présentent que les affinités lexicales. Par exemple les paroles *Dum rediens* (ode III,21) sont munies de commentaire:

> sol enim abit et redit. Sic in *Carmine saeculari*:
> Alme sol, curru nitido diem, qui
> Promis et celas aliusque et idem
> Nasceris . . . (donc v. 9–11)
> necessario autem sit, ut ex oriente sole sidera occultentur,
> temporis descriptionem ex consequenti necessario sumpsit.
> Quare.

Nous rencontrons des comparaisons plus longues. Un cycle particulièrment riche (c. 23–24) accompagne l'*incipit* de l'ode I,9: *Vides ut alta . . .* Après avoir rappelé

Anacréon et Archiloque dont le commentateur a traduit les citations en prose latine (*mensis adest december, nubes aquis gravantur procellae vehementer fremunt*, Ancr.; *Glauce, aspice ut iam profundum pelagus fluctibus commovetur, et nubes curva arboribus summis imminet. Tempestatis argumentum. Subitusque metus ex improviso ingruit*, Arch.) il cite les descriptions de la nature chez Horace: ode II,9, v. 1–8: *Non semper imbres* . . .; ode III,10, v. 5–8: *Audis, quo strepitu ianua* . . .; ode III,17, v. 9–12 à partir de *Cras foliis nemus* . . . jusqu'à *Sternet* . . .; ode III,27, v. 17–24: *Sed vides, quanto trepidet tumultu* . . .; ep. 2 v., 29–30: *At cum tonantis annus hibernus* . . .; ep. 10, v. 1–10: *Mala soluta navis* . . . Le contexte fut créé parfaitement.

Dans l'ode I,6 Horace nomme Varius (v. 1). Il est facile de montrer (voir c. 17 v.), combien de fois Horace rappelle cet auteur si peu connu, très souvent en le rapprochant de Virgile (*Sat.* I,5, 40; I,6, 55; I,10, 81; *Epist.* II,1, 247; *Ars poëtica* v. 53–55). Dans sa lettre poétique au souverain de Rome, Horace démontre que ce Varius est aussi aimé de l'empereur que Virgile, dans la lettre sur l'*Art poétique*, il en fait avec Virgile, le symbole de la nouvelle poésie qu'il a opposée à l'ancienne, donc vaincue:

> Quid autem
> Caesilio, Palutoque dabit Romanus ademptum
> Vergilio Varioque? (v. 53–55)

Une explication énorme (c. 156–158 v.) concerne l'*incipit* de l'ep. 2 (*Beatus ille* . . .) rendant l'atmosphère de toute l'épode. Virgile est cité plusieurs fois, ce qui est entièrement compréhensible: *Bucoliques, Géorgiques*. Par contre, le commentaire à l'épode 7 *Quo, quo scelesti ruitis?* nous étonne. L'éditeur l'a intitulé: *In bellum civile contra Brutum et Cassium*; nous le relisons aujourd'hui comme concernant certains événements historiques, mais dans le commentaire (c. 163 v.), on n'en dit pas un mot. On dit uniquement que *Quo, quo* est une *acerba increpatio*; ce qui est développé plus largement, pour le mot *ruitis* a été trouvé chez Virgile: *Per que hostes et tela ruit* (*Aen.* 12, 682);[6] *quo ruitis? quaene ista repens discordia surgit?* (*Aen.* 12, 313). Ainsi que pour l'expression *Aptantur enses* . . . (v. 2):

> Circumdat loricam humeris, simul aptat habenda
> Ensemque, clypeumque . . . (*Aen.* 12, 88–89)
> Laterique argivum accomodat ensem (*Aen.* 2, 393).
> Atque ensem collo suspendit eburnum (*Aen.* 11, 11).
> Laterique accinxerat ensem (*Aen.* 11, 489).

Le commentaire de l'ode II,30 (*Exegi monumentum* . . .) (c. 137 v.) diffère des autres par son caractère. Parthenio ne donne pas ici d'explications des différents mots, mais un cours *in continuo* sur cette ode. La note se rapproche par son caractère des fragments précédant les satires et les lettres. Un cours résumé consacré à l'ode III,30 commence par un rapprochement, très juste, avec l'ode II,20 (*Non usitata, nec tenui ferar* . . .). Évidemment, dans le vaste commentaire dont cette ode a été munie, après

---

[6] Texte correct: *Perque hostis, per tela ruit*. . . .

le rapprochement avec Hermogenes nous lisons (c. 98 v.):

Hoc apparet esse poetae propositum, ut de sua virtute glorietur. Qua comme-moratione se atque auditores delectat. In hoc eodem genere versatur totum illud carmen Exegi monumentum aere peremnius.

La présentation des idées contenues dans l'ode III,30 rapproche les paroles *Dicar qua violens ... Regnavit populorum ...* (v. 10–12) de la 4ᵉ et 5ᵉ strophe de l'ode II,20 (v. 13–20): *Iam Daedales ... Rhodanique potor,* et les vers:

Non omnis moriar, multaque pars mei
Vitabit Libitinam ... (v. 6–7)

de la 2ᵉ strophe de l'ode précédente (v. 5–8): *... Non ego pauperum cohibebor unda.*

Nous avons mentionné le problème de la littérature critique sur le sujet à laquelle l'éditeur se réfère parfois. Parmi les allusions nombreuses à Scaliger, il en faut citer une, importante pour son caractère polémique: Partenio professait le principe: *non iurare in verba magistri.* Dans le commentaire de l'ode I,15 (*Pastor cum traheret per freta navibus ...*), les paroles *Sublimi fugies mollis anhelitu ...* (v. 31) sont accompagnées d'une vaste explication commencée comme suit:

Scaliger existimat hunc locum considerandum. "Non intelligo—inquit—ex toto Galeno, quid sit sublimis anhelitus." Ego non puto consulandum Galenum aut quempiam alium medicum. Vox "sublimis" spectat ad modum ac morem cervi fugientis. Qui exagitatus, non demisso at sublimi atque alto capite fugit, ad quem poëta respiciens sublimem appellavit anhelitum cervi. Si enim fugiens anhelat ac si alto ac sublimi capite fugit, nonne et ipse anhelitus sublimi emittitur? ...

Le fragment le plus important concernant la littérature critique du sujet est donné par Parthenio dans le commentaire à l'ode I,24 (*Quis desiderio sit pudor ...*) (c. 45 v.– 46 r.). Il faut ajouter que l'ode est intitulée par le commentateur *Ad Virgilium,* et la matière est désignée par les mots: *Deflet Qunctilli mortem.* Il se réfère à la polémique très connue de Sigonius avec Robortello. Il prend nettement le parti de Sigonius, en commençant son commentaire par ces paroles:

Hanc oden Carolus Sigonius explicavit adversus Franciscum Robortellum, illius interpretationem reprehendens, cuius explicationem, quoniam erudita est, adscribendum exixtimavi. Sic ille.

Suit la citation de presque de deux pages de Sigonius. Il faut rappeler que Robor-tello avait contribué au commentaire de l'édition d'Horace élaborée par un travail collectif (1546 et plusieurs réimpressions), dans laquelle chaque ode avait reçu une mini-monographie. Il n'est pas clair au premier coup d'oeil, si cette "mini-mono-graphie" de l'ode I,24 est sortie entièrement de la plume de Robortello. Mais les pensées qui y sont exprimées sont répétées dans le traité *De arte sive ratione corrigendi antiquorum libros disputatio,* que le savant publia en 1557 avec un autre traité. En effet, certaines pensées y sont reprises de l'édition commentée de 1546. Sigonius parle de ce traité qui n'est pas consacré uniquement à l'ode I,24, dans sa longue oeuvre polémique *Emendatiorum adversus Franciscum Robortellum libri II.* Partenio cite ce traité assez fidèlement. Les changements, par ex. les altérations de *ostentaturum* en *monstruaturum*, de *artificium* en *officium*, de *autem eiusmodi* en *etiam huiusmodi*, ne provoquent pas de transformations du sens. Il en est de même des petites omissions.[7] La polémique entre les deux éminents humanistes italiens a déjà été largement traitée par la critique.

Après avoir terminé la citation, le commentateur de 1584 ajoute: *Hactenus Sigonius docte et vere*, après quoi il renvoie à la littérature historique du sujet; il rappelle que la mort de Quintilius Varus est décrite par Suétone qui témoigne de la tristesse d'Auguste à ce propos. Elle est mentionnée chez Suétone dans la biographie de Tibère (cap. 17).

Le nom de la Pologne, du roi puissant à qui le volume est dédié, apparaît une fois dans le commentaire dans un contexte honorable—dans les notes au *Carmen saeculare* (c. 172 v.). L'expression *iacentem lenis* (v. 51–52) est complétée de l'explication que savoir retenir sa colère envers ses ennemis est la plus grande vertu d'un souverain. Sont rappelés le livre I du *De officiis* et les paroles d'Euripide de la tragédie *Ion* (v. 1256) traduites en latin: *supplicem nefas occidere.* Ensuite nous lisons:

> Bis vincit, qui se vincit in victoria. De quo nos in Nuncupatoria Epistola Stephani Poloniae regis potentissimi pluribus agebamus, incredibilem illius Principis clementiam celebrantes, qua virtute omnibus imperatoribus merito est praeferendus.

University of Lodz

---

[7] Le texte de Sigonius est celui de l'édition *Opera omnia* . . . , V. 6 (Milan, 1737), 201–202, donc de l'édition posthume.

Petrarch and Boccaccio in Eighteenth-Century Finland: The Impact on H. G. Porthan

NINA VAN YZENDOORN

The subject of this study is the impact of Boccaccio and Petrarch in eighteenth-century Finland on the most important neo-humanist at the Turku Academy, Henrik Gabriel Porthan (1739–1804). The impulse for it was the existence of a manuscript in the Turku library collections containing Petrarch's *De viris illustribus* and Boccaccio's *De casibus virorum illustrium.*

Turku Royal Academy, founded during the expansion period of Sweden-Finland in the year 1640, was the only university in Finland, the eastern part of the kingdom. It was situated in the most important city of Finland, Turku, on the west coast. The initial period of the university was a time of Lutheran orthodoxy, which was still quite strong at the beginning of the eighteenth century.[1] The first neo-humanist influences, which reached their culmination during Porthan's activity, were already apparent during the period of Henrik Hassel (1700–1776), Porthan's predecessor as Professor of Eloquence (appointed 1728). He had stressed the importance of the humanities and rejected doctrines he considered too theoretical, like scholasticism, Cartesianism, and to some extent Wolfism. During this period, religious tolerance and freedom of thought increased.[2]

At the end of the eighteenth century, German *Neuhumanismus* (neo-humanism)

---

[1] On the history of the University, see I. A. Heikel, *Helsingfors Universitet 1640–1940* (Helsingfors, 1940) and M. Klinge, *Eine nordische Universität. Die Universität Helsinki 1640–1990* (Keuruu, 1992), which is an abridged version of the original, M. Klinge et al., *Helsingin yliopiston historia*, 3 vols. (Keuruu, 1987–1990). For the period of Porthan, see vol. I, *Kuninkaallinen Turun Akatemia 1640–1808* (Keuruu, 1987), also in Swedish, *Helsingfors Universitet 1640–1990*, vol. I, *Kungliga Akademien i Åbo 1640–1808* (Keuruu, 1988).

[2] On H. Hassel: I. A. Heikel, *Filologins studium vid Åbo Universitet*. Åbo Universitets lärdomshistoria, 5 (Helsingfors, 1894), 167–179; and I. Kajanto, *Porthan and Classical Scholarship. A Study of Classical Influences in Eighteenth-Century Finland*. Annales Academiae Scientiarum Fennicae, B 225 (Helsinki, 1984), 26–29.

reached Finland. Authors like J. A. Gesner (1691–1761) and Chr. Heyne (1729–1812) in Göttingen and J. A. Ernesti (1707–1781) in Leipzig renewed positive attitudes towards classical learning. They saw the classical authors as developers of taste, judgement, and the human mind. Classical studies, moral philosophy, and history gained more appreciation, and new disciplines like classical archaeology were founded.

H. G. Porthan was born in Middle Finland in the year 1739. He began his studies at the Academy of Turku in 1754 at the age of 15, obtaining the degree of *Magister Artium* in 1760.[3] He was appointed as *Docens Eloquentiae* in 1762, Assistant Librarian in 1764, Librarian in 1772, and finally as Professor of Eloquence in 1777. Porthan traveled within Finland, to Sweden (to Stockholm), and once abroad to Germany in 1779, where he visited many universities, especially Göttingen, the centre of German neo-humanism. Porthan was also one of the founders of the first Finnish literary society (*Aurora*) and the editor of the first Finnish newspaper (*Åbo Tidningar*).

We can distinguish different categories in Porthan's literary production, the most important ones being letters, his contributions to *Åbo Tidningar*, the dissertations, and the notes on his lectures at the Academy.

The letters to his contemporaries contain mostly regional news, descriptions of events and politics at the Academy, and also opinions on doctrines such as criticism of Immanuel Kant's philosophy. The letters to a former fellow-student, *Iuris Professor* Matthias Calonius, contain book orders for both the Academy Library and Porthan's private collection, and thus give information on Porthan's personal interest in literature.[4]

The contributions to the *Åbo Tidningar* handle current affairs, Finland's history and culture, and translating. Porthan's translations from both classical and modern languages into Swedish were also published in *Åbo Tidningar*.[5]

The 211 dissertations witness Porthan's activity as a university teacher.[6] Most of these dissertations consist of only sixteen pages, only a few exceeding thirty pages.[7] The authorship of the dissertations is often unclear. It has been claimed that the first

---

[3] With the dissertations on the relations of philosophy and Revelation, *Revelationi quid debeat philosophia nostra I–II*, 1758–1762.

[4] Porthan's letters are printed in *Bref från H. G. Porthan till Samtida I–II*, ed. W. Lagus. Skrifter utgifna av Svenska Litteratursällskapet (= SSLS) 38 (Helsingfors, 1898) and 102 (Helsingfors, 1912); *H. G. Porthan och Nath. Gerh. Schultén. Brevväxling 1784–1804*, ed. E. Lagus. SSLS 319 (Helsinki, 1948). Letters to Calonius: *Bref från H. G. Porthan till M. Calonius I–II*, ed. E. Lagus. SSLS 1 and 5 (Helsingfors, 1886). Porthan criticizes Kant's philosophy and terminology for being obscure; e.g., *Bref till M. Calonius I*, pp. 187–192.

[5] Printed in H. G. Porthan, *Opera selecta, V. Porthans skrifter i urval utg. af Finska Litteratursällskapet*. Suomalaisen Kirjallisuuden Seuran toimituksia (= SKS) 21, 5 (Helsingfors, 1873).

[6] Printed in H. G. Porthan, *Opera Omnia*, vol. I, ed. Porthan-seura (Turku, 1939); vol. V, eds. H. Koskenniemi, E. Matinolli, and M. Nyman (Turku, 1974); vol. VI, eds. H. Koskenniemi and E. Matinolli (Turku, 1978) and in H. G. Porthan, *Opera selecta. H. G. Porthans skrifter i urval, utg. af Finska litteratursällskapet I*. SKS:n toimituksia 21, 1 (Helsingfors, 1859); vol. II. SKS:n toimituksia 21, 2 (Helsingfors, 1862); vol. III. SKS:n toimituksia 21,3 (Helsingfors, 1867); vol. IV. SKS:n toimituksia 21,4 (Helsingfors, 1870).

[7] Kajanto, *Porthan and Classical Scholarship*, p. 14.

part of the dissertation, the *pro exercitio*, was usually written by Porthan. The second part, the *pro gradu*, was presumably often written by the *respondens*.[8] In some cases it is clear that Porthan has provided the footnotes to the work, and in some cases he may even have written the text. In any case Porthan provided the subject and thoroughly corrected the dissertation before it was presented, so that the dissertations inform us about Porthan's interests and opinions.[9]

Porthan is most famous for his dissertations concerning Finnish history and folklore (e.g., *De superstitione veterum Fennorum theoretica et practica*, 1782). Of the dissertations he supervised 25 deal with eloquence, 133 with history, 32 with moral philosophy and psychology, twelve with folklore and religion, seven with philology and two with education. Purely classical subjects were few, only six.[10] The dissertations show neo-humanistic influences; for instance, the educative value of the classical authors and subjects on Greek antiquity (e.g., *De Pandora Hesiodea*, 1795).

The majority of the extant notes on Porthan's lectures (approximately seventy-eight manuscripts) were written by his pupils. Porthan's own notes have survived on his *Horace Ars poetica* lecture and his *collegium logicum*. Porthan lectured on Roman authors (Horace, Virgil, Ovid, Cicero, Livy, Sallust), rhetoric (according to J. A. Ernesti's *Initia Rhetorica*), history of learning (according to Heumann's *Conspectus reipublicae literariae*), and on classical archaeology (according to Ernesti's *Archaeologia literaria*). As we can see, the impact of German neo-classicism can be observed in the themes and sources of Porthan's lectures.[11]

Porthan also produced a series of dissertations on the Library of the Academy of Turku, the *Historia Bibliothecae regiae Aboensis*, 1771–1795.[12] In this work Porthan describes the history and the collections of the Academy Library. As the library was destroyed in the fire of Turku in 1827, Porthan's inventory is of great importance to the history of the library. The library flourished during Porthan's time. An inventory dated 1755 indicates that the collections consisted of only 3,534 volumes, but by the time the fire occurred in 1827 there were no fewer than 40,000 volumes in the Library collection. Only 600 of these were saved.[13]

---

[8] The student had to present two dissertations. The first was mainly intended to prove the student's knowledge in Latin, the second to manifest specific learning in his field.

[9] On the authorship of the dissertations, see Kajanto, *Porthan and Classical Scholarship*, pp. 14–20.

[10] E. Matinolli, "H. G. Porthanin kirjallisesta jäämistöstä," *Turun Historiallinen arkisto 28* (Turku, 1973): 156–166.

[11] On the themes of Porthan's lectures, see Kajanto, *Porthan and Classical Scholarship*, pp. 66–69 and 89–97; and Heikel, *Filologins studium*, pp. 224–225. Notes in the lectures are printed in H. G. Porthan, *Opera Omnia*, vol. II, eds. H. Aaltonen, H. Koskenniemi and E. Matinolli (Turku, 1963); vol. III, ed. E. Matinolli (Turku, 1966); vol. IV, eds. H Koskenniemi and E. Matinolli (Turku, 1971).

[12] Facsimile printed in *Op. Omn.* V and *Op. Selecta* III.

[13] On the history of the Library, see J. Vallinkoski, *The History of the University Library at Turku*, vol. I, 1644–1722. Helsingin yliopiston julkaisuja, 21 (Helsinki, 1948) and vol. II, 1722–1772. Helsingin yliopiston julkaisuja, 37 (Helsinki, 1975). The inventories are described in Vallinkoski II, p. 182 and M. Klinge, vol. I, pp. 213–221.

In the *Historia Bibliothecae regiae Aboensis* of 1783 Porthan describes a manuscript in the following way:

XV. FRANCISCI PETRARCHAE, Poëtae laureati, quorundam clarissimorum heroum epythematis (Epitome), ad Generosissimum Patavi Dominum Franciscum de Carraria. Vitas continet virorum XXIII illustrium; (XIV tantum habet HAMBERGER Zuverlässige Nachricht. etc.;[14] mihi exemplum aliquod typis expressum hujus Omnium Operum Petrarchae inspicere ac cum nostro codice comparare, non contigit); quarum quae postremo loco comparet, Historia C. Julii Caesaris, reliquas omnes junctina sumtas mole superat.

Subjunctum est opus JOHANNIS BOCCACII (sic!) de Certaldo, de Casibus virorum (et foeminarum) illustrium (Libri IX), ad generosum Militem Dominum Machinardum de Cavalcantibus de Florencia, preclarum Regni Sicilie Marescallum.

Codex Membranaceus in Folio majore, eleganter scriptus. Opus utrumque hominibus eruditis non incognitum est; quamobrem plura addere nihil attinet.[15]

The manuscript contained Petrarch's *De viris illustribus*, often called the *Epitome* in its more common form. Thirteen of twenty-two existing manuscripts of *De viris illustribus* contain the twenty-two lives of illustrious Roman men from Romulus to Marcus Porcius Cato followed by the life of Julius Caesar.[16] Four of these manuscripts are preceded by a preface containing a dedication to Francesco da Carrara. The Turku Library manuscript contained the same preface.

In the same volume as Petrarch's work was Boccaccio's *De casibus virorum illustrium*. It has sometimes been falsely stated that the Academy Library would have owned both a copy of *De casibus virorum illustrium* and a copy of *De claris mulieribus*.[17]

---

[14] Hamberger, *Zuverlässige Nachrichten von den vornehmsten Schriftstellern bis 1300*, vol. IV (Lemgo, 1764), no. 589.

[15] *Op. Omn.* V, p. 178.

[16] Fr. Petrarca, *De viris illustribus*, ed. G. Martelotti. Edizione nazionale delle opere di Francesco Petrarca, II (Firenze, 1964), see pp. IX–CLIV.

[17] Vallinkoski, II, p. 158: "On the basis of Porthan's comments, the manuscript may even have included Boccaccio's *De claris mulieribus*." Prof. T. Nurmela writes about Boccaccio in Finland in his article "Boccaccio nell'area di lingua finnica," in *Il Boccaccio nelle culture e letterature nazionali*, ed. Fr. Mazzoni. Ente Nazionale "Giovanni Boccaccio," Pubblicazioni, 3 (Firenze, 1978), 445–452, and also in the Finnish language, "Boccaccio Suomessa," *Parnasso* 3 (Helsinki, 1977): 152–162. In the first (p. 446) he mentions that there were two works of Boccaccio at the Academy Library according to "a catalogue" dated 1783, the *De casibus virorum illustrium* and the *De claris mulieribus*. The catalogue referred to must be Porthan's *Historia Bibliothecae Regiae Aboensis*, which is the most important one and in which the description of the Petrarch-Boccaccio manuscript is dated to this year. Since Porthan describes only one manuscript of *De casibus virorum illustrium*, it is perhaps the mention of the women in the title of the book that causes this claim that a copy of the *De claris mulieribus* was in the collections. In the article in Finnish he states that there were two manuscripts of *De casibus virorum illustrium* at the Academy Library. Since he refers to Porthan, it is obvious that

Because these scholars quote Porthan, it is quite clear that they have misinterpreted Porthan's description of the manuscript. The illustrious women (*et foeminarum*) are very often mentioned in the title of *De casibus virorum illustrium*, because the work also contains lives of famous women. The indication *libri IX* states quite clearly that only *De casibus virorum illustrium* was meant.

The provenance of this manuscript has been established. It was donated to the Library in 1767 with the Hermelin collection of twenty-three manuscripts. Many of these manuscripts had belonged to the Bishop of Heilsberg's Library, which was plundered when Swedish troops invaded Ermeland in East Prussia in the year 1703. Petrarch's *De viris illustribus* appears both in a catalogue of the Heilsberg collections in the year 1578 and in a second one in the year 1633.[18]

The statement at the end of the description of the manuscript is remarkable. Porthan writes that both works are commonly known to scholars and that no further explanations about them are needed.

Otherwise the *corpus Porthanianum* contains only a few mentions of Petrarch and Boccaccio. The letters contain no reference at all, and only one of the 211 dissertations mentions Petrarch. This is in a dissertation on aesthetics, *De pulchro* of 1795, and it too only as an example of the various tastes of men. The author writes that Petrarch tells us about a man who prefers to listen to the croaking of frogs than the beautiful singing of a nightingale:

> Quod quotidiana docemur experientia, tantam esse de pulchro opinionum discrepantiam, ut haud raro eadem res aliis hominibus pulchra, aliis turpis ac foeda videatur. Sic de homine quodam commemorat Petrarcha, cui stridulus latrantium ranarum clamor magis placebat, quam dulcissimus cantus lusciniae.[19]

Among the authors quoted in this work are Montesquieu, Pope, and Baumgarten, no classical author being mentioned. Prof. Kajanto states in his study of classical influences in the *corpus Porthanianum* that this dissertation could hardly have been written by Porthan, because of its "sometimes awkward Latin."[20] It probably was written by the respondent Jonas Danielsson. I have not found this quotation in *De viris illustribus*, and since it is not a direct quotation of Petrarch as a scientific source it is of minor importance.

In Porthan's lectures we find some mentions of Boccaccio and Petrarch. In the *collegium logicum* (notes made by Porthan himself) Porthan states that Dante and

---

he misinterprets the two passages in which the manuscript is described (*Op. Omn.* V, p. 178; ibid., pp. 138–139) as meaning two different manuscripts.

[18] Vallinkoski II, pp. 154–156; O. Walde, *Storhetstidens litterära krigsbyten. En kulturhistorisk-biografisk studie*, vol. II (Uppsala and Stockholm, 1920), 178–193. The inventories have been printed in A. Possevinus, *Apparatus sacer* I–III (1606–1608), and E. Brachvogel, "Die Bibliothek der Burg Heilsberg," *Zeitschrift für die Geschichte und Altertumskunde Ermlands* 23,2 (Braunsberg, 1928): 274–358.

[19] *De Pulchro* (1795), resp. Jonas Danielsson.

[20] Kajanto, *Porthan and Classical Scholarship*, p. 102.

Petrarch inspired the new rise of literature and language by collecting manuscripts.[21] This was important for adapting to a new understanding of philosophy. Petrarch as a manuscript collector and a promoter of a new literary period had often been praised in the modern literature Porthan frequently used as basis for his lectures, for example, Ernesti and Heumann.[22]

In his lectures on classical archaeology Porthan mentions Petrarch as the reanimator of numismatics at the time when "all sciences began to reawaken out of their sleep."[23] Here Porthan follows his sourcebook, Ernesti's *Archaeologia literaria*.[24]

The lectures on the history of learning were based upon Heumann's *Conspectus reipublicae literariae*.[25] Petrarch and Boccaccio are mentioned in three passages. In the first one (chap. 4.26) Porthan criticises Heumann's source Maresius for using "ridiculous" terms.[26] He does not approve of the terms *interregnum ac velut litterarum deliquium* in describing the period between Boethius and Petrarch. He then states that this time is more accurately called "middle ages" or "*secula barbara*." In this passage we can observe that Petrarch means to Porthan the end of the dark and uncivilized Middle Ages.

Porthan discusses Petrarch and Boccaccio in chapter 4.45.[27] Petrarch is, according to Porthan, "a great man, who had a wide knowledge in *historia litteraria*." Even though he was a learned man, Porthan says, his main profession was poetry. Porthan states that no one has surpassed Petrarch in Italian poetry. Boccaccio is described in the following way: "Johan Boccaccius, from Florence, a lawyer, wrote beautiful Latin, and fine and elegant Italian, so that the language after him lived a new *saeculum*. He is considered one of the best *Auctores Classici* in Italian."[28] Porthan's source Heumann describes Petrarch in the same way as Porthan, but Boccaccio is only mentioned as a disciple of Petrarch.[29] The information Porthan gives on Boccaccio has its source elsewhere. Since the notes on the lectures are dated 1803 and the Academy Library description of Boccaccio's manuscript dates from 1783, this Latin work was known by this time to Porthan. It is likely that Porthan had read so much of Boccaccio's work as would allow evaluation of his Latin. Interestingly, Petrarch's Latin, clearly more classical than Boccaccio's, is not mentioned. Perhaps this is due to the fact that Petrarch is praised as an initiator of an entirely new period in erudition and is well known for his beautiful Latin. There is no need to praise it here.

---

[21] *Op. Omn.* II, pp. 1–128.

[22] J. A. Ernesti, *Archaeologia literaria* (Lipsiae, 1790); C. A. Heumann, *Conspectus reipublicae litterariae* (Hannover, 1763).

[23] Free translation from Swedish, "Annotationer öfver Ernesti Archaeologia Literaria (adnotavit E. E. Lagus)" in *Op. Omn.* III, pp. 123–218.

[24] Ernesti, *Archaeologia literaria*, chap. 4.22.

[25] "Föreläsningar öfver Heumanni Conspectus reipublicae literariae (adnotavit P. J. Alopaeus)," in *Op. Omn.* III, pp. 341–464.

[26] *Op. Omn.* III, p. 390.

[27] *Op. Omn.* III, p. 402.

[28] Free translation from Swedish.

[29] Heumann, op. cit., chap. 45.

The third remark (chap. 5.13) states only that Dante and Petrarch especially are the most celebrated Italian poets.[30]

There are thus only a few mentions of Petrarch and Boccaccio in the *corpus Porthanianum*. These are usually quoted directly from the modern source books used as a basis for the lectures. Some information on Boccaccio seems, however, to derive from the lecturer himself, and it is certain that the Petrarch-Boccaccio manuscript was known to Porthan. In the description of the Academy manuscript Porthan states that both works were well known. Porthan also owned a copy of Boccaccio's *Decameron*, as a catalogue of his personal library, sold by auction in 1812, proves.[31] It is worth mentioning that the first translation into Swedish of one of the short stories in the *Decameron*—the tale of the three rings—was published in the year 1795 in *Åbo Tidningar*, during Porthan's editorship.[32] It is therefore safe to presume that this translation too was known to him.

I must conclude that even though the manuscript, which had been placed in the Academy Library collection in 1767, was well known to the Professor of Eloquence Porthan, it had little use as a scientific sourcebook and is therefore not mentioned in the academic literature of Porthan's period. After Porthan's death (1804), the Academy had to face many changes. The Russians invaded the country in 1809, and the year of the fire in Turku, 1827, marked the end of the Academy Library collections and the manuscript of Petrarch's *De viris illustribus* and Boccaccio's *De casibus virorum illustrium* as well as of the Academy situated in Turku. The capital of the country and its university were moved to Helsinki.

Åbo Akademi, Finland

---

[30] *Op. Omn.* III, p. 440.

[31] *Catalogus librorum quos possedit H. G. Porthan.* (Aboae, 1812), p. 269 no. 250.

[32] J. Vallinkoski, *Italia Suomen kirjallisuudessa 1640–1953*, Helsingin yliopiston kirjaston julkaisuja, 25 (Helsinki, 1955), p. 16 no. 18.

Ad memoriam Claymundi:
An English Humanist, His College, and His Books

MARK VESSEY

Collegium Claymundi

When Bishop Richard Foxe founded the College of Corpus Christi at Oxford in 1517 he gave institutional reality to a cherished ideal of northern humanism: the ideal of a Christian community devoted to the study of good literature and the advancement of God's work on earth. The founder's first project had been for a monastic establishment, but he had changed his mind. "What, my lord," his fellow bishop, Hugh Oldham of Exeter, is reported to have said to him, "shall we build houses . . . for a company of bussing monks . . . ? No, no, it is more meet a great deal that we should have care to provide for the increase of learning, and for such as who by their learning shall do good in the church and commonwealth."[1] In Foxe's revised plan, the fellows of Corpus Christi would be seculars, their president (according to the Statutes) *neque episcopus nec religiosus*, neither a bishop nor a member of any religious order. In company with the students of the College these men would work like bees in a hive, *veluti ingeniosae apes, dies noctesque ceram ad Dei honorem et dulciflua mella confici[entes] ad suam et universorum Christianorum commoditatem.*[2] Buzzing scholars, then, not bussing monks.

Erasmus's approval of the new foundation was to be expected.[3] As a young man

---

[1] Raphael Holinshed (quoting John Hooker *alias* Vowell), cited by Thomas Fowler, *The History of Corpus Christi College* (Oxford: Printed for the Oxford Historical Society, 1893), 21, who suggests that the word "bussing" may "either have the meaning of 'kissing,' from the amatory propensities of the monks, or may be only another way of writing 'buzzing,' = mumbling, muttering, from the way they talked' or performed the services." Fowler, *History*, 60–63, gives an account of Foxe's earlier design for a monastic college.

[2] Fowler, *History*, 44, 38.

[3] For the founder's contacts with Erasmus, see the notice on Foxe by J. B. Trapp in *Contemporaries of Erasmus: A Biographical Register of the Renaissance and Reformation*, ed. Peter G. Bietenholz and Thomas B. Deutscher, 3 vols. (Toronto: University of Toronto Press, 1985–1987), 1:46–49.

living under religious rule he had labored to adapt the content and procedures of monastic *lectio divina* to the spirit of late fifteenth-century Italian humanism. Since leaving the cloister, he had improvised alternative forms of the solitary-convivial pursuit of sacred learning, in writing and in print.[4] He is unstinting in his praise of Foxe's beehive, describing it in a letter of 1519 as *collegium magnificum . . . tribus praecipuis linguis ac melioribus literis vetustisque autoribus proprie consecra[tum].* The founder would be remembered forever, *Nam . . . quo monumento rectius nomen suum aeternae hominum memoriae dedicare?* The library of the new college was another wonder of the world, to be compared with the Colossus at Rhodes, the tomb of Mausolus in Caria, or the pyramids of Egypt.[5]

Though buried in Winchester Cathedral, Richard Foxe would have been content for later generations to mistake Corpus Christi College for his mausoleum. His memorials have not been allowed to decay. A statue of the bishop, imposing if not colossal, has formed part of the north facade of the Library building since 1817, where it confronts every visitor to the College. And there are several copies of a contemporary portrait, including one now hanging in the Library, whence the founder's likeness looks down over the book collection he began and the scholars who, more or less faithful to his Statutes, still busy themselves like bees in a hive. Foxe's hold on living memory is secure. But what of the man to whom Erasmus addressed his encomium of the new college, the first president of Corpus Christi, John Claymond? What fame would he deserve in the republic of Christian letters simultaneously projected by the founder's statutes and the *Opus epistolarum Erasmi?*

Epitaphium Claymundi

Halfway through his letter of 1519, Erasmus turns from praise of Foxe as founder of Corpus Christi College to praise of Claymond as its first president, from the *collegium Foxii* to the *collegium Claymundi.*[6] Imitating him, we now turn our back on the portrait of the bishop that beckons us as we come into his library, to glance down through the glass screen at its east end, into the College Chapel. There, almost directly beneath us in the floor of the ante-chapel (though usually covered by a protective strip of carpet), lies a sixteenth-century memorial brass. At one time it was in the middle of the choir, at "that very place [according to Anthony à Wood] where

---

[4] Lisa Jardine, *Erasmus, Man of Letters: The Construction of Charisma in Print* (Princeton: Princeton University Press, 1993) offers important new insights into this process. It may be noted that Erasmus's promotion of a literary life-in-common remains centred on an eremitical ideal of study. For all his success as the animator of a humanist community of letters, Erasmus was never a "college" man in the ordinary sense.

[5] *Ep.* 990 (to John Claymond) in *Opus epistolarum Desiderii Erasmi Roterodami,* ed. P. S. Allen et al., 12 vols. (Oxford: Clarendon Press, 1906–1958). See also Epp. 965, 1661.

[6] The spelling of the first president's name varies in the early sources. I have preferred the Latin form found in the majority of manuscripts of John Schepreve's *Epicedion* (see below). For modern notices on Claymond's life and his presidency of Corpus Christi College, see Fowler, *History*, 79–89; A. B. Emden, *A Biographical Register of the University of Oxford A.D. 1501–1540* (Oxford: Clarendon Press, 1974), 428–430; *Contemporaries of Erasmus*, 1:307–308.

the rectors of the choir sing the psalm, entitled 'Venite, exultemus.'"[7] It comme-morates John Claymond, president of the College from its foundation in 1517 until his death in 1537. The ensemble has suffered some damage and now lacks part of the framing inscription. This inscription contained a prayer for Claymond's soul and those of other benefactors of the College. It had spaces for the day, month, and year of the first president's death, which for some reason were never inserted. Read from the top left-hand corner, punctuated, and with the abbreviations expanded, it would have run as follows:

[Hic iacet tumulatum corpus venerabilis] magistri Iohannis Claimond primi presidis huius collegii et precipui benefactoris qui [quidem Iohannes] obiit . . . die mensis . . . anno domini millesimo quingentesimo tricesimo. . . . Cuius anime et animabus Christi fidelium omnium benefactorum propicietur deus. Amen.][8]

Enclosed within the frame, and surmounted by an incised figure of the dead man in his winding-sheet, was an epitaph in the style of a *meditatio mortis*, in elegiac couplets. These elements of the memorial are still in place today.[9] The epitaph was devised by Claymond himself; it is headed *Epitaphium Ioannis Claimondi / Quod ipse incolumis* [sc. *composuit?*]. Punctuated, it reads:

> Quid praestatis opes blandae, quid ludicra pompa,
>   Quid validae vires, forma quid egregia,
> Cum vitae extremo confregit tempore fila
>   Atropos, et tenebris lumina clausa tegit?
> 5   Spes nulla auxilii, in nobis solatia nulla,
>   Quos ante ornastis deseritis famulos.
> Spes sola in Christo est, immenso fonte bonorum,
>   Ex quo prorumpit praesidium miseris.
> Ergo tibi commendo animam, Christe, accipe quaeso,
> 10   Atque tuis semper pascito delitiis.
> Terra tibi reddat corpus quando ante tribunal
>   Cuncti apparebunt terrificante tuba.

Although perfectly traditional in their piety, the verses are recognizably those of an adept of the New Learning: metrically assured, somewhat precious in their diction (note *terrificante* in line 12), leavened with a discreet paganism (line 4) of the kind that

---

[7] *Athenae oxonienses*, ed. Philip Bliss, 4 vols. (London: F.C. & J. Rivington, 1813–1820), 1:106. Claymond's monument was moved when the Chapel was refurbished in the late seventeenth century (Fowler, *History*, 76).

[8] The text within square brackets, now missing, is supplied from the transcription given by Anthony à Wood, *History and Antiquities of the University of Oxford*, ed. John Gutch, 2 vols. in 3 (Oxford: Printed for the editor, 1792–1796), 3:401.

[9] Fowler, *History*, 76. The whole brass, including epitaph and engraved figure, is conveniently reproduced as Plate XVa in *The History of the University of Oxford*, vol. 3: *The Collegiate University*, ed. James McConica (Oxford: Clarendon Press, 1986).

seems to have been fashionable among the fellows of Corpus Christi in Claymond's day. Beforehand in their consciousness of the Judgment of Christ, they also anticipate the future verdict of scholars gathered in the College Chapel, in whose mortal sight the sanctity of the first president's life would always be linked in some mysterious way to the quality of his Latin.

Thus, like his friend and patron Bishop Foxe, John Claymond took care to dictate the terms in which he would be remembered. Yet there is only so much a man can do to fix the course of his own posthumous career, and on the nineteenth day of November, 1537, the burden of this man's life and work fell on his corporate executors, the *Somatochristiani*.

Epicedion Claymundi

The *Epicedion Claymundi* is a poem of 325 elegiac couplets, written in 1538 or soon after by John Schepreve (or Shepery),[10] the College Reader in Greek and, on this and other evidence, an exceptionally fluent writer of classicizing Latin verse.[11] The poem falls into three unequal sections, the third of which can be further divided. The opening section (lines 1–74) strikes a balance between lament and celebration that is tilted towards the latter. The poet has two reasons for singing Claymond's *splendida facta*: to ensure that none may accuse him and his colleagues of neglecting their duty, and to inspire others to emulate the departed. There follows an invocation (lines 75–86), in which the classical Graces and Muses are spurned in favour of the Holy Trinity, "author" alike of Claymond's virtuous deeds and of these duteous verses. The whole of the remainder of the poem (lines 87–650) is headed *Narratio* in the manuscripts, but there is a break around the halfway mark. Lines 87–362, which might be subtitled "Vita Claymundi," recall the subject's career, his character, and his many works of charity. The poet then introduces a theatrical metaphor: "Thus far [he says] I have unfolded four acts of a play." Now he will stage the fifth and final act.

---

[10] It has never been printed or critically edited. There are four manuscript copies in the Library of Corpus Christi College, Oxford. In the list of the College's MSS made by H. O. Coxe, *Catalogus codicum MSS, qui in collegiis aulisque oxoniensibus hodie asservantur*, 2 vols. (Oxford: Printed by T. Combe, 1852), they are nos. 257 (fols. 12–18), 266 (fols. 235–244), 280 (fols. 204–210), and 303 (fols. 66–87). The last and most legible of these is in the hand of the antiquarian William Fulman (1632–1688). Coxe 257 contains an expurgated text with anti-Romanist marginalia. The earliest complete text of the poem is in Coxe 266, copied by Miles Windsor in the later sixteenth century. There it is entitled "Ioannis Claymundi viri clarissimi olimque somatochristianorum presidis epicedion per Iohannem Scheprevum," and dated 1555. The date may have been carried over from a copy made in the reign of Queen Mary while the College was celebrating its fidelity to the Roman Catholic observances so prominently displayed in Schepreve's account of the life of Claymond. Later copies seem to depend on Coxe 266. The date of 1530 given to the poem in Coxe 280 was perhaps derived from the lacunose inscription on the president's tomb. There are additional copies of the poem in Bodleian Library, MS Wood F. 30 and Rawlinson MS Misc. 335, the latter of which I have not seen.

[11] The best, as well as the most recent, survey of Schepreve's poetic oeuvre is by J. W. Binns, *Intellectual Culture in Elizabethan and Jacobean England: The Latin Writings of the Age* (Leeds: Francis Cairns, 1990), 12–18. For his career, see Emden, *Biographical Register*, 513–514.

This is the "Mors Claymundi," the moral and narrative sequel to the foregoing "Vita." The earthly drama of the president's death, played out entirely within the walls of the College and (except for a walk-on part for a *medicus*) entirely by College members, occupies almost two hundred lines (363–550). Then comes a kind of eschatological postlude, in which Christ as Judge welcomes his faithful servant Claymond to eternal rest (lines 565–594). It is the full script of the scene for which the stage-direction was given in the final couplet of the *Epitaphium Claymundi*. The cautious hope of the earlier poem is surer now. How can we doubt that he is in bliss whom the voice of Christ—in the morality play of the poem—calls blessed? Even so, the poet is careful to add a "college prayer" for the deceased before grief finally chokes his verse.

Unlike other poems by John Schepreve, this one was never printed. Nor is there any sign that it was intended for the press. It appears to have been written for the domestic comfort and edification of those who had known the departed (*Qui novere hominem*, line 392), above all for members of Corpus Christi College, the *nos* of the poem. Other persons and places might have their share in Claymond's memory, but his life and death excite a special grief and joy in the *Somatochristiani*.

> Sed nos prae cunctis mortalibus undique faustos
> Extasis attonitos undique magna tenet,
> Quos apud hic tanto tam clarus tempore vixit,
> Quos apud eiusdem viscera clausa iacent.
>
> (lines 605–608)

The mortal remains of John Claymond were shut in a tomb, and that tomb was shut inside the College of Corpus Christi. The allusion to the president's burial-place in the Chapel is doubled by another earlier in the poem where (in a macaronic pun scarcely worthy of the Reader in Greek) the dead man's name is interpreted to mean *kleos mundi* or universally known: *Cuius enim parvo tegitur sub marmore corpus, / Eius laus toto latior orbe patet* (lines 361–363). The claim to universal renown and the assurance of domestic possession are inseparably linked. General though Claymond's fame is supposed to be, the full import and spiritual benefit of his life and death are reserved to those who daily visit the place where his body is interred, there to gaze on the sepulchral text and figure he had composed.

Schepreve had already seen the *Epitaphium Claymundi* and was able to assume a knowledge of it on the part of his readers. Indeed there is a close literary relationship between the *Epitaphium* and the *Epicedion*. The *Epitaphium* provides part of the "plot" of the longer poem, while the *Epicedion* supplies a narrative within which the dead man's preposthumous self-commemoration acquires its full sense. The poet was saving the labour of the executors who omitted, perhaps deliberately, to fill in the dates around Claymond's tomb. For if the memory of the first president was properly cultivated, might not his charismatic presence endure *sine die*?

Libri Claymundi

As well as the marble slab and memorial brass in the Chapel, the author of the *Epicedion* will have had other memorials of Claymond under his eye. He probably

recalled the terms in which Erasmus had praised Foxe's new foundation twenty years
earlier. The Dutchman had suggested that the trilingual library of Corpus Christi
College would make it a place of resort to rival the City of Rome. An alternative analogy of City and College is urged in the narrative of the *Epicedion*, where Claymond
becomes the first in a line of kings whose task would be to corroborate and embellish
the founder's Romulean work.[12]

Perhaps mindful of Erasmus's high expectations of the literary learning of the
Somatochristiani, Schepreve also reserves a special place for Claymond's studies. The
passage is remarkably detailed and circumstantial:

> Legerat authores—quis credat?—legerat, inquam,
>   Omnes qui scriptis qualiacunque dabat.
> Legerat exacte, non tantum legerat illos,
>   Ut licet e sparsis undique scire notis:
> Aspicies toto scriptos in margine libros,
>   Sic ut in his raro scribere plura queas.
> Adde quod illorum multis accesserit index,
>   Quem bene digessit prompta vigilque manus.
>   (lines 149–156)

As the *Epicedion Claymundi* is addressed in the first instance to a reader who worships
in the College Chapel, so it envisages one who studies in the adjacent Library. The
poet's phrasing (*licet scire . . . Aspicies . . . raro scribere queas*) invites us to turn the pages
of Claymond's own books, pen in hand—as we could if we were fellows of his
college. The first president's gifts and bequests of books to Corpus Christi roughly
doubled the size of the library set up by Bishop Foxe.[13] They comprised a number
of Greek manuscripts formerly the property of William Grocin, and more than 70
printed editions classical, biblical, patristic, scholastic, and humanist. All but a very
few of these volumes are still in the collection today. The majority of them came
from Claymond's own working library and would have passed to the College on his
death. Many are annotated in the fashion described by Schepreve, if not quite as
densely as he implies, and carefully indexed.[14] It seems that the volumes of Claymond's that were first placed in the Library in 1538 were then uniformly inscribed on
the recto of the first folio with the following formula: *orate pro anima Ioannis Clay-*

---

[12] "Sic enim fortis valuissent splendida Romae / Moenia, quae struxit Romulus ille, nihil /
Ni decorasset eam claris Hostilius armis, / Divitiis Ancus, religione Numa: / Sic tua, sancte parens
[sc. Foxe], incassam tecta parasses, / Ni bonus ornasset nobile praeses opus." (lines 129–134).

[13] J. R. Liddell, "The Library of Corpus Christi College, Oxford, in the Sixteenth Century,"
The Library, 4th ser., 18 (1938): 385–416 at 389–391 (abbreviated from the corresponding section
of his unpublished Oxford M. Litt. thesis, a copy of which is kept in the College Archives [CCC
501]). Claymond's gifts and bequests are listed by Emden (n. 6 above). See also N. R. Ker, "The
Provision of Books," in *The History of the University of Oxford*, 3:458–462.

[14] These remarks are based on a sampling of the volumes given or left by Claymond to the
Library.

mundi primi praesidis collegii corporis christi qui hunc librum dedit eidem.[15] However, not all Claymond's books bear signs of his own use and it is clear that some of the unmarked ones entered the Library during his lifetime. One such, a copy of Erasmus's *Novum Testamentum* of 1519, carries a donation formula with a date at the end: *orate pro anima Ioannis Claymondi huius collegii primi praesidis qui hunc librum eidem dedit. 1526.* Since the inscription, though not in the president's hand, was no doubt placed there on his instruction, it is worth noting that the variant form *huius collegii* (for *collegii corporis christi* in the volumes added *post mortem*) matches the phrasing on the border inscription of Claymond's tomb. In both places, in the book as on the marble slab, prayers for the dead were solicited preposthumously. And in both cases, another hand—of the acting librarian, of the engraver—inscribed a text that we may suppose drafted or dictated by the benefactor and would-be beneficiary. If the analogy holds, we should perhaps imagine Claymond's commemorative brass laid down in the Chapel, as some of his commemorative books were chained in the Library, before his death in 1537.[16]

Of this much we can be sure: the process of commemorating John Claymond, *primus praeses huius collegii*, was a collaborative one; it involved multiple media; and it was under way by the mid-1520s, more than a decade before his passing. Schepreve's reputation as a ready versifier notwithstanding,[17] there could be little that was truly extemporary in his *Epicedion Claymundi*.

Opus Claymundi

Requests to pray for the authors, scribes or (increasingly in the print era) donors of books were a natural expression of the learned piety of pre-Reformation Europe. They have a particular resonance in the institutional context of a society dedicated, as Foxe's college was, to the combined pursuit of *virtus* and *scientia*.[18] In this case the line between monastic and humanist aspirations is hard to draw precisely. As prayer, reading, and writing succeeded and supported each other in the round of monastic observance, so were they associated in the life of the humanist college. According to Schepreve, whatever time Claymond could spare from his official functions he spent either over his books or on his knees:

> Nec magis austeras quisquam sibi cultor eremi
>   Leges imposuit, quam pius iste sibi.
> Quicquid erat spatii rebus tribuebat honestis,
>   Ne minimum frustra tempus abire sinens.
> Namque vel hos libros, quos diximus ante, revolvit
>   (Unum tam multos vix potuisse putes),

---

[15] An example of such an inscription, in a Hebrew manuscript left by Claymond, appears in Plate XIVa of Volume 3 of *The History of the University of Oxford.*

[16] A conjecture made by Liddell in his M. Litt. thesis (n. 13 above), 32.

[17] Binns, 14, quoting Schepreve's editor and former pupil, George Etherege; Wood, *Athenae,* 1:135.

[18] *Corpus Statutes,* cited by Fowler, *History,* 38.

> Vel sanctis Domini feriebat vocibus aures. . . .
>
> (lines 605–612)

We might regard the parenthesis as redundant, were it not plain that the magnitude of Claymond's literary labours, evoked in an earlier passage to which the reader is referred, was a topic of some importance to the poet and his first readers. As we have seen, the annotated *libri Claymundi*, the books left by the president to the College, offered a convenient measure of his exertions. But—a humanist critic might interject—what was the use of so much notemaking and indexing if it never issued in another kind of *liber Claymundi*, a literary work to which he could put his own name as author? The first generation of scholars of Corpus Christi, Schepreve included, had the kind of publication record that would justify the confidence even of so conspicuous an over-producer as Erasmus. Where was the president's contribution? Reading Schepreve's poem we discover, as members of the College ca. 1538 would have been reminded, that a great work was extant but still in manuscript.

> Quam doctus fuerat, posthac res ipsa docebit,
>   Quodque diu sudans evigilavit opus,
> Si tamen indignum blattarum dente volumen
>   In patulum tandem fata venire sinent.
>
> (lines 165–168)

The poet presumably did not need to name Claymond's *magnum opus* to the *Somatochristiani*. They shared his knowledge of it and his anxious hopes for its long delayed appearance in print.

As it turned out, this was one part of the president's testament that the fellows of his college were unable to execute satisfactorily. Claymond's life's work, in the narrow literary sense of that phrase, was a commentary on Pliny's *Naturalis Historia* (one of the texts of study specified in the College Statutes). An incomplete manuscript of more than two thousand folios written on both sides, heavily annotated and interlineated, with copious additions on odd scraps of paper inserted between the leaves, remains to this day in the College Library, safe alike from the beetle's tooth and the world's eye.[19] A fair copy is said to be at Basel where it was sent some time after the author's death, to be printed by Johannes Oporinus.[20] Claymond himself

---

[19] MS CCC 178–181. Coxe says that these four volumes contain commentary on Books 4–27 of the *Naturalis Historia*, but I could not find the commentary on Books 4–6. Wood, *Athenae* 1:106, cites the Cambridge antiquarian John Caius to the effect that "the scholia on the first two [sic] books were lost after [Claymond's] death."

[20] Wood and others cite M. Neander, *Orbis terra succincta explicatio* (Leipzig, 1597), 410: "Ioannes Claimundus, de quo nobis retulit aliquando Oporinus noster, qui in totum Plinij opus eruditos commentarios scripserit, & ad se excudendos iam pridem miserit, cur autem non fuerint excusi ab Oporino, puto sumtus ad tantum opus imprimendum defuisse." J. G. Milne, *The Early History of Corpus Christi College* (Oxford: B. Blackwell, 1946) suggests that "it would be worth while for a modern scholar to examine [the volumes at Corpus Christi College] and the fair copy at Basel, as Claimond seems to have had access to at least one manuscript [of Pliny] which cannot now be traced."

once thought of entrusting the printing to Johannes Bebelius. In a letter[21] to Simon Grynaeus, written in 1532, he remarked that Bebel planned to publish a series of classical texts (*autores*) in London, adding: *Quod si fecerit, limabo fortasse meas in Plinium ineptiunculas....* Rarely can a diminutive have been so ill applied! But Claymond's modesty was as boundless as the work he had in hand.[22] In the same letter he responded warily to a hint that Grynaeus meant to acknowledge him in print. "You say that you are going to insert a few words *ad mei nominis memoriam*. If you love me, Grynaeus, do not even consider doing such a thing. My sole desire is that, living without glory here below, I may deserve to have my name written in the book of life." Conventional and sincere, such a profession was nonetheless strikingly at odds with the new "typographic" humanism of men like Erasmus and Grynaeus.[23] It both reinforces the eschatology of the inscription in the College Chapel, confirming the portrait of John Claymund as a man of God, and helps us to understand why those fellows of Corpus Christi who wished to remember their first president as a man of letters would take the trouble to copy and recopy his other memorials.[24]

University of British Columbia, Vancouver

---

[21] Extant in Bodleian Library, MS Wood F. 30, fols. 42v–43v, with other materials commemorating Claymond (including Erasmus's *Ep.* 990 and Schepreve's *Epicedion*), said to have been collected by Henry Jackson (1586–1662), a fellow of Corpus Christi and one of the editors of Richard Hooker. The letter to Grynaeus is dated from Oxford, May 13; for the year, see P. S. Allen's headnote to Erasmus's *Ep.* 990.

[22] Cf. Jackson's (?) comment (ad loc.): "Iam vero D. *Claymundi* modestia in eo elucet, quod suos in Plinium commentarios, quos viri doctissimi doctissimos esse censuerunt, *ineptiunculas* appellet, imitatus autorem suum *Plinium*, [qui] sua quoque opera nugas vocat." The reference is to Pliny's preface to Vespasian, NH praef. 1, quoting Catullus 1.4.

[23] See now Jardine, *Erasmus, Man of Letters*.

[24] I wish to thank the College Librarian, Dr. David Cooper, and the Archivist, Mrs. Christine Butler, for their generous help in the research for this paper.

The Literary Patronage of
Heinrich Rantzau (1526–1598)

PETER ZEEBERG

Heinrich Rantzau (1526–1598) was a nobleman and major statesman in the service of three successive kings of Denmark. But he was also a patron of literature and science, and a writer himself.[1] And as such he is well worth studying. He is not only a characteristic, or even exaggerated, example of the learned nobleman, a type which—at least in Northern Europe—emerged at his time; he is also someone through whom we can also get a detailed insight into some of the social processes which underlie the books of humanists and scientists. His activities were widespread, and our sources for them are particularly good: in addition to the many and varied publications themselves, we possess hundreds of letters between Rantzau and humanists throughout Europe.[2]

---

[1] The only monograph on Heinrich Rantzau is Wiebke Steinmetz, *Heinrich Rantzau (1526–1598): Ein Vertreter des Humanismus in Nordeuropa und seine Wirkungen als Förderer der Künste* Europäische Hochschulschriften, Reihe XXVIII, Kunstgeschichte, 125 (Frankfurt a. M., 1991). This deals especially with his activities as a patron of art, but it also contains a detailed biographical introduction. To this should be added the biographies by Johannes Moller in his *Cimbria Literata* (Copenhagen, 1744), vol. 3, 567–581, and by Johanne Skovgaard in *Dansk biografisk Leksikon*, 2nd ed. (Copenhagen, 1933–1944) and 3rd ed. (Copenhagen, 1979–1984). A fine study of his literary activities in general is Dieter Lohmeier, "Heinrich Rantzau und die Adelskultur der frühen Neuzeit," in *Arte et Marte. Studien zur Adelskultur des Barockzeitalters in Schweden, Dänemark und Schleswig-Holstein*, ed. Dieter Lohmeier (Neumünster, 1978), 67–84. On his literary patronage with special attention to his relationship to the kingdom of Denmark, see Peter Zeeberg, "Heinrich Rantzau (1526–1598), a Literary Maecenas between Denmark and Germany," in *Reformation and Latin Literature in Northern Europe*, ed. Inger Ekrem, Minna Skafte Jensen, and Egil Kragerud (Oslo, 1996), 138–150.

[2] The principal collections of Rantzau letters are three volumes of original letters in the National Library of Vienna (Con. Vindob. 9737 ldn) and three volumes of copies at the University Library of Kiel (S. H. 388), at Breitenburg Castle and at the University Library of Göttingen (prid. 8, Bd. IX, 2. T) respectively. Nearly two hundred letters were printed in Georg Ludwig Froben (ed.), *Epistolae consolatoriae* (S.l., 1593. Frankfurt a. M., 1593. Frankfurt a. M., s.a. [c. 1595]).

Geographically we are in the border area between Denmark and Germany, in the duchies of Schleswig and Holstein, which were independent but in personal union with Denmark: the king of Denmark was also duke of Schleswig and Holstein. Heinrich Rantzau was a German (Holstein, as opposed to Schleswig, was a part of the German Reich) but a subject of the Danish king.

He has himself given a short account of his life. It was printed, but only several years after his death, as an addition to a reprint of one of his own works on astrology.[3] Here we learn that he was born in 1526 to noble parents and that "soon in my early youth, following the wish of my parents, I devoted myself to the study of the arts until my twentieth year."

These studies included several years spent at the University of Wittenberg, where he heard both Luther and Melanchthon and even "sat at Luther's table," as it is phrased. Already then he was an important person, as his father, Johann Rantzau (1492–1565), was the most important statesman and general in the realm of the Danish kings in the age of Reformation.

"After that," he proceeds, "I attended the court of the Emperor Charles V together with Duke Adolf of Holstein . . . until my 29th year. After my return to my native country in that year, I soon married a noble and honest virgin, whose marriage portion was more than 200.000 Taler, not including real property. In my view the secondary reason for this event, after God, is the fact that Jupiter and Venus were in conjunction in the seventh house. . . ."

The astrological reflections are an important feature in this text, for reasons which we shall see later. Then follow passages on his many children, on his health, and on his offices: "In the same year as I married my wife, I was made Prefect of the castle of Segeberg, and soon after, in the following year, which was my 30th, I became Governor or Viceroy in Holstein and the other duchies."

Here we have to do with a nobleman who had reached the highest possible position: official, permanent substitute for the king. At the same time he was extremely rich—through his marriage, as we heard, but also through inheritance. He did, as he says later in this text, spend large sums on buying property: "manors, castles, fields, houses and villages." In fact, he was able to lend huge sums to kings and princes.

But now to the topic of this paper, his hobbies:
"Hunting," he says, "is a great delight to me, and when I give that up, I do not feel well. The study of astrology and mathematics I value highly and I am a great lover of philosophy and a student of history."

Humanist interests are here mentioned together with the archetypal nobleman's occupation of hunting. And that is no coincidence: Heinrich Rantzau was an ardent advocate of the ideal that a nobleman should live *arte et Marte*—an ideal which was not yet fully recognized among his fellow noblemen, at least not in his part of the world.[4]

---

[3] Heinrich Rantzau, *Thematum coelestium directiones.* (Frankfurt a. M., 1611). All quotations, here and in the following, are my translations from Latin.

[4] See Lohmeier, "Heinrich Rantzau," 77ff.

On the other hand it must be admitted—as he did himself occasionally—that contrary to his warlike father, he himself did not meddle much with Mars. Heinrich's primary interest was *ars*. In fact we have an interesting graphical description of this position on a map of Denmark which Rantzau had made as one of many contributions for Georg Braunius' famous topographical work *Ciuitates Orbis Terrarum*. Here we see Mars and Pallas together, flanking the coat of arms of the Rantzau family: Mars to the right with his guns, drums, and other attributes, Pallas to the left with books and globes. But a closer look reveals that the books are all works by Heinrich Rantzau, whereas Mars is a portrait of his father, Johann, with his foot on the neck of one of his notorious opponents from the Danish civil war in the 1530s.[5]

Heinrich and his father each represented one side of the *Mars/ars* dichotomy—and we may safely assume that the father (though he himself had sent his son to Wittenberg before he sent him to the imperial court) would have felt that Heinrich overdid his interest in *studia*, had he lived to see what was to come. It is no coincidence, I believe, that Heinrich's first publication was a collection of *elogia* to his father, published shortly after the latter's death in 1566. In this book, furthermore, much had been done to conceal the fact that Heinrich Rantzau himself had anything to do with it: it did contain a Latin poem by him, published in his name, but in the preface the book as a whole is presented as published during Rantzau's absence by his librarian, Martinus Coroneus, who—it is said—had found certain prose texts about Johann Rantzau in the library at Breitenburg! Presumably, this strange story means that Heinrich had also written these, the main parts of the book.[6]

There is no reason to doubt that the book as a whole was planned and ordered by Heinrich Rantzau. An interesting detail pointing in that direction is a letter from another Holsatian nobleman in which he tells Heinrich Rantzau about his own (Rantzau's, that is) last conversation with his father. Heinrich obviously asked his friends to send him letters with specific contents, in order to print them in this book. His ambitions with the book can also be seen from the fact that he had it reprinted three times during 1566 and 1567—and most of it was reprinted again in his *Epistolae consolatoriae*, 1593—which in its turn was reprinted twice.[7]

Rantzau's second book, dating from 1570, was also concerned with his father. This was a historical description of the war against Dithmarschen which had been conducted by his father. This too was printed under another name—this time a pseudonym: Christianus Cilicius Cimber—but he dedicated it to himself. At this time

---

[5] Georg Braunius: *Ciuitates Orbis Terrarum*, vol. 4. (Köln, 1588). The map (by the Holsteiner Marcus Jordan) is dated 1585. Cf. Johanne Skovgaard, "Georg Braun und Heinrich Rantzau," *Nordelbingen* 15 (1939), 100–125.

[6] Friedrich Bertheau, "Heinrich Rantzau als Humanist," *Zeitschrift der Gesellschaft für Schleswig-Holsteinische Geschichte*, 18 (1888), 182.

[7] Martinus Coroneus (Martin Kreye) (ed.), *Vita et res gestae Johannis Rantzovii* (Rostock, 1566; Lübeck, 1566; Wittenberg, 1567; Frankfurt a. M., 1567). For the practice of ordering laudatory texts with specific contents, see P. Zeeberg, "Neo-Latin Poetry in Its Social Context. Some Statistics and Some Examples from Sixteenth Century Denmark," in *Mare Balticum–Mare Nostrum*, ed. Outi Merisalo and R. Sarasti-Wilenius (Helsinki, 1994), 9–21.

several other books had already been dedicated to him, and a certain Georgius Crusius had published a description of his castle, Breitenburg.[8]

This, then, is the beginning of an impressive production of books and prints written by him, about him, to his order or for him—a production which increased gradually during the following thirty years until his death in 1598.

I am currently preparing a bibliography of this material, and so far I have found close to 300 items, books as well as minor prints, including reprints. These are written by about sixty different main authors.

Over the years Rantzau gathered around him a wide circle of humanists, covering most of Germany and the Netherlands, with whom he kept up an extensive correspondence, and whom he very often supported, financially and otherwise. In return, of course, they would publish books in his honour.

A letter from Heinrich Meibom (1555–1625), Professor of Poetics in Helmstedt, is illustrative.[9] Meibom thanks Rantzau for a sum of money which he has received in return for a poem. He is dependent on this kind of money from remote patrons, he says, as there are no patrons in his own part of the country, and his pay as a professor is only 83 Joachimstaler, which is too little to live on.

In the same letter he also mentions another way in which Rantzau could reward his clients: Meibom regrets the death of King Frederik II of Denmark, as he had planned to use Rantzau's influence to be crowned poet laureate by the king. (In another instance that strategy succeeded: Peter Lindeberg was created poet laureate by Paulus Melissus as a result of Rantzau's influence.)[10]

Meibom's letter does not state the sum paid by Rantzau, but other sources give us a general impression: a professor who dedicated a book to Rantzau would receive 50 to 60 Taler, while a young man, a student for instance, who wrote him a poem would normally get 1 Taler. (And that is to be compared to the 83 Joachimstaler which Meibom had as a professor.) This can be deduced from the letters as well as from an account book which belonged to one of Rantzau's servants.[11]

The list of humanists who dedicated their books to Rantzau includes such well known authors as: Justus Lipsius, Janus Gruterus, David Chytraeus, Joachim Camerarius the younger, Georg Rollenhagen, Johannes Lauterbach, Nicolaus Reusner, and Matthias Dresser.

Their books, of course, will be the ones that are most remembered now. Some, such as the second edition of Joseph Scaliger's *De emendatione temporum*,[12] or Rollenhagen's German poem *Froschenmeuseler*, are very important within their different

---

[8] Christianus Cilicius Cimber (= Heinrich Rantzau), *Belli Dithmarsici descriptio* (Basel, 1570. Strassburg, 1573. Frankfurt, 1583). Georgius Crusius, *Descriptio Breenbergae* (s.l. 1569; Wittenberg, 1570).

[9] 12 September 1589, ms. Breitenburg, 636.

[10] Announced in Lindeberg's *Juvenilia* (Frankfurt a. M., 1595). Rantzau's role can be seen in a letter from Melissus (dated 9 April 1595), printed as a supplement to Frobenius' *Epistolae consolatoriae* (Frankfurt a.M., s.a. [c. 1595]).

[11] Published in Steinmetz, *Heinrich Rantzau*.

[12] Frankfurt a. M., 1593, dedicated to Rantzau by the printer Johannes Wechelus.

fields. Others—the ones that he himself ordered from less famous, local humanists (some of them directly employed by him as librarians or private teachers)—tend to be forgotten now. These works, on the other hand, are the ones that tell us most about the purpose of his activities.

The point which distinguishes Rantzau's activities from the patronage exercised by other noblemen is the fact that Rantzau himself took an active part in their production. As we have already seen, some books were written by him personally, although usually they would be edited by someone else. His production includes historical works, books on astrology and medicine, one on warfare, and even poetry: a didactic poem on dreams, epigrams, and much occasional poetry.

In some cases the contributions of the editors were substantial, and there are examples of entire books written by others but published under Rantzau's name.[13] In other cases he contributed texts for books written by others or took part in their planning. One particular group is the editions of ancient and medieval texts "ex bibliotheca Ranzoviana," that is from manuscripts in his possession. In his correspondence we can follow how he sent out manuscripts to scholars around Germany to find out whether they were worth printing.[14]

As to the contents, three topics are the most prominent: scientific books (not least on astrology), history and topography (about Schleswig-Holstein and about Denmark as a whole), and thirdly what one might call "Ranzoviana." The last group—which is not the smallest—includes occasional poetry about family members, genealogical works, and works about Heinrich Rantzau.

Among the last group, the books aiming at presenting Heinrich Rantzau to the public, are several descriptions of his castles and other buildings, including monuments of different kinds. The most ambitious of these is *Hypotyposis Arcium, Palatiorum, Librorum, Pyramidum, Obeliscorum, Molarum, Fontium, Monumentorum, & Epitaphiorum*, from 1590, written by one of his closest collaborators, his "court poet," so to speak, Peter Lindeberg from Rostock.[15] Through prose, poetry, and woodcuts, this work describes all his buildings and monuments, but in addition to this it also lists his literary and scientific production and prints an enormous amount of other material about Rantzau and his family, especially panegyrical poetry, presented to him—or ordered by him—from poets all over Germany. The *Hypotyposis* alone includes texts by forty-two different authors. Something similar is the case with Froben's *Epistolae Consolatoriae*, which in the course of its three editions evolved from a collection of letters of condolence on the death of some of his sons to a collection of all kinds of literary material about Heinrich Rantzau.

In general, this kind of material abounds in the books from Rantzau's circle. He

---

[13] Thomas Fincke's *Horoscopographia* (Strassburg, 1585; Wittenberg, 1588). The ed. Schleswig, 1591, had Fincke himself on the title page.

[14] E.g., letter from David Chytraeus: 14 May 1586, Cod. Vindob. 9736 l, 83. From Reiner Reineccius: 20 February 1589, ms. Breitenburg, 630. One example is Reineccius' edition of *Chronicon Alberti abbatis Stadensis* (Helmstedt, 1587).

[15] Rostock 1590; Hamburg 1591; Frankfurt a. M. 1592.

personally saw to it that selections of poetry about himself and his family were included in practically all the books that were published under his patronage. In his letters we can follow how he sends laudatory epigrams and printing blocks for portraits and coats of arms to the printers when a new book is going to be printed.

Naturally such texts are panegyric, their aim, from Rantzau's point of view, being publicity. They present him to the public in the way he wants to be seen. But that was not the only purpose of his activities; he was earnestly interested in science and *litterae*. Indeed, these two sides of his activity ought not to be separated.

The "autobiography" is a good example: it was originally written in 1571 in a letter to the astronomer Cyprianus Leovitius (1524–1574) in Augsburg. Rantzau writes that he has heard that Leovitius is planning a book about astrology, in which he is going to use actual horoscopes as examples, and that he is now searching for famous and distinguished persons for that purpose. Therefore, ". . . although I am no personal acquaintance of yours (apart from the fact that we are united by a common interest in the liberal arts, which are not alien to me—although perhaps some people would consider me born for something different), I assume that you would appreciate it if I too sent you my horoscope."[16]

Here follows the autobiography, which, in this connection, functions as an analysis of the horoscope. The letter ends: "I ask you to examine this horoscope, add my and your own judgment to it, and include it in your promised work in its proper place. As soon as I understand that you have received this letter and, I hope, finished your work, I shall remunerate you deservedly, and I shall see to it, with care and diligence, that you shall not be wanting anything from me, if my services can support you and your work in any way."[17]

This, I suppose, is what one might call an offer you can't refuse. Unfortunately no answer has been preserved, and I have not been able to identify the book in question, if indeed it ever appeared. But the text in itself is typical of Rantzau. Even at this rather early point in his career as a Maecenas he knew how to make use of the production of famous professional scientists or writers to his own ends. He not only asks Leovitius to use his horoscope as an example, he also sends him an analysis of it and asks him to print this along with his own.

That Leovitius would probably do as he was told can be seen from a similar example: in 1578 a certain Henricus Petreus in Frankfurt published a book about courts: *De Aulica vita*. In a letter from him to Rantzau we hear that Rantzau sent him a poem on the same topic and asked him to include it in his book. In fact he did not receive Rantzau's poem till after the book was printed, but he felt obliged to replace

---

[16] 10 October 1571, ms. Breitenburg, 17: *Visum est itaque, tametsi nulla tecum mihi intercedat familiaritas (nisi quod communia liberalium & ingenuarum artium studia, a quibus ego, quem fortassè non deerunt qui dicant ad alia à parentibus natum, non sum alienus, videantur nos coniungere) rem tibi non ingratam me facturum si & meam* γένεσιν *tecum communicarem.*

[17] *Peto autem ut hanc meam genesin diligenter examines, Judicium meum tuumque addas, & operi promisso suo loco inseras. Ego ubi intellexero, has meas te accepisse literas; & operam tuam, ut spero, studio præstitisse, digna te afficiam remuneratione: & in id incumbam diligenter & sedulo, Ut si officij aliquo genere tibi possim prodesse, & tuos iuuare conatus, nihil in me possis desiderare (ibid., 25).*

some pages with this new material—a fact which evidently annoyed the printers. As Petreus writes: "Printing house workers really are too rude and bad tempered for words—especially during the confusion of the fair."[18]

Examples such as these show how Rantzau could place his fingerprint upon academic books, presenting himself to the public at one and the same time as a humanist and a nobleman. At other times he would leave much more than a fingerprint. And of course he had the money and the influence to do what he liked in this respect.

But the clients, too, knew that they had something to offer to their patron: a certain Hermann Hamelmann sent to Rantzau a manuscript which he wanted to dedicate to him when it was published. In the accompanying letter he asked Rantzau to examine the contents and feel free to make alterations, and then see to it that it was printed in Rostock, Lübeck, or Hamburg—and pay for the printing. "That" Hamelmann adds "will benefit the public and add glory to your illustrious name." Hamelmann ends his letter by asking Rantzau also to pay the letter carrier. The book was printed the following year (1592) in Leipzig (!), at Rantzau's expense.[19]

This frankness about the financial side of the relationship is characteristic. Another example: as already mentioned, Rantzau supported Georg Braunius' work with his description of the cities of Europe. In return he had substantial influence on the treatment which Denmark received in the book. At one point Braunius writes that in fact many Danish towns are villages rather than great cities, but "because of my reverence for the magnificence of your name, and for your Danish kingdom, I shall nevertheless take care that the different localities in your country are included in the fifth *Theatrum* of the work. I shall do that the more readily if I know that either your illustrious highness or Denmark, will meet some part of the expenses."[20]

Glory is what Rantzau expects to receive in return for his money. But that can, of course, only be achieved if the books are seen by the right people. This is also apparent in the letters: firstly, a substantial percentage of the letters mention books sent as presents—to clients, to other noblemen, and not least to princes. (Many of the still existing copies bear handwritten dedications, occasionally even a binding with the dedication on the front.) Secondly, we have several letters from the people who arranged the printing—typically a professor at some university—presenting the terms of agreement with the printers. These agreements always mention a large number of copies reserved for Rantzau's own use. Such figures as fifty or sixty copies are common, but in some cases he received a hundred or more.

This goes not only for his own books and the ones about himself or his family, but also for other people's scientific publications. As an example I can mention the

---

[18] 28 March 1578, ms. Breitenburg, 165.

[19] Hermannus Hamelmannus (ed.), *De recordatione, consideratione et meditatione perpetua quatuor novissimorum, . . .* (Leipzig, 1592). The letter: 1 January 1591, Cod. Vindob. 9737 m, 98. Copy in Ms. Breitenburg, 736.

[20] . . . *tamen, pro mea, erga nominis tui splendorem et Danicum Regnum vestrum obseruantia, hoc mihi curæ erit, vt, diuersa loca vestra, Quinto Theatro nostro inserantur, quod tunc propensius faciam, si ad tam plausibile, gentique vestræ laudabile institutum, aliquam sumtuum partem vel Illustrem Dom. vestram, vel Daniam suppeditaturam, cognouero.* 6 September 1593. Frobenius, *Epistolae consolatoriae*, 289–290.

editio princeps of a Greek astrological treatise, Paulus Alexandrinus' *Eisagogika*, which was printed "Ex bibliotheca Ranzoviana" in Wittenberg in 1586. This book was reprinted two years later at the request of Rantzau. We have a letter from 1587 in which the editor, Andreas Schato in Wittenberg, answers Rantzau that the book is out of print and offers his services if Rantzau wants to have it reprinted.[21] In his next letter he can inform Rantzau that he has made an agreement with the printer about the reprinting. At a cost of 20 or 21 Taler the printer will print the book together with another astrological treatise, which Rantzau wants to have printed, and Rantzau will receive fifty copies.[22]

In order to ensure the widest distribution possible, he often made famous humanists such as David Chytraeus or Justus Lipsius, who could be expected to have the right connections, distribute the books among their friends.[23] This may also explain why several of his books were printed simultaneously in three or four different German cities.

Let me give one example of a clear-cut success in this respect—the right people getting the right impression of Rantzau through a book he had sent out as a present. Among the frequently recurring elements in Rantzau's books are depictions of two monuments which Rantzau had erected to the memory of King Frederik II of Denmark: a pyramid and an obelisk. According to Lindeberg's description of these, the model for the obelisk was the obelisk which Pope Sixtus V had had erected outside S. Maria Maggiore in Rome. This gave Rantzau's correspondent at the Roman Curia, the Secretary of State Minuccio Minuzzi, an opportunity to propose the ultimate piece of flattery: in a letter of 1590 he explains that a picture of Rantzau's obelisk had been shown to the pope, Sixtus V himself, who apart from the one at S. Maria Maggiore, had also erected the Vatican obelisk, the Lateran obelisk and the one at Piazza del Popolo. According to Minuzzi, the pope had declared that he, who erected old obelisks, was surpassed by this man, who at great cost had new ones made![24]

To sum up: Rantzau's literary activities exceed by far what noblemen would normally do in this field. He not only supported science and literature on a greater scale than ordinary noblemen, he also was directly involved in these activites. One purpose of these activities was the publicity they could get him, but it must be stressed that he did it also out of an earnest and deeply felt interest in the *studia*. He wished to see himself as a member of the academic world as well as the aristocratic. And he wished to appear to the surrounding world as a learned nobleman (with equal stress on both elements), through academic works—his own as well as those of others.

Institut for Græsk og Latin, Kobenhavn S

---

21 16 October 1587, ms. Breitenburg, 397ff. and 388.

22 2 January 1588, ms. Breitenburg, 417.

23 E.g., letters from Chytraeus: 22 July 1587, Cod. Vindob. 9736 l, 260ʳ. 30 April 1588, ms. Breitenburg, 429. From Lipsius: 3 November 1588, ms. Breitenburg, 437.

24 8 July 1590, Cod. Vindob. 9737 m, fol. 35v. Cf. Horst Fuhrmann: "Heinrich Rantzaus römische Korrespondenten," *Archiv für Kulturgeschichte* 41 (1959), 63–89. The obelisk is described by Lindeberg in his *Hypotyposis* (note 15).

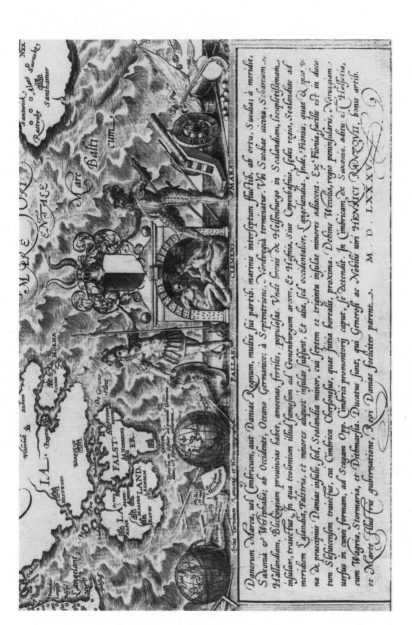

Map of Denmark from Braunius' *Theatrum Urbium* (1588), detail.
Royal Library, Copenhagen.

Index

ꟿRTS

ꟿEΔIEVAL & RENAISSANCE TEXTS & STUDIES
is the major publishing program of the
Arizona Center for Medieval and Renaissance Studies
at Arizona State University, Tempe, Arizona.

ꟿRTS emphasizes books that are needed —
texts, translations, and major research tools.

ꟿRTS aims to publish the highest quality scholarship
in attractive and durable format at modest cost.

'80 ● Virus New to Angola Kills 95: Travelers Told to Avoid North March 24, 2005 ● Angola: Deadly Disease's
eadly Virus Across Angola April 9, 2005 ● To Contain Virus in Angola, Group Wants Hospital Closed April 10,
ted Virus Carrier Dies Alone April 12, 2005 ● Stalking a Deadly Virus, Battling a Town's Fears April 17, 2005
1 May 20, 2005 ● New Vaccines Prevent Ebola and Marburg in Monkeys June 6, 2005 ● End of Deadly Epidemic
des Information on Deadly Health Threat March 17, 2003 ● Health Organization Stepping Up Efforts to Find
, but Seek Proof March 20, 2003 ● Asian Medics Stay Home, Imperiling Respiratory Patients March 21, 2003 ●
alls Ill March 25, 2003 ● China Raises Tally of Cases and Deaths in Mystery Illness March 27, 2003 ● Rise in
Asian Hub April 1, 2003 ● From Tourism to High Finance, Mysterious Illness Spreads Havoc April 3, 2003 ●
rise Quickly April 6, 2003 ● Fear Reigns as Dangerous Mystery Illness Spreads April 7, 2003 Asian Officials
Offer Little Defense Against Disease April 14, 2003 ● 12 More Die in Hong Kong from New Virus April 20, 2003
ronto Because of SARS April 24, 2003 ● Outbreak of a Disease Brings Big Drop-Off in China's Economy April
rk for a Riot in China April 29, 2003 ● W.H.O. Doubles Its Estimate of Death Rate From SARS May 8, 2003 ●
ks May 25, 2003 ● SARS Outbreak Fading Away Officials Say June 6, 2003 ● W.H.O. Lifts SARS Alert in China
d Contained, with No Cases in Past 20 Days July 6, 2003 ● Tracks of Mystery Disease Lead to New Form of Virus
Texas July 11, 1993 ● Mysterious Virus Feared Extensive August 13, 1993 ● Strain of Deadly Virus Found in
Student Death Is First Case of Rare Virus in the Northeast February 24, 1994 ● Indians Reject Name Linking
dging Up, Mostly in West April 12, 1996 ● Hantavirus Infection Claims a 4th Victim in Utah October 27, 1996 ●
Region September 21, 1997 ● Lethal Virus Borne by Mice Makes Return in the West June 25, 1998 ● Debate Over
Navajo Casts the Spotlight on a Rare Virus April 23, 2001 ● African Virus May Be the Culprit in
Dies of Mosquito-Borne Virus September 30, 1999 ● Mosquito Virus Exposes a Hole in the Safety Net October 4,
17, 1999 ● Traces of Deadly Virus Are Found in Hibernating Mosquitoes March 10, 2000 ● New Findings of Nile
Fight Against Fear as Well as Mosquitoes July 26, 2000 ● Mosquito Madness August 7, 2000 ● West Nile Virus
ust 19, 2000 ● Nile Virus Finding in Florida Bird Raises Concern About Fast Spread July 15, 2001 ● Ohio: New
2002 ● Experts Expect Rapid Rise in West Nile Virus Cases August 16, 2002 ● All 50 States Now Warn of West
ed Blood July 4, 2003 ● South Carolina: West Nile Virus Victim July 9, 2003 ● Spring Rains and Summer Heat
hs from West Nile Virus Climb to 14 in California September 11, 2004 ● Donor's Organs Are Linked to West Nile
003 ● Monkeypox Casts Light on Rule Gap for Exotic Pets June 10, 2003 ● Suspected Cases of Monkeypox Are
● Patient May Have Transmitted Monkeypox June 13, 2003 ● U.S. Health Official Is Optimistic on Containing
rms in Pennsylvania Quarantined November 6, 1983 ● Chicken Flocks with Flu December 16, 1983 ● Avian Flu
reads to Humans December 9, 1997 ● As Avian Flu spreads, China Is Seen as Its Epicenter December 21, 1997 ●
u Virus December 31, 1997 ● "Bird Flu" Reveals Gaps in Plans for Possible Global Outbreaks January 6, 1998 ●
s February 21, 2003 ● Cases of New Bird Flu in Hong Kong Prompt Worldwide Alerts February 22, 2003 ● Avian
Bird Flu: Virus Spreads January 24, 2004 ● Spread of Flu Across Asia Laid to Birds That Migrate January 27,
ported Found in Pigs in China August 21, 2004 ● Study Finds Bird-Flu Virus Can Spread Among Cats September
ely if the Asian Bird Flu Spreads Among People November 30, 2004 ● Tests Identify the First Human Case of
g Becomes a Monster: City and State Prepare an Overburdened System for the Threat of Avian Flu August 21,
October 15, 2005 ● Britain and Croatia Report Cases of Bird Flu October 22, 2005 ● Poverty and Superstition
ay 11, 1982 ● Infant Who Received Transfusion Dies of Immunodeficiency Illness December 10, 1982 ● Disease
struck 1,552 June 17, 1983 ● Virus Linked to AIDS Is Found in Hemophiliacs September 2, 1983 ● AIDS Now Seen
april 24, 1984 ● Increase in AIDS Cases Reported November 30, 1984 ● AIDS Strains Health Clinics
cts 10,000 in the Nation May 10, 1985 ● Help to AIDS Victims Brings Phone Threats May 12, 1985 ● Blood Supply
van AIDS Death Toll is 8 November 23, 1985 ● Soviet Acknowledges a Few Cases of AIDS December 8, 1985 ●
Victims of AIDS Predicted by 2000 March 4, 1987 ● AIDS Hits Western Europe, Mimicking Viral Path in
987 ● Surge in AIDS Cases in Congo Could Be an Omen for Africa January 22, 1988 ● U.S. Reports AIDS Deaths
, 1992 ● U.N. Agency Reports AIDS Virus Spreading Very Quickly in Africa December 13, 1993 ● Full-Blown
1996 ● U.N. Reports 3 Million New H.I.V. Cases Worldwide for '96 November 28, 1996 ● AIDS Deaths
AIDS Virus November 26, 1997 ● Parts of Africa Showing H.I.V. in 1 in 4 Adults June 24, 1998 Africa's
2001 ● Gains Made to Contain AIDS but Its Global Spread Goes On, U.N. Says June 3, 2005

Deadly
INVADERS